# Marketing Research
## AN APPLIED ORIENTATION

# Marketing Research

## AN APPLIED ORIENTATION

**Fourth Edition**

# Naresh K. Malhotra

*Georgia Institute of Technology*

**PEARSON**

Prentice
Hall

**Upper Saddle River, NJ 07458**

**Library of Congress Cataloging-in-Publication Data**

Malhotra, Naresh K.
    Marketing research: an applied orientation / Naresh K. Malhotra.—4th ed.
        p. cm
    Includes bibliographical references and indexes.
    ISBN 0-13-033716-1
        1. Marketing research. 2. Marketing research—Methodology. I. Title.
    HF5415.2 .M29 2003b

                                                    2002042467


Senior Editor: Wendy Craven
Editor-in-Chief: Jeff Shelstad
Assistant Editor: Melissa Pellerano
Editorial Assistant: Danielle Serra
Media Project Manager: Anthony Palmiotto
Marketing Manager: Michelle O'Brien
Senior Managing Editor (Production): Judy Leale
Production Editor: Marcela Maslanczuk
Production Assistant: Joseph DeProspero
Permissions Coordinator: Suzanne Grappi
Associate Director, Manufacturing: Vincent Scelta
Production Manager: Arnold Vila
Design Manager: Maria Lange
Interior Design: Michael Fruhbeis
Cover Design: Michael Fruhbeis
Cover Illustration/Photo: Corbis/Hannah Gal
Photo Researcher: Teri Stratford
Manager, Print Production: Christy Mahon
Composition: Carlisle Communications
Full-Service Project Management: Lynn Steines, Carlisle Communications
Printer/Binder: Courier Westford


Credits and acknowledgments borrowed from other sources and reproduced, with permission, in this textbook
appear on page C1.

Pearson Education LTD.
Pearson Education Singapore, Pte. Ltd
Pearson Education, Canada, Ltd
Pearson Education–Japan

Pearson Education Australia PTY, Limited
Pearson Education North Asia Ltd
Pearson Educación de Mexico, S.A. de C.V.
Pearson Education Malaysia, Pte. Ltd

10 9 8 7 6 5 4 3 2 1
ISBN 0-13-033716-1

*To the memory of my father*

*Mr. H. N. Malhotra*
*and*
*To my mother Mrs. Satya Malhotra*

*and*

*To my wife Veena and*
*children Ruth and Paul*

*The love, encouragement, and support of my parents,*
*wife, and children have been exemplary.*

*"The greatest of these is love."*

*I Corinthians 13:13*

# Brief Contents

# Contents

# Foreword

The world of business is moving more rapidly than ever. The intelligent and thoughtful use of research is critical to keeping pace. Undoubtedly, the most successful people will have a broad base of education, high levels of communication skills, and creative approaches to the opportunities that are racing toward us. It is marvelous when a textbook such as Dr. Malhotra's allows the classroom to become a source of these skills.

This text has already proven its worth as one of the most successful in the field, with well over 140 universities using it in the United States, translation into five languages, and four different English language editions. This text is unsurpassed in presenting the fundamentals that allow you to become researchers and intelligent users of research. The real-life examples bring you closer to the world businesspeople face daily. At every step, you can relate to the ongoing "Department Store Project" and to the practical vignettes that bring the educational material to a realistic and practical level. The success in keeping the material at the leading edge of research also can be seen in the integration of modern tools of research such as the Internet, computer analytic software, and the latest management practices.

We at Burke, Inc. are please to be asked to contribute further from our experiences for this fourth edition. We have shared these experiences as well as our philosophies, technical skill, and thoughts about the future of research. This fourth edition of *Marketing Research: An Applied Orientation* provides the foundation that we believe every student should have. We know you will find the combination of theory, practice, and sound advice to be of great value to you.

*Ron Tatham, Ph.D.*
**Chairman, Burke, Inc.**

# Preface

The motivation in writing this book was to provide a marketing research text that is comprehensive, practical, applied, and managerial and presents a balanced coverage of both qualitative and quantitative material. This book is written from the perspective of a marketing research user. It reflects the current trends in international marketing, ethics, and the integration of the Internet and computers, as well as a focus on the practice of marketing research by featuring Burke, Inc. and other marketing research organizations. Several unique features in terms of the content and presentation of the material make it distinctive.

The response to the first three editions has been truly gratifying with more than 144 universities adopting the book in the United States. The book has been translated into five languages: Chinese, Russian, Spanish, Portuguese, and Hungarian. Moreover, four English editions have been published: North American, International, European, and Australia and New Zealand. I want to express my sincere thanks and appreciation to all the professors and students who have contributed to the success of the book as adopters, users, reviewers, and providers of valuable feedback and encouragement. The fourth edition attempts to build on this success to make the book even more current, contemporary, illustrative, and sensitive to user needs.

## AUDIENCE

The book is suitable for use in graduate and upper-level undergraduate courses in marketing research and data analysis. This positioning is confirmed by the response to the first three editions that includes adoptions at these levels. However, my book, *Basic Marketing Research: Application to Contemporary Issues*, is more suitable for use in mainstream and lower-level undergraduate courses. The coverage of *Marketing Research: An Applied Orientation* is comprehensive and the material is presented in a manner that is easy to read and understand. There are several diagrams, tables, pictures, illustrations, and examples that explain the basic concepts. There are extensive exercises (questions, problems, and Internet and computer exercises) and activities (role playing, fieldwork, and group discussion). Not only is the book suitable for use in courses on **Marketing Research**, but it can also be effectively used in courses on **Marketing Data Analysis**. All the commonly used univariate and multivariate data analysis techniques are discussed extensively but simply and illustrated with manageable data sets that are presented in the book and enclosed as data files.

## ORGANIZATION

The book is organized into three parts, based on a six-step framework for conducting marketing research. Part one provides an introduction and discusses problem definition, the first and most important step. The nature and scope of research undertaken to develop an approach to the problem, the second step in the marketing research process, is also described. Part two covers research design, the third step, and describes in detail exploratory, descriptive, and causal research designs. We describe the types of information commonly obtained in marketing research and the appropriate scales for obtaining such information. We present several guidelines for designing questionnaires and explain the procedures, techniques, and statistical considerations involved in sampling. Part three presents a practical and managerially oriented discussion of fieldwork, the fourth step in the marketing research process. It also covers data preparation and analysis, the fifth step of the marketing research process. We discuss in detail basic and advanced statistical techniques with emphasis on explaining the procedures, interpreting the results, and discussing managerial implications, rather than on statistical elegance. Four statistical packages, SPSS, SAS, MINITAB, and EXCEL are featured. A student version of SPSS is enclosed. The SPSS files for all the input data sets used in this book can be downloaded from the Web site. This last part also contains guidelines for preparing and presenting a formal report, the sixth step in the marketing research process. It is also devoted to the complex process of international marketing research. Throughout the book, our orientation is applied and managerial.

# NEW FOR THE FOURTH EDITION

In addition to retaining many desirable features, the fourth edition contains major revisions. Several significant changes have been made. These changes were identified by conducting surveys of professors (users and nonusers) and students and by obtaining critical reviews and detailed evaluations. Major changes include:

1. Chapter modifications. Several of the chapters have been modified to present new ideas, to update existing materials, or in some instances to further clarify concepts. These modifications start with Chapter 1, which has been extensively rewritten, and are reflected throughout the text.

2. Integrated coverage of the Internet. The section on "Internet and Computer Applications" that appears in each chapter has been expanded and updated. This section discusses and illustrates how the Internet and computers can be used to implement the concepts in that chapter. In addition, use of the Internet is integrated throughout several of the chapters. Topics, URLs, and examples illustrating the use of the Internet appear throughout each chapter. The "Internet and Computer Exercises" that also appear in each chapter have been expanded. The data analysis chapters (15 to 21) feature several new computer exercises for which the data have been provided.

3. Added emphasis on SPSS. Although the data analysis chapters feature four statistical packages: SPSS, SAS, MINITAB, and EXCEL along with other popular programs, special emphasis has been placed on SPSS. The relevant chapters contain a special section on SPSS WINDOWS that illustrates the relevant SPSS programs and the steps required to run them. SPSS files have been provided for all input data sets that are featured at the beginning of all data analysis chapters (15 to 21), input data sets that appear in "Internet and Computer Exercises," input data sets for Cases (3.3, 3.4, 3.5, 4.1, and 4.2), as well as the corresponding output files. These data sets are also provided as Text (tab delimited) and EXCEL files. These data sets can be found online at *www.prenhall.com/malhotra*. The SPSS WINDOWS student version contains a tutorial that students can use to learn or refresh their knowledge of SPSS.

4. Video cases. Each part of the book contains video cases. These cases have been drawn from the Prentice Hall video library but have been written from a marketing research perspective. The questions at the end of each video case are all marketing research questions. The videotapes containing these cases are available to instructors who adopt the book. Solutions to these video cases are provided in the Instructor's Manual.

5. New figures, tables, exhibits, and text. Where appropriate, new material has been added to present a new idea, update the technology, or clarify the subject. Such additions have been made throughout the text.

6. New and updated examples and cases. Several new examples have been added, some old ones deleted, and the remaining examples have been updated as appropriate. Some new cases have been added and all the rest updated to reflect the current marketing and marketing research environment. Particularly noteworthy is the addition of two comprehensives cases (4.1 and 4.2) with data sets. These cases contain questions on each chapter of the book.

7. Updated references. The references have been updated. Each chapter contains many references that are from 2000 or later. However, some of the classic references have been retained.

8. Reorganized chapters. To conserve space, the capstone chapter titled "Ethics in Marketing Research" (Chapter 24 in the third edition) has been eliminated and the relevant material integrated throughout the text. Each chapter, except the data analysis chapters, has a section titled "Ethics in Marketing Research." Each data analysis chapter does have a blocked example on "Ethics in Marketing Research."

# KEY FEATURES OF THE TEXT

The book has several salient and unique features, both in terms of content and pedagogy.

## Content Features

1. A separate chapter has been devoted to defining the problem and developing an approach. These important steps in the marketing research process are discussed thoroughly and extensively (Chapter 2).

2. An overview of the different types of research designs is provided early in the book (Chapter 3). Exploratory, descriptive, and causal designs are introduced and illustrated.

3. A separate chapter covers secondary data analysis. In addition to the traditional sources, computerized databases and syndicate sources are also covered extensively. Use of the Internet for secondary data analysis is discussed in detail (Chapter 4).

4. Qualitative research is discussed in a separate chapter. Focus groups, depth interviews, and projective techniques are discussed in detail with emphasis on the applications of these procedures. Use of the Internet for qualitative research is discussed in detail (Chapter 5).

5. A separate chapter presents survey and observation methods (Chapter 6), and another discusses experimentation (Chapter 7). Thus, descriptive and causal designs are covered in detail.

6. Two chapters have been devoted to scaling techniques. One chapter is devoted to the fundamentals and comparative scaling techniques (Chapter 8). The other covers noncomparative techniques, including multiitem scales and procedures for assessing their reliability, validity, and generalizability (Chapter 9).

7. A separate chapter discusses questionnaire design. A step-by-step procedure and several guidelines are provided for constructing questionnaires (Chapter 10).

8. Two chapters cover sampling techniques. One chapter discusses the qualitative issues involved in sampling and the various nonprobability and probability sampling techniques (Chapter 11). The other chapter explains statistical issues, as well as final and initial sample size determination (Chapter 12).

9. A separate chapter presents fieldwork. We give several guidelines on training interviewers, interviewing, and supervising field workers (Chapter 13).

10. The book is unique in the treatment of marketing research data analysis. Separate chapters have been devoted to:

    a.  Data preparation (Chapter 14)

    b.  Frequency distribution, cross-tabulation, and hypothesis testing (Chapter 15)

    c.  Analysis of variance and covariance (Chapter 16)

    d.  Regression analysis (Chapter 17)

    e.  Discriminant analysis (Chapter 18)

    f.  Factor analysis (Chapter 19)

    g.  Cluster analysis (Chapter 20)

    h.  Multidimensional scaling and conjoint analysis (Chapter 21)

    The data set used to explain each technique is provided in the beginning of the chapter. Data analysis is illustrated for four statistical packages: SPSS, SAS, MINITAB, and EXCEL. There is a special emphasis on SPSS WINDOWS and the steps required to run each procedure are described.

11. A separate chapter has been devoted to report preparation and presentation. This chapter provides several guidelines for communicating the research findings (Chapter 22).

12. To supplement the discussions throughout the text, an additional chapter explains international marketing research. The environment in which international marketing research is conducted is described, followed by a discussion of some advanced concepts (Chapter 23).

# PEDAGOGICAL FEATURES

1. Scholarship is appropriately blended with a highly applied and managerial orientation. We illustrate in a pervasive manner the application of concepts and techniques by marketing researchers and implementation of findings by managers to improve marketing practice. Featuring Burke, Inc. in a significant way in each chapter further reinforces the emphasis on applied marketing research. The focus on Burke in each chapter of the book should not be interpreted as an endorsement for Burke over other marketing research firms. I have no business relationship with Burke and have not provided them with any consulting services. The primary intent is to show how a well-established marketing research firm practices the concepts discussed in each chapter.

2. Several real-life examples, titled "Real Research," are given and have been blocked for clarity and impact. These examples describe in some detail the kind of marketing research used to address a specific managerial problem and the decision that was based on the findings. Where appropriate, the sources cited have been supplemented by additional marketing research information to enhance the usefulness of these examples. Additional examples have been integrated throughout the text to further explain and illustrate the concepts in each chapter.

3. In addition, a real-life project is used as a running example to illustrate the various concepts throughout the text. These illustrations, entitled "Active Research: Department Store Project," have been blocked and highlighted using a colored background. To make the running example comprehensive so that it covers all aspects of marketing research, an actual department store

project that I conducted is supplemented with other similar projects that I was involved with, although several aspects of these projects have been disguised. In other instances, as in the case of causal research design, I show how the relevant concepts can be applied in a department store setting. Thus, the department store example spans the whole book and is easy to pick up in any chapter.

4. Another way in which a contemporary focus is achieved is by integrating the coverage of international marketing research and ethics in marketing research throughout the text. We show how the concepts discussed in each chapter can be applied in an international setting and discuss the ethical issues that may arise when implementing those concepts domestically and internationally.

5. The use of the Internet and computers has also been integrated throughout the text. Each chapter has a section entitled "Internet and Computer Applications." We show how the Internet and computers can be integrated in each step of the marketing research process and how they can be used to implement the concepts discussed in each chapter. Each chapter also contains "Internet and Computer Exercises" that present opportunities to apply these concepts in real-life settings. Where needed, relevant data sets have been provided.

6. Data analysis procedures are illustrated with respect to SPSS, SAS, MINITAB, and EXCEL, along with other popular programs. However, special emphasis has been placed on SPSS. A separate section entitled "SPSS WINDOWS" appears in the relevant chapters. This section discusses the appropriate SPSS programs and the steps required to run them. SPSS input data and output files have been provided.

7. Each part of the book contains video cases that have been written from a marketing research perspective. The questions at the end of each video case are all marketing research questions. The videotapes containing these cases are available to instructors who adopt the book.

8. Each part of the book contains some short real-life cases. These cases illustrate the concepts discussed. The conciseness of the cases will allow for their use in examinations. Some long cases are also provided, including some cases with statistical data. These cases are current and deal with topics of interest to students.

9. Extensive "Exercises" and "Activities," which include questions, problems, Internet and Computer Exercises, role playing, fieldwork, and group discussion, are found at the conclusion of each chapter. These sections provide ample opportunities for learning and testing the concepts covered in the chapter.

10. A complete set of learning aids, including a functional and useful Web site, an Instructor's Manual, PowerPoint slides, and Test Bank, has been provided.

11. The latest student version of SPSS WINDOWS is provided. All the SPSS data sets used in the beginning of each chapter and the corresponding SPSS output files, the SPSS data sets for the relevant "Internet and Computer Exercises," and cases can be downloaded from the Web site.

## INSTRUCTIONAL SUPPORT

A functional and useful Web site. The Web site can be accessed at *www.prenhall.com/ malhotra*. This site contains the following:

■ The entire Instructors' Manual

■ Test Item File

■ PowerPoint slides containing a chapter outline and all the figures, tables, and relevant content for each chapter. Additional material has been added and the PowerPoint slides have been enhanced as compared to those for the third edition.

- Data for Cases 3.3 (Matsushita), 3.4 (Pampers), 3.5 (DaimlerChrysler), 4.1 (Astec), and 4.2 (Children's Hospital) given in the book. These data can be downloaded with ease as either Text (tab delimited) files or SPSS files. SPSS data files are also provided for the data used to illustrate the statistical concepts in Chapters 15 through 21, as well as for the relevant Internet and Computer Exercises in these chapters.

- Two additional comprehensive cases with data. These cases are DuPont carpets (consumer products) and Gucci Catalog (direct marketing). Each case has associated with it: (1) questions for each of the 23 chapters, (2) questionnaire, (3) coding sheet, (4) file extract, (5) data that can be downloaded, and (6) answers to case questions that are contained in a password-protected directory.

- Links to other useful Web sites.

The Web site is being enhanced continually. Please contact your local Prentice Hall representative or me (*naresh.malhotra@mgt.gatech.edu*) to obtain the user id and password.

- Instructor's Manual. Personally written by me, the entire Instructor's Manual is very closely tied to the text. Each chapter contains transparency masters, chapter objectives, author's notes, chapter outlines, teaching suggestions, and answers to all end-of-chapter exercises and activities (questions, problems, Internet and Computer Exercises, role playing, fieldwork, and group discussion). In addition, solutions are provided to all the cases, including those that involve data analysis, as well as all the video cases. The Instructor's Manual also contains the two additional comprehensive cases with data: DuPont carpets (consumer products) and Gucci Catalog (direct marketing). The enclosed disk contains statistical data for Cases 3.3 (Matsushita), 3.4 (Pampers), 3.5 (DaimlerChrysler), 4.1 (Astec), and 4.2 (Children's Hospital) given in the book. It also contains SPSS data files for the data used to illustrate the statistical concepts in Chapters 15 through 21, as well as for the relevant Internet and Computer Exercises in these chapters. The relevant SPSS output files are also included.

- Test Item File. This valuable test item file contains a wide variety of tests for each chapter that allow you to 'create' your own exams.

# Acknowledgments

Several people have been extremely helpful in writing this textbook. I would like to acknowledge Professor Arun K. Jain (State University of New York at Buffalo) who taught me marketing research in a way I will never forget. My students, particularly former doctoral students (James Agarwal, Imad Baalbaki, Ashutosh Dixit, Dan McCort, Rick McFarland, Charla Mathwick, Gina Miller, Mark Peterson, Jamie Pleasant, and Cassandra Wells) as well as other doctoral students (Mark Leach and Tyra Mitchell), have been very helpful in many ways. I particularly want to acknowledge the assistance of Mark Leach and Gina Miller in writing the ethics sections and chapter, the assistance of Mark Peterson in writing the computer applications sections, and the assistance of James Agarwal with the international marketing research examples in the earlier two editions. MBA student David Ball and undergraduate student Charles Flanary provided helpful research assistance. The students in my marketing research courses have provided useful feedback as the material was class tested for several years. My colleagues at Georgia Tech, especially Fred Allvine, have been very supportive. I also want to thank Ronald L. Tatham (chairman, Burke, Inc.) for his encouragement and support and the many contributions from Burke that appear throughout the book. William D. Neal (founder and senior executive officer of SDR, Inc.) has been very helpful and supportive over the years. Roger L. Bacik (Elrick & Lavidge, Inc.) and the other practitioners have contributed to the earlier editions of this book.

The reviewers have provided many constructive and valuable suggestions. Among others, the help of the following reviewers is gratefully acknowledged.

### Reviewers for the fourth edition

Yong-Soon Kang, Binghamton University–SUNY

Curt Dommeyer, California State University–Northridge

John Tsalikis, Florida International University

Gerald Cavallo, Fairfield University–Connecticut

Charles Hofacker, Florida State University

### Reviewers for the third edition

Tom Anastasti, Boston University

John Weiss, Colorado State University

Subash Lonial, University of Louisville

Joel Herche, University of the Pacific

Paul Sauer, Canisius College

### Reviewers for the second edition

Rick Andrews, University of Delaware

Holland Blades, Jr., Missouri Southern State College

Sharmila Chatterjee, Santa Clara University

Rajshekhar Javalgi, Cleveland State University

Mushtaq Luqmani, Western Michigan University

Jeanne Munger, University of Southern Maine

Audesh Paswan, University of South Dakota

Venkatram Ramaswamy, University of Michigan

Gillian Rice, Thunderbird University

Paul L. Sauer, Canisius College

Hans Srinivasan, University of Connecticut

**Reviewers for the first edition**

David M. Andrus, Kansas State University

Joe Ballenger, Stephen F. Austin State University

Joseph D. Brown, Ball State University

Thomas E. Buzas, Eastern Michigan University

Rajendar K. Garg, Northeastern Illinois University

Lawrence D. Gibson, Consultant

Ronald E. Goldsmith, Florida State University

Rajshekhar G. Javalgi, Cleveland State University

Charlotte H. Mason, University of North Carolina

Kent Nakamoto, University of Colorado

Thomas J. Page, Jr., Michigan State University

William S. Perkins, Pennsylvania State University

Sudhi Seshadri, University of Maryland at College Park

David Shani, Baruch College

The team at Prentice Hall provided outstanding support. Special thanks are due to Jeff Shelstad, editor in chief; Wendy Craven, senior acquisitions editor; Anthony Palmiotto, media project manager; Melissa Pellerano, assistant editor; Michelle O'Brien, senior marketing manager; Marcela Maslanczuk, production editor; Danielle R. Serra, editorial assistant; Lynn Steines, copy editor; and Teri Stratford, photo editor. Special recognition is due to the several field representatives and sales people who have done an outstanding job in marketing the book.

I want to acknowledge with great respect my mother Mrs. Satya Malhotra and my departed father Mr. H. N. Malhotra. Their love, encouragement, support, and the sacrificial giving of themselves have been exemplary. My heartfelt love and gratitude go to my wife Veena and my children Ruth and Paul for their faith, hope, and love.

Most of all, I want to acknowledge and thank my Savior and Lord, Jesus Christ, for the many miracles He has performed in my life. This book is, truly, the result of His grace—"This is the Lord's doing; it is marvelous in our eyes" (Psalm 118: 23).

Naresh K. Malhotra

# Author Biography

Dr. Naresh K. Malhotra is Regents' Professor (highest academic rank in the university system of Georgia), DuPree College of Management, Georgia Institute of Technology. He has been listed in Marquis *Who's Who in America* continuously since the 51st edition in 1997, and in *Who's Who in the World* since 2000.

In an article by Wheatley and Wilson (1987 AMA Educators' Proceedings), Professor Malhotra was ranked number one in the country based on articles published in the *Journal of Marketing Research* during 1980 to 1985. He also holds the all-time record for the maximum number of publications in the *Journal of Health Care Marketing*. He is ranked number one based on publications in the *Journal of the Academy of Marketing Science* (JAMS) since its inception through Volume 23, 1995. He is also number one based on publications in JAMS during the ten-year period from 1986 to 1995.

He has published more than ninety (90) papers in major refereed journals, including the *Journal of Marketing Research, Journal of Consumer Research, Marketing Science, Journal of Marketing, Journal of Academy of Marketing Science, Journal of Retailing, Journal of Health Care Marketing,* and leading journals in statistics, management science, and psychology. In addition, he has also published numerous refereed articles in the proceedings of major national and international conferences. Several articles have received best paper research awards.

He was Chairman, Academy of Marketing Science Foundation, 1996 to 1998; President, Academy of Marketing Science, 1994 to 1996; and Chairman, Board of Governors, 1990 to 1992. He is a Distinguished Fellow of the Academy and Fellow, Decision Sciences Institute. He served as an Associate Editor of *Decision Sciences* for 18 years and has served as Section Editor, Health Care Marketing Abstracts, *Journal of Health Care Marketing*. Also, he serves on the editorial boards of eight (8) journals.

His book entitled *Marketing Research: An Applied Orientation* is a leader in the field. This book has been translated into five languages: Chinese, Russian, Spanish, Portuguese, and Hungarian. Moreover, it has been published in four English editions: North American, International, European, and Australian. The book has received widespread adoption at both the graduate and undergraduate levels with more than 144 schools using it in the United States. His latest book, *Basic Marketing Research: Application to Contemporary Issues,* was published by Prentice Hall in 2002.

Dr. Malhotra has consulted for business, nonprofit, and government organizations in the United States and abroad and has served as an expert witness in legal and regulatory proceedings. He has special expertise in data analysis and statistical methods. He is the winner of numerous awards and honors for research, teaching, and service to the profession.

Dr. Malhotra is a member and deacon, First Baptist Church, Atlanta. He lives in the Atlanta area with his wife Veena and children Ruth and Paul.

# Introduction and Early Phases of Marketing Research

*In this part we discuss the nature and scope of marketing research and explain its role in decision support systems. We describe the marketing research industry and the many exciting career opportunities in this field. We set out a six-step marketing research process and discuss problem definition, the first and the most important step, in detail. Finally, we describe the development of an approach to the problem, the second step in the marketing research process, and discuss in detail the various components of the approach. The perspective given in these chapters should be useful to both the decision maker and the marketing researcher.*

# CHAPTER 1

# Introduction to Marketing Research

"The role of a marketing researcher must include consulting skills, technical proficiency, and sound management. The focus of the role is to provide information to identify marketing problems and solutions in such a way that action can be taken."

*Ron Tatham, chairman,*
*Burke, Inc.*

## Objectives

After reading this chapter, the student should be able to:

1. Define marketing research and distinguish between problem identification and problem solving research.
2. Describe a framework for conducting marketing research as well as the six steps of the marketing research process.
3. Understand the nature and scope of marketing research and its role in designing and implementing successful marketing programs.
4. Discuss the types and roles of research suppliers including internal, external, full-service, and limited-service suppliers.
5. Describe careers available in marketing research and the backgrounds and skills needed to succeed in them.
6. Explain the role of marketing research in decision support systems in providing data, marketing models, and specialized software.
7. Acquire an appreciation of the international dimension and the complexity involved in international marketing research.
8. Gain an understanding of the ethical aspects of marketing research and the responsibilities each of the marketing research stakeholders have to themselves, each other, and the research project.
9. Explain how the Internet and computers can facilitate the marketing research process.

Marketing research comprises one of the most important and fascinating facets of marketing. In this chapter, we give a formal definition of marketing research and classify marketing research into two areas: problem identification and problem solving research. We provide several real-life examples to illustrate the basic concepts of marketing research. We describe the marketing research process and the six steps that are involved in conducting research and discuss the nature of marketing research, emphasizing its role of providing information for marketing decision making. Next we provide an overview of marketing research suppliers and services, along with guidelines for selecting a supplier. The demand for well-executed marketing research leads to many exciting career opportunities, which are presented. We show that marketing research is also an integral part of marketing information systems or decision support systems.

For the purpose of illustration, we examine the department store patronage project, which was an actual marketing research project conducted by the author, and it is used as a running example throughout the book. The topic of international marketing research is introduced and discussed systematically in the subsequent chapters. The ethical aspects of marketing research and the responsibilities each of the marketing research stakeholders have to themselves, each other, and the research project are presented and developed in more detail throughout the text. This chapter concludes with an applications-oriented discussion on the use of the Internet and computers in marketing research, another emphasis that pervades the entire book. Perhaps there is no better way to present an overview than to give a few examples that provide a flavor of the varied nature of marketing research.

## REAL RESEARCH

### IBM: Trekking on a Global Track

IBM (*www.ibm.com*), with 2001 revenues of $85.86 billion, conducts an international tracking study twice a year in 14 different languages across 27 different countries in Europe, North and South America, and Asia. The basic purpose of the study is to capture trend data on mainframe computing. It samples one out of every six sites where an IBM S/390 Enterprise Server is in use. The respondents surveyed are those responsible for IBM acquisition decisions at their respective companies. They are asked about their installed computing equipment, their future plans for acquiring equipment, and their views on various vendors. The survey allows IBM to track how they are doing on an ongoing basis. The questions are kept broad and are not used to determine a deeper understanding of customer wants but instead only to track overall trends. The information collected via this tracking survey becomes part of IBM's decision support system.

IBM utilizes the RONIN Corporation (*www.ronin.com*), a New Jersey-based research firm, to handle the interviewing and data collection process. RONIN conducts all interviews by telephone for this study at its international call center in London. Because the study is international, RONIN deals with such issues as accurate translations and receiving consistent results across countries and languages while rapidly turning results around. They must also communicate that results are representative only for specific countries, not for entire regions.

The results of such a study allow IBM to see how successful it is in penetrating key industries and how IBM equipment is used in large and small businesses across nations. These results are passed to the IBM sales force in each of the countries, where they provide their interpretation of the results and incorporate these results with their own field experiences to develop lists of the top 10 issues that they are experiencing in the field.

This tracking study is an example of Problem Identification Research. IBM is seeking to identify possible problems, such as respondents indicating that they have no plans for future equipment acquisitions from IBM, problems with maintenance service, or low customer satisfaction. Any problems that are identified are investigated further by using problem solving

International marketing research has enabled IBM to introduce innovative new products and services such as the eServer Z-series.

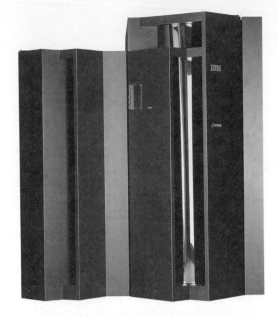

research with the objective of arriving at solutions. For example, low ratings on maintenance service, when investigated further, revealed that expectations of customers had increased, leading IBM to raise its service standards. The tracking study identified a new problem (or opportunity) when it revealed potential demand for Linux-driven mainframes. Based on subsequent problem solution research that investigated product preferences, in late January 2002, IBM introduced two new Linux-driven servers and a Linux-only mainframe computer that requires no traditional mainframe operating system. The eServer Z-Series uses the mainframe computer's ability to create up to hundreds of virtual Linux servers on only one physical box. IBM said the new mainframe will save energy and floor space and will reduce maintenance costs, thus addressing these needs identified in the tracking study. Non-Linux mainframe computers typically cost $750,000, whereas the new Z-Series mainframe computers cost $350,000.[1] ■

## REAL RESEARCH

### *Recipio Puts Research in Real Time*

Many of the nation's largest corporations are realizing that the information they can get from clients and customers through marketing research can best be used if it is provided each day. How about each minute? This is the basis upon which a company called Recipio (*www.recipio.com*) operates—real time. Recipio is a two-year-old application service provider that gives its clients the ability to view customer feedback the second it is entered on their Web sites. Not only can customers get online and submit complaints and suggestions to a company, but Recipio also hosts live chat sessions for users of certain products. All of this is done with the aim of capturing the true words and emotions of consumers, and in turn using this information to improve or develop products and services. Recipio capitalizes on the need for "live" marketing research.

As of 2003, the Internet continues to revolutionize the marketing research process. With the use of online services, there is no need for extra data input as is needed with traditional research methods. Recipio itself is not the traditional full-service supplier of marketing research. As a standardized limited-service provider, the company does not get involved with every aspect of the research process. The approach, design, and data preparation are the same for each customer, and these are the parts of the research process with which the company is involved.

Their service, however, aids clients in identifying any problems with products through customer feedback and with problem solving, especially if customers give suggestions. For example, the network station NBC (*www.nbc.com*) takes advantage of Recipio's services in order to obtain feedback from viewers. It helps the network to learn what viewers are looking for, their likes, and their dislikes. Ideally, the feedback is used and television shows are altered to more closely suit the tastes and desires of the viewers, thus leading to an increased number of people tuning in to watch the shows. NBC found that viewers wanted a sitcom that was lighthearted, clever, and humorous; therefore "Will and Grace" was created to fulfill viewers' tastes and premiered September 21, 1998. Viewer feedback provided by Recipio has been instrumental in composing and modifying scripts and storylines. As a result, in 2002, "Will and Grace" was a top-rated comedy show on NBC.[2]

As of March 13, 2002, Recipio became an acquired asset of Informative (*www.informative. com*). Informative was founded in 1996 and utilizes the Internet, e-mail, mobile communications, and other channels to obtain real-time feedback directly from customers and prospects. ■

### REAL RESEARCH

## *PortiCo Documents with Documentaries*

PortiCo Research (*www.porticoresearch.com*) specializes in observing individuals, recording them on videos, and selling these tapes for tens of thousands of dollars to its major clients, such as Honda, Delta, Lipton, and Procter & Gamble. They have fine-tuned the method of collecting observational data and have made it into a very profitable business.

"PortiCo's specialty is total immersion in the lives of consumers in an effort to document how they make purchasing decisions." Research teams of anthropologists, social psychologists, and ethnographers (professionals who comparatively study people) go into the subjects' homes with videographers. The teams tape the subjects in their homes and also take shopping trips with them to watch what they buy and get feedback on the reasons for their purchases. After filming, employees of PortiCo analyze the videos for their clients.

Their in-depth analysis is based on the research problem that the client intends to solve or get more information about. For example, PortiCo did an extensive study for Lipton (*www.lipton.com*) to determine people's attitudes towards tea. With the results of the study, Lipton would decide whether or not to invest more in advertising, develop new flavors, or market more iced tea instead of hot tea. The findings showed that Americans do not drink much hot tea. If and when they do drink hot tea, it is normally flavored herbal tea. Most of Lipton's hot tea was not available in special flavors, but subsequently they introduced more herbal teas to the market. The study also found that American consumers like iced tea. As a result of these findings, Lipton has done several creative developments in the area of iced tea. They vigorously marketed Brisk Iced Tea in the can, which has become the number one selling brand of ready-to-drink iced tea. Also, Lipton has created a Cold Brew Blend tea bag in both family size to make a whole pitcher and single glass size for one serving. This tea bag allows iced tea to be brewed with cold water instead of boiling water. Therefore, consumers can enjoy their tea faster with much less hassle. These marketing efforts, guided by the findings of PortiCo Research, have resulted in increased sales and market share for Lipton.[3] ■

Lipton developed the Cold Brew Blend when marketing research revealed that consumers wanted an iced tea that could be brewed with cold water instead of boiling water.

**REAL RESEARCH**

## Teens, Toejam, and P&G: Marketing and Marketing Research Go Hand in Hand

What do teens have to do with Toejam? Hopefully, a lot, according to the multinational giant Procter and Gamble (*www.pg.com*). In 2003, P&G marketed approximately 250 brands to five billion consumers in more than 130 countries worldwide, and its 2002 revenues exceeded $40 billion. Toejam (Teens Openly Expressing Just About Me) is a Web site created by P&G to target teens (*www.toejam.com*). This Web site was designed to assist with marketing research efforts, as well as with the marketing of products. P&G hopes to use these new approaches to marketing research to meet its goal of "identifying and leveraging the influence of 'teen chat leaders' to market products." The Toejam Web site has sections for members to submit essays and stories on particular topics. Members are selected to participate in both research and word-of-mouth marketing campaigns and rewarded with merchandise. Teens also receive prizes, including P&G product samples.

This Web site allows P&G executives to get into the minds of teenagers, a very lucrative market to penetrate. Through the essays and stories submitted on the Toejam site, the company is able to find out trends and topics of interest to young people. This way, the company can define marketing research problems with the help of teenagers. The Web site is very flexible as far as research methods are concerned. Surveys are offered, chat rooms act as focus groups, and other qualitative research is conducted. In a sense, teenagers are industry experts in their own right, and the information that P&G has, and will continue to receive, will be very beneficial to the company.

Additionally, P&G has received valuable feedback on the products that they send as prizes to the girls who register on the Toejam site. The company sent out samples of hairspray from its Physique line of hair care products. With the gift, the company sent a card requesting comments on the product's performance and packaging. The comments returned to the company revealed that most girls who tried the product liked the sleek silver styling of the package, but felt that the hairspray weighed their hair down too much and left flakes in the hair once the product dried. In response to the complaints, P&G recently introduced "new and improved" Physique products with "less flaking" and a lighter hold for the hairstyle. One extra benefit that P&G did not initially realize when sending the products as gifts is the influence girls have with their friends. Girls share their makeup and cosmetics. Once a girl likes a product and uses it, her friends will see it and most likely end up buying it for themselves, resulting in increased sales. Thus, for P&G, marketing research and marketing go hand in hand leading to innovative research, effective marketing, and increased sales.[4] ■

These examples illustrate the crucial role played by marketing research in designing and implementing successful marketing programs.[5] Note that marketing research is being used by all kinds of organizations, such as IBM, NBC, Lipton, and P&G. Furthermore, marketing research has become global (RONIN) and real time (Recipio), is being conducted in a specialized manner (PortiCo), and has become much more integrated with marketing (P&G). These examples illustrate only a few of the methods used to conduct marketing research: telephone, personal and Internet surveys, one-on-one depth interviews, and the use of the Internet as a source of information. This book will introduce you to the full complement of marketing research techniques and illustrate their applications in formulating effective marketing strategies. Perhaps the role of marketing research can be better understood in light of its definition.

# DEFINITION OF MARKETING RESEARCH

The American Marketing Association formally defines marketing research as:

**REAL RESEARCH**

## The American Marketing Association Redefines Marketing Research

The Board of Directors of the American Marketing Association has approved the following as the new definition of marketing research:

Marketing research is the function that links the consumer, customer, and public to the marketer through information—information used to identify and define marketing opportunities and problems; generate, refine, and evaluate marketing actions; monitor marketing performance; and improve understanding of marketing as a process.

Marketing research specifies the information required to address these issues, designs the method for collecting information, manages and implements the data collection process, analyzes the results, and communicates the findings and their implications.[6]

As of 2003, the American Marketing Association has implemented a Web site called MarketingPower (*www.marketingpower.com*). This Web site supplies marketing professionals with information on things such as marketing careers, "Best Practices" articles, and industry trends. ■

**marketing research**

The systematic and objective identification, collection, analysis, dissemination, and use of information for the purpose of assisting management in decision making related to the identification and solution of problems (and opportunities) in marketing.

For the purpose of this book, which emphasizes the need for information for decision making, marketing research is defined as follows:

***Marketing research*** is the systematic and objective identification, collection, analysis, dissemination, and use of information for the purpose of improving decision making related to the identification and solution of problems and opportunities in marketing.

Several aspects of this definition are noteworthy. First, marketing research is systematic. Thus, systematic planning is required at all stages of the *marketing research* process. The procedures followed at each stage are methodologically sound, well documented, and, as much as possible, planned in advance. Marketing research uses the scientific method in that data are collected and analyzed to test prior notions or hypotheses.

Marketing research attempts to provide accurate information that reflects a true state of affairs. It is objective and should be conducted impartially. Although research is always influenced by the researcher's philosophy, it should be free from the personal or political biases of the researcher or the management. Research that is motivated by personal or political gain involves a breach of professional standards. Such research is deliberately biased so as to result in predetermined findings. The motto of every researcher should be, "Find it and tell it like it is."

Marketing research involves the identification, collection, analysis, dissemination, and use of information. Each phase of this process is important. We identify or define the marketing research problem or opportunity and then determine what information is needed to investigate it. Because every marketing opportunity translates into a research problem to be investigated, the terms "problem" and "opportunity" are used interchangeably here. Next, the relevant information sources are identified and a range of data collection methods varying in sophistication and complexity are evaluated for their usefulness. The data are collected using the most appropriate method; they are analyzed and interpreted, and inferences are drawn. Finally, the findings, implications, and recommendations are provided in a format that allows the information to be used for marketing decision making and to be acted upon directly. The next section elaborates on this definition by classifying different types of marketing research.[7]

# A CLASSIFICATION OF MARKETING RESEARCH

Our definition states that organizations engage in marketing research for two reasons: (1) to identify and (2) to solve marketing problems. This distinction serves as a basis for classifying marketing research into problem identification research and problem solving research, as shown in Figure 1.1.

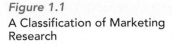

*Figure 1.1*
A Classification of Marketing
Research

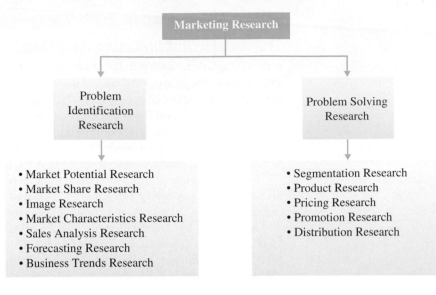

**problem identification research**
Research that is undertaken to help
identify problems that are not necessarily apparent on the surface and
yet exist or are likely to arise in the
future.

**Problem identification research** is undertaken to help identify problems that are, perhaps, not apparent on the surface and yet exist or are likely to arise in the future. Examples of problem identification research include market potential, market share, brand or company image, market characteristics, sales analysis, short-range forecasting, long-range forecasting, and business trends research. A survey of companies conducting marketing research indicated that 97 percent of those who responded were conducting market potential, market share, and market characteristics research. About 90 percent also reported that they were using other types of problem identification research. Research of this type provides information about the marketing environment and helps diagnose a problem. For example, a declining market potential indicates that the firm is likely to have a problem achieving its growth targets. Similarly, a problem exists if the market potential is increasing but the firm is losing market share. The recognition of economic, social, or cultural trends, such as changes in consumer behavior, may point to underlying problems or opportunities.[8]

**problem solving research**
Research undertaken to help solve
specific marketing problems.

Once a problem or opportunity has been identified, **problem solving research** is undertaken to arrive at a solution. The findings of problem solving research are used in making decisions that will solve specific marketing problems. Most companies conduct problem solving research.[9] Table 1.1 shows the different types of issues that are addressed

---

### TABLE 1.1

**Problem Solving Research**

*Segmentation Research*

determine basis of segmentation
establish market potential and responsiveness for various segments
select target markets and create lifestyle profiles, demography, media, and product image
    characteristics

| *Product Research* | *Promotional Research* |
| --- | --- |
| test concept | optimal promotional budget |
| optimal product design | sales promotion relationship |
| package tests | optimal promotional mix |
| product modification | copy decisions |
| brand positioning and repositioning | media decisions |
| test marketing | creative advertising testing |
| control store tests | claim substantiation |
| *Pricing Research* | evaluation of advertising effectiveness |
| importance of price in brand | *Distribution Research* |
|    selection | type of distribution |
| pricing policies | attitudes of channel members |
| product line pricing | intensity of wholesale and retail coverage |
| price elasticity of demand | channel margins |
| response to price changes | location of retail and wholesale outlets |

by problem solving research, including segmentation, product, pricing, promotion, and distribution research.

Classifying marketing research into two main types is useful from a conceptual as well as a practical viewpoint. However, problem identification research and problem solving research go hand in hand, and a given marketing research project may combine both types of research. This was illustrated in the opening IBM example. The tracking study identified potential demand for Linux-driven mainframes (problem identification). Subsequent research led to the introduction of two new Linux-driven servers and a Linux-only mainframe computer (problem solving). Kellogg's provides another example.

---

**REAL RESEARCH**

## Crunchy Nut Red Adds Color to Kellogg's Sales

Kellogg's (*www.kelloggs.com*), with 2001 annual revenues of $8.85 billion, was faced with a slump in the market and faced the challenge of reviving low cereal sales. Through problem identification research, Kellogg's was able to identify the problem, and through problem solving research, develop several solutions to increase cereal sales.

Kellogg's performed several tasks to identify the problem. The researchers spoke to decision makers within the company, interviewed industry experts, conducted analysis of available data, performed some qualitative research, and surveyed consumers about their perceptions and preferences for cereals. Several important issues or problems were identified by this research. Current products were being targeted to kids, bagels and muffins were winning for favored breakfast foods, and high prices were turning consumers to generic brands. Some other information also came to light during the research. Adults wanted quick foods that required very little or no preparation. These issues helped Kellogg's identify the problem. It was not being creative in introducing new products to meet the needs of the adult market.

After defining the problem, Kellogg's went to work on solutions. It developed and tested several new flavors of cereals using mall intercept interviews with adult consumers. Based on the results, Kellogg's introduced new flavors that were more suited to the adult palette but were not the tasteless varieties of the past. For example, it introduced Crunchy Nut Red in 2001. This new cereal includes cranberry fruit pieces, almonds, and yogurt flavored flakes. The new cereal was supported by a national television ad campaign, major in-store promotions, and 2 million specially produced sachets for a nationwide sampling campaign. Based on consumer trials, Kellogg's stated that the new cereal scored very high, returning one of the best research results ever for a new Kellogg's cereal.

Kellogg's partnered with the 2002 U.S. Olympic Team and the 2002 Olympic Winter Games. The company distributed Olympic-themed packages, products, and promotional offers in grocery stores as a way to welcome the Winter Games back to the United States. Through creative problem identification research followed by problem solving research, Kellogg's has not only seen an increase in sales, but also in increased consumption of cereal at times other than just breakfast.[10] ∎

Problem identification and problem solving research not only go hand in hand as shown by the Kellogg's example, but they also follow a common marketing research process.

# MARKETING RESEARCH PROCESS

**marketing research process**
A set of six steps that defines the tasks to be accomplished in conducting a marketing research study. These include problem definition, development of an approach to the problem, research design formulation, field work, data preparation and analysis, and report preparation and presentation.

We conceptualize the **marketing research process** as consisting of six steps. Each of these steps is discussed in great detail in the subsequent chapters; thus, the discussion here is brief.

## Step 1: Problem Definition

The first step in any marketing research project is to define the problem. In defining the problem, the researcher should take into account the purpose of the study, the relevant background information, the information needed, and how it will be used in decision making. Problem definition involves discussion with the decision makers, interviews with industry experts, analysis of secondary data, and, perhaps, some qualitative research, such as focus groups. Once the problem has been precisely defined, the research can be designed and conducted properly. (See Chapter 2.)

## Step 2: Development of an Approach to the Problem

Development of an approach to the problem includes formulating an objective or theoretical framework, analytical models, research questions, and hypotheses and identifying the information needed. This process is guided by discussions with management and industry experts, analysis of secondary data, qualitative research, and pragmatic considerations. (See Chapter 2.)

## Step 3: Research Design Formulation

A research design is a framework or blueprint for conducting the marketing research project. It details the procedures necessary for obtaining the required information, and its purpose is to design a study that will test the hypotheses of interest, determine possible answers to the research questions, and provide the information needed for decision making. Conducting exploratory research, precisely defining the variables, and designing appropriate scales to measure them are also a part of the research design. The issue of how the data should be obtained from the respondents (for example, by conducting a survey or an experiment) must be addressed. It is also necessary to design a questionnaire and a sampling plan to select respondents for the study. More formally, formulating the research design involves the following steps:

1. Definition of the information needed
2. Secondary data analysis
3. Qualitative research
4. Methods of collecting quantitative data (survey, observation, and experimentation)
5. Measurement and scaling procedures
6. Questionnaire design
7. Sampling process and sample size
8. Plan of data analysis

These steps are discussed in detail in Chapters 3 through 12.

## Step 4: Fieldwork or Data Collection

Data collection involves a field force or staff that operates either in the field, as in the case of personal interviewing (in-home, mall intercept, or computer-assisted personal interviewing), from an office by telephone (telephone or computer-assisted telephone interviewing), through mail (traditional mail and mail panel surveys with prerecruited households), or electronically (e-mail or Internet). Proper selection, training, supervision, and evaluation of the field force helps minimize data-collection errors. (See Chapter 13.)

## Step 5: Data Preparation and Analysis

Data preparation includes the editing, coding, transcription, and verification of data. Each questionnaire or observation form is inspected or edited and, if necessary, corrected. Number or letter codes are assigned to represent each response to each question in the questionnaire. The data from the questionnaires are transcribed or keypunched onto magnetic tape or disks, or input directly into the computer. The data are analyzed to derive information related to the components of the marketing research problem and, thus, provide input in to the management decision problem. (See Chapters 14 through 21.)

## Step 6: Report Preparation and Presentation

The entire project should be documented in a written report that addresses the specific research questions identified, describes the approach, the research design, data collection, and data analysis procedures adopted, and presents the results and the major findings. The findings should be presented in a comprehensible format so that management can readily use them in the decision making process. In addition, an oral presentation should be made to management using tables, figures, and graphs to enhance clarity and impact. (See Chapter 22.)

As indicated by the following example, our description of the marketing research process is fairly typical of the research being done by major corporations.

### REAL RESEARCH

### *Marketing Research at Marriott Corporation*

Marriott International (*www.marriott.com*) is a leading hospitality company with more than 2,100 properties located in 50 states and 59 countries as of 2003. Marriott functions in many areas that include brands such as Marriott, Renaissance, Courtyard, Residence Inn, Fairfield Inn, Towneplace Suites, Springhill Suites, and Ramada International.

Marketing research at Marriott is done at the corporate level through the Corporate Marketing Services (CMS). CMS's goals include providing managers of the different areas of Marriott with the information that they need to better understand the market and the customer.

CMS does many different types of research. It uses quantitative and qualitative research approaches such as telephone and mail surveys, focus groups, and customer intercepts to gain more information on market segmentation, product testing, price sensitivity of consumers, consumer satisfaction, and the like.

The process of research at Marriott is a simple stepwise progression. The first steps are to better define the problem to be addressed and the objectives of the client unit and to develop an approach to the problem. The next step is to design the study by formulating a formal research design. CMS must decide whether to do its own research or to buy it from an outside organization. Also it must decide whether or not to use multiple firms in the latter case. Once a decision is made, the data are collected and analyzed. Then CMS presents the study findings to the client unit in a formal report. The final step in the research process is to keep a constant dialogue between the client and CMS. During this stage, CMS may help explain the implications of the research findings, assist in decision making, or make suggestions for future research.[11] ▪

# THE NATURE OF MARKETING RESEARCH

The nature and role of marketing research can be better understood in light of the basic marketing paradigm depicted in Figure 1.2.

The emphasis in marketing is on the identification and satisfaction of customer needs. In order to determine customer needs and to implement marketing strategies and programs aimed at satisfying those needs, marketing managers need information. They need information about customers, competitors, and other forces in the marketplace. In recent years, many factors have increased the need for more and better information. As firms have become national and international in scope, the need for information on larger and more distant markets has increased. As consumers have become more affluent and sophisticated, marketing managers need better information on how they will respond to products and other marketing offerings. As competition has become more intense, managers need information on the effectiveness of their marketing tools. As the environment is changing more rapidly, marketing managers need more timely information.[12]

The task of marketing research is to assess the information needs and provide management with relevant, accurate, reliable, valid, and current information. Today's competitive marketing environment and the ever increasing costs attributed to poor decision making require marketing research to provide sound information. Sound

*Figure 1.2*
The Role of Marketing Research

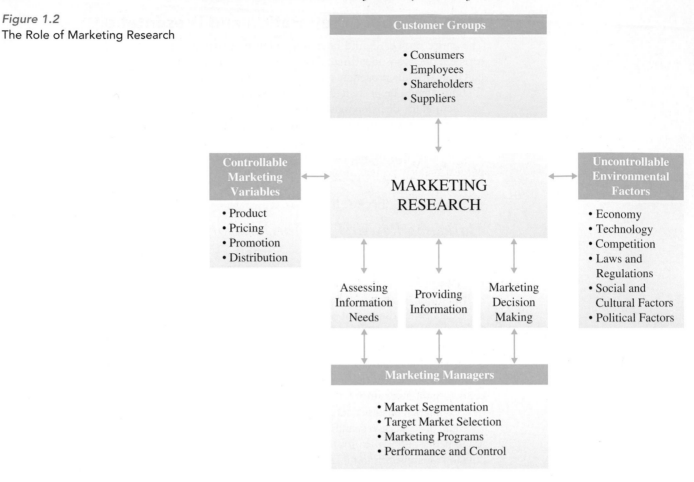

decisions are not based on gut feeling, intuition, or even pure judgment. In the absence of sound information, an incorrect management decision may result, as illustrated by the case of Johnson & Johnson baby aspirin.

### REAL RESEARCH

## J & J's Gentleness Could Not Handle Pain

Johnson & Johnson (*www.jnj.com*) is considered to be the world's most broadly based manufacturer of health care products with more than 190 operating companies selling products in more than 175 countries as of 2003. Despite its success in the industry, Johnson & Johnson's attempt to use its company name on baby aspirin proved to be unsuccessful. Johnson & Johnson products are perceived as gentle, but gentleness is not what people want in a baby aspirin. Although baby aspirin should be safe, gentleness per se is not a desirable feature. Rather, some people perceived that a gentle aspirin may not be effective enough. This is an example of what intuitively seemed to be a natural move but without proper marketing research turned out to be an incorrect decision.[13] ■

As indicated by the Johnson & Johnson example, marketing managers make numerous strategic and tactical decisions in the process of identifying and satisfying customer needs. As shown in Figure 1.2, they make decisions about potential opportunities, target market selection, market segmentation, planning and implementing marketing programs, marketing performance, and control. These decisions are complicated by interactions between the controllable marketing variables of product, pricing, promotion, and distribution. Further complications are added by uncontrollable environmental factors such as general economic conditions, technology, public policies and laws, political environment, competition, and social and cultural changes. Another factor in this mix is the complexity of the various customer groups: consumers, employees, shareholders, suppliers, etc. Marketing research helps the marketing manager link the marketing variables with the environment and the customer groups. It helps remove some of the uncertainty by providing relevant information about the marketing variables, environment, and consumers. In the absence of relevant information, consumers' response to marketing programs cannot be predicted reliably or accurately. Ongoing marketing research programs provide information on controllable and noncontrollable factors and consumers; this information enhances the effectiveness of decisions made by marketing managers.[14]

Traditionally, marketing researchers were responsible for assessing information needs and providing the relevant information, whereas marketing decisions were made by the managers. However, these roles are changing and marketing researchers are becoming more involved in decision making, whereas marketing managers are becoming more involved with research. This trend can be attributed to better training of marketing managers, the Internet and other advances in technology, and a shift in the marketing research paradigm where more and more marketing research is being undertaken on an ongoing basis rather than in response to specific marketing problems or opportunities. As illustrated by the P&G example in the overview and by the following example, marketing and marketing research are becoming more and more integrated.[15]

## REAL RESEARCH

### Reviving an Ailing Giant

DaimlerChrysler (*www.daimlerchrysler.com*) is the number three carmaker in the world with sales of $146.76 billion in 2001. In the early 1980s, Chrysler (*www.chrysler.com*) was fighting for survival. Fortunately, a few years earlier, two men had come to the company from Ford. These men were Lee Iacocca and Howard Sperlich, and they brought with them a revolutionary idea—the minivan.

Iacocca, a senior manager, and Sperlich, a designer, used marketing research to identify a need—better family transportation. Despite skyrocketing fuel prices in the early 1980s, "overpowering" research in the form of focus groups, mall intercept, and mail surveys suggested that consumers wanted a van that handled like a car. A Chrysler executive stated that "the people we're selling [the minivan] to don't tow. A very small percentage of Americans on a regular basis tow more than a Class 1 trailer; we can tow a Class 1 trailer." It was clear that the public did not need a workhorse vehicle, but a reliable, spacious, and convenient mode of transportation.

Marketing research revealed that a minivan met these characteristics. As a result, Chrysler stunned the competition with an innovative new product that eventually was dubbed an automotive "home run" for the company. Chrysler designed its product around the consumer rather than the internal perceptions of the organization. Marketing research

Marketing research helped Chrysler to identify the minivan market and develop and market products targeted at this segment.

gave the company the confidence to enter a market that GM and Ford considered too risky. GM and Ford missed the opportunity to bring the minivan to market. GM feared it would detract from its highly lucrative station wagon segment. Ford passed this opportunity and instead decided to focus on smaller, more fuel-efficient models.

Chrysler, in contrast, developed a strong linkage between the consumer problem and the product solution. About 25 years later, the company's product line still accounts for about one-quarter of Chrysler's sales and a significant portion of its profits. Marketing research that brought the minivan to market has revitalized the once ailing car manufacturer.

In 1998, Chrysler merged with Daimler-Benz creating a $35 billion company, DaimlerChrysler. However, the company continued to rely on marketing research to develop targeted products. In 2001, DaimlerChrysler introduced a power-operated rear liftgate for its minivans to aid shorter drivers. As of 2002, dual sliding doors were available on most mini-van models as well as power-operated sliding doors, and they were also offering pressure-based tire monitors for 2003 for those interested in safety and money conservation.[16] ∎

As shown by the experience of DaimlerChrysler, marketing research can greatly enhance the information available to management. In obtaining specific marketing information, management may also rely on marketing research suppliers and services.

## MARKETING RESEARCH SUPPLIERS AND SERVICES

**internal supplier**
Marketing research departments located within a firm.

Marketing research suppliers and services provide most of the information needed for making marketing decisions. Figure 1.3 classifies marketing research suppliers and services. Broadly, research suppliers can be classified as internal or external. An ***internal supplier*** is a marketing research department within the firm. Many firms, particularly the big ones, ranging from automobile companies (GM, Ford, DaimlerChrysler) to consumer products firms (Procter & Gamble, Colgate Palmolive, Coca-Cola) to banks (Citicorp, Bank of America) maintain in-house marketing research departments. The marketing research department's place in the organizational structure may vary considerably. At one extreme, the research function may be centralized and located at the corporate headquarters. At the other extreme is a decentralized structure in which the marketing research function is organized along divisional lines. In a decentralized scheme, the company may be organized into divisions by products, customers, or geographical regions, with marketing research personnel assigned to the various divisions. These personnel generally report to a division manager rather than to a corporate-level executive. In addition, between these two extremes, there are different types of organizations. The best organization for a firm

**Figure 1.3**
Marketing Research Suppliers and Services

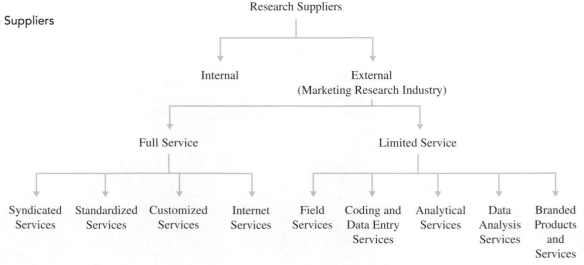

depends on its marketing research needs and the structure of marketing and other functions, although in recent years there has been a trend toward centralization and a trimming of the marketing research staff. Internal suppliers often rely on external suppliers to perform specific marketing research tasks. The following example illustrates the organization of the marketing research function at Oscar Mayer.

**REAL RESEARCH**

## Organization of Marketing Research at Oscar Mayer

Oscar Mayer (*www.oscarmayer.com*) is a division of Kraft Foods (*www.kraftfoods.com*). The Oscar Mayer Marketing Research department is organized into two functional areas: Brand Research and Marketing Systems and Analytics (MSA).

The Brand Research group has the following responsibilities:

- Conducting primary and secondary research
- Serving as marketing consultants
- Analyzing market trends
- Advancing the state of the art in marketing research

Researchers in the MSA group fulfill three main roles:

- Performing sales analysis based on shipment and store scanner data
- Supporting computer end users within the marketing department
- Serving as a source of marketing information

This organizational structure enabled the marketing research department to provide strong support to the marketing function, which also allowed Oscar Mayer to introduce several innovative products over the years and develop a strong bond with consumers. For example, based on market research, they discovered that as kids grow older, it becomes harder to satisfy their growing appetites and active lifestyles. Therefore, in 2001, Oscar Mayer introduced a new line of lunchables called Mega Pack Lunch Combinations. This new addition caters to 10-to-12-year-olds, and provides 40 percent more food than regular lunchables. The product met with instant success as it fulfilled a need in the marketplace.[17] ■

**external suppliers**
Outside marketing research companies hired to supply marketing research data.

**full-service suppliers**
Companies that offer the full range of marketing research activities.

**syndicated services**
Companies that collect and sell common pools of data designed to serve information needs shared by a number of clients.

**standardized services**
Companies that use standardized procedures to provide marketing research to various clients.

**External suppliers** are outside firms hired to supply marketing research data. These external suppliers, which collectively comprise the marketing research industry, range from small, one or a few persons, operations to very large global corporations.[18] Table 1.2 lists the top 50 U.S. research suppliers.[19] External suppliers can be classified as full-service or limited-service suppliers. **Full-service suppliers** offer the entire range of marketing research services, from problem definition, approach development, questionnaire design, sampling, data collection, data analysis, and interpretation, to report preparation and presentation. The services provided by these suppliers can be further broken down into syndicated services, standardized services, customized services, and Internet services (Figure 1.3).

**Syndicated services** collect information of known commercial value that they provide to multiple clients on a subscription basis. Surveys, diary panels, scanners, and audits are the main means by which these data are collected. For example, the Nielsen Television Index by Nielsen Media Research (*www.nielsenmedia.com*) provides information on audience size and demographic characteristics of households watching specific television programs. The ACNielsen Company (*www.acnielsen.com*) provides scanner volume tracking data, such as those generated by electronic scanning at checkout counters in supermarkets. The NPD group (*www.npd.com*) maintains one of the largest consumer panels in the United States. Syndicated services are discussed in more detail in Chapter 4.[20]

**Standardized services** are research studies conducted for different client firms but in a standard way. For example, procedures for measuring advertising effectiveness have been standardized so that the results can be compared across studies and evaluative norms can be established. The Starch Readership Survey conducted by RoperASW (*www.roperasw.com*) is the most widely used service for evaluating print advertisements; another well-known

## TABLE 1.2

### Top 50 U.S. Research Organizations

| U.S. Rank 2001 | U.S. Rank 2000 | Organization | Headquarters | Web Site | Worldwide Research Revenues* ($, in millions) | Non-U.S. Research Revenues* ($, in millions) | Percent Non-U.S. Revenues |
|---|---|---|---|---|---|---|---|
| 1 | 2 | VNU Inc. | New York | vnu.com | $2,400.0 | $1,100.0 | 45.8% |
| 2 | 3 | IMS Health Inc. | Fairfield, CT | imshealth.com | 1,171.0 | 702.0 | 60.0 |
| 3 | 4 | Information Resources Inc. | Chicago | infores.com | 555.9 | 135.6 | 24.4 |
| 4 | 6 | The Kantar Group | Fairfield, CT | kantargroup.com | 962.3 | 663.2 | 68.9 |
| 5 | 5 | Westat Inc. | Rockville, MD | westat.com | 285.8 | — | — |
| 6 | 7 | Arbitron Inc. | New York | arbitron.com | 227.5 | 7.9 | 3.5 |
| 7 | — | NOP World US | New York | nopworld.com | 224.1 | 17.5 | 7.8 |
| 8 | 8 | NFO WorldGroup | Greenwich, CT | nfow.com | 452.9 | 289.9 | 64.0 |
| 9 | 9 | Market Facts, Inc. | Arlington Heights, IL | marketfacts.com (synovate.com) | 189.7 | 33.5 | 17.7 |
| 10 | 11 | Taylor Nelson Sofres USA | London | tnsofres.com | 166.9 | 16.4 | 9.8 |
| 11 | 11 | Maritz Research | Fenton, MO | maritzresearch.com | 181.7 | 54.6 | 30.0 |
| 12 | 23 | Ipsos | New York | ipsos.com | 204.3 | 91.4 | 44.7 |
| 13 | 15 | J.D. Power and Associates | Westlake Village, CA | jdpa.com | 128.0 | 18.7 | 14.6 |
| 14 | 14 | Opinion Research Corp. | Princeton, NJ | opinionresearch.com | 133.6 | 42.2 | 31.6 |
| 15 | 10 | The NPD Group Inc. | Port Washington, NY | npd.com | 101.7 | 13.0 | 12.8 |
| 16 | 17 | Jupiter Media Metrix Inc. | New York | jupiterresearch.com | 85.8 | 17.2 | 20.0 |
| 17 | 18 | Harris Interactive Inc. | Rochester, NY | harrisinteractive.com | 75.4 | 10.5 | 13.9 |
| 18 | 20 | Abt Associates Inc. | Cambridge, MA | abtassociates.com | 62.8 | 9.4 | 15.0 |
| 19 | 19 | C&R Research Services Inc. | Chicago | crresearch.com | 43.6 | — | — |
| 20 | 22 | Wirthlin Worldwide | McLean, VA | wirthlin.com | 46.8 | 7.2 | 15.4 |
| 21 | 24 | Lieberman Research Worldwide | Los Angeles | lrwonline.com | 43.1 | 4.3 | 10.0 |
| 22 | 25 | Burke Inc. | Cincinnati | burke.com | 45.5 | 11.2 | 24.6 |
| 23 | 21 | MORPACE International Inc. | Farmington Hills, MI | morpace.com | 48.3 | 15.9 | 32.9 |
| 24 | 26 | Market Strategies Inc. | Livonia, MI | marketstrategies.com | 31.7 | 1.5 | 4.7 |
| 25 | 30 | GfK Custom Research Inc. | Minneapolis | customresearch.com | 29.8 | 0.9 | 3.0 |
| 26 | 32 | ICR/Int'l Communications Research | Media, PA | icrsurvey.com | 28.8 | 0.3 | 1.0 |
| 27 | 29 | M/A/R/C Research | Irving, TX | marcresearch.com | 24.5 | 0.5 | 2.0 |
| 28 | 31 | Elrick & Lavidge Marketing Research | Tucker, GA | elrickandlavidge.com | 22.9 | — | — |
| 29 | 36 | RDA Group Inc. | Bloomfield Hills, MI | rdagroup.com | 26.0 | 3.6 | 13.8 |
| 30 | 33 | Lieberman Research Group | Great Neck, NY | liebermanresearch.com | 22.3 | 0.5 | 2.2 |
| 31 | — | Knowledge Networks Inc. | Menlo Park, CA | knowledgenetworks.com | 21.4 | — | — |
| 32 | 34 | Walker Information | Indianapolis | walkerinfo.com | 26.8 | 5.5 | 20.5 |
| 33 | 37 | National Research Corp. | Lincoln, NE | nationalresearch.com | 17.7 | — | — |
| 34 | 38 | Directions Research Inc. | Cincinnati | directionsrsch.com | 16.7 | — | — |
| 35 | 48 | Marketing and Planning Systems Inc. | Waltham, MA | mapsnet.com | 19.7 | 3.2 | 16.2 |
| 36 | — | Alliance Research Inc. | Crestview Hills, KY | allianceresearch.com | 15.4 | — | — |
| 37 | 40 | Data Development Corp. | New York | datadc.com | 15.6 | 0.3 | 1.9 |
| 38 | 46 | Marketing Analysts Inc. | Charleston, SC | marketinganalysts.com | 15.1 | 0.4 | 2.6 |

*(Continued)*

## TABLE 1.2

**Top 50 U.S. Research Organizations** *(Continued)*

| U.S. RANK 2001 | U.S. RANK 2000 | ORGANIZATION | HEADQUARTERS | WEB SITE | WORLDWIDE RESEARCH REVENUES* ($, IN MILLIONS) | NON-U.S. RESEARCH REVENUES* ($, IN MILLIONS) | PERCENT NON-U.S. REVENUES |
|---|---|---|---|---|---|---|---|
| 39 | — | Marketing Research Services Inc. | Cincinnati | *mrsi.com* | 14.3 | — | — |
| 40 | 43 | Greenfield Online Inc. | Wilton, CT | *greenfield.com* | 14.2 | — | — |
| 41 | 42 | Greenfield Consulting Group Inc. | Westport, CT | *greenfieldgroup.com* | 14.0 | 0.1 | 1.0 |
| 42 | 45 | Savitz Research Companies | Dallas | *savitzresearch.com* | 13.2 | — | — |
| 43 | 44 | The PreTesting Co. Inc. | Tenafly, NJ | *pretesting.com* | 13.1 | 0.7 | 5.3 |
| 44 | 39 | Schulman, Ronca, & Bucuvalas Inc. | New York | *srbi.com* | 12.1 | 0.7 | 5.8 |
| 45 | 49 | Cheskin | Redwood Shores, CA | *cheskin.com* | 14.3 | 3.1 | 22.0 |
| 46 | — | The Marketing Workshop Inc. | Norcross, GA | *mwshop.com* | 10.6 | — | — |
| 47 | — | Symmetrical Holdings Inc. | Deerfield Beach, FL | *symmetrical.com* | 10.4 | — | — |
| 48 | — | comScore Networks Inc. | Reston, VA | *comscore.com* | 10.0 | — | — |
| 49 | — | MarketVision Research Inc. | Cincinnati | *marketvisionresearch.com* | 10.0 | — | — |
| 50 | 47 | The B/R/S Group Inc. | San Rafael, CA | *brsgroup.com* | 10.9 | 2.2 | 20.0 |
| | | | | Total top 50 | $8,318.2 | $3,285.1 | 39.5% |
| | | All other (130 CASRO companies not included in the Top 50)** | | | 563.1 | 52.5 | 9.3% |
| | | | | Total (180 companies) | $8,881.3 | $3,337.6 | 37.6% |

*U.S. and worldwide and non-U.S. revenues that include nonresearch activities for some companies are significantly higher. The companies are ranked according to U.S. research revenues.

**Total revenues of 130 survey research firms—beyond those in Top 50—that provide financial information, on a confidential basis, to the Council of American Survey Research Organizations (CASRO).

service is the Gallup and Robinson Magazine Impact Studies (*www.gallup-robinson.com*). These services are also sold on a syndicated basis.

**customized services**
Companies that tailor the research procedures to best meet the needs of each client.

*Customized services* offer a wide variety of marketing research services customized to suit a client's specific needs. Each marketing research project is treated uniquely. Some marketing research firms that offer these services include Burke, Inc. (*www.burke.com*), Market Facts, Inc. (*www.marketfacts.com*), and Elrick & Lavidge (*www.elavidge.com*).

**internet services**
Companies that have specialized in conducting marketing research on the Internet.

*Internet services* are offered by several marketing research firms including some who have specialized in conducting marketing research on the Internet. For example, Greenfield Online Research Center Inc., Westport, CT (*www.greenfieldonline.com*), a subsidiary of The Greenfield Consulting firm (*www.greenfieldgroup.com*), offers a broad range of customized qualitative and quantitative online marketing research for consumer, business-to-business, and professional markets. Using large, proprietary databases, studies are conducted within the company's secure Web site.

**limited-service suppliers**
Companies that specialize in one or a few phases of the marketing research project.

*Limited-service suppliers* specialize in one or a few phases of the marketing research project, as illustrated by Recipio in the overview. Services offered by such suppliers are classified as field services, coding and data entry, analytical services, data analysis, and branded products. *Field services* collect data through mail, personal, or telephone interviewing, and firms that specialize in interviewing are called field service organizations. These organizations may range from small proprietary organizations that operate locally to large multinational organizations. Some organizations maintain extensive interviewing facilities across the country for interviewing shoppers in malls. Many offer qualitative data collection services such as focus group interviewing (discussed in Chapter 5). Some firms that offer field services are Field Facts, Inc. (*www.fieldfacts.com*), Field Work Chicago, Inc. (*www.fieldwork.com*), Quality Controlled

**field services**
Companies whose primary service offering is their expertise in collecting data for research projects.

Services division of Maritz (*www.maritz.com*), and Survey America (*www.survey-america.com*).

**coding and data entry services**
Companies whose primary service offering is their expertise in converting completed surveys or interviews into a usable database for conducting statistical analysis.

*Coding and data entry services* include editing completed questionnaires, developing a coding scheme, and transcribing the data onto diskettes or magnetic tapes for input into the computer. Survey Service, Inc. (*www.surveyservice.com*) provides such services.

**analytical services**
Companies that provide guidance in the development of the research design.

*Analytical services* include designing and pretesting questionnaires, determining the best means of collecting data, designing sampling plans, and other aspects of the research design. Some complex marketing research projects require knowledge of sophisticated procedures, including specialized experimental designs (discussed in Chapter 7) and analytical techniques such as conjoint analysis and multidimensional scaling (discussed in Chapter 21). This kind of expertise can be obtained from firms and consultants specializing in analytical services, such as SDR Consulting (*www.sdr-consulting.com*).

**data analysis services**
Firms whose primary service is to conduct statistical analysis of quantitative data.

*Data analysis services* are offered by firms, also known as tab houses, that specialize in computer analysis of quantitative data such as those obtained in large surveys. Initially, most data analysis firms supplied only tabulations (frequency counts) and cross tabulations (frequency counts that describe two or more variables simultaneously). Now many firms, such as Beta Research Corporation (*www.nybeta.com*), offer sophisticated data analysis using advanced statistical techniques. With the proliferation of microcomputers and software, many firms now have the capability to analyze their own data, but data analysis firms are still in demand.

**branded marketing research products**
Specialized data collection and analysis procedures developed to address specific types of marketing research problems.

*Branded marketing research products* and services are specialized data collection and analysis procedures developed to address specific types of marketing research problems. These procedures are patented, given brand names, and marketed like any other branded product. Market Facts (*www.marketfacts.com*) offers several branded products under the TeleNation® family. One of their products, TeleNation, is a three-times-a-week multiclient telephone study among households selected at random from the U.S. population. Clients are charged based on the number of questions they ask. Each of the three weekly waves consists of 1,000 representative American adults.

There are certain guidelines that should be followed when selecting a research supplier, whether it is a full-service or a limited-service supplier.

## SELECTING A RESEARCH SUPPLIER

A firm that cannot conduct an entire marketing research project in house must select an external supplier for one or more phases of the project. The firm should compile a list of prospective suppliers from such sources as trade publications, professional directories, and word of mouth. When deciding on criteria for selecting an outside supplier, a firm should ask itself why it is seeking outside marketing research support. For example, a small firm that needs one project investigated may find it economically efficient to employ an outside source. A firm may not have the technical expertise to undertake certain phases of a project, or political conflict-of-interest issues may determine that a project be conducted by an outside supplier.

When developing criteria for selecting an outside supplier, a firm should keep some basics in mind. What is the reputation of the supplier? Do they complete projects on schedule? Are they known for maintaining ethical standards? Are they flexible? Are their research projects of high quality? What kind and how much experience does the supplier have? Has the firm had experience with projects similar to this one? Do the supplier's personnel have both technical and nontechnical expertise? In other words, in addition to technical skills, are the personnel assigned to the task sensitive to the client's needs and do they share the client's research ideology? Can they communicate well with the client?

Remember that the cheapest bid is not always the best one. Competitive bids should be obtained and compared on the basis of quality as well as price. A good practice is to get a written bid or contract before beginning the project. Decisions about marketing research suppliers, just like other management decisions, should be based on sound information. Career opportunities are available with marketing research suppliers as well as with marketing and advertising firms.

# CAREERS IN MARKETING RESEARCH

Promising career opportunities are available with marketing research firms (e.g., A. C. Nielsen, Burke, Inc., M/A/R/C). Equally appealing are careers in business and nonbusiness firms and agencies with in-house marketing research departments (e.g., Procter & Gamble, Coca-Cola, AT&T, the Federal Trade Commission, United States Census Bureau). Advertising agencies (e.g., BBDO International, Ogilvy & Mather, J. Walter Thompson, Young & Rubicam) also conduct substantial marketing research and employ professionals in this field. Some of the positions available in marketing research include vice president of marketing research, research director, assistant director of research, project manager, statistician/data processing specialist, senior analyst, analyst, junior analyst, field work director, and operational supervisor. Figure 1.4 lists job titles in marketing research and describes their accompanying responsibilities.[21]

The most common entry-level position in marketing research for people with bachelor's degrees (e.g., BBA) is an operational supervisor. These people are responsible for supervising a well-defined set of operations, including field work, data editing and coding, and may be involved in programming and data analysis. In the marketing research industry, however, there is a growing preference for people with master's degrees. Those with MBA or equivalent degrees are likely to be employed as project managers. In marketing research firms such as Elrick and Lavidge, the project manager works with the account director in managing the day-to-day operations of a marketing research project. The typical entry-level position in a business firm would be junior research analyst (for BBAs) or research analyst (for MBAs). The junior analyst and the research analyst learn about the particular industry and receive training from a senior staff member, usually the marketing research manager. The junior analyst position includes a training program to prepare individuals for the responsibilities of a research analyst, including coordinating with the marketing department and sales force to develop goals for product exposure. The research analyst responsibilities include checking all data for accuracy, comparing and contrasting new research with established norms, and analyzing primary and secondary data for the purpose of market forecasting.

As these job titles indicate, people with a variety of backgrounds and skills are needed in marketing research. Technical specialists such as statisticians obviously need strong

**Figure 1.4**
Selected Marketing Research
Job Descriptions

> 1. **Vice President of Marketing Research:** This is the senior position in marketing research. The VP is responsible for the entire marketing research operation of the company and serves on the top management team. The VP sets the objectives and goals of the marketing research department.
> 2. **Research Director:** Also a senior position, the director has the overall responsibility for the development and execution of all the marketing research projects.
> 3. **Assistant Director of Research:** This person serves as an administrative assistant to the director and supervises some of the other marketing research staff members.
> 4. **(Senior) Project Manager:** This person has overall responsibility for the design, implementation, and management of research projects.
> 5. **Statistician/Data Processing Specialist:** This person serves as an expert on theory and application of statistical techniques. Responsibilities include experimental design, data processing, and analysis.
> 6. **Senior Analyst:** This person participates in the development of projects and directs the operational execution of the assigned projects. A senior analyst works closely with the analyst, junior analyst, and other personnel in developing the research design and data collection. The senior analyst prepares the final report. The primary responsibility for meeting time and cost constraints rests with the senior analyst.
> 7. **Analyst:** An analyst handles the details involved in executing the project. The analyst designs and pretests the questionnaires and conducts a preliminary analysis of the data.
> 8. **Junior Analyst:** The junior analyst handles routine assignments such as secondary data analysis, editing and coding of questionnaires, and simple statistical analysis.
> 9. **Field Work Director:** This person is responsible for the selection, training, supervision, and evaluation of interviewers and other field workers.
> 10. **Operational Supervisor:** This person is responsible for supervising operations such as field work, data editing, and coding, and may be involved in programming and data analysis.

backgrounds in statistics and data analysis. Other positions, such as research director, call for managing the work of others and require more general skills. To prepare for a career in marketing research, you should:

- Take all the marketing courses you can.
- Take courses in statistics and quantitative methods.
- Acquire Internet and computer skills. Knowledge of programming languages is an added asset.
- Take courses in psychology and consumer behavior.
- Acquire effective written and verbal communication skills.
- Think creatively. Creativity and common sense command a premium in marketing research.

Marketing researchers should be liberally educated so that they can understand the problems confronting managers and address them from a broad perspective.[22] The following example shows what managers look for in entry-level employees.

### REAL RESEARCH

## *BPAmoco Digs for the Right Stuff*

In 1999, Amoco and BP merged their operations (*www.bpamoco.com*) and have remained successful with 2001 revenues amounting to $148 billion. As of 2003, BP was still in the process of changing all Amoco stores to the new BP name—BP Connect, which is the company's new version of a progressive convenience store for the new century. The new look includes a line of solar panels that form a canopy above the gas pumps, gourmet food in the café inside, Internet access for customers, and lower-pollution fuel. The company relies heavily on marketing research to determine consumer preferences and adapt its marketing accordingly. Abdul Azhari, marketing research director for BPAmoco, Chicago, looks for the following credentials when hiring new members for his department:

"It's essential that they know how to dig into the analytical matters, that they know how to analyze things. Also, it's essential that they know how to analyze data with an eye to practicality and application to marketing needs. It is also essential that they can communicate verbally and in writing to the various client departments that we have and also adjust communication to these various departments so that when they are with R&D people, they talk the language of scientists. When the client is the director of sales, they have to be able to speak 'marketingese.' Their written words as well as their presentation must be appropriate to the audience. They must look at the broad picture. They must see the forest—not only the trees. They must also understand that marketing research is one element of the process and is not the end itself."[23] ■

# THE ROLE OF MARKETING RESEARCH IN MIS AND DSS

Earlier, we defined marketing research as the systematic and objective identification, collection, analysis, and dissemination of information for use in marketing decision making.[24] The information obtained through marketing research and sources such as internal records and marketing intelligence becomes an integral part of the firm's marketing information system (MIS). A ***marketing information system*** (MIS) is a formalized set of procedures for generating, analyzing, storing, and distributing information to marketing decision makers on an ongoing basis. Note that the definition of MIS is similar to marketing research, except that MIS provide information continuously rather than on the basis of ad hoc research studies. The design of an MIS focuses on each decision maker's responsibilities, style, and information needs. Information gathered from various sources, such as invoices and marketing intelligence, including marketing research, is combined and presented in a format that can be readily used in decision making. More information can be obtained from MIS than from ad hoc marketing research projects, but MIS is limited in the amount and nature

*marketing information system (MIS)*
A formalized set of procedures for generating, analyzing, storing, and distributing pertinent information to marketing decision makers on an ongoing basis.

**Figure 1.5**

Management Information
Systems versus Decision
Support Systems

| MIS | DSS |
|---|---|
| • Structured Problems | • Unstructured Problems |
| • Use of Reports | • Use of Models |
| • Rigid Structure | • User-Friendly Interaction |
| • Information Displaying Restricted | • Adaptability |
| • Can Improve Decision Making by Clarifying Raw Data | • Can Improve Decision Making by Using "What If" Analysis |

***decision support systems (DSS)***
Information systems that enable
decision makers to interact directly
with both databases and analysis
models. The important components
of a DSS include hardware and a
communications network, database,
model base, software base, and the
DSS user (decision maker).

of information it provides and the way this information can be used by the decision maker. This is because the information is rigidly structured and cannot be easily manipulated.

Developed to overcome the limitations of MIS, decision support systems (DSS) enable decision makers to interact directly with databases and analysis models. ***Decision support systems*** (DSS) are integrated systems including hardware, communications network, database, model base, software base, and the DSS user (decision maker) that collect and interpret information for decision making. Marketing research contributes research data to the database, marketing models and analytical techniques to the model base, and specialized programs for analyzing marketing data to the software base. DSS differ from MIS in various ways (see Figure 1.5).[25] DSS combine the use of models or analytical techniques with the traditional access and retrieval functions of MIS. DSS are easier to use in an interactive mode and can adapt to changes in the environment as well as to the decision making approach of the user. In addition to improving efficiency, DSS can also enhance decision making effectiveness by using "what if" analysis.[26] DSS have been further developed to expert systems that utilize artificial intelligence procedures to incorporate expert judgment.

## REAL RESEARCH

### DSS Give FedEx an Exceptional Edge

Federal Express (*www.fedex.com*) has developed a reputation for being a reliable express service. With 2001 revenues exceeding $19.6 billion, it has become a technology leader in the highly competitive shipping market and aims to become the best worldwide. A major ingredient in FedEx's success has been the advanced worldwide decision support systems that provide information on customers. Such information includes detailed aspects of every shipment such as ordering, billing, tracking, and tracing. In 2001, FedEx Ground received a "Moby" award at the Go Mobile IT Wireless Conference. FedEx Ground was recognized for its ability to capture an electronic signature and pertinent information at the point of package delivery, which has resulted in a greatly enhanced transmission system for FedEx.

Its sophisticated DSS have enabled FedEx to become the first company to go from ". . . zero to 1 billion in sales in 10 years without the aid of mergers or acquisitions, and to dominate the fast-growing overnight-cargo field. . ." As one example of the several strategic ways in which the DSS are used, FedEx has implemented highly sophisticated "Segment Management Marketing" (SMM). FedEx has developed a "value quotient" formula that allows marketers to analyze individual customers on a case-by-case analysis. This value quotient includes weights for strategic/competitive value of customer and profitability through a survey of 30 questions. The objectives of FedEx help define the weight given to an individual customer and provide a more strategic perspective than simply using profit to pinpoint the value of a customer. FedEx has defined 14 highly specific customer segments based on consumer attitudes relating to price, reliability, urgency, safety of product, tracking, and proof of delivery. The current

Ongoing marketing research, which becomes a part of its DSS, has enabled FedEx to adopt an aggressive information oriented approach to competition.

SMM, which is a part of the company's DSS, includes family classifications and segments to help marketers further understand the customers they serve. Thus, FedEx has taken a very aggressive information-oriented approach to competition that will be the key to continued success.[27] ∎

The marketing research process outlined earlier in this chapter, which is followed by companies such as FedEx, was also adopted in the department store project.

---

**ACTIVE RESEARCH** | **DEPARTMENT STORE PROJECT**

A department store project conducted by the author is used as a running example throughout this text to illustrate concepts and data analysis procedures. The purpose of this project was to assess the relative strengths and weaknesses of a major department store, relative to a group of direct and indirect competitors. This store will be referred to as Sears; the true identity of the actual store has been disguised. The goal was to formulate marketing programs designed to boost the declining sales and profits of Sears. Ten major stores, including prestigious department stores (e.g., Saks Fifth Avenue, Neiman-Marcus), national chains (e.g., JC Penney), discount stores (e.g., K-Mart, Target), and some regional chains (e.g., Belk) were considered in this study. A questionnaire was designed and administered, using in-home personal interviews, to a convenience sample of 271 households drawn from a major metropolitan area. A six-point scale was used (subjects were asked to check a number from 1 to 6) whenever ratings were obtained. The following information was solicited:

1. Familiarity with the 10 department stores
2. Frequency with which household members shopped at each of the 10 stores
3. Relative importance attached to each of the eight factors selected as the choice criteria utilized in selecting a department store. These factors were quality of merchandise, variety and assortment of merchandise, returns and adjustment policy, service of store personnel, prices, convenience of location, layout of store, and credit and billing policies.
4. Evaluation of the 10 stores on each of the eight factors of the choice criteria
5. Preference ratings for each store
6. Rankings of the 10 stores (from most preferred to least preferred)
7. Degree of agreement with 21 lifestyle statements
8. Standard demographic characteristics (age, education, etc.)
9. Name, address, and telephone number

The study helped the sponsor to determine consumer perceptions of and preferences for the department store. Areas of weakness were identified in terms of specific factors influencing the

Marketing research can help depart-ment stores such as Sears to deter-mine relative strengths and weak-nesses and improve competitive positioning.

consumers' choice criteria and in terms of specific product categories. Appropriate marketing programs were designed to overcome these weaknesses. Finally, a positioning strategy was developed to attain a desirable store image.

Projects such as the department store project are routinely conducted on an international scale.

# INTERNATIONAL MARKETING RESEARCH

The United States accounts for only 39 percent of the marketing research expenditures worldwide. About 40 percent of all marketing research is conducted in Western Europe and 9 percent in Japan. Most of the European research is done in Germany, the United Kingdom, France, Italy, and Spain.[28] With the globalization of markets, marketing research has assumed a truly international character and this trend is likely to continue. Several U.S. firms conduct international marketing research, including VNU, IMS Health, Information Resources, and the Kantar Group (see Table 1.2). Foreign-based firms include Taylor Nelson Sofres (United Kingdom), Infratest, and GfK (Germany).

Conducting international marketing research (research for truly international products), foreign research (research carried out in a country other than the country of the research-commissioning organization), or multinational research (research conducted in all or all important countries where the company is represented) is much more complex than domestic marketing research. All research of this kind, including cross-cultural research, will be discussed under the broad rubric of international marketing research. The opening IBM example illustrated some of the complexities involved in conducting this type of research. The environment prevailing in the countries, cultural units, or international markets that are being researched influences the way the six steps of the marketing research process should be performed. These environmental factors and their impact on the marketing research process are discussed in detail in subsequent chapters. In addition, Chapter 23 is devoted exclusively to this topic.

Globalization of companies is the trend of today. Whether going online or setting up physical operations in a foreign country, research must be conducted so that relevant environmental factors are taken into consideration when going global. Many companies have faced global disaster because they did not take into account the differences between their country and the country with which they wish to do business.

Companies that are basing their business on the Web can run into problems. Many times the content on the Web page may be interpreted in a way that was unintended, such as in the case of a car manufacturer in Mexico. The Web page showed a hiker standing next to a car. In Mexico, hikers are poor people and they do not own cars. You also want local content to accommodate multiple languages in areas such as India where one region may have 20 different languages. Companies must take these environmental factors into account in order to gain sales and customers in other countries.

Despite the complexity involved, international marketing research is expected to grow at a faster rate than domestic research. A major contributing factor is that markets for many products in the United States are approaching saturation. In contrast, the markets for these products in other countries are in the early stages of development, as illustrated by the following example.

## REAL RESEARCH

### Unilever Taps Thai Lifestyles

Thanks to the rapid economic growth Thailand has experienced in the past few years, there are now millions of middle-class people looking for an international lifestyle and international products. For instance, Procter & Gamble (*www.pg.com*) and Unilever (*www.unilever.com*) dominate the hair care market with its different brands such as Sunsilk, Dimension, and Organic among others. Some Thai women seem to prefer brands directly imported from Western countries and this has become an interesting market segment for Unilever. In 2001, Unilever achieved revenues of approximately $46 billion, and the Asia and Pacific region generated 17 percent of Unilever's operating profit of over $4.7 billion.

Unilever conducted focus groups and surveys administered face to face and found that "metropolitan Thais are more eager to try new products than many other nationalities." Moreover, young women believe that changing their shampoo brands regularly makes their hair look better. The conservative appearance of many Thais has also recently changed to turn into "radical new looks," and there is an increasing number of people becoming "fashion conscious," especially regarding their hair. Last but not least, what happens in Thailand influences the consumer trends in neighboring countries such as Cambodia, Laos, and Vietnam that are looking at Thai people as a source of new lifestyle ideas.

International marketing research greatly helped Unilever to rethink both Thailand and its international strategy on hair products. It enabled the decision makers to take into account the cultural background and the cultural evolution of the Thai population. Having acquired so much information on the growing and quickly evolving Thai market, Unilever has reoriented its strategy. Thus, Thailand has become one of Unilever's key centers for the development of new hair products and Unilever's Organic shampoo was first launched in Thailand before being available worldwide.[29] ∎

## ETHICS IN MARKETING RESEARCH

Several aspects of marketing research have strong ethical implications. As explained earlier, marketing research is generally conducted by commercial (i.e., for-profit) firms that are either independent research organizations (external suppliers) or departments within corporations (internal suppliers). Most marketing research is conducted for clients representing commercial firms. The profit motive may occasionally cause researchers or clients to compromise the objectivity or professionalism associated with the marketing research process.

Marketing research has often been described as having four stakeholders: (1) the marketing researcher, (2) the client, (3) the respondent, and (4) the public. These stakeholders have certain responsibilities to each other and to the research project. Ethical issues arise when the interests of these stakeholders are in conflict and when one or more of the stakeholders are lacking in their responsibilities.[30] For example, if the researcher does not follow appropriate marketing research procedures, or if the client misrepresents the findings in the company's advertising, ethical norms are violated. Ethical issues are best resolved by the stakeholders behaving honorably. Codes of conduct, such as the American Marketing Association code of ethics, are available to guide behavior and help resolve ethical dilemmas. As indicated by the following example, reputable marketing research firms conform to such codes of ethics and openly disclose their ethical standards for scrutiny by others.

### REAL RESEARCH

## *Harris Online Is Right-On with Its Privacy Policy*

Harris Online Poll is an online poll dedicated to providing results of various surveys conducted over the Internet. Realizing its obligations to the survey respondents, Harris follows a strict privacy policy that is posted on its Web site (*www.harrispollonline.com*):

"We are committed to maintaining the privacy of our online and offline panel communities. Your identity and the replies you give to the Harris Poll, as well as to the Harris Poll Online are completely confidential. All our research reports contain only aggregated, not individual information about the panel. In our 40-year history, we have never violated our sacred trust with the public; the answers people have given to us have remained anonymous. The Harris Poll Online maintains that tradition by fiercely guarding your privacy. We never release individual information about our panel unless the individual expressly agrees to such disclosure. In addition, we do not 'spam' or send unsolicited commercial e-mails.

We are in conformance with the Council of American Survey Research Organizations (CASRO) Code of Standards and Ethics for Survey Research, as well as the American Association for Public Opinion Research (AAPOR) Code of Professional Ethics and Practices." ■

# INTERNET AND COMPUTER APPLICATIONS

The Internet, also known as the Information Super Highway, is possibly the greatest communication medium since the telephone. The World Wide Web (www or Web) is the dominant component of the Internet and many use the terms Web and Internet synonymously. Each document on the Web has a specific electronic address called a Uniform Resource Locator (URL). In this book we list the URLs of several sites useful for marketing research. These sites are not guaranteed to be available or to be at the same URL when you read this book, as the Internet changes rapidly.

There are many ways in which the Internet can be useful to marketing researchers. It can be used as a source of marketing research providers, a source of secondary data, a source for marketing research software, and a source for data gathering via focus groups, surveys, etc. It is another source of information that feeds into the firm's marketing information system. One of the great advantages of doing research on the Internet is that the data can be processed as fast as they come in. Internet data do not require the extra step of data input because the data are electronically sent from the respondent. The Internet is also very useful for project management. Internet e-mail combined with software such as Lotus Notes are being used for communication by researchers and clients, and for coordinating and managing the six steps of the marketing research process. The Internet is also being used to disseminate marketing research results and reports, which can be posted on the Web and made available to managers on a worldwide basis.

One way to determine what information is on the Internet is to use search engines to do queries for information. Search engines are provided free of charge by the Internet service provider. Yahoo! at *www.yahoo.com*, AltaVista at *www.altavista.com*, and Google at *www.google.com* are three well-known search engines.

The Internet is very efficient for identifying marketing research firms that supply specific services. Using a search engine, such as Yahoo!, several research firms can be identified. When selecting a research supplier, it is easy to find information on the suppliers at their Web sites. Many sites include information on company history, products, clients, and employees. For example, *www.greenbook.org* lists thousands of market research companies and specific firms can be conveniently located using their search procedures. To view specific Internet sites of well-known marketing research firms, visit Burke Marketing Research at *www.burke.com*. We give the URLs of important marketing research associations.

---

**REAL RESEARCH**

## Marketing Research Associations Online

### Domestic

AAPOR: American Association for Public Opinion Research (*www.aapor.org*)
AMA: American Marketing Association (*www.marketingpower.com*)
ARF: The Advertising Research Foundation (*www.arfsite.org*)
CASRO: The Council of American Survey Research Organizations (*www.casro.org*)
MRA: Marketing Research Association (*www.mra-net.org*)
QRCA: Qualitative Research Consultants Association (*www.qrca.org*)
RIC: Research Industry Coalition (*www.researchindustry.org*)
CMOR: Council for Marketing and Opinion Research (*www.cmor.org*)

### International

ESOMAR: European Society for Opinion and Marketing Research (*www.esomar.nl*)
MRS: The Market Research Society (UK) (*www.marketresearch.org.uk*)
MRSA: The Market Research Society of Australia (*www.mrsa.com.au*)
PMRS: The Professional Marketing Research Society (Canada) (*www.pmrs-aprm.com*) ■

---

Our earlier discussion on careers in marketing research gave job descriptions along with directions for preparing for such jobs. The Internet can be used to help find a job in marketing research. Research Info at *www.researchinfo.com* offers a research employment board where job postings and job wanted ads are placed. The Internet is quickly becoming a useful tool in the identification, collection, analysis, and dissemination of information related to marketing research. Throughout this book we show how the six steps of the marketing research process are facilitated by Internet research as well as by the use of computers.

## SPSS Windows

In this book we feature SPSS programs, not merely as a statistical package, but as an integrative package that can be used in the various stages of the marketing research process. We illustrate the use of SPSS for defining the problem, developing an approach, formulating the research design, data collection, data preparation and analysis, and report preparation and presentation. In addition to the BASE module, we also feature other SPSS programs such as Decision Time, What If?, Maps, Data Entry, SamplePower, Missing Values, TextSmart, and SmartViewer.

Data analysis is also illustrated with three other software packages: SAS, MINITAB, and EXCEL.[31]

In addition to SPSS windows, this book features Burke in a significant way with a section entitled 'Focus on Burke' appearing in each chapter. The intent is to show how the marketing research concepts discussed in this book are being practiced by a major research supplier.

**FOCUS ON BURKE**

Burke, Incorporated (*www.burke.com*) is headquartered in Cincinnati, Ohio. Founded in 1931, Burke is an independent, employee-owned company. Burke continues its strong alliance with Infratest Burke AG, Munich Germany (an NFO WorldGroup company), which owns a 50-percent interest. Burke operates internationally in more than 50 countries including 10 of the EU countries. International work is coordinated from Cincinnati, Munich, and London. U.S. work is managed from offices in 18 major markets. According to industry publications, Burke ranks among the top 50 U.S. research organizations.

Burke combines competencies across business units to offer a broad range of *decision support services* for marketing, operations, quality, and human resources. They acquire, integrate, analyze, and apply knowledge across the entire business enterprise. Current business units are:

- **Burke Customer Satisfaction Associates** offers specialized services in customer satisfaction and employee commitment measurement and business management systems to a wide range of business categories. The **Secure Customer Index**® and the **Employee Engagement Index**™ provides industry best-in-class standards for assessing and improving customer-driven business practices in order to improve customer retention and loyalty.

- **Burke Marketing Research** provides full-service custom marketing research, analysis and consulting for consumer and business-to-business companies to assess marketplace dynamics and maximize marketing ROI. BMR creates and applies sophisticated research protocols addressing a broad range of marketing issues.

- **Burke Strategic Consulting Group** helps clients optimize organizational effectiveness, improve financial performance, and establish sustainable growth. Services include executive selection, coaching, and assessment; succession planning, strategic planning, business process reengineering, organizational analysis/design, process mapping, process opportunity assessment, and change management.

- **Burke Linkage and Integration Services** helps clients make better, more informed decisions about where to invest limited resources to optimize customer retention, employee commitment, process effectiveness, and profitability. Critical business processes are linked and analyzed in a Burke-authored framework known as **Enterprise Value Management**™.

- **Burke Interactive** focuses on Internet research and consulting issues. Burke Interactive helps clients use the Internet and emerging media to connect with target markets, employees, and other stakeholders. Burke has developed tools and capabilities in the areas of Web data collection, online reporting, and Web site evaluation. Products include Burke's **Digital Dashboard**® and **Webnostics**®.

- **Burke Qualitative Services** offers state-of-the-art qualitative techniques, including international online focus groups and Web site assessment using **Blue Bear**™ technology.

**The Burke Institute** is the new joint venture of Burke, Inc. and ACNielsen Burke Institute combining the ACNielsen Burke Institute and The Training & Development Center to continue a tradition of excellence in educational seminars. This brings together the faculty and course content of both organizations to offer over 70 years of marketing research knowledge in such areas as data analysis, customer satisfaction, qualitative, international, and Internet research.

# SUMMARY

Marketing research involves the identification, collection, analysis, dissemination, and use of information. It is a systematic and objective process designed to identify and solve marketing problems. Thus, marketing research can be classified as problem identification research and problem solving research. The marketing research process consists of six steps that must be followed systematically. The role of marketing research is to assess information needs and provide relevant information in order to improve marketing decision making.

Marketing research may be conducted internally or may be purchased from external suppliers referred to as the marketing research industry. Full-service suppliers provide the entire range of marketing research services from problem definition to report preparation and presentation. The services provided by these suppliers can be classified as syndicated, standardized, customized, or Internet services. Limited-service suppliers specialize in one or a few phases of the marketing research project. Services offered by these suppliers can be classified as field services, coding and data entry, data analysis, analytical services, or branded products.

Due to the need for marketing research, attractive career opportunities are available with marketing research firms, business and nonbusiness firms, agencies with marketing research departments, and advertising agencies. Information obtained using marketing research becomes an integral part of the MIS and DSS. Marketing research contributes to the DSS by providing research data to the database, marketing models and analytical techniques to the model base, and specialized marketing research programs to the software base. International marketing research is much more complex than domestic research as the researcher must consider the environment prevailing in the international markets that are being researched. The ethical issues in marketing research involve four stakeholders: (1) the marketing researcher, (2) the client, (3) the respondent, and (4) the public. The Internet and microcomputers can be used at every step of the marketing research process.

# KEY TERMS AND CONCEPTS

marketing research, *7*
problem identification research, *8*
problem solving research, *8*
marketing research process, *9*
internal supplier, *14*
external suppliers, *15*
full-service suppliers, *15*

syndicated services, *15*
standardized services, *15*
customized services, *17*
internet services, *17*
limited-service suppliers, *17*
field services, *17*

coding and data entry services, *18*
analytical services, *18*
data analysis services, *18*
branded marketing research products, *18*
marketing information system (MIS), *20*
decision support systems (DSS), *21*

# EXERCISES

## Questions

1. Describe the task of marketing research.
2. What decisions are made by marketing managers? How does marketing research help in making these decisions?
3. Define marketing research.
4. Describe one classification of marketing research.
5. What is a marketing information system?
6. How is DSS different from MIS?
7. Explain one way to classify marketing research suppliers and services.
8. What are syndicated services?
9. What is the main difference between a full-service and a limited-service supplier?
10. What are branded products?
11. List five guidelines for selecting an external marketing research supplier.
12. What career opportunities are available in marketing research?
13. Discuss three ethical issues in marketing research that relate to (1) the client, (2) the supplier, and (3) the respondent.
14. Describe the steps in the marketing research process.

## Problems

1. Look through recent issues of newspapers and magazines to identify five examples of problem identification research and five examples of problem solving research.
2. List one kind of marketing research that would be useful to each of the following organizations:
   a. Your campus bookstore
   b. The public transportation authority in your city
   c. A major department store in your area
   d. A restaurant located near your campus
   e. A zoo in a major city

# INTERNET AND COMPUTER EXERCISES

1. Visit the Web sites of the top three marketing research firms in Table 1.2. Write a report on the services offered by these firms. Use the framework of Figure 1.3. What statements can you make about the structure of the marketing research industry?
2. Visit the Web site of Sears (*www.sears.com*). Write a report about the retailing and marketing activities of Sears. This will help you better understand the department store patronage project that is used as a running example throughout this book.
3. Visit the Web sites of MRA, ESOMAR, and MRSA (see the Real Research example for the URLs). Compare and contrast the information available at these sites. Of the three marketing research associations, which has the most useful Web site? Why?
4. Visit the Bureau of Labor Statistics at *www.bls.gov*. What is the employment potential for marketing researchers?

5. Examine recent issues of magazines such as *Marketing News, Quirk's Marketing Research Review,* and *Marketing Research: A Magazine of Management and Applications* to identify one mainframe or one microcomputer application in each of the following areas:
   a. Identification of information needs
   b. Collection of information
   c. Analysis of information
   d. Provision of information (report preparation)

# ACTIVITIES

## *Role Playing*

1. You are the research director for a major bank. You are to recruit a junior analyst who would be responsible for collecting and analyzing secondary data (data already collected by other agencies that are relevant to your operations). With a fellow student playing the role of an applicant for this position, conduct the interview. Does this applicant have the necessary background and skills? Reverse the roles and repeat the exercise.
2. You are a project director working for a major research supplier. You have just received a telephone call from an irate respondent who believes that an interviewer has violated her privacy by calling at an inconvenient time. The respondent expresses several ethical concerns. Ask a fellow student to play the role of this respondent. Address the respondent's concerns and pacify her.

## *Fieldwork*

1. Using your local newspaper and national newspapers such as *USA Today,* the *Wall Street Journal,* or the *New York Times,* compile a list of career opportunities in marketing research.

2. Interview someone who works for a marketing research supplier. What is this person's opinion about career opportunities in marketing research? Write a report of your interview.
3. Interview someone who works in the marketing research department of a major corporation. What is this person's opinion about career opportunities available in marketing research? Write a report of your interview.

## *Group Discussion*

As a small group of four or five, discuss the following issues.

1. What type of institutional structure is best for a marketing research department in a large business firm?
2. What is the ideal educational background for someone seeking a career in marketing research? Is it possible to acquire such a background?
3. Can ethical standards be enforced in marketing research? If so, how?

# CHAPTER

# 2

# Defining the Marketing Research Problem and Developing an Approach

"One of the most challenging tasks is defining the research problem such that the research yields information that directly addresses the management issue. The end result should be for management to understand the information fully and take action based on it."

*Jim Roberts,*
*vice president,*
*marketing services,*
*Burke, Inc.*

## Objectives

After reading this chapter, the student should be able to:

1. Understand the importance of and process used for defining the marketing research problem.
2. Describe the tasks involved in problem definition including discussions with decision maker(s), interviews with industry experts, secondary data analysis, and qualitative research.
3. Discuss the environmental factors affecting the definition of the research problem: past information and forecasts, resources and constraints, objectives of the decision maker, buyer behavior, legal environment, economic environment, and marketing and technological skills of the firm.
4. Clarify the distinction between the management decision problem and the marketing research problem.
5. Explain the structure of a well-defined marketing research problem including the broad statement and the specific components.
6. Discuss in detail the various components of the approach: objective/theoretical framework, analytical models, research questions, hypotheses, and specification of information needed.
7. Acquire an appreciation of the complexity involved and gain an understanding of the procedures for defining the problem and developing an approach in international marketing research.
8. Understand the ethical issues and conflicts that arise in defining the problem and developing the approach.
9. Explain how the Internet and computers can facilitate the process of defining the problem and developing an approach.

## Overview

This chapter covers the first two of the six steps of the marketing research process described in Chapter 1: defining the marketing research problem and developing an approach to the problem. Defining the problem is the most important step, because only when a problem has been clearly and accurately identified can a research project be conducted properly. Defining the marketing research problem sets the course of the entire project. In this chapter, we allow the reader to appreciate the complexities involved in defining a problem by identifying the factors to be considered and the tasks involved. Additionally, we provide guidelines for appropriately defining the marketing research problem and avoiding common types of errors. We also discuss in detail the components of an approach to the problem: objective/theoretical framework, analytical models, research questions, hypotheses, and specification of the information needed. The special considerations involved in defining the problem and developing an approach in international marketing research are discussed. Several ethical issues that arise at this stage of the marketing research process are considered. Finally, we discuss the use of the Internet and computers in defining the problem and developing an approach.

We introduce our discussion with an example from Harley Davidson, which needed specific information about its customers.

## REAL RESEARCH

### Harley Goes Whole Hog

The motorcycle manufacturer Harley Davidson (*www.harleydavidson.com*) made such an important comeback in the early 2000s that there was a long waiting list to get a bike. In 2001, Harley Davidson's revenues exceeded $3.3 billion. Although distributors urged Harley Davidson to build more motorcycles, the company was skeptical about investing in new production facilities.

The years of declining sales taught top management to be more risk averse than risk prone. Harley Davidson was now performing well again, and investing in new facilities meant taking risk. Would the demand follow in the long run or would customers stop wanting Harleys when the next fad came along? The decrease in motorcycles' quality linked to the fast growth of Harley had cost the company all its bad years. Top management was afraid that the decision to invest was too early. On the other hand, investing would help Harley Davidson expand and possibly become the market leader in the heavyweight segment. Discussions with industry experts indicated that brand loyalty was a major factor influencing the sales and repeat sales of motorcycles. Secondary data revealed that the vast majority of motorcycle owners also owned automobiles such as cars, SUVs, and trucks. Focus groups with motorcycle owners further indicated that motorcycles were not used primarily as a means of basic transportation but as a means of recreation. The focus groups also highlighted the role of brand loyalty in motorcycle purchase and ownership.

Forecasts called for an increase in consumer spending on recreation and entertainment well into the year 2010. Empowered by the Internet, consumers in the 21st century had become increasingly sophisticated and value conscious. Yet, brand image and brand loyalty played a significant role in buyer behavior with well-known brands continuing to command a premium. Clearly, Harley Davidson had the necessary resources and marketing and technological skills to achieve its objective of being the dominant motorcycle brand on a global basis.

This process and the findings that emerged helped define the management decision problem and the marketing research problem. The management decision problem was:

Should Harley Davidson invest to produce more motorcycles? The marketing research problem was to determine if customers would be loyal buyers of Harley Davidson in the long term. Specifically, the research had to address the following components:

1. Who are the customers? What are their demographic and psychographic characteristics?
2. Can different types of customers be distinguished? Is it possible to segment the market in a meaningful way?
3. How do customers feel regarding their Harleys? Are all customers motivated by the same appeal?
4. Are the customers loyal to Harley Davidson? What is the extent of brand loyalty?

One of the research questions (RQs) examined and the associated hypotheses (Hs) were:

RQ: Can the motorcycle buyers be segmented based on psychographic characteristics?
H1: There are distinct segments of motorcycle buyers.
H2: Each segment is motivated to own a Harley for a different reason.
H3: Brand loyalty is high among Harley Davidson customers in all segments.

This research was guided by the theory that brand loyalty is the result of positive beliefs, attitude, affect, and experience with the brand. Both qualitative research and quantitative research were conducted. First, focus groups of current owners, would-be owners, and owners of other brands were conducted to understand their feelings about Harley Davidson. Then, 16,000 surveys were mailed to get the psychological, sociological, and demographic profiles of customers and also their subjective appraisal of Harley.

Some of the major findings were as follows:

- Seven categories of customers could be distinguished: (1) the adventure-loving traditionalist, (2) the sensitive pragmatist, (3) the stylish status seeker, (4) the laid-back camper, (5) the classy capitalist, (6) the cool-headed loner, and (7) the cocky misfit. Thus, H1 was supported.
- All customers, however, had the same appeal to own a Harley: it was a symbol of independence, freedom, and power. (This uniformity across segments was surprising, contradicting H2.)
- All customers were long-term loyal customers of Harley Davidson, supporting H3.

Based on these findings, the decision was taken to invest and this way to increase the number of Harleys built. Harley continued to increase annual production at a double-digit rate with production in 2003 expected to be 289,444 units with sales of $4 billion.[1] ■

This example shows the importance of correctly defining the marketing research problem and developing an appropriate approach.

# IMPORTANCE OF DEFINING THE PROBLEM

*problem definition*
A broad statement of the general problem and identification of the specific components of the marketing research problem.

Although each step in a marketing research project is important, problem definition is the most important step. As mentioned in Chapter 1, for the purpose of marketing research, problems and opportunities are treated interchangeably. ***Problem definition*** involves stating the general problem and identifying the specific components of the marketing research problem. Only when the marketing research problem has been clearly defined can research be designed and conducted properly. Of all the tasks in a marketing research project, none is more vital to the ultimate fulfillment of a client's needs than a proper definition of the research problem. All the effort, time, and money spent from this point on will be wasted if the problem is misunderstood or ill defined.[2] This point is worth remembering, because inadequate problem definition is a leading cause of failure of marketing research projects. Further, better communication and more involvement in problem definition are the most frequently mentioned ways of improving the usefulness of research. These results lead to the conclusion that the importance of clearly identifying and defining the marketing research problem cannot be overstated. We cite an episode from personal experience to illustrate this point.

## REAL RESEARCH

### *Chain Restaurant Study*

One day I received a telephone call from a research analyst who introduced himself as one of our alumni. He was working for a restaurant chain in town and wanted help in analyzing the data he had collected while conducting a marketing research study. When we met, he presented me with a copy of the questionnaire and asked how he should analyze the data. My first question to him was, "What is the problem being addressed?" When he looked perplexed, I explained that data analysis was not an independent exercise. Rather, the goal of data analysis is to provide information related to the problem components. I was surprised to learn that he did not have a clear understanding of the marketing research problem and that a written definition of the problem did not exist. So, before proceeding any further, I had to define the marketing research problem. Once that was done, I found that much of the data collected were not relevant to the problem. In this sense, the whole study was a waste of resources. A new study had to be designed and implemented to address the problem identified. ■

Further insights on the difficulty involved in appropriately defining the problem are provided by the problem definition process.[3]

# THE PROCESS OF DEFINING THE PROBLEM AND DEVELOPING AN APPROACH

The problem definition and approach development process is shown in Figure 2.1. The tasks involved in problem definition consist of discussions with the decision makers, interviews with industry experts and other knowledgeable individuals, analysis of secondary data, and sometimes qualitative research. These tasks help the researcher to understand the background of the problem by analyzing the environmental context. Certain essential environmental factors bearing on the problem should be evaluated. Understanding of the environmental context facilitates the identification of the management decision problem. Then, the management decision problem is translated into a marketing research problem. Based on the definition of the marketing research problem, an appropriate approach is developed. The components of the approach consist of: objective/

*Figure 2.1*
The Process of Defining the
Problem and Developing an
Approach

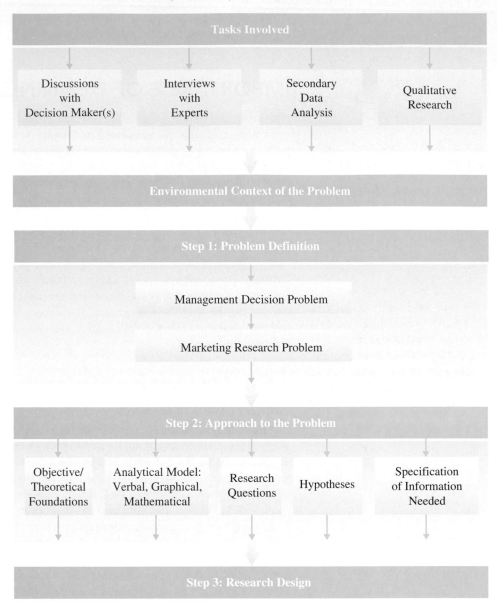

theoretical framework, analytical models, research questions, hypotheses, and specification of the information needed. Further explanation of the problem definition process begins with a discussion of the tasks involved.

# TASKS INVOLVED

## Discussions with Decision Makers

Discussions with decision makers are extremely important. The DM needs to understand the capabilities and limitations of research.[4] Research provides information relevant to management decisions, but it cannot provide solutions because solutions require managerial judgment. Conversely, the researcher needs to understand the nature that decision managers face and what they hope to learn from the research.

To identify the management problem, the researcher must possess considerable skill in interacting with the DM. Several factors may complicate this interaction. Access to the DM may be difficult, and some organizations have complicated protocols for access to top executives. The organizational status of the researcher or the research department may make it difficult to reach the key DM in the early stages of the project. Finally, there may be more than one key DM and meeting with them collectively or individually may be difficult. Despite these problems, it is necessary that the researcher interact directly with the key decision makers.[5]

**problem audit**
A comprehensive examination of a marketing problem to understand its origin and nature.

The **problem audit** provides a useful framework for interacting with the DM and identifying the underlying causes of the problem. The problem audit, like any other type of audit, is a comprehensive examination of a marketing problem with the purpose of understanding its origin and nature.[6] The problem audit involves discussions with the DM on the following issues that are illustrated with a problem facing McDonald's:

1. The events that led to the decision that action is needed, or the history of the problem. McDonald's, a long-time leader in the fast-food industry, was losing market share in 2001 and 2002 to competitors such as Burger King, Wendy's, and Subway in some of the key markets. This problem came into sharper focus as these competitors launched new products and aggressive promotional campaigns, whereas the recent campaigns of McDonald's were not as successful.

2. The alternative courses of action available to the DM. The set of alternatives may be incomplete at this stage, and qualitative research may be needed to identify the more innovative courses of action. The alternatives available to the management of McDonald's include: introducing new sandwiches and menu items, reducing prices, opening more restaurants, launching special promotions, and increasing advertising.

3. The criteria that will be used to evaluate the alternative courses of action. For example, new product offerings might be evaluated on the basis of sales, market share, profitability, return on investment, and so forth. McDonald's will evaluate the alternatives based on contributions to market share and profits.

4. The potential actions that are likely to be suggested based on the research findings. The research findings will likely call for a strategic marketing response by McDonald's.

5. The information that is needed to answer the DM's questions. The information needed includes a comparison of McDonald's and its major competitors on all the elements of the marketing mix (product, pricing, promotion, and distribution) in order to determine relative strengths and weaknesses.

6. The manner in which the DM will use each item of information in making the decision. The key decision makers will devise a strategy for McDonald's based on the research findings and their intuition and judgment.

7. The corporate culture as it relates to decision making.[7] In some firms, the decision making process is dominant; in others, the personality of the DM is more important. Awareness of corporate culture may be one of the most important factors that distinguishes researchers who affect strategic marketing decisions from those who do not. The corporate culture at McDonald's calls for a committee approach in which critical decisions are made by key decision makers.

It is important to perform a problem audit because the DM, in most cases, has only a vague idea of what the problem is. For example, the DM may know that the firm is losing market share but may not know why, because DMs tend to focus on symptoms rather than on causes. Inability to meet sales forecasts, loss of market share, and decline in profits are all symptoms. The researcher should treat the underlying causes, not merely address the symptoms. For example, loss of market share may be caused by a superior promotion by the competition, inadequate distribution of the company's products, or any number of other factors. Only when the underlying causes are identified can the problem be successfully addressed, as exemplified by the effort of Cingular.

### REAL RESEARCH

## Cingular: Singular Self-Expression

Cingular Wireless (*www.cingular.com*) was formed in October 2000, through a partnership of SBC Communications and BellSouth, with SBC owning 60 percent and BellSouth 40 percent. As of 2003, Cingular Wireless is the second largest wireless company in the United States dedicated to self-expression and customer-friendly service. Cingular controls 11 regional brands and offers service to 42 of the top 50 markets in the United States.

A problem audit helped Cingular Wireless identify the real problem that it lacked an image.

# cingular ᔕᴹ
## WIRELESS

## What do you have to say?

However, Cingular encountered difficulty in launching its products and services and initial sales did not meet management's expectation. A problem audit was conducted, which identified the real problem as a lack of image. So the marketing research problem was defined as measuring the awareness, perceptions, and image of Cingular. Focus groups were conducted followed by a telephone survey. The results indicated that awareness was low and consumers did not know what Cingular stood for, i.e., a lack of image. The results also indicated that a telecommunications company that enabled consumers to express themselves was perceived very positively.

To correct this situation, Cingular hired New York-based ad agency BBDO to launch their $300 million campaign in January 2001 during the Super Bowl with a focus on self-expression. Cingular decided that the main focus of their campaign should be image, rather than the differences in service. The company realized that it takes more than just service to win with a new brand in such a highly competitive market. Vance Overbey, executive advertising director at Cingular, contends, "While other carriers were trying to push their messages through a ghetto of competing technology and rate plans, Cingular decided to focus on human self-expression."

"We've been very, very pleased at the awareness levels, at the takeaway that Cingular is fun, creative, and expressive," said Virginia Vann, the company's chief marketing officer. "Everybody understands that Cingular is self-expression." Since the 2001 Super Bowl, Cingular has sponsored events such as the NCAA basketball tournament and Survivor II: The Australian Outback. Cingular is also running local advertisements in print as well as on television and radio. These advertisements put a little more emphasis on the heritage brands and talk more about the rates, but still stay well within the confines of self-expression. Not surprisingly, sales have been increasing at a healthy pace.[8] ■

As in the case of Cingular, a problem audit, which involves extensive interaction between the DM and the researcher, can greatly facilitate problem definition by determining the underlying causes. The interaction between the researcher and the DM is facilitated when one or more people in the client organization serve as a liaison and form a team with the marketing researcher. In order to be fruitful, the interaction between the DM and the researcher should be characterized by the seven Cs:

1. *Communication.* Free exchange of ideas between the DM and researcher is essential.
2. *Cooperation.* Marketing research is a team project in which both parties (DM and researcher) must cooperate.
3. *Confidence.* The interaction between the DM and the researcher should be guided by mutual trust.
4. *Candor.* There should not be any hidden agendas, and an attitude of openness should prevail.
5. *Closeness.* Feelings of warmth and closeness should characterize the relationship between the DM and the researcher.
6. *Continuity.* The DM and the researcher must interact continually rather than sporadically.
7. *Creativity.* The interaction between the DM and the researcher should be creative rather than formulaic.

# Interviews with Industry Experts

In addition to discussions with the DM, interviews with industry experts, individuals knowledgeable about the firm and the industry, may help formulate the marketing research problem.[9] These experts may be found both inside and outside the firm. Typically, expert information is obtained by unstructured personal interviews, without administering a formal questionnaire. It is helpful, however, to prepare a list of topics to be covered during the interview. The order in which these topics are covered and the questions to ask should not be predetermined but decided as the interview progresses. This allows greater flexibility in capturing the insights of the experts. The purpose of interviewing experts is to help define the marketing research problem rather than to develop a conclusive solution. Unfortunately, two potential difficulties may arise when seeking advice from experts:

1. Some individuals who claim to be knowledgeable and are eager to participate may not really possess expertise.
2. It may be difficult to locate and obtain the help from experts who are outside the client organization.

For these reasons, interviews with experts are more useful in conducting marketing research for industrial firms and for products of a technical nature, where it is relatively easy to identify and approach the experts. This method is also helpful in situations where little information is available from other sources, as in the case of radically new products. Experts can provide valuable insights in modifying or repositioning existing products, as illustrated by the repositioning of Diet Cherry Coke.

## REAL RESEARCH

### *Cherry Picking: The Repositioning of Diet Cherry Coke*

Coca-Cola (*www.cocacola.com*) is the world's leading manufacturer, marketer, and distributor of nonalcoholic beverage concentrates and syrups. As of 2003, Coca-Cola operates in more than 200 countries around the world and produces 230 brands. Sales of Diet Cherry Coke had been languishing, down from more than 8 million cases sold in the peak years. Coke system bottlers had begun to cut back distribution of Diet Cherry Coke. Faced with this issue, Coca-Cola had to determine the cause of such a decline in sales. When industry experts were consulted, the real problem was identified: Diet Cherry Coke was not positioned correctly. These experts emphasized that brand image was a key factor influencing soft drink sales and Diet Cherry Coke was perceived as conventional and old fashioned, an image inconsistent with that of Cherry Coke. Hence, the marketing research problem was identified as measuring the image and positioning of Diet Cherry Coke. The research undertaken confirmed the diagnosis of the industry experts and provided several useful insights.

Based on the research results, the product was repositioned to align it more closely to the image of Cherry Coke. The aim was to target younger drinkers. The packaging was remade to also be more consistent with the Cherry Coke packaging. Bolder, edgy graphics were used to appeal to the youth segment. Finally, Diet Cherry Coke was placed with Cherry Coke in a teen-targeted promotional giveaway. Positioning Diet Cherry Coke as a youthful soft drink and targeting the teenage segment led to a turnaround and increased sales in 2002. Sales have shown an upward trajectory since, thanks to the industry experts who helped identify the real problem.[10] ■

The Diet Cherry Coke example points to the key role of industry experts. However, information obtained from the DM and the industry experts should be supplemented with the available secondary data.

## Secondary Data Analysis

*secondary data*
Data collected for some purpose other than the problem at hand.

*primary data*
Data originated by the researcher specifically to address the research problem.

***Secondary data*** are data collected for some purpose other than the problem at hand. ***Primary data,*** on the other hand, are originated by the researcher for the specific purpose of addressing the research problem. Secondary data include information made available by business and government sources, commercial marketing research firms, and computerized databases. Secondary data are an economical and quick source of background information. Analysis of available secondary data is an essential step in the problem definition process: primary data should not be collected until the available secondary data have been fully analyzed. Given the tremendous importance of secondary data, this topic will be discussed in detail in Chapter 4, which also further discusses the differences between secondary and primary data. Here, we illustrate the use of secondary data in defining the marketing research problem.

### REAL RESEARCH

## *Vans Incorporated: The Maxi-Van of Skateboarding*

Skateboarding has hit the mainstream today as teens all over the country are trying tricks on their boards. Many different shoe companies have tried their hand at marketing to this crowd, but most have failed. Today, the brand of choice is Vans, Inc. (*www.vans.com*). This shoe company, based out of Santa Fe Springs, California, has pioneered the thick-soled, slip-on sneakers that have become a mainstay on the skateboarding front.

The company came across secondary data showing that a lot of skaters were getting in trouble with the law for skating around the city. The company collected additional secondary data that further revealed there were not too many places for their athletes to skate in this country safely. So Neal Lyons, president of retail for the company, wondered if Vans should open large skate parks next to shopping malls so that kids might have a safe place to skateboard. Accordingly, the marketing research problem was defined as assessing consumer preferences and the demand for large skate parks next to shopping malls. The research conducted resulted in affirmative findings, and so Lyons found a mall that agreed to let them build a park. That place was The Block in Orange County, California, which was known as a hip shopping space for teens to congregate. Luckily the Mills Corporation, known as a progressive entertainment mall developer, owned the property.

The park opened in November 1998 and attendance was booming. Attendance was close to 250,000 skaters at the end of the year, well over the projected attendance of 100,000. The park was a huge success and people from all over the world were coming to try their hand at the park. Subsequently, Vans continued to open more parks and on January 12, 2002, opened its 11th park in Orlando. It plans to open additional parks in Colorado, Virginia, Florida, and Milpitas, in northern California, by the year 2005. It all started with the analysis of secondary data that led to appropriate marketing research resulting in a successful expansion strategy.[11] ∎

Analysis of secondary data and subsequent research led Vans, Inc. to open large skate parks that have been very successful.

It is often helpful to supplement secondary data analysis with qualitative research.

## Qualitative Research

*qualitative research*
An unstructured, exploratory research methodology based on small samples intended to provide insight and understanding of the problem setting.

Information obtained from the DM, industry experts, and secondary data may not be sufficient to define the research problem. Sometimes qualitative research must be undertaken to gain an understanding of the problem and its underlying factors. *Qualitative research* is unstructured, exploratory in nature, based on small samples, and may utilize popular qualitative techniques such as focus groups (group interviews), word association (asking respondents to indicate their first responses to stimulus words), and depth interviews (one-on-one interviews that probe the respondents' thoughts in detail). Other exploratory research techniques, such as pilot surveys with small samples of respondents, may also be undertaken. Exploratory research is discussed in more detail in Chapter 3, and qualitative research techniques are discussed in detail in Chapter 5.

Although research undertaken at this stage may not be conducted in a formal way, it can provide valuable insights into the problem, as illustrated by Harley Davidson in the opening example. Industry experts indicated the importance of brand loyalty, which also emerged as a major factor in focus groups. Secondary data revealed that most motorcycle owners also owned automobiles such as cars, SUVs, and trucks. Focus groups further indicated that motorcycles were used primarily as a means of recreation.

The insights gained from qualitative research, along with discussions with decision maker(s), interviews with industry experts, and secondary data analysis help the researcher to understand the environmental context of the problem.

# ENVIRONMENTAL CONTEXT OF THE PROBLEM

*environmental context of the problem*
Consists of the factors that have an impact on the definition of the marketing research problem, including past information and forecasts, resources and constraints of the firm, objectives of the decision maker, buyer behavior, legal environment, economic environment, and marketing and technological skills of the firm.

To understand the background of a marketing research problem, the researcher must understand the client's firm and industry. In particular, the researcher should analyze the factors that have an impact on the definition of the marketing research problem. These factors, encompassing the *environmental context of the problem,* include past information and forecasts pertaining to the industry and the firm, resources and constraints of the firm, objectives of the decision maker, buyer behavior, legal environment, economic environment, and marketing and technological skills of the firm, as shown in Figure 2.2. Each of these factors is discussed briefly.[12]

*Figure 2.2*

Factors to be Considered in the Environmental Context of the Problem

- **P**ast Information and Forecasts
- **R**esources and Constraints
- **O**bjectives
- **B**uyer Behavior
- **L**egal Environment
- **E**conomic Environment
- **M**arketing and Technological Skills

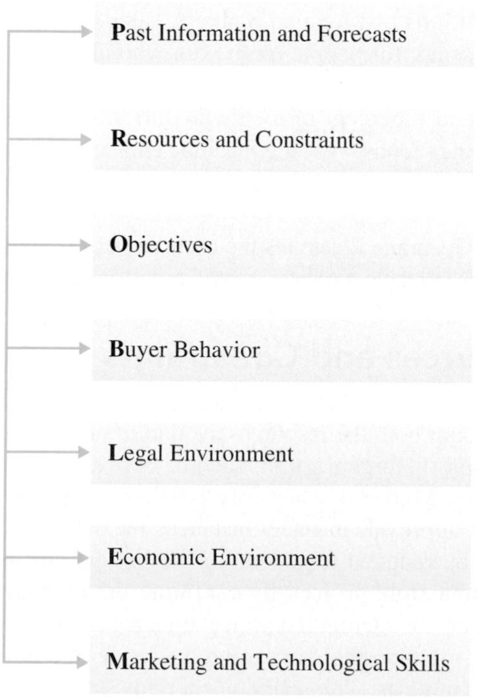

## Past Information and Forecasts

Past information and forecasts of trends with respect to sales, market share, profitability, technology, population, demographics, and lifestyle can help the researcher understand the underlying marketing research problem. Where appropriate, this kind of analysis should be carried out at the industry and firm levels. For example, if a firm's sales have decreased but industry sales have increased, the problems will be very different than if the industry sales have also decreased. In the former case, the problems are likely to be specific to the firm.[13]

Past information and forecasts can be valuable in uncovering potential opportunities and problems, as the fast-food industry has discovered. The following example shows how fast-food chains such as McDonald's have sought to exploit potential opportunities in the recent trend toward a shorter and vanishing lunch break in the office.

**REAL RESEARCH**

### *All Work and No Food*

In recent years, there has been a significant change in eating habits while people are at work. A study in 2001 by research firm Datamonitor (*www.datamonitor.com*) found that 31 percent of workers do not eat lunch at least once per week. The American work ethic has continued to put pressure on people to use their time wisely. The work environment change of having deadlines continuously throughout the day has affected people's perceptions about when to take lunch and what they choose to eat—if they eat at all.

Many people are also combining work and eating, which includes eating at one's desk or during meetings. Almost 24 percent of workers (23.9%) buy carryout at least once per week and about 10 percent (10.3%) have lunch delivered. Multitasking also involves using lunchtime for personal errands, such as going to the post office, carwash, gym, or shops. Workers aged 18 to 24 are more likely to take their lunch break than older workers, but they are also more likely to use that time for activities other than eating. On the other hand, it can be difficult for some people to take their full hour-long lunch because their coworkers may not do so, causing peer pressure. Over 40 percent of workers feel that they are not taking a proper lunch break. This trend will continue to grow according to the forecast.

From the marketer's perspective, convenience is very important in reaching "grab-it-and-go consumers." This also presents problems for sit-down restaurants and over-crowded fast-food restaurants during the typical lunchtime. More handheld food options will grow in popularity among workers. McDonald's (*www.mcdonalds.com*) introduced its three kinds of McSalad Shakers, salads in shakable containers for tossing the salad with dressing, for people on the run who also want to eat healthy. Now people have the option of ordering salad to eat in their vehicles, which is appealing to the 20 percent of women and 8 percent of men who currently eat salads for lunch. Companies that offer convenience foods, vending machine choices, and lunch on the go will continue to capture more share of the lunch market.[14] ▪

This example illustrates the usefulness of past information and forecasts, which can be especially valuable if resources are limited and there are other constraints on the organization.

## Resources and Constraints

To formulate a marketing research problem of appropriate scope, it is necessary to take into account both the resources available, such as money and research skills, and the constraints on the organization, such as cost and time. Proposing a large-scale project that would cost $100,000, when only $40,000 has been budgeted, obviously will not meet management approval. In many instances the scope of the marketing research problem may have to be reduced to accommodate budget constraints. This might be done, as in the department store project, by confining the investigation to major geographical markets rather than conducting the project on a national basis.

It is often possible to extend the scope of a project appreciably with only a marginal increase in costs. This can considerably enhance the usefulness of the project, thereby increasing the probability that management will approve it. Time constraints can be important when decisions must be made quickly.[15] A project for Fisher-Price, a major toy manufacturer, involving mall intercept interviews in six major cities (Chicago, Fresno, Kansas City, New York, Philadelphia, and San Diego) had to be completed in six weeks. Why this rush? The results had to be presented at an upcoming board meeting where a major (go/no go) decision was to be made about a new product introduction.[16]

Other constraints, such as those imposed by the client firm's personnel, organizational structure and culture, or decision-making styles, should be identified to determine the scope of the research project. However, constraints should not be allowed to diminish the value of the research to the decision maker or compromise the integrity of the research process. If a research project is worth doing, it is worth doing well. In instances where the resources are too limited to allow a high-quality project, the firm should be advised not to undertake formal marketing research. For this reason, it becomes necessary to identify resources and constraints, a task that can be better understood when examined in the light of the objectives of the organization and the decision maker.

## Objectives

**objectives**
Goals of the organization and of the decision maker must be considered in order to conduct successful marketing research.

Decisions are made to accomplish **objectives.** The formulation of the management decision problem must be based on a clear understanding of two types of objectives: (1) the organizational objectives (the goals of the organization), and (2) the personal objectives of the decision maker (DM). For the project to be successful, it must serve the objectives of the organization and of the DM. This, however, is not an easy task.

The decision maker rarely formulates personal or organizational objectives accurately. Rather, it is likely that these objectives will be stated in terms that have no operational significance, such as "to improve corporate image." Direct questioning of the DM is unlikely to reveal all of the relevant objectives. The researcher needs skill to extract these objectives. An effective technique is to confront the DM with each of the possible solutions to a problem and ask whether they would follow that course of action. If a "no" answer is received, use further probing to uncover objectives that are not served by the course of action.

## Buyer Behavior

**buyer behavior**
A body of knowledge that tries to understand and predict consumers' reactions based on an individual's specific characteristics.

**Buyer behavior** is a central component of the environmental context. In most marketing decisions, the problem can ultimately be traced to predicting the response of buyers to specific actions by the marketer. An understanding of the underlying buyer behavior can provide valuable insights into the problem. The buyer behavior factors that should be considered include:

1. The number and geographical location of the buyers and nonbuyers
2. Demographic and psychological characteristics
3. Product consumption habits and the consumption of related product categories
4. Media consumption behavior and response to promotions
5. Price sensitivity
6. Retail outlets patronized
7. Buyer preferences

The following example shows how an understanding of the relevant buyer behavior helps in identifying the causes underlying a problem.

### REAL RESEARCH

## *How 'Got Milk?' Got Sales*

Milk sales had declined in the 1980s and early 1990s, and the milk industry needed to find a way to increase sales. An advertising company was hired by the California Milk Processor Board, who in turn hired M/A/R/C Research (*www.marcresearch.com*) to conduct a telephone tracking survey of Californians over age 11. To identify the cause of low milk sales, the research company sought to understand the underlying behavior of consumers toward milk. Through extensive focus groups, household observations, and telephone surveys, M/A/R/C was able to understand consumer behavior underlying milk consumption. This research revealed how people used milk, what made them want it, with what foods they used it, and how they felt when they were deprived of it. They found that 88 percent of milk is consumed at home and that milk was not the central drink of the average person, but it was used in combination with certain foods such as cereal, cakes, pastries, etc. However, milk was strongly missed when there was none around. The advertising agency, Goodby, Silverstein & Partners, developed an ad campaign around consumer behavior with respect to milk, and launched the well-known "milk mustache" campaign with the "Got Milk?" tag line. This creative advertising was a real attention getter, showing celebrities from Joan Lunden to Rhea Perlman and Danny DeVito sporting the famous white mustache. Through marketing research and the advertising campaign, milk sales increased and continued to be stable through 2003. But beyond sales, "Got Milk?" has become part of the American language. Some consumers have even said that their kids walk into the kitchen with a cookie asking for a "glass of got milk?" In more recent ads, Cookie Monster and Snap Crackle Pop have experienced milk deprivation. The most recent addition to the ad campaign is the "Got Milk?" Web site at *www.gotmilk.com*, complete with merchandise, contests, games, and recipes.[17] ∎

The decline in milk consumption could be attributed to changes in the sociocultural environment, which includes demographic trends and consumer tastes. In addition, the legal environment and the economic environment can have an impact on the behavior of the consumers and the definition of the marketing research problem.

## Legal Environment

**legal environment**
Regulatory policies and norms within which organizations must operate.

The *legal environment* includes public policies, laws, government agencies, and pressure groups that influence and regulate various organizations and individuals in society. Important areas of law include patents, trademarks, royalties, trade agreements, taxes, and tariffs. Federal laws have an impact on each element of the marketing mix. In addition, laws have been passed to regulate specific industries. The legal environment can have an important bearing on the definition of the marketing research problem, as can the economic environment.

## Economic Environment

**economic environment**
The economic environment consists of income, prices, savings, credit, and general economic conditions.

Along with the legal environment, another important component of the environmental context is the *economic environment,* which is comprised of purchasing power, gross income, disposable income, discretionary income, prices, savings, credit availability, and general economic conditions. The general state of the economy (rapid growth, slow growth, recession, or stagflation) influences the willingness of consumers and businesses to take on credit and spend on big-ticket items. Thus, the economic environment can have important implications for marketing research problems.

## Marketing and Technological Skills

A company's expertise with each element of the marketing mix as well as its general level of marketing and technological skills affect the nature and scope of the marketing research project. For example, the introduction of a new product that requires sophisticated technology may not be a viable course if the firm lacks the skills to manufacture or market it.

A firm's marketing and technological skills greatly influence the marketing programs and strategies that can be implemented. At a broader level, other elements of the technological environment should be considered. Technological advances, such as the continuing development of computers, have had a dramatic impact on marketing research. To illustrate, computerized checkout lanes allow supermarkets to monitor daily consumer demand for products and make the scanner data available to the researcher. It is possible to obtain precise information on retail sales, not only of the firm's brands but also of competing brands. The speed and accuracy of data collection enable the researcher to investigate intricate problems such as the daily changes in market share during a promotion.

After gaining an adequate understanding of the environmental context of the problem, the researcher can define the management decision problem and the marketing research problem. This process was illustrated in the opening Harley Davidson example. Forecasts called for an increase in consumer spending on recreation and entertainment well into the year 2010. Empowered by the Internet, consumers in the 21st century became increasingly sophisticated and value conscious. Yet, brand image and brand loyalty played a significant role in buyer behavior with well-known brands continuing to command a premium. Clearly, Harley Davidson had the necessary resources and marketing and technological skills to achieve its objective of being the dominant motorcycle brand on a global basis. The management decision problem was: Should Harley Davidson invest to produce more motorcycles? The marketing research problem was to determine if the customers would be loyal buyers of Harley Davidson in the long term. The following section provides further understanding of the management decision problem and the marketing research problem.

# MANAGEMENT DECISION PROBLEM AND MARKETING RESEARCH PROBLEM

*management decision problem*
The problem confronting the decision maker. It asks what the decision maker needs to do.

*marketing research problem*
A problem that entails determining what information is needed and how it can be obtained in the most feasible way.

The ***management decision problem*** asks what the DM needs to do, whereas the ***marketing research problem*** asks what information is needed and how it can best be obtained (Table 2.1). Research can provide the necessary information to make a sound decision.[18] The management decision problem is action oriented. It is concerned with the possible actions the DM can take. How should the loss of market share be arrested? Should the market be segmented differently? Should a new product be introduced? Should the promotional budget be increased? In contrast, the marketing research problem is information oriented. It involves determining what information is needed and how that information can be obtained effectively and efficiently. Whereas the management decision problem focuses on symptoms, the marketing research problem focuses on underlying causes.

Consider, for example, the loss of market share for a particular product line. The DM's decision problem is how to recover this loss. Alternative courses of action include modifying existing products, introducing new products, changing other elements in the marketing mix, and segmenting the market. Suppose the DM and the researcher (R) believe that the problem is caused by inappropriate segmentation of the market and want research to provide information on this issue. The research problem would then become the identification and evaluation of an alternative basis for segmenting the market. Note that this process is interactive. The department store project example illustrates further the distinction between the management decision problem and the marketing research problem as well as the interactive nature of the problem definition process.

**TABLE 2.1**

**Management Decision Problem Versus the Marketing Research Problem**

| MANAGEMENT DECISION PROBLEM | MARKETING RESEARCH PROBLEM |
| --- | --- |
| Asks what the decision maker needs to do | Asks what information is needed and how it should be obtained |
| Action oriented | Information oriented |
| Focuses on symptoms | Focuses on the underlying causes |

**ACTIVE RESEARCH** | DEPARTMENT STORE PROJECT

### Defining the Problem

DM: We have seen a decline in the patronage of our store.
R: How do you know that?
DM: Well, it is reflected in our sales and market share.
R: Why do you think your patronage has declined?
DM: I wish I knew!
R: What about competition?
DM: I suspect we are better than competition on some factors and worse than them on others.
R: How do the customers view your store?
DM: I think most of them view it positively, although we may have a weak area or two.

After a series of dialogues with the DM and other key managers, analysis of secondary data, and qualitative research, the problem was identified as follows:

### Management Decision Problem
What should be done to improve the patronage of Sears?

### Marketing Research Problem
Determine the relative strengths and weaknesses of Sears, vis-à-vis other major competitors, with respect to factors that influence store patronage.

The following examples further distinguish between the management decision problem and the marketing research problem:

| Management decision problem | Marketing research problem |
|---|---|
| Should a new product be introduced? | To determine consumer preferences and purchase intentions for the proposed new product |
| Should the advertising campaign be changed? | To determine the effectiveness of the current advertising campaign |
| Should the price of the brand be increased? | To determine the price elasticity of demand and the impact on sales and profits of various levels of price changes |

This distinction between the management decision problem and the marketing research problem helps us in understanding how the marketing research problem should be defined.

# DEFINING THE MARKETING RESEARCH PROBLEM

The general rule to be followed in defining the marketing research problem is that the definition should (1) allow the researcher to obtain all the information needed to address the management decision problem, and (2) guide the researcher in proceeding with the project. Researchers make two common errors in problem definition. The first arises when the research problem is defined too broadly. A broad definition does not provide clear guidelines for the subsequent steps involved in the project. Some examples of overly broad marketing research problem definitions are: (1) developing a marketing strategy for the brand, (2) improving the competitive position of the firm, or (3) improving the company's image. These are not specific enough to suggest an approach to the problem or a research design.

The second type of error is just the opposite: the marketing research problem is defined too narrowly. A narrow focus may preclude consideration of some courses of

*Figure 2.3*
Proper Definition of the
Marketing Research Problem

action, particularly those that are innovative and may not be obvious. It may also prevent the researcher from addressing important components of the management decision problem. For example, in a project conducted for a major consumer products firm, the management problem was how to respond to a price cut initiated by a competitor. The alternative courses of action initially identified by the firm's research staff were: (1) decrease the price of the firm's brand to match the competitor's price cut; (2) maintain price but increase advertising heavily; (3) decrease the price somewhat, without matching the competitor's price and moderately increase advertising. None of these alternatives seemed promising. When outside marketing research experts were brought in, the problem was redefined as improving the market share and profitability of the product line. Qualitative research indicated that in blind tests consumers could not differentiate products offered under different brand names. Furthermore, consumers relied on price as an indicator of product quality. These findings led to a creative alternative: increase the price of the existing brand and introduce two new brands—one priced to match the competitor and the other priced to undercut it. This strategy was implemented, leading to an increase in market share and profitability.

The likelihood of committing either type of error in problem definition can be reduced by stating the marketing research problem in broad, general terms and identifying its specific components (see Figure 2.3). The ***broad statement*** provides perspective on the problem and acts as a safeguard against committing the second type of error. The ***specific components*** focus on the key aspects of the problem and provide clear guidelines on how to proceed further, thereby reducing the likelihood of the first type of error. Examples of appropriate marketing research problem definitions follow.

**broad statement**
The initial statement of the marketing research problem that provides an appropriate perspective on the problem.

**specific components**
The second part of the marketing research problem definition. The specific components focus on the key aspects of the problem and provide clear guidelines on how to proceed further.

## REAL RESEARCH

## *Research Serves* Tennis *Magazine*

*Tennis* magazine (*www.tennis.com*), a publication of the New York Times Co., wanted to obtain information about the readers. Though there were only 700,000 subscribers, the magazine had a readership of 1.6 million in 2003. They hired Signet Research, Inc. (*www.signetresearch.com*), an independent research company in Cliffside Park, NJ, to conduct marketing research. The management decision problem was what changes should be made in *Tennis* magazine to make it more appealing to its readers.

The broad marketing research problem was defined as gathering information about the subscribers of *Tennis* magazine. Specific components of the problem included the following:

1. Demographics. Who are the men and women who subscribe to the magazine?
2. Psychological characteristics and lifestyles. How did subscribers spend their money and their free time? Lifestyle indicators to be examined were fitness, travel, car rental, apparel, consumer electronics, credit cards, and financial investments.
3. Tennis activity. Where and how often do subscribers play tennis? What are their skill levels?
4. Relationship to *Tennis* magazine. How much time do subscribers spend with the issues? How long do they keep them? Do they share the magazine with other tennis players?

There should be a written statement of the marketing research problem that has been agreed to by the client. Burke consultant discussing the marketing research problem definition with the client.

Because the questions were so clearly defined, the information provided by this research helped management design specific features on tennis instruction, equipment, famous tennis players, and locations to play tennis to meet readers' specific needs. The changes that followed included the addition of Chris Evert as publisher in March 2001. She is one of the most influential people in the sport with 18 Grand Slam titles. As publisher, Evert writes a monthly column on various tennis issues and takes part in advertising events. These changes have made *Tennis* magazine more appealing to its readers.[19] ∎

In the *Tennis* magazine example, the broad statement of the problem focused on gathering information about the subscribers, and the specific components identified the particular items of information that should be obtained. This was also true in the opening Harley Davidson example, where a broad statement of the marketing research problem was followed by four specific components. Problem definition in the department store project followed a similar pattern.

Once the marketing research problem has been broadly stated and its specific components identified, the researcher is in a position to develop a suitable approach.

---

**ACTIVE RESEARCH** | DEPARTMENT STORE PROJECT

### *Problem Definition*

In the department store project, the marketing research problem is to determine the relative strengths and weaknesses of Sears, vis-à-vis other major competitors, with respect to factors that influence store patronage. Specifically, research should provide information on the following questions.

1. What criteria do households use when selecting department stores?
2. How do households evaluate Sears and competing stores in terms of the choice criteria identified in question 1?
3. Which stores are patronized when shopping for specific product categories?
4. What is the market share of Sears and its competitors for specific product categories?
5. What is the demographic and psychological profile of the customers of Sears? Does it differ from the profile of customers of competing stores?
6. Can store patronage and preference be explained in terms of store evaluations and customer characteristics?

# COMPONENTS OF THE APPROACH

In the process of developing an approach, we must not lose sight of the goal—the outputs. The outputs of the approach development process should include the following components: objective/theoretical framework, analytical models, research questions, hypotheses, and specification of information needed (see Figure 2.1). Each of these components is discussed in the following sections.

## Objective/Theoretical Framework

*theory*
A conceptual scheme based on foundational statements, or axioms, that are assumed to be true.

*objective evidence*
Unbiased evidence that is supported by empirical findings.

In general, research should be based on objective evidence and supported by theory. A *theory* is a conceptual scheme based on foundational statements called axioms, which are assumed to be true. *Objective evidence* (evidence that is unbiased and supported by empirical findings) is gathered by compiling relevant findings from secondary sources. Likewise, an appropriate theory to guide the research might be identified by reviewing academic literature contained in books, journals, and monographs. The researcher should rely on theory to determine which variables should be investigated. Furthermore, theoretical considerations provide information on how the variables should be operationalized and measured, as well as how the research design and sample should be selected. A theory also serves as a foundation on which the researcher can organize and interpret the findings. "Nothing is so practical as a good theory."[20]

Theory also plays a vital role in influencing the research procedures adopted in basic research. However, applying a theory to a marketing research problem requires creativity on the part of the researcher. A theory may not specify adequately how its abstract constructs (variables) can be embodied in a real-world phenomenon. Moreover, theories are incomplete. They deal with only a subset of variables that exist in the real world. Hence, the researcher must also identify and examine other, nontheoretical, variables.[21]

The department store patronage project illustrates how theory can be used to develop an approach. Review of the retailing literature revealed that the modeling of store patronage in terms of choice criteria had received considerable support.[22] Furthermore, as many as 42 choice criteria had been identified in the literature, and guidelines on operationalizing these variables were provided. This provided an initial pool from which the final eight characteristics included in the questionnaire were selected. Theoretical considerations also suggested that store behavior could be examined via a survey of respondents familiar with department store shopping. The theoretical framework also serves as a foundation for developing an appropriate analytical model.

## Analytical Model

*analytical model*
An explicit specification of a set of variables and their interrelationships designed to represent some real system or process in whole or in part.

*verbal models*
Analytical models that provide a written representation of the relationships between variables.

*graphical models*
Analytical models that provide a visual picture of the relationships between variables.

*mathematical models*
Analytical models that explicitly describe the relationships between variables, usually in equation form.

An *analytical model* is a set of variables and their interrelationships designed to represent, in whole or in part, some real system or process. Models can have many different forms. The most common are verbal, graphical, and mathematical structures. In *verbal models,* the variables and their relationships are stated in prose form. Such models may be mere restatements of the main tenets of a theory. *Graphical models* are visual. They are used to isolate variables and to suggest directions of relationships but are not designed to provide numerical results. They are logical preliminary steps to developing mathematical models. *Mathematical models* explicitly specify the relationships among variables, usually in equation form. These models can be used as guides for formulating the research design and have the advantage of being amenable to manipulation.[23] The different models are illustrated in the context of the department store project.

As can be seen from this example, the verbal, graphical, and mathematical models depict the same phenomenon or theoretical framework in different ways. The phenomenon of store patronage stated verbally is represented for clarity through a figure (graphical model) and is put in equation form (mathematical model) for ease of statistical estimation and testing. Graphical models are particularly helpful in conceptualizing an approach to the problem. In the opening Harley Davidson example, the underlying theory was that

### Model Building

*Verbal Model*

A consumer first becomes aware of a department store. That person then gains an understanding of the store by evaluating the store in terms of the factors comprising the choice criteria. Based on the evaluation, the consumer forms a degree of preference for the store. If preference is strong enough, the consumer will patronize the store.

*Graphical Model*

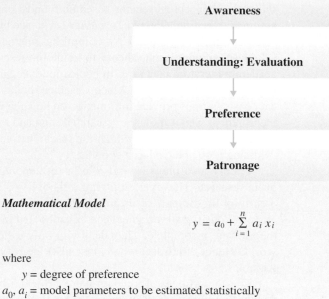

*Mathematical Model*

$$y = a_0 + \sum_{i=1}^{n} a_i x_i$$

where

   $y$ = degree of preference

$a_0, a_i$ = model parameters to be estimated statistically

   $x_i$ = store patronage factors that constitute the choice criteria

brand loyalty is the result of positive beliefs, attitude, affect, and experience with the brand. This theory may be represented by the following graphical model.

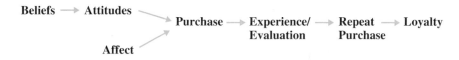

The verbal, graphical, and mathematical models complement each other and help the researcher identify relevant research questions and hypotheses.

## Research Questions

***Research questions*** (RQs) are refined statements of the specific components of the problem. Although the components of the problem define the problem in specific terms, further detail may be needed to develop an approach. Each component of the problem may have to be broken down into subcomponents or research questions. Research questions ask what specific information is required with respect to the problem components. If the research questions are answered by the research, then the information obtained should aid the decision maker. The formulation of the research questions should be guided not only by the problem definition, but also by the theoretical framework and the analytical model adopted. For a given problem component, there are likely to be several research questions, as in the case of the department store project.

The theoretical framework and the analytical model play a significant role in the operationalization and measurement of variables specified by the research questions. Whereas, in the department store project, the literature reviewed did not provide any

**ACTIVE RESEARCH** | DEPARTMENT STORE PROJECT

*Research Questions*

The fifth component of the research problem was the psychological profile of Sears' customers. In the context of psychological characteristics, several research questions were asked about the customers of Sears.

- Do they exhibit store loyalty?
- Are they heavy users of credit?
- Are they more conscious of personal appearance as compared to customers of competing stores?
- Do they combine shopping with eating out?

The research questions were then further refined by precisely defining the variables and determining how they were to be operationalized. To illustrate, how should the use of Sears credit be measured? It could be measured in any of the following ways.

1. Whether the customer holds a Sears credit card.
2. Whether the customer uses the Sears credit card.
3. The number of times the Sears credit card was used in a specified time period.
4. The dollar amount charged to the Sears credit card during a specified time period.

definitive measure of store credit, the mathematical model could incorporate any of the alternative measures. Thus, it was decided to include all four measures of store credit in the study. Research questions may be further refined into one or more hypotheses.

## Hypotheses

**hypothesis**
An unproven statement or proposition about a factor or phenomenon that is of interest to the researcher.

A *hypothesis* (H) is an unproven statement or proposition about a factor or phenomenon that is of interest to the researcher. It may, for example, be a tentative statement about relationships between two or more variables as stipulated by the theoretical framework or the analytical model. Often, a hypothesis is a possible answer to the research question. Hypotheses go beyond research questions because they are statements of relationships or propositions rather than merely questions to which answers are sought. Whereas research questions are interrogative, hypotheses are declarative and can be tested empirically (see Chapter 15). An important role of a hypothesis is to suggest variables to be included in the research design. The relationship between the marketing research problem, research questions, and hypotheses, along with the influence of the objective/theoretical framework and analytical models, is described in Figure 2.4 and illustrated by the following example from the department store project.[24]

Unfortunately, it may not be possible to formulate hypotheses in all situations. Sometimes sufficient information is not available to develop hypotheses. At other times,

*Figure 2.4*
Development of Research
Questions and Hypotheses

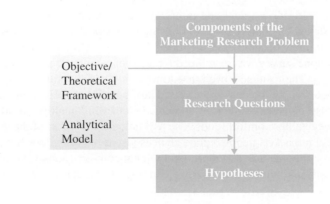

---

**ACTIVE RESEARCH**  |  DEPARTMENT STORE PROJECT

### *Hypotheses*

The following hypotheses were formulated in relation to the research question on store loyalty:[25]

H1: Customers who are store loyal are less knowledgeable about the shopping environment.
H2: Store-loyal customers are more risk averse than are nonloyal customers.

These hypotheses guided the research by ensuring that variables measuring knowledge of the shopping environment and propensity to take risks were included in the research design.

---

the most reasonable statement of a hypothesis may be a trivial restatement of the research question. For example:

RQ: Do customers of Sears exhibit store loyalty?
H: Customers of Sears are loyal.

Hypotheses are an important part of the approach to the problem. When stated in operational terms, as H1 and H2 in the department store example, they provide guidelines on what, and how, data are to be collected and analyzed. When operational hypotheses are stated using symbolic notation, they are commonly referred to as statistical hypotheses. A research question may have more than one hypothesis associated with it, as in the Harley Davidson example and the one that follows.

## REAL RESEARCH

### *The Taste of Comfort*

In the midst of an insecure economy in 2003, nothing is more comforting than trusted, familiar foods and treats. Do certain foods provide comfort under different situations in people's lives? For instance, does chicken soup make people feel better on a rainy day or when they have a cold, partially because they may have eaten chicken soup during the same situations when they were growing up? Marketing research was conducted to investigate comfort foods. The specific research questions and the associated hypotheses were:

RQ1: What foods are considered as comfort foods?
H1: Potato chips are considered comfort food.
H2: Ice cream is considered comfort food.
RQ2: When do people eat comfort foods?
H3: People eat comfort foods when they are in a good mood.
H4: People eat comfort foods when they are in a bad mood.
RQ3: How do people become attached to comfort foods?
H5: People are attached to comfort foods that are consistent with their personality.
H6: People are attached to comfort foods because of past associations.

In-depth telephone interviews were conducted with 411 people across the United States. The purpose was to find out what people's favorite comfort foods are and how these products became comfort foods. From the qualitative answers, a 20-minute quantitative phone survey was developed for a larger sample size of 1,005.

The results showed that America's favorite comfort food is potato chips, followed by ice cream, cookies, and candy. Thus, both H1 and H2 were supported. Many respondents also considered natural, homemade, or even "healthy" foods such as meats, soups, and vegetables comfort foods. The psychological comfort of these foods may provide a powerful impact on people's food choices just as the taste does for snack foods.

People are also more likely to eat comfort foods when they are in good moods than sad: jubilant (86 percent), celebrating (74 percent), got the blues (39 percent), the blahs

(52 percent), and lonely (39 percent). Thus, H3 had stronger support than H4, although both were supported.

The results also showed that past associations with products and personality identification are the two main reasons why foods become comfort foods, thus supporting H5 and H6. Foods often remind people of specific events during their lives, which is why they eat them for comfort. Some foods also help people form their identities because the products are consistent with their personality. For instance, meat and potatoes are staples for the macho, all-American male, which may explain why many males do not want to try healthier soy products.

The more marketers know about the psychology behind foods, at both the associative and personality levels, the better they will be at establishing new brands, as well as packaging and advertising existing brands that are already considered comfort foods and have their own brand personalities. For example, Frito-Lay's Baked Lays brand of low-fat potato chips has been very successful. Frito-Lay combined the fact that chips are fun to eat with the wave of health-conscious people in the United States. The slogan for the new brand was "Taste the Fun, Not the Fat." which affects one's concept of wanting a fun lifestyle. The fun product continues to be comforting while reducing people's guilt by its low fat content.[26] ■

## Specification of Information Needed

By focusing on each component of the problem and the analytical framework and models, research questions, and hypotheses, the researcher can determine what information should be obtained in the marketing research project. It is helpful to carry out this exercise for each component of the problem and make a list specifying all the information that should be collected. Let us consider the department store project and focus on the components of the problem identified earlier in this chapter to determine the information that should be obtained from the respondents selected for the survey.

**ACTIVE RESEARCH**  | DEPARTMENT STORE PROJECT

### *Specification of Information Needed*

**Component 1**
This component involves the criteria households use to select a department store. Based on the process outlined earlier in this chapter, the researcher identified the following factors as part of the choice criteria: quality of merchandise, variety and assortment of merchandise, returns and adjustment policy, service of store personnel, prices, convenience of location, layout of store, credit and billing policies. The respondents should be asked to rate the importance of each factor as it influences their store selection.

**Component 2**
This component is concerned with competition. The researcher identified nine department stores as competitors to Sears based on discussions with management. The respondents should be asked to evaluate Sears and its nine competitors on the eight choice criteria factors.

**Component 3**
Specific product categories are the focus of this component. Sixteen different product categories were selected, including women's dresses, women's sportswear, lingerie and body fashion, junior merchandise, men's apparel, cosmetics, jewelry, shoes, sheets and towels, furniture and bedding, and draperies. The respondents should be asked whether they shop at each of the 10 stores for each of the 16 product categories.

**Component 4**
No additional information needs to be obtained from the respondents.

*(continued)*

**ACTIVE RESEARCH** | DEPARTMENT STORE PROJECT *(continued)*

*Component 5*
Information on the standard demographic characteristics should be obtained from the respondents. Based on the process outlined earlier in this chapter, the researcher identified the following psychographic characteristics as relevant: store loyalty, credit use, appearance consciousness, and combining shopping with eating. Information on these variables should also be obtained from the respondents.

*Component 6*
No additional information needs to be obtained from the respondents.

This process is further illustrated by United Airlines.

### REAL RESEARCH

## *At United, Food Is Uniting the Airline with Travelers*

The airline industry was negatively affected by the September 11, 2001 terrorist hijackings. As of 2002, passenger traffic was still down. United Airlines (*www.ual.com*) had to deal with passenger loyalty (management decision problem: how should United attract more and more loyal passengers?). The broad marketing research problem was to identify the factors that influence loyalty of airline travelers. Exploratory research, theoretical framework, and empirical evidence revealed that the consumers' choice of an airline is influenced by safety, price of the ticket, frequent-flyer program, convenience of scheduling, and brand name.

A graphical model stipulated that consumers evaluate competing airlines based on factors of the choice criteria to select a preferred airline. The problem was that major airlines were quite similar on these factors. Indeed, airlines offered the same schedules, the same service, and the same fares. Consequently, United Airlines had to find a way to differentiate itself. Food turned out to be the solution.

Secondary data, like the J. D. Power & Associates' survey on "current and future trends in airline food industry," indicated that food service is a major contributor to customer loyalty. Qualitative and survey research conducted by United also emphasized the importance of food brands. The airline's Marketrak survey told United Airlines that customers wanted more varied and up-to-date food.

The following research questions and hypotheses were posed:

RQ1: How important is food for airline customers?
H1: Food is an important factor for airline travelers.
H2: Travelers value branded food.

A sound approach in the form of theoretical framework, graphical model, research questions, hypotheses, and specification of information needed helped United Airlines to discover the importance of food to airline customers.

H3: Travelers prefer larger food portions, but with consistent quality.
H4: Travelers prefer exotic food.

Information obtained from the respondents included evaluation of competing airlines (United, Delta, American, etc.) on food and other factors of the choice criteria and measurement of airline travel and loyalty.

This kind of research helped United Airlines to define their marketing research problem and develop the approach. Focus groups and surveys were conducted to check customers' perceptions of food in United Airlines' aircraft. The results provided support for all the hypotheses (H1 to H4). United Airlines then made a few changes: new "culinary menus," larger portions of food, new coffee, and branded products (e.g., Godiva chocolates). This resulted in better service, increasing customer satisfaction and fostering loyalty.[27] ■

# INTERNATIONAL MARKETING RESEARCH

The precise definition of the marketing research problem is more difficult in international marketing research than in domestic marketing research. Unfamiliarity with the environmental factors of the country where the research is being conducted can greatly increase the difficulty of understanding the problem's environmental context and uncovering its causes.

**REAL RESEARCH**

## *Heinz Ketchup Could Not Catch Up in Brazil*

In 2003, Heinz (*www.heinz.com*) was selling products in over 200 countries and sales were topping $10 billion with approximately 45 percent of revenue coming from overseas. Despite good track records inland and overseas, H. J. Heinz Co. failed in Brazil, a market that seemed to be South America's biggest and most promising. Heinz entered into a joint venture with Citrosuco Paulista, a giant orange juice exporter because of the future possibility of buying the profitable company. Yet, the sales of its products, including ketchup, did not take off. Where was the problem? A problem audit revealed that the company lacked a strong local distribution system. Heinz lost control of the distribution because it worked on consignment. Distribution could not reach 25 percent penetration. The other related problem was that Heinz concentrated on neighborhood shops because this strategy was successful in Mexico. However, the problem audit revealed that 75 percent of the grocery shopping in Sao Paulo is done in supermarkets and not the smaller shops. Although Mexico and Brazil may appear to have similar cultural and demographic characteristics, consumer behavior can vary greatly. A closer and intensive look at the Brazilian food distribution system and the behavior of consumers could have averted this failure. Heinz, however, is looking more closely at Asia, especially China, where the company markets baby food and where 22 million babies are born every year.[28] ■

As the Heinz example illustrates, many international marketing efforts fail, not because research was not conducted, but because the relevant environmental factors were not taken into account. Generally, this leads to a definition of the problem that is too narrow. Consider, for example, the consumption of soft drinks. In many Asian countries such as India, water is consumed with meals, and soft drinks are generally served to guests and on special occasions. Therefore, the management decision problem of increasing the market share of a soft drink brand would translate to a different marketing research problem in India than in the United States. Before defining the problem, the researcher must isolate and examine the impact of the **self-reference criterion** (SRC), or the unconscious reference to one's own cultural values. The following steps help researchers account for environmental and cultural differences when defining the problem in an international marketing context:[29]

**Step 1.** Define the marketing research problem in terms of domestic environmental and cultural factors. This involves an identification of relevant American (domestic country) traits, economics, values, needs, or habits.

**self-reference criterion**
The unconscious reference to one's own cultural values.

**Step 2.** Define the marketing research problem in terms of foreign environmental and cultural factors. Make no judgments. This involves an identification of the related traits, economics, values, needs, or habits in the proposed market culture. This task requires input from researchers familiar with the foreign environment.

**Step 3.** Isolate the self-reference criterion (SRC) influence on the problem and examine it carefully to see how it complicates the problem. Examine the differences between steps 1 and 2. The SRC can be seen to account for these differences.

**Step 4.** Redefine the problem without the SRC influence and address it for the foreign market situation. If the differences in step 3 are significant, the impact of the SRC should be carefully considered.

Consider the broad problem of the Coca-Cola Company trying to increase its penetration of the soft drink market in India. In step 1, the problem of increasing the market penetration in the United States would be considered. In the United States of America, virtually all households consume soft drinks, and the problem would be to increase the soft drink consumption of existing consumers. Furthermore, soft drinks are regularly consumed with meals and as thirst quenchers. So the problem of increasing marketing penetration would involve getting the consumers to consume more soft drinks with meals and at other times. In India, on the other hand (step 2), a much smaller percentage of households consume soft drinks, and soft drinks are not consumed with meals. Thus, in step 3, the SRC can be identified as the American notion that soft drinks are an all-purpose, all-meal, beverage. In step 4, the problem in the Indian context can be defined as how to get a greater percentage of the Indian consumers to consume soft drinks (Coca-Cola products) and how to get them to consume soft drinks (Coca-Cola products) more often for personal consumption.

While developing theoretical frameworks, models, research questions, and hypotheses, remember that differences in the environmental factors, especially the sociocultural environment, may lead to differences in the formation of perceptions, attitudes, preferences, and choice behavior. For example, orientation toward time varies considerably across cultures. In Asia, Latin America, and the Middle East, people are not as time conscious as Westerners. This influences their perceptions of and preferences for convenience foods such as frozen foods and prepared dinners. In developing an approach to the problem, the researcher should consider the equivalence of consumption and purchase behavior and the underlying factors that influence them. This is critical to the identification of the correct research questions, hypotheses, and information needed.

### REAL RESEARCH

## *Surf Superconcentrate Faces a Super Washout in Japan*

As of 2003, Unilever (*www.unilever.com*) sold consumer products in 150 countries. As much as 85 percent of their profits come from overseas, with 7 percent of their profits being attributed to Asia and the Pacific. Unilever attempted to break into the Japanese detergent market with Surf Superconcentrate. It achieved 14.5 percent of the market share initially during test marketing, which fell down to a shocking 2.8 percent when the product was introduced nationally. Where did they go wrong? Surf was designed to have a distinctive premeasured packet as in tea-bag-like sachets, joined in pairs because convenience was an important attribute to Japanese consumers. It also had a "fresh smell" appeal. However, Japanese consumers noticed that the detergents did not dissolve in the wash, partly because of weather conditions and also because of the popularity of low-agitation washing machines. Surf was not designed to work in the new washing machines. Unilever also found that the "fresh smell" positioning of new Surf had little relevance because most consumers hang their wash out in the fresh air. The research approach was certainly not without flaw as Unilever failed to identify critical attributes that are relevant in the Japanese detergent market. Furthermore, it identified factors such as "fresh smell" that had no relevance in the Japanese context. Appropriate qualitative research such as focus groups and depth interviews across samples from the target market could have revealed the correct characteristics or factors leading to a suitable research design.

Despite having to withdraw from the Japanese market, Surf continued to perform well in several markets including India through 2003. With the success and increasing popularity of its other detergent, Omo in Latin America and China, Unilever is looking to introduce the product to see how it fares in Japan.[30] ■

# ETHICS IN MARKETING RESEARCH

Ethical issues arise if the process of defining the problem and developing an approach is compromised by the personal agendas of the client (DM) or the researcher. This process is adversely affected when the DM has hidden objectives such as gaining a promotion or justifying a decision that has been already made. The DM has the obligation to be candid and disclose to the researcher all the relevant information that will enable a proper definition of the marketing research problem. Likewise, the researcher is ethically bound to define the problem so as to further the best interest of the client, rather than the interest of the research firm. At times this may mean making the interest of the research firm subservient to the client, leading to an ethical dilemma.

**REAL RESEARCH**

## *Ethical or More Profitable?*

A marketing research firm is hired by a major consumer electronics company (e.g., Philips) to conduct a large-scale segmentation study with the objective of improving market share. The researcher, after following the process outlined in this chapter, determines that the problem is not market segmentation but distribution. The company appears to be lacking an effective distribution system, which is limiting market share. However, the distribution problem requires a much simpler approach that will greatly reduce the cost of the project and the research firm's profits. What should the researcher do? Should the research firm conduct the research the client wants rather than the research the client needs? Ethical guidelines indicate that the research firm has an obligation to disclose the actual problem to the client. If, after the distribution problem has been discussed, the client still desires the segmentation research, the research firm should feel free to conduct the study. The reason is that the researcher cannot know for certain the motivations underlying the client's behavior.[31] ■

Several ethical issues are also pertinent in developing an approach. When a client solicits proposals, not with the intent of subcontracting the research, but with the intent of gaining the expertise of research firms without pay, an ethical breach has occurred. If the client rejects the proposal of a research firm, then the approach specified in that proposal should not be implemented by the client, unless the client has paid for the development of the proposal. Likewise, the research firm has the ethical obligation to develop an appropriate approach. If the approach is going to make use of models developed in another context, then this should be communicated to the client. For example, if the researcher is going to use a customer satisfaction model developed previously for an insurance company, in a customer satisfaction study for a bank, then this information should be disclosed. Proprietary models and approaches developed by a research firm are the property of that firm and should not be reused by the client in subsequent studies without the permission of the research firm.

Such ethical situations would be satisfactorily resolved if both the client and the researcher adhered to the seven Cs: communication, cooperation, confidence, candor, closeness, continuity, and creativity, as discussed earlier. This would lead to a relationship of mutual trust that would check any unethical tendencies.

# INTERNET AND COMPUTER APPLICATIONS

There are several ways in which the Internet can help in defining the problem and developing an approach, and add value to the traditional methods. Let us first consider the tasks involved.

## Discussions with Decision Makers

The Internet can help the researcher gain access to the DM or DMs. Thanks to e-mail, it is now possible to reach decision makers anywhere, at any time. The Internet can also provide chat rooms where the DM can go in their spare time to chat with the researcher and other DMs about the research project. A discussion could be developed around the problem audit. The audit issues could be introduced in the chat room by the researcher. The DMs could respond to the questions and to the thoughts of the other chat room respondents (other DMs, the researcher, etc.). The availability of the responses to be seen by whoever enters the chat room has the effect of getting all of the DMs together at one time without requiring that they be physically present at the same time. Because of the nature of the discussion (inside company correspondence), the participants could be given password access to the chat room, thus keeping the information secure from those without a need to know.

## Interviews with Industry Experts

The Internet can also be used to enhance the researcher's ability to obtain advice from experts. The Internet can be searched to find industry experts outside of the client's organization. By going to industry sites and newsgroups, one can find access to many knowledgeable industry experts. You could also do searches on the topic at hand and follow up on any postings or FAQs. For example, if you were looking for an expert in the computer hardware industry, these are the steps to take. Go to *www.usenet.com* (if you have a membership) or *groups.google.com* (free), and search for computer industry experts. They have a message board for this specific topic. By examining the postings, you can identify the experts. A search for Dell computers on Google resulted in several postings about Dell. The most recent posting was an e-mail asking a question about a Dell computer. Anyone can reply with information and have interactive chats. It seemed to be a very effective way to communicate with others and, thus, locate industry experts. One of the most effective links on Google is the advanced group search.

## Secondary Data Analysis and Qualitative Research

Search engines , mentioned in Chapter 1, can be used to collect secondary data quickly and economically. We will discuss the availability and acquisition of secondary information on the Internet in more detail in Chapter 4. The Internet is useful in doing qualitative research. We provide a detailed discussion of the use of chat rooms and listservers to do exploratory research in Chapter 3. Conducting qualitative research such as focus groups and depth interviews via the Internet is discussed in Chapter 5.

## Environmental Context of the Problem

Many of the factors to be considered in the environmental context of the problem can be researched via the Internet. Past information and forecasts of trends can be found by searching for the appropriate information with the search engines mentioned earlier.

For client-specific information, the user can go to the company home page and get the information from there. Generally, companies provide information about their products and services at their home page. Therefore, the home page of a company is a good starting point for information about the company. You can also go to *www.freeedgar.com* to download all the reports that a public company has ever created, including their annual report. Investor Communication Services (*ics.adp.com*) is another effective way to research a company and find information on financial reports, company news, corporate profiles, or annual reports. Finally, you can go to sites such as Yahoo Business or Finance or *www.quicken.com* to find out analyst views of the company. Firms such as Dun & Bradstreet (*www.dnb.com*) create company databases that can be accessed through a subscription, or reports that can be purchased on a one-time basis.

## Global Access Toolkit

In May 2001, Dun & Bradstreet (*www.dnb.com*) announced the introduction of their Global Access Toolkit, which provides businesses with D&B's world-class global business database and expands the way global data are delivered. Several Business Week 1000 companies have already adopted the new Toolkit, and it is easily customized for each customer based on decision support requirements and information technology environment. D&B's Toolkit can be used for global business practices that include global risk management, vendor management, and database marketing. The introduction of this new Toolkit reinforces D&B's commitment to dispersing business information in a way to make understanding companies easier. ■

Further, the user can also search for competitor information on the Internet. There are various ways of doing this; the easiest is to visit the competitor's homepage and get the information from there. For example, the user can go to the Pepsi homepage (*www.pepsico.com*) and get the relevant information.

The Dow Jones News/Retrieval Service (DJNR) is the full-text online service of Dow Jones and Company. It offers company and industry information on more than 10 million United States and international companies. Investor Communication Services provides a site where corporate information is available on many companies. The site can be found at *ics.adp.com*.

Several commercial marketing research firms, for example the Gallup organization (*www.gallup.com*), provide valuable information on buyer behavior and market trends. Many newsletters follow marketing, economic, and regulatory trends and are available through online databases. For example, NewsNet provides access to newsletters such as Congressional Activities and Congressional Research Report. All these sources can be very useful in understanding the environmental context of the problem and in developing a suitable approach.

In addition to the Internet, computers can be used in other ways to define the problem and develop an approach. The literature review could be conveniently conducted by examining, among other sources, online information about catalogs, books, and articles. Spreadsheet software packages such as Excel are effective managerial tools in developing and testing simple mathematical models. Data are stored in the cells of the spreadsheet and assigned a unique location code. By entering the variables of the model and specifying their relationships with a formula, the researcher can perform sensitivity analysis of key variables and study or graph their impact on other variables. The microcomputer and mainframe versions of four popular statistical packages, SPSS, SAS, MINITAB and EXCEL, can be used for developing and estimating mathematical models.

## SPSS Windows

In defining the problem and developing an approach, the researcher can make use of Decision Time and What If? distributed by SPSS. Forecasts of industry and company sales, and other relevant variables, can be aided by the use of Decision Time. Once the data are loaded into Decision Time, the program's interactive wizard asks you three simple questions. Based on the answers, Decision Time selects the best forecasting method and creates a forecast.

What If? uses the forecast by Decision Time to enable the researcher to explore different options to get a better understating of the problem situation. The researcher can generate answers to questions such as: How will an increase in advertising affect the sales of the product? How will a decrease (increase) in price affect the demand? How will an increase in the sales force affect the sales by region? and so on.

Forecasts and what-if analyses can help the researcher to isolate the underlying causes, identify the relevant variables that should be investigated, and formulate appropriate research questions and hypotheses.

The most difficult task in research, in the opinion of Burke, is coming to grips with the marketing research problem or objectives. Typically, a manager thinks in terms of the symptoms of a problem or the desired outcome of implementing decisions. For example, the manager might say, "Our level of repeat purchase among our customers is declining" (symptom). The manager might also say, "Would this new concept perform up to our expectations if introduced into the marketplace?" (desired outcome). It is the job of the researcher to aid the manager in taking these kinds of statements and creating a "researchable" definition, i.e., defining the marketing research problem. What Burke tries to achieve *before* designing the research is a statement of the marketing research problem that is based on:

1. Specific measurements that relate to the management decision problem
2. Details of the form the information is to take
3. Clear understanding of how the information is to be used

Each time Burke consultants meet with the key decision makers (DMs) to discuss a research issue, they fill out a brief form that includes:

1. Why the research is necessary, including the management issue and what decisions will be made
2. What specifically will be measured, e.g., purchase interest, price elasticity over a defined range of prices, etc.
3. How the information will be used by the DMs in decision making
4. What timing is required
5. What budget is appropriate

A manufacturer of a product for the treatment of athlete's foot was concerned that recent erosion in sales would lead eventually to distribution problems, as retailers would refuse to stock the product. To rejuvenate sales, the company planned to update the package and restage the product. The company asked Burke to bid on a telephone survey among recent users of the product, but the objectives of the proposed research were vague. After meeting with the decision makers of the company and its ad agency, Burke determined that the broad marketing research problem was "to determine the viability of the proposed restage." Burke also felt that focusing only on the users of the company's brand was a too narrow view of the problem. Recognizing that the restage would not succeed unless the product could draw users away from other brands, Burke recommended assessing the reaction of users of any athlete's foot remedy, not just users of the company's brand. The client agreed that Burke's definition of the marketing research problem would provide better information to help decision makers determine whether to proceed with the restage. This project was awarded to Burke.

# SUMMARY

Defining the marketing research problem is the most important step in a research project. It is a difficult step, because frequently management has not determined the actual problem or has only a vague notion about it. The researcher's role is to help management identify and isolate the problem.

The tasks involved in formulating the marketing research problem include discussions with management, including the key decision makers, interviews with industry experts, analysis of secondary data, and qualitative research. These tasks should lead to an understanding of the environmental context of the problem. The environmental context of the problem should be analyzed and certain essential factors evaluated. These factors include past information and forecasts about the industry and the firm, objectives of the DM, buyer behavior, resources and

constraints of the firm, the legal and economic environment, and marketing and technological skills of the firm.

Analysis of the environmental context should assist in the identification of the management decision problem, which should then be translated into a marketing research problem. The management decision problem asks what the DM needs to do, whereas the marketing research problem asks what information is needed and how it can be obtained effectively and efficiently. The researcher should avoid defining the marketing research problem either too broadly or too narrowly. An appropriate way of defining the marketing research problem is to make a broad statement of the problem and then identify its specific components.

Developing an approach to the problem is the second step in the marketing research process. The components of an approach consist of objective/theoretical framework, analytical models, research questions, hypotheses, and specification of information needed. It is necessary that the approach developed be based on objective or empirical evidence and be grounded in theory. The relevant variables and their interrelationships may be neatly summarized via an analytical model. The most common kinds of model structures are verbal, graphical, and mathematical. The research questions are refined statements of the specific components of the problem that ask what specific information is required with respect to the problem components. Research questions may be further refined into hypotheses. Finally, given the problem definition, research questions, and hypotheses, the information needed should be specified.

When defining the problem in international marketing research, the researcher must isolate and examine the impact of the self-reference criterion (SRC), or the unconscious reference to one's own cultural values. Likewise, when developing an approach, the differences in the environment prevailing in the domestic market and the foreign markets should be carefully considered. Several ethical issues that have an impact on the client and the researcher can arise at this stage but can be resolved by adhering to the seven Cs: communication, cooperation, confidence, candor, closeness, continuity, and creativity. The Internet and computers can be useful in the process of defining the problem and developing an approach.

# KEY TERMS AND CONCEPTS

problem definition, *33*
problem audit, *35*
secondary data, *37*
primary data, *37*
qualitative research, *39*
environmental context of the problem, *39*
objectives, *41*
buyer behavior, *41*

legal environment, *42*
economic environment, *42*
management decision problem, *43*
marketing research problem, *43*
broad statement, *45*
specific components, *45*
theory, *47*
objective evidence, *47*

analytical model, *47*
verbal models, *47*
graphical models, *47*
mathematical models, *47*
research questions, *48*
hypothesis, *49*
self-reference criterion, *53*

# EXERCISES

## Questions

1. What is the first step in conducting a marketing research project?
2. Why is it important to define the marketing research problem appropriately?
3. What are some reasons why management is often not clear about the real problem?
4. What is the role of the researcher in the problem definition process?
5. What is a problem audit?
6. What is the difference between a symptom and a problem? How can a skillful researcher differentiate between the two and identify a true problem?
7. What are some differences between a management decision problem and a marketing research problem?
8. What are the common types of errors encountered in defining a marketing research problem? What can be done to reduce the incidence of such errors?
9. How are the research questions related to components of the problem?
10. What are the differences between research questions and hypotheses?
11. Is it necessary for every research project to have a set of hypotheses? Why or why not?
12. What are the most common forms of analytical models?
13. Give an example of an analytical model that includes all the three major types.
14. Describe a microcomputer software program that can be used to assist the researcher in defining the research problem.

## Problems

1. State the research problems for each of the following management decision problems.
   a. Should a new product be introduced?
   b. Should an advertising campaign that has run for three years be changed?
   c. Should the in-store promotion for an existing product line be increased?
   d. What pricing strategy should be adopted for a new product?
   e. Should the compensation package be changed to motivate the sales force better?
2. State management decision problems for which the following research problems might provide useful information.
   a. Estimate the sales and market share of department stores in a certain metropolitan area.
   b. Determine the design features for a new product that would result in maximum market share.
   c. Evaluate the effectiveness of alternative TV commercials.
   d. Assess current and proposed sales territories with respect to their sales potential and workload.
   e. Determine the prices for each item in a product line so as to maximize total sales for the product line.

3. Identify five symptoms facing marketing decision makers and a plausible cause for each one.

4. For the first component of the department store project, identify the relevant research questions and develop suitable hypotheses. (Hint: Closely follow the example given in this chapter for the fifth component of the department store project.)

5. Suppose you are doing a project for Delta airlines. Identify, from secondary sources, the attributes or factors passengers consider when selecting an airline.

# INTERNET AND COMPUTER EXERCISES

1. You are a consultant to Coca-Cola USA working on a marketing research project for Diet Coke.
   a. Use the online databases in your library to compile a list of articles related to the Coca-Cola Company, Diet Coke, and the soft drink industry published during the past year.
   b. Visit the Coca-Cola and PepsiCo Web sites and compare the information available at each.
   c. Based on the information collected from the Internet, write a report on the environmental context surrounding Diet Coke.

2. Select any firm. Using secondary sources, obtain information on the annual sales of the firm and the industry for the last 10 years. Use a spreadsheet package, such as Excel, or any microcomputer or mainframe statistical package to develop a graphical model relating the firm's sales to the industry sales.

3. Visit the Web sites of competing sneaker brands (Nike, Reebok, Adidas). From an analysis of information available at these sites, determine the factors of the choice criteria used by consumers in selecting a sneaker brand.

4. Bank of America wants to know how it can increase its market share and has hired you as a consultant. Read the 10-K reports for Bank of America and three competing banks at *www. sec.gov/edgar.shtml* and analyze the environmental context of the problem.

# ACTIVITIES

## *Role Playing*

1. Ask a fellow student to play the role of decision maker (DM) for a local soft drink firm contemplating the introduction of a lemon-lime soft drink. This product would be positioned as a "change of pace" soft drink to be consumed by all soft drink users, including heavy cola drinkers. You act the role of a researcher. Hold discussions with the DM and identify the management decision problem. Translate the management problem into a written statement of the research problem. Does the DM agree with your definition? Develop an approach to the research problem that you have identified.

2. You are Vice President of Marketing for American Airlines and would like to increase your share of the business market. Make a list of relevant objectives for American Airlines. As the DM, what are your personal objectives?

## *Fieldwork*

1. Set up an appointment and visit the book store, a restaurant, or any business located on or near the university campus. Hold discussions with the decision maker. Can you identify a marketing research problem that could be fruitfully addressed?

2. Consider the field trip described in (1). For the problem you have defined, develop an analytical model, research question, and the appropriate hypotheses. Discuss these with the decision maker you visited earlier.

## *Group Discussion*

1. Form a small group of five or six people to discuss the following statement: "Correct identification and appropriate definition of the marketing research problem are more crucial to the success of a marketing research project than sophisticated research techniques." Did your group arrive at a consensus?

2. We are all aware that the Coca-Cola Company changed its flagship brand of 99 years to New Coke and subsequently returned to the old favorite, Coca-Cola Classic. Working in a group of four, read as much material as you can on this "marketing bungle." Identify the decision problem the Coke management faced. As a team of researchers, define the marketing research problem and its specific components.

3. Form a different group of five or six to discuss the following: "Theoretical research and applied research should not be mixed. Hence, it is wrong to insist that the approach to an applied marketing research problem be grounded in theory."

# CASES

## 1.1 Life in the Fast Lane: Fast-Food Chains Race to Be Number One

Limited menus, self-service, takeout orders, and high turnover have long characterized fast-food restaurants. The four market leaders include McDonald's, Burger King, Wendy's, and Taco Bell and they comprise about half of the 59,960 fast-food restaurants in the United States. In 2002, these four leaders collectively assumed 70 percent of the $45 billion market. For the fiscal year ending 2002, McDonald's achieved annual revenues of $15.4 billion. Since McDonald's is the world's leading foodservice retailer, they operate more than 29,000 restaurants in 121 countries, serving 45 million customers each day. In 2002, McDonald's owned a 43 percent stake in the fast-food market. Chief competitor Burger King had a 19 percent market share in 2002, achieved 2001 annual revenues of $8.6 billion and had 5,000 fewer stores than McDonald's. Wendy's 2001 revenues were $6.15 billion, with a 13.2 percent share.

While the domination of these market leaders was once thought to spell "doom" for local regional operators, smaller chains are, instead, rebounding and experiencing new levels of growth. Chains like Sonic and Carl's Jr. are invading markets that were formerly havens to their larger counterparts. With more and more chains competing for the consumer's fast-food buck, marketing is becoming increasingly important.

Concluding their three-year revitalization effort, McDonald's unveiled its $500 million "We love to see you smile" campaign in June 2000, which reinforced the chain's new ability to make sandwiches to order. The McDonald's 2001 marketing plan emphasized ongoing variety with the introduction of the New Tastes Menu. This is a permanent menu featuring 40 food items that franchises within the same co-op may choose to rotate for various periods. The new menu was backed by an estimated $60 million ad campaign by adult market agency, DDB Worldwide. By 2010, McDonald's intends to double domestic system-wide sales and triple franchisee cash flow. In order to achieve this 10-year growth plan, McDonald's new company brands—Boston Market, Chipotle Mexican Grill, and Donatos Pizza will have to play a big role in their growth picture.

Starting in 2002, Burger King introduced several new menu items that purposely were chosen to be in direct competition with McDonald's Big Mac, Quarter Pounder, and Egg McMuffin. Even though McDonald's long dominated the kids-meal market with its Happy Meals, Burger King set its sights on the fast-growing kiddies crowd. In 2001, Burger King was armed with an $80 million budget and new research ready to target kids. They picked a marketing agency exclusively specializing in kids marketing, Interpublic Group of Cos.' Campbell Mithun. Burger King aimed to leverage the space between kiddies and adults. While not abandoning the very young crowd, Burger King centered its kids program on its Big Kids brand meals. Now more than ever, marketing to consumers' tastes is key to competing in the increasingly intense fast-food restaurant war.

Capturing or retaining market position is intuitively tied to keeping up with the changing preferences of the American consumer. In a recent study conducted by Maritz Marketing Research, convenience of location, quality of food, menu selection, and then service are the most important influences on adults' fast-food choices. Surprisingly, low price was not among the top four reasons why Americans made their fast-food selections. Only 8 percent of those surveyed made a fast-food choice based on price.

Adults under the age of 65 cited proximity of location as the most important factor in their fast-food purchase, with 26 percent of those polled stating it to be the chief criterion influencing their dining choice. After convenience of location, quality of the fast-food itself was most important to consumers. This is interpreted to mean that not only do consumers want a superior product, but also they want a consistency in quality in each order at any location. Taco Bell recently shed its emphasis on low price for a focus on quality. The chain transformed its "Extra Value Meals" multi-menu item combination package into "Border Select" meal platters by upgrading and modifying the food offered and the image presented. Arby's, a chain specializing in roast beef sandwiches, holds the phrase "a cut above" not only as an advertising slogan but also as an intended view of its restaurants in general. "In everything we talk about—our uniforms, our buildings, our sandwiches—we want to be a little bit better than our competitors," proclaims the chain spokesman.

Moreover, customers are craving a variety of selections. According to 16 percent of American consumers, menu selection is the chief reason for choosing a fast-food restaurant. Knowing such important information, chains are offering diversified menus with unique items. For example, the Oklahoma City-based Sonic chain offers, in addition to the traditional sandwich, "things that you can't get at competitors like . . . onion rings and cherry limeades." Market leaders are also looking to capitalize on that one item that the competitor is not offering. In 2002, Wendy's restaurants introduced its new line of Garden Sensation Salads and racked up record sales according to the firm. Menu selection is important to senior citizens as well. One in four senior citizens feels that menu selection is the most important factor in their choice of dining establishments. Experts predicted that the number of menu items will continue to grow as all fast-food restaurants offer new items to avoid consumer boredom and maintain growth and market share. As a spokesman for Burger King said, "We'll stay with what we know best, but we have to add items to meet consumer preferences."

About 12 percent of adults feel that fast service is the basis of their choice for a fast-food restaurant. McDonald's strategy is to "attract customers with price and keep them with service" and become "recognized as the service leader in the nation," according to the corporation's USA president. To emphasize this aspect, McDonald's plans to extol its drive-thru operations in a series of television ads, showcasing the speed at which the hard-working staff diligently prepares the customers' orders. Taco Bell too exalts service qualities in its stores, with a mission summarized in the acronym FACT, which stands for "fast food, accurate orders, cleanliness, and food served at the right temperature." Wendy's has adopted the special acronym "MBA" which stands for a "Mop Bucket Attitude." This represents Wendy's "commitment to the traditional definition of customer satisfaction which places customer service (cleanliness, service, and atmosphere) before numbers and computer printouts." Wendy's maintains that this commitment is a major reason for their success. Burger King has long recognized the importance of providing good service and also creating a favorable and memorable dining experience. Burger King was the first fast-food restaurant to introduce dining rooms that allowed its customers to dine inside its facilities. In 1992, Burger King became the first fast-food restaurant to introduce table service and an expanded dinner menu in order to enhance the customer's dining experience.

The most recent trend in fast-food restaurants has been toward value pricing. This trend was ushered in by Taco Bell, which dropped prices and boosted system-wide sales by 18.5 percent in only two years. While it was a novelty for a short time, the value pricing has become a part of almost every major competitor. McDonald's offers its Extra Value Menu, Wendy's has a 99¢ Super Value Menu that emphasizes variety by offering items which range from ready-to-go Side Salads to a Country Fried Steak Sandwich. Burger King and Hardee's offer similar plans to that of McDonald's. Currently, McDonald's is bringing attention to its value menu by spending an estimated $10 million on a national advertising campaign focused on its Value Meals. In 2002, McDonald's introduced an Extra McValue Menu of items priced under $1.

In a further effort to expand the fast-food market, the industry looked overseas. Since Asian and European markets are at the stage of fast-food that America reached in 1960, American chains have a substantial competitive advantage internationally. Marketing experts predicted that it will be easier for established U.S. chains to expand overseas than at home. To illustrate, McDonald's realized about 40 percent of its operating profits outside the United States in 2000, as compared with 21 percent in 1990. In addition, Burger King focused on Japan as a wide open market for its burgers and gave much attention to the Eastern European market. It recently opened restaurants in Poland, the former East Germany, and Hungary, while at the same time establishing a training academy in London to service its European franchises.

Wendy's has also been recognized as a serious competitor in the international fast-food market. Wendy's has more than 8,000 restaurants located in more than 50 countries outside of the United States. Due to the loss of Wendy's founder and well-known spokesperson Dave Thomas in 2002, Wendy's marketing and advertising strategy will be undergoing some changes. Thomas made more than 800 commercials for Wendy's since 1989 and became a household name due to his regular guy persona and popularity. Wendy's has been preparing for Dave Thomas' passing since 1996 when his health began declining. However, the effects this will have on the company's strategy remains to be seen both nationally and internationally.

Given the stiff competition in the fast lane, the question remains whether McDonald's can continue to be the leader in the domestic fast-food race, as well as become the front-runner in the international fast-food race. The use of marketing research will be critical in achieving these goals.

## QUESTIONS

1. Describe the marketing information needs of the fast-food industry.
2. What role can marketing research play in providing the information needed?
3. Give some examples of problem identification research that McDonald's can undertake to ensure their continued leadership in the fast-food industry.
4. Describe the kinds of problem solution research that Wendy's might undertake to improve its sales and market share.
5. Given the market potential overseas, should fast-food chains conduct marketing research in foreign countries? What kind of opportunities and challenges will the fast-food chains encounter while conducting international marketing research?

## REFERENCES

Christopher Barton, "McDonald's to Try to Boost Service, Restaurant Investment," *Knight Ridder Tribune Business News* (January 9, 2002): 1

Ameet Sachdev, "Wendy's Founder Dave Thomas Dies at Age 69," *Knight Ridder Tribune Business News* (January 9, 2002): 1

Amy Zuber, "Listen up, Mac: BK Aims to Reign Supreme, Orders Menu Changes," *Nation's Restaurant News* 35 (51) (December 17, 2001): 3, 126

Bob Sperber, "McD Beefing up Value Meals," *Brandweek* 42 (45) (December 3, 2001): 3

Amy Zuber, "Skeptics Unsure McD Can Attain Sales Doubling," *Nation's Restaurant News* 35 (11) (March 12, 2001): 1, 96.

# 1.2 Nike Sprints Ahead of the Competition, Yet Has a Long Way to Run

Nike, Inc. (*www.nike.com*), located in Beaverton, Oregon, is the number one U.S. athletic footwear company and one of the most recognized American brands among foreign consumers. This high degree of recognition is one of the main reasons Nike has been so successful. For the 2001 fiscal year ended May 31, 2001, the company continued to soar, with sales of over $9.5 billion.

Perhaps such success could be attributed to its concept-based advertising campaigns. The company uses a process that is often called "image transfer." Nike ads traditionally did not specifically place a product—or mention the brand name. A mood or atmosphere was created and then the brand is associated with that mood. "We don't set out to make ads. The ultimate goal is to make a connection," states Dan Weiden, executive of one of Nike's ad agencies. One ad featured the Beatles and clips of Nike athletes, Michael Jordan and John McEnroe, juxtaposed with pictures of regular folks also engaged in sports. It was used to infer that real athletes prefer Nike and that perhaps if the general audience buys the brand they will play better too. Nike's unpredictable image-based ads have ranged from shocking, such as its portrayal of real blood and guts in a "Search and Destroy" campaign used during the 1996 Olympic games, to humorous, such as the first ad used to launch Michael Jordan's Jordan brand wear. The latter advertising made the tongue-in-cheek suggestion that Jordan himself had a hand in production by slipping away from a Bulls' game at half time to run over to his company and then return in time for the game's second half.

In 1998, Nike shifted to a new phase in its marketing strategy. Nike emphasized more of its product innovation skills than the jockey, edgy attitude that it displayed in previous years. "We recognize that our ads need to tell consumers that we're about product innovation and not just athletes and exposure. We need to prove to consumers that we're not just slapping a swoosh [the company trademark] on stuff to make a buck," said Chris Zimmerman, director of Nike's U.S. advertising. With the launch of the "I can" campaign, Nike showed less of the celebrity athletes that previously adorned its marketing output and showed more product usage than in the previous "Just Do It" campaign. Competitors Reebok and Adidas recently featured more product-focused ads and were met with a great deal of success. Despite this rearranged focus, Nike did not back away from innovative marketing.

Nike continues to excel in the advertising arena. Nike was named one of 2001's best in advertising by *Time Magazine* for its ad featuring expert dribblers doing trick moves. Time is quoted as saying the ad conveyed a message that "Sport is music. Sport is dance. Sport is art." Nike states that this ad was their most popular ad in 20 years. Another popular ad from 2001 was known as the "Take Me Out to the Ballgame" ad. This particular ad featured professional athletes from varying sports singing one line of the song "Take Me Out to the Ballgame" in their native language.

As the company looks ahead to 2010, at the heart of Nike's future strategy is the international arena, which could prove to be the most difficult element for Nike to undertake. There seemed to be a pretty strong recognition that by 2010, Nike would be larger outside of the U.S. than inside. As of 2003, international sales comprised one-third of Nike's business. Nike would like to expand into the soccer and international sports arena, but to do so, it would have to refocus its marketing and distribution in order to re-establish itself as an authentic, technically superior sports shoe.

In February 2001, Nike unveiled its latest technological revolution, the Nike Shox, to United Kingdom consumers. This shoe was in development for 16 years, and Nike hoped it would revolutionize the sports shoe market in much the same way that NikeAir did when it was launched in the UK in the 1980s. One reporter in London states that his pair of Nike Shox makes him feel like he is "walking on cloud nine with a spring in [his] step." The shoes are reported to provide support, comfort, shock absorbency, and style all at the same time. The Nike Shox line of athletic shoes is shaping up to be very popular in both the U.S. and the UK.

Most recently, Nike bought out many of its worldwide distribution centers in order to achieve greater control of its operations. In the future, Nike would like to build up its presence in the key markets of China, Germany, Mexico, and Japan. Nike will focus its advertising on sports, and will feature sports that are of a particular interest in specific regions. Nike realizes that while it is ahead of competition, it still has a long, long way to run.

## QUESTIONS

1. Should Nike switch from a focus on celebrities to a focus on its products in its advertising? Discuss the role of marketing research in helping Nike management make this decision. What kind of research should be undertaken?
2. How would you describe the buying behavior of consumers with respect to athletic footwear?
3. What is the management decision problem facing Nike as it attempts to retain its leadership position?
4. Define the marketing research problem facing Nike, given the management decision problem you have identified.
5. Develop two suitable research questions and formulate two hypotheses for each.
6. How can the Internet be used to help Nike in conducting marketing research, and in marketing its products?

## REFERENCES

Anonymous, "The 2001 Best & Worst: Advertising," *Time* 158 (27) (December 24, 2001): 88.

Sarah J. Heim, "Nike Champs Move to Gridiron," *Adweek* 51 (46) (November 12, 2001): 6.

Agnes Jumah, "Design Choice, Nike Shox," *Marketing* (March 22, 2001): 14.

*www.nikebiz.com/*

# 1.3 Lexus: Imparting Value to Luxury and Luxury to Value!

In the 1980s, Toyota developed a concept for a new car that was destined to be a success. The concept of the car, which was to be called Lexus, was based on the observation that there was a large, affluent market for cars that could boast exceptional performance. A significant portion of that market ranked value highly. However, they were unwilling to pay the extraordinary expensive prices that Mercedes charged for its high performance vehicles. Toyota planned to target this market by creating a car that matched Mercedes on the performance criteria but was priced much more reasonably, providing consumers the value they desired, and making them feel that they were smart buyers.

Toyota introduced the Lexus (*www.lexus.com*) in 1989 with much fanfare. A clever advertising campaign announced the arrival of this new car. For example, one ad showed the Lexus next to a Mercedes with the headline, "The First Time in History That Trading a $73,000 Car for a $36,000 Car Could Be Considered Trading Up." Of course, Lexus had all the detail that the Mercedes did: a sculptured form, a quality finish, and a plush interior. The detail was not, however, limited to the car. Separate dealerships were created that had the type of atmosphere that affluent consumers expected from a luxury carmaker, including a grand showroom, free refreshments, and professional salespeople.

Toyota placed a strong emphasis on the performance of the new car. A package was sent to potential customers that included a 12-minute video displaying Lexus' superior engineering. The video showed that when a glass of water was placed on the engine block of a Mercedes and a Lexus, the water shook on the Mercedes while the Lexus had a virtually still glass of water. This visually told the viewer that the stability of Lexus was far more extraordinary than even one of the most expensive cars around. Another video showed a Lexus making a sharp turn with a glass of water on its dashboard. The glass remained upright; again, the Lexus proved itself. These videos were successful in bringing in customers, whose expectations were surpassed.

As a result of its continued success, Lexus decided to raise the prices of their vehicles. However, this strategy did not work out as well as Lexus had hoped. Lexus realized that it lacked the heritage for prestige that European luxury cars command and that people are once again willing to pay extra for it. It has, as a result, turned to a new advertising campaign to inspire an emotional response to its cars. The campaign was exceptionally powerful because it also had to combat the decrease in growth of the luxury car market compared to the auto industry's overall growth. Partly responsible for this decline, the "near luxury" autos have skimmed away potential luxury auto consumers. Included in this group are the Toyota Avalon, the Nissan Maxima, and the Mazda Millennia. BMW and Mercedes also introduced products for this segment: the BMW 3 Series and the Mercedes C Class.

In response to this competition, Lexus emphasized nontraditional advertising and promotion, in addition to more mainstream luxury car advertisements. While many companies that rely heavily on commercial advertising are upset with TiVo (the new television viewing system that allows users to filter out commercials), Lexus positioned TiVo to its advantage. Lexus sponsored a "New World of Luxury" sweepstakes where the prize was a new ES300. TiVo users used their system to search for Lexus commercials for clues to questions that Lexus posted on TiVo's promotional page. The sweepstakes ran from November 12–December 14, 2001 and kept TiVo users watching Lexus commercials rather than filtering them out.

Lexus continues to show the automobile industry and its current customers that it is building vehicles with luxury, performance, and style. In 2001, JD Power & Associates ranked the Lexus luxury car number one in durability for the seventh year in a row. The award was based on the number of problems reported by 40,000 users of small trucks and passenger cars. Also in 2001, Lexus was ranked number one in retention of customers for the second year in a row and named number one in customer satisfaction with dealer service by JD Power & Associates.

As a result of Lexus' marketing efforts, in 2000 Lexus set a record of its own by selling a sizzling 206,037 units, which was an all-time sales record for the luxury automaker. With this, Lexus became the top-selling luxury brand, edging out Mercedes-Benz. In 2001, Lexus was named the best selling luxury brand for the second year in a row. The company sold 223,983 new vehicles, an increase of 8.7 percent over 2000.

Pre-owned vehicle sales were also up by 20.4 percent, totaling almost 58,000, and certified pre-owned vehicle sales were over 33,000—a 23.4 percent increase over 2000. At the end of 2001 the GX470, Lexus's third SUV, was introduced at the Detroit Auto Show. The SUV was priced from $45,000–$50,000, which positions it nicely between Lexus's two other SUV models.

For the future, Lexus is faced with the challenge of aiming for younger consumers for their vehicles. Denny Clements, group VP-general manager of Lexus, said the target group for the new luxury sedan has a median age between 47 and 55, while the current LS buyer's median age is 58 years old. "The exterior design is much more dramatic than the previous generation LS 400," said Mr. Clements, who admitted that past observations about the LS styling have included words such as "sedate" and "boring." Continued marketing plans will help Lexus attempt to attract younger consumers for their vehicles.

Lexus plans to expand marketing efforts in the future with the aim of not only gaining new customers, but also retaining present clients. While the company's plans are highly classified, their latest efforts hint that newer marketing tactics will follow in the unconventional style of ads past. For instance, Lexus' recent sponsorship of a skiing event in Colorado included an invitation to all Lexus owners to spend a luxurious all-expense-paid weekend in the mountains. These efforts are consistent with Lexus' philosophy of imparting value to luxury and luxury to value.

## QUESTIONS

1. Describe the management decision problem facing Lexus as it seeks to fight competition from other luxury car manufacturers such as Mercedes, BMW, and Jaguar, as well as competition from the "near luxury" autos like the Nissan Maxima and the Mazda Millennia.
2. Formulate the marketing research problem corresponding to the management decision problem you have identified in (1).
3. Develop a graphical model explaining the consumer choice process for luxury cars.
4. Identify two research questions based on the definition of the marketing research problem and the graphical model.
5. Develop at least one hypothesis for each research question you have identified in (4).
6. How would you conduct an Internet search for information on the luxury car market? Summarize the results of your search in a report.

## REFERENCES

Terry Box, "Demise of SUVs Certainly Looks Premature," *Knight Ridder Tribune Business News* (January 7, 2002): 1.

Jean Halliday, "Has Lincoln, Caddy Lux Run Out?" *Advertising Age* 72 (52) (December 31, 2001): 4.

Karl Greenburg, "Lexus looks for TiVo to up Commercial Viewing," *Brandweek* 42 (46) (December 10, 2001): 28.

"Toyota Lexus Top in U.S. Car Durability Study," *Jiji Press English News Service* (November 16, 2001): 1.

Anonymous, "Lexus Tops in Retention," *Automotive News* 76 (5956) (November 5, 2001): 26.

# CASES

# 1.1 Burke: Learning and Growing Through Marketing Research

Alberta Burke, who previously worked in the marketing department of Procter & Gamble Company, founded Burke, Inc. in 1931. At that time, there were few formalized marketing research companies not only in the United States but also in the world. Today, Burke is a decision-support company involved with helping its clients understand their business practices and making them more efficient. This video case traces the evolution of marketing research and how Burke implements the various phases of the marketing research process as of 2003.

## THE EVOLUTION OF MARKETING RESEARCH

The first recorded marketing research took place more than a century ago in 1895 or 1896. A professor sent out by telegram questions to advertising agencies about the future of advertising. He got back about 10 responses and he wrote a paper describing what was happening. In the first years most of the marketing research done was a spin-off of the Bureau of Census data and the analysis was basically limited to counting. The next wave of marketing research came in the early 1930s and can be described as the ladies with white gloves that were knocking on doors and checking pantries for cake mixes. The methodologies used were primarily door-to-door surveys; telephone was not a very widely utilized service at that time.

Then came World War II, which saw the introduction of the psychological side of marketing research. Through the 1950s and 1960s, television became more of an integral part of the public's lives, and with that came television advertising. So testing advertising commercials became the hot area of marketing research in the 1960s and 1970s. In the 1960s and 1970s, there came another fundamental change. The marketing research industry made a shift from just generating and testing new ideas and sharing them with their clients to working more with their clients on how to use those ideas to make decisions.

The emphasis on generating information to improve decision making increased in the 1980s and 1990s. The marketing research industry started developing processes that generated information to be used as input into management decision making. Thus, the marketing research industry has come a long way from the telegrams of 1895. As of 2003, the industry is trying to find creative ways to research consumers using methods such as telephone interviews, Web interviews, and multimode methods.

## HOW BURKE IMPLEMENTS THE MARKETING RESEARCH PROCESS

### Defining the Marketing Research Problem and Developing an Approach

Some companies need help when they have to make a decision. Any time there is a go or no go, a yes or no, or a decision to be made, they look at it and ask what information can help reduce the risk associated with the decision. At this point, Burke would like to talk with them to develop the information that would help reduce that risk.

The first step is to define the marketing research problem, and a lot of discovery takes place here. The account executive (AE) will sit down with a client and try to determine whether or not what the client believes is the problem really is the case or whether Burke needs to change or broaden the scope of the problem. Discussions with the key decision maker (DM) may reveal that the company has been focusing on too narrow an issue or that they have been focusing on the wrong problem altogether.

Burke believes that defining the marketing research problem is critical to a successful research project. The company will find out what the symptoms are and work with the client to identify the underlying causes. Considerable effort is devoted to examining the background or the environmental context of the problem. In at least half the cases, when they go through the process of exploring the problem, the problem will change. It will gain a new scope or direction. This process results in a precise definition of the marketing research problem, including an identification of its specific components.

Once the problem has been defined, Burke develops a suitable approach. The problem definition is refined to generate more specific research questions and sometimes hypotheses. Because of its vast experience, Burke has developed a variety of analytical models that are customized to the identified problem. This process also results in the identification of information that would help the client solve its problem.

## Research Design Formulation

*Qualitative Research.*    One of the pitfalls that Burke encounters comes with qualitative research. Qualitative research is nice because it is immediate. The information that you get tends to be extremely rich and in the customer's words. You get a lot of interaction in that you get to see what kinds of answers are being given and what kinds of questions and concerns your customers or potential customers might have. However, one of the dangers comes from thinking that all of your customers or potential customers might view your products or service offering in this manner, i.e., generalize the findings of qualitative research to the population. Burke also has the ability to do focus groups online.

*Survey Methods.*    Although Burke uses a variety of methods, telephone studies represent about 70 percent of the surveys. Other methods used include mall intercept, mail, and Internet or Web-based surveys. Burke carefully selects the method that is best suited to the problem. Burke predicts that telephone surveys will decrease, whereas Internet surveys will increase. If Burke is trying to interview customers around the globe, it sends an e-mail invitation to respondents to complete the survey via the Web. Burke likes the Internet's ability to show pictures of a particular product or concept to the survey respondents.

*Questionnaire Design.*    In designing the questionnaire, Burke pays particular attention to the content and wording of the questions. There are some questions that are well defined and can be easily framed. Then there may be other issues that need to be investigated, but the exact questions to ask may not be clear. The simpler the question and the more you know who needs to be asked, i.e., the target respondents, the better the information you are going to get.

*Sampling Design.*    Burke has a sampling department within data collection, and they consult with the senior account management team and account executives to determine the proper sample to use. The sampling frame is defined in terms of who the respondents are that can answer the questions that need to be addressed. The target population is defined by the marketing research problem and the research questions. Burke often buys the sampling lists from outside firms that specialize in this area.

## Data Collection and Analysis

Once the information has been collected, it will reside either in a computer-related format or a paper format that is entered into a computer format, and so essentially the results are tabulated and analyzed via computers. Through the "Digital Dashboard" product, Burke not only has the ability to disseminate the results to its clients when the project is finished, but it also has the ability to show them the data as they are being collected. Burke breaks down the data analysis by relevant groups. You might see information by total respondents, and you might see information broken out by gender or business size. Essentially, Burke looks at different breaks in the data to try to understand what is happening, to determine if there are differences that exist depending on different criteria, and to decide how to make decisions based on that data.

## Report Preparation and Presentation

Clients need information much faster than they have in the past, because decisions need to be made much more quickly than they were previously. So the idea of organizing large meetings to present data analysis results is not very practical anymore. Most of what Burke is doing in reporting and delivering data is again done over the Web. The report documents the entire research process. It discusses the management decision problem, the marketing research problem, the approach and research design, the information obtained to help management make the decision, and their recommendations.

The report-writing process starts from the first conversation with the client, and the report is written as the research proceeds, not simply when the project is almost done. The entire report is written and presented with a focus on improving management's decision making. Burke's goal is to help its clients have better decision-making abilities so that the clients are more valuable to their respected companies.

Burke believes that a successful research project often leads to a subsequent research project; the research process is a circular process. It is not one that typically has a finite beginning and end. Once you solve a problem, there is always another one to work on. Realizing this is what helps Burke and its clients constantly learn and grow.

## QUESTIONS

1. Describe the evolution of marketing research. How has the role of marketing research changed as this field has evolved?
2. What is Burke's view of the role of marketing research?
3. Visit www.burke.com and write a report about the various marketing research services offered by Burke.
4. What is Burke's view of the importance of defining the marketing research problem? What process does Burke follow and how does it compare to that given in Chapter 2?
5. What is Burke's view of the marketing research process? How does it compare with that given in Chapter 1?
6. If Burke were to offer you a position as an account executive with the responsibility of providing marketing research services to Procter & Gamble, would you accept this position? Why or why not?

## REFERENCES

*www.burke.com*

# 1.2 Accenture: The Accent Is in the Name

Accenture is the world's leading management and technology services organization. Through its network of businesses approach—in which the company enhances its consulting and outsourcing expertise through alliances, affiliated companies, and other capabilities—Accenture delivers innovations that help clients across all industries quickly realize their visions. With approximately 75,000 employees in 47 countries, Accenture can quickly mobilize its broad and deep global resources to accelerate results for clients. The company has extensive experience in 18 industry groups in key business areas, including customer relationship management, supply chain management, business strategy, technology, and outsourcing. Accenture also leverages its affiliates and alliances to help drive innovative solutions. Strong relationships within this network of businesses extend Accenture's knowledge of emerging business models and products, enabling the company to provide its clients with the best possible tools, technologies, and capabilities. Accenture uses these resources as a catalyst, helping clients anticipate and gain value from business and technology change. Accenture's clients include 89 of the *Fortune* Global 100 and more than half of the *Fortune* Global 500.

Accenture was originally named Andersen Consulting and was created in 1989 as a part of Arthur Andersen. In 2000, Andersen Consulting won the right to divorce itself from Arthur Andersen. However, this required that it change the company's name from Andersen Consulting to something else. This was an extremely significant event because Andersen Consulting had built up significant brand equity in its name, partly through the spending of approximately $7 billion over 10 years. Thus, the name change became a top priority, and it focused much of its time and effort on this task.

The first task was to pick a new name. Andersen Consulting challenged its employees to come up with suggestions for a new name by creating an internal contest. The contest resulted in a list of over 2,500 entries. After extensive marketing research on various names, which included surveys of target customers, the company decided to go with the name Accenture. It settled on this name because it believed it conveyed the message that it was focused on the future. It also spent a considerable amount of time creating a new logo. The final version of this was the company's name accented with a greater than (>) symbol, which it believes stressed its focus on the future.

Another task, which occurred simultaneously with the first task, was to get the word out and prepare the target market for the name change. The company began running ads notifying everyone that its name would change at the beginning of 2001. Accenture has a well-defined group of companies that comprise its target market and it had to focus its efforts on them.

Finally, on January 1, 2001, it announced its new name to the world. It used this opportunity not only to present its new name but also to sell its services and help people understand what it had to offer. In the end, Accenture spent a total of $175 million to rebrand itself, but it did not stop there. In February, it began a new campaign titled "Now it gets interesting." This campaign took the perspective that, despite all the incredible changes that have occurred recently due to technology, there are still even more challenges that lie ahead. The commercials showed how Accenture could help its clients capitalize on these challenges. It ran these ads throughout the winter months of 2001 and its success was evidenced by the increased traffic on its Web site. This is very important to Accenture because it believes that if it can get somebody to visit its site, then there is a better opportunity to tell its whole story.

Accenture has been successful in its quest of transferring the brand equity to its new name. Marketing research revealed that it has approximately 50 percent awareness with the public, which is essentially the same number it had under the old name. Accenture's marketing goes far beyond the name, as it is constantly challenged because the product it offers is consistently changing. To be successful, it must have good marketing research, creative marketing, a big budget, and an understanding of future trends.

## QUESTIONS

1. Discuss the role of marketing research in helping Andersen Consulting select a new name (Accenture).
2. Define Accenture's target market. Discuss the role of marketing research in helping Accenture understand the needs of its target customers.
3. Accenture would like to increase preference and loyalty for its services. Describe the management decision problem.
4. Define a suitable marketing research problem corresponding to the management decision problem that you have identified in (3).

## REFERENCES

*www.accenture.com*

Todd Wasserman, "Advertising Accenture Accents Idea Campaign," *Brandweek* (September 30, 2002).

# PART

# II

# Research Design Formulation

A research design (step 3) is formulated after the problem has been defined (step 1) and the approach developed (step 2). This part of the text describes in detail exploratory, descriptive, and causal research designs. Exploratory research involves secondary data and qualitative research, while descriptive research makes use of survey and observation methods. The major methodology used in causal designs is experimentation. We describe the primary scales of measurement and the comparative and noncomparative scaling techniques commonly used. We present several guidelines for designing questionnaires and explain the procedures, techniques, and statistical considerations involved in sampling. Managers and researchers should find this material helpful.

# 3

# Research Design

"When designing
research, one is faced with
a continual series of trade-
offs. Since there are typically numerous design
alternatives that will work,
the goal is to find the
design that enhances the
value of the information
obtained, while reducing
the cost of obtaining it."

*Mike Pietrangelo,*
*vice president,*
*client services,*
*Burke, Inc.*

## Objectives

After reading this chapter, the student should be able to:

1. Define research design, classify various research designs, and explain the differences between exploratory and conclusive designs.
2. Compare and contrast the basic research designs: exploratory, descriptive, and causal.
3. Describe the major sources of errors in a research design including random sampling error and the various sources of nonsampling error.
4. Discuss managerial aspects of coordinating research projects, particularly budgeting and scheduling.
5. Describe the elements of a marketing research proposal and show how it addresses the steps of the marketing research process.
6. Explain research design formulation in international marketing research.
7. Understand the ethical issues and conflicts that arise in formulating a research design.
8. Discuss the use of the Internet and computers in research design formulation.

## Overview

Chapter 2 discussed how to define a marketing research problem and develop a suitable approach. These first two steps are critical to the success of the entire marketing research project. Once they have been completed, attention should be devoted to designing the formal research project by formulating a detailed research design (see Figure 2.1 in Chapter 2).

This chapter defines and classifies research designs. We describe the two major types of research designs: exploratory and conclusive. We further classify conclusive research designs as descriptive or causal and discuss both types in detail. We then consider the differences between the two types of descriptive designs, cross-sectional and longitudinal, and identify sources of errors. We cover budgeting and scheduling of a research project and present guidelines for writing a marketing research proposal. The special considerations involved in formulating research designs in international marketing research are discussed. Several ethical issues that arise at this stage of the marketing research process are considered. Finally, we discuss the use of microcomputers and mainframes in formulating research designs. The reader can develop a better appreciation of the concepts presented in this chapter by first considering the following example, which illustrates exploratory and conclusive research designs.

## REAL RESEARCH

### *More Than Just Causes*

In a study of cause-related marketing, exploratory research in the form of secondary data analysis and focus groups was conducted to identify the social causes that American businesses should be concerned about. As a result, the following causes were identified as salient: childcare, drug abuse, public education, hunger, crime, environment, medical research, and poverty.

Then conclusive research in the form of a descriptive cross-sectional survey was undertaken to quantify how and why cause-related marketing influences consumers' perceptions of companies and brands and to determine the relative salience of the causes identified in exploratory research. A random sample of 2,000 Americans was surveyed by telephone. About 61 percent of respondents said that when price and quality are equal, they would switch brands or stores to companies that support good causes that help on the local or national level. The survey also revealed that 68 percent of consumers would pay more for a product that is linked to a good cause. Company support of good causes produces a more positive image and greater trust of the company according to 66 percent of those surveyed. The relative salience of the social causes that businesses should address is presented in the following table.

Social Issues Businesses Should Work the Hardest to Solve

| *Social Issue* | *Percent Saying It Is a Major Concern* |
| --- | --- |
| Public Education | 33 |
| Crime | 32 |
| Environment | 30 |
| Poverty | 24 |
| Medical Research | 23 |
| Hunger | 23 |
| Childcare | 22 |
| Drug Abuse | 18 |

Exploratory research followed by conclusive research helped Starbucks realize that the environment was an important cause influencing consumers' perceptions of companies and brands.

In keeping with these findings, Starbucks (*www.starbucks.com*) wants to help the environment by providing a new "eco-friendly" coffee cup, coffee composting, and burlap-bag recycling. The company also has initiatives to help small coffee bean farmers, local community programs, and charitable giving. There are even employee incentives and awards for volunteering for these causes. One of the newest social programs is to match its employees' volunteer hours with dollars to the same organization. In 2001, Starbucks, in conjunction with international specialty coffee organizations such as the National Federation of Coffee Growers of Colombia (*www.colombiacoffee.com*) and the Specialty Coffee Association of America (*www.scaa.org*), advised many environmental organizations about growing earth-friendly coffee. An extensive set of guidelines was established called the "Conservation Principles for Coffee Production." Thus, Starbucks has differentiated its brand and enhanced its image in a way that checkbook philanthropy never could.[1] ∎

As this example indicates, at a broad level, two main types of research designs are employed in marketing research: exploratory and conclusive. An understanding of the fundamentals of research design and its components enables the researcher to formulate a design that is appropriate for the problem at hand.

## RESEARCH DESIGN: DEFINITION

*research design*
A framework or blueprint for conducting the marketing research project. It specifies the details of the procedures necessary for obtaining the information needed to structure and/or solve marketing research problems.

A *research design* is a framework or blueprint for conducting the marketing research project. It details the procedures necessary for obtaining the information needed to structure and/or solve marketing research problems. Although a broad approach to the problem has already been developed, the research design specifies the details—the nuts and bolts—of implementing that approach. A research design lays the foundation for conducting the project. A good research design will ensure that the marketing research project is conducted effectively and efficiently. Typically, a research design involves the following components, or tasks:

1. Define the information needed (Chapter 2).
2. Design the exploratory, descriptive, and/or causal phases of the research (Chapters 3 through 7).
3. Specify the measurement and scaling procedures (Chapters 8 and 9).
4. Construct and pretest a questionnaire (interviewing form) or an appropriate form for data collection (Chapter 10).
5. Specify the sampling process and sample size (Chapters 11 and 12).
6. Develop a plan of data analysis (Chapter 14).

Each of these components will be discussed in great detail in the subsequent chapters. First, we must further our understanding of research design with a classification of the different types.

# RESEARCH DESIGN: CLASSIFICATION

**exploratory research**

One type of research design, which has as its primary objective the provision of insights into, and comprehension of, the problem situation confronting the researcher.

**conclusive research**

Research designed to assist the decision maker in determining, evaluating, and selecting the best course of action to take in a given situation.

Research designs may be broadly classified as exploratory or conclusive (see Figure 3.1). The differences between exploratory and conclusive research are summarized in Table 3.1. The primary objective of ***exploratory research*** is to provide insights into, and an understanding of, the problem confronting the researcher.[2] Exploratory research is used in cases when you must define the problem more precisely, identify relevant courses of action, or gain additional insights before an approach can be developed. The information needed is only loosely defined at this stage, and the research process that is adopted is flexible and unstructured. For example, it may consist of personal interviews with industry experts. The sample, selected to generate maximum insights, is small and nonrepresentative. The primary data are qualitative in nature and are analyzed accordingly. Given these characteristics of the research process, the findings of exploratory research should be regarded as tentative or as input to further research. Typically, such research is followed by further exploratory or conclusive research. Sometimes, exploratory research, particularly qualitative research, is all the research that is conducted. In these cases, caution should be exercised in utilizing the findings obtained. Exploratory research will be discussed in more detail in the next section.

The insights gained from exploratory research might be verified or quantified by conclusive research, as in the opening example. The importance of salient social causes that businesses should address identified through exploratory research was determined through a survey (conclusive research) that showed that public education was the most important cause of concern to 33 percent of the respondents. The objective of conclusive research is to test specific hypotheses and examine specific relationships. This requires that the researcher clearly specify the information needed.[3] ***Conclusive research*** is

**Figure 3.1**

A Classification of Marketing Research Designs

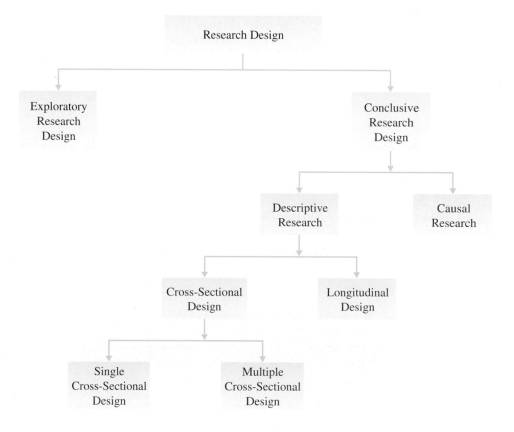

## TABLE 3.1

**Differences Between Exploratory and Conclusive Research**

|  | EXPLORATORY | CONCLUSIVE |
|---|---|---|
| Objective: | To provide insights and understanding | To test specific hypotheses and examine relationships |
| Characteristics: | Information needed is defined only loosely. | Information needed is clearly defined. |
|  | Research process is flexible and unstructured. | Research process is formal and structured. |
|  | Sample is small and nonrepresentative. | Sample is large and representative. |
|  | Analysis of primary data is qualitative. | Data analysis is quantitative. |
| Findings/Results: | Tentative | Conclusive |
| Outcome: | Generally followed by further exploratory or conclusive research | Findings used as input into decision making |

typically more formal and structured than exploratory research. It is based on large, representative samples, and the data obtained are subjected to quantitative analysis. The findings from this research are considered to be conclusive in nature in that they are used as input into managerial decision making. (However, it should be noted that from the perspective of the philosophy of science, nothing can be proven and nothing is conclusive.) As shown in Figure 3.1, conclusive research designs may be either descriptive or causal, and descriptive research designs may be either cross-sectional or longitudinal. Each of these classifications is discussed further, beginning with exploratory research.

# EXPLORATORY RESEARCH

As its name implies, the objective of exploratory research is to explore or search through a problem or situation to provide insights and understanding (Table 3.2). Exploratory research could be used for any of the following purposes:

- Formulate a problem or define a problem more precisely.
- Identify alternative courses of action.
- Develop hypotheses.
- Isolate key variables and relationships for further examination.[4]
- Gain insights for developing an approach to the problem.
- Establish priorities for further research.

The opening example in the overview section illustrated the use of exploratory research to identify the social causes that American businesses should be concerned about. As a result, the following causes were identified as salient: childcare, drug abuse, public education, hunger, crime, environment, medical research, and poverty. In general, exploratory research is meaningful in any situation where the researcher does not have enough understanding to proceed with the research project. Exploratory research is

## TABLE 3.2

**A Comparison of Basic Research Designs**

|  | EXPLORATORY | DESCRIPTIVE | CAUSAL |
|---|---|---|---|
| Objective: | Discover ideas and insights. | Describe market characteristics or functions. | Determine cause and effect relationships. |
| Characteristics: | Flexible | Marked by the prior formulation of specific hypotheses | Manipulation of one or more independent variables |
|  | Versatile | Preplanned and structured design | Control of other mediating variables |
|  | Often the front end of total research design |  |  |
| Methods: | Expert surveys | Secondary data | Experiments |
|  | Pilot surveys | Surveys |  |
|  | Secondary data | Panels |  |
|  | Qualitative research | Observational and other data |  |

characterized by flexibility and versatility with respect to the methods because formal research protocols and procedures are not employed. It rarely involves structured questionnaires, large samples, and probability sampling plans. Rather, researchers are alert to new ideas and insights as they proceed. Once a new idea or insight is discovered, they may redirect their exploration in that direction. That new direction is pursued until its possibilities are exhausted or another direction is found. For this reason, the focus of the investigation may shift constantly as new insights are discovered. Thus, the creativity and ingenuity of the researcher plays a major role in exploratory research. Yet, the abilities of the researcher are not the sole determinants of good exploratory research. Exploratory research can greatly benefit from use of the following methods (see Table 3.2):

> Survey of experts (discussed in Chapter 2)
> Pilot surveys (discussed in Chapter 2)
> Secondary data analyzed in a qualitative way (discussed in Chapter 4)
> Qualitative research (discussed in Chapter 5)

The use of exploratory research in defining the problem and developing an approach was discussed in Chapter 2. The advantages and disadvantages of exploratory research are further discussed in Chapter 4 (Secondary Data) and Chapter 5 (Qualitative Research). To aid the reader in visualizing the applications of exploratory research, we now consider the department store project, which employed the following types of exploratory studies:

- A review of academic and trade literature to identify the relevant demographic and psychographic factors that influence consumer patronage of department stores
- Interviews with retailing experts to determine trends, such as emergence of new types of outlets and shifts in consumer patronage patterns (e.g., shopping on the Internet)
- A comparative analysis of the three best and three worst stores of the same chain to gain some idea of the factors that influence store performance
- Focus groups to determine the factors that consumers consider important in selecting department stores

Further illustration of exploratory research is provided by the following example.

## REAL RESEARCH

### *Focus on Small Business Leads to Large Gains for Microsoft*

Statistics from the United States Small Business Administration (*www.sba.gov*) show that, as of 2003, small businesses represent 99 percent of all employers and provide about 75 percent of all new jobs. While most software manufacturers overlooked this potential market until recently, Microsoft Corporation had a head start and created a marketing research group in 1995 just to study the needs of small businesses.

Microsoft (*www.microsoft.com*) conducted exploratory research. The marketing research group spent more than 25,000 hours examining how small businesses can use technology to solve marketing, customer-service, and growth problems. It began with exploratory research analyzing available secondary data, conducting in-depth one-on-one interviews, and doing small-scale pilot surveys. This research helped Microsoft to understand the small business market. It was a market where the focus should be on selling business solutions, not just selling technology. Small business owners desired integrated tools that were easy to learn and allowed access to the Internet. Research also showed that the market was heterogeneous, with members having differing needs. The research allowed Microsoft to consider different factors in reaching solutions for a small business in order to meet these disparate needs. These factors include the PC-employee ratio, the amount of information processing the company does, and the computing expertise the company has.

Through exploratory research, Microsoft discovered insights about a market that had been virtually ignored before by software vendors. Additional descriptive research allowed Microsoft to create a product specifically tailored for small businesses: Office XP, Small Business Edition.

Microsoft still continues to develop solutions for the small business market through various services: a Web site just for small business, *www.bcentral.com*, Microsoft Small Business Manager, Microsoft Small Business Server 2000, Small Business Consultant Directory, Small Business Manager Partner Locator, and various newsgroups such as Microsoft XP Small Business newsgroup and Small Business Server Newsgroup. Through these efforts, Microsoft hopes to land more small business customers and remain the leader in this market segment whose potential and needs it identified through extensive exploratory research.[5] ■

Note that Microsoft did not rely exclusively on exploratory research. Once new positioning ideas were identified, they were further tested by descriptive research in the form of customer surveys. This example points to the importance of descriptive research in obtaining more conclusive findings.

# DESCRIPTIVE RESEARCH

**descriptive research**
A type of conclusive research that has as its major objective the description of something—usually market characteristics or functions.

As the name implies, the major objective of **descriptive research** is to describe something—usually market characteristics or functions (see Table 3.2). Descriptive research is conducted for the following reasons:

1. To describe the characteristics of relevant groups, such as consumers, salespeople, organizations, or market areas. For example, we could develop a profile of the "heavy users" (frequent shoppers) of prestigious department stores like Saks Fifth Avenue and Neiman Marcus.
2. To estimate the percentage of units in a specified population exhibiting a certain behavior. For example, we might be interested in estimating the percentage of heavy users of prestigious department stores who also patronize discount department stores.
3. To determine the perceptions of product characteristics. For example, how do households perceive the various department stores in terms of salient factors of the choice criteria?
4. To determine the degree to which marketing variables are associated. For example, to what extent is shopping at department stores related to eating out?
5. To make specific predictions. For example, what will be the retail sales of Neiman Marcus (specific store) for fashion clothing (specific product category) in the Dallas area (specific region)?

The example at the beginning of the chapter employed descriptive research in the form of a survey undertaken to quantify the salience of the different social causes for businesses. As this example shows, descriptive research assumes that the researcher has much prior knowledge about the problem situation.[6] In the opening example, the relevant social causes had already been identified through exploratory research before the descriptive survey was conducted. In fact, a major difference between exploratory and descriptive research is that descriptive research is characterized by the prior formulation of specific hypotheses. Thus, the information needed is clearly defined. As a result, descriptive research is preplanned and structured. It is typically based on large representative samples. A formal research design specifies the methods for selecting the sources of information and for collecting data from those sources. A descriptive design requires a clear specification of the who, what, when, where, why, and way (the six Ws) of the research. (It is interesting to note that news reporters use similar criteria for describing a situation.) We illustrate this in the context of the department store project.

**ACTIVE RESEARCH** | DEPARTMENT STORE PROJECT

### The Six Ws

1. Who—Who should be considered a patron of a particular department store? Some of the possibilities are:
   a. Anyone who enters the department store, whether or not they purchase anything
   b. Anyone who purchases anything from the store
   c. Anyone who makes purchases at the department store at least once a month
   d. The person in the household most responsible for department store shopping
2. What—What information should be obtained from the respondents? A wide variety of information could be obtained, including:
   a. Frequency with which different department stores are patronized for specific product categories
   b. Evaluation of the various department stores in terms of the salient choice criteria
   c. Information pertaining to specific hypotheses to be tested
   d. Psychographics and lifestyles, media consumption habits, and demographics
3. When—When should the information be obtained from the respondents? The available options include:
   a. Before shopping
   b. While shopping
   c. Immediately after shopping
   d. Some time after shopping to allow time for evaluation of their shopping experience
4. Where—Where should the respondents be contacted to obtain the required information? Possibilities include contacting the respondents:
   a. In the store
   b. Outside the store but in the shopping mall
   c. In the parking lot
   d. At home
5. Why—Why are we obtaining information from the respondents? Why is the marketing research project being conducted? Possible reasons could be to:
   a. Improve the image of the sponsoring store
   b. Improve patronage and market share
   c. Change the product mix
   d. Develop a suitable promotional campaign
   e. Decide on the location of a new store
6. Way—In what way are we going to obtain information from the respondents? The possible ways could be:
   a. Observe respondents' behavior
   b. Personal interviews
   c. Telephone interviews
   d. Mail interviews
   e. Electronic (e-mail or Internet) interviews

These, and other similar questions, should be asked until the information to be obtained has been clearly defined.

In summary, descriptive research, in contrast to exploratory research, is marked by a clear statement of the problem, specific hypotheses, and detailed information needs. The survey conducted in the department store patronage project, which involved personal interviews, is an example of descriptive research. Other examples of descriptive studies are:

- Market studies, which describe the size of the market, buying power of the consumers, availability of distributors, and consumer profiles
- Market share studies, which determine the proportion of total sales received by a company and its competitors
- Sales analysis studies, which describe sales by geographic region, product line, type and size of the account
- Image studies, which determine consumer perceptions of the firm and its products

- Product usage studies, which describe consumption patterns
- Distribution studies, which determine traffic flow patterns and the number and location of distributors
- Pricing studies, which describe the range and frequency of price changes and probable consumer response to proposed price changes
- Advertising studies, which describe media consumption habits and audience profiles for specific television programs and magazines

In the opening example, descriptive research in the form of a survey was undertaken to quantify the relative salience of various social causes to American businesses. All these examples demonstrate the range and diversity of descriptive research studies. A vast majority of marketing research studies involve descriptive research, which incorporates the following major methods:

Secondary data analyzed in a quantitative, as opposed to a qualitative, manner (discussed in Chapter 4)
Surveys (discussed in Chapter 6)
Panels (discussed in Chapters 4 and 6)
Observational and other data (discussed in Chapter 6)

Although the methods shown in Table 3.2 are typical, it should be noted that the researcher is not limited to these methods. For example, surveys can involve the use of exploratory (open-ended) questions, or causal studies (experiments) are sometimes administered by surveys. Descriptive research using the methods of Table 3.2 can be further classified into cross-sectional and longitudinal research (Figure 3.1).

## Cross-Sectional Designs

**cross-sectional design**
A type of research design involving the collection of information from any given sample of population elements only once.

**single cross-sectional design**
A cross-sectional design in which one sample of respondents is drawn from the target population and information is obtained from this sample once.

The cross-sectional study is the most frequently used descriptive design in marketing research. *Cross-sectional design* involves the collection of information from any given sample of population elements only once. They may be either single cross-sectional or multiple cross-sectional (Figure 3.1). In *single cross-sectional designs,* only one sample of respondents is drawn from the target population, and information is obtained from this sample only once. These designs are also called sample survey research designs.

### REAL RESEARCH

#### *Internet Healthcare Services*

Harris Interactive, with 2001 revenues of $130 million, is a worldwide marketing research and consulting firm that uses the Internet to conduct marketing research. Harris Interactive (*www.harrisinteractive.com*) conducted a study to determine the needs for online healthcare services and the best way to meet them. The research design consisted of an exploratory phase followed by a descriptive cross-sectional online survey of 1,000 U.S. healthcare consumers over the age of 18.

According to the survey, a visit to the doctor's office is not enough for most consumers. The average time a doctor spends with a patient has decreased to 15 minutes, which reduces the overall interpersonal healthcare communication. The survey revealed that consumers demand a range of options for accessing their doctors and nurses, which includes face-to-face, online, and telephone communication:

- 86% of respondents wanted to schedule appointments by phone with a person.
- 89% would like online or phone access to a nurse triage to help manage a chronic medical condition with availability after office hours.
- 40% expressed frustration at having to see their physicians in person to get answers to simple healthcare questions.
- 86% wanted electronic medical reminders.
- 83% wanted lab test procedures and results to be available online.
- 69% wanted online charts for monitoring chronic conditions.

In response to such findings, Kaiser Permanente (*www.kaiserpermanente.org*) redesigned its Web site in 2003 to enable members to access drug and medical encyclopedias, request appointments, ask confidential questions of advice nurses and pharmacists, and share health concerns with other members and physicians in discussion groups. The Kaiser site also provides access to information on health plan benefit options, local health education classes, physician directories, and directions to facilities. Members of the Kaiser site also have information on specific doctors and facilities at their fingertips. Alternative healthcare communication methods like Kaiser's will support the physician-patient relationship and make a physician's practice and an entire HMO more competitive when consumers make their decisions about doctors and healthcare providers.[7] ■

**multiple cross-sectional design**
A cross-sectional design in which there are two or more samples of respondents and information from each sample is obtained only once.

In **multiple cross-sectional designs,** there are two or more samples of respondents, and information from each sample is obtained only once. Often, information from different samples is obtained at different times over long intervals. Multiple cross-sectional designs allow comparisons at the aggregate level but not at the individual respondent level. As a different sample is taken each time a survey is conducted, there is no way to compare the measures on an individual respondent across surveys. One type of multiple cross-sectional design of special interest is cohort analysis.

**cohort analysis**
A multiple cross-sectional design consisting of a series of surveys conducted at appropriate time intervals. The cohort refers to the group of respondents who experience the same event within the same time interval.

*Cohort Analysis.* ***Cohort analysis*** consists of a series of surveys conducted at appropriate time intervals, where the cohort serves as the basic unit of analysis. A cohort is a group of respondents who experience the same event within the same time interval.[8] For example, a birth (or age) cohort is a group of people who were born during the same time interval, such as 1951 through 1960. The term cohort analysis refers to any study in which there are measures of some characteristics of one or more cohorts at two or more points in time.

It is unlikely that any of the individuals studied at time one will also be in the sample at time two. For example, the age cohort of people between 8 and 19 years was selected and their soft drink consumption was examined every 10 years for 30 years. In other words, every 10 years a different sample of respondents was drawn from the population of those who were then between 8 and 19 years old. This sample was drawn independently of any previous sample drawn in this study from the population of 8 to 19 years. Obviously, people who were selected once were unlikely to be included again in the same age cohort (8 to 19 years), as these people would be much older at the time of subsequent sampling. This study showed that this cohort had increased consumption of soft drinks over time. Similar findings were obtained for other age cohorts (20–29, 30–39, 40–49, and 50+). Further, the consumption of each cohort did not decrease as the cohort aged. These results are presented in Table 3.3, in which the consumption of the various age cohorts over time can be determined by reading down the diagonal. These findings contradicted the common belief that the consumption of soft drinks will decline with the graying of America. This common but erroneous belief was based on single cross-sectional studies. Note that if any column of

**TABLE 3.3**

**Consumption of Soft Drinks by Various Age Cohorts**
**(Percentage Consuming on a Typical Day)**

| Age | 1950 | 1960 | 1969 | 1979 | |
|-----|------|------|------|------|---|
| 8–19 | 52.9 | 62.6 | 73.2 | 81.0 | |
| 20–29 | 45.2 | 60.7 | 76.0 | 75.8 | C8 |
| 30–39 | 33.9 | 46.6 | 67.7 | 71.4 | C7 |
| 40–49 | 23.2 | 40.8 | 58.6 | 67.8 | C6 |
| 50+ | 18.1 | 28.8 | 50.0 | 51.9 | C5 |
| | C1 | C2 | C3 | C4 | |

C1: cohort born prior to 1900      C5: cohort born 1931–40

C2: cohort born 1901–10      C6: cohort born 1941–49

C3: cohort born 1911–20      C7: cohort born 1950–59

C4: cohort born 1921–30      C8: cohort born 1960–69

Table 3.3 is viewed in isolation, as a single cross-sectional study (reading down the column), the consumption of soft drinks declines with age, fostering the erroneous belief.[9]

Cohort analysis is also used to predict changes in voter opinions during a political campaign. Well-known marketing researchers such as Louis Harris (*www.harris interactive.com*) or George Gallup (*www.gallup.com*), who specialize in political opinion research, periodically question cohorts of voters (people with similar voting patterns during a given interval) about their voting preferences to predict election results. Thus, cohort analysis is an important cross-sectional design. The other type of descriptive design is longitudinal design.

## Longitudinal Designs

**longitudinal design**
A type of research design involving a fixed sample of population elements that is measured repeatedly. The sample remains the same over time, thus providing a series of pictures which, when viewed together, portray a vivid illustration of the situation and the changes that are taking place over time.

In **longitudinal designs,** a fixed sample (or samples) of population elements is measured repeatedly on the same variables. A longitudinal design differs from a cross-sectional design in that the sample (or samples) remain the same over time. In other words, the same people are studied over time and the same variables are measured. In contrast to the typical cross-sectional design, which gives a snapshot of the variables of interest at a single point in time, a longitudinal study provides a series of pictures that give an in-depth view of the situation and the changes that take place over time. For example, the question, "How did the American people rate the performance of George W. Bush immediately after the war in Afghanistan?" would be addressed using a cross-sectional design. However, a longitudinal design would be used to address the question, "How did the American people change their view of Bush's performance during the war in Afghanistan?"

**panel**
A sample of respondents who have agreed to provide information at specified intervals over an extended period.

Sometimes, the term panel is used interchangeably with the term longitudinal design. A **panel** consists of a sample of respondents, generally households that have agreed to provide information at specified intervals over an extended period. Syndicated firms maintain panels, and panel members are compensated for their participation with gifts, coupons, information, or cash. Panels are discussed further in Chapter 4. A panel design can be used to understand and monitor changes in women's attitudes toward golf, as illustrated in the following example.

### REAL RESEARCH

## Timeout. *Women's Golf Apparel Market Is in "Full Swing"*

In 2003, there were 27 million golfers in the United States, and of that number women comprised 20 percent. Although women comprise a smaller percent of all U.S. golfers, they purchase more than 50 percent of all golf products, excluding golf clubs, according to the Women's Sports Foundation. This trend has led traditional golf brands to introduce women's lines and open women's-only golf stores around the country to cater to the needs of neglected female golfers.

To meet this growing demand, TimeOut, a division of King Louie International (*www.kinglouie.com/timeoutforher*), now offers a full line of LPGA-licensed clothing (*www.lpga.com*). In order to ascertain what this large mass of women golfers expects and wants in their golf clothing, TimeOut created Fairway Forum, a panel of female golf enthusiasts that provides insight into women's apparel tastes. Women who have been recruited to this panel participate in focus groups and surveys. Because the women belong to the panel, multiple surveys measuring essentially the same variables can be conducted on the same set of respondents, thus implementing a longitudinal design.

What TimeOut has learned is that, with the passage of time, women are becoming more and more serious about their golf game and wish more LPGA events were televised. Additionally, TimeOut discovered that women are extremely eager for new brands to hit the market, as traditional brands do not offer enough selection to meet their tastes. These women do not want to wear reformulated versions of men's golf apparel, nor do they want to scamper about the course in "cutesy" clothing. Also, these women do not want to encounter other women wearing the same outfit. These ladies are hungry for more variety and are demanding it in the marketplace.

This research further indicates that female golfers want apparel that is both functional and attractive. For example, they want deep pockets to keep balls in while going around

Longitudinal designs implemented by using Timout's Fairway Forum panel have enabled manufacturers to design clothing for women golfers.

the course. The Forum also helped determine some of the underlying psychological factors that women link with their apparel. Although these women want to be treated as athletes, they also want to be treated with respect, and these feelings have become more intense over time. TimeOut's Fairway Forum panel has been an excellent panel in assisting sporting goods and apparel manufacturers in designing clothing to meet the needs of this growing and changing golf segment. The demand for women's golf apparel has grown over time, reaching about $200 million per year in 2003.[10] ■

Data obtained from panels not only provide information on market shares that are based on an extended period of time, but also allow the researcher to examine changes in market share over time.[11] As the following section explains, these changes cannot be determined from cross-sectional data.

## Relative Advantages and Disadvantages of Longitudinal and Cross-Sectional Designs

The relative advantages and disadvantages of longitudinal versus cross-sectional designs are summarized in Table 3.4. A major advantage of longitudinal design over the cross-sectional design is the ability to detect change as a result of repeated measurement of the same variables on the same sample.

Tables 3.5 and 3.6 demonstrate how cross-sectional data can mislead researchers about changes over time. The cross-sectional data reported in Table 3.5 reveal that purchases of brands A, B, and C remain the same in time periods 1 and 2. In each survey, 20 percent of the respondents purchase brand A, 30 percent brand B, and 50 percent

### TABLE 3.4

**Relative Advantages and Disadvantages of Longitudinal and Cross-Sectional Designs**

| EVALUATION CRITERIA | CROSS-SECTIONAL DESIGN | LONGITUDINAL DESIGN |
|---|---|---|
| Detecting change | − | + |
| Large amount of data collection | − | + |
| Accuracy | − | + |
| Representative sampling | + | − |
| Response bias | + | − |

Note: A + indicates a relative advantage over the other design, whereas a − indicates a relative disadvantage.

### TABLE 3.5

**Cross-Sectional Data May Not Show Change**

| | TIME PERIOD | |
|---|---|---|
| BRAND PURCHASED | PERIOD 1 SURVEY | PERIOD 2 SURVEY |
| Brand A | 200 | 200 |
| Brand B | 300 | 300 |
| Brand C | 500 | 500 |
| Total | 1,000 | 1,000 |

brand C. The longitudinal data presented in Table 3.6 show that substantial change, in the form of brand switching, occurred in the study period. For example, only 50 percent (100/200) of the respondents who purchased brand A in period 1 also purchased it in period 2. The corresponding repeat purchase figures for brands B and C are, respectively, 33.3 percent (100/300) and 55 percent (275/500). Hence, during this interval, brand C experienced the greatest loyalty and brand B the least. Table 3.6 provides valuable information on brand loyalty and brand switching. (Such a table is called a turnover table or a brand-switching matrix.[12])

Longitudinal data enable researchers to examine changes in the behavior of individual units and to link behavioral changes to marketing variables, such as changes in advertising, packaging, pricing, and distribution. Because the same units are measured repeatedly, variations caused by changes in the sample are eliminated and even small changes are apparent.

Another advantage of panels is that relatively large amounts of data can be collected. Because panel members are usually compensated for their participation, they are willing to participate in lengthy and demanding interviews. Yet another advantage is that panel data can be more accurate than cross-sectional data. A typical cross-sectional survey requires the respondent to recall past purchases and behavior; these data can be inaccurate because of memory lapses. Panel data, which rely on continuous recording of purchases in a diary, place less reliance on the respondent's memory. A comparison of panel and cross-sectional survey estimates of retail sales indicates that panel data give more accurate estimates.[13]

The main disadvantage of panels is that they may not be representative. Nonrepresentativeness may arise because of:

1. **Refusal to Cooperate.** Many individuals or households do not wish to be bothered with the panel operation and refuse to participate. Consumer panels requiring members to keep a record of purchases have a cooperation rate of 60 percent or less.
2. **Mortality.** Panel members who agree to participate may subsequently drop out because they move away or lose interest. Mortality rates can be as high as 20 percent per year.[14]
3. **Payment.** Payment may cause certain types of people to be attracted, making the group unrepresentative of the population.

Another disadvantage of panels is response bias. New panel members are often biased in their initial responses. They tend to increase the behavior being measured, such as food

### TABLE 3.6

**Longitudinal Data May Show Substantial Change**

| BRAND PURCHASED IN PERIOD 1 | BRAND PURCHASED IN PERIOD 2 | | | |
|---|---|---|---|---|
| | BRAND A | BRAND B | BRAND C | TOTAL |
| Brand A | 100 | 50 | 50 | 200 |
| Brand B | 25 | 100 | 175 | 300 |
| Brand C | 75 | 150 | 275 | 500 |
| Total | 200 | 300 | 500 | 1,000 |

purchasing. This bias decreases as the respondents overcome the novelty of being on the panel, so it can be reduced by initially excluding the data of new members. Seasoned panel members may also give biased responses because they believe they are experts or want to look good or give the "right" answer. Bias also results from boredom, fatigue, and incomplete diary entries.[15]

# CAUSAL RESEARCH

**causal research**
A type of conclusive research where the major objective is to obtain evidence regarding cause-and-effect (causal) relationships.

*Causal research* is used to obtain evidence of cause-and-effect (causal) relationships (see Table 3.2). Marketing managers continually make decisions based on assumed causal relationships. These assumptions may not be justifiable, and the validity of the causal relationships should be examined via formal research.[16] For example, the common assumption that a decrease in price will lead to increased sales and market share does not hold in certain competitive environments. Causal research is appropriate for the following purposes:

1. To understand which variables are the cause (independent variables) and which variables are the effect (dependent variables) of a phenomenon.
2. To determine the nature of the relationship between the causal variables and the effect to be predicted.

Like descriptive research, causal research requires a planned and structured design. Although descriptive research can determine the degree of association between variables, it is not appropriate for examining causal relationships. Such an examination requires a causal design, in which the causal, or independent, variables are manipulated in a relatively controlled environment. A relatively controlled environment is one in which the other variables that may affect the dependent variable are controlled or checked as much as possible. The effect of this manipulation on one or more dependent variables is then measured to infer causality. The main method of causal research is experimentation.[17]

Due to its complexity and importance, a separate chapter (Chapter 7) has been devoted to causal designs and experimental research. However, we give some examples here. In the context of the department store project, a researcher wishes to determine whether the presence and helpfulness of salespeople (causal variable) will influence the sales of housewares (effect variable). A causal design could be formulated in which two groups of otherwise comparable housewares departments of a particular chain are selected. For four weeks, trained salespeople are stationed in one group of housewares departments but not in the other. Sales are monitored for both groups, while controlling for other variables. A comparison of sales for the two groups will reveal the effect of salespeople on housewares sales in department stores. Alternatively, instead of selecting two groups of stores, the researcher could select only one set of department stores and carry out this manipulation for two comparable time periods: salespeople are present in one time period and absent in the other.

**REAL RESEARCH**

## *Does Merchandising Display Affect Sales?*

In 2000, the Mead Corporation and Westvaco Corporation announced that they had agreed to a merger of equals creating a $10 billion global company, MeadWestvaco (*www.mead westvaco.com*), with leading positions in packaging, coated and specialty papers, consumer and office products, and specialty chemicals. MeadWestvaco had developed a new merchandising display system for displaying its school and office stationary products such as notebooks, note pads, and other paper products. The question was whether the new system would increase sales of stationary items enough to pay for the increased cost of implementing this system. K-Mart stores (*www.kmart.com*) were a major outlet for MeadWestvaco stationary products. Therefore, an experiment was designed in which 12 K-Mart stores in a large metropolitan area were selected. Six stores were randomly assigned the new merchandising system, whereas six other stores were randomly selected to display the merchandise

Causal research in the form of an experiment helped MeadWestvaco determine the effectiveness of a new merchandising display system.

using the old system. This experiment was conducted for six months. During this time, the other marketing variables such as price, advertising, stock-outs, etc., were carefully controlled in all the 12 stores, and the sales of MeadWestvaco products were monitored. At the conclusion of the experiment, the sales of MeadWestvaco products, normalized for the effect of store size, were compared for the two groups of stores. It was found that the stores with the new system had sales that were 7 percent higher than the sales of the stores with the old system. Because a 7 percent increase in sales would more than offset the costs, the new merchandising display system was implemented nationwide. The new merchandising system also allowed the company to display an expanded line of products. As of 2003, MeadWestvaco also produced and distributed school and office supplies with highly recognized brand names such as Nike, Harry Potter, and M&M's/Mars. They also expanded their line through Five Star and Trapper Keeper notebooks for the classroom and At-A-Glance and Cambridge for the office.[18] ■

In the MeadWestvaco experiment, the causal (independent) variable was merchandising display, which was manipulated to have two levels: the old system and the new system. The effect (dependent) variable was sales, and the influence on sales of other variables, such as price, advertising, and store size, had to be controlled. Although the preceding example distinguished causal research from other types of research, causal research should not be viewed in isolation. Rather, the exploratory, descriptive, and causal designs often complement each other.

## RELATIONSHIPS AMONG EXPLORATORY, DESCRIPTIVE, AND CAUSAL RESEARCH

We have described exploratory, descriptive, and causal research as major classifications of research designs, but the distinctions among these classifications are not absolute. A given marketing research project may involve more than one type of research design and thus serve several purposes. Which combination of research designs should be employed depends on the nature of the problem. We offer the following general guidelines for choosing research designs:

1. When little is known about the problem situation, it is desirable to begin with exploratory research. Exploratory research is appropriate when the problem needs to be defined more precisely, alternative courses of action identified, research questions

or hypotheses developed, and key variables isolated and classified as dependent or independent.

2. Exploratory research is the initial step in the overall research design framework. It should, in most instances, be followed by descriptive or causal research. For example, hypotheses developed via exploratory research should be statistically tested using descriptive or causal research. This was illustrated in the cause-related marketing example given in the overview section. Exploratory research in the form of secondary data analysis and focus groups was conducted to identify the social causes that American businesses should be concerned about. Then a descriptive cross-sectional survey was undertaken to quantify the relative salience of these causes.

3. It is not necessary to begin every research design with exploratory research. It depends upon the precision with which the problem has been defined and the researcher's degree of certainty about the approach to the problem. A research design could well begin with descriptive or causal research. To illustrate, a consumer satisfaction survey that is conducted annually need not begin with or include an exploratory phase each year.

4. Although exploratory research is generally the initial step, it need not be. Exploratory research may follow descriptive or causal research. For example, descriptive or causal research results in findings that are hard for managers to interpret. Exploratory research may provide more insights to help understand these findings.

The relationship between exploratory, descriptive, and causal research is further illustrated by the department store project.

---

**ACTIVE RESEARCH** | DEPARTMENT STORE PROJECT

### Exploring and Describing Store Patronage

In the department store project, exploratory research, including secondary data analysis and qualitative research, was first conducted to define the problem and develop a suitable approach. This was followed by a descriptive study consisting of a survey in which a questionnaire was constructed and administered by personal interviews.

Suppose the patronage study was to be repeated after two years to determine if any changes had taken place. At that point, exploratory research would probably be unnecessary and the research design could begin with descriptive research.

Assume that the survey is repeated two years later and some unexpected findings are obtained. Management wonders why the store's ratings on in-store service have declined when the sales staff has increased. Exploratory research in the form of focus groups might be undertaken to probe the unexpected findings. The focus groups may reveal that although the salespeople are easy to find, they are not perceived to be friendly or helpful. This may suggest the need for training the sales staff.

---

This example involves the use of exploratory and descriptive research but not causal research. This reflects the fact that exploratory and descriptive research are frequently used in commercial marketing research, but causal research is not as popular. However, it is possible to combine exploratory, descriptive, and causal research, as demonstrated by Citibank.

**REAL RESEARCH**

## Citibank Groups Exploratory, Descriptive, and Causal Research

As of 2003, Citigroup (*www.citigroup.com*) provides a range of financial products and services, including banking, in more than 100 countries. In 2001, Citigroup achieved annual revenues of $80 billion. In order to maintain such high revenues, Citigroup must continually research target customers to better cater to their needs. Marketing Research at Citibank (*www.citibank.com*), a division of Citigroup, is typical in that it is used to measure consumer awareness of products, monitor their satisfaction and attitudes associated

Citibank makes use of exploratory, descriptive, and causal research in designing its marketing programs.

with the product, track product usage, and diagnose problems as they occur. To accomplish these tasks, Citibank makes extensive use of exploratory, descriptive, and causal research.

Often it is advantageous to offer special financial packages to specific groups of customers, in this case for senior citizens. Citibank followed the seven-step process to help in the design.

**Step 1.** A taskforce was created to better define the market parameters to include all the needs of the many Citibank branches. A final decision was made to include Americans 55 years of age or older, retired, and in the upper half of the financial strata of that market.

**Step 2.** Exploratory research in the form of secondary data analysis of the mature or older market was performed, and a study of competitive products was conducted. Exploratory qualitative research involving focus groups was also carried out in order to determine the needs and desires of the market and the level of satisfaction with the current products. In the case of senior citizens, a great deal of diversity was found in the market. This was determined to be due to such factors as affluence, relative age, and the absence or presence of a spouse.

**Step 3.** The next stage of exploratory research was brainstorming. This involved the formation of many different financial packages targeted for the target market. In this case, a total of 10 ideas were generated.

**Step 4.** The feasibility of each of the 10 ideas generated in step 3 was tested. The following list of questions was used as a series of hurdles that the ideas had to pass to continue on to the next step.
- Can the idea be explained in a manner that the target market will easily understand?
- Does the idea fit into the overall strategy of Citibank?
- Is there an available description of a specific target market for the proposed product?
- Does the research conducted so far indicate a potential match for target market needs, and is the idea perceived to have appeal to this market?
- Is there a feasible outline of the tactics and strategies for implementing the program?
- Have the financial impact and cost of the program been thoroughly evaluated and determined to be in line with company practices?

    In this study, only one idea generated from the brainstorming session made it past all the listed hurdles and on to step 5.

**Step 5.** A creative work plan was generated. This plan was to emphasize the competitive advantage of the proposed product as well as better delineate the specific features of the product.

**Step 6.** The previous exploratory research was followed up with descriptive research in the form of mall intercept surveys of people in the target market range. The survey showed that the list of special features was too long, and it was decided to drop the features more commonly offered by competitors.

**Step 7.** The product was test-marketed in six of the Citibank branches within the target market. Test-marketing is a form of causal research. Given successful test-marketing results, the product was introduced nationally.[19] ■

Regardless of the kind of research design employed, the researcher should attempt to minimize the potential sources of error.

# POTENTIAL SOURCES OF ERROR

Several potential sources of error can affect a research design. A good research design attempts to control the various sources of error. Although these errors are discussed in great detail in subsequent chapters, it is pertinent at this stage to give brief descriptions.

The *total error* is the variation between the true mean value in the population of the variable of interest and the observed mean value obtained in the marketing research project. For example, the average annual income of the target population is $75,871, as determined from latest census records, but the marketing research project estimates it as $67,157 based on a sample survey. As shown in Figure 3.2, total error is composed of random sampling error and nonsampling error.

## Random Sampling Error

*Random sampling error* occurs because the particular sample selected is an imperfect representation of the population of interest. Random sampling error is the variation between the true mean value for the population and the true mean value for the original sample. For example, the average annual income of the target population is $75,871, but it is only

---

**total error**
The variation between the true mean value in the population of the variable of interest and the observed mean value obtained in the marketing research project.

**random sampling error**
The error due to the particular sample selected being an imperfect representation of the population of interest. It may be defined as the variation between the true mean value for the sample and the true mean value of the population.

*Figure 3.2*
Potential Sources of Error in Research Designs

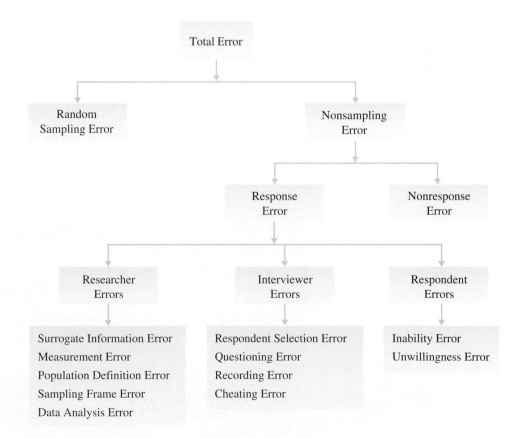

$71,382 for the original sample, as determined from the mail panel records that are believed to be accurate. Random sampling error is discussed further in Chapters 11 and 12.

## Nonsampling Error

*Nonsampling error* can be attributed to sources other than sampling, and they may be random or nonrandom. They result from a variety of reasons, including errors in problem definition, approach, scales, questionnaire design, interviewing methods, and data preparation and analysis. For example, the researcher designs a poor questionnaire, which contains several questions that lead the respondents to give biased answers. Nonsampling errors consist of nonresponse errors and response errors.

*Nonresponse Error.*   *Nonresponse error* arises when some of the respondents included in the sample do not respond. The primary causes of nonresponse are refusals and not-at-homes (see Chapter 12). Nonresponse will cause the net or resulting sample to be different in size or composition from the original sample. Nonresponse error is defined as the variation between the true mean value of the variable in the original sample and the true mean value in the net sample. For example, the average annual income is $71,382 for the original sample, but $69,467 for the net sample, both determined from the mail panel records that are believed to be accurate.

*Response Error.*   *Response error* arises when respondents give inaccurate answers or their answers are misrecorded or misanalyzed. Response error is defined as the variation between the true mean value of the variable in the net sample and the observed mean value obtained in the marketing research project. For example, the average annual income is $69,467 for the net sample, but is estimated as $67,157 in the marketing research project. Response errors can be made by researchers, interviewers, or respondents.[20]

Errors made by the researcher include surrogate information, measurement, population definition, sampling frame, and data analysis errors.

*Surrogate information error* may be defined as the variation between the information needed for the marketing research problem and the information sought by the researcher. For example, instead of obtaining information on consumer choice of a new brand (needed for the marketing research problem), the researcher obtains information on consumer preferences because the choice process cannot be easily observed.

*Measurement error* may be defined as the variation between the information sought and information generated by the measurement process employed by the researcher. Seeking to measure consumer preferences, the researcher employs a scale that measures perceptions rather than preferences.

*Population definition error* may be defined as the variation between the actual population relevant to the problem at hand and the population as defined by the researcher. The problem of appropriately defining the population may be far from trivial, as illustrated by the case of affluent households.

### REAL RESEARCH

## How Affluent Is Affluent?

In a recent study, the population of the affluent households was defined in four different ways: (1) households with income of $50,000 or more; (2) the top 20 percent of households, as measured by income; (3) households with net worth over $250,000; and (4) households with spendable discretionary income 30 percent higher than that of comparable households. The number and characteristics of the affluent households varied depending upon the definition, underscoring the need to avoid population definition error.[21] ■

As may be surmised, the results of this study would have varied markedly depending upon the way the population of affluent households was defined.

*Sampling frame error* may be defined as the variation between the population defined by the researcher and the population as implied by the sampling frame (list) used. For

---

**nonsampling error**
Nonsampling errors are errors that can be attributed to sources other than sampling, and they can be random or nonrandom.

**nonresponse error**
A type of nonsampling error that occurs when some of the respondents included in the sample do not respond. This error may be defined as the variation between the true mean value of the variable in the original sample and the true mean value in the net sample.

**response error**
A type of nonsampling error arising from respondents who do respond but give inaccurate answers, or their answers are misrecorded or misanalyzed. It may be defined as the variation between the true mean value of the variable in the net sample and the observed mean value obtained in the marketing research project.

example, the telephone directory used to generate a list of telephone numbers does not accurately represent the population of potential consumers due to unlisted, disconnected, and new numbers in service.

***Data analysis error*** encompasses errors that occur when raw data from questionnaires are transformed into research findings. For example, an inappropriate statistical procedure is used resulting in incorrect interpretation and findings.

Response errors made by the interviewer include respondent selection, questioning, recording, and cheating errors.

***Respondent selection error*** occurs when interviewers select respondents other than those specified by the sampling design or in a manner inconsistent with the sampling design. For example, in a readership survey, a nonreader is selected for the interview but classified as a reader of the *Wall Street Journal* in the 15 to 19 years category in order to meet a difficult quota requirement.

***Questioning error*** denotes errors made in asking questions of the respondents or in not probing when more information is needed. For example, while asking questions, an interviewer does not use the exact wording given in the questionnaire.

***Recording error*** arises due to errors in hearing, interpreting, and recording the answers given by the respondents. For example, a respondent indicates a neutral response (undecided) but the interviewer misinterprets that to mean a positive response (would buy the new brand).

***Cheating error*** arises when the interviewer fabricates answers to a part or all of the interview. For example, an interviewer does not ask the sensitive questions related to respondent's debt but later fills in the answers based on personal assessment.

Response errors made by the respondent are comprised of inability and unwillingness errors.

***Inability error*** results from the respondent's inability to provide accurate answers. Respondents may provide inaccurate answers because of unfamiliarity, fatigue, boredom, faulty recall, question format, question content, and other factors. For example, a respondent cannot recall the brand of yogurt purchased four weeks ago.

***Unwillingness error*** arises from the respondent's unwillingness to provide accurate information. Respondents may intentionally misreport their answers because of a desire to provide socially acceptable answers, avoid embarrassment, or please the interviewer. For example, a respondent intentionally misreports reading *Time* magazine in order to impress the interviewer.

These sources of error are discussed in more detail in the subsequent chapters; what is important here is that there are many sources of error. In formulating a research design, the researcher should attempt to minimize the total error, not just a particular source. This admonition is warranted by the general tendency among students and unsophisticated researchers to control sampling error with large samples. Increasing the sample size does decrease sampling error, but it may also increase nonsampling error by increasing interviewer errors.

Nonsampling error is likely to be more problematic than sampling error. Sampling error can be calculated, whereas many forms of nonsampling error defy estimation. Moreover, nonsampling error has been found to be the major contributor to total error, whereas random sampling error is relatively small in magnitude.[22] The point is that total error is important. A particular type of error is important only in that it contributes to total error.

Sometimes, researchers deliberately increase a particular type of error to decrease the total error by reducing other errors. For example, suppose a mail survey is being conducted to determine consumer preferences for purchasing fashion clothing from department stores. A large sample size has been selected to reduce sampling error. A response rate of 30 percent may be expected. Given the limited budget for the project, the selection of a large sample size does not allow for follow-up mailings. However, past experience indicates that the response rate could be increased to 45 percent with one follow-up and to 55 percent with two follow-up mailings. Given the subject of the survey, nonrespondents are likely to differ from respondents in terms of salient variables. Hence, it may be desirable to reduce the sample size to make money available for follow-up mailings. Although decreasing the sample size will increase random sampling error, the two follow-up mailings will more than offset this loss by decreasing nonresponse error.

# BUDGETING AND SCHEDULING THE PROJECT

**budgeting and scheduling**
Management tools needed to help ensure that the marketing research project is completed within the available resources.

Once a research design, appropriately controlling the total error, has been specified, the budgeting and scheduling decisions should be made. **Budgeting and scheduling** help to ensure that the marketing research project is completed within the available resources—financial, time, manpower, and other. By specifying the time parameters within which each task should be completed and the costs of each task, the research project can be effectively managed. A useful approach for managing a project is the **critical path method** (CPM), which involves dividing the research project into component activities, determining the sequence of these activities, and estimating the time required for each activity. These activities and time estimates are diagrammed in the form of a network flow chart. The critical path, the series of activities whose delay will hold up the project, can then be identified.

**critical path method (CPM)**
Management technique of dividing a research project into component activities, determining the sequence of these components and the time each activity will require.

An advanced version of CPM is the **program evaluation and review technique** (PERT), which is a probability-based scheduling approach that recognizes and measures the uncertainty of the project completion times.[23] An even more advanced scheduling technique is the **graphical evaluation and review technique** (GERT), in which both the completion probabilities and the activity costs can be built into a network representation.

**program evaluation and review technique (PERT)**
A more sophisticated critical path method that accounts for the uncertainty in project completion times.

**graphical evaluation and review technique (GERT)**
A sophisticated critical path method that accounts for both the completion probabilities and the activity costs.

# MARKETING RESEARCH PROPOSAL

**marketing research proposal**
The official layout of the planned marketing research activity for management. It describes the research problem, the approach, the research design, data collection methods, data analysis methods, and reporting methods.

Once the research design has been formulated, and budgeting and scheduling of the project accomplished, a written research proposal should be prepared. The **marketing research proposal** contains the essence of the project and serves as a contract between the researcher and management. The research proposal covers all phases of the marketing research process. It describes the research problem, the approach, the research design, and how the data will be collected, analyzed, and reported. It gives a cost estimate and a time schedule for completing the project. Although the format of a research proposal may vary considerably, most proposals address all steps of the marketing research process and contain the following elements:

1. Executive Summary. The proposal should begin with a summary of the major points from each of the other sections, presenting an overview of the entire proposal.
2. Background. The background to the problem, including the environmental context, should be discussed.
3. Problem Definition/Objectives of the Research. Normally, a statement of the problem, including the specific components, should be presented. If this statement has not been developed (as in the case of problem identification research), the objectives of the marketing research project should be clearly specified.
4. Approach to the Problem. At a minimum, a review of the relevant academic and trade literature should be presented, along with some kind of an analytical model. If research questions and hypotheses have been identified, then these should be included in the proposal.
5. Research Design. The research design adopted, whether exploratory, descriptive, or causal, should be specified. Information should be provided on the following components: (1) kind of information to be obtained, (2) method of administering the questionnaire (mail, telephone, personal, or electronic interviews), (3) scaling techniques, (4) nature of the questionnaire (type of questions asked, length, average interviewing time), and (5) sampling plan and sample size.
6. Field Work/Data Collection. The proposal should discuss how the data will be collected and who will collect it. If the field work is to be subcontracted to another supplier, this should be stated. Control mechanisms to ensure the quality of data collected should be described.
7. Data Analysis. The kind of data analysis that will be conducted (simple cross-tabulations, univariate analysis, multivariate analysis) and how the results will be interpreted should be described.

8. Reporting. The proposal should specify whether intermediate reports will be presented and at what stages, what will be the form of the final report, and whether a formal presentation of the results will be made.

9. Cost and Time. The cost of the project and a time schedule, broken down by phases, should be presented. A CPM or PERT chart might be included. In large projects, a payment schedule is also worked out in advance.

10. Appendices. Any statistical or other information that is of interest to only a few people should be contained in appendices.

Preparing a research proposal has several advantages. It ensures that the researcher and management agree about the nature of the project, and helps sell the project to management. As preparation of the proposal entails planning, it helps the researcher conceptualize and execute the marketing research project.

# INTERNATIONAL MARKETING RESEARCH

When conducting international marketing research, it is important to realize that given the environmental differences (see Chapter 23), the research design appropriate for one country may not be suitable in another. Consider the problem of determining household attitudes toward major appliances in the United States and Saudi Arabia. When conducting exploratory research in the United States, it is appropriate to conduct focus groups jointly with male and female heads of households. However, it would be inappropriate to conduct such focus groups in Saudi Arabia. Given the traditional culture, the wives are unlikely to participate freely in the presence of their husbands. It would be more useful to conduct one-on-one depth interviews with both male and female heads of households being included in the sample.

### REAL RESEARCH

## There's No Place Like Home

GfK (*www.gfk.it*), a European customer marketing research company, conducted a two-year, two-part study to determine the new trends in European youth and culture—what matters to European teenagers, and how international marketers should approach them. Exploratory research in the form of focus groups was conducted first to identify issues that are salient to European youth. The issues identified in focus groups were quantified by conducting a descriptive longitudinal survey. The survey was conducted in two parts spanning 16 different European countries including Denmark, Norway, Sweden, the U.K., Germany, Italy, Spain, and France, among others.

In each country, four groups of respondents were selected; 14-to-16-year-old girls, 14-to-16-year-old boys, 17-to-20-year-old girls, and 17-to-20-year-old boys. A descriptive survey was designed and administered in personal, face-to-face settings. Given the European youth culture, it was felt that the teens would feel more comfortable and be able to provide more candid responses in a personal setting. A total of 523 young people participated. Two years later, the same people were contacted in 9 of the 16 countries, with a total of 305 people participating in the longitudinal phase.

The results showed that tastes and opinions of teenagers in Europe have been changing dramatically over the past few years, and particularly during the last two years. It was discovered that European teens did not trust big companies. The concept of home included not only the family and actual home dwelling, but a sense of belonging and community, especially with friends. It is a symbol of coziness and warmth. The European teens did not see their families much during the week. Instead, friends filled this home function. Finally, they did put a lot of stock in a brand that has been around for a long time, feeling that if the brand has proven its existence over time that it must be good and worthy of its long stay.

The results proved very beneficial for McDonald's (*www.mcdonalds.com*) in developing their international advertising aimed at this market. McDonald's new campaign did not focus on its big company status, but localized its advertising to make it seem to be the local hamburger hangout joint for teens. Meeting up with friends at the local McDonald's made the McDonald's "home." It appeared to be fun, and the teens wanted to be there.

By using cross-sectional and longitudinal surveys, McDonald's has determined what appeals to European youth and positioned itself accordingly.

Additionally, McDonald's focused on the longevity and stability of the brand. It will always be around as a fun place where teens can hang out with their friends and have fun for a low price. The campaign resulted in increased market share in the lucrative European teenage market. As of 2003, McDonald's derived about 25 percent of its total sales from Europe.[24] ∎

In many countries, particularly developing countries, consumer panels have not been developed, making it difficult to conduct descriptive longitudinal research. Likewise, in many countries the marketing support infrastructure (i.e., retailing, wholesaling, advertising, and promotional infrastructure) is lacking, making it infeasible to implement a causal design involving a field experiment. In formulating a research design, considerable effort is required to ensure the equivalence and comparability of secondary and primary data obtained from different countries. In the context of collecting primary data, qualitative research, survey methods, scaling techniques, questionnaire design, and sampling considerations are particularly important. These topics are discussed in more detail in subsequent chapters.

# ETHICS IN MARKETING RESEARCH

During the research design stage, not only are the concerns of the researcher and the client involved, but the rights of the respondents must also be respected. Although there usually is no direct contact between the respondent and the other stakeholders (client and researcher) during research design, this is the stage when decisions with ethical ramifications, such as using hidden video or audio tape recorders are made.

The basic question of the type of research design that should be adopted (i.e., descriptive or causal, cross-sectional or longitudinal) has ethical overtones. For example, when studying brand switching in toothpaste purchases, a longitudinal design is the only actual way to assess changes in an individual respondent's brand choice. A research firm that has not conducted many longitudinal studies may try to justify the use of a cross-sectional design. Is this ethical?

The researchers must ensure that the research design utilized will provide the information needed to address the marketing research problem that has been identified. The client should have the integrity not to misrepresent the project, should describe the constraints under which the researcher must operate, and should not make unreasonable demands. Longitudinal research takes time. Descriptive research might require interviewing customers. If time is an issue, or if customer contact has to be restricted, the client should make these constraints known at the start of the project. Finally, the client should not take undue advantage of the research firm to solicit unfair concessions for the current project by making false promises of future research contracts.

**REAL RESEARCH**

## *Big Brother or Big Bully?*

Ethical dilemmas may arise due to the strong desire of marketing research firms to become suppliers to large business firms who are heavy users of marketing research. Take for example, Visa, Delta Airlines, Coca-Cola, or Ford Motor Company. Such firms have large marketing research budgets and regularly hire external marketing research suppliers. These large clients can manipulate the price for the current study or demand unreasonable concessions in the research design (e.g., the examination of additional variables, more focus groups, a larger, more targeted sample for the survey, or additional data analyses) by suggesting the potential for the marketing research firm to become a regular supplier. This may be considered just business, but it becomes unethical when there is no intention to follow up with a larger study or to use the research firm in the future.[25] ■

Equally important, the responsibilities to the respondents must not be overlooked. The researcher should design the study so as not to violate the respondents' right to safety, right to privacy, or right to choose. Furthermore, the client must not abuse power to jeopardize the anonymity of the respondents. These respondent-related issues are discussed in more detail in Chapters 4, 5, 6, and 7.

# INTERNET AND COMPUTER APPLICATIONS

The Internet can facilitate the implementation of different types of research designs.

## Exploratory Research

During the exploratory phase of the research, forums, chat rooms, or newsgroups can be used to generally discuss a topic with anyone who visits the chat room. Newsgroups focus on a particular topic and function like bulletin boards. Internet users stop by a newsgroup to read messages left by others and to post their own responses or comments. Chapter 2 discussed the use of *groups.google.com* to locate specific newsgroups. Newsgroups or chat rooms could be used to set up more formal focus groups with experts or individuals representing the target audience in order to obtain initial information on a subject. In Chapter 5, we discuss the use of the Internet for conducting focus groups in more detail.

Listservers could also be used to obtain the initial information needed to begin research design. Listservers make interactive discussion possible for special interest groups, user groups, customer service forums, etc., using Internet e-mail. Messages sent to the listserver are forwarded to all subscribers of that listserver. Broad or specific questions could be asked of listserver subscribers. The questions might not constitute a specifically developed survey, and the members of the listservers might not all represent the target audience precisely, but if the listservers are chosen based on their relationship to the area being researched, they should provide a means of quickly receiving responses that can begin to clarify the research area. Such responses would feed into more conclusive research. More information on listservers can be obtained at *www.cuenet.com/ml.html*.

## Conclusive Research

Many descriptive studies utilize secondary data, the methodology of which we describe in Chapter 4; surveys, which are discussed in Chapter 6; and panels, which are discussed in

Chapters 4 and 6. The use of the Internet for causal research designs is discussed in Chapter 7. The Internet, in its capacity as a source of information, can be useful in uncovering secondary data and collecting primary data needed in conclusive research, as illustrated by Greenfield Online Research Center, Inc.

**REAL RESEARCH**

## The Greenfield of Online Research

Greenfield Online Research Center, Inc. (*www.greenfieldonline.com*), based in Westport, Connecticut, is a subsidiary of the Greenfield Consulting Group. The Online Research Center conducts focus groups, surveys, and polls over the Internet. As of 2003, the company had built up a "panel" of close to 200,000 Internet users, from which it draws survey samples. The samples may be used for descriptive research designs such as single or multiple cross-sectional designs, as well as longitudinal designs. Causal designs can also be implemented. Respondents may also be chosen from the registered Internet users.

In addition to conducting conclusive research studies, Greenfield Online also offers a product called MindStorm that allows marketers to brainstorm with potential consumers on a new design for their product. MindStorm allows targeted participants to respond at their leisure to questions, concepts, and statements relating to brand, and projects can run for two days, two weeks, or two months, allowing for in-depth responses. This is great for exploratory research.

Cross Pen Computing Group (*www.cross.com*) had a problem. They needed to improve the customer appeal of their product, Cross Pad, and decided to use MindStorm to supplement other qualitative research. Cross Pad is an electronic notepad that comes in two sizes, letter size and six-by-nine inches. A special digital pen transmits handwriting electronically to the pad, allowing the user to draw or take notes that can be instantly uploaded into a personal computer.

Online respondents, who were users of high-end technology, joined together for the discussion in a password-protected area. The participants were all provided with an electronic look at Cross Pad. The group discussion went on for one week. The key finding was that marketing messages should emphasize the product's usefulness to consumers who were active note takers. When this finding was confirmed by a subsequent online survey, it became the platform for a new advertising campaign that was very successful. Thus, exploratory research followed by descriptive research led to a profitable marketing and advertising strategy for Cross Pad.[26] ∎

In addition to Internet applications, computers can also help control total error. By using computers, it is possible to understand how the various sources of error will affect the results and what levels of errors might be acceptable. It is relatively easy to estimate random sampling error when probability sampling schemes are used. Estimating the impact of various nonsampling errors, however, is much more problematic. Simulation can be conducted to determine how the distributions and levels of various nonsampling errors will affect final results.[27] This would indicate the acceptable levels of error, and the research design could be adjusted to contain these errors within the acceptable limits. The simulations provide only an indication, and considerable judgment on the part of the researcher is needed.

**FOCUS ON BURKE**

Burke starts the process of formulating a research design with a listing of the key information that the client needs. This is not a small task. Burke tries to clarify what information is critical and what is "nice to know," i.e., what information is "report card" and what is needed to allow a specific action. For example, in a study for a local blood bank a question was asked, "How convenient was the blood bank location?" This is a "report card" question. Thirty percent of the respondents said the location was inconvenient. What does management do? The question certainly does not imply any action. Some members of management jumped to the conclusion that this meant the blood bank was too far from the normal driving range of donors and a more suburban center should be considered. Follow-up research found that this was not at all the case. Those reporting that the blood bank location was inconvenient were those who had trouble finding a parking place when they donated. The proper action was improving the parking, not creating a new donation center. To ensure the usefulness of the information collected, Burke addresses the question of "what we are going to do with what we measure."

Once this has been done, Burke asks a series of questions: Who has the information? Do they really know the information? Are they willing to share the information? These are key questions in defining the relevant population for the study. The definition must be tight enough that any number of judges, when evaluating a respondent, would all agree as to whether the respondent is legitimately in the population or not. Another key question in formulating the research design is, "Will the respondents understand the measurement methods such that they can share the information accurately and reliably?" It is important that the researcher and the respondent use the same language. In the blood bank project, the word "convenient" was used. Is this defined the same way by all respondents and by the researcher? If you are going to ask a series of attribute ratings, are you sure that you are including the attributes the respondents really use and in the words they will understand?

Burke conducts exploratory, descriptive, and causal research. Generally, some combination of these basic designs is used in a particular study. When a new project is undertaken for a client, exploratory research is generally the first phase. This involves extensive analysis of available secondary data and some form of qualitative research, with focus groups being the most popular. The purpose of exploratory research is to understand the environmental context of the problem, particularly the underlying decision making process of the consumers or the customers with respect to the client's products. In the blood bank project, secondary data were analyzed and focus groups conducted to answer questions such as, "What factors do people consider in deciding to donate blood? What are the major motivations for donating blood? What are people's attitudes toward donating blood?" Exploratory research is in most instances followed by descriptive research, or sometimes by causal research if that is appropriate. In the blood bank project, exploratory research was followed by a single cross-sectional survey. The survey shed further light and quantified the findings of exploratory research. If unexpected or ambiguous findings are generated at the second phase, further exploratory or descriptive research may be undertaken, as in the blood bank project.

# SUMMARY

A research design is a framework or blueprint for conducting the marketing research project. It specifies the details of how the project should be conducted. Research designs may be broadly classified as exploratory or conclusive. The primary purpose of exploratory research is to provide insights into the problem. Conclusive research is conducted to test specific hypotheses and examine specific relationships. The findings from conclusive research are used as input into managerial decision making. Conclusive research may be either descriptive or causal.

The major objective of descriptive research is to describe market characteristics or functions. A descriptive design requires a clear specification of the who, what, when, where, why, and way of the research. Descriptive research can be fur-

ther classified into cross-sectional and longitudinal research. Cross-sectional designs involve the collection of information from a sample of population elements at a single point in time. In contrast, in longitudinal designs repeated measurements are taken on a fixed sample. Causal research is designed for the primary purpose of obtaining evidence about cause-and-effect (causal) relationships.

A research design consists of six components. Error can be associated with any of these components. The total error is composed of random sampling error and nonsampling error. Nonsampling error consists of nonresponse and response errors. Response error encompasses errors made by researchers, interviewers, and respondents. A written marketing research proposal including all the elements of the marketing research process should be prepared. In formulating a research design when conducting international marketing research, considerable effort is required to ensure the equivalence and comparability of secondary and primary data obtained from different countries.

In terms of ethical issues, the researchers must assure that the research design utilized will provide the information sought, and that the information sought is the information needed by the client. The client should have the integrity not to misrepresent the project, should describe the situation that the researcher must operate within, and should not make unreasonable demands. Every precaution should be taken to ensure the respondents' or subjects' right to safety, right to privacy, or right to choose. The Internet and computers can be usefully employed to aid the process of formulating a research design.

## KEY TERMS AND CONCEPTS

research design, *74*
exploratory research, *75*
conclusive research, *75*
descriptive research, *78*
cross-sectional design, *80*
single cross-sectional design, *80*
multiple cross-sectional design, *81*
cohort analysis, *81*
longitudinal design, *82*
panel, *82*
causal research, *85*
total error, *89*

random sampling error, *89*
nonsampling error, *90*
nonresponse error, *90*
response error, *90*
surrogate information error, *90*
measurement error, *90*
population definition error, *90*
sampling frame error, *90*
data analysis error, *91*
respondent selection error, *91*
questioning error, *91*
recording error, *91*

cheating error, *91*
inability error, *91*
unwillingness error, *91*
budgeting and scheduling, *92*
critical path method (CPM), *92*
program evaluation and review technique (PERT), *92*
graphical evaluation and review technique (GERT), *92*
marketing research proposal, *92*

## EXERCISES

### Questions

1. Define research design in your own words.
2. How does formulating a research design differ from developing an approach to a problem?
3. Differentiate between exploratory and conclusive research.
4. What are the major purposes for which descriptive research is conducted?
5. List the six Ws of descriptive research and give an example of each.
6. Compare and contrast cross-sectional and longitudinal designs.
7. Describe cohort analysis. Why is it of special interest?
8. Discuss the advantages and disadvantages of panels.
9. What is a causal research design? What is its purpose?
10. What are the relationships among exploratory, descriptive, and causal research?
11. List the major components of a research design.
12. What potential sources of error can affect a research design?
13. Why is it important to minimize total error rather than any particular source of error?

### Problems

1. Sweet Cookies is planning to launch a new line of cookies and wants to assess the market size. The cookies have a mixed chocolate-pineapple flavor and will be targeted at the premium end of the market. Discuss the six Ws of a descriptive research design that may be adopted.
2. Express each of the following types of error as an equation:
   a. Total error
   b. Random sampling error
   c. Nonresponse error
   d. Response error
3. Welcome, Inc. is a chain of fast-food restaurants located in major metropolitan areas in the South. Sales have been growing very slowly for the last two years. Management has decided to add some new items to the menu, but first they want to know more about their customers and their preferences.
   a. List two hypotheses.
   b. What kind of research design is appropriate? Why?

## INTERNET AND COMPUTER EXERCISES

1. Visit the Greenfield Online Research Center (*www.greenfield online.com*).
   a. What are the surveys being currently conducted by Greenfield?
   b. How are the respondents being recruited for these surveys?
   c. Discuss the different type of errors likely to arise, given the way the respondents are being recruited.
2. Visit the Web page of three of the marketing research firms listed in Table 1.2. What types of research designs have been implemented recently by these firms?

3. Obtain one of the CPM/PERT programs. Using this program, develop a schedule for the research project described in role play exercise 2.
4. You are conducting an image study for Carnival Cruise Lines. As part of exploratory research, analyze the messages posted to the newsgroup *rec.travel.cruises*, at *groups.google.com*, to determine the factors that consumers use in evaluating cruise companies.

# ACTIVITIES

## *Role Playing*

1. Assume the role of marketing manager of Sweet Cookies, Inc., and have your partner assume the role of a researcher hired by the firm (see problem 1). Discuss the issue and formulate the appropriate:
   a. management decision problem
   b. marketing research problem
   c. research design
2. You are a manager in charge of a marketing research project. Your goal is to determine what effects different levels of advertising have on consumption behavior. Based on the results of the project you will recommend the amount of money to be budgeted for advertising different products next year. Your supervisor will require strong justification for your recommendations, so your research design has to be as sound as possible. However, your resources (time, money, and labor) are limited. Develop a research project to address this problem. Focus on the kind of research designs you would use, why you would use them, and how you would conduct the research.

## *Fieldwork*

1. Contact a few marketing research organizations and ask them about the kind of research designs they have used during the last year, and the nature of the problems addressed. Write a report on your findings.

## *Group Discussion*

1. "If the research budget is limited, exploratory research can be dispensed with." Discuss this quote.
2. As a small group, discuss the following statement: "The researcher should always attempt to develop an optimal design for every marketing research project."
3. "There are many potential sources of error in a research project. It is impossible to control all of them. Hence, marketing research contains many errors and we cannot be confident of the findings." Discuss these statements as a small group. Did your group arrive at a consensus?

## CHAPTER 4

# Exploratory Research Design: Secondary Data

"Secondary data can be an immediate and cost effective means to gaining valuable insight into research issues; provided that the information comes from reliable and timely sources."

*Sandy Bautista, manager, corporate information center, Burke, Inc.*

## Objectives

After reading this chapter, the student should be able to:

1. Define the nature and scope of secondary data and distinguish secondary data from primary data.
2. Analyze the advantages and disadvantages of secondary data and their uses in the various steps of the marketing research process.
3. Evaluate secondary data using specifications, error, currency, objectives, nature, and dependability criteria.
4. Describe in detail the different sources of secondary data, including internal sources and external sources in the form of published materials, computerized databases, and syndicated services.
5. Discuss in detail the syndicated sources of secondary data, including household/consumer data obtained via surveys, purchase and media panels, and electronic scanner services, as well as institutional data related to retailers, wholesalers, and industrial/service firms.
6. Explain the need to use multiple sources of secondary data and describe single-source data.
7. Discuss applications of secondary data in computer mapping.
8. Identify and evaluate the sources of secondary data useful in international marketing research.
9. Understand the ethical issues involved in the use of secondary data.
10. Discuss the use of Internet and computers in researching secondary data.

# Overview

As mentioned in the previous chapters, analysis of secondary data helps define the marketing research problem and develop an approach (Chapter 2). Also, before the research design for collecting primary data is formulated (Chapter 3), the researcher should analyze the relevant secondary data. In some projects, particularly those with limited budgets, research may be largely confined to the analysis of secondary data because some routine problems may be addressed based only on secondary data.

This chapter discusses the distinction between primary and secondary data. The advantages and disadvantages of secondary data are considered, and criteria for evaluating secondary data are presented, along with a classification of secondary data. Internal secondary data are described, and major sources of external secondary data, such as published materials, online and offline databases, and syndicated services, are also discussed. We consider applications of secondary data in computer mapping. The sources of secondary data useful in international marketing research are discussed. Several ethical issues that arise in the use of secondary data are identified. Finally, we discuss the use of the Internet and computers in identifying and analyzing secondary data.[1]

We begin by citing several examples to give you a flavor of secondary data.

## REAL RESEARCH

### Boston Market: Someplace Like Home

According to secondary data, home meal replacement (HMR) will be the family dining business of the next century. HMR is portable, high-quality food that is meant for take-out, and it is the fastest growing and most significant opportunity in the food industry today. According to ACNielsen's consumer panel data (*acnielsen.com*), 55 percent of respondents purchased a meal for at-home consumption several times a month. Convenience and type of food were the two most influential factors when purchasing HMR. Also, 77 percent of the respondents preferred their meals ready to eat.

Another recent study by consultants McKinsey & Co. (*www.mckinsey.com*) projected that, between 2000 and 2005, virtually all growth in food sales will come from food service, defined as food prepared at least partially away from home. Estimates of total HMR market size, as well as future potential, vary widely. Numbers ranging from $25 billion to $100 billion have been given for the year 2005. It is the most important trend to hit the food industry since the advent of frozen food.

Most industry experts say the trend started when Boston Market (*www.boston market.com*) came to town, attracting consumers with promises of food just like mom used to make. Boston Market is now the HMR leader. As of 2003, Boston Market had more than 650 restaurants and operated in 30 states. The company is a wholly owned subsidiary of McDonald's Corporation (*www.mcdonalds.com*). The company constantly monitors HMR-related data available from secondary sources and uses them as inputs into its research and marketing programs. Currently, Boston Market is using such data to test new products that could be introduced in 2004. Tests being conducted include prepackaged "take-and-go" lunch boxes, expanded catering services, enhanced drive-thru operations, and call-ahead pick-up services.[2] ■

Secondary data indicating huge demand for home meal replacement spurred Boston Market to become the leader in this segment.

**REAL RESEARCH**

## *High Touch Goes High Tech*

According to the U.S. Department of Labor, more than 50 percent of the American workforce was over 40 years old in 2003. By 2010, women will account for 48 percent of the workforce. There will also be a decline in the number of young (age 16 to 24) workers available to fill entry-level positions. This potential shortage of young workers has caused many fast-food restaurants to switch from a "high-touch" to a "high-tech" service orientation. Many of the services formerly rendered by workers are now performed by consumers using high-tech equipment. The use of touch-screen kiosks is becoming a popular trend that provides a new avenue to cut labor costs and increase customer service. Fast-food companies that are deploying this new technology include Taco Bell, Arby's, and Pizza Hut.[3] ■

As these examples illustrate, research and consulting firms (ACNielsen, McKinsey & Co.) and government departments (U.S. Department of Labor) are only a few of the sources from which secondary data may be obtained. The nature and role of secondary data become clear when we understand the distinction between primary and secondary data.

# PRIMARY VERSUS SECONDARY DATA

**primary data**
Data originated by the researcher for the specific purpose of addressing the research problem.

**secondary data**
Data collected for some purpose other than the problem at hand.

*Primary data* are originated by a researcher for the specific purpose of addressing the problem at hand. The collection of primary data involves all six steps of the marketing research process (Chapter 1). Obtaining primary data can be expensive and time consuming. The department store patronage project cited in Chapter 1 is an example of primary data collection.

*Secondary data* are data that have already been collected for purposes other than the problem at hand. These data can be located quickly and inexpensively. In the department store project, secondary data on the criteria used by households to select department stores were obtained from marketing journals (*Journal of Retailing, Journal of Marketing, Journal of the Academy of Marketing Science,* and *Journal of Marketing Research*). Several other examples of secondary data were provided in the preceding section. The differences between primary and secondary data are summarized in Table 4.1. As compared to primary data, secondary data are collected rapidly and easily, at a relatively low cost, and in a short time.

These differences between primary and secondary data lead to some distinct advantages and uses of secondary data.

| TABLE 4.1 | | |
|---|---|---|
| **A Comparison of Primary and Secondary Data** | | |
| | PRIMARY DATA | SECONDARY DATA |
| Collection purpose | For the problem at hand | For other problems |
| Collection process | Very involved | Rapid and easy |
| Collection cost | High | Relatively low |
| Collection time | Long | Short |

# ADVANTAGES AND USES OF SECONDARY DATA

As can be seen from the foregoing discussion, secondary data offer several advantages over primary data. Secondary data are easily accessible, relatively inexpensive, and quickly obtained. Some secondary data, such as those provided by the U.S. Bureau of the Census, are available on topics where it would not be feasible for a firm to collect primary data. Although it is rare for secondary data to provide all the answers to a non-routine research problem, such data can be useful in a variety of ways.[4] Secondary data can help you:

1. Identify the problem
2. Better define the problem
3. Develop an approach to the problem
4. Formulate an appropriate research design (for example, by identifying the key variables)
5. Answer certain research questions and test some hypotheses
6. Interpret primary data more insightfully

Given these advantages and uses of secondary data, we state the following general rule:

> Examination of available secondary data is a prerequisite to the collection of primary data. Start with secondary data. Proceed to primary data only when the secondary data sources have been exhausted or yield marginal returns.

The rich dividends obtained by following this rule are illustrated by examples we have given in the introduction. These examples show that analysis of secondary data can provide valuable insights and lay the foundation for conducting primary data. However, the researcher should be cautious in using secondary data, because they have some limitations and disadvantages.

# DISADVANTAGES OF SECONDARY DATA

Because secondary data have been collected for purposes other than the problem at hand, their usefulness to the current problem may be limited in several important ways, including relevance and accuracy. The objectives, nature, and methods used to collect the secondary data may not be appropriate to the present situation. Also, secondary data may be lacking in accuracy, or they may not be completely current or dependable. Before using secondary data, it is important to evaluate them on these factors.

# CRITERIA FOR EVALUATING SECONDARY DATA

The quality of secondary data should be routinely evaluated, using the criteria of Table 4.2.

**TABLE 4.2**

### Criteria for Evaluating Secondary Data

| CRITERIA | ISSUES | REMARKS |
|---|---|---|
| Specifications/ Methodology | Data collection method<br>Response rate<br>Quality of data<br>Sampling technique<br>Sample size<br>Questionnaire design<br>Field work<br>Data analysis | Data should be reliable, valid, and generalizable to the problem at hand. |
| Error/Accuracy | Examine errors in: Approach, Research design, Sampling, Data collection, Data analysis, Reporting | Assess accuracy by comparing data from different sources. |
| Currency | Time lag between collection and publication<br>Frequency of updates | Census data are periodically updated by syndicated firms. |
| Objective | Why were the data collected? | The objective will determine the relevance of the data. |
| Nature | Definition of key variables<br>Units of measurement<br>Categories used<br>Relationships examined | Reconfigure the data to increase their usefulness, if possible. |
| Dependability | Expertise, credibility, reputation, and trustworthiness of the source | Data should be obtained from an original rather than an acquired source. |

## Specifications: Methodology Used to Collect the Data

The specifications, or the methodology used to collect the data, should be critically examined to identify possible sources of bias. Such methodological considerations include size and nature of the sample, response rate and quality, questionnaire design and administration, procedures used for field work, and data analysis and reporting procedures. These checks provide information on the reliability and validity of the data and help determine whether they can be generalized to the problem at hand. The reliability and validity can be further ascertained by an examination of the error, currency, objectives, nature, and dependability associated with secondary data.

**REAL RESEARCH**

### *Rating the Television Ratings Methodology*

WTVJ-TV, an NBC affiliate, uses the syndicated services of Nielsen Media Research (*www.nielsenmedia.com*), which provides television ratings and audience estimates. The television station feels that these data provided by Nielsen Media Research have been skewed as the methodology used was flawed. Specifically, they claim that Nielsen Media Research is putting too many meters into the homes of families that speak only Spanish, which is underestimating their ratings.

The problem is that the station is English speaking, and although 46 percent of its viewers were Hispanics in 2003, they all spoke English. By placing more Nielsen meters in homes that do not speak English, the information is not representative of the Miami community or the station's viewers. Also, because many decisions are based on the information provided by Nielsen, such as programming, advertising, and media buys, it is important that the station has accurate and reliable information about the market.

Although many support the actions of Nielsen Media Research and feel that the data do represent the community, it still raises a very important question. Can a company be confident that the information it receives is generated using appropriate methodology?[5] ■

## Error: Accuracy of the Data

The researcher must determine whether the data are accurate enough for the purposes of the present study. Secondary data can have a number of sources of error, or inaccuracy, including errors in the approach, research design, sampling, data collection, analysis, and reporting stages of the project. Moreover, it is difficult to evaluate the accuracy of secondary data, because the researcher did not participate in the research. One approach is to find multiple sources of data and compare them using standard statistical procedures.

The accuracy of secondary data can vary, particularly if they relate to phenomena that are subject to change. Moreover, data obtained from different sources may not agree. In these cases, the researcher should verify the accuracy of secondary data by conducting pilot studies or by other appropriate methods. Often, by exercising creativity, this can be done without much expense or effort.

**REAL RESEARCH**

## Detailing E-Tailing Revenues

In order to determine e-commerce sales, many research firms such as Forrester Research (*www.forrester.com*), ComScore (*www.comscore.com*), Nielsen/NetRatings (*www.net ratings.com*), and the U.S. Commerce Department (*www.commerce.gov*) conduct studies to determine such results. All four organizations have distinct methodologies of collecting and analyzing data to report results. The Forrester Research firm polls 5,000 online consumers every month during the first nine working days of each month. Responses from those polled consumers are adjusted to represent the U.S. population. Differing from Forrester Research, Nielsen/NetRatings' EcommercePulse polls a larger sample of 36,000 Internet users monthly and tracks how much money those consumers spend online. Differing once again is the U.S. Commerce Department, which randomly chooses 11,000 merchants to fill out survey forms about online sales. Finally, ComScore uses a passive response system that collects data from 1.5 million Internet users that allow ComScore to track their Internet traffic through the company's servers.

For the third quarter in 2001, Forrester Research reported $12 billion in online sales, Nielsen/NetRatings reported $14.5 billion, the Commerce Department reported $7.47 billion, and ComScore reported $7.24 billion. Unlike Forrester and NetRatings, the Commerce Department and ComScore exclude sales of travel services, event tickets, and auctions. According to ComScore, the total 2001 e-tail sales were $53 billion. Excluding travel services, event tickets, and auctions, the figures for 2001 were $33.7 billion. Such huge differences in online sales create problems for e-commerce companies, and even Federal Reserve Chairman, Alan Greenspan, has addressed this issue as a major problem. Comparing e-tail sales figures available from different sources can give marketing researchers an idea of the degree of error that may be present in the data.[6] ■

## Currency: When the Data Were Collected

Secondary data may not be current, and the time lag between data collection and publication may be long, as is the case with much census data. Moreover, the data may not be updated frequently enough for the purpose of the problem at hand. Marketing research requires current data; therefore the value of secondary data is diminished as they become dated. For instance, while the 2000 Census of Population data are comprehensive, they may not be applicable to a metropolitan area whose population has changed rapidly during the last two years. Fortunately, several marketing research firms update census data periodically and make the current information available on a syndicated basis.

## Objective: The Purpose for Which the Data Were Collected

Data are invariably collected with some objective in mind, and a fundamental question to ask is why the data were collected in the first place. The objective for collecting data will ultimately determine the purpose for which that information is relevant and useful. Data collected with a specific objective in mind may not be appropriate in another situation. As explained in more detail later in the chapter, scanner ***volume tracking data*** are collected with the objective of examining aggregate movement of brands, including shifts in market

***volume tracking data***
Scanner data that provide information on purchases by brand, size, price, and flavor or formulation.

shares. Such data on sales of orange juice, for example, would be of limited value in a study aimed at understanding how households select specific brands.

## Nature: The Content of the Data

The nature, or content, of the data should be examined with special attention to the definition of key variables, the units of measurement, categories used, and the relationships examined. If the key variables have not been defined or are defined in a manner inconsistent with the researcher's definition, then the usefulness of the data is limited. Consider, for example, secondary data on consumer preferences for TV programs. To use this information, it is important to know how preference for programs was defined. Was it defined in terms of the program watched most often, the one considered most needed, most enjoyable, most informative, or the program of greatest service to the community?

Likewise, secondary data may be measured in units that may not be appropriate for the current problem. For example, income may be measured by individual, family, household, or spending unit, and could be gross or net after taxes and deductions. Income may be classified into categories that are different from research needs. If the researcher is interested in high-income consumers with gross annual household incomes of over $90,000, secondary data with income categories of less than $15,000, $15,001–$35,000, $35,001–$50,000, and more than $50,000 will not be of much use. Determining the measurement of variables such as income may be a complex task. Finally, the relationships examined should be taken into account in evaluating the nature of data. If, for example, actual behavior is of interest, then data inferring behavior from self-reported attitudinal information may have limited usefulness. Sometimes it is possible to reconfigure the available data, for example, convert the units of measurement, so that the resulting data are more useful to the problem at hand.

## Dependability: How Dependable Are the Data?

An overall indication of the dependability of data may be obtained by examining the expertise, credibility, reputation, and trustworthiness of the source. This information can be obtained by checking with others who have used the information provided by the source. Data published to promote sales, to advance specific interests, or to carry on propaganda should be viewed with suspicion. The same may be said of data published anonymously or in a form that attempts to hide the details of the data collection methodology and process. It is also pertinent to examine whether the secondary data came from an original source, one that generated the data, or an acquired source, one that procured the data from an original source. For example, the Census of Population is an original source, whereas Statistical Abstracts of the United States is an acquired source. As a general rule, secondary data should be secured from an original rather than an acquired source. There are at least two reasons for this rule. First, an original source is the one that specifies the details of the data collection methodology. Second, an original source is likely to be more accurate and complete than a secondary source.

### REAL RESEARCH

### *Flying High on Secondary Data*

*Money* magazine published the results of a study conducted to uncover the airline characteristics consumers consider most important. In order of importance, these characteristics are safety, price, baggage handling, on-time performance, customer service, ease of reservations and ticketing, comfort, frequent flyer programs, and food. *Money* magazine then ranked the 10 largest U.S. airlines according to these characteristics.

This article would be a useful source of secondary data for American Airlines in conducting a market research study to identify characteristics of its service that should be improved. However, before using the data, American should evaluate them according to several criteria.

First, the methodology used to collect the data for this article should be examined. This *Money* magazine article includes a section that details the methodology used in the study. *Money* used a poll of 1,017 frequent fliers to determine important airline characteristics. The results of the survey had a 3 percent margin of error. American would need to decide whether a sample size of 1,017 was generalizable to the population and whether an error of 3 percent is acceptable. In addition, American should evaluate what type of response or nonresponse errors may have occurred in the data collection or analysis process.

The currency of the data and objective of the study would be important to American Airlines in deciding whether to utilize this article as a source of secondary data. This study was conducted before the airline hijackings of September 11, 2001. Perhaps, airline passengers' criteria have changed since these tragic events, which would diminish the usefulness of this study. The objective of the study was to rate airlines along choice criteria for a popular business magazine. The results are not likely to be biased towards any particular airline, as the magazine does not have a vested interest in any of the airline companies.

American would also need to look at the nature and dependability of the data. For instance, it would need to look at how the nine choice criteria are defined. For example, price is measured in terms of fare per mile. This may not be useful to American if it did not want to quantify price in that manner. In regards to dependability, American would need to research the reputation of *Money* magazine and of ICR, the company *Money* hired to administer the survey. American also needs to consider the fact that *Money* used some secondary research in its study. For instance, it used reports from the National Transportation Safety Board data on airline accidents and incident reports from the Federal Aviation Administration to rank the safety performance of the 10 airlines. It is always better to get information from the original source. Thus, American might want to acquire these reports themselves and do its own safety ranking. This would be more reliable than getting this information from the *Money* magazine report.

Though sales were almost $19 billion in 2001, American suffered a loss of income of $1.76 billion. Most of the loss was due to the residual effects of September 11th and the many security issues that airlines have to face. American Airlines decided to start adding back routes to its schedule in January 2002. The *Money* magazine article might be useful as a starting place for the marketing research project by American Airlines. For instance, it might be useful in formulating the problem definition. However, because of the article's limitation in regards to currency, nature, and dependability, this source should be supplemented by other sources of secondary research, as well as primary research.[7] ■

# CLASSIFICATION OF SECONDARY DATA

**internal data**
Internal data are data available within the organization for which the research is being conducted.

Figure 4.1 presents a classification of secondary data. Secondary data may be classified as either internal or external. ***Internal data*** are those generated within the organization for which the research is being conducted. This information may be available in a ready-to-use

*Figure 4.1*
A Classification of Secondary Data

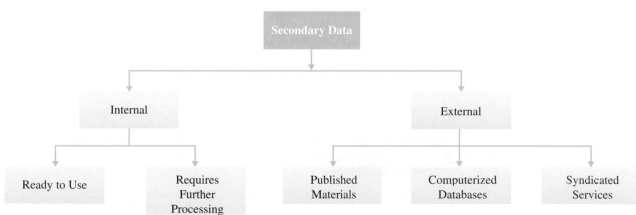

format, such as information routinely supplied by the management decision support system. On the other hand, these data may exist within the organization but may require considerable processing before they are useful to the researcher. For example, a variety of information can be found on sales invoices. Yet this information may not be easily accessible; further processing may be required to extract it. ***External data,*** on the other hand, are those generated by sources outside the organization. These data may exist in the form of published material, online databases, or information made available by syndicated services. Before collecting external secondary data, it is useful to analyze internal secondary data.

**external data**
Data that originate external to the organization.

# INTERNAL SECONDARY DATA

Internal sources should be the starting point in the search for secondary data. Because most organizations have a wealth of in-house information, some data may be readily available and provide useful insights. For example, sales and cost data are compiled in the regular accounting process. When internal data on sales showed Reebok (*www.reebok.com*) that Internet sales were a mere 0.7 percent of their total sales but were rousing bad feelings among retailers, the company discontinued online selling. It is also possible to process routinely collected sales data to generate a variety of useful information, as illustrated by the department store example.

Secondary internal data have two significant advantages. They are easily available and inexpensive. In fact, internal secondary sources are generally the least costly of any source of marketing research information; yet these data often are not fully exploited. However, this trend is changing with the increased popularity of database marketing.

## Database Marketing

**database marketing**
Database marketing involves the use of computers to capture and track customer profiles and purchase details.

***Database marketing*** involves the use of computers to capture and track customer profiles and purchase details. This secondary information serves as the foundation for marketing programs or as an internal source of information related to customer behavior. For many companies, the first step in creating a database is to transfer raw sales information, such as that found on sales call reports or on invoices, to a microcomputer. This consumer purchase information is then enhanced by overlaying it with demographic and psychographic information for the same customers, available from syndicated firms such as Donnelley Marketing (www.donnelleymarketing.com), Experian (www.experian.com), and R. L. Polk (www.rlpolk.com). This information can then be analyzed in terms of a customer's activity over the life of the business relationship. A profile of heavy versus light users, signs of change in the usage relationships, or significant "customer life cycle" events such as anniversaries can be identified and acted upon. These databases provide the essential tools needed to nurture, expand, and protect the customer relationship.[8]

---

**ACTIVE RESEARCH** | DEPARTMENT STORE PROJECT

***Internal Secondary Data***

Extensive analysis was conducted on internal secondary data in the department store project. This provided several rich insights. For example, sales were analyzed to obtain:

- Sales by product line
- Sales by major department (e.g., men's wear, housewares)
- Sales by specific stores
- Sales by geographical region
- Sales by cash versus credit purchases
- Sales in specific time periods
- Sales by size of purchase

Sales trends in many of these classifications were also examined.

CRM (Customer Relationship Management) is a unique type of database-driven marketing. As part of its CRM system, DaimlerChrysler (*www.daimlerchrysler.com*) implemented what they call Personal Information Centers. These PICs, as they are called, offer car owners an individualized Web site that creates direct links with the marketing research team. These PICs collect data on all aspects of buying a car, giving the company the ability to engage in customized marketing. If a prospect, on his completed online survey, indicated handling of minivans to be a concern, separate data could be included on a brochure sent only to that prospect. These data would show how the DaimlerChrysler minivan stood up against the competition in the minivan market. DaimlerChrysler believes that the customer relationship begins when a prospect first contacts the company and does not stop when a buyer purchases a vehicle. With this in mind, the company uses its CRM system to constantly track buyers' and prospects' opinions and desires. Its CRM has enabled the company to maintain its leadership in the automobile market. DaimlerChrysler is the number three carmaker in the world with sales of over $152 billion in 2001.[9]

Database marketing can lead to quite sophisticated and targeted marketing programs, as illustrated in the following example.

### REAL RESEARCH

## *The Colonel's Secret Weapon: A Massive Database*

As of 2003, there are over 11,000 KFC (*www.kfc.com*) outlets in more than 80 countries around the world that serve nearly eight million customers each day.

To better understand customer profiles and trends, KFC hired IBM (*www.ibm.com*) to develop "Metacube Software," which collects data from each of its 11,000 restaurants and compiles them in user-friendly spreadsheet format. According to Micki Thomas, KFC's director of information systems, "There's a day-and-a-half lag between when someone buys an order and when a record of that transaction is available in our data warehouse." These detail data provide market researchers a valuable tool in analyzing market research problems. This information can be used to help guide corporate marketing decisions and provide insight to individual stores that may not have the technology or expertise to complete their own market research. By using the data warehouse, customer profiles are developed, analyzing what and when purchases are made, including the percentage of customers eating in, going through the drive-through, and using home delivery.

By understanding consumer behavior, KFC could greatly improve the profitability and customer satisfaction within its individual franchisees. For example, the database is used to forecast sales by hour, day of the week, and by time of year based on stored historical data within the warehouse and economic trends in the geographic area. These forecasts are used to maximize the efficiency of employee scheduling and minimize food inventory. Thus, by using database marketing techniques, KFC helps franchisees anticipate customer needs, improve service and customer satisfaction, and maximize efficiency and profitability.[10] ■

### REAL RESEARCH

## *Type of Individual/Household Level Data Available from Syndicated Firms*

### I. Demographic Data

- Identification (name, address, telephone)
- Sex
- Marital status
- Names of family members
- Age (including ages of family members)
- Income
- Occupation
- Number of children present

- Home ownership
- Length of residence
- Number and make of cars owned

**II. Psychographic Lifestyle Data**

- Interest in golf
- Interest in snow skiing
- Interest in book reading
- Interest in running
- Interest in bicycling
- Interest in pets
- Interest in fishing
- Interest in electronics
- Interest in cable television

There are also firms such as Dun & Bradstreet (*www.dnb.com*) and American Business Information, a division of InfoUSA (*www.infousa.com*), that collect demographic data on businesses. ■

# PUBLISHED EXTERNAL SECONDARY SOURCES

Sources of published external secondary data include federal, state, and local governments, nonprofit organizations (e.g., chambers of commerce), trade associations and professional organizations, commercial publishers, investment brokerage firms, and professional marketing research firms. In fact, so much data are available that the researcher can be overwhelmed. Therefore, it is important to classify published sources. (See Figure 4.2.) Published external sources may be broadly classified as general business data or government data. General business sources are comprised of guides, directories, indexes, and statistical data. Government sources may be broadly categorized as census data and other publications.

## General Business Data

Businesses publish a lot of information in the form of books, periodicals, journals, newspapers, magazines, reports, and trade literature. This information can be located by using guides, directories, and indexes. Sources are also available for identifying statistical data.

*Guides.*    Guides are an excellent source of standard or recurring information. A guide may help identify other important sources such as directories, trade associations, and trade publications. Guides are one of the first sources a researcher should consult. Some of the most useful are the *American Marketing Association Bibliography Series, Business Information Sources, Data Sources for Business and Market Analysis,* and *Encyclopedia of Business Information Sources.*

*Figure 4.2*
A Classification of Published
Secondary Sources

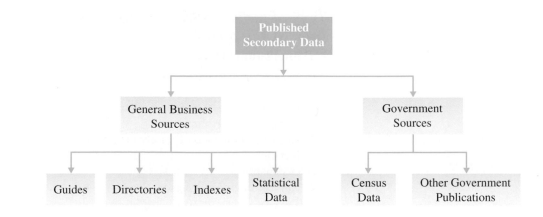

DEPARTMENT STORE PROJECT

**Data Search**

In addition to reviewing the theoretical literature, as discussed in Chapter 2, it was also necessary to identify the nonacademic sources of secondary data related to the factors considered in selecting department stores and other aspects of store patronage. The *Business Periodical Index,* the *Wall Street Journal Index,* and the *New York Times Index* were used to generate a list of relevant articles that had appeared in the last five years. The *Business Periodical Index* classifies articles by specific industries and firms, making it easy to locate articles of interest. Several articles obtained in this manner proved useful. One pointed to the tendency of people to combine shopping with eating out. Therefore, as discussed in Chapter 2, a specific research question was framed to investigate this behavior.

**Directories.**   Directories are helpful for identifying individuals or organizations that collect specific data. Some of the important directories include *Directories in Print, Consultants and Consulting Organizations Directory, Encyclopedia of Associations, FINDEX: The Directory of Market Research Reports, Studies and Surveys,* and *Research Services Directory.*

**Indexes.**   It is possible to locate information on a particular topic in several different publications by using an index. Indexes can, therefore, increase the efficiency of the search process. Several were used in the department store project.

As illustrated by this example, indexes greatly facilitate a directed search of the relevant literature. Several indexes are available for both academic and business sources. Some of the more useful business indexes are *Business Periodical Index, Business Index, Predicasts F & S Index: United States, Social Sciences Citation Index,* and the *Wall Street Journal Index.*

**Nongovernmental Statistical Data.**   Published statistical data are of great interest to researchers. Graphic and statistical analyses can be performed on these data to draw important insights. Important sources of nongovernmental statistical data include *A Guide to Consumer Markets, Predicasts Forecasts, Sales and Marketing Management Survey of Buying Power, Standard and Poor's Statistical Service,* and *Standard Rate and Data Service.*

## Government Sources

The U.S. government also produces large amounts of secondary data. Its publications may be divided into census data and other publications.[11]

**Census Data.**   The U.S. Bureau of the Census is the world's largest source of statistical data. Its monthly catalog lists and describes its various publications.[12] More convenient, however, is the *Guide to Economic Census.* The quality of census data is high and the data are often extremely detailed. Furthermore, one can purchase computer tapes or diskettes from the Bureau of the Census for a nominal fee and recast this information in a desired format.[13] Many private sources update census data at a detailed geographic level for the between-census years.[14] Important census data include Census of Housing, Census of Manufacturers, Census of Population, Census of Retail Trade, Census of Service Industries, and Census of Wholesale Trade.

**REAL RESEARCH**

## *The Changing Color of the American Marketplace*

According to Census 2000, there are 105.5 million households within the United States that included 281.4 million people. Census 2000 revealed a great deal on the makeup of our population including that 3.6 percent are Asian, 12.3 percent are African American, and 12.5 percent are Hispanic. This means that there are over 10.2 million Asians, over 34.7 million African Americans, and over 35.3 million Hispanics living within the United States. From 1990 to 2000, the minority races grew at a much faster pace than the rest of the population.

Such a dramatic difference in growth seriously changes the retailing landscape. Marketing companies must embrace these trends and determine how to best configure their marketing mix to meet the needs of these varying cultures. Their inclusion in the research process and marketing plans will be crucial to the long-term success of many organizations.

Mazda North America, though it had been making efforts to sell with diversity in mind, decided to put more money and effort into targeting Hispanics, Asians, and African Americans in the years 2002 to 2005. Univision, a Hispanic television network, is using the census results to pitch to CEOs to put more money into ethnic entertainment. Maintaining a close eye on the U.S. census data and understanding that the Asian American, African American, and Hispanic markets are not only different markets but also different cultures, each with vastly different histories, will help fuel America's growth for the next decade.[15] ■

***Other Government Publications.***   In addition to the census, the federal government collects and publishes a great deal of statistical data. The more useful publications are *Business America, Business Conditions Digest, Business Statistics, Index to Publications, Statistical Abstract of the United States,* and *Survey of Current Business.* The second example in the overview section showed how statistics from the U.S. Department of Labor helped fast-food restaurants switch from a high-touch to a high-tech orientation.

Most published information is also available in the form of computerized databases.

# COMPUTERIZED DATABASES

Computerized databases consist of information that has been made available in computer-readable form for electronic distribution. In the 2000s, the number of databases, as well as the vendors providing these services, has grown phenomenally.[16] Thus, a classification of computerized databases is helpful.

## Classification of Computerized Databases

**online databases**
Databases, stored in computers, which require a telecommunications network to access.

**Internet databases**
Internet databases can be accessed, searched, and analyzed on the Internet. It is also possible to download data from the Internet and store them in the computer or an auxiliary storage device.

**offline databases**
Databases that are available on diskette or CD-ROM.

Computerized databases may be classified as online, Internet, or offline, as shown in Figure 4.3. ***Online databases*** consist of a central data bank, which is accessed with a computer (or dumb terminal) via a telecommunications network. ***Internet databases*** can be accessed, searched, and analyzed on the Internet. It is also possible to download data from the Internet and store them in the computer or an auxiliary storage device.[17] ***Offline databases*** make the information available on diskettes and CD-ROM disks. Thus, offline databases can be accessed at the user's location without the use of an external telecommunications network. For example, the U.S. Bureau of the Census makes computer data files available on CD-ROM disks. These disks contain detailed information organized by census track or zip code. In the department store patronage project, this type of information was used in sample selection.[18] As indicated in the following example, several vendors are providing data in various forms.

**Figure 4.3**
A Classification of Computerized Databases

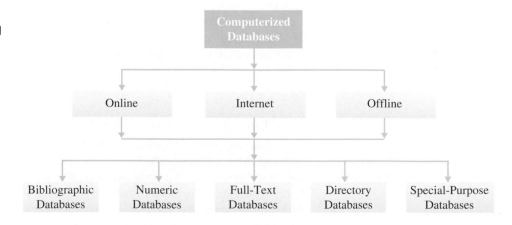

**REAL RESEARCH**

## InfoUSA: Here, There, and Everywhere

InfoUSA (*www.infousa.com*) is a leading provider of sales and marketing support data. The company also operates under various trade names such as Donnelley Marketing, American Business Information, Walter Karl, idEXEC, and infoCanada. Net sales in 2001 were $289 million. The company markets subsets of its data in a number of forms, including the professional online services (LEXISNEXIS and DIALOG), the general online services (CompuServe and Microsoft Network), the Internet (LookupUSA), and on CD-ROM. The underlying database on which all these products are based contains information on 113 million residential listings and 14 million business listings, as of 2003. These are verified with over 16 million phone calls annually. The products derived from these databases include sales leads, mailing lists, business directories, mapping products, and also delivery of data over the Internet.[19] ■

**bibliographic databases**
Databases composed of citations to articles in journals, magazines, newspapers, marketing research studies, technical reports, government documents, and the like. They often provide summaries or abstracts of the material cited.

**numeric databases**
Numeric databases contain numerical and statistical information that may be important sources of secondary data.

**full-text databases**
Databases containing the complete text of secondary source documents comprising the database.

**directory databases**
Directory databases provide information on individuals, organizations, and services.

**special-purpose databases**
Databases that contain information of a specific nature, e.g., data on a specialized industry.

Online, Internet, and offline databases may be further classified as bibliographic, numeric, full-text, directory, or special-purpose databases. ***Bibliographic databases*** are composed of citations to articles in journals, magazines, newspapers, marketing research studies, technical reports, government documents, and the like.[20] They often provide summaries or abstracts of the material cited. An example of bibliographic databases is ABI/Inform by ProQuest Information & Learning (*www.proquest.com*).

***Numeric databases*** contain numerical and statistical information. For example, some numeric databases provide time series data (data arranged in relation to time) about the economy and specific industries produced by vendors such as Boeing Computer Services Co. (*www.boeing.com*), and the Department of Commerce (*www.commerce.gov*). Census-based numeric databases that use the 2000 census of population and housing with proprietary updating to provide data at the census tract and zip code level are also available. Vendors providing these databases include the U.S. Bureau of the Census (*www.census.gov*), Donnelley Marketing Information Services (*www.donnelleymarketing.com*), and CACI, Inc. (*www.caci.com*).

***Full-text databases*** contain the complete text of the source documents comprising the database. The LexisNexis (*www.lexisnexis.com*) service provides full-text access to hundreds of business databases, including selected newspapers, periodicals, company annual reports, and investment firm reports.

***Directory databases*** provide information on individuals, organizations, and services. As an example, the national electronic Yellow Pages (*www.yellowpages.com*) directories of manufacturers, wholesalers, retailers, professionals, and service organizations provide the names, addresses, and North American Industrial Classification codes of numerous organizations.

Finally, there are ***special-purpose databases.*** For example, the Profit Impact of Market Strategies (PIMS) database is an ongoing database of research and analysis on business strategy conducted by the Strategic Planning Institute in Cambridge, Massachusetts. This database comprises more than 250 companies that provide data on over 2,000 businesses.[21] Virtually all libraries of major universities maintain computerized databases of management and related literature that students can access free of charge.

Because computerized databases are numerous and varied, their sheer number can be overwhelming, and locating a particular database may seem difficult. How, then, do you locate specific bibliographic, numeric, full-text, directory, or special-purpose databases? Directories of databases provide the needed help.

## Directories of Databases

There are numerous sources of information on databases. Perhaps the best way to obtain information about databases is to consult a directory. *Gale Directory of Databases* by Gale Research, Inc. (*www.gale.com*) is published every six months. Volume I covers online databases and Volume II covers CD-ROMs and other offline databases. Some of the other useful directories that are periodically updated are:

*Directory of On-line Databases.* Santa Monica, CA: Cuadra Associates, Inc.
(*www.cuadra.com*)
*Encyclopedia of Information System and Services.* Detroit: Gale Research Company
(*www.gale.com*)

# SYNDICATED SOURCES OF SECONDARY DATA

*syndicated sources (services)*
Information services offered by
marketing research organizations
that provide information from a
common database to different firms
that subscribe to their services.

In addition to published data or data available in the form of computerized databases,
syndicated sources constitute the other major source of external secondary data.
***Syndicated sources,*** also referred to as syndicated services, are companies that collect
and sell common pools of data of known commercial value, designed to serve information needs shared by a number of clients (see Chapter 1). These data are not collected for
the purpose of marketing research problems specific to individual clients, but the data and
reports supplied to client companies can be personalized to fit particular needs. For example, reports could be organized on the basis of the clients' sales territories or product lines.
Using syndicated sources is frequently less expensive than collecting primary data.
Figure 4.4 presents a classification of syndicated sources. Syndicated sources can be
classified based on the unit of measurement (households/consumers or institutions).
Household/consumer data may be obtained from surveys, purchase and media panels, or
electronic scanner services. Information obtained through surveys consists of values and
lifestyles, advertising evaluation, or general information related to preference, purchase,
consumption, and other aspects of behavior. Panels emphasize information on purchases
or media consumption. Electronic scanner services might provide scanner data only,
scanner data linked to panels, or scanner data linked to panels and (cable) TV. When institutions are the unit of measurement, the data may be obtained from retailers, wholesalers,
or industrial firms. An overview of the various syndicated sources is given in Table 4.3.
Each of these sources will be discussed.

Figure 4.4
A Classification of Syndicated
Services

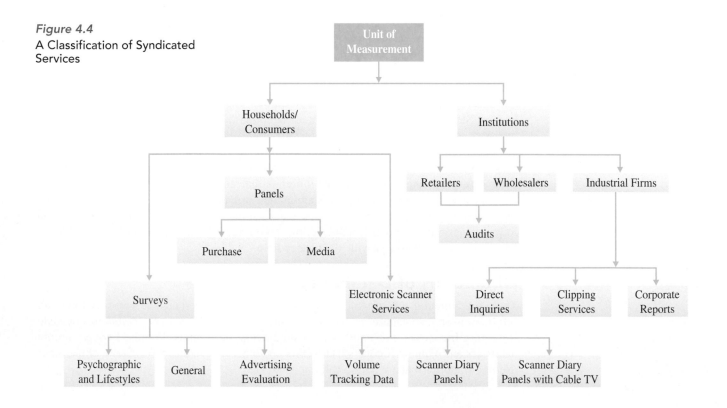

## TABLE 4.3

**Overview of Syndicated Services**

| Type | Characteristics | Advantages | Disadvantages | Uses |
|---|---|---|---|---|
| Surveys | Surveys conducted at regular intervals | Most flexible way of obtaining data; information on underlying motives | Interviewer errors; respondent errors | Market segmentation, advertising theme selection, and advertising effectiveness |
| Purchase Panels | Households provide specific information regularly over an extended period of time; respondents asked to record specific behaviors as they occur | Recorded purchase behavior can be linked to the demographic/ psychographic characteristics | Lack of representativeness; response bias; maturation | Forecasting sales, market share, and trends; establishing consumer profiles, brand loyalty, and switching; evaluating test markets, advertising, and distribution |
| Media Panels | Electronic devices automatically recording behavior, supplemented by a diary | Same as purchase panel | Same as purchase panel | Establishing advertising rates; selecting media program or air time; establishing viewer profiles |
| Scanner Volume Tracking Data | Household purchases recorded through electronic scanners in supermarkets | Data reflect actual purchases; timely data; less expensive | Data may not be representative; errors in recording purchases; difficult to link purchases to elements of marketing mix other than price | Price tracking, modeling, effectiveness of in-store modeling |
| Scanner Diary Panels with Cable TV | Scanner panels of households that subscribe to cable TV | Data reflect actual purchases; sample control; ability to link panel data to household characteristics | Data may not be representative; quality of data limited | Promotional mix analyses, copy testing, new-product testing, positioning |
| Audit Services | Verification of product movement by examining physical records or performing inventory analysis | Relatively precise information at the retail and wholesale levels | Coverage may be incomplete; matching of data on competitive activity may be difficult | Measurement of consumer sales and market share, competitive activity, analyzing distribution patterns: tracking of new products |
| Industrial Product Syndicated Services | Data banks on industrial establishments created through direct inquiries of companies, clipping services, and corporate reports | Important source of information in industrial firms, particularly useful in initial phases of the projects | Data is lacking in terms of content, quantity, and quality | Determining market potential by geographic area, defining sales territories, allocating advertising budget |

# SYNDICATED DATA FROM HOUSEHOLDS

## Surveys

**surveys**
Interviews with a large number of respondents using a predesigned questionnaire.

Various services regularly conduct **surveys,** which involve interviews with a large number of respondents using a predesigned questionnaire. Surveys may be broadly classified on the basis of their content as psychographics and lifestyles, advertising evaluation, or general surveys.

**psychographics**
Quantified psychological profiles of individuals.

***Psychographics and Lifestyles.*** *Psychographics* refer to the psychological profiles of individuals and to psychologically based measures of lifestyle. *Lifestyles* refer to the distinctive modes of living of a society or some of its segments. Together, these measures are generally referred to as Activities, Interest, and Opinions, or simply AIOs. The following example provides an application.

**REAL RESEARCH**

## Campbell Makes Sure AIOs Are in Its Alphabet Soup

Yankelovich Research and Consulting Services (*www.yankelovich.com*) provides the Yankelovich Monitor, a survey that contains data on lifestyles and social trends. The survey is conducted at the same time each year among a nationally projectable sample of 2,500 adults, 16 years of age or older, including a special sample of 300 college students living on campus. The sample is based on the most recent census data. Interviews are conducted in person at the respondent's home and take approximately 1.5 hours to complete. In addition, a questionnaire that takes about one hour to complete is left behind for the respondents to answer and mail back. Advertising agencies use the Yankelovich Monitor to discern changes in lifestyles and design advertising themes that reflect these trends. When the Monitor showed an adult craving for foods that cater to a healthy appetite, Campbell (*www.campbellsoup.com*) introduced their Chunky Soup in the winter of 2000 by using the NFL as a sponsor and stars Kurt Warner and Donovan McNabb in many of their commercials. These commercials showed that even soup can be hearty enough for the "big boys," in hopes of reaching a target market of adults who want a soup that can fill them up. The 2002 Winter Olympics featured advertisements that showed Olympic athletes trying to keep themselves warm and satisfied by eating Campbell's soup.[22] ■

SRI consulting, partner of SRI International and formerly Stanford Research Institute (*www.sric-bi.com*), conducts an annual survey of consumers that is used to classify persons into VALS-2 (Values and Lifestyles) types for segmentation purposes.[23] Information on specific aspects of consumers' lifestyles is also available. RoperASW (*www.roperasw.com*) conducts Green Gauge™, an annual survey of consumers' attitudes and behaviors related to environmental issues, with segmentation of consumer environmental behavior.

***Advertising Evaluation.***   The purpose of advertising evaluation surveys is to assess the effectiveness of advertising using print and broadcast media. A well-known survey is the Starch Readership Survey conducted by RoperASW (*www.roperasw.com*). Starch conducts over 50,000 interviews a year with magazine and newspaper readers. Interviews are conducted in person, using a through-the-book recognition technique, the closest approximation to "real-life" reading. Starch Ad Readership Reports measure ad readership within specific publications and each year measure over 25,000 ads in over 500 magazine issues. On the most basic level, the client will get raw readership scores—the percent of readers who saw the ad and read the copy. Then the data are put into a context: the ad is ranked not only against other ads in the issue, but also against other ads in its product category over the past two years. Starch Advertising Research also provides online impression studies that are customized to measure the effects of advertising. The Online Impress Study is conducted among a minimum of 100 people, randomly selected from AOL members in the client's target market. Such results are particularly important to heavy advertisers, such as Procter & Gamble, General Motors, Sears, PepsiCo, Eastman Kodak, and McDonald's, who are greatly concerned about how well their advertising dollars are spent.[24]

Evaluation of effectiveness is even more critical in the case of TV advertising. Television commercials are evaluated using either the recruited audience method or the in-home viewing method. In the former method, respondents are recruited and brought to a central viewing facility, such as a theater or mobile viewing laboratory. The respondents view the commercials and provide data regarding knowledge, attitudes, and preferences related to the product being advertised and the commercial itself. In the in-home viewing method, consumers evaluate commercials at home in their normal viewing environment. New commercials can be pretested at the network level or in local markets distributed via VCR cassettes. A survey of viewers is then conducted to assess the effectiveness of the commercials. Gallup & Robinson, Inc. (*www.gallup-robinson.com*) offers testing of television commercials using both these methods. These methods are also used for testing the effectiveness of advertising in other media such as magazines, radio, newspapers, and direct mail.

*General Surveys.*  Surveys are also conducted for a variety of other purposes, including examination of purchase and consumption behavior. For example, Harris Interactive (*www.harrisinteractive.com*) ShopperInsight is an Internet-based survey of 26,000 primary household shoppers nationwide asking for their reasons why they have chosen a particular supermarket, drugstore, or mass merchandiser. Shoppers are asked to rate their shopping experience based on 30 key factors that influence their choice of retailer, from checkout lines to store cleanliness, hours, and location. In addition, attributes such as product pricing and selection are evaluated across 45 individual product categories for every supermarket, drugstore, and mass merchandiser. These findings can help merchandisers such as Wal-Mart gauge their strengths and weaknesses. For example, the findings from a 2002 survey reinforced Wal-Mart's strategy of providing everyday low prices versus having frequent promotions on special items. The results showed that Wal-Mart's prices were perceived 3.8 percent lower than Target, its closest competitor.

*Uses of Surveys.*  Because a wide variety of data can be obtained, survey data have numerous uses. They can be used for market segmentation, as with psychographics and lifestyles data, and for establishing consumer profiles. Surveys are also useful for determining product image, measurement and positioning, and conducting price perception analysis. Other notable uses include advertising theme selection and evaluation of advertising effectiveness.

*Advantages and Disadvantages of Surveys.*  Surveys are the most flexible means of obtaining data from respondents. The researcher can focus on only a certain segment of the population—for example, teenagers, owners of vacation homes, or housewives between the age of 30 and 40. Surveys are the primary means of obtaining information about consumers' motives, attitudes, and preferences. A variety of questions can be asked, and visual aids, packages, products, or other props can be used during the interviews. Properly analyzed, survey data can be manipulated in many ways so that the researcher can look at intergroup differences, examine the effects of independent variables such as age or income, or even predict future behavior.

On the other hand, survey data may be limited in several significant ways. The researcher has to rely primarily on the respondents' self-reports. There is a gap between what people say and what they actually do. Errors may occur because respondents remember incorrectly or give socially desirable responses. Furthermore, samples may be biased, questions poorly phrased, interviewers not properly instructed or supervised, and results misinterpreted.

## Purchase and Media Panels

Often, survey data can be complemented with data obtained from purchase and media panels. Panels were discussed in Chapter 3 in the context of longitudinal research designs. Panels are samples of respondents who provide specified information at regular intervals over an extended period of time. These respondents may be organizations, households, or individuals, although household panels are most common. Panels are also maintained for conducting surveys; the distinguishing feature of purchase and media panels is that the respondents record specific behaviors as they occur. Previously, behavior was recorded in a diary, and the diary returned to the research organization every one to four weeks. Paper diaries have been gradually replaced by electronic diaries. Now, most of the panels are online and the behavior is recorded electronically, either entered online by the respondents or recorded automatically by electronic devices. Panel members are compensated for their participation with gifts, coupons, information, or cash. The content of information recorded is different for purchase panels or media panels.

**purchase panels**
A data gathering technique in which respondents record their purchases online or in a diary.

*Purchase Panels.*  In *purchase panels,* respondents record their purchases of a variety of different products, as in the NPD Panel.

A study using the NPD online panel indicated that women actually like shopping for swimwear.

### REAL RESEARCH

## *Information in These Diaries (Panels) Is No Secret*

The NPD Group (*www.npd.com*) is a leading provider of essential market information collected and delivered online for a wide range of industries and markets and operates in more than 20 countries as of 2003. NPD combines information obtained via surveys with that recorded by respondents about their behaviors to generate reports on consumption behaviors, industry sales, market share, and key demographic trends. NPD consumer information is collected from their Online Panel about a wide range of product categories including fashion, food, fun, house and home, tech, and auto. Respondents provide detailed information regarding the brand and amount purchased, price paid, whether any special deals were involved, the store where purchased, and intended use. The composition of the panel is representative of the U.S. population as a whole. For example, a study conducted by NPD in late 2001 revealed that women actually like shopping for swimwear. According to the survey, women rated their overall shopping experience for swimwear as excellent or very good, with 69 percent of satisfied shoppers being in the age range of 35 to 44. The results also showed that the biggest purchasing influences for a retail buyer are point-of-purchase display and the hang-tag description on the suit whereas for a catalog buyer the catalog layout is important. These findings have obvious implications for the marketing of swimwear.[25] ∎

Other organizations that maintain purchase panels include the NFO World Group (*www.nfow.com*). This group maintains a number of panels, including a large interactive panel. NFO special panels, such as Baby Panel, provide access to highly targeted groups of consumers. Each quarter, approximately 2,000 new mothers and 2,000 expectant mothers join the NFO Baby Panel.

**media panels**

A data gathering technique that is comprised of samples of respondents whose television viewing behavior is automatically recorded by electronic devices, supplementing the purchase information recorded online or in a diary.

***Media Panels.***    In ***media panels,*** electronic devices automatically record viewing behavior, thus supplementing a diary or an online panel. Perhaps the most familiar media panel is Nielsen Television Index by Nielsen Media Research (*www.nielsenmedia.com*), which provides television ratings and audience estimates. The heart of the Nielsen Media Research national ratings service is an electronic measurement system called the Nielsen People Meter. These meters are placed in a sample of 5,000 households (13,000 persons) in the United States, randomly selected and recruited by Nielsen Media so as to be representative of the population. The People Meter is placed on each TV in the sample household. The meter measures two things—what program or channel is being tuned and who is watching. Household tuning data for each day are stored in the in-home metering system

At the heart of Nielsen's television ratings are people meters that measure what programs or channels are being viewed and who is watching.

until they are automatically retrieved by Nielsen Media Research's computers each night. Nielsen Media Research's Operations Center in Dunedin, Florida processes this information each night for release to the television industry and other customers the next day.

To measure the audiences for local television, Nielsen Media Research gathers viewing information using TV diaries, booklets in which samples of viewers record their television viewing during a measurement week. They conduct diary measurement for each of the 210 television markets in the country four times each year, during February, May, July, and November. The diary requests that viewers write down not only who watched, but what program and what channel they watched. Once the diaries are filled out, viewers mail them back to Nielsen Media Research and the information is transferred into computers in order to calculate ratings.

Using these data, Nielsen estimates the number and percentage of all TV households viewing a given show. This information is also disaggregated by 10 demographic and socioeconomic characteristics, such as household income, education of head of house, occupation of head of house, household size, age of children, age of women, and geographical location. The Nielsen Television Index is useful to firms such as AT&T, Kellogg's Company, JC Penney, Pillsbury, and Unilever in selecting specific TV programs on which to air their commercials.[26]

Another index by the same company is the Nielsen Homevideo Index®—NHI. The NHI was established in 1980 and provides a measurement of cable, pay cable, VCRs, DVD players, satellite dishes, and other new television technologies. The data are collected through the use of People Meters, set-tuning meters, and paper diaries.

Given the growing popularity of the Internet, syndicated services are also geared to this medium. NetRatings, Inc. (*www.netratings.com*) tracks and collects Internet usage in real time from over 50,000 home and work users. It reports site and e-commerce activity: number of visits to properties, domains and unique sites, rankings by site and by category, time and frequency statistics, traffic patterns, and e-commerce transactions. It also reports banner advertising: audience response to banners, creative content, frequency, and site placement. This service has been launched in collaboration with ACNielsen.

## REAL RESEARCH

### Does Internet Usage Cannibalize Television Viewing?

In 2001, the U.S. Commerce Department conducted a study to determine how many people in the United States use the Internet. The report found that 54 percent of all U.S. citizens were using the Internet. In addition, the study also showed that Americans between the age of 5 and 17 comprise 90 percent of the total number of people that use computers. The rapid growth of home Internet access in the United States and the continued capability of television to reach mass audiences is naturally giving rise to efforts by key media players to better understand how these two powerful media affect one another and how they can be used in concert as communications and advertising vehicles. Research done by Nielsen Media Research (*www.nielsenmedia.com*) suggests that Internet homes are lighter TV viewers. Furthermore, analyses of the same homes before they had Internet access revealed that they were lighter TV viewers to begin with. Although Internet homes are lighter TV viewers, they seem to watch certain types of shows and outlets more than non-Internet homes. Internet access does not cannibalize television usage to any significant extent; instead, it offers a targeted vehicle to supplement advertising reach among these lighter television viewers. Therefore, firms like Procter & Gamble that spend heavily on advertising should make use of both these media in a complementary way to reach more consumers effectively.[27] ■

In addition to Nielsen, other services provide media panels. Arbitron (*www.arbitron.com*) maintains local and regional radio and TV media panels. The company is developing the Portable People Meter, a new technology for radio, TV, and cable ratings. Radio audience statistics are typically collected using diaries four times per year. An example of this is the Arbitron Radio Listening Diary.[28]

### *Uses of Purchase and Media Panels.*

Purchase panels provide information useful for forecasting sales, estimating market shares, assessing brand loyalty and brand switching behavior, establishing profiles of specific user groups, measuring promotional effectiveness, and conducting controlled store tests. Media panels yield information helpful for establishing advertising rates by radio and TV networks, selecting appropriate programming, and profiling viewer or listener subgroups. Advertisers, media planners, and buyers find panel information to be particularly useful.

### *Advantages and Disadvantages of Purchase and Media Panels.*

As compared to sample surveys, purchase and media panels offer certain distinct advantages.[29] Panels can provide longitudinal data (data can be obtained from the same respondents repeatedly). People who are willing to serve on panels may provide more and higher quality data than sample respondents. In purchase panels, information is recorded at the time of purchase, eliminating recall errors.[30] Information recorded by electronic devices is accurate because it eliminates human errors.

The disadvantages of purchase and media panels include lack of representativeness, maturation, and response biases. Most panels are not representative of the U.S. population. They underrepresent certain groups such as minorities and those with low education levels. This problem is further compounded by refusal to respond and attrition of panel members. Over time, maturation sets in and the panel members must be replaced (see Chapter 7). Response biases may occur, because simply being on the panel may alter behavior. Because purchase or media data are entered by hand, recording errors are also possible (see Chapter 3).

## Electronic Scanner Services

Although information provided by surveys and purchase and media panels is useful, electronic scanner services are becoming increasingly popular. **Scanner data** reflect some of the latest technological developments in the marketing research industry. Scanner data are collected by passing merchandise over a laser scanner, which optically reads the bar-coded description printed on the merchandise. This code is then linked to the current price held in the computer memory and used to prepare a sales slip. Information printed on the sales slip includes descriptions as well as prices of all items purchased. Checkout scanners, which are now used in many retail stores, are revolutionizing packaged-goods marketing research.

Three types of scanner data are available: volume tracking data, scanner panels, and scanner panels with cable TV. Volume tracking data provide information on purchases by brand, size, price, and flavor or formulation, based on sales data collected from the

*scanner data*
Data obtained by passing merchandise over a laser scanner that reads the UPC code from the packages.

checkout scanner tapes. This information is collected nationally from a sample of supermarkets with electronic scanners. Scanner services providing volume tracking data include National Scan Track (ACNielsen, *www.acnielsen.com*) and InfoScan (Information Resources, Inc., *www.infores.com*). The InfoScan tracking service collects scanner data weekly from more than 32,000 supermarket, drug, and mass merchandiser outlets across the United States. InfoScan store tracking provides detailed information on sales, share, distribution, pricing, and promotion.[31]

**scanner panels**
Scanner panel members are identified by an ID card, allowing each panel member's purchases to be stored with respect to her or his identity.

In **scanner panels,** each household member is given an ID card that can be read by the electronic scanner at the cash register. The scanner panel members simply present the ID card at the checkout counter each time they shop. In this way, consumer identity is linked to products purchased as well as the time and day of the shopping trip, and the firm can build a shopping record for that individual. Alternatively, some firms provide hand-held scanners to panel members. These members scan their purchases once they are home. The ACNielsen consumer panel called Homescan is used to record the purchases of approximately 125,000 households throughout the world. The consumer scans the bar codes on purchases with a hand-held scanner, which records the price, promotions, and quantity of each item. The information in the hand-held scanner is then transmitted to ACNielsen through telephone lines. ACNielsen uses the information from the scanner and additional information gathered from the consumer to determine such things as consumer demographics, quantity and frequency of purchases, percentage of households purchasing, shopping trips and expenditures, price paid, and usage information. Manufacturers and retailers use this information to better understand the purchasing habits of consumers. The Boston Market example given in the overview section provided an illustration. According to ACNielsen's consumer panel data, 55 percent of respondents purchased a meal for at-home consumption several times a month.[32]

**scanner panels with cable TV**
The combination of a scanner panel with manipulations of the advertising that is being broadcast by cable television companies.

An even more advanced use of scanning, **scanner panels with cable TV,** combines scanner panels with new technologies growing out of the cable TV industry. Households on these panels subscribe to one of the cable TV systems in their market. By means of a cable TV "split," the researcher targets different commercials into the homes of the panel members. For example, half the households may see test commercial A during the 6:00 P.M. newscast, while the other half see test commercial B. These panels allow researchers to conduct fairly controlled experiments in a relatively natural environment.[33]

## REAL RESEARCH

### *Using Total TV Households for Testing Total Advertising*

Based on cereal consumption research conducted in 2001, 73 percent of consumers eat cereal for breakfast and per capita consumption is very high. Results also indicated that cereal was the favorite breakfast item and was eaten regularly by three out of four adults. Therefore, General Mills (*www.generalmills.com*) has been promoting Total cereal on national television but is concerned about the effectiveness of its commercials.

Technology has been developed that allows transmission of advertising into participating households without the use of a cable TV system. Because the panel members can be selected from all available (total) TV households, not just those with cable TV, the bias of cable-only testing is eliminated. Using this type of system, General Mills can test which one of four test commercials for Total cereal results in the highest sales. Four groups of panel members are selected, and each receives a different test commercial. These households are monitored via scanner data to determine which group purchased the most Total cereal.[34] ∎

This example shows how scanner services incorporate advanced marketing research technology, which results in some advantages over survey and purchase panel data.

**Uses of Scanner Data.**   Scanner data are useful for a variety of purposes.[35] National volume tracking data can be used for tracking sales, prices, and distribution, modeling, and analyzing early warning signals. Scanner panels with cable TV can be used for testing new products, repositioning products, analyzing promotional mix, and making advertising decisions, including budget, copy and media, and pricing. These panels provide marketing researchers with a unique controlled environment for the manipulation of marketing variables.

*Advantages and Disadvantages of Scanner Data.*    Scanner data have an obvious advantage over surveys and purchase panels, because they reflect purchasing behavior that is not subject to interviewing, recording, memory, or expert biases. The record of purchases obtained by scanners is complete and unbiased by price sensitivity, because the panelist is not required to be overly conscious of price levels and changes. Another advantage is that in-store variables like pricing, promotions, and displays are part of the data set. The data are also likely to be current and can be obtained quickly. Finally, scanner panels with cable TV provide a highly controlled testing environment.

A major weakness of scanner data is lack of representativeness. National volume tracking data may not be projectable onto the total population, because only large supermarkets have scanners. Also, certain types of outlets, such as food warehouses and mass merchandisers, are excluded. Likewise, scanners have limited geographical dispersion and coverage.

The quality of scanner data may be limited by several factors. All products may not be scanned. For example, a clerk may use the register to ring up a heavy item to avoid lifting it. If an item does not scan on the first try, the clerk may key in the price and ignore the bar code. Sometimes a consumer purchases many flavors of the same item, but the clerk scans only one package and then rings in the number of purchases. Thus, the transaction is inaccurately recorded. With respect to scanner panels, the system provides information on TV sets in use rather than actual viewing behavior. Although scanner data provide behavioral and sales information, they do not provide information on underlying attitudes, preferences, and reasons for specific choices.

# SYNDICATED DATA FROM INSTITUTIONS

## Retailer and Wholesaler Audits

As Figure 4.4 shows, syndicated data are available for retailers and wholesalers as well as industrial firms. The most popular means of obtaining data from retailers and wholesalers is an audit. An *audit* is a formal examination and verification of product movement traditionally carried out by auditors who make in-person visits to retail and wholesale outlets and examine physical records or analyze inventory. Retailers and wholesalers who participate in the audit receive basic reports and cash payments from the audit service. Audit data focus on the products or services sold through the outlets or the characteristics of the outlets themselves. With the advent of scanner data, the need to perform audits has greatly decreased. Although audits are still being conducted, many do not collect data manually, but make use of computerized information.

The largest traditional retail audit service is the RoperASW National Retail Census that is conducted annually (*www.roperasw.com*). It is based on data gathered through in-person store visits to a national probability sample of 35,000 outlets of all kinds throughout the United States in more than 800 different geographical areas. Retail audit data can be useful to consumer product firms. For example, Colgate Palmolive is contemplating the introduction of a new toothpaste brand. A retail audit can help determine the size of the total market and distribution of sales by type of outlet and by different regions.

Another example of the traditional audit is the ACNielsen Convenience Track that is a retail audit of convenience stores in 30 local markets (*www.acnielsen.com*). For high speed and accuracy, the in-store auditors use hand-held computers to capture UPC information electronically. ACNielsen Convenience Track can integrate convenience store data with data from other channels including grocery, drug, and mass merchandisers.

Wholesale audit services, the counterpart of retail audits, monitor warehouse withdrawals. Participating operators, which include supermarket chains, wholesalers, and frozen-food warehouses, typically account for over 80 percent of the volume in the area.

*Uses of Audit Data.*    The uses of retail and wholesale audit data include: (1) determining the size of the total market and the distribution of sales by type of outlet, region, or city; (2) assessing brand shares and competitive activity; (3) identifying shelf space alloca-

---

**audit**
A data collection process derived from physical records or performing inventory analysis. Data are collected personally by the researcher or by representatives of the researcher, and the data are based upon counts usually of physical objects other than people.

tion and inventory problems; (4) analyzing distribution problems; (5) developing sales potentials and forecasts; and (6) developing and monitoring promotional allocations based on sales volume. Thus, audit data were particularly helpful in obtaining information on the environmental context of the problem in the department store patronage project.

***Advantages and Disadvantages of Audit Data.*** Audits provide relatively accurate information on the movement of many different products at the wholesale and retail levels. Furthermore, this information can be broken down by a number of important variables, such as brand, type of outlet, and size of market.

However, audits have limited coverage. Not all markets or operators are included. Also, audit information may not be timely or current, particularly compared to scanner data. Typically, there is a two-month gap between the completion of the audit cycle and the publication of reports. Another disadvantage is that, unlike scanner data, audit data cannot be linked to consumer characteristics. In fact, there may even be a problem in relating audit data to advertising expenditures and other marketing efforts. Some of these limitations are overcome in electronic (online) audits, as the following example illustrates.

**REAL RESEARCH**

*Online Audits for Tracking Online Shopping*

Ashford.com (*www.ashford.com*) is an online retailer that provides personal accessories including men and women's watches, women's purses, sunglasses, fragrances, etc. It combines over 300 brands and provides free same-day shipping. Obviously, for an online retailer, the holidays are a particularly important period. It is a time when many people shop online, so sales can really soar. Ashford.com was able to use electronic audit data about how their purchasers shop and how much they are buying.

Nielsen/NetRatings (*www.netratings.com*) constructed a Holiday e-Commerce Index, which measured Web shopping in eight different categories. Rather than gathering descriptive research about the customers from the customers, NetRatings gathered the data from the stores where the customers shopped. Because the orders were placed online, the store computers were able to track the purchases with ease. This computer tracking was then used to gather the purchasing information from the stores and to accumulate it into a collective report format. The survey told Ashford.com that a large portion of their customers were purchasing from the Web site while at work. This trend applied around the Web, as 46 percent of holiday online shopping in 2000 was conducted during work hours, versus the 54 percent that was conducted from consumers' homes. NetRatings determined that Ashford.com's customers were shopping during the lunch hour, or in small, 10 to 15 minute clips throughout the day.

Additionally, NetRatings demonstrated that online sales across the Web increased greatly in the first week of December as the holidays approached. Ashford.com's sales increased 385 percent during this period, so they did extremely well compared to other online companies. This information told Ashford.com that they should make sure their site is up and working during the workday. Promotions should be offered and flashed on the screen during this time. Additionally, the company might want to start advertising in corporate settings. Papers such as the *Wall Street Journal* and other corporate Web sites would be good places to advertise. A report from ComScore Networks revealed that $53 billion was generated in 2001 from online consumer sales at U.S. retail Web sites. With such a lucrative market at stake, online retailers like Ashford.com must take advantage of electronic audits and other types of marketing research in order to offer the products that online consumers want.[36] ■

## Industry Services

**industry services**
Industry services provide syndicated data about industrial firms, businesses, and other institutions.

***Industry services*** provide syndicated data about industrial firms, businesses, and other institutions. Financial, operating, and employment data are also collected by these syndicated research services for almost every North American Industry Classification System (NAICS) industrial category. These data are collected by making direct inquiries; from clipping services that monitor newspapers, the trade press, or broadcasts; and from corporate reports. The range and sources of syndicated data available for industrial goods firms are more limited than those available to consumer goods firms. Services available include Dun and Bradstreet's International Business Locator (*www.dnb.com*); Fortune Datastore that contains databases such as Fortune 500, Fortune 1000, and Global 500 and fastest growing companies database (*www.fortune.com*); and Standard & Poor's Information Services that includes Corporate Profiles (*www.standardpoor.com*).

The D&B® International Business Locator provides one-click access to over 28 million public/private companies in over 200 countries. After finding a business, the Locator will provide key business data including full address information, NAIC/line of business details, business size (sales, net worth, employees), names of key principals, and identification of this location's headquarters, domestic parent company, and/or global parent company.

### Uses of Industry Services.
Information provided by industrial services is useful for sales management decisions including identifying prospects, defining territories, setting quotas, and measuring market potential by geographic areas. It can also aid in advertising decisions such as targeting prospects, allocating advertising budgets, selecting media, and measuring advertising effectiveness. This kind of information is also useful for segmenting the market and designing custom products and services for important segments.

### Advantages and Disadvantages of Industry Services.
Industry services represent an important source of secondary information on industrial firms. The information they provide can be valuable in the initial phases of a marketing project. However, they are limited in the nature, content, quantity, and quality of information.

# COMBINING INFORMATION FROM DIFFERENT SOURCES: SINGLE-SOURCE DATA

**single-source data**
An effort to combine data from different sources by gathering integrated information on household and marketing variables applicable to the same set of respondents.

It is desirable to combine secondary information obtained from different sources. Combining data allows the researcher to compensate for the weakness of one method with the strengths of another. One outcome of the effort to combine data from different sources is **single-source data**. Single-source research follows a person's TV, reading, and shopping habits. After recruiting a test panel of households, the research firm meters each home's TV sets and surveys family members periodically on what they read. Their grocery purchases are tracked by UPC scanners. For background, most systems also track retail data, such as sales, advertising, and promotion. Thus, single-source data provide integrated information on household variables, including media consumption and purchases, and marketing variables, such as product sales, price, advertising, promotion, and in-store marketing effort.[37] An application of single-source data is illustrated by the Campbell Soup Company.

**REAL RESEARCH**

### Soaps Shed a "Guiding Light" on V8 Consumption
Still running after 65 years, "Guiding Light" aired its 16,293rd show on January 25, 2002. Although it originally started as a 15-minute radio show, it has been going strong and celebrated its 50th anniversary on television on June 30, 2002. During those years, it racked up 54 Daytime Emmy Awards and was inducted in the Soap Opera Hall of Fame. As of January 31, 2002, "General Hospital's" ratings were just behind "Guiding Light's" and they ranked 6 and 5, respectively, in overall soap opera viewership.

The Campbell Soup Company (*www.campbellsoupcompany.com*) used single-source data to target its advertising for V8 juice (*www.v8juice.com*). By obtaining single-source

Single-source data have enabled Campbell Soup to select appropriate television programs, such as "Guiding Light," for V8 commercials.

data on product consumption, media consumption, and demographic characteristics, Campbell found that demographically similar TV audiences consume vastly different amounts of V8. For example, on an index of 100 for the average household's V8 consumption, "General Hospital" had a below-average 80 index, whereas "Guiding Light" had an above-average 120 index. These results were surprising, because "General Hospital" actually had a slightly higher percentage of women 25 to 54 years old, the demographic group most predisposed to buy V8, and so would be expected to be a better medium to reach V8 drinkers. Using this information, Campbell rearranged its advertising schedule to raise the average index.

In 2001, V8 Juice introduced V8 Splash, a juicier version of its drink, to entice those who want a more fruity flavored drink. Although V8 is still doing well in the market, V8 Splash has done well enough in the market to launch two more Splash flavors and three Diet Splash flavors as of 2003.[38] ∎

*computer mapping*

Maps that solve marketing problems are called thematic maps. They combine geography with demographic information and a company's sales data or other proprietary information and are generated by a computer.

This example shows the usefulness of combining secondary information from different sources. As another example, **computer mapping** combines geography with demographic information and a company's sales data or other proprietary information to develop thematic maps. Marketers now routinely make decisions based on these color-coded maps. Mapping systems allow users to download geographically detailed demographic data supplied by vendors. The user can then draw a map that color codes neighborhoods in Dallas, for example, by the relative density of households headed by 35-to-45-year-olds with incomes of $50,000 or more. These systems allow users to add proprietary information to the downloaded data.[39]

Computer mapping combines geography with demographic and other proprietary data to generate thematic maps.

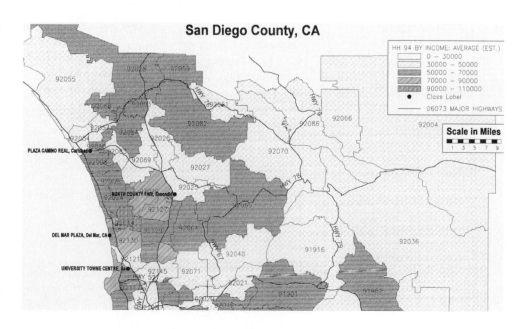

San Diego County, CA

*Figure 4.5*
Sources of International
Secondary Data

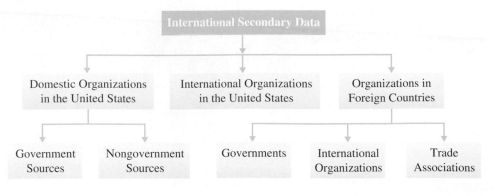

# INTERNATIONAL MARKETING RESEARCH

A wide variety of secondary data are available for international marketing research.[40] As in the case of domestic research, the problem is not a lack of data but rather a plethora of information available, and it is useful to classify the various sources (see Figure 4.5). Domestic organizations in the United States, both government and nongovernmental sources, can provide valuable secondary international data. The important government sources are the Department of Commerce, the Agency for International Development, the Small Business Administration, the Export-Import Bank of the United States, the Department of Agriculture, Department of State, Department of Labor, and the Port Authority of New York and New Jersey. The Department of Commerce offers not only a number of publications but also a variety of other services, such as the foreign buyer program, matchmaker events, trade missions, export contact list service, the foreign commercial service, and custom statistical service for exporters.

Nongovernmental organizations, including international organizations located in the United States, can provide information about international markets. These include the United Nations, the Organization for Economic Cooperation and Development (OECD), the International Monetary Fund (IMF), the World Bank, International Chambers of Commerce, the Commission of the European Community to the United States, and the Japanese External Trade Organization (JETRO). Finally, sources in foreign countries include governments, international organizations located abroad, trade associations, and private services, such as syndicated firms. When conducting a review of the literature, one could use directories, indexes, books, commercially produced reference material, and magazines and newspapers.

Evaluation of secondary data is even more critical for international than for domestic projects. Different sources report different values for a given statistic, such as GDP, because of differences in the way the unit is defined. Measurement units may not be equivalent across countries. In France, for example, workers are paid a 13th monthly salary each year as an automatic bonus, resulting in a measurement construct that is different from other countries.[41] The accuracy of secondary data may also vary from country to country. Data from highly industrialized countries like the United States are likely to be more accurate than those from developing countries. Business and income statistics are affected by the taxation structure and the extent of tax evasion. Population censuses may vary in frequency and year in which the data are collected. In the United States the census is conducted every 10 years, whereas in the People's Republic of China there was a 29-year gap between the censuses of 1953 and 1982. However, this situation is changing fast. Several syndicated firms are developing huge sources of international secondary data.

## REAL RESEARCH

### *Los Medios y Mercados de Latinoamérica*

Started in 1994 by RoperASW (*www.roperasw.com*), Los Medios y Mercados de Latinoamérica (The Markets & Media of Latin America) is the largest multinational sur-

Secondary data indicate that Latin America is on the brink of heavily adopting ATM terminals in the near future.

vey of media and consumer habits that is conducted in Latin America to provide managers with important information for their marketing strategies. The study that is repeated every year aims at tracking the development of media and consumer habits in Latin America.

A recent multinational survey was conducted in 18 Latin American countries including Argentina, Brazil, Colombia, Mexico, and Venezuela. It sampled 6,634 respondents between the ages of 12 and 64. Its probability sample representing urban as well as rural Latin America can be projected to 280 million people or, in other words, 79 million households.

The methodology for this survey involved two steps. First, the personal interview technique was used to measure the variety of media including newspapers, multinational and local magazines, television, and radio. Then, a 25-page self-administered booklet was passed on to the respondent to measure the product consumption and usage in over 100 categories and 800 brands. Demographic data gathered about the respondents include country/region, age, sex, employment status, occupation, education, household size, annual household income, automobile ownership, and household goods and services. Companies can easily use these data as the survey results are provided in a set of 14 printed volumes and in a computer database format that is accessible online or in SPSS format.

A recent survey found that Latin America is on the brink of heavily adopting ATM terminals in the near future due to the increasing demand for debit cards among consumers. It is expected that Latin America's ATM terminals will dramatically increase to 61,460 terminals in 2005, which is an increase in 34,890 terminals from 1999. With consumers having more readily available cash from ATM terminals, it is important for global retailers such as Wal-Mart (*www.walmart.com*), as well as global banks such as Citibank (*www.citibank.com*), to take such trends into account.[42] ∎

## ETHICS IN MARKETING RESEARCH

The researcher is ethically obligated to ensure the relevance and usefulness of secondary data to the problem at hand. The secondary data should be evaluated by the criteria discussed earlier in this chapter. Only data judged to be appropriate should be used. It is also important that the data were collected using procedures that are morally appropriate. Data can be judged unethical if they were gathered in a way that harms the respondents or invades their privacy. Ethical issues also arise if the users of secondary data are unduly critical of the data that do not support their interests and viewpoints.

## The Ethical Pill Can Be Bitter to Swallow

ABC, NBC, CBS, some advertising agencies, and major advertisers are at odds with Nielsen Media Research's (*www.nielsenmedia.com*) television ratings. They criticize Nielsen's sampling scheme and intrusive data recording methodologies. Instead, these companies appear to be supporting Statistical Research, Inc. (SRI) as a competitive service (*www.statisticalresearch.com*). SRI uses nonintrusive electronic data collection techniques, which will provide real time reports of viewership in the future.

A central issue in the criticisms against Nielsen is that the Big Three have received declining viewership ratings. As of the first half of 2001 television season, primetime viewership to the seven broadcast networks declined in every measure. The top seven broadcasters' collective U.S. household delivery dropped by almost 1 million homes, a decrease of 2.7 percent whereas cable had an increase of 9.8 percent. The top three broadcast networks (ABC, CBS, and NBC) each had across-the-board audience declines. During this period, primetime viewership for ad-supported cable averaged 26.2 million viewers, whereas the top seven networks averaged 33.8 million viewers. Rather than accept the idea that the broadcast network audience is shrinking, the networks would prefer a more flattering assessment of their audiences. Ratings translate directly into advertising revenues. The more viewers a television show draws, the higher fees a network can charge for airing advertising at that spot. Advertising charges can differ dramatically between timeslots, so accurate (or aggressive) viewer ratings are desirable from the network's perspective.

In defense of the networks, monopolies tend to resist innovation and lack incentive to improve processes. Complacency rules, as long as the money keeps coming. As a professional marketing research supplier, however, Nielsen Media Research is ethically bound to providing accurate and representative data—to the best of its ability.

Users also have the ethical responsibility of not criticizing secondary data simply because they do not support their own viewpoints. Eventually network executives will have to swallow the bitter pill of reality that cable TV, direct-broadcast satellite TV, and the Internet are all gaining ground over broadcast television viewership. Network executives find it difficult to swallow this pill.[43] ∎

Given the limitations of secondary data, it is often necessary to collect primary data in order to obtain the information needed to address the management decision problem. The use of secondary data alone, when the research problem requires primary data collection, could raise ethical concerns. Such concerns are heightened when the client is being billed a fixed fee for the project, and the proposal submitted to get the project did not adequately specify the data collection methodology. On the other hand, in some cases it may be possible to obtain the information needed from secondary sources alone, making it unnecessary to collect primary data. The unnecessary collection of expensive primary data, when the research problem can be addressed based on secondary data alone, may be unethical. These ethical issues become more salient if the research firm's billings go up, but at the expense of the client.

# INTERNET AND COMPUTER APPLICATIONS

## The World Wide Web as an Online Source of Secondary Data

The World Wide Web is an important source of secondary data for the marketing researcher. The search is facilitated by some generalist search engines, such as Yahoo! (*www.yahoo.com*) or Alta Vista (*www.altavista.com*), which require only some key words to get hundreds of sites related to one subject. One can also go directly to the Web sites of some traditional suppliers of secondary data. Many of those sites also have inside search engines that sort data from the supplier's internal database (see Chapter 1).

## Internal Secondary Data

Large organizations have intranets that greatly facilitate the search for access to internal secondary data. The Coca-Cola Company (*www.cocacola.com*), for example, has developed powerful intranet applications that enable Coca-Cola managers worldwide to search for past and current research studies and a wide variety of marketing-related information on the basis of key words. Once located, the information can be accessed online. Even sensitive and restricted information can be accessed by obtaining permission electronically. Organizations conducting business on the Internet have a natural advantage in building large customer databases and implementing database marketing programs, as illustrated in the following example.

**REAL RESEARCH**

### *The* New York Times *on the Web: A New Way to Target Consumers*

To handle alternate forms of interaction and updates, the *New York Times* created a separate unit, The New York Times Electronic Media Co. The *New York Times* on the Web (*www.nytimes.com*) has drawn over 10 million registrants as of 2003. It offers much more than the traditional newspaper with over 50,000 book reviews, up-to-date and breaking news, a premium archive service, as well as articles from the daily and Sunday newspaper. This helps to establish a sense of community among the readers and allows them to communicate and express their opinions regarding the services they receive.

The New York Times Electronic Media Company offers The *New York Times* on the Web database information to advertisers in a manner that enables firms to leverage the site's registrants. The database contains demographic information, such as age, gender, income, and zip code, which ties to an e-mail address. This new database marketing system can identify and customize user groups, target Web messages to specific segments of the population, and adjust the message based on audience reaction. It can also increase targeting opportunities through third-party data or additional information supplied by the user.

For example, the database enables an automobile firm to emphasize safety to older customers, luxury to affluent ones, and roominess to families. The system is set up so that near real time data can be received from the Web that indicates how well ads are performing relative to age, gender, and income characteristics. Thus, this system allows a firm to maintain up-to-date information on audiences in order to position its products effectively.[44] ∎

## General Business Sources

American business information can be obtained by visiting various business-related sites that provide sales leads, mailing lists, business profiles, and credit ratings. You can find reports on different industries at research firms' sites, such as: *www.jup.com*, *www.forrester.com*, *www.idc.com*, and *www.greenfield.com*, to name a few. However, other general publications also publish research results, such as: *www.wsj.com*, *www. businessweek.com*, *www. business20.com*, and *www.nytimes.com*.

## Government Data

One of the major sources of secondary data is the government. Several U.S. government sources can be reached from FedWorld (*www.fedworld.gov*). The researcher can visit the Government Information Location Service (GILS) at *www.gils.net*, or *www.doi.gov*. Extensive business statistics can be obtained from *www.stat-usa.gov*.

The U.S. Department of Commerce can be reached at *www.commerce.gov*. The Bureau of Census information can be reached via the Department of Commerce or directly at *www.census.gov*.

## Computerized Databases

The computerized databases that we have discussed may also be accessed via the Internet. For example, DIALOG (*www.dialog.com*) and LEXISNEXIS Communication Center (*www.lexisnexis.com*) are two of the popular database services that can be reached via the Internet.

## Syndicated Sources of Information

For syndicated sources of information, one can visit the home pages of the various marketing research companies and providers of syndicated information. The ACNielsen home page at *www.acnielsen.com* is a very good source. A company could also gather secondary syndicated data from sources such as: *www.nielsenmedia.com* (media), *www.mediamark.com* (psychographic), *www.yankelovich.com* (lifestyle), *www.surveys.com* (surveys), *www.sriresearch.com* (advertising), *www.gallup.com* (general), *www.nfow.com* (purchases), and *www.arbitron.com* (diaries).

## International Secondary Data

Several Web sites provide international secondary data. For example, *www.exporthotline.com* contains thousands of market research reports, a trade library, market intelligence on 80 countries, and plenty of links. The Global Information Locator Service is available at *www.gils.net*. One Internet site that is a good source of secondary data is the Central Intelligence Agency at *www.odci.gov* or *www.cia.gov*. The site lists every country in the world and gives detailed information about the following aspects of a country: general introduction, geography, people, government, economy, communications, transportations, military, and transnational issues. It also estimates the growth level of various fields and points out any interesting information about a specific country.

Computers can be used not only to access but also to analyze and store information available from online and offline databases. Several syndicated services make information available for use on microcomputers and mainframes. Given the sheer volume of scanner data that is available, software has been developed to process and repackage such data to user specifications. For example, Information Resources, Inc. (*www.infores.com*) has developed an expert system that extracts key information (sales, category volume, trend, and brand share) from large syndicated grocery scanner databases and delivers it in memo format.

## SPSS Windows

SPSS maps integrates seamlessly with SPSS base menus, enabling you to map a variety of data. You can choose from six base thematic maps or create other maps by combining map options. Maps can be further customized using the SPSS Syntax Editor. Such maps can be used for a variety of purposes, including interpreting sales and other data geographically to determine where the biggest customers are located, displaying sales trends for specific geographic locations, using buying trend information to determine the ideal location for new company stores, etc.

## FOCUS ON BURKE

Burke has found that secondary data available to companies is grossly underutilized. Often, an archive of previously conducted primary research for the company is not available for the project at hand. In addition, it may be difficult for the researcher to access the internal secondary data generated within the client firm. Data such as shipment returns, damage reports, customer complaints, lost customer reports, etc., are often maintained by widely separated parts of the company that do not facilitate movement of information across the departments. These data yield valuable insight into the relationships with customers but are simply not accessible in any coherent fashion in most companies.

Burke believes that the most valuable resource a company can have for planning and understanding its information needs is a functional database of all internal and purchased external data. The way Burke has organized its own internal data and the manner in which it uses secondary data could well serve as a model for client firms. The Corporate Information Center (CIC) at Burke, Inc. is the company's resource for secondary data. The CIC serves many different internal groups at varying stages of the marketing research process. Through the CIC, employees have access to internal and external secondary information. Internal secondary information refers to the information that has been collected by Burke in the past. This includes reports, analyses, and company information housed in the internal database. External secondary information refers to information published from other sources outside Burke.

Burke, Inc.'s Corporate Information Center (CIC) has a variety of resources that can help answer project, client, or industry-related questions. Internal secondary data include a File/Report archive dating back to 1988 and a database containing job information on studies dating back to 1986. The CIC also contains various sources of external secondary data. There are over 400 books in the corporate library. The collection includes various trade conference proceedings, marketing textbooks, and books on a variety of marketing research topics. Business directories, census publications, materials from marketing research seminars, manuals, and other reference materials can also be found in the corporate library. The CIC has a periodical collection that includes marketing research journals and general business publications.

In addition to the resources available in house, Burke employees have access to other external sources of information through the CIC. The CIC typically looks to one (or a combination) of the following resources to obtain pertinent and accurate data to gain knowledge and insight that can be applied throughout the various stages of the marketing research process: trade publications, industry associations, government agencies. syndicated market research reports, online databases, CD-ROM products, and the Internet.

At Burke, secondary data can be useful at all stages of the marketing research process. Some examples of typical applications where secondary data are utilized:

- Retrieving background information on a client, including latest news and company developments
- Providing a general overview of a client's industry
- Reviewing magazines, newspapers, newsletters, and other trade publications to keep abreast of new products and new technologies
- Obtaining demographic information for various geographical areas
- Conducting competitive intelligence
- Identifying new business opportunities
- Monitoring the regulatory environment for a particular industry

# SUMMARY

In contrast to primary data, which originate with the researcher for the specific purpose of the problem at hand, secondary data are data originally collected for other purposes. Secondary data can be obtained quickly and are relatively inexpensive. However, they have limitations and should be carefully evaluated to determine their appropriateness for the problem at hand. The evaluation criteria consist of specifications, error, currency, objectivity, nature, and dependability.

A wealth of information exists in the organization for which the research is being conducted. This information constitutes internal secondary data. External data are generated by sources outside the organization. These data exist in the form of published (printed) material, online, Internet, and offline databases, or information made available by syndicated services. Published external sources may be broadly classified as general business data or government data. General business sources comprise guides, directories, indexes, and statistical data. Government sources may be broadly categorized as census data and other data. Computerized databases may be online, Internet, or offline. These databases may be further classified as bibliographic, numeric, full-text, directory, or specialized databases.

Syndicated sources are companies that collect and sell common pools of data designed to serve a number of clients. Syndicated sources can be classified based on the unit of measurement (households/consumers or institutions). Household/consumer data may be obtained via surveys, purchase and media panels, or electronic scanner services. When institutions are the unit of measurement, the data may be obtained from retailers, wholesalers, or industrial firms. It is desirable to combine information obtained from different secondary sources.

There are several specialized sources of secondary data useful for conducting international marketing research. However, the evaluation of secondary data becomes even more critical as the usefulness and accuracy of these data can vary widely. Ethical dilemmas that can arise include the unnecessary collection of primary data, the use of only secondary data when primary data are needed, the use of secondary data that are not applicable, and the use of secondary data that have been gathered through morally questionable means. The Internet and computers can be used to access, analyze, and store information available from secondary sources.

# KEY TERMS AND CONCEPTS

primary data, *102*
secondary data, *102*
volume tracking data, *105*
internal data, *107*
external data, *108*
database marketing, *108*
online databases, *112*
Internet databases, *112*
offline databases, *112*

bibliographic databases, *113*
numeric databases, *113*
full-text databases, *113*
directory databases, *113*
special-purpose databases, *113*
syndicated sources (services), *114*
surveys, *115*
psychographics, *115*
lifestyles, *115*

purchase panels, *117*
media panels, *118*
scanner data, *120*
scanner panels, *121*
scanner panels with cable TV, *121*
audit, *122*
industry services, *123*
single-source data, *124*
computer mapping, *125*

# EXERCISES

## Questions

1. What are the differences between primary and secondary data?
2. Why is it important to obtain secondary data before primary data?
3. Differentiate between internal and external secondary data.
4. What are the advantages of secondary data?
5. What are the disadvantages of secondary data?
6. What are the criteria to be used when evaluating secondary data?
7. List the various sources of published secondary data.
8. What are the different forms of computerized databases?
9. What are the advantages of computerized databases?
10. List and describe the various syndicated sources of secondary data.
11. What is the nature of information collected by surveys?
12. How can surveys be classified?
13. Explain what a panel is. What is the difference between purchase panels and media panels?
14. What are relative advantages of purchase and media panels over surveys?
15. What kinds of data can be gathered through electronic scanner services?
16. Describe the uses of scanner data.
17. What is an audit? Discuss the uses, advantages, and disadvantages of audits.
18. Describe the information provided by industrial services.
19. Why is it desirable to use multiple sources of secondary data?

## Problems

1. Obtain automobile industry sales and sales of major automobile manufacturers for the last five years from secondary sources. (Hint: See Chapter 22, Table 22.1.)

2. Select an industry of your choice. Using secondary sources, obtain industry sales and the sales of the major firms in that industry for the past year. Estimate the market shares of each major firm. From another source, obtain information on the market shares of these same firms. Do the two estimates agree?

# INTERNET AND COMPUTER EXERCISES

1. Conduct an online data search to obtain background information on an industry of your choice (e.g., sporting goods). Your search should encompass both qualitative and quantitative information.

2. Visit the Web site of a company of your choice. Suppose the management decision problem facing this company was to expand its share of the market. Obtain as much secondary data from the Web site of this company and other sources on the Internet as are relevant to this problem.

3. Visit the Web site of the Bureau of Census (see one of the URLs given in the book). Write a report about the secondary data available from the bureau that would be useful to a fast-food firm such as McDonald's for the purpose of formulating domestic marketing strategy.

4. Visit *www.census.gov/statab*. Use State Rankings and Vital Statistics to identify the top six states for marketing products to the elderly.

5. For the department store project, Sears would like you to summarize the retail sales in the United States by visiting *www.census.gov*.

6. Visit *www.npd.com* and write a description of the panel maintained by NPD.

7. Visit *www.acnielsen.com* and write a report about the various services offered by ACNielsen.

# ACTIVITIES

## Role Playing

1. You are the marketing research manager of a local bank. Management has asked you to assess the demand potential for checking accounts in your metropolitan area. What sources of secondary data should you consult? What kind of information would you expect to obtain from each source? Ask a group of fellow students to play the role of management and explain to them the role of secondary data in this project.

2. You are the group product manager for Procter and Gamble in charge of laundry detergents. How would you make use of information available from a store audit? Ask another student to play the role of Vice President of Marketing. Explain to your boss the value of store audit information related to laundry detergents.

## Fieldwork

1. Make a trip to your local library. Write a report explaining how you would use the library to collect secondary data for a marketing research project assessing the demand potential for Cross soft tip pens. Please be specific.

## Group Discussion

1. Discuss the significance and limitations of the government census data as a major source of secondary data.

2. Discuss the growing use of computerized databases.

3. Discuss how the Nielsen TV ratings can affect the price advertisers pay for a commercial broadcast during a particular time.

# CHAPTER 5

# Exploratory Research Design: Qualitative Research

"Qualitative research provides the fundamental understanding of peoples' language, perceptions, and values. Qualitative research most often provides the understanding that allows us to decide on the information we must have to solve the research problem and how to properly interpret that information."

*Carol Raffel, vice president, qualitative services, Burke, Inc.*

## Objectives

After reading this chapter, the student should be able to:

1. Explain the difference between qualitative and quantitative research in terms of the objectives, sampling, data collection and analysis, and outcomes.
2. Understand the various forms of qualitative research including direct procedures such as focus groups and depth interviews and indirect methods such as projective techniques.
3. Describe focus groups in detail with an emphasis on planning and conducting focus groups and their advantages, disadvantages, and applications.
4. Describe depth interview techniques in detail citing their advantages, disadvantages, and applications.
5. Explain projective techniques in detail and compare association, completion, construction, and expressive techniques.
6. Discuss the considerations involved in conducting qualitative research in an international setting.
7. Understand the ethical issues involved in conducting qualitative research.
8. Discuss the use of the Internet and computers in obtaining and analyzing qualitative data.

## Overview

Like secondary data analysis (see Chapter 4), qualitative research is a major methodology used in exploratory research (Chapter 3). Researchers undertake qualitative research to define the problem or develop an approach (Chapter 2). In developing an approach, qualitative research is often used for generating hypotheses and identifying variables that should be included in the research. In cases where conclusive or quantitative research is not done, qualitative research and secondary data comprise the major part of the research project. In this chapter, we discuss the differences between qualitative and quantitative research and the role of each in the marketing research project. We present a classification of qualitative research and cover the major techniques, focus groups, and depth interviews in detail. We also consider the indirect procedures called projective techniques with emphasis on association, completion, construction, and expressive techniques. The considerations involved in conducting qualitative research when researching international markets are discussed. Several ethical issues that arise in qualitative research are identified. The chapter concludes with a discussion of the use of the Internet and computers in qualitative research. The following examples give a flavor of qualitative research and its applications in marketing research.

## REAL RESEARCH

### Qualitative Research Lights a Fire Under Sunfire

When Pontiac (*www.pontiac.com*) set out to introduce its sporty Sunfire, the company wanted to target younger drivers who wanted a sporty car but could not afford one: men and women between the ages of 21 to 34 who were intending to buy a car in the same class as the Sunfire and had incomes of $25,000+ with some college education. Pontiac hired D'arcy Masius Benton and Bowles, Inc. (DMB&B) of Bloomfield, Michigan (*www.darcyww. com.pl*) to research this market.

DMB&B utilized a combination of a traditional focus group and picture response technique making use of a collage to encourage the respondents to reveal their underlying beliefs and attitudes about Sunfire. The respondents were asked to create a collage out of the usual resources of magazines and construction paper at home about a week before the focus group. When assigning the collage, DMB&B asked the respondents to contemplate how cars fit into their lives and how they think and feel about cars. Then, they were asked to make a collage that would describe this relationship using anything from maps to family photographs to original artwork.

When the respondents met at a facility to begin the focus group, the moderator held up each collage and requested that the group talk about the creator of each collage and what they think the feelings the person who made the collage had for cars. After each collage was discussed in this manner, the respondents were shown photos of the Sunfire and were asked to discuss their feelings about the car and their beliefs and attitudes about it.

For Pontiac, this type of research helped identify many positioning ideas. They found that, for their particular target group, the car was a vehicle for adventure and discovery. The research uncovered that personal relationships were important to this target audience. They wanted to have a relationship with their car so that it could be the partner in their adventures. This group also had a very positive attitude about life.

From the findings of this research, Pontiac went on to develop an advertising campaign entitled "Sunfire Adventures." The television spots featured pictures of the Sunfire in adventurous places, such as the Great Wall of China and the Leaning Tower of Pisa. Pontiac Sunfire also sponsored ESPN's Extreme Games competition and marketed the car on the College Television Network and with health club displays. This campaign was instrumental in the successful launch of the Sunfire.

In 2001, Pontiac sold approximately 71,300 Sunfire automobiles. Continued focus group research has enabled Pontiac to remain successful and to introduce a restyled 2003 Sunfire. This newly designed model was introduced in Chicago because that geographic region is Pontiac's second largest market, with Sunfire being Pontiac's most popular selling model.[1] ■

## REAL RESEARCH

### *Feelings, Nothing More Than Feelings*

Qualitative research in the form of focus groups and individual depth interviews is used to discover what sensory feelings are important for customers. Such feelings cannot be uncovered by quantitative research. Depth interviews are conducted one on one and allow extensive probing of each respondent. Thus, it is possible to uncover underlying feelings (as well as values, beliefs, and attitudes). Several examples show how identifying consumers' sensory feelings are crucial in designing products.

**Ford**

Ford (*www.ford.com*) decided to redesign one of its Taurus models. They remodeled the dashboard buttons, the rear fenders, etc. They decided to change the door latches. However, there was a problem with the sound it made when somebody closed the door. It sounded weird. The latch made two thumps, which gave the impression to the user that something was going wrong even if there was no problem at all. Although consumers are not aware of their own perceptions, they are very sensitive to sounds a car makes.

**Whirlpool**

Whereas one might think that the perfect product would not make any noise, the case of Whirlpool (*www.whirlpool.com*) denies it. Whirlpool launched a new refrigerator, a quieter one. However, customers called the company to complain about "the softer, water-gurgling sounds" of the model. People had the impression that the new refrigerator was the noisiest they had ever heard, when it was actually the quietest ever manufactured.

**IBM**

IBM (*www.ibm.com*) focused on a new button in the middle of the keyboard that was to replace the mouse. Because people spend hours working on a computer, comfort for the finger used to touch the button was crucial. It took them nine years to "create the perfect cushion for a finger."

**Estee Lauder**

The cosmetic industry provides a lot of examples of qualitative research because cosmetic products are associated with female intimacy. For example, Estee Lauder (*www.esteelauder.com*) changed the shape of its blue compact so it appeals more to the customer. The shape was redesigned by rounding the edges to make it softer and thus create a link with the round shape of the female body.[2] ■

These examples illustrate the rich insights into the underlying behavior of consumers that can be obtained by using qualitative procedures.

# PRIMARY DATA: QUALITATIVE VERSUS QUANTITATIVE RESEARCH

As was explained in Chapter 4, primary data are originated by the researcher for the specific purpose of addressing the problem at hand. Primary data may be qualitative or quantitative in nature, as shown in Figure 5.1. The distinction between qualitative and

**Figure 5.1**
A Classification of Marketing
Research Data

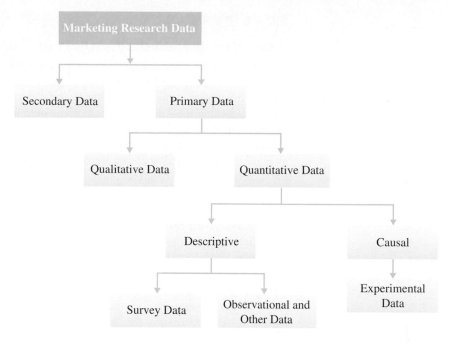

**qualitative research**
An unstructured, exploratory
research methodology based on
small samples that provides insights
and understanding of the problem
setting.

**quantitative research**
A research methodology that seeks
to quantify the data and, typically,
applies some form of statistical
analysis.

quantitative research closely parallels the distinction between exploratory and conclusive research discussed in Chapter 3. The differences between the two research methodologies are summarized in Table 5.1.[3] **Qualitative research** provides insights and understanding of the problem setting, whereas **quantitative research** seeks to quantify the data and, typically, applies some form of statistical analysis. Whenever a new marketing research problem is being addressed, quantitative research must be preceded by appropriate qualitative research. Sometimes qualitative research is undertaken to explain the findings obtained from quantitative research. However, the findings of qualitative research are misused when they are regarded as conclusive and are used to make generalizations to the population of interest.[4] It is a sound principle of marketing research to view qualitative and quantitative research as complementary, rather than in competition with each other.[5]

The story goes that Alfred Politz, a strong proponent of quantitative research, and Ernest Dichter, a strong proponent of qualitative research, were having their usual debate about the merits of the two methods. Politz stressed the importance of large-scale, projectable samples. Dichter answered: "But, Alfred, ten thousand times nothing is still nothing!" As Dichter argued, mere quantification, when the underlying behavior of interest is not well understood, will not lead to meaningful results. However, qualitative and quantitative research in combination can provide rich insights that can help in formulating successful marketing strategies, as in the case of Kraft Foods.

**TABLE 5.1**

**Qualitative Versus Quantitative Research**

|  | QUALITATIVE RESEARCH | QUANTITATIVE RESEARCH |
|---|---|---|
| Objective | To gain a qualitative understanding of the underlying reasons and motivations | To quantify the data and generalize the results from the sample to the population of interest |
| Sample | Small number of nonrepresentative cases | Large number of representative cases |
| Data collection | Unstructured | Structured |
| Data analysis | Nonstatistical | Statistical |
| Outcome | Develop an initial understanding | Recommend a final course of action |

### *Focus (Groups) on the Easiness of Easy Mac*

When Kraft Foods came out with its new product, Easy Mac, they thought it was going to be a great success. Easy Mac has the same taste as Kraft's original Macaroni and Cheese but it is prepared in a microwave oven using water. It comes in single-serving packages. They thought that the American population would love the convenience and the speed of preparing the product. However, the first year sales were disappointing.

Kraft conducted focus groups to figure out what went wrong. The focus groups revealed that consumers were aware of the product but perceptions of the product were low. Consumers were skeptical about the taste and quality of the product and were also confused about the steps involved in preparing the product. The focus groups also revealed that mothers liked the product because their older children could make it by themselves. This lightened their load and made kids more self-reliant.

When these findings were confirmed in a descriptive survey involving mall intercept interviews, Kraft launched ad campaigns stressing how older kids can make it themselves. They followed these up with a siblings campaign in which an older brother and younger sister are teasing one another because the sister cannot believe that the brother made the Easy Mac on his own. He later makes her a bowl and they talk about how good it tastes. They also included an easy three-step instruction process on the box to make it easier for consumers to understand how to make the product.

These ad campaigns were a hit and sales greatly increased for the new Kraft product. Focus groups (qualitative research) and the mall intercept survey (quantitative research) used in a complementary way allowed Kraft to discover what the consumer needed to know and to convey the correct message to them. In 2001, Kraft Foods (*www.kraft.com*) achieved annual sales of $33.8 billion with seven of its brands having more than $1 billion in sales each and a total of 61 brands having sales of $100 million each.[6] ∎

Whereas the Easy Mac example suggests the rationale behind qualitative research, we consider this topic in more detail.

# RATIONALE FOR USING QUALITATIVE RESEARCH

There are several reasons to use qualitative research. It is not always possible, or desirable, to use fully structured or formal methods to obtain information from respondents (see Chapter 3). People may be unwilling or unable to answer certain questions. People are unwilling to give truthful answers to questions that invade their privacy, embarrass them, or have a negative impact on their ego or status. Examples of such sensitive questions include: "Have you recently purchased sanitary napkins? Drugs for nervous tension? Pills for anxiety?" Second, people may be unable to provide accurate answers to questions that tap their subconscious. The values, emotional drives, and motivations residing at the subconscious level are disguised from the outer world by rationalization and other ego defenses. For example, a person may have purchased an expensive sports car to overcome feelings of inferiority. However, if asked, "Why did you purchase this sports car?" he may say, "I got a great deal," "My old car was falling apart," or "I need to impress my customers and clients." In such cases, the desired information can be best obtained through qualitative research. As illustrated in the "Feelings" examples in the overview section, qualitative research is also very useful to discover what sensory feelings are important for customers.[7]

# A CLASSIFICATION OF QUALITATIVE RESEARCH PROCEDURES

**direct approach**
One type of qualitative research in which the purposes of the project are disclosed to the respondent or are obvious, given the nature of the interview.

A classification of qualitative research procedures is presented in Figure 5.2. These procedures are classified as either direct or indirect, based on whether the true purpose of the project is known to the respondents. A **direct approach** is not disguised. The purpose of the

*Figure 5.2*
A Classification of Qualitative
Research Procedures

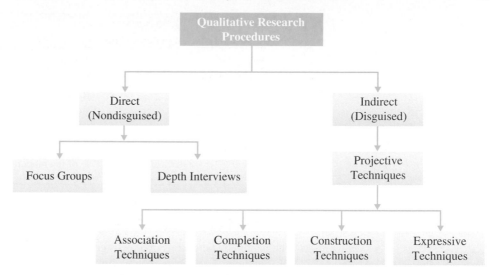

*Figure 5.2*
A Classification of Qualitative
Research Procedures

project is disclosed to the respondents or is otherwise obvious to them from the questions asked. Focus groups and depth interviews are the major direct techniques. In contrast, research that takes an ***indirect approach*** disguises the true purpose of the project. Projective techniques, the commonly used indirect techniques, consist of association, completion, construction, and expressive techniques. Each of these techniques is discussed in detail, beginning with focus groups.

**indirect approach**
A type of qualitative research in which the purposes of the project are disguised from the respondents.

# FOCUS GROUP INTERVIEWS

**focus group**
An interview conducted by a trained moderator among a small group of respondents in an unstructured and natural manner.

A *focus group* is an interview conducted by a trained moderator in a nonstructured and natural manner with a small group of respondents. The moderator leads the discussion. The main purpose of focus groups is to gain insights by listening to a group of people from the appropriate target market talk about issues of interest to the researcher. The value of the technique lies in the unexpected findings often obtained from a free-flowing group discussion.

Focus groups are the most important qualitative research procedure. They are so popular that many marketing research practitioners consider this technique synonymous with qualitative research.[8] Several hundred facilities around the country now conduct focus groups several times a week, and the typical focus group costs the client about $4,000. Given their importance and popularity, we describe the salient characteristics of focus groups in detail.[9]

A typical focus group session.

| TABLE 5.2 | |
| --- | --- |
| **Characteristics of Focus Groups** | |
| Group size | 8 to 12 |
| Group composition | Homogeneous; respondents prescreened |
| Physical setting | Relaxed, informal atmosphere |
| Time duration | 1 to 3 hours |
| Recording | Use of audiocassettes and videotapes |
| Moderator | Observational, interpersonal, and communication skills of the moderator |

## Characteristics

The major characteristics of a focus group are summarized in Table 5.2. A focus group generally includes 8 to 12 members. Groups of fewer than eight are unlikely to generate the momentum and group dynamics necessary for a successful session. Likewise, groups of more than 12 may be too crowded and may not be conducive to a cohesive and natural discussion.[10]

A focus group should be homogeneous in terms of demographic and socioeconomic characteristics. Commonalty among group members avoids interactions and conflicts among group members on side issues.[11] Thus, a women's group should not combine married homemakers with small children, young unmarried working women, and elderly divorced or widowed women, because their lifestyles are substantially different. Moreover, the participants should be carefully screened to meet certain criteria. The participants must have had adequate experience with the object or issue being discussed. People who have already participated in numerous focus groups should not be included. These so-called professional respondents are atypical and their participation leads to serious validity problems.[12]

The physical setting for the focus group is also important. A relaxed, informal atmosphere encourages spontaneous comments. Light refreshments should be served before the session and made available throughout. Although a focus group may last from 1 to 3 hours, a duration of 1.5 to 2 hours is typical. This period of time is needed to establish rapport with the participants and explore, in depth, their beliefs, feelings, ideas, attitudes, and insights regarding the topics of concern. Focus group interviews are invariably recorded, often on videotape, for subsequent replay, transcription, and analysis. Videotaping has the advantage of recording facial expressions and body movements, but it can increase the costs significantly. Frequently, clients observe the session from an adjacent room using a one-way mirror. Video transmission technology enables the clients to observe focus group sessions live from a remote location. For example, Stamford, Connecticut-based FocusVision Network, Inc. (*www.focusvision.com*) offers such a videoconferencing system.

The moderator plays a key role in the success of a focus group. The moderator must establish rapport with the participants, keep the discussion moving forward, and probe the respondents to elicit insights. In addition, the moderator may have a central role in the analysis and interpretation of the data. Therefore, the moderator should possess skill, experience, knowledge of the discussion topic, and an understanding of the nature of group dynamics. The key qualifications of the moderator are summarized.

### REAL RESEARCH

## Key Qualifications of Focus Group Moderators

1. Kindness with firmness: the moderator must combine a disciplined detachment with understanding empathy in order to generate the necessary interaction.
2. Permissiveness: the moderator must be permissive yet alert to signs that the group's cordiality or purpose is disintegrating.
3. Involvement: the moderator must encourage and stimulate intense personal involvement.

4. Incomplete understanding: the moderator must encourage respondents to be more specific about generalized comments by exhibiting incomplete understanding.
5. Encouragement: the moderator must encourage unresponsive members to participate.
6. Flexibility: the moderator must be able to improvise and alter the planned outline amid the distractions of the group process.
7. Sensitivity: the moderator must be sensitive enough to guide the group discussion at an intellectual as well as emotional level.[13] ■

## Planning and Conducting Focus Groups

The procedure for planning and conducting focus groups is described in Figure 5.3. Planning begins with an examination of the objectives of the marketing research project. In most instances, the problem has been defined by this stage and, if so, the general statement as well as the specific components of the problem should be carefully studied. Given the problem definition, the objectives of the qualitative research should be clearly specified, as illustrated by the department store project.

Note that these objectives are closely tied to the components of the department store problem defined in Chapter 2. The objectives must be specified before conducting any qualitative research, be it focus groups, depth interviews, or projective techniques.

The next step is to develop a detailed list of objectives for the focus group. This may take the form of a list of questions the researcher would like answered. Then a questionnaire to screen potential participants is prepared. Typical information obtained from the questionnaire includes product familiarity and knowledge, usage behavior, attitudes toward and participation in focus groups, and standard demographic characteristics.

A detailed moderator's outline for use during the focus group interview should be constructed. This involves extensive discussions among the researcher, client, and moderator. Because the moderator must be able to pursue important ideas when participants mention them, the moderator must understand the client's business, focus group objectives, and how the findings will be used. Use of a moderator's outline reduces

*Figure 5.3*

Procedure for Planning and Conducting Focus Groups

Determine the objectives of the marketing research project and define the problem.

↓

Specify the objectives of qualitative research.

↓

State the objectives/questions to be answered by focus groups.

↓

Write a screening questionnaire.

↓

Develop a moderator's outline.

↓

Conduct the focus group interviews.

↓

Review tapes and analyze the data.

↓

Summarize the findings and plan follow-up research or action.

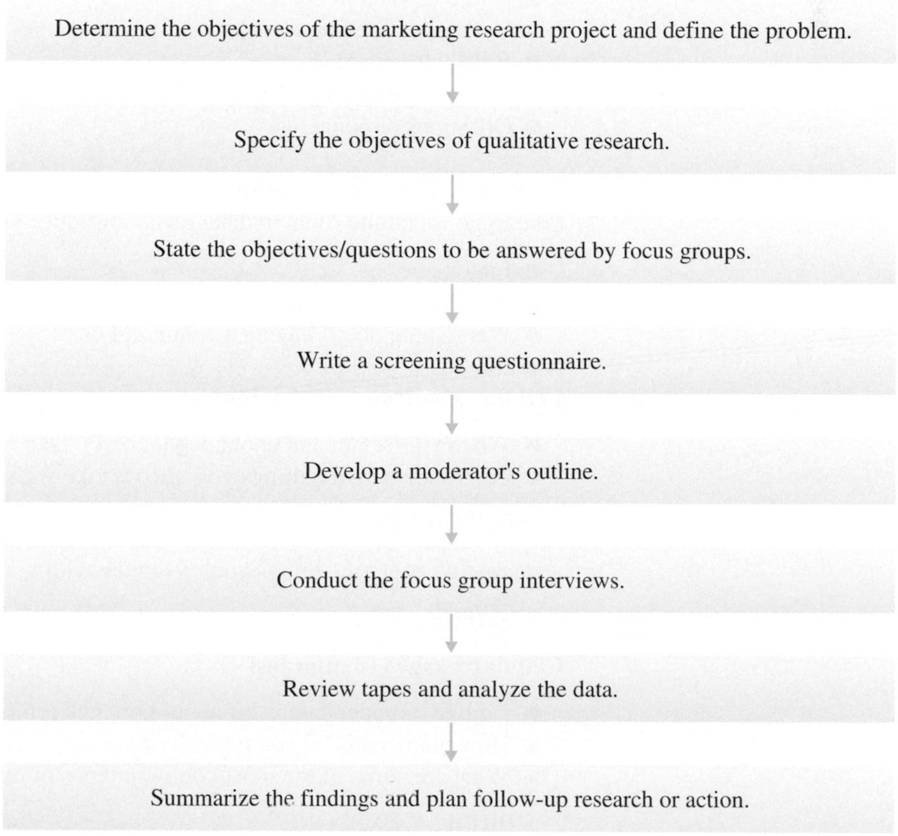

**ACTIVE RESEARCH** | DEPARTMENT STORE PROJECT

*Qualitative Research Objectives*

In the department store study, the objectives of qualitative research were as follows:

1. Identify the relevant factors (choice criteria) used by households in selecting department stores.
2. Identify what consumers consider to be competing stores for specific product categories.
3. Identify the psychological characteristics of consumers that are likely to influence store patronage behavior.
4. Identify any other aspects of consumer choice behavior that may be relevant to store patronage.

some of the reliability problems inherent in focus groups, such as those caused by different moderators not covering the same content areas in comparable ways. Given its importance, we illustrate how a moderator's outline should be constructed using a cellular handset replacement project conducted by the author.[14]

**REAL RESEARCH**

## *Focus Group Discussion Guide for Cellular Handsets*

### Pre-Amble (5 minutes)

- Thanks and welcome
- Nature of a focus group (informal, multiway, expansive, all views, disagree)
- May ask obvious questions—humor me (sometimes *actually* obvious, sometimes not)
- There are no right or wrong answers—all about finding out what people think
- Audio & video recording
- Colleagues viewing
- Help self to refreshments
- Going to be talking about cellular phone handsets
- Questions or concerns?

### Intros & Warm-Up (3 minutes)

Like to go round the room and have you introduce yourselves . . .

- First name
- Best thing about having a cellular phone
- Worst thing about having a cellular phone

### Cellular Environment (5 minutes)

- When you're out and about, what do you take with you?
- Let's start with the things you *always* take with you?

  FLIPCHART

- And what are the things you *often* take with you?

  FLIPCHART

### Cellular Usage (10 minutes)

- I'd like to understand a bit about how you typically use your cellular phone . . .
- How many calls do you typically make or receive in a week?
- What are some of the most common types of outgoing calls you make?

  BRIEFLY EXPLORE

■ What are the most common types of incoming calls you receive?
■ If we were to take away your cellular phone from you, what difference would that make to your life?

BRIEFLY EXPLORE

**Past Handset Purchase (20 minutes)**

■ Thinking now about your current handset, I'd like to talk about two different things . . .
■ First, how you actually went about the process of choosing the handset and, second, any criteria you had for the handset itself . . .

*Past Handset Selection Process*

■ So thinking first only about *how* you went about choosing your handset, *not* any features you wanted, how did you go about choosing one?

EXPLORE PROCESS
*Past Handset Criteria*

■ Ok, so now tell me what you actually looked for in a handset

EXPLORE

**Usage of Handset Features (10 minutes)**

■ Thinking now about handset features, I'd like to start by making a list of all the handset features you can think of—anything the handset can do, any settings you can change, etc.
■ We'll talk in a minute about which features you actually use, but I want to start with a list of everything your handset *could* do

FLIPCHART

■ Which features have you *ever* used, even if only once?

FLIPCHART

■ Are there any settings you only changed once, but are really glad you could change?
■ Why?

EXPLORE

■ And which features do you use regularly?
■ Why?

EXPLORE

**Desired Features (3 minutes)**

■ Are there any features your handset *doesn't* have but you wish that it did?

EXPLORE

**Motivations for Replacement (10 minutes)**

■ You've all been invited here because you've replaced your handset at least once . . .
■ What motivated you to replace your hand set?

EXPLORE

■ Was the hand set replacement tied to your switching or renewing your operator contract, i.e., contract with your wireless service provider?
■ What do you think are some of the reasons that people would replace their handsets?

EXPLORE

**Triggers to Past Upgrade (10 minutes)**

■ You've all been invited here because you've upgraded your handset at least once . . .

- What was it that made you want to upgrade to a better handset?

UNPROMPTED FIRST

- What were *ALL* the factors involved in that decision?
- What was the single *biggest* reason?

EXPLORE

### Barriers to Past Upgrade (5 minutes)

- How long was it from the first time you ever considered upgrading, however briefly, until the time you actually went ahead and bought the new handset?
- What were *all* the reasons you didn't do it immediately?

EXPLORE

- What was the *main* reason for leaving it a while?

EXPLORE

### Triggers & Barriers to Future Upgrade (20 minutes)

- What about the future—when do you think you will next upgrade your handset?

EXPLORE

- What would spur you to do that?
- Is there a killer feature that would have you upgrade immediately?

EXPLORE

- How would you go about choosing your next handset?

EXPLORE

- And what will you actually look for in your next handset?

EXPLORE

### Closing Exercise (10 minutes)

- Finally, I'd like your creativity for a few minutes—to come up with ideas . . .
- Don't worry about whether it's a good idea or a bad idea.
- The only word I'm going to ban is 'free'!
- Supposing a handset manufacturer wanted to encourage you to upgrade tomorrow . . .
- What could they do?
- Just call out anything at all that occurs to you—obvious, profound, serious, silly, whatever . . .

EXPLORE & REFINE

- Thank the respondents and close the session ■

As can be seen, theory (Chapter 2) played an important role in developing the moderator's outline in the department store project. After a detailed outline is formulated, participants are recruited and the focus group interview is conducted. During the interview, the moderator must (1) establish rapport with the group; (2) state the rules of group interaction; (3) set objectives; (4) probe the respondents and provoke intense discussion in the relevant areas; and (5) attempt to summarize the group's response to determine the extent of agreement.

Following the group discussion, either the moderator or an analyst reviews and analyzes the results. The analyst not only reports specific comments and findings but also looks for consistent responses, new ideas, concerns suggested by facial expressions and body language, and other hypotheses that may or may not have received confirmation from all of the participants.

Because the number of participants is small, frequencies and percentages are not usually reported in a focus group summary. Instead, reports typically include expressions like "most participants thought" or "participants were divided on this issue." Meticulous documentation and interpretation of the session lays the groundwork for the final step: taking action. This usually means doing additional research.

The number of focus groups that should be conducted on a single subject depends upon (1) the nature of the issue, (2) the number of distinct market segments, (3) the number of new ideas generated by each successive group, and (4) time and cost. Resources permitting, one should conduct additional discussion groups until the moderator can anticipate what will be said. This usually happens after three or four groups are conducted on the same topic.[15] It is recommended that at least two groups be conducted.[16] Properly conducted focus groups can generate important hypotheses that can serve as a basis for conducting quantitative research, as the following example indicates.

**REAL RESEARCH**

## *Making Kool-Aid Cool!*

Kool-Aid (*www.koolaid.com*) is a well-known product among moms and kids and is used in many households throughout America. Despite this, Kool-Aid sales had begun to decline. Kraft Foods wanted to find out why heavy users had slowed down their consumption of the product and how they could get Kool-Aid back into people's lifestyles.

Kool-Aid conducted focus groups, classifying the groups by product usage ranging from heavy users to light users. They found out a great deal about the different users. The heavy users like to drink Kool-Aid all year round and all family members drink it, not just the children. The heavy users also add more than just water to the mix; they add ingredients such as fruits, fruit juice, and club soda and drink Kool-Aid at home. On the other hand, the light users perceive Kool-Aid as a summer drink for kids. They are also more likely to head out of the house for socializing, and because Kool-Aid is not ready made and portable, they do not use it often. Hence the following hypotheses were formulated:

H1: The heavy users like and drink Kool-Aid all year round.
H2: Among the heavy users, all members of the family drink Kool-Aid.
H3: The heavy users regularly drink Kool-Aid at home.
H4: Among the light users, the kids are the primary users of Kool-Aid.
H5: The light users drink Kool-Aid primarily away from home.

A follow-up quantitative survey using telephone interviews supported these hypotheses. Therefore, Kool-Aid developed and tested different advertising executions for the heavy and light users. The heavy users were targeted with an execution showing people of all ages drinking Kool-Aid together in a home or a backyard. This is where the "How do you like your Kool-Aid" slogan came from, showing family and friends talking about the different ways they drink their Kool-Aid. The light users were targeted with advertising showing children and adults at a community dog wash enjoying summer fun and drinking Kool-Aid out of thermoses. This campaign was very successful in arresting the loss of Kool-Aid sales. As of 2003, beverages at Kraft accounted for approximately 20 percent of their revenue, Kool-Aid included.[17] ■

## Other Variations in Focus Groups

Focus groups can use several variations of the standard procedure. One variation was illustrated in the opening example where a traditional focus group and a picture response technique making use of a collage were combined to encourage the respondents to reveal their underlying beliefs and attitudes about Sunfire. Other variations include:

*Two-way focus group.* This allows one target group to listen to and learn from a related group. In one application, physicians viewed a focus group of arthritis patients discussing the treatment they desired. A focus group of these physicians was then held to determine their reactions.

*Dual-moderator group.* This is a focus group interview conducted by two moderators. One moderator is responsible for the smooth flow of the session, and the other ensures that specific issues are discussed.

*Dueling-moderator group.* Here also there are two moderators, but they deliberately take opposite positions on the issues to be discussed. This allows the researcher to explore both sides of controversial issues.

*Respondent-moderator group.* In this type of focus group, the moderator asks selected participants to play the role of moderator temporarily to improve group dynamics.

*Client-participant groups.* Client personnel are identified and made part of the discussion group. Their primary role is to offer clarifications that will make the group process more effective.

*Minigroups.* These groups consist of a moderator and only four or five respondents. They are used when the issues of interest require more extensive probing than is possible in the standard group of 8 to 12.

*Telesession groups.* These are focus group sessions conducted by phone using the conference call technique.[18]

Online focus groups are emerging as an important form of focus groups and are discussed in detail in the section on Internet and computer applications. We conclude our section on focus groups with a discussion of the various advantages and disadvantages.

## Advantages and Disadvantages of Focus Groups

Focus groups offer several advantages over other data collection techniques. These may be summarized by the 10 Ss:[19]

1. *Synergism:* Putting a group of people together will produce a wider range of information, insight, and ideas than will individual responses secured privately.
2. *Snowballing:* A bandwagon effect often operates in a group interview, in that one person's comment triggers a chain reaction from the other participants.
3. *Stimulation:* Usually after a brief introductory period, the respondents want to express their ideas and expose their feelings as the general level of excitement over the topic increases in the group.
4. *Security:* Because the participants' feelings are similar to those of other group members, they feel comfortable and are therefore willing to express their ideas and feelings.
5. *Spontaneity:* Because participants are not required to answer specific questions, their responses can be spontaneous and unconventional and should therefore provide an accurate idea of their views.
6. *Serendipity:* Ideas are more likely to arise out of the blue in a group than in an individual interview.
7. *Specialization:* Because a number of participants are involved simultaneously, use of a highly trained, but expensive, interviewer is justified.
8. *Scientific scrutiny:* The group interview allows close scrutiny of the data collection process, in that observers can witness the session and it can be recorded for later analysis.
9. *Structure:* The group interview allows for flexibility in the topics covered and the depth with which they are treated.
10. *Speed:* Because a number of individuals are being interviewed at the same time, data collection and analysis proceed relatively quickly.

The disadvantages of focus groups may be summarized by the five Ms:

1. *Misuse:* Focus groups can be misused and abused by considering the results as conclusive rather than exploratory.
2. *Misjudge:* Focus group results can be more easily misjudged than the results of other data-collection techniques. Focus groups are particularly susceptible to client and researcher biases.
3. *Moderation:* Focus groups are difficult to moderate. Moderators with all the desirable skills are rare. The quality of the results depends heavily on the skills of the moderator.
4. *Messy:* The unstructured nature of the responses makes coding, analysis, and interpretation difficult. Focus group data tend to be messy.

5. *Misrepresentation:* Focus group results are not representative of the general population and are not projectable. Consequently, focus group results should not be the sole basis for decision making, as the following example illustrates.

### Projecting the Unprojectable Projects Loss

A sophisticated insurance direct marketer conducted focus groups. The results were translated into clear-cut mail order marketing strategies. However, every single conclusion that grew out of the research flopped. What happened? The insurance company made the mistake of trying to project the unprojectable.[20] ■

This example illustrates a misuse and misrepresentation of focus groups. However, when properly conducted and used, focus groups have numerous applications.

## Applications of Focus Groups

Focus groups are being used extensively for profit, nonprofit, and all types of organizations.[21] They can be used in almost any situation requiring some preliminary understanding and insights, as illustrated in the Pontiac Sunfire, Easy Mac, and Kool-Aid examples. We will discuss some substantive and methodological applications that represent the wide range of use of this technique. Focus groups can be used to address substantive issues such as:

1. Understanding consumers' perceptions, preferences, and behaviors concerning a product category
2. Obtaining impressions of new product concepts
3. Generating new ideas about older products
4. Developing creative concepts and copy material for advertisements
5. Securing price impressions
6. Obtaining preliminary consumer reaction to specific marketing programs

The methodological applications of focus groups include:

1. Defining a problem more precisely
2. Generating alternative courses of action
3. Developing an approach to a problem
4. Obtaining information helpful in structuring consumer questionnaires
5. Generating hypotheses that can be tested quantitatively
6. Interpreting previously obtained quantitative results

# DEPTH INTERVIEWS

**depth interview**
An unstructured, direct, personal interview in which a single respondent is probed by a highly skilled interviewer to uncover underlying motivations, beliefs, attitudes, and feelings on a topic.

*Depth interviews* are another method of obtaining qualitative data. We describe the general procedure for conducting depth interviews and then illustrate some specific techniques. The advantages, disadvantages, and applications of depth interviews are also discussed.

## Characteristics

Like focus groups, depth interviews are an unstructured and direct way of obtaining information, but unlike focus groups, depth interviews are conducted on a one-on-one basis. Therefore, they are also called individual depth interviews or IDIs. A depth interview is an unstructured, direct, personal interview in which a single respondent is probed by a highly skilled interviewer to uncover underlying motivations, beliefs, attitudes, and feelings on a topic.[22]

A depth interview may take from 30 minutes to more than one hour. To illustrate the technique in the context of the department store example, the interviewer begins by asking a general question such as, "How do you feel about shopping at department stores?" The interviewer then encourages the subject to talk freely about their attitudes toward department stores. After asking the initial question, the interviewer uses an unstructured format. The subsequent direction of the interview is determined by the respondent's initial reply, the interviewer's probes for elaboration, and the respondent's answers. Suppose the respondent replies to the initial question by saying, "Shopping isn't fun anymore." The interviewer might then pose a question such as, "Why isn't it fun anymore?" If the answer is not very revealing ("Fun has just disappeared from shopping"), the interviewer may ask a probing question, such as, "Why was it fun before and what has changed?"

The interviewer attempts to follow a rough outline, similar to the moderator's outline for focus groups. The specific wording of the questions and the order in which they are asked is influenced by the subject's replies. Probing is of critical importance in obtaining meaningful responses and uncovering hidden issues. Probing is done by asking such questions as, "Why do you say that?," "That's interesting, can you tell me more?," or "Would you like to add anything else?"[23] Probing is further discussed in Chapter 13 on fieldwork. The value of information uncovered by probing is shown in the following example.

## REAL RESEARCH

### *Probing for Intelligence*

In a study designed to come up with new credit card features, respondents merely listed features of existing credit cards when questioned in a structured way. Then depth interviews were employed to probe the respondents. For example, the interviewer asked respondents to ask themselves, "What is important to me? What problems do I have? How do I wish I could live? What is my ideal world?" As a result of this method, consumers relayed information they had previously been unaware of and several new credit card features surfaced. The study uncovered the need for an "intelligent" credit card that could perform such tasks as keeping track of credit card and bank balances, investments, and emergency telephone numbers. Another concern of credit card users is the bulging wallet and annoyance from carrying too many credit cards. Research results found from such a focus group can help credit card companies offer new features while attracting new customers and satisfying existing customers. For example, in 2002, PrivaSys and First Data teamed up to introduce a battery-powered electronic credit card with an internal chip capable of holding an American Express, MasterCard, gas cards, and other debit cards all on one single piece of plastic that is the same size and shape as one credit card. The new card is expected to be a hit among today's convenience-driven consumers.[24] ■

Depth interviews identified the need for an "intelligent" card.

As this example indicates, probing is effective in uncovering underlying or hidden information. Probing is an integral part of depth interviews and is used in all depth interviewing techniques.

## Techniques

Three depth-interviewing techniques that have recently gained popularity are laddering, hidden issue questioning, and symbolic analysis. In *laddering,* the line of questioning proceeds from product characteristics to user characteristics. This technique allows the researcher to tap into the consumer's network of meanings. Laddering provides a way to probe into consumers' deep underlying psychological and emotional reasons that affect their purchasing decisions. When determining why a person buys a product, researchers want to know more then simply "quality" and "low price." Therefore, to examine the underlying motivators, a laddering technique should be used.

Laddering requires interviewers to be trained in specific probing techniques in order to develop a meaningful "mental map" of the consumer's view toward a target product. The ultimate goal is to combine mental maps of consumers who are similar, which will lead to the reasons why people purchase particular products. Probing is used to go beyond the initial responses interview participants give to a question. When asked why they prefer a product, responses are initially attribute related. Examples of responses would include color, taste, price, size, and product name. Each attribute, consequence, and value of the underlying motivators are found by "climbing the ladder" to the real reasons for purchasing products. Following initial responses with "why" questions leads to much more useful information for the marketer:

Answer: "I buy Maybelline cosmetics because it is a good brand name at a reasonable price."
Question: Why are reasonably priced cosmetics so important to you?
Answer: "Well, buying a quality product that isn't high priced makes me feel good about myself because I am spending my money wisely."

In *hidden issue questioning,* the focus is not on socially shared values but rather on personal "sore spots"; not on general lifestyles but on deeply felt personal concerns. *Symbolic analysis* attempts to analyze the symbolic meaning of objects by comparing them with their opposites. To learn what something is, the researcher attempts to learn what it is not. The logical opposites of a product that are investigated are nonusage of the product, attributes of an imaginary "nonproduct," and opposite types of products. The three techniques are illustrated in the following example.

**REAL RESEARCH**

## *Hidden Issues and Hidden Dimensions in Air Travel*

In this study, the researcher was investigating attitudes toward airlines among male middle-managers.

*Laddering.* Each airline attribute, such as wide-body aircrafts, was probed to determine why it was important (I can get more work done), and then that reason was probed (I accomplish more), and so on (I feel good about myself). Laddering indicated that managers preferred advanced seat reservation, wide-body aircraft, and first-class cabin seating (product characteristics), which resulted in greater physical comfort. This enabled them to get more work done while on the flight, leading to a sense of accomplishment and higher self-esteem (user characteristics). This technique showed that an advertising campaign, like the old United Airlines campaign of "You're The Boss," which bolsters the self-esteem of the managers, is worthy of consideration.

*Hidden issue questioning.* Respondents were questioned about fantasies, work lives, and social lives to identify hidden life issues. The answers indicated that glamorous, historic, elite, "masculine-camaraderie," competitive activities, such as Grand Prix car racing, fencing, and World War II airplane dog fighting, were of personal interest to the managers. These interests could be tapped with an advertising campaign like the one by

---

**laddering**
A technique for conducting depth interviews in which a line of questioning proceeds from product characteristics to user characteristics.

**hidden issue questioning**
A type of depth interview that attempts to locate personal sore spots related to deeply felt personal concerns.

**symbolic analysis**
A technique for conducting depth interviews in which the symbolic meaning of objects is analyzed by comparing them with their opposites.

Lufthansa German Airlines featuring a World War I-type "Red Baron" spokesperson. That campaign communicated the aggressiveness, high status, and competitive heritage of the airline.

*Symbolic analysis.* Questions asked included, "What would it be like if you could no longer use airplanes?" Responses like, "Without planes, I would have to rely on e-mail, letters, and long-distance calls" were received. This suggests that what airlines sell to the managers is face-to-face communication. Thus, an effective ad might be one that guarantees that the airline will do the same thing for a manager as Federal Express does for a package.

Information revealed by these techniques can be used to effectively position an airline and to design appropriate advertising and communication strategies. Advertising efforts following the U.S. terrorist attacks on September 11, 2001, have been very challenging for airline companies. In 2002, however, American Airlines created an advertising campaign that reminds consumers that they need planes to help them get to the people they love. Its television ad showed children wheeling suitcases around New York and showed icons such as the Statue of Liberty.[25] ■

The interviewer's role is critical to the success of the depth interview. The interviewer should (1) avoid appearing superior and put the respondent at ease; (2) be detached and objective, yet personable; (3) ask questions in an informative manner; (4) not accept brief "yes" or "no" answers; and (5) probe the respondent.

## Advantages and Disadvantages of Depth Interviews

Depth interviews can uncover greater depth of insights than focus groups. Also, depth interviews attribute the responses directly to the respondent, unlike focus groups where it is often difficult to determine which respondent made a particular response. Depth interviews result in free exchange of information that may not be possible in focus groups because there is no social pressure to conform to group response.

Depth interviews suffer from many of the disadvantages of focus groups and often to a greater extent. Skilled interviewers capable of conducting depth interviews are expensive and difficult to find. The lack of structure makes the results susceptible to the interviewer's influence, and the quality and completeness of the results depend heavily on the interviewer's skills. The data obtained are difficult to analyze and interpret, and the services of skilled psychologists are typically required for this purpose. The length of the interview combined with the high costs means that the number of depth interviews in a project will be small. Despite these disadvantages, depth interviews do have some applications.

## Applications of Depth Interviews

As with focus groups, the primary use of depth interviews is for exploratory research to gain insights and understanding. However, unlike focus groups, depth interviews are used infrequently in marketing research. Nevertheless, depth interviews can be effectively employed in special problem situations, such as:[26]

1. Detailed probing of the respondent (automobile purchase)
2. Discussion of confidential, sensitive, or embarrassing topics (personal finances, loose dentures)
3. Situations where strong social norms exist and the respondent may be easily swayed by group response (attitude of college students toward sports)
4. Detailed understanding of complicated behavior (department store shopping)
5. Interviews with professional people (industrial marketing research)
6. Interviews with competitors, who are unlikely to reveal the information in a group setting (travel agents' perceptions of airline package travel programs)
7. Situations where the product consumption experience is sensory in nature, affecting mood states and emotions (perfumes, bath soap)

The following example illustrates a case in which depth interviews were particularly helpful.

**REAL RESEARCH**

## *Climbing the Ladder to PlayStation 2 Success*

The laddering technique was used to determine consumer attitudes and purchasing motivations toward the Sony PlayStation 2 (*www.scea.com*). The key laddering insights for this product included:

- My friends come over and we spend an evening working together through a game or playing against each other.
- Challenging games require more critical thinking and decision making. It feels more like a puzzle rather than a game.
- Some games are suited to adults only, so I don't feel like I am playing a "kids' game," but taking part in a high-quality gaming experience.

Marketing implications from this information on the Sony PlayStation 2 include:

- Set up gaming kiosks in nightclubs in large cities such as Los Angeles and New York to attract adults.
- Advertise through sitcoms such as *Friends* with Joey and Chandler playing games on a PlayStation 2.
- Target magazines such as *Wired* and *Sports Illustrated* with more mature ads.

In 2001, Sony shipped more than 25 million PlayStations around the world. With such a high demand for Sony products, the company realizes that it must continue to learn more about consumer behavior patterns. The insights generated from laddering serve as a departure point for further research and hypothesis testing that can help develop new ideas for products, distribution, pricing, or promotion. [27] ■

This example illustrates the value of depth interviews in uncovering the hidden responses that underlie the clichés elicited in ordinary questioning.

# PROJECTIVE TECHNIQUES

**projective technique**
An unstructured and indirect form of questioning that encourages the respondents to project their underlying motivations, beliefs, attitudes, or feelings regarding the issues of concern.

Both focus groups and depth interviews are direct approaches in which the true purpose of the research is disclosed to the respondents or is otherwise obvious to them. Projective techniques are different from these techniques in that they attempt to disguise the purpose of the research. A **projective technique** is an unstructured, indirect form of questioning that encourages respondents to project their underlying motivations, beliefs, attitudes, or feelings regarding the issues of concern.[28] In projective techniques, respondents are asked to interpret the behavior of others rather than describe their own behavior. In interpreting the behavior of others, respondents indirectly project their own motivations, beliefs, attitudes, or feelings into the situation. Thus, the respondent's attitudes are uncovered by analyzing their responses to scenarios that are deliberately unstructured, vague, and ambiguous. The more ambiguous the situation, the more respondents project their emotions, needs, motives, attitudes, and values, as demonstrated by work in clinical psychology on which projective techniques are based.[29] As in psychology, these techniques are classified as association, completion, construction, and expressive. Each of these classifications is discussed.[30]

## Association Techniques

**association techniques**
A type of projective technique in which the respondent is presented with a stimulus and asked to respond with the first thing that comes to mind.

**word association**
A projective technique in which respondents are presented with a list of words, one at a time. After each word, they are asked to give the first word that comes to mind.

In **association techniques,** an individual is presented with a stimulus and asked to respond with the first thing that comes to mind. **Word association** is the best known of these techniques. In word association, respondents are presented with a list of words, one at a time, and asked to respond to each with the first word that comes to mind. The words of interest, called test words, are interspersed throughout the list that also contains some neutral, or filler, words to disguise the purpose of the study. For example, in the department store study, some of the test words might be: "location," "parking," "shopping," "quality," and "price." The subject's response to each word is recorded verbatim and responses are timed so that respondents who hesitate or reason out (defined as taking longer than three seconds to reply) can be identified. The interviewer, not the respondent, records the responses. This controls for the time required for the respondent to write the response.

The underlying assumption of this technique is that association allows respondents to reveal their inner feelings about the topic of interest. Responses are analyzed by calculating: (1) the frequency with which any word is given as a response; (2) the amount of time that elapses before a response is given; and (3) the number of respondents who do not respond at all to a test word within a reasonable period of time. Those who do not respond at all are judged to have an emotional involvement so high that it blocks a response. It is often possible to classify the associations as favorable, unfavorable, or neutral. An individual's pattern of responses and the details of the response are used to determine the person's underlying attitudes or feelings on the topic of interest, as shown in the following example.

### REAL RESEARCH

## *Dealing with Dirt*

Word association was used to study women's attitudes toward detergents. Below is a list of stimulus words used and the responses of two women of similar age and household status. The set of responses are quite different, suggesting that the women differ in personality and in their attitudes toward housekeeping. Mrs. M's associations suggest that she is resigned to dirt. She sees dirt as inevitable and does not want to do much about it. She does not do hard cleaning, nor does she get pleasure from her family. Mrs. C sees dirt too, but is energetic, factual minded, and less emotional. She is actively ready to combat dirt and uses soap and water as her weapons.

| *Stimulus* | *Mrs. M* | *Mrs. C* |
|---|---|---|
| washday | everyday | ironing |
| fresh | and sweet | clean |
| pure | air | soiled |
| scrub | don't; husband does | clean |
| filth | this neighborhood | dirt |
| bubbles | bath | soap and water |
| family | squabbles | children |
| towels | dirty | wash |

These findings suggest that the market for detergents could be segmented on the basis of attitudes. Firms like Procter & Gamble *(www.pg.com)* that market several different brands of detergents (Tide, Cheer, Gain, Bold, etc.) could benefit from positioning different brands for different attitudinal segments. In 2002, P&G was the laundry detergent market leader offering eight different brands and maintaining a 57 percent market share. Gain is P&G's lowest priced brand that is positioned as the low price leader. In 2001, it experienced a 20.9 percent sales increase and consequently beat out Tide's sales for the year. Research findings similar to those above can help P&G position other brands leading to increased sales.[31] ∎

There are several variations to the standard word association procedure illustrated here. Respondents may be asked to give the first two, three, or four words that come to mind rather than only the first word. This technique can also be used in controlled tests, as contrasted with free association. In controlled tests, respondents might be asked "What department stores come to mind first when I mention high-quality merchandise?" More detailed information can be obtained from completion techniques, which are a natural extension of association techniques.

## Completion Techniques

**completion technique**
A projective technique that requires the respondent to complete an incomplete stimulus situation.

In **completion techniques,** the respondent is asked to complete an incomplete stimulus situation. Common completion techniques in marketing research are sentence completion and story completion.

**ACTIVE RESEARCH** | DEPARTMENT STORE PROJECT

### Sentence Completion

In the context of the department store study, the following incomplete sentences may be used.

A person who shops at Sears is _____.

A person who receives a gift certificate redeemable at Sak's Fifth Avenue would be _____

_____.

JC Penney is most liked by _____.

When I think of shopping in a department store, I _____.

---

**sentence completion**

A projective technique in which respondents are presented with a number of incomplete sentences and asked to complete them.

### Sentence Completion. *Sentence completion* is similar to word association. Respondents are given incomplete sentences and asked to complete them. Generally, they are asked to use the first word or phrase that comes to mind, as illustrated in the department store project.

This example illustrates one advantage of sentence completion over word association: respondents can be provided with a more directed stimulus. Sentence completion may provide more information about the subjects' feelings than word association. However, sentence completion is not as disguised, and many respondents may be able to guess the purpose of the study. A variation of sentence completion is paragraph completion, in which the respondent completes a paragraph beginning with the stimulus phrase. A further expanded version of sentence completion and paragraph completion is story completion.

**story completion**

A projective technique in which the respondents are provided with part of a story and required to give the conclusion in their own words.

### Story Completion. In *story completion,* respondents are given part of a story— enough to direct attention to a particular topic but not to hint at the ending. They are required to give the conclusion in their own words. The respondents' completion of this story will reveal their underlying feeling and emotions, as in the following example.

### REAL RESEARCH

## Pantyhose Have Horror Stories?

Stories? Horror stories? That is one thing that DuPont (*www.dupont.com*), a manufacturer of pantyhose material, overlooked when doing their research to find out what customers like. DuPont conducted the same research that all other companies conduct, including focus groups and surveys. Unfortunately, that was not enough.

The problem with focus groups was the respondents' unwillingness to respond. Some felt ashamed or just were not interested in the subject. In other cases, customers had feelings and opinions they just were not comfortable discussing face-to-face. Then story completion was used.

Respondents were asked to bring in pictures and tell stories describing certain feelings, opinions, and reactions to wearing pantyhose. Surprisingly, many women showed up and had a lot to say. Women were freer in expressing their ideas. One woman brought in a picture of a spilled ice-cream sundae, capturing the rage she feels when she spots a run in her hose. Others brought in a picture of a Mercedes and Queen Elizabeth.

The analysis indicated that women felt more attractive and sexy to men when wearing pantyhose. The problem was not necessarily that women do not like to wear pantyhose, but more so that they have a feeling associated with wearing pantyhose, and when it gets a run, tear, or other defect in it, women lose the associated feeling they have (such as attractive, sexy, sensual). Pantyhose needed to be more durable and long lasting, so it can survive the "wear and tear" that may occur when women wear them all day.

Thus, DuPont was able to see what consumers' true feelings were about its products. When these findings were confirmed in a telephone survey, DuPont modified its pantyhose material to fit the consumers' needs. Furthermore, stocking manufacturers have begun to use these findings, tailoring ads to appeal less to women's executive personas and more towards their sexy, cocktail-dress side.

Story completion revealed that women felt more attractive and sexy to men when wearing pantyhose.

As of 2003, DuPont remains the world's largest maker of pantyhose material, and its marketing research efforts have proven successful with 2002 revenues exceeding $25 billion, thanks to its intensive use of qualitative research.[32] ■

## Construction Techniques

**construction technique**
A projective technique in which the respondent is required to construct a response in the form of a story, dialogue, or description.

*Construction techniques* are closely related to completion techniques. Construction techniques require the respondent to construct a response in the form of a story, dialogue, or description. In a construction technique, the researcher provides less initial structure to the respondent than in a completion technique. The two main construction techniques are (1) picture response and (2) cartoons.

**picture response technique**
A projective technique in which the respondent is shown a picture and asked to tell a story describing it.

### *Picture Response.*
The roots of *picture response techniques* can be traced to the Thematic Apperception Test (TAT) that consists of a series of pictures of ordinary as well as unusual events. In some of these pictures, the persons or objects are clearly depicted, whereas in others they are relatively vague. The respondent is asked to tell stories about these pictures. The respondent's interpretation of the pictures gives indications of that individual's personality. For example, an individual may be characterized as impulsive, creative, unimaginative, and so on. The term Thematic Apperception Test is used because themes are elicited based on the subject's perceptual interpretation (apperception) of pictures.

In marketing research uses of picture response techniques, respondents are shown a picture and asked to tell a story describing it. The responses are used to evaluate attitudes toward the topic and describe the respondents, as illustrated by the following.

### REAL RESEARCH

#### *"Gimme a Double Shake and a Lard on White"*

The light-and-healthy craze seems to be dying down for one segment of the population. In response to direct questioning, consumers are hesitant to say they want food that is bad for them. However, this finding emerged in a picture response test in which the respondents were asked to describe a picture depicting people consuming high-fat food rich in calories. A significant number of the respondents defended the behavior of the people in the picture, explaining that the increased stress in everyday life has caused people to turn from tasteless rice cakes to comfort foods, loaded with the ingredients that make life worth living.

Many marketers have capitalized upon this finding by introducing products that contain large amounts of fat and calories. Pepperidge Farm recently introduced its own bid for the comfort food market, no-calories-barred soft-baked cookies with about 40 percent

The picture response technique revealed that many people view high-fat food rich in calories as comfort food meant to counteract the stress of everyday life.

of the calories coming from fat. The new line is already the third biggest seller for the company.

In 2002, McDonald's rolled out several new products that were extremely high in fat and calories for the New Tastes Menu. Such new products included the fried Chicken Parmesan sandwich smothered with cheese and tomato sauce and a portable breakfast sandwich that had a sausage patty surrounded by two pancakes.[33] ■

**cartoon tests**

Cartoon characters are shown in a specific situation related to the problem. The respondents are asked to indicate the dialogue that one cartoon character might make in response to the comment(s) of another character.

*Cartoon Tests.*   In *cartoon tests,* cartoon characters are shown in a specific situation related to the problem. The respondents are asked to indicate what one cartoon character might say in response to the comments of another character. The responses indicate the respondents' feelings, beliefs, and attitudes toward the situation. Cartoon tests are simpler to administer and analyze than picture response techniques. An example is shown in Figure 5.4.

## Expressive Techniques

**expressive techniques**

Projective techniques in which the respondent is presented with a verbal or visual situation and asked to relate the feelings and attitudes of other people to the situation.

In *expressive techniques,* respondents are presented with a verbal or visual situation and asked to relate the feelings and attitudes of other people to the situation. The respondents express not their own feelings or attitudes, but those of others. The two main expressive techniques are role playing and third-person technique.

Figure 5.4
A Cartoon Test

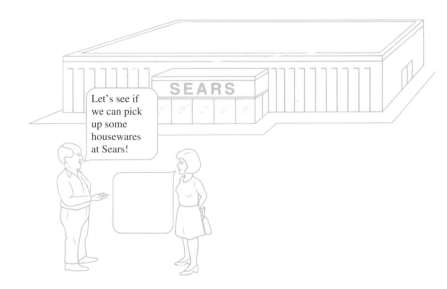

**role playing**
Respondents are asked to assume the behavior of someone else.

*Role Playing.*   In *role playing,* respondents are asked to play the role or assume the behavior of someone else. The researcher assumes that the respondents will project their own feelings into the role. These can then be uncovered by analyzing the responses.[34]

## REAL RESEARCH

### What Is Privacy?

When focus groups revealed that privacy was a major concern of apartment residents, an apartment builder became concerned with how people view privacy. The research company, Cossette Communication Group (*www.cossette.com*), used the role playing technique to gain the required information. Respondents were asked to play the role of an architect and design their own apartment homes using the boards provided. After the homes were designed, a series of research questions were asked. These questions addressed how the participants perceived privacy. For example, the respondents were asked how much space was needed between rooms to make them feel like their privacy would not be invaded, and how much sound should be audible through walls. The marketing research company felt that it would be more effective to have subjects become involved in a role-playing activity followed by questions on why they did what they did, rather than simply asking subjects what they would do in a certain situation. "We had people show us what privacy meant to them, rather than assuming they could explain it to us in words." The results helped the building company in designing and building apartments so that occupants would be more comfortable and feel more private. Walls between bedrooms were made to be more absorbent of sounds so that voices would not carry as easily. Additionally, bedrooms were set further apart instead of directly adjacent to each other. Apartments were built so that bedrooms were on opposite sides of the building. This way, roommates would not feel that their privacy was being compromised. The construction company benefited greatly from these creative methods of research, as demonstrated by the increased customer satisfaction that resulted from individuals feeling more confident about maintaining their privacy.[35] ∎

**third-person technique**
A projective technique in which the respondent is presented with a verbal or visual situation and asked to relate the beliefs and attitudes of a third person to the situation.

*Third-Person Technique.*   In *third-person technique,* the respondent is presented with a verbal or visual situation and asked to relate the beliefs and attitudes of a third person rather than directly expressing personal beliefs and attitudes. This third person may be a friend, neighbor, colleague, or a "typical" person. Again, the researcher assumes that the respondent will reveal personal beliefs and attitudes while describing the reactions of a third party. Asking the individual to respond in the third person reduces the social pressure to give an acceptable answer, as the following example shows.

## REAL RESEARCH

### What Will the Neighbors Say?

A study was performed for a commercial airline to understand why some people do not fly. When the respondents were asked, "Are you afraid to fly?," very few people said yes. The major reasons given for not flying were cost, inconvenience, and delays caused by bad weather. However, it was suspected that the answers were heavily influenced by the need to give socially desirable responses. Therefore, a follow-up study was done. In the second study, the respondents were asked, "Do you think your neighbor is afraid to fly?" The answers indicated that most of the neighbors who traveled by some other means of transportation were afraid to fly.

The fear of flying increased after the highjackings of September 11, 2001. As of January 2002, the Air Transport Association (ATA) reported that passenger enplanements, the number of ticketed passengers that board the airplane, on average were down 14.2 percent in December 2001 compared to December 2000. Also, the number of enplanements declined 14.7 percent domestically and 9.9 percent internationally. However, Continental Airlines, addressing the fear of flying by stressing heightened security measures and enhanced cabin comforts for passengers, suffered a much lower drop in passenger enplanements.[36] ■

Note that asking the question in the first person ("Are you afraid to fly?") did not elicit the true response. Phrasing the same question in the third person ("Do you think your neighbor is afraid to fly?") lowered the respondent's defenses and resulted in truthful answers. In a popular version of the third-person technique, the researcher presents the respondent with a description of a shopping list and asks for a characterization of the purchaser.[37]

## Advantages and Disadvantages of Projective Techniques

Projective techniques have a major advantage over the unstructured direct techniques (focus groups and depth interviews): they may elicit responses that subjects would be unwilling or unable to give if they knew the purpose of the study. At times, in direct questioning, the respondent may intentionally or unintentionally misunderstand, misinterpret, or mislead the researcher. In these cases, projective techniques can increase the validity of responses by disguising the purpose. This is particularly true when the issues to be addressed are personal, sensitive, or subject to strong social norms. Projective techniques are also helpful when underlying motivations, beliefs, and attitudes are operating at a subconscious level.[38]

Projective techniques suffer from many of the disadvantages of unstructured direct techniques, but to a greater extent. These techniques generally require personal interviews with highly trained interviewers. Skilled interpreters are also required to analyze the responses. Hence, they tend to be expensive. Furthermore, there is a serious risk of interpretation bias. With the exception of word association, all techniques are open ended, making the analysis and interpretation difficult and subjective.

Some projective techniques, such as role playing, require respondents to engage in unusual behavior. In such cases, the researcher may assume that respondents who agree to participate are themselves unusual in some way. Therefore, they may not be representative of the population of interest. As a result, it is desirable to compare findings generated by projective techniques with the findings of the other techniques that permit a more representative sample. Table 5.3 gives a relative comparison of focus groups, depth interviews, and projective techniques.

## Applications of Projective Techniques

Projective techniques are used less frequently than unstructured direct methods (focus groups and depth interviews). A possible exception may be word association, which is

## TABLE 5.3

### A Comparison of Focus Groups, Depth Interviews, and Projective Techniques

| CRITERIA | FOCUS GROUPS | DEPTH INTERVIEWS | PROJECTIVE TECHNIQUES |
|---|---|---|---|
| Degree of structure | Relatively high | Relatively medium | Relatively low |
| Probing of individual respondents | Low | High | Medium |
| Moderator bias | Relatively medium | Relatively high | Low to high |
| Interpretation bias | Relatively low | Relatively medium | Relatively high |
| Uncovering subconscious information | Low | Medium to high | High |
| Discovering innovative information | High | Medium | Low |
| Obtaining sensitive information | Low | Medium | High |
| Involve unusual behavior/questioning | No | To a limited extent | Yes |
| Overall usefulness | Highly useful | Useful | Somewhat useful |

used commonly to test brand names and occasionally to measure attitudes about particular products, brands, packages, or advertisements. As the examples have shown, projective techniques can be used in a variety of situations. The usefulness of these techniques is enhanced when the following guidelines are observed.

1. Projective techniques should be used because the required information cannot be accurately obtained by direct methods.
2. Projective techniques should be used for exploratory research to gain initial insights and understanding.
3. Given their complexity, projective techniques should not be used naively.

Given these guidelines, projective techniques, along with other qualitative techniques, can yield valuable information.

# INTERNATIONAL MARKETING RESEARCH

Because the researcher is often not familiar with the foreign product market to be examined, qualitative research is crucial in international marketing research. In the initial stages of cross-national research, qualitative research can provide insights into the problem and help in developing an approach by generating relevant research questions and hypotheses, models, and characteristics that influence the research design. Thus, qualitative research may reveal the differences between the foreign and domestic markets. Focus groups can be used in many settings, particularly in industrialized countries. The moderator should not only be trained in focus group methodology but should also be familiar with the language, culture, and patterns of social interaction prevailing in that country. The focus group findings should be derived not only from the verbal contents but also from nonverbal cues such as voice intonations, inflections, expressions, and gestures.[39]

The size of the focus group could also vary. For example, in Asia, seven respondents produce the highest level of interaction among group members. In some regions, such as in the Middle or Far East, people are hesitant to discuss their feelings in a group setting. In other countries such as Japan, people think it is impolite to disagree with others publicly. In these cases, depth interviews should be used. Moreover, qualitative data that are generated should be interpreted in the context of the culture. The following example highlights the importance of cultural differences in qualitative research.

**REAL RESEARCH**

## *Bugs Bug British*

Culture is a very important determinant of how qualitative research, such as focus groups, should be conducted. In focus group discussions in Britain, it is not easy to make a housewife admit she has cockroaches. To do this, the moderator must reassure her that everyone else has the problem too. In France, just the opposite occurs: the respondents start to chatter away about cockroaches within seconds of sitting down. These cultural attitudes greatly influence which qualitative research techniques should be used, how they should be implemented, and how the data should be interpreted.[40] ■

The use of projective techniques in international marketing research should be carefully considered. Association techniques (word association), completion techniques (sentence completion, story completion), and expressive techniques (role playing, third-person technique) involve the use of verbal cues. Construction techniques (picture response and cartoon tests) employ nonverbal stimuli (pictures). Whether verbal or nonverbal stimuli are used, the equivalence of meaning across the cultures should be established. This can be a difficult task if the sociocultural environments in which the research is conducted vary greatly. Establishing the equivalence of pictures can be particularly problematic. Line drawings are subject to fewer problems of interpretation than photographs. However, techniques employing verbal cues, such as word association, can be applied with greater ease, as illustrated in the following example.

---

**REAL RESEARCH**

## *Whirlpool Whirls Qualitative Research Around the World*

Whirlpool (*www.whirlpool.com*) has become a giant in the appliance industry, currently doing business in every corner of the world including the United States, Canada, and expanding markets in Asia, Europe, and Latin America. Whirlpool produces products under 12 brand names in over 140 countries. In 2001, Whirlpool recorded revenues of $10.3 billion.

How does Whirlpool intend to prosper in these very diverse markets? Whirlpool has heavily invested in cross-cultural market research. Through the expertise of local staff members, qualitative research in the form of focus groups, depth interviews, and various forms of projective techniques is undertaken around the world. The selection of a particular qualitative research technique in a country is strongly influenced by cultural considerations. For example, in Japan, depth interviews are favored over focus groups, given the reluctance of the Japanese to openly disagree in public. In refrigerator research in Europe, Whirlpool found that British consumers want strong construction, French consumers want fresh fruit and vegetables, and the Spanish want fresh meat. For ovens, the research revealed that Italians want childproof features and the Spanish favor accurate timers. Overall, Germans were the only group concerned about environmental features. The Japanese prefer low-agitation washing machines. In Latin America, gas ranges are favored because of high electric prices. Whirlpool strives to understand cultural factors so that they can take advantage of growing markets. For example, Latin America's economy is expected to grow at over five percent annually in the next decade. Whirlpool is well educated on different consumers from their global qualitative research and well equipped to compete in a global market.

In 2002, Whirlpool unveiled several new products at the International Builders Show that are geared toward an international market. New products included Internet-enabled appliances that allow family communication, cooking, shopping, and washing assistance via a Web Tablet. The Web Tablet serves as a central control station matched with the refrigerator, oven, dishwasher, and dryer. Countries such as Japan and the United States, where Internet access and usage is prevalent, will be target markets for these new products.[41] ■

---

The usual limitations of qualitative techniques also apply in the international context, perhaps to a greater extent. It is often difficult to find trained moderators and interviewers overseas. The development of appropriate coding, analysis, and interpretation procedures poses additional difficulties.

# ETHICS IN MARKETING RESEARCH

When conducting qualitative research, ethical issues related to the respondents and the general public are of primary concern. These issues include disguising the purpose of the research and the use of deceptive procedures, videotaping and recording the proceedings, comfort level of the respondents, and misusing the findings of qualitative research.[42]

All indirect procedures require disguising the purpose of the research, at least to some extent. Often, a cover story is used to camouflage the true purpose. This can not only violate the respondents right to know but also result in psychological harm. For example, respondents may be upset if, after responding to a series of completion techniques, they discovered that they had spent their time on a trivial issue such as what should be the color of the can of a new orange drink, when they had been recruited to participate in a study on nutrition. To minimize such negative effects, the respondents should be informed up front that the true purpose of the research is being disguised so as not to bias the responses. After completing the research tasks, debriefing sessions should be held in which the respondents are informed about the true purpose and given opportunities to make comments or ask questions. Deceptive procedures that violate respondents' right to privacy and informed consent should be avoided, for example, allowing clients to observe focus groups or in-depth interviews by introducing them as colleagues helping with the project.

An ethical dilemma involves videotaping or recording the focus group or the depth interview. Videotaping or audiotaping the respondents without their prior knowledge or consent raises ethical concerns. Ethical guidelines suggest that respondents should be informed and their consent obtained prior to the start of the proceedings, preferably at the time of recruitment. Furthermore, at the end of the meeting, participants should be asked to sign a written statement conveying their permission to use the recording. This statement should disclose the true purpose of the research and all people who will have access to the recording. Participants should be given an opportunity to refuse signing. The tapes should be edited to completely omit the identity and comments of the respondents who have refused.

Another concern that needs to be addressed is the comfort level of the respondents. During qualitative research, particularly during depth interviews, respondents should not be pushed beyond a point so as to make them uncomfortable. Respect for the respondent's welfare should warrant restraint on the part of the moderator or interviewer. If a respondent feels uncomfortable and does not wish to answer more questions on a particular topic, the interviewer should not aggressively probe further. A final issue relates to the general public and deals with the ethics of using qualitative research results for questionable purposes, as in the political campaigns profiled below.

### REAL RESEARCH

## *Focusing on Mudslinging in Presidential Campaigns*

The ethics of negative or "attack" ads has been under debate for some time. However, the focus has shifted from the ads themselves to the ethics of employing marketing research techniques to design the ad message. Nowhere, perhaps, is this phenomenon more prevalent than in political "mudslinging" in presidential campaigns. In particular, the Bush campaign against Dukakis in the 1988 presidential election has been cited. In designing negative ads about Dukakis, the Bush campaign leaders tested negative information about Dukakis in focus groups. The idea was to develop some insight into how the American public would react if this negative information were released in the form of advertisements. Negative issues that elicited very negative emotions from the focus groups were chosen to be incorporated into Bush's political advertising. The result? Painted ". . . as an ineffectual, weak, liberal, do-gooder lacking in common sense. . . ," Dukakis lost the election by a wide margin. Similar (mis)use of qualitative research was observed in the 1992 and 1996 presidential elections that Bill Clinton won in part by negatively attacking the Republicans. In the 2000 presidential election, Gore unfairly attacked Bush as lacking in experience when focus groups revealed that experience was an important criterion for voters.[43] ∎

# INTERNET AND COMPUTER APPLICATIONS

The use of forums, newsgroups, and chat rooms to conduct exploratory research was discussed in Chapter 3. Here we discuss the use of the Internet for conducting focus groups, depth interviews, and projective techniques.[44]

## The Internet and Focus Group Interviews

Online focus group participation is by invitation only. The respondents are prerecruited, generally from an online list of people who have expressed an interest in participating. A screening questionnaire is administered online to qualify the respondents. Those who qualify are invited to participate in a focus group; they receive a time, a URL, a room name, and a password via e-mail. Generally, four to six people participate in the online group. There are fewer people in an online focus group than in a face-to-face meeting because too many voices can confuse the discussion.

Before the focus group begins, participants receive information about the focus group that covers such things as how to express emotions when typing. Electronic emotion indicators are produced using keyboard characters and are standard in their use on the Internet. For example, :-) and :-( are examples of smiling and sad faces. The emotions are usually inserted in the text at the point in which the emotion is meant. Emotions can also be expressed using a different font or color. There is a wide range of emotions to choose such as: I'm frowning, I'm laughing to myself, I'm embarrassed, I'm mad now, I'm responding passionately now, etc. This is then followed by the response. The participants can also preview information about the focus group topic by visiting a Web site and reading information or downloading and viewing an actual TV ad on their PCs. Then, just before the focus group begins, participants visit a Web site where they log on and get some last-minute instructions.

When it is time for the group to begin, they move into a Web-based chat room. They go to the focus group location (URL) and click on the "Enter Focus Room" icon. To enter, they must supply the room name, user name, and password that was e-mailed to them earlier. In the chatroom, the moderator and the participants type to each other in real time. The general practice is for the moderators to always pose their questions in all capital letters and the respondents are asked to use upper and lower case. The respondents are also asked to always start their response with the question number, so the moderator can quickly tie the response to the proper question. This makes it fast and easy to transcribe a focus group session. The group interaction lasts for about an hour. A raw transcript is available as soon as the group is completed, and a formatted transcript is available within 48 hours. The whole process is much faster than the traditional method. An example of companies that provide online focus groups is Surveysite (*www.surveysite.com*).

## Advantages

People from all over the country or even the world can participate, and the client can observe the group from the convenience of the home or office. Geographical constraints are removed and time constraints are lessened. Unlike traditional focus groups, you have the unique opportunity to recontact group participants at a later date, to either revisit issues, or introduce them to modifications in material presented in the original focus group. The Internet enables the researcher to reach segments that are usually hard to survey: doctors, lawyers, professional people, working mothers, and others who lead busy lives and are not interested in taking part in traditional focus groups.

Moderators may also be able to carry on side conversations with individual respondents, probing deeper into interesting areas. People are generally less inhibited in their responses and are more likely to fully express their thoughts. A lot of online focus groups go well past their allotted time because so many responses are expressed. Finally, as there is no travel, videotaping, or facilities to arrange, the cost is much lower than traditional focus groups. Firms are able to keep costs between one-fifth and one-half the cost of traditional focus groups.

## Disadvantages

Only people that have and know how to use a computer can be surveyed online. Because the name of an individual on the Internet is often private, actually verifying that a respondent is a member of a target group is difficult. This is illustrated in a cartoon in *The New Yorker,* where two dogs are seated at a computer and one says to the other, "On the Internet, nobody knows you are a dog!" To overcome this limitation, other traditional methods such as telephone calls, are used for recruitment and verification of respondents.

Another factor that must be considered is the lack of general control over the respondent's environment and their potential exposure to distracting external stimuli. Because online focus groups could potentially have respondents scattered all over the world, the researchers and moderator(s) have no idea what else the respondents may be doing while participating in the group. Only audio and visual stimuli can be tested. Products cannot be touched (e.g., clothing) or smelled (e.g., perfumes).

## Uses

There are instances in which traditional focus groups will continue to be preferred. For instance, you really cannot explore highly emotional issues or subject matters online. Because the reach for online focus groups is currently limited to people with Internet access, online focus groups are not appropriate for every research situation. However, they are very suitable for companies who use the Internet to sell products or services and want to either gain market share or gather intelligence. Applications include banner ads, copy testing, concept testing, usability testing, multimedia evaluation, and comparisons of icons or graphic images. Another potential use for online focus groups or surveys is for corporations who want to gather feedback on workplace issues such as downsizing, job changes, and diversity. Employees can be referred to a Web site where they can participate anonymously in discussions with management. Companies such as Fulcrum Analytics (*www.fulcrumanalytics.com*) specialize in online focus groups, e-mail surveys, and Web surveys.

---

**REAL RESEARCH**

### *Enhancing the Utility of Sports Utility Vehicles*

One industry that has taken advantage of online focus groups is the automobile industry, specifically Nissan North America. While designing the Xterra sports utility vehicle (SUV), Nissan conducted several online focus groups to get feedback on designs, as well as find out what their target market wanted to see in an SUV. The market, consisting of young, active, athletic people, was eager to participate. They wanted an SUV that could carry sporting and camping equipment inside the vehicle or on racks, but they wanted it to be offered at a reasonable price. The focus groups discussed topics such as the features they were looking for, such as racks on the top and the back of the SUV, four doors, a sporty design, trendy colors, and lots of room inside the vehicle. Nissan delivered in all of these areas and has been successful. The 2001 Xterra being named the top SUV for 2001 by AAA demonstrates the company's success.

Online focus groups revealed that many automobile buyers wanted custom-built vehicles. Therefore, in 2002 Nissan became the first major automaker to announce Web-enabled, build-to-order manufacturing. Although other major automakers such as Ford and GM offer Web vehicle services, Nissan claims that its Web engine configuration will be similar to Dell's custom manufacturing Web engine. In 2003, Nissan plans to roll out its customization technology that will be initially limited to the Altima, Frontier, and Xterra models that are made in Nissan's Tennessee plant in North America.[45] ∎

---

In a similar manner, depth interviews can also be conducted over the Internet, with the interviewer and the respondent being at separate locations. Virtually all of the projective techniques that we have discussed can be implemented over the Internet. Picture response techniques are being effectively used by various companies and market researchers, e.g., Coca-Cola can provide a picture and ask the respondents to write a story about it. The demographic data of the person coupled with the story can provide valuable insights into the psychographics and the consumption pattern of the respondent.

Microcomputers and mainframes can be used to select and screen respondents in qualitative research. A computerized system can maintain and manage respondent files, storing information on a large number of demographic and other characteristics for each respondent. Thus, respondents who meet stated criteria can be easily and quickly identified, and recruiting forms, confirmation letters, and sign-in sheets can be automatically generated. A problem common to all qualitative research techniques is the coding and analysis of responses to open-ended questions. Microcomputers and mainframes are increasingly being utilized for this purpose. With the artificial intelligence program such as CATPAC from The Galileo Company (*www.thegalileocompany.com*), the difficulties of qualitative data analysis can be reduced dramatically.

## FOCUS ON BURKE

The dominant use of qualitative research conducted by Burke worldwide is through focus groups. In using focus groups, two very practical issues have to be addressed. The first results from the question most clients ask: "How many groups should we do and where should they be?" The second is of prime importance to the researcher but almost never voiced by the client: "How can the client be a contributing participant to focus-group-based research?"

*Number and Location*

For most groups, the question of number and location is really one of definition of the populations of interest. Are there different market segments that should be explored in different groups? Should those who are likely "very knowledgeable" be separated from the "less knowledgeable" to avoid dominance? Should groups be conducted in different regions where the level of market development is different? These decisions can be made only with secondary research or internal data to help support a position. The only clear rule of thumb is that if Burke decides on a particular composition of groups by character or location, at least two focus groups are done for each composition. The reasoning behind this is that each of these groups has its own dynamic and a second, confirmatory group will help assure that conclusions are not drawn prematurely from one group's composition and group dynamic.

One of the largest casual-dining restaurant chains in the United States wanted to determine what types of desserts are "irresistible" to customers. The company hoped to boost sales by fine-tuning its dessert menu. Burke conducted a series of 10 focus groups split among four constituencies or segments:

1. People who usually order dessert when eating at a casual-dining restaurant
2. The company's own customers who usually order dessert
3. The company's own customers who rarely order dessert
4. The company's servers

Participants discussed what types of desserts they like, how many desserts should be offered on a restaurant menu, and how desserts should be "presented" by servers to entice people to order one. In each group the Burke moderator read descriptions of more than 25 different desserts and showed photos of more than 50 desserts. The moderator asked participants to evaluate the overall appeal of each dessert. Burke used this exercise to identify irresistible desserts that appealed to a broad range of customers. The restaurant chain used this qualitative information and subsequent quantitative research to improve its dessert menu.

*The Client as a Contributor to the Process*

Burke takes great pains in training its clients properly in the evaluation of focus groups. When a group of managers sits behind a one-way glass observing a focus group, they have to be coached in what to do and what not to do. The first thing they are told to avoid is counting responses and thinking in terms of quantitative results. The issue is not how many people say something, but whether general agreement among the group seems apparent or if there are divergent opinions.

Burke coaches client observers to listen to all opinions and not just to those that support a preconceived position. If the researcher does not manage the observation process correctly, the observing managers will often walk away from the session having already drawn their own conclusions and not fully understanding what actually happened. The final report will typically be ignored under these circumstances. Moreover, Burke focuses on managing the total communication process, not just the groups.

# SUMMARY

Qualitative and quantitative research should be viewed as complementary. Qualitative research methods may be direct or indirect. In direct methods, respondents are able to discern the true purpose of the research, whereas indirect methods disguise the purpose of the research. The major direct methods are focus groups and depth interviews. Focus groups are conducted in a group setting, whereas depth interviews are done one on one. Focus group interviews are the most widely used qualitative research technique.

The indirect techniques are called projective techniques as they aim to project the respondent's motivations, beliefs, attitudes, and feelings onto ambiguous situations. The projective techniques may be classified as association (word association), completion (sentence completion, paragraph completion, story completion), construction (picture response, cartoon tests), and expressive (role playing, third-person) techniques. Projective techniques are particularly useful when respondents are unwilling or unable to provide the required information by direct methods.

Qualitative research can reveal the salient differences between the domestic and foreign markets. Whether focus groups or depth interviews should be conducted and how the findings should be interpreted depends heavily on the cultural differences. When conducting qualitative research, the researcher and the client must respect the respondents. This should include protecting the anonymity of respondents, honoring all statements and promises used to ensure participation, and conducting research in a way not to embarrass or harm the respondents. Focus groups, depth interviews, and projective techniques can also be conducted via the Internet. Microcomputers and mainframes can be used to select and screen respondents, and in coding and analyzing qualitative data.

# KEY TERMS AND CONCEPTS

qualitative research, *137*
quantitative research, *137*
direct approach, *138*
indirect approach, *139*
focus group, *139*
depth interview, *147*
laddering, *149*

hidden issue questioning, *149*
symbolic analysis, *149*
projective technique, *151*
association techniques, *151*
word association, *151*
completion techniques, *152*
sentence completion, *153*

story completion, *153*
construction technique, *154*
picture response technique, *154*
cartoon tests, *155*
expressive techniques, *155*
role playing, *156*
third-person technique, *156*

# EXERCISES

## Questions

1. What are the primary differences between qualitative and quantitative research techniques?
2. What is qualitative research and how is it conducted?
3. Differentiate between direct and indirect qualitative research. Give an example of each.
4. Why is the focus group the most popular qualitative research technique?
5. Why is the focus group moderator so important in obtaining quality results?
6. What are some key qualifications of focus group moderators?
7. Why should one safeguard against professional respondents?
8. Give two ways in which focus groups can be misused.
9. What is the difference between a dual-moderator and a dueling-moderator group?
10. What is the conference call technique? What are the advantages and disadvantages of this technique?
11. What is a depth interview? Under what circumstances is it preferable to focus groups?
12. What are the major advantages of depth interviews?
13. What are projective techniques? What are the four types of projective techniques?

14. Describe the term association technique. Give an example of a situation in which this technique is especially useful.
15. When should projective techniques be employed?

## Problems

1. Following the methods outlined in the text, develop a plan for conducting a focus group to determine consumers' attitudes toward, and preferences for, imported automobiles. Specify the objectives of the focus group, write a screening questionnaire, and develop a moderator's outline.
2. Suppose Baskin Robbins wants to know why some people do not eat ice cream regularly. Develop a cartoon test for this purpose.

## Internet and Computer Exercises

1. The Coca-Cola Company has asked you to conduct Internet focus groups with heavy users of soft drinks. Explain how you would identify and recruit such respondents.
2. Could a depth interview be conducted via the Internet? What are the advantages and disadvantages of this procedure over conventional depth interviews?

3. Visit the Web site of Qualitative Research Consultants Association (*www.qrca.org*). Write a report about the current state of the art in qualitative research.

4. *Tennis* magazine would like to recruit participants for online focus groups. How would you make use of a newsgroup (Usenet: *rec.sport.tennis*) to recruit participants?

5. Obtain the CATPAC program discussed in the text. Use it to analyze the data from a depth interview that you have conducted with a fellow student (as the respondent) to determine attitudes toward sports.

# ACTIVITIES

## Role Playing

1. You are a marketing research consultant hired to organize focus groups for an innovative German-style fast-food restaurant. What kind of people would you select to participate in focus groups? What screening criteria would you use? What questions would you ask?

2. As a marketing researcher, persuade your boss (a fellow student) not to bypass quantitative research once the qualitative research has been conducted.

## Fieldwork

1. The campus athletic center is trying to determine why more students do not use its facilities. Conduct a series of focus groups to determine what could be done to attract more students to the athletic center. Based on the focus group results, generate the relevant hypotheses.

2. A cosmetics firm would like to increase its penetration of the female student market. It hires you as a consultant to obtain an understanding and preliminary insights into the attitudes, purchases, and use of cosmetics by female students. Conduct at least five depth interviews. Employ the construction technique as well. Do your findings from the two techniques agree? If not, try to reconcile the discrepancy.

## Group Discussion

1. In a group of five or six, discuss whether qualitative research is scientific.

2. If the focus group findings confirm prior expectations, the client should dispense with quantitative research. Discuss this statement in a small group.

3. As a small group of five or six, discuss the following statement: "Quantitative research is more important than qualitative research because it results in statistical information and conclusive findings."

# CHAPTER

# 6

# Descriptive Research Design: Survey and Observation

The key to good descriptive research is knowing exactly what you want to measure and selecting a survey method in which every respondent is willing to cooperate and capable of giving you complete and accurate information efficiently.

*Joe Ottaviani, senior vice president, general manager, Burke, Inc.*

## Objectives

After reading this chapter, the student should be able to:

1. Discuss and classify survey methods and describe the various telephone, personal, and mail interviewing methods.
2. Identify the criteria for evaluating survey methods, compare the different methods, and evaluate which is best suited for a particular research project.
3. Explain and classify the different observation methods used by marketing researchers and describe personal observation, mechanical observation, audit, content analysis, and trace analysis.
4. Identify the criteria for evaluating observation methods, compare the different methods, and evaluate which, if any, is suited for a particular research project.
5. Describe the relative advantages and disadvantages of observational methods and compare them to survey methods.
6. Discuss the considerations involved in implementing surveys and observation methods in an international setting.
7. Understand the ethical issues involved in conducting survey and observation research.
8. Discuss the use of the Internet and computers in surveys and observation methods.

## Overview

In previous chapters we have explained that once the marketing research problem has been defined (step 1 of the marketing research process) and an appropriate approach developed (step 2), the researcher is in a position to formulate the research design (step 3). As was discussed in Chapter 3, the major types of research designs are exploratory and conclusive. Exploratory designs employ secondary data analysis (Chapter 4) and qualitative research (Chapter 5) as the major methodologies. Conclusive research designs may be classified as causal or descriptive. Causal designs will be explained in Chapter 7.

In this chapter we focus on the major methods employed in descriptive research designs: survey and observation. As was explained in Chapter 3, descriptive research has as its major objective the description of something—usually market characteristics or functions. Survey, or communication, methods may be classified by mode of administration as traditional telephone interviews, computer-assisted telephone interviews, personal in-home interviews, mall intercept interviews, computer-assisted personal interviews, mail interviews, mail panels, e-mail, and Internet surveys. We describe each of these methods and present a comparative evaluation of all the survey methods. Next, we consider the major observational methods: personal observation, mechanical observation, audit, content analysis, and trace analysis. The relative advantages and disadvantages of observation over survey methods are discussed. The considerations involved in conducting survey and observation research when researching international markets are discussed. Several ethical issues that arise in survey research and observation methods are identified. The chapter concludes with a discussion of the use of microcomputers and mainframes in survey and observation research.

## REAL RESEARCH

### Who Is the Next President?

Internet surveys are gaining in popularity, and the November 2000 U.S. elections provided market researchers with a unique opportunity to test online survey methods, their accuracy, and also their ability to predict elections. Harris Interactive (*www.harrisinteractive.com*) took the initiative to conduct online research in 73 different political races including nationwide votes for president, statewide votes in 38 states, and several senator and governor elections in many different states. Interactive online interviews conducted between October 31 and November 6, 2000 polled a total of 240,666 adults who were characterized as likely voters. The results turned out to be almost identical to those used in the nationwide Harris Interactive telephone poll, which happened to be the only other poll to have Bush and Gore tied in its final prediction. The results are shown in the table on the following page.

The accuracy of the other 72 races turned out quite favorable as well. The accuracy of these online polls in predicting the results of 73 races proved that well-designed Internet surveys can reliably predict election results. Therefore, the popularity of Internet surveys for election polling and other uses is expected to continue to grow.[1] ■

2000 Presidential Elections: The Nationwide Vote

| | Gore % | Bush % | Nader % | Errors Bush/Gore Spread % | Errors Nader % |
|---|---|---|---|---|---|
| Election Results | 48 | 48 | 3 | — | — |
| Harris Interactive (Online) | 47 | 47 | 4 | 0 | 1 |
| Harris Interactive (Phone) | 47 | 47 | 5 | 0 | 2 |
| CBS | 45 | 44 | 4 | 1 | 1 |
| Gallup/CNN/USA Today | 46 | 48 | 4 | 2 | 1 |
| Pew Research | 47 | 49 | 4 | 2 | 1 |
| 18D/CSM/TIPP | 46 | 48 | 4 | 2 | 1 |
| Zogby | 48 | 46 | 5 | 2 | 2 |
| ICR/Politics Now | 44 | 46 | 7 | 2 | 4 |
| NBC/WSJ | 44 | 47 | 3 | 3 | 0 |
| ABC/WashPost | 45 | 48 | 3 | 3 | 0 |
| Battleground | 45 | 50 | 4 | 5 | 1 |
| Rasmussen (Automated Telephone) | 49 | 40 | 4 | 9 | 1 |

Notes:
1. Undecided and others omitted.
2. The National Council on Published Polls (NCPP) has calculated the error on the spread as being half the difference between the actual spread (i.e., the result) and the spread in the poll. We show it here as the difference (i.e., our estimates of error are twice those shown by NCPP).
*Source: National Council on Published Poils.*

**REAL RESEARCH**

## *Marketing Research: The Japanese Way*

Japanese companies rely heavily on personal observation as a means of obtaining information. When Canon Cameras (*www.canon.com*) was losing market share in the United States to Minolta (*www.minolta.com*), Canon decided that its distributor, Bell & Howell, was not giving adequate support. However, Canon did not use data from a broad survey of consumers or retailers to make this decision. Instead, it relied on personal observation and sent three managers to the United States to look into the problem.

Canon's head of the team, Tatehiro Tsuruta, spent almost six weeks in America. Upon entering a camera store, he would act just like a customer. He would note how the cameras were displayed and how the clerks served customers. He observed that the dealers were not enthusiastic about Canon. He also observed that it would not be advantageous for Canon to use drugstores and other discount outlets. This led Canon to open its own sales subsidiary, resulting in increased sales and market share. Its own sales subsidiary was also a major asset in expanding the sales of its digital cameras in the early 2000s. As of 2003, Canon sold its products in over 115 countries worldwide through direct sales and resellers with worldwide sales exceeding $22 billion.[2] ∎

Telephone and Internet interviews, as well as other survey methods, are becoming increasingly popular for predicting election results and have many other applications. Observation methods are employed less frequently, but they too have important uses in marketing research, as indicated by the Canon example.

## SURVEY METHODS

**survey method**
A structured questionnaire given to respondents and designed to elicit specific information.

The **survey method** involves a structured questionnaire given to respondents and designed to elicit specific information. Thus, this method of obtaining information is based on the questioning of respondents. Respondents are asked a variety of questions regarding their behavior, intentions, attitudes, awareness, motivations, and demographic and lifestyle characteristics. These questions may be asked verbally, in writing, or via computer, and the responses may be obtained in any of these forms. Typically, the ques-

**structured data collection**
Use of a formal questionnaire that presents questions in a prearranged order.

tioning is structured. Structured here refers to the degree of standardization imposed on the data-collection process. In **structured data collection,** a formal questionnaire is prepared and the questions are asked in a prearranged order; thus the process is also direct. Whether research is classified as direct or indirect is based on whether the true purpose is known to the respondents. As explained in Chapter 5, a direct approach is nondisguised, in that the purpose of the project is disclosed to the respondents or is otherwise obvious to them from the questions asked.

The structured direct survey, the most popular data-collection method, involves administering a questionnaire. In a typical questionnaire, most questions are **fixed-alternative questions** that require the respondent to select from a predetermined set of responses. Consider, for example, the following question designed to measure attitude toward department stores:

**fixed-alternative questions**
Questions that require respondents to choose from a set of predetermined answers.

|  | *Disagree* |  |  |  | *Agree* |
|---|---|---|---|---|---|
| Shopping in department stores is fun. | 1 | 2 | 3 | 4 | 5 |

The survey method has several advantages. First, the questionnaire is simple to administer. Second, the data obtained are reliable because the responses are limited to the alternatives stated. The use of fixed-response questions reduces the variability in the results that may be caused by differences in interviewers. Finally, coding, analysis, and interpretation of data are relatively simple.[3]

Disadvantages are that respondents may be unable or unwilling to provide the desired information. For example, consider questions about motivational factors. Respondents may not be consciously aware of their motives for choosing specific brands or shopping at specific department stores. Therefore, they may be unable to provide accurate answers to questions about their motives. Respondents may be unwilling to respond if the information requested is sensitive or personal. Also, structured questions and fixed-response alternatives may result in loss of validity for certain types of data such as beliefs and feelings. Finally, wording questions properly is not easy (see Chapter 10 on questionnaire design). Yet, despite these disadvantages, the survey approach is by far the most common method of collecting primary quantitative data in marketing research, as illustrated by the political polling example in the overview section.

## REAL RESEARCH

### Survey Supports Customer Support

Ariba (*www.ariba.com*), a B2B software provider, utilizes both the Internet and sophisticated computer applications to collect survey data. Ariba has integrated its Vantive Enterprise Customer Relationship Management platform (a proprietary software system) with the Web Survey System from CustomerSat.com. With this setup, Ariba has the ability to gain real time feedback, track trends, and obtain immediate notification about unsatisfied customers. Other advantages that Ariba receives from this system are the ability to distribute positive data figures to build company morale and to implement best practices procedures as a result of the data.

The system works by administering an online survey to each customer (respondent) who asks for customer support. This survey gathers not only specifics about the problem customers are experiencing but also data that can be used to make executive decisions down the road (e.g., current product needs, likes/dislikes). The system then analyzes the responses and routes the respondent to an appropriate specialist. Customers can rate and comment on their customer support experience within 24 hours of the case being closed. Ariba can use this survey data not only to improve its customer support system but also to utilize the non-problem-related data to make executive decisions about the direction and offerings of the company. As a result of implementing this system, Ariba's growth has been phenomenal.[4] ■

Survey methods can be classified based on the mode used to administer the questionnaire. These classification schemes help distinguish among survey methods.

*Figure 6.1*
A Classification of Survey
Methods

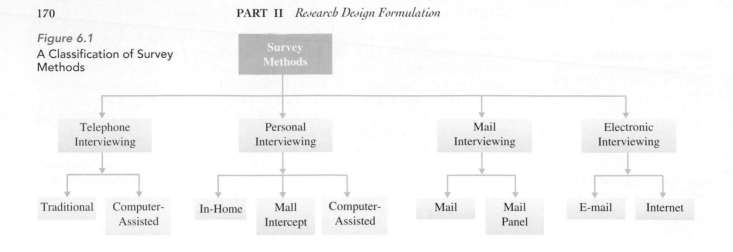

# SURVEY METHODS CLASSIFIED BY MODE OF ADMINISTRATION

Survey questionnaires may be administered in four major modes: (1) telephone interviews, (2) personal interviews, (3) mail interviews, and (4) electronic interviews (see Figure 6.1). Telephone interviews may be further classified as traditional telephone interviews or computer-assisted telephone interviews (CATI). Personal interviews may be conducted in home, as mall intercept interviews, or as computer-assisted personal interviews (CAPI). The third major method, mail interviewing, takes the form of ordinary mail surveys or surveys conducted using mail panels. Finally, electronic interviews can be conducted via e-mail or administered on the Internet. Of these methods, telephone interviews are the most popular, followed by personal interviews and mail surveys. The use of electronic methods, especially Internet surveys, is growing at a fast pace. We now describe each of these methods.

# TELEPHONE METHODS

As stated earlier, telephone interviews can be traditional or computer assisted.

## Traditional Telephone Interviews

Traditional telephone interviews involve phoning a sample of respondents and asking them a series of questions. The interviewer uses a paper questionnaire and records the responses with a pencil. Advances in telecommunications and technology have made nationwide telephone interviewing from a central location practical. Consequently, the use of local telephone interviewing has decreased in recent years.[5]

## Computer-Assisted Telephone Interviewing

Computer-assisted telephone interviewing from a central location is now more popular than the traditional telephone method. Computer-assisted telephone interviewing (CATI) uses a computerized questionnaire administered to respondents over the telephone. A computerized questionnaire may be generated using a mainframe computer, a minicomputer, or a personal computer. The interviewer sits in front of a computer terminal and wears a miniheadset. The computer replaces a paper and pencil questionnaire and the miniheadset substitutes for a telephone. Upon command, the computer dials the telephone number to be called. When contact is made, the interviewer reads questions posed on the computer screen and records the respondent's answers directly into the computer memory bank.

In computer-assisted telephone interviewing, the computer systematically guides the interviewer.

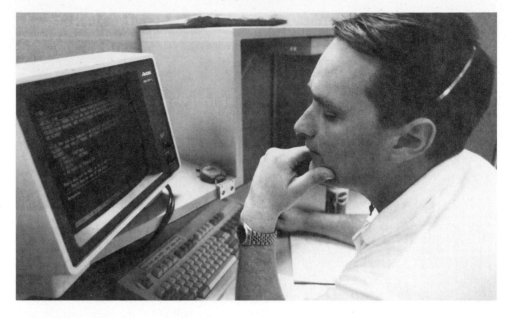

The computer systematically guides the interviewer. Only one question at a time appears on the screen. The computer checks the responses for appropriateness and consistency. It uses the responses as they are obtained to personalize the questionnaire. The data collection flows naturally and smoothly. Interviewing time is reduced, data quality is enhanced, and the laborious steps in the data-collection process, coding questionnaires, and entering the data into the computer, are eliminated. Because the responses are entered directly into the computer, interim and update reports on data collection or results can be provided almost instantaneously. The Harris Interactive phone survey in the presidential election polling example in the overview section made use of CATI, as does the following example.

### REAL RESEARCH

## Telephone Surveys: The Hallmark of Hallmark

As females control more than half of the purchasing decisions in their homes, Hallmark, Inc. (*www.hallmark.com*) did some research on this target market—women. Qualitative research revealed the importance of girlfriends in the life of women. A national telephone survey was conducted, asking women aged 18 to 39 how they first became acquainted with their girlfriends and how often they kept in touch with their girlfriends. Respondents were asked to rate how likely (or unlikely) they were to share secrets, surprises, disagreements with spouses, and personal (pregnancy) information with their girlfriends. The results showed that 45 percent of women felt that there was an occasion in which they would rather share the information with a female friend than a male friend. It was also found that 81 percent of women "calmly discuss topics when they have a difference in opinion with their girlfriends." Both of these percentages illustrate a higher probability for females to share information and engage in correspondence.

Forty-two percent of the women in the study stated that they have one woman they consider their "best friend." Thirty-three percent of women live within 10 miles of their best friend, and 28 percent live more than 100 miles away from their best friends. Based on this information, Hallmark launched its new line of cards, "Hallmark Fresh Ink," that enable women to keep in touch with their girlfriends. Knowing that females were their target market, and how much they kept in touch with one another, enabled the company to launch a successful new line. Telephone surveys have become the hallmark of Hallmark's marketing research, enabling the company to formulate successful marketing strategies. As of 2003, Hallmark holds 55 percent of the market share in the United States for greeting cards sales and their cards are sold in over 47,000 retail outlets. They also publish products in more than 30 languages that are sold in over 100 countries.[6] ∎

# PERSONAL METHODS

Personal interviewing methods may be categorized as in-home, mall intercept, or computer assisted.

## Personal In-Home Interviews

In personal in-home interviews, respondents are interviewed face-to-face in their homes. The interviewer's task is to contact the respondents, ask the questions, and record the responses. In recent years, the use of personal in-home interviews has declined due to its high cost. Nevertheless, they are still used, particularly by syndicated firms (see Chapter 4) such as the Roper Organization.

### REAL RESEARCH

### *Limobus: A Limo or a Bus Ride into American Homes*

The Roper Organization's (*www.roperasw.com*) omnibus panel, Limobus, conducts personal in-home interviews with 2,000 adult Americans every month and makes the results available four weeks after the survey. The sample size and composition of the panel for a specific project are tailored to the client's needs: all or some of the panel members may be asked questions of interest to a specific client. Limobus can be used for checking advertising and brand awareness, conducting pre- and postcampaign measurements, checking ad impact, recall, and communication, assessing brand penetration, testing new or altered packaging, evaluating new product performance, and other marketing research problems.[7] ■

Despite their many applications, the use of personal in-home interviews is declining, whereas mall intercepts are becoming more frequent.

## Mall Intercept Personal Interviews

In mall intercept personal interviews, respondents are intercepted while they are shopping in malls and brought to test facilities in the malls. The interviewer then administers a questionnaire as in the in-home personal survey. The advantage of mall intercept interviews is that it is more efficient for the respondent to come to the interviewer than for the interviewer to go to the respondent.[8] This method has become increasingly popular and there are several hundred permanent mall research facilities. As the following example shows, mall intercepts are especially appropriate when the respondents need to see, handle, or consume the product before they can provide meaningful information.

A mall intercept interview in progress.

*Same Name, New Number*

Stepping into the new millennium, AT&T (*www.att.com*) had moved from just providing long-distance phone service to offering cable television services, wireless cellular services, and Internet services. However, most people still viewed the firm purely as an old-fashioned, boring telephone company. Therefore, the company wanted to create a new image of fun and trendy. Their ad agency, Young & Rubicam (*www.yr.com*), had an idea to use the logo of AT&T, the blue and white globe, and animate it to be the spokesperson in the ads. In order to determine if the logo was recognizable enough, AT&T conducted a survey. The researchers conducted 500 mall intercept personal interviews in 15 markets to address AT&T's problem. Mall intercept interviewing was selected over other survey methods so that the respondents could be shown a picture of the AT&T logo before responding. The consumers were asked if they recognized the logo, which was pictured without the company name. The survey results showed that 75 percent of the entire sample recognized the logo as being representative of AT&T without any help, whereas 77 percent of the 18- to 24-year-olds, and 80 percent of the "high-value, active networkers" recognized the logo. High-value, active networkers are those who spend $75 or more on wireless services or long distance.

Given these positive results, commercials were made that showed the animated logo bouncing around on the screen demonstrating how AT&T's various services can help an individual or a business. The 2002 Winter Olympic Games provided ample exposure to AT&T's new animated logo, which has definitely helped to promote the company's services and to establish a dynamic and fun image. Since then, awareness and perceptions of AT&T's services have remained high.[9] ■

## Computer-Assisted Personal Interviewing (CAPI)

In computer-assisted personal interviewing (CAPI), the third form of personal interviewing, the respondent sits in front of a computer terminal and answers a questionnaire on the computer screen by using the keyboard or a mouse. There are several user-friendly electronic packages that design questions that are easy for the respondent to understand. Help screens and courteous error messages are also provided. The colorful screens and on- and off-screen stimuli add to the respondent's interest and involvement in the task. This method has been classified as a personal interview technique because an interviewer is usually present to serve as a host or hostess and to guide the respondent as needed.

CAPI has been used to collect data at shopping malls, product clinics, conferences, and trade shows. However, you may wonder, how does CAPI compare with the traditional method of conducting personal interviews, using paper-and-pencil questionnaires? The experience of Bank One of Chicago provides some insight.[10]

## *Banking on Computers Creates Interest*

Bank One Corporation (*www.bankone.com*), headquartered in Chicago, is one of the nation's largest banks with assets of more than $265 billion in 2003. Bank One compared CAPI with interviewer-assisted paper-and-pencil questionnaires. It was found that computer questionnaires took longer to complete, although the respondents underestimated the time they spent on the computer. Respondents found the computer-assisted surveys more interesting and expressed more positive predispositions toward them. Greater variance and less-inhibited answers were obtained with CAPI. Computer-assisted interviews resulted, in certain instances, in 33 to 40 percent cost savings over interviewer-assisted paper-and-pencil questionnaires. Therefore, Bank One has continued to use CAPI in many of its ongoing marketing research programs. ■

# MAIL METHODS

Mail interviews, the third major form of survey administration, can be conducted via ordinary mail or the mail panel.

## Mail Interviews

In the traditional mail interview, questionnaires are mailed to preselected potential respondents. A typical mail interview package consists of the outgoing envelope, cover letter, questionnaire, return envelope, and possibly an incentive. The respondents complete and return the questionnaires. There is no verbal interaction between the researcher and the respondent.[11]

However, before data collection can begin, the respondents need to be at least broadly identified. Therefore, an initial task is to obtain a valid mailing list. Mailing lists can be compiled from telephone directories, customer rosters, or association membership rolls or purchased from publication subscription lists or commercial mailing list companies.[12] Regardless of its source, a mailing list should be current and closely related to the population of interest. The researcher must also make decisions about the various elements of the mail interview package (see Table 6.1). Mail surveys are used for a variety of purposes including measurement of consumer preferences, as illustrated by the following example.

---

**TABLE 6.1**

**Some Decisions Related to the Mail Interview Package**

*Outgoing Envelope*
Outgoing envelope: size, color, return address
Postage
Method of addressing

| *Cover Letter* | |
| --- | --- |
| Sponsorship | Signature |
| Personalization | Postscript |
| Type of appeal | |

| *Questionnaire* | |
| --- | --- |
| Length | Layout |
| Content | Color |
| Size | Format |
| Reproduction | Respondent anonymity |

*Return Envelope*
Type of envelope
Postage

*Incentives*
Monetary versus nonmonetary
Prepaid versus promised famount

A mail questionnaire with return envelope.

|  | VERY SATIS-FIED | SATIS-FIED | NEU-TRAL | DIS-SATIS-FIED | VERY DIS-SATIS-FIED |
|---|---|---|---|---|---|
| 1. THE QUALITY OF YOUR EQUIPMENT | 1 | 2 | 3 | 4 | 5 |
| 2. THE RESPONSE TIME TO YOUR CALL | 1 | 2 | 3 | 4 | 5 |
| 3. THE QUALITY OF SERVICE PERFORMED | 1 | 2 | 3 | 4 | 5 |
| 4. THE COURTESY OF MY SERVICE PERSON | 1 | 2 | 3 | 4 | 5 |
| 5. MEETING OUR SERVICE COMMITMENTS TO YOU | 1 | 2 | 3 | 4 | 5 |
| 6. MY OVERALL SERVICE | 1 | 2 | 3 | 4 | 5 |

||||| (TEAR HERE)

**BUSINESS REPLY CARD**
FIRST CLASS    PERMIT NO. 832    ATLANTA, GA.
POSTAGE WILL BE PAID BY ADDRESSEE

ELRICK AND LAVIDGE, INC.
P.O. Box 4402
Atlanta, GA 30302

NO POSTAGE
NECESSARY
IF MAILED
IN THE
UNITED STATES

## REAL RESEARCH

### *Mint to Be Together*

The Mint Museum of Art (*www.mintmuseum.org*) is located in Charlotte, North Carolina and has a reputation as one of the Southeast's leading cultural institutions. Due to recent changes in the area's population, the Mint began to wonder if its diverse and vast collection was the best way to present art to the public, and just who this public was. Additionally, the Mint wanted to create a Mint Museum of Craft + Design, but they were not sure this is what the public would want, or if they would understand the concept. So they hired InterActive Research of Atlanta.

InterActive Research created a two-phase study to discover the information desired by the Mint. The goal of the research was to measure awareness, usage, and attitudes towards the existing museum, as well as the plan for the new Museum of Craft + Design. The first phase of the study was qualitative and consisted of 15 focus groups, followed by

Mail surveys helped the Mint Museum of Art to design effective marketing strategies.

a quantitative phase that was composed of a detailed questionnaire mailed to approximately 10,000 Charlotte-area residents; 1,300 responses were received.

The results showed that the Mint was perceived as elitist. Respondents also felt that the current collection was too diverse and did not present a coherent theme. People supported the new Craft + Design museum, but they felt a large educational initiative was needed to inform the public about what exactly this entailed. Pricing and parking were seen as two barriers that currently prevented people from attending, so it was decided this needed to be kept in mind when developing the new building. Entrance fees of $5 to $7 were found to be acceptable, but people did not think they would pay to go to the new museum if it cost more than that. The research also implied that the Mint should consider offering a joint membership into both of its museums to encourage attendance. Many of these research findings were implemented as of 2003. Based on the research results provided, the Mint decided to consolidate its current collection into a more focused theme—Art in the Americas—and organize it in chronological order. It will occasionally have a European piece, but most of the art will have originated in either North or South America. The maximum admission price was $6 per person and tickets purchased were good for admission to both the Mint Museum of Art and the Mint Museum of Craft + Design as long as they were used on the same day.[13] ∎

## Mail Panels

**mail panel**
A large and nationally representative sample of households who have agreed to periodically participate in mail questionnaires and product tests.

Mail panels were introduced in Chapters 3 and 4. A ***mail panel*** consists of a large, nationally representative sample of households that have agreed to participate in periodic mail questionnaires and product tests. The households are compensated with various incentives. Data on the panel members is updated every year. Because of the panel members' commitment, the response rates can approach 80 percent. The Consumer Mail Panel maintained by Market Facts (*www.marketfacts.com* or *www.synovate.com*) consists of a representative sample of 600,000 households in the United States and 60,000 in Canada. Several marketing research companies are moving from mail panels to online panels. The NFO World Group (*www.nfow.com*) claims that one out of every 200 households is a member of their online consumer panel.

Mail panels can be used to obtain information from the same respondents repeatedly. Thus, they can be used to implement a longitudinal design.

# ELECTRONIC METHODS

As mentioned earlier, electronic surveys can be conducted by e-mail or administered on the Internet or the Web.

## E-mail Interviews

To conduct an e-mail survey, a list of e-mail addresses is obtained. The survey is written within the body of the e-mail message. The e-mails are sent out over the Internet. E-mail surveys use pure text (ASCII) to represent questionnaires and can be received and responded to by anyone with an e-mail address, whether or not they have access to the Web. Respondents type the answers to either closed-ended or open-ended questions at designated places, and click on "reply." Responses are data entered and tabulated. Note that data entry is typically required.

E-mail surveys have several limitations. Given the technical limitations of most e-mail systems, questionnaires cannot utilize programmed skip patterns, logic checks, or randomization. The limited intelligence of ASCII text cannot keep a respondent from, say, choosing both "yes" and "no" to a question where only one response is meaningful. Skipping instructions (e.g., "If the answer to question 5 is yes, go to question 9") must appear explicitly, just as on paper. These factors can reduce the quality of data from an e-mail survey and can require postsurvey data cleaning. Another limitation is that some e-mail software products limit the length of the body of an e-mail message.[14]

**REAL RESEARCH**

## Sample E-mail Survey

To: respondent@xyz.com
From: survey@analysis.net
Subject: Employee survey

Hello,

We have been commissioned by Jane Smith of the Human Resources department to conduct a survey of XYZ company employees. The results will be used to give senior management a better understanding of what issues are important to employees.

Please be assured that ALL responses to ALL questions will be held completely confidential by Analysis.Net. We will provide only summarized or anonymous comments in our final report.

For each of the following questions, please place your answer in the appropriate [ ] box, like this:

[x ] or this: [3]

_____

1. How long have you been working at XYZ company?
[ ] years.

_____

2. Overall, would you say you are very satisfied, satisfied, neutral, dissatisfied, or very dissatisfied with your job at XYZ company?

[ ] very satisfied
[ ] satisfied
[ ] neutral
[ ] dissatisfied
[ ] very dissatisfied

_____

3. What would you say is the biggest challenge facing XYZ company today?
[               ]

Note that we are able to collect comments as well as numeric or "multiple-choice" responses. ■

## Internet Interviews

**hypertext markup language (HTML)**
Hypertext markup language (HTML) is the language of the Web.

In contrast to e-mail surveys, Internet or Web surveys use **hypertext markup language** (HTML), the language of the Web, and are posted on a Web site. Respondents may be recruited over the Internet from potential respondent databases maintained by the marketing research firm or they can be recruited by conventional methods (mail, telephone). Respondents are asked to go to a particular Web location to complete the survey. Many times, respondents are not recruited but those who happen to be visiting the Web site where the survey is posted (or other popular Web sites) are invited to participate in the survey. Either all or every *i*th Web site visitor is allowed to participate. Web surveys offer several advantages as compared to e-mail surveys. It is possible in HTML, but not in ASCII text, to construct buttons, check boxes, and data-entry fields that prevent respondents from selecting more than one response where only one is intended, or from otherwise typing where no response is required. Skip patterns can be programmed and performed automatically as in CATI or CAPI. It is possible to validate responses as they are entered. Finally, additional survey stimuli such as graphs, images, animations, and links to other Web pages may be integrated into or around the survey. The responses are collected in an adjoining database. The data require some processing before they can be tabulated or used in a statistical package. All these factors contribute to higher quality data. The Harris Interactive online survey in the presidential election polling example in the overview section was an example of an Internet survey.

Limitations of e-mail surveys include possible cleanup from the messages, limited forms that must be strictly adhered to by the user to ensure no cleanup is required, and e-mail system compatibility issues. For Web surveys that recruit respondents who are browsing or by placing banner ads, there is inherent self-selection bias. This can be alleviated by using a validated sample, where individuals are preselected from a set of e-mail addresses and sent an invitation to the Web site. Web surveys do offer an advantage over e-mail surveys by the fact that they can have graphics and sound, can be sent over a secured server, and provide instantaneous feedback. Web surveys can also employ alert systems that can trigger when certain thresholds are met. For instance, if a hotel site reaches its trigger limit for subpar performance, a manager can be immediately notified and can act quickly. Problems, of course, with any Web survey include the fact that bias may be introduced if the respondents answer more than once and, also for nonvalidated samples, there may not be statistical representativeness of the sample frame.

Basically, Internet research can be just as representative and effective as other traditional methods, especially as the Internet population continues to grow. Problems of conducting research over the Internet must be effectively addressed and resolved, just as the problems with traditional research have been and continue to be.[15]

Remember, however, that not all survey methods are appropriate in a given situation. Therefore, the researcher should conduct a comparative evaluation to determine which methods are appropriate.

# A COMPARATIVE EVALUATION OF SURVEY METHODS

Table 6.2 compares the different survey methods across a variety of factors. For any particular research project, the relative importance attached to these factors will vary.

## Flexibility of Data Collection

The flexibility of data collection is determined primarily by the extent to which the respondent can interact with the interviewer and the survey questionnaire. The personal interview, whether conducted in home or as mall intercept interview, allows the highest flexibility of data collection. Because the respondent and the interviewer meet face to face, the interviewer can administer complex questionnaires, explain and clarify difficult questions, and even utilize unstructured techniques.

The traditional telephone interview, by contrast, allows only moderate flexibility, because it is more difficult to use unstructured techniques, ask complex questions, or obtain in-depth answers to open-ended questions over the telephone. CATI, CAPI, and Internet surveys allow somewhat greater flexibility because the questionnaire is administered in an interactive mode. The researcher can use various question formats, personalize the questionnaire, and handle complex skip patterns (directions for skipping questions in the questionnaire based on the subject's responses). Because these modes do not allow for interaction between the interviewer and the respondent, mail surveys, mail panels, and e-mail surveys have low flexibility.

An often overlooked benefit of Internet survey research is the ease with which an Internet survey can be quickly modified. For example, early data returns may suggest additional questions that should be asked. Changing or adding questions on the fly would be nearly impossible with a mail questionnaire and difficult with personal or telephone questionnaires, but can be achieved in a matter of minutes with some Internet survey systems.

## Diversity of Questions

The diversity of questions that can be asked in a survey depends upon the degree of interaction the respondent has with the interviewer and the questionnaire, as well as the ability to actually see the questions. A wide variety of questions can be asked in a personal inter-

## TABLE 6.2

A Comparative Evaluation of Survey Methods

| CRITERIA | TELEPHONE/ CATI | IN-HOME INTERVIEWS | MALL INTERCEPT INTERVIEWS | CAPI | MALL SURVEYS | MALL PANELS | E-MAIL | INTERNET |
|---|---|---|---|---|---|---|---|---|
| Flexibility of data collection | Moderate to high | High | High | Moderate to high | Low | Low | Low | Moderate to high |
| Diversity of questions | Low | High | High | High | Moderate | Moderate | Moderate | Moderate to high |
| Use of physical stimuli | Low | Moderate to high | High | High | Moderate | Moderate | Low | Moderate |
| Sample control | Moderate to high | Potentially high | Moderate | Moderate | Low | Moderate to high | Low | Low to moderate |
| Control of data-collection environment | Moderate | Moderate to high | High | High | Low | Low | Low | Low |
| Control of field force | Moderate | Low | Moderate | Moderate | High | High | High | High |
| Quantity of data | Low | High | Moderate | Moderate | Moderate | High | Moderate | Moderate |
| Response rate | Moderate | High | High | High | Low | Moderate | Low | Very low |
| Perceived anonymity of the respondent | Moderate | Low | Low | Low | High | High | Moderate | High |
| Social desirability | Moderate | High | High | Moderate to high | Low | Low | Moderate | Low |
| Obtaining sensitive information | High | Low | Low | Low to moderate | High | Moderate to high | Moderate | High |
| Potential for interviewer bias | Moderate | High | High | Low | None | None | None | None |
| Speed | High | Moderate | Moderate to high | Moderate to high | Low | Low to moderate | High | Very high |
| Cost | Moderate | High | Moderate to high | Moderate to high | Low | Low to moderate | Low | Low |

view because the respondents can see the questionnaire and an interviewer is present to clarify ambiguities. Thus, in-home, mall intercept, and CAPI surveys allow for diversity. In Internet surveys, multimedia capabilities can be utilized, and so the ability to ask a diversity of questions is moderate to high, despite the absence of an interviewer. In mail surveys, mail panels, and e-mail surveys, less diversity is possible. In traditional telephone interviews and CATI, the respondent cannot see the questions while answering and this limits the diversity of questions. For example, in a telephone interview or CATI, one could not ask respondents to rank 15 brands of automobiles in terms of preference.

## Use of Physical Stimuli

Often it is helpful or necessary to use physical stimuli such as the product, a product prototype, commercials, or promotional displays during the interview. For the most basic example, a taste test involves tasting the product. In other cases, photographs, maps, or other audiovisual cues are helpful. In these cases, personal interviews conducted at central locations (mall intercept and CAPI) are preferable to in-home interviews. Mail surveys and mail panels are moderate on this dimension, because sometimes it is possible to mail the facilitating aids or even product samples. Internet surveys are also moderately suitable. Because they are Web-based, the questionnaires can include multimedia elements such as prototype Web pages and advertisements. The use of physical stimuli is limited in traditional telephone interviews, CATI, and also in e-mail surveys.

## Sample Control

**sample control**
The ability of the survey mode to reach the units specified in the sample effectively and efficiently.

**Sample control** is the ability of the survey mode to reach the units specified in the sample effectively and efficiently.[16] At least in principle, in-home personal interviews offer the best sample control. It is possible to control which sampling units are interviewed, who is interviewed, the degree of participation of other members of the household, and many other aspects of data collection. In practice, to achieve a high degree of control, the researcher has to overcome several problems. It is difficult to find respondents at home during the day, as most people work outside the home. Also, for safety reasons, interviewers are reluctant to venture into certain neighborhoods and people have become cautious of responding to strangers at their door.

Mall intercept interviews allow only a moderate degree of sample control. Although the interviewer has control over which respondents to intercept, the choice is limited to mall shoppers, and frequent shoppers have a greater probability of being included. Also, potential respondents can intentionally avoid or initiate contact with the interviewer. Compared to mall intercept, CAPI offers slightly better control, as sampling quotas can be set and respondents randomized automatically.

**sampling frame**
A representation of the elements of the target population. It consists of a list or set of directions for identifying the target population.

Moderate to high sampling control can be achieved with traditional telephone interviews and CATI. Telephones offer access to geographically dispersed respondents and hard-to-reach areas. These procedures depend upon a **sampling frame**—a list of population units with their telephone numbers.[17] The sampling frames normally used are telephone directories, but telephone directories are limited in that: (1) not everyone has a phone, (2) some people have unlisted numbers, and (3) directories do not reflect new phones in service or recently disconnected phones. Although the telephone has achieved an almost total penetration of households in the United States, there are some variations by region and within regions. The percentage of households with unlisted numbers is about 31 percent and varies considerably by geographical region. In large metropolitan areas, it may be as high as 60 percent. The total of unpublished numbers and new phones in service since the directory was published can account for as much as 40 percent of total telephone households in some metropolitan areas.[18]

**random digit dialing (rdd)**
A technique used to overcome the bias of unpublished and recent telephone numbers by selecting all telephone number digits at random.

The **random digit dialing** (rdd) technique is used to overcome the bias of unpublished and recent numbers. RDD consists of selecting all ten (area code, prefix or exchange, suffix) telephone number digits at random. Although this approach gives all households with telephones an approximately equal chance of being included in the sample, it suffers from limitations. It is costly and time consuming to implement, because not all possible

*Figure 6.2*
Random Digit Directory Designs

**Addition of a Constant to the Last Digit**

An integer between 1 and 9 is added to the telephone number selected from the directory. In plus-one sampling the number added to the last digit is 1.

Number selected from directory: 404–953–3004 (area code-exchange-block). Add 1 to the last digit to form 404–953–3005. This is the number to be included in the sample.

**Randomization on the *r* Last Digits**

Replace the *r* (*r* = 2, 3, or 4) last digits with an equal number of randomly selected digits.

Number selected from directory: 212–881–1124. Replace the last four digits of block with randomly selected numbers 5, 2, 8, and 6 to form 212–881–5286.

**Two-Stage Procedure**

The first stage consists of selecting an exchange and telephone number from the directory. In the second stage, the last three digits of the selected number are replaced with a three digit random number between 000 and 999.

**Cluster 1**

Selected exchange: 202–636
Selected number: 202–636–3230
Replace the last three digits (230) with randomly selected 389 to form 202–636–3389.
Repeat this process until the desired number of telephone numbers from this cluster is obtained.

---

telephone numbers are in service: although there are 10 billion possible telephone numbers, there are only about 100 million actual household telephone numbers. Also, RDD does not distinguish between telephone numbers that are of interest and those that are not (in a consumer survey, for example, business and government numbers are not of interest). There are several variations of RDD that reduce wasted effort. One variation randomly selects a working exchange and adds a block of four-digit random numbers. In ***random digit directory designs*** a sample of numbers is drawn from the directory. These numbers are modified to allow unpublished numbers a chance of being included in the sample. The popular approaches for modification of numbers include: (1) adding a constant to the last digit, (2) randomizing the last *r* digits, and (3) a two-stage procedure. These procedures are described and illustrated in Figure 6.2. Of these three methods, adding a constant to the last digit, particularly plus-one sampling, results in high contact rates and representative samples.[19]

Mail surveys require a list of addresses of individuals or households eligible for inclusion in the sample. Mail surveys can reach geographically dispersed respondents in hard-to-reach areas.[20] However, mailing lists are sometimes unavailable, outdated, or incomplete. Typically, telephone and street directories are used for a listing of the general population. Problems with these types of lists have been discussed already. Catalogs of mailing lists contain thousands of lists that can be purchased.

Another factor outside the researcher's control is whether the questionnaire is answered and who answers it. Some subjects refuse to respond because of lack of interest or motivation; others cannot respond because they are illiterate. For these reasons, the degree of sample control in mail surveys is low.[21]

Mail panels, on the other hand, provide moderate to high control over the sample. They provide samples matched to U.S. Bureau of the Census statistics on key demographic variables. It is also possible to identify specific user groups within a panel and to direct the survey to households with specific characteristics. Specific members of households in the panel can be questioned. Finally, low-incidence groups, groups that occur infrequently in the population, can be reached with panels, but there is a question of the extent to which a panel can be considered to be representative of the entire population.

Not all populations are candidates for Internet survey research. The general consumer population is often a poor fit, because many U.S. households do not regularly use Internet services. Although the respondents can be screened to meet qualifying criteria and quotas imposed, the ability to meet quotas is limited by the number and characteristics of

**random digit directory designs**
A research design for telephone surveys in which a sample of numbers is drawn from the telephone directory and modified to allow unpublished numbers a chance of being included in the sample.

respondents who visit the Web site. However, there are some exceptions to this broad statement. For example, computer products purchasers and users of Internet services are both ideal populations. Business and professional users of Internet services are also an excellent population to reach with Internet surveys. Over 90 percent of businesses are currently estimated to have Internet connections. It can be difficult to prevent respondents from completing an Internet survey multiple times. Thus, sample control is low to moderate for Internet surveys. E-mail surveys suffer from many of the limitations of mail surveys and thus offer low sample control.

## Control of the Data-Collection Environment

The degree of control a researcher has over the environment in which the respondent answers the questionnaire is another factor that differentiates the various survey modes. Personal interviews conducted at central locations (mall intercept and CAPI) offer the greatest degree of environmental control. For example, the researcher can set up a special facility for demonstrating the product. In-home personal interviews offer moderate to good control because the interviewer is present. Traditional telephone and CATI offer moderate control. The interviewer cannot see the environment in which the interview is being conducted, but he or she can sense the background conditions and encourage the respondent to be attentive and involved. In mail surveys and panels, e-mail, and Internet surveys, the researcher has little control over the environment.

## Control of Field Force

*field force*
The field force is made up of both the actual interviewers and the supervisors involved in data collection.

The *field force* consists of interviewers and supervisors involved in data collection. Because they require no such personnel, mail surveys, mail panels, e-mail, and Internet surveys eliminate field force problems. Traditional telephone interviews, CATI, mall intercept, and CAPI all offer moderate degrees of control because the interviews are conducted at a central location, making supervision relatively simple. In-home personal interviews are problematic in this respect. Because many interviewers work in many different locations, continual supervision is impractical.[22]

## Quantity of Data

In-home personal interviews allow the researcher to collect large amounts of data. The social relationship between the interviewer and the respondent, as well as the home environment, motivates the respondent to spend more time in the interview. Less effort is required of the respondent in a personal interview than in a telephone or mail interview. The interviewer records answers to open-ended questions and provides visual aids to help with lengthy and complex scales. Some personal interviews last for as long as 75 minutes. In contrast to in-home interviews, mall intercept and CAPI provide only moderate amounts of data. Because these interviews are conducted in shopping malls and other central locations, the respondents' time is more limited. Typically, the interview time is 30 minutes or less. For example, in recent mall intercept interviews conducted by General Foods, the interview time was limited to 25 minutes.[23]

Mail surveys also yield moderate amounts of data. Fairly long questionnaires can be used, because short questionnaires have not been shown to generate higher response rates than long ones. The same is true for e-mail and Internet surveys, although the Internet is a better medium in this respect. Mail panels, on the other hand, can generate large amounts of data because of the special relationship between the panel members and the sponsoring organization. For example, the author has used the Market Facts panel to administer a questionnaire that took two hours to complete.

Traditional telephone interviews and CATI result in the most limited quantities of data. They tend to be shorter than other surveys, because respondents can easily terminate the telephone conversation at their own discretion. These interviews commonly last about 15 minutes, although longer interviews may be conducted when the subject matter is of interest to the respondents.[24] Studies indicate that respondents tend to underestimate the length of telephone interviews by as much as 50 percent. This suggests that telephone interviews may be conducted for a longer duration than is currently the practice.

## Response Rate

**response rate**
The percentage of the total attempted interviews that are completed.

Survey **response rate** is broadly defined as the percentage of the total attempted interviews that are completed. Personal, in-home, mall intercept, and computer-assisted interviews yield the highest response rate (typically more than 80 percent). Problems caused by not-at-homes can often be resolved by calling back at different times. Telephone interviews, traditional and CATI, yield response rates between 60 and 80 percent. These modes also suffer from not-at-homes or no-answers. Higher response rates are obtained by callbacks. Many telephone surveys attempt to call back at least three times.

Mail surveys have poor response rates. In a mail survey of randomly selected respondents, without any pre- or postmailing contact, the response rate is typically less than 15 percent. Such low response rate can lead to serious bias (nonresponse bias), because whether a person responds to a mail survey is related to his or her interest in the topic. The magnitude of **nonresponse bias** increases as the response rate decreases. However, use of appropriate response-inducement procedures can increase the response rate in mail surveys to 80 percent or more. Response rates in mail panels are typically in the 70 to 80 percent range, because of assured respondent cooperation.

**nonresponse bias**
When actual respondents differ from those who refuse to participate.

Internet surveys have the poorest response rates, even lower than e-mail surveys. This is due to the fact that some respondents may have access to e-mail but not to the Web, and accessing the Web requires more effort and skill. Furthermore, respondents generally need to be connected to the Internet while completing a Web survey; they may not be offline, as with e-mail surveys. If the respondents are prerecruited, they have to log onto a Web site. Many are unwilling to undertake this effort.

A comprehensive review of the literature covering 497 response rates in 93 journal articles found weighted average response rates of 81.7, 72.3, and 47.3 percent for, respectively, personal, telephone, and mail surveys.[25] The same review also found that response rates increase with:

- either prepaid or promised monetary incentives
- increase in the amount of monetary incentive
- nonmonetary premiums and rewards (pens, pencils, books)
- preliminary notification
- foot-in-the door techniques. These are multiple request strategies. The first request is relatively small, and all or most people agree to comply. The small request is followed by a larger request, called the **critical request,** which is actually the target behavior.
- personalization (sending letters addressed to specific individuals)
- follow-up letters

**critical request**
The target behavior that is being researched.

A further discussion of improving response rates is found in Chapter 12.

## Perceived Anonymity

**perceived anonymity**
The respondent's perceptions that their identities will not be discerned by the interviewer or the researcher.

**Perceived anonymity** refers to the respondents' perceptions that the interviewer or the researcher will not discern their identities. Perceived anonymity of the respondent is high in mail surveys, mail panels, and Internet surveys because there is no contact with an interviewer while responding. It is low in personal interviews (in home, mall intercept, and computer assisted) due to face-to-face contact with the interviewer. Traditional telephone interviews and CATI fall in the middle. It is also moderate with e-mail. Although there is no contact with the interviewer, respondents know that their names can be located on the return e-mail.

## Social Desirability/Sensitive Information

**social desirability**
The tendency of the respondents to give answers that may not be accurate but that may be desirable from a social standpoint.

**Social desirability** is the tendency of the respondents to give answers that are socially acceptable, whether or not they are true. As mail surveys, mail panels, and Internet surveys do not involve any social interaction between the interviewer and the respondent, they are least susceptible to social desirability. Evidence suggests that such methods are good for obtaining sensitive information such as that related to financial or personal behavior. Traditional telephone interviews and CATI are moderately good at avoiding socially desirable responses. They are good for obtaining sensitive information, as the respondents have the perception that they are not committing to anything in writing over the telephone.[26] E-mail is only moderately good for controlling social desirability and obtaining sensitive information, given the respondents' awareness that their names can be located on the return e-mail. Personal interviews, whether in home, mall intercept, or computer assisted, are limited in this respect, although the problem is somewhat mitigated in the case of computer-assisted interviews.[27]

## Potential for Interviewer Bias

Interviewers can bias the results of a survey by the manner in which they (1) select respondents (interviewing somebody else when required to interview the male head of household), (2) ask research questions (omitting questions), and (3) record answers (recording an answer incorrectly or incompletely). The extent of the interviewer's role determines the potential for bias.[28] In-home and mall intercept personal interviews are highly susceptible to interviewer bias. Traditional telephone interviews and CATI are less susceptible, although the potential is still there. For example, with inflection and tone of voice, interviewers can convey their own attitudes and thereby suggest answers. Computer-assisted interviews have a low potential for bias. Mail surveys, mail panels, e-mail, and Internet surveys are free of it.

## Speed

The Internet is by far the fastest method of obtaining data from a large number of respondents. First, there is the speed with which a questionnaire can be created, distributed to respondents, and the data returned. Because printing, mailing, and data keying delays are eliminated, the researcher can have data in hand within hours of writing an Internet questionnaire. Data are obtained in electronic form, so statistical analysis software can be programmed to process standard questionnaires and return statistical summaries and charts automatically. The e-mail survey is also fast, although slower than Internet surveys because greater time is needed to compile an e-mail list, and data entry is also required.

Traditional telephone interviews and CATI are also fast ways of obtaining information. When a central telephone facility is used, several hundred telephone interviews can be done per day. Data for even large national surveys can be collected in one week or less. Next in speed are mall intercept and computer-assisted interviews that reach potential respondents in central locations. In-home personal interviews are slower, because there is dead time between interviews while the interviewer travels to the next respondent. To expedite data collection, interviews can be conducted in different markets or regions simultaneously. Mail surveys are typically the slowest. It usually takes several weeks to receive completed questionnaires; follow-up mailings take even longer. In a recent study comparing two survey methods, the mean number of days respondents took for the e-mail surveys was a mere 4.3, compared with 18.3 for the mail survey. Mail panels are faster than mail surveys, as little follow-up is required.[29]

## Cost

For large samples, the cost of Internet surveys is the lowest. Printing, mailing, keying, and interviewer costs are eliminated, and the incremental costs of each respondent are typically low, so studies with large numbers of respondents can be done at substantial savings compared to mail, telephone, or personal surveys. Personal interviews tend to be the most expensive mode of data collection per completed response. In general, Internet, e-mail, mail surveys, mail panel, traditional telephone, CATI, CAPI, mall intercept, and personal in-home interviews require progressively larger field staff and greater supervision and

| ACTIVE RESEARCH | DEPARTMENT STORE PROJECT |

**Personal In-Home Interviews**

In the department store project, personal in-home interviews were utilized for a number of reasons. Many diverse questions were asked. Some questions were complex and a relatively large amount of data had to be collected. The information obtained was not sensitive or threatening. Trained students were used as interviewers, thereby reducing the cost. Another critical consideration was that the personal interviews could be conducted without subcontracting the data collection to a field service organization.

Telephone methods were not chosen, due to the complexity of the questions and amount of data needed. Mall intercept and CAPI were not appropriate either, because so much data were needed. The use of a central location facility would have necessitated subcontracting with a field service organization. Mail surveys were ruled out, due to low response rate and the complexity of the information needed. Mail panels were inappropriate, given the complexity of information needed; and a self-administered questionnaire was not considered to be appropriate. The electronic methods were not chosen, as many people in the target market did not have access to e-mail or the Internet when the survey was conducted.

control. Hence, the cost increases in this order. However, relative costs depend on the subject of inquiry and the procedures adopted.[30]

# SELECTION OF SURVEY METHOD(S)

As is evident from Table 6.2 and the preceding discussion, no survey method is superior in all situations. Depending upon such factors as information requirements, budgetary constraints (time and money), and respondent characteristics, none, one, two, or even all methods may be appropriate.[31] Remember that the various data-collection modes are not mutually exclusive. Rather, they can be employed in a complementary fashion to build on each other's strengths and compensate for each other's weaknesses. The researcher can employ these methods in combination and develop creative methods. To illustrate, in a classic project, interviewers distributed the product, self-administered questionnaires, and return envelopes to respondents. Traditional telephone interviews were used for follow-up. Combining the data-collection modes resulted in telephone cooperation from 97 percent of the respondents. Furthermore, 82 percent of the questionnaires were returned by mail.[32] In the introduction we illustrated how election polling successfully used telephone and Internet interviewing. The following example illustrate the selection of survey modes.

## REAL RESEARCH

### *Crossing Surveys Helps BlueCross*

BlueCross (*www.bluecross.com*) wanted to know where to concentrate their advertising dollars and therefore wanted to determine the recognition of advertisements placed in different types of media (seven print ads, six TV commercials, and two radio commercials). In order to keep the cost of the survey down, personal interviews were not used. First, BlueCross conducted telephone interviews throughout their Minnesota marketing area. The radio advertisement with the company's name bleeped out was played and respondents were asked to identify the company. At the end of the phone interview, the participant was asked if they would be willing to answer similar questions pertaining to some print ads and television commercials. The 650 respondents who agreed were sent a mail survey. Similar procedures were used in the mail survey. The company's name was blocked out and a storyboard approach was used to recreate the television commercials on paper. These, along with the print ads and a questionnaire, were mailed to the respondents. After one follow-up phone call, 405 surveys were returned.

The results from the study were rather interesting. Print ads were recognized by 23 percent of the survey participants, TV ads by 41 percent, and the radio ads by 40 percent. By dividing the percent recognition rate and the reach by the cost of producing ads in that particular medium, BlueCross was able to determine the payoff from each medium. Print was the most effective medium, followed closely by radio and then TV. This analysis enabled BlueCross to concentrate their advertising in the most effective medium, while still using the other two in a complementary way.[33] ■

# OBSERVATION METHODS

*observation*
The recording of behavioral patterns of people, objects, and events in a systematic manner to obtain information about the phenomenon of interest.

Observation methods are the second type of methodology used in descriptive research. *Observation* involves recording the behavioral patterns of people, objects, and events in a systematic manner to obtain information about the phenomenon of interest. The observer does not question or communicate with the people being observed. Information may be recorded as the events occur or from records of past events. Observational methods may be structured or unstructured, direct or indirect. Furthermore, observation may be conducted in a natural or contrived environment.[34]

## Structured Versus Unstructured Observation

*structured observation*
Observation techniques where the researcher clearly defines the behaviors to be observed and the methods by which they will be measured.

In *structured observation,* the researcher specifies in detail what is to be observed and how the measurements are to be recorded. An example would be an auditor performing inventory analysis in a store. This reduces the potential for observer bias and enhances the reliability of the data. Structured observation is appropriate when the marketing research problem has been clearly defined and the information needed has been specified. In these circumstances, the details of the phenomenon to be observed can be clearly identified. Structured observation is suitable for use in conclusive research.

*unstructured observation*
Observation that involves a researcher monitoring all aspects of the phenomenon without specifying the details in advance.

In *unstructured observation,* the observer monitors all aspects of the phenomenon that seem relevant to the problem at hand, for example, observing children playing with new toys. This form of observation is appropriate when the problem has yet to be formulated precisely and flexibility is needed in observation to identify key components of the problem and to develop hypotheses. In unstructured observation, potential for observer bias is high. For this reason, the observation findings should be treated as hypotheses to be tested, rather than as conclusive findings. Thus, unstructured observation is most appropriate for exploratory research.

## Disguised Versus Undisguised Observation

In disguised observation, the respondents are unaware that they are being observed. Disguise enables respondents to behave naturally, because people tend to behave differently when they know they are being observed. Disguise may be accomplished by using one-way mirrors, hidden cameras, or inconspicuous mechanical devices. Observers may be disguised as shoppers or sales clerks or in other appropriate roles.

In undisguised observation, the respondents are aware that they are under observation. For example, they may be aware of the presence of the observer. Researchers disagree on how much effect the presence of an observer has on behavior. One viewpoint is that the observer effect is minor and short lived. The other position is that the observer can seriously bias the behavior patterns.[35]

## Natural Versus Contrived Observation

*natural observation*
Observing behavior as it takes place in the environment.

*contrived observation*
The behavior is observed in an artificial environment.

*Natural observation* involves observing behavior as it takes places in the environment. For example, one could observe the behavior of respondents eating fast food in Burger King. In *contrived observation,* respondents' behavior is observed in an artificial environment, such as a test kitchen.

The advantage of natural observation is that the observed phenomenon will more accurately reflect the true phenomenon. The disadvantages are the cost of waiting for the phenomenon to occur and the difficulty of measuring the phenomenon in a natural setting.

**Figure 6.3**
A Classification of
Observation Methods

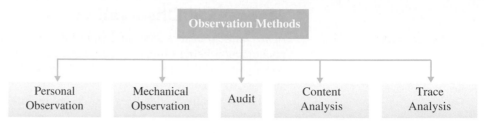

The Canon Cameras example in the overview section presented an example of unstructured, disguised observation in a natural setting.

# OBSERVATION METHODS CLASSIFIED BY MODE OF ADMINISTRATION

As shown in Figure 6.3, observation methods may be classified by mode of administration as personal observation, mechanical observation, audit, content analysis, and trace analysis.

## Personal Observation

**personal observation**
An observational research strategy in which human observers record the phenomenon being observed as it occurs.

In *personal observation,* a researcher observes actual behavior as it occurs, as in the Canon Cameras example in the overview section. The observer does not attempt to control or manipulate the phenomenon being observed. The observer merely records what takes place. For example, a researcher might record traffic counts and observe traffic flows in a department store. This information could aid in designing store layout and determining the location of individual departments, shelf locations, and merchandise displays.

### REAL RESEARCH

## *The Mystery Behind Mystery Shopping*

The Bose Corporation (*www.bose.com*) is one of the world's leading audio brands, selling a variety of audio products, including home theater speakers, auto sound systems, and portable items for musicians. As of 2003, Bose relied on an array of sales channels, such as retail stores, direct-mail operations, and online sales, to drive about $1.5 billion in annual sales. One strategy that Bose uses effectively is selling directly to consumers through its own retail shops around the country with its own employees who know the products and can explain them to customers. Bose uses mystery shopping to ensure that its customers get the best customer service available. This method combines the use of personal observation with questioning to evaluate different features of the retail shops. Shoppers are recruited and trained in the observation and questioning process.

The mystery shopping process begins with a telephone call to the retail shop. Shoppers ask questions about products and record how helpful the employee was in answering questions. Customers also rate the employee's friendliness and other factors on an excellent-satisfactory-unsatisfactory scale. Next, there is the in-person visit where the shopper, pretending to be a buyer, gives a more in-depth look at the employee's people skills and knowledge of the product. The process is more involved during the in-person visit. The employees are graded on their language, the store environment, and their demonstrations of the products. Shoppers are instructed to complete the observation form immediately after the experience, while everything is still fresh in their mind. This feedback is used to make changes in the personal selling and marketing strategy. When mystery shopping revealed that some salespeople were not very knowledgeable about the products, Bose strengthened its basic technical training program and made it mandatory for all its salespeople. Moreover, salespeople are also required to participate in an ongoing training program so that they keep up to date with Bose products and technology. As a result, shopper satisfaction is very high.[36] ∎

# Mechanical Observation

**mechanical observation**
An observational research strategy in which mechanical devices, rather than human observers, record the phenomenon being observed.

In *mechanical observation,* mechanical devices, rather than human observers, record the phenomenon being observed. These devices may or may not require the respondents' direct participation. They are used for continuously recording ongoing behavior for later analysis.

Of the mechanical devices that do not require respondents' direct participation, the ACNielsen audimeter is best known. The audimeter is attached to a television set to continually record what channel the set is tuned to. Recently, people meters have been introduced. People meters attempt to measure not only the channels to which a set is tuned but also who is watching.[37] Other common examples include turnstiles that record the number of people entering or leaving a building, and traffic counters placed across streets to determine the number of vehicles passing certain locations. On-site cameras (still, motion picture, or video) are increasingly used by retailers to assess package designs, counter space, floor displays, and traffic flow patterns. Technological advances such as the universal product code (UPC) have made a major impact on mechanical observation. The UPC system, together with optical scanners, allows for mechanized information collection regarding consumer purchases by product category, brand, store type, price, and quantity (see Chapter 4).

In contrast, many mechanical observation devices do require respondent involvement. These mechanical devices may be classified into five groups: (1) eye-tracking monitors, (2) pupilometers, (3) psychogalvanometers, (4) voice pitch analyzers, and (5) devices measuring response latency. Eye-tracking equipment, such as oculometers, eye cameras, or eye view minuters, records the gaze movements of the eye. These devices can be used to determine how a respondent reads an advertisement or views a TV commercial and for how long the respondent looks at various parts of the stimulus. Such information is directly relevant to assessing advertising effectiveness. The pupilometer measures changes in the diameter of the pupils of the respondent's eyes. Respondents are asked to look at a screen on which an advertisement or other stimulus is projected. Image brightness and distance from the respondents' eyes are held constant. Changes in pupil size are interpreted as changes in cognitive (thinking) activity resulting from exposure to the stimulus. The underlying assumption is that increased pupil size reflects interest and positive attitudes toward the stimulus.[38]

**psychogalvanometer**
An instrument that measures a respondent's galvanic skin response.

**galvanic skin response (GSR)**
Changes in the electrical resistance of the skin that relate to a respondent's affective state.

**voice pitch analysis**
Measurement of emotional reactions through changes in the respondent's voice.

**response latency**
The amount of time it takes to respond.

The *psychogalvanometer* measures *galvanic skin response* (GSR) or changes in the electrical resistance of the skin.[39] The respondent is fitted with small electrodes that monitor electrical resistance and is shown stimuli such as advertisements, packages, and slogans. The theory behind this device is that physiological changes, such as increased perspiration, accompany emotional reactions. Excitement leads to increased perspiration, which increases the electrical resistance of the skin. From the strength of the response, the researcher infers the respondent's interest level and attitudes toward the stimuli.

*Voice pitch analysis* measures emotional reactions through changes in the respondent's voice. Changes in the relative vibration frequency of the human voice that accompany emotional reaction are measured with audio-adapted computer equipment.[40]

*Response latency* is the time a respondent takes before answering a question. It is used as a measure of the relative preference for various alternatives.[41] Response time is thought to be directly related to uncertainty. Therefore, the longer a respondent takes to choose between two alternatives, the closer the alternatives are in terms of preference. On the other hand, if the respondent makes a quick decision, one alternative is clearly preferred. With the increased popularity of computer-assisted data collection, response latency can be recorded accurately and without the respondent's awareness.

Use of eye-tracking monitors, pupilometers, psychogalvanometers, and voice pitch analyzers assumes that physiological reactions are associated with specific cognitive and affective responses. This has yet to be clearly demonstrated. Furthermore, calibration of these devices to measure physiological arousal is difficult and they are expensive to use. Another limitation is that respondents are placed in an artificial environment and know that they are being observed.

**REAL RESEARCH**

## *Mirro: "Nonsticking" Itself from a Sticky Situation*

Mirro Company, a division of NewellRubbermaid (*www.newellco.com*), manufactures inexpensive cookware and conducted exploratory research to try to increase market share by introducing a new product. The objective of the research was to determine what characteristics could be added to their kitchenware in order to be more beneficial to the user. The company hired Metaphase Design Group (*www.metaphase.com*) to conduct observational market research by using in-home personal meeting with female heads of households. The cities that Metaphase targeted were St. Louis, Boston, and San Francisco. All in-home observations were videotaped for later analysis. The results showed that the most problematic activities involving kitchenware was its pouring characteristics, its storage problems, and its difficulty to clean. More specifically, the company found that, "Pouring was a problem, as was moving food in and out of the pan. And people didn't know what to do with their lids while they were cooking. They complained about the mess that lids leave when you have to set them on the counter or on the stove top." Metaphase also noted that most consumers were unhappy with the ability of "non-stick" pans to not stick.

After analyzing the results, Mirro Company, along with Metaphase, designed a new pot, Allegro, that had a square top with a circular bottom. The square top allowed for easier storage, the ability to pour more carefully, and added volume. All three of these features were directly related to the exploratory research results that the company obtained. The results of the new product were explained by president Gerry Paul, "Allegro sales have topped expectations, and production has finally caught up with the overwhelming demand generated by the early infomercials. Consumer reaction is very good." As of 2003, the Allegro Collection is part of the Wearever product line (*www.wearever.com*) produced by Mirro.[42] ■

## Audit

In an audit, the researcher collects data by examining physical records or performing inventory analysis. Audits have two distinguishing features. First, data are collected personally by the researcher. Second, the data are based upon counts, usually of physical objects. Retail and wholesale audits conducted by marketing research suppliers were discussed in the context of secondary data (see Chapter 4). Here we focus on the role of audits in collecting primary data. In this respect, an important audit conducted at the consumer level, is the pantry audit. In a **pantry audit,** the researcher takes an inventory of brands, quantities, and package sizes in a consumer's home, perhaps in the course of a personal interview. Pantry audits greatly reduce the problem of untruthfulness or other forms of response bias. However, obtaining permission to examine consumers' pantries can be difficult, and the fieldwork is expensive. Furthermore, the brands in the pantry may not reflect the most preferred brands or the brands purchased most often. For these reasons, audits are most common at the retail and wholesale level, and these audits were discussed in Chapter 4.

*pantry audit*
A type of audit where the researcher inventories the brands, quantities, and package sizes of products in a consumer's home.

## Content Analysis

*content analysis*
The objective, systematic, and quantitative description of the manifest content of a communication.

**Content analysis** is an appropriate method when the phenomenon to be observed is communication, rather than behavior or physical objects. It is defined as the objective, systematic, and quantitative description of the manifest content of a communication.[43] It includes observation as well as analysis. The unit of analysis may be words (different words or types of words in the message), characters (individuals or objects), themes (propositions), space and time measures (length or duration of the message), or topics (subject of the message). Analytical categories for classifying the units are developed and the communication is broken down according to prescribed rules. Marketing research applications involve observing and analyzing the content or message of advertisements, newspaper articles, television and radio programs, and the like. For example, the frequency of appearance of blacks, women, and members of other minority groups in mass media has been studied using content analysis. In the department store patronage project, content analysis may be used to analyze magazine advertisements of the sponsoring and competing stores to compare their projected images. Content analysis has also been used in cross-cultural advertising research.

### REAL RESEARCH

## *Cross-Cultural Content Makes Ad Agencies Content*

As of 2003, the United States accounts for half of the world's advertising expenditures, followed by Japan, which accounts for 10 percent. Content analysis was used to compare the information content in American and Japanese magazine advertising. Six categories of magazines (general, women's, men's, professional, sports, and entertainment) were chosen from each country. Advertisements from these magazines were selected for analysis resulting in a total of 1,440 advertisements: 832 from American magazines and 608 from Japanese magazines. Three judges independently noted whether each advertisement was informative or uninformative, which criteria for information content were satisfied by the advertisement, the size of the ad, and the product category being advertised. Japanese magazine advertising was found to be consistently more informative than U.S. magazine advertising. For example, more than 85 percent of the Japanese ads analyzed satisfied at least one criterion for information content and thus were perceived to be informative, compared to only 75 percent of the American ads. Likewise, Japanese ads had an average of 1.7 information cues per ad, compared to 1.3 cues per ad for the American ads. This information is useful for multinational companies and advertising agencies including Young & Rubicam, Saatchi & Saatchi Worldwide, McCann Erickson Worldwide, Ogilvy & Mather Worldwide, BBDO Worldwide, and others with global operations conducting cross-cultural advertising campaigns.[44] ∎

Content analysis can involve tedious coding and analysis. However, microcomputers and mainframes can be used to facilitate coding and analysis. The manifest content of the object can be computer coded. The observed frequencies of category codes can be aggregated and compared on the criteria of interest using computers. Although content analysis has not been widely used in marketing research, the technique offers great potential. For example, it could be profitably employed in the analysis of open-ended questions.

## Trace Analysis

**trace analysis**
An approach in which data collection is based on physical traces, or evidence, of past behavior.

An observation method that can be inexpensive if used creatively is trace analysis. In **trace analysis,** data collection is based on physical traces, or evidence, of past behavior. These traces may be left intentionally or unintentionally by the respondents. To illustrate, in the context of the department store project, store charge card slips are traces shoppers leave behind that can be analyzed to examine their store credit usage behavior.

Several other innovative applications of trace analysis have been made in marketing research.

- The selective erosion of tiles in a museum, indexed by the replacement rate, was used to determine the relative popularity of exhibits.
- The number of different fingerprints on a page was used to gauge the readership of various advertisements in a magazine.
- The position of the radio dials in cars brought in for service was used to estimate share of listening audience of various radio stations. Advertisers used the estimates to decide on which stations to advertise.
- The age and condition of cars in a parking lot were used to assess the affluence of customers.

■ The magazines people donated to charity were used to determine people's favorite magazines.

■ Internet visitors leave traces that can be analyzed to examine browsing and usage behavior, by using cookies.

**REAL RESEARCH**

### Have a Cookie

Many users do not realize it, but they have been served a cookie or two while on the Internet. A cookie is not a culinary delight in this case. It is a sophisticated means by which a Web site can collect information on visitors. Often this process takes place without the knowledge of the Web surfer.

The cookie is a group of letters and numbers stored in a Web surfer's browser that identify the user. Companies and individuals that host Web sites use cookies to collect marketing research information on visitors. Cookies follow the traveler through the Web site and record the pages accessed by the visitor and the number of minutes spent on each page. Your name, address, phone number, and access site can be collected by the cookie and saved into a database if the visitor enters any information. During a follow-up visit, the cookie accesses this information and has the ability to repeat it to the visitor. In essence, the cookie collects data on the user during every visit to the site.

Hotwired's *Packet* (*www.hotwired.com*) uses cookies to collect information about site traffic. The information helps marketing personnel at the electronic and print magazine to collect demographics on the reader. Also, the company can monitor "hits" on particular topics and gain valuable feedback on user interest. Data collection is based upon visitor behavior. This disguised technique enables Hotwired to monitor use patterns and to eliminate socially acceptable response bias. Information collected in this manner has been used to modify editorial content and format to make the magazine more appealing.[45] ■

Although trace analysis has been creatively applied, it has limitations. Current evidence indicates that it should be used only when no other approach is possible. Moreover, ethical issues, such as the use of cookies, should be duly addressed.

## A COMPARATIVE EVALUATION OF OBSERVATION METHODS

A comparative evaluation of the observation methods is given in Table 6.3. The different observation methods are evaluated in terms of the degree of structure, degree of disguise, ability to observe in a natural setting, observation bias, measurement and analysis bias, and additional general factors.

**TABLE 6.3**

**A Comparative Evaluation of Observation Methods**

| CRITERIA | PERSONAL OBSERVATION | MECHANICAL OBSERVATION | AUDIT | CONTENT ANALYSIS | TRACE ANALYSIS |
|---|---|---|---|---|---|
| Degree of structure | Low | Low to high | High | High | Medium |
| Degree of disguise | Medium | Low to high | Low | High | High |
| Ability to observe in natural setting | High | Low to high | High | Medium | Low |
| Observation bias | High | Low | Low | Medium | Medium |
| Analysis bias | High | Low to medium | Low | Low | Medium |
| General remarks | Most flexible | Can be intrusive | Expensive | Limited to communications | Method of last resort |

Structure relates to the specification of what is to be observed and how the measurements are to be recorded. As can be seen from Table 6.3, personal observation is low, trace analysis is medium, and audit and content analysis are high on the degree of structure. Mechanical observation can vary widely from low to high depending upon on the methods used. Methods such as optical scanners are very structured in that the characteristics to be measured, e.g., characteristics of items purchased scanned in supermarket checkouts, are precisely defined. Thus, these methods are high in the degree of structure. In contrast, mechanical methods, such as use of hidden cameras to observe children at play with toys, tend to be unstructured.

The degree of disguise is low in the case of audits, as it is difficult to conceal the identity of auditors. Personal observation offers a medium degree of disguise, as there are limitations on the extent to which the observer can be disguised as a shopper, sales clerk, employee, etc. Trace analysis and content analysis offer a high degree of disguise, as the data are collected "after the fact," i.e., after the phenomenon to be observed has taken place. Some mechanical observations, such as hidden cameras, offer excellent disguise, whereas the use of others, such as psychogalvanometers, is very difficult to disguise.

The ability to observe in a natural setting is low in trace analysis because the observation takes place after the behavior has occurred. It is medium in the case of content analysis because the communication being analyzed is only a limited representation of the natural phenomenon. Personal observation and audits are excellent on this score, as human observers can observe people or objects in a variety of natural settings. Mechanical observation methods vary from low (e.g., use of psychogalvanometers) to high (e.g., use of turnstiles).

Observation bias is low in the case of mechanical observation because a human observer is not involved. It is also low for audits. Although the auditors are humans, the observation usually takes place on objects and the characteristics to be observed are well defined, leading to low observation bias. Observation bias is medium for trace analysis and content analysis. In both of these methods, human observers are involved and the characteristics to be observed are not that well defined. However, the observers typically do not interact with human respondents during the observation process, thus lessening the degree of bias. It is high for personal observation due to the use of human observers who interact with the phenomenon being observed.

Data analysis bias is low for audits and content analysis because the variables are precisely defined, the data are quantitative, and statistical analysis is conducted. Trace analysis has a medium degree of bias, as the definition of variables is not very precise. Mechanical observation methods can have a low (e.g., scanner data) to medium (e.g., hidden camera) degree of analysis bias depending on the method. Unlike personal observation, the bias in mechanical observation is limited to the medium level, due to improved measurement and classification because the phenomenon to be observed can be recorded continuously using mechanical devices.

In addition, personal observation is the most flexible, as human observers can observe a wide variety of phenomenon in a wide variety of settings. Some mechanical observation methods, such as use of psychogalvanometers, can be very intrusive, leading to artificiality and bias. Audits using human auditors tend to be expensive. Content analysis is well suited for and limited to the observation of communications. As mentioned earlier, trace analysis is a method of last resort. The application of these criteria will lead to the identification of an appropriate method, if observation is at all suitable in the given situation.

# A COMPARISON OF SURVEY AND OBSERVATION METHODS

Only about one percent of the marketing research projects rely solely on observational methods to obtain primary data.[46] This implies that observational methods have some major disadvantages as compared to survey methods. Yet these methods offer some advantages that make their use in conjunction with survey methods quite fruitful.

## Relative Advantages of Observation

The greatest advantage of observational methods is that they permit measurement of actual behavior rather than reports of intended or preferred behavior. There is no reporting bias, and potential bias caused by the interviewer and the interviewing process is eliminated or reduced. Certain types of data can be collected only by observation. These include behavior patterns that the respondent is unaware of or unable to communicate. For example, information on babies' toy preferences is best obtained by observing babies at play because they are unable to express themselves adequately. Moreover, if the observed phenomenon occurs frequently or is of short duration, observational methods may be cheaper and faster than survey methods.

## Relative Disadvantages of Observation

The most serious disadvantage of observation is that the reasons for the observed behavior may not be determined because little is known about the underlying motives, beliefs, attitudes, and preferences. For example, people observed buying a brand of cereal may or may not like it themselves. They may be purchasing that brand for someone else in the household. Another limitation of observation is that selective perception (bias in the researcher's perception) can bias the data. In addition, observational data is often time consuming and expensive and it is difficult to observe certain forms of behavior such as personal activities. Finally, in some cases the use of observational methods may be unethical, as in monitoring the behavior of people without their knowledge or consent.

To sum up, observation has the potential to provide valuable information when properly used. From a practical standpoint, it is best to view observation as a complement to survey methods, rather than as being in competition with them.

### REAL RESEARCH

### *How Do You Like Your Beef?*

When people shop for meat at the grocery store, they tend to stick with what they know. This is what was found when PortiCo Research (*www.porticoresearch.com*) conducted research for the National Cattlemen's Beef Association (NCBA). The research was performed to help the NCBA figure out why the sales of certain cuts of beef had been dropping by 20 percent over a period of four years. PortiCo Research used mechanical observation along with customer interviews. PortiCo researchers stationed themselves at the meat cases of stores in order to record the buying behavior of consumers. The consumers were video taped while shopping for beef. These observations showed that many consumers were not purchasing certain cuts of beef even when they looked good and were less fattening than the more popular sirloin or ground beef. When these consumers were asked why they did not buy certain cuts of beef, the overwhelming response was that they did not know how to cook them.

The NCBA took several steps to address this situation. Appropriate cooking instructions for the cut of meat are now clearly printed on the package. Additionally, the NCBA worked with grocers to change the store layout to display the beef according to the cooking method. There are labels above each section that state not only the nutritional facts, but also the ways in which a cut of beef may be prepared. Small recipe cards have also been placed alongside the beef cuts.

In 2001, consumers spent more money on beef compared to any other year in history (*www.beef.org*). Total consumer expenditures were estimated at $57 billion in 2001, which is $4.3 billion more than total expenditures in 2000.[47] ∎

# INTERNATIONAL MARKETING RESEARCH

Global marketing research presents several challenges to collecting data using surveys. It is unlikely that a single data-collection methodology will be effective in a multicountry research study. For instance, mail surveys are popular in the United States and Canada. However, mail surveys in Europe are less popular, and they are rare in most other parts of the world. Several reasons account for this difference, including lower literacy rates, excessive time for mail to reach its destination, and cultures where people do not believe in writing replies that will be read by a stranger.

A similar problem occurs with telephone surveys. Phone interviewing has grown in Europe recently, but is still not widely used outside the United States. Response rates for mail and telephone surveys are much lower in marketing studies abroad. Personal interview techniques remain the most popular internationally used marketing field research techniques. It is very important to instruct field workers who are collecting the data how they may be affecting the results of a face-to-face study in an international setting. In selecting interviewers, it is also useful to consider the nationalities of the interviewers compared with the participants because of cultural relations that may bias the responses.

Selection of appropriate interviewing methods is much more difficult because of the challenges of conducting research in foreign countries. Given the differences in the economic, structural, informational and technological, and sociocultural environment, the feasibility and popularity of the different interviewing methods vary widely. In the United States and Canada, the telephone has achieved almost total penetration of households. As a result, telephone interviewing is the dominant mode of questionnaire administration. The same situation exists in some European countries, such as Sweden. However, in many of the other European countries, telephone penetration is still not complete. In developing countries, only very few households have telephones.

In-home personal interviews are the dominant mode of collecting survey data in many European countries, such as Switzerland, newly industrialized countries (NICs), and developing countries. Although mall intercepts are being conducted in some European countries, such as Sweden, they are not popular in Europe or developing countries. In contrast, central location/street interviews constitute the dominant method of collecting survey data in France and the Netherlands.

Because of their low cost, mail interviews continue to be used in most developed countries where literacy is high and the postal system is well developed: United States, Canada, Denmark, Finland, Iceland, Norway, Sweden, and the Netherlands, for example. In Africa, Asia, and South America, however, the use of mail surveys and mail panels is low because of illiteracy and the large proportion of the population living in rural areas. Mail panels are extensively used only in a few countries outside the United States, such as Canada, the United Kingdom, France, Germany, and the Netherlands. However, the use of panels may increase with the advent of new technology. Likewise, although a Web site can be accessed from anywhere in the world, access to the Web or e-mail is limited in many countries, particularly developing countries. Hence, the use of electronic surveys is not feasible, especially for interviewing households. The different methods of survey administration are discussed in more detail in Chapter 23.

## Selection of Survey Methods

No questionnaire administration method is superior in all situations. Table 6.4 presents a comparative evaluation of the major modes of collecting quantitative data in the context of international marketing research. In this table, the survey methods are discussed only under the broad headings of telephone, personal, mail, and electronic interviews. The use of CATI, CAPI, and mail panels depends heavily on the state of technological development in the country. Likewise, the use of mall intercept interviewing is contingent upon the dominance of shopping malls in the retailing environment. The same is true for e-mail and Internet surveys, which rely on access to computers and the Internet. The major methods of interviewing should be carefully evaluated on the criteria given in Table 6.4.

Another very important consideration in selecting the methods of administering questionnaires is to ensure equivalence and comparability across countries. Different methods may have different reliabilities in different countries. In collecting data from different countries, it is desirable to use survey methods with equivalent levels of reliability, rather than the same method, as illustrated in the following example.[48]

## TABLE 6.4

### A Comparative Evaluation of Survey Methods for International Marketing Research

| CRITERIA | TELEPHONE | PERSONAL | MAIL | ELECTRONIC |
|---|---|---|---|---|
| High sample control | + | + | − | − |
| Difficulty in locating respondents at home | + | − | + | + |
| Inaccessibility of homes | + | − | + | + |
| Unavailability of a large pool of trained interviewers | + | − | + | + |
| Large population in rural areas | − | + | − | − |
| Unavailability of maps | + | − | + | + |
| Unavailability of current telephone directory | − | + | − | + |
| Unavailability of mailing lists | + | + | − | + |
| Low penetration of telephones | − | + | + | − |
| Lack of an efficient postal system | + | + | − | + |
| Low level of literacy | − | + | − | − |
| Face-to-face communication culture | − | + | − | − |
| Poor access to computers and Internet | ? | + | ? | − |

Note: A + denotes an advantage, and a − denotes a disadvantage.

**REAL RESEARCH**

### Using Dominant Survey Methods to Gain Dominant Market Share

Reebok International Ltd. (*www.reebok.com*) had an 11.9 percent share of the over $8 billion U.S. athletic footwear market, whereas Nike had 42.6 percent and Adidas had 11.3 percent. With worldwide sales accounting for 44 percent of its total, Reebok is marketed in over 170 countries as of 2003. Currently, Reebok is seeking to expand in Europe. Rather than strictly compete with Nike, Adidas, and Puma in Europe for the athletic market, Reebok would like to institute strong marketing programs to sell street sneakers to the European masses. A survey of consumer preferences for sneakers is to be undertaken in three countries: Sweden, France, and Switzerland. Comparability of results can best be achieved by using the dominant mode of interviewing in each country: telephone interviews in Sweden, central location/street interviews in France, and in-home personal interviews in Switzerland.[49] ∎

As in the case of surveys, the selection of an appropriate observation method in international marketing research should also take into account the differences in the economic, structural, informational and technological, and sociocultural environment.

## ETHICS IN MARKETING RESEARCH

The unethical use of survey research as a guise for selling or fundraising was discussed in Chapter 1. Another ethical issue that is salient in survey and observation research is respondents' anonymity. Researchers have an obligation to not disclose respondents' names to outside parties, including the client. This is all the more critical if the respondents were promised anonymity in order to obtain their participation. The client is not entitled to the names of respondents. Only when respondents are notified in advance, and their consent is obtained prior to administering the survey, can their names be disclosed to the client. Even in such situations, the researcher should have the assurance that the client will not use respondents' names in sales efforts or misuse them in other ways. The following example highlights the battle being waged by the marketing research industry in the ethical arena.

## REAL RESEARCH

### *The Signal Is Busy for Telephone Research*

The Council for Marketing and Opinion Research (CMOR) (*www.cmor.org*) recently identified the "major threats to research vitality." At the top of the list was telephone research, due to concern over proposed legislation. About half of the states have introduced bills to regulate unsolicited telephone calls and the remaining are considering similar legislation. A California law, designed to limit eavesdropping, makes it illegal to listen in on an extension, and this might limit supervisory monitoring of telephone interviewers.

Another issue facing the marketing research industry is image, as the general public does not distinguish between telephone research and telemarketing. This identity crisis is exacerbated by the action of some firms to commit "sugging and frugging," industry terms for selling or fund-raising under the guise of a survey.

All of these barriers raise the cost of telephone research and make it difficult for researchers to obtain representative samples. Recent statistics released in September 2001 by CMOR confirm that the industry still faces an increasing trend in the number of people refusing to participate in surveys each year. The study surveyed 3,700 U.S. consumers, and nearly 45 percent stated they had refused to participate in a survey during the last year. CMOR's definition of a survey refusal does not include cases where consumers avoid phone calls by means of caller ID or answering machines. Such factors would actually push the true refusal rate much higher. Consumers' concern about privacy is the number one reason that survey refusal rate is so high. In addition, the widespread use of the Internet and the publicized awareness of fraudulent use has made consumers more hesitant about participating in interviews. The study also reveals that only 30 percent of respondents "agree" or "strongly agree" that researchers can be trusted to protect consumers' right to privacy, which has decreased from 40 percent in 1999 and 50 percent in 1995. The CMOR is fighting back and has hired the Washington law firm of Covington and Burling to lobby Congress and coordinate state-level lobbying. Another action under consideration is a "seal of approval" from the CMOR to raise the public's image perceptions of responsible research firms. The battle to save telephone research must be waged; all it takes is a phone call.[50] ■

Researchers should not place respondents in stressful situations. Disclaimers such as "there are no right or wrong answers, we are interested only in your opinion" can relieve much of the stress inherent in a survey.

Often the behavior of people is observed without their knowledge because informing the respondents may alter their behavior.[51] However, this can violate the respondents' privacy. One guideline is that people should not be observed for research in situations where they would not expect to be observed by the public. However, observing people in public places like a mall or a grocery store is appropriate if certain procedures are followed. Notices should be posted in these areas stating that they are under observation for marketing research purposes. After the data have been collected, the researcher should obtain the necessary permission from the respondents. If any of the respondents refuse to grant permission, the observation records pertaining to them should be destroyed. These guidelines should also be applied when using cookies on the Internet.[52]

# INTERNET AND COMPUTER APPLICATIONS

Internet surveys are gaining in popularity. One reason is that the cost, in most cases, is less than that of phone and mail surveys or personal interviews. Also, the Internet survey is not as inconvenient as the phone call in the middle of dinner. The online survey can be completed in one's own time and place. Quick response time is another advantage cited by those producing online surveys. Greenfield Online Research Center cited a case where they placed a survey online "Good Friday and had 2,400 competed forms on Monday morning." Greenfield has a panel of nearly 200,000 people via the Internet. Thus, the speed of response is a definite advantage of online marketing research.

Another advantage of Internet marketing research is the ability to target specific populations. For example, the purchasers of a specific model home-office product, purchased over a specific time interval, were needed to conduct some market research. Several months of traditional research was conducted via telephone and several thousands of dollars were spent to land very few individuals. Then using the Internet, hundreds of potential candidates were found in only a few weeks at comparatively little cost. Thus online market research aids those researchers attempting to find specific target markets.

There are limitations to electronic surveys. The Internet or e-mail users are not representative of the general population. Burke Marketing Research is trying to improve the randomness of those participating in online surveys by designing suitable Internet sampling programs. Other limitations of such market research is the verification of who is actually responding to the survey. The absence of a human facilitator to motivate participants, security, and privacy are also areas of concern. The research company can receive "flame" messages from recipients who consider receiving an online survey as an invasion of their privacy.

One company, Decisive Technology Corporation (*www.doubleclick.com*), created two software tools to help users create and analyze e-mail and Web-based surveys. One product, Decisive Survey, allows users to create, administer, and analyze Web-based and e-mail surveys. Their other product, Decisive Feedback, is used for e-mail surveys only. The software is a forms-based tool that gives users a graphical way to design surveys. Once the completed surveys are returned, the software then allows the easy porting of data to databases and statistical software packages such as SPSS and SAS. Previously, marketing research companies would use text-based surveys for the Internet. However, this meant that the data had to be rekeyed once they were returned. Decisive Survey and Decisive Feedback allow for automatic tabulation and graphical outputs such as pie and line charts. The system also allows for the full range of responses, such as Choose One, Choose All that Apply, and Fill in the Blank. Other companies, such as Centrac (*www.centrac.com*) also provide services to design and field online surveys.

## REAL RESEARCH

### From E-Commerce to M-Commerce

Telephia (*www.telephia.com*) provides data-gathering services in the areas of marketing and network quality for the wireless telephone industry. The company formed the largest nationwide panel of wireless data and Internet users to research customers' needs in the wireless market as we move from an e-commerce to an m-commerce (mobile-commerce) world. An Internet survey was conducted with 3,500 respondents who used PDA, two-way pager, wireless laptop, or wireless data-enabled phones. The objective of this survey was to gain insight into customers' attitudes and usage of wireless technology, especially wireless Internet and related services. A survey conducted by InStat revealed that m-commerce will not be a booming market until at least 2003, due to the small number of wireless Web users and because providers are still tackling pricing options. PCIA/Yankelovich conducted a Global M-User Study that showed 27 percent of consumers in the United States strongly agreed with the following statement: "I wish that I could do the same thing on my mobile phone that I can now do only with a computer." Globally speaking, other countries' consumers that strongly agreed with this statement were Japan (28%), Italy (21%), United Kingdom (20%), South Korea (17%), and Germany (15%). These statistics definitely show that there is great potential for the m-commerce market.

Telephia's survey results provided information on customers' perceptions and usage of wireless data devices, service providers, wireless Internet usage, customer satisfaction, interest in new product offerings, purchase behavior using wireless data devices, and factors affecting loyalty and switching. Almost half of the survey respondents agreed that data services were "very" to "extremely" important when making decisions about which wireless service provider to choose. There were also some insights regarding voice-activated devices, location-based services, and wireless advertising. For example, 50 percent of wireless users were interested in location-based services, such as directional maps, addresses, yellow pages, and ATM location information.

Companies such as Verizon, Motorola, Cingular, and Sprint can use this information about early wireless adopters in planning their marketing strategies. Verizon could offer more location-based services in order to expand the features of its wireless service. In 2002, Motorola and America Online teamed up to make the AOL Instant Messenger service a standard feature in mobile phone handsets.[53] ■

The Internet can be a very good source for observation and can provide valuable information. The observations can be made in a variety of ways. Primary observations can be made by the number of times the Web page is visited; the time spent on the page can also be measured by advanced techniques of starting a timer when the person visiting the page clicks on a certain icon and stopping the timer when they click on the next button. Further, various other links can be provided by the researcher on the Web page, and it can be observed as to which links are accessed more often. This will provide the researcher with important information about the information needs of the individuals and also about the interests of the target segment. The analysis of the links from where the company site is being approached by the individuals will provide the market researcher important information regarding the consumer's related interests, and an in-depth analysis of the link sites will provide information on advertising, competitors, consumers, target market demographics, and psychographics.

The use of microcomputers and mainframes has already been discussed in the context of CATI, CAPI, content analysis, audits, and trace analysis. Software for implementing these and other survey and observation methods is available. Computer-automated telephone surveys (CATS) systems are capable of dialing and interviewing respondents without any human intervention, other than the digital recording of questions to be asked during the phone survey. A handheld computer can replace paper questionnaires used in personal interviewing. Using pen-based computing technology, this system uses the display memory as a software keypad. A variety of software is also available for conducting mail surveys. Conquest Direct Express by Donnelley Marketing Information Services (*www.donnelleymarketing.com*) defines market areas and obtains counts and consumer lists for only those households or individuals in the block group or enumeration districts, census tracts, or zip codes in a desired area (geometric or geographic).

## FOCUS ON BURKE

Burke uses all the major interviewing methods (telephone, mail, personal, and electronic). The use of multiple methods is illustrated in customer satisfaction research.

Burke generally uses telephone interviews, mail surveys, or a combination of the two to collect customer satisfaction data. Telephone interviews are most appropriate when:

- Customers must be screened to identify the person best qualified to answer the questions.
- The project requires fast turnaround.
- The questionnaire has complex skip patterns or a number of open-ended questions.
- The number of customers eligible to participate in the survey is relatively small.

Burke operates three data-collection centers with a total of 250 CATI stations.

Mail surveys tend to cost less than telephone surveys and are therefore most appropriate for large-scale projects. For example, Burke uses mail surveys to collect data from customers of a nationwide fast-food restaurant chain.

Interactive voice-recognition systems have gained popularity in recent years. Burke uses this technology for a large financial institution. Both customers and employees use their touch-tone phone to key in answers to Burke's satisfaction questions.

In a typical customer satisfaction study, Burke's client provides the list of customer names, addresses, and phone numbers. Client-supplied lists are particularly common for business-to-business studies. Clients generally ask Burke to interview current customers, though it is not unusual to interview former customers.

Mall intercept surveys are also conducted frequently when it is advantageous to administer the questionnaire using personal interviewing. For this purpose, Burke has contacts with a network of more than 200 mall agencies. Opinion One is a specialized mall intercept survey offered by Burke. It is computer administered (CAPI), using a fully interactive multimedia platform designed to collect data based on a variety of visual and audio stimuli. All the mall locations offering Opinion One are electronically linked to ensure fast transmission of data to and from Burke's Cincinnati headquarters.

For the Internet, Burke has designed WEBNOSTICS, a survey that is administered at the client's Web site to every $n$th visitor to obtain a systematic evaluation of the Web site. The Secure Surfer Index is an Internet survey that evaluates the impact of the client's Web site on the commitment and loyalty of Web visitors. As people visit the Client's Web site, they are randomly presented with a link to the Burke Secure Surfer Index questions. If they do not want to participate, they press the "Decline" button and continue surfing unhindered. If they agree to participate, they press the "Accept" button and are tracked from the exact location and subdirectory of the client's Web site.

The bulk of worldwide research is done by face-to-face interviews and self-administered interviews. The United States and Canada are the only countries with high levels of telephone interviewing. Among Burke's international affiliates, Sweden is the third highest in percent of interviews conducted by telephone at about 18 percent. Therefore, when conducting international marketing research, Burke designs surveys so that they may be administered by different modes in different countries.

Burke conducted a study for a software vendor in 14 countries. The range of feasible data-collection methods included telephone, mail, face to face, and fax. A major consideration for research design was creating questions that could be legitimately administered using any of these methods and produce comparable results. Burke's procedure is to involve a research professional in each country to give a perspective on how the data could best be collected in their country and how the questions should be modified for their country. At this point, key budget and timing decisions have to be made, as a change of data-collection method to allow greater comparability across countries can seriously affect the cost and time of completion of the study. These are the types of decisions and trade-offs that only experienced professionals in the different cultures can manage. By building expertise in different survey methods at a global level, Burke has the resources to select the survey method that is best suited for a given study in a specific country, and that will result in data comparable to those collected in other countries where different survey methods may be used.

# SUMMARY

The two basic means of obtaining primary quantitative data in descriptive research are survey and observation. Survey involves the direct questioning of respondents, whereas observation entails recording respondent behavior.

Surveys involve the administration of a questionnaire and may be classified, based on the method or mode of administration, as (1) traditional telephone interviews, (2) CATI, (3) in-home personal interviews, (4) mall intercept interviews, (5) CAPI, (6) mail surveys, (7) mail panels, (8) e-mail surveys, and (9) Internet surveys. Of these methods, traditional telephone interviews and CATI are the most popular. However, each method has some general advantages and disadvantages. The various methods may be compared in terms of flexibility of data collection, diversity of questions, use of physical stimuli, sample control, control of the data-collection environment, control of field force, quantity of data, social desirability, obtaining sensitive information, potential for interviewer bias, response rate, perceived anonymity, speed, and cost. Although these data-collection methods are usually thought of as distinct and competitive, they should not be considered mutually exclusive. It is possible to employ them productively in combination.

Observational methods may be classified as structured or unstructured, disguised or undisguised, and natural or con-trived. The major methods are personal observation, mechanical observation, audit, content analysis, and trace analysis. As compared to surveys, the relative advantages of observational methods are: (1) they permit measurement of actual behavior, (2) there is no reporting bias, and (3) there is less potential for interviewer bias. Also, certain types of data can be obtained best, or only, by observation. The relative disadvantages of observation are: (1) very little can be inferred about motives, beliefs, attitudes, and preferences, (2) there is potential for observer bias, (3) most methods are time consuming and expensive, (4) it is difficult to observe some forms of behavior, and (5) there is potential for being unethical. Observation is rarely used as the sole method of obtaining primary data, but it can be usefully employed in conjunction with survey methods.

In collecting data from different countries, it is desirable to use survey methods with equivalent levels of reliability, rather than the same method. Respondents' anonymity should be protected and their names should not be turned over to the clients. People should not be observed without consent for research in situations where they would not expect to be observed by the public. Internet and computers are used extensively in survey research. They also facilitate observation methods, particularly content analysis, audits, and trace analysis.

# KEY TERMS AND CONCEPTS

survey method, *168*
structured data collection, *169*
fixed-alternative questions, *169*
mail panel, *176*
hypertext markup language (HTML), *177*
sample control, *180*
sampling frame, *180*
random digit dialing (rdd), *180*
random digit directory designs, *181*

field force, *182*
response rate, *183*
nonresponse bias, *183*
critical request, *183*
perceived anonymity, *183*
social desirability, *183*
observation, *186*
structured observation, *186*
unstructured observation, *186*
natural observation, *186*

contrived observation, *186*
personal observation, *187*
mechanical observation, *188*
psychogalvanometer, *188*
galvanic skin response (GSR), *188*
voice pitch analysis, *188*
response latency, *188*
pantry audit, *189*
content analysis, *189*
trace analysis, *190*

# EXERCISES

## *Questions*

1. Explain briefly how the topics covered in this chapter fit into the framework of the marketing research process.
2. What are the advantages and disadvantages of the structured direct survey method?
3. Name the major modes for obtaining information via a survey.
4. What are the relevant factors for evaluating which survey method is best suited to a particular research project?
5. What would be the most appropriate survey method for a project in which control of field force and cost are critical factors?
6. Name the types of mechanical observation and explain how they work.

7. Explain how content analysis could be employed in the analysis of open-ended questions. Comment on the relative advantages and disadvantages of using such a method.
8. Why is trace analysis used as a means of last resort?
9. What are the relative advantages and disadvantages of observation?

## *Problems*

1. Describe a marketing research problem in which both survey and observation methods could be used for obtaining the information needed.

2. Collect 30 advertisements featuring women from recent issues of popular magazines. Do a content analysis of these ads to examine the different roles in which women are portrayed in advertising.

3. The campus food service would like to determine how many people eat in the student cafeteria. List the survey method ways in which this information could be obtained. Which method is best?

# INTERNET AND COMPUTER EXERCISES

1. Ask your instructor or other faculty members if you could serve as a respondent in a computer-assisted personal interview. Then answer the same questionnaire in a pencil-and-paper format. Compare the two experiences.
2. Use simple spreadsheet software, such as EXCEL, or any appropriate microcomputer or mainframe program, to conduct the content analysis described in problem 2 above.
3. Locate an Internet survey for which you would qualify as a respondent. Answer this survey. How would you evaluate this survey based on the criteria factors of Table 6.2.
4. Locate an Internet survey. Examine the content of the questionnaire carefully. What are the relative advantages and disadvantages of administering the same survey using CATI or mall intercept interviewing?
5. Design an e-mail survey to measure students' attitudes toward credit cards. E-mail the survey to 10 students. Summarize, in a qualitative way, the responses received. Are student attitudes toward credit cards positive or negative?
6. Visit the Gallup organization's Web site at *www.gallup.com*. What survey methods have been used by Gallup in some of the recent surveys posted at this site? Why were these survey methods selected?

# ACTIVITIES

## Role Playing

1. You work for a high-tech company and are asked to do a study of people's responses to your advertising. Specifically, your boss wants to know which ads in a series are especially appealing or interesting to consumers. Your recommendations will be used to determine the product's copy mix. Explain how you will obtain this information. What methods will you use and why? Be specific.
2. You have been hired by the campus bookstore to determine how students make purchase decisions while shopping. You are to use the method of personal observation. Disguise yourself as a shopper and observe the behavior of other students in the bookstore. Write a report about your findings.

## Fieldwork

1. Visit a local marketing research firm engaged in survey research. Take a tour of their CATI facilities. Write a report describing how this firm conducts CATI.

2. Contact a marketing research firm with mall intercept interviewing facilities. Arrange to visit these facilities when mall intercept interviews are being conducted. Write a report about your experience.

## Group Discussion

1. As a small group, discuss the ethical issues involved in disguised observation. How can such issues be addressed?
2. "With advances in technology, observation methods are likely to become popular." Discuss this statement as a small group.

# CHAPTER 7

# Causal Research Design: Experimentation

*Our experiments cannot prove causality. They can, however, go a long way toward eliminating all the possible causes other than the ones we are interested in.*

*Michael Baumgardner,*
*president,*
*Burke, Inc.*

## Objectives

After reading this chapter, the student should be able to:

1. Explain the concept of causality as defined in marketing research and distinguish between the ordinary meaning and the scientific meaning of causality.
2. Define and differentiate the two types of validity: internal validity and external validity.
3. Discuss the various extraneous variables that can affect the validity of results obtained through experimentation and explain how the researcher can control extraneous variables.
4. Describe and evaluate experimental designs and the differences among preexperimental, true experimental, quasi-experimental, and statistical designs.
5. Compare and contrast the use of laboratory versus field experimentation and experimental versus nonexperimental designs in marketing research.
6. Describe test marketing and its various forms: standard test market, controlled test market, and simulated test market.
7. Understand why the internal and external validity of field experiments conducted overseas is generally lower than in the United States.
8. Describe the ethical issues involved in conducting causal research and the role of debriefing in addressing some of these issues.
9. Discuss the use of the Internet and computers in causal research.

## Overview

We introduced causal designs in Chapter 3, where we discussed their relationship to exploratory and descriptive designs and defined experimentation as the primary method employed in causal designs. This chapter explores the concept of causality further. We identify the necessary conditions for causality, examine the role of validity in experimentation, and consider the extraneous variables and procedures for controlling them. We present a classification of experimental designs and consider specific designs, along with the relative merits of laboratory and field experiments. An application in the area of test marketing is discussed in detail. The considerations involved in conducting experimental research when researching international markets are discussed. Several ethical issues that arise in experimentation are identified. The chapter concludes with a discussion of the use of the Internet and computers in causal research.

## REAL RESEARCH

### *It's in the Bag*

LeSportsac, Inc. (*www.lesportsac.com*) filed a suit against Kmart Corporation (*www.kmart.com*) after Kmart introduced a "di Paris sac" line of bags, which LeSportsac claimed looked like its bags. According to LeSportsac, Kmart led consumers to believe that they were purchasing LeSportsac bags when they were not. To prove its point, LeSportsac undertook causal research.

Two groups of women were selected. One group was shown two LeSportsac lightweight soft-sided bags from which all tags were removed and all words and designs were printed over within the distinctive LeSportsac ovals. The second group of women were shown two "di Paris sac" bags with the brand name visible and bearing the tags and labels these bags carry in Kmart stores. Information was obtained from both groups of women to learn whether or not these women perceive a single company or source and/or brand identification of masked bags, what identifications they make, if any, and the reasons they give for doing so. The sample consisted of 200 women in each group selected by mall intercept interviews conducted in Chicago, Los Angeles, and New York. Rather than utilizing a probability sample, the respondents were selected in accordance with age quotas.

The study indicated that many consumers could not distinguish the origin of the two makes of bags, supporting the position of LeSportsac. This experiment helped LeSportsac convince the court of appeals to affirm the issuance of an injunction against Kmart. Kmart agreed to stop selling its "di Paris sac." LeSportsac was founded in 1974 and as of 2003 its products are sold in over 15 countries worldwide including the United States of America, Italy, United Kingdom, France, Sweden, Japan, Hong Kong, Korea, Taiwan, Singapore, Australia, Colombia, and Saudi Arabia.[1] ∎

Drugstores such as Eckerd are increasingly experimenting with in-store advertising to determine its effect on sales.

## POP Buys

Eckerd Drug Co. (*www.eckerd.com*) conducted an experiment to examine the effectiveness of in-store radio advertisements to induce point-of-purchase (POP) buys. Twenty statistically compatible stores were selected based on store size, geographical location, traffic flow count, and age. Half of these were randomly selected as test stores, whereas the other half served as control stores. The test stores aired the radio advertisements, whereas the control stores' POP radio systems were removed. Tracking data in the form of unit volume and dollar sales were obtained for seven days before the experiment, during the course of the four-week experiment, and seven days after the experiment. The products monitored varied from inexpensive items to small kitchen appliances. Results indicated that sales of the advertised products in the test stores at least doubled. Based on this evidence, Eckerd concluded that in-store radio advertising was highly effective in inducing POP buys and decided to continue it.

In 2001, Point of Purchase Advertising International (*www.popai.com*) conducted a study to determine the growth effects of in-store advertising in the soft drink beverage category in grocery stores. Results revealed that sales increased at an estimated 11 percent when soft drinks were displayed with freestanding promotional items, and more than 20 percent when standing promo items were tied to a themed display. Anheuser-Busch, Pepsi/Frito-Lay, Pfizer, Procter & Gamble, and Ralston-Purina sponsored this study, with the data gathered by Information Resources from 250 grocery stores. All these companies sell products that can benefit from point-of-purchase advertising, and based on these results decided to increase their POP promotional budget.[2] ■

# CONCEPT OF CAUSALITY

**causality**
When the occurrence of X increases the probability of the occurrence of Y.

Experimentation is commonly used to infer causal relationships. The concept of **causality** requires some explanation. The scientific concept of causality is complex. "Causality" means something very different to the average person on the street than to a scientist.[3] A statement such as "*X* causes *Y* " will have different meanings to an ordinary person and to a scientist, as seen in the table on the following page.

The scientific meaning of causality is more appropriate to marketing research than is the everyday meaning. Marketing effects are caused by multiple variables, and the relationship between cause and effect tends to be probabilistic. Moreover, we can never prove causality (i.e., demonstrate it conclusively); we can only infer a cause-and-effect relationship. In other words, it is possible that the true causal relation, if one exists, may

| *Ordinary Meaning* | *Scientific Meaning* |
|---|---|
| X is the only cause of Y. | X is only one of a number of possible causes of Y. |
| X must always lead to Y (X is a deterministic cause of Y). | The occurrence of X makes the occurrence of Y more probable (X is a probabilistic cause of Y). |
| It is possible to prove that X is a cause of Y. | We can never prove that X is a cause of Y. At best, we can infer that X is a cause of Y. |

not have been identified. We further clarify the concept of causality by discussing the conditions for causality.

# CONDITIONS FOR CAUSALITY

Before making causal inferences, or assuming causality, three conditions must be satisfied. These are: (1) concomitant variation, (2) time order of occurrence of variables, and (3) elimination of other possible causal factors. These conditions are necessary but not sufficient to demonstrate causality. No one of these three conditions, or all three conditions combined, can demonstrate decisively that a causal relationship exists.[4]

## Concomitant Variation

**concomitant variation**
A condition for inferring causality that requires that the extent to which a cause, *X*, and an effect, *Y*, occur together or vary together is predicted by the hypothesis under consideration.

*Concomitant variation* is the extent to which a cause, *X*, and an effect, *Y*, occur together or vary together in the way predicted by the hypothesis under consideration. Evidence pertaining to concomitant variation can be obtained in a qualitative or quantitative manner.

For example, in the qualitative case, the management of a department store believes that sales are highly dependent upon the quality of in-store service. This hypothesis could be examined by assessing concomitant variation. Here, the causal factor *X* is in-store service, and the effect factor *Y* is sales. A concomitant variation supporting the hypothesis would imply that stores with satisfactory in-store service would also have satisfactory sales. Likewise, stores with unsatisfactory service would exhibit unsatisfactory sales. If, on the other hand, the opposite pattern was found, we would conclude that the hypothesis is untenable.

For a quantitative example, consider a random survey of 1,000 respondents regarding purchase of fashion clothing from department stores. This survey yields the data in Table 7.1. The respondents have been classified into high- and low-education groups based on a median or even split. This table suggests that the purchase of fashion clothing is influenced by education level. Respondents with high education are likely to purchase more fashion clothing. Seventy-three percent of the respondents with high education have a high purchase level, whereas only 64 percent of those with low education have a high purchase level. Furthermore, this is based on a relatively large sample of 1,000 people.

Based on this evidence, can we conclude that high education causes high purchase of fashion clothing? Certainly not! All that can be said is that association makes the hypothesis more tenable; it does not prove it. What about the effect of other possible causal factors such as income? Fashion clothing is expensive, so people with higher incomes can buy more of it. Table 7.2 shows the relationship between purchase of fashion clothing and education for different income segments. This is equivalent to holding the effect of income constant. Here again, the sample has been split at the median to produce high- and low-income

| **TABLE 7.1** | | | |
|---|---|---|---|
| **Evidence of Concomitant Variation Between Purchase of Fashion Clothing and Education** | | | |
| EDUCATION - X | PURCHASE OF FASHION CLOTHING - Y | | |
| | HIGH | LOW | TOTAL |
| High | 363 (73%) | 137 (27%) | 500 (100%) |
| Low | 322 (64%) | 178 (36%) | 500 (100%) |

## TABLE 7.2

**Purchase of Fashion Clothing by Income and Education**

| | LOW INCOME | | | | HIGH INCOME | | |
| | PURCHASE | | | | PURCHASE | | |
| EDUCATION | HIGH | LOW | TOTAL | EDUCATION | HIGH | LOW | TOTAL |
|---|---|---|---|---|---|---|---|
| High | 122 (61%) | 78 (39%) | 200 (100%) | High | 241 (80%) | 59 (20%) | 300 (100%) |
| Low | 171 (57%) | 129 (43%) | 300 (100%) | Low | 151 (76%) | 49 (24%) | 200 (100%) |

groups of equal size. Table 7.2 shows that the difference in purchase of fashion clothing between high- and low-education respondents has been reduced considerably. This suggests that the association indicated by Table 7.1 may be spurious.

We could give you similar examples to show why the absence of initial evidence of concomitant variation does not imply that there is no causation. It is possible that considering a third variable may crystallize an association that was originally obscure. The time order of the occurrence of variables provides additional insights into causality.

## Time Order of Occurrence of Variables

The time order of occurrence condition states that the causing event must occur either before or simultaneously with the effect; it cannot occur afterwards. By definition, an effect cannot be produced by an event that occurs after the effect has taken place. However, it is possible for each event in a relationship to be both a cause and an effect of the other event. In other words, a variable can be both a cause and an effect in the same causal relationship. To illustrate, customers who shop frequently in a department store are more likely to have the charge or credit card for that store. Also, customers who have the charge card for a department store are likely to shop there frequently.

Consider the in-store service and sales of a department store. If in-store service is the cause of sales, then improvements in service must be made before, or at least simultaneously with, an increase in sales. These improvements might consist of training or hiring more sales personnel. Then, in subsequent months, the sales of the department store should increase. Alternatively, the sales might increase simultaneously with the training or hiring of additional sales personnel. On the other hand, suppose a store experienced an appreciable increase in sales and then decided to use some of that money to retrain its sales personnel, leading to an improvement in service. In this case, in-store service cannot be a cause of increased sales. Rather, just the opposite hypothesis might be plausible.

## Absence of Other Possible Causal Factors

The absence of other possible causal factors means that the factor or variable being investigated should be the only possible causal explanation. In-store service may be a cause of sales if we can be sure that changes in all other factors affecting sales, such as pricing, advertising, level of distribution, product quality, competition, etc., were held constant or otherwise controlled.

In an after-the-fact examination of a situation, we can never confidently rule out all other causal factors. In contrast, with experimental designs, it is possible to control for some of the other causal factors. It is also possible to balance the effects of some of the uncontrolled variables so that only random variations resulting from these uncontrolled variables will be measured. These aspects are discussed in more detail later in this chapter. The difficulty of establishing a causal relationship is illustrated by the following example.

### REAL RESEARCH

*Which Comes First?*

Recent statistical data show that consumers increasingly make buying decisions in the store while they are shopping. Some studies indicate that as much as 80 percent of buying decisions are made at point of purchase (POP). POP buying decisions have increased concurrently with increased advertising efforts in the stores. These include radio advertisements, ads on shopping carts and grocery bags, ceiling signs, and shelf displays. It is estimated that brand and retail owners spent roughly one billion dollars in 2002 trying to influence the consumer at the point of purchase. It is difficult to ascertain from these data whether the increased POP decision making is the result of increased advertising efforts in the store, or whether the increase in store advertising results from attempts to capture changing consumer attitudes toward purchasing and to capture sales from the increase in POP decision making. It is also possible that both variables may be both causes and effects in this relationship.[5] ■

If, as the preceding example indicates, it is difficult to establish cause-and-effect relationships, what is the role of evidence obtained in experimentation?

## Role of Evidence

Evidence of concomitant variation, time order of occurrence of variables, and elimination of other possible causal factors, even if combined, still do not demonstrate conclusively that a causal relationship exists. However, if all the evidence is strong and consistent, it may be reasonable to conclude that there is a causal relationship. Accumulated evidence from several investigations increases our confidence that a causal relationship exists. Confidence is further enhanced if the evidence is interpreted in light of intimate conceptual knowledge of the problem situation. Controlled experiments can provide strong evidence on all three conditions.

# DEFINITIONS AND CONCEPTS

In this section, we define some basic concepts and illustrate them using examples, including the LeSportsac and Eckerd examples given at the beginning of this chapter.

**Independent Variables.**  *Independent variables* are variables or alternatives that are manipulated (i.e., the levels of these variables are changed by the researcher) and whose effects are measured and compared. These variables, also known as treatments, may include price levels, package designs, and advertising themes. In the two examples given at the beginning of this chapter, the treatments consisted of LeSportsac versus the "di Paris sac" bags in the first example and in-store radio advertising (present versus absent) in the second.

**Test Units.**  *Test units* are individuals, organizations, or other entities whose response to the independent variables or treatments is being examined. Test units may include consumers, stores, or geographic areas. The test units were women in the LeSportsac case and stores in the Eckerd example.

**Dependent Variables.**  *Dependent variables* are the variables that measure the effect of the independent variables on the test units. These variables may include sales, profits, and market shares. The dependent variable was brand or source identification in the LeSportsac example and sales in the Eckerd example.

**Extraneous Variables.**  *Extraneous variables* are all variables other than the independent variables that affect the response of the test units. These variables can confound the dependent variable measures in a way that weakens or invalidates the results of the experiment. Extraneous variables include store size, store location, and competitive effort. In the Eckerd example, store size, geographical location, traffic flow count, and age of the stores were extraneous variables that had to be controlled.

**Experiment.**  An *experiment* is formed when the researcher manipulates one or more independent variables and measures their effect on one or more dependent variables, while

---

**independent variables**
Variables that are manipulated by the researcher and whose effects are measured and compared.

**test units**
Individuals, organizations, or other entities whose response to independent variables or treatments is being studied.

**dependent variables**
Variables that measure the effect of the independent variables on the test units.

**extraneous variables**
Variables, other than the independent variables, that influence the response of the test units.

**experiment**
The process of manipulating one or more independent variables and measuring their effect on one or more dependent variables, while controlling for the extraneous variables.

controlling for the effect of extraneous variables.[6] Both the LeSportsac and Eckerd research projects qualify as experiments based on this definition.

**Experimental Design.**   An *experimental design* is a set of procedures specifying (1) the test units and how these units are to be divided into homogeneous subsamples, (2) what independent variables or treatments are to be manipulated, (3) what dependent variables are to be measured, and (4) how the extraneous variables are to be controlled.[7]

**experimental design**
The set of experimental procedures specifying (1) the test units and sampling procedures, (2) independent variables, (3) dependent variables, and (4) how to control the extraneous variables.

### REAL RESEARCH

## Taking Coupons at Face Value

An experiment was conducted to test the effects of the face value of coupons on the likelihood of coupon redemption, controlling for the frequency of brand usage. Personal interviews were conducted in greater New York with 280 shoppers who were entering or leaving a supermarket. Subjects were randomly assigned to two treatment groups, one offered 15-cent coupons and the other 50-cent coupons for four products: Tide detergent, Kellogg's Corn Flakes, Aim toothpaste, and Joy liquid detergent. During the interviews, the respondents answered questions about which brands they used and how likely they were to cash coupons of the given face value the next time they shopped. An interesting finding was that higher face value coupons produced higher likelihood of redemption among infrequent or nonbuyers of the promoted brand but had little effect on regular buyers. A study conducted in 2002 showed that U.S. businesses distributed approximately 259 billion coupons in 2001, with an average face value of 74 cents. According to the Promotion Marketing Association (*www.pmalink.org*), consumers redeemed 200 million fewer coupons in 2000 compared to 1999. Contributing to the lower number of redeemers were young adults (Generation Y) who use the least amount of coupons and account for a large part of the population.[8] ∎

In the preceding experiment, the independent variable that was manipulated was the value of the coupon (15-cent coupon versus 50-cent coupon). The dependent variable was the likelihood of cashing the coupon. The extraneous variable that was controlled was brand usage. The test units were individual shoppers. The experimental design required the random assignment of test units (shoppers) to treatment groups (15-cent coupon or 50-cent coupon).

Experimental evidence shows that infrequent buyers of the promoted brand have a higher likelihood of redeeming coupons of higher face value, as compared to regular buyers.

# DEFINITION OF SYMBOLS

To facilitate our discussion of extraneous variables and specific experimental designs, we define a set of symbols that are now commonly used in marketing research.

> $X$ = the exposure of a group to an independent variable, treatment, or event, the effects of which are to be determined.
>
> $O$ = the process of observation or measurement of the dependent variable on the test units or group of units.
>
> $R$ = the random assignment of test units or groups to separate treatments.

In addition, the following conventions are adopted:

- Movement from left to right indicates movement through time.
- Horizontal alignment of symbols implies that all those symbols refer to a specific treatment group.
- Vertical alignment of symbols implies that those symbols refer to activities or events that occur simultaneously.

For example, the symbolic arrangement

$$X \qquad O_1 \qquad O_2$$

means that a given group of test units was exposed to the treatment variable ($X$) and the response was measured at two different points in time, $O_1$ and $O_2$.

Likewise, the symbolic arrangement

$$R \qquad X_1 \qquad O_1$$
$$R \qquad X_2 \qquad O_2$$

means that two groups of test units were randomly assigned to two different treatment groups at the same time, and the dependent variable was measured in the two groups simultaneously.

# VALIDITY IN EXPERIMENTATION

When conducting an experiment, a researcher has two goals: (1) draw valid conclusions about the effects of independent variables on the study group and (2) make valid generalizations to a larger population of interest. The first goal concerns internal validity, the second, external validity.[9]

## Internal Validity

**internal validity**
A measure of accuracy of an experiment. It measures whether the manipulation of the independent variables, or treatments, actually caused the effects on the dependent variable(s).

*Internal validity* refers to whether the manipulation of the independent variables or treatments actually caused the observed effects on the dependent variables. Thus, internal validity examines whether the observed effects on the test units could have been caused by variables other than the treatment. If the observed effects are influenced or confounded by extraneous variables, it is difficult to draw valid inferences about the causal relationship between the independent and dependent variables. Internal validity is the basic minimum that must be present in an experiment before any conclusion about treatment effects can be made. Without internal validity, the experimental results are confounded. Control of extraneous variables is a necessary condition for establishing internal validity.

## External Validity

**external validity**
A determination of whether the cause-and-effect relationships found in the experiment can be generalized.

*External validity* refers to whether the cause-and-effect relationships found in the experiment can be generalized. In other words, can the results be generalized beyond the experimental situation and, if so, to what populations, settings, times, independent variables, and dependent variables can the results be projected?[10] Threats to external validity arise when the specific set of experimental conditions does not realistically take into account the interactions of other relevant variables in the real world.

It is desirable to have an experimental design that has both internal and external validity, but in applied marketing research often we have to trade one type of validity for another.[11] To control for extraneous variables, a researcher may conduct an experiment in an artificial environment. This enhances internal validity, but it may limit the generalizability of the results, thereby reducing external validity. For example, fast-food chains test customers' preferences for new formulations of menu items in test kitchens. Can the effects measured in this environment be generalized to fast-food outlets? (Further discussion on the influence of artificiality on external validity may be found in the section of this chapter on laboratory versus field experimentation.) In spite of these deterrents to external validity, if an experiment lacks internal validity, it may not be meaningful to generalize the results. Factors that threaten internal validity may also threaten external validity, the most serious of these being extraneous variables.

# EXTRANEOUS VARIABLES

In this section, we classify extraneous variables in the following categories: history, maturation, testing, instrumentation, statistical regression, selection bias, and mortality.

## History

**history (H)**
Specific events that are external to the experiment but occur at the same time as the experiment.

Contrary to what the name implies, **history** (H) does not refer to the occurrence of events before the experiment. Rather, history refers to specific events that are external to the experiment but occur at the same time as the experiment. These events may affect the dependent variable. Consider the following experiment

$$O_1 \qquad X_1 \qquad O_2$$

where $O_1$ and $O_2$ are measures of sales of a department store chain in a specific region, and $X_1$ represents a new promotional campaign. The difference $(O_2 - O_1)$ is the treatment effect. Suppose the experiment revealed that there was no difference between $O_2$ and $O_1$. Can we then conclude that the promotional campaign was ineffective? Certainly not! The promotional campaign $(X_1)$ is not the only possible explanation of the difference between $O_2$ and $O_1$. The campaign might well have been effective. What if general economic conditions declined during the experiment, and the local area was particularly hard hit by layoffs and plant closings (history)? Conversely, even if there was some difference between $O_2$ and $O_1$, it may be incorrect to conclude that the campaign was effective if history was not controlled, because the experimental effects might have been confounded by history. The longer the time interval between observations, the greater the possibility that history will confound an experiment of this type.[12]

## Maturation

**maturation (MA)**
An extraneous variable attributable to changes in the test units themselves that occur with the passage of time.

**Maturation** (MA) is similar to history except that it refers to changes in the test units themselves. These changes are not caused by the impact of independent variables or treatments but occur with the passage of time. In an experiment involving people, maturation takes place as people become older, more experienced, tired, bored, or uninterested. Tracking and market studies that span several months are vulnerable to maturation, because it is difficult to know how respondents are changing over time.

Maturation effects also extend to test units other than people. For example, consider the case in which the test units are department stores. Stores change over time in terms of physical layout, decor, traffic, and composition.

## Testing Effects

Testing effects are caused by the process of experimentation. Typically, these are the effects on the experiment of taking a measure on the dependent variable before and after the presentation of the treatment. There are two kinds of testing effects: (1) main testing effect (MT) and (2) interactive testing effect (IT).

The ***main testing effect*** (MT) occurs when a prior observation affects a latter observation. Consider an experiment to measure the effect of advertising on attitudes toward a certain brand. The respondents are given a pretreatment questionnaire measuring background information and attitude toward the brand. They are then exposed to the test commercial embedded in an appropriate program. After viewing the commercial, the respondents again answer a questionnaire measuring, among other things, attitude toward the brand. Suppose that there is no difference between the pre- and posttreatment attitudes. Can we conclude that the commercial was ineffective? An alternative explanation might be that the respondents tried to maintain consistency between their pre- and posttreatment attitudes. As a result of the main testing effect, posttreatment attitudes were influenced more by pretreatment attitudes than by the treatment itself. The main testing effect may also be reactive, causing the respondents to change their attitudes simply because these attitudes have been measured. The main testing effect compromises the internal validity of the experiment.

In the ***interactive testing effect*** (IT), a prior measurement affects the test unit's response to the independent variable. Continuing with our advertising experiment, when people are asked to indicate their attitudes toward a brand, they become aware of that brand: they are sensitized to that brand and become more likely to pay attention to the test commercial than people who were not included in the experiment. The measured effects are then not generalizable to the population; therefore, the interactive testing effects influence the experiment's external validity.

## Instrumentation

***Instrumentation*** (I) refers to changes in the measuring instrument, in the observers, or in the scores themselves. Sometimes, measuring instruments are modified during the course of an experiment. In the advertising experiment, if a newly designed questionnaire was used to measure the posttreatment attitudes, this could lead to variations in the responses obtained. Consider an experiment in which dollar sales are being measured before and after exposure to an in-store display (treatment). If there is a nonexperimental price change between $O_1$ and $O_2$, this results in a change in instrumentation because dollar sales will be measured using different unit prices. In this case, the treatment effect ($O_2 - O_1$) could be attributed to a change in instrumentation.

Instrumentation effects are likely when interviewers make pre- and posttreatment measurements. The effectiveness of interviewers can be different at different times.

## Statistical Regression

***Statistical regression*** (SR) effects occur when test units with extreme scores move closer to the average score during the course of the experiment. In the advertising experiment, suppose that some respondents had either very favorable or very unfavorable attitudes. On posttreatment measurement, their attitudes might have moved toward the average. People's attitudes change continuously. People with extreme attitudes have more room for change, so variation is more likely. This has a confounding effect on the experimental results, because the observed effect (change in attitude) may be attributable to statistical regression rather than to the treatment (test commercial).

## Selection Bias

***Selection bias*** (SB) refers to the improper assignment of test units to treatment conditions. This bias occurs when selection or assignment of test units results in treatment groups that differ on the dependent variable before the exposure to the treatment condition. If test units self-select their own groups or are assigned to groups on the basis of the researchers' judgment, selection bias is possible. For example, consider a merchandising experiment in which two different merchandising displays (old and new) are assigned to different department stores. The stores in the two groups may not be equivalent to begin with. They may vary with respect to a key characteristic, such as store size. Store size is likely to affect sales regardless of which merchandising display was assigned to a store.

---

**main testing effect (MN)**
An effect of testing occurring when a prior observation affects a latter observation.

**interactive testing effect (IT)**
An effect in which a prior measurement affects the test unit's response to the independent variable.

**instrumentation (I)**
An extraneous variable involving changes in the measuring instrument or in the observers or scores themselves.

**statistical regression (SR)**
An extraneous variable that occurs when test units with extreme scores move closer to the average score during the course of the experiment.

**selection bias (SB)**
An extraneous variable attributable to the improper assignment of test units to treatment conditions.

## Mortality

*Mortality* (MO) refers to the loss of test units while the experiment is in progress. This happens for many reasons, such as test units refusing to continue in the experiment. Mortality confounds results because it is difficult to determine if the lost test units would respond in the same manner to the treatments as those that remain. Consider again the merchandising display experiment. Suppose that during the course of the experiment, three stores in the new display treatment condition drop out. The researcher could not determine whether the average sales for the new display stores would have been higher or lower if these three stores had continued in the experiment.

The various categories of extraneous variables are not mutually exclusive. They can occur jointly and also interact with each other. To illustrate, testing—maturation—mortality refers to a situation where, because of pretreatment measurement, the respondents' beliefs and attitudes change over time and there is a differential loss of respondents from the various treatment groups.

# CONTROLLING EXTRANEOUS VARIABLES

Extraneous variables represent alternative explanations of experimental results. They pose a serious threat to the internal and external validity of an experiment. Unless they are controlled for, they affect the dependent variable and thus confound the results. For this reason, they are also called *confounding variables.* There are four ways of controlling extraneous variables: randomization, matching, statistical control, and design control.

## Randomization

*Randomization* refers to the random assignment of test units to experimental groups by using random numbers. Treatment conditions are also randomly assigned to experimental groups. For example, respondents are randomly assigned to one of three experimental groups. One of the three versions of a test commercial, selected at random, is administered to each group. As a result of random assignment, extraneous factors can be represented equally in each treatment condition. Randomization is the preferred procedure for ensuring the prior equality of experimental groups.[13] However, randomization may not be effective when the sample size is small, because randomization merely produces groups that are equal on average. It is possible, though, to check whether randomization has been effective by measuring the possible extraneous variables and comparing them across the experimental groups.

## Matching

*Matching* involves comparing test units on a set of key background variables before assigning them to the treatment conditions. In the merchandising display experiment, stores could be matched on the basis of annual sales, size, or location. Then one store from each matched pair would be assigned to each experimental group.

Matching has two drawbacks. First, test units can be matched on only a few characteristics, so the test units may be similar on the variables selected but unequal on others. Second, if the matched characteristics are irrelevant to the dependent variable, then the matching effort has been futile.[14]

## Statistical Control

*Statistical control* involves measuring the extraneous variables and adjusting for their effects through statistical analysis. This was illustrated in Table 7.2, which examined the relationship (association) between purchase of fashion clothing and education, controlling for the effect of income. More advanced statistical procedures, such as analysis of covariance (ANCOVA), are also available. In ANCOVA, the effects of the extraneous variable on the dependent variable are removed by an adjustment of the dependent variable's mean value within each treatment condition. (ANCOVA is discussed in more detail in Chapter 16.)

## Design Control

**design control**
One method of controlling extraneous variables that involves using specific experimental designs.

**Design control** involves the use of experiments designed to control specific extraneous variables. The types of controls possible by suitably designing the experiment are illustrated in the following example.

### REAL RESEARCH

### *Experimenting with New Products*

Controlled-distribution electronic test markets are used increasingly to conduct experimental research on new products. This method makes it possible to control for several extraneous factors that affect new product performance and manipulate the variables of interest. It is possible to ensure that a new product: (1) obtains the right level of store acceptance and all commodity volume distribution, (2) is positioned in the correct aisle in each store, (3) receives the right number of facings on the shelf, (4) has the correct everyday price, (5) never has out-of-stock problems, and (6) obtains the planned level of trade promotion, display, and price features on the desired time schedule. Thus, a high degree of internal validity can be obtained.[15] ∎

The preceding example shows that controlled-distribution electronic test markets can be effective in controlling for specific extraneous variables. Extraneous variables can also be controlled by adopting specific experimental designs, as described in the next section.

# A CLASSIFICATION OF EXPERIMENTAL DESIGNS

**preexperimental designs**
Designs that do not control for extraneous factors by randomization.

**true experimental designs**
Experimental designs distinguished by the fact that the researcher can randomly assign test units to experimental groups and also randomly assign treatments to experimental groups.

**quasi-experimental designs**
Designs that apply part of the procedures of true experimentation but lack full experimental control.

Experimental designs may be classified as preexperimental, true experimental, quasi-experimental, or statistical (Figure 7.1). **Preexperimental designs** do not employ randomization procedures to control for extraneous factors. Examples of these designs include the one-shot case study, the one-group pretest-posttest design, and the static group. In **true experimental designs,** the researcher can randomly assign test units and treatments to experimental groups. Included in this category are the pretest-posttest control group design, the posttest-only control group design, and the Solomon four-group design. **Quasi-experimental designs** result when the researcher is unable to achieve full manipulation of scheduling or allocation of treatments to test units but can still apply part of the apparatus

**Figure 7.1**
A Classification of Experimental Designs

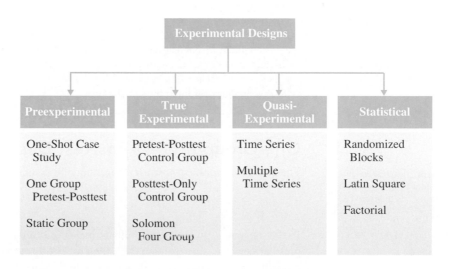

| Experimental Designs | | | |
|---|---|---|---|
| **Preexperimental** | **True Experimental** | **Quasi-Experimental** | **Statistical** |
| One-Shot Case Study | Pretest-Posttest Control Group | Time Series | Randomized Blocks |
| One Group Pretest-Posttest | Posttest-Only Control Group | Multiple Time Series | Latin Square |
| Static Group | Solomon Four Group | | Factorial |

of true experimentation. Two such designs are time series and multiple time series designs. A ***statistical design*** is a series of basic experiments that allows for statistical control and analysis of external variables. The basic designs used in statistical designs include preexperimental, true experimental, and quasi-experimental. Statistical designs are classified on the basis of their characteristics and use. The important statistical designs include randomized block, Latin square, and factorial. These designs are illustrated in the context of measuring the effectiveness of a test commercial for a department store.[16]

**statistical design**
Designs that allow for the statistical control and analysis of external variables.

# PREEXPERIMENTAL DESIGNS

These designs are characterized by an absence of randomization. Three specific designs are described: the one-shot case study, the one-group pretest-posttest design, and the static group.

## One-Shot Case Study

**one-shot case study**
A preexperimental design in which a single group of test units is exposed to a treatment *X*, and then a single measurement on the dependent variable is taken.

Also known as the after-only design, the ***one-shot case study*** may be symbolically represented as

$$X \qquad O_1$$

A single group of test units is exposed to a treatment *X*, and then a single measurement on the dependent variable is taken ($O_1$). There is no random assignment of test units. Note that the symbol *R* is not used, because the test units are self-selected or selected arbitrarily by the researcher.

The danger of drawing valid conclusions from experiments of this type can be easily seen. It does not provide a basis of comparing the level of $O_1$ to what would happen when *X* was absent. Also, the level of $O_1$ might be affected by many extraneous variables, including history, maturation, selection, and mortality. Lack of control for these extraneous variables undermines the internal validity. For these reasons, the one-shot case study is more appropriate for exploratory than for conclusive research.

---

**ACTIVE RESEARCH** | DEPARTMENT STORE PROJECT

### *One-Shot Case Study*

A one-shot case study to measure the effectiveness of a test commercial for a department store, e.g., Sears, would be conducted as follows. Telephone interviews are conducted with a national sample of respondents who report watching a particular TV program the previous night. The program selected is the one that contains the test commercial, e.g., Sears commercial (*X*). The dependent variables (*O*s) are unaided and aided recall. First, unaided recall is measured by asking the respondents whether they recall seeing a commercial for a department store, e.g., "do you recall seeing a commercial for a department store last night?" If they recall the test commercial, details about commercial content and execution are solicited. Respondents who do not recall the test commercial are asked about it specifically, e.g., "do you recall seeing a commercial for Sears last night?" (aided recall). The results of aided and unaided recall are compared to norm scores to develop an index for interpreting the scores.

---

## One-Group Pretest-Posttest Design

**one-group pretest-posttest design**
A preexperimental design in which a group of test units is measured twice.

The ***one-group pretest-posttest design*** may be symbolized as

$$O_1 \qquad X \qquad O_2$$

In this design, a group of test units is measured twice. There is no control group. First, a pretreatment measure is taken ($O_1$), then the group is exposed to the treatment (*X*). Finally, a posttreatment measure is taken ($O_2$). The treatment effect is computed as $O_2 - O_1$, but the validity of this conclusion is questionable because extraneous variables are largely uncontrolled. History, maturation, testing (both main and interactive testing effects), instrumentation, selection, mortality, and regression could possibly be present.

---

**ACTIVE RESEARCH** | DEPARTMENT STORE PROJECT

### One-Group Pretest-Posttest Design

A one-group pretest-posttest design to measure the effectiveness of a test commercial for a department store, e.g., Sears, would be implemented as follows. Respondents are recruited to central theater locations in different test cities. At the central location, respondents are first administered a personal interview to measure, among other things, attitudes towards the store, Sears ($O_1$). Then they watch a TV program containing the test (Sears) commercial ($X$). After viewing the TV program, the respondents are again administered a personal interview to measure attitudes towards the store, Sears ($O_2$). The effectiveness of the test commercial is measured as $O_2 - O_1$.

---

## Static Group Design

**static group**

A preexperimental design in which there are two groups: the experimental group (EG), which is exposed to the treatment, and the control group (CG). Measurements on both groups are made only after the treatment, and test units are not assigned at random.

The *static group* is a two-group experimental design. One group, called the experimental group (EG), is exposed to the treatment, and the other, called the control group (CG), is not. Measurements on both groups are made only after the treatment, and test units are not assigned at random. This design may be symbolically described as

EG:   $X$   $O_1$
CG:       $O_2$

The treatment effect would be measured as $O_1 - O_2$. Note that this difference could also be attributed to at least two extraneous variables (selection and mortality). Because test units are not randomly assigned, the two groups (EG and CG) may differ before the treatment, and selection bias may be present. There may also be mortality effects, as more test units may withdraw from the experimental group than from the control group. This would be particularly likely to happen if the treatment was unpleasant.

In practice, a control group is sometimes defined as the group that receives the current level of marketing activity, rather than a group that receives no treatment at all. The control group is defined this way because it is difficult to reduce current marketing activities, such as advertising and personal selling, to zero.

---

**ACTIVE RESEARCH** | DEPARTMENT STORE PROJECT

### Static Group

A static group comparison to measure the effectiveness of a test commercial for a department store would be conducted as follows. Two groups of respondents would be recruited on the basis of convenience. Only the experimental group would be exposed to the TV program containing the test (Sears) commercial. Then, attitudes toward the department store (Sears) of both the experimental and control group respondents would be measured. The effectiveness of the test commercial would be measured as $O_1 - O_2$.

---

# TRUE EXPERIMENTAL DESIGNS

The distinguishing feature of the true experimental designs, as compared to preexperimental designs, is randomization. In true experimental designs, the researcher randomly assigns test units to experimental groups and treatments to experimental groups. True experimental designs include the pretest-posttest control group design, the posttest-only control group design, and the Solomon four-group design.

## Pretest-Posttest Control Group Design

In the **pretest-posttest control group design,** test units are randomly assigned to either the experimental or the control group, and a pretreatment measure is taken on each group. This design is symbolized as

$$\text{EG:} \quad R \quad O_1 \quad X \quad O_2$$
$$\text{CG:} \quad R \quad O_3 \quad \quad O_4$$

The treatment effect (*TE*) is measured as

$$(O_2 - O_1) - (O_4 - O_3)$$

This design controls for most extraneous variables. Selection bias is eliminated by randomization. The other extraneous effects are controlled as follows

$$O_2 - O_1 = TE + H + MA + MT + IT + I + SR + MO$$
$$O_4 - O_3 = H + MA + MT + I + SR + MO$$
$$= EV \text{ (Extraneous Variables)}$$

where the symbols for the extraneous variables are as defined previously. The experimental result is obtained by

$$(O_2 - O_1) - (O_4 - O_3) = TE + IT$$

Interactive testing effect is not controlled, because of the effect of the pretest measurement on the reaction of units in the experimental group to the treatment.

As this example shows, the pretest-posttest control group design involves two groups and two measurements on each group. A simpler design is the posttest-only control group design.

---

**ACTIVE RESEARCH**    DEPARTMENT STORE PROJECT

### Pretest-Posttest Control Group

In the context of measuring the effectiveness of a test commercial for a department store, e.g., Sears, a pretest-posttest control group design would be implemented as follows. A sample of respondents would be selected at random. Half of these would be randomly assigned to the experimental group, and the other half would form the control group. Respondents in both groups would be administered a questionnaire to obtain a pretest measurement on attitudes toward the department store (Sears). Only the respondents in the experimental group would be exposed to the TV program containing the test commercial. Then, a questionnaire would be administered to respondents in both groups to obtain posttest measures on attitudes toward the store (Sears).

---

## Posttest-Only Control Group Design

The **posttest-only control group design** does not involve any premeasurement. It may be symbolized as

$$\text{EG :} \quad R \quad X \quad O_1$$
$$\text{CG :} \quad R \quad \quad O_2$$

The treatment effect is obtained by

$$TE = O_1 - O_2$$

This design is fairly simple to implement. Because there is no premeasurement, the testing effects are eliminated, but this design is sensitive to selection bias and mortality. It is assumed that the two groups are similar in terms of pretreatment measures on the dependent variable, because of the random assignment of test units to groups. However, because there is no pretreatment measurement, this assumption cannot be checked. This design is also sensitive to mortality. It is difficult to determine whether those in the experimental group who discontinue the experiment are similar to their counterparts in the control group. Yet another limitation is that this design does not allow the researcher to examine changes in individual test units.

It is possible to control for selection bias and mortality through carefully designed experimental procedures. Examination of individual cases is often not of interest. On the other hand, this design possesses significant advantages in terms of time, cost, and sample size requirements. It involves only two groups and only one measurement per group. Because of its simplicity, the posttest-only control group design is probably the most popular in marketing research. Note that, except for premeasurement, the implementation of this design is very similar to that of the pretest-posttest control group design.

---

**ACTIVE RESEARCH** | DEPARTMENT STORE PROJECT

*Posttest-Only Control Group*

To measure the effectiveness of a test commercial for a department store, the posttest-only control group design would be implemented as follows. A sample of respondents would be selected at random. The sample would be randomly split, with half the subjects forming the experimental group and the other half constituting the control group. Only the respondents in the experimental group would be exposed to the TV program containing the test (Sears) commercial. Then, a questionnaire would be administered to both groups to obtain posttest measures on attitudes toward the department store (Sears). The difference in the attitudes of the experimental group and the control group would be used as a measure of the effectiveness of the test commercial.

---

**Solomon four-group design**
A true experimental design that explicitly controls for interactive testing effects, in addition to controlling for all the other extraneous variables.

In this example, the researcher is not concerned with examining the changes in the attitudes of individual respondents. When this information is desired, the Solomon four-group design should be considered. The **Solomon four-group design** overcomes the limitations of the pretest-posttest control group and posttest-only control group designs in that it explicitly controls for interactive testing effect, in addition to controlling for all the other extraneous variables (EV). However, this design has practical limitations: it is expensive and time consuming to implement. Hence, it is not considered further.[17]

In all true experimental designs, the researcher exercises a high degree of control. In particular, the researcher can control when the measurements are taken, on whom they are taken, and the scheduling of the treatments. Moreover, the researcher can randomly select the test units and randomly expose test units to the treatments. In some instances, the researcher cannot exercise this kind of control, and then quasi-experimental designs should be considered.

# QUASI-EXPERIMENTAL DESIGNS

A quasi-experimental design results under the following conditions. First, the researcher can control when measurements are taken and on whom they are taken. Second, the researcher lacks control over the scheduling of the treatments and also is unable to expose test units to the treatments randomly.[18] Quasi-experimental designs are useful because they can be used in cases when true experimentation cannot, and because they are quicker and less expensive. However, because full experimental control is lacking, the researcher must take into account the specific variables that are not controlled. Popular forms of quasi-experimental designs are time series and multiple time series designs.

## Time Series Design

**time series design**
A quasi-experimental design that involves periodic measurements on the dependent variable for a group of test units. Then, the treatment is administered by the researcher or occurs naturally. After the treatment, periodic measurements are continued in order to determine the treatment effect.

The **time series design** involves a series of periodic measurements on the dependent variable for a group of test units. The treatment is then administered by the researcher or occurs naturally. After the treatment, periodic measurements are continued to determine the treatment effect. A time series experiment may be symbolized as

$$O_1 \; O_2 \; O_3 \; O_4 \; O_5 \; X \; O_6 \; O_7 \; O_8 \; O_9 \; O_{10}$$

This is a quasi-experiment, because there is no randomization of test units to treatments, and the timing of treatment presentation, as well as which test units are exposed to the treatment, may not be within the researcher's control.

Taking a series of measurements before and after the treatment provides at least partial control for several extraneous variables. Maturation is at least partially controlled, because it would not affect $O_5$ and $O_6$ alone but would influence other observations. By similar reasoning, main testing effect, instrumentation, and statistical regression are controlled as well. If the test units are selected randomly or by matching, selection bias can be reduced. Mortality may pose a problem, but it can be largely controlled by paying a premium or offering other incentives to respondents.

The major weakness of the time series design is the failure to control history. Another limitation is that the experiment may be affected by the interactive testing effect, because multiple measurements are being made on the test units. Nevertheless, time series designs are useful. The effectiveness of a test commercial ($X$) may be examined by broadcasting the commercial a predetermined number of times and examining the data from a preexisting test panel. Although the marketer can control the scheduling of the test commercial, it is uncertain when or whether the panel members are exposed to it. The panel members' purchases before, during, and after the campaign are examined to determine whether the test commercial has a short-term effect, a long-term effect, or no effect.

## Multiple Time Series Design

*multiple time series design*
A time series design that includes another group of test units to serve as a control group.

The ***multiple time series design*** is similar to the time series design except that another group of test units is added to serve as a control group. Symbolically, this design may be described as

$$\text{EG}: \quad O_1 \quad O_2 \quad O_3 \quad O_4 \quad O_5 \quad X \quad O_6 \quad O_7 \quad O_8 \quad O_9 \quad O_{10}$$
$$\text{CG}: \quad O_1 \quad O_2 \quad O_3 \quad O_4 \quad O_5 \quad\;\; \quad O_6 \quad O_7 \quad O_8 \quad O_9 \quad O_{10}$$

If the control group is carefully selected, this design can be an improvement over the simple time series experiment. The improvement lies in the ability to test the treatment effect twice: against the pretreatment measurements in the experimental group and against the control group. To use the multiple time series design to assess the effectiveness of a commercial, the test panel example would be modified as follows. The test commercial would be shown in only a few of the test cities. Panel members in these cities would comprise the experimental group. Panel members in cities where the commercial was not shown would constitute the control group.

### REAL RESEARCH

### *Splitting Commercials Shows Their Strength*

A multiple time series design was used to examine the buildup effect of increased advertising. The data were obtained from ACNielsen BASES (*www.acnielsenbases.com*) split-cable TV advertising field experiment. In the split-cable system, one group of households was assigned to the experimental panel and an equivalent group to the control panel. The two groups were matched on demographic variables. Data were collected for 76 weeks. Both panels received the same level of advertising for the first 52 weeks for the brand in question. For the next 24 weeks, the experimental panel was exposed to twice as much advertising as the control panel. The results indicated that the buildup effect of advertising was immediate with a duration of the order of the purchase cycle. Information of this type can be useful in selecting advertising timing patterns (allocating a set of advertising exposures over a specified period to obtain maximum impact).

An experimental study, conducted in 2000, showed a new approach to relating advertising exposures of TV media schedules to sales-related market performance. These measures included cumulative sales volume, number of purchases, penetration, and repeat-

**TABLE 7.3**

**Sources of Invalidity of Experimental Designs**

| DESIGN | SOURCE OF INVALIDITY | | | | | | | |
|---|---|---|---|---|---|---|---|---|
| | INTERNAL | | | | | | | EXTERNAL |
| | History | Maturation | Testing | Instrumentation | Regression | Selection | Mortality | Interaction of testing and of X |
| *Preexperimental designs:* | | | | | | | | |
| One-shot case study  X  O | – | – | | | | – | – | |
| One-group pretest-posttest design  O  X  O | – | – | – | – | ? | | | – |
| Static group comparison  X  O  O | + | ? | + | + | + | – | – | |
| *True experimental designs:* | | | | | | | | |
| Pretest-posttest control  R  O  X  O  R  O  O | + | + | + | + | + | + | + | – |
| Posttest-only control group design  R  X  O  R  O | + | + | + | + | + | + | + | + |
| *Quasi-experimental designs:* | | | | | | | | |
| Time series  O  O  O  X  O  O  O | – | + | + | ? | + | + | + | – |
| Multiple time series  O  O  O  X  O  O  O  O  O  O  O  O  O | + | + | + | + | + | + | + | – |

purchase patterns. The approach was derived from a matched split-cable experimental design methodology. Consumer panel companies such as ACNielsen BASES can provide the data needed to implement such an approach. In the future, it is expected that companies like ACNielsen BASES will be at the forefront of using technological advances to measure consumer advertising exposure and purchase behavior simultaneously.[19] ■

In concluding our discussion of preexperimental, true experimental, and quasi-experimental designs, we summarize in Table 7.3 the potential sources of invalidity that may affect each of these designs. In this table, a minus sign indicates a definite weakness, a plus sign indicates that the factor is controlled, a question mark denotes a possible source of concern, and a blank means that the factor is not relevant. It should be remembered that potential sources of invalidity are not the same as actual errors.

# STATISTICAL DESIGNS

Statistical designs consist of a series of basic experiments that allow for statistical control and analysis of external variables. In other words, several basic experiments are conducted simultaneously. Thus, statistical designs are influenced by the same sources of invalidity that affect the basic designs being used. Statistical designs offer the following advantages:

1. The effects of more than one independent variable can be measured.
2. Specific extraneous variables can be statistically controlled.
3. Economical designs can be formulated when each test unit is measured more than once.

The most common statistical designs are the randomized block design, the Latin square design, and the factorial design.

## Randomized Block Design

**randomized block design**
A statistical design in which the test units are blocked on the basis of an external variable to ensure that the various experimental and control groups are matched closely on that variable.

A **randomized block design** is useful when there is only one major external variable, such as sales, store size, or income of the respondent, that might influence the dependent variable. The test units are blocked, or grouped, on the basis of the external variable. The researcher must be able to identify and measure the blocking variable. By blocking, the researcher ensures that the various experimental and control groups are matched closely on the external variable.

As this example illustrates, in most marketing research situations, external variables, such as sales, store size, store type, location, income, occupation, and social class of the respondent, can influence the dependent variable. Therefore, generally speaking, randomized block designs are more useful than completely random designs. Their main limitation is that the researcher can control for only one external variable. When more than one variable must be controlled, the researcher must use Latin square or factorial designs.

---

**ACTIVE RESEARCH** | DEPARTMENT STORE PROJECT

### *Randomized Block Design*

Let us extend the department store (Sears) test commercial example to measure the impact of humor on the effectiveness of advertising.[20] Three test commercials, A, B, and C, have, respectively, no humor, some humor, and high levels of humor. Which of these would be the most effective? Management feels that the respondents' evaluation of the commercials will be influenced by the extent of their store patronage, so store patronage is identified as the blocking variable, and the randomly selected respondents are classified into four blocks (heavy, medium, light, or nonpatrons of the department store). Respondents from each block are randomly assigned to the treatment groups (test commercials A, B, and C). The results reveal that the some-humor commercial (B) was the most effective overall (see Table 7.4).

---

## Latin Square Design

**Latin square design**
A statistical design that allows for the statistical control of two noninteracting external variables in addition to the manipulation of the independent variable.

A **Latin square design** allows the researcher to statistically control two noninteracting external variables as well as to manipulate the independent variable. Each external or

---

| TABLE 7.4 | | | | |
|---|---|---|---|---|
| **An Example of a Randomized Block Design** | | | | |
| BLOCK NO. | STORE PATRONAGE | TREATMENT GROUPS | | |
| | | COMMERCIAL A | COMMERCIAL B | COMMERCIAL C |
| 1 | Heavy | A | B | C |
| 2 | Medium | A | B | C |
| 3 | Low | A | B | C |
| 4 | None | A | B | C |

**TABLE 7.5**

**An Example of Latin Square Design**

| STORE PATRONAGE | INTEREST IN THE STORE | | |
|---|---|---|---|
| | HIGH | MEDIUM | LOW |
| High | B | A | C |
| Medium | C | B | A |
| Low and none | A | C | B |

Note: A, B, and C denote the three test commercials, which have, respectively, no humor, some humor, and high humor.

blocking variable is divided into an equal number of blocks or levels. The independent variable is also divided into the same number of levels. A Latin square is conceptualized as a table (see Table 7.5), with the rows and the columns representing the blocks in the two external variables. The levels of the independent variable are then assigned to the cells in the table. The assignment rule is that each level of the independent variable should appear only once in each row and each column, as shown in Table 7.5.

**ACTIVE RESEARCH** | **DEPARTMENT STORE PROJECT**

*Latin Square Design*

To illustrate the Latin square design, suppose that in the previous example, in addition to controlling for store patronage, the researcher also wanted to control for interest in the store (defined as high, medium, or low). To implement a Latin square design, store patronage would also have to be blocked at three rather than four levels (e.g., by combining the low and nonpatrons into a single block). Assignments of the three test commercials could then be made as shown in Table 7.5. Note that each of the commercials, A, B, and C, appears once, and only once, in each row and each column.

Although Latin square designs are popular in marketing research, they are not without limitations. They require an equal number of rows, columns, and treatment levels, which is sometimes problematic. Note that in the previous example, the low and nonpatrons had to be combined to satisfy this requirement. Also, only two external variables can be controlled simultaneously. An additional variable can be controlled with an expansion of this design into a Graeco-Latin square. Finally, Latin squares do not allow the researcher to examine interactions of the external variables with each other or with the independent variable. To examine interactions, factorial designs should be used.

## Factorial Design

*factorial design*
A statistical experimental design that is used to measure the effects of two or more independent variables at various levels and to allow for interactions between variables.

A *factorial design* is used to measure the effects of two or more independent variables at various levels. Unlike the randomized block design and the Latin square, factorial designs allow for interactions between variables.[21] An interaction is said to take place when the simultaneous effect of two or more variables is different from the sum of their separate effects. For example, an individual's favorite drink might be coffee and favorite temperature level might be cold, but this individual might not prefer cold coffee, leading to an interaction.

A factorial design may also be conceptualized as a table. In a two-factor design, each level of one variable represents a row and each level of another variable represents a column. Multidimensional tables can be used for three or more factors. Factorial designs involve a cell for every possible combination of treatment variables. Suppose that in the previous example, in addition to examining the effect of humor, the researcher was also interested in simultaneously examining the effect of amount of store information. Further, the amount of store information was also varied at three levels (high, medium, and low). As shown in Table 7.6, this would require $3 \times 3 = 9$ cells. Thus, nine different commercials would be produced, each having a specific level of store information and

**TABLE 7.6**

**An Example of a Factorial Design**

| AMOUNT OF STORE INFORMATION | AMOUNT OF HUMOR | | |
|---|---|---|---|
| | NO HUMOR | MEDIUM HUMOR | HIGH HUMOR |
| Low | A | B | C |
| Medium | D | E | F |
| High | G | H | I |

amount of humor. The respondents would be randomly selected and randomly assigned to the nine cells. Respondents in each cell would receive a specific treatment combination. For example, respondents in the upper left-hand corner cell would view a commercial that had no humor and low store information. The results revealed a significant interaction between the two factors or variables. Respondents in the low amount of store information condition preferred the high humor commercial (C). However, those in the high amount of store information condition preferred the no humor commercial (G). Note that although Table 7.6 may appear somewhat similar to Table 7.4, the random assignment of respondents and data analysis are very different for the randomized block design and the factorial design.[22]

The main disadvantage of a factorial design is that the number of treatment combinations increases multiplicatively with an increase in the number of variables or levels. In our example of Table 7.6, if the amount of humor and store information had five levels each instead of three, the number of cells would have jumped from 9 to 25. All the treatment combinations are required if all the main effects and interactions are to be measured. If the researcher is interested in only a few of the interactions or main effects, fractional factorial designs may be used. As their name implies, these designs consist of only a fraction, or portion, of the corresponding full factorial design.

# LABORATORY VERSUS FIELD EXPERIMENTS

**laboratory environment**
An artificial setting for experimentation in which the researcher constructs the desired conditions.

**field environment**
An experimental location set in actual market conditions.

Experiments may be conducted in laboratory or field environments. A **laboratory environment** is an artificial one, which the researcher constructs with the desired conditions specific to the experiment. The term **field environment** is synonymous with actual market conditions. The Eckerd example in the overview section presented a field experiment. Our experiment to measure the effectiveness of a test commercial could be conducted in a laboratory environment by showing the test commercial embedded in a TV program to respondents in a test theater. The same experiment could also be conducted in a field environment by running the test commercial on actual TV stations. The differences between the two environments are summarized in Table 7.7.

Laboratory experiments have some advantages over field experiments. The laboratory environment offers a high degree of control because it isolates the experiment in a carefully monitored environment. Therefore, the effects of history can be minimized. A laboratory experiment also tends to produce the same results if repeated with similar subjects, leading to high internal validity. Laboratory experiments tend to use a small number of test units, last for a shorter time, be more restricted geographically, and be easier to conduct than field experiments. Hence, they are generally less expensive as well.

**demand artifacts**
The respondents attempt to guess the purpose of the experiment and respond accordingly.

As compared to field experiments, laboratory experiments suffer from some disadvantages. The artificiality of the environment may cause reactive error, in that the respondents react to the situation itself, rather than to the independent variable.[23] Also, the environment may cause **demand artifacts,** a phenomenon in which the respondents attempt to guess the purpose of the experiment and respond accordingly. For example, while viewing the test commercial, the respondents may recall pretreatment questions about the brand and guess that the commercial is trying to change their attitudes toward the

**TABLE 7.7**

**Laboratory Versus Field Experiments**

| FACTOR | LABORATORY | FIELD |
|---|---|---|
| Environment | Artificial | Realistic |
| Control | High | Low |
| Reactive error | High | Low |
| Demand artifacts | High | Low |
| Internal validity | High | Low |
| External validity | Low | High |
| Time | Short | Long |
| Number of units | Small | Large |
| Ease of implementation | High | Low |
| Cost | Low | High |

brand.[24] Finally, laboratory experiments are likely to have lower external validity than field experiments. Because a laboratory experiment is conducted in an artificial environment, the ability to generalize the results to the real world may be diminished.

It has been argued that artificiality, or lack of realism, in a laboratory experiment need not lead to lower external validity. One must be aware of the aspects of the laboratory experiment that differ from the situation to which generalizations are to be made. External validity will be reduced only if these aspects interface with the independent variables explicitly manipulated in the experiment, as is often the case in applied marketing research. However, another consideration is that laboratory experiments allow for more complex designs than field experiments. Hence, the researcher can control for more factors or variables in the laboratory setting, increasing external validity.[25]

The researcher must consider all of these factors when deciding whether to conduct laboratory or field experiments. Field experiments are less common in marketing research than laboratory experiments, although laboratory and field experiments play complementary roles.[26]

# EXPERIMENTAL VERSUS NONEXPERIMENTAL DESIGNS

In Chapter 3, we discussed three types of research designs: exploratory, descriptive, and causal. Of these, only causal designs are truly appropriate for inferring cause-and-effect relationships. Although descriptive survey data are often used to provide evidence of "causal" relationships, these studies do not meet all the conditions required for causality. For example, it is difficult in descriptive studies to establish the prior equivalence of the respondent groups with respect to both the independent and dependent variables. On the other hand, an experiment can establish this equivalence by random assignment of test units to groups. In descriptive research, it is also difficult to establish time order of occurrence of variables. However, in an experiment, the researcher controls the timing of the measurements and the introduction of the treatment. Finally, descriptive research offers little control over other possible causal factors.

We do not wish to undermine the importance of descriptive research designs in marketing research. As we mentioned in Chapter 3, descriptive research constitutes the most popular research design in marketing research, and we do not want to imply that it should never be used to examine causal relationships. Indeed, some authors have suggested procedures for drawing causal inferences from descriptive (nonexperimental) data.[27] Rather, our intent is to alert the reader to the limitations of descriptive research for examining causal relationships. Likewise, we also want to make the reader aware of the limitations of experimentation.[28]

# LIMITATIONS OF EXPERIMENTATION

Experimentation is becoming increasingly important in marketing research, but there are limitations of time, cost, and administration of an experiment.

## Time

Experiments can be time consuming, particularly if the researcher is interested in measuring the long-term effects of the treatment, such as the effectiveness of an advertising campaign. Experiments should last long enough so that the posttreatment measurements include most or all the effects of the independent variables.

## Cost

Experiments are often expensive. The requirements of experimental group, control group, and multiple measurements significantly add to the cost of research.

## Administration

Experiments can be difficult to administer. It may be impossible to control for the effects of the extraneous variables, particularly in a field environment. Field experiments often interfere with a company's ongoing operations, and obtaining cooperation from the retailers, wholesalers, and others involved may be difficult. Finally, competitors may deliberately contaminate the results of a field experiment.

# APPLICATION: TEST MARKETING

*test marketing*
An application of a controlled experiment done in limited, but carefully selected, test markets. It involves a replication of the planned national marketing program for a product in the test markets.

*test markets*
A carefully selected part of the marketplace that is particularly suitable for test marketing.

*standard test market*
A test market in which the product is sold through regular distribution channels. For example, no special considerations are given to products simply because they are being test-marketed.

*Test marketing,* also called market testing, is an application of a controlled experiment, done in limited but carefully selected parts of the marketplace called ***test markets.*** It involves a replication of a planned national marketing program in the test markets. Often, the marketing mix variables (independent variables) are varied in test marketing, and the sales (dependent variable) are monitored so that an appropriate national marketing strategy can be identified. The two major objectives of test marketing are: (1) to determine market acceptance of the product, and (2) to test alternative levels of marketing mix variables. Test-marketing procedures may be classified as standard test markets, controlled and minimarket tests, and simulated test marketing.

## Standard Test Market

In a ***standard test market,*** test markets are selected and the product is sold through regular distribution channels. Typically, the company's own sales force is responsible for distributing the product. Sales personnel stock the shelves, restock, and take inventory at regular intervals. One or more combinations of marketing mix variables (product, price, distribution, and promotional levels) are employed.

Designing a standard test market involves deciding what criteria are to be used for selecting test markets, how many test markets to use, and the duration of the test. Test markets must be carefully selected. The criteria for selection of test markets are described in the literature.[29] In general, the more test markets that can be used, the better. If resources are limited, at least two test markets should be used for each program variation to be tested. However, where external validity is important, at least four test markets should be used.

The duration of the test depends on the repurchase cycle for the product, the probability of competitive response, cost considerations, the initial consumer response, and company philosophy. The test should last long enough for repurchase activity to be observed. This indicates the long-term impact of the product. If competitive reaction to the test is anticipated, the duration should be short. The cost of the test is also an important factor. The longer a test, the more it costs, and at some point the value of additional information is outweighed by its costs. Recent evidence suggests that tests of new brands should run for at least 10 months. An empirical analysis found that the final test market share was reached in 10 months 85 percent of the time and in 12 months 95 percent of the time.[30] Test marketing can be very beneficial to a product's successful introduction, but is not without risk.

## REAL RESEARCH

### Test Marketing: Wow!

Olestra, marketed under the name Olean, developed and researched by Procter & Gamble (*www.pg.com*) over 25 years at a cost of more than $200 million, is an amazing new cooking oil that adds zero calories and no fat to the snacks people love. During April 22 to June 21, 1996, Frito-Lay's (*www.fritolay.com*) Max chips with Olean were test-marketed in three cities in 31 supermarkets. Researchers collected sales data and customer reports of any effects that they associated with eating Frito-Lay's Max chips. The key findings were encouraging: (1) sales exceeded expectations; both the initial purchase and repurchase rates were very high; (2) most people responded positively that snacks made with Olean offered a good way to reduce fat in their diets; and (3) the reporting rate of any side effects was lower than the small reporting rate anticipated prior to FDA approval.

Because the initial findings were encouraging, it was decided to expand the test marketing to Columbus, Ohio in September 1996, and Indianapolis, Indiana, in February 1997. The product in these test markets was changed in packaging design, price, and the name, called WOW!, which better described the product with its great taste and no- and low-fat/calorie reduced attributes versus the MAX product name used in the initial test markets. The test market results were again positive. Based on favorable results, the decision was made in February 1998 to launch nationally Frito-Lay's "WOW!" line of Ruffles, Lay's, and Doritos chips, all made with Olestra. Despite the initial success of products made with Olestra, consumer concern about the possible side effects of such fat-free products caused Olestra products to be unpopular. Consequently, in 2001, Procter & Gamble decided to drop Olestra as a consumer brand, but it will still be used in some of Pepsi's Frito-Lay snacks. P&G's chief executive, Alan Lafley, said the company plans to phase out failing brands, such as Olestra, more rapidly in the future despite the amount of marketing expenditures behind such brands.[31] ∎

A standard test market constitutes a one-shot case study. In addition to the problems associated with this design, test marketing faces two unique problems. First, competitors often take actions such as increasing their promotional efforts to contaminate the test-marketing program. When Procter & Gamble test-marketed its hand-and-body lotion, Wondra, the market leader, Cheeseborough Ponds, started a competitive buy-one-get-one-free promotion for its flagship brand, Vaseline Intensive Care lotion. This encouraged

Test marketing played a crucial role in Frito-Lay's decision to launch nationally the "WOW!" line of Ruffles, Lay's, and Doritos chips, all made with Olestra.

consumers to stock up on Vaseline Intensive Care lotion, and as a result, Wondra did poorly in the test market. In spite of this, Procter & Gamble launched the Wondra line nationally. Ponds again countered with the same promotional strategy. Today, Wondra has about 4 percent of the market, and Vaseline Intensive Care has 22 percent.[32]

Another problem is that while a firm's test marketing is in progress, competitors have an opportunity to beat it to the national market. Hills Bros. High Yield Coffee was test-marketed and introduced nationally, but only after Procter & Gamble introduced Folger's Flakes. Procter & Gamble skipped test marketing Folger's Flakes and beat Hills Bros. to the national market. P&G also launched Ivory shampoo without test marketing.

Sometimes it is not feasible to implement a standard test market using the company's personnel. Instead, the company must seek help from an outside supplier, in which case a controlled test market may be an attractive option.

## Controlled Test Market

**controlled test market**
A test-marketing program conducted by an outside research company in field experimentation. The research company guarantees distribution of the product in retail outlets that represent a predetermined percentage of the market.

In a **controlled test market,** the entire test-marketing program is conducted by an outside research company. The research company guarantees distribution of the product in retail outlets that represent a predetermined percentage of the market. It handles warehousing and field sales operations, such as shelf stocking, selling, and inventory control. The controlled test market includes both minimarket (or forced distribution) tests and the smaller controlled store panels. This service is provided by a number of research firms, including RoperASW (*www.roperasw.com*) and ACNielsen (*www.acnielsen.com*).

## Simulated Test Market

**simulated test market**
A quasi test market in which respondents are preselected, then interviewed and observed on their purchases and attitudes toward the product.

Also called a laboratory test or test market simulation, a **simulated test market** yields mathematical estimates of market share based on initial reaction of consumers to a new product. The procedure works as follows. Typically, respondents are intercepted in high-traffic locations, such as shopping malls, and prescreened for product usage. The selected individuals are exposed to the proposed new product concept and given an opportunity to buy the new product in a real-life or laboratory environment. Those who purchase the new product are interviewed about their evaluation of the product and repeat-purchase intentions. The trial and repeat-purchase estimates so generated are combined with data on proposed promotion and distribution levels to project a share of the market.

Simulated test markets can be conducted in 16 weeks or less. The information they generate is confidential and the competition cannot get hold of it. They are also relatively inexpensive. Whereas a standard test market can cost as much as $1 million, simulated test markets cost less than 10 percent as much. One of the major firms supplying this service is ACNielsen BASES (*www.acnielsenbases.com*). Simulated test markets are becoming increasingly popular.[33]

# INTERNATIONAL MARKETING RESEARCH

If field experiments are difficult to conduct in the United States, the challenge they pose is greatly increased in the international arena. In many countries, the marketing, economic, structural, information, and technological environment (see Chapter 23) is not developed to the extent that it is in the United States. For example, in many countries, the TV stations are owned and operated by the government with severe restrictions on television advertising. This makes field experiments manipulating advertising levels extremely difficult. Consider, for example, M&M/Mars that has set up massive manufacturing facilities in Russia and advertises its candy bars on television. Yet, the sales potential has not been realized. Is Mars advertising too much, too little, or just right? Although the answer could be determined by conducting a field experiment that manipulated the level of advertising, such causal research is not feasible, given the tight control of the Russian government on television stations. Despite their troubles, Mars has continued to invest in Russia. A pet food factory started was in Novosibirsk in August 2002.

Likewise, the lack of major supermarkets in the Baltic states makes it difficult for P&G to conduct field experiments to determine the effect of in-store promotions on the sales of its detergents. In some countries in Asia, Africa, and South America, a majority of the population lives in small towns and villages. Yet, basic infrastructures such as roads, transportation, and warehouse facilities are lacking, making it difficult to achieve desired levels of distribution. Even when experiments are designed, it is difficult to control for the time order of occurrence of variables and the absence of other possible causal factors, two of the necessary conditions for causality. Because the researcher has far less control over the environment, control of extraneous variables is particularly problematic. Furthermore, it may not be possible to address this problem by adopting the most appropriate experimental design, as environmental constraints may make that design infeasible.

Thus, the internal and external validity of field experiments conducted overseas is generally lower than in the United States. By pointing to the difficulties of conducting field experiments in other countries, we do not wish to imply that such causal research can not or should not be conducted. Some form of test marketing is generally possible, as the following example indicates.

## REAL RESEARCH

### *Flawless Quality and Exclusivity at $87,000 a Piece*

Watchmaker Lange Uhren (*www.langeuhren.com*) has succeeded in the struggling eastern German economy. The reason is their market savvy. Simulated test marketing was done in the United States, Japan, and France to determine an effective positioning and pricing strategy for the watches. In each country, the price and the positioning strategy were varied and consumer response assessed. The results, which were similar across countries, indicated that a prestige positioning with a premium price would be most effective. The eastern Germany area was well known for superior craftsmanship prior to the rise of communism. Lange Uhren used a well-trained workforce and the new marketing platform to rekindle this tradition. The new positioning strategy is based on flawless quality and exclusivity, which are portrayed uniquely in each cultural context. The watches are sold by only 22 retailers worldwide for as much as $87,000 each. The strategy has been successful. In 2002, about 4,000 of these exclusive watches were sold.

German jewelry industry officials were "cautiously optimistic" when discussing the 2003 to 2005 industry outlook. Officials believed that the Euro, launched in January 2002, would provide an increase in demand from European union-member states for German-made jewelry such as watches. Europe is the primary sales market for German-made goods, and accounts for an estimated 70 percent of all jewelry and watch exports. Given these predictions and statistics, Lange Uhren is positioned to continue its success in this industry.[34] ∎

## ETHICS IN MARKETING RESEARCH

It is often necessary to disguise the purpose of the experiment in order to produce valid results. Consider, for example, a project conducted to determine the effectiveness of television commercials for Kellogg's Rice Krispies cereal. The respondents are recruited and brought to a central facility. They are told that they will be watching a television program on nutrition and then will be asked some questions. Interspersed in the program is the commercial for Rice Krispies (test commercial), as well as commercials for some other products (filler commercials). After viewing the program and the commercials, the respondents are administered a questionnaire. The questionnaire obtains evaluations on the program content, the test commercial, and some of the filler commercials. Note, the evaluations of the program content and the filler commercials are not of interest but are obtained to reinforce the nature of the disguise. If the respondents knew the true purpose was to determine the effectiveness of the Rice Krispies commercial, their responses might be biased.

Disguising the purpose of the research should be done in a manner that does not violate the rights of the respondents. One way to handle this ethical dilemma is to inform the respondents, at the beginning, that the experiment has been disguised. They should also

*debriefing*
After the experiment, informing test subjects what the experiment was about and how the experimental manipulations were performed.

be given a description of the research task and told that they can leave the experiment at any time. After the data have been collected, the true purpose of the study and the nature of the disguise should be fully explained to the respondents and they should be given an opportunity to withdraw their information. The procedure is called ***debriefing.*** Disclosure in this way does not bias the results. There is evidence indicating that data collected from subjects informed of the disguise and those not informed are similar.[35] Debriefing can alleviate stress and make the experiment a learning experience for the respondents. However, if not properly handled, debriefing itself can be stressful. In the Rice Krispies cereal example, respondents may find it disheartening that they spent their time on a trivial task, evaluating a cereal commercial. The researcher should anticipate and address this issue in the debriefing session.

One further ethical concern is the responsibility of the researcher to use an appropriate experimental design for the problem so as to control errors caused by extraneous variables. As the following example illustrates, determining the most appropriate experimental design for the problem requires not only an initial evaluation but also continuous monitoring.

### REAL RESEARCH

## *Correcting Errors Early: A Stitch in Time Saves Nine*

A marketing research firm specializing in advertising research is examining the effectiveness of a television commercial for Nike (*www.nike.com*) athletic shoes. In 2001, Nike's revenues totaled $9.5 billion. A one-group pretest-posttest design was used. Attitudes held by the respondents toward Nike athletic shoes were obtained prior to being exposed to a sports program and several commercials, including the one for Nike. Attitudes were again measured after viewing the program and the commercials. Initial evaluation based on a small sample found the one-group pretest-posttest design adopted in this study to be susceptible to demand artifacts: respondents attempt to guess the purpose of the experiment and respond accordingly. Because time and financial constraints make redesigning the study difficult at best, the research continues without correction. Continuing a research project after knowing errors were made in the early stages is not ethical behavior. Experimental design problems should be disclosed immediately to the client. Decisions whether to redesign the study or accept the flaw should be made jointly by the researcher and the client.[36] ∎

# INTERNET AND COMPUTER APPLICATIONS

The Internet can also be a useful vehicle for conducting causal research. Different experimental treatments can be displayed at different Web sites. Respondents can then be recruited to visit these sites and respond to a questionnaire that obtains information on the dependent and extraneous variables. Thus, the Internet can provide a mechanism for controlled experimentation, although in a laboratory type of environment.

Let us continue with the example of testing advertising effectiveness considered in this chapter. Different advertisements or commercials can be posted at different Web sites. Matched or randomly selected respondents can be recruited to visit these sites, with each group visiting only one site. If any pretreatment measures have to be obtained, the respondents answer a questionnaire posted on the site. Then they are exposed to a particular advertisement or a commercial at that site. After viewing the advertisement or commercial, the respondents answer additional questions providing posttreatment measures. Control groups can also be implemented in a similar way. Thus, all types of experimental designs that we have considered can be implemented in this manner.

Experimental research can help Barnes & Noble to determine the optimal value of Internet coupons in its effort to get online customers to visit its stores.

## Internet Experimentation: A Noble Effort

Barnes & Noble (*www.bn.com*) sells books, video games, and entertainment software products and is also engaged in the online retailing of books. As of 2003, it is in competition with many Internet sites (*www.amazon.com* and *www.campusbooks.com*) as well as retail outlets (Borders Books and also campus/university bookstores). Barnes & Noble has recently launched an Internet couponing service with Interactive Coupon Network (*www.coolsavings.com*). These coupons can be used with printed books or e-books that were launched in 2001. The goal of Internet couponing was to establish complementary promotional programs, reach more consumers, and gain additional data about these consumers. Barnes & Noble wanted to link online customers to the ones actually getting to the store. What should be the face value of these coupons? An experimental design can be adopted where coupons of different face values can be offered to different Internet users and the results monitored to determine the optimal value.[37] ■

To complement the Internet, microcomputers and mainframe software can be used in the design and analysis of experiments. The comprehensive statistical analysis software package MINITAB can be used to design experiments. Although similar in use to SPSS, or SAS, MINITAB includes functions and documentation specifically for quality control work where factorial designs are encountered. For example, researchers for a destination-type specialty retail outlet, such as Niketown, might want to investigate some of the interactions of independent variables, such as elements of store atmospherics in one section of their store. The dependent variable in this experiment would be the subjects' rating of the store section for browsing. Three factors would be included in this $2 \times 2 \times 2$ study. Assuming two lighting levels (i.e., low or medium), two sound types (i.e., outdoor stadium noise or indoor arena noise), and two olfactory stimuli (i.e., hot chocolate or hot popcorn smell), the best combinations of store atmospherics can be examined.

**FOCUS ON BURKE**

Burke has the capabilities to implement a variety of experimental designs, including those discussed in this chapter. Due consideration is given to factors that will affect internal and external validity. However, from a practical standpoint, Burke has to give careful consideration to cost and efficiency. To illustrate, Burke had to design a very simple experiment with two factors in order to examine the potential of a premixed liquid cake mix. Basically, consumers pour the mix from a carton into a pan and put it in the oven. Historically, products from the refrigerator case are judged "fresher" by respondents than products found on the grocery shelf. Also, there has been some resistance (among people who are heavy users of cake mix) to low involvement with the final product. It seems psychologically more appealing to have added something to the mix, as opposed to just dumping it in a pan. To examine these premises, the new liquid cake mix was tested with two factors:

Refrigeration (Refrig): refrigeration required versus no refrigeration required
Ingredients: Eggs must be added by the baker versus no ingredients added

The simplest design, requiring the fewest assumptions, would call for selecting four random samples and giving each sample group a different cake mix, as illustrated here. This, however, was the most expensive design. With a sample size of 100 people per group, we would need 400 people. This was also a statistically inefficient design.

|         | *Refrig*         | *No Refrig*      |
|---------|------------------|------------------|
| Eggs    | Random Group 1   | Random Group 3   |
| No Eggs | Random Group 2   | Random Group 4   |

An alternate design was used with only two random samples. Each sample got two different storage methods but the same ingredients.

|         | *Refrig*         | *No Refrig*      |
|---------|------------------|------------------|
| Eggs    | Random Group 1   | Random Group 1   |
| No Eggs | Random Group 2   | Random Group 2   |

Thus, the major benefits of Burke's approach to experimental design is that it saves money and it enables the researcher to make sensitive measures on the most important factor. Of course, Burke has to make sure that the respondents are capable of handling the experimental task, i.e., handing two types of cake mix rather than one. Also, the design should not negatively affect the internal validity of the experiment.

Burke occasionally uses an experimental design to determine the order in which respondents evaluate stimuli such as products or concepts. For example, a leading manufacturer of juice drinks asked Burke to measure the appeal of five different juice blends. Burke recommended a sip test conducted in shopping malls. To avoid sensory overload, respondents were asked to evaluate only three of the five products. Burke used an experimental design to determine how the products should be grouped. Each product was evaluated an equal number of times in the first, second, and third positions. Each product was positioned an equal number of times before and after each of the other four products. This design helped minimize order bias.

# SUMMARY

The scientific notion of causality implies that we can never prove that *X* causes *Y*. At best, we can only infer that *X* is one of the causes of *Y* in that it makes the occurrence of *Y* probable. Three conditions must be satisfied before causal inferences can be made: (1) concomitant variation, which implies that *X* and *Y* must vary together in a hypothesized way; (2) time order of occurrence of variables, which implies that *X* must precede *Y;* and (3) elimination of other possible causal factors, which implies that competing explanations must be ruled out. Experiments provide the most convincing evidence of all three conditions. An experiment is formed when one or more independent variables are manipulated or controlled by the researcher, and their effect on one or more dependent variables is measured.

In designing an experiment, it is important to consider internal and external validity. Internal validity refers to whether the manipulation of the independent variables actually caused the effects on the dependent variables. External validity refers to the generalizability of experimental results. For the experiment to be valid, the researcher must control the threats imposed by extraneous variables, such as history, maturation, testing (main and interactive testing effects), instru-

mentation, statistical regression, selection bias, and mortality. There are four ways of controlling extraneous variables: randomization, matching, statistical control, and design control.

Experimental designs may be classified as preexperimental, true experimental, quasi-experimental, or statistical. An experiment may be conducted in a laboratory environment or under actual market conditions in a real-life setting. Only causal designs encompassing experimentation are appropriate for inferring cause-and-effect relationships.

Although experiments have limitations in terms of time, cost, and administration, they are becoming increasingly popular in marketing. Test marketing is an important application of experimental design.

The internal and external validity of field experiments conducted overseas is generally lower than in the United States. The level of development in many countries is lower, and the researcher lacks control over many of the marketing variables. The ethical issues involved in conducting causal research include disguising the purpose of the experiment. Debriefing can be used to address some of these issues. The Internet and computers are very useful in the design and implementation of experiments.

# KEY TERMS AND CONCEPTS

causality, *204*
concomitant variation, *205*
independent variables, *207*
test units, *207*
dependent variables, *207*
extraneous variables, *207*
experiment, *207*
experimental design, *208*
internal validity, *209*
external validity, *209*
history (H), *210*
maturation (MA), *210*
main testing effect (MN), *211*
interactive testing effect (IT), *211*
instrumentation (I), *211*
statistical regression (SR), *211*

selection bias (SB), *211*
mortality (MO), *212*
confounding variables, *212*
randomization, *212*
matching, *212*
statistical control, *212*
design control, *213*
preexperimental designs, *213*
true experimental designs, *213*
quasi-experimental designs, *213*
statistical design, *214*
one-shot case study, *214*
one-group pretest-posttest design, *214*
static group, *215*
pretest-posttest control group design, *216*
posttest-only control group design, *216*

Solomon four-group design, *217*
time series design, *217*
multiple time series design, *218*
randomized block design, *220*
Latin square design, *220*
factorial design, *221*
laboratory environment, *222*
field environment, *222*
demand artifacts, *222*
test marketing, *224*
test markets, *224*
standard test market, *224*
controlled test market, *226*
simulated test market, *226*
debriefing, *228*

# EXERCISES

## Questions

1. What are the requirements for inferring a causal relationship between two variables?
2. Differentiate between internal and external validity.
3. List any five extraneous variables and give an example to show how each can reduce internal validity.
4. Describe the various methods for controlling extraneous sources of variation.
5. What is the key characteristic that distinguishes true experimental designs from preexperimental designs?
6. List the steps involved in implementing the posttest-only control group design. Describe the design symbolically.
7. What is a time series experiment? When is it used?
8. How is a multiple time series design different from a basic time series design?
9. What advantages do statistical designs have over basic designs?
10. What are the limitations of the Latin square design?
11. Compare laboratory and field experimentation.
12. Should descriptive research be used for investigating causal relationships? Why or why not?
13. What is test marketing? What are the three types of test marketing?
14. What is the main difference between a standard test market and a controlled test market?
15. Describe how simulated test marketing works.

## Problems

1. A pro-life group wanted to test the effectiveness of an antiabortion commercial. Two random samples, each of 250 respondents, were recruited in Atlanta. One group was shown the antiabortion commercial. Then, attitudes toward abortion were measured for respondents in both groups.
   a. Identify the independent and dependent variables in this experiment.
   b. What type of design was used?
   c. What are the potential threats to internal and external validity in this experiment?

2. In the experiment just described, suppose the respondents had been selected by convenience rather than randomly. What type of design would result?
3. Consider the following table in which 500 respondents have been classified based on product use and income.

| Product Use | Income High | Medium | Low |
|---|---|---|---|
| High | 40 | 30 | 40 |
| Medium | 35 | 70 | 60 |
| Low | 25 | 50 | 150 |

   a. Does this table indicate concomitant variation between product use and income?
   b. Describe the relationship between product use and income, based on the above table.

4. State the type of experiment being conducted in the following situations. In each case, identify the potential threat to internal and external validity.
   a. A major distributor of office equipment is considering a new sales presentation program for its salespersons. The largest sales territory is selected, the new program is implemented, and the effect on sales is measured.
   b. Procter & Gamble wants to determine if a new package design for Tide is more effective than the current design. Twelve supermarkets are randomly selected in Chicago. In six of them, randomly selected, Tide is sold in the new packaging. In the other six, the detergent is sold in the old package. Sales for both groups of supermarkets are monitored for three months.

5. Describe a specific situation for which each of the following experimental designs is appropriate. Defend your reasoning.
   a. One-group pretest-posttest design
   b. Pretest-posttest control group design
   c. Posttest-only control group design
   d. Multiple time series design
   e. Factorial design

# INTERNET AND COMPUTER EXERCISES

1. Survey the relevant literature and write a short paper on the role of the computer in controlled experiments in marketing research.
2. Design an experiment for determining the effectiveness of online coupons based on relevant information obtained from *www.coupons-online.com.*
3. Coca-Cola has developed three alternative package designs for its flagship product, Coke. Design an Internet-based experiment to determine which, if any, of these new package designs is superior to the current one.
4. Microsoft has developed a new version of its spreadsheet EXCEL but is not sure what the user reaction will be. Design an Internet-based experiment to determine user reaction to the new and the previous versions of EXCEL.
5. Explain how you would implement a posttest-only control group design on the Internet to measure the effectiveness of a new print ad for Toyota Camry.

# ACTIVITIES

## *Role Playing*

1. You are a marketing research manager for the Coca-Cola Company. The company would like to determine whether it should increase, decrease, or maintain the current level of advertising dollars spent on Coke Classic. Design a field experiment to address this issue.

2. What potential difficulties do you see in conducting the experiment just described? What assistance would you require from the Coca-Cola management to overcome these difficulties?

## *Fieldwork*

1. Select two different perfume advertisements for any brand of perfume. Design and conduct an experiment to determine which ad is more effective. Use a student sample with 10 students being exposed to each ad (treatment condition). Develop your own measures of advertising effectiveness in this context.

## *Group Discussion*

1. "Whereas one cannot prove a causal relationship by conducting an experiment, experimentation is unscientific for examining cause-and-effect relationships." Discuss this statement as a small group.

# Measurement and Scaling: Fundamentals and Comparative Scaling

"When we analyze research results, we must believe that the measurements provide realistic representations of opinions and behaviors and properly capture how a respondent's data relates to all other respondents."

*Greg VanScoy, senior account executive, client services, Burke, Inc.*

## Objectives

After reading this chapter, the student should be able to:

1. Introduce the concepts of measurement and scaling and show how scaling may be considered an extension of measurement.
2. Discuss the primary scales of measurement and differentiate nominal, ordinal, interval, and ratio scales.
3. Classify and discuss scaling techniques as comparative and noncomparative, and describe the comparative techniques of paired comparison, rank order, constant sum, and Q-sort scaling.
4. Discuss the considerations involved in implementing the primary scales of measurement in an international setting.
5. Understand the ethical issues involved in selecting scales of measurement.
6. Discuss the use of the Internet and computers in implementing the primary scales of measurement.

## Overview

Once the type of research design has been determined (Chapters 3 through 7), and the information to be obtained specified, the researcher can move on to the next phase of the research design: deciding on measurement and scaling procedures. This chapter describes the concepts of scaling and measurement and discusses four primary scales of measurement: nominal, ordinal, interval, and ratio. We next describe both comparative and noncomparative scaling techniques and explain comparative techniques in detail. Noncomparative techniques are covered in Chapter 9. The considerations involved in implementing the primary scales of measurement when researching international markets are discussed. Several ethical issues that arise in measurement and scaling are identified. The chapter concludes with a discussion of the use of the Internet and computers in implementing the primary scales of measurement.

## REAL RESEARCH

### The World's and America's Most Admired Companies

The value of the World's Most Admired Companies rankings, as with *Fortune's* list of America's most admired, lies in their having been bestowed by the people who are closest to the action: senior executives and outside directors in each industry, and financial analysts who are in a position to study and compare the competitors in each field. *Fortune* asked them to rate companies on the eight criteria used to rank America's most admired: innovativeness, overall quality of management, value as a long-term investment, responsibility to the community and the environment, ability to attract and keep talented people, quality of products or services, financial soundness, and wise use of corporate assets. For global ranking, *Fortune* added another criteria to reflect international scope: a company's effectiveness in doing business globally. A company's overall ranking is based on the average of the scores of all criteria attributes. The March 4, 2002, issue featured the top two world's most admired companies as General Electric and Wal-Mart Stores in that order. Also, as of March 2002, here are America's Most Admired Companies:

| ID | Company | Rank | Total Return in 2001 |
|----|---------|------|----------------------|
| A | General Electric | 1 | −15.1% |
| B | Southwest Airlines | 2 | −17.3% |
| C | Wal-Mart Stores | 3 | 9.0% |
| D | Microsoft | 4 | 52.7% |
| E | Berkshire Hathaway | 5 | 6.5% |
| F | Home Depot | 6 | 12.1% |
| G | Johnson & Johnson | 7 | 14.0% |
| H | FedEx | 8 | 29.8% |
| I | Citigroup | 9 | 0.1% |
| J | Intel | 10 | 4.9% |

General Electric is the World's and America's most admired company.

In this example, the ID alphabets used to identify the companies represent a nominal scale. Thus, "B" denotes Southwest Airlines and "F" refers to Home Depot. The ranks represent an ordinal scale. Thus, Berkshire Hathaway, ranked 5, received higher evaluations than FedEx, ranked 8. The company score, the average rating on all the criteria attributes, represents an interval scale. These scores are not shown in the table, but General Electric had an average score of 8.01. Finally, the 2001 rate of return represents a ratio scale. Thus, Microsoft had more than four times the rate of return of Home Depot.[1] ■

## MEASUREMENT AND SCALING

**measurement**

The assignment of numbers or other symbols to characteristics of objects according to certain prespecified rules.

*Measurement* means assigning numbers or other symbols to characteristics of objects according to certain prespecified rules.[2] Note that what we measure is not the object, but some characteristic of it. Thus, we do not measure consumers—only their perceptions, attitudes, preferences, or other relevant characteristics. In marketing research, numbers are usually assigned for one of two reasons. First, numbers permit statistical analysis of the resulting data. Second, numbers facilitate the communication of measurement rules and results.

The most important aspect of measurement is the specification of rules for assigning numbers to the characteristics. The assignment process must be isomorphic: there must be one-to-one correspondence between the numbers and the characteristics being measured. For example, the same dollar figures are assigned to households with identical annual incomes. Only then can the numbers be associated with specific characteristics of the measured object, and vice versa. In addition, the rules for assigning numbers should be standardized and applied uniformly. They must not change over objects or time.

**scaling**

The generation of a continuum upon which measured objects are located.

Scaling may be considered an extension of measurement. *Scaling* involves creating a continuum upon which measured objects are located. To illustrate, consider a scale from 1 to 100 for locating consumers according to the characteristic "attitude toward department stores." Each respondent is assigned a number from 1 to 100 indicating the degree of (un)favorableness, with 1 = extremely unfavorable, and 100 = extremely favorable. Measurement is the actual assignment of a number from 1 to 100 to each respondent. Scaling is the process of placing the respondents on a continuum with respect to their attitude toward department stores. In the opening example of most admired companies, the assignment of numbers to reflect the rate of return was an example of measurement. The placement of individual companies on the rate of return continuum was scaling.

## PRIMARY SCALES OF MEASUREMENT

There are four primary scales of measurement: nominal, ordinal, interval, and ratio.[3] These scales are illustrated in Figure 8.1, and their properties are summarized in Table 8.1 and discussed in the following sections.

### Nominal Scale

**nominal scale**

A scale whose numbers serve only as labels or tags for identifying and classifying objects with a strict one-to-one correspondence between the numbers and the objects.

A *nominal scale* is a figurative labeling scheme in which the numbers serve only as labels or tags for identifying and classifying objects. For example, the numbers assigned to the

**Figure 8.1**
An Illustration of Primary Scales
of Measurement

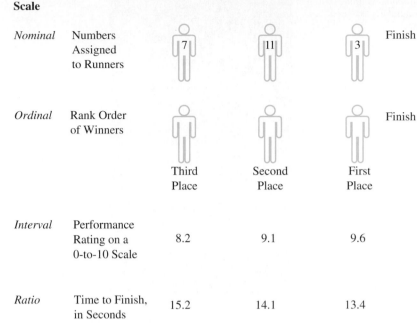

**Scale**

respondents in a study constitute a nominal scale. When a nominal scale is used for the purpose of identification, there is a strict one-to-one correspondence between the numbers and the objects. Each number is assigned to only one object and each object has only one number assigned to it. Common examples include Social Security numbers and numbers assigned to football players. In marketing research, nominal scales are used for identifying respondents, brands, attributes, stores, and other objects.

When used for classification purposes, the nominally scaled numbers serve as labels for classes or categories. For example, you might classify the control group as group 1 and the experimental group as group 2. The classes are mutually exclusive and collectively exhaustive. The objects in each class are viewed as equivalent with respect to the characteristic represented by the nominal number. All objects in the same class have the same number and no two classes have the same number. However, a nominal scale need not involve the assignment of numbers; alphabets or symbols could be assigned as well. In the opening example, alphabets were assigned to denote specific companies.

## TABLE 8.1

### Primary Scales of Measurement

| SCALE | BASIC CHARACTERISTICS | COMMON EXAMPLES | MARKETING EXAMPLES | PERMISSIBLE STATISTICS | |
|---|---|---|---|---|---|
| | | | | DESCRIPTIVE | INFERENTIAL |
| Nominal | Numbers identify and classify objects | Social Security numbers, numbering of football players | Brand numbers, store types, sex classification | Percentages, mode | Chi-square, binomial test |
| Ordinal | Numbers indicate the relative positions of the objects but not the magnitude of differences between them | Quality rankings, rankings of teams in a tournament | Preference rankings, market position, social class | Percentile, median | Rank-order correlation, Friedman ANOVA |
| Interval | Differences between objects can be compared; zero point is arbitrary | Temperature (Fahrenheit, Centigrade) | Attitudes, opinions, index numbers | Range, mean, standard deviation | Product-moment correlations, t-tests, ANOVA, regression, factor analysis |
| Ratio | Zero point is fixed; ratios of scale values can be computed | Length, weight | Age, income, costs, sales, market shares | Geometric mean, harmonic mean | Coefficient of variation |

A common and popular example of a nominal scale is numbers assigned to football players.

The numbers in a nominal scale do not reflect the amount of the characteristic possessed by the objects. For example, a high Social Security number does not imply that the person is in some way superior to those with lower Social Security numbers or vice versa. The same applies to numbers assigned to classes. The only permissible operation on the numbers in a nominal scale is counting. Only a limited number of statistics, all of which are based on frequency counts, are permissible. These include percentages, mode, chi-square, and binomial tests (see Chapter 15). It is not meaningful to compute an average Social Security number, the average sex of the respondents in a survey, or the number assigned to an average department store, as in the following example.

---

**ACTIVE RESEARCH** | DEPARTMENT STORE PROJECT

***Nominal Scale***

In the department store project, numbers 1 through 10 were assigned to the 10 stores considered in the study (see Table 8.2). Thus store number 9 referred to Sears. This did not imply that Sears was in any way superior or inferior to Neiman-Marcus, which was assigned the number 6. Any reassignment of the numbers, such as transposing the numbers assigned to Sears and Neiman-Marcus, would have no effect on the numbering system, because the numerals did not reflect any characteristics of the stores. It is meaningful to make statements such as "75 percent of the respondents patronized store 9 (Sears) within the last month." Although the average of the assigned numbers is 5.5, it is not meaningful to state that the number of the average store is 5.5.

---

## Ordinal Scale

*ordinal scale*
A ranking scale in which numbers are assigned to objects to indicate the relative extent to which some characteristic is possessed. Thus it is possible to determine whether an object has more or less of a characteristic than some other object.

An ***ordinal scale*** is a ranking scale in which numbers are assigned to objects to indicate the relative extent to which the objects possess some characteristic. An ordinal scale allows you to determine whether an object has more or less of a characteristic than some other object, but not how much more or less. Thus an ordinal scale indicates relative position, not the magnitude of the differences between the objects. The object ranked first has more of the characteristic as compared to the object ranked second, but whether the object ranked second is a close second or a poor second is not known. Common examples of ordinal scales include quality rankings, rankings of teams in a tournament, socioeconomic class, and occupational status. In marketing research, ordinal scales are used to measure relative attitudes, opinions, perceptions, and preferences. In the opening example, the rank order of the most admired companies represented an ordinal scale. General Electric, with a rank of 1, was America's most admired company. Measurements of this type include "greater than" or "less than" judgments from the respondents.

# Everything happens Instantly!

**Instant Credit** - It only takes seconds to be approved

**Instant Coupon** - If you're approved, you'll get $30 off the first order you pay for with the card

**Instant Rewards** - You'll earn points for all your card purchases and triple points for purchases at Amazon.com.[1]

**Instant Savings** - You'll enjoy no annual fee and a low introductory APR for up to 12 months

amazon.com
and you're done.™

amazon.com
and you're done.™
PLATINUM
4840 1234 5678
VALID THRU
GOOD THRU
VISA

Visit
## www.amazon.com/getmycard
Save $30 instantly on your first purchase with the card!

BUC_wr56659

# Apply, Buy, and Save Instantly!

## Save $30 on your next order!

Thanks for shopping at Amazon.com®! Did you know that if you pay with the Amazon.com Platinum Visa® Card, you earn **triple points** towards **free rewards**? Look at all these great benefits:

- Instant use of the card after approval so you can apply today, use today, and save today!
- **Save $30** on your first purchase with the card at Amazon.com
- 3 reward points earned for every dollar spent at Amazon.com
- 1 reward point earned for every dollar spent on purchases elsewhere
- For every 2,500 points you accrue, you'll receive a $25 Amazon.com Reward Certificate
- Low introductory APR for up to 12 months
- No annual fee

**amazon**.com®
and you're done.™

Visit
## www.amazon.com/getmycard
**Save $30 instantly** on your first purchase with the card!

**TABLE 8.2**

**Illustration of Primary Scales of Measurement**

| NOMINAL SCALE | | ORDINAL SCALE | INTERVAL SCALE | | RATIO SCALE |
|---|---|---|---|---|---|
| No. | Store | PREFERENCE RANKINGS | PREFERENCE RATINGS 1–7 | 11–17 | $ SPENT LAST 3 MONTHS |
| 1. | Lord & Taylor | 7    79 | 5 | 15 | 0 |
| 2. | Macy's | 2    25 | 7 | 17 | 200 |
| 3. | Kmart | 8    82 | 4 | 14 | 0 |
| 4. | Rich's | 3    30 | 6 | 16 | 100 |
| 5. | JC Penney | 1    10 | 7 | 17 | 250 |
| 6. | Neiman-Marcus | 5    53 | 5 | 15 | 35 |
| 7. | Target | 9    95 | 4 | 14 | 0 |
| 8. | Saks Fifth Ave | 6    61 | 5 | 15 | 100 |
| 9. | Sears | 4    45 | 6 | 16 | 0 |
| 10. | Wal-Mart | 10    115 | 2 | 12 | 10 |

In an ordinal scale, as in a nominal scale, equivalent objects receive the same rank. Any series of numbers can be assigned that preserves the ordered relationships between the objects. For example, ordinal scales can be transformed in any way as long as the basic ordering of the objects is maintained.[4] In other words, any monotonic positive (order-preserving) transformation of the scale is permissible, because the differences in numbers are void of any meaning other than order (see the following example). For these reasons, in addition to the counting operation allowable for nominal scale data, ordinal scales permit the use of statistics based on centiles. It is meaningful to calculate percentile, quartile, median (Chapter 15), rank-order correlation (Chapter 17) or other summary statistics from ordinal data.

**ACTIVE RESEARCH** | **DEPARTMENT STORE PROJECT**

***Ordinal Scale***

Table 8.2 gives a particular respondent's preference rankings. Respondents ranked 10 department stores in order of preference by assigning a rank 1 to the most preferred store, rank 2 to the second most preferred store, and so on. Note that JC Penney (ranked 1) is preferred to Macy's (ranked 2), but how much it is preferred we do not know. Also, it is not necessary that we assign numbers from 1 to 10 to obtain a preference ranking. The second ordinal scale, which assigns a number 10 to JC Penney, 25 to Macy's, 30 to Rich's, and so on, is an equivalent scale, as it was obtained by a monotonic positive transformation of the first scale. The two scales result in the same ordering of the stores according to preference.

## Interval Scale

*interval scale*
A scale in which the numbers are used to rate objects such that numerically equal distances on the scale represent equal distances in the characteristic being measured.

In an ***interval scale,*** numerically equal distances on the scale represent equal values in the characteristic being measured. An interval scale contains all the information of an ordinal scale, but it also allows you to compare the differences between objects. The difference between any two scale values is identical to the difference between any other two adjacent values of an interval scale. There is a constant or equal interval between scale values. The difference between 1 and 2 is the same as the difference between 2 and 3, which is the same as the difference between 5 and 6. A common example in everyday life is a temperature scale. In marketing research, attitudinal data obtained from rating scales are often treated as interval data. In the opening example of the most admired companies, the ratings on all the criteria attributes represented an interval scale.[5]

**ACTIVE RESEARCH | DEPARTMENT STORE PROJECT**

*Interval Scale*

In Table 8.2, a respondent's preferences for the 10 stores are expressed on a seven-point rating scale. We can see that although Sears received a preference rating of 6 and Wal-Mart a rating of 2, this does not mean that Sears is preferred three times as much as Wal-Mart. When the ratings are transformed to an equivalent 11-to-17 scale (next column), the ratings for these stores become 16 and 12, and the ratio is no longer 3 to 1. In contrast, the ratios of preference differences are identical on the two scales. The ratio of the preference difference between JC Penney and Wal-Mart to the preference difference between Neiman-Marcus and Wal-Mart is 5 to 3 on both the scales.

In an interval scale, the location of the zero point is not fixed. Both the zero point and the units of measurement are arbitrary. Hence, any positive linear transformation of the form $y = a + bx$ will preserve the properties of the scale. Here, $x$ is the original scale value, $y$ is the transformed scale value, b is a positive constant, and a is any constant. Therefore, two interval scales that rate objects A, B, C, and D as 1, 2, 3, and 4, or as 22, 24, 26, and 28, are equivalent. Note that the latter scale can be derived from the former by using $a = 20$ and $b = 2$ in the transforming equation. Because the zero point is not fixed, it is not meaningful to take ratios of scale values. As can be seen, the ratio of D to B values changes from 2:1 to become 7:6 when the scale is transformed. Yet, ratios of differences between scale values are permissible. In this process, the constants a and b in the transforming equation drop out in the computations. The ratio of the difference between D and B to the difference between C and B is 2:1 in both the scales.

Statistical techniques that may be used on interval scale data include all of those that can be applied to nominal and ordinal data. In addition, you can calculate the arithmetic mean, standard deviation (Chapter 15), product moment correlations (Chapter 17), and other statistics commonly used in marketing research. However, certain specialized statistics such as geometric mean, harmonic mean, and coefficient of variation are not meaningful on interval scale data.

As a further illustration, Federation Internationale de Football Association (FIFA) uses ordinal and interval scaling to rank football teams of various countries.

**REAL RESEARCH**

## Scaling the Football World

According to Federation Internationale de Football Association (FIFA) (*www.fifa.com*) 2002 rankings, world champion France was at the top with 807 points and Argentina was in the second spot with 793 points. The top 13 countries in football (known as soccer in the United States) were:

| | | Ranking as of 20 March 2002 | | |
|------|---------------|------------------|-------------------|--------------------|
| ID | Team: | Rank: March 02 | Points: March 02 | Rank: December 01 |
| A | France | 1 | 807 | 1 |
| B | Argentina | 2 | 793 | 2 |
| C | Brazil | 3 | 788 | 3 |
| D | Italy | 4 | 738 | 6 |
| E | Colombia | 5 | 735 | 5 |
| F | Portugal | 6 | 733 | 4 |
| G | Spain | 7 | 728 | 7 |
| H | Mexico | 8 | 719 | 9 |
| I | Netherlands | 9 | 718 | 8 |
| J | Germany | 10 | 710 | 12 |
| K | Yugoslavia | 11 | 708 | 11 |
| L | England | 12 | 704 | 10 |
| M | United States | 13 | 702 | 24 |

The alphabets assigned to countries constitute a nominal scale, the rankings represent an ordinal scale, whereas the points awarded denote an interval scale. Thus country G refers to Spain, which was ranked 7 and received 728 points. Note that the alphabets assigned to denote the countries simply serve the purpose of identification and are not in any way related to their football-playing capabilities. Such information can be obtained only by looking at the ranks. Thus, Colombia, ranked 5, played better than Germany, ranked 10. The lower the rank, the better the performance. The ranks do not give any information on the magnitude of the differences between countries, which can be obtained only by looking at the points. Based on the points awarded, it can be seen that Mexico, with 719 points, played only marginally better than Netherlands, with 718 points. The points help us to discern the magnitude of difference between countries receiving different ranks.[6] ∎

## Ratio Scale

**ratio scale**
The highest scale. It allows the researcher to identify or classify objects, rank order the objects, and compare intervals or differences. It is also meaningful to compute ratios of scale values.

A *ratio scale* possesses all the properties of the nominal, ordinal, and interval scales and, in addition, an absolute zero point. Thus, in ratio scales we can identify or classify objects, rank the objects, and compare intervals or differences. It is also meaningful to compute ratios of scale values. Not only is the difference between 2 and 5 the same as the difference between 14 and 17, but also 14 is seven times as large as 2 in an absolute sense. Common examples of ratio scales include height, weight, age, and money. In marketing, sales, costs, market share, and number of customers are variables measured on a ratio scale. In the opening example, the rate of return of the most admired companies represented a ratio scale.

Ratio scales allow only proportionate transformations of the form $y = bx$, where b is a positive constant. One cannot add an arbitrary constant, as in the case of an interval scale. An example of this transformation is provided by the conversion of yards to feet (b = 3). The comparisons between the objects are identical whether made in yards or feet.

All statistical techniques can be applied to ratio data. These include specialized statistics such as geometric mean, harmonic mean, and coefficient of variation.

The four primary scales (discussed here) do not exhaust the measurement level categories. It is possible to construct a nominal scale that provides partial information on order (the partially ordered scale). Likewise, an ordinal scale can convey partial information on distance, as in the case of an ordered metric scale. A discussion of these scales is beyond the scope of this text.[7]

**ACTIVE RESEARCH** | DEPARTMENT STORE PROJECT

*Ratio Scale*

In the ratio scale illustrated in Table 8.2, a respondent is asked to indicate the dollar amounts spent in each of the 10 stores during the last two months. Note that whereas this respondent spent $200 in Macy's and only $10 in Wal-Mart, this person spent 20 times as much in Macy's as Wal-Mart. Also, the zero point is fixed, because 0 means that the respondent did not spend anything at that store. Multiplying these numbers by 100 to convert dollars to cents results in an equivalent scale.

## A COMPARISON OF SCALING TECHNIQUES

**comparative scales**
One of two types of scaling techniques in which there is direct comparison of stimulus objects with one another.

The scaling techniques commonly employed in marketing research can be classified into comparative and noncomparative scales (see Figure 8.2). *Comparative scales* involve the direct comparison of stimulus objects. For example, respondents might be asked whether they prefer Coke or Pepsi. Comparative scale data must be interpreted in relative terms and have only ordinal or rank order properties. For this reason, comparative scaling is also referred to as nonmetric scaling. As shown in Figure 8.2, comparative scales include paired comparisons, rank order, constant sum scales, Q-Sort, and other procedures.

*Figure 8.2*
A Classification of Scaling
Techniques

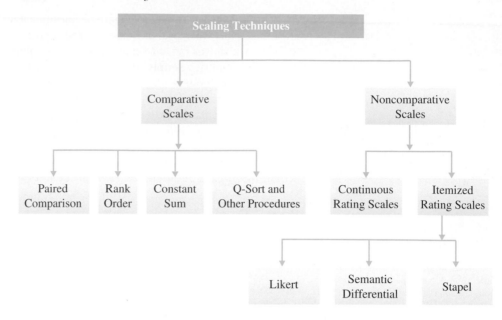

The major benefit of comparative scaling is that small differences between stimulus objects can be detected. As they compare the stimulus objects, respondents are forced to choose between them. In addition, respondents approach the rating task from the same known reference points. Consequently, comparative scales are easily understood and can be applied easily. Other advantages of these scales are that they involve fewer theoretical assumptions, and they also tend to reduce halo or carryover effects from one judgment to another. The major disadvantages of comparative scales include the ordinal nature of the data and the inability to generalize beyond the stimulus objects scaled. For instance, to compare RC Cola to Coke and Pepsi, the researcher would have to do a new study. These disadvantages are substantially overcome by the noncomparative scaling techniques.

In ***noncomparative scales,*** also referred to as monadic or metric scales, each object is scaled independently of the others in the stimulus set. The resulting data are generally assumed to be interval or ratio scaled.[8] For example, respondents may be asked to evaluate Coke on a 1-to-6 preference scale (1 = not at all preferred, 6 = greatly preferred). Similar evaluations would be obtained for Pepsi and RC Cola. As can be seen in Figure 8.2, noncomparative scales can be continuous rating or itemized rating scales. The itemized rating scales can be further classified as Likert, semantic differential, or Stapel scales. Noncomparative scaling is the most widely used scaling technique in marketing research. Given its importance, Chapter 9 is devoted to noncomparative scaling. The rest of this chapter focuses on comparative scaling techniques.

**noncomparative scales**
One of two types of scaling techniques in which each stimulus object is scaled independently of the other objects in the stimulus set.

# COMPARATIVE SCALING TECHNIQUES

## Paired Comparison Scaling

**paired comparison scaling**
A comparative scaling technique in which a respondent is presented with two objects at a time and asked to select one object in the pair according to some criterion. The data obtained are ordinal in nature.

As its name implies, in ***paired comparison scaling,*** a respondent is presented with two objects and asked to select one according to some criterion. The data obtained are ordinal in nature. A respondent may state that they shop in JC Penney more than in Sears, like Total cereal better than Kellogg's Product 19, or like Crest more than Colgate. Paired comparison scales are frequently used when the stimulus objects are physical products. Coca-Cola is reported to have conducted more than 190,000 paired comparisons before introducing New Coke.[9] Paired comparison scaling is the most widely used comparative scaling technique.

**Figure 8.3**
Obtaining Shampoo Preferences
Using Paired Comparisons

---

***Instructions***

We are going to present you with 10 pairs of shampoo brands. For each pair, please indicate which one of the two brands of shampoo in the pair you would prefer for personal use.

***Recording Form***

| | *Jhirmack* | *Finesse* | *Vidal Sassoon* | *Head & Shoulders* | *Pert* |
|---|---|---|---|---|---|
| Jhirmack | | 0 | 0 | 1 | 0 |
| Finesse | 1[a] | | 0 | 1 | 0 |
| Vidal Sassoon | 1 | 1 | | 1 | 1 |
| Head & Shoulders | 0 | 0 | 0 | | 0 |
| Pert | 1 | 1 | 0 | 1 | |
| Number of times preferred[b] | 3 | 2 | 0 | 4 | 1 |

[a]A 1 in a particular box means that the brand in that column was preferred over the brand in the corresponding row. A 0 means that the row brand was preferred over the column brand.
[b]The number of times a brand was preferred is obtained by summing the 1's in each column.

---

Figure 8.3 shows paired comparison data obtained to assess a respondent's shampoo preferences. As can be seen, this respondent made 10 comparisons to evaluate five brands. In general, with *n* brands, $[n(n - 1)/2]$ paired comparisons are required to include all possible pairings of objects.[10]

Paired comparison data can be analyzed in several ways.[11] The researcher can calculate the percentage of respondents who prefer one stimulus to another by summing the matrices of Figure 8.3 for all the respondents, dividing the sum by the number of respondents, and multiplying by 100. Simultaneous evaluation of all the stimulus objects is also possible. Under the assumption of transitivity, it is possible to convert paired comparison data to a rank order. ***Transitivity of preference*** implies that if brand A is preferred to B, and brand B is preferred to C, then brand A is preferred to C. To arrive at a rank order, the researcher determines the number of times each brand is preferred by summing the column entries in Figure 8.3. Therefore, this respondent's order of preference, from most to least preferred, is Head and Shoulders, Jhirmack, Finesse, Pert, and Vidal Sassoon. It is also possible to derive an interval scale from paired comparison data using the Thurstone case V procedure. Refer to the appropriate literature for a discussion of this procedure.[12]

*transitivity of preference*
An assumption made in order to convert paired comparison data to rank order data. It implies that if brand A is preferred to brand B and brand B is preferred to brand C, then brand A is preferred to brand C.

Several modifications of the paired comparison technique have been suggested. One involves the inclusion of a neutral/no difference/no opinion response. Another extension is graded paired comparisons. In this method, respondents are asked which brand in the pair is preferred and how much it is preferred. The degree of preference may be expressed by how much more the respondent is willing to pay for the preferred brand. The resulting scale is a dollar metric scale. Another modification of paired comparison scaling is widely used in obtaining similarity judgments in multidimensional scaling (see Chapter 21).

Paired comparison scaling is useful when the number of brands is limited, because it requires direct comparison and overt choice. However, with a large number of brands, the number of comparisons becomes unwieldy. Other disadvantages are that violations of the assumption of transitivity may occur, and order in which the objects are presented may bias the results. Paired comparisons bear little resemblance to the marketplace situation that involves selection from multiple alternatives. Also, respondents may prefer one object to certain others, but they may not like it in an absolute sense.

When taste tests showed that several consumers preferred white cranberries to red cranberries, Ocean Spray added White Cranberry drinks to its product line.

**REAL RESEARCH**

## *Paired Comparison Scaling*

The most common method of taste testing is paired comparison. The consumer is asked to sample two different products and select the one with the most appealing taste. The test is done in private, either in homes or other predetermined sites. A minimum of 1,000 responses is considered an adequate sample.

Ocean Spray (*www.oceanspray.com*), North America's top producer of bottled and canned juices/juice drinks, makes extensive use of taste tests in developing new products. Respondents are asked to sample new drinks presented in pairs and evaluate them on taste and flavor and choose the one they like more than the other.

Taste tests showed that several consumers preferred white cranberries to the strong, tart taste of red cranberries. Therefore, in early 2002, Ocean Spray added White Cranberry drinks, made with natural white cranberries harvested a few weeks earlier than the red variety, and Juice Spritzers, lightly carbonated juice drinks, to its product line in an effort to appeal to a broader range of consumers.[13] ■

## Rank Order Scaling

After paired comparisons, the most popular comparative scaling technique is rank order scaling. In **rank order scaling,** respondents are presented with several objects simultaneously and asked to order or rank them according to some criterion. For example, respondents may be asked to rank brands of toothpaste according to overall preference. As shown in Figure 8.4, these rankings are typically obtained by asking the respondents to assign a rank of 1 to the most preferred brand, 2 to the second most preferred, and so on, until a rank of *n* is assigned to the least preferred brand. Like paired comparison, this approach is also comparative in nature, and it is possible that the respondent may dislike the brand ranked 1 in an absolute sense. Furthermore, rank order scaling also results in ordinal data. See Table 8.2, which uses rank order scaling to derive an ordinal scale.

Rank order scaling is commonly used to measure preferences for brands as well as attributes. Rank order data are frequently obtained from respondents in conjoint analysis (see Chapter 21), because rank order scaling forces the respondent to discriminate among the stimulus objects. Moreover, as compared to paired comparisons, this type of scaling process more closely resembles the shopping environment. It also takes less time and eliminates intransitive responses. If there are *n* stimulus objects, only $(n - 1)$ scaling decisions need be made in rank order scaling. However, in paired comparison scaling,

---

**rank order scaling**
A comparative scaling technique in which respondents are presented with several objects simultaneously and asked to order or rank them according to some criterion.

*Figure 8.4*
Preference for Toothpaste Brands
Using Rank Order Scaling

**Instructions**

Rank the various brands of toothpaste in order of preference. Begin by picking out the one brand that you like most and assign it a number 1. Then find the second most preferred brand and assign it a number 2. Continue this procedure until you have ranked all the brands of toothpaste in order of preference. The least preferred brand should be assigned a rank of 10.

*No two brands should receive the same rank number.*

The criterion of preference is entirely up to you. There is no right or wrong answer. Just try to be consistent.

| *Brand* | *Rank Order* |
|---|---|
| 1. Crest | _____ |
| 2. Colgate | _____ |
| 3. Aim | _____ |
| 4. Gleem | _____ |
| 5. Macleans | _____ |
| 6. Ultra Brite | _____ |
| 7. Close Up | _____ |
| 8. Pepsodent | _____ |
| 9. Plus White | _____ |
| 10. Stripe | _____ |

$[n(n-1)/2]$ decisions would be required. Another advantage is that most respondents easily understand the instructions for ranking. The major disadvantage is that this technique produces only ordinal data.

Finally, under the assumption of transitivity, rank order data can be converted to equivalent paired comparison data, and vice versa. Figure 8.3 illustrated this point. It is possible to derive an interval scale from rankings using the Thurstone case V procedure. Other approaches for deriving interval scales from rankings have also been suggested.[14] The following example shows how rank order scaling is used to determine the world's top brands.

### REAL RESEARCH

## World's Best-Known Brands

To be a strong competitor in today's American marketplace, companies rely heavily on brand recognition. When consumers recognize a company or a product as a household name, preferably for good reasons rather than as a result of bad publicity, brand equity is increased. Core Brand (*www.corebrand.com*), a firm specializing in brand strategy and communications, conducts an annual survey to determine which brands are the most recognized by consumers. They release a list of the 10 best-known brands. Their "top 10" list is an example of rank order scaling. Their 2001 Corporate Brand Index reveals the relative strength of the world's best-known brands. Here are the top 10:[15]

**1.** Coca-Cola Co.
**2.** United Parcel Service (UPS)
**3.** Microsoft Corp.
**4.** Walt Disney
**5.** Johnson & Johnson
**6.** Campbell Soup
**7.** FedEx
**8.** Harley-Davidson
**9.** IBM
**10.** MasterCard ■

**Figure 8.5**
Importance of Toilet Soap
Attributes Using a Constant
Sum Scale

**Instructions**

Below are eight attributes of toilet soaps. Please allocate 100 points among the attributes so that your allocation reflects the relative importance you attach to each attribute. The more points an attribute receives, the more important the attribute is. If an attribute is not at all important, assign it zero points. If an attribute is twice as important as some other attribute, it should receive twice as many points.

**Form**

| | *Average Responses of Three Segments* | | |
|---|---|---|---|
| *Attribute* | *Segment I* | *Segment II* | *Segment III* |
| 1. Mildness | 8 | 2 | 4 |
| 2. Lather | 2 | 4 | 17 |
| 3. Shrinkage | 3 | 9 | 7 |
| 4. Price | 53 | 17 | 9 |
| 5. Fragrance | 9 | 0 | 19 |
| 6. Packaging | 7 | 5 | 9 |
| 7. Moisturizing | 5 | 3 | 20 |
| 8. Cleaning power | 13 | 60 | 15 |
| Sum | 100 | 100 | 100 |

Another example of rank order scaling was America's most admired companies given in the overview.

## Constant Sum Scaling

In *constant sum scaling*, respondents allocate a constant sum of units, such as points, dollars, or chips, among a set of stimulus objects with respect to some criterion. As shown in Figure 8.5, respondents may be asked to allocate 100 points to attributes of a toilet soap in a way that reflect the importance they attach to each attribute. If an attribute is unimportant, the respondent assigns it zero points. If an attribute is twice as important as some other attribute, it receives twice as many points. The sum of all the points is 100. Hence, the name of the scale.

The attributes are scaled by counting the points assigned to each one by all the respondents and dividing by the number of respondents. These results are presented for three groups, or segments, of respondents in Figure 8.5. Segment I attaches overwhelming

Use of constant sum scaling to determine the relative importance of bathing soap attributes has enabled Irish Spring to develop a superior product.

importance to price. Segment II considers basic cleaning power to be of prime importance. Segment III values lather, fragrance, moisturizing, and cleaning power. Such information cannot be obtained from rank order data unless they are transformed into interval data. Note that the constant sum also has an absolute zero—10 points are twice as many as 5 points, and the difference between 5 and 2 points is the same as the difference between 57 and 54 points. For this reason, constant sum scale data are sometimes treated as metric. Although this may be appropriate in the limited context of the stimuli scaled, these results are not generalizable to other stimuli not included in the study. Hence, strictly speaking, the constant sum should be considered an ordinal scale because of its comparative nature and the resulting lack of generalizability. It can be seen that the allocation of points in Figure 8.5 is influenced by the specific attributes included in the evaluation task.

The main advantage of the constant sum scale is that it allows for fine discrimination among stimulus objects without requiring too much time. However, it has two primary disadvantages. Respondents may allocate more or fewer units than those specified. For example, a respondent may allocate 108 or 94 points. The researcher must modify such data in some way or eliminate this respondent from analysis. Another potential problem is rounding error if too few units are used. On the other hand, the use of a large number of units may be too taxing on the respondent and cause confusion and fatigue.

## Q-Sort and Other Procedures

*Q-sort scaling*

A comparative scaling technique that uses a rank order procedure to sort objects based on similarity with respect to some criterion.

*Q-sort scaling* was developed to discriminate among a relatively large number of objects quickly. This technique uses a rank order procedure in which objects are sorted into piles based on similarity with respect to some criterion. For example, respondents are given 100 attitude statements on individual cards and asked to place them into 11 piles, ranging from "most highly agreed with" to "least highly agreed with." The number of objects to be sorted should not be less than 60 nor more than 140; 60 to 90 objects is a reasonable range. The number of objects to be placed in each pile is prespecified, often to result in a roughly normal distribution of objects over the whole set.

Another comparative scaling technique is magnitude estimation.[16] In this technique, numbers are assigned to objects such that ratios between the assigned numbers reflect ratios on the specified criterion. For example, respondents may be asked to indicate whether they agree or disagree with each of a series of statements measuring attitude toward department stores. Then they assign a number between 0 to 100 to each statement to indicate the intensity of their agreement or disagreement. Providing this type of numbers imposes a cognitive burden on the respondents. Finally, mention must be made of Guttman scaling, or scalogram analysis, which is a procedure for determining whether a set of objects can be ordered into an internally consistent, unidimensional scale.

# INTERNATIONAL MARKETING RESEARCH

In the four primary scales, the level of measurement increases from nominal to ordinal to interval to ratio scale. This increase in measurement level is obtained at the cost of complexity. From the viewpoint of the respondents, nominal scales are the simplest to use, whereas the ratio scales are the most complex. Respondents in many developed countries, due to higher education and consumer sophistication levels, are quite used to providing responses on interval and ratio scales. However, it has been argued that opinion formation may not be well crystallized in some developing countries. Hence, these respondents experience difficulty in expressing the gradation required by interval and ratio scales. Preferences can, therefore, be best measured by using ordinal scales. In particular, the use of binary scales (e.g., preferred/not preferred), the simplest type of ordinal scale, has been recommended.[17] For example, when measuring preferences for jeans in the United States, Levi Strauss & Co. could ask consumers to rate their preferences for wearing jeans on specified occasions using a seven-point interval scale. However, consumers in Papua New Guinea could be shown a pair of jeans and simply asked whether or not they would prefer to wear it for a specific occasion (e.g., when shopping, working, relaxing on a holiday, etc.). The advantage of selecting the primary scales to match the profile of the target respondents is well illustrated by the Japanese survey of automobile preferences in Europe.

**REAL RESEARCH**

*Car War—Japan Making a Spearhead*

For the first time, European journalists had given their car-of-the-year award to a Japanese model—Nissan's new British-made Micra, a $10,000 subcompact. This came as a big blow to the European automakers that have been trying to keep the Japanese onslaught at bay. "They will change the competitive balance," warns Bruce Blythe, Ford of Europe Inc.'s head of business strategy. How did the Japanese do it?

Nissan conducted a survey of European consumers' preferences for automobiles using interval scales to capture the magnitude of preference differences. The use of interval scales enabled Nissan to compare the differences between automobile features and determine which features were preferred. The findings revealed distinct consumer preferences. So the Japanese made inroads by transplanting their production and building technical centers in Europe to customize their cars to local styling tastes and preferences. Nissan also forged an alliance with French auto manufacturer Renault in 1999 and sold 483,990 cars in Europe in 2001. Nissan introduced new models in Europe in 2003 in hopes of lifting recent sagging sales in that market. The European automakers need to be on guard against such fierce competition.[18] ∎

It should also be noted that comparative scales, except for paired comparisons, require comparisons of multiple stimulus objects and are, therefore, taxing on the respondents. In contrast, in noncomparative scales, each object is scaled independently of others in the stimulus set, i.e., objects are scaled one at a time. Hence, noncomparative scales are simpler to administer and more appropriate in cultures were the respondents are less educated or unfamiliar with marketing research.

# ETHICS IN MARKETING RESEARCH

The researcher has the responsibility to use the appropriate type of scales to get the data needed to answer the research questions and test the hypotheses. Take, for example, a newspaper such as the *Wall Street Journal* wanting information on the personality profiles of its readers and nonreaders. Information on the personality characteristics might best be obtained by giving respondents (readers and nonreaders) several cards, each listing one personality characteristic. The respondents are asked to sort the cards and to rank order the personality characteristics, listing, in order, those they believe describe their personality best first and those that do not describe themselves last. This process will provide rich insight into the personality characteristics by allowing respondents to compare and shuffle the personality cards. However, the resulting data are ordinal and cannot be easily used in multivariate analysis. To examine differences in the personality characteristics of readers and nonreaders and relate them to marketing strategy variables, interval scale data are needed. It is the obligation of the researcher to obtain the data that are most appropriate, given the research questions, as the following example illustrates.

**REAL RESEARCH**

*Scaling Ethical Dilemmas*

In a study designed to measure ethical judgments of marketing researchers, scale items from a previously developed and tested scale were used. After a pretest was conducted on a convenience sample of 65 marketing professionals, however, it became apparent that some original scale items were worded in a way that did not reflect current usage. Therefore, these items were updated. For example, an item that was gender specific, such as, "He pointed out that . . ." was altered to read "The project manager pointed out that. . . ." Subjects were requested to show their approval or disapproval of the stated action (item) of a marketing research director with regard to specific scenarios. Realizing that a binary or dichotomous scale would be too restrictive, approval or disapproval was indicated by having respondents supply interval-level data via five-point scales with descriptive anchors of 1 = disapprove, 2 = disapprove somewhat, 3 = neither approve or disapprove, 4 = approve somewhat, and 5 = approve. In this way, scaling dilemmas were resolved.[19] ■

After the data have been collected, they should be analyzed correctly. If nominal scaled data are gathered, then statistics permissible for nominal scaled data must be used. Likewise, when ordinal scaled data are collected, statistical procedures developed for use with interval or ratio data should not be used. Conclusions based on the misuse of statistics are misleading. Using the personality example above, if it were decided to gather data by the rank order technique described, ordinal data would be collected. If, after collection, the client wishes to know how the readers and the nonreaders differed, the researcher should treat these data correctly and use nonmetric techniques for analysis (discussed in Chapter 15). When the researcher lacks the expertise to identify and use the appropriate statistical techniques, help should be sought from other sources, for example, from statisticians.

# INTERNET AND COMPUTER APPLICATIONS

All the primary scales of measurement that we have considered can be implemented on the Internet. The same is true for the commonly used comparative scales. Paired comparisons involving verbal, visual, or auditory comparisons can be implemented with ease. However, taste, smell, and touch comparisons are difficult to implement. It may also be difficult to implement specialized scales such as the Q-sort. The process of implementing comparative scales may be facilitated by searching the Internet for similar scales that have been implemented by other researchers.

**REAL RESEARCH**

## *Primary Scales Help Domino's to Become a Primary Competitor*

Domino's Pizza builds Web sites to communicate its image and give information on its products. It also sees its Web site as a medium to collect information on customers and therefore conduct marketing research. Although no pizza is sold online, the company has one national Web site (*www.dominos.com*) in addition to Web sites for each of its local subsidiaries.

For local subsidiaries, the customer is asked to fill in a comment form on the Web site. This posted survey, which is different on each Domino's Pizza's Web site, helps the local team to better understand its customers' needs and better service them. Different scales are utilized to obtain the following information.

■ name, phone number, and (e-mail) address (nominal scale)
■ preference for pizza restaurants in the local area (ordinal scale)
■ impressions on the service offered by Domino's Pizza as a whole (interval scale)
■ assessments on the products and price (interval scale)
■ customer satisfaction (interval scale)
■ amount spent on pizza and fast foods (ratio scale)

This enables the company to set up a database of clients for target marketing and to know what to improve in its marketing mix (product/price/delivery). It also enables

Domino's to measure customer satisfaction and to use it for a variety of purposes, such as linking it to salaries. In 2001, Domino's launched its advertising campaign entitled, "Get the Door. It's Domino's," and it opened its 7,000th store. Following the September 11, 2001, terrorist attacks, Domino's provided more than 12,000 pizzas to relief workers at Ground Zero.[20] ■

Database managers allow researchers to develop and test several different scales to determine their appropriateness for a particular application. Several off-the-shelf packages are also available. Microcomputers have been used to administer paired comparison scales in taste tests. Several programs are available for designing and administering paired comparison and other types of scales.

## SPSS Windows

Using SPSS Data Entry, the researcher can design any of the primary type of scales: nominal, ordinal, interval, or ratio. Either the question library can be used or customized scales can be designed. Moreover, paired comparison, rank order, and constant sum scales can be easily implemented. We show the use of SPSS Data Entry to design ordinal scales to measure education and income (Figure 8.6). This software is not included but may be purchased separately from SPSS.

*Figure 8.6*
Ordinal Scales for Measuring Education and Income

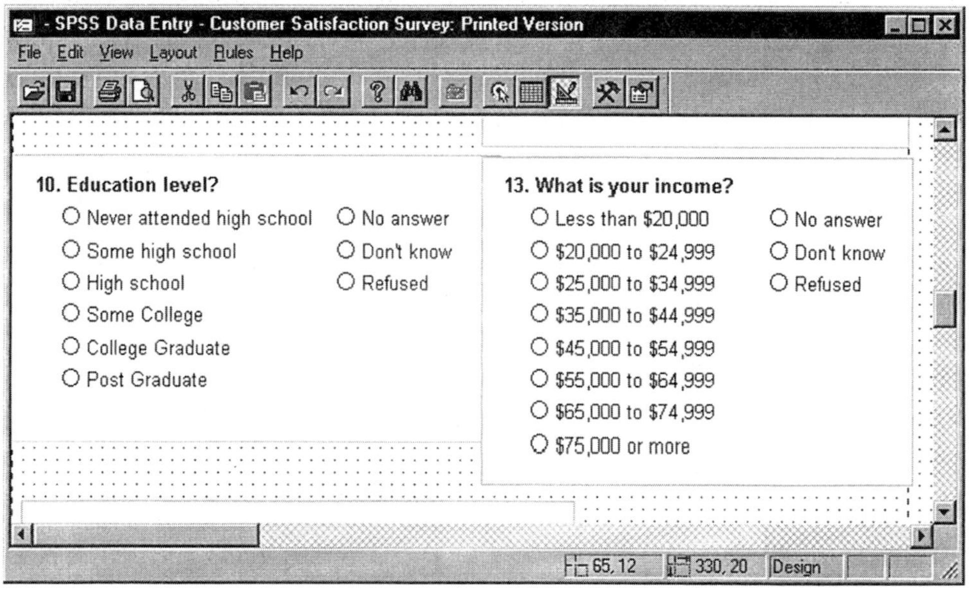

## FOCUS ON BURKE

Given the diverse nature of projects conducted by Burke, it employs all the four basic types of scales. Nominal scales are employed to denote subjects, brands, stores, advertisements, and virtually any type of marketing stimuli. Rank order scales are used to rank new product names, packages, competing brands, and other choice alternatives in terms of preference and purchase intent. Interval scales are widely used. Most of the projects will employ some form of interval scale measurement. For example, customer satisfaction is measured on a four-point scale (1 = very dissatisfied, 2 = somewhat dissatisfied, 3 = somewhat satisfied, and 4 = very satisfied). Ratio scales are also used to measure sales potential, sales, and market share. An illustration of the use of a ratio scale is provided by the Burke Integrated Concept Evaluation System (ICES). The ICES evaluates new product concepts by estimating for each concept a potential score in terms of the number of units of that product (concept) that could be sold per 100 households. This measure, called the Concept Potential Score (CPS) constitutes a ratio scale. Based on the CPS, concepts with the greatest potential can be identified.

A major dog food manufacturer had identified 13 new product opportunities and needed to find a way to set priorities for product development. Burke's ICES was chosen for its ability to efficiently screen multiple concepts and estimate sales potential using the Concept Potential Score (CPS). Based on the CPS, several high-potential products were accelerated, a few low-potential ideas were shelved, and the remaining were scheduled for subsequent development. ICES helped this manufacturer solve its immediate problem of setting priorities. The real value became evident when concept and product testing, as well as in-market sales performance, validated these early screening results. In addition, this manufacturer has established a database of concept screening results against which to compare future waves of ICES-tested concepts.

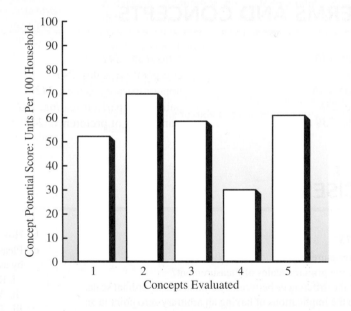

Finally, Burke is very cautious about using comparative scales. To illustrate Burke's concerns, imagine this scenario in which the category manager reports to the president of the company:

Category Manager: "We had 100 people try our two product concepts and 70 percent said that they preferred concept A! Let's start production."
President, after a moment's thought, asks: "Do you think anyone will buy this new product?"
Category Manager: "We didn't ask that, but 70 percent prefer A over B!"
President: "Is it possible that A is the best of two bad products . . . the 'king of the pigs'?"

This conversation could continue, but it points out why Burke is very careful with comparative scales. When you ask respondents to compare, rank order, allocate points, or state a relative preference, you are asking for their judgments internal to the set of objects. You have little or no measurement that has validity external to the set.

# CHAPTER 9

# Measurement and Scaling: Noncomparative Scaling Techniques

"The purpose of a scale is to allow us to represent respondents with the highest possible accuracy and reliability. We can't have one without the other and still believe in our data."

*Bart Gamble,*
*vice president,*
*client services,*
*Burke, Inc.*

## Objectives

After reading this chapter, the student should be able to:

1. Describe the noncomparative scaling techniques, distinguish between continuous and itemized rating scales, and explain Likert, semantic differential, and Stapel scales.
2. Discuss the decisions involved in constructing itemized rating scales with respect to the number of scale categories, balanced versus unbalanced scales, odd or even number of categories, forced versus nonforced choice, degree of verbal description, and the physical form of the scale.
3. Discuss the criteria used for scale evaluation and explain how to assess reliability, validity, and generalizability.
4. Discuss the considerations involved in implementing noncomparative scales in an international setting.
5. Understand the ethical issues involved in developing noncomparative scales.
6. Discuss the use of the Internet and computers in implementing continuous and itemized rating scales.

## Overview

As discussed in Chapter 8, scaling techniques are classified as comparative or noncomparative. The comparative techniques, consisting of paired comparison, rank order, constant sum, and Q-sort scaling were discussed in the last chapter. The subject of this chapter is noncomparative techniques, which are comprised of continuous and itemized rating scales. We discuss the popular itemized rating scales, the Likert, semantic differential, and Stapel scales, as well as the construction of multiitem rating scales. We show how scaling techniques should be evaluated in terms of reliability and validity and consider how the researcher selects a particular scaling technique. Mathematically derived scales are also presented. The considerations involved in implementing noncomparative scales when researching international markets are discussed. Several ethical issues that arise in rating scale construction are identified. The chapter concludes with a discussion of the use of the Internet and computers in developing continuous and itemized rating scales.

## REAL RESEARCH

 **New York City Transit**

The New York City Transit (NYCT) (*www.mta.nyc.ny.us/nyct/subway*) does not have a wholly captive audience as some people believe. Many people do not use the mass transit system when they have a choice. A much needed rate hike brought fears that more people would avoid taking the bus or subway. Therefore, research was undertaken to uncover ways to increase ridership.

In a telephone survey, respondents were asked to rate different aspects of the transit system using five-point Likert scales. Likert scales were chosen as they are easy to administer over the telephone and the respondents merely indicate their degree of (dis)agreement (1 = strongly disagree, 5 = strongly agree).

The results showed that personal safety was the major concern on subways. New Yorkers were afraid to use a subway station in their own neighborhoods. The factor that contributed most to riders' fears was the lack of a way to contact someone in case of trouble. NYCT was able to respond to riders' concerns by increasing police presence, having a more visible NYCT staff, increasing lighting, and repositioning walls, columns, and stairways for better visibility throughout the station.

Telephone surveys also revealed that cleanliness of subway stations and subway cars is related to the perception of crime. In response, NYCT was able to concentrate more on ways to maintain a cleaner appearance. Action was also taken to reduce the number of homeless people and panhandlers. They are asked to leave, and sometimes transportation to shelters is provided.

Results of marketing research efforts have helped NYCT improve perceptions surrounding the system, leading to increased ridership. As of 2003, the NYCT was ranked as the fifth largest subway system in the world and the largest in North America with an annual ridership of 1.3 billion.[1]

**TABLE 9.1**

**Basic Noncomparative Scales**

| SCALE | BASIC CHARACTERISTICS | EXAMPLES | ADVANTAGES | DISADVANTAGES |
|---|---|---|---|---|
| Continuous rating scale | Place a mark on a continuous line | Reaction to TV commercials | Easy to construct | Scoring can be cumbersome unless computerized |
| ITEMIZED RATING SCALES | | | | |
| Likert scale | Degree of agreement on a 1 (strongly disagree) to 5 (strongly agree) scale | Measurement of attitudes | Easy to construct, administer, and understand | More time consuming |
| Semantic differential | Seven-point scale with bipolar labels | Brand, product, and company images | Versatile | Controversy as to whether the data are interval |
| Stapel scale | Unipolar ten-point scale, −5 to +5, without a neutral point (zero) | Measurement of attitudes and images | Easy to construct; administered over telephone | Confusing and difficult to apply |

# NONCOMPARATIVE SCALING TECHNIQUES

**noncomparative scale**
One of two types of scaling techniques in which each stimulus object is scaled independently of the other objects in the stimulus set.

Respondents using a **noncomparative scale** employ whatever rating standard seems appropriate to them. They do not compare the object being rated either to another object or to some specified standard, such as "your ideal brand." They evaluate only one object at a time, and for this reason noncomparative scales are often referred to as monadic scales. Noncomparative techniques consist of continuous and itemized rating scales, which are described in Table 9.1 and discussed in the following sections.

## Continuous Rating Scale

**continuous rating scale**
Also referred to as graphic rating scale, this measurement scale has the respondents rate the objects by placing a mark at the appropriate position on a line that runs from one extreme of the criterion variable to the other.

In a **continuous rating scale,** also referred to as a graphic rating scale, respondents rate the objects by placing a mark at the appropriate position on a line that runs from one extreme of the criterion variable to the other. Thus, the respondents are not restricted to selecting from marks previously set by the researcher. The form of the continuous scale may vary considerably. For example, the line may be vertical or horizontal; scale points, in the form of numbers or brief descriptions, may be provided; and, if provided, the scale points may be few or many. Three versions of a continuous rating scale are illustrated.

---

**ACTIVE RESEARCH** | DEPARTMENT STORE PROJECT

*Continuous Rating Scales*

How would you rate Sears as a department store?

Version 1
Probably the worst - - - - - - -I - - - - - - - - - - - - - - - - - - - - - - - - - - - - - Probably the best

Version 2
Probably the worst - - - - - - -I - - - - - - - - - - - - - - - - - - - - - - - - - Probably the best
                0   10  20  30  40  50  60  70  80  90  100

Version 3
               Very bad     Neither good    Very good
                          nor bad

Probably the worst - - - - - - -I - - - - - - - - - - - - - - - - - - - - - - - - - Probably the best
                0   10  20  30  40  50  60  70  80  90  100

---

Once the respondent has provided the ratings, the researcher divides the line into as many categories as desired and assigns scores based on the categories into which the ratings fall. In the department store project example, the respondent exhibits an unfavorable attitude toward Sears. These scores are typically treated as interval data.

The advantage of continuous scales is that they are easy to construct. However, scoring is cumbersome and unreliable. Moreover, continuous scales provide little new information. Hence, their use in marketing research has been limited. Recently, however, with the increased popularity of computer-assisted personal interviewing and other technologies, their use is becoming more frequent.

**REAL RESEARCH**

## Continuous Measurement and Analysis of Perceptions: The Perception Analyzer

The Perception Analyzer (*www.perceptionanalyzer.com*) by MSInteractive is a computer-supported, interactive, feedback system composed of wireless or wired handheld dials for each participant, a console (computer interface), and special software that edits questions, collects data, and analyzes participant responses. Members of focus groups use it to record their emotional response to television commercials, instantly and continuously. Each participant is given a dial and instructed to continuously record their reaction to the material being tested. As the respondents turn the dials, the information is fed to a computer. Thus, the researcher can determine the second-by-second response of the respondents as the commercial is run. Furthermore, this response can be superimposed on the commercial to see the respondents' reactions to the various frames and parts of the commercial.

The analyzer was recently used to measure responses to a series of "slice-of-life" commercials for McDonald's. The researchers found that mothers and daughters had different responses to different aspects of the commercial. Using the emotional response data, the researchers could determine which commercial had the greatest emotional appeal across mother-daughter segments. McDonald's marketing efforts proved successful with 2001 revenues of $14.8 billion.[2] ■

Companies such as McDonald's have used the Perception Analyzer to measure consumers' reactions to commercials, company videos, and other audio/visual materials.

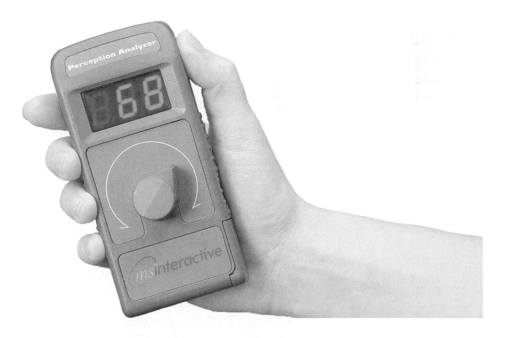

# ITEMIZED RATING SCALES

**itemized rating scale**
A measurement scale having numbers and/or brief descriptions associated with each category. The categories are ordered in terms of scale position.

In an **itemized rating scale**, the respondents are provided with a scale that has a number or brief description associated with each category. The categories are ordered in terms of scale position; and the respondents are required to select the specified category that best describes the object being rated. Itemized rating scales are widely used in marketing research and form the basic components of more complex scales, such as multiitem rating scales. We first describe the commonly used itemized rating scales, the Likert, semantic differential, and Stapel scales, and then examine the major issues surrounding the use of these scales.

## Likert Scale

Named after its developer, Rensis Likert, the **Likert scale** is a widely used rating scale that requires the respondents to indicate a degree of agreement or disagreement with each of a series of statements about the stimulus objects.[3] Typically, each scale item has five response categories, ranging from "strongly disagree" to "strongly agree." We illustrate with a Likert scale for evaluating attitudes toward Sears in the context of the Department Store Project.

---

**ACTIVE RESEARCH** | DEPARTMENT STORE PROJECT

### Likert Scale

#### Instructions

Listed below are different opinions about Sears. Please indicate how strongly you agree or disagree with each by using the following scale:

1 = Strongly disagree
2 = Disagree
3 = Neither agree nor disagree
4 = Agree
5 = Strongly agree

|  | Strongly disagree | Disagree | Neither agree nor disagree | Agree | Strongly agree |
|---|---|---|---|---|---|
| 1. Sears sells high-quality merchandise. | 1 | 2X | 3 | 4 | 5 |
| 2. Sears has poor in-store service. | 1 | 2X | 3 | 4 | 5 |
| 3. I like to shop at Sears. | 1 | 2 | 3X | 4 | 5 |
| 4. Sears does not offer a good mix of different brands within a product category. | 1 | 2 | 3 | 4X | 5 |
| 5. The credit policies at Sears are terrible. | 1 | 2 | 3 | 4X | 5 |
| 6. Sears is where America shops. | 1X | 2 | 3 | 4 | 5 |
| 7. I do not like the advertising done by Sears. | 1 | 2 | 3 | 4X | 5 |
| 8. Sears sells a wide variety of merchandise. | 1 | 2 | 3 | 4X | 5 |
| 9. Sears charges fair prices. | 1 | 2X | 3 | 4 | 5 |

---

To conduct the analysis, each statement is assigned a numerical score, ranging either from −2 to +2 or 1 to 5. The analysis can be conducted on an item-by-item basis (profile analysis), or a total (summated) score can be calculated for each respondent by summing across items. Suppose the Likert scale in the department store example was used to measure attitudes toward Sears as well as JC Penney. Profile analysis would involve comparing the two stores in terms of the average respondent ratings for each item, such as quality of merchandise, in-store service, and brand mix. The summated approach is most frequently used and, as a result, the Likert scale is also referred to as a summated scale.[4] When using this approach to determine the total score for each respondent on each store, it is important to use a consistent scoring procedure so that a high (or low) score consistently reflects a favorable response. This requires that the categories assigned to the negative statements by the respondents be scored by reversing the scale. Note that for a negative statement, an agreement reflects an unfavorable response, whereas for a positive statement, agreement represents a favorable response. Accordingly, a "strongly agree" response to a favorable statement and a "strongly disagree" response to an unfavorable statement would both receive scores of five. In the scale shown above, if a higher score is to denote a more favorable attitude, the scoring of items 2, 4, 5, and 7 will be reversed. Thus, the respondent in the department store project example has an attitude score of 22. Each respondent's total score for each store is calculated. A respondent will have the most favorable attitude toward the store with the highest score. The procedure for developing summated Likert scales is described later in the section on multiitem scales.

The Likert scale has several advantages. It is easy to construct and administer. Respondents readily understand how to use the scale, making it suitable for mail, telephone, or personal interviews. Therefore, this scale was used in the NYCT telephone survey in the opening example. The major disadvantage of the Likert scale is that it takes longer to complete than other itemized rating scales because respondents have to read each statement. The following example shows another use of a Likert scale in marketing research.

## REAL RESEARCH

### *Job Satisfaction—Intrinsic or Extrinsic?*

A study investigated the hypothesis that salespeople's intrinsic job satisfaction (IJS) is related positively to the length of time they will stay in a company. Intrinsic job satisfaction was measured using the standard Likert scale.[5] One of the items used to measure IJS is as follows:

| | Strongly Disagree | Disagree | Neutral | Agree | Strongly Agree |
|---|---|---|---|---|---|
| I get a feeling of accomplishment from the work I am doing. | 1 | 2 | 3 | 4 | 5 |

Empirical data provided support for the hypothesis. The study concluded that sales managers should spend more effort on recruiting, training, and supporting salespeople so as to increase intrinsic job satisfaction and thereby reduce salesforce turnover. A study conducted in 2002 revealed that overall job satisfaction and perceptions of organizational support are key to maintaining commitment in the workplace. ■

To reduce salesforce turnover, it is very important to increase intrinsic job satisfaction, as measured by Likert scales.

## Semantic Differential Scale

**semantic differential**
A seven-point rating scale with endpoints associated with bipolar labels that have semantic meaning.

The **semantic differential** is a seven-point rating scale with endpoints associated with bipolar labels that have semantic meaning. In a typical application, respondents rate objects on a number of itemized, seven-point rating scales bounded at each end by one of two bipolar adjectives, such as "cold" and "warm."[6] We illustrate this scale by presenting a respondent's evaluation of Sears on five attributes.

The respondents mark the blank that best indicates how they would describe the object being rated.[7] Thus, in our example, Sears is evaluated as somewhat weak, reliable, very old fashioned, warm, and careful. The negative adjective or phrase sometimes appears at the left side of the scale and sometimes at the right. This controls the tendency of some respondents,

**ACTIVE RESEARCH** | DEPARTMENT STORE PROJECT

### Semantic Differential Scale

#### Instructions

This part of the study measures what certain department stores mean to you by having you judge them on a series of descriptive scales bounded at each end by one of two bipolar adjectives. Please mark (X) the blank that best indicates how accurately one or the other adjective describes what the store means to you. Please be sure to mark every scale; do not omit any scale.

#### Form

Sears is:

| | | |
|---|---|---|
| Powerful | —:—:—:—:-X-:—:—: | Weak |
| Unreliable | —:—:—:—:—:-X-:—: | Reliable |
| Modern | —:—:—:—:—:—:-X-: | Old fashioned |
| Cold | —:—:—:—:—:-X-:—: | Warm |
| Careful | —:-X-:—:—:—:—:—: | Careless |

particularly those with very positive or very negative attitudes, to mark the right- or left-hand sides without reading the labels. The methods for selecting the scale labels and constructing a semantic differential scale have been described elsewhere by the author. A general semantic differential scale for measuring self-concepts, person concepts, and product concepts is shown.

**REAL RESEARCH**

## A Semantic Differential Scale for Measuring Self-Concepts, Person Concepts, and Product Concepts[8]

|  |  |  |
|---|---|---|
| **1.** Rugged | :—:—:—:—:—:—: | Delicate |
| **2.** Excitable | :—:—:—:—:—:—: | Calm |
| **3.** Uncomfortable | :—:—:—:—:—:—: | Comfortable |
| **4.** Dominating | :—:—:—:—:—:—: | Submissive |
| **5.** Thrifty | :—:—:—:—:—:—: | Indulgent |
| **6.** Pleasant | :—:—:—:—:—:—: | Unpleasant |
| **7.** Contemporary | :—:—:—:—:—:—: | Noncontemporary |
| **8.** Organized | :—:—:—:—:—:—: | Unorganized |
| **9.** Rational | :—:—:—:—:—:—: | Emotional |
| **10.** Youthful | :—:—:—:—:—:—: | Mature |
| **11.** Formal | :—:—:—:—:—:—: | Informal |
| **12.** Orthodox | :—:—:—:—:—:—: | Liberal |
| **13.** Complex | :—:—:—:—:—:—: | Simple |
| **14.** Colorless | :—:—:—:—:—:—: | Colorful |
| **15.** Modest | :—:—:—:—:—:—: | Vain ∎ |

Individual items on a semantic differential scale may be scored on either a −3-to-+3 or a 1-to-7 scale. The resulting data are commonly analyzed through profile analysis. In profile analysis, means or median values on each rating scale are calculated and compared by plotting or statistical analysis. This helps determine the overall differences and similarities among the objects. To assess differences across segments of respondents, the researcher can compare mean responses of different segments. Although the mean is most often used as a summary statistic, there is some controversy as to whether the data obtained should be treated as an interval scale.[9] On the other hand, in cases when the researcher requires an overall comparison of objects, such as to determine store preference, the individual item scores are summed to arrive at a total score.

Its versatility makes the semantic differential a popular rating scale in marketing research. It has been widely used in comparing brand, product, and company images. It has also been used to develop advertising and promotion strategies and in new product development studies.[10] Several modifications of the basic scale have been proposed.

## Stapel Scale

The *Stapel scale,* named after its developer, Jan Stapel, is a unipolar rating scale with 10 categories numbered from −5 to +5, without a neutral point (zero).[11] This scale is usually presented vertically. Respondents are asked to indicate how accurately or inaccurately each term describes the object by selecting an appropriate numerical response category. The higher the number, the more accurately the term describes the object, as shown in the department store project. In this example, Sears is evaluated as not having high quality and having somewhat poor service.

---

**ACTIVE RESEARCH** | DEPARTMENT STORE PROJECT

*Stapel Scale*

*Instructions*

Please evaluate how accurately each word or phrase describes each of the department stores. Select a plus number for the phrases you think describe the store accurately. The more accurately you think the phrase describes the store, the larger the plus number you should choose. You should select a minus number for phrases you think do not describe it accurately. The less accurately you think the phrase describes the store, the larger the minus number you should choose. You can select any number, from +5 for phrases you think are very accurate, to −5 for phrases you think are very inaccurate.

*Form*

|  | **Sears** |  |
|---|---|---|
|  | +5 | +5 |
|  | +4 | +4 |
|  | +3 | +3 |
|  | +2 | +2X |
|  | +1 | +1 |
| **High Quality** |  | **Poor Service** |
| −1 |  | −1 |
| −2 |  | −2 |
| −3 |  | −3 |
| −4X |  | −4 |
| −5 |  | −5 |

---

The data obtained by using a Stapel scale can be analyzed in the same way as semantic differential data. The Stapel scale produces results similar to the semantic differential. The Stapel scale's advantages are that it does not require a pretest of the adjectives or phrases to ensure true bipolarity, and it can be administered over the telephone. However, some researchers believe the Stapel scale is confusing and difficult to apply. Of the three itemized rating scales considered, the Stapel scale is used least. However, this scale merits more attention than it has received.

# NONCOMPARATIVE ITEMIZED RATING SCALE DECISIONS

As is evident from the discussion so far, noncomparative itemized rating scales need not be used as originally proposed but can take many different forms. The researcher must make six major decisions when constructing any of these scales.

1. The number of scale categories to use
2. Balanced versus unbalanced scale
3. Odd or even number of categories
4. Forced versus nonforced choice
5. The nature and degree of the verbal description
6. The physical form of the scale

## Number of Scale Categories

Two conflicting considerations are involved in deciding the number of scale categories. The greater the number of scale categories, the finer the discrimination among stimulus objects that is possible. On the other hand, most respondents cannot handle more than a few categories. Traditional guidelines suggest that the appropriate number of categories should be seven plus or minus two: between five and nine.[12] Yet, there is no single optimal number of categories. Several factors should be taken into account in deciding on the number of categories.

If the respondents are interested in the scaling task and are knowledgeable about the objects, a larger number of categories may be employed. On the other hand, if the respondents are not very knowledgeable or involved with the task, fewer categories should be used. Likewise, the nature of the objects is also relevant. Some objects do not lend themselves to fine discrimination, so a small number of categories is sufficient. Another important factor is the mode of data collection. If telephone interviews are involved, many categories may confuse the respondents. Likewise, space limitations may restrict the number of categories in mail questionnaires.

How the data are to be analyzed and used should also influence the number of categories. In situations where several scale items are added together to produce a single score for each respondent, five categories are sufficient. The same is true if the researcher wishes to make broad generalizations or group comparisons. If, however, individual responses are of interest or the data will be analyzed by sophisticated statistical techniques, seven or more categories may be required. The size of the correlation coefficient, a common measure of relationship between variables (Chapter 17), is influenced by the number of scale categories. The correlation coefficient decreases with a reduction in the number of categories. This, in turn, has an impact on all statistical analysis based on the correlation coefficient.[13]

## Balanced Versus Unbalanced Scales

**balanced scale**
A scale with an equal number of favorable and unfavorable categories.

In a ***balanced scale,*** the number of favorable and unfavorable categories are equal; in an unbalanced scale, they are unequal.[14] Examples of balanced and unbalanced scales are given in Figure 9.1. In general, the scale should be balanced in order to obtain objective data. However, if the distribution of responses is likely to be skewed, either positively or negatively, an unbalanced scale with more categories in the direction of skewness may be appropriate. If an unbalanced scale is used, the nature and degree of unbalance in the scale should be taken into account in data analysis.

## Odd or Even Number of Categories

With an odd number of categories, the middle scale position is generally designated as neutral or impartial. The presence, position, and labeling of a neutral category can have a significant influence on the response. The Likert scale is a balanced rating scale with an odd number of categories and a neutral point.[15]

The decision to use an odd or even number of categories depends on whether some of the respondents may be neutral on the response being measured. If a neutral or indifferent response is possible from at least some of the respondents, an odd number of categories should

*Figure 9.1*
Balanced and Unbalanced Scales

| Balanced Scale | | Unbalanced Scale | |
|---|---|---|---|
| Jovan Musk for Men is | | Jovan Musk for Men is | |
| Extremely good | _____ | Extremely good | _____ |
| Very good | _____ | Very good | _____ |
| Good | _____ | Good | _____ |
| Bad | _____ | Somewhat good | _____ |
| Very bad | _____ | Bad | _____ |
| Extremely bad | _____ | Very bad | _____ |

be used. If, on the other hand, the researcher wants to force a response or believes that no neutral or indifferent response exists, a rating scale with an even number of categories should be used. A related issue is whether the scale should be forced or nonforced.

## Forced Versus Nonforced Scales

**forced rating scales**
A rating scale that forces the respondents to express an opinion because "no opinion" or "no knowledge" option is not provided.

On *forced rating scales,* the respondents are forced to express an opinion, because a "no opinion" option is not provided. In such a case, respondents without an opinion may mark the middle scale position. If a sufficient proportion of the respondents do not have opinions on the topic, marking the middle position will distort measures of central tendency and variance. In situations where the respondents are expected to have no opinion, as opposed to simply being reluctant to disclose it, the accuracy of data may be improved by a nonforced scale that includes a "no opinion" category.[16]

## Nature and Degree of Verbal Description

The nature and degree of verbal description associated with scale categories varies considerably and can have an effect on the responses. Scale categories may have verbal, numerical, or even pictorial descriptions. Furthermore, the researcher must decide whether to label every scale category, some scale categories, or only extreme scale categories. Surprisingly, providing a verbal description for each category may not improve the accuracy or reliability of the data. Yet, an argument can be made for labeling all or many scale categories to reduce scale ambiguity. The category descriptions should be located as close to the response categories as possible.

The strength of the adjectives used to anchor the scale may influence the distribution of the responses. With strong anchors (1 = completely disagree, 7 = completely agree), respondents are less likely to use the extreme scale categories. This results in less variable and more peaked response distributions. Weak anchors (1 = generally disagree, 7 = generally agree), in contrast, produce uniform or flat distributions. Procedures have been developed to assign values to category descriptors so as to result in balanced or equal-interval scales.[17]

## Physical Form or Configuration

A number of options are available with respect to scale form or configuration. Scales can be presented vertically or horizontally. Categories can be expressed by boxes, discrete lines, or units on a continuum and may or may not have numbers assigned to them. If numerical values are used, they may be positive, negative, or both. Several possible configurations are presented in Figure 9.2.

Two unique rating scale configurations used in marketing research are the thermometer scale and the smiling face scale. For the thermometer scale, the higher the temperature, the more favorable the evaluation. Likewise, happier faces indicate more favorable evaluations. These scales are especially useful for children.[18] Examples of these scales are shown in Figure 9.3. Table 9.2 summarizes the six decisions in designing rating scales.

# MULTIITEM SCALES

The development of multiitem rating scales requires considerable technical expertise.[19] Figure 9.4 is a paradigm for constructing multiitem scales. The characteristic to be measured is frequently called a construct. Scale development begins with an underlying theory of the construct being measured. A theory is necessary not only for constructing the scale but also for interpreting the resulting scores. The next step is to generate an initial pool of scale items. Typically, this is done based on theory, analysis of secondary data, and qualitative research. From this pool, a reduced set of potential scale items is generated by the judgment of the researcher and other knowledgeable individuals. Some qualitative criterion is adopted to aid their judgment. The reduced set of items is still too large to constitute a scale. Thus, further reduction is achieved in a quantitative manner.

**Figure 9.2**

Rating Scale Configurations

A variety of scale configurations may be employed to measure the gentleness of Cheer detergent. Some examples include:

Cheer detergent is:

1. Very harsh — — — — — — — Very gentle

2. Very harsh   1   2   3   4   5   6   7   Very gentle

3. ☐ Very harsh
   ☐
   ☐
   ☐ Neither harsh nor gentle
   ☐
   ☐
   ☐ Very gentle

4.

| ___ | ___ | ___ | ___ | ___ | ___ | ___ |
|---|---|---|---|---|---|---|
| Very harsh | Harsh | Somewhat harsh | Neither harsh nor gentle | Somewhat gentle | Gentle | Very gentle |

5.

| $-3$ | $-2$ | $-1$ | $0$ | $+1$ | $+2$ | $+3$ |
|---|---|---|---|---|---|---|
| Very harsh | | | Neither harsh nor gentle | | | Very gentle |

**Figure 9.3**

Some Unique Rating Chart Configurations

*Thermometer Scale*
**Instructions**
Please indicate how much you like McDonald's hamburgers by coloring in the thermometer with your blue pen. Start at the bottom and color up to the temperature level that best indicates how strong your preference is for McDonald's hamburgers.
**Form**

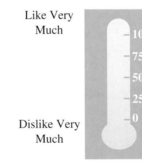

Like Very Much

100°
75
50
25
0

Dislike Very Much

*Smiling Face Scale*
**Instructions**
Please tell me how much you like the Barbie Doll by pointing to the face that best shows how much you like it. If you did not like the Barbie Doll at all, you would point to Face 1. If you liked it very much, you would point to Face 5. Now tell me, how much did you like the Barbie Doll?
**Form**

1    2    3    4    5

### TABLE 9.2

**Summary of Itemized Rating Scale Decisions**

| | |
|---|---|
| **1.** Number of categories | Although there is no single, optimal number, traditional guidelines suggest that there should be between five and nine categories. |
| **2.** Balanced versus unbalanced | In general, the scale should be balanced to obtain objective data. |
| **3.** Odd or even number of categories | If a neutral or indifferent scale response is possible from at least some of the respondents, an odd number of categories should be used. |
| **4.** Forced versus nonforced | In situations where the respondents are expected to have no opinion, the accuracy of data may be improved by a nonforced scale. |
| **5.** Verbal description | An argument can be made for labeling all or many scale categories. The category descriptions should be located as close to the response categories as possible. |
| **6.** Physical form | A number of options should be tried and the best one selected. |

Data are collected on the reduced set of potential scale items from a large pretest sample of respondents. The data are analyzed using techniques such as correlations, factor analysis, cluster analysis, discriminant analysis, and statistical tests discussed later in this book. As a result of these statistical analyses, several more items are eliminated, resulting in a purified scale. The purified scale is evaluated for reliability and validity by collecting more data from a different sample (see the following section). On the basis of these assessments, a final set of scale items is selected. As can be seen from Figure 9.4, the scale development process is an iterative one with several feedback loops.[20]

**Figure 9.4**

Development of a Multiitem Scale

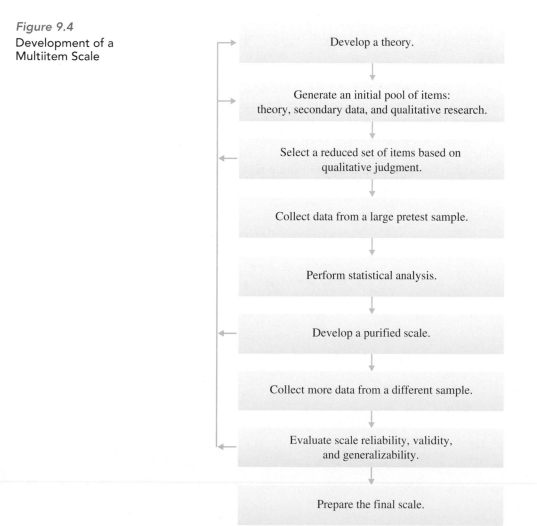

## *Measuring Technical Sophistication with a Technically Sophisticated Scale*

The following multiitem scale measures the technical sophistication of a product line.[21]

| 1. Technical | 1 | 2 | 3 | 4 | 5 | 6 | 7 | Nontechnical |
| 2. Low engineering content | 1 | 2 | 3 | 4 | 5 | 6 | 7 | High engineering content |
| 3. Fast changing | 1 | 2 | 3 | 4 | 5 | 6 | 7 | Slowly changing |
| 4. Unsophisticated | 1 | 2 | 3 | 4 | 5 | 6 | 7 | Sophisticated |
| 5. Commodity | 1 | 2 | 3 | 4 | 5 | 6 | 7 | Customized |
| 6. Unique | 1 | 2 | 3 | 4 | 5 | 6 | 7 | Common |
| 7. Complex | 1 | 2 | 3 | 4 | 5 | 6 | 7 | Simple |

Items 1, 3, 6, and 7 are reversed when scoring. This scale can be used in industrial marketing to measure the technical sophistication of a customer's product line and suggest changes to improve technical quality. ■

# SCALE EVALUATION

A multiitem scale should be evaluated for accuracy and applicability.[22] As shown in Figure 9.5, this involves an assessment of reliability, validity, and generalizability of the scale. Approaches to assessing reliability include test-retest reliability, alternative-forms reliability, and internal consistency reliability. Validity can be assessed by examining content validity, criterion validity, and construct validity.

Before we can examine reliability and validity, we need an understanding of measurement accuracy, because it is fundamental to scale evaluation.

## Measurement Accuracy

As was mentioned in Chapter 8, a measurement is a number that reflects some characteristic of an object. A measurement is not the true value of the characteristic of interest but rather an observation of it. A variety of factors can cause ***measurement error,*** which results in the measurement or observed score being different from the true score of the characteristic being measured (see Fig. 9.6). The ***true score model*** provides a framework for understanding the accuracy of measurement. According to this model,

$$X_O = X_T + X_S + X_R$$

where

$X_O$ = the observed score or measurement
$X_T$ = the true score of the characteristic
$X_S$ = systematic error
$X_R$ = random error

**measurement error**
The variation in the information sought by the researcher and the information generated by the measurement process employed.

**true score model**
A mathematical model that provides a framework for understanding the accuracy of measurement.

**Figure 9.5**
Evaluation of a Multiitem Scale

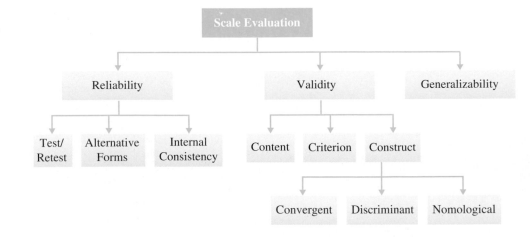

*Figure 9.6*
Potential Sources of Error
in Measurement

> 1. Other relatively stable characteristics of the individual that influence the test score, such as intelligence, social desirability, and education
> 2. Short-term or transient personal factors, such as health, emotions, fatigue
> 3. Situational factors, such as the presence of other people, noise, and distractions
> 4. Sampling of items included in the scale: addition, deletion, or changes in the scale items
> 5. Lack of clarity of the scale, including the instructions or the items themselves
> 6. Mechanical factors, such as poor printing, overcrowding of items in the questionnaire, and poor design
> 7. Administration of the scale, such as differences among interviewers
> 8. Analysis factors, such as differences in scoring and statistical analysis

**systematic error**
Systematic error affects the measurement in a constant way and represents stable factors that affect the observed score in the same way each time the measurement is made.

**random error**
Measurement error that arises from random changes or differences in respondents or measurement situations.

**reliability**
The extent to which a scale produces consistent results if repeated measurements are made on the characteristic.

**test-retest reliability**
An approach for assessing reliability in which respondents are administered identical sets of scale items at two different times under as nearly equivalent conditions as possible.

Note that the total measurement error includes the systematic error, $X_S$, and the random error, $X_R$. **Systematic error** affects the measurement in a constant way. It represents stable factors that affect the observed score in the same way each time the measurement is made, such as mechanical factors (see Fig. 9.6). **Random error,** on the other hand, is not constant. It represents transient factors that affect the observed score in different ways each time the measurement is made, such as transient personal or situational factors. The distinction between systematic and random error is crucial to our understanding of reliability and validity.

# Reliability

**Reliability** refers to the extent to which a scale produces consistent results if repeated measurements are made.[23] Systematic sources of error do not have an adverse impact on reliability, because they affect the measurement in a constant way and do not lead to inconsistency. In contrast, random error produces inconsistency, leading to lower reliability. Reliability can be defined as the extent to which measures are free from random error, $X_R$. If $X_R = 0$, the measure is perfectly reliable.

Reliability is assessed by determining the proportion of systematic variation in a scale. This is done by determining the association between scores obtained from different administrations of the scale. If the association is high, the scale yields consistent results and is therefore reliable. Approaches for assessing reliability include the test-retest, alternative-forms, and internal consistency methods.

**Test-Retest Reliability.**  In **test-retest reliability,** respondents are administered identical sets of scale items at two different times under as nearly equivalent conditions as possible. The time interval between tests or administrations is, typically, two to four weeks. The degree of similarity between the two measurements is determined by computing a correlation coefficient (see Chapter 17). The higher the correlation coefficient, the greater the reliability.

There are several problems associated with the test-retest approach to determining reliability. First, it is sensitive to the time interval between testing. Other things being equal, the longer the time interval, the lower the reliability. Second, the initial measurement may alter the characteristic being measured. For example, measuring respondents' attitude toward low-fat milk may cause them to become more health conscious and develop a more positive attitude toward low-fat milk. Third, it may be impossible to make repeated measurements (for example, the research topic may be the respondent's initial reaction to a new product). Fourth, the first measurement may have a carryover effect to the second or subsequent measurements. Respondents may attempt to remember answers they gave the first time. Fifth, the characteristic being measured may change between measurements. For example, favorable information about an object between measurements may make a respondent's attitude more positive. Finally, the test-retest reliability coefficient can be inflated by the correlation of each item with itself. These correlations tend to be higher than correlations between different scale items across administrations. Hence, it is possible to have high test-retest correlations because of the high correlations between the same scale items measured at different times even though the correlations between different scale items are quite low. Because of these problems, a test-retest approach is best applied in conjunction with other approaches, such as alternative forms.[24]

### Alternative-Forms Reliability.

**alternative-forms reliability**
An approach for assessing reliability that requires two equivalent forms of the scale to be constructed and then the same respondents are measured at two different times.

In *alternative-forms reliability,* two equivalent forms of the scale are constructed. The same respondents are measured at two different times, usually two to four weeks apart, with a different scale form being administered each time. The scores from the administration of the alternative-scale forms are correlated to assess reliability.[25]

There are two major problems with this approach. First, it is time consuming and expensive to construct an equivalent form of the scale. Second, it is difficult to construct two equivalent forms of a scale. The two forms should be equivalent with respect to content. In a strict sense, this requires that the alternative sets of scale items should have the same means, variances, and intercorrelations. Even if these conditions are satisfied, the two forms may not be equivalent in content. Thus, a low correlation may reflect either an unreliable scale or nonequivalent forms.

### Internal Consistency Reliability.

**internal consistency reliability**
An approach for assessing the internal consistency of the set of items when several items are summated in order to form a total score for the scale.

**split-half reliability**
A form of internal consistency reliability in which the items constituting the scale are divided into two halves and the resulting half scores are correlated.

**coefficient alpha**
A measure of internal consistency reliability that is the average of all possible split-half coefficients resulting from different splittings of the scale items.

*Internal consistency reliability* is used to assess the reliability of a summated scale where several items are summed to form a total score. In a scale of this type, each item measures some aspect of the construct measured by the entire scale, and the items should be consistent in what they indicate about the characteristic. This measure of reliability focuses on the internal consistency of the set of items forming the scale.

The simplest measure of internal consistency is **split-half reliability.** The items on the scale are divided into two halves and the resulting half scores are correlated. High correlations between the halves indicate high internal consistency. The scale items can be split into halves based on odd- and even-numbered items or randomly. The problem is that the results will depend on how the scale items are split. A popular approach to overcoming this problem is to use the coefficient alpha.

The **coefficient alpha,** or Cronbach's alpha, is the average of all possible split-half coefficients resulting from different ways of splitting the scale items. This coefficient varies from 0 to 1, and a value of 0.6 or less generally indicates unsatisfactory internal consistency reliability. An important property of coefficient alpha is that its value tends to increase with an increase in the number of scale items. Therefore, coefficient alpha may be artificially, and inappropriately, inflated by including several redundant scale items.[26] Another coefficient that can be employed in conjunction with coefficient alpha is coefficient beta. Coefficient beta assists in determining whether the averaging process used in calculating coefficient alpha is masking any inconsistent items.

Some multiitem scales include several sets of items designed to measure different aspects of a multidimensional construct. For example, store image is a multidimensional construct that includes quality of merchandise, variety and assortment of merchandise, returns and adjustment policy, service of store personnel, prices, convenience of location, layout of the store, and credit and billing policies. Hence, a scale designed to measure store image would contain items measuring each of these dimensions. Because these dimensions are somewhat independent, a measure of internal consistency computed across dimensions would be inappropriate. However, if several items are used to measure each dimension, internal consistency reliability can be computed for each dimension.

### REAL RESEARCH

### The Technology Behind Technology Opinion Leadership

In a study of technology adoption, opinion leadership was measured using the following seven-point Likert type scales (1 = strongly agree, 7 = strongly disagree).

#### Opinion Leadership

1. My opinions on hardware/software products seem not to count with other people.
2. When other people choose to adopt a hardware/software product, they turn to me for advice.
3. Other people select hardware/software products rarely based on what I have suggested to them.
4. I often persuade other people to adopt the hardware/software products that I like.

**5.** Other people rarely come to me for advice about choosing hardware/software products.

**6.** I often influence other people's opinions about hardware/software products.

The alpha value for opinion leadership was 0.88, indicating good internal consistency. It was found that early adopters of technology products tend to be younger males who are opinion leaders, seek novel information, and have a lot of computer experience. Information technology companies like Microsoft need to ensure positive reactions from early product adopters and should focus marketing efforts on these individuals in the new product introduction stage.[27] ■

# Validity

The **validity** of a scale may be defined as the extent to which differences in observed scale scores reflect true differences among objects on the characteristic being measured, rather than systematic or random error. Perfect validity requires that there be no measurement error ($X_O = X_T$, $X_R = 0$, $X_S = 0$). Researchers may assess content validity, criterion validity, or construct validity.[28]

*Content Validity.* *Content validity,* sometimes called face validity, is a subjective but systematic evaluation of how well the content of a scale represents the measurement task at hand. The researcher or someone else examines whether the scale items adequately cover the entire domain of the construct being measured. Thus, a scale designed to measure store image would be considered inadequate if it omitted any of the major dimensions (quality, variety and assortment of merchandise, etc.). Given its subjective nature, content validity alone is not a sufficient measure of the validity of a scale, yet it aids in a common-sense interpretation of the scale scores. A more formal evaluation can be obtained by examining criterion validity.

*Criterion Validity.* *Criterion validity* reflects whether a scale performs as expected in relation to other variables selected as meaningful criteria (criterion variables). Criterion variables may include demographic and psychographic characteristics, attitudinal and behavioral measures, or scores obtained from other scales. Based on the time period involved, criterion validity can take two forms, concurrent and predictive validity.

Concurrent validity is assessed when the data on the scale being evaluated and on the criterion variables are collected at the same time. To assess concurrent validity, a researcher may develop short forms of standard personality instruments. The original instruments and the short versions would be administered simultaneously to a group of respondents and the results compared. To assess predictive validity, the researcher collects data on the scale at one point in time and data on the criterion variables at a future time. For example, attitudes toward cereal brands could be used to predict future purchases of cereals by members of a scanner panel. Attitudinal data are obtained from the panel members, and then their future purchases are tracked with scanner data. The predicted and actual purchases are compared to assess the predictive validity of the attitudinal scale.

*Construct Validity.* *Construct validity* addresses the question of what construct or characteristic the scale is, in fact, measuring. When assessing construct validity, the researcher attempts to answer theoretical questions about why the scale works and what deductions can be made concerning the underlying theory. Thus, construct validity requires a sound theory of the nature of the construct being measured and how it relates to other constructs. Construct validity is the most sophisticated and difficult type of validity to establish. As Figure 9.5 shows, construct validity includes convergent, discriminant, and nomological validity.

*Convergent validity* is the extent to which the scale correlates positively with other measures of the same construct. It is not necessary that all these measures be obtained by using conventional scaling techniques. *Discriminant validity* is the extent to which a measure does not correlate with other constructs from which it is supposed to differ. It involves demonstrating a lack of correlation among differing constructs. *Nomological validity* is the extent to which the scale correlates in theoretically predicted ways with measures of different but related constructs. A theoretical model is formulated that leads to further deductions, tests, and inferences. Gradually, a nomological net is built in which

---

**validity**
The extent to which differences in observed scale scores reflect true differences among objects on the characteristic being measured, rather than systematic or random errors.

**content validity**
A type of validity, sometimes called face validity, that consists of a subjective but systematic evaluation of the representativeness of the content of a scale for the measuring task at hand.

**criterion validity**
A type of validity that examines whether the measurement scale performs as expected in relation to other variables selected as meaningful criteria.

**construct validity**
A type of validity that addresses the question of what construct or characteristic the scale is measuring. An attempt is made to answer theoretical questions of why a scale works and what deductions can be made concerning the theory underlying the scale.

**convergent validity**
A measure of construct validity that measures the extent to which the scale correlates positively with other measures of the same construct.

**discriminant validity**
A type of construct validity that assesses the extent to which a measure does not correlate with other constructs from which it is supposed to differ.

**nomological validity**
A type of validity that assesses the relationship between theoretical constructs. It seeks to confirm significant correlations between the constructs as predicted by theory.

several constructs are systematically interrelated. We illustrate construct validity in the context of a multiitem scale designed to measure self-concept.[29]

### To Thine Own Self Be True

The following findings would provide evidence of construct validity for a multiitem scale to measure self-concept.

- High correlations with other scales designed to measure self-concepts and with reported classifications by friends (convergent validity)
- Low correlations with unrelated constructs of brand loyalty and variety seeking (discriminant validity)
- Brands that are congruent with the individual's self-concept are more preferred, as postulated by the theory (nomological validity)
- A high level of reliability ■

Notice that a high level of reliability was included as an evidence of construct validity in this example. This illustrates the relationship between reliability and validity.

## Relationship Between Reliability and Validity

The relationship between reliability and validity can be understood in terms of the true score model. If a measure is perfectly valid, it is also perfectly reliable. In this case $X_O = X_T$, $X_R = 0$, and $X_S = 0$. Thus, perfect validity implies perfect reliability. If a measure is unreliable, it cannot be perfectly valid, because at a minimum $X_O = X_T + X_R$. Furthermore, systematic error may also be present, i.e., $X_S \neq 0$. Thus, unreliability implies invalidity. If a measure is perfectly reliable, it may or may not be perfectly valid, because systematic error may still be present ($X_O = X_T + X_S$). Although lack of reliability constitutes negative evidence for validity, reliability does not in itself imply validity. Reliability is a necessary, but not sufficient, condition for validity.

## Generalizability

**generalizability**
The degree to which a study based on a sample applies to a universe of generalization.

*Generalizability* refers to the extent to which one can generalize from the observations at hand to a universe of generalizations. The set of all conditions of measurement over which the investigator wishes to generalize is the universe of generalization. These conditions may include items, interviewers, situations of observation, etc. A researcher may wish to generalize a scale developed for use in personal interviews to other modes of data collection, such as mail and telephone interviews. Likewise, one may wish to generalize from a sample of items to the universe of items, from a sample of times of measurement to the universe of times of measurement, from a sample of observers to a universe of observers, and so on.[30]

In generalizability studies, measurement procedures are designed to investigate the universes of interest by sampling conditions of measurement from each of them. For each universe of interest, an aspect of measurement called a facet is included in the study. Traditional reliability methods can be viewed as single-facet generalizability studies. A test-retest correlation is concerned with whether scores obtained from a measurement scale are generalizable to the universe scores across all times of possible measurement. Even if the test-retest correlation is high, nothing can be said about the generalizability of the scale to other universes. To generalize to other universes, generalizability theory procedures must be employed.

# CHOOSING A SCALING TECHNIQUE

In addition to theoretical considerations and evaluation of reliability and validity, certain practical factors should be considered in selecting scaling techniques for a particular marketing research problem.[31] These include the level of information (nominal, ordinal, interval, or ratio) desired, the capabilities of the respondents, the characteristics of the stimulus objects, method of administration, the context, and cost.

As a general rule, using the scaling technique that will yield the highest level of information feasible in a given situation will permit the use of the greatest variety of statistical analyses. Also, regardless of the type of scale used, whenever feasible, several scale items should measure the characteristic of interest. This provides more accurate measurement than a single-item scale. In many situations, it is desirable to use more than one scaling technique or to obtain additional measures using mathematically derived scales.

# MATHEMATICALLY DERIVED SCALES

All the scaling techniques discussed in this chapter require the respondents to evaluate directly various characteristics of the stimulus objects. In contrast, mathematical scaling techniques allow researchers to infer respondents' evaluations of characteristics of stimulus objects. These evaluations are inferred from the respondents' overall judgments of the objects. Two popular mathematically derived scaling techniques are multidimensional scaling and conjoint analysis. These techniques are discussed in detail in Chapter 21.

# INTERNATIONAL MARKETING RESEARCH

In designing the scale or response format, respondents' educational or literacy levels should be taken into account.[32] One approach is to develop scales that are pan-cultural, or free of cultural biases. Of the scaling techniques we have considered, the semantic differential scale may be said to be pan-cultural. It has been tested in a number of countries and has consistently produced similar results.

## REAL RESEARCH

### *Copying the Name Xerox*

Xerox (*www.xerox.com*) was a name well received in the former Soviet Union for the past 30 years. In fact, the act of copying documents was called Xeroxing, a term coined after the name of the company. It was a brand name people equated with quality. However, with the disintegration of Soviet Union into the Commonwealth of Independent States, sales of Xerox started to fall. The management initially considered this problem to be the result of intense competition with strong competitors such as Canon, Ricoh Co., Mitsubishi Electric Corp., and Minolta Camera Co. First attempts at making the product more competitive did not help. Subsequently, marketing research was undertaken to measure the image of Xerox and its competitors. Semantic differential scales were used, as this type of scale is considered pan-cultural. The bipolar labels used were carefully tested to ensure that they had the intended semantic meaning in the Russian context.

Semantic differential scales were used to measure the image of Xerox and its competitors in Russia.

The results of the study revealed that the real problem was a growing negative perception of Russian customers toward Xerox products. What could have gone wrong? The problem was not with Xerox, but with several independent producers of copying machines that had illegally infringed on Xerox's trademark rights. With the disintegration of the Soviet Union, the protection of these trademarks was unclear and trademark infringement kept growing. As a result, customers developed a misconception that Xerox was selling low-quality products. Among other courses of action, Xerox ran a corporate campaign on the national Russian TV and radio networks as well as in local print media. The campaign emphasized Xerox's leadership position in the commonwealth countries where quality demands were very high. This was a positive step in removing some misconceptions of Russian consumers toward Xerox. Xerox also registered its trademark separately in each republic. Xerox saw its first-quarter 2000 revenues grow in Russia and other developing markets by 15 percent. In 2001, Xerox achieved annual revenues of $16.5 billion.[33] ∎

Although the semantic differential worked well in the Russian context, an alternative approach is to develop scales that use a self-defined cultural norm as a base referent. For example, respondents may be required to indicate their own anchor point and position relative to a culture-specific stimulus set. This approach is useful for measuring attitudes that are defined relative to cultural norms (e.g., attitude toward marital roles). In developing response formats, verbal rating scales appear to be the most suitable. Even less-educated respondents can readily understand and respond to verbal scales. Special attention should be devoted to determining equivalent verbal descriptors in different languages and cultures. The endpoints of the scale are particularly prone to different interpretations. In some cultures, 1 may be interpreted as best, whereas in others, it may be interpreted as worst, regardless of how it is scaled. It is important that the scale endpoints and the verbal descriptors be employed in a manner that is consistent with the culture.

Finally, in international marketing research, it is critical to establish the equivalence of scales and measures used to obtain data from different countries. This topic is complex and is discussed in some detail in Chapter 23.

## ETHICS IN MARKETING RESEARCH

The researcher has the ethical responsibility to use scales that have reasonable reliability, validity, and generalizability. The findings generated by scales that are unreliable, invalid, or not generalizable to the target population are questionable at best and raise serious ethical issues. Moreover, the researcher should not bias the scales so as to slant the findings in any particular direction. This is easy to do by either biasing the wording of the statements (Likert type scales), the scale descriptors, or other aspects of the scales. Consider the use of scale descriptors. The descriptors used to frame a scale can be chosen to bias results in a desired direction, for example, generate a positive view of the client's brand or a negative view of a competitor's brand. To project the client's brand favorably, respondents are asked to indicate their opinion of the brand on several attributes using seven-point scales anchored by the descriptors extremely poor to good. In such a case, respondents are reluctant to rate the product extremely poorly. In fact, respondents who believe the product to be only mediocre will end up responding favorably. Try this yourself. How would you rate BMW automobiles on the following attributes?

| Reliability | Horrible | 1 | 2 | 3 | 4 | 5 | 6 | 7 | Good |
| Performance | Very poor | 1 | 2 | 3 | 4 | 5 | 6 | 7 | Good |
| Quality | One of the worst | 1 | 2 | 3 | 4 | 5 | 6 | 7 | Good |
| Prestige | Very low | 1 | 2 | 3 | 4 | 5 | 6 | 7 | Good |

Did you find yourself rating BMW cars positively? Using this same technique, it is possible to negatively bias evaluations of competitors' brands by providing a mildly negative descriptor (somewhat poor) against a strong positive descriptor (extremely good).

Thus, we see how important it is to use balanced scales with comparable positive and negative descriptors. When this guideline is violated, responses are biased and should be interpreted accordingly. The researcher has a responsibility to both the client and respondents to ensure the applicability and usefulness of the scale. Similarly, client companies have a responsibility to treat their customers and the general public in an ethical manner. The following example proposes an appropriate scale for evaluating the conduct of direct marketers.

**REAL RESEARCH**

## A Direct Measure of the Ethics of Direct Marketers

In this day and age, many types of businesses are marketing to people over the phone, by e-mail, and by direct mail without any consideration for the individuals they are trying to persuade to purchase their products. Many direct-marketing companies, including insurance, healthcare, and telecommunication companies, have paid billions of dollars in fines for unethical marketing practices. Denny Hatch has proposed the following honesty scale for companies using direct marketing.

1. Overall, my offer is, in Dick Benson's words, "scrupulously honest."
   0    1    2    3    4    5
2. I would be proud to make this offer to my mother or my daughter.
   0    1    2    3    4    5
3. My guarantee is clearly stated and ironclad. I will live up to it.
   0    1    2    3    4    5
4. I believe from my toes to my nose every promise I make in the offer.
   0    1    2    3    4    5
5. All the type in my promotion is easy to read and the copy is clear.
   0    1    2    3    4    5
6. All testimonials are absolutely real and have been freely given.
   0    1    2    3    4    5
7. Merchandise will arrive at the time promised. I do not live on float.
   0    1    2    3    4    5
8. I slavishly adhere to all industry opt-in/opt-out guidelines.
   0    1    2    3    4    5
9. I make it very easy to cancel or return the merchandise.
   0    1    2    3    4    5
10. I issue prompt refunds to unsatisfied customers.
   0    1    2    3    4    5

This is a self-rate scale of 0 to 5, where 0 is failing and 5 is excellent. Direct marketers should apply this to themselves to find out just how ethical their practices are. If your score is less than 50, you are not being scrupulously honest.[34] ■

# INTERNET AND COMPUTER APPLICATIONS

Continuous rating scales may be easily implemented on the Internet. The cursor can be moved on the screen in a continuous fashion to select the exact position on the scale that best describes the respondent's evaluation. Moreover, the scale values can be automatically scored by the computer, thus increasing the speed and accuracy of processing the data.

It is also easy to implement all the three itemized rating scales on the Internet. Moreover, using the Internet, one can search for and locate similar scales used by other researchers. It is also possible that other researchers have reported reliability and validity assessments for multiitem scales. Before generating new scales, a researcher should first examine similar scales used by other researchers and use them if they meet the measurement objectives. The Office of Scales Research at Southern Illinois University–Carbondale, best known for the production of the Marketing Scales Handbook, has posted its technical reports on the Internet (*www.siu.edu/departments/coba/mktg/osr*).

**REAL RESEARCH**

## *How Private Is Your Online Privacy?*

In spite of the enormous potential of e-commerce, its share compared to the total portion of the economy still remained small: less than 1 percent worldwide as of 2002. The lack of consumer confidence in online privacy is a major problem hampering growth of e-commerce. A recent report showed that practically all Americans (94.5%), including Internet users and non-Internet users, are concerned about "the privacy of their personal information when or if they buy online." Therefore, researchers have developed a scale for measuring Internet users' information privacy concerns. This is a ten-item, three-dimensional scale. The three dimensions are control, knowledge, and collection. Each of the 10 items is scored on a seven-point Likert type agree-disagree scale. The scale has been shown to have good reliability and construct validity. This scale should enable online marketers and policy makers to measure and address Internet users' information privacy concerns, which should result in increased e-commerce.[35] ■

Microcomputers are useful for developing and testing continuous and itemized rating scales, particularly multiitem scales. SURVENT by Computers for Marketing Corporation (CfMC) of San Francisco (*www.cfmc.com*) can customize scales for printed questionnaires or for use by telephone interviewers at computer screens in a fraction of the time this would take without automation. Other specialized programs are also available for constructing itemized rating scales. Several of the questionnaire design packages, discussed in Chapter 10, can construct comparative and noncomparative scales. Idea Works (*www.ideaworks.com*) sells Measurement & Scaling Strategist. It identifies existing scales for key concepts. It aids in the design of new measures and scales while maximizing validity and reliability. This software also avoids common pitfalls in questionnaire development. Some other features are a context-sensitive help, detailed reporting, and a built-in editor.

## SPSS Windows

Using SPSS Data Entry, the researcher can design any of the three noncomparative scales: Likert, semantic differential, or Stapel. Moreover, multiitem scales can be easily accommodated. Either the question library can be used or customized scales can be designed. We show the use of SPSS Data Entry to design Likert type scales for rating sales people and product characteristics in Figure 9.7.

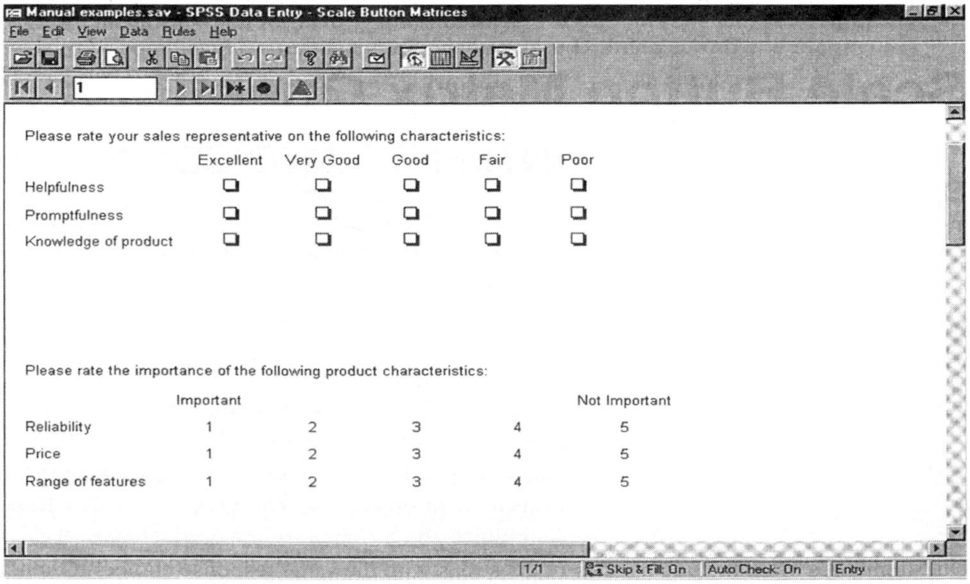

*Figure 9.7*
Likert Type Scales for Rating
Salespeople and Product
Characteristics

## FOCUS ON BURKE

Burke tailors each study to address the client's needs and, thus, the use of scales varies considerably. The different forms of scales discussed in this chapter are used, although Likert type scales are the most popular. For its branded products, Burke generally adheres to a standard protocol and the same set of scales are used across clients. Consider the scales designed to measure the percentage of "secure" customers and to provide a strategic blueprint that highlights improvement priorities. Burke's protocol uses the following three criterion measures to create a composite measure known as the Secure Customer Index®:

***Overall Satisfaction***

4 = Very satisfied
3 = Somewhat satisfied
2 = Somewhat dissatisfied
1 = Very dissatisfied

***Willingness to Recommend***

5 = Definitely would recommend
4 = Probably would recommend
3 = Might or might not recommend
2 = Probably would not recommend
1 = Definitely would not recommend

***Likelihood to Use Again***

5 = Definitely will use again
4 = Probably will use again
3 = Might or might not use again
2 = Probably will not use again
1 = Definitely will not use again

The Secure Customer Index™ is the percentage of customers who are "very satisfied" *and* "definitely would recommend" *and* "definitely will use the client's product or service again."

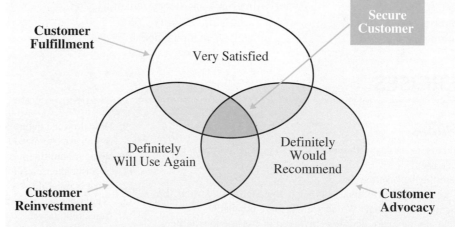

Burke has found that the Secure Customer Index™ is more discriminating than an overall satisfaction question alone. Burke has also documented a strong correlation between the Secure Customer Index™ and actual performance measures such as margin, market share, and customer retention rates. For example, in a study among commercial purchasers of computer hardware and software, Burke found that retention rates increased as the level of customer "security" increased:

| Level of Security | Retention Rate |
| --- | --- |
| Secure | 88% |
| Still favorable | 57% |
| Indifferent | 30% |
| Dissatisfied | 25% |

In addition to the Secure Customer Index™, Burke generally collects ratings on a battery of attributes. Again, Likert type scales are used. Burke analyzes the data to determine which attributes "drive" customer security, thus identifying attributes the client should target for improvements.

# SUMMARY

In noncomparative scaling, each object is scaled independently of the other objects in the stimulus set. The resulting data are generally assumed to be interval or ratio scaled. Noncomparative rating scales can be either continuous or itemized. The itemized rating scales are further classified as Likert, semantic differential, or Stapel scales. When using noncomparative itemized rating scales, the researcher must decide on the number of scale categories, balanced versus unbalanced scales, odd or even number of categories, forced versus nonforced scales, nature and degree of verbal description, and the physical form or configuration.

Multiitem scales consist of a number of rating scale items. These scales should be evaluated in terms of reliability and validity. Reliability refers to the extent to which a scale produces consistent results if repeated measurements are made. Approaches to assessing reliability include test-retest,

alternative-forms, and internal consistency. Validity, or accuracy of measurement, may be assessed by evaluating content validity, criterion validity, and construct validity.

The choice of particular scaling techniques in a given situation should be based on theoretical and practical considerations. As a general rule, the scaling technique used should be the one that will yield the highest level of information feasible. Also, multiple measures should be obtained.

In international marketing research, special attention should be devoted to determining equivalent verbal descriptors in different languages and cultures. The researcher has a responsibility to both the client and respondents to ensure the applicability and usefulness of the scales. The Internet and computers are useful for developing and testing continuous and itemized rating scales, particularly multiitem scales.

# KEY TERMS AND CONCEPTS

noncomparative scale, *256*
continuous rating scale, *256*
itemized rating scale, *257*
Likert scale, *258*
semantic differential, *259*
Stapel scale, *261*
balanced scale, *262*
forced rating scales, *263*
measurement error, *266*

true score model, *266*
systematic error, *267*
random error, *267*
reliability, *267*
test-retest reliability, *267*
alternative-forms reliability, *268*
internal consistency reliability, *268*
split-half reliability, *268*
coefficient alpha, *268*

validity, *269*
content validity, *269*
criterion validity, *269*
construct validity, *269*
convergent validity, *269*
discriminant validity, *269*
nomological validity, *269*
generalizability, *270*

# EXERCISES

## *Questions*

1. What is a semantic differential scale? For what purposes is this scale used?
2. Describe the Likert scale.
3. What are the differences between the Stapel scale and the semantic differential? Which scale is more popular?
4. What are the major decisions involved in constructing an itemized rating scale?
5. How many scale categories should be used in an itemized rating scale? Why?
6. What is the difference between balanced and unbalanced scales?
7. Should an odd or even number of categories be used in an itemized rating scale?
8. What is the difference between forced and nonforced scales?
9. How does the nature and degree of verbal description affect the response to itemized rating scales?
10. What are multiitem scales?
11. Describe the true score model.
12. What is reliability?
13. What are the differences between test-retest and alternative-forms reliability?
14. Describe the notion of internal consistency reliability.
15. What is validity?
16. What is criterion validity? How is it assessed?
17. How would you assess the construct validity of a multiitem scale?
18. What is the relationship between reliability and validity?
19. How would you select a particular scaling technique?

## Problems

1. Develop a Likert, semantic differential, and a Stapel scale for measuring store loyalty.
2. Develop a multiitem scale to measure students' attitudes toward internationalization of the management curriculum. How would you assess the reliability and validity of this scale?
3. Develop a Likert scale for measuring the attitude of students toward the Internet as a source of general information. Administer your scale to a small sample of 10 students and refine it.
4. The following scale was used in a recent study to measure attitude toward new technology. Please tell me how much you agree or disagree with the following statements as they describe how you view new technology. Use a scale of 1 to 5, where 1 = strongly disagree and 5 = strongly agree.

I'm a person who avoids new technology.
I'm a technology buff who keeps up with the latest equipment.
I take a "wait-and-see" approach to new technology until it is proven.
I'm the kind of person friends turn to for advice on buying new technology.

   **a.** How would you score this scale to measure attitude toward new technology?
   **b.** Develop an equivalent semantic differential scale to measure attitude toward new technology.
   **c.** Develop an equivalent Stapel scale to measure attitude toward new technology.
   **d.** Which scale form is most suited for a telephone survey?

# INTERNET AND COMPUTER EXERCISES

1. Design Likert scales to measure the usefulness of Ford Motor Company's Web site. Visit the site at *www.ford.com* and rate it on the scales that you have developed.
2. Design semantic differential scales to measure the perception of FedEx overnight delivery service and compare it to that offered by UPS. Relevant information may be obtained by visiting the Web sites of these two companies (*www.fedex.com*, *www.ups.com*).
3. Visit the Office of Scales Research Web site (*www.siu.edu/departments/coba/mktg/osr*). Identify one application of the Likert scale and one application of the semantic differential scale. Write a report describing the context in which these scales have been used.
4. Visit the Web sites of two marketing research firms conducting surveys. Analyze one survey of each firm to critically evaluate the itemized rating scales being used.
5. Surf the net to find two examples each of Likert, semantic differential, and Stapel scales. Write a report describing the context in which these scales are being used.

# ACTIVITIES

## Role Playing

1. You work in the marketing research department of a firm specializing in developing decision support systems (DSS) for the health care industry. Your firm would like to measure the attitudes of hospital administrators toward DSS. The interviews would be conducted by telephone. You have been asked to develop an appropriate scale for this purpose. Management would like you to explain and justify your reasoning in constructing this scale.

## Fieldwork

1. Develop a semantic differential scale to measure the images of two major airlines that fly to your city. Administer this scale to a pilot sample of 20 students. Based on your pilot study, which airline has a more favorable image?

## Group Discussion

1. "It really does not matter which scaling technique you use. As long as your measure is reliable, you will get the right results." Discuss this statement as a small group.
2. "One need not be concerned with reliability and validity in applied marketing research." Discuss this statement as a small group.

# 10

# Questionnaire and Form Design

"A good questionnaire must engage the respondent and stimulate their interest in providing complete and accurate answers. It must do this while creating a common understanding of both the questions and answers among all respondents."

*Bobbi Brantley,*
*training manger,*
*research services,*
*Burke, Inc.*

## Objectives

After reading this chapter, the student should be able to:

1. Explain the purpose of a questionnaire and its objectives of asking questions that the respondents can and will answer, encouraging respondents, and minimizing response error.
2. Describe the process of designing a questionnaire, the steps involved, and guidelines that must be followed at each step.
3. Discuss the observational form of data collection and specify the who, what, when, where, why, and way of behavior to be observed.
4. Discuss the considerations involved in designing questionnaires for international marketing research.
5. Understand the ethical issues involved in questionnaire design.
6. Discuss the use of the Internet and computers in designing questionnaires.

## Overview

Questionnaire or form design is an important step in formulating a research design. Once the researcher has specified the nature of research design (Chapters 3 through 7) and determined the scaling procedures (Chapters 8 and 9), they can develop a questionnaire or an observational form. This chapter discusses the importance of questionnaires and observational forms. Next, we describe the objectives of a questionnaire and the steps involved in designing questionnaires. We provide several guidelines for developing sound questionnaires. We also consider the design of observation forms. The considerations involved in designing questionnaires when conducting international marketing research are discussed. Several ethical issues that arise in questionnaire design are identified. The chapter concludes with a discussion of the use of the Internet and computers in designing questionnaires.

## REAL RESEARCH

### The Consensus on Census 2000 Questionnaires

Every 10 years, the United States Census Bureau (*www.census.gov*) conducts a survey to determine how many people are in the country, as well as the various demographics of these individuals. This survey is done using questionnaires. Because the forms have been long and hard to understand in the past, there has been a decline in mail responses for the census. As a result, the questionnaires were redesigned for the 2000 census. The goal was to make them more user friendly and shorter in hopes of increasing the response rates.

The questionnaire was considerably shortened. Whereas the 1990 short form contained 12 subjects, the 2000 short form had only seven subjects (name, sex, age, relationship, Hispanic origin, and race for each household member, as well as whether the home was owned or rented). Likewise, the long form for 2000 had 34 subjects instead of 38 for 1990.

Once the content of the questionnaire was determined, it was time to work on the structure and actual wording of the statements. The hard part of the process was making the questions short enough to keep respondents interested, but long enough to obtain the necessary data. Each question had to be clearly defined using unambiguous words. A review was conducted of the 1990 census questions to determine which ones needed to be revised. After determining the content, structure, wording, and sequence of questions, the Bureau looked to a New York design firm, Two Twelve Associates (*www.twotwelve.com*), to improve form and layout and develop visual imagery for the questionnaire, including a logo and slogan.

The revised questionnaire was thoroughly pretested. The most extensive pretest was the 1996 National Content Survey (formally known as the U.S. Census 2000 Test), which was designed to test new and revised question wording, formatting, and sequencing.

As a result of improved design, mail response rates to the Census 2000 questionnaires were about 10 percent higher than in 1990.

During actual data collection, a card was first mailed before the questionnaire was sent and respondents were given the option to request the questionnaire in English, Spanish, Chinese, Korean, Vietnamese, or Tagalog. Then the questionnaire package was sent in an official envelope with the Census logo on the front. A note on the envelopes reminded the recipients that their response was required by law.

As a result of the user-friendly format of the 2000 questionnaires, mail response rates were about 10 percent higher than in 1990. The consensus was that the 2000 questionnaires were much improved over those used a decade earlier.[1] ■

# QUESTIONNAIRES AND OBSERVATION FORMS

As was discussed in Chapter 5, survey and observation are the two basic methods for obtaining quantitative primary data in descriptive research. Both of these methods require some procedure for standardizing the data-collection process so that the data obtained are internally consistent and can be analyzed in a uniform and coherent manner. If 40 different interviewers conduct personal interviews or make observations in different parts of the country, the data they collect will not be comparable unless they follow specific guidelines and ask questions and record answers in a standard way. A standardized questionnaire or form will ensure comparability of the data, increase speed and accuracy of recording, and facilitate data processing.

## Questionnaire Definition

**questionnaire**
A structured technique for data collection that consists of a series of questions, written or verbal, that a respondent answers.

A *questionnaire,* whether it is called a schedule, interview form, or measuring instrument, is a formalized set of questions for obtaining information from respondents. Typically, a questionnaire is only one element of a data-collection package that might also include (1) fieldwork procedures, such as instructions for selecting, approaching, and questioning respondents (see Chapter 13); (2) some reward, gift, or payment offered to respondents, and (3) communication aids, such as maps, pictures, advertisements, and products (as in personal interviews) and return envelopes (in mail surveys). Regardless of the form of administration, a questionnaire is characterized by some specific objectives.

## Objectives of a Questionnaire

Any questionnaire has three specific objectives. First, it must translate the information needed into a set of specific questions that the respondents can and will answer. Developing questions that respondents can and will answer and that will yield the desired information is difficult. Two apparently similar ways of posing a question may yield different information. Hence, this objective is a challenge.

Second, a questionnaire must uplift, motivate, and encourage the respondent to become involved in the interview, to cooperate, and to complete the interview. Incomplete interviews have limited usefulness at best. In designing a questionnaire, the researcher should strive to minimize respondent fatigue, boredom, incompleteness, and nonresponse. A well-designed questionnaire can motivate the respondents and increase the response rate, as illustrated by the Census 2000 questionnaire in the opening example.

Third, a questionnaire should minimize response error. The potential sources of error in research designs were discussed in Chapter 3, where response error was defined as the error that arises when respondents give inaccurate answers or their answers are misrecorded or misanalyzed. A questionnaire can be a major source of response error. Minimizing this error is an important objective of questionnaire design.

# QUESTIONNAIRE DESIGN PROCESS

The great weakness of questionnaire design is lack of theory. Because there are no scientific principles that guarantee an optimal or ideal questionnaire, questionnaire design is a skill acquired through experience. It is an art rather than a science. Stanley Payne's The Art of Asking Questions, published in 1951, is still a basic work in the field.[2] This section presents guidelines useful to beginning researchers in designing questionnaires. Although these rules can help you avoid major mistakes, the fine-tuning of a questionnaire comes from the creativity of a skilled researcher.

Questionnaire design will be presented as a series of steps (see Figure 10.1). These steps are: (1) specify the information needed, (2) specify the type of interviewing method, (3) determine the content of individual questions, (4) design the questions to overcome the respondent's inability and unwillingness to answer, (5) decide on the question structure, (6) determine the question wording, (7) arrange the questions in proper order, (8) identify the form and layout, (9) reproduce the questionnaire, and (10) pretest the questionnaire. We will present guidelines for each step. In practice, the steps are interrelated and the development of a questionnaire will involve some iteration and looping. For example, the researcher may discover that respondents misunderstand all the possible wordings of a question. This may require a loop back to the earlier step of deciding on the question structure.[3]

# SPECIFY THE INFORMATION NEEDED

The first step in questionnaire design is to specify the information needed. This is also the first step in the research design process. Note that as the research project progresses, the information needed becomes more and more clearly defined. It is helpful to review components of the problem and the approach, particularly the research questions, hypotheses, and the information needed. To further ensure that the information obtained fully addresses all the components of the problem, the researcher should prepare a set of dummy tables. A dummy table is a blank table used to catalog data. It describes how the analysis will be structured once the data have been collected.

It is also important to have a clear idea of the target population. The characteristics of the respondent group have a great influence on questionnaire design. Questions that are

**Figure 10.1**
Questionaire Design Process

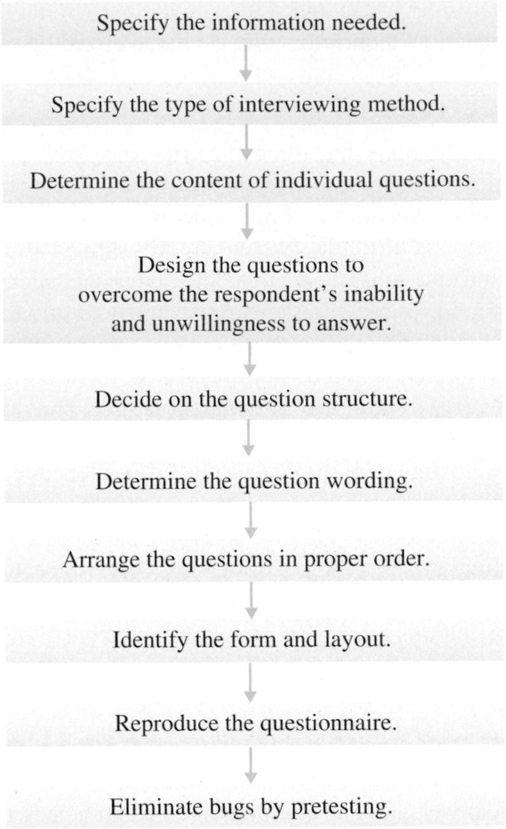

| Specify the information needed. |
|---|

| Specify the type of interviewing method. |
|---|

| Determine the content of individual questions. |
|---|

| Design the questions to overcome the respondent's inability and unwillingness to answer. |
|---|

| Decide on the question structure. |
|---|

| Determine the question wording. |
|---|

| Arrange the questions in proper order. |
|---|

| Identify the form and layout. |
|---|

| Reproduce the questionnaire. |
|---|

| Eliminate bugs by pretesting. |
|---|

appropriate for college students may not be appropriate for housewives. Understanding is related to respondent socioeconomic characteristics. Furthermore, poor understanding is associated with a high incidence of uncertain or no-opinion responses. The more diversified the respondent group, the more difficult it is to design a single questionnaire that is appropriate for the entire group.

# TYPE OF INTERVIEWING METHOD

An appreciation of how the type of interviewing method influences questionnaire design can be obtained by considering how the questionnaire is administered under each method (see Chapter 6). In personal interviews, respondents see the questionnaire and interact face to face with the interviewer. Thus, lengthy, complex, and varied questions can be asked. In telephone interviews, the respondents interact with the interviewer, but they do not see the questionnaire. This limits the type of questions that can be asked to short and simple ones (see the department store project). Mail questionnaires are self-administered, so the questions must be simple and detailed instructions must be provided. In computer-assisted interviewing (CAPI and CATI), complex skip patterns and randomization of questions to eliminate order bias can be easily accommodated. Internet questionnaires share many of the characteristics of CAPI, but e-mail questionnaires have to be simpler. Questionnaires designed for personal and telephone interviews should be written in a conversational style.

In the department store project example, ranking 10 stores is too complex a task to be administered over the telephone. Instead, the simpler rating task, where the stores are rated one at a time, is selected to measure preferences. Note the use of cards to facilitate the ranking task in the personal interview. Interviewer instructions (typed in capital letters) are much more extensive in the personal interview. Another difference is that whereas the

### Effect of Interviewing Method on Questionnaire Design

#### Mail Questionnaire

Please rank order the following department stores in order of your preference to shop at these stores. Begin by picking out the one store that you like most and assign it a number 1. Then find the second most preferred department store and assign it a number 2. Continue this procedure until you have ranked all the stores in order of preference. The least preferred store should be assigned a rank of 10. No two stores should receive the same rank number. The criterion of preference is entirely up to you. There is no right or wrong answer. Just try to be consistent.

| Store | Rank Order |
|---|---|
| 1. Lord & Taylor | _____ |
| 2. Macy's | _____ |
| 3. Kmart | _____ |
| 4. Rich's | _____ |
| 5. JC Penney | _____ |
| 6. Neiman-Marcus | _____ |
| 7. Target | _____ |
| 8. Saks Fifth Ave | _____ |
| 9. Sears | _____ |
| 10. Wal-Mart | _____ |

#### Telephone Questionnaire

I will read to you the names of some department stores. Please rate them in terms of your preference to shop at these stores. Use a ten-point scale, where 1 denotes not so preferred and 10 denotes greatly preferred. Numbers between 1 and 10 reflect intermediate degrees of preference. Again, Please remember that the higher the number, the greater the degree of preference. Now, please tell me your preference to shop at.....(READ ONE STORE AT A TIME)

| Store | Not So Preferred | | | | | | | | | Greatly Preferred |
|---|---|---|---|---|---|---|---|---|---|---|
| 1. Lord & Taylor | 1 | 2 | 3 | 4 | 5 | 6 | 7 | 8 | 9 | 10 |
| 2. Macy's | 1 | 2 | 3 | 4 | 5 | 6 | 7 | 8 | 9 | 10 |
| 3. Kmart | 1 | 2 | 3 | 4 | 5 | 6 | 7 | 8 | 9 | 10 |
| 4. Rich's | 1 | 2 | 3 | 4 | 5 | 6 | 7 | 8 | 9 | 10 |
| 5. JC Penney | 1 | 2 | 3 | 4 | 5 | 6 | 7 | 8 | 9 | 10 |
| 6. Neiman-Marcus | 1 | 2 | 3 | 4 | 5 | 6 | 7 | 8 | 9 | 10 |
| 7. Target | 1 | 2 | 3 | 4 | 5 | 6 | 7 | 8 | 9 | 10 |
| 8. Saks Fifth Ave | 1 | 2 | 3 | 4 | 5 | 6 | 7 | 8 | 9 | 10 |
| 9. Sears | 1 | 2 | 3 | 4 | 5 | 6 | 7 | 8 | 9 | 10 |
| 10. Wal-Mart | 1 | 2 | 3 | 4 | 5 | 6 | 7 | 8 | 9 | 10 |

#### Personal Questionnaire

(HAND DEPARTMENT STORE CARDS TO THE RESPONDENT.) Here is a set of department store names, each written on a separate card. Please examine these cards carefully. (GIVE RESPONDENT TIME). Now, please examine these cards again and pull out the card that has the name of the store you like the most, that is, your most preferred store for shopping. (RECORD THE STORE NAME AND KEEP THIS CARD WITH YOU.) Now, please examine the remaining nine cards. Of these remaining nine stores, what is your most preferred store for shopping? (REPEAT THIS PROCEDURE SEQUENTIALLY UNTIL THE RESPONDENT HAS ONLY ONE CARD LEFT.)

| Store Rank | Name of the Store |
|---|---|
| 1. ___1___ | _____ |
| 2. ___2___ | _____ |
| 3. ___3___ | _____ |
| 4. ___4___ | _____ |
| 5. ___5___ | _____ |
| 6. ___6___ | _____ |
| 7. ___7___ | _____ |
| 8. ___8___ | _____ |
| 9. ___9___ | _____ |
| 10. ___10___ | _____ |

This question for e-mail and Internet questionnaires will be very similar to that for the mail questionnaire; in all these methods, the questionnaire is self-administered by the respondent.

respondent records the ranks in mail and electronic surveys, the interviewer records the store names in the personal interview. The type of interviewing method also influences the content of individual questions.

# INDIVIDUAL QUESTION CONTENT

Once the information needed is specified and the type of interviewing method decided, the next step is to determine individual question content: what to include in individual questions.

## Is the Question Necessary?

Every question in a questionnaire should contribute to the information needed or serve some specific purpose. If there is no satisfactory use for the data resulting from a question, that question should be eliminated. As illustrated in the opening example, a hard look at the 1990 Census of Population short form resulted in the elimination of questions pertaining to five subjects.

In certain situations, however, questions may be asked that are not directly related to the information that is needed. It is useful to ask some neutral questions at the beginning of the questionnaire to establish involvement and rapport, particularly when the topic of the questionnaire is sensitive or controversial. Sometimes filler questions are asked to disguise the purpose or sponsorship of the project. Rather than limiting the questions to the brand of interest, questions about competing brands may also be included to disguise the sponsorship. For example, a survey on personal computers sponsored by IBM may also include filler questions related to Dell and Apple. Questions unrelated to the immediate problem may sometimes be included to generate client support for the project. At times, certain questions may be duplicated for the purpose of assessing reliability or validity.[4]

## Are Several Questions Needed Instead of One?

Once we have ascertained that a question is necessary, we must make sure that it is sufficient to get the desired information. Sometimes, several questions are needed to obtain the required information in an unambiguous manner. Consider the question,

> "Do you think Coca-Cola is a tasty and refreshing soft drink?"  (Incorrect)

A "yes" answer will presumably be clear, but what if the answer is "no"? Does this mean that the respondent thinks that Coca-Cola is not tasty, that it is not refreshing, or that it is neither tasty nor refreshing? Such a question is called a ***double-barreled question,*** because two or more questions are combined into one. To obtain the required information, two distinct questions should be asked:

> "Do you think Coca-Cola is a tasty soft drink?" and
> "Do you think Coca-Cola is a refreshing soft drink?"  (Correct)

Another example of multiple questions embedded in a single question is the "why" question. In the context of the department store study, consider the question,

> "Why do you shop at Nike Town?"  (Incorrect)

The possible answers may include: "to buy athletic shoes," "it is more conveniently located than other stores," and "it was recommended by my best friend." Each of these answers relates to a different question embedded in the "why" question. The first answer tells why the respondent shops in the athletic merchandise store, the second answer reveals what the respondent likes about Nike Town as compared to other stores, and the third answer tells how the respondent learned about Nike Town. The three answers are not

---

**double-barreled question**
A single question that attempts to cover two issues. Such questions can be confusing to respondents and result in ambiguous responses.

A question such as "What do you like about Nike Town as compared to other stores?" will reveal several positive features of Nike Town.

comparable and any one answer may not be sufficient. Complete information may be obtained by asking two separate questions:

> "What do you like about Nike Town as compared to other stores?" and
>
> "How did you first happen to shop in Nike Town?"                              (Correct)

Most "why" questions about the use of a product or choice alternative involve two aspects: (1) attributes of the product, and (2) influences leading to knowledge of it.[5]

# OVERCOMING INABILITY TO ANSWER

Researchers should not assume that respondents can provide accurate or reasonable answers to all questions. The researcher should attempt to overcome the respondents' inability to answer. Certain factors limit the respondents' ability to provide the desired information. The respondents may not be informed, may not remember, or may be unable to articulate certain types of responses.

## Is the Respondent Informed?

Respondents are often asked about topics on which they are not informed. A husband may not be informed about monthly expenses for groceries and department store purchases if it is the wife who makes these purchases, or vice versa. Research has shown that respondents will often answer questions even though they are uninformed, as the following example shows.

### REAL RESEARCH

### *The Complaint About Consumer Complaints*

In one study, respondents were asked to express their degree of agreement or disagreement with the following statement: "The National Bureau of Consumer Complaints provides an effective means for consumers who have purchased a defective product to obtain relief." As many as 96.1 percent of the lawyers and 95 percent of the general public who responded expressed an opinion. Even with a "don't know" option in the response set, 51.9 percent of the lawyers and 75.0 percent of the public still expressed an opinion about the National Bureau of Consumer Complaints. Why should these high response rates be problematic? Because there is no such entity as the National Bureau of Consumer Complaints![6] ■

**filter questions**
An initial question in a question-naire that screens potential respondents to ensure they meet the requirements of the sample.

In situations where not all respondents are likely to be informed about the topic of interest, *filter questions* that measure familiarity, product use, and past experience should be asked before questions about the topics themselves.[7] Filter questions enable the researcher to filter out respondents who are not adequately informed.

The department store questionnaire included questions related to 10 different department stores, ranging from prestigious stores to discount stores. It was likely that many respondents would not be sufficiently informed about all the stores, so information on familiarity and frequency of patronage was obtained for each store (see Chapter 1). This allowed for separate analysis of data on stores about which the respondents were not informed. A "don't know" option appears to reduce uninformed responses without reducing the overall response rate or the response rate for questions about which the respondents have information. Hence, this option should be provided when the researcher expects that respondents may not be adequately informed about the subject of the question.[8]

## Can the Respondent Remember?

Many things that we might expect everyone to know are remembered by only a few. Test this out on yourself. Can you answer the following?

What is the brand name of the shirt you were wearing two weeks ago?

What did you have for lunch a week ago?

What were you doing a month ago at noon?

How many gallons of soft drinks did you consume during the last four weeks?        (Incorrect)

These questions are incorrect as they exceed the ability of the respondents to remember. Evidence indicates that consumers are particularly poor at remembering quantities of products consumed. In situations where factual data were available for comparison, it was found that consumer reports of product usage exceeded actual usage by 100 percent or more.[9] Thus, soft drink consumption may be better obtained by asking:

How often do you consume soft drinks in a typical week?

i. _____ Less than once a week
ii. _____ 1 to 3 times per week
iii. _____ 4 to 6 times per week
iv. _____ 7 or more times per week                                        (Correct)

**telescoping**
A psychological phenomenon that takes place when an individual telescopes or compresses time by remembering an event as occurring more recently than it actually occurred.

The inability to remember leads to errors of omission, telescoping, and creation. *Omission* is the inability to recall an event that actually took place. *Telescoping* takes place when an individual telescopes or compresses time by remembering an event as occurring more recently than it actually occurred.[10] For example, a respondent reports three trips to the supermarket in the last two weeks when, in fact, one of these trips was made 18 days ago. *Creation* error takes place when a respondent "remembers" an event that did not actually occur.

The ability to remember an event is influenced by (1) the event itself, (2) the time elapsed since the event, and (3) the presence or absence of events that would aid memory. We tend to remember events that are important or unusual or that occur frequently. People remember their wedding anniversary and birthday. Likewise, more recent events are remembered better. A grocery shopper is more likely to remember what was purchased on the last shopping trip as compared to what was bought three shopping trips ago.

Research indicates that questions that do not provide the respondent with cues to the event, and rely on unaided recall, can underestimate the actual occurrence of an event. For example, unaided recall of soft drink commercials could be measured by questions like, "What brands of soft drinks do you remember being advertised last night on TV?" The aided recall approach attempts to stimulate the respondent's memory by providing cues related to the event of interest. The aided recall approach would list a number of soft drink brands and then ask, "Which of these brands were advertised last night on TV?" In presenting cues, the researcher must guard against biasing the responses by employing several successive levels of stimulation. The influence of stimulation on responses can then be analyzed to select an appropriate level of stimulation.

## Can the Respondent Articulate?

Respondents may be unable to articulate certain types of responses. For example, if asked to describe the atmosphere of the department store they would prefer to patronize, most respondents may be unable to phrase their answers. On the other hand, if the respondents are provided with alternative descriptions of store atmosphere, they will be able to indicate the one they like the best. If the respondents are unable to articulate their responses to a question, they are likely to ignore that question and may refuse to respond to the rest of the questionnaire. Thus respondents should be given aids, such as pictures, maps, and descriptions to help them articulate their responses.

# OVERCOMING UNWILLINGNESS TO ANSWER

Even if respondents are able to answer a particular question, they may be unwilling to do so, either because too much effort is required, the situation or context may not seem appropriate for disclosure, no legitimate purpose or need for the information requested is apparent, or the information requested is sensitive.

## Effort Required of the Respondents

Most respondents are unwilling to devote a lot of effort to provide information. Hence, the researcher should minimize the effort required of the respondents. Suppose the researcher is interested in determining from which departments in a store the respondent purchased merchandise on the most recent shopping trip. This information can be obtained in at least two ways. The researcher could ask the respondent to list all the departments from which merchandise was purchased on the most recent shopping trip, or the researcher could provide a list of departments and ask the respondent to check the applicable ones:

> Please list all the departments from which you purchased merchandise
> on your most recent shopping trip to a department store.          (Incorrect)

> In the list that follows, please check all the departments from which you purchased
> merchandise on your most recent shopping trip to a department store.

>  **1.** Women's dresses        _____
>  **2.** Men's apparel          _____
>  **3.** Children's apparel     _____
>  **4.** Cosmetics              _____
>     .
>     .
>     .
>  **17.** Jewelry               _____
>  **18.** Other (please specify) _____          (Correct)

The second option is preferable, because it requires less effort from respondents.

## Context

Some questions may seem appropriate in certain contexts but not in others. For example, questions about personal hygiene habits may be appropriate when asked in a survey sponsored by the American Medical Association, but not in one sponsored by a fast-food restaurant. Respondents are unwilling to respond to questions that they consider to be inappropriate for the given context. Sometimes, the researcher can manipulate the context in which the questions are asked so that the questions seem appropriate. For example, before asking for information on personal hygiene in a survey for a fast-food restaurant, the context could be manipulated by making the following statement. "As a fast-food restaurant, we are very concerned about providing a clean and hygienic environment for our customers. Therefore, we would like to ask you some questions related to personal hygiene."

## Legitimate Purpose

Respondents are also unwilling to divulge information that they do not see as serving a legitimate purpose. Why should a firm marketing cereals want to know their age, income, and occupation? Explaining why the data are needed can make the request for the information seem legitimate and increase the respondents' willingness to answer. A statement such as, "To determine how the consumption of cereal and preferences for cereal brands vary among people of different ages, incomes, and occupations, we need information on . . ." can make the request for information seem legitimate.

## Sensitive Information

Respondents are unwilling to disclose, at least accurately, sensitive information because this may cause embarrassment or threaten the respondent's prestige or self-image. If pressed for the answer, respondents may give biased responses, especially during personal interviews (see Chapter 6, Table 6.2).[11] Sensitive topics include money, family life, political and religious beliefs, and involvement in accidents or crimes. The techniques described in the following section can be adopted to increase the likelihood of obtaining information that respondents are unwilling to give.

## Increasing the Willingness of Respondents

Respondents may be encouraged to provide information that they are unwilling to give by the following techniques.[12]

1. Place sensitive topics at the end of the questionnaire. By then, initial mistrust has been overcome, rapport has been created, legitimacy of the project has been established, and respondents are more willing to give information.
2. Preface the question with a statement that the behavior of interest is common. For example, before requesting information on credit card debt, say, "Recent studies show that most Americans are in debt." This technique, called the use of counterbiasing statements, is further illustrated by the following example.[13]

---

**REAL RESEARCH**

### *Public versus Private*

A recent poll conducted by RoperASW (*www.roperasw.com*) for *U.S. News & World Report* sought to obtain information on whether personal information about political candidates or ordinary citizens should be disclosed to the public. This question was prefaced with the following statement: "The question of where to draw the line on the matter of privacy has been much debated, with some saying that the standards should be different for candidates for important public office than for ordinary citizens." This statement increased the willingness of the people to respond. ■

3. Ask the question using the third-person technique (see Chapter 5): phrase the question as if it referred to other people.
4. Hide the question in a group of other questions that respondents are willing to answer. The entire list of questions can then be asked quickly.
5. Provide response categories rather than asking for specific figures. Do not ask, "What is your household's annual income?" Instead, ask the respondent to check the appropriate income category: under $25,000, $25,001–$50,000, $50,001–$75,000, or over $75,000. In personal interviews, give the respondents cards that list the numbered choices. The respondents then indicate their responses by number.

**6.** Use randomized techniques. In these techniques, respondents are presented with two questions, one sensitive and the other a neutral question with a known probability of a "yes" response (e.g., "Is your birthday in March?"). They are asked to select one question randomly, for example by flipping a coin. The respondent then answers the selected question "yes" or "no," without telling the researcher which question is being answered. Given the overall probability of a "yes" response, the probability of selecting the sensitive question, and the probability of a "yes" response to the neutral question, the researcher can determine the probability of "yes" response to the sensitive question using the law of probability. However, the researcher cannot determine which respondents have answered "yes" to the sensitive question.[14]

# CHOOSING QUESTION STRUCTURE

A question may be unstructured or structured. In the following sections, we define unstructured questions and discuss their relative advantages and disadvantages and then consider the major types of structured questions: multiple-choice, dichotomous, and scales.[15]

## Unstructured Questions

**unstructured questions**
Open-ended questions that respondents answer in their own words.

*Unstructured questions* are open-ended questions that respondents answer in their own words. They are also referred to as free-response or free-answer questions. The following are some examples:

- What is your occupation?
- What do you think of people who patronize discount department stores?
- Who is your favorite political figure?

Open-ended questions are good as first questions on a topic. They enable the respondents to express general attitudes and opinions that can help the researcher interpret their responses to structured questions. Unstructured questions have a much less biasing influence on response than structured questions. Respondents are free to express any views. Their comments and explanations can provide the researcher with rich insights. Hence, unstructured questions are useful in exploratory research.

A principal disadvantage is that potential for interviewer bias is high. Whether the interviewers record the answers verbatim or write down only the main points, the data depend on the skills of the interviewers. Tape recorders should be used if verbatim reporting is important.

Another major disadvantage of unstructured questions is that the coding of responses is costly and time consuming.[16] The coding procedures required to summarize responses in a format useful for data analysis and interpretation can be extensive. Implicitly, unstructured or open-ended questions give extra weight to respondents who are more articulate. Also, unstructured questions are not suitable for self-administered questionnaires (mail, CAPI, e-mail, and Internet), because respondents tend to be more brief in writing than in speaking.

Precoding can overcome some of the disadvantages of unstructured questions. Expected responses are recorded in multiple-choice format, although the question is presented to the respondents as an open-ended question. Based on the respondent's reply, the interviewer selects the appropriate response category. This approach may be satisfactory when the respondent can easily formulate the response and it is easy to develop precoded categories as the response alternatives are limited. For example, this approach may be used to obtain information on ownership of appliances. It has also been used successfully in business surveys, as shown by the following example.

### REAL RESEARCH

*Assessing Access Attitudes*

A major telecommunications firm conducted a national telephone survey to determine the attitudes of businesses toward equal access. One of the questions was asked as an open-ended question with precoded responses.[17]

Which company or companies is your business presently using for long-distance telephone service? If more than one, please indicate the names of all the companies. (ASK AS AN OPEN-ENDED QUESTION. ALLOW FOR MULTIPLE RESPONSES AND SCORE AS FOLLOWS.)

1. _____ MCI

2. _____ US SPRINT

3. _____ CONTEL

4. _____ AT&T

5. _____ Regional Bell operating co. (insert name)

6. _____ Other (specify)

7. _____ Don't know/no answer ■

In general, open-ended questions are useful in exploratory research and as opening questions. Otherwise, their disadvantages outweigh their advantages in a large survey.[18]

## Structured Questions

**structured questions**
Questions that prespecify the set of response alternatives and the response format. A structured question could be multiple choice, dichotomous, or a scale.

*Structured questions* specify the set of response alternatives and the response format. A structured question may be multiple choice, dichotomous, or a scale.

### *Multiple-Choice Questions.*
In multiple-choice questions, the researcher provides a choice of answers and respondents are asked to select one or more of the alternatives given. Consider the following question.

Do you intend to buy a new car within the next six months?

_____ Definitely will not buy

_____ Probably will not buy

_____ Undecided

_____ Probably will buy

_____ Definitely will buy

_____ Other (please specify)

Several of the issues discussed in Chapter 9 with respect to itemized rating scales also apply to multiple-choice answers. Two additional concerns in designing multiple-choice questions are the number of alternatives that should be included and order or position bias.

The response alternatives should include the set of all possible choices. The general guideline is to list all alternatives that may be of importance and include an alternative labeled "Other (please specify)," as shown above. The response alternatives should be mutually exclusive. Respondents should also be able to identify one, and only one, alternative, unless the researcher specifically allows two or more choices (for example, "Please indicate all the brands of soft drinks that you have consumed in the past week"). If the response alternatives are numerous, consider using more than one question to reduce the information-processing demands on the respondents.

**order or position bias**
A respondent's tendency to check an alternative merely because it occupies a certain position or is listed in a certain order.

*Order or position bias* is the respondents' tendency to check an alternative merely because it occupies a certain position or is listed in a certain order. Respondents tend to check the first or the last statement in a list, particularly the first. For a list of numbers (quantities or prices), there is a bias toward the central value on the list. To control for order bias, several forms of the questionnaire should be prepared with the order in which the alternatives are listed varied from form to form. Each alternative should appear once in each of the extreme positions, once in the middle, and once somewhere in between.[19]

Multiple-choice questions overcome many of the disadvantages of open-ended questions, because interviewer bias is reduced and these questions are administered quickly. Also, coding and processing of data are much less costly and time consuming. In self-administered questionnaires, respondent cooperation is improved if the majority of the questions are structured.

Multiple-choice questions are not without disadvantages. Considerable effort is required to design effective multiple-choice questions. Exploratory research using open-ended questions may be required to determine the appropriate response alternatives. It is difficult to obtain information on alternatives not listed. Even if an "Other (please specify)" category is included, respondents tend to choose among the listed alternatives. In addition, showing respondents the list of possible answers produces biased responses.[20] There is also the potential for order bias.

*dichotomous question*
A structured question with only two response alternatives, such as yes and no.

### Dichotomous Questions.
A *dichotomous question* has only two response alternatives: yes or no, agree or disagree, and so on. Often, the two alternatives of interest are supplemented by a neutral alternative, such as "no opinion," "don't know," "both" or "none."[21] The question asked before about intentions to buy a new car as a multiple-choice question can also be asked as a dichotomous question.

Do you intend to buy a new car within the next six months?

_____ Yes
_____ No
_____ Don't know

The decision to use a dichotomous question should be guided by whether the respondents approach the issue as a yes-or-no question. Although decisions are often characterized as series of binary or dichotomous choices, the underlying decision-making process may reflect uncertainty, which can best be captured by multiple-choice responses. For example, two individuals may be equally likely to buy a new car within the next six months if the economic conditions remain favorable. However, one individual, who is being optimistic about the economy, will answer "yes," whereas the other, feeling pessimistic, will answer "no."

Another issue in the design of dichotomous questions is whether to include a neutral response alternative. If it is not included, respondents are forced to choose between "yes" and "no" even if they feel indifferent. On the other hand, if a neutral alternative is included, respondents can avoid taking a position on the issue, thereby biasing the results. We offer the following guidelines. If a substantial proportion of the respondents can be expected to be neutral, include a neutral alternative. If the proportion of neutral respondents is expected to be small, avoid the neutral alternative.

The general advantages and disadvantages of dichotomous questions are very similar to those of multiple-choice questions. Dichotomous questions are the easiest type of questions to code and analyze, but they have one acute problem. The response can be influenced by the wording of the question. To illustrate the statement, "Individuals are more to blame than social conditions for crime and lawlessness in this country," produced agreement from 59.6 percent of the respondents. However, on a matched sample that responded to the opposite statement, "Social conditions are more to blame than individuals for crime and lawlessness in this country," 43.2 percent (as opposed to 40.4 percent) agreed.[22] To overcome this problem, the question should be framed in one way on one-half of the questionnaires and in the opposite way on the other half. This is referred to as the split ballot technique.

### Scales.
Scales were discussed in detail in Chapters 8 and 9. To illustrate the difference between scales and other kinds of structured questions, consider the question about intentions to buy a new car. One way of framing this using a scale is as follows:

Do you intend to buy a new car within the next six months?

| Definitely will not buy | Probably will not buy | Undecided | Probably will buy | Definitely will buy |
|---|---|---|---|---|
| 1 | 2 | 3 | 4 | 5 |

This is only one of several scales that could be used to ask this question (see Chapters 8 and 9). As shown in the following example, a survey may contain different types of questions.

**REAL RESEARCH**

## Question Structure in GAP

The Global Airline Performance (GAP) study is a survey conducted to measure the opinions of air travelers on 22 airlines departing from 30 airports across the world. It reaches 240,000 passengers each year and is conducted in seven languages. This survey uses different types of structured questions, including multiple choice, dichotomous, and scales, as illustrated in the following.[23]

Q. How did you make your reservation? (Please pick ONE only)

\_\_\_\_\_ Airline Web site

\_\_\_\_\_ Airline phone reservations or ticket office

\_\_\_\_\_ Through travel agent

\_\_\_\_\_ Other

Q. Are you using an e-ticket (electronic paperless ticket) on this trip?

\_\_\_\_\_ Yes

\_\_\_\_\_ No

Q. Based on your experience of today's flight, would you select this airline for your next trip on this route?

\_\_\_\_\_ Definitely would (5)

\_\_\_\_\_ Probably would (4)

\_\_\_\_\_ Might/might not (3)

\_\_\_\_\_ Probably not (2)

\_\_\_\_\_ Definitely not (1) ■

# CHOOSING QUESTION WORDING

Question wording is the translation of the desired question content and structure into words that respondents can clearly and easily understand. Deciding on question wording is perhaps the most critical and difficult task in developing a questionnaire, as illustrated by the Census 2000 questionnaire in the opening example. If a question is worded poorly, respondents may refuse to answer it or may answer it incorrectly. The first condition, known as item nonresponse, can increase the complexity of data analysis.[24] The second condition leads to response error, discussed earlier. Unless the respondents and the researcher assign exactly the same meaning to the question, the results will be seriously biased.[25]

To avoid these problems, we offer the following guidelines: (1) define the issue, (2) use ordinary words, (3) avoid ambiguous words, (4) avoid leading questions, (5) avoid implicit alternatives, (6) avoid implicit assumptions, (7) avoid generalizations and estimates, and (8) use positive and negative statements.

## Define the Issue

A question should clearly define the issue being addressed. Beginning journalists are admonished to define the issue in terms of who, what, when, where, why, and way (the six

A well-defined question is needed to determine which brand of shampoo a person uses.

Ws).[26] These can also serve as guidelines for defining the issue in a question. (See Chapter 3 for an application of these guidelines to descriptive research.) Consider the following question:

> Which brand of shampoo do you use? (Incorrect)

On the surface, this may seem to be a well-defined question, but we may reach a different conclusion when we examine it under the microscope of who, what, when, and where. "Who" in this question refers to the respondent. It is not clear, though, whether the researcher is referring to the brand the respondent uses personally or the brand used by the household. "What" is the brand of shampoo. However, what if more than one brand of shampoo is being used? Should the respondent mention the most preferred brand, the brand used most often, the brand used most recently, or the brand that comes to mind first? "When" is not clear; does the researcher mean last time, last week, last month, last year, or ever? As for "where," it is implied that the shampoo is used at home, but this is not stated clearly. A better wording for this question would be:

> Which brand or brands of shampoo have you personally used at home during the last month? In case of more than one brand, please list all the brands that apply. (Correct)

## Use Ordinary Words

Ordinary words should be used in a questionnaire and they should match the vocabulary level of the respondents.[27] When choosing words, keep in mind that the average person in the United States has a high school, not a college, education. For certain respondent groups, the education level is even lower. For example, the author did a project for a major telecommunications firm that operates primarily in rural areas. The average educational level in these areas is less than high school, and many respondents had only fourth to sixth grade education. Technical jargon should also be avoided. Most respondents do not understand technical marketing words. For example, instead of asking,

> "Do you think the distribution of soft drinks is adequate?" (Incorrect)

ask,

> "Do you think soft drinks are readily available when you want to buy them?" (Correct)

Assessing the distribution of soft drinks requires the use of words as ordinary and common place as soft drinks themselves.

## Use Unambiguous Words

The words used in a questionnaire should have a single meaning that is known to the respondents. A number of words that appear to be unambiguous have different meanings to different people.[28] These include "usually," "normally," "frequently," "often," "regularly," "occasionally," and "sometimes." Consider the following question:

In a typical month, how often do you shop in department stores?

|            |             |
|------------|-------------|
| _____ | Never       |
| _____ | Occasionally |
| _____ | Sometimes   |
| _____ | Often       |
| _____ | Regularly   |

(Incorrect)

The answers to this question are fraught with response bias, because the words used to describe category labels have different meanings for different respondents. Three respondents who shop once a month may check three different categories: occasionally, sometimes, and often. A much better wording for this question would be the following:

In a typical month, how often do you shop in department stores?

|            |                  |
|------------|------------------|
| _____ | Less than once   |
| _____ | 1 or 2 times     |
| _____ | 3 or 4 times     |
| _____ | More than 4 times |

(Correct)

Note that this question provides a consistent frame of reference for all respondents. Response categories have been objectively defined, and respondents are no longer free to interpret them in their own way.

In deciding on the choice of words, researchers should consult a dictionary and thesaurus and ask the following questions of each word used:

1. Does it mean what we intended?
2. Does it have any other meanings?
3. If so, does the context make the intended meaning clear?
4. Does the word have more than one pronunciation?
5. Is there any word of similar pronunciation that might be confused with this word?
6. Is a simpler word or phrase suggested?

The U.S. Census Bureau took great pains to use ordinary and unambiguous words in the Census 2000 questionnaires, which not only improved the response rate but also resulted in more accurate data (see opening example).

## Avoid Leading or Biasing Questions

**leading question**
A question that gives the respondent a clue as to what answer is desired or leads the respondent to answer in a certain way.

A *leading question* is one that clues the respondent to what answer is desired or leads the respondent to answer in a certain way, as in the following:

Do you think that patriotic Americans should buy imported automobiles when that would put American labor out of work?

| | | |
|---|---|---|
| _____ | Yes | |
| _____ | No | |
| _____ | Don't know | (Incorrect) |

This question would lead respondents to a "No" answer. After all, how can patriotic Americans put American labor out of work? Therefore, this question would not help determine the preferences of Americans for imported versus domestic automobiles. A better question would be:

Do you think that Americans should buy imported automobiles?

| | | |
|---|---|---|
| _____ | Yes | |
| _____ | No | |
| _____ | Don't know | (Correct) |

Bias may also arise when respondents are given clues about the sponsor of the project. Respondents tend to respond favorably toward the sponsor. The question, "Is Colgate your favorite toothpaste?" is likely to bias the responses in favor of Colgate. A more unbiased way of obtaining this information would be to ask, "What is your favorite toothpaste brand?" Likewise, the mention of a prestigious or nonprestigious name can bias the response, as in, "Do you agree with the American Dental Association that Colgate is effective in preventing cavities?" An unbiased question would be to ask, "Is Colgate effective in preventing cavities?"[29]

## Avoid Implicit Alternatives

**implicit alternative**
An alternative that is not explicitly expressed.

An alternative that is not explicitly expressed in the options is an *implicit alternative.* Making an implied alternative explicit may increase the percentage of people selecting that alternative, as in the two following questions.

1. Do you like to fly when traveling short distances? (Incorrect)
2. Do you like to fly when traveling short distances, or would you rather drive? (Correct)

In the first question, the alternative of driving is only implicit, but in the second question, it is explicit. The first question is likely to yield a greater preference for flying than the second question.

Questions with implicit alternatives should be avoided unless there are specific reasons for including them.[30] When the alternatives are close in preference or large in number, the alternatives at the end of the list have a greater chance of being selected. To overcome this bias, the split ballot technique should be used to rotate the order in which the alternatives appear.

## Avoid Implicit Assumptions

Questions should not be worded so that the answer is dependent upon implicit assumptions about what will happen as a consequence. Implicit assumptions are assumptions that are not stated in the question, as in the following example.[31]

1. Are you in favor of a balanced budget? (Incorrect)
2. Are you in favor of a balanced budget if it would result in an increase in the personal income tax? (Correct)

Implicit in question 1 are the consequences that will arise as a result of a balanced budget. There might be a cut in defense expenditures, increase in personal income tax, cut in social programs, and so on. Question 2 is a better way to word this question. Question 1's failure to make its assumptions explicit would result in overestimating the respondents' support for a balanced budget.

## Avoid Generalizations and Estimates

Questions should be specific, not general. Moreover, questions should be worded so that the respondent does not have to make generalizations or compute estimates. Suppose we were interested in households' annual per capita expenditure on groceries. If we asked respondents

"What is the annual per capita expenditure on groceries in your
household?"                                                                                      (Incorrect)

they would first have to determine the annual expenditure on groceries by multiplying the monthly expenditure on groceries by 12 or the weekly expenditure by 52. Then they would have to divide the annual amount by the number of persons in the household. Most respondents would be unwilling or unable to perform these calculations. A better way of obtaining the required information would be to ask the respondents two simple questions:

"What is the monthly (or weekly) expenditure on groceries in your household?"
and
"How many members are there in your household?"                                                   (Correct)

The researcher can then perform the necessary calculations.

## Dual Statements: Positive and Negative

Many questions, particularly those measuring attitudes and lifestyles, are worded as statements to which respondents indicate their degree of agreement or disagreement. Evidence indicates that the response obtained is influenced by the directionality of the statements: whether they are stated positively or negatively. In these cases, it is better to use dual statements, some of which are positive and the others negative. Two different questionnaires could be prepared. One questionnaire would contain half negative and half positive statements in an interspersed way. The direction of these statements would be reversed in the other questionnaire. An example of dual statements was provided in the summated Likert scale in Chapter 9 designed to measure attitudes toward Sears.

# DETERMINING THE ORDER OF QUESTIONS

## Opening Questions

The opening questions can be crucial in gaining the confidence and cooperation of respondents. The opening questions should be interesting, simple, and nonthreatening. Questions that ask respondents for their opinions can be good opening questions, because most people like to express their opinions. Sometimes such questions are asked even though they are unrelated to the research problem and their responses are not analyzed.[32]

### REAL RESEARCH

*Opening Opinion Question Opens the Door to Cooperation*

The American Chicle Youth Poll was commissioned by the American Chicle Group, Pfizer Company (*www.pfizer.com*), and conducted by RoperASW (*www.roperasw.com*). A nationwide cross-section of 1,000 American young people, aged 8 to 17 and attending school, was interviewed. The questionnaire contained a simple opening question, asking an opinion about living in the local town or city.

To begin with, I'd like to know, how much do you like living in this (town/city)? Would you say you like it a *lot,* a *little,* or *not too much?*

| | |
|---|---|
| A lot | _____ |
| A little | _____ |
| Not too much | _____ |
| Don't know | _____ ■ |

In some instances, it is necessary to qualify the respondents, or determine whether the respondent is eligible to participate in the interview. In these cases, the qualifying questions serve as the opening questions.

---

**ACTIVE RESEARCH** | DEPARTMENT STORE PROJECT

### *Opening Question*

In the department store project, the questionnaire was to be answered by the male or female head of the household who did most of the shopping in department stores. The first question asked was, "Who in your household does most of the shopping in department stores?" Thus the opening question helped in identifying the eligible respondents. It also gained cooperation because of its simple and nonthreatening nature.

---

## Type of Information

The type of information obtained in a questionnaire may be classified as: (1) basic information, (2) classification information, and (3) identification information. Basic information relates directly to the research problem. *Classification information,* consisting of socioeconomic and demographic characteristics, is used to classify the respondents and understand the results. *Identification information* includes name, address, and telephone number. Identification information may be obtained for a variety of purposes, including verifying that the respondents listed were actually interviewed, remitting promised incentives, and so on. As a general guideline, basic information should be obtained first, followed by classification and, finally, identification information. The basic information is of greatest importance to the research project and should be obtained first, before we risk alienating the respondents by asking a series of personal questions. The questionnaire given in problem 7 (see Exercises for this chapter) incorrectly obtains identification (name) and some classification (demographic) information in the beginning.

> **classification information**
> Socioeconomic and demographic characteristics used to classify respondents.
>
> **identification information**
> A type of information obtained in a questionnaire that includes name, address, and phone number.

## Difficult Questions

Difficult questions or questions that are sensitive, embarrassing, complex, or dull should be placed late in the sequence. After rapport has been established and the respondents become involved, they are less likely to object to these questions. Thus in the department store project, information about credit card debt was asked at the end of the section on basic information. Likewise, income should be the last question in the classification section, and telephone number the final item in the identification section.

## Effect on Subsequent Questions

Questions asked early in a sequence can influence the responses to subsequent questions. As a rule of thumb, general questions should precede specific questions. This prevents specific questions from biasing responses to general questions. Consider the following sequence of questions:

Q1: "What considerations are important to you in selecting a department store?"

Q2: "In selecting a department store, how important is convenience of location?"                                                    (Correct)

Note that the first question is general, whereas the second is specific. If these questions were asked in the reverse order, respondents would be clued about convenience of location and would be more likely to give this response to the general question. (Incorrect)

Going from general to specific is called the ***funnel approach.*** The funnel approach is particularly useful when information has to be obtained about respondents' general choice behavior and their evaluations of specific products.[33] Sometimes the inverted funnel approach may be useful. In this approach, questioning begins with specific questions and concludes with the general questions. The respondents are compelled to provide specific information before making general evaluations. This approach is useful when respondents have no strong feelings or have not formulated a point of view.

## Logical Order

Questions should be asked in a logical order. All of the questions that deal with a particular topic should be asked before beginning a new topic. When switching topics, brief transitional phrases should be used to help respondents switch their train of thought.

Branching questions should be designed carefully.[34] ***Branching questions*** direct respondents to different places in the questionnaire based on how they respond to the question at hand. These questions ensure that all possible contingencies are covered. They also help reduce interviewer and respondent error and encourage complete responses. Skip patterns based on the branching questions can become quite complex. A simple way to account for all contingencies is to prepare a flow chart of the logical possibilities and then develop branching questions and instructions based on it. A flow chart used to assess the use of credit in store purchases is shown in Figure 10.2.

Placement of branching questions is important and the following guidelines should be followed: (1) the question being branched (the one to which the respondent is being directed) should be placed as close as possible to the question causing the branching, and (2) the branching questions should be ordered so that the respondents cannot anticipate what additional information will be required. Otherwise, the respondents may discover that they can avoid detailed questions by giving certain answers to branching questions. For example, the respondents should first be asked if they have seen any of the listed commercials before they are asked to evaluate commercials. Otherwise, the respondents will quickly discover that stating they have seen a commercial leads to detailed questions about that commercial and that they can avoid detailed questions by stating that they have not seen the commercial.

# FORM AND LAYOUT

The format, spacing, and positioning of questions can have a significant effect on the results, as illustrated by the Census 2000 questionnaire in the opening example. This is particularly important for self-administered questionnaires. Experiments on mail questionnaires for census of population revealed that questions at the top of the page

---

**funnel approach**
A strategy for ordering questions in a questionnaire in which the sequence starts with the general questions that are followed by progressively specific questions, in order to prevent specific questions from biasing general questions.

**branching questions**
Question used to guide an interviewer through a survey by directing the interviewer to different spots on the questionnaire depending on the answers given.

---

| ACTIVE RESEARCH | DEPARTMENT STORE PROJECT |

### Form and Layout

In the department store project, the questionnaire was divided into several parts. Part A contained the qualifying question, information on familiarity, frequency of shopping, evaluation of the 10 stores on each of the eight factors of the choice criteria, and preference ratings for the 10 stores. Part B contained questions on the relative importance attached to each factor of the choice criteria and the preference rankings of the 10 stores. Part C obtained information on lifestyles. Finally, part D obtained standard demographic and identification information. Identification information was obtained along with classification information, rather than in a separate part, so as to minimize its prominence. Dividing the questionnaire into parts in this manner provided natural transitions. It also alerted the interviewer and the respondent that, as each part began, a different kind of information was being solicited.

**Figure 10.2**
Flow Chart for Questionnaire
Design

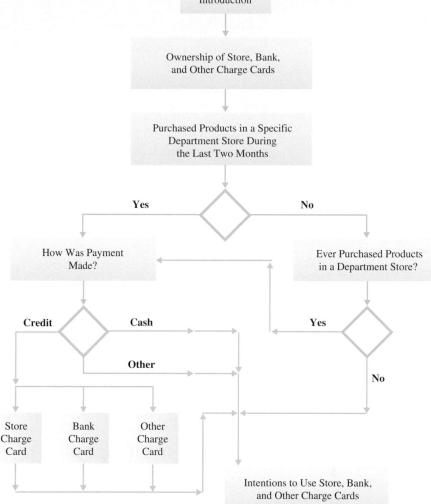

received more attention than those placed at the bottom. Instructions printed in red made little difference except that they made the questionnaire appear more complicated to the respondents.

It is a good practice to divide a questionnaire into several parts. Several parts may be needed for questions pertaining to the basic information.

The questions in each part should be numbered, particularly when branching questions are used. Numbering of questions also makes the coding of responses easier. The questionnaires should preferably be precoded. In **precoding,** the codes to enter in the computer are printed on the questionnaire. Typically, the code identifies the line number and the column numbers in which a particular response will be entered. Note that when CATI or CAPI is used, the precoding is built into the software. Coding of questionnaires is explained in more detail in Chapter 14 on data preparation. Here we give an example of a precoded questionnaire. To conserve space, only part of the questionnaire is reproduced.

**precoding**
In questionnaire design, assigning a code to every conceivable response before data collection.

## REAL RESEARCH

### *Example of a Precoded Survey from* The American Lawyer *Magazine (www.americanlawyer.com)*

**The American Lawyer**
A Confidential Survey of Our Subscribers

1. Considering all the times you pick it up, about how much time, in total, do you spend in reading or looking through a typical issue of *The American Lawyer?*

Less than 30 minutes. . . . . . . . . . ☐ -1          1 1/2 hours to 1 hour 59 minutes . . ☐ -4
30 to 59 minutes . . . . . . . . . . . . . ☐ -2          2 hours to 2 hours 59 minutes. . . . . ☐ -5
1 hour to 1 hour 29 minutes . . . . . ☐ -3          3 hours or more . . . . . . . . . . . . . . . ☐ -6

**2.** After you have finished reading an issue of *The American Lawyer,* what do you usually do with it?

Save entire issue for firm library   ☐ -1          Place in a waiting room/
Save entire issue for home use . . . ☐ -2             public area. . . . . . . . . . . . . . . . . ☐ -5
Pass it along (route it) to others                    Discard it. . . . . . . . . . . . . . . . . . . . ☐ -6
   in my company  . . . . . . . . . . . . ☐ -3          Other _____  ☐ -7
Clip and save items of interest . . . ☐ -4          (Please specify)

**3.** *Not including yourself,* how many other people, on the average, would you estimate read or look through your personal copy (not the office copy) of *The American Lawyer,*

Number of additional readers per copy:

One . . . . . . . . . ☐ -1          Five . . . . . . . . . ☐ -5          10–14 . . . . . . . ☐ -9
Two. . . . . . . . . ☐ -2          Six. . . . . . . . . . ☐ -6          15 or more  . . . ☐ -x
Three. . . . . . . . ☐ -3          Seven  . . . . . . . ☐ -7          None . . . . . . . . ☐ -0
Four  . . . . . . . . ☐ -4          8–9  . . . . . . . . ☐ -8          ■

The questionnaires themselves should be numbered serially. This facilitates the control of questionnaires in the field as well as the coding and analysis. Numbering makes it easy to account for the questionnaires and to determine if any have been lost. A possible exception to this rule is mail questionnaires. If these are numbered, respondents assume that a given number identifies a particular respondent. Some respondents may refuse to participate or may answer differently under these conditions. However, recent research suggests that this loss of anonymity has little, if any, influence on the results.[35]

# REPRODUCTION OF THE QUESTIONNAIRE

How a questionnaire is reproduced for administration can influence the results. For example, if the questionnaire is reproduced on poor-quality paper or is otherwise shabby in appearance, the respondents will think the project is unimportant and the quality of response will be adversely affected. Therefore, the questionnaire should be reproduced on good-quality paper and have a professional appearance.

When a printed questionnaire runs to several pages, it should take the form of a booklet rather than a number of sheets of paper clipped or stapled together. Booklets are easier for the interviewer and the respondents to handle and do not come apart with use as do clipped and stapled papers. They allow the use of double-page format for questions and look more professional.

Each question should be reproduced on a single page (or double-page spread). A researcher should avoid splitting a question, including its response categories. Split questions can mislead the interviewer or the respondent into thinking that the question has ended at the end of a page. This will result in answers based on incomplete questions.

Vertical response columns should be used for individual questions. It is easier for interviewers and respondents to read down a single column rather than sideways across several columns. Sideways formatting and splitting, done frequently to conserve space, should be avoided. This problem can be observed in *The American Lawyer* questionnaire (Real Research).

The tendency to crowd questions together to make the questionnaire look shorter should be avoided. Overcrowded questions with little blank space between them can lead to errors in data collection and yield shorter and less informative replies. Moreover, they give the impression that the questionnaire is complex and can result in lower cooperation and completion rates. Although shorter questionnaires are more desirable than longer ones, the reduction in size should not be obtained at the expense of crowding.

Directions or instructions for individual questions should be placed as close to the questions as possible. Instructions relating to how the question should be administered or answered by the respondent should be placed just before the question. Instructions concerning how the answer should be recorded or how the probing should be done should be placed after the question (for more information on probing and other interviewing procedures, see Chapter 13). It is a common practice to distinguish instructions from questions by using distinctive type, such as capital letters. (See the department store project in the section entitled "Type of Interviewing Method.")

Although color does not influence response rates to questionnaires, it can be employed advantageously in some respects. Color coding is useful for branching questions. The next question to which the respondent is directed is printed in a color that matches the space in which the answer to the branching question was recorded. Surveys directed at different respondent groups can be reproduced on different colored paper. In a mail survey conducted for a major telecommunications firm, the business questionnaire was printed on white paper, whereas the household questionnaire was printed on yellow paper.

The questionnaire should be reproduced in such a way that it is easy to read and answer. The type should be large and clear. Reading the questionnaire should not impose a strain. Several technologies allow researchers to obtain better print quality and simultaneously reduce costs. One effort along these lines resulted in a lowering of printing costs from $1,150 to $214.[36]

# PRETESTING

*pretesting*
The testing of the questionnaire on a small sample of respondents for the purpose of improving the questionnaire by identifying and eliminating potential problems.

*Pretesting* refers to the testing of the questionnaire on a small sample of respondents to identify and eliminate potential problems. Even the best questionnaire can be improved by pretesting. As a general rule, a questionnaire should not be used in the field survey without adequate pretesting. A pretest should be extensive, as illustrated by the Census 2000 questionnaire in the opening example. All aspects of the questionnaire should be tested, including question content, wording, sequence, form and layout, question difficulty, and instructions. The respondents in the pretest should be similar to those who will be included in the actual survey in terms of background characteristics, familiarity with the topic, and attitudes and behaviors of interest.[37] In other words, respondents for the pretest and for the actual survey should be drawn from the same population.

Pretests are best done by personal interviews, even if the actual survey is to be conducted by mail, telephone, or electronic means, because interviewers can observe respondents' reactions and attitudes. After the necessary changes have been made, another pretest could be conducted by mail, telephone, or electronic means if those methods are to be used in the actual survey. The latter pretests should reveal problems peculiar to the interviewing method. To the extent possible, a pretest should involve administering the questionnaire in an environment and context similar to that of the actual survey.

A variety of interviewers should be used for pretests. The project director, the researcher who developed the questionnaire, and other key members of the research team should conduct some pretest interviews. This will give them a good feel for potential problems and the nature of the expected data. Regular interviewers, however, should conduct most of the pretest interviews. It is good practice to employ both experienced and new interviewers. The experienced interviewers can easily perceive uneasiness, confusion, and resistance in the respondents. New interviewers can help the researcher identify interviewer-related problems. Ordinarily, the pretest sample size is small, varying from 15 to 30 respondents for the initial testing, depending on the heterogeneity of the target population. The sample size can increase substantially if the pretesting involves several stages.

Protocol analysis and debriefing are two commonly used procedures in pretesting. In protocol analysis the respondent is asked to "think aloud" while answering the questionnaire. Typically, the respondent's remarks are tape-recorded and analyzed to determine the reactions invoked by different parts of the questionnaire. Debriefing occurs after the questionnaire has been completed. Respondents are told that the questionnaire they just completed was a pretest and the objectives of pretesting are described to them. They are then asked to describe the meaning of each question, to explain their answers, and to state any problems they encountered while answering the questionnaire.

Editing involves correcting the questionnaire for the problems identified during pretesting. After each significant revision of the questionnaire, another pretest should be conducted, using a different sample of respondents. Sound pretesting involves several stages. One pretest is a bare minimum. Pretesting should be continued until no further changes are needed.

Finally, the responses obtained from the pretest should be coded and analyzed. The analysis of pretest responses can serve as a check on the adequacy of the problem definition and the data and analysis required to obtain the necessary information. The dummy tables prepared before developing the questionnaire will point to the need for the various sets of data. If the response to a question cannot be related to one of the preplanned dummy tables, either those data are superfluous, or some relevant analysis has not been foreseen. If part of a dummy table remains empty, a necessary question may have been omitted. Analysis of pretest data helps to ensure that all data collected will be utilized and that the questionnaire will obtain all the necessary data.[38]

Table 10.1 on page 304 summarizes the questionnaire design process in the form of a checklist.

# OBSERVATIONAL FORMS

Forms for recording observational data are easier to construct than questionnaires. The researcher need not be concerned with the psychological impact of the questions and the way they are asked. The researcher need only develop a form that identifies the required information clearly, makes it easy for the field worker to record the information accurately, and simplifies the coding, entry, and analysis of data.

Observational forms should specify the who, what, when, where, why, and way of behavior to be observed. In the department store project, an observational form for the study of purchases would include space for all of the following information.

---

**ACTIVE RESEARCH**  |  DEPARTMENT STORE PROJECT

### *Observation*

Who: Purchasers, browsers, males, females, parents with children, children alone
What: Products/brands considered, products/brands purchased, size, price of package inspected, influence of children or other family members
When: Day, hour, date of observation
Where: Inside the store, checkout counter, or type of department within the store
Why: Influence of price, brand name, package size, promotion, or family members on the purchase
Way: Personal observer disguised as sales clerk, undisguised personal observer, hidden camera, or obtrusive mechanical device

---

The form and layout as well as the reproduction of observational forms should follow the same guidelines discussed for questionnaires. A well-designed form permits field workers to record individual observations, but not to summarize observations as that could lead to error. Finally, like questionnaires, observational forms also require adequate pretesting.

# INTERNATIONAL MARKETING RESEARCH

The questionnaire or research instrument should be adapted to the specific cultural environment and should not be biased in terms of any one culture. This requires careful attention to each step of the questionnaire design process. The information needed should be clearly specified. It is important to take into account any differences in underlying consumer behavior, decision-making process, psychographic, lifestyle, and demographic variables. In the context of demographic characteristics, information on marital status, education, household size, occupation, income, and dwelling unit may have to be specified differently for different countries, as these variables may not be directly comparable across countries. For example, household definition and size varies greatly, given the extended family structure in some countries and the practice of two or even three families living under the same roof.

Although personal interviewing is the dominant survey method in international marketing research, different interviewing methods may be used in different countries. Hence, the questionnaire may have to be suitable for administration by more than one method. For ease of comprehension and translation, it is desirable to have two or more simple questions rather than a single complex question. In overcoming the inability to answer, the variability in the extent to which respondents in different cultures are informed about the subject matter of the survey should be taken into account. Respondents in some countries, for example in the Far East and the CIS (former Soviet Union), may not be as well informed as those in the United States.

The use of unstructured or open-ended questions may be desirable if the researcher lacks knowledge about the determinants of response in other countries. Unstructured questions also reduce cultural bias, because they do not impose any response alternatives. However, unstructured questions are more affected by differences in educational levels than structured questions. They should be used with caution in countries with high illiteracy rates. Unstructured and structured questions can be employed in a complementary way to provide rich insights, as in the following example.

### REAL RESEARCH

## *The Theme: Singapore's Theme Restaurants*

Singapore is comprised of over 60 surrounding islets and has a population of about 4 million people as of 2003 (*www.tourismsingapore.com*). Globally, it is known for its diverse restaurant industry. Out of the 22,000 food-service establishments, 21 percent are classified as restaurants. A study was conducted on the following four theme restaurants in Singapore: Hard Rock Café (*www.hardrock.com*), Planet Hollywood (*www.planethollywood.com*), Celebrities Asia, and House of Mao.

The questionnaire was pretested with 20 diners who had eaten at all four of the theme restaurants. Some revisions were made to the questionnaire based on the comments from those people. The survey was then administered to 300 participants in a questionnaire format that was designed to find out the participants' perceptions of the theme restaurants. The participants were chosen at random using a mall intercept method and by asking the participant if they had been a customer in a theme restaurant in the past year. If their answer was yes, they were asked to participate and then fill out a four-page survey. The survey was divided into two sections: section A asked about the participant's general perception of the theme restaurants, and section B asked the respondent to rate the four restaurants on a five-point scale on nine different attributes. Respondents were also asked several open-ended questions at the end of the questionnaire, such as if they thought more theme restaurants would open in Singapore in the future and if they thought these restaurants would be successful.

Most respondents felt more theme restaurants would open in Singapore and most were neutral about their success. House of Mao received the highest rating in theme concept and Hard Rock Café received the highest rating in overall experience meeting expectations. Hard Rock Café had the best overall ratings on the nine attributes. Based on this survey, there is room for growth in the theme restaurant industry in Singapore.

Theme restaurants have taken a hit in the United States the last few years, with Planet Hollywood filing for Chapter 11 bankruptcy in April 1999. Neither the Fashion Café nor the All-Star Café theme restaurants fared well after high expectations upon opening in the early 90s. These restaurants should look to countries such as Singapore in order to expand.[39] ∎

The questionnaire may have to be translated for administration in different cultures. The researcher must ensure that the questionnaires in different languages are equivalent. The special procedures designed for this purpose are discussed in Chapter 23.

## TABLE 10.1

### Questionnaire Design Checklist

Step 1    Specify the information needed.

1. Ensure that the information obtained fully addresses all the components of the problem. Review components of the problem and the approach, particularly the research questions, hypotheses, and the information needed.

2. Prepare a set of dummy tables.

3. Have a clear idea of the target population.

Step 2    Specify the type of interviewing method.

1. Review the type of interviewing method determined based on considerations discussed in Chapter 6.

Step 3    Determine the content of individual questions.

1. Is the question necessary?

2. Are several questions needed instead of one to obtain the required information in an unambiguous manner?

3. Do not use double-barreled questions.

Step 4    Design the questions to overcome the respondent's inability and unwillingness to answer.

1. Is the respondent informed?

2. If respondents are not likely to be informed, filter questions that measure familiarity, product use, and past experience should be asked before questions about the topics themselves.

3. Can the respondent remember?

4. Avoid errors of omission, telescoping, and creation.

5. Questions that do not provide the respondent with cues can underestimate the actual occurrence of an event.

6. Can the respondent articulate?

7. Minimize the effort required of the respondents.

8. Is the context in which the questions are asked appropriate?

9. Make the request for information seem legitimate.

10. If the information is sensitive:

    a. Place sensitive topics at the end of the questionnaire.

    b. Preface the question with a statement that the behavior of interest is common.

    c. Ask the question using the third-person technique.

    d. Hide the question in a group of other questions that respondents are willing to answer.

    e. Provide response categories rather than asking for specific figures.

    f. Use randomized techniques, if appropriate.

Step 5    Decide on the question structure.

1. Open-ended questions are useful in exploratory research and as opening questions.

2. Use structured questions whenever possible.

3. In multiple-choice questions, the response alternatives should include the set of all possible choices and should be mutually exclusive.

4. In a dichotomous question, if a substantial proportion of the respondents can be expected to be neutral, include a neutral alternative.

5. Consider the use of the split ballot technique to reduce order bias in dichotomous and multiple-choice questions.

6. If the response alternatives are numerous, consider using more than one question to reduce the information processing demands on the respondents.

Step 6    Determine the question wording.

1. Define the issue in terms of who, what, when, where, why, and way (the six Ws).

2. Use ordinary words. Words should match the vocabulary level of the respondents.

3. Avoid ambiguous words: usually, normally, frequently, often, regularly, occasionally, sometimes, etc.

4. Avoid leading questions that clue the respondent to what the answer should be.

5. Avoid implicit alternatives that are not explicitly expressed in the options.

6. Avoid implicit assumptions.

7. Respondent should not have to make generalizations or compute estimates.

8. Use positive and negative statements.

*(Continued)*

| TABLE 10.1 | |
|---|---|

**Questionnaire Design Checklist** *(Continued)*

Step 7    Arrange the questions in proper order.

  **1.** The opening questions should be interesting, simple, and nonthreatening.

  **2.** Qualifying questions should serve as the opening questions.

  **3.** Basic information should be obtained first, followed by classification, and, finally, identification information.

  **4.** Difficult, sensitive, or complex questions should be placed late in the sequence.

  **5.** General questions should precede the specific questions.

  **6.** Questions should be asked in a logical order.

  **7.** Branching questions should be designed carefully to cover all possible contingencies.

  **8.** The question being branched should be placed as close as possible to the question causing the branching, and the branching questions should be ordered so that the respondents cannot anticipate what additional information will be required.

Step 8    Identify the form and layout.

  **1.** Divide a questionnaire into several parts.

  **2.** Questions in each part should be numbered.

  **3.** The questionnaire should be precoded.

  **4.** The questionnaires themselves should be numbered serially.

Step 9    Reproduce the questionnaire.

  **1.** The questionnaire should have a professional appearance.

  **2.** Booklet format should be used for long questionnaires.

  **3.** Each question should be reproduced on a single page (or double-page spread).

  **4.** Vertical response columns should be used.

  **5.** Grids are useful when there are a number of related questions that use the same set of response categories.

  **6.** The tendency to crowd questions to make the questionnaire look shorter should be avoided.

  **7.** Directions or instructions for individual questions should be placed as close to the questions as possible.

Step 10    Eliminate bugs by pretesting.

  **1.** Pretesting should be done always.

  **2.** All aspects of the questionnaire should be tested, including question content, wording, sequence, form and layout, question difficulty, and instructions.

  **3.** The respondents in the pretest should be similar to those who will be included in the actual survey.

  **4.** Begin the pretest by using personal interviews.

  **5.** Pretest should also be conducted by mail or telephone if those methods are to be used in the actual survey.

  **6.** A variety of interviewers should be used for pretests.

  **7.** The pretest sample size is small, varying from 15 to 30 respondents for the initial testing.

  **8.** Use protocol analysis and debriefing to identify problems.

  **9.** After each significant revision of the questionnaire, another pretest should be conducted, using a different sample of respondents.

  **10.** The responses obtained from the pretest should be coded and analyzed.

Pretesting of the questionnaire is complicated in international research, because the linguistic equivalence must be pretested. Two sets of pretests are recommended. The translated questionnaire should be pretested on monolingual subjects in their native language. The original and translated versions should also be administered to bilingual subjects. The pretest data from administration of the questionnaire in different countries or cultures should be analyzed and the pattern of responses compared to detect any cultural biases.

# ETHICS IN MARKETING RESEARCH

Several ethical issues related to the researcher-respondent relationship and the researcher-client relationship may have to be addressed in questionnaire design. Of particular concern are the use of overly long questionnaires, asking sensitive questions, combining questions of more than one client in the same questionnaire or survey (piggybacking), and deliberately biasing the questionnaire.

Respondents are volunteering their time and should not be overburdened by soliciting too much information. The researcher should avoid overly long questionnaires. An overly long questionnaire may vary in length or completion time depending upon variables such as the topic of the survey, the effort required, the number of open-ended questions, the frequency of use of complex scales, and the method of administration. According to the guidelines of the Professional Marketing Research Society of Canada (*www.pmrs-aprm. com*), with the exception of in-home personal interviews, questionnaires that take more than 30 minutes to complete are generally considered "overly long." Personal in-home interviews can take up to 60 minutes without overloading the respondents. Overly long questionnaires are burdensome on the respondents and adversely affect the quality of responses. Similarly, questions that are confusing, exceed the respondents' ability, are difficult, or are otherwise improperly worded should be avoided.

Sensitive questions deserve special attention. On one hand, candid and honest responses are needed to generate meaningful findings. On the other hand, the researcher should not invade respondents' privacy or cause them undue stress. The guidelines we have given in this chapter should be followed. To minimize discomfort, it should be made clear at the beginning of the interview that respondents are not obligated to answer any question that makes them uncomfortable.

An important researcher-client issue is piggybacking, which occurs when a questionnaire contains questions pertaining to more than one client. This is often done in omnibus panels (see Chapters 3 and 4) that different clients can use to field their questions. Piggybacking can substantially reduce costs and can be a good way for clients to collect primary data they would not be able to afford otherwise. In these cases, all clients must be aware of and consent to the arrangement. Unfortunately, piggybacking is sometimes used without the client's knowledge for the sole purpose of increasing the research firm's profit. This is unethical.

Finally, the researcher has the ethical responsibility of designing the questionnaire so as to obtain the required information in an unbiased manner. Deliberately biasing the questionnaire in a desired direction—for example, by asking leading questions—cannot be condoned. In deciding the question structure, the most appropriate rather than the most convenient option should be adopted, as illustrated by the next example. Also, the questionnaire should be thoroughly pretested before fieldwork begins, or an ethical breach has occurred.

## REAL RESEARCH

### *Questioning International Marketing Ethics*

In designing a questionnaire, open-ended questions may be most appropriate if the response categories are not known. In a study designed to identify ethical problems in international marketing, a series of open-ended questions was used. The objective of the survey was to elicit the three most frequently encountered ethical problems, in order of priority, to Australian firms that engage in international marketing activities. After reviewing the results, the researcher tabulated and categorized them into 10 categories that occurred most often: traditional small-scale bribery; large-scale bribery; gifts, favors, and entertainment; pricing; inappropriate products or technology; tax evasion practices; illegal or immoral activities; questionable commissions to channel members; cultural differences; and involvement in political affairs. The sheer number of categories indicates that international marketing ethics should probably be questioned more closely! The use of structured questions in this case, although more convenient, would have been inappropriate, raising ethical concerns.[40] ∎

## INTERNET AND COMPUTER APPLICATIONS

The questionnaire design process outlined in this chapter also applies to Internet questionnaires. Several firms, such as Sawtooth Software (*www.sawtoothsoftware.com*) supply software and services for designing internet questionnaires. Internet questionnaires share many of the features of CAPI questionnaires. The questionnaire can be designed using a wide variety of stimuli such as graphics, pictures, advertisements, animations, sound clips, and full-motion video. Moreover, the researcher can control the amount of time that the stimuli are available to the respondents and the number of times a respondent can access each stimulus. This greatly increases the range and complexity of questionnaires that can be administered over the Internet. As in the case of CATI and CAPI, complicated skip patterns can be programmed into the questionnaire. The questions can be personalized and answers to previous questions can be inserted into subsequent questions. See, for example, *www.customersat.com*.

**REAL RESEARCH**

## *SurveySite for Web Site Evaluation*

Online marketers and Web site designers are increasingly concerned with what design features and experiences make visitors return to a site. An equally important concern is knowing what features and experiences are *undesirable* so that they can avoid including them in their site. SurveySite (*www.surveysite.com*), an online marketing research company, conducted an extensive study to address these questions.

It recruited 87 American and Canadian Web sites to participate in the study. Each site was equipped with a feedback icon so visitors could participate in a standardized survey that asked evaluative questions about the visit. The questionnaire consisted of 12 questions that fell into two broad areas: design/technical evaluation and emotional experience during the site visit. The design/technical questions were kept simple so that even respondents who were not technically savvy could answer them. These questions were asked first, in part A, and followed a logical order. Then, in part B, questions related to emotional experience were asked. All the questions were asked using seven-point rating scales except one, which was open ended. That question asked respondents what factors were most important in their decisions to return or not return to the site. The final part, part C, obtained Web usage and demographic information. The questionnaire had been extensively pretested before it was used in the study.

The results of the survey found that content was the most important factor in determining whether or not a site would receive repeat visitors. Correspondingly, "frivolous content" was the most cited reason for not returning to a site. The second most important factor in determining the repeat visit rate was whether or not the respondent found the visit enjoyable. Enjoyment may mean that visitors found the information they were looking for. Next, quality of the organization of the site and its degree of uniqueness also influence repeat visit rates. Based on the results of this survey, marketers and site designers should consider content, layout, and uniqueness when developing Web sites. Doing so will help improve the number of repeat visitors to their site.[41] ■

Many questionnaire design packages are available, especially for microcomputers. One of the well-known packages is Ci3 (*www.sawtoothsoftware.com*). Another recent release, SURVENT, by Computers for Marketing Corporation (*www.cfmc.com*), can also create, test, and prepare questionnaires and pass the completed questionnaires to compatible interviewing systems for the fieldwork. SURVEYPRO by Apian Software (*www.apian.com*) of Menlo Park, CA brings ease of use and desktop publishing capabilities to printed questionnaire design. Recent SURVEYPRO add-ons such as NetCollect or DirectCollect allow for Web publishing of surveys and automated telephone surveys respectively.[42]

## SPSS Windows

SPSS Data Entry can help the researcher in designing the questionnaire, facilitated by the drag-and-drop feature of the program.

## FOCUS ON BURKE

In developing a questionnaire, Burke ensures that it will obtain all the information specified by the marketing research problem. Certain procedures are followed to achieve this end.

1. Develop a flow chart of the information required based on the marketing research problem (see Figure 10.2).
   a. Once the entire sequence of information is laid out, the interrelationships should become clear.
   b. Match up the actual data you would expect to collect from the questionnaire against the information needs listed in the flow chart.
   c. Be specific in the objective for each area of information and data. You should be able to write an objective for each area so specifically that it guides your construction of the questions.
2. At this stage, put on your "critic's" hat and go back over the flowchart and ask:
   a. Do I need to know it and know exactly what I am going to do with it? or
   b. It would be nice to know it but I do not have to have it.

You will constantly run into the situation where the client says, "while we have the respondent's attention, this is a great opportunity to ask _____!" Burke argues strongly against adding "nice-to-know" questions.

Once the need for a question is established, Burke decides on the structure. A majority of the questions are structured questions employing multiple choices or scales. The use of unstructured questions is limited, especially in surveys administered to a large number of respondents. Considerable attention is devoted to choosing question wording. The goal is to frame questions that are simple and precise, will be understood by all respondents in the manner intended by the researcher, and will elicit accurate and unbiased responses. In deciding on the order, screening questions meant to qualify the respondents are asked first, and the demographic and personal information is obtained last. In between are questions related to the marketing research problem, arranged in a logical order. The form and layout is such that a questionnaire is often divided into parts, with each part containing questions about a specific topic. Consider the WEBNOSTICS survey questionnaire designed to assess the tactical performance of a Web site. The type of information obtained, and the order in which it is obtained, is as follows:

- Content of the Web site (informative, relevant, entertaining)
- Technical performance (time to download Web pages, use of plug-ins)
- Design/layout (cool, easy to navigate, intuitive, quality of graphics)
- Downloads (usefulness, speed, reliability, updated often)
- Links (suitability, were links explored, incoming hits)
- Purchasing (security, ease of transactions, price, quality)
- Advertising (appeal, were "click me" ads clicked?)
- Chats/threaded newsgroups (relevance, frequency of use)
- Games/contests (interest, prizes, frequency of participation)
- Privacy (trustworthiness of site, personal information requests)

Note that privacy, being a sensitive issue, is asked last.

Finally, Burke is very particular about pretesting. Every questionnaire is thoroughly pretested using the same respondents and interviewing procedures that will be used in the actual survey. If problems are discovered, the questionnaire will undergo another wave of pretesting. Superior questionnaire design has enabled Burke to generate valuable findings for its clients.

# SUMMARY

To collect quantitative primary data, a researcher must design a questionnaire or an observation form. A questionnaire has three objectives. It must translate the information needed into a set of specific questions the respondents can and will answer. It must motivate respondents to complete the interview. It must also minimize response error.

Designing a questionnaire is an art rather than a science. The process begins by specifying (1) the information needed and (2) the type of interviewing method. The next step (3) is to decide on the content of individual questions. The question should overcome the respondents' inability and unwillingness to answer (step 4). Respondents may be unable to answer if they are not informed, cannot remember, or cannot articulate the response. The unwillingness of the respondents to answer must also be overcome. Respondents may be unwilling to answer if the question requires too much effort, is asked in a situation or context deemed inappropriate, does not serve a legitimate purpose, or solicits sensitive information. Then comes the decision regarding the question structure (step 5). Questions can be unstructured (open ended) or structured to a varying degree. Structured questions include multiple-choice, dichotomous questions, and scales.

Determining the wording of each question (step 6) involves defining the issue, using ordinary words, using unambiguous words, and using dual statements. The researcher should avoid leading questions, implicit alternatives, implicit assumptions, and generalizations and estimates. Once the questions have been worded, the order in which they will appear in the questionnaire must be decided (step 7). Special consideration should be given to opening questions, type of information, difficult questions, and the effect on subsequent questions. The questions should be arranged in a logical order.

The stage is now set for determining the form and layout of the questions (step 8). Several factors are important in reproducing the questionnaire (step 9). These include: appearance, use of booklets, fitting entire question on a page, response category format, avoiding overcrowding, placement of directions, color coding, easy-to-read format, and cost. Last but not least is pretesting (step 10). Important issues are the extent of pretesting, nature of respondents, type of interviewing method, type of interviewers, sample size, protocol analysis and debriefing, and editing and analysis.

The design of observational forms requires explicit decisions about what is to be observed and how that behavior is to be recorded. It is useful to specify the who, what, when, where, why, and way of the behavior to be observed.

The questionnaire should be adapted to the specific cultural environment and should not be biased in terms of any one culture. Also, the questionnaire may have to be suitable for administration by more than one method as different interviewing methods may be used in different countries. Several ethical issues related to the researcher-respondent relationship and the researcher-client relationship may have to be addressed. The Internet and computers can greatly assist the researcher in designing sound questionnaires and observational forms.

# KEY TERMS AND CONCEPTS

questionnaire, *280*
double-barreled question, *284*
filter questions, *286*
telescoping, *286*
unstructured questions, *289*
structured questions, *290*

order or position bias, *290*
dichotomous question, *291*
leading question, *295*
implicit alternative, *295*
classification information, *297*

identification information, *297*
funnel approach, *298*
branching questions, *298*
precoding, *299*
pretesting, *301*

# EXERCISES

## *Questions*

1. What is the purpose of questionnaires and observation forms?
2. Explain how the mode of administration affects questionnaire design.
3. How would you determine whether a specific question should be included in a questionnaire?
4. What is a double-barreled question?
5. What are the reasons that respondents are unable to answer the question asked?
6. Explain the errors of omission, telescoping, and creation. What can be done to reduce such errors?

7. Explain the concepts of aided and unaided recall.
8. What are the reasons that respondents are unwilling to answer specific questions?
9. What can a researcher do to make the request for information seem legitimate?
10. Explain the use of randomized techniques in obtaining sensitive information.
11. What are the advantages and disadvantages of unstructured questions?
12. What are the issues involved in designing multiple-choice questions?

13. What are the guidelines available for deciding on question wording?
14. What is a leading question? Give an example.
15. What is the proper order for questions intended to obtain basic, classification, and identification information?
16. What guidelines are available for deciding on the form and layout of a questionnaire?
17. Describe the issues involved in pretesting a questionnaire.
18. What are the major decisions involved in designing observational forms?

## Problems

1. Develop three double-barreled questions related to flying and passengers' airline preferences. Also develop corrected versions of each question.
2. List at least 10 ambiguous words that should not be used in framing questions.
3. Do the following questions define the issue? Why or why not?
   a. What is your favorite brand of toothpaste?
   b. How often do you go on a vacation?
   c. Do you consume orange juice?
      1. Yes  2. No

4. Design an open-ended question to determine whether households engage in gardening. Also develop a multiple-choice and a dichotomous question to obtain the same information. Which form is the most desirable?
5. Formulate five questions that ask respondents to provide generalizations or estimates.
6. Develop a series of questions for determining the proportion of households with children under age 10 where child abuse takes place. Use the randomized response technique.
7. A new graduate hired by the marketing research department of a major telephone company is asked to prepare a questionnaire to determine household preferences for telephone calling cards. The questionnaire is to be administered in mall intercept interviews. Using the principles of questionnaire design, critically evaluate this questionnaire, which follows.

Household Telephone Calling Card Survey

---

**HOUSEHOLD TELEPHONE CALLING CARD SURVEY**

1. Your name _____

2. Age _____

3. Marital status _____

4. Income _____

5. Which, if any, of the following telephone calling cards do you have?
   a. _____ AT&T          b. _____ MCI
   c. _____ US Sprint      d. _____ Others

6. How frequently do you use a telephone calling card?

   Infrequently                                              Very frequently
   
   　　　1　　　2　　　3　　　4　　　5　　　6　　　7

7. What do you think of the telephone calling card offered by AT&T?

   _____

8. Suppose your household were to select a telephone calling card. Please rate the importance of the following factors in selecting a card.

   |  | Not important |  |  |  | Very important |
   |---|---|---|---|---|---|
   | a. Cost per call | 1 | 2 | 3 | 4 | 5 |
   | b. Easy of use | 1 | 2 | 3 | 4 | 5 |
   | c. Local and long-distance charges included in the same bill | 1 | 2 | 3 | 4 | 5 |
   | d. Rebates and discounts on calls | 1 | 2 | 3 | 4 | 5 |
   | e. Quality of telephone service | 1 | 2 | 3 | 4 | 5 |
   | f. Quality of customer service | 1 | 2 | 3 | 4 | 5 |

9. How important is it for a telephone company to offer a calling card?

   Not important                                            Very important
   
   　　　1　　　2　　　3　　　4　　　5　　　6　　　7

10. Do you have children living at home? _____

   Thank you for your help.

# INTERNET AND COMPUTER EXERCISES

1. IBM would like to conduct an Internet survey to determine the image of IBM PCs and the image of its major competitors (Apple, Dell, and Hewlett Packard). Develop such a questionnaire. Relevant information may be obtained by visiting the Web sites of these companies (*www.ibm.com, www.applecomputer. com, www.dell.com, www.hp.com*).

2. Develop the questionnaire in Fieldwork problem 1 using an electronic questionnaire design package such as the Ci3 System. Administer this questionnaire to 10 students using a microcomputer.

3. Develop the questionnaire in Fieldwork problem 2 using an electronic questionnaire design package. Compare your experiences in designing this questionnaire electronically and manually.

4. Visit the Web site of one of the online marketing research firms (e.g., Greenfield Online Research Center, Inc. at *www.green fieldonline.com*). Locate a survey being currently administered at this site. Critically analyze the questionnaire using the principles discussed in this chapter.

# ACTIVITIES

## *Role Playing*

1. You have just been hired as a management trainee by a firm that manufactures major appliances. Your boss has asked you to develop a questionnaire to determine how households plan, purchase, and use major appliances. This questionnaire is to be used in a nationwide study. However, you feel that you do not have the expertise or the experience to construct such a complex questionnaire. Explain this to your boss (role played by a fellow student).

2. You are working as an assistant marketing research manager with a national department store chain. Management, represented by a group of students, is concerned about the extent of shoplifting by the employees. You are assigned the task of developing a questionnaire to determine the extent of shoplifting by the employees. This questionnaire would be mailed to employees nationwide. Explain your approach to designing the questionnaire to management. (Hint: use the randomized response technique.)

## *Fieldwork*

1. Develop a questionnaire for determining how students select restaurants. Pretest the questionnaire by administering it to 10 students using personal interviews. How would you modify the questionnaire based on the pretest?

2. Develop a questionnaire for determining household preferences for popular brands of cold cereals. Administer the questionnaire to 10 female head of households using personal interviews. How would you modify the questionnaire if it was to be administered by telephone? What changes would be necessary if it was to be administered by mail?

## *Group Discussion*

1. "Because questionnaire design is an art, it is useless to follow a rigid set of guidelines. Rather, the process should be left entirely to the creativity and ingenuity of the researcher." Discuss as a small group.

2. Discuss as a small group the role of questionnaire design in minimizing total research error.

3. Discuss the importance of form and layout in questionnaire construction.

# 11

# Sampling: Design and Procedures

## Objectives

After reading this chapter, the student should be able to:

1. Differentiate a sample from a census and identify the conditions that favor the use of a sample versus a census.
2. Discuss the sampling design process: definition of the target population, determination of the sampling frame, selection of sampling technique(s), determination of sample size, and execution of the sampling process.
3. Classify sampling techniques as nonprobability and probability sampling techniques.
4. Describe the nonprobability sampling techniques of convenience, judgmental, quota, and snowball sampling.
5. Describe the probability sampling techniques of simple random, systematic, stratified, and cluster sampling.
6. Identify the conditions that favor the use of nonprobability sampling versus probability sampling.
7. Understand the sampling design process and the use of sampling techniques in international marketing research.
8. Identify the ethical issues related to the sampling design process and the use of appropriate sampling techniques.
9. Explain the use of the Internet and computers in sampling design.

Sampling is one of the components of a research design. The formulation of the research design is the third step of the marketing research process. At this stage, the information needed to address the marketing research problem has been identified and the nature of the research design (exploratory, descriptive, or causal) has been determined (Chapters 3 through 7). Furthermore, the scaling and measurement procedures have been specified (Chapters 8 and 9), and the questionnaire has been designed (Chapter 10). The next step is to design suitable sampling procedures. Sampling design involves several basic questions: (1) Should a sample be taken? (2) If so, what process should be followed? (3) What kind of sample should be taken? (4) How large should it be? and (5) What can be done to control and adjust for nonresponse errors?

This chapter introduces the fundamental concepts of sampling and the qualitative considerations necessary to answer these questions. We address the question of whether or not to sample and describe the steps involved in sampling. Next, we present nonprobability and probability sampling techniques. We discuss the use of sampling techniques in international marketing research, identify the relevant ethical issues, and describe the use of the Internet and computers for sampling. Statistical determination of sample size and the causes for, control of, and adjustments for nonresponse error are discussed in Chapter 12.

## REAL RESEARCH

### Reviving a Lame Duck

The sale of Duck Stamps by the U.S. Fish and Wildlife Service (USFWS) (*www.fws.gov*) to pay the cost of preserving the wetlands was declining. So, the USFWS brought in The Ball Group (*www.ballgroup.com*), a marketing research and advertising firm based in Lancaster, Pennsylvania, to conduct research to discover who else might be interested in purchasing the stamps and why these groups would want to purchase the stamps—what marketing should take place and what benefits the stamps were perceived as providing. The Ball Group decided to conduct focus groups and a telephone survey to determine the answers to these questions. The sampling process for the telephone survey was as follows. Duck stamps are available throughout the United States, and all U.S. citizens are affected by the preservation of the wetlands, so the population was defined to include all U.S. citizens. The sampling frame consisted of computer software for randomly and efficiently generating telephone numbers. The sample size, determined by resource constraints and sample size used in similar studies, was 1,000.

The steps in the sampling design process were as follows:

1. *Target population:* Male or female head of household; *Sampling unit:* Working telephone numbers; *Extent:* United States; *Time:* Period of the survey
2. *Sampling frame:* Computer program for randomly and efficiently generating telephone numbers excluding nonworking and business numbers
3. *Sampling technique:* Simple random sampling with modification to exclude nonworking and business telephone numbers
4. *Sample size:* 1,000
5. *Execution:* Use a computer program to randomly generate a list of household telephone numbers. Select the male or female head of household using the next birthday method. Conduct the interviews using a computer-assisted telephone interviewing (CATI) system.

An appropriate sampling design helped the U.S. Fish and Wildlife Service create effective marketing strategies for the Duck Stamp program.

The result of this research showed that people did want to help the effort, but they wanted something to show for and demonstrate their generosity. Therefore, the U.S. Fish and Wildlife Service decided to start marketing the stamps to the American public as a great way to "donate" money to help save the wetlands. For $30, in addition to receiving a stamp, the purchaser also receives a certificate saying that they helped to save the wetlands. As of 2003, the Duck Stamp program was a great success.[1] ■

This example illustrates the various steps in the sampling design process. However, before we discuss these aspects of sampling in detail, we will address the question of whether the researcher should sample or take a census.

## SAMPLE OR CENSUS

**population**
The aggregate of all the elements, sharing some common set of characteristics, that comprises the universe for the purpose of the marketing research problem.

**census**
A complete enumeration of the elements of a population or study objects.

**sample**
A subgroup of the elements of the population selected for participation in the study.

The objective of most marketing research projects is to obtain information about the characteristics or parameters of a population. A **population** is the aggregate of all the elements that share some common set of characteristics and that comprise the universe for the purpose of the marketing research problem. The population parameters are typically numbers, such as the proportion of consumers who are loyal to a particular brand of toothpaste. Information about population parameters may be obtained by taking a census or a sample. A **census** involves a complete enumeration of the elements of a population. The population parameters can be calculated directly in a straightforward way after the census is enumerated. A **sample,** on the other hand, is a subgroup of the population selected for participation in the study. Sample characteristics, called statistics, are then used to make inferences about the population parameters. The inferences that link sample characteristics and population parameters are estimation procedures and tests of hypotheses. These inference procedures are considered later in Chapters 15 through 21.

Table 11.1 summarizes the conditions favoring the use of a sample versus a census. Budget and time limits are obvious constraints favoring the use of a sample. A census is both costly and time consuming to conduct. A census is unrealistic if the population is large, as it is for most consumer products. In the case of many industrial products, however, the population is small, making a census feasible as well as desirable. For example, in investigating the use of certain machine tools by U.S. automobile manufacturers, a census would be preferred to a sample. Another reason for preferring a census in this case is that variance in the characteristic of interest is large. For example, machine tool usage of Ford

**TABLE 11.1**

**Sample versus Census**

| | CONDITIONS FAVORING THE USE OF | |
| | SAMPLE | CENSUS |
|---|---|---|
| 1. Budget | Small | Large |
| 2. Time available | Short | Long |
| 3. Population size | Large | Small |
| 4. Variance in the characteristic | Small | Large |
| 5. Cost of sampling errors | Low | High |
| 6. Cost of nonsampling errors | High | Low |
| 7. Nature of measurement | Destructive | Nondestructive |
| 8. Attention to individual cases | Yes | No |

will vary greatly from the usage of Honda. Small population sizes as well as high variance in the characteristic to be measured favor a census.

If the cost of sampling errors is high (e.g., if the sample omitted a major manufacturer such as Ford, the results could be misleading), a census, which eliminates such errors, is desirable. High cost of nonsampling errors, on the other hand, would favor sampling. A census can greatly increase nonsampling error to the point that these errors exceed the sampling errors of a sample. Nonsampling errors are found to be the major contributor to total error, whereas random sampling errors have been relatively small in magnitude (see Chapter 3).[2] Hence, in most cases, accuracy considerations would favor a sample over a census. This is one of the reasons that the U. S. Bureau of the Census checks the accuracy of various censuses by conducting sample surveys.[3] However, it is not always possible to reduce nonsampling error sufficiently to compensate for sampling error, as in the case of a study involving U.S. automobile manufacturers.

A sample may be preferred if the measurement process results in the destruction or contamination of the elements sampled. For example, product usage tests result in the consumption of the product. Therefore, taking a census in a study that requires households to use a new brand of photographic film would not be feasible. Sampling may also be necessary to focus attention on individual cases, as in the case of depth interviews. Finally, other pragmatic considerations, such as the need to keep the study secret, may favor a sample over a census.

# THE SAMPLING DESIGN PROCESS

The sampling design process includes five steps that are shown sequentially in Figure 11.1. These steps are closely interrelated and relevant to all aspects of the marketing research project, from problem definition to the presentation of the results. Therefore, sample design decisions should be integrated with all other decisions in a research project.[4]

## Define the Target Population

**target population**
The collection of elements or objects that possess the information sought by the researcher and about which inferences are to be made.

**element**
Objects that possess the information sought by the researcher and about which inferences are to be made.

**sampling unit**
The basic unit containing the elements of the population to be sampled.

Sampling design begins by specifying the target population. The ***target population*** is the collection of elements or objects that possess the information sought by the researcher and about which inferences are to be made. The target population must be defined precisely. Imprecise definition of the target population will result in research that is ineffective at best and misleading at worst. Defining the target population involves translating the problem definition into a precise statement of who should and should not be included in the sample.

The target population should be defined in terms of elements, sampling units, extent, and time. An ***element*** is the object about which or from which the information is desired. In survey research, the element is usually the respondent. A ***sampling unit*** is an element, or

*Figure 11.1*
The Sampling Design Process

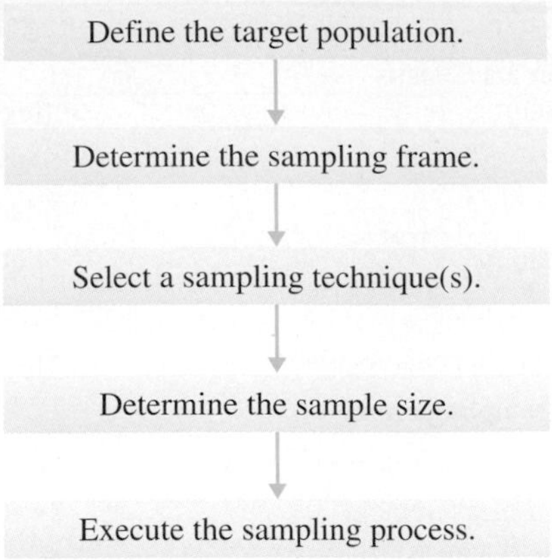

Define the target population.

↓

Determine the sampling frame.

↓

Select a sampling technique(s).

↓

Determine the sample size.

↓

Execute the sampling process.

a unit containing the element, that is available for selection at some stage of the sampling process. Suppose that Revlon wanted to assess consumer response to a new line of lipsticks and wanted to sample females over 18 years of age. It may be possible to sample females over 18 directly, in which case a sampling unit would be the same as an element. Alternatively, the sampling unit might be households. In the latter case, households would be sampled and all females over 18 in each selected household would be interviewed. Here, the sampling unit and the population element are different. Extent refers to the geographical boundaries, and the time factor is the time period under consideration. The opening duck stamps example showed an appropriate definition of a population. We use the department store project to provide another illustration.

---

**ACTIVE RESEARCH** | DEPARTMENT STORE PROJECT

***Target Population***

The target population for the department store project was defined as follows:

Elements—male or female head of the household responsible for most of the shopping at
    department stores
Sampling units—households
Extent—metropolitan Atlanta
Time—2003

---

Defining the target population may not be as easy as it was in this example. Consider a marketing research project assessing consumer response to a new brand of men's cologne. Who should be included in the target population? All men? Men who have used a cologne during the last month? Men 17 or older? Should females be included, because some women buy colognes for their husbands? These and similar questions must be resolved before the target population can be appropriately defined.[5]

## Determine the Sampling Frame

A *sampling frame* is a representation of the elements of the target population. It consists of a list or set of directions for identifying the target population. Examples of a sampling frame include the telephone book, an association directory listing the firms in an industry, a mailing list purchased from a commercial organization, a city directory, or a map. If a list cannot be compiled, then at least some directions for identifying the target population should be specified, such as random digit dialing procedures in telephone surveys (see Chapter 6). In the opening duck stamp example, the sampling frame consisted of a computer program for randomly and efficiently generating telephone numbers excluding non-working and business numbers.

Often it is possible to compile or obtain a list of population elements, but the list may omit some elements of the population or include other elements that do not belong.

Therefore, the use of a list will lead to sampling frame error, which was discussed in Chapter 3.[6]

In some instances, the discrepancy between the population and the sampling frame is small enough to ignore. However, in most cases, the researcher should recognize and treat the sampling frame error. This can be done in at least three ways. One approach is to redefine the population in terms of the sampling frame. If the telephone book is used as a sampling frame, the population of households could be redefined as those with a correct listing in the telephone book in a given area. Although this approach is simplistic, it does prevent the researcher from being misled about the actual population being investigated.[7]

Another way is to account for sampling frame error by screening the respondents in the data-collection phase. The respondents could be screened with respect to demographic characteristics, familiarity, product usage, and other characteristics to ensure that they satisfy the criteria for the target population. Screening can eliminate inappropriate elements contained in the sampling frame, but it cannot account for elements that have been omitted.

Yet another approach is to adjust the data collected by a weighting scheme to counterbalance the sampling frame error. This is discussed in Chapter 12 and also in Chapter 14. Regardless of which approach is adopted, it is important to recognize any sampling frame error that exists, so that inappropriate population inferences can be avoided.

## Select a Sampling Technique

Selecting a sampling technique involves several decisions of a broader nature. The researcher must decide whether to use a Bayesian or traditional sampling approach, to sample with or without replacement, and to use nonprobability or probability sampling.

*Bayesian approach*

A selection method where the elements are selected sequentially. The Bayesian approach explicitly incorporates prior information about population parameters as well as the costs and probabilities associated with making wrong decisions.

In the ***Bayesian approach,*** the elements are selected sequentially. After each element is added to the sample, the data are collected, sample statistics computed, and sampling costs determined. The Bayesian approach explicitly incorporates prior information about population parameters as well as the costs and probabilities associated with making wrong decisions. This approach is theoretically appealing. Yet, it is not used widely in marketing research because much of the required information on costs and probabilities is not available. In the traditional sampling approach, the entire sample is selected before data collection begins. Because the traditional approach is most commonly used, this is the approach assumed in the following sections.

*sampling with replacement*

A sampling technique in which an element can be included in the sample more than once.

*sampling without replacement*

A sampling technique in which an element cannot be included in the sample more than once.

In ***sampling with replacement,*** an element is selected from the sampling frame and appropriate data are obtained. Then the element is placed back in the sampling frame. As a result, it is possible for an element to be included in the sample more than once. In ***sampling without replacement,*** once an element is selected for inclusion in the sample, it is removed from the sampling frame and, therefore, cannot be selected again. The calculation of statistics is done somewhat differently for the two approaches, but statistical inference is not very different if the sampling frame is large relative to the ultimate sample size. Thus the distinction is important only when the sampling frame is not large compared to the sample size.

The most important decision about the choice of sampling technique is whether to use probability or nonprobability sampling. Given its importance, the issues involved in this decision are discussed in great detail in this chapter.

If the sampling unit is different from the element, it is necessary to specify precisely how the elements within the sampling unit should be selected. In in-home personal interviews and telephone interviews, merely specifying the address or the telephone number may not be sufficient. For example, should the person answering the doorbell or the telephone be interviewed, or someone else in the household? Often, more than one person in a household may qualify. For example, both the male and female heads of household may be eligible to participate in a study examining family leisure-time activities. When a probability sampling technique is being employed, a random selection must be made from all the eligible persons in each household. A simple procedure for random selection is the next birthday method. The interviewer asks which of the eligible persons in the household has the next birthday and includes that person in the sample, as in the opening duck stamps example.

## Determine the Sample Size

*Sample size* refers to the number of elements to be included in the study. Determining the sample size is complex and involves several qualitative and quantitative considerations. The qualitative factors are discussed in this section, and the quantitative factors are considered in Chapter 12. Important qualitative factors that should be considered in determining the sample size include: (1) the importance of the decision, (2) the nature of the research, (3) the number of variables, (4) the nature of the analysis, (5) sample sizes used in similar studies, (6) incidence rates, (7) completion rates, and (8) resource constraints.

In general, for more important decisions, more information is necessary and the information should be obtained more precisely. This calls for larger samples, but as the sample size increases, each unit of information is obtained at greater cost. The degree of precision may be measured in terms of the standard deviation of the mean. The standard deviation of the mean is inversely proportional to the square root of the sample size. The larger the sample, the smaller the gain in precision by increasing the sample size by one unit.

The nature of the research also has an impact on the sample size. For exploratory research designs, such as those using qualitative research, the sample size is typically small. For conclusive research, such as descriptive surveys, larger samples are required. Likewise, if data are being collected on a large number of variables, larger samples are required. The cumulative effects of sampling error across variables are reduced in a large sample.

If sophisticated analysis of the data using multivariate techniques is required, the sample size should be large. The same applies if the data are to be analyzed in great detail. Thus, a larger sample would be required if the data are being analyzed at the subgroup or segment level than if the analysis is limited to the aggregate or total sample.

Sample size is influenced by the average size of samples in similar studies. Table 11.2 gives an idea of sample sizes used in different marketing research studies. These sample sizes have been determined based on experience and can serve as rough guidelines, particularly when nonprobability sampling techniques are used.

Finally, the sample size decision should be guided by a consideration of the resource constraints. In any marketing research project, money and time are limited. Other constraints include the availability of qualified personnel for data collection. In the opening duck stamp example, the sample size of 1,000 was determined by resource constraints and the sample size used in similar studies. The sample size required should be adjusted for the incidence of eligible respondents and the completion rate, as explained in the next chapter.

### TABLE 11.2

**Sample Sizes Used in Marketing Research Studies**

| TYPE OF STUDY | MINIMUM SIZE | TYPICAL RANGE |
|---|---|---|
| Problem identification research (e.g., market potential) | 500 | 1,000–2,500 |
| Problem solving research (e.g., pricing) | 200 | 300–500 |
| Product tests | 200 | 300–500 |
| Test-marketing studies | 200 | 300–500 |
| TV/Radio/Print advertising (per commercial or ad tested) | 150 | 200–300 |
| Test-market audits | 10 stores | 10–20 stores |
| Focus groups | 6 groups | 10–15 groups |

## Execute the Sampling Process

Execution of the sampling process requires a detailed specification of how the sampling design decisions with respect to the population, sampling frame, sampling unit, sampling technique, and sample size are to be implemented. If households are the sampling unit, an operational definition of a household is needed. Procedures should be specified for vacant housing units and for callbacks in case no one is at home. Detailed information must be provided for all sampling design decisions.

---

**REAL RESEARCH**

### *Tourism Department Telephones Birthday Boys and Girls*

A telephone survey was conducted for the Florida Department of Tourism (*www.myflorida.com*) to gain an understanding of the travel behavior of in-state residents. In 2003, there were approximately 16 million Florida residents. The households were stratified by north, central, and south Florida regions. A computerized random-digit sample was used to reach these households. Households were screened to locate family members who met four qualifications:

1. Age 25 or older
2. Live in Florida at least seven months of the year
3. Have lived in Florida for at least two years
4. Have a Florida driver's license

To obtain a representative sample of qualified individuals, a random method was used to select the respondent from within a household. All household members meeting the four qualifications were listed and the person with the next birthday was selected. Repeated callbacks were made to reach that person. The steps in the sampling design process were as follows.

1. *Target population:* adults meeting the four qualifications (element) in a household with a working telephone number (sampling unit) in the state of Florida (extent) during the survey period (time)
2. *Sampling frame:* computer program for generating random telephone numbers
3. *Sampling technique:* stratified sampling. The target population was geographically stratified into three regions: north, central, and south Florida.
4. *Sample size:* 868
5. *Execution:* Allocate the sample among strata; use computerized random-digit dialing; list all the members in the household who meet the four qualifications; select one member of the household using the next birthday method.[8] ▪

Surveys based on sound sampling designs have helped the Florida Department of Tourism market the state to in-state as well as out-of-state customers.

An appropriate sampling design process enabled the Florida Department of Tourism to gain valuable insights into the travel behavior of in-state residents. The opening duck stamp example provides another illustration of the sampling design process.

## A CLASSIFICATION OF SAMPLING TECHNIQUES

*nonprobability sampling*
Sampling techniques that do not use chance selection procedures. Rather, they rely on the personal judgment of the researcher.

Sampling techniques may be broadly classified as nonprobability and probability (see Figure 11.2). ***Nonprobability sampling*** relies on the personal judgment of the researcher rather than chance to select sample elements. The researcher can arbitrarily or consciously decide what elements to include in the sample. Nonprobability samples may yield good estimates of the population characteristics. However, they do not allow for objective evaluation of the precision of the sample results. Because there is no way of determining the probability of selecting any particular element for inclusion in the sample, the estimates obtained are not statistically projectable to the population. Commonly used nonprobability sampling techniques include convenience sampling, judgmental sampling, quota sampling, and snowball sampling.

*probability sampling*
A sampling procedure in which each element of the population has a fixed probabilistic chance of being selected for the sample.

In ***probability sampling,*** sampling units are selected by chance. It is possible to prespecify every potential sample of a given size that could be drawn from the population, as well as the probability of selecting each sample. Every potential sample need not have the same probability of selection, but it is possible to specify the probability of selecting any particular sample of a given size. This requires not only a precise definition of the target population, but also a general specification of the sampling frame. Because sample elements are selected by chance, it is possible to determine the precision of the sample

*Figure 11.2*
A Classification of Sampling Techniques

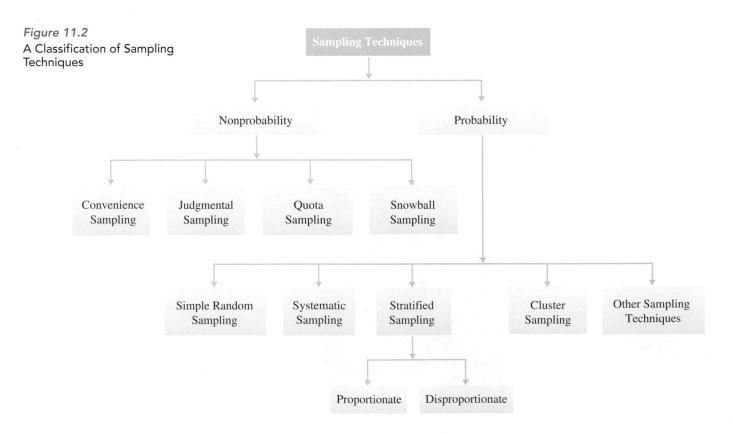

estimates of the characteristics of interest. Confidence intervals, which contain the true population value with a given level of certainty, can be calculated. This permits the researcher to make inferences or projections about the target population from which the sample was drawn. Probability sampling techniques are classified based on:

- Element versus cluster sampling
- Equal unit probability versus unequal probabilities
- Unstratified versus stratified selection
- Random versus systematic selection
- Single-stage versus multistage techniques

All possible combinations of these five aspects result in 32 different probability sampling techniques. Of these techniques, we consider simple random sampling, systematic sampling, stratified sampling, and cluster sampling in depth and briefly touch on some others. First, however, we discuss nonprobability sampling techniques.

# NONPROBABILITY SAMPLING TECHNIQUES

## Convenience Sampling

**convenience sampling**
A nonprobability sampling technique that attempts to obtain a sample of convenient elements. The selection of sampling units is left primarily to the interviewer.

*Convenience sampling* attempts to obtain a sample of convenient elements. The selection of sampling units is left primarily to the interviewer. Often, respondents are selected because they happen to be in the right place at the right time. Examples of convenience sampling include: (1) use of students, church groups, and members of social organizations, (2) mall intercept interviews without qualifying the respondents, (3) department stores using charge account lists, (4) tear-out questionnaires included in a magazine, and (5) "people on the street" interviews.[9]

Convenience sampling is the least expensive and least time consuming of all sampling techniques. The sampling units are accessible, easy to measure, and cooperative. In spite of these advantages, this form of sampling has serious limitations. Many potential sources of selection bias are present, including respondent self-selection. Convenience samples are not representative of any definable population. Hence, it is not theoretically meaningful to generalize to any population from a convenience sample, and convenience samples are not appropriate for marketing research projects involving population inferences. Convenience samples are not recommended for descriptive or causal research, but they can be used in exploratory research for generating ideas, insights, or hypotheses. Convenience samples can be used for focus groups, pretesting questionnaires, or pilot studies. Even in these cases, caution should be exercised in interpreting the results. Nevertheless, this technique is sometimes used even in large surveys.

### REAL RESEARCH

## *Olympic Convenience*

The International Olympic Committee (IOC—*www.olympic.org*) used surveys at the 2000 Summer Olympics in Sydney to find out what visitors thought about the level of commercialism in Sydney. One survey was given to a convenience sample of 200 visitors to the games and they were asked about the level of commercialism they find appropriate, whether they thought the event was too commercial, and whether company sponsorship of the Games was perceived to be positive. The survey, conducted by Performance Research (*www.performanceresearch.com*), revealed that 77 percent of the visitors found the presence of large corporations such as Coca-Cola (*www.cocacola.com*) and McDonald's (*www.mcdonalds.com*) to be appropriate. Furthermore, 88 percent of the visitors thought the sponsors contributed to the Olympics positively. About 33 percent said that they thought that a company's involvement in Sydney made them feel more positive about that company in general.

Performance Research continued their study of Olympic sponsorship by conducting 900 telephone, 1,500 Internet, and 300 on-site surveys using convenience samples in conjunction with the 2002 Winter Olympics in Salt Lake City, Utah. The results with respect to

When surveys based on convenience sampling indicated positive perceptions of sponsoring companies, Visa advertised in conjunction with the 2002 Winter Olympics in Salt Lake City, Utah.

companies' sponsorship and involvement in the Olympics were again positive. The IOC used this formation to enhance sponsorship revenues. For the 2002 Games, 30-second advertising spots were priced at roughly $600,000. Some companies that advertised were Coca-Cola, Visa, Kodak, McDonald's, Panasonic, Sports Illustrated, and Xerox.[10] ■

## Judgmental Sampling

**judgmental sampling**
A form of convenience sampling in which the population elements are purposively selected based on the judgment of the researcher.

*Judgmental sampling* is a form of convenience sampling in which the population elements are selected based on the judgment of the researcher. The researcher, exercising judgment or expertise, chooses the elements to be included in the sample, because he or she believes that they are representative of the population of interest or are otherwise appropriate. Common examples of judgmental sampling include: (1) test markets selected to determine the potential of a new product, (2) purchase engineers selected in industrial marketing research because they are considered to be representative of the company, (3) bellwether precincts selected in voting behavior research, (4) expert witnesses used in court, and (5) department stores selected to test a new merchandising display system.

**ACTIVE RESEARCH**    DEPARTMENT STORE PROJECT

*Sampling Technique*

In the department store study, 20 census tracts in the metropolitan area were selected based on judgment. Tracts with very poor people and those with undesirable (high-crime-rate) areas were excluded. In each tract, blocks judged to be representative or typical were selected. Finally, households located 10 houses apart from each other were selected within each block. The interviewer instructions were as follows.

"Start at the southeast corner of the designated block. Go around the entire block in a clockwise manner. After completing an interview, skip 10 households to select the next one. However, go to the next dwelling unit if you encounter any of following situations: respondent not at home, respondent refuses to cooperate, or no qualified respondent is available. After completing a block, go to the next assigned block and follow the same procedure until you obtain the required number of completed interviews."

In this example, judgment was used to select specific tracts, blocks, and households. Judgmental sampling is low cost, convenient, and quick, yet it does not allow direct generalizations to a specific population, usually because the population is not defined explicitly. Judgmental sampling is subjective and its value depends entirely on the researcher's judgment, expertise, and creativity. It may be useful if broad population inferences are not required. As in the department store example, judgment samples are frequently used in commercial marketing research projects. An extension of this technique involves the use of quotas.

## Quota Sampling

*quota sampling*
A nonprobability sampling technique that is a two-stage restricted judgmental sampling. The first stage consists of developing control categories or quotas of population elements. In the second stage, sample elements are selected based on convenience or judgment.

*Quota sampling* may be viewed as two-stage restricted judgmental sampling. The first stage consists of developing control categories, or quotas, of population elements. To develop these quotas, the researcher lists relevant control characteristics and determines the distribution of these characteristics in the target population. The relevant control characteristics, which may include sex, age, and race, are identified on the basis of judgment. Often, the quotas are assigned so that the proportion of the sample elements possessing the control characteristics is the same as the proportion of population elements with these characteristics. In other words, the quotas ensure that the composition of the sample is the same as the composition of the population with respect to the characteristics of interest. In the second stage, sample elements are selected based on convenience or judgment. Once the quotas have been assigned, there is considerable freedom in selecting the elements to be included in the sample. The only requirement is that the elements selected fit the control characteristics.[11]

### REAL RESEARCH

### *Does Metropolitan Magazine Readership Measure Up?*

A study is undertaken to determine the readership of certain magazines by the adult population of a metropolitan area with a population of 350,000. A quota sample of 1,000 adults is selected. The control characteristics are sex, age, and race. Based on the composition of the adult population of the community, the quotas are assigned as follows.

| Control Characteristic | Population Composition Percentage | Sample Composition Percentage | Number |
|---|---|---|---|
| Sex | | | |
| Male | 48 | 48 | 480 |
| Female | 52 | 52 | 520 |
| | 100 | 100 | 1,000 |
| Age | | | |
| 18–30 | 27 | 27 | 270 |
| 31–45 | 39 | 39 | 390 |
| 45–60 | 16 | 16 | 160 |
| Over 60 | 18 | 18 | 180 |
| | 100 | 100 | 1,000 |
| Race | | | |
| White | 59 | 59 | 590 |
| Black | 35 | 35 | 350 |
| Other | 6 | 6 | 60 |
| | 100 | 100 | 1,000 ∎ |

Quota sampling can be highly effective in determining magazine readership.

In this example, quotas are assigned such that the composition of the sample is the same as that of the population. In certain situations, however, it is desirable either to under- or oversample elements with certain characteristics. To illustrate, it may be desirable to oversample heavy users of a product so that their behavior can be examined in detail. Although this type of sample is not representative, it may nevertheless be very relevant.

Even if the sample composition mirrors that of the population with respect to the control characteristics, there is no assurance that the sample is representative. If a characteristic that is relevant to the problem is overlooked, the quota sample will not be representative. Relevant control characteristics are often omitted, because there are practical difficulties associated with including many control characteristics. Because the elements within each quota are selected based on convenience or judgment, many sources of selection bias are potentially present. The interviewers may go to selected areas where eligible respondents are more likely to be found. Likewise, they may avoid people who look unfriendly, are not well dressed, or live in undesirable locations. Quota sampling does not permit assessment of sampling error.

Quota sampling attempts to obtain representative samples at a relatively low cost. Its advantages are the lower costs and greater convenience to the interviewers in selecting elements for each quota. Recently, tighter controls have been imposed on interviewers and interviewing procedures that tend to reduce selection bias, and guidelines have been suggested for improving the quality of mall intercept quota samples. Under certain conditions, quota sampling obtains results close to those for conventional probability sampling.[12]

## Snowball Sampling

**snowball sampling**
A nonprobability sampling technique in which an initial group of respondents is selected randomly. Subsequent respondents are selected based on the referrals or information provided by the initial respondents. This process may be carried out in waves by obtaining referrals from referrals.

In **snowball sampling,** an initial group of respondents is selected, usually at random. After being interviewed, these respondents are asked to identify others who belong to the target population of interest. Subsequent respondents are selected based on the referrals. This process may be carried out in waves by obtaining referrals from referrals, thus leading to a snowballing effect. Even though probability sampling is used to select the initial respondents, the final sample is a nonprobability sample. The referrals will have demographic and psychographic characteristics that are more similar to the persons referring them than would occur by chance.[13]

A major objective of snowball sampling is to estimate characteristics that are rare in the population. Examples include users of particular government or social services, such as food stamps, whose names cannot be revealed; special census groups, such as widowed males under 35; and members of a scattered minority population. Snowball sampling is used in industrial buyer-seller research to identify buyer-seller pairs. The major advantage of snowball sampling is that it substantially increases the likelihood of locating the desired characteristic in the population. It also results in relatively low sampling variance and costs.[14]

### Knowledge Is Power

Everyday there are hundreds of people who are infected with HIV and contract the AIDS virus. A study was undertaken to examine the risk behavior of Indo-Chinese drug users (IDUs). A structured questionnaire was administered to 184 IDUs aged 15 to 24. Respondents were recruited using snowball sampling techniques "based on social and street networks." This technique was used because drug users know other drug users and can easily provide referrals for research purposes. Respondents were asked numerous questions regarding their drug use, injection-related risk behaviors, and perceived susceptibility to HIV. Interviews were held in Melbourne and in Sydney. Locations of interviews varied from on the streets, to restaurants and coffee shops, and even in people's homes.

The results showed that heroin was the first drug injected for 98 percent of the respondents, and 86 percent of them stated they smoked the drug prior to intravenous use. Age for the first injection varied from 11 years to 23 years, averaging 17 years. Thirty-six percent "ever shared" a needle, 23 percent of those shared with a close friend, and 1 percent shared with a partner or lover. The awareness of blood-borne viruses and related complications was low. Based on these results, the public health officials in Australia decided to launch a vigorous campaign to educate the IDUs of the risks they faced and what they could do to reduce them.[15] ■

In this example, snowball sampling was more efficient than random selection. In other cases, random selection of respondents through probability sampling techniques is more appropriate.

# PROBABILITY SAMPLING TECHNIQUES

Probability sampling techniques vary in terms of sampling efficiency. Sampling efficiency is a concept that reflects a tradeoff between sampling cost and precision. Precision refers to the level of uncertainty about the characteristic being measured. Precision is inversely related to sampling errors but positively related to cost. The greater the precision, the greater the cost, and most studies require a tradeoff. The researcher should strive for the most efficient sampling design, subject to the budget allocated. The efficiency of a probability sampling technique may be assessed by comparing it to that of simple random sampling.

## Simple Random Sampling

**simple random sampling (SRS)**
A probability sampling technique in which each element in the population has a known and equal probability of selection. Every element is selected independently of every other element and the sample is drawn by a random procedure from a sampling frame.

In *simple random sampling* (SRS), each element in the population has a known and equal probability of selection. Furthermore, each possible sample of a given size ($n$) has a known and equal probability of being the sample actually selected. This implies that every element is selected independently of every other element. The sample is drawn by a random procedure from a sampling frame. This method is equivalent to a lottery system in which names are placed in a container, the container is shaken, and the names of the winners are then drawn out in an unbiased manner.

To draw a simple random sample, the researcher first compiles a sampling frame in which each element is assigned a unique identification number. Then random numbers are generated to determine which elements to include in the sample. The random numbers may be generated with a computer routine or a table (see Table 1 shown in the Appendix of Statistical Tables). Suppose that a sample of size 10 is to be selected from a sampling frame containing 800 elements. This could be done by starting with row 1 and column 1 of Table 1, considering the three rightmost digits, and going down the column until 10 numbers between 1 and 800 have been selected. Numbers outside this range are ignored. The elements corresponding to the random numbers generated constitute the sample. Thus, in our example, elements 480, 368, 130, 167, 570, 562, 301, 579, 475, and 553 would be selected. Note that the last three digits of row 6 (921) and row 11 (918) were ignored, because they were out of range.

SRS has many desirable features. It is easily understood. The sample results may be projected to the target population. Most approaches to statistical inference assume that the data have been collected by simple random sampling. However, SRS suffers from at least four significant limitations. First, it is often difficult to construct a sampling frame that will permit a simple random sample to be drawn. Second, SRS can result in samples that are very large or spread over large geographic areas, thus increasing the time and cost of data collection. Third, SRS often results in lower precision with larger standard errors than other probability sampling techniques. Fourth, SRS may or may not result in a representative sample. Although samples drawn will represent the population well on average, a given simple random sample may grossly misrepresent the target population. This is more likely if the size of the sample is small. For these reasons, SRS is not widely used in marketing research. Procedures such as systematic sampling are more popular.

## Systematic Sampling

**systematic sampling**
A probability sampling technique in which the sample is chosen by selecting a random starting point and then picking every *i*th element in succession from the sampling frame.

In *systematic sampling,* the sample is chosen by selecting a random starting point and then picking every *i*th element in succession from the sampling frame. The sampling interval, *i,* is determined by dividing the population size *N* by the sample size *n* and rounding to the nearest integer. For example, there are 100,000 elements in the population and a sample of 1,000 is desired. In this case, the sampling interval, *i,* is 100. A random number between 1 and 100 is selected. If, for example, this number is 23, the sample consists of elements 23, 123, 223, 323, 423, 523, and so on.[16]

Systematic sampling is similar to SRS in that each population element has a known and equal probability of selection. However, it is different from SRS in that only the permissible samples of size *n* that can be drawn have a known and equal probability of selection. The remaining samples of size *n* have a zero probability of being selected.

For systematic sampling, the researcher assumes that the population elements are ordered in some respect. In some cases, the ordering (for example, alphabetic listing in a telephone book) is unrelated to the characteristic of interest. In other instances, the ordering is directly related to the characteristic under investigation. For example, credit card customers may be listed in order of outstanding balance, or firms in a given industry may be ordered according to annual sales. If the population elements are arranged in a manner unrelated to the characteristic of interest, systematic sampling will yield results quite similar to SRS.

On the other hand, when the ordering of the elements is related to the characteristic of interest, systematic sampling increases the representativeness of the sample. If firms in an industry are arranged in increasing order of annual sales, a systematic sample will include some small and some large firms. A simple random sample may be unrepresentative because it may contain, for example, only small firms or a disproportionate number of small firms. If the ordering of the elements produces a cyclical pattern, systematic sampling may decrease the representativeness of the sample. To illustrate, consider the use of systematic sampling to generate a sample of monthly department store sales from a sampling frame containing monthly sales for the last 60 years. If a sampling interval of 12 is chosen, the resulting sample would not reflect the month-to-month variation in sales.[17]

Systematic sampling is less costly and easier than SRS, because random selection is done only once. Moreover, the random numbers do not have to be matched with individual elements as in SRS. Because some lists contain millions of elements, considerable time can be saved. This reduces the costs of sampling. If information related to the characteristic of interest is available for the population, systematic sampling can be used to obtain a more representative and reliable (lower sampling error) sample than SRS. Another relative advantage is that systematic sampling can even be used without knowledge of the composition (elements) of the sampling frame. For example, every *i*th person leaving a department store or mall can be intercepted. For these reasons, systematic sampling is often employed in consumer mail, telephone, mall intercept, and Internet interviews.

### REAL RESEARCH

### *Autos.msn.com Equips Autos with Cell Phone Accessories*

Autos.msn.com is a Microsoft-owned Web site (*autos.msn.com*) that gives auto pricing and other vehicle research information to consumers. It conducted a poll to find out if people currently use or would consider using the cell phone hands-free devices. *Autos.msn.com* conducted an Internet survey using systematic random sampling that popped up on a separate screen when every 50th visitor stopped at the Web site. Of the 879 individuals who were presented with the survey, 836 responded.

The results indicated that 62 percent of the respondents had never used a hands-free device, and only 54 percent were willing to use one in the future. In light of the realization that individuals are not too receptive to the idea of attaching hands-free devices to their cellular phones, it is predicted that by the year 2006, 65 percent of the vehicles in the country will be equipped with cell phone accessories. This will take place as a result of state laws that will increasingly be passed in the next few years. In some states, such as New York, where the law went into effect in November, 2001, handheld cell phone use while driving has already been banned completely.[18] ■

## Stratified Sampling

**stratified sampling**

A probability sampling technique that uses a two-step process to partition the population into subpopulations, or strata. Elements are selected from each stratum by a random procedure.

*Stratified sampling* is a two-step process in which the population is partitioned into subpopulations, or strata. The strata should be mutually exclusive and collectively exhaustive in that every population element should be assigned to one and only one stratum and no population elements should be omitted. Next, elements are selected from each stratum by a random procedure, usually SRS. Technically, only SRS should be employed in selecting the elements from each stratum. In practice, sometimes systematic sampling and other probability sampling procedures are employed. Stratified sampling differs from quota sampling in that the sample elements are selected probabilistically rather than based on convenience or judgment. A major objective of stratified sampling is to increase precision without increasing cost.[19]

The variables used to partition the population into strata are referred to as stratification variables. The criteria for the selection of these variables consist of homogeneity, heterogeneity, relatedness, and cost. The elements within a stratum should be as homogeneous as possible, but the elements in different strata should be as heterogeneous as possible. The stratification variables should also be closely related to the characteristic of interest. The more closely these criteria are met, the greater the effectiveness in controlling extraneous sampling variation. Finally, the variables should decrease the cost of the stratification process by being easy to measure and apply. Variables commonly used for stratification include demographic characteristics (as illustrated in the example for quota sampling), type of customer (credit card versus non-credit card), size of firm, or type of industry. It is possible to use more than one variable for stratification, although more than two are seldom used because of pragmatic and cost considerations. The number of strata to use is a matter of judgment, but experience suggests the use of no more than six. Beyond six strata, any gain in precision is more than offset by the increased cost of stratification and sampling.

### REAL RESEARCH

### *Online Retirement Plans Are On*

CIGNA Retirement and Investment Services (*www.cigna.com*) achieved revenues of $19 billion in 2001. CIGNA conducted a national stratified marketing research survey to learn more about online users' demands for additional Internet retirement services. CIGNA contracted RoperASW (*www.roperasw.com*) to survey by telephone 659 full-time employees over the age of 18 with a quota of 80 percent of those surveyed to be participants in a retirement plan, such as a pension or 401(k) plan through their employer. The sample was stratified by income and age because of differences in the use of the Internet and possible varying concerns on retirement services. The sampling design adopted is shown in the table.

The survey revealed that results did vary by income and age, confirming the usefulness of these variables for stratification. For example, 75 percent of those with annual income less than $20,000 had not conducted at least one e-commerce Internet transaction, whereas only 30 percent of those with income of $50,000 or more had not done so. Age was an important factor in users' preferences for online retirement plan information, with those over 65 expressing the least preference.

Overall, the results of the survey showed that there is an increasing interest in employees having access to their retirement programs and funds online, which gives them greater control in their retirement planning. CIGNA used the survey results to offer AnswerNet and CIGNATrade, Web sites that allow customers to access their retirement plans and brokerage accounts, respectively. In Spring 2002, CIGNA and Yahoo! offered CIGNA health care members and retirement plan participants the opportunity to have personalized benefits Web sites based on the My Yahoo! interface.[20]

### Sampling Design

| | |
|---|---|
| **Target population** | Adults meeting qualifications: over 18 years old, full-time employment in the United States, working telephone number, 80 percent currently participate in retirement plan during the survey period |
| **Sampling frame** | Commercial phone list provided by RoperASW |
| **Sampling technique** | Stratified sampling by age and income |
| **Sample size** | 659 |
| **Execution** | Allocate sample by strata, select random phone number from list, survey first qualified household member subject to quota requirements ■ |

Another important decision involves the use of proportionate or disproportionate sampling (see Figure 11.2). In proportionate stratified sampling, the size of the sample drawn from each stratum is proportionate to the relative size of that stratum in the total population. In disproportionate stratified sampling, the size of the sample from each stratum is proportionate to the relative size of that stratum and to the standard deviation of the distribution of the characteristic of interest among all the elements in that stratum. The logic behind disproportionate sampling is simple. First, strata with larger relative sizes are more influential in determining the population mean, and these strata should also exert a greater influence in deriving the sample estimates. Consequently, more elements should be drawn from strata of larger relative size. Second, to increase precision, more elements should be drawn from strata with larger standard deviations and fewer elements should be drawn from strata with smaller standard deviations. (If all the elements in a stratum are identical, a sample size of one will result in perfect information.) Note that the two methods are identical if the characteristic of interest has the same standard deviation within each stratum.

Disproportionate sampling requires that some estimate of the relative variation, or standard deviation of the distribution of the characteristic of interest, within strata be known. As this information is not always available, the researcher may have to rely on intuition and logic to determine sample sizes for each stratum. For example, large retail stores might be expected to have greater variation in the sales of some products as compared to small stores. Hence, the number of large stores in a sample may be disproportionately large. When the researcher is primarily interested in examining differences between strata, a common sampling strategy is to select the same sample size from each stratum.

Stratified sampling can ensure that all the important subpopulations are represented in the sample. This is particularly important if the distribution of the characteristic of interest in the population is skewed. For example, because most households have annual incomes of less than $50,000, the distribution of household incomes is skewed. Very few households have annual incomes of $125,000 or more. If a simple random sample is taken, households with incomes of $125,000 or more may not be adequately represented. Stratified sampling would guarantee that the sample contains a certain number of these households. Stratified sampling combines the simplicity of SRS with potential gains in precision. Therefore, it is a popular sampling technique.

## Cluster Sampling

In *cluster sampling,* the target population is first divided into mutually exclusive and collectively exhaustive subpopulations, or clusters. Then a random sample of clusters is selected, based on a probability sampling technique such as SRS. For each selected cluster, either all the elements are included in the sample or a sample of elements is drawn

**cluster sampling**
First, the target population is divided into mutually exclusive and collectively exhaustive subpopulations called clusters. Then, a random sample of clusters is selected based on a probability sampling technique such as simple random sampling. For each selected cluster, either all the elements are included in the sample or a sample of elements is drawn probabilistically.

*Figure 11.3*
Types of Cluster Sampling

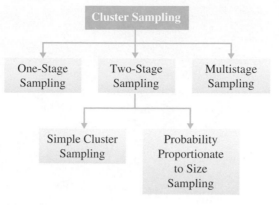

probabilistically. If all the elements in each selected cluster are included in the sample, the procedure is called one-stage cluster sampling. If a sample of elements is drawn probabilistically from each selected cluster, the procedure is two-stage cluster sampling. As shown in Figure 11.3, two-stage cluster sampling can be either simple two-stage cluster sampling involving SRS, or probability proportionate to size (PPS) sampling. Furthermore, a cluster sample can have multiple (more than two) stages, as in multistage cluster sampling.

The key distinction between cluster sampling and stratified sampling is that in cluster sampling, only a sample of subpopulations (clusters) is chosen, whereas in stratified sampling, all the subpopulations (strata) are selected for further sampling. The objectives of the two methods are also different. The objective of cluster sampling is to increase sampling efficiency by decreasing costs. The objective of stratified sampling is to increase precision. With respect to homogeneity and heterogeneity, the criteria for forming clusters are just the opposite of that for forming strata. Elements within a cluster should be as heterogeneous as possible, but clusters themselves should be as homogeneous as possible. Ideally, each cluster should be a small-scale representation of the population. In cluster sampling, a sampling frame is needed only for those clusters selected for the sample.

**area sampling**
A common form of cluster sampling in which the clusters consist of geographic areas such as counties, housing tracts, blocks, or other area descriptions.

A common form of cluster sampling is ***area sampling***, in which the clusters consist of geographic areas, such as counties, housing tracts, or blocks. If only one level of sampling takes place in selecting the basic elements (for example, the researcher samples blocks and then all the households within the selected blocks are included in the sample), the design is called single-stage area sampling. If two (or more) levels of sampling take place before the basic elements are selected (the researcher samples blocks, and then samples households within selected blocks), the design is called two (multi)-stage area sampling. The distinguishing feature of the one-stage area sample is that all of the households in the selected blocks (or geographic areas) are included in the sample.

There are two types of two-stage designs, as shown in Figure 11.3. One type involves SRS at the first stage (e.g., sampling blocks) as well as the second stage (e.g., sampling households within blocks). This design is called simple two-stage cluster sampling. In this design, the fraction of elements (e.g., households) selected at the second stage is the same for each sample cluster (e.g., selected blocks).

## REAL RESEARCH

### Blocks with Bucks

A marketing research project investigated the behavior of affluent consumers. A simple random sample of 800 block groups was selected from a listing of neighborhoods with average incomes exceeding $50,000 in the states ranked in the top half by income according to census data. Commercial list organizations supplied head-of-household names and addresses for approximately 95 percent of the census-tabulated homes in these 800 block groups. From the 213,000 enumerated households, 9,000 were selected by simple random sampling.[21] ∎

Two-stage area sampling has been used to select affluent households.

This design is appropriate when the clusters are equal in size, i.e., the clusters contain approximately the same number of sampling units. However, if they differ greatly in size, simple two-stage cluster sampling can lead to biased estimates. Sometimes, the clusters can be made of equal size by combining clusters. When this option is not feasible, probability proportionate to size (PPS) sampling can be used.

*probability proportionate to size sampling*
A selection method where the clusters are selected with probability proportional to size and the probability of selecting a sampling unit in a selected cluster varies inversely with the size of the cluster.

In *probability proportionate to size sampling,* the clusters are sampled with probability proportional to size. The size of a cluster is defined in terms of the number of sampling units within that cluster. Thus, in the first stage, large clusters are more likely to be included than small clusters. In the second stage, the probability of selecting a sampling unit in a selected cluster varies inversely with the size of the cluster. Thus, the probability that any particular sampling unit will be included in the sample is equal for all units, because the unequal first-stage probabilities are balanced by the unequal second-stage probabilities. The numbers of sampling units included from the selected clusters are approximately equal.

Cluster sampling has two major advantages: feasibility and low cost. In many situations, the only sampling frames readily available for the target population are clusters, not population elements. It is often impossible to compile a list of all consumers in a population, given the resources and constraints. However, lists of geographical areas, telephone exchanges, and other clusters of consumers can be constructed relatively easily. Cluster sampling is the most cost-effective probability sampling technique. This advantage must be weighed against several limitations. Cluster sampling results in relatively imprecise samples and it is difficult to form heterogeneous clusters, because, for example, households in a block tend to be similar rather than dissimilar.[22] It can be difficult to compute and interpret statistics based on clusters. The strengths and weaknesses of cluster sampling and the other basic sampling techniques are summarized in Table 11.3. Exhibit 11.1 describes the procedures for drawing probability samples.

## Other Probability Sampling Techniques

In addition to the four basic probability sampling techniques, there are a variety of other sampling techniques. Most of these may be viewed as extensions of the basic techniques and were developed to address complex sampling problems. Two techniques with some relevance to marketing research are sequential sampling and double sampling.

*sequential sampling*
A probability sampling technique in which the population elements are sampled sequentially, data collection and analysis are done at each stage, and a decision is made as to whether additional population elements should be sampled.

In *sequential sampling,* the population elements are sampled sequentially, data collection and analysis are done at each stage, and a decision is made as to whether additional population elements should be sampled. The sample size is not known in advance, but a decision rule is stated before sampling begins. At each stage, this rule indicates whether sampling should be continued or whether enough information has been

## TABLE 11.3

**Strengths and Weaknesses of Basic Sampling Techniques**

| TECHNIQUE | STRENGTHS | WEAKNESSES |
|---|---|---|
| *Nonprobability Sampling* | | |
| Convenience sampling | Least expensive, least time consuming, most convenient | Selection bias, sample not representative, not recommended for descriptive or causal research |
| Judgmental sampling | Low cost, convenient, not time consuming | Does not allow generalization, subjective |
| Quota sampling | Sample can be controlled for certain characteristics | Selection bias, no assurance of representativeness |
| Snowball sampling | Can estimate rare characteristics | Time consuming |
| *Probability Sampling* | | |
| Simple random sampling (SRS) | Easily understood, results projectable | Difficult to construct sampling frame, expensive, lower precision, no assurance of representativeness |
| Systematic sampling | Can increase representativeness, easier to implement than SRS, sampling frame not necessary | Can decrease representativeness |
| Stratified sampling | Includes all important subpopulations, precision | Difficult to select relevant stratification variables, not feasible to stratify on many variables, expensive |
| Cluster sampling | Easy to implement, cost effective | Imprecise, difficult to compute and interpret results |

obtained. Sequential sampling has been used to determine preferences for two competing alternatives. In one study, respondents were asked which of two alternatives they preferred, and sampling was terminated when sufficient evidence was accumulated to validate a preference. It has also been used to establish the price differential between a standard model and a deluxe model of a consumer durable.[23]

**double sampling**
A sampling technique in which certain population elements are sampled twice.

In **double sampling,** also called two-phase sampling, certain population elements are sampled twice. In the first phase, a sample is selected and some information is collected from all the elements in the sample. In the second phase, a subsample is drawn from the original sample and additional information is obtained from the elements in the subsample. The process may be extended to three or more phases, and the different phases may take place simultaneously or at different times. Double sampling can be useful when no sampling frame is readily available for selecting final sampling units but when the elements of the frame are known to be contained within a broader sampling frame. For example, a researcher wants to select households that consume apple juice in a given city. The households of interest are contained within the set of all households, but the researcher does not know which they are. In applying double sampling, the researcher would obtain a sampling frame of all households in the first phase. This would be constructed from the city directory or purchased. Then a sample of households would be drawn, using systematic random sampling to determine the amount of apple juice consumed. In the second phase, households that consume apple juice would be selected and stratified according to the amount of apple juice consumed. Then a stratified random sample would be drawn and detailed questions regarding apple juice consumption asked.[24]

# CHOOSING NONPROBABILITY VERSUS PROBABILITY SAMPLING

The choice between nonprobability and probability samples should be based on considerations such as the nature of the research, relative magnitude of nonsampling versus sampling errors, variability in the population, as well as statistical and operational considerations (see Table 11.4). For example, in exploratory research, the findings are treated as preliminary and the use of probability sampling may not be warranted. On the other hand,

Exhibit 11.1

Procedures for Drawing
Probability Samples

*Simple Random Sampling*

1. Select a suitable sampling frame.
2. Each element is assigned a number from 1 to $N$ (population size).
3. Generate $n$ (sample size) different random numbers between 1 and $N$. This can be done using a microcomputer or mainframe software package or using a table of simple random numbers (Table 1 in the Appendix of Statistical Tables). To use Table 1, select the appropriate number of digits (e.g., if $N = 900$, select three digits). Arbitrarily select a beginning number. Then proceed either up or down until $n$ different numbers between 1 and $N$ have been selected. Note, discard 0, duplicate numbers, and numbers greater than $N$.
4. The numbers generated denote the elements which should be included in the sample.

*Systematic Sampling*

1. Select a suitable sampling frame.
2. Each element is assigned a number from 1 to $N$ (population size).
3. Determine the sampling interval, $i$, $i = \dfrac{N}{n}$. If $i$ is a fraction, round to the nearest integer.
4. Select a random number, $r$, between 1 and $i$, as explained in simple random sampling.
5. The elements with the following numbers will comprise the systematic random sample: $r, r + i, r + 2i, r + 3i, r + 4i, \ldots, r + (n-1)i$.

*Stratified Sampling*

1. Select a suitable sampling frame.
2. Select the stratification variable(s) and the number of strata ($H$).
3. Divide the entire population into $H$ strata. Based on the classification variable, each element of the population is assigned to one of the $H$ strata.
4. In each stratum, number the elements from 1 to $N_h$ (the population size of stratum $h$).
5. Determine the sample size of each stratum, $n_h$, based on proportionate or disproportionate stratified sampling. Note, $\displaystyle\sum_{h=1}^{H} n_h = n$
6. In each stratum, select a simple random sample of size $n_h$.

*Cluster Sampling*

We describe the procedure for selecting a two-stage PPS sample, because this represents the most commonly used general case.

1. Assign a number, from 1 to $N$, to each element in the population.
2. Divide the population into C clusters, of which $c$ will be included in the sample.
3. Calculate the sampling interval, $i$, $i = \dfrac{N}{c}$. If $i$ is a fraction, round to the nearest integer.
4. Select a random number, $r$, between 1 and $i$, as explained in simple random sampling.
5. Identify elements with the following numbers: $r, r + i, r + 2i, r + 3i, \ldots, r + (c-1)i$.
6. Select the clusters which contain the identified elements.
7. Select sampling units within each selected cluster based on SRS or systematic sampling. The number of sampling units selected from each sample cluster is approximately the same and equal to $\dfrac{n}{c}$.
8. If the population of a cluster exceeds the sampling interval, $i$, that cluster is selected with certainty. That cluster is removed from further consideration. Calculate the new population size, $N^*$, number of clusters to be selected, $c^*$ ($= c - 1$), and the new sampling interval, $i^*$. Repeat this process until each of the remaining clusters has a population less than the relevant sampling interval. If $b$ clusters have been selected with certainty, select the remaining $c - b$ clusters according to steps 1 through 7. The fraction of units to be sampled from each cluster selected with certainty is the overall sampling fraction = $n/N$. Thus, for clusters selected with certainty we would select
$$n_s = \frac{n}{N}(N_1 + N_2 + \ldots + N_b)$$ units. The units selected from clusters selected under PPS sampling will therefore be $n^* = n - n_s$.

**TABLE 11.4**

**Choosing Nonprobability versus Probability Sampling**

| FACTORS | CONDITIONS FAVORING THE USE OF | |
| --- | --- | --- |
| | NONPROBABILITY SAMPLING | PROBABILITY SAMPLING |
| Nature of research | Exploratory | Conclusive |
| Relative magnitude of sampling and nonsampling errors | Nonsampling errors are larger | Sampling errors are larger |
| Variability in the population | Homogeneous (low) | Heterogeneous (high) |
| Statistical considerations | Unfavorable | Favorable |
| Operational considerations | Favorable | Unfavorable |

in conclusive research where the researcher wishes to use the results to estimate overall market shares or the size of the total market, probability sampling is favored. Probability samples allow statistical projection of the results to a target population. For these reasons, probability sampling was used in the opening duck stamp example.

For some research problems, highly accurate estimates of population characteristics are required. In these situations, the elimination of selection bias and the ability to calculate sampling error make probability sampling desirable. However, probability sampling will not always result in more accurate results. If nonsampling errors are likely to be an important factor, then nonprobability sampling may be preferable, as the use of judgment may allow greater control over the sampling process.

Another consideration is the homogeneity of the population with respect to the variables of interest. A more heterogeneous population would favor probability sampling, because it would be more important to secure a representative sample. Probability sampling is preferable from a statistical viewpoint, as it is the basis of the most common statistical techniques.

However, probability sampling is sophisticated and requires statistically trained researchers. It generally costs more and takes longer than nonprobability sampling. In many marketing research projects, it is difficult to justify the additional time and expense. Therefore, in practice, the objectives of the study dictate which sampling method will be used, as in the following example.

**REAL RESEARCH**

## *Laboring Labor Statistics*

The Bureau of Labor Statistics (*www.bls.gov*) publishes employment measurements on a monthly basis. The BLS traditionally used a quota sampling method, which cut off the sample when a certain number of responses were met for each type of employer in a specific industry or labor sector. In June 2000, the bureau applied a new technique for estimating jobs in the wholesale trade sector, which included suppliers for large retailers, construction contractors, hospitals, and farms. The new technique was stratified sampling that stratified employers by labor sectors. Within each stratum, employers were selected at random so that a true representation of the employment numbers could be obtained. The quota method was not adapted every year to account for the actual percentage of each type of employer within the sector. For instance, the number of farming employers is decreasing, whereas hospital and medical-related employers are on the rise, which would require changes in the quota percentages. The quota method is scheduled to be phased out for all sectors by June 2003.

Probabilistic sampling provides better estimates of employment statistics because it selects employers at random within each labor sector. The sampling estimates can be projected to the population and sampling errors estimated. Patricia M. Getz, division chief for the bureau's Current Employment Statistics division, describes probabilistic sampling as "the recognized standard—more scientifically based."[25] ∎

# USES OF NONPROBABILITY AND PROBABILITY SAMPLING

Nonprobability sampling is used in concept tests, package tests, name tests, and copy tests, where projections to the populations are usually not needed. In such studies, interest centers on the proportion of the sample that gives various responses or expresses various attitudes. Samples for these studies can be drawn using methods such as mall intercept quota sampling. On the other hand, probability sampling is used when there is a need for highly accurate estimates of market share or sales volume for the entire market. National market tracking studies, which provide information on product category and brand usage rates, as well as psychographic and demographic profiles of users, use probability sampling. Studies that use probability sampling generally employ telephone interviews. Stratified and systematic sampling are combined with some form of random-digit dialing to select the respondents.

# INTERNATIONAL MARKETING RESEARCH

Implementing the sampling design process in international marketing research is seldom an easy task. Several factors should be considered in defining the target population. The relevant element (respondent) may differ from country to country. In the United States, children play an important role in the purchase of children's cereals. However, in countries with authoritarian child-rearing practices, the mother may be the relevant element. Women play a key role in the purchase of automobiles and other durables in the United States; in male-dominated societies, such as in the Middle East, such decisions are made by men. Accessibility also varies across countries. In Mexico, houses cannot be entered by strangers because of boundary walls and servants. Additionally, dwelling units may be unnumbered and streets unidentified, making it difficult to locate designated households.[26]

Developing an appropriate sampling frame is a difficult task. In many countries, particularly in developing countries, reliable information about the target population may not be available from secondary sources. Government data may be unavailable or highly biased. Population lists may not be available commercially. The time and money required to compile these lists may be prohibitive. For example, in Saudi Arabia, there is no officially recognized census of population, no elections, and hence no voter registration records, and no accurate maps of population centers. In this situation, the interviewers could be instructed to begin at specified starting points and to sample every $n$th dwelling, until the specified number of units has been sampled.

Given the lack of suitable sampling frames, the inaccessibility of certain respondents, such as women in some cultures, and the dominance of personal interviewing, probability sampling techniques are uncommon in international marketing research. Quota sampling has been used widely in the developed and developing countries in both consumer and industrial surveys. Snowball sampling is also appealing when the characteristic of interest is rare in the target population or when respondents are hard to reach. For example, it has been suggested that in Saudi Arabia graduate students be employed to hand-deliver questionnaires to relatives and friends. These initial respondents can be asked for referrals to other potential respondents, and so on. This approach would result in a large sample size and a high response rate.

Sampling techniques and procedures vary in accuracy, reliability, and cost from country to country. If the same sampling procedures are used in each country, the results may not be comparable. To achieve comparability in sample composition and representativeness, it may be desirable to use different sampling techniques in different countries.

## REAL RESEARCH

### *Achieving Sample Comparability Through Diversity*

Research in the United States has shown that most consumers feel that a purchase is accompanied by a degree of risk when they choose among alternative brands. A study was conducted to compare the U.S. results with those from Mexico, the Netherlands, Turkey, Thailand, and Saudi Arabia. The targeted respondent in each culture was an upper-middle-income woman residing in a major city. However, differences in sampling occurred across the countries. In the United States, random sampling from the telephone directory was used. In Mexico, judgmental sampling was used by having experts identify neighborhoods where the target respondent lived; homes were then randomly selected for personal interviews. In Thailand, judgmental sampling was also used, but the survey took place in major urban centers and a store intercept technique was used to select respondents. Finally, in Saudi Arabia, convenience sampling employing the snowball procedure was used, because there were no lists from which sampling frames could be drawn and social customs prohibited spontaneous personal interviews. Thus, comparability in sample composition and representativeness was achieved by using different sampling procedures in different countries.[27] ■

# ETHICS IN MARKETING RESEARCH

The researcher has several ethical responsibilities to both the client and the respondents in the sampling process. Pertaining to the client, the researcher must develop a sampling design that is appropriate for controlling the sampling and nonsampling errors (see Chapter 3). When appropriate, probability sampling should be used. When nonprobability sampling is used, effort should be made to obtain a representative sample. It is unethical and misleading to treat nonprobability samples as probability samples and to project the results to a target population. As the following example demonstrates, appropriate definition of the population and the sampling frame and application of the correct sampling techniques are essential if the research is to be conducted and the findings used ethically.

**REAL RESEARCH**

*Systematic Sampling Reveals Systematic Gender Differences in Ethical Judgments*

In an attempt to explore differences in research ethics judgments between male and female marketing professionals, data were obtained from 420 respondents. The population was defined as marketing professionals, and the sampling frame was the American Marketing Association directory. The respondents were selected based on a systematic sampling plan from the directory. Attempts were made to overcome nonresponse by not only mailing a cover letter and a stamped preaddressed return envelope along with the questionnaire, but also by promising to provide each respondent with a copy of the research study results. Results of the survey showed that female marketing professionals, in general, demonstrated higher levels of research ethical judgments than their male counterparts.[28] ■

Researchers must be sensitive to preserving the anonymity of the respondents when conducting business-to-business research, employee research, and other projects in which the population size is small. When the population size is small, it is easier to discern the identities of the respondents than when the samples are drawn from a large population. Sampling details that are too revealing or verbatim quotations in reports to the client can compromise the anonymity of the respondents. In such situations, the researcher has the ethical obligation to protect the identities of the respondents, even if it means limiting the level of sampling detail that is reported to the client and other parties.

# INTERNET AND COMPUTER APPLICATIONS

Sampling potential respondents who are surfing the Internet is meaningful if the sample that is generated is representative of the target population. More and more industries are meeting this criterion. In software, computers, networking, technical publishing, semiconductors, and graduate education, it is rapidly becoming feasible to use the Internet for sampling respondents for quantitative research, such as surveys. For internal customer surveys, where the client's employees share a corporate e-mail system, an Intranet survey is practical even if workers have no access to the external Internet. However, sampling on the Internet is not yet practical for many noncomputer-oriented consumer products.

To avoid sampling errors, the researcher must be able to control the pool from which the respondents are selected. Also, it must be ensured that the respondents do not respond multiple times ("stuff the ballot box"). These requirements are met by e-mail surveys, where the researcher selects specific respondents. Furthermore, the surveys can be encoded to match the returned surveys with their corresponding outbound e-mailings. This can also be accomplished with Web surveys by e-mailing invitations to selected respondents and asking them to visit the Web site where the survey is posted. In this case, the survey is posted in a hidden location on the Web that is protected by a password. Hence, uninvited Web surfers are unable to access it.

Nonprobability as well as probability sampling techniques can be implemented on the Internet. Moreover, the respondents can be prerecruited or tapped online. Tapping visitors to a Web site is obviously an example of convenience sampling. Based on the researcher's judgment, certain qualifying criteria can be introduced to prescreen the respondents. Even quotas can be imposed. However, the extent to which the quotas will be met is limited by the number as well as the characteristics of the visitors to the site.

Likewise, simple random sampling is commonly used. To prevent gathering information always from the same professional respondents (here, professional means that respondents take a lot of online surveys to get points), and so not to have a nonrepresentative sample, some companies, such as Millward Brown Intelliquest (*www.intelliquest.com*), use a "click-stream intercept." In this method, online users are randomly sampled and given the opportunity to participate or decline. Various other forms of probability sampling can also be implemented, some techniques, such as systematic random sampling, with relative ease.

## REAL RESEARCH

## Random Sampling and Pop-Up Surveys

SurveySite is a full-service research firm based out of Ontario, Canada (*www.surveysite. com*). SurveySite's mission is to provide "leading-edge and innovative Web site evaluation systems and market research to the Internet community." Its goal is to be the "undisputed leader in quality Web site research and visitor analysis." In 2001, SurveySite conducted a survey to determine Canada's perception of the high-tech industry compared to the United States. Three thousand Canadian IT managers were surveyed and the results revealed that Canadians perceive themselves to have fallen behind in technology compared to the United States. Many respondents noted that Australia was a more realistic country to compare Canada to, instead of the United States.

One research program SurveySite offers is the "Pop-Up Survey." The product counts the number of people that visit a Web site and selects visitors at a predetermined interval. For example, every 100th person to click on a client's Web site is selected based on systematic random sampling. When this happens, a small Java script pops up. The script requests the user to complete a short online survey. If the visitor clicks no, the Java script disappears and the person continues browsing. If the visitor clicks yes, a client-designed survey appears.

The advantage to this "pop-up" model is that it significantly increases the user response rate. The typical survey method offers a banner that asks visitors to take the survey. The banners, however, tend to have a very poor response rate. In general, the rate is about 0.02 percent or 1 out of every 500 visitors. The SurveySite "pop-up" dramatically improves the response rate, and it enables data collection to be reduced from weeks to days.

As a result, SurveySite's Internet research strategy has helped the Internet research firm to land corporate clients such as Timex, Delta Hotels, Toronto-Dominion Bank, Kellogg's, and Canadian Tire.[29] ▪

Microcomputers and mainframes can make the sampling design process more effective and efficient. Computers can be used for specifying the sampling frame, because they can handle lists of population elements as well as geographical maps.

Microcomputers and mainframes may be employed to select the sample needed, using either nonprobability or probability techniques. Once the sampling frame has been determined, simulations can be used to generate random numbers and select the sample directly from the database. Software such as SPSS, SAS, MINITAB, or EXCEL can be used for this purpose. Specialized programs, such as GENESYS sampling systems for telephone interviewing, provide the market researcher the power to compose an accurate Random Digit Dialing (RDD) sample, avoiding the waste of dialing nonproductive numbers during surveys.

## FOCUS ON BURKE

Burke makes use of a variety of sampling techniques depending on the nature and objectives of the project. Of the nonprobability sampling techniques, quota sampling is used most often, primarily in conjunction with mall intercept interviews, such as Opinion One surveys (see Focus on Burke in Chapter 6). In these projects, the interest is mainly in the relative evaluation of stimuli (e.g., different advertisements) rather than in projecting the results to the population. When the projections are of interest, as in estimating sales and market shares of specific brands, probability techniques are used to select the sample. Simple random sampling is used to select respondents from a mailing list and for generating telephone numbers for CATI surveys using modified forms of random-digit dialing. Burke has developed efficient procedures for eliminating nonproductive telephone numbers generated in this manner (e.g., eliminating nonworking numbers, duplicates, business numbers from household surveys). Systematic sampling has been used to select respondents for Internet surveys. Burke's WEBNOSTICS surveys assessing the tactical performance of a Web site make use of the randomized $n$th ($i$th in terms of the terminology used in the book) visitor methodology to sample Internet respondents. For every $n$th ($i$th) visitor to the client's Web site, a frame pops into view on the visitor's browser, requesting participation in a survey and offering incentives to do so. As is the case with physical world research, the Web visitor has the opportunity to decline participation. By using systematic sampling, Burke is able to avoid respondent self-selection bias, which plagues a simple "click me" button placed on a site to collect online information.

Another probability sampling technique that Burke uses widely is stratified sampling. In several projects the population is stratified by demographic or other variables to ensure that certain segments are included in the sample and to increase precision. A key issue that Burke faces in such projects is whether to select proportionate or disproportionate stratified sampling. Burke recently conducted a project for a company that had developed an annuity investment product targeted to women. The client had decided to stratify the women using two variables: age (under 35 years old, and 35 and over), and marital status (never married, and ever married). The client's original specification called for 100 respondents in each of the four resulting strata. By looking at census data, Burke found these groups to be distributed in the population as:

| | |
|---|---|
| women 15 to 34 and never married: | 10.4% |
| women 35 plus and never married: | 3.4% |
| women 15 to 34 and ever married: | 22.3% |
| women 35 plus and ever married: | 64.0% |

Clearly, the cost of finding a sample of 35 plus and never married would be considerable, given the very low incidence of such women in the population (3.4%). Secondly, the weighting considerations for analyzing the data would be very complicating (see Chapter 14). Without going into statistical details, it is sufficient to say that this degree of weighting would seriously increase the variance of the final estimate compared to a proportionately selected representative sample. Therefore, Burke recommended to the client that proportionate stratified sampling be used, because the client was interested in making projections to the overall women's market, not to any specific segments. Burke is very sensitive to the client's needs. Suppose in this case, the client considered the 3.4 percent of 35-plus and never-married women as an important niche market for which separate estimates were needed. In that case, the client's need would have taken priority over cost savings and the negative consequences of extreme weighting, and Burke would have gone along with the client's original specification. In sum, Burke adopts a sampling design that is in the best interest of the client.

# SUMMARY

Information about the characteristics of a population may be obtained by conducting either a sample or a census. Budget and time limits, large population size, and small variance in the characteristic of interest favor the use of a sample. Sampling is also preferred when the cost of sampling error is low, the cost of nonsampling error is high, the nature of measurement is destructive, and attention must be focused on individual cases. The opposite set of conditions favor the use of a census.

Sampling design begins by defining the target population in terms of elements, sampling units, extent, and time. Then the sampling frame should be determined. A sampling frame is a representation of the elements of the target population. It consists of a list of directions for identifying the target population. At this stage, it is important to recognize any sampling frame errors that may exist. The next steps involve selecting a sampling technique and determining the sample size. In addition to quantitative analysis, several qualitative considerations should be taken into account in determining the sample size. Finally, execution of the sampling process requires detailed specifications for each step in the sampling process.

Sampling techniques may be classified as nonprobability and probability techniques. Nonprobability sampling techniques rely on the researcher's judgment. Consequently, they do not permit an objective evaluation of the precision of the sample results, and the estimates obtained are not statistically projectable to the population. The commonly used nonprobability sampling techniques include convenience sampling, judgmental sampling, quota sampling, and snowball sampling.

In probability sampling techniques, sampling units are selected by chance. Each sampling unit has a nonzero chance of being selected and the researcher can prespecify every potential sample of a given size that could be drawn from the population, as well as the probability of selecting each sample. It is also possible to determine the precision of the sample estimates and inferences and make projections to the target population. Probability sampling techniques include simple random sampling, systematic sampling, stratified sampling, cluster sampling, sequential sampling, and double sampling. The choice between probability and nonprobability sampling should be based on the nature of the research, the degree of error tolerance, the relative magnitude of sampling and nonsampling errors, the variability in the population, and statistical and operational considerations.

When conducting international marketing research, it is desirable to achieve comparability in sample composition and representativeness even though this may require the use of different sampling techniques in different countries. It is unethical and misleading to treat nonprobability samples as probability samples and project the results to a target population. The Internet and computers can be used to make the sampling design process more effective and efficient.

# KEY TERMS AND CONCEPTS

population, *314*
census, *314*
sample, *314*
target population, *315*
element, *315*
sampling unit, *315*
sampling frame, *316*
Bayesian approach, *317*
sampling with replacement, *317*

sampling without replacement, *317*
sample size, *318*
nonprobability sampling, *320*
probability sampling, *320*
convenience sampling, *321*
judgmental sampling, *322*
quota sampling, *323*
snowball sampling, *324*
simple random sampling (SRS), *325*

systematic sampling, *326*
stratified sampling, *327*
cluster sampling, *328*
area sampling, *329*
probability proportionate to size sampling, *330*
sequential sampling, *330*
double sampling, *331*

# EXERCISES

## Questions

1. What is the major difference between a sample and a census?
2. Under what conditions would a sample be preferable to a census? A census preferable to a sample?
3. Describe the sampling design process.
4. How should the target population be defined?
5. What is a sampling unit? How is it different from the population element?
6. What qualitative factors should be considered in determining the sample size?
7. What are incidence rates? How do they affect the sample size?
8. How do probability sampling techniques differ from nonprobability sampling techniques?
9. What is the least expensive and least time consuming of all sampling techniques? What are the major limitations of this technique?
10. What is the major difference between judgmental and convenience sampling?
11. What is the relationship between quota sampling and judgmental sampling?
12. What are the distinguishing features of simple random sampling?
13. Describe the procedure for selecting a systematic random sample.

14. Describe stratified sampling. What are the criteria for the selection of stratification variables?
15. What are the differences between proportionate and disproportionate stratified sampling?
16. Describe the cluster sampling procedure. What is the key distinction between cluster sampling and stratified sampling?
17. What factors should be considered in choosing between probability and nonprobability sampling?
18. What strategies are available for adjusting for nonresponse?

## Problems

1. Define the appropriate target population and the sampling frame in each of the following situations:
   a. The manufacturer of a new cereal brand wants to conduct in-home product usage tests in Chicago.
   b. A national chain store wants to determine the shopping behavior of customers who have its store charge card.
   c. A local TV station wants to determine households' viewing habits and programming preferences.
   d. The local chapter of the American Marketing Association wants to test the effectiveness of its new member drive in Atlanta.
2. A manufacturer would like to survey users to determine the demand potential for a new power press. The new press has a capacity of 500 tons and costs $225,000. It is used for forming products from lightweight and heavyweight steel and can be used by automobile, construction equipment, and major appliance manufacturers.
   a. Identify the population and sampling frame that could be used.
   b. Describe how a simple random sample can be drawn using the identified sampling frame.
   c. Could a stratified sample be used? If so, how?
   d. Could a cluster sample be used? If so, how?
   e. Which sampling technique would you recommend? Why?

# INTERNET AND COMPUTER EXERCISES

1. P&G would like to conduct a survey of consumer preferences for toothpaste brands in California. Stratified random sampling will be used. Visit *www.census.gov* to identify information that will be relevant in determining income and age strata.
2. Using software such as GENESYS, generate a random-digit telephone sample of 1,000 people in your metropolitan area.
3. Generate the quota sample described in Role Playing question 1 using a microcomputer.
4. Using a microcomputer or mainframe program, generate a set of 1,000 random numbers for selecting a simple random sample.
5. Visit the SurveySite Web site. Examine the Internet surveys being conducted. Write a report about the sampling plans being used.

# ACTIVITIES

## Role Playing

1. The alumni office of your university would like to conduct a survey to determine alumni's attitudes toward a new fund-raising program. As a consultant, you must develop a quota sample. What quota variables and levels of variables should be used? How many alumni should be included in each cell? Obtain the necessary information from the alumni office or the library on your campus and present your results to a group of students representing the alumni office.
2. You work as a marketing research manager for a major New York City bank. Management would like to know if the banking habits of different ethnic groups differ. They wonder whether, given the varied population of New York City, it is meaningful to segment the market according to ethnic background. A survey will be conducted. You have been asked to design an appropriate sampling process. Complete the assignment and make a presentation of your results to a group of students representing the bank management.

## Fieldwork

1. A major software firm wants to determine the use of spreadsheets by: (1) manufacturing firms, (2) service organizations, and (3) educational institutions located in the state of California. Using the resources available in your library, develop an appropriate sampling plan.
2. Visit a local marketing research firm. Determine what procedures the firm uses for online sample control in telephone interviews. Summarize your findings in a report.

## Group Discussion

1. "Given that the U.S. Bureau of the Census uses sampling to check on the accuracy of various censuses, a constitutional amendment should be passed replacing the decennial census with a sample." Discuss as a small group.
2. "Because nonsampling errors are greater in magnitude than sampling errors, it really does not matter which sampling technique is used." Discuss this statement.

# Sampling: Final and Initial Sample Size Determination

"The size of the sample you ultimately take will depend on your budget, the economic importance of the decisions, and the variability in the population. Two of the three are managerial issues for you to determine, only the third (variability) is outside your control."

Brenda Landy,
senior account executive,
client services,
Burke, Inc.

## Objectives

After reading this chapter, the student should be able to:

1. Define key concepts and symbols pertinent to sampling.
2. Understand the concepts of the sampling distribution, statistical inference, and standard error.
3. Discuss the statistical approach to determining sample size based on simple random sampling and the construction of confidence intervals.
4. Derive the formulas to statistically determine the sample size for estimating means and proportions.
5. Discuss the nonresponse issues in sampling and the procedures for improving response rates and adjusting for nonresponse.
6. Understand the difficulty of statistically determining the sample size in international marketing research.
7. Identify the ethical issues related to sample size determination, particularly the estimation of population variance.
8. Explain the use of the Internet and computers in statistically determining the sample size.

In the last chapter (11), we considered the role of sampling in research design formulation, described the sampling process, and presented the various nonprobability and probability sampling techniques.

This chapter focuses on the determination of sample size in simple random sampling. We define various concepts and symbols and discuss the properties of the sampling distribution. Additionally, we describe statistical approaches to sample size determination based on confidence intervals. We present the formulas for calculating the sample size with these approaches and illustrate their use. We briefly discuss the extension to determining sample size in other probability sampling designs. The sample size determined statistically is the final or net sample size, i.e., it represents the completed number of interviews or observations. However, to obtain this final sample size, a much larger number of potential respondents have to be contacted initially. We describe the adjustments that need to be made to the statistically determined sample size to account for incidence and completion rates and calculate the initial sample size. We also cover the nonresponse issues in sampling, with a focus on improving response rates and adjusting for nonresponse. We discuss the difficulty of statistically determining the sample size in international marketing research, identify the relevant ethical issues, and explain the role of the Internet and computers.

Statistical determination of sample size requires knowledge of the normal distribution and the use of normal probability tables. The normal distribution is bell shaped and symmetrical. Its mean, median, and mode are identical (see Chapter 15). Information on the normal distribution and the use of normal probability tables is presented in Appendix 12.1.

## REAL RESEARCH

### Bicycling Reduces Accidents Due to Error

The sample size in *Bicycling* (*www.bicycling.com*) magazine's survey of U.S. retail bicycle stores was influenced by statistical considerations. The allowance for sampling error was limited to 5 percentage points.

The table that follows was used to determine the allowances that should be made for sampling error. The computed confidence intervals took into account the effect of the sample design on sampling error. These intervals indicate the range (plus or minus the figure shown) within which the results of repeated samplings in the same time period could be

Like the cyclists who read it, *Bicycling* magazine attempts to limit the error due to chance (Sampling) factors.

expected to vary, 95 percent of the time, assuming that the sample procedure, survey execution, and questionnaire used were the same.[1]

Recommended Allowance for Sampling Error of a Percentage

| In Percentage Points | (At 95% Confidence Level for a Sample Size of 456) |
|---|---|
| Percentage near 10 | 3 |
| Percentage near 20 | 4 |
| Percentage near 30 | 4 |
| Percentage near 40 | 5 |
| Percentage near 50 | 5 |
| Percentage near 60 | 5 |
| Percentage near 70 | 4 |
| Percentage near 80 | 4 |
| Percentage near 90 | 3 |

The table should be used as follows: If a reported percentage is 43, look at the row labeled "percentages near 40." The number in this row is 5, which means that the 43 percent obtained in the sample is subject to a sampling error of plus or minus 5 percentage points. Another way of saying this is that very probably (95 times out of 100) the average of repeated samplings would be somewhere between 38 percent and 48 percent, with the most likely figure being 43 percent. A recent survey conducted by *Bicycling* magazine to gauge interest in a fundraiser called "United We Ride," a way to generate money for families of victims of the September 11, 2001 terrorist attacks, made use of this table for estimating sampling errors. ■

To grasp the statistical aspects of sampling, it is important to understand certain basic definitions and symbols.

# DEFINITIONS AND SYMBOLS

Confidence intervals and other statistical concepts that play a central role in sample size determination are defined in the following list.

**Parameter:** A *parameter* is a summary description of a fixed characteristic or measure of the target population. A parameter denotes the true value that would be obtained if a census rather than a sample was undertaken.

**Statistic:** A *statistic* is a summary description of a characteristic or measure of the sample. The sample statistic is used as an estimate of the population parameter.

**Finite Population Correction:** The *finite population correction* (fpc) is a correction for overestimation of the variance of a population parameter, e.g., a mean or proportion, when the sample size is 10 percent or more of the population size.

**Precision level:** When estimating a population parameter by using a sample statistic, the *precision level* is the desired size of the estimating interval. This is the maximum permissible difference between the sample statistic and the population parameter.

**Confidence interval:** The *confidence interval* is the range into which the true population parameter will fall, assuming a given level of confidence.

**Confidence level:** The *confidence level* is the probability that a confidence interval will include the population parameter.

The symbols used in statistical notation for describing population and sample characteristics are summarized in Table 12.1.

# THE SAMPLING DISTRIBUTION

**sampling distribution**
The distribution of the values of a sample statistic computed for each possible sample that could be drawn from the target population under a specified sampling plan.

The *sampling distribution* is the distribution of the values of a sample statistic computed for each possible sample that could be drawn from the target population under a specified sampling plan.[2] Suppose a simple random sample of five hospitals is to be drawn from a

| **TABLE 12.1** | | |
|---|---|---|
| **Symbols for Population and Sample Variables** | | |
| VARIABLE | POPULATION | SAMPLE |
| Mean | $\mu$ | $\overline{X}$ |
| Proportion | $\pi$ | $p$ |
| Variance | $\sigma^2$ | $s^2$ |
| Standard deviation | $\sigma$ | $s$ |
| Size | $N$ | $n$ |
| Standard error of the mean | $\sigma_{\overline{x}}$ | $S_{\overline{x}}$ |
| Standard error of the proportion | $\sigma_p$ | $S_p$ |
| Standardized variate ($z$) | $\dfrac{X - \mu}{\sigma}$ | $\dfrac{X - \overline{X}}{S}$ |
| Coefficient of variation ($C$) | $\dfrac{\sigma}{\mu}$ | $\dfrac{S}{\overline{X}}$ |

population of 20 hospitals. There are $(20 \times 19 \times 18 \times 17 \times 16)/(1 \times 2 \times 3 \times 4 \times 5)$, or 15,504 different samples of size 5 that can be drawn. The relative frequency distribution of the values of the mean of these 15,504 different samples would specify the sampling distribution of the mean.

An important task in marketing research is to calculate statistics, such as the sample mean and sample proportion, and use them to estimate the corresponding true population values. This process of generalizing the sample results to the population results is referred to as **statistical inference.** In practice, a single sample of predetermined size is selected and the sample statistics (such as mean and proportion) are computed. Hypothetically, in order to estimate the population parameter from the sample statistic, every possible sample that could have been drawn should be examined. If all possible samples were actually to be drawn, the distribution of the statistic would be the sampling distribution. Although in practice only one sample is actually drawn, the concept of a sampling distribution is still relevant. It enables us to use probability theory to make inferences about the population values.

The important properties of the sampling distribution of the mean, and the corresponding properties for the proportion, for large samples (30 or more) are as follows:

*statistical inference*
The process of generalizing the sample results to the population results.

1. The sampling distribution of the mean is a **normal distribution** (see Appendix 12.1). Strictly speaking, the sampling distribution of a proportion is a binomial. However, for large samples ($n = 30$ or more), it can be approximated by the normal distribution.

*normal distribution*
A basis for classical statistical inference that is bell-shaped and symmetrical in appearance. Its measures of central tendency are all identical.

2. The mean of the sampling distribution of the mean $\left( \overline{X} = \dfrac{\sum_{i=1}^{n} X_i}{n} \right)$ or of the proportion ($p$) equals the corresponding population parameter value, $\mu$ or $\pi$, respectively.

3. The standard deviation is called the **standard error** of the mean or the proportion to indicate that it refers to a sampling distribution of the mean or the proportion, and not to a sample or a population. The formulas are:

*standard error*
The standard deviation of the sampling distribution of the mean or proportion.

$$\text{Mean} \qquad\qquad\qquad \text{Proportion}$$

$$\sigma_{\overline{x}} = \frac{\sigma}{\sqrt{n}} \qquad\qquad \sigma_p = \sqrt{\frac{\pi(1 - \pi)}{n}}$$

4. Often the population standard deviation, $\sigma$, is not known. In these cases, it can be estimated from the sample by using the following formula:

$$s = \sqrt{\frac{\sum\limits_{i=1}^{n}(X_i - \overline{X})^2}{n-1}}$$

or

$$s = \sqrt{\frac{\left(\sum\limits_{i=1}^{n}X_i^2\right) - \left(\sum\limits_{i=1}^{n}X_i\right)^2}{n-1}}{n-1}}$$

In cases where $\sigma$ is estimated by $s$, the standard error of the mean becomes

$$\text{est. } \sigma_{\overline{x}} = \frac{s}{\sqrt{n}}$$

"est." denotes the fact that $s$ has been used as an estimate of $\sigma$.

    Assuming no measurement error, the reliability of an estimate of a population parameter can be assessed in terms of its standard error.

5. Likewise, the standard error of the proportion can be estimated by using the sample proportion $p$ as an estimator of the population proportion, $\pi$, as:

$$\text{est. } s_p = \sqrt{\frac{p(1-p)}{n}}$$

6. The area under the sampling distribution between any two points can be calculated in terms of **z *values.*** The $z$ value for a point is the number of standard errors a point is away from the mean. The $z$ values may be computed as follows:

$$z = \frac{\overline{X} - \mu}{\sigma_{\overline{x}}}$$

For example, the areas under one side of the curve between the mean and points that have $z$ values of 1.0, 2.0, and 3.0 are, respectively, 0.3413, 0.4772, and 0.4986. (See Table 2 in the Appendix of Statistical Tables.) In the case of proportion, the computation of $z$ values is similar.

7. When the sample size is 10 percent or more of the population size, the standard error formulas will overestimate the standard deviation of the population mean or proportion. Hence, these should be adjusted by a finite population correction factor defined by:

$$\sqrt{\frac{N-n}{N-1}}$$

In this case

$$\sigma_{\overline{x}} = \frac{\sigma}{\sqrt{n}} \sqrt{\frac{N-n}{N-1}}$$

# STATISTICAL APPROACH TO DETERMINING SAMPLE SIZE

Several qualitative factors should also be taken into consideration when determining the sample size (see Chapter 11). These include the importance of the decision, the nature of the research, the number of variables, the nature of the analysis, sample sizes used in similar studies, incidence rates, completion rates, and resource constraints. The statistically determined sample size is the net or final sample size—the sample remaining after eliminating potential respondents who do not qualify or who do not complete the interview. Depending on incidence and completion rates, the size of the initial sample may have to be much larger. In commercial marketing research, limits on time, money, and expert resources can exert an overriding influence on sample size determination. In the department store project, the sample size was determined based on these considerations.

The statistical approach to determining sample size that we consider is based on traditional statistical inference.[3] In this approach the precision level is specified in advance. This approach is based on the construction of confidence intervals around sample means or proportions.

# THE CONFIDENCE INTERVAL APPROACH

The confidence interval approach to sample size determination is based on the construction of confidence intervals around the sample means or proportions using the standard error formula. This was illustrated in the opening *Bicycling* magazine example where the sampling errors were related to the sample size and to the confidence level. As another example, suppose that a researcher has taken a simple random sample of 300 households to estimate the monthly expenses on department store shopping and found that the mean household monthly expense for the sample is $182. Past studies indicate that the population standard deviation $\sigma$ can be assumed to be $55.

We want to find an interval within which a fixed proportion of the sample means would fall. Suppose we want to determine an interval around the population mean that will include 95 percent of the sample means, based on samples of 300 households. The 95 percent could be divided into two equal parts, half below and half above the mean, as shown in Figure 12.1. Calculation of the confidence interval involves determining a distance below ($\overline{X}_L$) and above ($\overline{X}_U$) the population mean ($\overline{X}$) that contains a specified area of the normal curve.

The $z$ values corresponding to $\overline{X}_L$ and $\overline{X}_U$ may be calculated as

$$z_L = \frac{\overline{X}_L - \mu}{\sigma_{\overline{x}}}$$

$$z_U = \frac{\overline{X}_U - \mu}{\sigma_{\overline{x}}}$$

where $z_L = -z$ and $z_U = +z$. Therefore, the lower value of $\overline{X}$ is

$$\overline{X}_L = \mu - z\sigma_{\overline{x}}$$

and the upper value of $\overline{X}$ is

$$\overline{X}_U = \mu + z\sigma_{\overline{x}}$$

Note that $\mu$ is estimated by $\overline{X}$. The confidence interval is given by

$$\overline{X} \pm z\sigma_{\overline{x}}$$

We can now set a 95 percent confidence interval around the sample mean of $182. As a first step, we compute the standard error of the mean:

$$\sigma_{\overline{x}} = \frac{\sigma}{\sqrt{n}} = \frac{55}{\sqrt{300}} = 3.18$$

*Figure 12.1*
95 Percent Confidence Interval

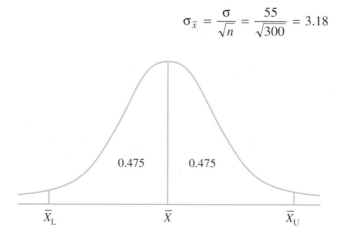

0.475        0.475

$\overline{X}_L$          $\overline{X}$          $\overline{X}_U$

From Table 2 in the Appendix of Statistical Tables, it can be seen that the central 95 percent of the normal distribution lies within ± 1.96 $z$ values. The 95 percent confidence interval is given by

$$\overline{X} \pm 1.96\sigma_{\overline{x}}$$
$$= 182.00 \pm 1.96(3.18)$$
$$= 182.00 \pm 6.23$$

Thus the 95 percent confidence interval ranges from \$175.77 to \$188.23. The probability of finding the true population mean to be between \$175.77 and \$188.23 is 95 percent.

## Sample Size Determination: Means

The approach used here to construct a confidence interval can be adapted to determine the sample size that will result in a desired confidence interval.[4] Suppose the researcher wants to estimate the monthly household expense on department store shopping more precisely so that the estimate will be within ±\$5.00 of the true population value. What should be the size of the sample? The following steps, summarized in Table 12.2, will lead to an answer.

1. Specify the level of precision. This is the maximum permissible difference ($D$) between the sample mean and the population mean. In our example, $D = \pm\$5.00$.
2. Specify the level of confidence. Suppose that a 95% confidence level is desired.
3. Determine the $z$ value associated with the confidence level using Table 2 in the Appendix of Statistical Tables. For a 95% confidence level, the probability that the population mean will fall outside one end of the interval is 0.025(0.05/2). The associated $z$ value is 1.96.
4. Determine the standard deviation of the population. The standard deviation of the population may be known from secondary sources. If not, it might be estimated by conducting a pilot study. Alternatively, it might be estimated on the basis of the researcher's judgment. For example, the range of a normally distributed variable is approximately equal to plus or minus three standard deviations, and one can thus estimate the standard deviation by dividing the range by six. The researcher can often estimate the range based on knowledge of the phenomenon.
5. Determine the sample size using the formula for the standard error of the mean.

$$z = \frac{\overline{X} - \mu}{\sigma_{\overline{x}}}$$
$$= \frac{D}{\sigma_{\overline{x}}}$$

## TABLE 12.2

**Sample Size Determination for Means and Proportions**

| STEPS | MEANS | PROPORTIONS |
|---|---|---|
| 1. Specify the level of precision. | $D = \pm\$5.00$ | $D = p - \pi = \pm0.05$ |
| 2. Specify the confidence level (CL). | $CL = 95\%$ | $CL = 95\%$ |
| 3. Determine the $z$ value associated with the CL. | $z$ value is 1.96 | $z$ value is 1.96 |
| 4. Determine the standard deviation of the population. | Estimate $\sigma$:<br>$\sigma = 55$ | Estimate $\pi$:<br>$\pi = 0.64$ |
| 5. Determine the sample size using the formula for the standard error. | $n = \dfrac{\sigma^2 z^2}{D^2}$ | $n = \dfrac{\pi(1-\pi)z^2}{D^2}$ |
| | $n = \dfrac{55^2(1.96)^2}{5^2}$ | $n = \dfrac{0.64(1-0.64)(1.96)^2}{(0.05)^2}$ |
| | $= 465$ | $= 355$ |
| 6. If the sample size represents 10 percent of the population, apply the finite population correction (fpc). | $n_c = \dfrac{nN}{N+n-1}$ | $n_c = \dfrac{nN}{N+n-1}$ |
| 7. If necessary, reestimate the confidence interval by employing $s$ to estimate $\sigma$. | $= \bar{X} \pm zs_{\bar{x}}$ | $= p \pm zs_p$ |
| 8. If precision is specified in relative rather than absolute terms, then use these equations to determine the sample size. | $D = R\mu$<br>$n = \dfrac{C^2 z^2}{R^2}$ | $D = R\pi$<br>$n = \dfrac{z^2(1-\pi)}{R^2\pi}$ |

or

$$\sigma_{\bar{x}} = \frac{D}{z}$$

or

$$\frac{\sigma}{\sqrt{n}} = \frac{D}{z}$$

or

$$n = \frac{\sigma^2 z^2}{D^2}$$

In our example,

$$n = \frac{55^2(1.96)^2}{5^2}$$
$$= 464.83$$
$$= 465 \text{ (rounded to the next higher integer)}$$

It can be seen from the formula for sample size that sample size increases with an increase in the population variability, degree of confidence, and the precision level required of the estimate. Because the sample size is directly proportional to $\sigma^2$, the larger the population variability, the larger the sample size. Likewise, a higher degree of confidence implies a larger value of $z$, and thus a larger sample size. Both $\sigma^2$ and $z$ appear in the numerator. Greater precision means a smaller value of $D$, and thus a larger sample size because $D$ appears in the denominator.

6. If the resulting sample size represents 10 percent or more of the population, the finite population correction (fpc) should be applied.[5] The required sample size should then be calculated from the formula

$$n_c = nN/(N + n - 1)$$

where

$$n = \text{sample size without fpc}$$
$$n_c = \text{sample size with fpc}$$

7. If the population standard deviation, $\sigma$, is unknown and an estimate is used, it should be reestimated once the sample has been drawn. The sample standard deviation, $s$, is used as an estimate of $\sigma$. A revised confidence interval should then be calculated to determine the precision level actually obtained.

   Suppose that the value of 55.00 used for $\sigma$ was an estimate because the true value was unknown. A sample of $n = 465$ is drawn, and these observations generate a mean $\overline{X}$ of 180.00 and a sample standard deviation $s$ of 50.00. The revised confidence interval then is

$$\overline{X} \pm z s_{\overline{x}}$$
$$= 180.00 \pm 1.96(50.0/\sqrt{465})$$
$$= 180.00 \pm 4.55$$

or

$$175.45 \leq \mu \leq 184.55$$

   Note that the confidence interval obtained is narrower than planned, because the population standard deviation was overestimated, as judged by the sample standard deviation.

8. In some cases, precision is specified in relative rather than absolute terms. In other words, it may be specified that the estimate be within plus or minus $R$ percentage points of the mean. Symbolically,

$$D = R\mu$$

In these cases, the sample size may be determined by

$$n = \frac{\sigma^2 z^2}{D^2}$$
$$= \frac{C^2 z^2}{R^2}$$

where the coefficient of variation $C = (\sigma/\mu)$ would have to be estimated.

The population size, $N$, does not directly affect the size of the sample, except when the finite population correction factor has to be applied. Although this may be counterintuitive, upon reflection it makes sense. For example, if all the population elements are identical on the characteristics of interest, then a sample size of one will be sufficient to estimate the mean perfectly. This is true whether there are 50, 500, 5,000, or 50,000 elements in the population. What directly affects the sample size is the variability of the characteristic in the population. This variability enters into the sample size calculation by way of population variance $\sigma^2$ or sample variance $s^2$.

## Sample Size Determination: Proportions

If the statistic of interest is a proportion, rather than a mean, the approach to sample size determination is similar. Suppose that the researcher is interested in estimating the proportion of households possessing a department store credit card. The following steps should be followed.

1. Specify the level of precision. Suppose the desired precision is such that the allowable interval is set as $D = p - \pi = \pm 0.05$.
2. Specify the level of confidence. Suppose that a 95% confidence level is desired.
3. Determine the $z$ value associated with the confidence level. As explained in the case of estimating the mean, this will be $z = 1.96$.
4. Estimate the population proportion $\pi$. As explained earlier, the population proportion may be estimated from secondary sources, estimated from a pilot study, or based on the judgment of the researcher. Suppose that, based on secondary data, the researcher

estimates that 64 percent of the households in the target population possess a department store credit card. Hence, $\pi = 0.64$.

5. Determine the sample size using the formula for the standard error of the proportion.

$$\sigma_p = \frac{p - \pi}{z}$$
$$= \frac{D}{z}$$
$$= \sqrt{\frac{\pi(1 - \pi)}{n}}$$

or

$$n = \frac{\pi(1 - \pi)z^2}{D^2}$$

In our example,

$$n = \frac{0.64(1 - 0.64)(1.96)^2}{(0.05)^2}$$
$$= 354.04$$
$$= 355 \text{ (rounded to the next higher integer)}$$

6. If the resulting sample size represents 10 percent or more of the population, the finite population correction (fpc) should be applied. The required sample size should then be calculated from the formula:

$$n_c = nN/(N + n - 1)$$

where

$$n = \text{sample size without fpc}$$
$$n_c = \text{sample size with fpc}$$

7. If the estimate of $\pi$ turns out to be poor, the confidence interval will be more or less precise than desired. Suppose that after the sample has been taken, the proportion $p$ is calculated to have a value of 0.55. The confidence interval is then reestimated by employing $s_p$ to estimate the unknown $\sigma_p$ as

$$p \pm z s_p$$

where

$$s_p = \sqrt{\frac{p(1 - p)}{n}}$$

In our example,

$$s_p = \sqrt{\frac{0.55(1 - 0.55)}{355}}$$
$$= 0.0264$$

The confidence interval, then, is

$$= 0.55 \pm 1.96(0.0264)$$
$$= 0.55 \pm 0.052$$

which is wider than that specified. This could be attributed to the fact that the sample standard deviation based on $p = 0.55$ was larger than the estimate of the population standard deviation based on $\pi = 0.64$.

If a wider interval than specified is unacceptable, the sample size can be determined to reflect the maximum possible variation in the population. This occurs when the product $\pi(1 - \pi)$ is the greatest, which happens when $\pi$ is set at 0.5. This result can also be seen intuitively. Because one-half the population has one value of the characteristic and the other half the other value, more evidence would be required to obtain a valid inference than if the situation was more clear-cut and the majority had one particular value. In our example, this leads to a sample size of

$$n = \frac{0.5(0.5)(1.96)^2}{(0.05)^2}$$
$$= 384.16$$
$$= 385 \text{ rounded to the next higher integer}$$

8. Sometimes, precision is specified in relative rather than absolute terms. In other words, it may be specified that the estimate be within plus or minus $R$ percentage points of the population proportion. Symbolically,

$$D = R\pi$$

In such a case, the sample size may be determined by

$$n = \frac{z^2(1 - \pi)}{R^2\pi}$$

## REAL REASEARCH

## *Statistical Sampling: Not Always an Emergency*

The city of Los Angeles, California hired PriceWaterhouseCoopers (PWC) to evaluate customer demand for nonemergency city services and investigate customer services usage patterns. The goal was to implement a new system that would alleviate some of the strain on the city's 9-1-1 phone system. A telephone survey of 1,800 randomly selected Los Angeles City residents was conducted.

The random-digit dialing telephone survey was stratified into two groups of 900 each: city resident customers who had contacted the city for service in the past six months and a group of other residents. The sample size was determined by using a 95% confidence interval and a margin of error of 3.5 percent. At this confidence level, one would expect that if all the residents of Los Angeles were asked the same survey, that responses to the survey would change no more than ±3.5 percent.

To confirm that the sample size of 900 was adequate, calculations for sample size determination by proportions were made as follows, using the maximum possible population variation ($\pi = 0.5$). The precision of $D$ in this study is 0.035 for a 95% confidence level.

$$n = \frac{\pi(1 - \pi)z^2}{D^2}$$
$$n = [(0.5)(1 - 0.5)(1.96^2)]/(0.035)^2 = 784$$

Therefore, the 900 sample size was more than sufficient.

Findings from the telephone survey revealed that the Department of Water and Power, the Sanitation Bureau, the Bureau of Parking Violations, and the Police Department received about one-half of the city's nonemergency customer contact volume. The main method of contacting the city was by phone, which accounted for about 74 percent of the contacts, compared to 18 percent who made personal visits. Despite high Internet usage rates in Los Angeles, very few residents accessed city services through the Web. By Web enabling many of the city's services, there was a potential for large cost savings by reducing the call volume and improving customer service. The survey also identified specific services and functionality residents would like to see available online. Therefore, the city of Los Angeles launched a 3-1-1/Internet customer service in 1999 to alleviate some of the strain on the city's 9-1-1 phone system. As of 2003, this service had become popular, handling a large share of the city's nonemergency customer contacts.[6] ∎

# MULTIPLE CHARACTERISTICS AND PARAMETERS

In the preceding examples, we focused on the estimation of a single parameter. In commercial marketing research, several characteristics, not just one, are of interest in any project. The researcher is required to estimate several parameters, not just one. The calculation of sample size in these cases should be based on a consideration of all the parameters that must be estimated, as illustrated in the department store example.

| ACTIVE RESEARCH | DEPARTMENT STORE PROJECT |
|---|---|

### Sample Size Estimation

Suppose that in addition to the mean household monthly expenses on department store shopping, it was decided to estimate the mean household monthly expense on clothes and on gifts. The sample sizes needed to estimate each of the three mean monthly expenses are given in Table 12.3 and are 465 for department store shopping, 246 for clothes, and 217 for gifts. If all the three variables were equally important, the most conservative approach would be to select the largest value of $n = 465$ to determine the sample size. This will lead to each variable being estimated at least as precisely as specified. However, if the researcher was most concerned with the mean household monthly expense on clothes, a sample size of $n = 246$ could be selected.

## TABLE 12.3

**Sample Size for Estimating Multiple Parameters**

| | MEAN HOUSEHOLD MONTHLY EXPENSE ON: | | |
|---|---|---|---|
| | DEPARTMENT STORE SHOPPING | CLOTHES | GIFTS |
| Confidence level | 95% | 95% | 95% |
| $z$ value | 1.96 | 1.96 | 1.96 |
| Precision level ($D$) | $5 | $5 | $4 |
| Standard deviation of the population ($\sigma$) | $55 | $40 | $30 |
| Required sample size ($n$) | 465 | 246 | 217 |

So far, the discussion of sample size determination has been based on the methods of traditional statistical inference and has assumed simple random sampling. Next, we discuss the determination of sample size when other sampling techniques are used.

# OTHER PROBABILITY SAMPLING TECHNIQUES

The determination of sample size for other probability sampling techniques is based on the same underlying principles. The researcher must specify the level of precision and the degree of confidence and estimate the sampling distribution of the test statistic.

In simple random sampling, cost does not enter directly into the calculation of sample size. However, in the case of stratified or cluster sampling, cost has an important influence. The cost per observation varies by strata or cluster and the researcher needs some initial estimates of these costs. In addition, the researcher must take into account within-strata variability or within- and between-cluster variability. Once the overall sample size is determined, the sample is apportioned among strata or clusters. This increases the complexity of the sample size formulas. The interested reader is referred to standard works on sampling theory for more information.[7] In general, to provide the same reliability as simple random sampling, sample sizes are the same for systematic sampling, smaller for stratified sampling, and larger for cluster sampling.

# ADJUSTING THE STATISTICALLY DETERMINED SAMPLE SIZE

The sample size determined statistically represents the final or net sample size that must be achieved in order to ensure that the parameters are estimated with the desired degree of precision and the given level of confidence. In surveys, this represents the number of interviews that must be completed. In order to achieve this final sample size, a much greater number of potential respondents have to be contacted. In other words, the initial sample size has to be much larger because typically the incidence rates and completion rates are less than 100 percent.[8]

*incidence rate*
The rate of occurrence of persons eligible to participate in the study expressed as a percentage.

*Incidence rate* refers to the rate of occurrence or the percentage of persons eligible to participate in the study. Incidence rate determines how many contacts need to be screened for a given sample size requirement. Suppose a study of floor cleaners calls for a sample of female heads of households aged 25 to 55. Of the women between the ages of 20 and 60 who might reasonably be approached to see if they qualify, approximately 75 percent are heads of households between 25 and 55. This means that, on average, 1.33 women would be approached to obtain one qualified respondent. Additional criteria for qualifying respondents (for example, product usage behavior) will further increase the number of contacts. Suppose that an added eligibility requirement is that the women should have used a floor cleaner during the last two months. It is estimated that 60 percent of the women contacted would meet this criteria. Then the incidence rate is $0.75 \times 0.60 = 0.45$. Thus the final sample size will have to be increased by a factor of $(1/0.45)$ or 2.22.

*completion rate*
The percentage of qualified respondents who complete the interview. It enables researchers to take into account anticipated refusals by people who qualify.

Similarly, the determination of sample size must take into account anticipated refusals by people who qualify. The *completion rate* denotes the percentage of qualified respondents who complete the interview. If, for example, the researcher expects an interview completion rate of 80 percent of eligible respondents, the number of contacts should be increased by a factor of 1.25. The incidence rate and the completion rate together imply that the number of potential respondents contacted, i.e., the initial sample size, should be $2.22 \times 1.25$ or 2.77 times the sample size required. In general, if there are $c$ qualifying factors with an incidence of $Q_1, Q_2, Q_3, \ldots Q_c$, each expressed as a proportion,

$$\text{Incidence rate} = Q_1 \times Q_2 \times Q_3 \ldots \times Q_c$$

$$\text{Initial sample size} = \frac{\text{Final sample size}}{\text{Incidence rate} \times \text{Completion rate}}$$

The number of units that will have to be sampled will be determined by the initial sample size. Often, as in the symphony example, a number of variables are used for qualifying potential respondents, thereby decreasing the incidence rate.

## REAL REASEARCH

### Tuning Up a Symphony Sample

A telephone survey was conducted to determine the consumer's awareness of and attitudes toward the Jacksonville Symphony Orchestra (*www.jaxsymphony.org*). The screening qualifications for a respondent included in the survey were: (1) has lived in the Jacksonville area for more than one year; (2) 25 years old or older; (3) listens to classical or pop music; and (4) attends live performances of classical or pop music. These qualifying criteria decreased the incidence rate to less than 15 percent, leading to a substantial increase in the number of contacts. Although having four qualifying factors resulted in a highly targeted or tuned sample, it also made the interviewing process inefficient, as several people who were called could not qualify. The survey indicated that parking was a problem and people wanted greater involvement with the symphony. Therefore, the Jacksonville Symphony Orchestra advertised the Conductor's Club in 2002. Annual fund donors who join can enjoy the perks of membership including complimentary valet parking at all Jacksonville Symphony Masterworks and Pops concerts. All membership levels include complimentary admission to intermission receptions in the Davis Gallery at selected concerts (including open bar and hors d'oeuvres).[9] ■

The Jacksonville Symphony Orchestra tuned up the right sample by appropriately screening the respondents.

Completion rates are affected by nonresponse. Hence, nonresponse issues deserve attention.

# NONRESPONSE ISSUES IN SAMPLING

The two major nonresponse issues in sampling are improving response rates and adjusting for nonresponse. Nonresponse error arises when some of the potential respondents included in the sample do not respond (see Chapter 3). This is one of the most significant problems in survey research. Nonrespondents differ from respondents in terms of demographic, psychographic, personality, attitudinal, motivational, and behavioral variables.[10] For a given study, if the nonrespondents differ from the respondents on the characteristics of interest, the sample estimates will be seriously biased. Higher response rates, in general, imply lower rates of nonresponse bias, yet response rate may not be an adequate indicator of nonresponse bias. Response rates themselves do not indicate whether the respondents are representative of the original sample.[11] Increasing the response rate may not reduce nonresponse bias if the additional respondents are not different from those who have already responded but differ from those who still do not respond. Because low response rates increase the probability of nonresponse bias, an attempt should always be made to improve the response rate.[12]

## Improving the Response Rates

The primary causes of low response rates are refusals and not-at-homes, as shown in Figure 12.2.

*Refusals.*   Refusals, which result from the unwillingness or inability of people included in the sample to participate, result in lower response rates and increased potential for nonresponse bias. Refusal rates, the percentage of contacted respondents who refuse to participate, range from 0 to 50 percent or more in telephone surveys. Refusal rates for mall intercept interviews are even higher, and they are highest of all for mail surveys. Most refusals occur immediately after the interviewer's opening remarks or when the potential respondent first opens the mail package. In a national telephone survey, 40 percent of those contacted refused at the introduction stage, but only 6 percent refused during the interview. The following example gives further information on refusals, terminations, and completed interviews.

**Figure 12.2**
Improving Response Rates

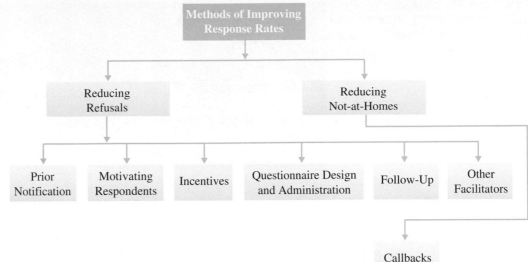

## Reasons for Refusal

In a study investigating the refusal problem in telephone surveys, telephone interviews were conducted with responders and nonresponders to a previous survey, using quotas of 100 for each subsample. The results are presented in the following table:

Refusals, Terminations, and Completed Interviews

| Property | Total Sample | Responders | Nonresponders |
| --- | --- | --- | --- |
| Number of refusals (1) | 224 | 31 | 193 |
| Number of terminations (2) | 100 | 33 | 67 |
| Number of completed interviews (3) | 203 | 102 | 101 |
| Total number of contacts $(1 + 2 + 3)^a$ | 527 | 166 | 361 |
| Refusal rate $(1/[1 + 2 + 3])^b$ | 42.5% | 18.7% | 53.5% |
| Termination rate $(2/[1 + 2 + 3])$ | 19.0% | 19.9% | 18.5% |
| Completion rate $(3/[1 + 2 + 3])^b$ | 38.5% | 61.4% | 28.0% |

[a] A total of 1,388 attempts was required to make these contacts: the 166 responder contacts required 406 attempts (with one callback per respondent), and the 361 nonresponder contacts required 982 attempts (with two callbacks per respondent). The sampling frame contained 965 phone numbers—313 responders and 652 nonresponders.

[b] Responder/nonresponder differences were significant at $\alpha = 0.05$ (two-tail test).

The study found that people who are likely to participate in a telephone survey (responders) differ from those who are likely to refuse (nonresponders) in the following ways: (1) confidence in survey research, (2) confidence in the research organization, (3) demographic characteristics, and (4) beliefs and attitudes about telephone surveys.

A 2002 study conducted by CMOR indicated that consumers prefer Internet surveys versus the telephone method of surveys. Statistically speaking, out of 1,753 U.S. consumers, 78.9 percent of respondents chose the Internet as their first choice of survey method, whereas only 3.2 percent chose the telephone method of surveys.[13] ■

Given the differences between responders and nonresponders that this study demonstrated, researchers should attempt to lower refusal rates. This can be done by prior notification, motivating the respondents, incentives, good questionnaire design and administration, and follow-up.

*Prior notification.* In prior notification, potential respondents are sent a letter notifying them of the imminent mail, telephone, personal, or Internet survey. Prior notification increases response rates for samples of the general public because it reduces surprise and uncertainty and creates a more cooperative atmosphere.[14]

*Motivating the respondents.* Potential respondents can be motivated to participate in the survey by increasing their interest and involvement. Two of the ways this can be done are the foot-in-the-door and door-in-the-face strategies. Both strategies attempt to obtain participation through the use of sequential requests. As explained briefly in Chapter 6, in the foot-in-the-door strategy, the interviewer starts with a relatively small request, such as "Will you please take five minutes to answer five questions?", to which a large majority of people will comply. The small request is followed by a larger request, the critical request, that solicits participation in the survey or experiment. The rationale is that compliance with an initial request should increase the chances of compliance with the subsequent request. The door-in-the-face is the reverse strategy. The initial request is relatively large and a majority of people refuse to comply. The large request is followed by a smaller request, the critical request, soliciting participation in the survey. The underlying reasoning is that the concession offered by the subsequent critical request should increase the chances of compliance. Foot-in-the-door is more effective than door-in-the-face.[15]

*Incentives.* Response rates can be increased by offering monetary as well as nonmonetary incentives to potential respondents. Monetary incentives can be prepaid or promised. The prepaid incentive is included with the survey or questionnaire. The promised incentive is sent to only those respondents who complete the survey. The most commonly used nonmonetary incentives are premiums and rewards, such as pens, pencils, books, and offers of survey results.[16]

Prepaid incentives have been shown to increase response rates to a greater extent than promised incentives. The amount of incentive can vary from 10 cents to $50 or more. The amount of incentive has a positive relationship with response rate, but the cost of large monetary incentives may outweigh the value of additional information obtained.

*Questionnaire design and administration.* A well-designed questionnaire can decrease the overall refusal rate as well as refusals to specific questions (see Chapter 10). Likewise, the skill used to administer the questionnaire in telephone and personal interviews can increase the response rate. Trained interviewers are skilled in refusal conversion or persuasion. They do not accept a "no" response without an additional plea. The additional plea might emphasize the brevity of the questionnaire or importance of the respondent's opinion. Skilled interviewers can decrease refusals by about 7 percent on average. Interviewing procedures are discussed in more detail in Chapter 13.

*Follow-up.* Follow-up, or contacting the nonrespondents periodically after the initial contact, is particularly effective in decreasing refusals in mail surveys. The researcher might send a postcard or letter to remind nonrespondents to complete and return the questionnaire. Two or three mailings are needed, in addition to the original one. With proper follow-up, the response rate in mail surveys can be increased to 80 percent or more. Follow-ups can also be done by telephone, e-mail, or personal contacts.[17]

*Other facilitators.* Personalization, or sending letters addressed to specific individuals, is effective in increasing response rates.[18] The next example illustrates the procedure employed by Arbitron to increase its response rate.

## REAL RESEARCH

### Arbitron's Response to Low Response Rates

Arbitron, (*www.arbitron.com*), a major marketing research supplier, achieved annual 2001 revenues of $227 million. Recently, Arbitron was trying to improve response rates in order to get more meaningful results from its surveys. Arbitron created a special cross-functional team of employees to work on the response rate problem. Their method was named the "breakthrough method" and the whole Arbitron system concerning the response rates was questioned and changed. The team suggested six major strategies for improving response rates:

1. Maximize the effectiveness of placement/follow-up calls.
2. Make materials more appealing and easier to complete.
3. Increase Arbitron name awareness.

**4.** Improve survey participant rewards.

**5.** Optimize the arrival of respondent materials.

**6.** Increase usability of returned diaries.

Eighty initiatives were launched to implement these six strategies. As a result, response rates improved significantly. However, in spite of those encouraging results, people at Arbitron remain very cautious. They know that they are not done yet and that it is an everyday fight to keep those response rates high. Arbitron's response rates for winter and spring 2001 were 37.6 and 36.9 percent, respectively.[19] ■

*Not-at-Homes.*   The second major cause of low response rates is not-at-homes. In telephone and in-home personal interviews, low response rates can result if the potential respondents are not at home when contact is attempted. A study analyzing 182 commercial telephone surveys involving a total sample of over one million consumers revealed that a large percentage of potential respondents was never contacted. The median noncontact rate was 40 percent. In nearly 40 percent of the surveys, only a single attempt was made to contact potential respondents. The results of 259,088 first-call attempts, using the sophisticated random-digit dialing M/A/R/C Telno System (*www.marcgroup.com*), shows that less than 10 percent of the calls resulted in completed interviews.[20]

The likelihood that potential respondents will not be at home varies with several factors. People with small children are more likely to be at home than single or divorced people. Consumers are more likely to be at home on weekends than on weekdays, and in the evening as opposed to during the afternoon. Prenotification and appointments increase the likelihood that the respondent will be at home when contact is attempted.

The percentage of not-at-homes can be substantially reduced by employing a series of callbacks, or periodic follow-up attempts to contact nonrespondents. The decision about the number of callbacks should weigh the benefits of reducing nonresponse bias against the additional costs. As callbacks are completed, the callback respondents should be compared to those who have already responded to determine the usefulness of making further callbacks. In most consumer surveys, three to four callbacks may be desirable. Whereas the first call yields the most responses, the second and third calls have a higher response per call. It is important that callbacks be made and controlled according to a prescribed plan.

## Adjusting for Nonresponse

High response rates decrease the probability that nonresponse bias is substantial. Nonresponse rates should always be reported and, whenever possible, the effects of nonresponse should be estimated. This can be done by linking the nonresponse rate to estimated differences between respondents and nonrespondents. Information on differences between the two groups may be obtained from the sample itself. For example, differences found through callbacks could be extrapolated, or a concentrated follow-up could be conducted on a subsample of the nonrespondents. Alternatively, it may be possible to estimate these differences from other sources.[21] To illustrate, in a survey of owners of major appliances, demographic and other information may be obtained for respondents and nonrespondents from the warranty cards. For a mail panel, a wide variety of information is available for both groups from syndicate organizations. If the sample is supposed to be representative of the general population, then comparisons can be made with census figures. Even if it is not feasible to estimate the effects of nonresponse, some adjustments should still be made during data analysis and interpretation.[22] The strategies available to adjust for nonresponse error include subsampling of nonrespondents, replacement, substitution, subjective estimates, trend analysis, simple weighting, and imputation.

*Subsampling of Nonrespondents.*   Subsampling of nonrespondents, particularly in the case of mail surveys, can be effective in adjusting for nonresponse bias. In this technique, the researcher contacts a subsample of the nonrespondents, usually by means of telephone or personal interviews. This often results in a high response rate within that subsample. The values obtained for the subsample are then projected to all the nonrespondents, and the survey results are adjusted to account for nonresponse. This method can estimate the effect of nonresponse on the characteristic of interest.

### Replacement.
In replacement, the nonrespondents in the current survey are replaced with nonrespondents from an earlier, similar survey. The researcher attempts to contact these nonrespondents from the earlier survey and administer the current survey questionnaire to them, possibly by offering a suitable incentive. It is important that the nature of nonresponse in the current survey be similar to that of the earlier survey. The two surveys should use similar kinds of respondents, and the time interval between them should be short. As an example, if the department store survey is being repeated one year later, the nonrespondents in the present survey may be replaced by the nonrespondents in the earlier survey.

**substitution**
A procedure that substitutes for nonrespondents other elements from the sampling frame that are expected to respond.

### Substitution.
In *substitution,* the researcher substitutes for nonrespondents other elements from the sampling frame that are expected to respond. The sampling frame is divided into subgroups that are internally homogeneous in terms of respondent characteristics, but heterogeneous in terms of response rates. These subgroups are then used to identify substitutes who are similar to particular nonrespondents but dissimilar to respondents already in the sample. Note that this approach would not reduce nonresponse bias if the substitutes are similar to respondents already in the sample.

### REAL RESEARCH

## Exit Polling of Voters: Substituting Nonrespondents

Planning exit interviews for a presidential election begins as early as two years before the big day. Research firms such as Gallup (*www.gallup.com*) and Harris Interactive (*www.harrisinteractive.com*) systematically recruit and train workers.

The questions are short and pointed. Certain issues are well-known determinants of a voter's choice, whereas other questions deal with last-minute events such as political scandal. The questionnaires are written at the last possible moment and are designed to determine not only whom people voted for but on what basis.

Uncooperative pollsters are a problem among exit polling. Interviewers are told to record a basic demographic profile for noncompliers. From this demographic data, a voter profile is developed to replace the uncooperative pollster using the method of substitution. Age, sex, race, and residence are strong indicators of how Americans vote. For example, younger voters are more likely to be swayed by moral issues, whereas older voters are more likely to consider a candidate's personal qualities. Therefore, researchers substitute for nonrespondents other potential respondents who are similar in age, sex, race, and residence. The broad coverage of exit interviews and the substitution technique for noncompliant pollsters allow researchers to obtain margins of error close to 3 to 4 percent.[23] ∎

### Subjective Estimates.
When it is no longer feasible to increase the response rate by subsampling, replacement, or substitution, it may be possible to arrive at subjective estimates of the nature and effect of nonresponse bias. This involves evaluating the likely effects of nonresponse based on experience and available information. For example, married adults with young children are more likely to be at home than single or divorced adults or married adults with no children. This information provides a basis for evaluating the effects of nonresponse due to not-at-homes in personal or telephone surveys.

**trend analysis**
A method of adjusting for nonresponse in which the researcher tries to discern a trend between early and late respondents. This trend is projected to nonrespondents to estimate their characteristic of interest.

### Trend Analysis.
*Trend analysis* is an attempt to discern a trend between early and late respondents. This trend is projected to nonrespondents to estimate where they stand on the characteristic of interest. For example, Table 12.4 presents the results of several waves of a mail survey. The characteristic of interest is dollars spent on shopping in department stores during the last two months. The known value of the characteristic for the total sample is given at the bottom of the table. The value for each successive wave of respondents becomes closer to the value for nonrespondents. For example, those responding to the second mailing spent 79 percent of the amount spent by those who responded to the first mailing. Those responding to the third mailing spent 85 percent of the amount spent by those who responded to the second mailing. Continuing this trend, one might estimate that those

**TABLE 12.4**

Use of Trend Analysis in Adjusting for Nonresponse

|  | PERCENTAGE RESPONSE | AVERAGE DOLLAR EXPENDITURE | PERCENTAGE OF PREVIOUS WAVE'S RESPONSE |
|---|---|---|---|
| First mailing | 12 | 412 | — |
| Second mailing | 18 | 325 | 79 |
| Third mailing | 13 | 277 | 85 |
| Nonresponse | (57) | (230) | 91 |
| Total | 100 | 275 |  |

who did not respond spent 91 percent [85 + (85 − 79)] of the amount spent by those who responded to the third mailing. This results in an estimate of $252(277 × 0.91) spent by nonrespondents and an estimate of $288(0.12 × 412 + 0.18 × 325 + 0.13 × 277 + 0.57 × 252) for the average amount spent in shopping at department stores during the last two months for the overall sample. Note that the actual amount spent by the nonrespondents was $230 rather than the $252, and the actual sample average was $275 rather than the $288 estimated by trend analysis. Although the trend estimates are wrong, the error is smaller than the error that would have resulted from ignoring the nonrespondents. Had the nonrespondents been ignored, the average amount spent would have been estimated at $335(0.12 × 412 + 0.18 × 325 + 0.13 × 277)/(0.12 + 0.18 + 0.13) for the sample.

**weighting**

Statistical procedure that attempts to account for nonresponse by assigning differential weights to the data depending on the response rates.

*Weighting.*    *Weighting* attempts to account for nonresponse by assigning differential weights to the data depending on the response rates.[24] For example, in a survey on personal computers, the sample was stratified according to income. The response rates were 85, 70, and 40 percent, respectively, for the high-, medium-, and low-income groups. In analyzing the data, these subgroups are assigned weights inversely proportional to their response rates. That is, the weights assigned would be (100/85), (100/70), and (100/40), respectively, for the high-, medium-, and low-income groups. Although weighting can correct for the differential effects of nonresponse, it destroys the self-weighting nature of the sampling design and can introduce complications. Weighting is further discussed in Chapter 14 on data preparation.

**imputation**

A method to adjust for nonresponse by assigning the characteristic of interest to the nonrespondents based on the similarity of the variables available for both nonrespondents and respondents.

*Imputation.*    *Imputation* involves imputing, or assigning, the characteristic of interest to the nonrespondents based on the similarity of the variables available for both nonrespondents and respondents.[25] For example, a respondent who does not report brand usage may be imputed the usage of a respondent with similar demographic characteristics. Often there is a high correlation between the characteristic of interest and some other variables. In such cases, this correlation can be used to predict the value of the characteristic for the nonrespondents (see Chapter 17).

# INTERNATIONAL MARKETING RESEARCH

When conducting marketing research in foreign countries, statistical estimation of sample size may be difficult, as estimates of the population variance may be unavailable. Hence, the sample size is often determined by qualitative considerations, as discussed in Chapter 11: (1) the importance of the decision, (2) the nature of the research, (3) the number of variables, (4) the nature of the analysis, (5) sample sizes used in similar studies, (6) incidence rates, (7) completion rates, and (8) resource constraints. If statistical estimation of sample size is at all attempted, it should be realized that the estimates of the population variance may vary from country to country. For example, in measuring consumer preferences, a greater degree of heterogeneity may be encountered in countries where consumer preferences are not that well developed. Thus, it may be a mistake to assume that the population variance is the same or to use the same sample size in different countries.

For millions of Chinese, travel is a relatively new experience and Chinese preferences for air travel are likely to exhibit much more variability as compared to preferences of Americans.

### REAL REASEARCH

## *The Chinese Take to the Sky and the Sky Is the Limit*

The airline industry seems to have a strong and promising market potential in China, where the airline market is growing rapidly. With billions of dollars spent, China is trying to satisfy surging demand and to catch up with the rest of the world. Strong economic growth, surging foreign trade, and a revival in tourism have helped to fuel the boom. In 2000, China's airlines carried 67,217,000 passengers, up 10.3 percent from 1999. Boeing (*www.boeing.com*) forecasts a total market for approximately 1,764 commercial jet airplane sales in China (including Hong Kong and Macau) worth U.S. $144 billion over the next 20 years to 2020, making China the largest forecasted aviation market outside the United States.

Yet, for millions of Chinese, air travel is a relatively new experience, and many more millions have never flown. Hence, Chinese preferences for air travel are likely to exhibit much more variability as compared to Americans. In a survey by Delta Airlines to compare the attitude toward air travel in China and the United States of America, the sample size of the Chinese survey would have to be larger than the American survey in order for the two survey estimates to have comparable precision.[26] ■

It is important to realize that the response rates to surveys can vary widely across countries. In a 2000 business mail survey conducted in 22 countries, the response rates varied from a low of 7.1 percent in Hong Kong to a high of 42.1 percent in Denmark, with the overall response rate being 20 percent. The study also analyzed factors to help explain the differences in response rates. Factors that were looked at included cultural and geographic distance from the Netherlands, where the survey was mailed. Other factors were foreign sales, Export GNP, number of employees, power distance, and size of corporation.[27]

## ETHICS IN MARKETING RESEARCH

Although the statistical determination of sample size is usually objective, it is, nonetheless, susceptible to ethical concerns. As can be seen from the formula, the sample size is dependent on the standard deviation of the variable, and there is no way of precisely knowing the standard deviation until the data have been collected. An estimate of the standard deviation is used to calculate the sample size. This estimate is based on secondary data, judgment, or a small pilot study. By inflating the standard deviation, it is possible to increase the sample size and thus the project revenue for the research firm. Using the sample size formula, it can be seen that increasing the standard deviation by 20 percent, for example, will increase the sample size by 44 percent. It is clearly unethical to inflate the standard deviation, and thereby increase the sample size, simply to enhance the revenue of the marketing research firm.

Ethical dilemmas can arise even when the standard deviation is estimated honestly. Often, the standard deviation in the actual study is different than that estimated initially. When the standard deviation is larger than the initial estimate, the confidence interval will also be larger than desired. In such a situation, the researcher has the responsibility to discuss this with the client and jointly decide on a course of action. The ethical ramifications of miscommunicating the confidence intervals of survey estimates based on statistical samples are underscored in political polling.

**REAL REASEARCH**

### Surveys Serve Up Elections

The dissemination of some survey results has been strongly criticized as manipulative and unethical. In particular, the ethics of releasing political poll results before and during elections have been questioned. Opponents of such surveys claim that the general public is mislead by these results. First, before the election, voters are influenced by who the polls predict will win. If they see that the candidate they favor is trailing, they may decide not to vote; they assume that there is no way their candidate can win. The attempt to predict the election results while the election is in progress has come under even harsher criticism. Opponents of this practice feel that this predisposes voters to vote for the projected winner for their state, or that it may even discourage voters from voting. Even though the polls have not closed in their state, many will not vote because the media projects that there is already a winner. Furthermore, not only are the effects of these projections questionable, but frequently the accuracy of the projections is questionable as well. Although voters may be told a candidate has a certain percentage of the votes within ±1%, the confidence interval may be much larger, depending on the sample size.[28] ∎

Researchers also have the ethical responsibility to investigate the possibility of nonresponse bias and make a reasonable effort to adjust for nonresponse. The methodology adopted and the extent of nonresponse bias found should be clearly communicated.

# INTERNET AND COMPUTER APPLICATIONS

There are a number of Web sites on the Internet that offer free use of sample size and confidence interval calculators, for example, Survey System (*www.surveysystem.com*). You can use this calculator to determine how many people you need to interview in order to get results that reflect the target population as precisely as needed. You can also find the level of precision you have in an existing sample. The Discovery Research Group also has a sample size calculator (*www.drgutah.com*).

**REAL RESEARCH**

### Opinion Place *Bases Its Opinions on 1,000 Respondents*

Marketing research firms are now turning to the Web to conduct online research. Recently, four leading market research companies (ASI Market Research, Custom Research, Inc., M/A/R/C Research, and RoperASW) partnered with Digital Marketing Services (DMS), Dallas, to conduct custom research on AOL.

DMS and AOL will conduct online surveys on AOL's *Opinion Place* (*www.opinion place.com*) with an average base of 1,000 respondents by survey. This sample size was determined based on statistical considerations as well as sample sizes used in similar research conducted by traditional methods. AOL will give reward points (that can be traded in for prizes) to respondents. Users will not have to submit their e-mail addresses. The surveys will help measure response to advertiser's online campaigns. The primary objective of these researches is to gauge consumers' attitudes and other subjective information that can help media buyers plan their campaigns.

Another advantage of online surveys is that you are sure to reach your target (sample control), and that they are quicker to turn around than traditional surveys such as mall intercepts or home interviews. They also are cheaper (DMS charges $20,000 for an online survey, whereas it costs between $30,000 and $40,000 to conduct a mall intercept survey of 1,000 respondents). ■

## Improving Response Rates

Use of the Internet itself is thought to increase response rates to surveys because surveys on the Internet are easy to access and can be completed in multiple sessions if necessary. Because the length of a survey on the Internet is hidden from respondents, they are less inclined not to respond due to survey length. The inclusion of electronic skip patterns in the questionnaire design also help promote higher response rates by making it easier for the respondent to maneuver through the survey. Internet surveys can also use attractive design and plug-ins, such as music and video, to make the process of responding more interesting.

For electronic mail surveys, prior e-mails sent by the sponsor to announce the survey are strongly suggested by many of the Internet marketing research firms. These firms also send reminder e-mails to nonrespondents a few days after the initial survey has been sent. Another way to motivate respondents to complete surveys is to tell them whether the results will be used to enhance service. According to the Georgia Tech Graphics Visualization and Usability Center survey of Web users, 85 percent of Web browsers are willing to complete a survey if they are told that the results will be used to enhance service.

Another motivator is to provide incentives for completion of surveys. One respondent to a Research Info Chat Board request on how to recruit respondents for Web-based interviewing noted that he had participated in a survey because he would be entered into a cash drawing for participating. Another technique cited was to give points redeemable for merchandise or discounts to survey respondents. To visit the Research Info chat room to find other responses on how to recruit respondents for Web-based research, go to *www.researchinfo.com*.

Microcomputers and mainframes can determine the sample size for various sampling techniques. For simple applications, appropriate sample size formulas can be entered using spreadsheet programs. The researcher specifies the desired precision level, confidence level, and population variance, and the program determines the appropriate sample size for the study. By incorporating the cost of each sampling unit, the sample size can be adjusted based on budget considerations. Statchek by Data Vision Research (*www.dvrinc.com*) calculates confidence intervals and can be used to determine sample sizes. Several marketing research firms supply sample design software and services, including statistical determination of sample sizes and estimation of sample statistics. Survey Sampling (*www.surveysampling.com*) has a line of sampling products. Their Contact and Cooperation Rate Adjustment software statistically adjusts sample sizes by taking into account the expected incidence and completion rates.

## SPSS Windows

SamplePower by SPSS can be used to calculate confidence intervals and statistically adjust the sample size. The sample size calculations are available for means as well as proportions.

## FOCUS ON BURKE

Before recommending an appropriate sample size, Burke considers the following factors:

- What is the size of the "universe"? That is, how many customers qualify to participate in the study? The size of the universe is not a consideration when the population is known to be large, as in the case of household or consumers. However, this becomes an important factor when the universe is small, as in some business-to-business and industrial marketing situations.
- How much precision does the client need? The more precision required, the larger the sample size must be.
- Will any subgroups by analyzed? If so, the sample size must be adequate to draw reliable conclusions for each subgroup.
- How often does the client want to collect data? Because customers may object to participating in repeat studies, clients sometimes have to limit the number of customers Burke can interview in each wave.
- What is the client's budget?

When statistically determining the sample size, Burke uses the approaches discussed in this chapter for means and proportions. Estimates of the population standard deviation needed to calculate sample size are based on similar studies conducted by Burke in the past.

The chamber of commerce for a large city in the southeastern United States asked Burke to conduct a quality-of-life survey among residents of the 10-county metropolitan area. The chamber asked Burke to recommend the appropriate sample size based on the following three criteria:

- The chamber wanted to analyze data for the area as a whole and for each of the 10 individual counties.
- The chamber wanted to be 90 percent confident that the opinions expressed by the residents in the sample represented the views of all residents.
- The chamber would tolerate an error range of no more than 5 percent around the sample proportion.

Burke used these criteria to recommend a sample size of 270 per county. This sample size was statistically determined using the formula for proportions with $\pi = 0.5$, $D = 0.05$, and $z = 1.645$. Burke could say with 90 percent certainty that, in theory, the survey results for each county represented the views of all residents in the county within plus or minus 5 percentage points.

Burke calculates the initial incidence rate based on past studies conducted by Burke or other secondary sources. Burke has found that the completion rate for telephone interviews is about 25 percent, and so it uses the following formula to estimate how many telephone numbers may be required to complete the interviewing quota (final sample size): (quota ÷ estimated incidence) × 4. To complete a quota of 1,000 at an incidence of 37 percent, Burke would start with about 10,800 telephone numbers.

Burke offers monetary incentives in many business-to-business studies. Incentives may range from $10 to as much as $100, depending on what the respondent's job entails, whether there is a "gatekeeper" to screen calls, and how long the interview takes to complete. For example, a 20-minute interview with a cardiologist may require a $100 incentive.

Burke rarely offers incentives for consumers to complete telephone interviews. Exceptions are sometimes made when the interview is long (45 minutes or longer) or the incidence is low (5 percent or less). Burke may offer incentives for consumers prerecruited by phone to complete a follow-up survey by phone or mail. For example, a regional telecommunications company asked Burke to collect evaluations of several new products and services that the company had developed for residential customers. Burke screened people by phone to recruit qualified respondents for a follow-up mail survey. To encourage participation, Burke used a sweepstakes, entering the names of participants in a drawing for several high-ticket items. Burke also enclosed a $2 bill in the package of materials mailed to respondents.

When Burke conducts "blind" mail surveys (i.e., without prerecruiting respondents by phone), incentives are almost mandatory to achieve an acceptable response rate. When one of the largest banks in the United States asked Burke to conduct a mail survey among accountholders, Burke used a $2 bill, enclosed with the eight-page questionnaire, to achieve a response rate of about 60 percent. Mall intercepts generally require a monetary incentive only when the interview length exceeds 20 minutes or the incidence drops below 20 percent. Incentives for mall intercepts typically range from $2 to $5.

# SUMMARY

The statistical approaches to determining sample size are based on confidence intervals. These approaches may involve the estimation of the mean or proportion. When estimating the mean, determination of sample size using the confidence interval approach requires the specification of precision level, confidence level, and population standard deviation. In the case of proportion, the precision level, confidence level, and an estimate of the population proportion must be specified. The sample size determined statistically represents the final or net sample size that must be achieved. In order to achieve this final sample size, a much greater number of potential respondents have to be contacted to account for reduction in response due to incidence rates and completion rates.

Nonresponse error arises when some of the potential respondents included in the sample do not respond. The primary causes of low response rates are refusals and not-at-homes. Refusal rates may be reduced by prior notification, motivating the respondents, incentives, proper questionnaire design and administration, and follow-up. The percentage of not-at-homes can be substantially reduced by callbacks. Adjustments for nonresponse can be made by subsampling nonrespondents, replacement, substitution, subjective estimates, trend analysis, weighting, and imputation.

The statistical estimation of sample size is even more complicated in international marketing research, as the population variance may differ from one country to the next. The preliminary estimation of population variance for the purpose of determining the sample size also has ethical ramifications. The Internet and computers can assist in determining the sample size and adjusting it to account for expected incidence and completion rates.

# KEY TERMS AND CONCEPTS

parameter, *342*
statistic, *342*
finite population correction (fpc), *342*
precision level, *342*
confidence interval, *342*
confidence level, *342*

sampling distribution, *342*
statistical inference, *343*
normal distribution, *343*
standard error, *343*
z values, *344*
incidence rate, *352*

completion rate, *352*
substitution, *357*
trend analysis, *357*
weighting, *358*
imputation, *358*

# EXERCISES

## Questions

1. Define the sampling distribution.
2. What is the standard error of the mean?
3. Define finite population correction.
4. Define a confidence interval.
5. What is the procedure for constructing a confidence interval around a mean?
6. Describe the difference between absolute precision and relative precision when estimating a population mean.
7. How do the degree of confidence and the degree of precision differ?
8. Describe the procedure for determining the sample size necessary to estimate a population mean, given the degree of precision and confidence and a known population variance. After the sample is selected, how is the confidence interval generated?
9. Describe the procedure for determining the sample size necessary to estimate a population mean, given the degree of precision and confidence, but the population variance is unknown. After the sample is selected, how is the confidence interval generated?
10. How is the sample size affected when the absolute precision with which a population mean is estimated is doubled?
11. How is the sample size affected when the degree of confidence with which a population mean is estimated is increased from 95 percent to 99 percent?
12. Define what is meant by absolute precision and relative precision when estimating a population proportion.

13. Describe the procedure for determining the sample size necessary to estimate a population proportion, given the degree of precision and confidence. After the sample is selected, how is the confidence interval generated?
14. How can the researcher ensure that the generated confidence interval will be no larger than the desired interval when estimating a population proportion?
15. When several parameters are being estimated, what is the procedure for determining the sample size?
16. Define incidence rate and completion rate. How do these rates affect the determination of the final sample size?
17. What strategies are available for adjusting for nonresponse?

## Problems

1. Using Table 2 of the Appendix of Statistical Tables, calculate the probability that:
   a. $z$ is less than 1.48
   b. $z$ is greater than 1.90
   c. $z$ is between 1.48 and 1.90
   d. $z$ is between $-1.48$ and 1.90
2. What is the value of $z$ if:
   a. 60 percent of all values of $z$ are larger
   b. 10 percent of all values of $z$ are larger
   c. 68.26 percent of all possible $z$ values (symmetrically distributed around the mean) are to be contained in this interval

3. The management of a local restaurant wants to determine the average monthly amount spent by households in restaurants. Some households in the target market do not spend anything at all, whereas other households spend as much as $300 per month. Management wants to be 95 percent confident of the findings and does not want the error to exceed plus or minus $5.

   a. What sample size should be used to determine the average monthly household expenditure?

   b. After the survey was conducted, the average expenditure was found to be $90.30 and the standard deviation was $45. Construct a 95 percent confidence interval. What can be said about the level of precision?

4. To determine the effectiveness of the advertising campaign for a new VCR, management would like to know what percentage of

the households are aware of the new brand. The advertising agency thinks that this figure is as high as 70 percent. The management would like a 95 percent confidence interval and a margin of error no greater than plus or minus 2 percent.

   a. What sample size should be used for this study?

   b. Suppose that management wanted to be 99 percent confident but could tolerate an error of plus or minus 3 percent. How would the sample size change?

5. Assuming that $n = 100$ and $N = 1,000$, $\sigma = 5$, compute the standard error of the mean with and without the finite population correction factor.

# INTERNET AND COMPUTER EXERCISES

1. Using a spread sheet (e.g., EXCEL), program the formulas for determining the sample size under the various approaches. (This is very simple to do.)

2. Solve problems 1 through 4 using the programs that you have developed.

3. Visit the Gallup organization Web site (*www.gallup.com*). Identify some of the surveys recently completed by the Gallup organization. What were the sample sizes in these surveys and how were they determined?

# ACTIVITIES

## Role Playing

1. You work in the marketing research department of Burger King. Burger King has developed a new cooking process that makes the hamburgers taste better. However, before the new hamburger is introduced in the market, taste tests will be conducted. How should the sample size for these taste tests be determined? What approach would you recommend? Justify your recommendations to a group of students representing Burger King management.

2. A major electric utility would like to determine the average amount spent per household for cooling during the summer. The management believes that a survey should be conducted. You are appointed as a consultant. What procedure would you recommend for determining the sample size? Make a presentation about this project to three students who represent the Chief

Operating Officer, Chief Financial Officer, and the Chief Marketing Officer of this utility.

## Fieldwork

1. Visit a local marketing research firm. Find out how the sample sizes were determined in some recent surveys or experiments. Write a report about your findings.

## Group Discussion

1. "Quantitative considerations are more important than qualitative considerations in determining the sample size." Discuss as a small group.

2. Discuss the relative advantages and disadvantages of the confidence interval approach.

# APPENDIX 12.1

## The Normal Distribution

In this appendix we provide a brief overview of the normal distribution and the use of the normal distribution table. The normal distribution is used in calculating the sample size and it serves as the basis for classical statistical inference. Many continuous phenomena follow the normal distribution or can be approximated by it. The normal distribution can, likewise, be used to approximate many discrete probability distributions.[1]

The *normal distribution* has some important theoretical properties. It is bell-shaped and symmetrical in appearance. Its measures of central tendency (mean, median, and mode) are all identical. Its associated random variable has an infinite range ($-\infty < x < +\infty$).

The normal distribution is defined by the population mean $\mu$ and population standard deviation $\sigma$. Because an infinite number of combination of $\mu$ and $\sigma$ exist, an infinite number of normal distributions exist, and an infinite number of tables would be required. However, by standardizing the data, we need only one table, such as Table 2 given in the Appendix of Statistical Tables. Any normal random variable $X$ can be

---

[1] This material is drawn from Mark L. Berenson, David M. Levine, and Timothy Krehbiel, *Basic Business Statistics: Concepts and Applications,* 8th ed. (Englewood Cliffs, NJ: Prentice Hall, 2002).

converted to a standardized normal random variable $z$ by the formula:

$$z = \frac{X - \mu}{\sigma}$$

Note that the random variable $z$ is always normally distributed with a mean of 0 and a standard deviation of 1. The normal probability tables are generally used for two purposes: (1) finding probabilities corresponding to known values of $X$ or $z$, and (2) finding values of $X$ or $z$ corresponding to known probabilities. Each of these uses is discussed.

## Finding Probabilities Corresponding to Known Values

Suppose Figure 12A.1 represents the distribution of the number of engineering contracts received per year by an engineering firm. Because the data span the entire history of the firm, Figure 12A.1 represents the population. Therefore, the probabilities, or proportion of area under the curve, must add up to 1.0. The vice president of marketing wishes to determine the probability that the number of contracts received next year will be between 50 and 55. The answer can be determined by using Table 2 of the Appendix of Statistical Tables.

Table 2 gives the probability, or area under the standardized normal curve from the mean (zero) to the standardized value of interest, $z$. Only positive entries of $z$ are listed in the table. For a symmetrical distribution with zero mean, the area from the mean to $+z$ (i.e., $z$ standard deviations above the mean) is identical to the area from the mean to $-z$ ($z$ standard deviations below the mean).

Note that the difference between 50 and 55 corresponds to a $z$ value of 1.00. Note that to use Table 2, all $z$ values must be recorded to two decimal places. To read the probability or area under the curve from the mean to $z = +1.00$, scan down

the $z$ column of Table 2 until the $z$ value of interest (in tenths) is located. In this case, stop in the row $z = 1.0$. Then, read across this row until you intersect the column containing the hundredths place of the $z$ value. Thus, in Table 2, the tabulated probability for $z = 1.00$ corresponds to the intersection of the row $z = 1.0$ with the column $z = 0.00$. This probability is 0.3413. As shown in Figure 12A.1, the probability is 0.3413 that the number of contracts received by the firm next year will be between 50 and 55. It can also be concluded that the probability is 0.6826 (2 × 0.3413) that the number of contracts received next year will be between 45 and 55.

This result could be generalized to show that for any normal distribution, the probability is 0.6826 that a randomly selected item will fall within ±1 standard deviations above or below the mean. Also, it can be verified from Table 2 that there is a 0.9544 probability that any randomly selected normally distributed observation will fall within ±2 standard deviations above or below the mean, and a 0.9973 probability that the observation will fall within 3 standard deviations above or below the mean.

## Finding Values Corresponding to Known Probabilities

Suppose the vice president of marketing wishes to determine how many contracts must come in so that 5 percent of the contracts for the year have come in. If 5 percent of the contracts have come in, 95 percent of the contracts have yet to come. As shown in Figure 12A.2, this 95 percent can be broken down into two parts—contracts above the mean (i.e., 50 percent) and contracts between the mean and the desired $z$ value (i.e., 45 percent). The desired $z$ value can be determined from Table 2, because the area under the normal curve from the standardized mean, 0, to this $z$ must be 0.4500. From Table 2, we search for the area or probability 0.4500. The closest value is 0.4495 or 0.4505. For 0.4495, we see that the $z$ value corresponding to the particular $z$ row (1.6) and $z$ column (0.04) is 1.64. However, the $z$ value must be recorded as negative (i.e., $z = -1.64$), because it is below the standardized mean of 0. Similarly, the $z$ value corresponding to the area of 0.4505 is $-1.65$. Because 0.4500 is midway between 0.4495 and 0.4505, the appropriate $z$ value could be midway between the two $z$ values and estimated as $-1.645$. The corresponding

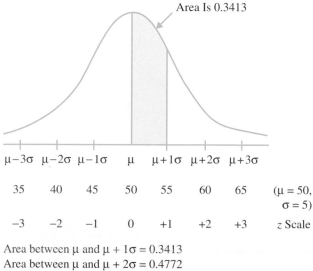

Area Is 0.3413

| $\mu-3\sigma$ | $\mu-2\sigma$ | $\mu-1\sigma$ | $\mu$ | $\mu+1\sigma$ | $\mu+2\sigma$ | $\mu+3\sigma$ | |
| --- | --- | --- | --- | --- | --- | --- | --- |
| 35 | 40 | 45 | 50 | 55 | 60 | 65 | ($\mu = 50$, $\sigma = 5$) |
| $-3$ | $-2$ | $-1$ | 0 | $+1$ | $+2$ | $+3$ | $z$ Scale |

Area between $\mu$ and $\mu + 1\sigma = 0.3413$
Area between $\mu$ and $\mu + 2\sigma = 0.4772$
Area between $\mu$ and $\mu + 3\sigma = 0.4986$

**Figure 12A.1**
Finding Probability Corresponding to a Known Value

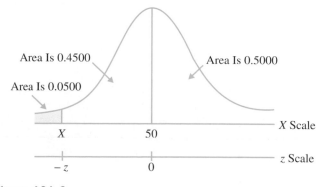

Area Is 0.4500          Area Is 0.5000

Area Is 0.0500

$X$          50          X Scale

$-z$          0          $z$ Scale

**Figure 12A.2**
Finding Values Corresponding to Known Probabilities

*X* value can then be calculated from the standardization formula, as follows:

$$X = \mu + z\sigma$$

or

$$X = 50 + (-1.645)5 = 41.775$$

Suppose the vice president wanted to determine the interval in which 95 percent of the contracts for next year are expected to lie. As can be seen from Figure 12A.3, the corresponding *z* values are ±1.96. This corresponds to *X* values of 50 ± (1.96)5, or 40.2 and 59.8. This range represents the 95 percent confidence interval.

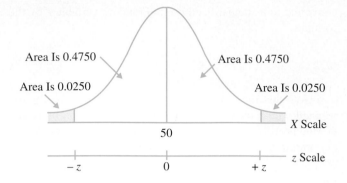

Area Is 0.4750　　Area Is 0.4750

Area Is 0.0250　　Area Is 0.0250

*X* Scale

50

*z* Scale

$-z$　　0　　$+z$

**Figure 12A.3**

Finding Values Corresponding to Known Probabilities: Confidence Intervals

# CASES

## 2.1 The Forecast Is Sunny for The Weather Channel!

When The Weather Channel, the first 24-hour all-weather network, began broadcasting in 1982, it quickly became the object of mockery. "Many in the industry ridiculed us, suggesting that the only type of advertiser we would attract would be a raincoat company or a galoshes company," remembers Michael Eckert, The Weather Channel's CEO. Besides pondering where advertising support would come from, critics questioned what kind of audience was going to tune in to a channel that boasts wall-to-wall weather, a topic that sounds as interesting as staring at wallpaper.

So far, the answers to these questions have been quite surprising. In its over twenty years of broadcasting, the channel has gained support from a cadre of deep-pocket advertisers, which include Buick, Motorola, and Campbell's Soup. In 2003, the Weather Channel reached more than 83 million U.S. households and covered more than 95 percent of cable homes. In addition, their exposure goes beyond U.S. shores to reach 8.2 million households in Latin America under the name, El Canal del Tiempo.

According to The Weather Channel's vice-president of strategic marketing, Steven Clapp, "There might have been a time when people weren't willing to admit that they were viewers. Now people are proud to say they watch us. Research shows that we are [gaining ratings], although it's difficult to isolate why." A major event linked to the increase in popularity of the network is the extensive brand building effort that started in the spring of 1995. Although some viewers will always see the weather as just a commodity, promise for making the presentation of weather forecasts into something brandable lies in a growing segment of "weather-engaged" viewers, viewers who tune in regularly and ones that the network wants to reach. "Viewers know that they can turn to us for quality forecasts and weather expertise. What we're trying to do is take it one step further and emotionally bond with the viewer," says Clapp. Hayes Roth, a branding expert, agrees that branding the channel helps build stronger ties to viewers and advertisers. The company's efforts have spanned from improving the network's products, extending The Weather Channel name to related products, and a promotional blitz.

The network, whose slogan declares that "no place on Earth has better weather," went beyond providing just expert forecasts to create lines of programming tailored to retaining viewer interest. The network uses a staff of more than 100 meteorologists to analyze National Weather Service data and prepare 4,000 localized forecasts. While these local reports are the channel's mainstays, new features have crept in that have had the effect of stretching the average viewing time from 11 minutes to approximately 14 minutes, with some fanatical individuals watching for hours at a time. These new features act to expand what constitutes the channel's weather information and spark the interest of the average viewer beyond the routine weather topics. For example, "The Skiers Forecast" spotlights conditions on ski slopes. The Weather Channel has worked with the National Football League to prepare specialized game day forecasts. Playing off a recent upsurge in interest in the weather among audiences, the network has presented features such as *The Chase,* a program about people who chase tornadoes, and *Forecast for Victory,* a one-hour long show that looked at the role of weather in deciding significant battles of World War II. These features keep certain segments of the market glued to the station for more than just the weather forecast.

In order to create more brand awareness and to keep weather forecasts and weather updates as accurate as possible, The Weather Channel and the U.S. Navy teamed up to share information in 2001. The Weather Channel now has access to the Navy's sophisticated technology in order to assist in predicting and presenting the weather. Also, in January 2002, The Weather Channel became the weather forecaster for USA Today's domestic and international issues as well as for *USAToday.com.* The two companies shared the weather coverage for the 2002 Winter Olympics in Salt Lake City.

The Weather Channel worked to extend its boundaries beyond just the television format. Customized Weather Channel reports are available for over 30 online services, 250 radio stations, a hugely popular 900-number phone service, and 64 newspapers across the U.S.—all with The Weather Channel tagline or logo. Just recently, The Weather Channel began to offer wireless weather delivered to handheld devices. This project is in conjunction with Verizon, AT&T, Sprint, and Palm Pilot. "If a consumer sees The Weather Channel name in the newspaper, that just reinforces the brand," says Hayes Roth. In addition to these partnerships, The Weather Channel has worked to package weather in creative ways including books, home videos, calendars, educational material for elementary schools, and a CD-ROM titled *Everything Weather.* In fact, after a hugely positive response on a test mailing, the network started a mail-order catalog of company-themed merchandise. One of the most widely popular line extensions is the company's web site, *www.weather.com,* which enables users to create a personalized weather page. In only 40 minutes after its launch, 1,000 users had already created a customized web page.

In late 2000, Weather.com re-launched its site in an effort to refresh the look, feel, and organization of content. The goal is also to enable the site to accommodate more traffic and content, as well as incorporate database functions. Now, Weather.com is delivering even more-highly personalized weather content. The re-launch is part of the site's ongoing strategy to make the weather relevant. It is also a continuation of Weather.com's positioning of itself as a lifestyle site. According to Debora Wilson, President and CEO of Weather.com, the company is going to launch new country specific sites to draw more of an audience. The company is hoping the new sites, targeting the UK, France, and Germany, will help to boost online revenue. The company began launching the new sites in late 2001 and 2002. There has also been a report about Weather.com including a "portfolio of subscription-based services" on its site but Wilson declined to give estimates of how this would affect revenue.

In an effort to transform itself into a lifestyle destination Web site, Weather.com launched a 4-city test marketing campaign in 2001, that featured its first offline advertisement. The test cities included Houston, Nashville, Philadelphia, and Columbus, Ohio. This campaign was expected to cost between $2 million and $10 million depending on the results from the test cities. Weather.com felt the need to explore advertising in different medias; therefore, their promotional test included offline advertisements from a variety of television, radio, and outdoor sources. Additionally, Weather.com tested unconventional ad schemes on dry-cleaner bags and packages of airline peanuts. Weather.com's non-traditional campaigns featured such taglines as, "Forget about what they are wearing in Paris, think Anchorage" and "Don't you have your own Doppler?" Vice President of Marketing, Alan Kaminsky, said, "The test campaigns were a part of a larger strategy to give weather forecasts a higher profile."

Even though Weather.com's promotional campaign contributed to their overall strategy, the network still had a few problems to overcome despite their potential, according to branding expert Hayes Roth. He said, "They have a great brand name but it's boring as toast. They're doing a mediocre job of on-air branding. If you're surfing channels, it's so dull that you tend to flick by it." Roth also sees that the brand lacks a cool or hip image. He said, "People wear clothes with MTV's logo because they've decided that it's a cool logo. I don't know if people want to see The Weather Channel on their jacket." Despite some gray clouds, Weather.com does have a very sunny spot. The network has a large loyal audience, something of which other networks are envious. Furthermore, Weather.com really knows what they're talking about, and that is a very marketable commodity. It has the vast potential of owning the weather and could become the official brand of weather. So watch out gray clouds, it is clearing up and the forecast is sunny for The Weather Channel!

## QUESTIONS

1. Visit the Web site of The Weather Channel (*www.weather.com*). Write a report about the type of information available at this site.
2. Identify other potential sources of information about the weather.
3. Discuss the role of qualitative research in identifying consumer's needs for weather-related information. Which qualitative research techniques should be used?
4. If a survey were to be conducted to determine consumer preferences for weather-related information, which interviewing method would you recommend? Why?
6. Can observation methods be used to determine consumer preferences for weather-related information? If so, which observational methods would you use? Why?

## REFERENCES

"E-Business: The Weather Channel, Inc.," *Internetweek* (877) (September 10, 2001): 48.

Anonymous, "The Weather Channel gets Navy Data," *Broadcasting and Cable* 131 (25) (June 11, 2001): 67.

Kim McAvoy, "Changing With the Weather.com," *Broadcasting & Cable* 131 (7) (February 12, 2001): 38–39.

Keith Flamer, "Eye of the Storm," *Broadcasting & Cable* 130 (40) (September 25, 2000): 84–86.

# 2.2 Who Is the Host with the Most?

The once traditionally complacent hotel industry had to learn to market its services due to the increase in the number of hotels and the accompanying drop in occupancy rates. The hotel industry generated $110 billion in 2001, and every chain is continually trying to segment to gain a bigger share of the market. Perhaps the most troublesome problem the industry faced is the lack of customer loyalty. Most hotels provide similar facilities, and most customers do not travel enough to recognize distinctions between them. For this reason, many companies opted to differentiate their hotels through multiple branding, or moving into different market segments. The major chains continue to use broad market reach techniques, because many feel that future success can be gained in targeting certain segments of the market and catering to their needs better than the competitor. Three important segments that have gained importance for hotel chains in the 1990s are business travelers, senior citizens, and extended-stay travelers.

The importance of business travelers to more luxury hotel chains has not gone unnoticed. Marketing research showed that 75 percent of stays at these types of facilities are business related. It is, therefore, no wonder why certain chains have gone out of their way to court business travelers. In early 1990, Marriott (*www.marriott.com*) began to offer hotel rooms designed to meet the needs of business travelers. Marriott felt that it could enter the moderately priced market by targeting business travelers with the Courtyard Hotel concept. To better meet the needs of business travelers, Marriott began installing high-speed Internet access in their hotels during October 2000. Marriott also has an ExecuStay Division designed for extended-stay business travelers. The division has 6,500 fully furnished apartment style units across the United States. Finally, Marriott provides conference centers to business travelers. These centers have state-of-the-art audiovisual communications equipment to give business travelers a meeting area away from the home office.

Some chains, like Holiday Inn, have made attempts at direct business-to-business marketing. Holiday Inn uses trade shows, direct marketing, and traditional media with a special narrow emphasis to penetrate members of the business sector. "Twenty-five percent of our corporate marketing budget is earmarked for business-to-business," says CEO Bryan Langton. Holiday Inn is also adapting rooms to make them more oriented to business travelers. Between 1994 and 1999, the chain spent more than $1.5 billion on hotel renovations. Six Continents Hotels (*www.sixcontinentshotels.com*), the owner of the Holiday Inn chain, offered its Crowne Plaza and Embassy Suites chains to appeal to the up-scale business traveler and to compete with Courtyard Hotels. The company used the name Holiday Inn for its middle-class image hotels and the name Holiday Inn Express to compete with such economy chains as Motel 6, Red Roof, Days Inn, Super 8, and Econo Lodge. However, Holiday Inn still experienced difficulties in differentiating its various brands, especially when more than one was located in the same city. In order to keep customers coming back to its hotels, Six Continental Hotels started "Priority Club Worldwide," which the company calls the "world's first and largest multi-brand hotel loyalty program." Members of the club receive special promotions as well as points anytime they stay in one of the 3,200 Six Continental Hotels around the world. The points can be redeemed for free hotel stays, airline miles, brand name goods, and vacation packages. During November 2001, Holiday Inn held a "Next Night Free" promotion. This gave guests a chance to earn one free night for every night they paid for, up to five free nights! Holiday Inn held the promotion to encourage travelers to stay at Holiday Inn Hotels for extended periods of time during the holiday season.

Hyatt's (*www.hyatt.com*) research showed that 58 percent of business travelers were spending more time working in their rooms, and 72 percent stated that they felt pressure to show work while on the road. As a result, Hyatt began marketing its Business Plan program, which includes office style conveniences in the rooms such as complimentary local, toll-free, and credit-card telephone access; and 24-hour printer, copier, and fax availability. Hyatt also offers its business travelers cutting edge technology such as high-speed Ethernet access and videoconferencing equipment. In addition, a complimentary breakfast is provided to help business travelers stay productive on the road. In 2000, Hyatt was on the forefront of developing faster, more efficient check-in options, which included 1-800-CHECKIN, allowing guests to check in to their hotel rooms in the U.S. and Canada by telephone. Taking advantage of this propensity, hotels have tailored their Web sites, facilitating online reservations and developing special advertising for this media. Firms are also attempting to address other needs of the traveler beyond just the work-related ones. When Hilton Hotels found that approximately 50 percent of business travelers suffer from some form of insomnia, the chain, in conjunction with the National Sleep Foundation, designed special rooms. The Sleep-Tight Rooms project is claimed to provide the "ultimate sleep environment" and features top-quality mattresses, synthetic down pillows, a music system with a CD player all to soothe the weary business traveler to sleep and a clock and special lamp which gently awaken the traveler 30 minutes before commute time.

Another segment of the market that hotel chains are courting are senior citizens. A study by RoperASW shows that the number of Americans over 50 will increase by 47.3 million in the next 25 years. In the United States alone, someone turns 50 every seven seconds. Marketing research also show that men and women over 50 travel more and stay longer in hotels than do their younger counterparts, spending more than $30 billion in travel in 2000 alone. Choice Hotels adapted accommodations for this segment in 1995 and continue to be successful today. Select Choice chains feature the Senior Room package in 10 percent of the rooms, which features comforts seniors indicated are similar to those in their own homes. Brighter lighting, large button phones, and standard TV remote controls are amenities that are intrinsic to these special rooms. Bathrooms were given special attention, featuring special lever door handles and grab bars. With these rooms generating $5 million in annual revenues, other chains are looking into addressing concerns of this segment. One aspect of catering to seniors that is gaining importance by hotel chains is assisted living. Assisted living facilities, which are in the middle of the spectrum of independent living and nursing homes, allow seniors to live as they wish while providing certain extra services such as meals and housekeeping. Hyatt, which operates Classic Residence facilities, and Marriott, which offers Brighton Gardens facilities among other operations, are leaders in this segment.

The fastest growing segment of the market, extended-stay travelers, has traditionally been the most neglected. In

2000, extended-stay hotels comprised roughly 30 to 35 percent of the entire hotel market. Extended stay travelers are guests who wish to stay five days or longer and require special facilities, such as 24-hour staffed front desks and sometimes kitchen amenities. Unfortunately, demand for this type of hotel room far exceeds supply. In 2000, only 3 percent to 5 percent of the lodging supply—or just more than 100,000 rooms—were dedicated to extended-stay facilities.

In 2000, a study conducted by PricewaterhouseCoopers for Extended StayAmerica indicated that approximately 300,000 new rooms could be supported by the demand that existed. Hotel chains realized the missed opportunity, and began pouring resources into developing and marketing these facilities. Marriott's Residence Inn dominates the market, but newer entrants to this segment are trying to capitalize on the widespread interest in extended-stay rooms. In 1997, Holiday Inn launched a new extension, Staybridge Suites by Holiday Inn, specifically designed for this market. These suites feature such amenities as 24-hour self-serve laundry facilities, a 24-hour convenience store, high-speed Internet access, a personal telephone number, and voice-mail box for each suite. As of 2000, they had 25 successful new hotels and 25 hotels that were under construction. Holiday Inn's extension proved to be a success.

Hotels are attempting to segment the market and offer enhanced services to attract customers. For a hotel to be successful in attracting customers, it must be the "host with the most." Marketing research will be a key driver for success in this industry.

## QUESTIONS

1. Identify some possible sources of secondary data for the hotel industry. What types of data are available on the Internet?
2. The hotel industry has faced the troublesome problem of differentiation. Holiday Inn would like to undertake marketing research to determine how it can differentiate itself from its competitors. What research design would you recommend?
3. What information is needed for Holiday Inn to develop a program to differentiate itself from competition?
4. Design a questionnaire to obtain the relevant information.
5. What research design would be appropriate for monitoring consumers' changing needs and preferences for hotels?
6. Marriott would like to know what is the best way to segment the hotel market. What type of research design would you recommend and why?

## REFERENCES

Edward R. DeLome, "Hotel Industry Slowly Sees Light at the End of a Recession Tunnel," *The Real Estate Finance Journal* 17 (3) (Winter 2002): 36–37

Julie Forster, Andrew and Christopher Palmeri, "Making Hay While it Rains," *Business Week* (January 14, 2002): 32–33

Eryn Brown, "Heartbreak Hotel," *Fortune* 144 (11) (November 26, 2001): 161–165.

Paul Davidson and Doug Carroll, "Marriott Chief Says Travel Industry Is in Recession; Occupancy Rate Down, but It Has Risen Since Sept. 11," *USA Today* (November 20, 2001): B10.

Daniel Northington and Sheridan Prasso, "Holiday Inn Has Just the Ticket," *Business Week* (3720) (February 19, 2001): 16.

# 2.3 Candy Is Dandy for Hershey

The battle was on! Hershey and Mars, the two candy giants, dueling over the number one spot in the $73-billion-a-year candy industry. Hershey (*www.hersheys.com*) lost its throne in the early 1970s, and it took the company time to get back into the competitive arena. By 1985, however, Mars and Hershey were the manufacturers of the top 10 candy bars, and together they shared 70 percent of the market. Cadbury held about 9 percent of the market and Nestle only 6 percent. Then in 1988, Hershey acquired Cadbury and its share jumped from 36 percent to 44 percent of the candy market. The addition of brands such as Cadbury Dairy Milk Chocolate, Peter Paul Mounds, Almond Joy, and York Peppermint Pattie enabled Hershey to regain its throne in the candy market.

The late 1980s and early 1990s produced the introduction of such products as Hershey's Kisses with Almonds, Hugs, Hugs with Almonds, Amazin' Fruit gummy bears, and the Cookies 'n' Mint Chocolate bar. In 1994, Hershey Food Corp. celebrated its 100th year in business. In 1996, Hershey addressed its lack of strong showing products in the non-chocolate sector of the industry by acquiring Leaf North American brand, which produces such strong sellers as Jolly Rancher and Good & Plenty. Also in 1996, Hershey unveiled its low-fat Sweet Escapes line, which brought in over $100 million in 1997.

After problems in implementing a new distribution system in 1999, Hershey restored sales, market share, and earnings growth in 2000, marking its best year volume-wise since 1996. For the fiscal year ending 2001, total sales were $4.5 billion, which were 8 percent higher than the same time period for the previous year. As of 2002, Hershey was dominating the candy market with a 30.3 percent market share. The number two player M&M/Mars, Inc.'s market share was 16.8 percent, while the number three competitor, Nestle, had 6.3 percent of the market. The decisions over the past 100 years have been both diverse and profitable. (See Tables 1 & 2.)

One factor that helped Hershey in their battle with M&M/Mars was its excellent marketing research department. Hershey's research showed that the typical consumer viewed candy as a luxury good or as a self-indulgence. Because of these attitudes and beliefs, 70 percent of all candy sales were attributed to impulse buying. In 1999, Hershey introduced

## TABLE 1

**Hershey's Timeline**

| | |
|---|---|
| 1895 | First Hershey's Chocolate Bar is sold. |
| 1907 | Hershey's Kisses are introduced. |
| 1908 | Hershey's Milk Chocolate Bar with Almonds is introduced. |
| 1911 | Sales reach $5 million. |
| 1925 | Mr. Goodbar chocolate bar is introduced. |
| 1938 | The Hershey's Krakel bar is introduced. |
| 1939 | Hershey's Miniatures are introduced. |
| 1945 | Milton Hershey dies at the age of 88. |
| 1963 | Reese Candy Co., producer of Reese's peanut butter cups, is purchased. |
| 1966 | Hershey purchases San Giorgio Macaroni Co. |
| 1968 | Hershey Chocolate Corp. changes its name to Hershey Food Corp. |
| 1977 | Y & S Candies, Inc., manufacturer of licorice and licorice-type products such as Twizzlers and Nibs, is purchased. |
| 1986 | Luden's and 5th Avenue trademarks are added through acquisition of the Dietrich Corporations confectionery operations. |
| 1988 | Hershey Foods Corp. acquires Peter Paul/Cadbury U.S. confectionery operations. Brands acquired include Peter Paul Mounds and Almond Joy bars and York Peppermint Patties. |
| 1990 | Hershey's Kisses with Almonds are introduced. |
| 1991 | Fluid milk plant used to produce a chocolate drink is purchased. |
| 1992 | Hershey's Cookies 'n' Mint bar and Amazin' Fruit gummy bears are introduced. |
| 1993 | Hershey's Hugs and Hershey's Hugs with Almonds are introduced. |
| 1994 | Hershey's Nuggets chocolates and Reese's Peanut Butter Puffs brand cereal are introduced. |
| 1996 | Hershey launches the Sweet Escapes low-fat chocolate line. Hershey acquires Leaf North American brand to strengthen its non-chocolate line. |
| 1997 | Reese's Crunchy Cookie Cups are introduced. |
| 1998 | Reese Sticks are launched. |
| 1999 | Hershey's Bites are introduced in flavors such as Almond Joy, Reese's Peanut Butter Cups, Hershey's Milk Chocolate with Almonds, and Hershey's Cookies and Crème. |
| 2000 | Hershey acquires the breath mint and chewing gum business of Nabisco for $135 million. |
| 2001 | Hershey's Bites secured the #10 spot of 2000s Top 10 list of best new product introductions. |

## TABLE 2

**Top 10 Chocolate Brands**

| RANK | BRAND | SHARE (IN PERCENTAGE) |
|---|---|---|
| 1 | Snickers | 10.20 |
| 2 | Reese's | 9.33 |
| 3 | M&M Peanut | 6.31 |
| 4 | M&M Plain | 5.26 |
| 5 | Kit Kat | 4.97 |
| 6 | Butterfinger | 4.71 |
| 7 | Hershey Almond | 3.39 |
| 8 | Crunch | 3.33 |
| 9 | Milky Way | 3.25 |
| 10 | Hershey Milk | 2.91 |

Hershey Bites, which are miniature bite-size versions of their candy bars. As of 2002, the bite-size candy flavors included 7 of their most popular regular sized candy bars. The success of the Hershey Bites line was great, increasing the unwrapped packaged candy segment by 33.4 percent. Consumers were obviously ready for the bite-sized candies. Candy customers also tended to be fickle, rarely purchasing the same candy bar twice in a row.

A consumer's age was also shown to influence buying habits. Market research also informed Hershey that the population was getting older. In the 1970s and early 1980s, young people from age 13 to the late 20s were the dominant age group. In the 1990s, it was becoming the 35 to 50 age group. For this reason, the candy industry decided to move upscale to attract the baby-boom adults. For the year 2000, the median age for Americans was 40. The National Confectioners Association believes that as Americans get older, they tend to favor the better things in life. Among these better things are quality confections. A multiple cross-sectional analysis of consumption patterns revealed that adults were consuming an ever-increasing percentage of candy (Table 3). The adult market has therefore proven to be increasingly lucrative.

Additionally, to gain market share, Hershey decided to become a fearless product innovator. For example, in 1998, Reese's NutRageous candy bar was initially tested under the name *Acclaim.* Unfortunately, when Hershey's marketing

## TABLE 3

### Candy Consumption by Age Group (percent)

| Age Group | 1980 | 1990 | 2000 (Est.) |
| --- | --- | --- | --- |
| 0–17 yrs | 46 percent | 38 percent | 33 percent |
| 18–34 yrs | 22 percent | 23 percent | 24 percent |
| 35–45 yrs | 20 percent | 24 percent | 26 percent |
| 46+ yrs | 12 percent | 15 percent | 17 percent |

staff showed consumers the name *Acclaim* typed on a plain white piece of paper and asked them what came to mind, their biggest association was with the Acclaim automobile made by Plymouth. This showed marketers they needed to create a new name so they tested the name NutRageous. The name fit the product's description perfectly! Introduced in February 1998, ReeseSticks combines three ingredients consumers love: Reese's peanut butter, crispy wafers, and milk chocolate. ReeseSticks proved to be so successful that demand initially exceeded Hershey's ability to produce all the usual packtypes. To appeal to adults with larger appetites, Hershey introduced the Kit Kat Big Kat in May 2000. This bigger version of an old favorite is two times as wide and three times as thick as one section of the traditional Kit Kat. To appeal to children, Hershey introduced a new candy creation product called the Hershey's Candy Bar Factory. The product entered the market in June 2000, allowed kids to use their creativity and imagination to create their own, unique chocolate candy.

For many reasons, Hershey, like its competitors, has been looking toward the snack industry with the insight that sweets do not just consist of candy. Today's more sophisticated consumers look at ice cream bars, cookies, and chocolate covered granola bars when they crave something sweet. In 1999, Hershey and Breyers Ice cream teamed up to launch a two-item candy flavors line: Breyers Hershey's Milk Chocolate with Almonds Chocolate Ice Cream with Fudge Swirls, and Breyers Reese's Peanut Butter Cup Ice Cream with Fudge Swirls. Hershey has already entered the granola market with New Trail granola bars. Hershey also produces other non-candy items such as baking chocolate and candy, chocolate syrup, chocolate drinks, ice cream toppings, hot cocoa mix, and peanut butter. They have also entered the non-chocolate candy market with their acquisition of Y&S Candies, which produces Twizzlers and Nibs. In an effort to reemphasize the Twizzler brand's playful qualities, a new campaign was launched during the spring of 2001. Commercials featured a 30-second, live-action spot, which marked a departure from 15 years of animated executions. The new Twizzler's TWIST-n-FILL

candy, introduced in June 2000, also emphasized Twizzler's playful qualities. The candy combines flavors and is available in two combinations, watermelon/cherry and raspberry/tropical.

In late 2000, Hershey acquired the breath mint and chewing gum business of Nabisco for $135 million. The brands affected by the acquisition include Ice Breakers, Breath Savers Cool Blasts intense mints, Care*free, Stick*free, Bubble Yum and Fruit Stripe gums, and Nabisco's gum factory in Puerto Rico. While candy is dandy for Hershey, there is the shrewd realization that candy bars alone may not give the company its sweetest bottom line.

## QUESTIONS

1. Search the Internet and compile information related to the candy market.
2. Describe the kind of market research that could have led to the introduction of Kit Kat Big Kat. Discuss the kind of research design that would be appropriate.
3. Describe the target audience for Kit Kat Big Kat. What kind of information about their preferences, purchase intentions, behaviors, lifestyles, psychographics, and demographics had to be obtained?
4. Discuss the scaling techniques which should be used to measure preferences, purchase intentions, lifestyles, attitudes, and knowledge about candy. What is the nature (nominal, ordinal, interval, or ratio) of information obtained from each of these scales?
5. Design part of a questionnaire that could be used to obtain this information.
6. What would be the best way to administer the questionnaire? Which interviewing method should be used? Why?
7. Recommend an appropriate sampling technique for this survey. How should the sample size be determined?
8. Could the observation method be used to determine consumer preferences for different kinds of candy bars? If so, which observation method would you use? Why?

## REFERENCES

Bill Sulon, "Hershey Foods Tops Candy-Selling Rivals," *Knight Ridder Tribune Business News* (January 19, 2002): 1.

Stephanie Thompson, "Hershey to Increase Ad Budgets for Key Brands," *Advertising Age* (72) 44 (October 29, 2001): 1, 40.

Anonymous, "Rite Aid Names Hershey to Supplier of the Year List," *Drug Store News* (23) 15 (October 22, 2001): 26.

Anonymous, "Hershey's Bites Make IRI's Top New Products List," *Candy Industry* 2 (February 2001): 11.

Anonymous, "Hershey Takes On Nabisco Mint, Gum Business," *Candy Industry* 165 (12) (December 2000): 10.

# 2.4 Fragrances Are Sweet, But Competition Is Bitter

The mature fragrance industry has become a marketing war zone. Every manufacturer is battling for its piece of market share. In the 1970s, fragrances ranked in the top 20 among items with the highest dollar expenditures. However, by the mid 1990s they had dropped to the top 50. As a result, manufacturers relied heavily on new product introductions to stimulate consumer interest, sometimes at the price of older brands. The number of new product introductions shot up from 20–25 per year in the early 1980s to 30–40 in the mid 1990s. However, new product introductions failed to increase total bottle sales. Since 1981, purchases of women's fragrances in the United States tumbled by about 34 percent in total bottle sales.

In the twenty-first century, the fragrance industry continues to face rising price competition, price transparency, and fundamental changes in distribution. In 2000, the global market for fragrances in seven countries was valued at approximately $15 billion. The fragrance market is heavily influenced by prevailing fashion trends and is characterized by a low-level of brand loyalty. All of these factors contribute to the limited growth prospects for the fragrance industry in the future. However, competition among fragrance companies still continues. Fragrance companies have to attempt to portray their brand as a "dream in a bottle." In 2001, fragrance companies spent a total of $46.8 million on advertising in an attempt to portray the "dream-like" quality of their fragrance.

A major theme in perfume advertising is sex. The reduced sales suggest that the sex angle did not have as much appeal as some fragrance makers had hoped. A report by Euromonitor in 2000, the London-based marketing research consultancy, said that despite the fragrance industry's emphasis on unisex products, the market has peaked and more traditional, gender-specific fragrances are back in vogue. The competitive nature of the industry forced several manufacturers to explore new distribution outlets. One of these was the drugstore market (see Table 1). Consolidation among department stores reduced the number of distribution outlets for fragrances. Marketing research indicated that drugstore consumers were purchasing more non-drug items, such as makeup and fragrances. Pharmacy and drugstore fragrance sales accounted for 47 percent of value share in 2000. However, this is expected to decrease as competition from grocery chains becomes heated. Consumers between the ages of 30 and 60 were found to go to the drugstore for prescriptions more often than younger consumers. Women in their 20s and 30s who had small children also made frequent trips to drugstores. Women under 25, who accounted for 8 to 9 percent of fragrance purchases, preferred shopping for fragrances in drugstores to department stores. On the other hand, women who were 45 and over, had high incomes, and discretionary buying power purchased 33 percent of fragrances. These women generally bought from department stores. Apparel specialty stores had also gained attention, since their total overall sales increased at twice the rate compared to the increase in department and discount department store sales. The move to drugstore and discount markets has allowed fine fragrances to be available to more consumers who are price conscious. However, it has also led to a lessening of the image of the fine fragrance. Since many brands are now available in multiple types of retail outlets, a gap has been created for exclusive brands sold at a higher price in a limited number of stores. Table 2 lists the major brands in terms of market share.

Minorities represented another potential market segment. The spending of Blacks, Hispanics, and Asian Americans on perfumes is expected to grow at a much faster rate than the rest of the population. Due to a decline in the U.S. fragrance market, marketers have chosen to tap into new markets such as the Latin

---

**TABLE 1**

**Sales Through Drug Stores**

*Top Fine Fragrances:*
- Calvin Klein
- Yves Saint Laurent
- Estee Lauder
- Chanel
- Hugo Boss
- Christian Dior

*Top Mass Fragrances:*
- Lynx
- Gillette Series
- Coty
- Yves Rocher
- Revlon
- Old Spice

---

**TABLE 2**

**Market Share of the Major Brands: 2000 Market Share (percent)**

| | | |
|---|---|---|
| 1. | LVMH Moet Hennessy Louis Vuitton SA | 8.2 |
| 2. | L'Oreal SA | 7.6 |
| 3. | Estee Lauder Company, Inc. | 7.0 |
| 4. | Unilever Group | 6.5 |
| 5. | Avon Products, Inc. | 5.8 |
| 6. | Coty, Inc. | 4.7 |

American countries. Since Latin American countries continue to integrate with the global economy and the rise of Latin culture has increased worldwide, marketers thought these countries would be a great growth opportunity. This attitude has been generated by overall market success posted by Peru, Venezuela, Argentina, and Chile. Datamonitor anticipated that through a decrease in inflation, an increase in privatization, and lower existing trade barriers through bilateral and comprehensive agreements, Latin American countries would continue to improve their economic stature and serve as a strong marketplace for fragrance in the future. In addition, the male segment is predicted to gain a stronger focus. Since the 1990s was the era of developing a positive image for the female, it is believed that the next decades will be the era of developing a positive image for the male. Women's fragrance sales had a total value of $478 million in 2000. As of 2003, the men's market for fragrances was approximately half the size of the women's market. There was an upswing in men's fragrance use when men's lifestyle and fashion magazines first emerged, but this area of the market only grew by 1.3 percent between 1999 and 2000. It has been reported that around 30 percent of men receive cologne, aftershave, or other fragrance as a gift, and that 39 percent of men stick to one brand when purchasing a fragrance. In addition, 36 percent of men are reported to have one brand of fragrance that they wear all the time. Another segment that perfume manufacturers cannot afford to overlook is the older American. By the year 2003, more than one-third of the population was over 50.

In 2003, e-commerce in the fragrance industry turned out to be very promising and profitable for already existing brands and new brands that were otherwise unobtainable. Experts suggest that fragrance marketers tie in e-commerce to boost brand recognition. However, fragrance marketers must realize the rise of the Internet has increased price transparency, which makes it easier to shop around online for the best bargain.

Marketers must also increasingly learn the importance of marketing research. The keys to success have been in defining the market, truly understanding the consumers' preferences, creating a brand that consistently meets these expectations, and communicating these brand attributes to the consumer. Beyond discerning the popular trends, it is important to match the brand image to the fragrance. Even the most brilliant fragrance will not sell if it does not meet the perceptions of the brands' traits. Consumer testing is used to make sure that the product meets its image and has been increasingly vital to the industry.

A survey by the NPD Group found that women buy perfume instead of waiting for someone else to buy it for them. Among those who do use fragrances, 49 percent have purchased three or more bottles for themselves within the past year. Likewise, the small boom in sales of perfume gift sets is largely due to women buying these gifts for themselves. Due to these purchases, "most women who wear a fragrance own six bottles of scent or more." A 2002 study found that big names are increasingly important. To reinforce this idea, 63 percent of fragrance users admitted that designer and celebrity names influenced their brand decisions. That was truer of women age 15 to 34 than their elders, who remain "more loyal to classic scents."

Today's consumers have a diverse lifestyle and the goal for fragrance marketers is to meet these very different needs. One important trend is consumer interest in the inner-directed search for peace and relief from stress. There has been a distinct move away from the heavy scents of the early 1990s toward fresher, lighter fragrances in the 2000s. Comforting home scents such as vanilla, chocolate, and coffee are becoming popular. The healthy lifestyle trend is still popular and scents such as flowers and fruits, which connote health and vitality, are popular. Quest, a leading fragrance supplier, is using the most up-to-date techniques to capture the scents in nature and turn them into invigorating body fragrances. Meanwhile, consumers are showing a renewed interest in glamour and dressing up for the evening. To accommodate these differing lifestyles, consumers are looking for fragrances that can accommodate the look or feel of a particular day or evening. Brands that can offer a gentle attitude combined with an elegant luxury, and can successfully communicate and deliver on a popular image, will be profitable. It is up to marketers to meet consumer expectations if they wish to revitalize sales in the next millennium and mask the bitter taste of competition with the sweet fragrance of success.

## QUESTIONS

1. Identify some possible sources of secondary data for the fragrance industry. What sources can be located on the Internet and how should an Internet search be conducted.
2. Discuss the kind of market research fragrance manufacturers could conduct to determine if there is a demand for a new fragrance.
3. Once an audience for a new fragrance has been targeted, what kind of information is needed about their attitudes, preferences, purchase intentions, behaviors, motivations, psychographics, and demographics?
4. Which techniques would you recommend for collecting the information needed above? Discuss.
5. Design appropriate scales for obtaining the information identified above.
6. For a marketing research project aimed at assessing the demand for a new fragrance, a junior analyst designed the enclosed questionnaire (Exhibit 1). Is this a well-designed questionnaire? If not, how could it be improved?

## REFERENCES

Peter Landau, "Euromonitor Finds That Unisex Fragrances Are Losing Appeal," *Chemical Market Reporter* 257 (10) (March 6, 2000): 31.

Mark Dolliver, "Taking Fragrant Matters Into Their Own Hands," *Adweek* 41 (50) (December 11, 2000): 61.

Bill Schmitt, "Making Scents of Demand and Technology Trends," *Chemical Week* (163) 43 (November 21–28, 2001): 36.

Glenn Koser, "Retail Scents," *Global Cosmetic Industry* (169) 6 (November 2001): 50.

Anonymous, "Message in a Bottle," *Chemist & Druggist* (October 13, 2001): 40.

Taylor Nelson Sofres, *www.tnsofres.com*, July 29, 2001—top brands in pharmacies.

EXHIBIT 1
New Fragrance Survey

Please fill out the following survey, answering the questions as accurately as possible.

**Part I**

1. What is your sex?
   _____ Male
   _____ Female

2. What age group are you in?
   _____ 18–24      _____ 35–44
   _____ 25–29      _____ 45 and over
   _____ 30–34

3. What category of income do you fit into?
   _____ 0–$15,000      _____ $35,000–$45,000
   _____ $15,000–$25,000      _____ $45,000 and above
   _____ $25,000–$35,000

4. What is your marital status?
   _____ Married
   _____ Single

5. If you are married, how many children do you have?
   _____ one      _____ three
   _____ two      _____ four or more

6. How often do you go to the mall?
   _____ once a week (or more)
   _____ once a month
   _____ once every 6 months
   _____ once a year

7. If you shop at department stores, which one do you frequent?
   _____ Target
   _____ J. C. Penney
   _____ Sears
   _____ Sak's Fifth Avenue/Neiman-Marcus

**Part II**

8. I usually buy my fragrances in a department store.

| 1 | 2 | 3 | 4 | 5 |
|---|---|---|---|---|
| Strongly agree | agree | don't know | disagree | Strongly disagree |

9. I usually buy my fragrances in a drugstore.

| 1 | 2 | 3 | 4 | 5 |
|---|---|---|---|---|
| Strongly agree | agree | don't know | disagree | Strongly disagree |

10. I only buy one brand of fragrance.

| 1 | 2 | 3 | 4 | 5 |
|---|---|---|---|---|
| Strongly agree | agree | don't know | disagree | Strongly disagree |

11. Department store fragrances are worth the extra cost.

| 1 | 2 | 3 | 4 | 5 |
|---|---|---|---|---|
| Strongly agree | agree | don't know | disagree | Strongly disagree |

12. Free gift packages are a definite incentive to buy a fragrance product.

| 1 | 2 | 3 | 4 | 5 |
|---|---|---|---|---|
| Strongly agree | agree | don't know | disagree | Strongly disagree |

13. Celebrity endorsement of a fragrance gives it more appeal.

| 1 | 2 | 3 | 4 | 5 |
|---|---|---|---|---|
| Strongly agree | agree | don't know | disagree | Strongly disagree |

14. Fragrances endorsed by celebrities are higher in quality.

| 1 | 2 | 3 | 4 | 5 |
|---|---|---|---|---|
| Strongly agree | agree | don't know | disagree | Strongly disagree |

15. I would be interested in a new fragrance.

| 1 | 2 | 3 | 4 | 5 |
|---|---|---|---|---|
| Strongly agree | agree | don't know | disagree | Strongly disagree |

16. I frequently try new fragrances.

| 1 | 2 | 3 | 4 | 5 |
|---|---|---|---|---|
| Strongly agree | agree | don't know | disagree | Strongly disagree |

**Part III**

17. How often do you buy fragrances?

_____

18. What is your favorite fragrance?

_____

19. What are the qualities you look for in a fragrance?

_____
_____

20. Are you happy with the fragrances currently on the market?

_____
_____

Thank you for your time. Your assistance will help us in better meeting your fragrance needs.

# 2.5 Is Super Bowl Advertising Super Effective?

About 140 million Americans and 700 million total global viewers tune in to Super Bowl Sunday, making the event one of the largest occasions for home entertainment. Advertising time during the Super Bowl is limited and priced at a premium. The fight for the prime spots starts months in advance of the actual airtime. In 1993, the cost for a 30-second time slot was a high $850,000, but by 1997 the cost had shot to $1.2 million for the same short time frame. In 1998, a 30-second spot during the Super Bowl cost $1.3 million. In 2000, a 30-second spot during the Super Bowl cost companies a record average of $2.2 million. Dot.com companies that have since failed or are struggling to keep their heads above water purchased forty percent of the Super Bowl ad slots in 2000. For the 2001 Super Bowl XXXVI, the average rate for an advertising spot was approximately 2.1 million.

In 2002, during Super Bowl XXXVI, Fox Network offered 60 commercial spots for a total of 30 minutes of advertising time. The average selling price for each 30-second spot was just under $2 million, at $1.9 million each. Companies who paid for commercial time during Super Bowl XXXVI included Anheuser-Busch, who purchased ten 30-second spots, PepsiCo, who featured one 90-second commercial starring Britney Spears, E-Trade, M&M/Mars, AT&T Wireless, Levi Strauss, Yahoo!, Visa, and fast food chains Quizno's, Taco Bell, and Subway are among others.

Although Fox did end up selling all of the available ad spots, the network did not sell the final ad until the Thursday before the game. There are several reasons for the selling delay and for the reduced rates in 2002. First, marketers were facing the "worst advertising recession in recent memory." This caused companies to carefully monitor how they spent their advertising budgets and many decided that the money could be better applied elsewhere. Many companies chose to advertise during other prime time events that were more affordable. The average rate for a 30-second spot during the early evening news in 2002 was $45,900. Even events such as the Golden Globes (estimated price $45,000 per 30-second spot), the Grammies (estimated price $57,000 per 30-second spot), and the Academy Awards (estimated price $1.6 million per 30-second spot) offer companies ad time at lower rates. However, these events do not draw as many viewers as the Super Bowl. Secondly, the NFL, for the first time, sponsored a pre-game show on the Friday night before the Super Bowl. Some companies, such as AOL Time Warner, Phillip Morris, Miller Brewing Co., and Motorola chose to avoid paying "television's highest commercial prices" and bought ad time for lower rates during the pre-game show. A final reason for lower rates and less marketer interest in Super Bowl ad time was competition from the 2002 Olympic Winter Games. The games began just five days after the Super Bowl and offered 17 days of events during which advertisers could buy commercial time. The average selling rate for a 30-second prime time spot during the Olympics was only $600,000, a bargain compared to the Super Bowl.

Is Super Bowl advertising worth the cost? For many advertisers who bought time slots in previous games, the answer was a resounding no. Nissan, Porsche, Fila, and MCI passed on the chance to advertise during the game. According to marketing consultant Jack Trout, the increasing rates made buying Super Bowl ad time difficult to justify. Nissan marketing chief Brad Bradshaw stated that although the company had intended to advertise during the game, it came to the conclusion that the resources could be better used to sell its vehicles in other ways.

In addition to the cost factor, many question what effect advertising actually has on the audience. The purpose of an advertisement is to increase customer awareness for a particular brand. For Super Bowl ads, however, the brand name often becomes secondary to the commercial itself in terms of viewer attention. Super Bowl ads have become events in and of themselves, with each firm trying to put out the next earth-shattering commercial that will stir talk about the commercial itself. Ever since Apple computer's classic "1984" ad, firms have been trying to top previous years' ads. Ad agencies and clients often seem to shoot for ads that are extraordinary for the sake of creativity, rather than their intended purpose, with many attention-getting promotions not translating into product purchases. It is questionable whether brand name is retained, and so despite having an incredible commercial, many advertisers' ad dollars possibly go into just providing new fodder for water cooler conversation for the week instead of forming a lasting brand image in the minds of consumers. Without new research into the effectiveness of Super Bowl advertising and its effect on consumers, many advertisers may be better off avoiding buying Super Bowl ad time and abandoning the world's biggest television audience.

Some advertisers like Purina Cat Chow have taken a slightly different approach by purchasing airtime on the show directly following the Super Bowl. They obtained airtime at one-sixth of the cost during the game and they believe that they retain approximately 40 percent of the audience. Which advertiser got the biggest bang for the bucks: M&M/Mars that advertised during Super Bowl 2002, or Purina Cat Chow that advertised after the game? Without systematic marketing research aimed at measuring Super Bowl advertising effectiveness, questions such as these beg answers. It remains to be established that Super Bowl advertising is super effective!

## QUESTIONS

1. What kind of research design would you recommend for determining the effectiveness of M&M/Mars' advertising during the Super Bowl?
2. If the research design involves a survey of households, which survey method would you recommend and why?
3. What kind of measures and scales will you employ in your survey?
4. Can the observation method be used to determine the effectiveness of M&M/Mars' advertising during the Super Bowl? If so, which observation method would you recommend and why?
5. Which syndicated services discussed in the book can provide useful information?

## REFERENCES

"Super Bowl Ads Sold Out," *CNNMoney* (February 1, 2002) money.cnn.com/2002/02/01/news/wires/superbowl_ads_ap/

Vanessa O'Connell and Joe Flint, "Super Bowl Gets Competition," *The Wall Street Journal* (January 28, 2002): B1

"Super Bowl Veteran Scrambling to Score," *The Wall Street Journal* 237 (14) (January 19, 2001): B5.

# CASES

# 2.1 Starbucks: Staying Local While Going Global Through Marketing Research

Starbucks Corporation purchases and roasts high-quality whole coffee beans and sells them, along with fresh, rich-brewed coffees, Italian-style espresso beverages, cold blended beverages, a variety of pastries and confections, coffee-related accessories and equipment, a selection of premium teas, and a line of compact discs, primarily through company-operated retail stores. In addition to sales through its company-operated retail stores, Starbucks sells coffee and tea products through other channels of distribution including its Business Alliances business unit and other specialty operations (collectively, Specialty Operations). Starbucks, through its joint venture partnerships, also produces and sells bottled Frappuccino coffee drink and a line of premium ice creams.

Over the last two decades, Starbucks has revitalized the coffee industry. The inspiration behind Starbucks was conceived when CEO Howard Schultz visited Italy. He noticed the atmosphere of the coffee shops there and wanted to recreate that experience in the United States.

Starbucks' objective is to establish Starbucks as the most recognized and respected brand in the world. It expects to achieve this by continuing with rapid expansion of its retail stores and growing its specialty sales and other operations. It will also continually pursue other opportunities to leverage the Starbucks brand through new products and new distribution channels that meet consumer needs determined by marketing research.

Starbucks has shown tremendous growth over recent years. In 2001, it had $3 billion in total revenues. This was a 31 percent increase from the previous year. Most of the increase can be attributed to the opening of an additional 1,208 stores in 2001. New store locations are determined based on marketing research. Approximately 84 percent of net revenues come from company-operated retail stores. Specialty operations accounted for the remaining 16 percent. Currently, one-third of all the coffee sold in coffee shops comes from either a corporate-owned or licensed Starbucks store. These stores account for 26.5 percent of the coffee shops in the United States, and there are 4,247 stores throughout North America.

The major challenge for Starbucks in achieving its massive growth goals was to capture the essence of the European coffeehouse culture while appealing to a broad range of Americans. Marketing research determined four strategic pillars for expressing the Starbucks brand. The four pillars are coffee, coffee-related products, environment, and experience. Even though the coffee and the products are important, the key to Starbucks' success has been the latter two. It has designed an environment that is warm and welcoming and has provided an experience that makes it part of the community or local culture. It has been able to achieve this success by emphasizing the Starbucks culture.

Marketing research has shown that it is important for Starbucks to stay connected to the local community. As it has grown, Starbucks' biggest concern has been that its stores would not stay locally relevant. It was, and is, important that there be consistency among its stores in order to maintain its brand quality. It does this by maintaining tight connections with its employees within each of these coffee shops. In turn, these employees strive to keep their connections with their clientele. To help preserve its connections with local employees, Starbucks treats them as partners and makes them feel like a vital part of the company, because they are.

Starbucks uses experience and culture as its key sources of marketing. Thus, it is extremely important to develop, train, and appease its employees because these people help provide this experience and they add to the Starbucks' culture. Starbucks has spent much more money on developing its employees than it has on traditional marketing methods. Therefore, its strategy has been to grow by word of mouth, and this has proven extremely successful. It also draws upon its customers for ideas by conducting extensive marketing research. Many of the products and services it provides are a direct result of suggestions from patrons or local employees.

Due to the success of its brand building with the coffeehouses, Starbucks has been able to move into other important markets. Syndicated data from ACNielsen show that grocery stores sell two-thirds of the coffee in the United

States, and Starbucks has been able to enter this lucrative market. It has also used partnerships in other industries to increase its revenues.

Starbucks has been extremely successful in achieving its objectives. It has been able to maintain a local feel despite massive growth around the globe. Even more surprising, it has been able to achieve this despite the lack of a widespread marketing campaign, and without a technology component that would make it unique. Starbucks has done this by stressing its culture and placing the focus on its employees and customers through marketing research.

## QUESTIONS

1. Using the Internet, identify secondary sources of information pertaining to coffee consumption in the United States.
2. What are consumers looking for in a coffeehouse experience? How do they view the Starbucks coffee shop experience? How can Starbucks determine answers to these questions?
3. A survey is to be conducted to determine the image coffee drinkers have of Starbucks and other coffee shop chains. Which survey method should be used and why?
4. Starbucks is thinking of introducing a new gourmet coffee with a strong aroma. Can the observation method be used to determine the consumer reaction to this coffee prior to national introduction? If so, which observation method should be used?
5. What type of scale would be appropriate for measuring the image of Starbucks? Design such a scale.
6. Design a sampling plan for administering the survey of question 3.

## REFERENCES

www.starbucks.com

Robert V. Kozinets, "The Field Behind the Screen: Using Netnography for Marketing Research in Online Communities," *Journal of Marketing Research* (Winter, 2002): 61.

Dina ElBoghdady, "Pouring It On; The Starbucks Strategy? Locations, Locations, Locations," *The Washington Post* (August 25, 2002): H01.

Terry Pristin, "Veni, Venti, Grande; Starbucks Strikes Deep in a Wary Land of Pushcarts and Delis," *The New York Times* (April 29, 2002): B1.

# 2.2 Nike: Associating Athletes, Performance, and the Brand

Nike, Inc. designs, develops, and markets footwear, apparel, equipment, and accessory products. Nike is the largest seller of athletic footwear and athletic apparel in the world, with 30 percent market share worldwide. Nike sells its products to approximately 17,000 retail accounts in the United States and approximately 140 countries around the world. Nike has grown from an $8,000 company in 1963 to a $9.9 billion company in 2002.

In 2002, Nike spent an enormous amount of money, approximately $1.3 billion, on advertising, endorsements, and sales promotion. In order to make sure that this money is being spent properly, Nike relies on marketing research. It has shown a history of innovation and inspiration in its marketing and is quick to adapt to the changing consumer and the world of sports. Nike has used marketing research in understanding where its future growth lies. A recent example is Nike's shift from marketing in its more traditional sports (basketball and running) to other sports (golf and soccer) where it has not been as strong traditionally. Marketing research revealed that the awareness of Nike among soccer and golf players was low and it has decided to work on increasing these numbers. Nike has decided that the money needed for licenses in its strong areas can be better spent in other areas where Nike does not have the brand awareness.

Today the Nike Swoosh is recognized around the world. This is the result of 40 years of work and innovation. Nike signed its first athletes to wear its shoes in 1973. Early on, Nike realized the importance of associating athletes with its products. The partnership helps relate the excellence of the athlete with the perception of the brand. Nike discovered through marketing research the pyramid influence, which shows that the mass market can be influenced by the preference of a small group of top athletes. After it realized this effect, it began to spend millions on celebrity endorsements. The association with the athlete also helps dimensionalize who the company is and what they believe in. With Nike this was, and is, extremely important. It wants to convey a message that its company's goal is to bring innovation to every athlete in the world. Nike also uses the athletes to design its products by attempting to meet their individual goals.

The company also realized that in order to achieve its lofty growth goals, it must appeal to multiple market segments. Based on marketing research, Nike divided the market into three different groups. There is the ultimate athlete, the athletics participant, and the consumer that is influenced by the sports culture.

Nike has always been an aggressive user of marketing research and this has been shown in its attack on the European market. It decided that it had to concentrate on different sports in order to reach European consumers. It placed its focus on major sporting events (World Cups and Olympics) and celebrity athletes that are relevant to the European consumer. Marketing research, in the form of focus groups and survey research, revealed that the best positioning for Nike shoes was one that enhanced performance in the sport. Through massive advertising campaigns, Nike has been able to change the perception of its products from fashion to performance and in the process increase its sales dramatically.

Another technique Nike has used is to specifically design a product line for a certain market. Nike uses marketing research to determine the lifestyles and product usage characteristics of a particular market segment and then designs products for that segment. An example is its Presto line, which was designed for a certain lifestyle of youths. It put this lifestyle first and designed the products around this group, hoping to reach them. It also used marketing research to determine the most effective mediums to communicate with its targeted market.

All of these methods have allowed Nike to become recognizable by 97 percent of U.S. citizens, and its sales have soared in the process. However, Nike faces a new concern. This concern is that it has gotten away from its traditional image of a smaller innovative company. It also faces future obstacles in maintaining its brand equity and brand meaning. Continued reliance on marketing research will help Nike to associate its brand with top athletes and performance, thus enhancing its image.

## QUESTIONS

1. Nike would like to increase its share of the athletic shoe market. Define the management decision problem.

2. Define an appropriate marketing research problem corresponding to the management decision problem you have identified.

3. Develop a graphical model explaining consumers' selection of a brand of athletic shoes.

4. How can qualitative research be used to strengthen the image of Nike? Which qualitative research technique(s) should be used and why?

5. Should Nike invest by opening more upscale company retail stores such as Nike Town? Management is wondering if survey research can provide an answer. How should such a survey be administered?

6. Develop Likert, semantic differential, and Stapel scales for evaluating the durability of Nike running shoes.

7. Develop a questionnaire for measuring the image of Nike, Reebok, and Adidas.

8. Develop a sampling plan for administering the survey in question 5.

## REFERENCES

www.nike.com

Kristen Vinakmens, "Brands Draw on Art in Lifestyle Campaigns," *Brunico Communications, Inc.* (August 26, 2002): 1.

Boaz Herzog, "Marketing That Stings," *The Oregonian* (April 12, 2002): D01.

Leah Beth Ward, "Private Sector; At Nike, Function Over Fashion," *The New York Times* (April 28, 2002), section 3: 2.

# 2.3 Intel: Building Blocks Inside Out

The Intel Corporation was founded in 1968 to build semiconductor memory products. It introduced the world's first microprocessor in 1971. Microprocessors, also referred to as central processing units (CPUs), are often described as the "brain" of a computer. Today, Intel supplies the building blocks for the computing and communications industries. These building blocks include chips, boards, systems, and software, and they are used in computers, servers, and networking/communications products. As stated on its Web site, "Intel's mission is to be the preeminent building block supplier to the Internet economy."

Intel is organized into four separate operating units. These units are the Intel Architecture business, the Intel Communications Group, the Wireless Communications and Computing Group, and the New Business Group. The Intel Architecture business develops platform solutions for the desktop, server, and mobile market segments. The Intel Communication Group develops products for the networking and communications platform, focusing on three areas. These three areas are Ethernet connectivity, optical components, and network processing components. The Wireless Communication and Computing Group provides component hardware and software for digital cellular communications and related areas. The New Business Group is designed to develop new business around the company's core capabilities.

Most of Intel's customers fall into two separate groups, the original equipment manufacturers (OEMs) and the PC and network communications products users. The OEMs manufacture computer systems, cellular handsets and handheld computing devices, telecommunications and networking communications equipment, and peripherals. The PC and network communications products users include individuals, large and small businesses, and service providers, who buy Intel's PC enhancements, networking products, and business communications products through reseller, retail, e-business, and OEM channels. Intel is also an increasingly global company. In 2001, only 35 percent of revenues were from North America, whereas Asia and Europe accounted for 31 percent and 25 percent, respectively.

Intel has shown phenomenal growth as a company, especially throughout the 1990s. Its net revenues increased from approximately $6 billion in 1992 to as high as $34 billion in 2000 before falling with the entire market to $26.8 billion in

2002. Much of Intel's success can be attributed to innovation within its marketing department based upon marketing research. This innovation was required to overcome several obstacles that Intel had. The main problem Intel faced was trying to sell an ingredient brand, which is a component of a larger product. Thus, the difficulty is in reaching consumers that will never see your product and may not even know what it does or why it is there.

Intel began its marketing research in the 1980s because it was having difficulty with its customers not upgrading from the 286 to the 386 microprocessor. Marketing research showed that this was due to a lack of customer awareness, and Intel set out to change that. It conducted a small but effective advertising campaign. In fact, in the process, it realized that it had inadvertently created a brand in Intel. After success in this small campaign, Intel began to realize the importance of marketing and marketing research and it focused more effort and money into these areas.

Marketing research revealed that in order to be effective in their overall marketing campaign, Intel would have to reach the consumers and convince them that what was inside the computer was as important as the outside. This became the key element of the "Intel Inside" campaign conducted during the early 1990s. This slogan helped Intel put a name with its products, and it helped Intel encompass several of its products under one title.

Furthermore, marketing research showed that it would be most effective to cross-market with its technology partners. This would help consumers understand the products that Intel helped make up. It did this by including its "Intel Inside" logo in the ads of its partners. It also helped fund these advertisements. A problem with including its slogan in other ads is that it did not want to intrude on the commercials. Intel decided to help make the small logo sink in by accompanying it with a jingle every time it was displayed. This jingle has become extremely recognizable and synonymous with Intel's slogan. All of this helped Intel realize its goal of increased consumer awareness. Continuous measurement of advertising effectiveness via marketing research revealed that the "Intel Inside" campaign was very effective so that it was still running as of 2003.

Intel's next idea was to come up with a name for its microprocessor. This would allow Intel to avoid using the numbering scheme, which was nonpatentable, and find a name that consumers could identify its processors with. After extensive marketing research, Intel chose the name Pentium, which it found generated positive reactions with its consumers. It has been marketing its processors under this name ever since.

Between 1990 and 1993, Intel invested $500 million in advertising to build its brand equity. By 1993, 80 percent of people in the United States recognized Intel and 75 percent had positive feelings about the brand. Most importantly, 50 percent of consumers looked for the brand when they were shopping.

By 1994, Intel had captured 95 percent of the microprocessor market due in large part to its marketing efforts. Its market share for microprocessors has slipped to 82.8 percent in 2002, which is a result of increased competition from its main competitor, AMD. This increased competition makes Intel's marketing research efforts more important than ever as it attempts to preserve its dominant place in the market. Intel has been very successful by placing importance on technology, brand image, and brand equity. There are still future challenges that Intel faces. These include increased competition, the opening of new markets, and the development of new products. Intel will continue to rely on marketing research to meet these challenges and, thus, enhance its image as a preeminent building block supplier inside out.

## QUESTIONS

1. Discuss the role of marketing research in helping Intel devise the "Intel Inside" campaign.
2. Intel would like to increase the preference for Intel chips amongst PC users in the individual user as well as business user segments. Define the management decision problem.
3. Define an appropriate marketing research problem corresponding to the management decision problem you have identified in question 2.
4. Intel would like to gain a better understanding of how businesses select PC and network communications products. What type of research design should be adopted?
5. Discuss the role of the Internet in obtaining secondary data relevant to the marketing research problem you have defined in question 3.
6. Discuss the role of qualitative research in understanding how businesses select PC and network communications products. Which qualitative research techniques should be used and why?
7. If a survey is to be conducted to determine businesses' selection criterion for choosing PC and network communications products, which survey method should be used and why?
8. Design a questionnaire for determining businesses' selection criterion for choosing PC and network communications products.
9. Develop a suitable sampling plan for conducting the survey identified in question 7.

## REFERENCES

*www.intel.com*

Olga Kharif, "Intel Is Kicking Silicon at AMD," *Business Week Online* (September 24, 2002).

Kirk Ladendorf, "AMD Takes on Intel with Its Hammer," *Cox News Service* (August 18, 2002): Financial pages.

Michael Kanellos, "Intel Gains Market Share on AMD's Back," CNET News.com (July 30, 2002).

# 2.4 Nivea: Marketing Research Leads to Consistency in Marketing

Nivea skin care products are part of the German company Beiersdorf. Nivea's line of skin care products is marketed in 94 countries. The product line has been around for eight decades, originating with a scientific breakthrough with the first skin cream that did not separate into water and oil. That, coupled with intelligent marketing, led to a strong positive brand image that accounts for much of Nivea's success. The company's continual success is due to the marriage of marketing and research and development within the company. Research and development are continual, and the latest findings in dermatology, product technology, and raw materials are applied to existing products. The goal of improved product performance and quality is central to the Nivea product line. Nivea helps ensure this quality through constant testing and consumer feedback obtained via marketing research.

Nivea began marketing in the 1920s when it changed its logo and began selling its product around the world. Early on, it established its brand identity as a pure and gentle product on which families could rely. It advertised with a picture of the Nivea Girl. In 1924, the company broke from tradition and began advertising with the Nivea Boys. This helped to convey the message that Nivea was made for the entire family. Its brand image has transcended decades with the help of a foundation built upon advertising that stresses family relationships and values.

In the 1970s, Nivea had to defend itself against true competition for the first time. It relied heavily on marketing research, which helped to formulate a two-pronged strategy. The first part was the defense of its core business through a new advertising campaign—Crème de la Crème. The second part was the introduction of new products, which helped keep the brand fresh and introduced new sources of sales.

In the 1980s, when marketing research indicated brand differentiation was becoming increasingly important, Nivea began branding with sub-brands. These sub-brands included skincare, bath products, sun protection, baby care, facial care, hair care, and care for men. Nivea used an umbrella strategy with the sub-brands, which means that it was using its core brand to encompass all of the sub-brands. The goal was to establish individual images that were distinct but consistent with the core image of Nivea. It was focused on not diluting the brand name and wanting to link the new sub-brands with the traditional values of the core brand. The result was an explosion in sales.

Nivea was able to continue its success in the 1990s as its sales grew rapidly throughout the decade. The growth was due in large part to the introduction of new products, each based on extensive marketing research. The most successful products were an antiwrinkle cream and an entire line of cosmetics.

Nivea entered the new millennium as the number one skincare and cosmetics company in the world with $2.7 billion in revenues. However, it is not void of challenges. Its greatest challenge is in the U.S. market, where its brand is not as strong as it is in other parts of the world. The U.S. market poses many obstacles because it is the largest and most dynamic market in the world. Nivea hopes to overcome these obstacles through the use of extensive marketing research. This research will lead Nivea to conduct more product launches and to develop focused marketing strategies. Nivea focuses on consistency in their marketing, which is another difficulty because it can be troublesome to communicate the same message across various cultures. However, Nivea will do whatever it takes to maintain this consistency because it believes this gives it an edge over competitors. It helps consumers relate all its products to its core brand and identity. Nivea will continue to rely on marketing research to retain and refine the consistency in its marketing across global markets.

## QUESTIONS

1. Nivea would like to increase its share of the U.S. market. Define the management decision problem.
2. Define an appropriate marketing research problem based on the management decision problem you have identified in question 1.
3. Nivea would like to undertake research to understand the preferences of American consumers for skin care products. What type of research design should be adopted and why?
4. Discuss the role of qualitative research in understanding the preferences of American consumers for skin care products. Which qualitative research techniques should be used and why?
5. If a survey is to be conducted to understand the preferences of American consumers for skin care products, which survey method should be used and why?
6. Develop Likert, semantic differential, and Stapel scales for determining consumers' evaluation of foreign skin care products.
7. Develop a sampling plan for administering the survey in question 5.

## REFERENCES

*www.nivea.com*

Anonymous, "World's Top 100 Brands—Are They Fact or Fiction?" *Brand Strategy* (August 21, 2002): 10.

Anonymous, "Beauty Is in the Eye of the Brand Holder," *Marketing Week* (May 30, 2002): 19.

# PART

III

# Data Collection, Preparation, Analysis, and Reporting

This part presents a practical and managerially oriented discussion of fieldwork, the fourth step in the marketing research process. We offer several guidelines for selecting, training, supervising, validating, and evaluating field workers. When the fieldwork is complete, the researcher moves on to data preparation and analysis, the fifth step of the marketing research process. In this part we emphasize the importance and discuss the process of preparing data to make them suitable for analysis. Then we describe the various data analysis techniques. We cover not only the basic techniques of frequency distribution, cross-tabulation, and hypothesis testing, but also the commonly used multivariate techniques of analysis of variance and regression. Then, we describe the more advanced techniques: discriminant, factor, and cluster analysis, as well as multidimensional scaling and conjoint analysis. In the discussion of each statistical technique, the emphasis is on explaining the procedure, interpreting the results, and drawing managerial implications, rather than on statistical elegance. Three of the cases with statistical data sets provide ample opportunities to practice these techniques.

Communicating the research by preparing and presenting a formal report constitutes the sixth step in a marketing research project. Using a practical orientation, we provide guidelines for writing reports and preparing tables and graphs and also discuss oral presentation of the report. We focus on the international dimensions of marketing research. Although this topic has been discussed in a pervasive way in the previous chapters, this part presents additional details. We present a conceptual framework for international marketing research and illustrate, in detail, how the environment prevailing in the countries, cultural units, or international markets being researched influences the way the marketing research process should be performed.

# Fieldwork

"No matter how well you design the research process, the persons actually doing the work have control of the quality. The key to good fieldwork is founded in careful selection, thorough training, and continuous evaluation . . . always with an eye to quality."

*Trenton Haack,*
*senior qualitative specialist,*
*Burke, Inc.*

## Objectives

After reading this chapter, the student should be able to:

1. Describe the fieldwork process and explain the selection, training, and supervision of field workers, the validation of fieldwork, and the evaluation of field workers.
2. Discuss the training of field workers in making the initial contact, asking the questions, probing, recording the answers, and terminating the interview.
3. Discuss the supervision of field workers in terms of quality control and editing, sampling control, control of cheating, and central office control.
4. Describe the evaluation of field workers in areas of cost and time, response rates, quality of interviewing, and the quality of data.
5. Explain the issues related to fieldwork when conducting international marketing research.
6. Discuss the ethical aspect of fieldwork.
7. Illustrate the use of the Internet and computers in fieldwork.

Fieldwork is the fourth step in the marketing research process. It follows problem definition, development of the approach (Chapter 2), and formulation of the research design (Chapters 3 through 12). During this phase the field workers make contact with the respondents, administer the questionnaires or observation forms, record the data, and turn in the completed forms for processing. A personal interviewer administering questionnaires door-to-door, an interviewer intercepting shoppers in a mall, a telephone interviewer calling from a central location, a worker mailing questionnaires from an office, an observer counting customers in a particular section of a store, and others involved in data collection and supervision of the process are all field workers.

This chapter describes the nature of fieldwork and the general fieldwork/data-collection process. This process involves the selection, training, and supervision of field workers, the validation of fieldwork, and the evaluation of field workers. We briefly discuss fieldwork in the context of international marketing research, identify the relevant ethical issues, and explain the role of the Internet and computers.

## ACTIVE RESEARCH | DEPARTMENT STORE PROJECT

### Fieldwork

In the department store project, in-home personal interviews were conducted by interviewers who were graduate and undergraduate students enrolled in marketing research courses taught by the author. The field workers' training included having each interviewer (1) act as a respondent and self-administer the questionnaire and (2) administer the questionnaire to a few other students not involved in the project (dummy respondents). Detailed guidelines for interviewing were developed and provided to each interviewer. The supervision of interviewers was carried out by graduate students who monitored the fieldwork activities on a day-to-day basis. All the respondents were called back to verify that the interviewer had actually administered the questionnaire to them and to thank them for participating in the survey. A 100 percent validation check was performed. All the field workers, interviewers, and supervisors were evaluated by the author.

## REAL RESEARCH

### Refusing Refusals

The Council for Marketing and Opinion Research (CMOR) is a national nonprofit research industry trade group (*www.cmor.org*). In a CMOR survey that interviewed over 3,700 U.S. consumers in May 2001, nearly 45 percent said they had refused to participate in a survey over the past year, up from 40 percent in 1999. Several guidelines offered by CMOR for reducing refusal rates relate to fieldwork:

- Interviewer training programs should be routinely administered so that field workers will be effective at their jobs.
- Courtesy should be exercised when deciding what hours of the day to call respondents. Calling between 9 A.M. and 9 P.M. is recommended.
- If mall respondents indicate the time is not convenient, an appointment should be made to conduct the interview later.

Guidelines by CMOR help reduce refusal rates in surveys.

■ The subject matter should be disclosed to the respondents if this can be done without biasing the data. The more information people are given, the less reason they have to be suspicious.

■ Field workers should make the interviews as pleasant and appealing as possible.[1] ■

## THE NATURE OF FIELDWORK

Marketing research data are rarely collected by the persons who design the research. Researchers have two major options for collecting their data. They can develop their own organizations or they can contract with a fieldwork agency. In either case, data collection involves the use of some kind of field force. The field force may operate either in the field (personal in-home, mall intercept, computer-assisted personal interviewing, and observation) or from an office (telephone, mail, e-mail, and Internet surveys). The field workers who collect the data typically have little research background or training. Ethical concerns are particularly germane to fieldwork. Although there is ample opportunity for violation of ethical standards, clients need not be overly concerned when dealing with reputable fieldwork agencies. Michael Redington, senior vice president for corporate development at Marketing and Research Counselors Group (M/A/R/C Group, *www.marcgroup.com*), is an aggressive advocate of field quality. His evaluation of the quality of fieldwork in the marketing research industry is as follows: "I was very pleased to help shoot down the myth that data collection is characterized by a bunch of people out there attempting to bend the rules, to rip you off, and to cheat on interviews. There are a lot of people on the client side who believe just that. Quite frankly, we were out trying to find it, but we didn't. That was a revelation to us. We were afraid that there were more unethical practices in the field than there really were."[2] The quality of fieldwork is high because the fieldwork/data-collection process is streamlined and well controlled.

## FIELDWORK/DATA-COLLECTION PROCESS

All fieldwork involves the selection, training, and supervision of persons who collect data.[3] The validation of fieldwork and the evaluation of field workers are also parts of the process. Figure 13.1 represents a general framework for the fieldwork/data-collection

*Figure 13.1*
Fieldwork/Data-Collection Process

Selection of field workers.

↓

Training of field workers.

↓

Supervision of field workers.

↓

Validation of fieldwork.

↓

Evaluation of field workers.

process. Whereas we describe a general process, it should be recognized that the nature of fieldwork varies with the mode of data collection, and the relative emphasis on the different steps will be different for telephone, personal, mail, and electronic interviews.

# SELECTION OF FIELD WORKERS

The first step in the fieldwork process is the selection of field workers. The researcher should: (1) develop job specifications for the project, taking into account the mode of data collection; (2) decide what characteristics the field workers should have; and (3) recruit appropriate individuals. Interviewers' background characteristics, opinions, perceptions, expectations, and attitudes can affect the responses they elicit.[4]

For example, the social acceptability of a field worker to the respondent may affect the quality of data obtained, especially in personal interviewing. Researchers generally agree that the more characteristics the interviewer and the respondent have in common, the greater the probability of a successful interview.

## REAL RESEARCH

### *Searching for Common Ground*

In a survey dealing with emotional well-being and mental health, older interviewers got better cooperation from respondents than younger interviewers. However, this performance appeared to be independent of years of experience. Differences in nonresponse rates also appeared between black and white interviewers. Black interviewers produced higher nonresponse rates with white respondents than did white interviewers. The more the interviewer and the respondent had in common, the greater the cooperation and the better the quality of the data.[5] ■

Thus, to the extent possible, interviewers should be selected to match respondents' characteristics. The job requirements will also vary with the nature of the problem and the type of data-collection method. However, there are some general qualifications of field workers:

■ **Healthy.** Fieldwork can be strenuous and the workers must have the stamina required to do the job.

■ **Outgoing.** The interviewers should be able to establish rapport with the respondents. They should be able to relate to strangers.

■ **Communicative.** Effective speaking and listening skills are a great asset.

■ **Pleasant appearance.** If the field worker's physical appearance is unpleasant or unusual, the data collected may be biased.

■ **Educated.** Interviewers must have good reading and writing skills. A majority of fieldwork agencies require a high school education and many prefer some college education.

■ **Experienced.** Experienced interviewers are likely to do a better job in following instructions, obtaining respondent cooperation, and conducting the interview.

## REAL RESEARCH

### *Your Experience Counts*

Research has found the following effects of interviewer experience on the interviewing process.

■ Inexperienced interviewers are more likely to commit coding errors, to misrecord responses, and to fail to probe.

■ Inexperienced interviewers have a particularly difficult time filling quotas of respondents.

■ Inexperienced interviewers have larger refusal rates. They also accept more "don't know" responses and refusals to answer individual questions.[6] ■

Field workers are generally paid an hourly rate or on a per-interview basis. The typical interviewer is a married woman age 35 to 54, with an above-average education and an above-average household income.

# TRAINING OF FIELD WORKERS

Training of field workers is critical to the quality of data collected. Training may be conducted in person at a central location or, if the interviewers are geographically dispersed, by mail. Training ensures that all interviewers administer the questionnaire in the same manner so that the data can be collected uniformly. Training should cover making the initial contact, asking the questions, probing, recording the answers, and terminating the interview.[7]

## Making the Initial Contact

The initial contact can result in cooperation or the loss of potential respondents.[8] Interviewers should be trained to make opening remarks that will convince potential respondents that their participation is important.

---

**ACTIVE RESEARCH**  | DEPARTMENT STORE PROJECT

### *Initial Contact Statement*

Hello, my name is _____. I represent the Marketing Department of Georgia Tech. We are conducting a survey about household preferences for department stores. You are one of the select group of respondents who have been scientifically chosen to participate in this survey. We highly value your opinion and would like to ask you a few questions.[9]

---

Note that the interviewer did not specifically ask the respondent's permission. Questions that directly ask permission, such as "May I have some of your valuable time?" or "Would you like to answer a few questions?" should be avoided. Interviewers should also be instructed on handling objections and refusals. For example, if the respondent says, "This is not a convenient time for me," the interviewer should respond, "What would be a more convenient time for you? I will call back then." If the foot-in-the-door or door-in-the-face techniques discussed in Chapter 12 are being employed, interviewers should be trained accordingly.

## Asking the Questions

Even a slight change in the wording, sequence, or manner in which a question is asked can distort its meaning and bias the response. Asking questions is an art. Training in asking questions can yield high dividends in eliminating potential sources of bias. Changing the phrasing or order of questions during the interview can make significant differences in the response obtained. "While we could be faulted for not writing as perfect a questionnaire as we possibly could, still it must be asked in the exact way it was written. It's a challenge for us to try to get the interviewers more conversational, but despite this, the field force absolutely must ask questions as they are written."[10] The following are guidelines for asking questions.[11]

1. Be thoroughly familiar with the questionnaire.
2. Ask the questions in the order in which they appear in the questionnaire.
3. Use the exact wording given in the questionnaire.
4. Read each question slowly.
5. Repeat questions that are not understood.
6. Ask every applicable question.
7. Follow instructions and skip patterns, probing carefully.

## Probing

*probing*
A motivational technique used when asking survey questions to induce the respondents to enlarge on, clarify, or explain their answers and to help the respondents to focus on the specific content of the interview.

*Probing* is intended to motivate respondents to enlarge on, clarify, or explain their answers. Probing also helps respondents focus on the specific content of the interview and provide only relevant information. Probing should not introduce any bias. Listed below are some commonly used probing techniques.[12]

1. Repeating the question. Repeating the question in the same words can be effective in eliciting a response.
2. Repeating the respondent's reply. Respondents can be stimulated to provide further comments by repeating verbatim their replies. This can be done as the interviewer records the replies.

3. Using a pause or silent probe. A silent probe, or an expectant pause or look, can cue the respondent to provide a more complete response. However, the silence should not become embarrassing.

4. Boosting or reassuring the respondent. If the respondent hesitates, the interviewer should reassure the respondent with comments like, "There are no right or wrong answers. We are just trying to get your opinions." If the respondent needs an explanation of a word or phrase, the interviewer should not offer an interpretation. Rather, the responsibility for the interpretation should be returned to the respondent. This can be done with a comment such as, "Just whatever it means to you."

5. Eliciting clarification. The respondent's motivation to cooperate with the interviewer and provide complete answers can be aroused with a question like, "I don't quite understand what you mean by that—could you please tell me a little more?"

6. Using objective/neutral questions or comments. Some common questions or comments used as probes and the corresponding abbreviations are: Any other reason? (AO?), Anything else? (AE or Else?), What do you mean? (What mean?), and Why do you feel that way? (Why?).[13] The interviewer should record the abbreviations on the questionnaire in parentheses next to the question asked.

## Recording the Answers

Although recording respondent answers seems simple, several mistakes are common.[14] All interviewers should use the same format and conventions to record the interviews and edit completed interviews. Although the rules for recording answers to structured questions vary with each specific questionnaire, the general rule is to check the box that reflects the respondent's answer. The general rule for recording answers to unstructured questions is to record the responses verbatim. The Interviewer's Manual of the Survey Research Center provides the following specific guidelines for recording answers to unstructured questions.

1. Record responses during the interview.
2. Use the respondent's own words.
3. Do not summarize or paraphrase the respondent's answers.
4. Include everything that pertains to the question objectives.
5. Include all probes and comments.
6. Repeat the response as it is written down.

## Terminating the Interview

The interview should not be closed before all the information is obtained. Any spontaneous comments the respondent offers after all the formal questions have been asked should be recorded. The interviewer should answer the respondent's questions about the project. The respondent should be left with a positive feeling about the interview. It is important to thank the respondent and express appreciation.

### REAL RESEARCH

### *The Center for Disease Control Controls Training*

The Center for Disease Control and Prevention (CDC) (*www.cdc.gov*) has conducted the state-based Behavioral Risk Factor Surveillance System (BRFSS), the largest continuously conducted telephone health survey in the world, to collect data on risk behaviors and preventive health practices every month since 1984. Field workers who are trained in their respective states conduct these standardized questionnaires. The CDC receives health data on hypertension, high cholesterol, smoking, and drinking behaviors from individual states and publishes a report every year. To increase standardization in the training of field workers and data collection, the CDC implemented a computer-assisted telephone interviewing (CATI) system.

The CDC understands that its field interviewers are the only link between the survey participants and the researchers conducting the survey. The CDC therefore requires states to spend a lot of time and effort training its interviewers. In training, an effort is made to ensure that the interviewer:

- Understands the nature and content of the questions
- Understands how to record responses, code questionnaires, and edit interviews

- Ensures respondents' confidentiality
- Ensures that the correct respondents are interviewed
- Records a true picture
- Executes the work clearly and accurately
- Is prepared to deal with problem situations that may arise during interviews
- Is persuasive and minimizes the number of selected households and respondents who refuse to participate
- Makes quality a priority in all aspects of interviewing
- Is courteous and friendly
- Strives for maximum efficiency without sacrificing quality

With the nature of the BRFSS, interviewers must also sign a confidentiality agreement. Respondents are sometimes concerned about confidentiality with their health information. Measures are taken to eliminate the possibility of ever identifying the specific person who has taken a survey. For instance, the last two digits of the telephone number are deleted in the final survey results. Interviewers are trained to relay this information to people who are concerned when they call them.

Other training procedures are useful in obtaining valid responses for the questionnaire and for being courteous to the participants. The table summarizes the tips for telephone interviewing that CDC uses as part of its training program. This extensive training is vital to providing the accurate information the CDC needs for its analysis of locally relevant data on risk behaviors and preventive health practices. The data are used in a variety of ways by states and health agencies for planning, implementing, and measuring the progress of their risk-reduction programs, and for developing appropriate policies and legislation.[15]

Tips for Telephone Interviewing

| *Voice Personality* | *Handling Difficult Respondents* |
|---|---|
| Be courteous and polite. | Answer respondents. |
| Sound confident. | Alleviate confidentiality concerns. |
| Do not sound bored. | Encourage responses from reluctant respondents. |
| Sound interested in the responses. | Alleviate concerns about length of interview. |
| Put a smile in your voice. | *General Knowledge of the BRFSS* |
| *Probing and Clarification* | Recognize need for data quality. |
| Probe for accurate information. | Know survey objectives. |
| Know when to probe. | Know rationale for the questions. |
| Use neutral probes. | *Interviewing Techniques* |
| *Enunciation of Questionnaire* | Read questions verbatim. |
| Speak clearly. | Verify telephone number. |
| Pronounce words properly. | Follow skip patterns smoothly. |
| | Go from introduction to questions smoothly. |
| | Close interview smoothly. |
| | Make appointments properly. |
| | Provide neutral feedback. ■ |

# SUPERVISION OF FIELD WORKERS

Supervision of field workers means making sure that they are following the procedures and techniques in which they were trained. Supervision involves quality control and editing, sampling control, control of cheating, and central office control.

## Quality Control and Editing

Quality control of field workers requires checking to see if the field procedures are being properly implemented.[16] If any problems are detected, the supervisor should discuss them with the field workers and provide additional training if necessary. To understand the interviewers' problems, the supervisors should also do some interviewing. Supervisors should collect questionnaires and other forms and edit them daily. They should examine the questionnaires to make sure all appropriate questions have been completed, unsatisfactory or incomplete answers have not been accepted, and the writing is legible.

Supervisors should also keep a record of hours worked and expenses. This will allow a determination of the cost per completed interview, whether the job is moving on schedule, and if any interviewers are having problems.

## Sampling Control

An important aspect of supervision is **sampling control,** which attempts to ensure that the interviewers are strictly following the sampling plan rather than selecting sampling units based on convenience or accessibility. Interviewers tend to avoid dwellings or sampling units that they perceive as difficult or undesirable. If the sampling unit is not at home, the interviewers may be tempted to substitute the next available unit rather than call back. Interviewers sometimes stretch the requirements of quota samples. For example, a 58-year-old person may be placed in the 46-to-55 age category and interviewed to fulfill quota requirements.

To control these problems, supervisors should keep daily records of the number of calls made, number of not-at-homes, number of refusals, number of completed interviews for each interviewer, and the total for all interviewers under their control.

## Control of Cheating

Cheating involves falsifying part of a question or the entire questionnaire. An interviewer may falsify part of an answer to make it acceptable or may fake answers. The most blatant form of cheating occurs when the interviewer falsifies the entire questionnaire, merely filling in fake answers without contacting the respondent. Cheating can be minimized through proper training, supervision, and validation of fieldwork.[17]

## Central Office Control

Supervisors provide quality and cost-control information to the central office so that a total progress report can be maintained. In addition to the controls initiated in the field, other controls may be added at the central office to identify potential problems. Central office control includes tabulation of quota variables, important demographic characteristics, and answers to key variables.

# VALIDATION OF FIELDWORK

Validation of fieldwork means verifying that the field workers are submitting authentic interviews. To validate the study, the supervisors call 10 to 25 percent of the respondents to inquire whether the field workers actually conducted the interviews. The supervisors ask about the length and quality of the interview, reaction to the interviewer, and basic demographic data. The demographic information is cross-checked against the information reported by the interviewers on the questionnaires.

# EVALUATION OF FIELD WORKERS

It is important to evaluate field workers to provide them with feedback on their performance as well as to identify the better field workers and build a better, high-quality field force. The evaluation criteria should be clearly communicated to the field workers during their training. The evaluation of field workers should be based on the criteria of cost and time, response rates, quality of interviewing, and quality of data.[18]

## Cost and Time

The interviewers can be compared in terms of the total cost (salary and expenses) per completed interview. If the costs differ by city size, comparisons should be made only among field workers working in comparable cities. The field workers should also be evaluated on how they spend their time. Time should be broken down into categories such as actual interviewing, travel, and administration.

## Response Rates

It is important to monitor response rates on a timely basis so that corrective action can be taken if these rates are too low.[19] Supervisors can help interviewers with an inordinate number of refusals by listening to the introductions they use and providing immediate feedback. When all the interviews are over, different field workers' percentage of refusals can be compared to identify the better ones.

## Quality of Interviewing

To evaluate interviewers on the quality of interviewing, the supervisor must directly observe the interviewing process. The supervisor can do this in person, or the field worker can tape-record the interview. The quality of interviewing should be evaluated in terms of (1) the appropriateness of the introduction, (2) the precision with which the field worker asks questions, (3) the ability to probe in an unbiased manner, (4) the ability to ask sensitive questions, (5) interpersonal skills displayed during the interview, and (6) the manner in which the interview is terminated.

## Quality of Data

The completed questionnaires of each interviewer should be evaluated for the quality of data. Some indicators of quality data are: (1) the recorded data are legible; (2) all instructions, including skip patterns, are followed; (3) the answers to unstructured questions are recorded verbatim; (4) the answers to unstructured questions are meaningful and complete enough to be coded; and (5) item nonresponse occurs infrequently.

### REAL RESEARCH

### Guidelines on Interviewing: The Council of American Survey Research Organizations

Each interviewer is to follow these techniques for good interviewing:

1. Provide his or her full name, if asked by the respondent, as well as a phone number for the research firm.
2. Read each question exactly as written. Report any problems to the supervisor as soon as possible.
3. Read the questions in the order indicated on the questionnaire, following the proper skip sequences.
4. Clarify any question by the respondent in a neutral way.
5. Do not mislead respondents as to the length of the interview.
6. Do not reveal the identity of the ultimate client unless instructed to do so.
7. Keep a tally on each terminated interview and the reason for each termination.
8. Remain neutral in interviewing. Do not indicate agreement or disagreement with the respondent.
9. Speak slowly and distinctly so that words will be understood.
10. Record all replies verbatim, not paraphrased.
11. Avoid unnecessary conversations with the respondent.
12. Probe and clarify for additional comments on all open-end questions, unless otherwise instructed. Probe and clarify in a neutral way.
13. Write neatly and legibly.
14. Check all work for thoroughness before turning in to the supervisor.
15. When terminating a respondent, do so in a neutral way such as, "Thank you," or "Our quota has already been filled in this area, but thank you anyway."
16. Keep all studies, materials, and findings confidential.
17. Do not falsify any interviews or any answers to any question.
18. Thank the respondent for participating in the study. ∎

# INTERNATIONAL MARKETING RESEARCH

The selection, training, supervision, and evaluation of field workers are critical in international marketing research. Local fieldwork agencies are unavailable in many countries. Therefore, it may be necessary to recruit and train local field workers or import trained foreign workers. The use of local field workers is desirable, as they are familiar with the local language and culture. They can thus create an appropriate climate for the interview and be sensitive to the concerns of the respondents. Extensive training may be required and close supervision may be necessary. As observed in many countries, interviewers tend to help the respondent with the answers and select household or sampling units based on personal considerations rather than the sampling plan. Finally, interviewer cheating may be more of a problem in many foreign countries than in the United States. Validation of fieldwork is critical. Proper application of fieldwork procedures can greatly reduce these difficulties and result in consistent and useful findings.

International marketing research studies add more complexity regardless of how simple a survey may seem. Collecting data that is comparable between countries may be difficult, but it can be done using some standard methodologies with adaptations when needed. Equivalent marketing research procedures allow researchers to detect, analyze, and better understand the world's sociocultural differences. A global approach to marketing research is desired, which may require changing several methodologies for studies conducted in the United States so that U.S. data can be compared to other countries.

## REAL RESEARCH

### *Americanism Unites Europeans*

An image study conducted by Research International (*www.research-int.com*), a U.K. market research company, showed that despite unification of the European market, European consumers still increasingly favor U.S. products. It is expected that Americanism will unite the consumers in Europe. The survey was conducted in France, Germany, United Kingdom, Italy, and the Netherlands. In each country, local interviewers and supervisors were used, as it was felt they would be able to identify better with the respondents. However, the field workers were trained extensively and supervised closely in order to ensure quality results and minimize the variability in country-to-country results due to differences in interviewing procedures.

A total of 6,724 personal interviews were conducted. Some of the findings were that Europeans gave U.S products high marks for being innovative and some countries also regarded them as fashionable and of high quality. Interestingly, France, considered as anti-American, also emerged as pro-American. Among the 1,034 French consumers surveyed, 40 percent considered U.S. products fashionable, 38 percent believed they were innovative, and 15 percent said U.S. products were of high quality. In addition, when asked what nationality they preferred for a new company in their area, a U.S. company was the first choice. These findings were comparable and consistent across the four countries. A key to the discovery of these findings was the use of local field workers and extensive training and supervision that resulted in high-quality data.

This study is very useful for marketers to drum up and overplay the American brand name in the European market. "Rather than trying to hide the fact that they are American, we think companies ought to stress or try to exploit their American heritage," says Mr. Eric Salama, director of European operations for the Henley Center, the U.K. economic forecasting consultancy. U.S. firms have, in fact, capitalized on the "made in America" equity. As a result, exports to Europe have been soaring in recent years. U.S. exports for 2001 to western Europe were $701 million. The top three countries to whom the United States exported goods included: the United Kingdom at $166 million, Germany at $154 million, and France at $70 million.[20] ∎

# ETHICS IN MARKETING RESEARCH

The data, whether collected by the internal marketing research department or by an external fieldwork agency, should be obtained by following high ethical standards. The researchers and field workers should make the respondents feel comfortable by addressing their apprehensions. One way in which the comfort level of the respondents can be increased is by providing them with adequate information about the research firm, the project, addressing their questions, and clearly stating the responsibilities and expectations of the field workers and the respondents at the start of the interview. Moreover, the respondents should be told that they are not obligated to answer questions that make them uncomfortable, and that they can terminate the interview at any point should they experience discomfort. The researcher and field workers have an ethical responsibility to respect the respondents' privacy, feelings, and dignity."[21] Moreover, the respondents should be left with a positive and pleasant experience. This will enhance goodwill and future cooperation from respondents.

The researchers and the fieldwork agencies are also responsible to the clients for following the accepted procedures for the selection, training, supervision, validation, and evaluation of field workers. They must ensure the integrity of the data-collection process. The fieldwork procedures should be carefully documented and made available to the clients. Appropriate actions by researchers and fieldwork agencies can go a long way in addressing ethical concerns associated with fieldwork.

## REAL RESEARCH

### *Fielding Respondents' Ethical Concerns During Fieldwork*

Information provided while responding to an 800 number, using a credit card, or purchasing a product is often used to compile lists of customers and potential customers. These lists are rarely sold to telemarketing and direct marketing organizations. The public perception is different, however, and many people feel that marketers and marketing researchers misuse the information they collect. This misperception is giving marketing research a negative image.

In an effort to fight back, many marketing researchers and fieldwork agencies are addressing this issue head-on at the start of the interview. For example, when contacting potential respondents, the Gallup Organization (*www.gallup.com*) provides them with information about the firm (Gallup) and the marketing research project. The respondents are assured that Gallup operates within a code of ethics. Some marketing research firms and fieldwork agencies provide potential respondents with toll-free numbers that can be called to obtain more information or verify the information given by the field workers. Such actions make the respondents more comfortable and informed, and result in higher quality data for the clients.[22] ■

## INTERNET AND COMPUTER APPLICATIONS

Regardless of which method is used for interviewing (telephone, personal, mail, or electronic), the Internet can play a valuable role in all the phases of fieldwork: selection, training, supervision, validation, and evaluation of field workers. As far as selection is concerned, interviewers can be located, interviewed, and hired by using the Internet. This process can be initiated, for example, by posting job vacancy notices for interviewers at the company Web site, bulletin boards, and other suitable locations. Although this would confine the search to only Internet-savvy interviewers, this may well be a qualification to look for in the current marketing research environment.

Similarly, the Internet, with its multimedia capabilities, can be a good supplementary tool for training the field workers in all aspects of interviewing. Training in this manner can complement personal training programs and add value to the process. Supervision is enhanced by facilitating communication between the supervisors and the interviewers via e-mail and secured chatrooms. Central office control can be strengthened by posting progress reports, quality, and cost-control information on a secured location at a Web site, so that it is easily available to all the relevant parties.

Validation of fieldwork, especially for personal and telephone interviews, can be easily accomplished for those respondents who have an e-mail address or access to the Internet. These respondents can be sent a short verification survey by e-mail or asked to visit a Web site where the survey is posted. Finally, the evaluation criteria can be communicated to the field workers during the training stage by using the Internet, and performance feedback can also be provided to them by using this medium.

Microcomputers and mainframes, such as the Ci3 System by Sawtooth Software, Inc. (*www.sawtoothsoftware.com*), can be used in fieldwork for respondent selection, interviewer planning, and supervision and control. Ci3 CATI's ability to guide the interview process makes it a valuable asset in marketing research. Computers can also be used to manage mailing lists. For example, the mailing lists can be sorted according to zipcodes, geographical regions, or other prespecified characteristics. Computers can also electronically monitor mail survey nonresponse. Computers can generate accurate and timely reports for supervision and control purposes. These include quota reports, call disposition (outcome) reports, incidence reports, top-line reports of respondent data, and interviewer productivity reports. Automatic reporting enhances supervision and control and increases the overall quality of data collection. Because less time is spent compiling reports, more time can be spent on data interpretation and on supervision. Several Web-based services are also available for fielding online surveys.

**REAL RESEARCH**

## *Create Your Own Online Survey*

CreateSurvey (*www.createsurvey.com*) is an online international company that allows anyone to create and administer online surveys to whomever they want. It distributes the survey, monitors participation and participants, and then collects and analyzes the data, all for free. It is sponsored by Web advertising in the form of online banners that appear on the site and the questionnaires, so respondents as well as the survey creators see the advertisements. If an individual does not wish to have the advertising banners appear on their page, they can be removed, but then a fee of at least $5 per 1,000 respondents is charged to the creator to support the service. CreateSurvey does not provide respondents. This is done by the users at their discretion. For instance, they may create a Web page and have the survey as a link from the Web page, or they may send out an e-mail with the link requesting people to participate in the survey. CreateSurvey provides a valuable service for creating and administering online surveys that have been used by many individuals, companies, universities, and even marketing research organizations. ■

Another Web-based service that also lets you create your own surveys is (*www.zoomerang.com*) by MarketTools, an Internet-based, technology-enabled, full-service marketing research company (*www.markettools.com*).

## SPSS Windows

SPSS offers several programs to assist in the fieldwork or data collection. Moreover, a number of different methods of administering the survey can be accommodated, including telephone, electronic, mail, and personal interviewing.

1. SPSS Data Entry Station: This deployment method will put a copy of the questionnaire on a computer so that a data-entry operator or respondent can enter the answers on the screen using the keyboard and mouse (without giving them the ability to edit the form). In this way, to some extent, data entry can simulate a proper CATI system because you can prepopulate the data with the phone number and basic details of the respondent so the information appears as the operator moves through the list. However, this system completely lacks the ability to keep a call log and a callback list, which most good, true CATI systems should do.

2. SPSS Data Entry Enterprise Server (DEES): This deployment method will upload a copy of the questionnaire to a Web server so that data-entry operators or respondents can log on using a password and enter their results without having to install anything to their local machine. DEES can be used on both Intranet and Internet settings. This software also includes technology that prevents ballot stuffing (a respondent answering the survey multiple times).

3. Printing the form: This can be done by using SPSS DE Builder to simply print the form after it has been designed for a mail survey or personal interviewing. This is the least sophisticated because the researcher will not be able to take advantage of space-saving pull-down menus or any of the rules that were included. The rules can be used when the follow-up data entry is done, but in many situations if there is an error, it may be too late to correct it. For a personal interview it may be a better option for the interviewer to use a laptop with the form in DE Station, as the rules would "fire" as the questions are answered, thus allowing for quick corrections if required.

## FOCUS ON BURKE

Burke makes sure that the interviewers assigned to each and every project have the proper training, motivation, supervision, and evaluation to make the research effective and efficient. How does it manage this process? The first step is to have good managers. Burke recruits to its management trainee program from the ranks of successful interviewers and universities. The employment of new recruits starts with a 6-to-12-month training program, depending on background and rate of completing 24 two-to-three-hour training modules and supervised (under a senior data-collection manager) implementation of what they have learned. The focus is on data-collection standard operating procedures. Additionally, the manager trainees are cross-trained in:

- Customer service procedures
- Sample management procedures and systems
- Human resources management
- Interaction management (employee relations, evaluation procedures, conflict resolution, etc.)

Burke's data-collection area has full-time human resource professionals assigned to maintain the recruiting and training activities both for management and interviewers. To maintain a highly professional interviewing staff, Burke recruits from three basic target populations: college students, second-income workers, and career interviewers.

Burke has adopted rigorous procedures for the selection and training of its field workers. As part of the initial screening, the applicants are given simple literacy and numeracy tests. It is sad to say that a very high proportion of the applicants either fail these tests or pass marginally. In Burke's training process, attention is given to improving these skills. At an early stage the applicants are put into a group discussion session and observed in this exercise to determine their ability to listen and react logically and coherently to what they hear. After passing these checks, the final hiring decision is based on:

- Practice dialing under close supervision
- Listening and evaluation by supervisors
- Classroom drills and discussions of effective interviewing
- Ability to read and sound conversational
- Apparent professionalism
- Skill at implementing standard procedures and guidelines

The interviewers attend workshops on:

- Handling respondent refusals and interview terminations
- Efficiency in the interviewing process
- Vocalization workshop (enunciation, pronunciation, etc.)
- Typing skills
- Customer satisfaction training (interviewing as an identified representative of an organization)

To ensure the integrity of data collection for each project, Burke continually monitors for quality and consistency across interviewers through:

- Daily listening and evaluating on every project, every interviewer
- Standardized reports generated by the CATI system
- Interview length by interviewer
- Termination rate by interviewer
- Dialing disposition by interviewer
- Online time, open-end detail report
- Senior management involvement through open monitoring program in which managers listen at random to interviewers

# SUMMARY

Researchers have two major options for collecting data: developing their own organizations or contracting with field-work agencies. In either case, data collection involves the use of a field force. Field workers should be healthy, outgoing, communicative, pleasant, educated, and experienced. They should be trained in important aspects of fieldwork, including making the initial contact, asking the questions, probing, recording the answers, and terminating the interview.

Supervision of field workers involves quality control and editing, sampling control, control of cheating, and central office control. Validation of fieldwork can be accomplished by calling 10 to 25 percent of those who have been identified as interviewees and inquiring whether the interviews took place. Field workers should be evaluated on the basis of cost and time, response rates, quality of interviewing, and quality of data collection.

The selection, training, supervision, and evaluation of field workers is even more critical in international marketing research, as local fieldwork agencies are not available in many countries. Ethical issues include making the respondents feel comfortable in the data-collection process so that their experience is positive. Every effort must be undertaken to ensure that the data are of high quality. The Internet and computers can greatly facilitate and improve the quality of fieldwork.

# KEY TERMS AND CONCEPTS

probing, *390*

sampling control, *393*

# EXERCISES

## Questions

1. What options are available to researchers for collecting data?
2. Describe the fieldwork/data-collection process.
3. What qualifications should field workers possess?
4. What are the guidelines for asking questions?
5. What is probing?
6. How should the answers to unstructured questions be recorded?
7. How should the field worker terminate the interview?
8. What aspects are involved in the supervision of field workers?
9. How can respondent selection problems be controlled?
10. What is validation of fieldwork? How is this done?
11. Describe the criteria that should be used for evaluating field workers.
12. Describe the major sources of error related to fieldwork.

## Problems

1. Write some interviewer instructions for in-home personal interviews to be conducted by students.
2. Comment on the following field situations, making recommendations for corrective action.
   a. One of the interviewers has an excessive rate of refusals in in-home personal interviewing.
   b. In a CATI situation, many phone numbers are giving a busy signal during the first dialing attempt.
   c. An interviewer reports that, at the end of the interviews, many respondents asked if they had answered the questions correctly.
   d. While validating the fieldwork, a respondent reports that she cannot remember being interviewed over the telephone, but the interviewer insists that the interview was conducted.

# INTERNET AND COMPUTER EXERCISES

1. Visit the Web sites of some marketing research suppliers. Make a report of all the material related to fieldwork that is posted on these sites.
2. Visit the Marketing Research Association Web site (*www.mra-net.org*) and examine the ethical codes relating to data collection. Write a brief report.

3. Using PERT/CPM software such as MacProject, Timeline, Harvard Project Manager, Microsoft Project, or Category PERTmaster, develop a fieldwork schedule for conducting a national survey of consumer preferences for fast foods involving 2,500 mall intercept interviews in Los Angeles, Salt Lake City, Dallas, St. Louis, Milwaukee, New Orleans, Cincinnati, Orlando, Atlanta, New York City, and Boston.

# ACTIVITIES

## Role Playing

1. You are a field supervisor. Ask a fellow student to assume the role of an interviewer and another student the role of a respondent. Train the interviewer to conduct in-home personal interviews by giving a live demonstration.
2. Exchange the roles of interviewer and supervisor in the role-playing situation described in activity 1.

## Fieldwork

1. Arrange a field trip to a marketing research firm or data-collection agency. Ask the fieldwork supervisor to describe the agency's fieldwork process. How does it compare to the one described in this book?
2. Arrange a visit to a mall intercept interviewing facility when interviews are being conducted. Observe the interviewing process. Write a report about your visit.

## Group Discussion

1. Discuss the impact of women's changing lifestyles on fieldwork during the last decade.
2. Discuss the notion of interviewer cheating. Why do interviewers cheat? How can cheating be detected and prevented?

# CHAPTER 14

# Data Preparation

"No matter how often you hear 'garbage in . . . garbage out', this must be your mantra when working with data."

*Mary Beth Mapstone,*
*vice president, finance,*
*Burke, Inc.*

## Objectives

After reading this chapter, the student should be able to:

1. Discuss the nature and scope of data preparation, and the data-preparation process.

2. Explain questionnaire checking and editing, and treatment of unsatisfactory responses by returning to the field, assigning missing values, and discarding unsatisfactory responses.

3. Describe the guidelines for coding questionnaires including the coding of structured and unstructured questions.

4. Discuss the data-cleaning process and the methods used to treat missing responses: substitution of a neutral value, imputed response, casewise deletion, and pairwise deletion.

5. State the reasons for and methods of statistically adjusting data: weighting, variable respecification, and scale transformation.

6. Describe the procedure for selecting a data analysis strategy and the factors influencing the process.

7. Classify statistical techniques and give a detailed classification of univariate techniques as well as a classification of multivariate techniques.

8. Understand the intracultural, pancultural, and cross-cultural approaches to data analysis in international marketing research.

9. Identify the ethical issues related to data processing, particularly the discarding of unsatisfactory responses, violation of the assumptions underlying the data analysis techniques, and evaluation and interpretation of results.

10. Explain the use of the Internet and computers in data preparation and analysis.

After the research problem has been defined and a suitable approach developed (Chapter 2), an appropriate research design formulated (Chapters 3 to 12), and the fieldwork conducted (Chapter 13), the researcher can move on to data preparation and analysis, the fifth step of the marketing research process. Before the raw data contained in the questionnaires can be subjected to statistical analysis, they must be converted into a form suitable for analysis. The quality of statistical results depends on the care exercised in the data-preparation phase. Paying inadequate attention to data preparation can seriously compromise statistical results, leading to biased findings and incorrect interpretation.

This chapter describes the data-collection process, which begins with checking the questionnaires for completeness. Then, we discuss the editing of data and provide guidelines for handling illegible, incomplete, inconsistent, ambiguous, or otherwise unsatisfactory responses. We also describe coding, transcribing, and data cleaning, emphasizing the treatment of missing responses and statistical adjustment of data. We discuss the selection of a data analysis strategy and classify statistical techniques. The intracultural, pancultural, and cross-cultural approaches to data analysis in international marketing research are explained. The ethical issues related to data processing are identified with emphasis on the discarding of unsatisfactory responses, violation of the assumptions underlying the data analysis techniques, and evaluation and interpretation of results. Finally, we explain the use of microcomputers and mainframes in data preparation and analysis.

---

**ACTIVE RESEARCH** | DEPARTMENT STORE PROJECT

### Data Preparation

In the department store project, the data were obtained through in-home personal interviews. The supervisors edited the questionnaires as the interviewers turned them in. The questionnaires were checked for incomplete, inconsistent, and ambiguous responses. Questionnaires with unsatisfactory responses were returned to the field and the interviewers were asked to recontact the respondents to obtain the required information. Nine questionnaires were discarded because the proportion of unsatisfactory responses was large. This resulted in a final sample size of 271.

A codebook was developed for coding the questionnaires. Coding was relatively simple because there were no open-ended questions. The data were transcribed onto a computer tape via keypunching. About 25 percent of the data were verified for keypunching errors. The data were cleaned by identifying out-of-range and logically inconsistent responses. Most of the rating information was obtained using six-point scales, so responses of 0, 7, and 8 were considered out of range and a code of 9 was assigned to missing responses.

Any missing responses were treated by casewise deletion, in which respondents with any missing values were dropped from the analysis. Casewise deletion was selected because the number of cases (respondents) with missing values was small and the sample size was sufficiently large. In statistically adjusting the data, dummy variables were created for the categorical variables. New variables that were composites of original variables were also created. For example, the familiarity ratings of the 10 department stores were summed to create a familiarity index. Finally, a data analysis strategy was developed.

---

**REAL RESEARCH**

## Custom Cleaning

According to Joann Harristhal of Gfk Custom Research (*www.cresearch.com*), completed questionnaires from the field often have many small errors because of the inconsistent quality of interviewing. For example, qualifying responses are not circled, or skip patterns are not followed accurately.

These small errors can be costly. When responses from such questionnaires are put into a computer, Custom Research runs a cleaning program that checks for completeness and logic. Discrepancies are identified on a computer printout, which is checked by the tabulation supervisors. Once the errors are identified, appropriate corrective action is taken before data analysis is carried out. Custom Research has found that this procedure substantially increases the quality of statistical results.[1] ■

The department store example describes the various phases of the data-preparation process. Note that the process is initiated while the fieldwork is still in progress. The Custom Research example describes the importance of cleaning data and identifying and correcting errors before the data are analyzed. A systematic description of the data-preparation process follows.

# THE DATA-PREPARATION PROCESS

The data-preparation process is shown in Figure 14.1. The entire process is guided by the preliminary plan of data analysis that was formulated in the research design phase (Chapter 3). The first step is to check for acceptable questionnaires. This is followed by editing, coding, and transcribing the data. The data are cleaned and a treatment for missing responses prescribed. Often, statistical adjustment of the data may be necessary to make them representative of the population of interest. The researcher should then select an appropriate data analysis strategy. The final data analysis strategy differs from the preliminary plan of data analysis due to the information and insights gained since the preliminary plan was formulated. Data preparation should begin as soon as the first batch of questionnaires is received from the field, while the fieldwork is still going on. Thus if any problems are detected, the fieldwork can be modified to incorporate corrective action.

*Figure 14.1*
Data-Preparation Process

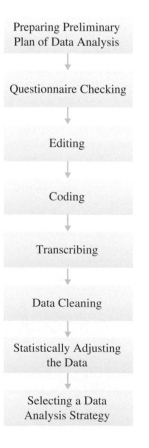

Preparing Preliminary
Plan of Data Analysis

Questionnaire Checking

Editing

Coding

Transcribing

Data Cleaning

Statistically Adjusting
the Data

Selecting a Data
Analysis Strategy

# QUESTIONNAIRE CHECKING

The initial step in questionnaire checking involves a check of all questionnaires for completeness and interviewing quality. Often these checks are made while fieldwork is still underway. If the fieldwork was contracted to a data-collection agency, the researcher should make an independent check after it is over. A questionnaire returned from the field may be unacceptable for several reasons.

1. Parts of the questionnaire may be incomplete.
2. The pattern of responses may indicate that the respondent did not understand or follow the instructions. For example, skip patterns may not have been followed.
3. The responses show little variance. For example, a respondent has checked only 4s on a series of seven-point rating scales.
4. The returned questionnaire is physically incomplete: one or more pages are missing.
5. The questionnaire is received after the preestablished cutoff date.
6. The questionnaire is answered by someone who does not qualify for participation.

If quotas or cell group sizes have been imposed, the acceptable questionnaires should be classified and counted accordingly. Any problems in meeting the sampling requirements should be identified and corrective action taken, such as conducting additional interviews in the underrepresented cells, before the data are edited.

# EDITING

**editing**
A review of the questionnaires with the objective of increasing accuracy and precision.

*Editing* is the review of the questionnaires with the objective of increasing accuracy and precision. It consists of screening questionnaires to identify illegible, incomplete, inconsistent, or ambiguous responses.

Responses may be illegible if they have been poorly recorded. This is particularly common in questionnaires with a large number of unstructured questions. The data must be legible if they are to be properly coded. Likewise, questionnaires may be incomplete to varying degrees. A few or many questions may be unanswered.

At this stage, the researcher makes a preliminary check for consistency. Certain obvious inconsistencies can be easily detected. For example, a respondent reports an annual income of less than $20,000, yet indicates frequent shopping at prestigious department stores such as Saks Fifth Avenue and Neiman-Marcus.

Responses to unstructured questions may be ambiguous and difficult to interpret clearly. The answer may be abbreviated, or some ambiguous words may have been used. For structured questions, more than one response may be marked for a question designed to elicit a single response. Suppose a respondent circles 2 and 3 on a five-point rating scale. Does this mean that 2.5 was intended? To complicate matters further, the coding procedure may allow for only a single-digit response.

## Treatment of Unsatisfactory Responses

Unsatisfactory responses are commonly handled by returning to the field to get better data, assigning missing values, or discarding unsatisfactory respondents.

***Returning to the Field.*** The questionnaires with unsatisfactory responses may be returned to the field, where the interviewers recontact the respondents. This approach is particularly attractive for business and industrial marketing surveys, where the sample sizes are small and the respondents are easily identifiable. However, the data obtained the second time may be different from those obtained during the original survey. These differences may be attributed to changes over time or differences in the mode of questionnaire administration (e.g., telephone versus in-person interview).

***Assigning Missing Values.*** If returning the questionnaires to the field is not feasible, the editor may assign missing values to unsatisfactory responses. This approach may be desirable if (1) the number of respondents with unsatisfactory responses is small, (2) the proportion of unsatisfactory responses for each of these respondents is small, or (3) the variables with unsatisfactory responses are not the key variables.

***Discarding Unsatisfactory Respondents.***   In this approach, the respondents with unsatisfactory responses are simply discarded. This approach may have merit when (1) the proportion of unsatisfactory respondents is small (less than 10%), (2) the sample size is large, (3) the unsatisfactory respondents do not differ from satisfactory respondents in obvious ways (e.g., demographics, product usage characteristics), (4) the proportion of unsatisfactory responses for each of these respondents is large, or (5) responses on key variables are missing. However, unsatisfactory respondents may differ from satisfactory respondents in systematic ways and the decision to designate a respondent as unsatisfactory may be subjective. Both these factors bias the results. If the researcher decides to discard unsatisfactory respondents, the procedure adopted to identify these respondents and their number should be reported.

## REAL RESEARCH

### Declaring Discards

In a cross-cultural survey of marketing managers from English-speaking African countries, questionnaires were mailed to 565 firms. A total of 192 completed questionnaires were returned, of which four were discarded because respondents suggested that they were not in charge of overall marketing decisions. The decision to discard the four questionnaires was based on the consideration that the sample size was sufficiently large and the proportion of unsatisfactory respondents was small.[2] ■

# CODING

**coding**
The assignment of a code to represent a specific response to a specific question along with the data record and column position that code will occupy.

*Coding* means assigning a code, usually a number, to each possible response to each question. The code includes an indication of the column position (field) and data record it will occupy. For example, sex of respondents may be coded as 1 for females and 2 for males. A field represents a single item of data, such as sex of the respondent. A record consists of related fields, such as sex, marital status, age, household size, occupation, etc. Often all the data for a respondent will be contained in a single record, although a number of records may be used for each respondent. A convenient way for entering data is to use a spreadsheet such as EXCEL, where specific columns can be easily designated for specific questions and responses. Each row contains the data for one respondent.

The data (all the records) for all the respondents are stored in a computer file, as illustrated in Table 14.1. This table demonstrates the more general case of coding where more than one record may be used for each respondent. In this table, the columns represent the fields and the rows the records. Table 14.1 presents coded data for part of the first record for respondents in the department store project. These data have been coded according to the coding scheme specified in Figure 14.2. Columns 1 to 3 represent a single field and contain the respondent numbers coded 001 to 271. Column 4 contains the record number. This column has a value of 1 for all the rows because only the first record of the respondents

## TABLE 14.1

**Illustrative Computer File: Department Store Project**

| RECORDS | FIELDS COLUMN NUMBERS | | | | | |
|---------|-----|---|-----|-----|-----|----|
| | 1–3 | 4 | 5–6 | 7–8 . . . . . . . . . . . 26 . . . . . 35 . . . . . . . . . . 77 | | |
| Record #1 | 001 | 1 | 31 | 01 | 6544234553 | 5 |
| Record #11 | 002 | 1 | 31 | 01 | 5564435433 | 4 |
| Record #21 | 003 | 1 | 31 | 01 | 4655243324 | 4 |
| Record #31 | 004 | 1 | 31 | 01 | 5463244645 | 6 |
| Record #2701 | 271 | 1 | 31 | 55 | 6652354435 | 5 |

**Figure 14.2**

Codebook Excerpt Showing Information for the First Record: Department Store Project

| Column Number | Variable Number | Variable Name | Question Number | Coding Instructions |
|---|---|---|---|---|
| 1–3 | 1 | Respondent ID | | 001 to 890 add leading zeros as necessary |
| 4 | 2 | Record number | | 1 (same for all respondents) |
| 5–6 | 3 | Project code | | 31 (same for all respondents) |
| 7–8 | 4 | Interview code | | As coded on the questionnaire |
| 9–14 | 5 | Date code | | As coded on the questionnaire |
| 15–20 | 6 | Time code | | As coded on the questionnaire |
| 21–22 | 7 | Validation code | | As coded on the questionnaire |
| 23–24 | | Blank | | Leave these columns blank |
| 25 | 8 | Who shops | I | Male head = 1 |
| | | | | Female head = 2 |
| | | | | Other = 3 |
| | | | | **input the number circled** |
| | | | | Missing values = 9 |
| 26 | 9 | Familiarity with store 1 | IIa | For question II parts a through j, **input the number circled** |
| 27 | 10 | Familiarity with store 2 | IIb | Not so familiar = 1 |
| | | | | Very familiar = 6 |
| | | | | Missing values = 9 |
| 28 | 11 | Familiarity with store 3 | IIc | |
| 35 | 18 | Familiarity with store 10 | IIj | |
| 36 | 19 | Frequency: Store 1 | IIIa | For question III parts a through j, **input the number circled** |
| 37 | 20 | Frequency: Store 2 | IIIb | Not at all = 1 |
| | | | | Very frequently = 6 |
| | | | | Missing values = 9 |
| 45 | 28 | Frequency: Store 10 | IIIj | |
| 46–47 | | Blank | | Leave these columns blank |
| 48 | 29 | Rating of store 1 on quality | IVa1 | For questions IV through XI, **input the number circled** |
| 57 | 38 | Rating of store 10 on quality | IVa10 | |
| 58 | 39 | Rating of store 1 on variety | IVb1 | |
| 67 | 48 | Rating of store 10 on variety | IVb10 | |
| 68 | 49 | Rating of store 1 on prices | IVc1 | |
| 77 | 58 | Rating of store 10 on prices | IVc10 | |
| 78–80 | | Blank | | Leave these columns blank |

is displayed. Columns 5 to 6 contain the project code, which is 31. The next two columns, 7 to 8, display the interviewer code that varies from 01 to 55, as 55 interviewers were used. Columns 26 to 35, each representing one field, contain familiarity ratings for the 10 stores, with values ranging from 1 to 6. Finally, column 77 represents the rating of store 10 on prices. Note that columns 78 to 80 are blank. There are 10 records for each respondent. There are 2710 rows, indicating that data for 271 respondents are stored in this file.

If the questionnaire contains only structured questions or very few unstructured questions, it is precoded. This means that codes are assigned before fieldwork is conducted. If the questionnaire contains unstructured questions, codes are assigned after the questionnaires have been returned from the field (postcoding). Precoding was briefly discussed in Chapter 10 on questionnaire design, and we provide further guidelines here.[3]

## Coding Questions

The respondent code and the record number should appear on each record in the data. However, the record code can be dispensed if there is only one record for each respondent. The following additional codes should be included for each respondent: project code, interviewer code, date and time codes, and validation code. *Fixed-field codes,* which mean that the number of records for each respondent is the same and the same data appear in the same column(s) for all respondents, are highly desirable. If possible, standard codes should be used for missing data. For example, a code of 9 could be used for a single-column variable, 99 for a double-column variable, and so on. The missing value codes should be distinct from the codes assigned to the legitimate responses.

**fixed-field codes**

A code in which the number of records for each respondent are the same, and the same data appear in the same columns for all respondents.

Coding of structured questions is relatively simple, because the response options are predetermined. The researcher assigns a code for each response to each question and specifies the appropriate record and columns in which the response codes are to appear. For example,

Do you have a currently valid passport?
1. Yes   2. No   (1/54)

For this question, a "Yes" response is coded 1 and a "No" response 2. The numbers in parentheses indicate that the code assigned will appear on the first record for this respondent in column 54. Because only one response is allowed and there are only two possible responses (1 or 2), a single column is sufficient. In general, a single column is sufficient to code a structured question with a single response if there are less than nine possible responses.

In questions that permit a large number of responses, each possible response option should be assigned a separate column. Such questions include those about brand ownership or usage, magazine readership, and television viewing. For example,

Which accounts do you *now* have at this bank? ("X" as many as apply)

| | | |
|---|---|---|
| Regular savings account | ☐ | (162) |
| Regular checking account | ☐ | (163) |
| Mortgage | ☐ | (164) |
| Now account | ☐ | (165) |
| Club account (Christmas, etc.) | ☐ | (166) |
| Line of credit | ☐ | (167) |
| Term savings account (time deposits, etc.) | ☐ | (168) |
| Savings bank life insurance | ☐ | (169) |
| Home improvement loan | ☐ | (170) |
| Auto loan | ☐ | (171) |
| Other services | ☐ | (172) |

In this example, suppose a respondent checked regular savings, regular checking, and term savings accounts. On record #9, a 1 will be entered in the column numbers 162, 163, and 168. All the other columns (164, 165, 166, 167, 169, 170, 171, and 172) will receive a 0. Since there is only one record per respondent, the record has been omitted.

The coding of unstructured or open-ended questions is more complex. Respondents' verbatim responses are recorded on the questionnaire. Codes are then developed and assigned to these responses. Sometimes, based on previous projects or theoretical considerations, the researcher can develop the codes before beginning fieldwork. Usually, this must wait until the completed questionnaires are received. Then the researcher lists 50 to 100 responses to an unstructured question to identify the categories suitable for coding. Once codes are developed, the coders should be trained to assign the correct codes to the verbatim responses. The following guidelines are suggested for coding unstructured questions and questionnaires in general.[4]

Category codes should be mutually exclusive and collectively exhaustive. Categories are mutually exclusive if each response fits into one and only one category code. Categories should not overlap. Categories are collectively exhaustive if every response fits into one of the assigned category codes. This can be achieved by adding an additional category code of "other" or "none of the above." However, only a few (10% or less) of the responses should fall into this category. The vast majority of the responses should be classified into meaningful categories.

Category codes should be assigned for critical issues even if no one has mentioned them. It may be important to know that no one has mentioned a particular response. For example, the management of a major consumer goods company was concerned about the packaging for a new brand of toilet soap. Hence, packaging was included as a separate category in coding responses to the question, "What do you like least about this toilet soap?"

Data should be coded to retain as much detail as possible. For example, if data on the exact number of trips made on commercial airlines by business travelers have been obtained, they should be coded as such, rather than grouped into two category codes of "infrequent fliers" and "frequent fliers." Obtaining information on the exact number of trips allows the researcher to later define categories of business travelers in several different ways. If the categories were predefined, the subsequent analysis of data would be limited by those categories.

## Codebook

A *codebook* contains coding instructions and the necessary information about variables in the data set. A codebook guides the coders in their work and helps the researcher to properly identify and locate the variables. Even if the questionnaire has been precoded, it is helpful to prepare a formal codebook. A codebook generally contains the following information: (1) column number, (2) record number, (3) variable number, (4) variable name, (5) question number, and (6) instructions for coding. Figure 14.2 is an excerpt from a coding book developed for the department store project. Figure 14.3 is an example of questionnaire coding, showing the coding of demographic data typically obtained in consumer surveys. This questionnaire was precoded.

# TRANSCRIBING

Transcribing data involves transferring the coded data from the questionnaires or coding sheets onto disks or magnetic tapes or directly into computers by keypunching. If the data have been collected via CATI or CAPI, this step is unnecessary as the data are entered directly into the computer, as they are collected. Besides keypunching, the data can be transferred by using mark sense forms, optical scanning, or computerized sensory analysis (see Figure 14.4). Mark sense forms require responses to be recorded with a special pencil in a predesignated area coded for that response. The data can then be read by a machine. Optical scanning involves direct machine reading of the codes and simultaneous transcription. A familiar example of optical scanning is the transcription of UPC (universal product code) data at supermarket checkout counters. Technological advances have resulted in computerized sensory analysis systems, which automate the data-collection process. The questions appear on a computerized gridpad, and responses are recorded directly into the computer using a sensing device.

If keypunching is used, errors can occur, and it is necessary to verify the data set, or at least a portion of it, for keypunching errors. A verifier machine and a second operator are utilized for data verification. The second operator repunches the data from the coded questionnaires. The transcribed data from the two operators are compared record by record. Any discrepancy between the two sets of transcribed data is investigated to identify and correct for keypunching errors. Verification of the entire data set will double the time and cost of data transcription. Given the time and cost constraints, as well as the fact that experienced keypunch operators are quite accurate, it is sufficient to verify only 25 to 50 percent of the data.

When CATI or CAPI are employed, data are verified as they are collected. In the case of inadmissible responses, the computer will prompt the interviewer or respondent. In case of admissible responses, the interviewer or the respondent can see the recorded response on the screen and verify it before proceeding.

The selection of a data-transcription method is guided by the type of interviewing method used and the availability of equipment. If CATI or CAPI are used, the data are entered directly into the computer. Keypunching via CRT terminal is most frequently used for ordinary telephone, in-home, mall intercept, and mail interviews. However, the use of computerized sensory analysis systems in personal interviews is increasing with the increasing use of gridpads and hand-held computers. Optical scanning can be used in structured and repetitive surveys, and mark sense forms are used in special cases.[5]

**Figure 14.3**

Example of Questionnaire Coding Showing Coding of Demographic Data

Finally, in this part of the questionnaire we would like to ask you some background information for classification purposes.

**PART D**

1. This questionnaire was answered by                                                     (229)
   1. _____ Primarily the male head of household
   2. _____ Primarily the female head of household
   3. _____ Jointly by the male and female heads of household

2. Marital Status                                                                         (230)
   1. _____ Married
   2. _____ Never married
   3. _____ Divorced/separated/widowed

3. What is the total number of family members living at home? _____      (231–232)

4. Number of children living at home:
   1. Under six years _____                                                          (233)
   2. Over six years _____                                                           (234)

5. Number of children not living at home _____                                       (235)

6. Number of years of formal education which you (and your spouse,
   if applicable) have completed. (please circle)

   |  |  | College |  |  |
   |---|---|---|---|---|
   |  | High School | Undergraduate | Graduate |  |
   | 1. You | 8 or less 9 10 11 12 | 13 14 15 16 | 17 18 19 20 21 22 or more | (236–237) |
   | 2. Spouse | 8 or less 9 10 11 12 | 13 14 15 16 | 17 18 19 20 21 22 or more | (238–239) |

7. 1. Your age _____                                                                  (240–241)
   2. Age of spouse (if applicable) _____                                            (242–243)

8. If employed, please indicate your household's occupations by checking
   the appropriate category.

   |  | (244) Male head | (245) Female head |
   |---|---|---|
   | 1. Professional and technical | _____ | _____ |
   | 2. Managers and administrators | _____ | _____ |
   | 3. Sales workers | _____ | _____ |
   | 4. Clerical and kindred workers | _____ | _____ |
   | 5. Craftsman/operative/laborers | _____ | _____ |
   | 6. Homemakers | _____ | _____ |
   | 7. Others (please specify) | _____ | _____ |
   | 8. Not applicable | _____ | _____ |

9. Is your place of residence presently owned by household?                               (246)
   1. Owned _____
   2. Rented _____

10. How many years have you been residing in the greater Atlanta area?
    _____ years.                                                                      (247–248)

11. What is the approximate combined annual income of your household
    before taxes? Please check.                                                           (249–250)

    | 1. Less than $10,000 _____ | 8. $40,000 to 44,999 _____ |
    |---|---|
    | 2. $10,000 to 14,999 _____ | 9. $45,000 to 49,999 _____ |
    | 3. $15,000 to 19,999 _____ | 10. $50,000 to 54,999 _____ |
    | 4. $20,000 to 24,999 _____ | 11. $55,000 to 59,999 _____ |
    | 5. $25,000 to 29,999 _____ | 12. $60,000 to 69,999 _____ |
    | 6. $30,000 to 34,999 _____ | 13. $70,000 to 89,999 _____ |
    | 7. $35,000 to 39,999 _____ | 14. $90,000 and over _____ |

**Note:** Columns 1 through 228 contain the respondent ID, project information, and information pertaining to parts A, B, and C of the questionnaire. There is only one record per respondent.

*Figure 14.4*
Data Transcription

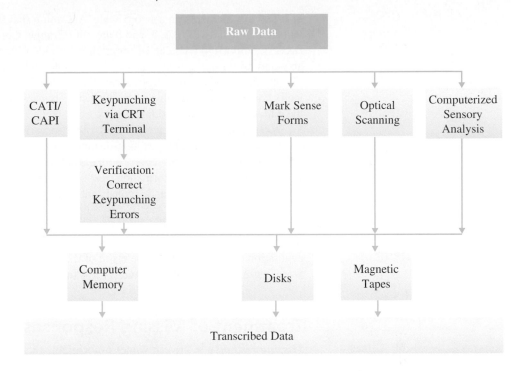

## REAL RESEARCH

### Scanning the Seas

Princess Cruises Incorporated (*www.princess.com*), based in London, operates large cruise ships across the world. They are the third largest cruise line that annually carries approximately 700,000 passengers with revenues of more than $2 billion. In 2002, Princess had 18 ships and planned to add nine more by 2004.

Princess wished to know what passengers thought of the cruise experience, but wanted to determine this information in a cost-effective way. A scannable questionnaire was developed that allowed the cruise line to quickly transcribe the data from thousands of surveys, thus expediting data preparation and analysis. This questionnaire is distributed to measure customer satisfaction on all voyages.

In addition to saving time as compared to keypunching, scanning has also increased the accuracy of the survey results. The senior market researcher for Princess Cruises, Jaime Goldfarb, commented, "When we compared the data files from the two methods, we found that although the scanned system occasionally missed marks because they had not been filled in properly, the scanned data file was still more accurate than the keypunched file."

A monthly report by cruise destination and ship is produced. This report identifies any specific problems that have been noticed and steps are taken to make sure these problems are addressed. Recently, these surveys have led to changes in the menu and the various buffets located around the ship.[6] ■

# DATA CLEANING

**data cleaning**
Thorough and extensive checks for consistency and treatment of missing responses.

*Data cleaning* includes consistency checks and treatment of missing responses. Although preliminary consistency checks have been made during editing, the checks at this stage are more thorough and extensive, because they are made by computer.

## Consistency Checks

**consistency checks**
A part of the data-cleaning process that identifies data that are out of range, logically inconsistent, or have extreme values. Data with values not defined by the coding scheme are inadmissible.

*Consistency checks* identify data that are out of range, logically inconsistent, or have extreme values. Out-of-range data values are inadmissible and must be corrected. For example, respondents have been asked to express their degree of agreement with a series of lifestyle statements on a 1-to-5 scale. Assuming that 9 has been designated for missing values, data values of 0, 6, 7, and 8 are out of range. Computer packages like SPSS, SAS, EXCEL, and MINITAB can be programmed to identify out-of-range values for each variable and print out the respondent code, variable code, variable name, record number, column number, and out-of-range value.[7] This makes it easy to check each variable systematically for out-of-range values. The correct responses can be determined by going back to the edited and coded questionnaire.

Responses can be logically inconsistent in various ways. For example, a respondent may indicate that she charges long-distance calls to a calling card, although she does not have one. Or a respondent reports both unfamiliarity with, and frequent usage of, the same product. The necessary information (respondent code, variable code, variable name, record number, column number, and inconsistent values) can be printed to locate these responses and take corrective action.

Finally, extreme values should be closely examined. Not all extreme values result from errors, but they may point to problems with the data. For example, an extremely low evaluation of a brand may be the result of the respondent indiscriminately circling 1s (on a 1-to-7 rating scale) on all attributes of this brand.

## Treatment of Missing Responses

**missing responses**
Values of a variable that are unknown, as these respondents did not provide unambiguous answers to the question.

*Missing responses* represent values of a variable that are unknown, either because respondents provided ambiguous answers or their answers were not properly recorded. Treatment of missing responses poses problems, particularly if the proportion of missing responses is more than 10 percent. The following options are available for the treatment of missing responses.[8]

1. **Substitute a Neutral Value.** A neutral value, typically the mean response to the variable, is substituted for the missing responses. Thus, the mean of the variable remains unchanged and other statistics, such as correlations, are not affected much. Although this approach has some merit, the logic of substituting a mean value (say 4) for respondents who, if they had answered, might have used either high ratings (6 or 7) or low ratings (1 or 2) is questionable.[9]

2. **Substitute an Imputed Response.** The respondents' pattern of responses to other questions are used to impute or calculate a suitable response to the missing questions. The researcher attempts to infer from the available data the responses the individuals would have given if they had answered the questions. This can be done statistically by determining the relationship of the variable in question to other variables, based on the available data. For example, product usage could be related to household size for respondents who have provided data on both variables. The missing product usage response for a respondent could then be calculated, given that respondent's household size. However, this approach requires considerable effort and can introduce serious bias. Sophisticated statistical procedures have been developed to calculate imputed values for missing responses.

### REAL RESEARCH

### *Imputation Increases Integrity*

A project was undertaken to assess the willingness of households to implement the recommendations of an energy audit (dependent variable), given the financial implications. The independent variables consisted of five financial factors that were manipulated at known levels, and their values were always known by virtue of the design adopted. However, several values of the dependent variable were missing. These missing values were replaced with imputed values. The imputed values were statistically calculated, given the corresponding values of the independent variables. The treatment of missing responses in this manner greatly increased the simplicity and validity of subsequent analysis.[10] ∎

**casewise deletion**
A method for handling missing responses in which cases or respondents with any missing responses are discarded from the analysis.

3. **Casewise Deletion.** In *casewise deletion,* cases, or respondents, with any missing responses are discarded from the analysis. Because many respondents may have some missing responses, this approach could result in a small sample. Throwing away large amounts of data is undesirable, because it is costly and time consuming to collect data. Furthermore, respondents with missing responses could differ from respondents with complete responses in systematic ways. If so, casewise deletion could seriously bias the results.

**pairwise deletion**
A method of handling missing values in which all cases, or respondents, with any missing values are not automatically discarded, rather, for each calculation only the cases or respondents with complete responses are considered.

4. **Pairwise Deletion.** In *pairwise deletion,* instead of discarding all cases with any missing values, the researcher uses only the cases or respondents with complete responses for each calculation. As a result, different calculations in an analysis may be based on different sample sizes. This procedure may be appropriate when (1) the sample size is large, (2) there are few missing responses, and (3) the variables are not highly related. Yet, this procedure can produce results that are unappealing or even infeasible.

The different procedures for the treatment of missing responses may yield different results, particularly when the responses are not missing at random and the variables are related. Hence, missing responses should be kept to a minimum. The researcher should carefully consider the implications of the various procedures before selecting a particular method for the treatment of nonresponse.

# STATISTICALLY ADJUSTING THE DATA

Procedures for statistically adjusting the data consist of weighting, variable respecification, and scale transformations. These adjustments are not always necessary but can enhance the quality of data analysis.

## Weighting

**weighting**
A statistical adjustment to the data in which each case or respondent in the database is assigned a weight to reflect its importance relative to other cases or respondents.

In *weighting,* each case or respondent in the database is assigned a weight to reflect its importance relative to other cases or respondents. The value 1.0 represents the unweighted case. The effect of weighting is to increase or decrease the number of cases in the sample that possess certain characteristics. (See Chapter 12 which discussed the use of weighting to adjust for nonresponse).

Weighting is most widely used to make the sample data more representative of a target population on specific characteristics. For example, it may be used to give greater importance to cases or respondents with higher quality data. Yet another use of weighting is to adjust the sample so that greater importance is attached to respondents with certain characteristics. If a study is conducted to determine what modifications should be made to an existing product, the researcher might want to attach greater weight to the opinions of heavy users of the product. This could be accomplished by assigning weights of 3.0 to heavy users, 2.0 to medium users, and 1.0 to light users and nonusers. Weighting should be applied with caution, as it destroys the self-weighting nature of the sample design.[11]

### REAL RESEARCH

#### *Determining the Weight of Fast-Food Customers*

A mail survey was conducted in the Los Angeles–Long Beach area to determine consumer patronage of fast-food restaurants. The resulting sample composition differed in educational level from the area population distribution as compiled from recent census data. Therefore, the sample was weighted to make it representative in terms of educational level. The weights applied were determined by dividing the population percentage by the corresponding sample percentage. The distribution of education for the sample and population, as well as the weights applied, are given in the following table.

The patronage of fast-food restaurants is influenced by demographic characteristics such as education. Thus, weighting may be necessary.

Use of Weighting for Representativeness

| Years of Education | Sample Percentage | Population Percentage | Weight |
|---|---|---|---|
| *Elementary School* | | | |
| 0 to 7 years | 2.49 | 4.23 | 1.70 |
| 8 years | 1.26 | 2.19 | 1.74 |
| *High School* | | | |
| 1 to 3 years | 6.39 | 8.65 | 1.35 |
| 4 years | 25.39 | 29.24 | 1.15 |
| *College* | | | |
| 1 to 3 years | 22.33 | 29.42 | 1.32 |
| 4 years | 15.02 | 12.01 | 0.80 |
| 5 to 6 years | 14.94 | 7.36 | 0.49 |
| 7 years or more | 12.18 | 6.90 | 0.57 |
| Totals | 100.00 | 100.00 | |

Categories underrepresented in the sample received higher weights, whereas overrepresented categories received lower weights. Thus, the data for a respondent with 1 to 3 years of college education should be overweighted by multiplying by 1.32, whereas the data for a respondent with 7 or more years of college education should be underweighted by multiplying by 0.57. ■

If used, the weighting procedure should be documented and made a part of the project report.

### REAL RESEARCH

## Nielsen's Internet Survey: Does It Carry Any Weight?

In a potentially large, new revenue business, Internet surveying, ACNielsen (*www.acnielsen.com*) is encountering questions concerning the validity of its survey results. Due to the tremendous impact of electronic commerce on the business world, advertisers need to know how many people are doing business on the Internet in order to decide if it would be lucrative to place their ads online.

Nielsen performed a survey for CommerceNet (*www.commerce.net*), a group of companies that includes Sun Microsystems and American Express, to help determine the total number of users on the Internet. Nielsen's research stated that 37 million people over the age of 16 have access to the Internet, and 24 million have used the Internet in the last three months. Where statisticians believe the numbers are flawed is in the weighting used to help match the sample to the population. Weighting must be used to prevent research from being skewed towards any demographic group.

The Nielsen survey was weighted for gender but not for education; that may have skewed the population towards educated adults. Nielsen then proceeded to weight the survey by age and income after they had already weighted it for gender. Statisticians also feel that this is incorrect because weighting must occur simultaneously, not in separate calculations. Nielsen does not believe the concerns about their sample are legitimate and feels that they have not erred in weighting the survey. However, due to the fact that most third parties have not endorsed Nielsen's methods, the validity of their research remains to be established. Nielsen currently measures 225,000 Internet users at home and at work. Nielsen/NetRatings, their Web site devoted to Internet research, can be accessed at *www.netratings.com*. In 2001, NetRatings achieved annual revenues of $23.5 million, which is a 15-percent increase from the previous year.[12] ■

## Variable Respecification

**variable respecification**
The transformation of data to create new variables or the modification of existing variables so that they are more consistent with the objectives of the study.

*Variable respecification* involves the transformation of data to create new variables or modify existing variables. The purpose of respecification is to create variables that are consistent with the objectives of the study. For example, suppose the original variable was product usage, with 10 response categories. These might be collapsed into four categories: heavy, medium, light, and nonuser. Or, the researcher may create new variables that are composites of several other variables. For example, the researcher may create an Index of Information Search (IIS), which is the sum of information customers seek from dealers, promotional materials, the Internet, and other independent sources. Likewise, one may take the ratio of variables. If the amount of purchases at department stores $(X_1)$ and the amount of purchases charged $(X_2)$ have been measured, the proportion of purchases charged can be a new variable created by taking the ratio of the two $(X_2/X_1)$. Other respecifications of variables include square root and log transformations, which are often applied to improve the fit of the model being estimated.

**dummy variables**
A respecification procedure using variables that take on only two values, usually 0 or 1.

An important respecification procedure involves the use of dummy variables for respecifying categorical variables. *Dummy variables* are also called *binary, dichotomous, instrumental,* or *qualitative* variables. They are variables that may take on only two values, such as 0 or 1. The general rule is that to respecify a categorical variable with $K$ categories, $K - 1$ dummy variables are needed. The reason for having $K - 1$, rather than $K$, dummy variables is that only $K - 1$ categories are independent. Given the sample data, information about the $K$th category can be derived from information about the other $K - 1$ categories. Consider sex, a variable having two categories. Only one dummy variable is needed. Information on the number or percentage of males in the sample can be readily derived from the number or percentage of females.

### REAL RESEARCH

#### *"Frozen" Consumers Treated as Dummies*

In a study of consumer preferences for frozen foods, the respondents were classified as heavy, medium, light, and nonusers and originally assigned codes of 4, 3, 2, and 1, respectively. This coding was not meaningful for several statistical analyses. In order to conduct these analyses, product usage was represented by three dummy variables, $X_1$, $X_2$, and $X_3$, as shown.

| *Product Usage Category* | *Original Variable Code* | *Dummy Variable Code* | | |
|---|---|---|---|---|
| | | $X_1$ | $X_2$ | $X_3$ |
| Nonusers | 1 | 1 | 0 | 0 |
| Light users | 2 | 0 | 1 | 0 |
| Medium users | 3 | 0 | 0 | 1 |
| Heavy users | 4 | 0 | 0 | 0 |

Note that $X_1 = 1$ for nonusers and 0 for all others. Likewise, $X_2 = 1$ for light users and 0 for all others, and $X_3 = 1$ for medium users and 0 for all others. In analyzing the data, $X_1$, $X_2$, and $X_3$ are used to represent all user/nonuser groups. ■

## Scale Transformation

*Scale transformation* involves a manipulation of scale values to ensure comparability with other scales or otherwise make the data suitable for analysis. Frequently, different scales are employed for measuring different variables. For example, image variables may be measured on a seven-point semantic differential scale, attitude variables on a continuous rating scale, and lifestyle variables on a five-point Likert scale. Therefore, it would not be meaningful to make comparisons across the measurement scales for any respondent. To compare attitudinal scores with lifestyle or image scores, it would be necessary to transform the various scales. Even if the same scale is employed for all the variables, different respondents may use the scale differently. For example, some respondents consistently use the upper end of a rating scale, whereas others consistently use the lower end. These differences can be corrected by appropriately transforming the data.

### REAL RESEARCH

### *Health Care Services—Transforming Consumers*

In a study examining preference segmentation of health care services, respondents were asked to rate the importance of 18 factors affecting preferences for hospitals on a three-point scale (very, somewhat, or not important). Before analyzing the data, each individual's ratings were transformed. For each individual, preference responses were averaged across all 18 items. Then this mean was subtracted from each item rating and a constant was added to the difference. Thus, the transformed data, $X_t$, were obtained by:

$$X_t = X_i - \overline{X} + C$$

Subtraction of the mean value corrected for uneven use of the importance scale. The constant C was added to make all the transformed values positive, because negative importance ratings are not meaningful conceptually. This transformation was desirable because some respondents, especially those with low incomes, had rated almost all the preference items as very important. Others, high-income respondents in particular, had assigned the very important rating to only a few preference items. Thus, subtraction of the mean value provided a more accurate idea of the relative importance of the factors.[13] ■

In this example, the scale transformation is corrected only for the mean response. A more common transformation procedure is *standardization.* To standardize a scale $X_i$, we first subtract the mean, $\overline{X}$, from each score and then divide by the standard deviation, $s$. Thus, the standardized scale will have a mean of zero and a standard deviation of 1. This is essentially the same as the calculation of $z$ scores (see Chapter 12). Standardization allows the researcher to compare variables that have been measured using different types of scales.[14] Mathematically, standardized scores, $z_i$, may be obtained as:

$$z_i = (X_i - \overline{X})/s$$

## SELECTING A DATA ANALYSIS STRATEGY

The process of selecting a data analysis strategy is described in Figure 14.5. The selection of a data analysis strategy should be based on the earlier steps of the marketing research process, known characteristics of the data, properties of statistical techniques, and the background and philosophy of the researcher.

Data analysis is not an end in itself. Its purpose is to produce information that will help address the problem at hand. The selection of a data analysis strategy must begin with a consideration of the earlier steps in the process: problem definition (Step I), development of an approach (Step II), and research design (Step III). The preliminary plan of data analysis prepared as part of the research design should be used as a springboard. Changes may be necessary in light of additional information generated in subsequent stages of the research process.

The next step is to consider the known characteristics of the data. The measurement scales used exert a strong influence on the choice of statistical techniques (see Chapter 8). In addition,

**ACTIVE RESEARCH** | DEPARTMENT STORE PROJECT

### Data Analysis Strategy

As part of the analysis conducted in the department store project, store choice was modeled in terms of store image characteristics or the factors influencing the choice criteria. The sample was split into halves. The respondents in each half were clustered on the basis of the importance attached to the store image characteristics. Statistical tests for clusters were conducted and four segments were identified. Store preference was modeled in terms of the evaluations of the stores on the image variables. The model was estimated separately for each segment. Differences between segment preference functions were statistically tested. Finally, model validation and cross-validation were conducted for each segment. The data analysis strategy adopted is depicted in the following.[15]

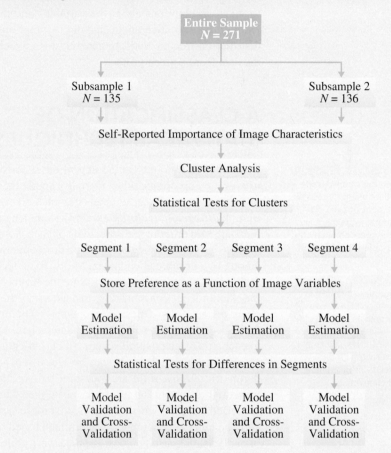

**Figure 14.5**
Selecting a Data Analysis Strategy

the research design may favor certain techniques. For example, analysis of variance (see Chapter 16) is suited for analyzing experimental data from causal designs. The insights into the data obtained during data preparation can be valuable for selecting a strategy for analysis.

It is also important to take into account the properties of the statistical techniques, particularly their purpose and underlying assumptions. Some statistical techniques are appropriate for examining differences in variables, others for assessing the magnitudes of the relationships between variables, and others for making predictions. The techniques also involve different assumptions, and some techniques can withstand violations of the underlying assumptions better than others. A classification of statistical techniques is presented in the next section.

Finally, the researcher's background and philosophy affect the choice of a data analysis strategy. The experienced, statistically trained researcher will employ a range of techniques, including advanced statistical methods. Researchers differ in their willingness to make assumptions about the variables and their underlying populations. Researchers who are conservative about making assumptions will limit their choice of techniques to distribution-free methods. In general, several techniques may be appropriate for analyzing the data from a given project.

# A CLASSIFICATION OF STATISTICAL TECHNIQUES

**univariate techniques**
Statistical techniques appropriate for analyzing data when there is a single measurement of each element in the sample or, if there are several measurements on each element, each variable is analyzed in isolation.

**multivariate techniques**
Statistical techniques suitable for analyzing data when there are two or more measurements on each element and the variables are analyzed simultaneously. Multivariate techniques are concerned with the simultaneous relationships among two or more phenomena.

**metric data**
Data that are interval or ratio in nature.

**nonmetric data**
Data derived from a nominal or ordinal scale.

**independent**
The samples are independent if they are drawn randomly from different populations.

**paired**
The samples are paired when the data for the two samples relate to the same group of respondents.

**dependence techniques**
Multivariate techniques appropriate when one or more of the variables can be identified as dependent variables and the remaining as independent variables.

Statistical techniques can be classified as univariate or multivariate. ***Univariate techniques*** are appropriate when there is a single measurement of each element in the sample, or there are several measurements of each element but each variable is analyzed in isolation. ***Multivariate techniques,*** on the other hand, are suitable for analyzing data when there are two or more measurements of each element and the variables are analyzed simultaneously. Multivariate techniques are concerned with the simultaneous relationships among two or more phenomena. Multivariate techniques differ from univariate techniques in that they shift the focus away from the levels (averages) and distributions (variances) of the phenomena, concentrating instead upon the degree of relationships (correlations or covariances) among these phenomena.[16] The univariate and multivariate techniques are described in detail in subsequent chapters; here we show how the various techniques relate to each other in an overall scheme of classification.

Univariate techniques can be classified based on whether the data are metric or nonmetric. ***Metric data*** are measured on an interval or ratio scale. ***Nonmetric data*** are measured on a nominal or ordinal scale (see Chapter 8). These techniques can be further classified based on whether one, two, or more samples are involved. It should be noted that here the number of samples is determined based on how the data are treated for the purpose of analysis, not based on how the data were collected. For example, the data for males and females may well have been collected as a single sample, but if the analysis involves an examination of sex differences, two sample techniques will be used. The samples are ***independent*** if they are drawn randomly from different populations. For the purpose of analysis, data pertaining to different groups of respondents, e.g., males and females, are generally treated as independent samples. On the other hand, the samples are ***paired*** when the data for the two samples relate to the same group of respondents.

For metric data, when there is only one sample, the $z$ test and the $t$ test can be used. When there are two or more independent samples, the $z$ test and $t$ test can be used for two samples, and one-way analysis of variance (one-way ANOVA) for more than two samples. In the case of two or more related samples, the paired $t$ test can be used. For nonmetric data involving a single sample, frequency distribution, chi-square, Kolmogorov-Smirnov, runs, and binomial tests can be used. For two independent samples with nonmetric data, the chi-square, Mann-Whitney, Median, K-S, and Kruskal-Wallis one-way analysis of variance (K-W ANOVA) can be used. In contrast, when there are two or more related samples, the sign, McNemar, and Wilcoxon tests should be used (see Figure 14.6).

Multivariate statistical techniques can be classified as dependence techniques or interdependence techniques (see Figure 14.7). ***Dependence techniques*** are appropriate when one or more variables can be identified as dependent variables and the remaining as inde-

*Figure 14.6*
A Classification of Univariate
Techniques

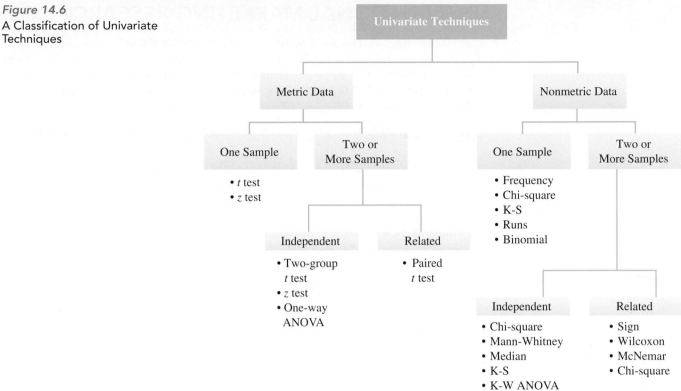

pendent variables. When there is only one dependent variable, cross-tabulation, analysis of variance and covariance, regression, two-group discriminant analysis, and conjoint analysis can be used. However, if there is more than one dependent variable, the appropriate techniques are multivariate analysis of variance and covariance, canonical correlation, and multiple discriminant analysis. In *interdependence techniques,* the variables are not classified as dependent or independent; rather, the whole set of interdependent relationships is examined. These techniques focus on either variable interdependence or interobject similarity. The major technique for examining variable interdependence is factor analysis. Analysis of interobject similarity can be conducted by cluster analysis and multidimensional scaling.[17]

**interdependence techniques**
Multivariate statistical techniques that attempt to group data based on underlying similarity, and thus allow for interpretation of the data structures. No distinction is made as to which variables are dependent and which are independent.

*Figure 14.7*
A Classification of Multivariate
Techniques

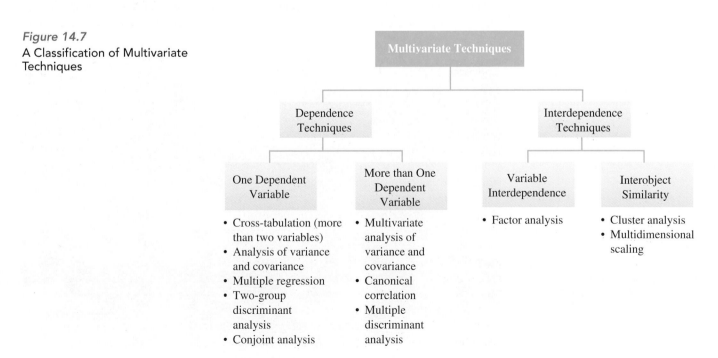

# INTERNATIONAL MARKETING RESEARCH

Before analyzing the data, the researcher should ensure that the units of measurement are comparable across countries or cultural units. For example, the data may have to be adjusted to establish currency equivalents or metric equivalents. Furthermore, standardization or normalization of the data may be necessary to make meaningful comparisons and achieve consistent results.

### REAL RESEARCH

## *A Worldwide Scream for Ice Cream*

Häagen-Dazs (*www.haagen-dazs.com*), the hyperrich U.S. ice cream, is the latest hot American export. Its sales in Asia, Britain, France, and Germany are increasing at a phenomenal rate. In 2001, Häagen-Dazs achieved annual revenues of $183 million from the $4 billion ice cream market. Over half the sales were coming from the international market. In December 2001, General Mills, Inc. sold its 50 percent stake in Häagen-Dazs to the Swiss company Nestle for $641 million. How did this come about? The strategy for whetting foreign appetites is simple. Marketing research conducted in several European (e.g., Britain, France, and Germany) and several Asian (e.g., Japan, Singapore, and Taiwan) countries revealed that consumers were hungry for a high-quality ice cream with a premium image and were willing to pay a premium price for it. These consistent findings emerged after the price of ice cream in each country was standardized to have a mean of zero and a standard deviation of unity. Standardization was desirable, as the prices were specified in different local currencies and a common basis was needed for comparison across countries. Also, in each country, the premium price had to be defined in relation to the prices of competing brands. Standardization accomplished both these objectives.

Based on these findings, Häagen-Dazs first introduced the brand at a few high-end retailers; then built company-owned stores in high-traffic areas; and finally rolled into convenience stores and supermarkets. Hungry for a quality product, British consumers shelled out $5 a pint—double or triple the price of some home brands. "It is easily the largest selling ice cream shop in the world under a trademark name," says John Riccitiello, senior vice president for international sales. Back home in the United States, Häagen-Dazs remains popular although faced with intense competition and health consciousness. This added to the impetus to enter the foreign markets.[18] ∎

The data analysis could be conducted at three levels: (1) individual, (2) within country or cultural unit, and (3) across countries or cultural units. Individual-level analysis requires that the data from each respondent be analyzed separately. For example, one might

Appropriate transformation and analysis of data collected in several countries have enabled Häagen-Dazs to effectively market its products worldwide.

compute a correlation coefficient or run a regression analysis for each respondent. This means that enough data must be obtained from each individual to allow analysis at the individual level, which is often not feasible. Yet it has been argued that in international marketing or cross-cultural research, the researcher should possess a sound knowledge of the consumer in each culture. This can best be accomplished by individual-level analysis.[19]

In within-country or cultural-unit analysis, the data are analyzed separately for each country or cultural unit. This is also referred to as ***intracultural analysis.*** This level of analysis is quite similar to that conducted in domestic marketing research. The objective is to gain an understanding of the relationships and patterns existing in each country or cultural unit. In across-countries analysis, the data of all the countries are analyzed simultaneously. Two approaches to this method are possible. The data for all respondents from all the countries can be pooled and analyzed. This is referred to as ***pancultural analysis.*** Alternatively, the data can be aggregated for each country and these aggregate statistics analyzed. For example, one could compute means of variables for each country, and then compute correlations on these means. This is referred to as ***cross-cultural analysis.*** The objective of this level of analysis is to assess the comparability of findings from one country to another. The similarities as well as the differences between countries should be investigated. When examining differences, not only differences in means but also differences in variance and distribution should be assessed. All the statistical techniques that have been discussed in this book can be applied to within-country or across-country analysis and, subject to the amount of data available, to individual-level analysis as well.[20]

## ETHICS IN MARKETING RESEARCH

Ethical issues that arise during the data-preparation and analysis step of the marketing research process pertain mainly to the researcher. While checking, editing, coding, transcribing, and cleaning, researchers should try to get some idea about the quality of the data. An attempt should be made to identify respondents who have provided data of questionable quality. Consider, for example, a respondent who checks the "7" response to all the 20 items measuring attitude toward spectator sports on a 1-to-7 Likert-type scale. Apparently, this respondent did not realize that some of the statements were negative whereas the others were positive. Thus, this respondent indicates an extremely favorable attitude toward spectator sports on all the positive statements and an extremely negative attitude on the statements that were reversed. Decisions whether such respondents should be discarded, i.e., not included in the analysis, can raise ethical concerns. A good rule of thumb is to make such decisions during the data-preparation phase before conducting any analysis.

In contrast, suppose the researcher conducted the analysis without first attempting to identify unsatisfactory respondents. The analysis, however, does not reveal the expected relationship, i.e., the analysis does not show that attitude toward spectator sports influences attendance of spectator sports. The researcher then decides to examine the quality of data obtained. In checking the questionnaires, a few respondents with unsatisfactory data are identified. In addition to the type of unsatisfactory responses mentioned earlier, there were other questionable patterns as well. To illustrate, some respondents had checked all responses as "4," the "neither agree nor disagree" response, to all the 20 items measuring attitude toward spectator sports. When these respondents are eliminated and the reduced data set analyzed, the expected results are obtained showing a positive influence of attitude on attendance of spectator sports. Discarding respondents after analyzing the data raises ethical concerns, particularly if the report does not state that the initial analysis was inconclusive. Moreover, the procedure used to identify unsatisfactory respondents and the number of respondents discarded should be clearly disclosed.

### REAL RESEARCH

## *The Ethics of Downsizing*

The effects of a softened economy in 2002 forced many U.S. companies to downsize. A study was recently conducted on the differences of employee and CEO perceptions on whether downsizing is ethical or not. There were a total of 410 surveys mailed to employees of U.S. corporations and 231 completed surveys were returned, but 53 were determined to

---

*intracultural analysis*
Within-country analysis of international data.

*pancultural analysis*
Across-countries analysis in which the data for all respondents from all the countries are pooled and analyzed.

*cross-cultural analysis*
A type of across-countries analysis in which the data could be aggregated for each country and these aggregate statistics analyzed.

be unusable. The surveys were unusable because they either contained incomplete responses to questions or were filled by unqualified respondents. This resulted in an employee sample size of 178. The survey was also mailed to 179 CEOs of companies that had been identified as going through at least one downsizing during the last five years. Out of the 179, only 36 surveys were returned of which, five CEOs indicated they had never actually been with a company during a downsizing. Therefore, only 31 CEO surveys were determined to be usable in the study. This is an example of ethical editing of the data. The criterion for unusable or unsatisfactory responses is clearly stated, the unsatisfactory respondents are identified before the analysis, and the number of respondents eliminated is disclosed.

The findings of this study were that the employees and CEOs hold different perceptions about downsizing, and different factors can influence someone's perceptions of downsizing. The employees found the downsizing to be unethical when they had been a casualty of the downsizing, when information was withheld, and when the downsizing was done around the holiday season. These perceptions may often affect an employee's work if they cause the employee to view the company in a negative manner.[21] ■

While analyzing the data, the researcher may also have to deal with ethical issues. The assumptions underlying the statistical techniques used to analyze the data must be satisfied to obtain meaningful results. Any departure from these assumptions should be critically examined to determine the appropriateness of the technique for analyzing the data at hand. The researcher has the responsibility of justifying the statistical techniques used for analysis. When this is not done, ethical questions can be raised. Moreover, there should be no intentional or deliberate misrepresentation of research methods or results. Similarly, ethical issues can arise in interpreting the results, drawing conclusions, making recommendations, and in implementation. Although interpretations, conclusions, recommendations, and implementations necessarily involve subjective judgment, this judgment must be exercised honestly, free from personal biases or agendas of the researcher or the client.

# INTERNET AND COMPUTER APPLICATIONS

Major statistical packages such as SPSS (*www.spss.com*), SAS (*www.sas.com*), MINITAB (*www.minitab.com*), and EXCEL (*www.microsoft.com/office/excel/*) have Internet sites that can be accessed for a variety of information. Exhibit 14.1 details the use of these packages

**Exhibit 14.1**
Computer Programs for Data Preparation

> ### SPSS
> Out-of-range values can be selected using the SELECT IF or PROCESS IF statements. These cases, with the identifying information (subject ID, record no., variable name, variable value), can then be printed using the PRINT or WRITE commands. As a further check, the LIST command can be used to display the values of variables for each case. SPSS Data Entry simplifies the process of entering new data files. It facilitates data cleaning and checking for logical inconsistencies.
>
> ### SAS
> The IF, IF-THEN, and IF-THEN/ELSE statements can be used to select cases with missing or out-of-range values. The SELECT statement executes one of several statements or groups of statements. The LIST statement is useful for printing suspicious input lines. The LOSTCARD statement can be used to identify missing records in the data. The PRINT and PRINTTO procedures can be used to identify cases and print variable names and variable values. In addition, the OUTPUT and PUT statements can be used to write the values of variables.
>
> ### Minitab
> There are control statements that permit the control of the order of commands in a macro. The IF command allows implementation of different blocks of commands. This includes IF, ELSEIF, ELSE, and ENDIF.
>
> ### Excel
> The IF statement can be used to make logical checks and check out of range values. The IF statement can be accessed under the INSERT>FUNCTION>ALL>IF.

to make consistency checks. These packages also contain options for handling missing responses and for statistically adjusting the data. In addition, a number of statistical packages can now be found on the Internet. Although some of these programs may not offer integrated data analysis and management, they can nevertheless be very useful for conducting specific statistical analyses.

Information useful for formulating a data analysis strategy is readily available on the Internet. A lot of information can be obtained about the appropriateness of using certain statistical techniques in specific settings. It is possible to surf the Net for new statistical techniques that are not yet available in commonly used statistical packages. News groups and special-interest groups are useful sources for a variety of statistical information.

## SPSS Windows

Using the Base module, out-of-range values can be selected using the SELECT IF command. These cases, with the identifying information (subject ID, record number, variable name, and variable value), can then be printed using the LIST or PRINT commands. The PRINT command will save active cases to an external file. If a formatted list is required, the SUMMARIZE command can be used.

SPSS Data Entry can facilitate data preparation. You can verify respondents have answered completely by setting rules. These rules can be used on existing data sets to validate and check the data, whether or not the questionnaire used to collect the data was constructed in Data Entry. Data Entry allows you to control and check the entry of data through three types of rules: validation, checking, and skip and fill rules.

Although the missing values can be treated within the context of the Base module, SPSS Missing Values Analysis can assist in diagnosing missing values and replacing missing values with estimates.

TextSmart by SPSS can help in the coding and analysis of open-ended responses.

---

## FOCUS ON BURKE

Burke places a lot of emphasis on appropriately preparing the data before conducting any analysis. The completed questionnaires are thoroughly checked and edited as they are returned from the field. Where possible, the respondents are recontacted to obtain information on missing or unsatisfactory responses. Standard procedures are followed for coding and transcribing the data. Extensive computer checks are made to identify out-of-range, logically inconsistent, or extreme responses.

Transforming data to meet a research objective is common. However, Burke has often found that the transformation, although appearing logical, may create problems for the researcher. Consider the research Burke conducted for a client that wanted to examine reported incidence of setup problems for new computers. Two key questions were:

1. How many new computers were delivered to this site in the past 30 days?
2. How many of those computers had a problem that required returning them or some components of the computer to the vendor?

Burke has seen several questionable transformations used to handle these kinds of data. One approach is to weight the number of returns by dividing by the number of deliveries. This creates a new variable, which is simply the proportion of deliveries generating a return. Clearly, when you would treat this as your "observed data," any summing or averaging of these numbers totally ignores the base from which each was calculated. For example, one respondent had 1 return from 4 deliveries or 1/4, a second respondent had 10/30 or 1/3. These would be treated exactly as the same measurement, and an "average" would be 7/24 or .29. Of course, the real average returns is 11/34 or .32. Thus, Burke is very careful about using the appropriate transformations.

With some transformation, certain statistical techniques, such as cross-tabulations, are not appropriate in their common form. Burke has created special statistical software to analyze the data in such cases. A detailed data analysis strategy is formulated for each project. Burke makes extensive use of simple univariate as well as sophisticated multivariate techniques in analyzing marketing research data. Burke has created customized software for analyzing data in special situations involving uncommon transformations.

# SUMMARY

Data preparation begins with a preliminary check of all questionnaires for completeness and interviewing quality. Then more thorough editing takes place. Editing consists of screening questionnaires to identify illegible, incomplete, inconsistent, or ambiguous responses. Such responses may be handled by returning questionnaires to the field, assigning missing values, or discarding the unsatisfactory respondents.

The next step is coding. A numerical or alphanumeric code is assigned to represent a specific response to a specific question, along with the column position that code will occupy. It is often helpful to prepare a codebook containing the coding instructions and the necessary information about the variables in the data set. The coded data are transcribed onto disks or magnetic tapes or entered into computers via keypunching. Mark sense forms, optical scanning, or computerized sensory analysis may also be used.

Cleaning the data requires consistency checks and treatment of missing responses. Options available for treating missing responses include substitution of a neutral value such as the mean, substitution of an imputed response, casewise deletion, and pairwise deletion. Statistical adjustments such as weighting, variable respecification, and scale transformations often enhance the quality of data analysis. The selection of a data analysis strategy should be based on the earlier steps of the marketing research process, known characteristics of the data, properties of statistical techniques, and the background and philosophy of the researcher. Statistical techniques may be classified as univariate or multivariate.

Before analyzing the data in international marketing research, the researcher should ensure that the units of measurement are comparable across countries or cultural units. The data analysis could be conducted at three levels: (1) individual, (2) within country or cultural unit (intracultural analysis), and (3) across countries or cultural units: pancultural or cross-cultural analysis. Several ethical issues are related to data processing, particularly the discarding of unsatisfactory responses, violation of the assumptions underlying the data analysis techniques, and evaluation and interpretation of results. The Internet and computers play a significant role in data preparation and analysis.

# KEY TERMS AND CONCEPTS

editing, *403*
coding, *404*
fixed-field codes, *405*
codebook, *407*
data cleaning, *409*
consistency checks, *409*
missing responses, *410*
casewise deletion, *411*
pairwise deletion, *411*

weighting, *411*
variable respecification, *413*
dummy variables, *413*
scale transformation, *414*
standardization, *414*
univariate techniques, *416*
multivariate techniques, *416*
metric data, *416*

nonmetric data, *416*
independent, *416*
paired, *416*
dependence techniques, *416*
interdependence techniques, *417*
intracultural analysis, *419*
pancultural analysis, *419*
cross-cultural analysis, *419*

# EXERCISES

## Questions

1. Describe the data-preparation process.
2. What activities are involved in the preliminary checking of questionnaires that have been returned from the field?
3. What is meant by editing a questionnaire?
4. How are unsatisfactory responses that are discovered in editing treated?
5. What is the difference between precoding and postcoding?
6. Describe the guidelines for the coding of unstructured questions.
7. What does transcribing the data involve?
8. What kinds of consistency checks are made in cleaning the data?
9. What options are available for the treatment of missing data?
10. What kinds of statistical adjustments are sometimes made to the data?
11. Describe the weighting process. What are the reasons for weighting?
12. What are dummy variables? Why are such variables created?
13. Explain why scale transformations are made.

14. Which scale transformation procedure is most commonly used? Briefly describe this procedure.
15. What considerations are involved in selecting a data analysis strategy?

## Problems

1. Develop dummy variable coding schemes for the following variables.
   - Sex
   - Marital status consisting of the following four categories: never married, now married, divorced, other (separated, widowed, etc.)
   - Frequency of international travel, measured as:
     1. Do not travel abroad
     2. Travel abroad 1 or 2 times a year
     3. Travel abroad 3 to 5 times a year
     4. Travel abroad 6 to 8 times a year
     5. Travel abroad more than 8 times a year

2. Shown below is part of a questionnaire used to determine consumer preferences for cameras. Set up a coding scheme for these three questions.

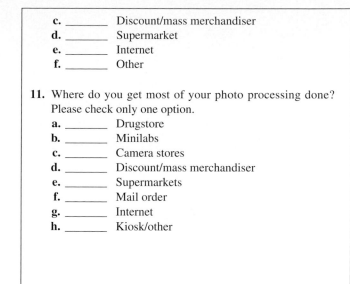

9. Please rate the importance of the following features you would consider when shopping for a new camera.

|  | Not so important | | | Very important |
|---|---|---|---|---|
| Film speed setting | 1 | 2 | 3 | 4 | 5 |
| Auto-film advance | 1 | 2 | 3 | 4 | 5 |
| Autofocus | 1 | 2 | 3 | 4 | 5 |
| Autoloading | 1 | 2 | 3 | 4 | 5 |

10. If you were to buy a new camera, which of the following outlets would you visit? Please check as many as apply.
   a. _____ Drugstore
   b. _____ Camera store
   c. _____ Discount/mass merchandiser
   d. _____ Supermarket
   e. _____ Internet
   f. _____ Other

11. Where do you get most of your photo processing done? Please check only one option.
   a. _____ Drugstore
   b. _____ Minilabs
   c. _____ Camera stores
   d. _____ Discount/mass merchandiser
   e. _____ Supermarkets
   f. _____ Mail order
   g. _____ Internet
   h. _____ Kiosk/other

# INTERNET AND COMPUTER EXERCISES

1. Explain how you would make consistency checks for the questionnaire given in problem #2 above using SPSS, SAS, MINITAB, or EXCEL.
2. Use an electronic questionnaire design and administration package such as Ci3 to program the camera preference questionnaire given in problem #2. Add one or two questions of your own. Administer the questionnaire to five students and prepare the data for analysis. Does computer administration of the questionnaire facilitate data preparation?

# ACTIVITIES

## *Role Playing*

1. You are a project supervisor with SDR, Inc., a data analysis firm based in Atlanta. You are supervising the data-preparation process for a large survey conducted for a leading manufacturer of paper towels. The data are being collected via in-home personal interviews and 1,823 questionnaires have been returned from the field. In cleaning the data, you find that 289 questionnaires have missing responses. The data analyst preparing the data (a student in your class), not knowing how to deal with these missing responses, approaches you for help and instructions. Please explain to the data analyst how the missing responses should be handled.
2. You are the marketing research manager for General Electric. GE has developed a luxury refrigerator model that has several innovative features and will be sold for a premium price of $1,995. A national survey was conducted to determine consumer response to the proposed model. The data were obtained by conducting mall intercept interviews in 10 major U.S. cities. Although the resulting sample of 2,639 respondents is fairly representative on all other demographic characteristics, it underrepresents the upper-income households. The marketing research analyst, who reports to you, feels that weighting is not necessary. Discuss this question with the analyst (a student in your class).

## *Fieldwork*

1. Visit a marketing research firm or a business firm with an in-house marketing research department. Investigate the data-preparation process this firm followed in a recently completed project. How does this process compare with the one described in the book?
2. Obtain a codebook or coding instructions used by a marketing research firm for a completed project. Examine the codebook or coding instructions carefully. Can you improve on the coding scheme followed by the firm?

## *Group Discussion*

1. As a small group, discuss the following statements. "Data preparation is a time-consuming process. In projects with severe time constraints, data preparation should be circumvented."
2. As a group, discuss the following: "The researcher should always use computer-assisted interviewing (CATI or CAPI) to collect the data, as these methods greatly facilitate data preparation."

# CHAPTER 15

# Frequency Distribution, Cross-Tabulation, and Hypothesis Testing

"Cross-tabulations and frequency distributions are the fundamental building blocks of analysis. They offer a simple and quick look at the data. This simplicity is both a virtue and a problem. They are a great starting point but not sufficient, in most cases, for a complete analysis."

*Betty Fraley,*
*vice president,*
*account management,*
*Burke, Inc.*

## Objectives

At the end of this chapter, the student should be able to:

1. Describe the significance of preliminary data analysis and the insights that can be obtained from such an analysis.
2. Discuss data analysis associated with frequencies including measures of location, measures of variability, and measures of shape.
3. Explain data analysis associated with cross-tabulations and the associated statistics: chi-square, phi coefficient, contingency coefficient, Cramer's *V*, and lambda coefficient.
4. Describe data analysis associated with parametric hypothesis testing for one sample, two independent samples, and paired samples.
5. Understand data analysis associated with nonparametric hypothesis testing for one sample, two independent samples, and paired samples.

# Overview

Once the data have been prepared for analysis (Chapter 14), the researcher should conduct some basic analysis. This chapter describes basic data analysis including frequency distribution, cross-tabulation, and hypothesis testing. First, we describe the frequency distribution and explain how it provides both an indication of the number of out-of-range, missing, or extreme values as well as insights into the central tendency, variability, and shape of the underlying distribution. Next, we introduce hypothesis testing by describing the general procedure. Hypothesis testing procedures are classified as tests of associations or tests of differences. We consider the use of cross-tabulation for understanding the associations between variables taken two or three at a time. Although the nature of the association can be observed from tables, statistics are available for examining the significance and strength of the association. Finally, we present tests for examining hypotheses related to differences based on one or two samples.

Many commercial marketing research projects do not go beyond basic data analysis. These findings are often displayed using tables and graphs, as discussed further in Chapter 22. Although the findings of basic analysis are valuable in their own right, they also provide guidance for conducting multivariate analysis. The insights gained from the basic analysis are also invaluable in interpreting the results obtained from more sophisticated statistical techniques. To provide the reader with a flavor of these techniques, we illustrate the use of cross-tabulation, chi-square analysis, and hypothesis testing.

**ACTIVE RESEARCH** | DEPARTMENT STORE PROJECT

### Basic Data Analysis

In the department store project, basic data analysis formed the foundation for conducting subsequent multivariate analysis. Data analysis began by obtaining a frequency distribution and descriptive statistics for each variable. In addition to identifying possible problems with the data (see Chapter 14), this information provided a good feel for the data and insights into how specific variables should be treated in subsequent analyses. For example, should some variables be treated as categorical, and, if so, how many categories should there be? Several two- and three-variable cross-tabulations were also conducted to identify associations in the data. The effects of variables with two categories on the metric dependent variables of interest were examined by means of *t* tests and other hypotheses-testing procedures.

**REAL RESEARCH**

## Commercial Battle of the Sexes

A comparison of television advertising in Australia, Mexico, and the United States focused on the analysis of sex roles in advertising. Results showed differences in the portrayal of the sexes in different countries. Australian advertisements revealed somewhat fewer, and Mexican advertisements slightly more, sex-role differences than U.S. advertisements. Cross-tabulation and chi-square analysis provided the following information for Mexico.

| Product Advertised | Persons Appearing in the AD (%) | |
| Used by | Women | Men |
| --- | --- | --- |
| Females | 25.0 | 4.0 |
| Males | 6.8 | 11.8 |
| Either | 68.2 | 84.2 |

$\chi^2 = 19.73$, $p \leq 0.001$

These results indicate that in Mexican commercials, women appeared in commercials for products used by women or by either sex but rarely in commercials for men's products. Men appeared in commercials for products used by either sex. These differences were also found in the U.S. ads, although to a lesser extent, but were not found in Australian ads. In the United States, the increasing population of Hispanic Americans has turned many advertisers' attention to Spanish-language television advertising. Sex roles in the Hispanic culture show women as traditional homemakers, conservative and dependent upon men for support, but many Hispanic families in the United States do not fit this traditionally held view. In 2003, more than half of Hispanic women work outside of the home, which almost matches the proportion of women in the Anglo population that work outside the home in the United States. Therefore, many U.S. consumer products companies appear to be advertising the same ways in which they advertise to the general U.S. market.[1] ■

## REAL RESEARCH

### *Catalogs Are Risky Business*

Twelve product categories were examined to compare catalog to store shopping. The null hypothesis that there is no significant difference in the overall amount of risk perceived when buying products by catalog compared to buying the same products in a retail store was rejected. The hypothesis was tested by computing 12 (one for each product) paired-observations *t* tests. Mean scores for overall perceived risk for some of the products in both buying situations are presented in the following table, with higher scores indicating greater risk.

Catalog shopping is perceived more risky than shopping at retail stores as revealed by paired *t* tests.

Mean Scores of Overall Perceived Risk for Products by Purchase Mode

| | Overall Perceived Risk | |
|---|---|---|
| *Product* | *Catalog* | *Retail Store* |
| Stereo hi-fi | 48.89 | 41.98[*] |
| Record albums | 32.65 | 28.74[*] |
| Dress shoes | 58.60 | 50.80[*] |
| 13-inch color TV | 48.53 | 40.91[*] |
| Athletic socks | 35.22 | 30.22[*] |
| Pocket calculator | 49.62 | 42.00[*] |
| 35-mm camera | 48.13 | 39.52[*] |
| Perfume | 34.85 | 29.79[*] |

[*]Significant at 0.01 level

As can be seen, a significantly ($p < 0.01$) higher overall amount of perceived risk was attached to products purchased by catalog as compared to those purchased from a retail store. Although this study reveals risk associated with catalog purchasing, terrorist attacks of September 11, 2001, and the continued threats have increased the amount of products that are purchased from catalogs. Security concerns have made ordering from a catalog a more attractive means of purchasing products for consumers.[2] ■

The department store example illustrates the role of basic data analysis used in conjunction with multivariate procedures, whereas the other two examples show how such analysis can be useful in its own right. The cross-tabulation and chi-square analysis in the international television advertising example, and the paired *t* tests in the catalog shopping example, enabled us to draw specific conclusions from the data. These and other concepts discussed in this chapter are illustrated in the context of explaining Internet usage for personal (nonprofessional) reasons. Table 15.1 contains data for 30 respondents giving the sex (1 = male, 2 = female), familiarity with the Internet (1 = very unfamiliar, 7 = very familiar), Internet usage in hours per week, attitude toward Internet and toward technology, both measured on a seven-point scale (1 = very unfavorable, 7 = very favorable), and whether the respondents have done shopping or banking on the Internet (1 = yes, 2 = no). As a first step in the analysis, it is often useful to examine the frequency distributions of the relevant variables.

# FREQUENCY DISTRIBUTION

Marketing researchers often need to answer questions about a single variable. For example:

- How many users of the brand may be characterized as brand loyal?
- What percentage of the market consists of heavy users, medium users, light users, and nonusers?
- How many customers are very familiar with a new product offering? How many are familiar, somewhat familiar, and unfamiliar with the brand? What is the mean familiarity rating? Is there much variance in the extent to which customers are familiar with the new product?
- What is the income distribution of brand users? Is this distribution skewed toward low-income brackets?

**frequency distribution**
A mathematical distribution whose objective is to obtain a count of the number of responses associated with different values of one variable and to express these counts in percentage terms.

The answers to these kinds of questions can be determined by examining frequency distributions. In a *frequency distribution,* one variable is considered at a time. The objective is to obtain a count of the number of responses associated with different values of the variable. The relative occurrence, or frequency, of different values of the variable is expressed in percentages. A frequency distribution for a variable produces a table of frequency counts, percentages, and cumulative percentages for all the values associated with that variable.

Table 15.2 gives the frequency distribution of familiarity with the Internet. In the table, the first column contains the labels assigned to the different categories of the variable, and the second column indicates the codes assigned to each value. Note that a code of 9 has been

## TABLE 15.1

### Internet Usage Data

| RESPONDENT NUMBER | SEX | FAMILIARITY | INTERNET USAGE | ATTITUDE TOWARD INTERNET | ATTITUDE TOWARD TECHNOLOGY | USAGE OF INTERNET: SHOPPING | USAGE OF INTERNET: BANKING |
|---|---|---|---|---|---|---|---|
| 1 | 1.00 | 7.00 | 14.00 | 7.00 | 6.00 | 1.00 | 1.00 |
| 2 | 2.00 | 2.00 | 2.00 | 3.00 | 3.00 | 2.00 | 2.00 |
| 3 | 2.00 | 3.00 | 3.00 | 4.00 | 3.00 | 1.00 | 2.00 |
| 4 | 2.00 | 3.00 | 3.00 | 7.00 | 5.00 | 1.00 | 2.00 |
| 5 | 1.00 | 7.00 | 13.00 | 7.00 | 7.00 | 1.00 | 1.00 |
| 6 | 2.00 | 4.00 | 6.00 | 5.00 | 4.00 | 1.00 | 2.00 |
| 7 | 2.00 | 2.00 | 2.00 | 4.00 | 5.00 | 2.00 | 2.00 |
| 8 | 2.00 | 3.00 | 6.00 | 5.00 | 4.00 | 2.00 | 2.00 |
| 9 | 2.00 | 3.00 | 6.00 | 6.00 | 4.00 | 1.00 | 2.00 |
| 10 | 1.00 | 9.00 | 15.00 | 7.00 | 6.00 | 1.00 | 2.00 |
| 11 | 2.00 | 4.00 | 3.00 | 4.00 | 3.00 | 2.00 | 2.00 |
| 12 | 2.00 | 5.00 | 4.00 | 6.00 | 4.00 | 2.00 | 2.00 |
| 13 | 1.00 | 6.00 | 9.00 | 6.00 | 5.00 | 2.00 | 1.00 |
| 14 | 1.00 | 6.00 | 8.00 | 3.00 | 2.00 | 2.00 | 2.00 |
| 15 | 1.00 | 6.00 | 5.00 | 5.00 | 4.00 | 1.00 | 2.00 |
| 16 | 2.00 | 4.00 | 3.00 | 4.00 | 3.00 | 2.00 | 2.00 |
| 17 | 1.00 | 6.00 | 9.00 | 5.00 | 3.00 | 1.00 | 1.00 |
| 18 | 1.00 | 4.00 | 4.00 | 5.00 | 4.00 | 1.00 | 2.00 |
| 19 | 1.00 | 7.00 | 14.00 | 6.00 | 6.00 | 1.00 | 1.00 |
| 20 | 2.00 | 6.00 | 6.00 | 6.00 | 4.00 | 2.00 | 2.00 |
| 21 | 1.00 | 6.00 | 9.00 | 4.00 | 2.00 | 2.00 | 2.00 |
| 22 | 1.00 | 5.00 | 5.00 | 5.00 | 4.00 | 2.00 | 1.00 |
| 23 | 2.00 | 3.00 | 2.00 | 4.00 | 2.00 | 2.00 | 2.00 |
| 24 | 1.00 | 7.00 | 15.00 | 6.00 | 6.00 | 1.00 | 1.00 |
| 25 | 2.00 | 6.00 | 6.00 | 5.00 | 3.00 | 1.00 | 2.00 |
| 26 | 1.00 | 6.00 | 13.00 | 6.00 | 6.00 | 1.00 | 1.00 |
| 27 | 2.00 | 5.00 | 4.00 | 5.00 | 5.00 | 1.00 | 1.00 |
| 28 | 2.00 | 4.00 | 2.00 | 3.00 | 2.00 | 2.00 | 2.00 |
| 29 | 1.00 | 4.00 | 4.00 | 5.00 | 3.00 | 1.00 | 2.00 |
| 30 | 1.00 | 3.00 | 3.00 | 7.00 | 5.00 | 1.00 | 2.00 |

## TABLE 15.2

### Frequency Distribution of Familiarity with the Internet

| VALUE LABEL | VALUE | FREQUENCY (N) | PERCENTAGE | VALID PERCENTAGE | CUMULATIVE PERCENTAGE |
|---|---|---|---|---|---|
| Very unfamiliar | 1 | 0 | 0.0 | 0.0 | 0.0 |
| | 2 | 2 | 6.7 | 6.9 | 6.9 |
| | 3 | 6 | 20.0 | 20.7 | 27.6 |
| | 4 | 6 | 20.0 | 20.7 | 48.3 |
| | 5 | 3 | 10.0 | 10.3 | 58.6 |
| | 6 | 8 | 26.7 | 27.6 | 86.2 |
| Very familiar | 7 | 4 | 13.3 | 13.8 | 100.0 |
| Missing | 9 | 1 | 3.3 | | |
| | TOTAL | 30 | 100.0 | 100.0 | |

*Figure 15.1*
Frequency Histogram

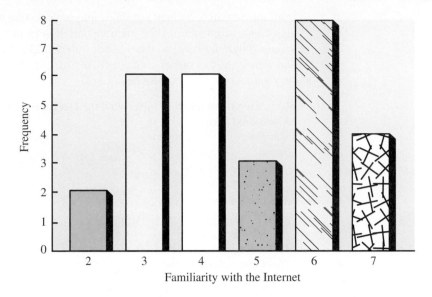

*Figure 15.1*
Frequency Histogram

assigned to missing values. The third column gives the number of respondents checking each value. For example, three respondents checked value 5, indicating that they were somewhat familiar with the Internet. The fourth column displays the percentage of respondents checking each value. The next column shows percentages calculated by excluding the cases with missing values. If there are no missing values, columns 4 and 5 are identical. The last column represents cumulative percentages after adjusting for missing cases. As can be seen, of the 30 respondents who participated in the survey, 10.0 percent checked value 5. If the one respondent with a missing value is excluded, this percentage changes to 10.3. The cumulative percentage corresponding to the value of 5 is 58.6. In other words, 58.6 percent of the respondents with valid responses indicated a familiarity value of 5 or less.

A frequency distribution helps determine the extent of item nonresponse (1 respondent out of 30 in Table 15.1). It also indicates the extent of illegitimate responses. Values of 0 and 8 would be illegitimate responses, or errors. The cases with these values could be identified and corrective action taken. The presence of outliers or cases with extreme values can also be detected. In the case of a frequency distribution of household size, a few isolated families with household sizes of 9 or more might be considered outliers. A frequency distribution also indicates the shape of the empirical distribution of the variable. The frequency data may be used to construct a histogram, or a vertical bar chart, in which the values of the variable are portrayed along the *X*-axis and the absolute or relative frequencies of the values are placed along the *Y*-axis. Figure 15.1 is a histogram of the frequency data in Table 15.1. From the histogram, one could examine whether the observed distribution is consistent with an expected or assumed distribution, such as the normal distribution.

## REAL RESEARCH

### *Basic Analysis Yields Olympic Results*

For the 1996 Olympic games in Atlanta, more than 2 million unique visitors came to the games and more than 11 million tickets were sold. In Sydney, at the 2000 Olympic games, more than 5.5 million tickets were available to be sold. It is obvious that this is a potential target market that cannot be ignored. Researchers at the University of Colorado at Boulder decided to find what motivated the international and domestic travelers to come to the Olympic games in Atlanta. A survey was developed and administered to visitors via personal interviews during a nine-day period surrounding the completion of the 1996 Olympic games. Three hundred twenty surveys were actually completed correctly and were used in the data analysis.

The results (see the following table) showed that the top three factors that motivated people to attend the games were: a once-in-a-lifetime opportunity, availability of housing, and availability of tickets. The results of this study helped planners for the 2000 Olympic games in Sydney find what specific characteristics the city needed to improve. For instance, from this research, Sydney put funds into projects that added hotel rooms to the city. They also constructed state-of-the-art transportation (a new elevated rail system) and unique venues (Olympic Park) so that visitors truly felt like they were getting a once-in-a-lifetime experience. As this survey continues to evolve over the years, the data received will become very valuable to the next host city.[3]

Motivational Factors that Influenced the Decision to Attend the Olympic Games

| *Motivational Factor* | *Frequency* | *Percentage* |
|---|---|---|
| Once-in-a-lifetime opportunity | 95 | 29.7 |
| Availability of housing | 36 | 11.2 |
| Availability of tickets | 27 | 8.4 |
| Distance away from home | 24 | 7.5 |
| Business/employment | 17 | 5.3 |
| Availability of money—overall expenses | 17 | 5.3 |
| Availability of time | 12 | 3.8 |
| Personal relationship with participant or official | 8 | 2.5 |
| Other motivational factor | 8 | 2.5 |
| Visit Atlanta | 4 | 1.3 |
| Security | 3 | 0.9 |
| Did not respond | 69 | 21.6 |
| Total | 320 | 100.0 |

Note that the numbers and percentages in the preceding example indicate the extent of the various motivational factors that attract individuals to the Olympic games. Because numbers are involved, a frequency distribution can be used to calculate descriptive or summary statistics.

# STATISTICS ASSOCIATED WITH FREQUENCY DISTRIBUTION

As illustrated in the previous section, a frequency distribution is a convenient way of looking at different values of a variable. A frequency table is easy to read and provides basic information, but sometimes this information may be too detailed and the researcher must summarize it by the use of descriptive statistics. The most commonly used statistics associated with frequencies are measures of location (mean, mode, and median), measures of variability (range, interquartile range, standard deviation, and coefficient of variation), and measures of shape (skewness and kurtosis).[4]

## Measures of Location

**measures of location**
A statistic that describes a location within a data set. Measures of central tendency describe the center of the distribution.

The **measures of location** that we discuss are measures of central tendency because they tend to describe the center of the distribution. If the entire sample is changed by adding a fixed constant to each observation, then the mean, mode, and median change by the same fixed amount.

***Mean.***    The **mean,** or average value, is the most commonly used measure of central tendency. It is used to estimate the mean when the data have been collected using an interval or ratio scale. The data should display some central tendency, with most of the responses distributed around the mean.

**mean**
The average; that value obtained by summing all elements in a set and dividing by the number of elements.

The mean, $\overline{X}$, is given by

$$\overline{X} = \sum_{i=1}^{n} X_i/n$$

where

$$X_i = \text{Observed values of the variable } X$$
$$n = \text{Number of observations (sample size)}$$

If there are no outliers, the mean is a robust measure and does not change markedly as data values are added or deleted. For the frequencies given in Table 15.2, the mean value is calculated as follows:

$$\bar{X} = (2 \times 2 + 6 \times 3 + 6 \times 4 + 3 \times 5 + 8 \times 6 + 4 \times 7)/29$$
$$= (4 + 18 + 24 + 15 + 48 + 28)/29$$
$$= 137/29$$
$$= 4.724$$

**mode**
A measure of central tendency given as the value that occurs the most in a sample distribution.

*Mode.*   The *mode* is the value that occurs most frequently. It represents the highest peak of the distribution. The mode is a good measure of location when the variable is inherently categorical or has otherwise been grouped into categories. The mode in Table 15.2 is 6.000.

**median**
A measure of central tendency given as the value above which half of the values fall and below which half of the values fall.

*Median.*   The *median* of a sample is the middle value when the data are arranged in ascending or descending order. If the number of data points is even, the median is usually estimated as the midpoint between the two middle values—by adding the two middle values and dividing their sum by 2. The median is the 50th percentile. The median is an appropriate measure of central tendency for ordinal data. In Table 15.2, the median is 5.000.

As can be seen from Table 15.1, the three measures of central tendency for this distribution are different (mean = 4.724, mode = 6.000, median = 5.000). This is not surprising, because each measure defines central tendency in a different way. So which measure should be used? If the variable is measured on a nominal scale, the mode should be used. If the variable is measured on an ordinal scale, the median is appropriate. If the variable is measured on an interval or ratio scale, the mode is a poor measure of central tendency. This can be seen from Table 15.2. Although the modal value of 6.000 has the highest frequency, it represents only 27.6% of the sample. In general, for interval or ratio data, the median is a better measure of central tendency, although it too ignores available information about the variable. The actual values of the variable above and below the median are ignored. The mean is the most appropriate measure of central tendency for interval or ratio data. The mean makes use of all the information available because all of the values are used in computing it. However, the mean is sensitive to extremely small or extremely large values (outliers). When there are outliers in the data, the mean is not a good measure of central tendency and it is useful to consider both the mean and the median.

## Measures of Variability

**measures of variability**
A statistic that indicates the distribution's dispersion.

The *measures of variability,* which are calculated on interval or ratio data, include the range, interquartile range, variance or standard deviation, and coefficient of variation.

**range**
The difference between the largest and smallest values of a distribution.

*Range.*   The *range* measures the spread of the data. It is simply the difference between the largest and smallest values in the sample. As such, the range is directly affected by outliers.

$$\text{Range} = X_{\text{largest}} - X_{\text{smallest}}$$

If all the values in the data are multiplied by a constant, the range is multiplied by the same constant. The range in Table 15.2 is $7 - 2 = 5.000$.

**interquartile range**
The range of a distribution encompassing the middle 50% of the observations.

*Interquartile Range.*   The *interquartile range* is the difference between the 75th and 25th percentile. For a set of data points arranged in order of magnitude, the pth percentile is the value that has $p$ percent of the data points below it and $(100 - p)$ percent above it. If all the data points are multiplied by a constant, the interquartile range is multiplied by the same constant. The interquartile range in Table 15.2 is $6 - 3 = 3.000$.

**variance**
The mean squared deviation of all the values from the mean.

*Variance and Standard Deviation.*   The difference between the mean and an observed value is called the deviation from the mean. The *variance* is the mean squared deviation from the mean. The variance can never be negative. When the data points are clustered around the mean, the variance is small. When the data points are scattered, the

*standard deviation*
The square root of the variance.

variance is large. If all the data values are multiplied by a constant, the variance is multiplied by the square of the constant. The **standard deviation** is the square root of the variance. Thus, the standard deviation is expressed in the same units as the data, rather than in squared units. The standard deviation of a sample, *s,* is calculated as:

$$s = \sqrt{\frac{\sum_{i=1}^{n}(X_i - \overline{X})^2}{n-1}}$$

We divide by $n-1$ instead of $n$ because the sample is drawn from a population and we are trying to determine how much the responses vary from the mean of the entire population. However, the population mean is unknown; therefore the sample mean is used instead. The use of the sample mean makes the sample seem less variable than it really is. By dividing by $n-1$, instead of $n$, we compensate for the smaller variability observed in the sample. For the data given in Table 15.2, the variance is calculated as follows:

$$s^2 = \frac{\{2\times(2-4.724)^2 + 6\times(3-4.724)^2 + 6\times(4-4.724)^2 + 3\times(5-4.724)^2 + 8\times(6-4.724)^2 + 4\times(7-4.724)^2\}}{28}$$

$$= \frac{\{14.840 + 17.833 + 3.145 + 0.229 + 13.025 + 20.721\}}{28}$$

$$= \frac{69.793}{28}$$

$$= 2.493$$

The standard deviation, therefore, is calculated as:

$$s = \sqrt{2.493}$$
$$= 1.579$$

*coefficient of variation*
A useful expression in sampling theory for the standard deviation as a percentage of the mean.

***Coefficient of Variation.*** The **coefficient of variation** is the ratio of the standard deviation to the mean, expressed as a percentage, and it is a unitless measure of relative variability. The coefficient of variation, *CV,* is expressed as:

$$CV = \frac{s}{\overline{X}}$$

The coefficient of variation is meaningful only if the variable is measured on a ratio scale. It remains unchanged if all the data values are multiplied by a constant. Because familiarity with the Internet is not measured on a ratio scale, it is not meaningful to calculate the coefficient of variation for the data in Table 15.2.

## Measures of Shape

In addition to measures of variability, measures of shape are also useful in understanding the nature of the distribution. The shape of a distribution is assessed by examining skewness and kurtosis.

*skewness*
A characteristic of a distribution that assesses its symmetry about the mean.

***Skewness.*** Distributions can be either symmetric or skewed. In a symmetric distribution, the values on either side of the center of the distribution are the same, and the mean, mode, and median are equal. The positive and corresponding negative deviations from the mean are also equal. In a skewed distribution, the positive and negative deviations from the mean are unequal. **Skewness** is the tendency of the deviations from the mean to be larger in one direction than in the other. It can be thought of as the tendency for one tail of the distribution to be heavier than the other (see Figure 15.2). The skewness value for the data of Table 15.2 is $-0.094$, indicating a slight negative skew.

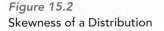

**Figure 15.2**
Skewness of a Distribution

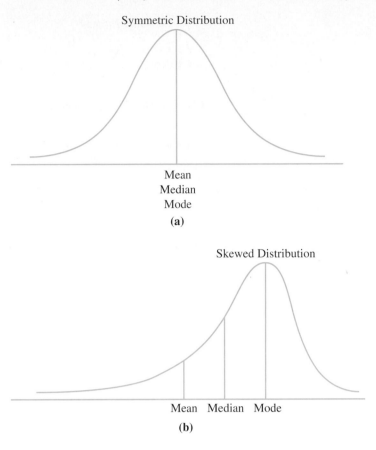

**kurtosis**
A measure of the relative peaked-ness or flatness of the curve defined by the frequency distribution.

**Kurtosis.** *Kurtosis* is a measure of the relative peakedness or flatness of the curve defined by the frequency distribution. The kurtosis of a normal distribution is zero. If the kurtosis is positive, then the distribution is more peaked than a normal distribution. A negative value means that the distribution is flatter than a normal distribution. The value of this statistic for Table 15.2 is $-1.261$, indicating that the distribution is flatter than a normal distribution.

# INTRODUCTION TO HYPOTHESIS TESTING

Basic analysis invariably involves some hypothesis testing. Examples of hypotheses generated in marketing research abound:

- The department store is being patronized by more than 10 percent of the households.
- The heavy and light users of a brand differ in terms of psychographic characteristics.
- One hotel has a more upscale image than its close competitor.
- Familiarity with a restaurant results in greater preference for that restaurant.

Chapter 12 covered the concepts of the sampling distribution, standard error of the mean or the proportion, and the confidence interval.[5] All these concepts are relevant to hypothesis testing and should be reviewed. Now we describe a general procedure for hypothesis testing that can be applied to test hypotheses about a wide range of parameters.

# A GENERAL PROCEDURE FOR HYPOTHESIS TESTING

The following steps are involved in hypothesis testing (Figure 15.3).

1. Formulate the null hypothesis $H_0$ and the alternative hypothesis $H_1$.
2. Select an appropriate statistical technique and the corresponding test statistic.
3. Choose the level of significance, $\alpha$.

*Figure 15.3*
A General Procedure for
Hypothesis Testing

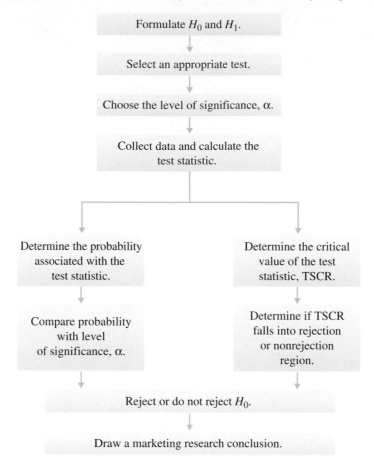

4. Determine the sample size and collect the data. Calculate the value of the test statistic.
5. Determine the probability associated with the test statistic under the null hypothesis, using the sampling distribution of the test statistic. Alternatively, determine the critical values associated with the test statistic that divide the rejection and nonrejection region.
6. Compare the probability associated with the test statistic with the level of significance specified. Alternatively, determine whether the test statistic has fallen into the rejection or the nonrejection region.
7. Make the statistical decision to reject or not reject the null hypothesis.
8. Express the statistical decision in terms of the marketing research problem.

## Step 1: Formulate the Hypotheses

**null hypothesis**
A statement in which no difference or effect is expected. If the null hypothesis is not rejected, no changes will be made.

**alternative hypothesis**
A statement that some difference or effect is expected. Accepting the alternative hypothesis will lead to changes in opinions or actions.

The first step is to formulate the null and alternative hypothesis. A ***null hypothesis*** is a statement of the status quo, one of no difference or no effect. If the null hypothesis is not rejected, no changes will be made. An ***alternative hypothesis*** is one in which some difference or effect is expected. Accepting the alternative hypothesis will lead to changes in opinions or actions. Thus, the alternative hypothesis is the opposite of the null hypothesis.

The null hypothesis is always the hypothesis that is tested. The null hypothesis refers to a specified value of the population parameter (e.g., $\mu$, $\sigma$, $\pi$), not a sample statistic (e.g., $\bar{X}$). A null hypothesis may be rejected, but it can never be accepted based on a single test. A statistical test can have one of two outcomes. One is that the null hypothesis is rejected and the alternative hypothesis accepted. The other outcome is that the null hypothesis is not rejected based on the evidence. However, it would be incorrect to conclude that because the null hypothesis is not rejected, it can be accepted as valid. In classical hypothesis testing, there is no way to determine whether the null hypothesis is true.

In marketing research, the null hypothesis is formulated in such a way that its rejection leads to the acceptance of the desired conclusion. The alternative hypothesis represents the conclusion for which evidence is sought. For example, a major department store is considering the introduction of an Internet shopping service. The new service will be introduced if more than 40 percent of the Internet users shop via the Internet. The appropriate way to formulate the hypotheses is:

$$H_0: \pi \leq 0.40$$
$$H_1: \pi > 0.40$$

If the null hypothesis $H_0$ is rejected, then the alternative hypothesis $H_1$ will be accepted and the new Internet shopping service introduced. On the other hand, if $H_0$ is not rejected, then the new service should not be introduced unless additional evidence is obtained.

**one-tailed test**
A test of the null hypothesis where the alternative hypothesis is expressed directionally.

This test of the null hypothesis is a ***one-tailed test,*** because the alternative hypothesis is expressed directionally: the proportion of Internet users who use the Internet for shopping is greater than 0.40. On the other hand, suppose the researcher wanted to determine whether the proportion of Internet users who shop via the Internet is different than 40 percent. Then a ***two-tailed test*** would be required, and the hypotheses would be expressed as:

**two-tailed test**
A test of the null hypothesis where the alternative hypothesis is not expressed directionally.

$$H_0: \pi = 0.40$$
$$H_1: \pi \neq 0.40$$

In commercial marketing research, the one-tailed test is used more often than a two-tailed test. Typically, there is some preferred direction for the conclusion for which evidence is sought. For example, the higher the profits, sales, and product quality, the better. The one-tailed test is more powerful than the two-tailed test. The power of a statistical test is discussed further in step 3.

## Step 2: Select an Appropriate Test

To test the null hypothesis, it is necessary to select an appropriate statistical technique. The researcher should take into consideration how the test statistic is computed and the sampling distribution that the sample statistic (e.g., the mean) follows. The ***test statistic*** measures how close the sample has come to the null hypothesis. The test statistic often follows a well-known distribution, such as the normal, *t*, or chi-square distribution. Guidelines for selecting an appropriate test or statistical technique are discussed later in this chapter. In our example, the *z* statistic, which follows the standard normal distribution, would be appropriate. This statistic would be computed as follows:

**test statistic**
A measure of how close the sample has come to the null hypothesis. It often follows a well-known distribution, such as the normal, *t*, or chi-square distribution.

$$z = \frac{p - \pi}{\sigma_p}$$

where

$$\sigma_p = \sqrt{\frac{\pi(1 - \pi)}{n}}$$

## Step 3: Choose Level of Significance, $\alpha$

Whenever we draw inferences about a population, there is a risk that an incorrect conclusion will be reached. Two types of errors can occur.

**type I error**
Also known as alpha error, occurs when the sample results lead to the rejection of a null hypothesis that is in fact true.

***Error.*** ***Type I error*** occurs when the sample results lead to the rejection of the null hypothesis when it is in fact true. In our example, a Type I error would occur if we concluded, based on the sample data, that the proportion of customers preferring the new service plan was greater than 0.40, when in fact it was less than or equal to 0.40. The probability of Type I error ($\alpha$) is also called the ***level of significance.*** The Type I error is controlled by establishing the tolerable level of risk of rejecting a true null hypothesis. The selection of a particular risk level should depend on the cost of making a Type I error.

**level of significance**
The probability of making a type I error.

Figure 15.4
Type I Error ($\alpha$) and Type II
Error ($\beta$)

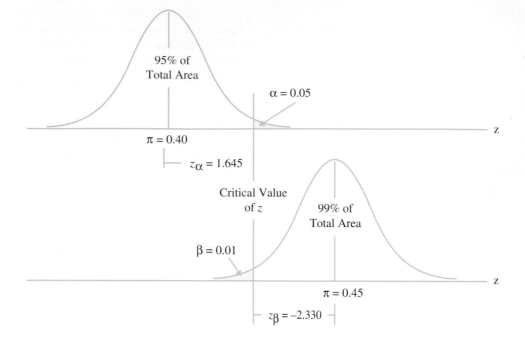

---

**type II error**
Also known as beta error, occurs
when the sample results lead to the
nonrejection of a null hypothesis
that is in fact false.

***Type II Error.***   ***Type II error*** occurs when, based on the sample results, the null
hypothesis is not rejected when it is in fact false. In our example, the Type II error would
occur if we concluded, based on sample data, that the proportion of customers preferring
the new service plan was less than or equal to 0.40 when, in fact, it was greater than 0.40.
The probability of Type II error is denoted by $\beta$. Unlike $\alpha$, which is specified by the
researcher, the magnitude of $\beta$ depends on the actual value of the population parameter
(proportion). The probability of Type I error ($\alpha$) and the probability of Type II error ($\beta$) are
shown in Figure 15.4. The complement ($1 - \beta$) of the probability of a Type II error is
called the power of a statistical test.

**power of a test**
The probability of rejecting the null
hypothesis when it is in fact false
and should be rejected.

***Power of a Test.***   The ***power of a test*** is the probability ($1 - \beta$) of rejecting the null
hypothesis when it is false and should be rejected. Although $\beta$ is unknown, it is related
to $\alpha$. An extremely low value of $\alpha$ (e.g., $= 0.001$) will result in intolerably high $\beta$ errors.
So it is necessary to balance the two types of errors. As a compromise, $\alpha$ is often set at
0.05; sometimes it is 0.01; other values of $\alpha$ are rare. The level of $\alpha$, along with the sample
size, will determine the level of $\beta$ for a particular research design. The risk of both $\alpha$ and $\beta$
can be controlled by increasing the sample size. For a given level of $\alpha$, increasing the sample size will decrease $\beta$, thereby increasing the power of the test.

## Step 4: Collect Data and Calculate Test Statistic

Sample size is determined after taking into account the desired $\alpha$ and $\beta$ errors and other
qualitative considerations, such as budget constraints. Then the required data are collected
and the value of the test statistic computed. In our example, 30 users were surveyed and 17
indicated that they used the Internet for shopping. Thus the value of the sample proportion
is $p = 17/30 = 0.567$.

The value of $\sigma_p$ can be determined as follows:

$$\sigma_p = \sqrt{\frac{\pi(1 - \pi)}{n}}$$

$$= \sqrt{\frac{(0.40)(0.60)}{30}}$$

$$= 0.089$$

**Figure 15.5**
Probability of *z* with a One-Tailed
Test

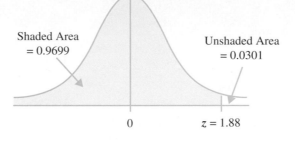

The test statistic *z* can be calculated as follows:

$$z = \frac{p - \pi}{\sigma_p}$$

$$= \frac{0.567 - 0.40}{0.089}$$

$$= 1.88$$

## Step 5: Determine the Probability (Critical Value)

Using standard normal tables (Table 2 of the Statistical Appendix), the probability of obtaining a *z* value of 1.88 can be calculated (see Figure 15.5). The shaded area between $-\infty$ and 1.88 is 0.9699. Therefore, the area to the right of $z = 1.88$ is $1.0000 - 0.9699 = 0.0301$. Alternatively, the critical value of *z*, which will give an area to the right side of the critical value of 0.05, is between 1.64 and 1.65 and equals 1.645. Note that in determining the critical value of the test statistic, the area to the right of the critical value is either $\alpha$ or $\alpha/2$. It is $\alpha$ for a one-tail test and $\alpha/2$ for a two-tail test.

## Steps 6 and 7: Compare the Probability (Critical Value) and Make the Decision

The probability associated with the calculated or observed value of the test statistic is 0.0301. This is the probability of getting a *p* value of 0.567 when $\pi = 0.40$. This is less than the level of significance of 0.05. Hence, the null hypothesis is rejected. Alternatively, the calculated value of the test statistic $z = 1.88$ lies in the rejection region, beyond the value of 1.645. Again, the same conclusion to reject the null hypothesis is reached. Note that the two ways of testing the null hypothesis are equivalent but mathematically opposite in the direction of comparison. If the probability associated with the calculated or observed value of the test statistic ($TS_{CAL}$) is <u>less than</u> the level of significance ($\alpha$), the null hypothesis is rejected. However, if the calculated value of the test statistic is <u>greater than</u> the critical value of the test statistic ($TS_{CR}$), the null hypothesis is rejected. The reason for this sign shift is that the larger the value of $TS_{CAL}$, the smaller the probability of obtaining a more extreme value of the test statistic under the null hypothesis. This sign shift can be easily seen:

if probability of $TS_{CAL}$ < significance level ($\alpha$), then reject $H_0$,

but

if $TS_{CAL} > TS_{CR}$, then reject $H_0$.

## Step 8: Marketing Research Conclusion

The conclusion reached by hypothesis testing must be expressed in terms of the marketing research problem. In our example, we conclude that there is evidence that the proportion of Internet users who shop via the Internet is significantly greater than 0.40. Hence, the recommendation to the department store would be to introduce the new Internet shopping service.

*Figure 15.6*
A Broad Classification of
Hypothesis Tests

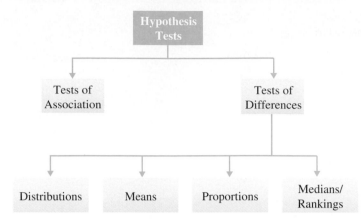

As can be seen from Figure 15.6, hypotheses testing can be related to either an examination of associations, or an examination of differences. In tests of associations, the null hypothesis is that there is no association between the variables ($H_0$: . . . is NOT related to . . . ). In tests of differences, the null hypothesis is that there is no difference ($H_0$: . . . is NOT different than . . .). Tests of differences could relate to distributions, means, proportions, medians, or rankings. First, we discuss hypotheses related to associations in the context of cross-tabulations.

# CROSS-TABULATIONS

Although answers to questions related to a single variable are interesting, they often raise additional questions about how to link that variable to other variables. To introduce the frequency distribution, we posed several representative marketing research questions. For each of these, a researcher might pose additional questions to relate these variables to other variables. For example:

- How many brand-loyal users are males?
- Is product use (measured in terms of heavy users, medium users, light users, and nonusers) related to interest in outdoor activities (high, medium, and low)?
- Is familiarity with a new product related to age and education levels?
- Is product ownership related to income (high, medium, and low)?

**cross-tabulation**
A statistical technique that describes two or more variables simultaneously and results in tables that reflect the joint distribution of two or more variables that have a limited number of categories or distinct values.

The answers to such questions can be determined by examining cross-tabulations. Whereas a frequency distribution describes one variable at a time, a **cross-tabulation** describes two or more variables simultaneously. A cross-tabulation is the merging of the frequency distribution of two or more variables in a single table. It helps us to understand how one variable such as brand loyalty relates to another variable such as sex. Cross-tabulation results in tables that reflect the joint distribution of two or more variables with a limited number of categories or distinct values. The categories of one variable are cross-classified with the categories of one or more other variables. Thus, the frequency distribution of one variable is subdivided according to the values or categories of the other variables.

Suppose we are interested in determining whether Internet usage is related to sex. For the purpose of cross-tabulation, respondents are classified as light or heavy users. Those reporting 5 hours or less usage are classified as light users, and the remaining are heavy users. The cross-tabulation is shown in Table 15.3. A cross-tabulation includes a cell for every combination of the categories of the two variables. The number in each cell shows how many respondents gave that combination of responses. In Table 15.3, 10 respondents were females who reported light Internet usage. The marginal totals in this table indicate that of the 30 respondents with valid responses on both the variables, 15 reported light usage and 15 were heavy users. In terms of sex, 15 respondents were females and 15 were males. Note that this information could have been obtained from a separate frequency distribution for each variable. In general, the margins of a cross-tabulation show the same

| TABLE 15.3 | | | |
|---|---|---|---|
| **Sex and Internet Usage** | | | |
| | SEX | | |
| INTERNET USAGE | MALE | FEMALE | ROW TOTAL |
| Light (1) | 5 | 10 | 15 |
| Heavy (2) | 10 | 5 | 15 |
| Column total | 15 | 15 | |

| TABLE 15.4 | | |
|---|---|---|
| **Sex by Internet Usage** | | |
| | SEX | |
| INTERNET USAGE | MALE | FEMALE |
| Light | 33.3% | 66.7% |
| Heavy | 66.7% | 33.3% |
| Column total | 100.0% | 100.0% |

| TABLE 15.5 | | |
|---|---|---|
| **Internet Usage by Sex** | | |
| | INTERNET USAGE | |
| SEX | LIGHT | HEAVY | TOTAL |
| Male | 33.3% | 66.7% | 100.0% |
| Female | 66.7% | 33.3% | 100.0% |

**contingency table**

A cross-tabulation table. It contains a cell for every combination of categories of the two variables.

information as the frequency tables for each of the variables. Cross-tabulation tables are also called **contingency tables.** The data are considered to be qualitative or categorical data, because each variable is assumed to have only a nominal scale.[6]

Cross-tabulation is widely used in commercial marketing research, because (1) cross-tabulation analysis and results can be easily interpreted and understood by managers who are not statistically oriented; (2) the clarity of interpretation provides a stronger link between research results and managerial action; (3) a series of cross-tabulations may provide greater insights into a complex phenomenon than a single multivariate analysis; (4) cross-tabulation may alleviate the problem of sparse cells, which could be serious in discrete multivariate analysis; and (5) cross-tabulation analysis is simple to conduct and appealing to less sophisticated researchers.[7]

## Two Variables

Cross-tabulation with two variables is also known as bivariate cross-tabulation. Consider again the cross-classification of Internet usage with sex given in Table 15.3. Is usage related to sex? It appears to be from Table 15.3. We see that disproportionately more of the respondents who are males are heavy Internet users as compared to females. Computation of percentages can provide more insights.

Because two variables have been cross-classified, percentages could be computed either columnwise, based on column totals (Table 15.4), or rowwise, based on row totals (Table 15.5). Which of these tables is more useful? The answer depends on which variable will be considered as the independent variable and which as the dependent variable. The general rule is to compute the percentages in the direction of the independent variable, across the dependent variable. In our analysis, sex may be considered as the independent variable, and Internet usage as the dependent variable, and the correct way of calculating percentages is as shown in Table 15.4. Note that whereas 66.7 percent of the males are

*Figure 15.7*
The Introduction of a Third
Variable in Cross-Tabulation

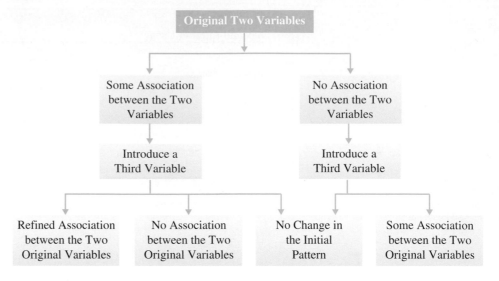

heavy users, only 33.3 percent of females fall into this category. This seems to indicate that males are more likely to be heavy users of the Internet as compared to females.

Note that computing percentages in the direction of the dependent variable across the independent variable, as shown in Table 15.5, is not meaningful in this case. Table 15.5 implies that heavy Internet usage causes people to be males. This latter finding is implausible. It is possible, however, that the association between Internet usage and sex is mediated by a third variable, such as age or income. This kind of possibility points to the need to examine the effect of a third variable.

## Three Variables

Often the introduction of a third variable clarifies the initial association (or lack of it) observed between two variables. As shown in Figure 15.7, the introduction of a third variable can result in four possibilities.

1. It can refine the association observed between the two original variables.
2. It can indicate no association between the two variables, although an association was initially observed. In other words, the third variable indicates that the initial association between the two variables was spurious.
3. It can reveal some association between the two variables, although no association was initially observed. In this case, the third variable reveals a suppressed association between the first two variables.
4. It can indicate no change in the initial association.[8]

These cases are explained with examples based on a sample of 1,000 respondents. Although these examples are contrived to illustrate specific cases, such cases are not uncommon in commercial marketing research.

*Refine an Initial Relationship.*    An examination of the relationship between the purchase of fashion clothing and marital status resulted in the data reported in Table 15.6. The respondents were classified into either high or low categories based on their purchase of fashion clothing. Marital status was also measured in terms of two categories: currently married or unmarried. As can be seen from Table 15.6, 52 percent of unmarried respondents fell in the high-purchase category, as opposed to 31 percent of the married respondents. Before concluding that unmarried respondents purchase more fashion clothing than those who are married, a third variable, the buyer's sex, was introduced into the analysis.

The buyer's sex was selected as the third variable based on past research. The relationship between purchase of fashion clothing and marital status was reexamined in light of the third variable, as shown in Table 15.7. In the case of females, 60 percent of the unmarried fall in the high-purchase category, as compared to 25 percent of those who are

**TABLE 15.6**

**Purchase of Fashion Clothing by Marital Status**

| PURCHASE OF FASHION CLOTHING | CURRENT MARITAL STATUS | |
| --- | --- | --- |
| | MARRIED | UNMARRIED |
| High | 31% | 52% |
| Low | 69% | 48% |
| Column | 100% | 100% |
| Number of respondents | 700 | 300 |

**TABLE 15.7**

**Purchase of Fashion Clothing by Marital Status and Sex**

| PURCHASE OF FASHION CLOTHING | SEX | | | |
| --- | --- | --- | --- | --- |
| | MALE MARITAL STATUS | | FEMALE MARITAL STATUS | |
| | MARRIED | UNMARRIED | MARRIED | UNMARRIED |
| High | 35% | 40% | 25% | 60% |
| Low | 65% | 60% | 75% | 40% |
| Column totals | 100% | 100% | 100% | 100% |
| Number of cases | 400 | 120 | 300 | 180 |

**TABLE 15.8**

**Ownership of Expensive Automobiles by Education Level**

| OWN EXPENSIVE AUTOMOBILE | EDUCATION | |
| --- | --- | --- |
| | COLLEGE DEGREE | NO COLLEGE DEGREE |
| Yes | 32% | 21% |
| No | 68% | 79% |
| Column total | 100% | 100% |
| Number of cases | 250 | 750 |

married. On the other hand, the percentages are much closer for males, with 40 percent of the unmarried and 35 percent of the married falling in the high-purchase category. Hence, the introduction of sex (third variable) has refined the relationship between marital status and purchase of fashion clothing (original variables). Unmarried respondents are more likely to fall in the high-purchase category than married ones, and this effect is much more pronounced for females than for males.

*Initial Relationship Was Spurious.*    A researcher working for an advertising agency promoting a line of automobiles costing more than $30,000 was attempting to explain the ownership of expensive automobiles (see Table 15.8). The table shows that 32 percent of those with college degrees own an expensive automobile, as compared to 21 percent of those without college degrees. The researcher was tempted to conclude that education influenced ownership of expensive automobiles. Realizing that income may also be a factor, the researcher decided to reexamine the relationship between education and ownership of expensive automobiles in light of income level. This resulted in Table 15.9. Note that the percentages of those with and without college degrees who own expensive automobiles are the same for each of the income groups. When the data for the high-income and low-income groups are examined separately, the association between education and ownership of expensive automobiles disappears, indicating that the initial relationship observed between these two variables was spurious.

### TABLE 15.9

**Ownership of Expensive Automobiles by Education and Income Levels**

| OWN EXPENSIVE AUTOMOBILE | INCOME | | | |
| | LOW INCOME EDUCATION | | HIGH INCOME EDUCATION | |
| | COLLEGE DEGREE | NO COLLEGE DEGREE | COLLEGE DEGREE | NO COLLEGE DEGREE |
|---|---|---|---|---|
| Yes | 20% | 20% | 40% | 40% |
| No | 80% | 80% | 60% | 60% |
| Column totals | 100% | 100% | 100% | 100% |
| Number of respondents | 100 | 700 | 150 | 50 |

### TABLE 15.10

**Desire to Travel Abroad by Age**

| DESIRE TO TRAVEL ABROAD | AGE | |
| | LESS THAN 45 | 45 OR MORE |
|---|---|---|
| Yes | 50% | 50% |
| No | 50% | 50% |
| Column total | 100% | 100% |
| Number of respondents | 500 | 500 |

### TABLE 15.11

**Desire to Travel Abroad by Age and Sex**

| DESIRE TO TRAVEL ABROAD | SEX | | | |
| | MALE AGE | | FEMALE AGE | |
| | < 45 | ≥ 45 | < 45 | ≥ 45 |
|---|---|---|---|---|
| Yes | 60% | 40% | 35% | 65% |
| No | 40% | 60% | 65% | 35% |
| Column total | 100% | 100% | 100% | 100% |
| Number of cases | 300 | 300 | 200 | 200 |

***Reveal Suppressed Association.***   A researcher suspected desire to travel abroad may be influenced by age. However, a cross-tabulation of the two variables produced the results in Table 15.10, indicating no association. When sex was introduced as the third variable, Table 15.11 was obtained. Among men, 60 percent of those under 45 indicated a desire to travel abroad, as compared to 40 percent of those 45 or older. The pattern was reversed for women, where 35 percent of those under 45 indicated a desire to travel abroad, as opposed to 65 percent of those 45 or older. Because the association between desire to travel abroad and age runs in the opposite direction for males and females, the relationship between these two variables is masked when the data are aggregated across sex, as in Table 15.10. But when the effect of sex is controlled, as in Table 15.11, the suppressed association between desire to travel abroad and age is revealed for the separate categories of males and females.

***No Change in Initial Relationship.***   In some cases, the introduction of the third variable does not change the initial relationship observed, regardless of whether the original variables were associated. This suggests that the third variable does not influence the

**TABLE 15.12**

**Eating Frequently in Fast-Food Restaurants by Family Size**

| EAT FREQUENTLY IN FAST-FOOD RESTAURANTS | FAMILY SIZE | |
| --- | --- | --- |
| | SMALL | LARGE |
| Yes | 65% | 65% |
| No | 35% | 35% |
| Column total | 100% | 100% |
| Number of cases | 500 | 500 |

**TABLE 15.13**

**Eating Frequently in Fast-Food Restaurants by Family Size and Income**

| EAT FREQUENTLY IN FAST-FOOD RESTAURANTS | INCOME | | | |
| --- | --- | --- | --- | --- |
| | LOW INCOME | | HIGH INCOME | |
| | FAMILY SIZE | | FAMILY SIZE | |
| | SMALL | LARGE | SMALL | LARGE |
| Yes | 65% | 65% | 65% | 65% |
| No | 35% | 35% | 35% | 35% |
| Column total | 100% | 100% | 100% | 100% |
| Number of respondents | 250 | 250 | 250 | 250 |

relationship between the first two. Consider the cross-tabulation of family size and the tendency to eat out frequently in fast-food restaurants, as shown in Table 15.12. The respondents were classified into small and large family size categories based on a median split of the distribution, with 500 respondents in each category. No association is observed. The respondents were further classified into high- or low-income groups based on a median split. When income was introduced as a third variable in the analysis, Table 15.13 was obtained. Again, no association was observed.

## General Comments on Cross-Tabulation

More than three variables can be cross-tabulated, but the interpretation is quite complex. Also, because the number of cells increases multiplicatively, maintaining an adequate number of respondents or cases in each cell can be problematic. As a general rule, there should be at least five expected observations in each cell for the statistics computed to be reliable. Thus, cross-tabulation is an inefficient way of examining relationships when there are several variables. Note that cross-tabulation examines association between variables, not causation. To examine causation, the causal research design framework should be adopted (see Chapter 7).

# STATISTICS ASSOCIATED WITH CROSS-TABULATION

We will discuss the statistics commonly used for assessing the statistical significance and strength of association of cross-tabulated variables. The statistical significance of the observed association is commonly measured by the chi-square statistic. The strength of association, or degree of association, is important from a practical or substantive perspective. Generally, the strength of association is of interest only if the association is statistically significant. The strength of the association can be measured by the phi correlation coefficient, the contingency coefficient, Cramer's *V*, and the lambda coefficient.

## Chi-Square

The **chi-square statistic** ($\chi^2$) is used to test the statistical significance of the observed association in a cross-tabulation. It assists us in determining whether a systematic association exists between the two variables. The null hypothesis, $H_0$, is that there is no association between the variables. The test is conducted by computing the cell frequencies that would be expected if no association were present between the variables, given the existing row and column totals. These expected cell frequencies, denoted $f_e$, are then compared to the actual observed frequencies, $f_o$, found in the cross-tabulation to calculate the chi-square statistic. The greater the discrepancies between the expected and actual frequencies, the larger the value of the statistic. Assume that a cross-tabulation has $r$ rows and $c$ columns and a random sample of $n$ observations. Then the expected frequency for each cell can be calculated by using a simple formula:

$$f_e = \frac{n_r n_c}{n}$$

where

$$n_r = \text{total number in the row}$$
$$n_c = \text{total number in the column}$$
$$n = \text{total sample size}$$

For the data in Table 15.3, the expected frequencies for the cells going from left to right and from top to bottom, are:

$$\frac{15 \times 15}{30} = 7.50 \qquad \frac{15 \times 15}{30} = 7.50$$

$$\frac{15 \times 15}{30} = 7.50 \qquad \frac{15 \times 15}{30} = 7.50$$

Then the value of $\chi^2$ is calculated as follows:

$$\chi^2 = \sum_{\substack{\text{all} \\ \text{cells}}} \frac{(f_o - f_e)^2}{f_e}$$

For the data in Table 15.3, the value of $\chi^2$ is calculated as:

$$\chi^2 = \frac{(5 - 7.5)^2}{7.5} + \frac{(10 - 7.5)^2}{7.5} + \frac{(10 - 7.5)^2}{7.5} + \frac{(5 - 7.5)^2}{7.5}$$
$$= 0.833 + 0.833 + 0.833 + 0.833$$
$$= 3.333$$

To determine whether a systematic association exists, the probability of obtaining a value of chi-square as large or larger than the one calculated from the cross-tabulation is estimated. An important characteristic of the chi-square statistic is the number of degrees of freedom (df) associated with it. In general, the number of degrees of freedom is equal to the number of observations less the number of constraints needed to calculate a statistical term. In the case of a chi-square statistic associated with a cross-tabulation, the number of degrees of freedom is equal to the product of number of rows ($r$) less one and the number of columns ($c$) less one. That is, df $= (r - 1) \times (c - 1)$.[9] The null hypothesis ($H_0$) of no association between the two variables will be rejected only when the calculated value of the test statistic is greater than the critical value of the chi-square distribution with the appropriate degrees of freedom, as shown in Figure 15.8.

The **chi-square distribution** is a skewed distribution whose shape depends solely on the number of degrees of freedom.[10] As the number of degrees of freedom increases, the chi-square distribution becomes more symmetrical. Table 3 in the Statistical Appendix contains upper-tail areas of the chi-square distribution for different degrees of freedom. In this table, the value at the top of each column indicates the area in the upper portion (the right side, as shown in Figure 15.8) of the chi-square distribution. To illustrate, for 1 degree of freedom, the value for an upper-tail area of 0.05 is 3.841. This indicates that for 1 degree

Figure 15.8
Chi-Square Test of Association

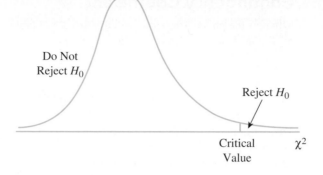

of freedom, the probability of exceeding a chi-square value of 3.841 is 0.05. In other words, at the 0.05 level of significance with 1 degree of freedom, the critical value of the chi-square statistic is 3.841.

For the cross-tabulation given in Table 15.3, there are $(2 - 1) \times (2 - 1) = 1$ degree of freedom. The calculated chi-square statistic had a value of 3.333. Because this is less than the critical value of 3.841, the null hypothesis of no association can not be rejected, indicating that the association is not statistically significant at the 0.05 level.

The chi-square statistic can also be used in goodness-of-fit tests to determine whether certain models fit the observed data. These tests are conducted by calculating the significance of sample deviations from assumed theoretical (expected) distributions, and can be performed on cross-tabulations as well as on frequencies (one-way tabulations). The calculation of the chi-square statistic and the determination of its significance is the same as illustrated above.

The chi-square statistic should be estimated only on counts of data. When the data are in percentage form, they should first be converted to absolute counts or numbers. In addition, an underlying assumption of the chi-square test is that the observations are drawn independently. As a general rule, chi-square analysis should not be conducted when the expected or theoretical frequencies in any of the cells is less than five. If the number of observations in any cell is less than 10, or if the table has two rows and two columns (a 2 × 2 table), a correction factor should be applied.[11] With the correction factor, the value is 2.133, which is not significant at the 0.05 level. In the case of a 2 × 2 table, the chi-square is related to the phi coefficient.

## Phi Coefficient

**phi coefficient**
A measure of the strength of association in the special case of a table with two rows and two columns (a 2 × 2 table).

The ***phi coefficient*** ($\phi$) is used as a measure of the strength of association in the special case of a table with two rows and two columns (a 2 × 2 table). The phi coefficient is proportional to the square root of the chi-square statistic. For a sample of size $n$, this statistic is calculated as:

$$\phi = \sqrt{\frac{\chi^2}{n}}$$

It takes the value of 0 when there is no association, which would be indicated by a chi-square value of 0 as well. When the variables are perfectly associated, phi assumes the value of 1 and all the observations fall just on the main or minor diagonal. (In some computer programs, phi assumes a value of $-1$ rather than 1 when there is perfect negative association). In our case, because the association was not significant at the 0.05 level, we would not normally compute the phi value. However, for the purpose of illustration, we show how the values of phi and other measures of the strength of association would be computed. The value of phi is:

$$\phi = \sqrt{\frac{3.333}{30}}$$
$$= 0.333$$

Thus, the association is not very strong. In the more general case involving a table of any size, the strength of association can be assessed by using the contingency coefficient.

## Contingency Coefficient

contingency coefficient (C)
A measure of the strength of association in a table of any size.

Whereas the phi coefficient is specific to a 2 × 2 table, the **contingency coefficient** (*C*) can be used to assess the strength of association in a table of any size. This index is also related to chi-square, as follows:

$$C = \sqrt{\frac{\chi^2}{\chi^2 + n}}$$

The contingency coefficient varies between 0 and 1. The 0 value occurs in the case of no association (i.e., the variables are statistically independent), but the maximum value of 1 is never achieved. Rather, the maximum value of the contingency coefficient depends on the size of the table (number of rows and number of columns). For this reason, it should be used only to compare tables of the same size. The value of the contingency coefficient for Table 15.3 is:

$$C = \sqrt{\frac{3.333}{3.333 + 30}}$$
$$= 0.316$$

This value of *C* indicates that the association is not very strong. Another statistic that can be calculated for any table is Cramer's *V*.

## Cramer's *V*

Cramer's V
A measure of the strength of association used in tables larger than 2 × 2.

***Cramer's* V** is a modified version of the phi correlation coefficient, ϕ, and is used in tables larger than 2 × 2. When phi is calculated for a table larger than 2 × 2, it has no upper limit. Cramer's *V* is obtained by adjusting phi for either the number of rows or the number of columns in the table, based on which of the two is smaller. The adjustment is such that *V* will range from 0 to 1. A large value of *V* merely indicates a high degree of association. It does not indicate how the variables are associated. For a table with *r* rows and *c* columns, the relationship between Cramer's *V* and the phi correlation coefficient is expressed as:

$$V = \sqrt{\frac{\phi^2}{\min(r-1),(c-1)}}$$

or

$$V = \sqrt{\frac{\chi^2/n}{\min(r-1),(c-1)}}$$

The value of Cramer's *V* for Table 15.3 is:

$$V = \sqrt{\frac{3.333/30}{1}}$$
$$= 0.333$$

Thus, the association is not very strong. As can be seen, in this case *V* = ϕ. This is always the case for a 2 × 2 table. Another statistic commonly estimated is the lambda coefficient.

## Lambda Coefficient

asymmetric lambda
A measure of the percentage improvement in predicting the value of the dependent variable, given the value of the independent variable in contingency table analysis. Lambda also varies between 0 and 1.

symmetric lambda
The symmetric lambda does not make an assumption about which variable is dependent. It measures the overall improvement when prediction is done in both directions.

Lambda assumes that the variables are measured on a nominal scale. ***Asymmetric lambda*** measures the percentage improvement in predicting the value of the dependent variable, given the value of the independent variable. Lambda also varies between 0 and 1. A value of 0 means no improvement in prediction. A value of 1 indicates that the prediction can be made without error. This happens when each independent variable category is associated with a single category of the dependent variable.

Asymmetric lambda is computed for each of the variables (treating it as the dependent variable). In general, the two asymmetric lambdas are likely to be different because the marginal distributions are not usually the same. A ***symmetric lambda*** is also computed, which is a kind of average of the two asymmetric values. The symmetric lambda does not make an assumption about which variable is dependent. It measures the overall improvement when prediction is done in both directions.[12] The value of asymmetric lambda in Table 15.3, with usage as the dependent variable, is 0.333. This indicates that knowledge of sex increases our predictive ability by the proportion of 0.333, i.e., a 33.3 percent improvement. The symmetric lambda is also 0.333.

## Other Statistics

Note that in the calculation of the chi-square statistic, the variables are treated as being measured on only a nominal scale. Other statistics such as tau *b,* tau *c,* and gamma are available to measure association between two ordinal-level variables. All these statistics use information about the ordering of categories of variables by considering every possible pair of cases in the table. Each pair is examined to determine if its relative ordering on the first variable is the same as its relative ordering on the second variable (concordant), if the ordering is reversed (discordant), or if the pair is tied. The manner in which the ties are treated is the basic difference between these statistics. Both tau *b* and tau *c* adjust for ties. ***Tau* b** is the most appropriate with square tables, in which the number of rows and the number of columns are equal. Its value varies between $+1$ and $-1$. Thus the direction (positive or negative) as well as the strength (how close the value is to 1) of the relationship can be determined. For a rectangular table in which the number of rows is different than the number of columns, ***tau* c** should be used. ***Gamma*** does not make an adjustment for either ties or table size. Gamma also varies between $+1$ and $-1$ and generally has a higher numerical value than tau *b* or tau *c.* For the data in Table 15.3, as sex is a nominal variable, it is not appropriate to calculate ordinal statistics. All these statistics can be estimated by using the appropriate computer programs for cross-tabulation. Other statistics for measuring the strength of association, namely product moment correlation and nonmetric correlation, are discussed in Chapter 17.

*tau* **b**
Test statistic that measures the association between two ordinal-level variables. It makes an adjustment for ties and is most appropriate when the table of variables is square.

*tau* **c**
Test statistic that measures the association between two ordinal-level variables. It makes an adjustment for ties and is most appropriate when the table of variables is not square but a rectangle.

*gamma*
Test statistic that measures the association between two ordinal-level variables. It does not make an adjustment for ties.

# CROSS-TABULATION IN PRACTICE

When conducting cross-tabulation analysis in practice, it is useful to proceed along the following steps.

1. Test the null hypothesis that there is no association between the variables using the chi-square statistic. If you fail to reject the null hypothesis, then there is no relationship.
2. If $H_0$ is rejected, then determine the strength of the association using an appropriate statistic (phi coefficient, contingency coefficient, Cramer's *V,* lambda coefficient, or other statistics).
3. If $H_0$ is rejected, interpret the pattern of the relationship by computing the percentages in the direction of the independent variable, across the dependent variable.
4. If the variables are treated as ordinal rather than nominal, use tau *b,* tau *c,* or gamma as the test statistic. If $H_0$ is rejected, then determine the strength of the association using the magnitude, and the direction of the relationship using the sign of the test statistic.

# HYPOTHESES TESTING RELATED TO DIFFERENCES

The previous section considered hypotheses testing related to associations. We now focus on hypotheses testing related to differences. A classification of hypothesis-testing procedures for examining differences is presented in Figure 15.9. Note that Figure 15.9 is consistent with the classification of univariate techniques presented in Figure 14.6. The major difference is that Figure 14.6 also accommodates more than two samples and thus deals

*Figure 15.9*
Hypothesis Tests Related
to Differences

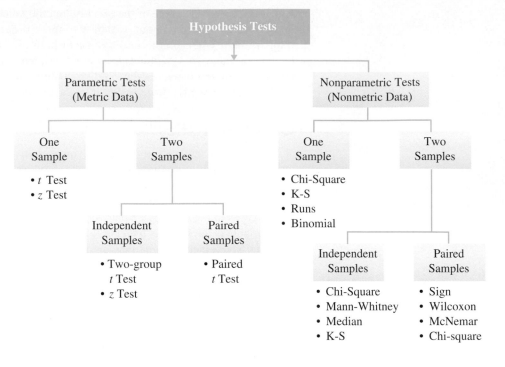

with techniques such as one-way ANOVA and K-W ANOVA (Chapter 14), whereas Figure 15.9 is limited to no more than two samples. Also, one-sample techniques such as frequencies, which do not involve statistical testing, are not covered in Figure 15.9. Hypothesis-testing procedures can be broadly classified as parametric or nonparametric, based on the measurement scale of the variables involved. ***Parametric tests*** assume that the variables of interest are measured on at least an interval scale. ***Nonparametric tests*** assume that the variables are measured on a nominal or ordinal scale. These tests can be further classified based on whether one, two, or more samples are involved. As explained in Chapter 14, the number of samples is determined based on how the data are treated for the purpose of analysis, not based on how the data were collected. The samples are **independent** if they are drawn randomly from different populations. For the purpose of analysis, data pertaining to different groups of respondents, e.g., males and females, are generally treated as independent samples. On the other hand, the samples are **paired** when the data for the two samples relate to the same group of respondents.

The most popular parametric test is the *t* test, conducted for examining hypotheses about means. The *t* test could be conducted on the mean of one sample or two samples of observations. In the case of two samples, the samples could be independent or paired. Nonparametric tests based on observations drawn from one sample include the Kolmogorov-Smirnov test, the chi-square test, the runs test, and the binomial test. In case of two independent samples, the Mann-Whitney *U* test, the median test, and the Kolmogorov-Smirnov two-sample test are used for examining hypotheses about location. These tests are nonparametric counterparts of the two-group *t* test. For paired samples, nonparametric tests include the Wilcoxon matched-pairs signed-ranks test and the sign test. These tests are the counterparts of the paired *t* test. Parametric as well as nonparametric tests are also available for evaluating hypotheses relating to more than two samples. These tests are considered in later chapters.

## PARAMETRIC TESTS

Parametric tests provide inferences for making statements about the means of parent populations. A **t** *test* is commonly used for this purpose. This test is based on the Student's *t* statistic. The **t** *statistic* assumes that the variable is normally distributed and the mean is known (or assumed to be known) and the population variance is estimated from the sam-

*parametric tests*
Hypothesis testing procedures that assume that the variables of interest are measured on at least an interval scale.

*nonparametric tests*
Hypothesis testing procedures that assume that the variables are measured on a nominal or ordinal scale.

**t** *test*
A univariate hypothesis test using the *t* distribution, which is used when the standard deviation is unknown and the sample size is small.

**t** *statistic*
A statistic that assumes that the variable has a symmetric bell-shaped distribution and the mean is known (or assumed to be known) and the population variance is estimated from the sample.

ple. Assume that the random variable $X$ is normally distributed, with mean $\mu$ and unknown population variance $\sigma^2$, which is estimated by the sample variance $s^2$. Recall that the standard deviation of the sample mean, $\overline{X}$, is estimated as $s_{\overline{X}} = s/\sqrt{n}$. Then $t = (\overline{X} - \mu)/s_{\overline{X}}$ is $t$ distributed with $n - 1$ degrees of freedom.

The **t** *distribution* is similar to the normal distribution in appearance. Both distributions are bell shaped and symmetric. However, as compared to the normal distribution, the $t$ distribution has more area in the tails and less in the center. This is because population variance $\sigma^2$ is unknown and is estimated by the sample variance $s^2$. Given the uncertainty in the value of $s^2$, the observed values of $t$ are more variable than those of $z$. Thus, we must go a larger number of standard deviations from 0 to encompass a certain percentage of values from the $t$ distribution than is the case with the normal distribution. Yet, as the number of degrees of freedom increases, the $t$ distribution approaches the normal distribution. In fact, for large samples of 120 or more, the $t$ distribution and the normal distribution are virtually indistinguishable. Table 4 in the Statistical Appendix shows selected percentiles of the $t$ distribution. Although normality is assumed, the $t$ test is quite robust to departures from normality.

The procedure for hypothesis testing, for the special case when the $t$ statistic is used, is as follows.

1. Formulate the null ($H_0$) and the alternative ($H_1$) hypotheses.
2. Select the appropriate formula for the $t$ statistic.
3. Select a significance level, $\alpha$, for testing $H_0$. Typically, the 0.05 level is selected.[13]
4. Take one or two samples and compute the mean and standard deviation for each sample.
5. Calculate the $t$ statistic assuming $H_0$ is true.
6. Calculate the degrees of freedom and estimate the probability of getting a more extreme value of the statistic from Table 4. (Alternatively, calculate the critical value of the $t$ statistic.)
7. If the probability computed in step 6 is smaller than the significance level selected in step 3, reject $H_0$. If the probability is larger, do not reject $H_0$. (Alternatively, if the value of the calculated $t$ statistic in step 5 is larger than the critical value determined in step 6, reject $H_0$. If the calculated value is smaller than the critical value, do not reject $H_0$.) Failure to reject $H_0$ does not necessarily imply that $H_0$ is true. It only means that the true state is not significantly different than that assumed by $H_0$.[14]
8. Express the conclusion reached by the $t$ test in terms of the marketing research problem.

## One Sample

In marketing research, the researcher is often interested in making statements about a single variable against a known or given standard. Examples of such statements include: the market share for a new product will exceed 15 percent, at least 65 percent of customers will like a new package design, and 80 percent of dealers will prefer the new pricing policy. These statements can be translated to null hypotheses that can be tested using a one-sample test, such as the $t$ test or the $z$ test. In the case of a $t$ test for a single mean, the researcher is interested in testing whether the population mean conforms to a given hypothesis ($H_0$). For the data in Table 15.2, suppose we wanted to test the hypothesis that the mean familiarity rating exceeds 4.0, the neutral value on a seven-point scale. A significance level of $\alpha = 0.05$ is selected. The hypotheses may be formulated as:

$$H_0: \mu \leq 4.0$$
$$H_1: \mu > 4.0$$

$$t = \frac{(\overline{X} - \mu)}{s_{\overline{X}}}$$

$$s_{\overline{X}} = \frac{s}{\sqrt{n}}$$

$$s_{\overline{X}} = 1.579/\sqrt{29} = 1.579/5.385 = 0.293$$
$$t = (4.724 - 4.0)/0.293 = 0.724/0.293 = 2.471$$

The degrees of freedom for the $t$ statistic to test hypothesis about one mean are $n - 1$. In this case, $n - 1 = 29 - 1$ or 28. From Table 4 in the Statistical Appendix, the probability of getting a more extreme value than 2.471 is less than 0.05. (Alternatively, the critical $t$ value for 28 degrees of freedom and a significance level of 0.05 is 1.7011, which is less than the calculated value.) Hence, the null hypothesis is rejected. The familiarity level does exceed 4.0.

Note that if the population standard deviation was assumed to be known as 1.5, rather than estimated from the sample, a **z test** would be appropriate. In this case, the value of the $z$ statistic would be:

$$z = (\overline{X} - \mu)/\sigma_{\overline{X}}$$

where

$$\sigma_{\overline{X}} = 1.5/\sqrt{29} = 1.5/5.385 = 0.279$$

and

$$z = (4.724 - 4.0)/0.279 = 0.724/0.279 = 2.595$$

From Table 2 in the Statistical Appendix, the probability of getting a more extreme value of $z$ than 2.595 is less than 0.05. (Alternatively, the critical $z$ value for a one-tailed test and a significance level of 0.05 is 1.645, which is less than the calculated value.) Therefore, the null hypothesis is rejected, reaching the same conclusion arrived at earlier by the $t$ test.

The procedure for testing a null hypothesis with respect to a proportion was illustrated earlier in this chapter when we introduced hypothesis testing.

## Two Independent Samples

Several hypotheses in marketing relate to parameters from two different populations: for example, the users and nonusers of a brand differ in terms of their perceptions of the brand, the high-income consumers spend more on entertainment than low-income consumers, or the proportion of brand-loyal users in segment I is more than the proportion in segment II. Samples drawn randomly from different populations are termed *independent samples*. As in the case for one sample, the hypotheses could relate to means or proportions.

***Means.***   In the case of means for two independent samples, the hypotheses take the following form.

$$H_0: \mu_1 = \mu_2$$
$$H_1: \mu_1 \neq \mu_2$$

The two populations are sampled and the means and variances computed based on samples of sizes $n_1$ and $n_2$. If both populations are found to have the same variance, a pooled variance estimate is computed from the two sample variances as follows:

$$s^2 = \frac{\sum_{i=1}^{n_1}(\chi_{i1} - \overline{\chi}_1)^2 + \sum_{i=1}^{n_2}(\chi_{i2} - \overline{\chi}_2)^2}{n_1 + n_2 - 2}$$

or

$$s^2 = \frac{(n_1 - 1)s_1^2 + (n_2 - 1)s_2^2}{n_1 + n_2 - 2}$$

The standard deviation of the test statistic can be estimated as:

$$s_{\overline{\chi}_1 - \overline{\chi}_2} = \sqrt{s^2\left(\frac{1}{n_1} + \frac{1}{n_2}\right)}$$

The appropriate value of $t$ can be calculated as:

$$t = \frac{(\overline{\chi}_1 - \overline{\chi}_2) - (\mu_1 - \mu_2)}{s_{\overline{\chi}_1 - \overline{\chi}_2}}$$

The degrees of freedom in this case are $(n_1 + n_2 - 2)$.

If the two populations have unequal variances, an exact $t$ cannot be computed for the difference in sample means. Instead, an approximation to $t$ is computed. The number of degrees of freedom in this case is usually not an integer, but a reasonably accurate probability can be obtained by rounding to the nearest integer.[15]

An **F *test*** of sample variance may be performed if it is not known whether the two populations have equal variance. In this case the hypotheses are:

$$H_0: \sigma_1^2 = \sigma_2^2$$
$$H_1: \sigma_1^2 \neq \sigma_2^2$$

The **F *statistic*** is computed from the sample variances as follows:

$$F_{(n_1 - 1),\ (n_2 - 1)} = \frac{s_1^2}{s_2^2}$$

where

$$n_1 = \text{size of sample 1}$$
$$n_2 = \text{size of sample 2}$$
$$n_1 - 1 = \text{degrees of freedom for sample 1}$$
$$n_2 - 1 = \text{degrees of freedom for sample 2}$$
$$s_1^2 = \text{sample variance for sample 1}$$
$$s_2^2 = \text{sample variance for sample 2}$$

**F *test***
A statistical test of the equality of the variances of two populations.

**F *statistic***
The $F$ statistic is computed as the ratio of two sample variances.

**F *distribution***
A frequency distribution that depends upon two sets of degrees of freedom—the degrees of freedom in the numerator and the degrees of freedom in the denominator.

As can be seen, the critical value of the **F *distribution*** depends upon two sets of degrees of freedom—those in the numerator and those in the denominator. The critical values of $F$ for various degrees of freedom for the numerator and denominator are given in Table 5 of the Statistical Appendix. If the probability of $F$ is greater than the significance level $\alpha$, $H_0$ is not rejected, and $t$ based on the pooled variance estimate can be used. On the other hand, if the probability of $F$ is less than or equal to $\alpha$, $H_0$ is rejected and $t$ based on a separate variance estimate is used.

Using the data of Table 15.1, suppose we wanted to determine whether Internet usage was different for males as compared to females. A two-independent-samples $t$ test was conducted. The results are presented in Table 15.14. Note that the $F$ test of sample variances has a probability that is less than 0.05. Accordingly, $H_0$ is rejected, and the $t$ test based on the "equal variances not assumed" should be used. The $t$ value is $-4.492$ and, with 18.014 degrees of freedom, this gives a probability of 0.000, which is less than the significance level of 0.05. Therefore, the null hypothesis of equal means is rejected. Because the mean usage for males (sex = 1) is 9.333 and that for females (sex = 2) is 3.867, males use the Internet to a significantly greater extent than females. We also show the $t$ test assuming equal variances because most computer programs automatically conduct the $t$ test both ways.

**REAL RESEARCH**

## Stores Seek to Suit Elderly to a "t"

A study based on a national sample of 789 respondents who were age 65 or older attempted to determine the effect that lack of mobility has on patronage behavior. A major research question related to the differences in the physical requirements of dependent and self-reliant elderly persons. That is, did the two groups require different things to get to the store or after they arrived at the store? A more detailed analysis of the physical requirements conducted by two-independent-sample $t$ tests (shown in the table) indicated that dependent elderly persons are more likely to look for stores that offer home delivery and phone orders, and stores to which they have accessible transportation. They are also more likely to look for a variety of stores located close together. Retailers, now more than ever, are realizing the sales potential in the elderly market. With the Baby Boomer generation nearing retirement in 2005, stores such as Wal-Mart, Coldwater Creek, and Williams-Sonoma see "the icing on the cake." The elderly shoppers are more likely to spend more money and become patrons of a store.[16]

Differences in Physical Requirements Between Dependent and Self-Reliant Elderly

| | *Mean*[a] | | |
|---|---|---|---|
| *Physical Requirement Items* | *Self-reliant* | *Dependent* | *t Test Probability* |
| Delivery to home | 1.787 | 2.000 | 0.023 |
| Phone-in order | 2.030 | 2.335 | 0.003 |
| Transportation to store | 2.188 | 3.098 | 0.000 |
| Convenient parking | 4.001 | 4.095 | 0.305 |
| Location close to home | 3.177 | 3.325 | 0.137 |
| Variety of stores close together | 3.456 | 3.681 | 0.023 |

[a]Measured on a five-point scale from not important (1) to very important (5). ■

In this example, we tested the difference between means. A similar test is available for testing the difference between proportions for two independent samples.

***Proportions.***    The case involving proportions for two independent samples is also illustrated using the data of Table 15.1, which gives the number of males and females who use the Internet for shopping. Is the proportion of respondents using the Internet for shopping the same for males and females? The null and alternative hypotheses are:

$$H_0: \pi_1 = \pi_2$$
$$H_1: \pi_1 \neq \pi_2$$

A $z$ test is used as in testing the proportion for one sample. However, in this case the test statistic is given by:

$$z = \frac{P_1 - P_2}{s_{P_1 - P_2}}$$

**TABLE 15.14**

**Two-Independent-Samples *t* Test**

SUMMARY STATISTICS

| | NUMBER OF CASES | MEAN | STANDARD ERROR MEAN |
|---|---|---|---|
| Male | 15 | 9.333 | 1.137 |
| Female | 15 | 3.867 | 0.435 |

*F* TEST FOR EQUALITY OF VARIANCES

| *F* VALUE | 2-TAIL PROBABILITY |
|---|---|
| 15.507 | 0.000 |

*T* TEST

| EQUAL VARIANCES ASSUMED | | | EQUAL VARIANCES NOT ASSUMED | | |
|---|---|---|---|---|---|
| *T* VALUE | DEGREES OF FREEDOM | 2-TAIL PROBABILITY | *T* VALUE | DEGREES OF FREEDOM | 2-TAIL PROBABILITY |
| −4.492 | 28 | 0.000 | −4.492 | 18.014 | 0.000 |

In the test statistic, the numerator is the difference between the proportions in the two samples, $P_1$ and $P_2$. The denominator is the standard error of the difference in the two proportions and is given by

$$s_{P_1-P_2} = \sqrt{P(1-P)\left(\frac{1}{n_1} + \frac{1}{n_2}\right)}$$

where

$$P = \frac{n_1 P_1 + n_2 P_2}{n_1 + n_2}$$

A significance level of $\alpha = 0.05$ is selected. Given the data of Table 15.1, the test statistic can be calculated as:

$$P_1 - P_2 = (11/15) - (6/15)$$
$$= 0.733 - 0.400 = 0.333$$

$$P = (15 \times 0.733 + 15 \times 0.4)/(15 + 15) = 0.567$$

$$s_{P_1-P_2} = \sqrt{0.567 \times 0.433\left(\frac{1}{15} + \frac{1}{15}\right)} = 0.181$$

$$z = 0.333/0.181 = 1.84$$

Given a two-tail test, the area to the right of the critical value is $\alpha/2$ or 0.025. Hence, the critical value of the test statistic is 1.96. Because the calculated value is less than the critical value, the null hypothesis can not be rejected. Thus, the proportion of users (0.733) for males and (0.400) for females is not significantly different for the two samples. Note that although the difference is substantial, it is not statistically significant due to the small sample sizes (15 in each group).

## Paired Samples

*paired samples*

In hypothesis testing, the observations are paired so that the two sets of observations relate to the same respondents.

*paired samples t test*

A test for differences in the means of paired samples.

In many marketing research applications, the observations for the two groups are not selected from independent samples. Rather, the observations relate to *paired samples* in that the two sets of observations relate to the same respondents. A sample of respondents may rate two competing brands, indicate the relative importance of two attributes of a product, or evaluate a brand at two different times. The difference in these cases is examined by a *paired samples t test.* To compute *t* for paired samples, the paired difference variable, denoted by *D,* is formed and its mean and variance calculated. Then the *t* statistic is computed. The degrees of freedom are $n - 1$, where *n* is the number of pairs. The relevant formulas are:

$$H_0: \mu_D = 0$$
$$H_1: \mu_D \neq 0$$

$$t_{n-1} = \frac{\overline{D} - \mu_D}{\frac{s_D}{\sqrt{n}}}$$

where

$$\overline{D} = \frac{\sum_{i=1}^{n} D_i}{n}$$

$$s_D = \sqrt{\frac{\sum_{i=1}^{n} (D_i - \overline{D})^2}{n-1}}$$

$$S_{\overline{D}} = \frac{S_D}{\sqrt{n}}$$

## TABLE 15.15

**Paired Samples *t* Test**

| Variable | Number of Cases | Mean | Standard Deviation | Standard Error |
|---|---|---|---|---|
| Internet Attitude | 30 | 5.167 | 1.234 | 0.225 |
| Technology Attitude | 30 | 4.100 | 1.398 | 0.255 |

Difference = Internet − Technology

| Difference Mean | Standard Deviation | Standard Error | Correlation | 2-Tail Probability | *T* Value | Degrees of Freedom | 2-Tail Probability |
|---|---|---|---|---|---|---|---|
| 1.067 | 0.828 | 0.1511 | 0.809 | 0.000 | 7.059 | 29 | 0.000 |

In the Internet usage example (Table 15.1), a paired *t* test could be used to determine if the respondents differed in their attitude toward the Internet and attitude toward technology. The resulting output is shown in Table 15.15. The mean attitude toward the Internet is 5.167 and that toward technology is 4.10. The mean difference between the variables is 1.067, with a standard deviation of 0.828 and a standard error of 0.1511. This results in a *t* value of (1.067/0.1511) 7.06, with 30 − 1 = 29 degrees of freedom and a probability of less than 0.001. Therefore, the respondents have a more favorable attitude toward the Internet as compared to technology in general. Another application is provided in the context of determining the relative effectiveness of 15-second versus 30-second television commercials.

## REAL RESEARCH

### *Seconds Count*

A survey of 83 media directors of the largest Canadian advertising agencies was conducted to determine the relative effectiveness of 15-second versus 30-second commercial advertisements. Using a five-point rating scale (1 being excellent and 5 being poor), 15- and 30-second commercials were rated by each respondent for brand awareness, main idea recall, persuasion, and ability to tell an emotional story. The table indicates that 30-second commercials were rated more favorably on all the dimensions. Paired *t* tests indicated that these differences were significant, and the 15-second commercials were evaluated as less effective. Today, the problem may not be how effective are television commercials, but will the consumers actually be watching the commercials. One in five users never watched a commercial in 2002, and there is a threat that this number will increase in the future. Heavy advertisers such as General Motors will have to come up with more effective and creative ways to show their commercials.[17]

Mean Rating of 15- and 30-Second Commercials on the Four Communication Variables

| Brand Awareness | | Main Idea Recall | | Persuasion | | Ability to Tell Emotional Story | |
|---|---|---|---|---|---|---|---|
| *15* | *30* | *15* | *30* | *15* | *30* | *15* | *30* |
| 2.5 | 1.9 | 2.7 | 2.0 | 3.7 | 2.1 | 4.3 | 1.9 |

The difference in proportions for paired samples can be tested by using the McNemar test or the chi-square test, as explained in the following section on nonparametric tests.

## NONPARAMETRIC TESTS

Nonparametric tests are used when the independent variables are nonmetric. Like parametric tests, nonparametric tests are available for testing variables from one sample, two independent samples, or two related samples.

# One Sample

Sometimes the researcher wants to test whether the observations for a particular variable could reasonably have come from a particular distribution, such as the normal, uniform, or Poisson distribution. Knowledge of the distribution is necessary for finding probabilities corresponding to known values of the variable or variable values corresponding to known probabilities (see Appendix 12A). The **Kolmogorov-Smirnov (K-S) one-sample test** is one such goodness-of-fit test. The K-S compares the cumulative distribution function for a variable with a specified distribution. $A_i$ denotes the cumulative relative frequency for each category of the theoretical (assumed) distribution, and $O_i$ the comparable value of the sample frequency. The K-S test is based on the maximum value of the absolute difference between $A_i$ and $O_i$. The test statistic is

$$K = \text{Max} \mid A_i - O_i \mid$$

The decision to reject the null hypothesis is based on the value of $K$. The larger the $K$ is, the more confidence we have that $H_0$ is false. For $\alpha = 0.05$, the critical value of $K$ for large samples (over 35) is given by $1.36/\sqrt{n}$.[18] Alternatively, $K$ can be transformed into a normally distributed $z$ statistic and its associated probability determined.

In the context of the Internet usage example, suppose we wanted to test whether the distribution of Internet usage was normal. A K-S one-sample test is conducted, yielding the data shown in Table 15.16. The largest absolute difference between the observed and normal distribution was $K = 0.222$. Although our sample size is only 30 (less than 35), we can use the approximate formula and the critical value for $K$ is $1.36/\sqrt{30} = 0.248$. Because the calculated value of $K$ is smaller than the critical value, the null hypothesis cannot be rejected. Alternatively, Table 15.16 indicates that the probability of observing a $K$ value of 0.222, as determined by the normalized $z$ statistic, is 0.103. Because this is more than the significance level of 0.05, the null hypothesis can not be rejected, leading to the same conclusion. Hence, the distribution of Internet usage does not deviate significantly from the normal distribution.

As mentioned earlier, the chi-square test can also be performed on a single variable from one sample. In this context, the chi-square serves as a goodness-of-fit test. It tests whether a significant difference exists between the observed number of cases in each category and the expected number. Other one-sample nonparametric tests include the runs test and the binomial test. The **runs test** is a test of randomness for the dichotomous variables. This test is conducted by determining whether the order or sequence in which observations are obtained is random. The **binomial test** is also a goodness-of-fit test for dichotomous variables. It tests the goodness of fit of the observed number of observations in each category to the number expected under a specified binomial distribution. For more information on these tests, refer to standard statistical literature.[19]

# Two Independent Samples

When the difference in the location of two populations is to be compared based on observations from two independent samples, and the variable is measured on an ordinal scale, the **Mann-Whitney U test** can be used.[20] This test corresponds to the two-independent-sample $t$ test for interval scale variables, when the variances of the two populations are assumed equal.

**Kolmogorov-Smirnov one-sample test**
A one-sample nonparametric goodness-of-fit test that compares the cumulative distribution function for a variable with a specified distribution.

**runs test**
A test of randomness for a dichotomous variable.

**binomial test**
A goodness-of-fit statistical test for dichotomous variables. It tests the goodness of fit of the observed number of observations in each category to the number expected under a specified binomial distribution.

**Mann-Whitney U test**
A statistical test for a variable measured on an ordinal scale comparing the difference in the location of two populations based on observations from two independent samples.

**TABLE 15.16**

**K-S One-Sample Test for Normality for Internet Usage**

TEST DISTRIBUTION—NORMAL

| | |
|---|---|
| Mean: | 6.600 |
| Standard Deviation: | 4.296 |
| Cases: | 30 |

MOST EXTREME DIFFERENCES

| ABSOLUTE | POSITIVE | NEGATIVE | K-S z | 2-TAILED P |
|---|---|---|---|---|
| 0.222 | 0.222 | −0.142 | 1.217 | 0.103 |

## TABLE 15.17

**Mann-Whitney *U* Test**

MANN-WHITNEY *U*—WILCOXON RANK SUM *W* TEST

INTERNET USAGE BY SEX

| SEX | MEAN RANK | CASES |
|---|---|---|
| Male | 20.93 | 15 |
| Female | 10.07 | 15 |
| Total | | 30 |

| *U* | *W* | *z* | CORRECTED FOR TIES 2-TAILED *P* |
|---|---|---|---|
| 31.000 | 151.000 | −3.406 | 0.001 |

Note
*U* = Mann-Whitney test statistic
*W* = Wilcoxon *W* Statistic
*z* = *U* transformed into a normally distributed *z* statistic

In the Mann-Whitney *U* test, the two samples are combined and the cases are ranked in order of increasing size. The test statistic, *U,* is computed as the number of times a score from sample 1 or group 1 precedes a score from group 2. If the samples are from the same population, the distribution of scores from the two groups in the rank list should be random. An extreme value of *U* would indicate a nonrandom pattern, pointing to the inequality of the two groups. For samples of less than 30, the exact significance level for *U* is computed. For larger samples, *U* is transformed into a normally distributed *z* statistic. This *z* can be corrected for ties within ranks.

We examine again the difference in the Internet usage of males and females. This time, though, the Mann-Whitney *U* test is used. The results are given in Table 15.17. Again, a significant difference is found between the two groups, corroborating the results of the two-independent-samples *t* test reported earlier. Because the ranks are assigned from the smallest observation to the largest, the higher mean rank (20.93) of males indicates that they use the Internet to a greater extent than females (mean rank = 10.07).

Researchers often wish to test for a significant difference in proportions obtained from two independent samples. As an alternative to the parametric *z* test considered earlier, one could also use the cross-tabulation procedure to conduct a chi-square test.[21] In this case, we will have a 2 × 2 table. One variable will be used to denote the sample and will assume the value 1 for sample 1 and the value of 2 for sample 2. The other variable will be the binary variable of interest.

Two other independent-samples nonparametric tests are the median test and Kolmogorov-Smirnov test. The ***two-sample median test*** determines whether the two groups are drawn from populations with the same median. It is not as powerful as the Mann-Whitney *U* test because it merely uses the location of each observation relative to the median, and not the rank, of each observation. The ***Kolmogorov-Smirnov two-sample test*** examines whether the two distributions are the same. It takes into account any differences between the two distributions, including the median, dispersion, and skewness, as illustrated by the following example.

**two-sample median test**
Nonparametric test statistic that determines whether two groups are drawn from populations with the same median. This test is not as powerful as the Mann-Whitney *U.*

**Kolmogorov-Smirnov two-sample test**
Nonparametric test statistic that determines whether two distributions are the same. It takes into account any differences in the two distributions including median, dispersion, and skewness.

## REAL RESEARCH

### Directors Change Direction

How do marketing research directors and users in Fortune 500 manufacturing firms perceive the role of marketing research in initiating changes in marketing strategy formulation? It was found that the marketing research directors were more strongly in favor of initiating changes in strategy and less in favor of holding back than were users of marketing research. The users of marketing research had become even more reluctant to initiate marketing strategy changes during the economic slowdown of 2002 and 2003. In today's business climate, however, the reluctance of these marketing research users must be overcome to help gain a better understanding of the buyer's power. The percentage responses to one of the items, "Initiate change in the marketing strategy of the firm whenever possible," are given below. Using the Kolmogorov-Smirnov (K-S) test, these differences of role definition were statistically significant at the 0.05 level, as shown in the table.[22]

The Role of Marketing Research in Strategy Formulation

| | | Responses (%) | | | | |
|---|---|---|---|---|---|---|
| Sample | n | Absolutely Must | Preferably Should | May or May Not | Preferably Should Not | Absolutely Must Not |
| D | 77 | 7 | 26 | 43 | 19 | 5 |
| U | 68 | 2 | 15 | 32 | 35 | 16 |

K-S Significance = 0.05
*D = Directors, U = users ▪

In this example, the marketing research directors and users comprised two independent samples. However, the samples are not always independent. In the case of paired samples, a different set of tests should be used.

## Paired Samples

An important nonparametric test for examining differences in the location of two populations based on paired observations is the ***Wilcoxon matched-pairs signed-ranks test.*** This test analyzes the differences between the paired observations, taking into account the magnitude of the differences. It computes the differences between the pairs of variables and ranks the absolute differences. The next step is to sum the positive and negative ranks. The test statistic, $z$, is computed from the positive and negative rank sums. Under the null hypothesis of no difference, $z$ is a standard normal variate with mean 0 and variance 1 for large samples. This test corresponds to the paired $t$ test considered earlier.[23]

The example considered for the paired $t$ test, whether the respondents differed in terms of attitude toward the Internet and attitude toward technology, is considered again. Suppose we assume that both these variables are measured on ordinal rather than interval scales. Accordingly, we use the Wilcoxon test. The results are shown in Table 15.18. Again, a significant difference is found in the variables, and results are in accordance with the conclusion reached by the paired $t$ test. There are 23 negative differences (attitude toward technology is less favorable than attitude toward Internet). The mean rank of these negative differences is 12.72. On the other hand, there is only one positive difference (attitude toward technology is more favorable than attitude toward Internet). The mean rank of this difference is 7.50. There are six ties, or observations with the same value for both variables. These numbers indicate that the attitude toward the Internet is more favorable than toward technology. Furthermore, the probability associated with the $z$ statistic is less than 0.05, indicating that the difference is indeed significant.

Another paired sample nonparametric test is the ***sign test.***[24] This test is not as powerful as the Wilcoxon matched-pairs signed-ranks test, as it compares only the signs of

**TABLE 15.18**

**Wilcoxon Matched-Pairs Signed-Rank Test**

| | INTERNET WITH TECHNOLOGY | |
|---|---|---|
| (TECHNOLOGY—INTERNET) | CASES | MEAN RANK |
| − Ranks | 23 | 12.72 |
| + Ranks | 1 | 7.50 |
| Ties | 6 | |
| Total | 30 | |
| $z = -4.207$ | | 2-tailed $p = 0.0000$ |

## TABLE 15.19

**A Summary of Hypothesis Tests Related to Differences**

| SAMPLE | APPLICATION | LEVEL OF SCALING | TEST/COMMENTS |
|---|---|---|---|
| **ONE SAMPLE** | | | |
| One sample | Distributions | Nonmetric | K-S and chi-square for goodness of fit<br>Runs test for randomness<br>Binomial test for goodness of fit for dichotomous variables |
| One sample | Means | Metric | $t$ test, if variance is unknown<br>$z$ test, if variance is known |
| One Sample | Proportions | Metric | $z$ test |
| **TWO INDEPENDENT SAMPLES** | | | |
| Two independent samples | Distributions | Nonmetric | K-S two-sample test for examining the equivalence of two distributions |
| Two independent samples | Means | Metric | Two-group $t$ test<br>$F$ test for equality of variances |
| Two independent samples | Proportions | Metric<br>Nonmetric | $z$ test<br>Chi-square test |
| Two independent samples | Rankings/Medians | Nonmetric | Mann-Whitney $U$ test is more powerful than the median test |
| **PAIRED SAMPLES** | | | |
| Paired samples | Means | Metric | Paired $t$ test |
| Paired samples | Proportions | Nonmetric | McNemar test for binary variables<br>Chi-square test |
| Paired samples | Rankings/Medians | Nonmetric | Wilcoxon matched-pairs ranked-signs test is more powerful than the sign test |

the differences between pairs of variables without taking into account the ranks. In the special case of a binary variable where the researcher wishes to test differences in proportions, the McNemar test can be used. Alternatively, the chi-square test can also be used for binary variables. The various parametric and nonparametric tests for differences are summarized in Table 15.19. The tests in Table 15.19 can be easily related to those in Figure 15.9. Table 15.19 classifies the tests in more detail as parametric tests (based on metric data) are classified separately for means and proportions. Likewise, nonparametric tests (based on nonmetric data) are classified separately for distributions and rankings/medians. The next example illustrates the use of hypothesis testing in international branding strategy, and the example after that cites the use of descriptive statistics in research on ethics.

### REAL RESEARCH

## International Brand Equity—The Name of the Game

In the 2000s, the trend is toward global marketing. How can marketers market a brand abroad where there exists diverse historical and cultural differences? A study conducted in 2001 showed that, in general, a firm's international brand structure includes firm-based characteristics, product market characteristics, and market dynamics. More specifically, according to Bob Kroll, the former president of Del Monte International, uniform packaging may be an asset to marketing internationally, yet catering to individual countries' culinary taste preferences is more important. One recent survey on international product marketing makes this clear. Marketing executives now believe it is best to think globally but act locally. Respondents included 100 brand and product managers and marketing people from some of the nation's largest food, pharmaceutical, and personal product companies. Thirty-nine percent said that it would not be a good idea to use uniform packaging in foreign markets, whereas 38 percent were in favor of it. Those in favor of regionally

Colgate toothpaste has followed a mixed strategy of standardized branding with customized packaging in some foreign markets. A two independent samples *t* test can be used to assess the effectiveness of this strategy.

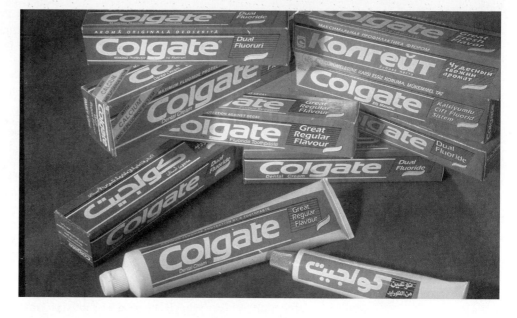

targeted packaging, however, mentioned the desirability of maintaining as much brand equity and package consistency as possible from market to market. But they also believed it was necessary to tailor the package to fit the linguistic and regulatory needs of different markets. Based on this finding, a suitable research question can be: Do consumers in different countries prefer to buy global name brands with different packaging customized to suit their local needs? Based on this research question, one can frame a hypothesis that, other things being constant, standardized branding with customized packaging for a well-established name brand will result in greater market share. The hypotheses may be formulated as follows:

$H_0$: Standardized branding with customized packaging for a well-established name brand will not lead to greater market share in the international market.

$H_1$: Other factors remaining equal, standardized branding with customized packaging for a well-established name brand will lead to greater market share in the international market.

To test the null hypothesis, a well-established brand such as Colgate toothpaste, which has followed a mixed strategy, can be selected. The market share in countries with standardized branding and standardized packaging can be compared with market share in countries with standardized branding and customized packaging, after controlling for the effect of other factors. A two-independent-samples *t* test can be used.[25] ∎

## REAL RESEARCH

### Statistics Describe Distrust

Descriptive statistics indicate that the public perception of ethics in business, and thus ethics in marketing, is poor. In a poll conducted by *Business Week,* 46 percent of those surveyed said that the ethical standards of business executives are only fair. A *Time* magazine survey revealed that 76 percent of Americans felt that business managers (and thus researchers) lacked ethics and this lack contributes to the decline of moral standards in the United States. However, the general public is not alone in its disparagement of business ethics. In a Touche Ross survey of businesspersons, results showed that the general feeling was that ethics were a serious concern and media portrayal of the lack of ethics in business has not been exaggerated. However, a research study conducted in late 2000 by the Ethics Resource Center of Washington, D.C., found that 90 percent of American businesspersons expected their organization to do what is right, not just what is profitable. Twelve percent of those polled said they felt pressure to compromise their organization's ethical standards. Twenty-six percent of those polled cited the most common ethical slip in the workplace to be lying to customers, other employees, vendors, or the public, whereas 25 percent cited withholding needed information from those parties. A mere 5 percent of those polled have seen people giving or taking bribes or inappropriate gifts. Despite the fact that American businesspersons expect their organization to conduct business in an ethical manner, these studies reveal that unethical behavior remains a common practice in the workplace.[26] ■

# INTERNET AND COMPUTER APPLICATIONS

The major programs for frequency distribution are FREQUENCIES (SPSS) and UNIVARIATE (SAS). Other programs provide only the frequency distribution (FREQ in SAS) or only some of the associated statistics (Exhibit 15.1).[27] In MINITAB, the main function is Stats>Descriptive Statistics. The output values include the mean, median, standard deviation, minimum, maximum, and quartiles. Histograms in a bar chart or graph can be produced from the Graph>Histogram selection. Several of the spreadsheets can also be used to obtain frequencies and descriptive statistics. In EXCEL, the Tools>Data Analysis function computes the descriptive statistics. The output produces the mean, standard error, median, mode, standard deviation, variance, kurtosis, skewness, range, minimum, maximum, sum, count, and confidence level. Frequencies can be selected under the Histogram function. A histogram can be produced in bar format.

The major cross-tabulation programs are CROSSTABS (SPSS) and FREQ (SAS). All these programs will display the cross-classification tables and provide cell counts, row and column percentages, the chi-square test for significance, and all the measures of the strength of the association that have been discussed. In addition, the TABULATE (SAS) program can be used for obtaining cell counts and row and column percentages, although it does not provide any of the associated statistics. In MINITAB, cross-tabulations (cross tabs) and chi-square are under the Stats>Tables function. Each of these features must be selected separately under the Tables function. The Data>Pivot Table function performs cross tabs in EXCEL. To do additional analysis or customize data, select a different summary function

*Exhibit 15.1*

Computer Programs for Frequencies

### SPSS

The main program in SPSS is FREQUENCIES. It produces a table of frequency counts, percentages, and cumulative percentages for the values of each variable. It gives all of the associated statistics except for the coefficient of variation. If the data are interval scaled and only the summary statistics are desired, the DESCRIPTIVES procedure can be used. All of the statistics computed by DESCRIPTIVES are available in FREQUENCIES. However, DESCRIPTIVES is more efficient because it does not sort values into a frequency table. An additional program, MEANS, computes means and standard deviations for a dependent variable over subgroups of cases defined by independent variables.

### SAS

The main program in SAS is UNIVARIATE. In addition to providing a frequency table, this program provides all of the associated statistics. Another procedure available is FREQ. For a one-way frequency distribution, FREQ does not provide any associated statistics. If only summary statistics are desired, procedures such as MEANS, SUMMARY, and TABULATE can be used. It should be noted that FREQ is not available as an independent program in the microcomputer version.

### Minitab

The main function is Stats>Descriptive Statistics. The output values include the mean, median, mode, standard deviation, minimum, maximum, and quartiles. Histograms in a bar chart or graph can be produced from the Graph>Histogram selection.

### Excel

The Tools>Data Analysis function computes the descriptive statistics. The output produces the mean, standard error, median, mode, standard deviation, variance, kurtosis, skewness, range, minimum, maximum, sum, count, and confidence level. Frequencies can be selected under the Histogram function. A histogram can be produced in bar format.

such as max, min, average, or standard deviation. In addition, a custom calculation can be selected to perform values based on other cells in the data plane. ChiTest can be accessed under the Insert>Function>Statistical>ChiTest function.

The major program for conducting *t* tests in SPSS is T-TEST. This program can be used to conduct *t* tests on independent as well as paired samples. All the nonparametric tests that we have discussed can be conducted by using the NPAR TESTS program. In SAS, the program T TEST can be used. The nonparametric tests may be conducted by using NPAR1WAY. This program will conduct the two-independent-samples tests (Mann-Whitney, median, and K-S) as well as the Wilcoxon test for paired samples. Parametric tests available in MINITAB in descriptive stat function are *z* test mean, *t* test of the mean, and 2-sample *t* test. The nonparametric tests can be accessed under the Stat>Time Series function. The output includes the one-sample sign, one-sample Wilcoxon, Mann-Whitney, Kruskal-Wallis, Mood's Median test, Friedman, runs test, pairwise average, pairwise differences, and pairwise slopes. The available parametric tests in EXCEL and other spreadsheets include the *t* test: paired two sample for means, *t* test: two independent samples assuming equal variances, *t* test: two independent samples assuming unequal variances, *z* test: two samples for means, and *F* test two samples for variances. Nonparametric tests are not available.

## SPSS Windows

The main program in SPSS is FREQUENCIES. It produces a table of frequency counts, percentages, and cumulative percentages for the values of each variable. It gives all of the associated statistics. If the data are interval scaled and only the summary statistics are desired, the DESCRIPTIVES procedure can be used. All of the statistics computed by DESCRIPTIVES are available in FREQUENCIES. However, DESCRIPTIVES is more efficient because it does not sort values into a frequency table. Moreover, the DESCRIPTIVES procedure displays summary statistics for several variables in a single table and can also calculate standardized values (*z* scores). The EXPLORE procedure produces summary statistics and graphical displays, either for all of cases or separately for groups of cases. Mean, median, variance, standard deviation, minimum, maximum, and range are some of the statistics that can be calculated.

To select these procedures, click:

Analyze>Descriptive Statistics>Frequencies
Analyze>Descriptive Statistics>Descriptives
Analyze>Descriptive Statistics>Explore

The major cross-tabulation program is CROSSTABS. This program will display the cross-classification tables and provide cell counts, row and column percentages, the chi-square test for significance, and all the measures of the strength of the association that have been discussed.

To select these procedures, click:

Analyze>Descriptive Statistics>Crosstabs

The major program for conducting parametric tests in SPSS is COMPARE MEANS. This program can be used to conduct *t* tests on one sample or independent or paired samples. To select these procedures using SPSS for Windows, click:

Analyze>Compare Means>Means . . .
Analyze>Compare Means>One-Sample T Test . . .
Analyze>Compare Means>Independent-Samples T Test . . .
Analyze>Compare Means>Paired-Samples T Test . . .

The nonparametric tests discussed in this chapter can be conducted using NONPARAMETRIC TESTS. To select these procedures using SPSS for Windows, click:

Analyze>Nonparametric Tests>Chi-Square . . .
Analyze>Nonparametric Tests>Binomial . . .
Analyze>Nonparametric Tests>Runs . . .
Analyze>Nonparametric Tests>1-Sample K-S . . .
Analyze>Nonparametric Tests>2 Independent Samples . . .
Analyze>Nonparametric Tests>2 Related Samples . . .

## FOCUS ON BURKE

The basic tool used by most researchers to examine their data is the cross-tabulation. It affords a quick look at the distribution of responses and may show any data problems. However, it can be misleading unless care is taken.

Burke completed a study for a client, which caused great concern for the client. The results from the Burke tables were very different from previous results from another research company. We use contrived data to illustrate the situation (the actual data are proprietary). This study was conducted among small businesses (fewer than 20 employees) concerning their use of temporary worker ("temp") agencies. A sample of 100 businesses with one employee was taken as well as a sample of 100 businesses with 2 to 19 employees. The following tabulation was created.

This was the type of table the client was accustomed to seeing. Do you believe that 52 percent of businesses used temporary assistance agencies? The Burke Corporate Information Center had census records that show that in the population there are 9.2 million one-person businesses and only 2.5 million businesses with 2 to 19 employees (from county business patterns). The weighted total column should look like the table below:

|  |  | *Number of Full-Time Employees* | | |
|---|---|---|---|---|
|  |  | *1* | *2 to 19* | *Total* |
|  | Base | 100 | 100 | 200 |
|  | Yes | 40 | 65 | 105 |
| Used |  | 40% | 65% | 52% |
| Temps? |  |  |  |  |
|  |  | 60 | 35 | 95 |
|  | No | 60% | 35% | 48% |

- A representative sample would have had 157 businesses with one employee and 43 with 2 to 19 employees.
- The weights are then 1.57 and 0.43 to create the total column.

The proper table would be as follows:

|  |  | *Number of Full-Time Employees* | | *Weighed* |
|---|---|---|---|---|
|  |  | *1* | *2 to 19* | *Total* |
|  | Base | 100 | 100 | 200 |
|  | Yes | 40 | 65 | 91 |
| Used |  | 40% | 65% | 45% |
| Temps? |  |  |  |  |
|  |  | 60 | 35 | 109 |
|  | No | 60% | 35% | 55% |

% sampled population = 1 emp. is 0.79

% sampled population = 2 to 19 emp. is 0.2

Now the client is told that 45 percent rather than 52 percent of companies with fewer than 20 employees use temporary employee agencies. This may not sound like a big change, but when the client saw the proper table, they realized that all of their historical trending had to be reconstructed. Never construct total columns in tabulations without considering the true distribution in the population.

# SUMMARY

Basic data analysis provides valuable insights and guides the rest of the data analysis as well as the interpretation of the results. A frequency distribution should be obtained for each variable in the data. This analysis produces a table of frequency counts, percentages, and cumulative percentages for all the values associated with that variable. It indicates the extent of out-of-range, missing, or extreme values. The mean, mode, and median of a frequency distribution are measures of central tendency. The variability of the distribution is described by the range, the variance or standard deviation, coefficient of variation, and interquartile range. Skewness and kurtosis provide an idea of the shape of the distribution.

Cross-tabulations are tables that reflect the joint distribution of two or more variables. In cross-tabulation, the percentages can be computed either columnwise, based on column totals, or rowwise, based on row totals. The general rule is to compute the percentages in the direction of the independent variable, across the dependent variable. Often the introduction of a third variable can provide additional insights. The chi-square statistic provides a test of the statistical significance of the observed association in a cross-tabulation. The phi coefficient, contingency coefficient, Cramer's *V,* and the lambda coefficient provide measures of the strength of association between the variables.

Parametric and nonparametric tests are available for testing hypotheses related to differences. In the parametric case, the *t* test is used to examine hypotheses related to the population mean. Different forms of the *t* test are suitable for testing hypotheses based on one sample, two independent samples, or paired samples. In the nonparametric case, popular one-sample tests include the Kolmogorov-Smirnov, chi-square, runs test, and the binomial test. For two independent nonparametric samples, the Mann-Whitney *U* test, median test, and the Kolmogorov-Smirnov test can be used. For paired samples, the Wilcoxon matched-pairs signed-ranks test and the sign test are useful for examining hypotheses related to measures of location.

# KEY TERMS AND CONCEPTS

frequency distribution, *427*
measures of location, *430*
mean, *430*
mode, *431*
median, *431*
measures of variability, *431*
range, *431*
interquartile range, *431*
variance, *431*
standard deviation, *432*
coefficient of variation, *432*
skewness, *432*
kurtosis, *433*
null hypothesis, *434*
alternative hypothesis, *434*
one-tailed test, *435*
two-tailed test, *435*
test statistic, *435*
type I error, *435*

level of significance, *435*
type II error, *436*
power of a test, *436*
cross-tabulation, *438*
contingency tables, *439*
chi-square statistic, *444*
chi-square distribution, *444*
phi coefficient, *445*
contingency coefficient (C), *446*
Cramer's *V, 446*
asymmetric lambda, *446*
symmetric lambda, *446*
tau *b, 447*
tau *c, 447*
gamma, *447*
parametric tests, *448*
nonparametric tests, *448*
*t* test, *448*
*t* statistic, *448*

*t* distribution, *449*
*z* test, *450*
independent samples, *450*
*F* test, *451*
*F* statistic, *451*
*F* distribution, *451*
paired samples, *453*
paired samples *t* test, *453*
Kolmogorov-Smirnov (K-S) one-sample test, *455*
runs test, *455*
binomial test, *455*
Mann-Whitney *U* test, *455*
two-sample median test, *456*
Kolmogorov-Smirnov two-sample test, *456*
Wilcoxon matched-pairs signed-ranks test, *457*
sign test, *457*

# EXERCISES

## *Questions*

1. Describe the procedure for computing frequencies.
2. What measures of location are commonly computed?
3. Define the interquartile range. What does it measure?
4. What is meant by the coefficient of variation?
5. How is the relative flatness or peakedness of a distribution measured?
6. What is a skewed distribution? What does it mean?
7. What is the major difference between cross-tabulation and frequency distribution?
8. What is the general rule for computing percentages in cross-tabulation?
9. Define a spurious correlation.
10. What is meant by a suppressed association? How is it revealed?
11. Discuss the reasons for the frequent use of cross-tabulations. What are some of its limitations?

12. Present a classification of hypothesis testing procedures.
13. Describe the general procedure for conducting a *t* test.
14. What is the major difference between parametric and nonparametric tests?
15. Which nonparametric tests are the counterparts of the two-independent-samples *t* test for parametric data?
16. Which nonparametric tests are the counterparts of the paired samples *t* test for parametric data?

## *Problems*

1. In each of the following situations, indicate the statistical analysis you would conduct and the appropriate test or test statistic that should be used.
   a. Consumer preferences for Camay bathing soap were obtained on an 11-point Likert scale. The same consumers were then shown a commercial about Camay. After the

commercial, preferences for Camay were again measured. Has the commercial been successful in inducing a change in preferences?

b. Does the preference for Camay soap follow a normal distribution?

c. Respondents in a survey of 1,000 households were classified as heavy, medium, light, or nonusers of ice cream. They were also classified as being in high-, medium-, or low-income categories. Is the consumption of ice cream related to income level?

d. In a survey using a representative sample of 2,000 households from the Market Facts consumer mail panel, the respondents were asked to rank 10 department stores, including Sears, in order of preference. The sample was divided into small and large households based on a median split of the household size. Does preference for shopping in Sears vary by household size?

2. The current advertising campaign for a major soft drink brand would be changed if less than 30 percent of the consumers like it.
   a. Formulate the null and alternative hypotheses.
   b. Discuss the type I and type II errors that could occur in hypothesis testing.
   c. Which statistical test would you use? Why?
   d. A random sample of 300 consumers was surveyed, and 84 respondents indicated that they liked the campaign. Should the campaign be changed? Why?

3. A major department store chain is having an end-of-season sale on refrigerators. The number of refrigerators sold during this sale at a sample of 10 stores was:

   80   110   0   40   70   80   100   50   80   30

   a. Is there evidence that an average of more than 50 refrigerators per store were sold during this sale? Use $\alpha = 0.05$.
   b. What assumption is necessary to perform this test?

# INTERNET AND COMPUTER EXERCISES

1. In a pretest, data were obtained from 45 respondents on Nike. These data are given in the following table, which gives the usage, sex, awareness, attitude, preference, intention, and loyalty toward Nike of a sample of Nike users. Usage has been coded as 1, 2, or 3, representing light, medium, or heavy users. The sex has been coded as 1 for females and 2 for males. Awareness, attitude, preference, intention, and loyalty are measured on seven-point Likert type scales (1 = very unfavorable, 7 = very favorable). Note that five respondents have missing values that are denoted by 9.

| Number | Usage | Sex | Awareness | Attitude | Preference | Intention | Loyalty |
|---|---|---|---|---|---|---|---|
| 1 | 3 | 2 | 7 | 6 | 5 | 5 | 6 |
| 2 | 1 | 1 | 2 | 2 | 4 | 6 | 5 |
| 3 | 1 | 1 | 3 | 3 | 6 | 7 | 6 |
| 4 | 3 | 2 | 6 | 5 | 5 | 3 | 2 |
| 5 | 3 | 2 | 5 | 4 | 7 | 4 | 3 |
| 6 | 2 | 2 | 4 | 3 | 5 | 2 | 3 |
| 7 | 2 | 1 | 5 | 4 | 4 | 3 | 2 |
| 8 | 1 | 1 | 2 | 1 | 3 | 4 | 5 |
| 9 | 2 | 2 | 4 | 4 | 3 | 6 | 5 |
| 10 | 1 | 1 | 3 | 1 | 2 | 4 | 5 |
| 11 | 3 | 2 | 6 | 7 | 6 | 4 | 5 |
| 12 | 3 | 2 | 6 | 5 | 6 | 4 | 4 |
| 13 | 1 | 1 | 4 | 3 | 3 | 1 | 1 |
| 14 | 3 | 2 | 6 | 4 | 5 | 3 | 2 |
| 15 | 1 | 2 | 4 | 3 | 4 | 5 | 6 |
| 16 | 1 | 2 | 3 | 4 | 2 | 4 | 2 |
| 17 | 3 | 1 | 7 | 6 | 4 | 5 | 3 |
| 18 | 2 | 1 | 6 | 5 | 4 | 3 | 2 |
| 19 | 1 | 1 | 1 | 1 | 3 | 4 | 5 |
| 20 | 3 | 1 | 5 | 7 | 4 | 1 | 2 |
| 21 | 3 | 2 | 6 | 6 | 7 | 7 | 5 |
| 22 | 2 | 2 | 2 | 3 | 1 | 4 | 2 |
| 23 | 1 | 1 | 1 | 1 | 3 | 2 | 2 |
| 24 | 3 | 1 | 6 | 7 | 6 | 7 | 6 |
| 25 | 1 | 2 | 3 | 2 | 2 | 1 | 1 |
| 26 | 2 | 2 | 5 | 3 | 4 | 4 | 5 |
| 27 | 3 | 2 | 7 | 6 | 6 | 5 | 7 |
| 28 | 2 | 1 | 6 | 4 | 2 | 5 | 6 |
| 29 | 1 | 1 | 9 | 2 | 3 | 1 | 3 |
| 30 | 2 | 2 | 5 | 9 | 4 | 6 | 5 |
| 31 | 1 | 2 | 1 | 2 | 9 | 3 | 2 |
| 32 | 1 | 2 | 4 | 6 | 5 | 9 | 3 |
| 33 | 2 | 1 | 3 | 4 | 3 | 2 | 9 |
| 34 | 2 | 1 | 4 | 6 | 5 | 7 | 6 |
| 35 | 3 | 1 | 5 | 7 | 7 | 3 | 3 |
| 36 | 3 | 1 | 6 | 5 | 7 | 3 | 4 |
| 37 | 3 | 2 | 6 | 7 | 5 | 3 | 4 |
| 38 | 3 | 2 | 5 | 6 | 4 | 3 | 2 |
| 39 | 3 | 2 | 7 | 7 | 6 | 3 | 4 |
| 40 | 1 | 1 | 4 | 3 | 4 | 6 | 5 |
| 41 | 1 | 1 | 2 | 3 | 4 | 5 | 6 |
| 42 | 1 | 1 | 1 | 3 | 2 | 3 | 4 |
| 43 | 1 | 1 | 2 | 4 | 3 | 6 | 7 |
| 44 | 1 | 1 | 3 | 3 | 4 | 6 | 5 |
| 45 | 1 | 1 | 1 | 1 | 4 | 5 | 3 |

Analyze the Nike data to answer the following questions. In each case, formulate the null and the alternative hypotheses and conduct the appropriate statistical test(s).

a. Obtain a frequency distribution for each of the following variables and calculate the relevant statistics: awareness, attitude, preference, intention, and loyalty toward Nike.

b. Conduct a cross-tabulation of the usage with sex. Interpret the results.

c. Does the awareness for Nike exceed 3.0?

d. Do the males and females differ in their awareness for Nike? Their attitude toward Nike? Their loyalty for Nike?

e. Do the respondents in the pretest have a higher level of awareness than loyalty?

f. Does awareness of Nike follow a normal distribution?

g. Is the distribution of preference for Nike normal?

h. Assume that awareness toward Nike was measured on an ordinal scale rather than an interval scale. Do males and females differ in their awareness toward Nike?

i. Assume that loyalty toward Nike was measured on an ordinal scale rather than an interval scale. Do males and females differ in their loyalty toward Nike?

j. Assume that attitude and loyalty toward Nike were measured on an ordinal scale rather than an interval scale. Do the respondents have greater awareness of Nike than loyalty for Nike?

2. In a pretest, respondents were asked to express their preference for an outdoor lifestyle using a seven-point scale, 1 = not at all preferred, 7 = greatly preferred (V1). They were also asked to

indicate the importance of the following variables on a seven-point scale, 1 = not at all important, 7 = very important.

V2 = enjoying nature
V3 = relating to the weather
V4 = living in harmony with the environment
V5 = exercising regularly
V6 = meeting other people

The sex of the respondent (V7) was coded as 1 for females and 2 for males. The location of residence (V8) was coded as: 1 = midtown/downtown, 2 = suburbs, and 3 = countryside. The data obtained are given in the following.

| V1 | V2 | V3 | V4 | V5 | V6 | V7 | V8 |
|------|------|------|------|------|------|------|------|
| 7.00 | 3.00 | 6.00 | 4.00 | 5.00 | 2.00 | 1.00 | 1.00 |
| 1.00 | 1.00 | 1.00 | 2.00 | 1.00 | 2.00 | 1.00 | 1.00 |
| 6.00 | 2.00 | 5.00 | 4.00 | 4.00 | 5.00 | 1.00 | 1.00 |
| 4.00 | 3.00 | 4.00 | 6.00 | 3.00 | 2.00 | 1.00 | 1.00 |
| 1.00 | 2.00 | 2.00 | 3.00 | 1.00 | 2.00 | 1.00 | 1.00 |
| 6.00 | 3.00 | 5.00 | 4.00 | 6.00 | 2.00 | 1.00 | 1.00 |
| 5.00 | 3.00 | 4.00 | 3.00 | 4.00 | 5.00 | 1.00 | 1.00 |
| 6.00 | 4.00 | 5.00 | 4.00 | 5.00 | 1.00 | 1.00 | 1.00 |
| 3.00 | 3.00 | 2.00 | 2.00 | 2.00 | 2.00 | 1.00 | 1.00 |
| 2.00 | 4.00 | 2.00 | 6.00 | 2.00 | 2.00 | 1.00 | 1.00 |
| 6.00 | 4.00 | 5.00 | 3.00 | 5.00 | 5.00 | 1.00 | 2.00 |
| 2.00 | 3.00 | 1.00 | 4.00 | 2.00 | 1.00 | 1.00 | 2.00 |
| 7.00 | 2.00 | 6.00 | 4.00 | 5.00 | 6.00 | 1.00 | 2.00 |
| 4.00 | 6.00 | 4.00 | 5.00 | 3.00 | 3.00 | 1.00 | 2.00 |
| 1.00 | 3.00 | 1.00 | 2.00 | 1.00 | 4.00 | 1.00 | 2.00 |
| 6.00 | 6.00 | 6.00 | 3.00 | 4.00 | 5.00 | 2.00 | 2.00 |
| 5.00 | 5.00 | 6.00 | 4.00 | 4.00 | 6.00 | 2.00 | 2.00 |
| 7.00 | 7.00 | 4.00 | 4.00 | 7.00 | 7.00 | 2.00 | 2.00 |
| 2.00 | 6.00 | 3.00 | 7.00 | 4.00 | 3.00 | 2.00 | 2.00 |
| 3.00 | 7.00 | 3.00 | 6.00 | 4.00 | 4.00 | 2.00 | 2.00 |
| 1.00 | 5.00 | 2.00 | 6.00 | 3.00 | 3.00 | 2.00 | 3.00 |
| 5.00 | 6.00 | 4.00 | 7.00 | 5.00 | 6.00 | 2.00 | 3.00 |
| 2.00 | 4.00 | 1.00 | 5.00 | 4.00 | 4.00 | 2.00 | 3.00 |
| 4.00 | 7.00 | 4.00 | 7.00 | 4.00 | 6.00 | 2.00 | 3.00 |
| 6.00 | 7.00 | 4.00 | 2.00 | 1.00 | 7.00 | 2.00 | 3.00 |
| 3.00 | 6.00 | 4.00 | 6.00 | 4.00 | 4.00 | 2.00 | 3.00 |
| 4.00 | 7.00 | 7.00 | 4.00 | 2.00 | 5.00 | 2.00 | 3.00 |
| 3.00 | 7.00 | 2.00 | 6.00 | 4.00 | 3.00 | 2.00 | 3.00 |
| 4.00 | 6.00 | 3.00 | 7.00 | 2.00 | 7.00 | 2.00 | 3.00 |
| 5.00 | 6.00 | 2.00 | 6.00 | 7.00 | 2.00 | 2.00 | 3.00 |

Using a statistical package of your choice, please answer the following questions. In each case, formulate the null and the alternative hypotheses and conduct the appropriate statistical test(s).

a. Does the mean preference for an outdoor lifestyle exceed 3.0?
b. Does the mean importance of enjoying nature exceed 3.5?
c. Does the mean preference for an outdoor lifestyle differ for males and females?
d. Does the importance attached to V2 to V6 differ for males and females?
e. Do the respondents attach more importance to enjoying nature than they do to relating to the weather?
f. Do the respondents attach more importance to relating to the weather than they do to meeting other people?
g. Do the respondents attach more importance to living in harmony with the environment than they do to exercising regularly?
h. Does the importance attached to V2 to V6 differ for males and females if these variables are treated as ordinal rather than interval scaled?
i. Do the respondents attach more importance to relating to the weather than they do to meeting other people if these variables are treated as ordinal rather than interval?

3. Use one of the mainframe statistical packages (SPSS, SAS, MINITAB, or EXCEL) to conduct the following analysis for the soft drink data that you have collected as part of your fieldwork (described later).

a. Obtain a frequency distribution of the weekly soft drink consumption.
b. Obtain the summary statistics related to the weekly amount spent on soft drinks.
c. Conduct a cross-tabulation of the weekly consumption of soft drinks with sex of the respondent. Does your data show any association?
d. Do a two-independent-sample *t* test to determine whether the weekly amount spent on soft drinks is different for males and females.
e. Conduct a test to determine whether there is any difference between the weekly amount spent on soft drinks and that spent on other nonalcoholic beverages. What is your conclusion?

# ACTIVITIES

## Role Playing

1. You have been hired as a marketing research analyst by a major industrial marketing company in the country. Your boss, the market research manager, is a high-powered statistician who does not believe in using rudimentary techniques such as frequency distributions, cross-tabulations, and simple *t* tests. Convince your boss (a student in your class) of the merits of conducting these analyses.

## Fieldwork

1. Develop a questionnaire to obtain the following information from students on your campus.
   a. Average amount per week spent on the consumption of soft drinks.
   b. Average amount per week spent on the consumption of other nonalcoholic beverages (milk, coffee, tea, fruit juices, etc.).
   c. Frequency of weekly soft drink consumption. Measure this as categorical variable with the following question: "How often do you consume soft drinks? (1) once a week or less often, (2) two or three times a week, (3) four to six times a week, and (4) more than six times a week."
   d. Sex of the respondent.
      Administer this questionnaire to 40 students. Code the data and transcribe them for computer analysis.

## Group Discussion

1. "Because cross-tabulation has certain basic limitations, this technique should not be used extensively in commercial marketing research." Discuss as a small group.
2. "Why waste time doing basic data analysis? Why not just conduct sophisticated multivariate data analysis?" Discuss.

# CHAPTER 16

# Analysis of Variance and Covariance

"Analysis of variance is a necessity in the researcher's tool kit. It is a straightforward way to look at differences between groups of responses measured on interval or ratio scales."

*Tammy Wise,
vice president,
client services,
Burke, Inc.*

## Objectives

After reading this chapter, the student should be able to:

1. Discuss the scope of the analysis of variance (ANOVA) technique and its relationship to the *t* test and regression.
2. Describe one-way analysis of variance including decomposition of the total variation, measurement of effects, significance testing, and interpretation of results.
3. Describe *n*-way analysis of variance and the testing of the significance of the overall effect, the interaction effect, and the main effect of each factor.
4. Describe analysis of covariance and show how it accounts for the influence of uncontrolled independent variables.
5. Explain key factors pertaining to the interpretation of results with emphasis on interactions, relative importance of factors, and multiple comparisons.
6. Discuss specialized ANOVA techniques applicable to marketing such as repeated measures ANOVA, nonmetric analysis of variance, and multivariate analysis of variance (MANOVA).

## Overview

In Chapter 15, we examined tests of differences between two means or two medians. In this chapter, we discuss procedures for examining differences between more than two means or medians. These procedures are called analysis of variance and analysis of covariance. Although these procedures have traditionally been used for analyzing experimental data, they are also used for analyzing survey or observational data.

We describe the analysis of variance and covariance procedures and discuss their relationship to other techniques. Then we describe one-way analysis of variance, the simplest of these procedures, followed by *n*-way analysis of variance and analysis of covariance. Special attention is given to issues in interpretation of results as they relate to interactions, relative importance of factors, and multiple comparisons. Some specialized topics, such as repeated measures analysis of variance, nonmetric analysis of variance, and multivariate analysis of variance, are briefly discussed.

**ACTIVE RESEARCH** | DEPARTMENT STORE PROJECT
### *Analysis of Variance*

In the department store project, several independent variables were examined as categorical variables having more than two categories. For example, familiarity with the department stores considered was respecified as high, medium, or low. The effects of these independent variables on metric dependent variables were examined using analysis of variance procedures. Several useful insights were obtained that guided subsequent data analysis and interpretation. For example, a three-category respecification of familiarity produced results that were not significant, whereas treating familiarity as a binary variable (high or low) produced significant results. This, along with the frequency distribution, indicated that treating familiarity as having only two categories was most appropriate.

## REAL RESEARCH

### *Analysis of Tourism Destinations*

A marketing research survey conducted by EgeBank in Istanbul, Turkey, focused on the importance of U.S. tour operators and travel agent's perceptions of selected Mediterranean tourist destinations (Egypt, Greece, Italy, and Turkey). This study was conducted with the help of the Department of Tourism and Convention Administration at the University of Nevada–Las Vegas (*www.unlv.edu*).

Operators/travel agents were mailed surveys based on the locations of tours, broken down as follows: Egypt (53), Greece (130), Italy (150), and Turkey (65). The survey consisted of questions on affective and perceptual/cognitive evaluations of the four destinations. The four affective questions were asked on a seven-point semantic differential scale, whereas the 14 perceptual/cognitive evaluations were measured on a five-point Likert scale (1 = offers very little, 2 = offers somewhat little, 3 = offers neither little nor much, 4 = offers somewhat much, and 5 = offers very much). The differences in the evaluations of the four locations were examined using one-way analysis of variance (ANOVA) as seen in the following table.

Image Variations of Destinations Promoted to Tour Operators and Travel Agencies

| Image Items | Turkey (n = 36) | Egypt (n = 29) | Greece (n = 37) | Italy (n = 34) | Significance |
|---|---|---|---|---|---|
| **Affective (Scale 1–7)** | | | | | |
| Unpleasant-pleasant | 6.14 | 5.62 | 6.43 | 6.50 | 0.047[a] |
| Sleepy-arousing | 6.24 | 5.61 | 6.14 | 6.56 | 0.053 |
| Distressing-relaxing | 5.60 | 4.86 | 6.05 | 6.09 | 0.003[a] |
| Gloomy-exciting | 6.20 | 5.83 | 6.32 | 6.71 | 0.061 |
| **Perceptual (Scale 1–5)** | | | | | |
| Good value for money | 4.62 | 4.32 | 3.89 | 3.27 | 0.000[a] |
| Beautiful scenery and natural attractions | 4.50 | 4.04 | 4.53 | 4.70 | 0.011[a] |
| Good climate | 4.29 | 4.00 | 4.41 | 4.35 | 0.133 |
| Interesting cultural attractions | 4.76 | 4.79 | 4.67 | 4.79 | 0.781 |
| Suitable accommodations | 4.17 | 4.28 | 4.35 | 4.62 | 0.125 |
| Appealing local food (cuisine) | 4.44 | 3.57 | 4.19 | 4.85 | 0.000[a] |
| Great beaches and water sports | 3.91 | 3.18 | 4.27 | 3.65 | 0.001[a] |
| Quality of infrastructure | 3.49 | 2.97 | 3.68 | 4.09 | 0.000[a] |
| Personal safety | 3.83 | 3.28 | 4.19 | 4.15 | 0.000[a] |
| Interesting historical attractions | 4.71 | 4.86 | 4.81 | 4.82 | 0.650 |
| Unpolluted and unspoiled environment | 3.54 | 3.34 | 3.43 | 3.59 | 0.784 |
| Good nightlife and entertainment | 3.44 | 3.15 | 4.06 | 4.27 | 0.000[a] |
| Standard hygiene and cleanliness | 3.29 | 2.79 | 3.76 | 4.29 | 0.000[a] |
| Interesting and friendly people | 4.34 | 4.24 | 4.35 | 4.32 | 0.956 |

[a]Significant at 0.05 level

The ANOVA table shows that "unpleasant-pleasant" and "distressing-relaxing" affective factors have significant differences among the four destinations. For instance, Greece and Italy were perceived as being significantly more relaxing than Egypt. As for the perceptual factors, eight of the 14 factors were significant. Turkey was perceived as a significantly better value for the money than Greece and Italy. Turkey's main strength appears to be "good value," and the country's tourism agencies should promote this in their marketing strategies. On the other hand, Turkey needs to improve the perception of its infrastructure, cleanliness, and entertainment to attract more tour operators and travel agencies in the United States to start offering travel packages to Turkey.[1] ■

One-way analysis of variance indicated that Turkey needs to improve the perception of its infrastructure, cleanliness, and entertainment to attract more tourists.

## Electronic Shopping Risks

Analysis of variance was used to test differences in preferences for electronic shopping for products with different economic and social risks. In a $2 \times 2$ design, economic risk and social risk were varied at two levels each (high, low). Preference for electronic shopping served as the dependent variable. The results indicated a significant interaction of social risk with economic risk. Electronic shopping was not perceived favorably for high-social-risk products, regardless of the level of economic product risk, but it was preferred for low-economic-risk products over high-economic-risk products when the level of social risk was low.

Despite the results of this study, in 2002, the number of online shoppers increased significantly compared to 2001. The increase in shoppers can be attributed to bargain-seeking consumers, convenience of using the Internet and, surprisingly as of 2002, an added sense of safety associated with purchasing online. Improved Web sites, streamlined order taking and delivery, and assurances of more secure payment systems have increased the flow of new shoppers to the Internet while decreasing the traditional risk associated with online transaction purchases.[2] ■

In the department store example, when familiarity had three categories, the *t* test was not appropriate to examine the overall difference in category means, so analysis of variance was used instead. The tourist destination example presented a similar situation with four categories. The electronic shopping study involved a comparison of means when there were two factors (independent variables), each of which was varied at two levels. In this example, *t* tests were not appropriate, because the effect of each factor was not independent of the effect of other factor (in other words, interactions were significant). Analysis of variance provided meaningful conclusions in these studies. The relationship of analysis of variance to the *t* test and other techniques is considered in the next section.

# RELATIONSHIP AMONG TECHNIQUES

Analysis of variance and analysis of covariance are used for examining the differences in the mean values of the dependent variable associated with the effect of the controlled independent variables, after taking into account the influence of the uncontrolled independent variables. Essentially, ***analysis of variance*** (ANOVA) is used as a test of means for two or more populations. The null hypothesis, typically, is that all means are equal. For example, suppose the researcher was interested in examining whether heavy, medium, light, and nonusers of cereals differed in their preference for Total cereal, measured on a nine-point Likert scale. The null hypothesis that the four groups were not different in preference for Total could be tested using analysis of variance.

In its simplest form, analysis of variance must have a dependent variable (preference for Total cereal) that is metric (measured using an interval or ratio scale). There must also be one or more independent variables (product use: heavy, medium, light, and nonusers). The independent variables must be all categorical (nonmetric). Categorical independent variables are also called ***factors***. A particular combination of factor levels, or categories, is called a ***treatment***. ***One-way analysis of variance*** involves only one categorical variable, or a single factor. The differences in preference of heavy, medium, light, and nonusers would be examined by one-way ANOVA. In one-way analysis of variance, a treatment is the same as a factor level (medium users constitute a treatment). If two or more factors are involved, the analysis is termed **n-*way analysis of variance***. If, in addition to product use, the researcher also wanted to examine the preference for Total cereal of customers who are loyal and those who are not, an *n*-way analysis of variance would be conducted.

If the set of independent variables consists of both categorical and metric variables, the technique is called ***analysis of covariance*** (ANCOVA). For example, analysis of covariance would be required if the researcher wanted to examine the preference of product use groups and loyalty groups, taking into account the respondents' attitudes toward nutrition and the importance they attached to breakfast as a meal. The latter two variables would be measured on nine-point Likert scales. In this case, the categorical independent variables (product use and brand loyalty) are still referred to as factors,

**analysis of variance (ANOVA)**
A statistical technique for examining the differences among means for two or more populations.

**factors**
Categorical independent variables. The independent variables must be all categorical (nonmetric) to use ANOVA.

**treatment**
In ANOVA, a particular combination of factor levels or categories.

**one-way analysis of variance**
An ANOVA technique in which there is only one factor.

**n-*way analysis of variance***
An ANOVA model where two or more factors are involved.

**analysis of covariance (ANCOVA)**
An advanced analysis of variance procedure in which the effects of one or more metric-scaled extraneous variables are removed from the dependent variable before conducting the ANOVA.

**Figure 16.1**
Relationship Between *t* Test,
Analysis of Variance, Analysis of
Covariance, and Regression

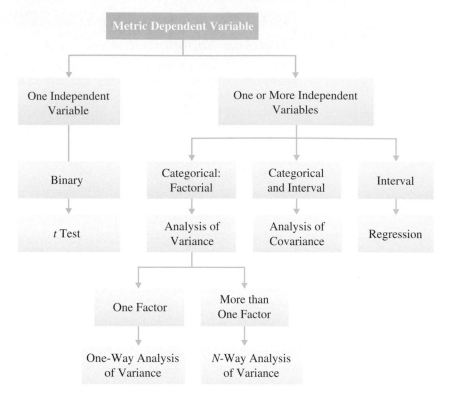

*covariate*
A metric independent variable used
in ANCOVA.

whereas the metric-independent variables (attitude toward nutrition and importance attached to breakfast) are referred to as *covariates.*

The relationship of analysis of variance to *t* tests and other techniques, such as regression (see Chapter 17), is shown in Figure 16.1. All of these techniques involve a metric dependent variable. ANOVA and ANCOVA can include more than one independent variable (product use, brand loyalty, attitude, and importance). Furthermore, at least one of the independent variables must be categorical, and the categorical variables may have more than two categories (in our example, product use has four categories). A *t* test, on the other hand, involves a single, binary independent variable. For example, the difference in the preferences of loyal and nonloyal respondents could be tested by conducting a *t* test. Regression analysis, like ANOVA and ANCOVA, can also involve more than one independent variable. However, all the independent variables are generally interval scaled, although binary or categorical variables can be accommodated using dummy variables. For example, the relationship between preference for Total cereal, attitude toward nutrition, and importance attached to breakfast could be examined via regression analysis, with preference for Total serving as the dependent variable and attitude and importance as independent variables.

## ONE-WAY ANALYSIS OF VARIANCE

Marketing researchers are often interested in examining the differences in the mean values of the dependent variable for several categories of a single independent variable or factor. For example:

- Do the various segments differ in terms of their volume of product consumption?
- Do the brand evaluations of groups exposed to different commercials vary?
- Do retailers, wholesalers, and agents differ in their attitudes toward the firm's distribution policies?
- How do consumers' intentions to buy the brand vary with different price levels?
- What is the effect of consumers' familiarity with the store (measured as high, medium, and low) on preference for the store?

The answer to these and similar questions can be determined by conducting one-way analysis of variance. Before describing the procedure, we define the important statistics associated with one-way analysis of variance.[3]

# STATISTICS ASSOCIATED WITH ONE-WAY ANALYSIS OF VARIANCE

**eta²** ($\eta^2$). The strength of the effects of $X$ (independent variable or factor) on $Y$ (dependent variable) is measured by *eta²* ($\eta^2$). The value of $\eta^2$ varies between 0 and 1.

**F statistic.** The null hypothesis that the category means are equal in the population is tested by an F statistic based on the ratio of mean square related to $X$ and mean square related to error.

**Mean square.** The mean square is the sum of squares divided by the appropriate degrees of freedom.

**$SS_{between}$.** Also denoted as $SS_x$, this is the variation in $Y$ related to the variation in the means of the categories of $X$. This represents variation between the categories of $X$, or the portion of the sum of squares in $Y$ related to $X$.

**$SS_{within}$.** Also referred to as $SS_{error}$, this is the variation in $Y$ due to the variation within each of the categories of $X$. This variation is not accounted for by $X$.

**$SS_y$.** The total variation in $Y$ is $SS_y$.

# CONDUCTING ONE-WAY ANALYSIS OF VARIANCE

The procedure for conducting one-way analysis of variance is described in Figure 16.2. It involves identifying the dependent and independent variables, decomposing the total variation, measuring effects, testing significance, and interpreting results. We consider these steps in detail and illustrate them with some applications.

## Identify the Dependent and Independent Variables

The dependent variable is denoted by $Y$ and the independent variable by $X$. $X$ is a categorical variable having $c$ categories. There are $n$ observations on $Y$ for each category of $X$, as shown in Table 16.1. As can be seen, the sample size in each category of $X$ is $n$, and the total sample size $N = n \times c$. Although the sample sizes in the categories of $X$ (the group sizes) are assumed to be equal for the sake of simplicity, this is not a requirement.

## Decompose the Total Variation

**decomposition of the total variation**

In one-way ANOVA, separation of the variation observed in the dependent variable into the variation due to the independent variables plus the variation due to error.

In examining the differences among means, one-way analysis of variance involves the **decomposition of the total variation** observed in the dependent variable. This variation is measured by the sums of squares corrected for the mean (*SS*). Analysis of variance is so named because it examines the variability or variation in the sample (dependent variable) and, based on the variability, determines whether there is reason to believe that the population means differ.

**Figure 16.2**
Conducting One-Way ANOVA

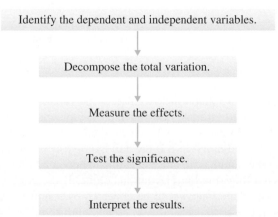

Identify the dependent and independent variables.

Decompose the total variation.

Measure the effects.

Test the significance.

Interpret the results.

**TABLE 16.1**

**Decomposition of the Total Variation: One-Way ANOVA**

| | | INDEPENDENT VARIABLE | | X | | |
|---|---|---|---|---|---|---|

(Table content)

Within-Category Variation = $SS_{within}$

| | $X_1$ | $X_2$ | $X_3$ | $\cdots$ | $X_c$ | TOTAL SAMPLE |
|---|---|---|---|---|---|---|
| | $Y_1$ | $Y_1$ | $Y_1$ | | $Y_1$ | $Y_1$ |
| | $Y_2$ | $Y_2$ | $Y_2$ | | $Y_2$ | $Y_2$ |
| | $\bullet$ | | | | | $\bullet$ |
| | $\bullet$ | | | | | $\bullet$ |
| | $\bullet$ | | | | | $\bullet$ |
| | $Y_n$ | $Y_n$ | $Y_n$ | | $Y_n$ | $Y_N$ |
| Category Mean | $\overline{Y}_1$ | $\overline{Y}_2$ | $\overline{Y}_3$ | | $\overline{Y}_c$ | $\overline{Y}$ |

Total Variation = $SS_y$

Between-Category Variation = $SS_{between}$

The total variation in $Y$, denoted by $SS_y$, can be decomposed into two components:

$$SS_y = SS_{between} + SS_{within}$$

where the subscripts *between* and *within* refer to the categories of $X$. $SS_{between}$ is the variation in $Y$ related to the variation in the means of the categories of $X$. It represents variation between the categories of $X$. In other words, $SS_{between}$ is the portion of the sum of squares in $Y$ related to the independent variable or factor $X$. For this reason, $SS_{between}$ is also denoted as $SS_x$. $SS_{within}$ is the variation in $Y$ related to the variation within each category of $X$. $SS_{within}$ is not accounted for by $X$. Therefore it is referred to as $SS_{error}$. The total variation in $Y$ may be decomposed as:

$$SS_y = SS_x + SS_{error}$$

where

$$SS_y = \sum_{i=1}^{N} (Y_i - \overline{Y})^2$$

$$SS_x = \sum_{j=1}^{c} n(\overline{Y}_j - \overline{Y})^2$$

$$SS_{error} = \sum_{j}^{c}\sum_{i}^{n} (Y_{ij} - \overline{Y}_j)^2$$

$Y_i$ = individual observation

$\overline{Y}_j$ = mean for category $j$

$\overline{Y}$ = mean over the whole sample, or grand mean

$Y_{ij}$ = $i$th observation in the $j$th category

The logic of decomposing the total variation in $Y$, $SS_y$, into $SS_{between}$ and $SS_{within}$ in order to examine differences in group means can be intuitively understood. Recall from Chapter 15 that if the variation of the variable in the population was known or estimated, one could estimate how much the sample mean should vary because of random variation alone. In analysis of variance, there are several different groups (e.g., heavy, medium, light, and nonusers). If the null hypothesis is true and all the groups have the same mean in the population, one can estimate how much the sample means should vary because of sampling (random) variations alone. If the observed variation in the sample means is more than what would be expected by sampling variation, it is reasonable to conclude that this extra variability is related to differences in group means in the population.

In analysis of variance, we estimate two measures of variation: within groups ($SS_{within}$) and between groups ($SS_{between}$). Within-group variation is a measure of how much the observations, $Y$ values, within a group vary. This is used to estimate the variance within a group in the population. It is assumed that all the groups have the same variation in the population. However, because it is not known that all the groups have the same mean, we cannot calculate the variance of all the observations together. The variance for each of the groups must be calculated individually, and these are combined into an "average" or "overall" variance. Likewise, another estimate of the variance of the $Y$ values may be obtained by examining the variation between the means. (This process is the reverse of determining the variation in the means, given the population variances.) If the population mean is the same in all the groups, then the variation in the sample means and the sizes of the sample groups can be used to estimate the variance of $Y$. The reasonableness of this estimate of the $Y$ variance depends on whether the null hypothesis is true. If the null hypothesis is true and the population means are equal, the variance estimate based on between-group variation is correct. On the other hand, if the groups have different means in the population, the variance estimate based on between-group variation will be too large. Thus, by comparing the $Y$ variance estimates based on between-group and within-group variation, we can test the null hypothesis. Decomposition of the total variation in this manner also enables us to measure the effects of $X$ on $Y$.

## Measure the Effects

The effects of $X$ on $Y$ are measured by $SS_x$. Because $SS_x$ is related to the variation in the means of the categories of $X$, the relative magnitude of $SS_x$ increases as the differences among the means of $Y$ in the categories of $X$ increase. The relative magnitude of $SS_x$ also increases as the variations in $Y$ within the categories of $X$ decrease. The strength of the effects of $X$ on $Y$ are measured as follows:

$$\eta^2 = \frac{SS_x}{SS_y} = \frac{(SS_y - SS_{error})}{SS_y}$$

The value of $\eta^2$ varies between 0 and 1. It assumes a value of 0 when all the category means are equal, indicating that $X$ has no effect of $X$ on $Y$. The value of $\eta^2$ will be 1 when there is no variability within each category of $X$ but there is some variability between categories. Thus, $\eta^2$ is a measure of the variation in $Y$ that is explained by the independent variable $X$. Not only can we measure the effects of $X$ on $Y$, but we can also test for their significance.

## Test the Significance

In one-way analysis of variance, the interest lies in testing the null hypothesis that the category means are equal in the population.[4] In other words,

$$H_0: \mu_1 = \mu_2 = \mu_3 = \ldots = \mu_c$$

Under the null hypothesis, $SS_x$ and $SS_{error}$ come from the same source of variation. In such a case, the estimate of the population variance of $Y$ can be based on either between-category variation or within-category variation. In other words, the estimate of the population variance of $Y$,

$$S_y^2 = \frac{SS_x}{(c-1)}$$
$$= \text{mean square due to } X$$
$$= MS_x$$

or

$$S_y^2 = \frac{SS_{error}}{(N-c)}$$
$$= \text{mean square due to error}$$
$$= MS_{error}$$

The null hypothesis may be tested by the $F$ statistic based on the ratio between these two estimates:

$$F = \frac{SS_x/(c-1)}{SS_{error}/(N-c)} = \frac{MS_x}{MS_{error}}$$

This statistic follows the $F$ distribution, with $(c-1)$ and $(N-c)$ degrees of freedom (df). A table of the $F$ distribution is given as Table 5 in the Statistical Appendix at the end of the book. As mentioned in Chapter 15, the $F$ distribution is a probability distribution of the ratios of sample variances. It is characterized by degrees of freedom for the numerator and degrees of freedom for the denominator.[5]

## Interpret the Results

If the null hypothesis of equal category means is not rejected, then the independent variable does not have a significant effect on the dependent variable. On the other hand, if the null hypothesis is rejected, then the effect of the independent variable is significant. In other words, the mean value of the dependent variable will be different for different categories of the independent variable. A comparison of the category mean values will indicate the nature of the effect of the independent variable. Other salient issues in the interpretation of results, such as examination of differences among specific means, are discussed later.

# ILLUSTRATIVE DATA

We illustrate the concepts discussed in this chapter using the data presented in Table 16.2. These data were generated by an experiment in which a major department store chain wanted to examine the effect of the level of in-store promotion and storewide coupon on sales. In-store promotion was varied at three levels: high (1), medium (2), and low (3). Couponing was manipulated at two levels. Either a 20-dollar storewide coupon was distributed to potential shoppers (denoted by 1) or it was not (denoted by 2 in Table 16.2). In-store promotion and couponing were crossed, resulting in a $3 \times 2$ design with six cells. Thirty stores were randomly selected, and five stores were randomly assigned to each treatment condition, as shown in Table 16.2. The experiment was run for two months. Sales in each store were measured, normalized to account for extraneous factors (store size, traffic, etc.), and converted to a 1-to-10 scale. In addition, a qualitative assessment was made of the relative affluence of the clientele of each store, again using a 1-to-10 scale. In these scales, higher numbers denote higher sales or more affluent clientele.

# ILLUSTRATIVE APPLICATIONS OF ONE-WAY ANALYSIS OF VARIANCE

We illustrate one-way ANOVA first with an example showing calculations done by hand and then using computer analysis. Suppose that only one factor, namely in-store promotion was manipulated, i.e., let us ignore couponing for the purpose of this illustration. The department store is attempting to determine the effect of in-store promotion $(X)$ on sales $(Y)$. For the purpose of illustrating hand calculations, the data of Table 16.2 are transformed in Table 16.3 to show the store $(Y_{ij})$ for each level of promotion.

The null hypothesis is that the category means are equal:

$$H_0: \mu_1 = \mu_2 = \mu_3$$

To test the null hypothesis, the various sums of squares are computed as follows:

$$\begin{aligned}
SS_y = {} & (10-6.067)^2 + (9-6.067)^2 + (10-6.067)^2 + (8-6.067)^2 + (9-6.067)^2 \\
& + (8-6.067)^2 + (9-6.067)^2 + (7-6.067)^2 + (7-6.067)^2 + (6-6.067)^2 \\
& + (8-6.067)^2 + (8-6.067)^2 + (7-6.067)^2 + (9-6.067)^2 + (6-6.067)^2
\end{aligned}$$

## TABLE 16.2

### Coupon Level, In-Store Promotion, Sales, and Clientele Rating

| Store Number | Coupon Level | In-Store Promotion | Sales | Clientele Rating |
|---|---|---|---|---|
| 1 | 1 | 1 | 10 | 9 |
| 2 | 1 | 1 | 9 | 10 |
| 3 | 1 | 1 | 10 | 8 |
| 4 | 1 | 1 | 8 | 4 |
| 5 | 1 | 1 | 9 | 6 |
| 6 | 1 | 2 | 8 | 8 |
| 7 | 1 | 2 | 8 | 4 |
| 8 | 1 | 2 | 7 | 10 |
| 9 | 1 | 2 | 9 | 6 |
| 10 | 1 | 2 | 6 | 9 |
| 11 | 1 | 3 | 5 | 8 |
| 12 | 1 | 3 | 7 | 9 |
| 13 | 1 | 3 | 6 | 6 |
| 14 | 1 | 3 | 4 | 10 |
| 15 | 1 | 3 | 5 | 4 |
| 16 | 2 | 1 | 8 | 10 |
| 17 | 2 | 1 | 9 | 6 |
| 18 | 2 | 1 | 7 | 8 |
| 19 | 2 | 1 | 7 | 4 |
| 20 | 2 | 1 | 6 | 9 |
| 21 | 2 | 2 | 4 | 6 |
| 22 | 2 | 2 | 5 | 8 |
| 23 | 2 | 2 | 5 | 10 |
| 24 | 2 | 2 | 6 | 4 |
| 25 | 2 | 2 | 4 | 9 |
| 26 | 2 | 3 | 2 | 4 |
| 27 | 2 | 3 | 3 | 6 |
| 28 | 2 | 3 | 2 | 10 |
| 29 | 2 | 3 | 1 | 9 |
| 30 | 2 | 3 | 2 | 8 |

$$+ (4 - 6.067)^2 + (5 - 6.067)^2 + (5 - 6.067)^2 + (6 - 6.067)^2 + (4 - 6.067)^2$$
$$+ (5 - 6.067)^2 + (7 - 6.067)^2 + (6 - 6.067)^2 + (4 - 6.067)^2 + (5 - 6.067)^2$$
$$+ (2 - 6.067)^2 + (3 - 6.067)^2 + (2 - 6.067)^2 + (1 - 6.067)^2 + (2 - 6.067)^2$$

$$= (3.933)^2 + (2.933)^2 + (3.933)^2 + (1.933)^2 + (2.933)^2$$
$$+ (1.933)^2 + (2.933)^2 + (0.933)^2 + (0.933)^2 + (-0.067)^2$$
$$+ (1.933)^2 + (1.933)^2 + (0.933)^2 + (2.933)^2 + (-0.067)^2$$
$$+ (-2.067)^2 + (-1.067)^2 + (-1.067)^2 + (-0.067)^2 + (-2.067)^2$$
$$+ (-1.067)^2 + (0.933)^2 + (-0.067)^2 + (-2.067)^2 + (-1.067)^2$$
$$+ (-4.067)^2 + (-3.067)^2 + (-4.067)^2 + (-5.067)^2 + (-4.067)^2$$
$$= 185.867$$

$$SS_x = 10(8.3 - 6.067)^2 + 10(6.2 - 6.067)^2 + 10(3.7 - 6.067)^2$$
$$= 10(2.233)^2 + 10(0.133)^2 + 10(-2.367)^2$$
$$= 106.067$$

## TABLE 16.3

**Effect of In-Store Promotion on Sales**

| STORE | LEVEL OF IN-STORE PROMOTION | | |
|---|---|---|---|
| No. | HIGH | MEDIUM | Low |
| | | NORMALIZED SALES | |
| 1 | 10 | 8 | 5 |
| 2 | 9 | 8 | 7 |
| 3 | 10 | 7 | 6 |
| 4 | 8 | 9 | 4 |
| 5 | 9 | 6 | 5 |
| 6 | 8 | 4 | 2 |
| 7 | 9 | 5 | 3 |
| 8 | 7 | 5 | 2 |
| 9 | 7 | 6 | 1 |
| 10 | 6 | 4 | 2 |
| Column Totals | 83 | 62 | 37 |
| Category means: $\overline{Y}_j$ | $\dfrac{83}{10}$ | $\dfrac{62}{10}$ | $\dfrac{37}{10}$ |
| | = 8.3 | = 6.2 | = 3.7 |
| Grand mean, $\overline{Y}$ | | $= \dfrac{(83 + 62 + 37)}{30} = 6.067$ | |

$$
\begin{aligned}
SS_{error} = \ & (10 - 8.3)^2 + (9 - 8.3)^2 + (10 - 8.3)^2 + (8 - 8.3)^2 + (9 - 8.3)^2 \\
& + (8 - 8.3)^2 + (9 - 8.3)^2 + (7 - 8.3)^2 + (7 - 8.3)^2 + (6 - 8.3)^2 \\
& + (8 - 6.2)^2 + (8 - 6.2)^2 + (7 - 6.2)^2 + (9 - 6.2)^2 + (6 - 6.2)^2 \\
& + (4 - 6.2)^2 + (5 - 6.2)^2 + (5 - 6.2)^2 + (6 - 6.2)^2 + (4 - 6.2)^2 \\
& + (5 - 3.7)^2 + (7 - 3.7)^2 + (6 - 3.7)^2 + (4 - 3.7)^2 + (5 - 3.7)^2 \\
& + (2 - 3.7)^2 + (3 - 3.7)^2 + (2 - 3.7)^2 + (1 - 3.7)^2 + (2 - 3.7)^2
\end{aligned}
$$

$$
\begin{aligned}
= \ & (1.7)^2 + (0.7)^2 + (1.7)^2 + (-0.3)^2 + (0.7)^2 \\
& + (-0.3)^2 + (0.7)^2 + (-1.3)^2 + (-1.3)^2 + (-2.3)^2 \\
& + (1.8)^2 + (1.8)^2 + (0.8)^2 + (2.8)^2 + (-0.2)^2 \\
& + (-2.2)^2 + (-1.2)^2 + (-1.2)^2 + (-0.2)^2 + (-2.2)^2 \\
& + (1.3)^2 + (3.3)^2 + (2.3)^2 + (0.3)^2 + (1.3)^2 \\
& + (-1.7)^2 + (-0.7)^2 + (-1.7)^2 + (-2.7)^2 + (-1.7)^2 \\
= \ & 79.80
\end{aligned}
$$

It can be verified that

$$
SS_y = SS_x + SS_{error}
$$

as follows:

$$
185.867 = 106.067 + 79.80
$$

The strength of the effects of $X$ on $Y$ are measured as follows:

$$
\begin{aligned}
\eta^2 &= \frac{SS_x}{SS_y} \\
&= \frac{106.067}{185.867} \\
&= 0.571
\end{aligned}
$$

**TABLE 16.4**

**One-Way ANOVA: Effect of In-Store Promotion on Store Sales**

| SOURCE OF VARIATION | SUM OF SQUARES | DF | MEAN SQUARE | F RATIO | F PROB. |
|---|---|---|---|---|---|
| Between groups (In-store promotion) | 106.067 | 2 | 53.033 | 17.944 | 0.000 |
| Within groups (Error) | 79.800 | 27 | 2.956 | | |
| TOTAL | 185.867 | 29 | 6.409 | | |

| CELL MEANS | | |
|---|---|---|
| Level of In-store promotion | Count | Mean |
| High (1) | 10 | 8.300 |
| Medium (2) | 10 | 6.200 |
| Low (3) | 10 | 3.700 |
| TOTAL | 30 | 6.067 |

In other words, 57.1 percent of the variation in sales ($Y$) is accounted for by in-store promotion ($X$), indicating a modest effect. The null hypothesis may now be tested.

$$F = \frac{SS_x/(c-1)}{SS_{error}/(N-c)} = \frac{MS_X}{MS_{error}}$$

$$F = \frac{106.067/(3-1)}{79.800/(30-3)}$$

$$= 17.944$$

From Table 5 in the Statistical Appendix, we see that for 2 and 27 degrees of freedom, the critical value of $F$ is 3.35 for $\alpha = 0.05$. Because the calculated value of $F$ is greater than the critical value, we reject the null hypothesis. We conclude that the population means for the three levels of in-store promotion are indeed different. The relative magnitudes of the means for the three categories indicate that a high level of in-store promotion leads to significantly higher sales.

We now illustrate the analysis-of-variance procedure using a computer program. The results of conducting the same analysis by computer are presented in Table 16.4. The value of $SS_x$ denoted by main effects is 106.067 with 2 df; that of $SS_{error}$ is denoted by residual is 79.80 with 27 df. Therefore, $MS_x = 106.067/2 = 53.033$, and $MS_{error} = 79.80/27 = 2.956$. The value of $F = 53.033/2.956 = 17.944$ with 2 and 27 degrees of freedom, resulting in a probability of 0.000. Because the associated probability is less than the significance level of 0.05, the null hypothesis of equal population means is rejected. Alternatively, it can be seen from Table 5 in the Statistical Appendix that the critical value of $F$ for 2 and 27 degrees of freedom is 3.35. Because the calculated value of $F$ (17.944) is larger than the critical value, the null hypothesis is rejected. As can be seen from Table 16.4, the sample means, with values of 8.3, 6.2, and 3.7, are quite different. Stores with a high level of in-store promotion have the highest average sales (8.3) and stores with a low level of in-store promotion have the lowest average sales (3.7). Stores with a medium level of in-store promotion have an intermediate level of average sales (6.2). These findings seem plausible.

The procedure for conducting one-way analysis of variance and the illustrative application help us understand the assumptions involved.

## ASSUMPTIONS IN ANALYSIS OF VARIANCE

The salient assumptions in analysis of variance can be summarized as follows.

1. Ordinarily, the categories of the independent variable are assumed to be fixed. Inferences are made only to the specific categories considered. This is referred to as the

*fixed-effects model.* Other models are also available. In the *random-effects model,* the categories or treatments are considered to be random samples from a universe of treatments. Inferences are made to other categories not examined in the analysis. A *mixed-effects model* results if some treatments are considered fixed and others random.[6]

2. The error term is normally distributed, with a zero mean and a constant variance. The error is not related to any of the categories of *X*. Modest departures from these assumptions do not seriously affect the validity of the analysis. Furthermore, the data can be transformed to satisfy the assumption of normality or equal variances.

3. The error terms are uncorrelated. If the error terms are correlated (i.e., the observations are not independent), the *F* ratio can be seriously distorted.

In many data analysis situations, these assumptions are reasonably met. Analysis of variance is therefore a common procedure, as illustrated by the following example.

### REAL RESEARCH

## *Videologs Put Marketers in the Picture*

Although the videolog, a shop-at-home video catalog, is still in its infancy, many direct marketers have shown an interest in its use. Companies such as Spiegel (*www.spiegel.com*) and Neiman-Marcus (*www.neimanmarcus.com*) either plan to or already have offered video catalogs to consumers.

A study was designed to investigate the effectiveness of videolog retailing as a form of direct marketing. Subjects were randomly assigned to one of three treatments: (a) videolog only; (b) both videolog and catalog; or (c) catalog only. The dependent variables of interest, consisting of attitudes and opinions, were: (1) assessments of product (clothing) attributes; (2) assessments of the videolog/catalog sponsoring company; (3) assessments of price information; and (4) intentions to purchase.

One-way analysis of variance was conducted separately for each dependent variable. The results showed that respondents exposed to the videolog, or videolog and catalog, perceived the clothing more positively than did those exposed only to the catalog. Although the videolog-only treatment enhanced perceptions of the sponsoring company, the results were not as striking as were those for clothing perceptions. No significant differences were found in price perceptions and intentions to purchase. Yet the mean number of items respondents said they were likely to purchase was greater for those viewing both the videolog and catalog than those seeing just the videolog or the catalog.

Although this study was an exploratory effort, the positive results found in assessments of clothing seen in the videolog suggest that this is an area that may have potential for direct marketers.[7] ∎

## *N*-WAY ANALYSIS OF VARIANCE

In marketing research, one is often concerned with the effect of more than one factor simultaneously.[8] For example:

- How do the consumers' intentions to buy a brand vary with different levels of price and different levels of distribution?
- How do advertising levels (high, medium, and low) interact with price levels (high, medium, and low) to influence a brand's sale?
- Do educational levels (less than high school, high school graduate, some college, and college graduate) and age (less than 35, 35–55, more than 55) affect consumption of a brand?
- What is the effect of consumers' familiarity with a department store (high, medium, and low) and store image (positive, neutral, and negative) on preference for the store?

In determining such effects, *n*-way analysis of variance can be used. A major advantage of this technique is that it enables the researcher to examine interactions between the factors. *Interactions* occur when the effects of one factor on the dependent variable depend on the level (category) of the other factors. The procedure for conducting *n*-way analysis of vari-

**interaction**
When assessing the relationship between two variables, an interaction occurs if the effect of $X_1$ depends on the level of $X_2$, and vice versa.

ance is similar to that for one-way analysis of variance. The statistics associated with $n$-way analysis of variance are also defined similarly. Consider the simple case of two factors, $X_1$ and $X_2$, having categories, $c_1$ and $c_2$. The total variation in this case is partitioned as follows:

$$SS_{total} = SS \text{ due to } X_1 + SS \text{ due to } X_2 + SS \text{ due to interaction of } X_1 \text{ and } X_2 + SS_{within}$$

or

$$SS_y = SS_{x_1} + SS_{x_2} + SS_{x_1 x_2} + SS_{error}$$

A larger effect of $X_1$ will be reflected in a greater mean difference in the levels of $X_1$ and a larger $SS_{x_1}$. The same is true for the effect of $X_2$. The larger the interaction between $X_1$ and $X_2$, the larger $SS_{x_1 x_2}$ will be. On the other hand, if $X_1$ and $X_2$ are independent, the value of $SS_{x_1 x_2}$ will be close to zero.[9]

**multiple η²**
The strength of the joint effect of two (or more) factors, or the overall effect.

The strength of the joint effect of two factors, called the overall effect, or **multiple η²,** is measured as follows:

$$\text{multiple } \eta^2 = \frac{(SS_{x_1} + SS_{x_2} + SS_{x_1 x_2})}{SS_y}$$

**significance of the overall effect**
A test that some differences exist between some of the treatment groups.

The **significance of the overall effect** may be tested by an $F$ test, as follows:

$$F = \frac{(SS_{x_1} + SS_{x_2} + SS_{x_1 x_2})/\text{df}_n}{SS_{error}/\text{df}_d}$$

$$= \frac{SS_{x_1, x_2, x_1 x_2}/\text{df}_n}{SS_{error}/\text{df}_d}$$

$$= \frac{MS_{x_1, x_2, x_1 x_2}}{MS_{error}}$$

where

$$
\begin{aligned}
\text{df}_n &= \text{degrees of freedom for the numerator} \\
&= (c_1 - 1) + (c_2 - 1) + (c_1 - 1)(c_2 - 1) \\
&= c_1 c_2 - 1 \\
\text{df}_d &= \text{degrees of freedom for the denominator} \\
&= N - c_1 c_2 \\
MS &= \text{mean square}
\end{aligned}
$$

**significance of the interaction effect**
A test of the significance of the interaction between two or more independent variables.

If the overall effect is significant, the next step is to examine the **significance of the interaction effect.** Under the null hypothesis of no interaction, the appropriate $F$ test is:

$$F = \frac{SS_{x_1 x_2}/\text{df}_n}{SS_{error}/\text{df}_d}$$

$$= \frac{MS_{x_1 x_2}}{MS_{error}}$$

where

$$\text{df}_n = (c_1 - 1)(c_2 - 1)$$
$$\text{df}_d = N - c_1 c_2$$

If the interaction effect is found to be significant, then the effect of $X_1$ depends on the level of $X_2$, and vice versa. Because the effect of one factor is not uniform, but varies with the level of the other factor, it is not generally meaningful to test the significance of the main effects. However, it is meaningful to test the significance of each main effect of each factor if the interaction effect is not significant.[10]

**significance of the main effect**
A test of the significance of the main effect for each individual factor.

The **significance of the main effect** of each factor may be tested as follows for $X_1$:

$$F = \frac{SS_{x_1}/\text{df}_n}{SS_{error}/\text{df}_d}$$

$$= \frac{MS_{x_1}}{MS_{error}}$$

where

$$df_n = c_1 - 1$$
$$df_d = N - c_1 c_2$$

The foregoing analysis assumes that the design was orthogonal, or balanced (the number of cases in each cell was the same). If the cell size varies, the analysis becomes more complex.

# ILLUSTRATIVE APPLICATION OF *N*-WAY ANALYSIS OF VARIANCE

Returning to the data of Table 16.2, let us now examine the effect of the level of in-store promotion and couponing on store sales. The results of running a $3 \times 2$ ANOVA on the computer are presented in Table 16.5. For the main effect of level of promotion, the sum of squares $SS_{xp}$, degrees of freedom, and mean square $MS_{xp}$ are the same as earlier determined in Table 16.4. The sum of squares for couponing $SS_{xc} = 53.333$ with 1 df, resulting in an identical value for the mean square $MS_{xc}$. The combined main effect is determined by adding the sum of squares due to the two main effects ($SS_{xp} + SS_{xc} = 106.067 + 53.333 = 159.400$) as well as adding the degrees of freedom ($2 + 1 = 3$). For the promotion and coupon interaction effect, the sum of squares $SS_{xpxc} = 3.267$ with $(3 - 1)(2 - 1) = 2$ degrees of freedom, resulting in $MS_{xpxc} = 3.267/2 = 1.633$. For the overall (model) effect, the sum of squares is the addition of sum of squares for promotion main effect, coupon main effect, and interaction effect $= 106.067 + 53.333 + 3.267 = 162.667$ with $2 + 1 + 2 = 5$ degrees of freedom, resulting in a mean square of $162.667/5 = 32.533$. Note, however, the error statistics are now different than in Table 16.4. This is due to the fact that we now have two factors instead of one. $SS_{error} = 23.2$ with $(30 - 3 \times 2)$ or 24 degrees of freedom resulting in $MS_{error} = 23.2/24 = 0.967$.

The test statistic for the significance of the overall effect is

$$F = \left( \frac{32.533}{0.967} \right)$$

$$= 33.655$$

with 5 and 24 degrees of freedom, which is significant at the 0.05 level.

The test statistic for the significance of the interaction effect is

$$F = \left( \frac{1.633}{0.967} \right)$$

$$= 1.690$$

with 2 and 24 degrees of freedom, which is not significant at the 0.05 level.

As the interaction effect is not significant, the significance of the main effects can be evaluated. The test statistic for the significance of the main effect of promotion is

$$F = \left( \frac{53.033}{0.967} \right)$$

$$= 54.862$$

with 2 and 24 degrees of freedom, which is significant at the 0.05 level.

The test statistic for the significance of the main effect of coupon is

$$F = \left( \frac{53.333}{0.967} \right)$$

$$= 55.172$$

with 1 and 24 degrees of freedom, which is significant at the 0.05 level. Thus, a higher level of promotion results in higher sales. The distribution of a storewide coupon results in higher sales. The effect of each is independent of the other.

**TABLE 16.5**

Two-Way Analysis of Variance

| SOURCE OF VARIATION | SUM OF SQUARES | DF | MEAN SQUARE | F | SIG. OF F | $\omega^2$ |
|---|---|---|---|---|---|---|
| Main Effects | | | | | | |
|   In-store promotion | 106.067 | 2 | 53.033 | 54.862 | 0.000 | 0.557 |
|   Coupon | 53.333 | 1 | 53.333 | 55.172 | 0.000 | 0.280 |
|   Combined | 159.400 | 3 | 53.133 | 54.966 | 0.000 | |
| Two-way interaction | 3.267 | 2 | 1.633 | 1.690 | 0.206 | |
| Model | 162.667 | 5 | 32.533 | 33.655 | 0.000 | |
| Residual (Error) | 23.200 | 24 | 0.967 | | | |
| TOTAL | 185.867 | 29 | 6.409 | | | |

CELL MEANS

| IN-STORE PROMOTION | COUPON | COUNT | MEAN |
|---|---|---|---|
| High | Yes | 5 | 9.200 |
| High | No | 5 | 7.400 |
| Medium | Yes | 5 | 7.600 |
| Medium | No | 5 | 4.800 |
| Low | Yes | 5 | 5.400 |
| Low | No | 5 | 2.000 |

FACTOR LEVEL MEANS

| PROMOTION | COUPON | COUNT | MEAN |
|---|---|---|---|
| High | | 10 | 8.300 |
| Medium | | 10 | 6.200 |
| Low | | 10 | 3.700 |
| | Yes | 15 | 7.400 |
| | No | 15 | 4.733 |
| Grand Mean | | 30 | 6.067 |

## REAL RESEARCH

### Country Affiliation Affects TV Reception

A study examined the impact of country affiliation on the credibility of product-attribute claims for TVs. The dependent variables were the following product-attribute claims: good sound, reliability, crisp-clear picture, and stylish design. The independent variables that were manipulated consisted of price, country affiliation, and store distribution. A $2 \times 2 \times 2$ between-subjects design was used. Two levels of price, $349.95 (low) and $449.95 (high), two levels of country affiliation, Korea and the United States, and two levels of store distribution, Hudson's and without Hudson's, were specified.

Data were collected from two suburban malls in a large midwestern city. Thirty respondents were randomly assigned to each of the eight treatment cells for a total of 240 subjects. Table 1 presents the results for manipulations that had significant effects on each of the dependent variables.

TABLE 1   Analyses for Significant Manipulations

| Effect | Dependent Variable | *Univariate* F | df | p |
|---|---|---|---|---|
| Country × price | Good sound | 7.57 | 1,232 | 0.006 |
| Country × price | Reliability | 6.57 | 1,232 | 0.011 |
| Country × distribution | Crisp-clear picture | 6.17 | 1,232 | 0.014 |
| Country × distribution | Reliability | 6.57 | 1,232 | 0.011 |
| Country × distribution | Stylish design | 10.31 | 1,232 | 0.002 |

The directions of country-by-distribution interaction effects for the three dependent variables are shown in Table 2. Whereas the credibility ratings for the crisp-clear picture, reliability, and stylish design claims are improved by distributing the Korean-made TV set through Hudson's, rather than some other distributor, the same is not true of a U.S.-made set. Similarly, the directions of country-by-price interaction effects for the two dependent variables are shown in Table 3. At $449.95, the credibility ratings for the "good sound" and "reliability" claims are higher for the U.S.-made TV set than for its Korean counterpart, but there is little difference related to country affiliation when the product is priced at $349.95.

**TABLE 2**    Country-by-Distribution Interaction Means

| *Country* × *Distribution* | Crisp-Clear Picture | *Reliability* | Stylish Design |
|---|---|---|---|
| *Korea* | | | |
| Hudson's | 3.67 | 3.42 | 3.82 |
| Without Hudson's | 3.18 | 2.88 | 3.15 |
| *United States* | | | |
| Hudson's | 3.60 | 3.47 | 3.53 |
| Without Hudson's | 3.77 | 3.65 | 3.75 |

**TABLE 3**    Country-by-Price Interaction Means

| *Country* × *Price* | *Good Sound* | *Reliability* |
|---|---|---|
| $349.95 | | |
| Korea | 3.75 | 3.40 |
| United States | 3.53 | 3.45 |
| $449.95 | | |
| Korea | 3.15 | 2.90 |
| United States | 3.73 | 3.67 |

This study demonstrates that credibility of attribute claims, for products traditionally exported to the United States by a company in a newly industrialized country, can be significantly improved if the same company distributes the product through a prestigious U.S. retailer and considers making manufacturing investments in the United States. Specifically, three product attribute claims (crisp-clear picture, reliability, and stylish design) are perceived as more credible when the TVs are made in Korea if they are also distributed through a prestigious U.S. retailer. Also, the "good sound" and "reliability" claims for TVs are perceived to be more credible for a U.S-made set sold at a higher price, possibly offsetting the potential disadvantage of higher manufacturing costs in the United States. Thus,

N-way analysis of variance indicated that Thomson, the manufacturer of RCA products, may be better off manufacturing its TV sets in the United States and selling them at a higher price.

Thomson multimedia, the manufacturer of RCA products (*www.rca.com*), may be better off manufacturing its TV sets in the United States and selling them at a higher price.[11] ■

# ANALYSIS OF COVARIANCE

When examining the differences in the mean values of the dependent variable related to the effect of the controlled independent variables, it is often necessary to take into account the influence of uncontrolled independent variables. For example:

- In determining how consumers' intentions to buy a brand vary with different levels of price, attitude toward the brand may have to be taken into consideration.
- In determining how different groups exposed to different commercials evaluate a brand, it may be necessary to control for prior knowledge.
- In determining how different price levels will affect a household's cereal consumption, it may be essential to take household size into account.

In such cases, analysis of covariance should be used. Analysis of covariance includes at least one categorical independent variable and at least one interval or metric independent variable. The categorical independent variable is called a factor, whereas the metric independent variable is called a *covariate*. The most common use of the covariate is to remove extraneous variation from the dependent variable, because the effects of the factors are of major concern. The variation in the dependent variable due to the covariates is removed by an adjustment of the dependent variable's mean value within each treatment condition. An analysis of variance is then performed on the adjusted scores.[12] The significance of the combined effect of the covariates, as well as the effect of each covariate, is tested by using the appropriate $F$ tests. The coefficients for the covariates provide insights into the effect that the covariates exert on the dependent variable. Analysis of covariance is most useful when the covariate is linearly related to the dependent variable and is not related to the factors.[13]

We again use the data of Table 16.2 to illustrate analysis of covariance. Suppose that we wanted to determine the effect of in-store promotion and couponing on sales while controlling for the effect of clientele. It is felt that the affluence of the clientele may also have an effect on sales of the department store. The dependent variable consists of store sales. As before, promotion has three levels and couponing has two. Clientele measured on an interval scale serves as the covariate. The results are shown in Table 16.6. As can be seen, the sum of squares attributable to the covariate is very small (0.838) with 1 df resulting in an identical value for the mean square. The associated $F$ value is $0.838/0.972 = 0.862$, with 1 and 23 degrees of freedom, which is not significant at the 0.05 level. Thus,

## TABLE 16.6

**Analysis of Covariance**

| Source of Variation | Sum of Squares | DF | Mean Square | F | Sig. of F |
|---|---|---|---|---|---|
| Covariates | | | | | |
| Clientele | 0.838 | 1 | 0.838 | 0.862 | 0.363 |
| Main effects | | | | | |
| Promotion | 106.067 | 2 | 53.033 | 54.546 | 0.000 |
| Coupon | 53.333 | 1 | 53.333 | 54.855 | 0.000 |
| Combined | 159.400 | 3 | 53.133 | 54.649 | 0.000 |
| 2-way interaction | | | | | |
| Promotion × Coupon | 3.267 | 2 | 1.633 | 1.680 | 0.208 |
| Model | 163.505 | 6 | 27.251 | 28.028 | 0.000 |
| Residual (Error) | 22.362 | 23 | 0.972 | | |
| TOTAL | 185.867 | 29 | 6.409 | | |
| Covariate | Raw coefficient | | | | |
| Clientele | −0.078 | | | | |

the conclusion is that the affluence of the clientele does not have an effect on the sales of the department store. If the effect of the covariate is significant, the sign of the raw coefficient can be used to interpret the direction of the effect on the dependent variable.

# ISSUES IN INTERPRETATION

Important issues involved in the interpretation of ANOVA results include interactions, relative importance of factors, and multiple comparisons.

## Interactions

The different interactions that can arise when conducting ANOVA on two or more factors are shown in Figure 16.3. One outcome is that ANOVA may indicate that there are no interactions (the interaction effects are not found to be significant). The other possibility is that the interaction is significant. An *interaction effect* occurs when the effect of an independent variable on a dependent variable is different for different categories or levels of another independent variable. The interaction may be ordinal or disordinal. In ***ordinal interaction,*** the rank order of the effects related to one factor does not change across the levels of the second factor. ***Disordinal interaction,*** on the other hand, involves a change in the rank order of the effects of one factor across the levels of another. If the interaction is disordinal, it could be of a noncrossover or crossover type.[14]

These interaction cases are displayed in Figure 16.4, which assumes that there are two factors, $X_1$ with three levels ($X_{11}$, $X_{12}$, and $X_{13}$), and $X_2$ with two levels ($X_{21}$ and $X_{22}$). Case 1 depicts no interaction. The effects of $X_1$ on $Y$ are parallel over the two levels of $X_2$. Although there is some departure from parallelism, this is not beyond what might be expected from chance. Parallelism implies that the net effect of $X_{22}$ over $X_{21}$ is the same across the three levels of $X_1$. In the absence of interaction, the joint effect of $X_1$ and $X_2$ is simply the sum of their individual main effects.

Case 2 depicts an ordinal interaction. The line segments depicting the effects of $X_1$ and $X_2$ are not parallel. The difference between $X_{22}$ and $X_{21}$ increases as we move from $X_{11}$ to $X_{12}$ and from $X_{12}$ to $X_{13}$, but the rank order of the effects of $X_1$ is the same over the two levels of $X_2$. This rank order, in ascending order, is $X_{11}$, $X_{12}$, $X_{13}$, and it remains the same for $X_{21}$ and $X_{22}$.

Disordinal interaction of a noncrossover type is displayed by case 3. The lowest effect of $X_1$ at level $X_{21}$ occurs at $X_{11}$, and the rank order of effects is $X_{11}$, $X_{12}$, and $X_{13}$. However, at level $X_{22}$, the lowest effect of $X_1$ occurs at $X_{12}$, and the rank order is changed to $X_{12}$, $X_{11}$, $X_{13}$. Because it involves a change in rank order, disordinal interaction is stronger than ordinal interaction.

In disordinal interactions of a crossover type, the line segments cross each other, as shown by case 4 in Figure 16.4. In this case, the relative effect of the levels of one factor changes with the levels of the other. Note that $X_{22}$ has a greater effect than $X_{21}$ when the levels of $X_1$ are $X_{11}$ and $X_{12}$. When the level of $X_1$ is $X_{13}$, the situation is reversed, and $X_{21}$ has a greater effect than $X_{22}$. (Note that in cases 1, 2, and 3, $X_{22}$ had a greater impact than $X_{21}$ across all three levels of $X_1$.) Hence, disordinal interactions of a crossover type represent the strongest interactions.[15]

---

**ordinal interaction**
An interaction where the rank order of the effects attributable to one factor does not change across the levels of the second factor.

**disordinal interaction**
The change in the rank order of the effects of one factor across the levels of another.

---

*Figure 16.3*
A Classification of Interaction Effects

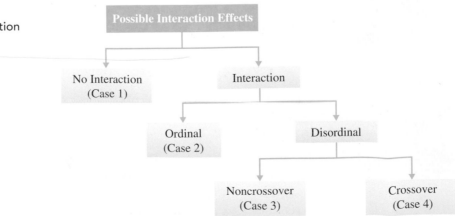

*Figure 16.4*
**Patterns of Interaction**

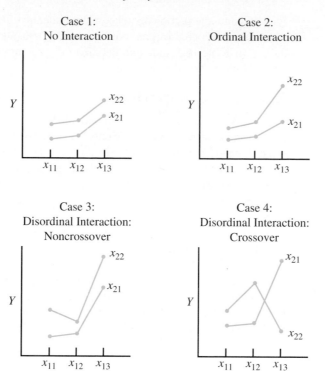

Case 1:
No Interaction

Case 2:
Ordinal Interaction

Case 3:
Disordinal Interaction:
Noncrossover

Case 4:
Disordinal Interaction:
Crossover

## Relative Importance of Factors

*omega squared ($\omega^2$)*
A measure indicating the proportion of the variation in the dependent variable explained by a particular independent variable or factor.

Experimental designs are usually balanced, in that each cell contains the same number of respondents. This results in an orthogonal design in which the factors are uncorrelated. Hence, it is possible to determine unambiguously the relative importance of each factor in explaining the variation in the dependent variable. The most commonly used measure in ANOVA is *omega squared,* $\omega^2$. This measure indicates what proportion of the variation in the dependent variable is related to a particular independent variable or factor. The relative contribution of a factor $X$ is calculated as follows:[16]

$$\omega_x^2 = \frac{SS_x - (df_x \times MS_{error})}{SS_{total} + MS_{error}}$$

Normally, $\omega^2$ is interpreted only for statistically significant effects.[17] In Table 16.5, $\omega^2$ associated with the level of in-store promotion is calculated as follows:

$$\omega_p^2 = \frac{106.067 - (2 \times 0.967)}{185.867 + 0.967}$$

$$= \frac{104.133}{186.834}$$

$$= 0.557$$

Note, in Table 16.5, that

$$SS_{total} = 106.067 + 53.333 + 3.267 + 23.2$$
$$= 185.867$$

Likewise, the $\omega^2$ associated with couponing is:

$$\omega_c^2 = \frac{53.333 - (1 \times 0.967)}{185.867 + 0.967}$$

$$= \frac{52.366}{186.834}$$

$$= 0.280$$

As a guide to interpreting $\omega^2$, a large experimental effect produces an $\omega^2$ of 0.15 or greater, a medium effect produces an index of around 0.06, and a small effect produces an index of 0.01.[18] In Table 16.5, although the effect of promotion and couponing are both large, the effect of promotion is much larger.

## Multiple Comparisons

The ANOVA $F$ test examines only the overall difference in means. If the null hypothesis of equal means is rejected, we can conclude only that not all of the group means are equal. However, only some of the means may be statistically different and we may wish to examine differences among specific means. This can be done by specifying appropriate **contrasts**, or comparisons used to determine which of the means are statistically different. Contrasts may be a priori or a posteriori. *A priori contrasts* are determined before conducting the analysis, based on the researcher's theoretical framework. Generally, a priori contrasts are used in lieu of the ANOVA $F$ test. The contrasts selected are orthogonal (they are independent in a statistical sense).

*A posteriori contrasts* are made after the analysis. These are generally ***multiple comparison tests.*** They enable the researcher to construct generalized confidence intervals that can be used to make pairwise comparisons of all treatment means. These tests, listed in order of decreasing power, include least significant difference, Duncan's multiple range test, Student-Newman-Keuls, Tukey's alternate procedure, honestly significant difference, modified least significant difference, and Scheffe's test. Of these tests, least significant difference is the most powerful, Scheffe's the most conservative. For further discussion on a priori and a posteriori contrasts, refer to the literature.[19]

Our discussion so far has assumed that each subject is exposed to only one treatment or experimental condition. Sometimes subjects are exposed to more than one experimental condition, in which case repeated measures ANOVA should be used.

**contrasts**
In ANOVA, a method of examining differences among two or more means of the treatment groups.

**a priori contrasts**
Contrasts that are determined before conducting the analysis, based on the researcher's theoretical framework.

**a posteriori contrasts**
Contrasts made after the analysis. These are generally multiple comparison tests.

**multiple comparison test**
A posteriori contrasts that enable the researcher to construct generalized confidence intervals that can be used to make pairwise comparisons of all treatment means.

# REPEATED MEASURES ANOVA

In marketing research there are often large differences in the background and individual characteristics of respondents. If this source of variability can be separated from treatment effects (effects of the independent variable) and experimental error, then the sensitivity of the experiment can be enhanced. One way of controlling the differences between subjects is by observing each subject under each experimental condition (see Table 16.7). In this sense, each subject serves as its own control. For example, in a survey attempting to determine differences in evaluations of various airlines, each respondent evaluates all the major competing airlines. Because repeated measurements are obtained from each respondent, this design is referred to as within-subjects design or ***repeated measures analysis of variance.*** This differs from the assumption we made in our earlier discussion that each respondent is exposed to only one treatment condition, also referred to as between-subjects design.[20] Repeated measures analysis of variance may be thought of as an extension of the paired-samples $t$ test to the case of more than two related samples.

**repeated measures ANOVA**
An ANOVA technique used when respondents are exposed to more than one treatment condition and repeated measurements are obtained.

In the case of a single factor with repeated measures, the total variation, with $nc-1$ degrees of freedom, may be split into between-people variation and within-people variation.

$$SS_{total} = SS_{between\ people} + SS_{within\ people}$$

The between-people variation, which is related to the differences between the means of people, has $n - 1$ degrees of freedom. The within-people variation has $n(c - 1)$ degrees of freedom. The within-people variation may, in turn, be divided into two different sources of variation. One source is related to the differences between treatment means, and the second consists of residual or error variation. The degrees of freedom corresponding to the treatment variation are $c - 1$, and those corresponding to residual variation are $(c - 1)(n - 1)$. Thus,

$$SS_{within\ people} = SS_x + SS_{error}$$

A test of the null hypothesis of equal means may now be constructed in the usual way:

$$F = \frac{SS_x/(c - 1)}{SS_{error}/(n - 1)(c - 1)} = \frac{MS_x}{MS_{error}}$$

**TABLE 16.7**

**Decomposition of the Total Variation: Repeated Measures ANOVA**

INDEPENDENT VARIABLE        X

<table>
<tr><td></td><td colspan="6">SUBJECT No.       CATEGORIES        TOTAL SAMPLE</td></tr>
<tr><td></td><td>$X_1$</td><td>$X_2$</td><td>$X_3$</td><td>... $X_c$</td><td></td></tr>
<tr><td>1</td><td>$Y_{11}$</td><td>$Y_{12}$</td><td>$Y_{13}$</td><td>$Y_{1c}$</td><td>$Y_1$</td></tr>
<tr><td>2</td><td>$Y_{21}$</td><td>$Y_{22}$</td><td>$Y_{23}$</td><td>$Y_{2c}$</td><td>$Y_2$</td></tr>
<tr><td>n</td><td>$Y_{n1}$</td><td>$Y_{n2}$</td><td>$Y_{n3}$</td><td>$Y_{nc}$</td><td>$Y_N$</td></tr>
<tr><td></td><td>$\bar{Y}_1$</td><td>$\bar{Y}_2$</td><td>$\bar{Y}_3$</td><td>$\bar{Y}_c$</td><td>$\bar{Y}$</td></tr>
</table>

Between-People Variation $= SS_{between\ people}$

Total Variation $= SS_y$

Category Mean

Within-People Variation $= SS_{within\ people}$

So far we have assumed that the dependent variable is measured on an interval or ratio scale. If the dependent variable is nonmetric, however, a different procedure should be used.

# NONMETRIC ANALYSIS OF VARIANCE

**nonmetric ANOVA**
An ANOVA technique for examining the difference in the central tendencies of more than two groups when the dependent variable is measured on an ordinal scale.

**k-sample median test**
Nonparametric test that is used to examine differences among groups when the dependent variable is measured on an ordinal scale.

**Kruskal-Wallis one-way analysis of variance**
A nonmetric ANOVA test that uses the rank value of each case, not merely its location relative to the median.

*Nonmetric analysis of variance* examines the difference in the central tendencies of more than two groups when the dependent variable is measured on an ordinal scale. One such procedure is the **k-sample median test.** As its name implies, this is an extension of the median test for two groups, which was considered in Chapter 15. The null hypothesis is that the medians of the $k$ populations are equal. The test involves the computation of a common median over the $k$ samples. Then a $2 \times k$ table of cell counts based on cases above or below the common median is generated. A chi-square statistic is computed. The significance of the chi-square implies a rejection of the null hypothesis.

A more powerful test is the **Kruskal-Wallis one-way analysis of variance.** This is an extension of the Mann-Whitney test (Chapter 15). This test also examines the difference in medians. The null hypothesis is the same as in the $k$-sample median test, but the testing procedure is different. All cases from the $k$ groups are ordered in a single ranking. If the $k$ populations are the same, the groups should be similar in terms of ranks within each group. The rank sum is calculated for each group. From these, the Kruskal-Wallis $H$ statistic, which has a chi-square distribution, is computed.

The Kruskal-Wallis test is more powerful than the $k$-sample median test as it uses the rank value of each case, not merely its location relative to the median. However, if there are a large number of tied rankings in the data, the $k$-sample median test may be a better choice.

Nonmetric analysis of variance is not popular in commercial marketing research. Another procedure, which is also only rarely used, is multivariate analysis of variance.

# MULTIVARIATE ANALYSIS OF VARIANCE

**multivariate analysis of variance (MANOVA)**
An ANOVA technique using two or more metric dependent variables.

*Multivariate analysis of variance* (MANOVA) is similar to analysis of variance (ANOVA), except that instead of one metric dependent variable, we have two or more. The objective is the same; MANOVA is also concerned with examining differences between groups. Whereas ANOVA examines group differences on a single dependent variable, MANOVA examines group differences across multiple dependent variables simultaneously. In ANOVA, the null hypothesis is that the means of the dependent variable are equal across the groups. In MANOVA, the null hypothesis is that the vectors of means on multiple dependent variables are equal across groups. Multivariate analysis of variance is appropriate when there are two or more dependent variables that are correlated. If there are multiple dependent variables that are uncorrelated or orthogonal, ANOVA on each of the dependent variables is more appropriate than MANOVA.[21]

As an example, suppose that four groups, each consisting of 100 randomly selected individuals, were exposed to four different commercials about Tide detergent. After seeing the commercial, each individual provided ratings on preference for Tide, preference for Procter & Gamble (the company marketing Tide), and preference for the commercial itself. Because these three preference variables are correlated, multivariate analysis of variance should be conducted to determine which commercial is the most effective (produced the highest preference across the three preference variables). The next example illustrates the application of ANOVA and MANOVA in international marketing research, and the example after that shows an application of these techniques in examining ethics in marketing research.

### REAL RESEARCH

## *The Commonality of Unethical Research Practices Worldwide*

As of 2003, mass media is continuing to focus more attention on the highly visible practices of unethical marketing research and this poses a serious threat to marketing research practitioners. A study examined marketing professionals' perceptions of the commonality of unethical marketing research practices on a cross-national basis. The sample of marketing professionals was drawn from Australia, Canada, Great Britain, and the United States.

Respondents' evaluations were analyzed using computer programs for MANOVA and ANOVA. Country of respondent comprised the predictor variable in the analysis, and 15 commonality evaluations served as the criterion variables. The $F$ values from the ANOVA analyses indicated that only two of the 15 commonality evaluations achieved significance ($p < 0.05$ or better). Further, the MANOVA $F$ value was not statistically significant, implying the lack of overall differences in commonality evaluations across respondents of the four countries. Therefore, it was concluded that marketing professionals in the four countries evince similar perceptions of the commonality of unethical research practices. This finding is not surprising, given research evidence that organizations in the four countries reflect similar corporate cultures. Thus, the marketing research industry in these four countries should adopt a common platform in fighting unethical practices.[22] ■

### REAL RESEARCH

## *"MAN"OVA Demonstrates That Man Is Different from Woman*

In order to investigate differences between research ethics judgments in men and women, the statistical techniques of MANOVA and ANOVA were used. Respondents were asked to indicate their degree of approval with regard to a series of scenarios involving decisions of an ethical nature. These evaluations served as the dependent variable in the analysis, and sex of the respondent served as the independent variable. MANOVA was used for multivariate analysis and its resultant $F$ value was significant at the $p < 0.001$ level—indicating that there was an "overall" difference between males and females in research ethics judgments. Univariate analysis was conducted via ANOVA, and $F$ values indicated that three items were the greatest contributors to the overall gender difference in ethical evaluations: the use of ultraviolet ink to precode a mail questionnaire, the use of an ad that encourages consumer misuse of a product, and unwillingness by researcher to offer data help to an inner-city advisory group. A similar study was conducted in 2001, which examined how ethical beliefs are related to age and gender of business professionals. The results of this particular study indicated that overall, younger business professionals exhibited a lower standard of ethical beliefs. In the younger age group, females demonstrated a higher level of ethical beliefs compared to males. However, in the older age group, results showed that males had a slightly higher level of ethical beliefs. Thus, companies should emphasize ethical values and training to the younger professionals, especially men.[23] ■

# INTERNET AND COMPUTER APPLICATIONS

The major computer packages (SPSS and SAS) have programs for conducting analysis of variance and covariance available in the microcomputer and mainframe versions. In addition to the basic analysis that we have considered, these programs can also perform more complex analysis. MINITAB and EXCEL also offer some programs. Exhibit 16.1 contains a description of the relevant programs. Refer to the user manuals for these packages for more details.

## SPSS Windows

One-way ANOVA can be efficiently performed using the program COMPARE MEANS and then ONE-WAY ANOVA. To select this procedure using SPSS for Windows, click:

>    Analyze>Compare Means>One-Way ANOVA . . .

*N*-way analysis of variance, analysis of covariance, MANOVA, and repeated measures ANOVA can be performed using GENERAL LINEAR MODEL. To select this procedure using SPSS for Windows, click:

>    Analyze>General Linear Model>Univariate . . .
>    Analyze>General Linear Model>Multivariate . . .
>    Analyze>General Linear Model>Repeated Measures . . .

For nonmetric analysis of variance, including the *k* sample median test and Kruskal-Wallis one way analysis of variance, the program Nonparametric Tests should be used

>    Analyze>Nonparametric Tests>K Independent Samples . . .
>    Analyze>Nonparametric Tests>K Related Samples . . .

*EXHIBIT 16.1*

Computer Programs for ANOVA and ANCOVA

---

Given the importance of analysis of variance and covariance, several programs are available in each package.

### SPSS

One-way ANOVA can be efficiently performed using the program ONEWAY. This program also allows the user to test a priori and a posteriori contrasts, which cannot be done in other SPSS programs. For performing *n*-way analysis of variance, the program ANOVA can be used. Although covariates can be specified, ANOVA does not perform a full analysis of covariance. For comprehensive analysis of variance or analysis of covariance, including repeated measures and multiple dependent measures, the MANOVA procedure is recommended. For nonmetric analysis of variance, including the *k*-sample median test and Kruskal-Wallis one-way analysis of variance, the program NPAR TESTS should be used.

### SAS

The main program for performing analysis of variance in the case of a balanced design is ANOVA. This program can handle data from a wide variety of experimental designs, including multivariate analysis of variance and repeated measures. Both a priori and a posteriori contrasts can be tested. For unbalanced designs, the more general GLM procedure can be used. This program performs analysis of variance, analysis of covariance, repeated measures analysis of variance, and multivariate analysis of variance. It also allows the testing of a priori and a posteriori contrasts. Although GLM can also be used for analyzing balanced designs, it is not as efficient as ANOVA for such models. The VARCOMP procedure computes variance components. For nonmetric analysis of variance, the NPAR1WAY procedure can be used. For constructing designs and randomized plans, the PLAN procedure can be used.

### Minitab

Analysis of variance and covariance can be assessed from the Stats>ANOVA function. This function performs one-way ANOVA, two-way ANOVA, analysis of means, balanced ANOVA, analysis of covariance, general linear model, main effects plot, interactions plot, and residual plots. In order to compute the mean and standard deviation, the CROSSTAB function must be used. To obtain *F* and *p* values, use the balanced ANOVA.

### Excel

Both a one-way ANOVA and two-way ANOVA can be performed under the Tools>DATA ANALYSIS function. The two-way ANOVA has the features of a two-factor with replication and a two-factor without replication. The two-factor with replication includes more than one sample for each group of data. The two-factor without replication does not include more than one sampling per group.

### FOCUS ON BURKE

Often problems for which ANOVA would be used have predictor variables that are correlated. This mandates great care in interpreting the results. Although the overall significance test for the model is unaffected, the manner in which you look at the contribution of the individual predictors will be impacted. Analysis of a Burke study in which the two categorical predictor variables were correlated illustrates this point with this small data set (the real data are proprietary).

| Purchase Intent | Performance Rating | Gender |
|---|---|---|
| 2 | 1 | 0 |
| 4 | 2 | 1 |
| 6 | 3 | 1 |
| 4 | 4 | 0 |
| 5 | 5 | 0 |
| 6 | 6 | 1 |
| 2 | 1 | 0 |
| 3 | 2 | 0 |
| 4 | 3 | 0 |
| 5 | 4 | 1 |
| 6 | 5 | 1 |
| 8 | 6 | 1 |

As the two predictors are somewhat correlated ($r^2 = 0.24$), the interpretation of the contribution of each predictor becomes an issue of concern.

The first ANOVA table (from SPSS) shows the sum of squares running the model under the assumptions that the sum of squares for each predictor should be adjusted for the presence of the other predictor (i.e., as if each had been entered second). The second ANOVA table shows the result run hierarchically with Rating first to "enter." The third ANOVA table shows the result run hierarchically with Gender first to "enter."

**ANOVA**[a, b]

| | | | Sum of Squares | df | Unique Method Mean Square | F | Significance |
|---|---|---|---|---|---|---|---|
| PI | Main | (Combined) | 32.542 | 6 | 5.424 | 11.418 | 0.009 |
| | Effects | RATING | 13.792 | 5 | 2.758 | 5.807 | 0.038 |
| | | GENDER | 3.125 | 1 | 3.125 | 6.579 | 0.050 |
| | Model | | 32.542 | 6 | 5.424 | 11.418 | 0.009 |
| | Residual | | 2.375 | 5 | 0.475 | | |
| | Total | | 34.917 | 11 | 3.174 | | |

[a]PI by RATING, GENDER

[b]All effects entered simultaneously

# SUMMARY

In ANOVA and ANCOVA, the dependent variable is metric and the independent variables are all categorical, or combinations of categorical and metric variables. One-way ANOVA involves a single independent categorical variable. Interest lies in testing the null hypothesis that the category means are equal in the population. The total variation in the dependent variable is decomposed into two components: variation related to the independent variable and variation related to

error. The variation is measured in terms of the sum of squares corrected for the mean (*SS*). The mean square is obtained by dividing the *SS* by the corresponding degrees of freedom (df). The null hypothesis of equal means is tested by an *F* statistic, which is the ratio of the mean square related to the independent variable to the mean square related to error.

*N*-way analysis of variance involves the simultaneous examination of two or more categorical independent vari-

*ANOVA*[a]

| | | | Sum of Squares | df | Hierarchical Method Mean Square | F | Significance |
|---|---|---|---|---|---|---|---|
| PI | Main | (Combined) | 32.542 | 6 | 5.424 | 11.418 | 0.009 |
| | Effects | RATING | 29.417 | 5 | 5.883 | 12.386 | 0.008 |
| | | GENDER | 3.125 | 1 | 3.125 | 6.579 | 0.050 |
| | Model | | 32.542 | 6 | 5.424 | 11.418 | 0.009 |
| | Residual | | 2.375 | 5 | 0.475 | | |
| | Total | | 34.917 | 11 | 3.174 | | |

[a]PI by RATING, GENDER

*ANOVA*[a]

| | | | Sum of Squares | df | Hierarchical Method Mean Square | F | Significance |
|---|---|---|---|---|---|---|---|
| PI | Main | (Combined) | 32.542 | 6 | 5.424 | 11.418 | 0.009 |
| | Effects | GENDER | 18.750 | 1 | 18.750 | 39.474 | 0.002 |
| | | RATING | 13.792 | 5 | 2.758 | 5.807 | 0.038 |
| | Model | | 32.542 | 6 | 5.424 | 11.418 | 0.009 |
| | Residual | | 2.375 | 5 | 0.475 | | |
| | Total | | 34.917 | 11 | 3.174 | | |

[a]PI by GENDER, RATING

Summarizing the results:

| | | Hierarchical | |
|---|---|---|---|
| Sum of Squares | Regression | Rating First | Gender First |
| Rating | 13.792 | 29.417 | 18.750 |
| Gender | 3.125 | 3.125 | 13.792 |
| Total of predictors | 16.917 | 32.542 | 32.542 |
| Total explained | 32.542 | 32.542 | 32.542 |

Now the issue is obvious, what portion of the sum of squares does each predictor explain? As the predictors are correlated, the hierarchical approach shows the sum of squares for the predictors entered in a specified order. The unique solution shows the explained sum of squares for each predictor as if it had been entered second (that is why it does not add up to the proper total . . . both predictors cannot be entered second). The three solutions give a complete picture of the contribution of each variable if it was the only predictor and what its marginal contribution would be as the second predictor.

ables. A major advantage is that the interactions between the independent variables can be examined. The significance of the overall effect, interaction terms, and main effects of individual factors are examined by appropriate $F$ tests. It is meaningful to test the significance of main effects only if the corresponding interaction terms are not significant.

ANCOVA includes at least one categorical independent variable and at least one interval or metric independent variable. The metric independent variable, or covariate, is commonly used to remove extraneous variation from the dependent variable.

When analysis of variance is conducted on two or more factors, interactions can arise. An interaction occurs when the effect of an independent variable on a dependent variable is different for different categories or levels of another independent variable. If the interaction is significant, it may be ordinal or disordinal. Disordinal interaction may be of a noncrossover or crossover type. In balanced designs, the relative importance of factors in explaining the variation in the dependent variable is measured by omega squared ($\omega^2$). Multiple comparisons in the form of a priori or a posteriori contrasts can be used for examining differences among specific means.

In repeated measures analysis of variance, observations on each subject are obtained under each treatment condition. This design is useful for controlling for the differences in subjects that exist prior to the experiment. Nonmetric analysis of variance involves examining the differences in the central tendencies of two or more groups when the dependent variable is measured on an ordinal scale. Multivariate analysis of variance (MANOVA) involves two or more metric dependent variables.

# KEY TERMS AND CONCEPTS

analysis of variance (ANOVA), *469*
factors, *469*
treatment, *469*
one-way analysis of variance, *469*
*n*-way analysis of variance, *469*
analysis of covariance (ANCOVA), *469*
covariates, *470*
eta$^2$ ($\eta^2$), *471*
*F* statistic, *471*
mean square, *471*
$SS_{between}$ ($SS_x$), *471*
$SS_{within}$ ($SS_{error}$), *471*

$SS_y$, *471*
decomposition of the total variation, *471*
interactions, *478*
multiple $\eta^2$, *479*
significance of the overall effect, *479*
significance of the interaction effect, *479*
significance of the main effect, *479*
ordinal interaction, *484*
disordinal interaction, *484*
omega squared ($\omega^2$), *485*
contrasts, *486*
a priori contrasts, *486*

a posteriori contrasts, *486*
multiple comparison tests, *486*
repeated measures analysis of variance, *486*
nonmetric analysis of variance, *487*
*k*-sample median test, *487*
Kruskal-Wallis one-way analysis of variance, *487*
multivariate analysis of variance (MANOVA), *487*

# EXERCISES

## Questions

1. Discuss the similarities and differences between analysis of variance and analysis of covariance.
2. What is the relationship between analysis of variance and the *t* test?
3. What is total variation? How is it decomposed in a one-way analysis of variance?
4. What is the null hypothesis in one-way ANOVA? What basic statistic is used to test the null hypothesis in one-way ANOVA? How is this statistic computed?
5. How does *n*-way analysis of variance differ from the one-way procedure?
6. How is the total variation decomposed in *n*-way analysis of variance?
7. What is the most common use of the covariate in ANCOVA?
8. Define an interaction.
9. What is the difference between ordinal and disordinal interaction?
10. How is the relative importance of factors measured in a balanced design?
11. What is an a priori contrast?
12. What is the most powerful test for making a posteriori contrasts? Which test is the most conservative?
13. What is meant by repeated measures ANOVA? Describe the decomposition of variation in repeated measures ANOVA.
14. What are the differences between metric and nonmetric analyses of variance?
15. Describe two tests used for examining differences in central tendencies in nonmetric ANOVA.
16. What is multivariate analysis of variance? When is it appropriate?

## Problems

1. After receiving some complaints from the readers, your campus newspaper decides to redesign its front page. Two new formats, B and C, were developed and tested against the current format, A. A total of 75 students were randomly selected and

25 students were randomly assigned to each of three format conditions. The students were asked to evaluate the effectiveness of the format on a 11-point scale (1 = poor, 11 = excellent).
   a. State the null hypothesis.
   b. What statistical test should you use?
   c. What are the degrees of freedom associated with the test statistic?

2. A marketing researcher wants to test the hypothesis that, in the population, there is no difference in the importance attached to shopping by consumers living in the northern, southern, eastern, and western United States. A study is conducted and analysis of variance is used to analyze the data. The results obtained are presented in the following table.

| Source | df | Sum of Squares | Mean Squares | F Ratio | F Probability |
|---|---|---|---|---|---|
| Between groups | 3 | 70.212 | 23.404 | 1.12 | 0.3 |
| Within groups | 996 | 20812.416 | 20.896 | | |

   a. Is there sufficient evidence to reject the null hypothesis?
   b. What conclusion can be drawn from the table?
   c. If the average importance was computed for each group, would you expect the sample means to be similar or different?
   d. What was the total sample size in this study?

3. In a pilot study examining the effectiveness of three commercials (A, B, and C), 10 consumers were assigned to view each commercial and rate it on a nine-point Likert scale. The data obtained from the 30 respondents are shown in the table.

| Commercial | | | Commercial | | |
|---|---|---|---|---|---|
| *A* | *B* | *C* | *A* | *B* | *C* |
| 4 | 7 | 8 | 4 | 6 | 7 |
| 5 | 4 | 7 | 4 | 5 | 8 |
| 3 | 6 | 7 | 3 | 5 | 8 |
| 4 | 5 | 6 | 5 | 4 | 5 |
| 3 | 4 | 8 | 5 | 4 | 6 |

a. Calculate the category means and the grand mean.
b. Calculate $SS_y$, $SS_x$, and $SS_{error}$.
c. Calculate $\eta^2$.
d. Calculate the value of $F$.
e. Are the three commercials equally effective?

4. An experiment tested the effects of package design and shelf display on the likelihood of purchase of Product 19 cereal. Package design and shelf display were varied at two levels each, resulting in a 2 × 2 design. Purchase likelihood was measured on a seven-point scale. The results are partially described in the following table.

| Source of Variation | Sum of Squares | df | Mean Square | F | Significance of F | $\omega^2$ |
|---|---|---|---|---|---|---|
| Package design | 68.76 | 1 | | | | |
| Shelf display | 320.19 | 1 | | | | |
| Two-way interaction | 55.05 | 1 | | | | |
| Residual error | 176.00 | 40 | | | | |

a. Complete the table by calculating the mean square, $F$, significance of $F$, and $\omega^2$ values.
b. How should the main effects be interpreted?

# INTERNET AND COMPUTER EXERCISES

1. Analyze the Nike data given in Internet and Computer Exercises 1 of Chapter 15. Do the three usage groups differ in terms of awareness, attitude, preference, intention, and loyalty toward Nike when these variables are considered individually, i.e., one at a time?

2. Conduct the following analyses for the outdoor lifestyle data given in Internet and Computer Exercises 2 of Chapter 15.
   a. Do the three groups based on location of residence differ in their preference for an outdoor lifestyle?
   b. Do the three groups based on location of residence differ in terms of the importance attached to enjoying nature?
   c. Do the three groups based on location of residence differ in terms of the importance attached to living in harmony with the environment?
   d. Do the three groups based on location of residence differ in terms of the importance attached to exercising regularly?

3. In an experiment designed to measure the effect of sex and frequency of travel on preference for foreign travel a 2 (sex) × 3 (frequency of travel) between-subjects design was adopted. Five respondents were assigned to each cell for a total sample size of 30. Preference for foreign travel was measured on a nine-point scale (1 = no preference, 9 = strong preference). Sex was coded as male = 1 and female = 2. Frequency of travel was coded as light = 1, medium = 2, and heavy = 3. The data obtained are shown.

| Number | Sex | Travel Group | Preference |
|---|---|---|---|
| 1 | 1 | 1 | 2 |
| 2 | 1 | 1 | 3 |
| 3 | 1 | 1 | 4 |
| 4 | 1 | 1 | 4 |
| 5 | 1 | 1 | 2 |
| 6 | 1 | 2 | 4 |
| 7 | 1 | 2 | 5 |
| 8 | 1 | 2 | 5 |
| 9 | 1 | 2 | 3 |
| 10 | 1 | 2 | 3 |
| 11 | 1 | 3 | 8 |
| 12 | 1 | 3 | 9 |
| 13 | 1 | 3 | 8 |
| 14 | 1 | 3 | 7 |
| 15 | 1 | 3 | 7 |
| 16 | 2 | 1 | 6 |
| 17 | 2 | 1 | 7 |
| 18 | 2 | 1 | 6 |
| 19 | 2 | 1 | 5 |
| 20 | 2 | 1 | 7 |
| 21 | 2 | 2 | 3 |
| 22 | 2 | 2 | 4 |
| 23 | 2 | 2 | 5 |
| 24 | 2 | 2 | 4 |
| 25 | 2 | 2 | 5 |
| 26 | 2 | 3 | 6 |
| 27 | 2 | 3 | 6 |
| 28 | 2 | 3 | 6 |
| 29 | 2 | 3 | 7 |
| 30 | 2 | 3 | 8 |

Using software of your choice, perform the following analysis.
   a. Do the males and the females differ in their preference for foreign travel?
   b. Do the light, medium, and heavy travelers differ in their preference for foreign travel?
   c. Conduct a 2 × 3 analysis of variance with preference for foreign travel as the dependent variable and sex and travel frequency as the independent variables or factors. Interpret the results.

4. Using the appropriate microcomputer and mainframe programs in the package of your choice (SPSS, SAS, MINITAB, or EXCEL), analyze the data collected in Fieldwork assignment 1. Should the campus newspaper change the format of the cover page? What is your conclusion?

# ACTIVITIES

## Fieldwork

1. Contact your campus newspaper. Collect data for the experiment described in problem 1. Because this may be too much work for one student, this project may be handled in teams of three.

## Group Discussion

1. Which procedure is more useful in marketing research—analysis of variance or analysis of covariance? Discuss as a small group.

# CHAPTER 17

# Correlation and Regression

## Objectives

After reading this chapter, the student should be able to:

1. Discuss the concepts of product moment correlation, partial correlation, and part correlation and show how they provide a foundation for regression analysis.
2. Explain the nature and methods of bivariate regression analysis and describe the general model, estimation of parameters, standardized regression coefficient, significance testing, prediction accuracy, residual analysis, and model cross-validation.
3. Explain the nature and methods of multiple regression analysis and the meaning of partial regression coefficients.
4. Describe specialized techniques used in multiple regression analysis, particularly stepwise regression, regression with dummy variables, and analysis of variance and covariance with regression.
5. Discuss nonmetric correlation and measures such as Spearman's rho and Kendall's tau.

"For a researcher, correlation is the most convenient and understandable way to look at the association between two metric variables. When extended to multiple regression, the relationship between one variable and several others becomes more understandable."

*Jim Kershaw,*
*group manager,*
*consulting & analytical,*
*Burke, Inc.*

Chapter 16 examined the relationship among the *t* test, analysis of variance and covariance, and regression. This chapter describes regression analysis, which is widely used for explaining variation in market share, sales, brand preference, and other marketing results in terms of marketing management variables such as advertising, price, distribution, and product quality. However, before discussing regression, we describe the concepts of product moment correlation and partial correlation coefficient, which lay the conceptual foundation for regression analysis.

In introducing regression analysis, we discuss the simple bivariate case first. We describe estimation, standardization of the regression coefficients, testing and examination of the strength and significance of association between variables, prediction accuracy, and the assumptions underlying the regression model. Next, we discuss the multiple regression model, emphasizing the interpretation of parameters, strength of association, significance tests, and examination of residuals.

Then we cover topics of special interest in regression analysis, such as stepwise regression, multicollinearity, relative importance of predictor variables, and cross-validation. We describe regression with dummy variables and the use of this procedure to conduct analysis of variance and covariance.

---

**ACTIVE RESEARCH** | DEPARTMENT STORE PROJECT

### *Multiple Regression*

In the department store project, multiple regression analysis was used to develop a model that explained store preference in terms of respondents' evaluations of the store on the eight choice criteria. The dependent variable was preference for each store. The independent variables were the evaluations of each store on quality of merchandise, variety and assortment of merchandise, returns and adjustment policy, service of store personnel, prices, convenience of location, layout of store, and credit and billing policies. The results indicated that all the factors of the choice criteria, except service of store personnel, were significant in explaining store preference. The coefficients of all the variables were positive, indicating that higher evaluations on each of the significant factors led to higher preference for that store. The model had a good fit and good ability to predict store preference.

---

**REAL RESEARCH**

## *Regression Rings the Right Bell for Avon*

Avon Products, Inc. (*www.avon.com*), was having significant problems with the sales staff. The company's business, dependent on sales representatives, was facing a shortage of sales reps without much hope of getting new ones. Regression models, operating on microcomputers, were developed to reveal the possible variables that were fueling this situation. The models revealed that the most significant variable was the level of the appointment fee that reps pay for materials and second was the employee benefits. With data to back up its actions, the company lowered the fee. The company also hired senior manager Michele Schneider in 2001 to improve the way Avon informed new hires of their employee benefits program. Schneider revamped Avon's benefits program information packet, which

Good products, well-trained sales reps, and sophisticated regression models have opened the doors for Avon, enabling it to penetrate the cosmetics market.

yielded an informative and easy to navigate "Guide to Your Personal Benefits." These changes resulted in an improvement in the recruitment and retention of sales reps. As of 2003, Avon was operating in over 100 countries.[1] ■

### REAL RESEARCH

## *Retailing Revolution*

Many retailing experts suggest that electronic shopping will be the next revolution in retailing. Whereas many traditional retailers experienced sluggish, single-digit sales growth in 2001, online sales records were off the charts with sales of $10 billion for that same year. According to market researcher, comScore Networks, Inc. online sales in 2001 were 12 percent higher than in 2000. Although e-tailing continues to make up a very small portion of overall retail sales (just 2 percent in 2001), the trend looks very promising for the future. A research project investigating this trend looked for correlates of consumers' preferences for electronic shopping services via home videotex (computerized in-home shopping services). The explanation of consumers' preferences was sought in psychographic, demographic, and communication variables suggested in the literature. The study was conducted in south Florida where Viewtron, a videotex service, has been offered since 1983. Viewtron, a subsidiary of Knight-Ridder Corporation (*www.knightridder.com*), spent millions on advertising in the area. All the respondents were familiar with the concept of computerized shopping from home.

Multiple regression was used to analyze the data. The overall multiple regression model was significant at 0.05 level. Univariate *t* tests indicated that the following variables in the model were significant at 0.05 level or better: price orientation, sex, age, occupation, ethnicity, and education. None of the three communication variables (mass media, word of mouth, and publicity) was significantly related to consumer preference, the dependent variable.

The results suggest that electronic shopping is preferred by white females who are older, better educated, working in supervisory or higher level occupations, and price-oriented shoppers. Information of this type is valuable in targeting marketing effort to electronic shoppers.[2] ■

These examples illustrate some of the uses of regression analysis in determining which independent variables explain a significant variation in the dependent variable of interest, the structure and form of the relationship, the strength of the relationship, and predicted values of the dependent variable. Fundamental to regression analysis is an understanding of the product moment correlation.

# PRODUCT MOMENT CORRELATION

In marketing research we are often interested in summarizing the strength of association between two metric variables, as in the following situations:

- How strongly are sales related to advertising expenditures?
- Is there an association between market share and size of the sales force?
- Are consumers' perceptions of quality related to their perceptions of prices?

*product moment correlation* (r)
A statistic summarizing the strength of association between two metric variables.

In situations like these, the ***product moment correlation,*** **r**, is the most widely used statistic, summarizing the strength of association between two metric (interval or ratio scaled) variables, say $X$ and $Y$. It is an index used to determine whether a linear, or straight-line, relationship exists between $X$ and $Y$. It indicates the degree to which the variation in one variable, $X$, is related to the variation in another variable, $Y$. Because it was originally proposed by Karl Pearson, it is also known as the *Pearson correlation coefficient*. It is also referred to as *simple correlation*, *bivariate correlation*, or merely the *correlation coefficient*. From a sample of $n$ observations, $X$ and $Y$, the product moment correlation, $r$, can be calculated as:

$$ r = \frac{\sum_{i=1}^{n} (X_i - \overline{X})(Y_i - \overline{Y})}{\sqrt{\sum_{i=1}^{n} (X_i - \overline{X})^2 \sum_{i=1}^{n} (Y_i - \overline{Y})^2}} $$

Division of the numerator and denominator by $n - 1$ gives

$$ r = \frac{\sum_{i=1}^{n} \dfrac{(X_i - \overline{X})(Y_i - \overline{Y})}{n - 1}}{\sqrt{\sum_{i=1}^{n} \dfrac{(X_i - \overline{X})^2}{n - 1} \sum_{i=1}^{n} \dfrac{(Y_i - \overline{Y})^2}{n - 1}}} $$

$$ = \frac{COV_{xy}}{S_x S_y} $$

*covariance*
A systematic relationship between two variables in which a change in one implies a corresponding change in the other ($COV_{xy}$).

In these equations, $\overline{X}$ and $\overline{Y}$ denote the sample means, and $S_x$ and $S_y$ the standard deviations. $COV_{xy}$, the ***covariance*** between $X$ and $Y$, measures the extent to which $X$ and $Y$ are related. The covariance may be either positive or negative. Division by $S_x S_y$ achieves standardization, so that $r$ varies between $-1.0$ and $+1.0$. Note that the correlation coefficient is an absolute number and is not expressed in any unit of measurement. The correlation coefficient between two variables will be the same regardless of their underlying units of measurement.

As an example, suppose a researcher wants to explain attitudes toward a respondent's city of residence in terms of duration of residence in the city. The attitude is measured on an 11-point scale (1 = do not like the city, 11 = very much like the city), and the duration of residence is measured in terms of the number of years the respondent has lived in the city. In a pretest of 12 respondents, the data shown in Table 17.1 are obtained.

The correlation coefficient may be calculated as follows:

$$ \overline{X} = \frac{(10 + 12 + 12 + 4 + 12 + 6 + 8 + 2 + 18 + 9 + 17 + 2)}{12} $$

$$ = 9.333 $$

$$ \overline{Y} = \frac{(6 + 9 + 8 + 3 + 10 + 4 + 5 + 2 + 11 + 9 + 10 + 2)}{12} $$

$$ = 6.583 $$

## TABLE 17.1

### Explaining Attitude Toward the City of Residence

| RESPONDENT No. | ATTITUDE TOWARD THE CITY | DURATION OF RESIDENCE | IMPORTANCE ATTACHED TO WEATHER |
|:---:|:---:|:---:|:---:|
| 1 | 6 | 10 | 3 |
| 2 | 9 | 12 | 11 |
| 3 | 8 | 12 | 4 |
| 4 | 3 | 4 | 1 |
| 5 | 10 | 12 | 11 |
| 6 | 4 | 6 | 1 |
| 7 | 5 | 8 | 7 |
| 8 | 2 | 2 | 4 |
| 9 | 11 | 18 | 8 |
| 10 | 9 | 9 | 10 |
| 11 | 10 | 17 | 8 |
| 12 | 2 | 2 | 5 |

$$
\begin{aligned}
\sum_{i=1}^{n} (X_i - \overline{X})(Y_i - \overline{Y}) &= (10 - 9.33)(6 - 6.58) + (12 - 9.33)(9 - 6.58) \\
&\quad + (12 - 9.33)(8 - 6.58) + (4 - 9.33)(3 - 6.58) \\
&\quad + (12 - 9.33)(10 - 6.58) + (6 - 9.33)(4 - 6.58) \\
&\quad + (8 - 9.33)(5 - 6.58) + (2 - 9.33)(2 - 6.58) \\
&\quad + (18 - 9.33)(11 - 6.58) + (9 - 9.33)(9 - 6.58) \\
&\quad + (17 - 9.33)(10 - 6.58) + (2 - 9.33)(2 - 6.58) \\
&= -0.3886 + 6.4614 + 3.7914 + 19.0814 \\
&\quad + 9.1314 + 8.5914 + 2.1014 + 33.5714 \\
&\quad + 38.3214 - 0.7986 + 26.2314 + 33.5714 \\
&= 179.6668
\end{aligned}
$$

$$
\begin{aligned}
\sum_{i=1}^{n} (X_i - \overline{X})^2 &= (10 - 9.33)^2 + (12 - 9.33)^2 + (12 - 9.33)^2 + (4 - 9.33)^2 \\
&\quad + (12 - 9.33)^2 + (6 - 9.33)^2 + (8 - 9.33)^2 + (2 - 9.33)^2 \\
&\quad + (18 - 9.33)^2 + (9 - 9.33)^2 + (17 - 9.33)^2 + (2 - 9.33)^2 \\
&= 0.4489 + 7.1289 + 7.1289 + 28.4089 \\
&\quad + 7.1289 + 11.0889 + 1.7689 + 53.7289 \\
&\quad + 75.1689 + 0.1089 + 58.8289 + 53.7289 \\
&= 304.6668
\end{aligned}
$$

$$
\begin{aligned}
\sum_{i=1}^{n} (Y_i - \overline{Y})^2 &= (6 - 6.58)^2 + (9 - 6.58)^2 + (8 - 6.58)^2 + (3 - 6.58)^2 \\
&\quad + (10 - 6.58)^2 + (4 - 6.58)^2 + (5 - 6.58)^2 + (2 - 6.58)^2 \\
&\quad + (11 - 6.58)^2 + (9 - 6.58)^2 + (10 - 6.58)^2 + (2 - 6.58)^2 \\
&= 0.3364 + 5.8564 + 2.0164 + 12.8164 \\
&\quad + 11.6964 + 6.6564 + 2.4964 + 20.9764 \\
&\quad + 19.5364 + 5.8564 + 11.6964 + 20.9764 \\
&= 120.9168
\end{aligned}
$$

Thus,

$$r = \frac{179.6668}{\sqrt{(304.6668)(120.9168)}}$$

$$= 0.9361$$

In this example, $r = 0.9361$, a value close to 1.0. This means that respondents' duration of residence in the city is strongly associated with their attitude toward the city. Furthermore, the positive sign of $r$ implies a positive relationship; the longer the duration of residence, the more favorable the attitude and vice versa.

Because $r$ indicates the degree to which variation in one variable is related to variation in another, it can also be expressed in terms of the decomposition of the total variation (see Chapter 16). In other words,

$$r^2 = \frac{\text{Explained variation}}{\text{Total variation}}$$

$$= \frac{SS_x}{SS_y}$$

$$= \frac{\text{Total variation} - \text{Error variation}}{\text{Total variation}}$$

$$= \frac{SS_y - SS_{error}}{SS_y}$$

Hence, $r^2$ measures the proportion of variation in one variable that is explained by the other. Both $r$ and $r^2$ are symmetric measures of association. In other words, the correlation of $X$ with $Y$ is the same as the correlation of $Y$ with $X$. It does not matter which variable is considered to be the dependent variable and which the independent. The product moment coefficient measures the strength of the linear relationship and is not designed to measure nonlinear relationships. Thus, $r = 0$ merely indicates that there is no linear relationship between $X$ and $Y$. It does not mean that $X$ and $Y$ are unrelated. There could well be a nonlinear relationship between them, which would not be captured by $r$ (see Figure 17.1).

When it is computed for a population rather than a sample, the product moment correlation is denoted by $\rho$, the Greek letter rho. The coefficient $r$ is an estimator of $\rho$. Note that the calculation of $r$ assumes that $X$ and $Y$ are metric variables whose distributions have the same shape. If these assumptions are not met, $r$ is deflated and underestimates $\rho$. In marketing research, data obtained by using rating scales with a small number of categories may not be strictly interval. This tends to deflate $r$, resulting in an underestimation of $\rho$.[3]

The statistical significance of the relationship between two variables measured by using $r$ can be conveniently tested. The hypotheses are:

$$H_0: \rho = 0$$
$$H_1: \rho \neq 0$$

The test statistic is:

$$t = r\left[\frac{n-2}{1-r^2}\right]^{1/2}$$

Figure 17.1

A Nonlinear Relationship for Which $r = 0$

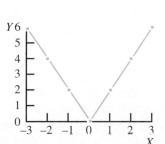

which has a $t$ distribution with $n - 2$ degrees of freedom.[4] For the correlation coefficient calculated based on the data given in Table 17.1,

$$t = 0.9361 \left[ \frac{12 - 2}{1 - (0.9361)^2} \right]^{1/2}$$

$$= 8.414$$

and the degrees of freedom $= 12 - 2 = 10$. From the $t$ distribution table (Table 4 in the Statistical Appendix), the critical value of $t$ for a two-tailed test and $\alpha = 0.05$ is 2.228. Hence, the null hypothesis of no relationship between $X$ and $Y$ is rejected. This, along with the positive sign of $r$, indicates that attitude toward the city is positively related to the duration of residence in the city. Moreover, the high value of $r$ indicates that this relationship is strong.

In conducting multivariate data analysis, it is often useful to examine the simple correlation between each pair of variables. These results are presented in the form of a correlation matrix, which indicates the coefficient of correlation between each pair of variables. Usually, only the lower triangular portion of the matrix is considered. The diagonal elements all equal 1.00, because a variable correlates perfectly with itself. The upper triangular portion of the matrix is a mirror image of the lower triangular portion, because $r$ is a symmetric measure of association. The form of a correlation matrix for five variables, $V_1$ through $V_5$, is as follows.

|       | $V_1$ | $V_2$ | $V_3$ | $V_4$ | $V_5$ |
|-------|-------|-------|-------|-------|-------|
| $V_1$ |       |       |       |       |       |
| $V_2$ | 0.5   |       |       |       |       |
| $V_3$ | 0.3   | 0.4   |       |       |       |
| $V_4$ | 0.1   | 0.3   | 0.6   |       |       |
| $V_5$ | 0.2   | 0.5   | 0.3   | 0.7   |       |

Although a matrix of simple correlations provides insights into pairwise associations, sometimes researchers want to examine the association between two variables after controlling for one or more other variables. In the latter case, partial correlation should be estimated.

# PARTIAL CORRELATION

**partial correlation coefficient**
A measure of the association between two variables after controlling or adjusting for the effects of one or more additional variables.

Whereas the product moment or simple correlation is a measure of association describing the linear association between two variables, a ***partial correlation coefficient*** measures the association between two variables after controlling for or adjusting for the effects of one or more additional variables. This statistic is used to answer the following questions:

- How strongly are sales related to advertising expenditures when the effect of price is controlled?
- Is there an association between market share and size of the sales force after adjusting for the effect of sales promotion?
- Are consumers' perceptions of quality related to their perceptions of prices when the effect of brand image is controlled?

As in these situations, suppose one wanted to calculate the association between $X$ and $Y$ after controlling for a third variable, $Z$. Conceptually, one would first remove the effect of $Z$ from $X$. To do this, one would predict the values of $X$ based on a knowledge of $Z$ by using the product moment correlation between $X$ and $Z$, $r_{xz}$. The predicted value of $X$ is then subtracted from the actual value of $X$ to construct an adjusted value of $X$. In a similar manner, the values of $Y$ are adjusted to remove the effects of $Z$. The product moment correlation between the adjusted values of $X$ and the adjusted values of $Y$ is the partial correlation coefficient between $X$ and $Y$, after controlling for the effect of $Z$, and is denoted by $r_{xy.z}$. Statistically, because the simple correlation between two variables completely describes the linear relationship between them, the partial correlation coefficient can be calculated by a knowledge of the simple correlations alone, without using individual observations.

$$r_{xy.z} = \frac{r_{xy} - (r_{xz})(r_{yz})}{\sqrt{1 - r_{xz}^2}\sqrt{1 - r_{yz}^2}}$$

To continue our example, suppose the researcher wanted to calculate the association between attitude toward the city, $Y$, and duration of residence, $X_1$, after controlling for a third variable, importance attached to weather, $X_2$. These data are presented in Table 17.1. The simple correlations between the variables are:

$$r_{yx_1} = 0.9361 \qquad r_{yx_2} = 0.7334 \qquad r_{x_1x_2} = 0.5495$$

The required partial correlation be calculated as follows:

$$r_{yx_1.x_2} = \frac{0.9361 - (0.5495)(0.7334)}{\sqrt{1 - (0.5495)^2}\sqrt{1 - (0.7334)^2}}$$
$$= 0.9386$$

As can be seen, controlling for the effect of importance attached to weather has little effect on the association between attitude toward the city and duration of residence.

Partial correlations have an *order* associated with them. The order indicates how many variables are being adjusted or controlled. The simple correlation coefficient, $r$, has a zero-order, as it does not control for any additional variables when measuring the association between two variables. The coefficient $r_{xy.z}$ is a first-order partial correlation coefficient, as it controls for the effect of one additional variable, $Z$. A second-order partial correlation coefficient controls for the effects of two variables, a third-order for the effects of three variables, and so on. The higher-order partial correlations are calculated similarly. The $(n + 1)$th-order partial coefficient may be calculated by replacing the simple correlation coefficients on the right side of the preceding equation with the $n$th-order partial coefficients.

Partial correlations can be helpful for detecting spurious relationships (see Chapter 15). The relationship between $X$ and $Y$ is spurious if it is solely due to the fact that $X$ is associated with $Z$, which is indeed the true predictor of $Y$. In this case, the correlation between $X$ and $Y$ disappears when the effect of $Z$ is controlled. Consider a case in which consumption of a cereal brand ($C$) is positively associated with income ($I$), with $r_{ci} = 0.28$. Because this brand was popularly priced, income was not expected to be a significant factor. Therefore, the researcher suspected that this relationship was spurious. The sample results also indicated that income is positively associated with household size ($H$), $r_{hi} = 0.48$, and that household size is associated with cereal consumption, $r_{ch} = 0.56$. These figures seem to indicate that the real predictor of cereal consumption is not income but household size. To test this assertion, the first-order partial correlation between cereal consumption and income is calculated, controlling for the effect of household size. The reader can verify that this partial correlation, $r_{ci.h}$, is 0.02, and the initial correlation between cereal consumption and income vanishes when the household size was controlled. Therefore, the correlation between income and cereal consumption is spurious. The special case when a partial correlation is larger than its respective zero-order correlation involves a supressor effect (see Chapter 15).[5]

Another correlation coefficient of interest is the ***part correlation coefficient.*** This coefficient represents the correlation between $Y$ and $X$ when the linear effects of the other independent variables have been removed from $X$ but not from $Y$. The part correlation coefficient, $r_{y(x.z)}$, is calculated as follows:

$$r_{y(x.z)} = \frac{r_{xy} - r_{yz}r_{xz}}{\sqrt{1 - r_{xz}^2}}$$

**part correlation coefficient**
A measure of the correlation between $Y$ and $X$ when the linear effects of the other independent variables have been removed from $X$ but not from $Y$.

The part correlation between attitude toward the city and the duration of residence, when the linear effects of the importance attached to weather have been removed from the duration of residence, can be calculated as:

$$r_{y(x_1.x_2)} = \frac{0.9361 - (0.5495)(0.7334)}{\sqrt{1 - (0.5495)^2}}$$
$$= 0.63806$$

**REAL RESEARCH**

## *Selling Ads to Home Shoppers*

Advertisements play a very important role in forming attitudes/preferences for brands. Often advertisers use celebrity spokespersons as a credible source to influence consumers' attitudes and purchase intentions. Another type of source credibility is corporate credibility, which can also influence consumer reactions to advertisements and shape brand attitudes. In general, it has been found that for low-involvement products, attitude toward the advertisement mediates brand cognition (beliefs about the brand) and attitude toward the brand. What would happen to the effect of this mediating variable when products are purchased through a home shopping network? Home Shopping Budapest in Hungary conducted research to assess the impact of advertisements toward purchase. A survey was conducted where several measures were taken, such as attitude toward the product, attitude toward the brand, attitude toward the ad characteristics, brand cognitions, and so on. It was hypothesized that in a home shopping network, advertisements largely determined attitude toward the brand. In order to find the degree of association of attitude toward the ad with both attitude toward the brand and brand cognition, a partial correlation coefficient could be computed. The partial correlation would be calculated between attitude toward the brand and brand cognitions after controlling for the effects of attitude toward the ad on the two variables. If attitude toward the ad is significantly high, then the partial correlation coefficient should be significantly less than the product moment correlation between brand cognition and attitude toward the brand. Research was conducted that supported this hypothesis. Then, Saatchi & Saatchi (*www.saatchi.com*) designed the ads aired on Home Shopping Budapest to generate positive attitude toward the advertising and this turned out to be a major competitive weapon for the network.[6] ■

The partial correlation coefficient is generally viewed as more important than the part correlation coefficient. The product moment correlation, partial correlation, and the part correlation coefficients all assume that the data are interval or ratio scaled. If the data do not meet these requirements, the researcher should consider the use of nonmetric correlation.

## NONMETRIC CORRELATION

*nonmetric correlation*
A correlation measure for two nonmetric variables that relies on rankings to compute the correlation.

At times, the researcher may have to compute the correlation coefficient between two variables that are nonmetric. It may be recalled that nonmetric variables do not have interval or ratio scale properties and do not assume a normal distribution. If the nonmetric variables are ordinal and numeric, Spearman's rho, $\rho_s$, and Kendall's tau, $\tau$, are two measures of **nonmetric correlation** that can be used to examine the correlation between them. Both these measures use rankings rather than the absolute values of the variables and the basic concepts underlying them are quite similar. Both vary from $-1.0$ to $+1.0$ (see Chapter 15).

In the absence of ties, Spearman's $\rho_s$ yields a closer approximation to the Pearson product moment correlation coefficient, $\rho$, than Kendall's $\tau$. In these cases, the absolute magnitude of $\tau$ tends to be smaller than Pearson's $\rho$. On the other hand, when the data contain a large number of tied ranks, Kendall's $\tau$ seems more appropriate. As a rule of thumb, Kendall's $\tau$ is to be preferred when a large number of cases fall into a relatively small number of categories (thereby leading to a large number of ties). Conversely, the use of Spearman's $\rho_s$ is preferable when we have a relatively larger number of categories (thereby having fewer ties).[7]

The product moment as well as the partial and part correlation coefficients provide a conceptual foundation for bivariate as well as multiple regression analysis.

## REGRESSION ANALYSIS

*regression analysis*
A statistical procedure for analyzing associative relationships between a metric dependent variable and one or more independent variables.

**Regression analysis** is a powerful and flexible procedure for analyzing associative relationships between a metric dependent variable and one or more independent variables. It can be used in the following ways:

1. Determine whether the independent variables explain a significant variation in the dependent variable: whether a relationship exists.
2. Determine how much of the variation in the dependent variable can be explained by the independent variables: strength of the relationship.
3. Determine the structure or form of the relationship: the mathematical equation relating the independent and dependent variables.
4. Predict the values of the dependent variable.
5. Control for other independent variables when evaluating the contributions of a specific variable or set of variables.

Although the independent variables may explain the variation in the dependent variable, this does not necessarily imply causation. The use of the terms *dependent* or *criterion* variables, and *independent* or *predictor* variables in regression analysis arises from the mathematical relationship between the variables. These terms do not imply that the criterion variable is dependent on the independent variables in a causal sense. Regression analysis is concerned with the nature and degree of association between variables and does not imply or assume any causality.

# BIVARIATE REGRESSION

**bivariate regression**
A procedure for deriving a mathematical relationship, in the form of an equation, between a single metric dependent variable and a single metric independent variable.

*Bivariate regression* is a procedure for deriving a mathematical relationship, in the form of an equation, between a single metric dependent or criterion variable and a single metric independent or predictor variable. The analysis is similar in many ways to determining the simple correlation between two variables. However, because an equation has to be derived, one variable must be identified as the dependent and the other as the independent variable. The examples given earlier in the context of simple correlation can be translated into the regression context.

■ Can variation in sales be explained in terms of variation in advertising expenditures? What is the structure and form of this relationship, and can it be modeled mathematically by an equation describing a straight line?
■ Can the variation in market share be accounted for by the size of the sales force?
■ Are consumers' perceptions of quality determined by their perceptions of price?

Before discussing the procedure for conducting bivariate regression, we define some important statistics.

# STATISTICS ASSOCIATED WITH BIVARIATE REGRESSION ANALYSIS

The following statistics and statistical terms are associated with bivariate regression analysis.

*Bivariate regression model.* The basic regression equation is $Y_i = \beta_0 + \beta_1 X_i + e_i$, where $Y$ = dependent or criterion variable, $X$ = independent or predictor variable, $\beta_0$ = intercept of the line, $\beta_1$ = slope of the line, and $e_i$ is the error term associated with the $i$th observation.

*Coefficient of determination.* The strength of association is measured by the coefficient of determination, $r^2$. It varies between 0 and 1 and signifies the proportion of the total variation in $Y$ that is accounted for by the variation in $X$.

*Estimated or predicted value.* The estimated or predicted value of $Y_i$ is $\hat{Y}_i = a + bx$, where $\hat{Y}_i$ is the predicted value of $Y_i$, and $a$ and $b$ are estimators of $\beta_0$ and $\beta_1$, respectively.

*Regression coefficient.* The estimated parameter $b$ is usually referred to as the nonstandardized regression coefficient.

*Scattergram.* A scatter diagram, or scattergram, is a plot of the values of two variables for all the cases or observations.

***Standard error of estimate.*** This statistic, *SEE*, is the standard deviation of the actual *Y* values from the predicted $\hat{Y}$ values.

***Standard error.*** The standard deviation of *b*, $SE_b$, is called the standard error.

***Standardized regression coefficient.*** Also termed the beta coefficient or beta weight, this is the slope obtained by the regression of *Y* on *X* when the data are standardized.

***Sum of squared errors.*** The distances of all the points from the regression line are squared and added together to arrive at the sum of squared errors, which is a measure of total error, $\Sigma e_j^2$.

**t *statistic.*** A *t* statistic with $n - 2$ degrees of freedom can be used to test the null hypothesis that no linear relationship exists between *X* and *Y*, or $H_0$: $\beta_1 = 0$, where $t = \dfrac{b}{SE_b}$.

# CONDUCTING BIVARIATE REGRESSION ANALYSIS

The steps involved in conducting bivariate regression analysis are described in Figure 17.2. Suppose the researcher wants to explain attitudes toward the city of residence in terms of the duration of residence (see Table 17.1). In deriving such relationships, it is often useful to first examine a scatter diagram.

## Plot the Scatter Diagram

A scatter diagram, or scattergram, is a plot of the values of two variables for all the cases or observations. It is customary to plot the dependent variable on the vertical axis and the independent variable on the horizontal axis. A scatter diagram is useful for determining the form of the relationship between the variables. A plot can alert the researcher to pat-

*Figure 17.2*
Conducting Bivariate
Regression Analysis

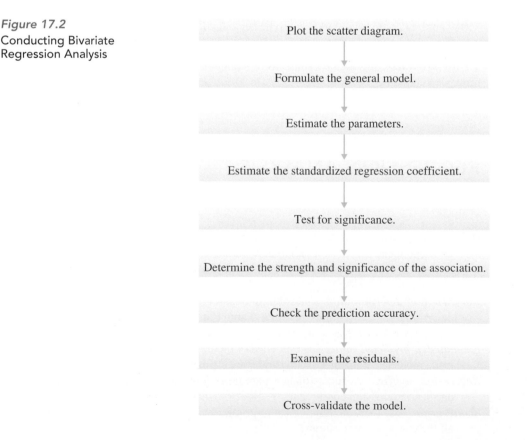

*Figure 17.3*
Plot of Attitude with Duration

*Figure 17.3*
Plot of Attitude with Duration

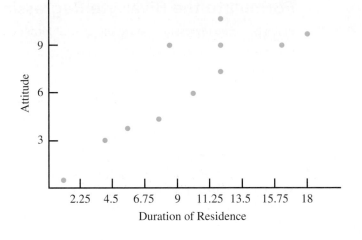

terns in the data, or to possible problems. Any unusual combinations of the two variables can be easily identified. A plot of $Y$ (attitude toward the city) against $X$ (duration of residence) is given in Figure 17.3. The points seem to be arranged in a band running from the bottom left to the top right. One can see the pattern: as one variable increases, so does the other. It appears from this scattergram that the relationship between $X$ and $Y$ is linear and could be well described by a straight line. How should the straight line be fitted to best describe the data?

The most commonly used technique for fitting a straight line to a scattergram is the **least-squares procedure.** This technique determines the best-fitting line by minimizing the square of the vertical distances of all the points from the line. The best-fitting line is called the *regression line.* Any point that does not fall on the regression line is not fully accounted for. The vertical distance from the point to the line is the error, $e_j$ (see Figure 17.4). The distances of all the points from the line are squared and added together to arrive at the sum of squared errors, which is a measure of total error, $\Sigma e_j^2$. In fitting the line, the least-squares procedure minimizes the sum of squared errors. If $Y$ is plotted on the vertical axis and $X$ on the horizontal axis, as in Figure 17.4, the best-fitting line is called the regression of $Y$ on $X$, because the vertical distances are minimized. The scatter diagram indicates whether the relationship between $Y$ and $X$ can be modeled as a straight line and, consequently, whether the bivariate regression model is appropriate.

**least-squares procedure**

A technique for fitting a straight line to a scattergram by minimizing the square of the vertical distances of all the points from the line.

*Figure 17.4*
Bivariate Regression

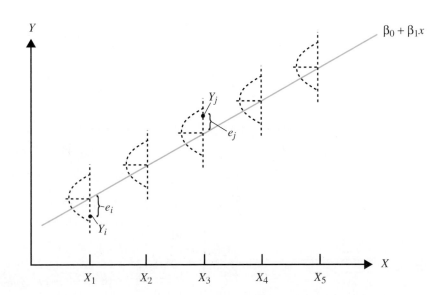

## Formulate the Bivariate Regression Model

In the bivariate regression model, the general form of a straight line is:

$$Y = \beta_0 + \beta_1 X$$

where

$$
\begin{aligned}
Y &= \text{dependent or criterion variable} \\
X &= \text{independent or predictor variable} \\
\beta_0 &= \text{intercept of the line} \\
\beta_1 &= \text{slope of the line}
\end{aligned}
$$

This model implies a deterministic relationship, in that $Y$ is completely determined by $X$. The value of $Y$ can be perfectly predicted if $\beta_0$ and $\beta_1$ are known. In marketing research, however, very few relationships are deterministic. So the regression procedure adds an error term to account for the probabilistic or stochastic nature of the relationship. The basic regression equation becomes:

$$Y_i = \beta_0 + \beta_1 X_i + e_i$$

where $e_i$ is the error term associated with the $i$th observation.[8] Estimation of the regression parameters, $\beta_0$ and $\beta_1$, is relatively simple.

## Estimate the Parameters

In most cases, $\beta_0$ and $\beta_1$ are unknown and are estimated from the sample observations using the equation

$$\hat{Y}_i = a + bx_i$$

where $\hat{Y}_i$ is the estimated or predicted value of $Y_i$, and $a$ and $b$ are estimators of $\beta_0$ and $\beta_1$, respectively. The constant $b$ is usually referred to as the nonstandardized regression coefficient. It is the slope of the regression line and it indicates the expected change in $Y$ when $X$ is changed by one unit. The formulas for calculating $a$ and $b$ are simple.[9] The slope, $b$, may be computed in terms of the covariance between $X$ and $Y$ ($COV_{xy}$) and the variance of $X$ as:

$$
\begin{aligned}
b &= \frac{COV_{xy}}{S_x^2} \\
&= \frac{\sum_{i=1}^{n}(X_i - \overline{X})(Y_i - \overline{Y})}{\sum_{i=1}^{n}(X_i - \overline{X})^2} \\
&= \frac{\sum_{i=1}^{n} X_i Y_i - n\overline{XY}}{\sum_{i=1}^{n} X_i^2 - n\overline{X}^2}
\end{aligned}
$$

The intercept, $a$, may then be calculated using:

$$a = \overline{Y} - b\overline{X}$$

For the data in Table 17.1, the estimation of parameters may be illustrated as follows:

$$
\begin{aligned}
\sum_{i=1}^{12} X_i Y_i &= (10)(6) + (12)(9) + (12)(8) + (4)(3) + (12)(10) + (6)(4) \\
&\quad + (8)(5) + (2)(2) + (18)(11) + (9)(9) + (17)(10) + (2)(2) \\
&= 917
\end{aligned}
$$

$$
\begin{aligned}
\sum_{i=1}^{12} X_i^2 &= 10^2 + 12^2 + 12^2 + 4^2 + 12^2 + 6^2 \\
&\quad + 8^2 + 2^2 + 18^2 + 9^2 + 17^2 + 2^2 \\
&= 1,350
\end{aligned}
$$

It may be recalled from earlier calculations of the simple correlation that

$$\overline{X} = 9.333$$
$$\overline{Y} = 6.583$$

Given $n = 12$, $b$ can be calculated as:

$$b = \frac{917 - (12)(9.333)(6.583)}{1350 - (12)(9.333)^2}$$
$$= 0.5897$$

$$a = \overline{Y} - b\overline{X}$$
$$= 6.583 - (0.5897)(9.333)$$
$$= 1.0793$$

Note that these coefficients have been estimated on the raw (untransformed) data. Should standardization of the data be considered desirable, the calculation of the standardized coefficients is also straightforward.

## Estimate Standardized Regression Coefficient

*Standardization* is the process by which the raw data are transformed into new variables that have a mean of 0 and a variance of 1 (Chapter 14). When the data are standardized, the intercept assumes a value of 0. The term *beta coefficient* or *beta weight* is used to denote the standardized regression coefficient. In this case, the slope obtained by the regression of Y on X, $B_{yx}$, is the same as the slope obtained by the regression of X on Y, $B_{xy}$. Moreover, each of these regression coefficients is equal to the simple correlation between X and Y.

$$B_{yx} = B_{xy} = r_{xy}$$

There is a simple relationship between the standardized and nonstandardized regression coefficients:

$$B_{yx} = b_{yx}(S_x/S_y)$$

For the regression results given in Table 17.2, the value of the beta coefficient is estimated as 0.9361. Note that this is also the value of $r$ calculated earlier in this chapter.

Once the parameters have been estimated, they can be tested for significance.

### TABLE 17.2

**Bivariate Regression**

| | |
|---|---|
| Multiple $R$ | 0.93608 |
| $R^2$ | 0.87624 |
| Adjusted $R^2$ | 0.86387 |
| Standard error | 1.22329 |

**ANALYSIS OF VARIANCE**

| | DF | SUM OF SQUARES | MEAN SQUARE |
|---|---|---|---|
| Regression | 1 | 105.95222 | 105.95222 |
| Residual | 10 | 14.96444 | 1.49644 |

$F = 70.80266$     Significance of $F = 0.0000$

**VARIABLES IN THE EQUATION**

| VARIABLE | B | SE$_B$ | BETA (B) | T | SIGNIFICANCE OF T |
|---|---|---|---|---|---|
| DURATION | 0.58972 | 0.07008 | 0.93608 | 8.414 | 0.0000 |
| (Constant) | 1.07932 | 0.74335 | | 1.452 | 0.1772 |

## Test for Significance

The statistical significance of the linear relationship between $X$ and $Y$ may be tested by examining the hypotheses:

$$H_0: \beta_1 = 0$$
$$H_1: \beta_1 \neq 0$$

The null hypothesis implies that there is no linear relationship between $X$ and $Y$. The alternative hypothesis is that there is a relationship, positive or negative, between $X$ and $Y$. Typically, a two-tailed test is done. A $t$ statistic with $n - 2$ degrees of freedom can be used, where

$$t = \frac{b}{SE_b}$$

$SE_b$ denotes the standard deviation of $b$ and is called the *standard error*.[10] The $t$ distribution was discussed in Chapter 15.

Using a computer program, the regression of attitude on duration of residence, using the data shown in Table 17.1, yielded the results shown in Table 17.2. The intercept, $a$, equals 1.0793, and the slope, $b$, equals 0.5897. Therefore, the estimated equation is:

$$\text{Attitude } (\hat{Y}) = 1.0793 + 0.5897 \text{ (Duration of residence)}$$

The standard error or standard deviation of $b$ is estimated as 0.07008, and the value of the $t$ statistic, $t = 0.5897/0.0700 = 8.414$, with $n - 2 = 10$ degrees of freedom. From Table 4 in the Statistical Appendix, we see that the critical value of $t$ with 10 degrees of freedom and $\alpha = 0.05$ is 2.228 for a two-tailed test. Because the calculated value of $t$ is larger than the critical value, the null hypothesis is rejected. Hence, there is a significant linear relationship between attitude toward the city and duration of residence in the city. The positive sign of the slope coefficient indicates that this relationship is positive. In other words, those who have resided in the city for a longer time have more positive attitudes toward the city.

## Determine the Strength and Significance of Association

A related inference involves determining the strength and significance of the association between $Y$ and $X$. The strength of association is measured by the coefficient of determination, $r^2$. In bivariate regression, $r^2$ is the square of the simple correlation coefficient obtained by correlating the two variables. The coefficient $r^2$ varies between 0 and 1. It signifies the proportion of the total variation in $Y$ that is accounted for by the variation in $X$. The decomposition of the total variation in $Y$ is similar to that for analysis of variance (Chapter 16). As shown in Figure 17.5, the total variation, $SS_y$, may be decomposed into

**Figure 17.5**

Decomposition of the Total Variation in Bivariate Regression

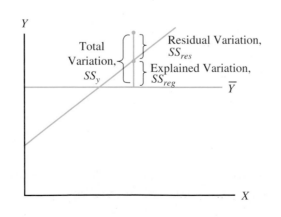

the variation accounted for by the regression line, $SS_{reg}$, and the error or residual variation, $SS_{error}$ or $SS_{res}$, as follows:

$$SS_y = SS_{reg} + SS_{res}$$

where

$$SS_y = \sum_{i=1}^{n} (Y_i - \overline{Y})^2$$

$$SS_{reg} = \sum_{i=1}^{n} (\hat{Y}_i - \overline{Y})^2$$

$$SS_{res} = \sum_{i=1}^{n} (Y_i - \hat{Y}_i)^2$$

The strength of association may then be calculated as follows:

$$r^2 = \frac{SS_{reg}}{SS_y}$$
$$= \frac{SS_y - SS_{res}}{SS_y}$$

To illustrate the calculations of $r^2$, let us consider again the regression of attitude toward the city on the duration of residence. It may be recalled from earlier calculations of the simple correlation coefficient that:

$$SS_y = \sum_{i=1}^{n} (Y_i - \overline{Y})^2$$
$$= 120.9168$$

The predicted values $(\hat{Y})$ can be calculated using the regression equation:

$$\text{Attitude } (\hat{Y}) = 1.0793 + 0.5897 \text{ (Duration of residence)}$$

For the first observation in Table 17.1, this value is:

$$(\hat{Y}) = 1.0793 + 0.5897 \times 10 = 6.9763$$

For each successive observation, the predicted values are, in order, 8.1557, 8.1557, 3.4381, 8.1557, 4.6175, 5.7969, 2.2587, 11.6939, 6.3866, 11.1042, and 2.2587. Therefore,

$$
\begin{aligned}
SS_{reg} = \sum_{i=1}^{n} (\hat{Y}_i - \overline{Y})^2 = {} & (6.9763 - 6.5833)^2 + (8.1557 - 6.5833)^2 \\
& + (8.1557 - 6.5833)^2 + (3.4381 - 6.5833)^2 \\
& + (8.1557 - 6.5833)^2 + (4.6175 - 6.5833)^2 \\
& + (5.7969 - 6.5833)^2 + (2.2587 - 6.5833)^2 \\
& + (11.6939 - 6.5833)^2 + (6.3866 - 6.5833)^2 \\
& + (11.1042 - 6.5833)^2 + (2.2587 - 6.5833)^2 \\
= {} & 0.1544 + 2.4724 + 2.4724 + 9.8922 + 2.4724 \\
& + 3.8643 + 0.6184 + 18.7021 + 26.1182 \\
& + 0.0387 + 20.4385 + 18.7021 \\
= {} & 105.9524
\end{aligned}
$$

$$
\begin{aligned}
SS_{res} = \sum_{i=1}^{n} (Y_i - \hat{Y}_i)^2 = {} & (6 - 6.9763)^2 + (9 - 8.1557)^2 + (8 - 8.1557)^2 \\
& + (3 - 3.4381)^2 + (10 - 8.1557)^2 + (4 - 4.6175)^2 \\
& + (5 - 5.7969)^2 + (2 - 2.2587)^2 + (11 - 11.6939)^2 \\
& + (9 - 6.3866)^2 + (10 - 11.1042)^2 + (2 - 2.2587)^2 \\
= {} & 14.9644
\end{aligned}
$$

It can be seen that $SS_y = SS_{reg} + SS_{res}$. Furthermore,

$$r^2 = \frac{SS_{reg}}{SS_y}$$

$$= \frac{105.9524}{120.9168}$$

$$= 0.8762$$

Another equivalent test for examining the significance of the linear relationship between $X$ and $Y$ (significance of $b$) is the test for the significance of the coefficient of determination. The hypotheses in this case are:

$$H_0: R^2_{pop} = 0$$
$$H_1: R^2_{pop} > 0$$

The appropriate test statistic is the $F$ statistic:

$$F = \frac{SS_{reg}}{SS_{res}/(n-2)}$$

which has an $F$ distribution with 1 and $n-2$ degrees of freedom. The $F$ test is a generalized form of the $t$ test (see Chapter 15). If a random variable is $t$ distributed with $n$ degrees of freedom, then $t^2$ is $F$ distributed with 1 and $n$ degrees of freedom. Hence, the $F$ test for testing the significance of the coefficient of determination is equivalent to testing the following hypotheses:

$$H_0: \beta_1 = 0$$
$$H_1: \beta_1 \neq 0$$

or

$$H_0: \rho = 0$$
$$H_1: \rho \neq 0$$

From Table 17.2, it can be seen that:

$$r^2 = \frac{105.9524}{(105.9524 + 14.9644)}$$

$$= 0.8762$$

which is the same as the value calculated earlier. The value of the $F$ statistic is:

$$F = \frac{105.9524}{(14.9644/10)}$$

$$= 70.8027$$

with 1 and 10 degrees of freedom. The calculated $F$ statistic exceeds the critical value of 4.96 determined from Table 5 in the Statistical Appendix. Therefore, the relationship is significant at $\alpha = 0.05$, corroborating the results of the $t$ test. If the relationship between $X$ and $Y$ is significant, it is meaningful to predict the values of $Y$ based on the values of $X$ and to estimate prediction accuracy.

## Check Prediction Accuracy

To estimate the accuracy of predicted values, $\hat{Y}$, it is useful to calculate the standard error of estimate, *SEE*. This statistic is the standard deviation of the actual $Y$ values from the predicted $\hat{Y}$ values.

$$SEE = \sqrt{\frac{\sum_{i=1}^{n}(Y_i - \hat{Y})^2}{n-2}}$$

or

$$SEE = \sqrt{\frac{SS_{res}}{n - 2}}$$

or more generally, if there are $k$ independent variables,

$$SEE = \sqrt{\frac{SS_{res}}{n - k - 1}}$$

*SEE* may be interpreted as a kind of average residual or average error in predicting $Y$ from the regression equation.[11]

Two cases of prediction may arise. The researcher may want to predict the mean value of $Y$ for all the cases with a given value of $X$, say $X_0$, or predict the value of $Y$ for a single case. In both situations, the predicted value is the same and is given by $\hat{Y}$, where

$$\hat{Y} = a + bX_0$$

However, the standard error is different in the two situations, although in both situations it is a function of *SEE*. For large samples, the standard error for predicting mean value of $Y$ is $SEE/\sqrt{n}$, and for predicting individual $Y$ values it is *SEE*. Hence, the construction of confidence intervals (see Chapter 12) for the predicted value varies, depending upon whether the mean value or the value for a single observation is being predicted.

For the data given in Table 17.2, the *SEE* is estimated as follows:

$$SEE = \sqrt{\frac{14.9644}{(12 - 2)}}$$
$$= 1.22329$$

The final two steps in conducting bivariate regression, namely examination of residuals and model cross-validation, are considered later.

## Assumptions

The regression model makes a number of assumptions in estimating the parameters and in significance testing, as shown in Figure 17.4:

1. The error term is normally distributed. For each fixed value of $X$, the distribution of $Y$ is normal.[12]
2. The means of all these normal distributions of $Y$, given $X$, lie on a straight line with slope $b$.
3. The mean of the error term is 0.
4. The variance of the error term is constant. This variance does not depend on the values assumed by $X$.
5. The error terms are uncorrelated. In other words, the observations have been drawn independently.

Insights into the extent to which these assumptions have been met can be gained by an examination of residuals, which is covered in the next section on multiple regression.[13]

# MULTIPLE REGRESSION

**multiple regression**
A statistical technique that simultaneously develops a mathematical relationship between two or more independent variables and an interval-scaled dependent variable.

*Multiple regression* involves a single dependent variable and two or more independent variables. The questions raised in the context of bivariate regression can also be answered via multiple regression by considering additional independent variables.

■ Can variation in sales be explained in terms of variation in advertising expenditures, prices, and level of distribution?
■ Can variation in market shares be accounted for by the size of the sales force, advertising expenditures, and sales promotion budgets?

- Are consumers' perceptions of quality determined by their perceptions of prices, brand image, and brand attributes?

Additional questions can also be answered by multiple regression.

- How much of the variation in sales can be explained by advertising expenditures, prices, and level of distribution?
- What is the contribution of advertising expenditures in explaining the variation in sales when the levels of prices and distribution are controlled?
- What levels of sales may be expected, given the levels of advertising expenditures, prices, and level of distribution?

### REAL RESEARCH

## *Global Brands—Local Ads*

Europeans welcome brands from other countries, but when it comes to advertising, they prefer the homegrown variety. A survey done by Yankelovich and Partners (*www.yankelovich.com*) and its affiliates finds that most European consumers' favorite commercials are for local brands even though they are more than likely to buy foreign brands. Respondents in France, Germany, and the United Kingdom named Coca-Cola as the most often purchased soft drink. However, the French selected the famous award-winning spot for France's Perrier bottled water as their favorite commercial. Similarly, in Germany, the favorite advertising was for a German brand of nonalcoholic beer—Clausthaler. However, in the United Kingdom, Coca-Cola was the favorite soft drink and also the favorite advertising. In light of such findings, the important question is—does advertising help? Does it help increase the purchase probability of the brand or does it merely maintain the brand recognition rate high. One way of finding out is by running multiple regressions where the dependent variable is the likelihood of brand purchase and the independent variables are brand attribute evaluations and advertising evaluations. Separate models with and without advertising can be run to assess any significant difference in the contribution. Individual *t* tests could also be examined to find out the significant contribution of both the brand attributes and advertising. The results will indicate the degree to which advertising plays an important part in brand purchase decisions. In conjunction with these results, a study conducted in late 2000 revealed that attempting to build brand loyalty purchases by means of a sales promotion is not a desirable way to achieve such an objective. According to the study, sales promotions only encourage momentary brand switching and merely enhance short-term performance for companies. Furthermore, over the long run, a sales promotion may imply a low quality or unstable brand image to consumers or it may confuse consumers, which could also lead to a decline in brand loyalty. The results of this study show that sacrificing advertising and relying on sales promotions reduce brand associations, which ultimately leads to a decrease in brand loyalty purchases.[14] ■

**multiple regression model**
An equation used to explain the results of multiple regression analysis.

The general form of the **multiple regression model** is as follows:

$$Y = \beta_0 + \beta_1 X_1 + \beta_2 X_2 + \beta_3 X_3 + \ldots + \beta_k X_k + e$$

which is estimated by the following equation:

$$\hat{Y} = a + b_1 X_1 + b_2 X_2 + b_3 X_3 + \ldots + b_k X_k$$

As before, the coefficient *a* represents the intercept, but the *b*s are now the partial regression coefficients. The least-squares criterion estimates the parameters in such a way as to minimize the total error, $SS_{res}$. This process also maximizes the correlation between the actual values of $Y$ and the predicted values, $\hat{Y}$. All the assumptions made in bivariate regression also apply in multiple regression. We define some associated statistics and then describe the procedure for multiple regression analysis.[15]

# STATISTICS ASSOCIATED WITH MULTIPLE REGRESSION

Most of the statistics and statistical terms described under bivariate regression also apply to multiple regression. In addition, the following statistics are used:

*Adjusted* **R²**. $R^2$, coefficient of multiple determination, is adjusted for the number of independent variables and the sample size to account for diminishing returns. After the first few variables, the additional independent variables do not make much contribution.

*Coefficient of multiple determination.* The strength of association in multiple regression is measured by the square of the multiple correlation coefficient, $R^2$, which is also called the coefficient of multiple determination.

**F** *test.* The $F$ test is used to test the null hypothesis that the coefficient of multiple determination in the population, $R^2_{pop}$, is zero. This is equivalent to testing the null hypothesis $H_0: \beta_1 = \beta_2 = \beta_3 = \ldots = \beta_k = 0$. The test statistic has an $F$ distribution with $k$ and $(n - k - 1)$ degrees of freedom.

*Partial* **F** *test.* The significance of a partial regression coefficient, $\beta_i$, of $X_i$ may be tested using an incremental $F$ statistic. The incremental $F$ statistic is based on the increment in the explained sum of squares resulting from the addition of the independent variable $X_i$ to the regression equation after all the other independent variables have been included.

*Partial regression coefficient.* The partial regression coefficient, $b_1$, denotes the change in the predicted value, $\hat{Y}$, per unit change in $X_1$ when the other independent variables, $X_2$ to $X_k$, are held constant.

# CONDUCTING MULTIPLE REGRESSION ANALYSIS

The steps involved in conducting multiple regression analysis are similar to those for bivariate regression analysis. The discussion focuses on partial regression coefficients, strength of association, significance testing, and examination of residuals.

## Partial Regression Coefficients

To understand the meaning of a partial regression coefficient, let us consider a case in which there are two independent variables, so that:

$$\hat{Y} = a + b_1 X_1 + b_2 X_2$$

First, note that the relative magnitude of the partial regression coefficient of an independent variable is, in general, different from that of its bivariate regression coefficient. In other words, the partial regression coefficient, $b_1$, will be different from the regression coefficient, $b$, obtained by regressing $Y$ on only $X_1$. This happens because $X_1$ and $X_2$ are usually correlated. In bivariate regression, $X_2$ was not considered, and any variation in $Y$ that was shared by $X_1$ and $X_2$ was attributed to $X_1$. However, in the case of multiple independent variables, this is no longer true.

The interpretation of the partial regression coefficient, $b_1$, is that it represents the expected change in $Y$ when $X_1$ is changed by one unit but $X_2$ is held constant or otherwise controlled. Likewise, $b_2$ represents the expected change in $Y$ for a unit change in $X_2$, when $X_1$ is held constant. Thus, calling $b_1$ and $b_2$ partial regression coefficients is appropriate. It can also be seen that the combined effects of $X_1$ and $X_2$ on $Y$ are additive. In other words, if $X_1$ and $X_2$ are each changed by one unit, the expected change in $Y$ would be $(b_1 + b_2)$.

Conceptually, the relationship between the bivariate regression coefficient and the partial regression coefficient can be illustrated as follows. Suppose one was to remove the effect of $X_2$ from $X_1$. This could be done by running a regression of $X_1$ on $X_2$. In other words, one would estimate the equation $\hat{X}_1 = a + bX_2$ and calculate the residual $X_r = (X_1 - \hat{X}_1)$. The partial regression coefficient, $b_1$, is then equal to the bivariate regression coefficient, $b_r$, obtained from the equation $\hat{Y} = a + b_r X_r$. In other words, the partial regression coefficient, $b_1$, is equal to the regression coefficient, $b_r$, between $Y$ and the residuals of $X_1$ from which the effect of $X_2$ has been removed. The partial coefficient, $b_2$, can also be interpreted along similar lines.

Extension to the case of $k$ variables is straightforward. The partial regression coefficient, $b_1$, represents the expected change in $Y$ when $X_1$ is changed by one unit and $X_2$ through $X_k$ are held constant. It can also be interpreted as the bivariate regression coefficient, $b$, for the regression of $Y$ on the residuals of $X_1$, when the effect of $X_2$ through $X_k$ has been removed from $X_1$.

The beta coefficients are the partial regression coefficients obtained when all the variables ($Y, X_1, X_2, \ldots X_k$) have been standardized to a mean of 0 and a variance of 1 before estimating the regression equation. The relationship of the standardized to the nonstandardized coefficients remains the same as before:

$$B_1 = b_1 \left( \frac{S_{x1}}{S_y} \right)$$

$$\cdot$$
$$\cdot$$

$$B_k = b_k \left( \frac{S_{xk}}{S_y} \right)$$

The intercept and the partial regression coefficients are estimated by solving a system of simultaneous equations derived by differentiating and equating the partial derivatives to 0. Because these coefficients are automatically estimated by the various computer programs, we will not present the details. Yet it is worth noting that the equations cannot be solved if: (1) the sample size, $n$, is smaller than or equal to the number of independent variables, $k$; or (2) one independent variable is perfectly correlated with another.

Suppose that in explaining the attitude toward the city, we now introduce a second variable, importance attached to the weather. The data for the 12 pretest respondents on attitude toward the city, duration of residence, and importance attached to the weather are given in Table 17.1. The results of multiple regression analysis are depicted in Table 17.3. The partial regression coefficient for duration ($X_1$) is now 0.4811, different from what it was in the bivariate case. The corresponding beta coefficient is 0.7636. The partial

## TABLE 17.3

### Multiple Regression

| Multiple $R$ | 0.97210 |
|---|---|
| $R^2$ | 0.94498 |
| Adjusted $R^2$ | 0.93276 |
| Standard error | 0.85974 |

| ANALYSIS OF VARIANCE | | | |
|---|---|---|---|
| | DF | SUM OF SQUARES | MEAN SQUARE |
| Regression | 2 | 114.26425 | 57.13213 |
| Residual | 9 | 6.65241 | 0.73916 |

$F = 77.29364$        Significance of $F = 0.0000$

| VARIABLES IN THE EQUATION | | | | | |
|---|---|---|---|---|---|
| VARIABLE | B | $SE_B$ | BETA ($B$) | $T$ | SIGNIFICANCE OF $T$ |
| IMPOR | 0.28865 | 0.08608 | 0.31382 | 3.353 | 0.0085 |
| DURATION | 0.48108 | 0.05895 | 0.76363 | 8.160 | 0.0000 |
| (Constant) | 0.33732 | 0.56736 | | 0.595 | 0.5668 |

regression coefficient for importance attached to weather ($X_2$) is 0.2887, with a beta coefficient of 0.3138. The estimated regression equation is:

$$(\hat{Y}) = 0.33732 + 0.48108X_1 + 0.28865X_2$$

or

$$\text{Attitude} = 0.33732 + 0.48108 \text{ (Duration)} + 0.28865 \text{ (Importance)}$$

This equation can be used for a variety of purposes, including predicting attitudes toward the city, given a knowledge of the respondents' duration of residence in the city and the importance they attach to weather.

## Strength of Association

The strength of the relationship stipulated by the regression equation can be determined by using appropriate measures of association. The total variation is decomposed as in the bivariate case:

$$SS_y = SS_{reg} + SS_{res}$$

where

$$SS_y = \sum_{i=1}^{n} (Y_i - \overline{Y})^2$$

$$SS_{reg} = \sum_{i=1}^{n} (\hat{Y}_i - \overline{Y})^2$$

$$SS_{res} = \sum_{i=1}^{n} (Y_i - \hat{Y}_i)^2$$

The strength of association is measured by the square of the multiple correlation coefficient, $R^2$, which is also called the coefficient of multiple determination.

$$R^2 = \frac{SS_{reg}}{SS_y}$$

The multiple correlation coefficient, $R$, can also be viewed as the simple correlation coefficient, $r$, between $Y$ and $\hat{Y}$. Several points about the characteristics of $R^2$ are worth noting. The coefficient of multiple determination, $R^2$, cannot be less than the highest bivariate, $r^2$, of any individual independent variable with the dependent variable. $R^2$ will be larger when the correlations between the independent variables are low. If the independent variables are statistically independent (uncorrelated), then $R^2$ will be the sum of bivariate $r^2$ of each independent variable with the dependent variable. $R^2$ cannot decrease as more independent variables are added to the regression equation. Yet diminishing returns set in, so that after the first few variables, the additional independent variables do not make much of a contribution.[16] For this reason, $R^2$ is adjusted for the number of independent variables and the sample size by using the following formula:

$$\text{Adjusted } R^2 = R^2 - \frac{k(1 - R^2)}{n - k - 1}$$

For the regression results given in Table 17.3, the value of $R^2$ is:

$$R^2 = \frac{114.2643}{(114.2643 + 6.6524)}$$

$$= 0.9450$$

This is higher than the $r^2$ value of 0.8762 obtained in the bivariate case. The $r^2$ in the bivariate case is the square of the simple (product moment) correlation between attitude toward the city and duration of residence. The $R^2$ obtained in multiple regression is also higher than the square of the simple correlation between attitude and importance attached to weather (which can be estimated as 0.5379). The adjusted $R^2$ is estimated as:

$$\text{Adjusted } R^2 = 0.9450 - \frac{2(1.0 - 0.9450)}{(12 - 2 - 1)}$$

$$= 0.9328$$

Note that the value of adjusted $R^2$ is close to $R^2$ and both are higher than $r^2$ for the bivariate case. This suggests that the addition of the second independent variable, importance attached to weather, makes a contribution in explaining the variation in attitude toward the city.

## Significance Testing

Significance testing involves testing the significance of the overall regression equation as well as specific partial regression coefficients. The null hypothesis for the overall test is that the coefficient of multiple determination in the population, $R^2_{pop}$, is zero.

$$H_0: R^2_{pop} = 0$$

This is equivalent to the following null hypothesis:

$$H_0: \beta_1 = \beta_2 = \beta_3 = \ldots = \beta_k = 0$$

The overall test can be conducted by using an $F$ statistic:

$$F = \frac{SS_{reg}/k}{SS_{res}/(n - k - 1)}$$

$$= \frac{R^2/k}{(1 - R^2)/(n - k - 1)}$$

which has an $F$ distribution with $k$ and $(n - k - 1)$ degrees of freedom.[17] For the multiple regression results given in Table 17.3,

$$F = \frac{114.2643/2}{6.6524/9} = 77.2936$$

which is significant at $\alpha = 0.05$.

If the overall null hypothesis is rejected, one or more population partial regression coefficients have a value different from 0. To determine which specific coefficients ($\beta_i$s) are nonzero, additional tests are necessary. Testing for the significance of the $\beta_i$s can be done in a manner similar to that in the bivariate case by using $t$ tests. The significance of the partial coefficient for importance attached to weather may be tested by the following equation:

$$t = \frac{b}{SE_b}$$

$$= \frac{0.2887}{0.08608}$$

$$= 3.353$$

which has a $t$ distribution with $n - k - 1$ degrees of freedom. This coefficient is significant at $\alpha = 0.05$. The significance of the coefficient for duration of residence is tested in a similar way and found to be significant. Therefore, both the duration of residence and importance attached to weather are important in explaining attitude toward the city.

Some computer programs provide an equivalent $F$ test, often called the partial $F$ test. This involves a decomposition of the total regression sum of squares, $SS_{reg}$, into components related to each independent variable. In the standard approach, this is done by assuming that each independent variable has been added to the regression equation after all the other independent variables have been included. The increment in the explained sum of squares, resulting from the addition of an independent variable, $X_i$, is the component of the variation attributed to that variable and is denoted by $SS_{x_i}$.[18] The significance of the partial regression coefficient for this variable, $b_i$, is tested using an incremental $F$ statistic:

$$F = \frac{SS_{x_i}/1}{SS_{res}/(n - k - 1)}$$

which has an $F$ distribution with 1 and $(n - k - 1)$ degrees of freedom.

Although high $R^2$ and significant partial regression coefficients are comforting, the efficacy of the regression model should be evaluated further by an examination of the residuals.

## Examination of Residuals

**residual**

The difference between the observed value of $Y_i$ and the value predicted by the regression equation, $Y_i$.

A *residual* is the difference between the observed value of $Y_i$ and the value predicted by the regression equation, $\hat{Y}_i$. Residuals are used in the calculation of several statistics associated with regression. In addition, scattergrams of the residuals, in which the residuals are plotted against the predicted values, $\hat{Y}_i$, time, or predictor variables, provide useful insights in examining the appropriateness of the underlying assumptions and regression model fitted.[19]

The assumption of a normally distributed error term can be examined by constructing a histogram of the residuals. A visual check reveals whether the distribution is normal. Additional evidence can be obtained by determining the percentages of residuals falling within $\pm 1$ *SE* or $\pm 2$ *SE*. These percentages can be compared with what would be expected under the normal distribution (68% and 95%, respectively). More formal assessment can be made by running the K-S one-sample test.

The assumption of constant variance of the error term can be examined by plotting the residuals against the predicted values of the dependent variable, $\hat{Y}_i$. If the pattern is not random, the variance of the error term is not constant. Figure 17.6 shows a pattern whose variance is dependent upon the $\hat{Y}_i$ values.

A plot of residuals against time, or the sequence of observations, will throw some light on the assumption that the error terms are uncorrelated. A random pattern should be seen if this assumption is true. A plot like the one in Figure 17.7 indicates a linear relationship between residuals and time. A more formal procedure for examining the correlations between the error terms is the Durbin-Watson test.[20]

Plotting the residuals against the independent variables provides evidence of the appropriateness or inappropriateness of using a linear model. Again, the plot should result in a random pattern. The residuals should fall randomly, with relatively equal distribution dispersion about 0. They should not display any tendency to be either positive or negative.

**Figure 17.6**
Residual Plot Indicating That Variance Is Not Constant

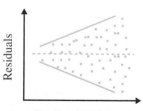

Predicted *Y* Values

**Figure 17.7**
Plot Indicating a Linear Relationship Between Residuals and Time

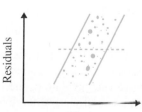

Time

Predicted *Y* Values

To examine whether any additional variables should be included in the regression equation, one could run a regression of the residuals on the proposed variables. If any variable explains a significant proportion of the residual variation, it should be considered for inclusion. Inclusion of variables in the regression equation should be strongly guided by the researcher's theory. Thus, an examination of the residuals provides valuable insights into the appropriateness of the underlying assumptions and the model that is fitted. Figure 17.8 shows a plot that indicates that the underlying assumptions are met and that the linear model is appropriate. If an examination of the residuals indicates that the assumptions underlying linear regression are not met, the researcher can transform the variables in an attempt to satisfy the assumptions. Transformations, such as taking logs, square roots, or reciprocals can stabilize the variance, make the distribution normal, or make the relationship linear.

## REAL RESEARCH

### At No "Ad"ditional Cost

Due to the decline in the economy in 2001 and 2002, the survival of many companies has been questioned. Despite troubled times, analysts predict calmer seas ahead for the companies in the magazine industry in 2003. Forecasters such as Zenith Media predict magazine spending to be $17 billion in 2003. However, due to a decrease in automotive, dot-com, and tobacco spending, magazine advertisement spending is expected to slow down during the following five years. It is widely believed that consumer magazines' prices are subsidized by the advertising carried within the magazines. A study examined the contribution of advertising to the price per copy of magazines.

Multiple regression analysis was used to examine the relationships among price per copy and editorial pages, circulation, percentage of newsstand circulation, promotional expenditures, percentage of color pages, and per-copy advertising revenues. The form of the analysis was:

$$\text{PPC} = b_0 + b_1 \,(\text{Ed Pages}) + b_2 \,(\text{Circ}) + b_3 \,(\% \text{ News Circ}) + b_4 \,(\text{PE}) + b_5 \,(\% \text{ Color}) + b_6 \,(\text{Ad Revs})$$

where

$$\text{PPC} = \text{price per copy (in \$)}$$
$$\text{Ed Pages} = \text{editorial pages per average issue}$$
$$\text{Circ} = \text{the log of average paid circulation (in 000s)}$$
$$\% \text{ News Circ} = \text{percentage newsstand circulation}$$
$$\text{PE} = \text{promotional expenditures (in \$)}$$
$$\% \text{ Color} = \text{percentage of pages printed in color}$$
$$\text{Ad Revs} = \text{per-copy advertising revenues (in \$)}$$

The result of regression analysis using price per copy as the dependent variable is given in the table. Of the six independent variables, three were significant ($p < 0.05$): the number of editorial pages, average circulation, and percentage newsstand circulation. The three variables accounted for virtually all of the explained variance ($R^2 = 0.51$; adjusted $R^2 = 0.48$). The direction of the coefficients was consistent with prior expectations: the number of editorial pages was positive; circulation was negative; and percentage news-

Multiple regression analysis shows that advertising is provided free to consumers but does not subsidize prices of magazines.

stand circulation was positive. This was expected, given the structure of the magazine publishing industry, and confirmed the hypothesized relationship.

Promotional expenditures, use of color, and per-copy advertising revenues were found to have no relationship with price per copy, after the effects of circulation, percentage newsstand circulation, and editorial pages were controlled in the regression analysis.

Because the effect of per-copy advertising revenue was not significant, no support was found for the contention that advertising decreases the price per copy of consumer magazines. It was concluded that advertising in magazines is provided free to consumers, but does not subsidize prices.[21]

Regression Analysis Using Price per Copy as Dependent Variable

**Dependent Variable: Price per Copy**
**Independent Variables:**

|  | *b* | *SE* | *F* |
|---|---|---|---|
| Editorial pages | 0.0084 | 0.0017 | 23.04* |
| Circulation | −0.4180 | 0.1372 | 9.29* |
| Percentage newsstand circulation | 0.0067 | 0.0016 | 18.46* |
| Promotional expenditures | 0.13-04** | 0.0000 | 0.59 |
| Percentage color pages | 0.0227 | 0.0092 | 0.01 |
| Per-copy ad revenues | 0.1070 | 0.0412 | 0.07 |
| Overall $R^2 = 0.51$ | df = 6, 93 | Overall $F = 16.19$* | |

*$p < 0.05$. **decimal moved in by four zeros ■

In the preceding example, promotional expenditures, percentage of color pages, and per-copy advertising revenues were not found to be significantly related to the price per copy of magazines. Some independent variables considered in a study often turn out to be nonsignificant. When there are a large number of independent variables and the researcher suspects that not all of them are significant, stepwise regression should be used.

## STEPWISE REGRESSION

**stepwise regression**
A regression procedure in which the predictor variables enter or leave the regression equation one at a time.

The purpose of **stepwise regression** is to select, from a large number of predictor variables, a small subset of variables that account for most of the variation in the dependent or criterion variable. In this procedure, the predictor variables enter or are removed from the regression equation one at a time.[22] There are several approaches to stepwise regression.

1. *Forward inclusion.* Initially, there are no predictor variables in the regression equation. Predictor variables are entered one at a time, only if they meet certain criteria specified in terms of the $F$ ratio. The order in which the variables are included is based on the contribution to the explained variance.
2. *Backward elimination.* Initially, all the predictor variables are included in the regression equation. Predictors are then removed one at a time based on the $F$ ratio.
3. *Stepwise solution.* Forward inclusion is combined with the removal of predictors that no longer meet the specified criterion at each step.

Stepwise procedures do not result in regression equations that are optimal, in the sense of producing the largest $R^2$, for a given number of predictors. Because of the correlations between predictors, an important variable may never be included, or less important variables may enter the equation. To identify an optimal regression equation, one would have to compute combinatorial solutions in which all possible combinations are examined. Nevertheless, stepwise regression can be useful when the sample size is large in relation to the number of predictors, as shown in the following example.

## REAL RESEARCH

### *Stepping Out . . . to the Mall*

Even in the 21st century, browsing is a fundamental part of shopping—whether it is online or in the mall. Customers like to consider their purchase decisions before actually carrying them out. Many consider store-based retailers to have an advantage over Web-based retailers when it comes to browsing because store-based retailers are larger in size and product offerings. Although the Web appeals to younger shoppers, the mall will remain ahead of the game especially with so many entertainment factors now being built inside malls. A profile of browsers in regional shopping malls was constructed using three sets of independent variables: demographics, shopping behavior, and psychological and attitudinal variables. The dependent variable consisted of a browsing index. In a stepwise regression including all three sets of variables, demographics were found to be the most powerful predictors of browsing behavior. The final regression equation, which contained 20 of the possible 36 variables, included all of the demographics. The table presents the regression coefficients, standard errors of the coefficients, and their significance levels.

Stepwise regression indicates that browsers are more likely to be employed females, somewhat younger, and exhibit lower levels of education and income.

Regression of Browsing Index on Descriptive and Attitudinal Variables
by Order of Entry into Stepwise Regression

| Variable Description | Coefficient | SE | Significance |
|---|---|---|---|
| Sex (0 = Male, 1 = Female) | −0.485 | 0.164 | 0.001 |
| Employment status (0 = Employed) | 0.391 | 0.182 | 0.003 |
| Self-confidence | −0.152 | 0.128 | 0.234 |
| Education | 0.079 | 0.072 | 0.271 |
| Brand intention | −0.063 | 0.028 | 0.024 |
| Watch daytime TV? (0 = Yes) | 0.232 | 0.144 | 0.107 |
| Tension | −0.182 | 0.069 | 0.008 |
| Income | 0.089 | 0.061 | 0.144 |
| Frequency of mall visits | −0.130 | 0.059 | 0.028 |
| Fewer friends than most | 0.162 | 0.084 | 0.054 |
| Good shopper | −0.122 | 0.090 | 0.174 |
| Others' opinions important | −0.147 | 0.065 | 0.024 |
| Control over life | −0.069 | 0.069 | 0.317 |
| Family size | −0.086 | 0.062 | 0.165 |
| Enthusiastic person | −0.143 | 0.099 | 0.150 |
| Age | 0.036 | 0.069 | 0.603 |
| Number purchases made | −0.068 | 0.043 | 0.150 |
| Purchases per store | 0.209 | 0.152 | 0.167 |
| Shop on tight budget | −0.055 | 0.067 | 0.412 |
| Excellent judge of quality | −0.070 | 0.089 | 0.435 |
| CONSTANT | 3.250 | | |

Overall $R^2 = 0.477$

In interpreting the coefficients, it should be recalled that the smaller the browsing index (the dependent variable), the greater the tendency to exhibit behaviors associated with browsing. The two predictors with the largest coefficients are sex and employment status. Browsers are more likely to be employed females. They also tend to be somewhat downscale, compared to other mall patrons, exhibiting lower levels of education and income, after accounting for the effects of sex and employment status. Although browsers tend to be somewhat younger than nonbrowsers, they are not necessarily single; those who reported larger family sizes tended to be associated with smaller values of the browsing index.

The downscale profile of browsers relative to other mall patrons indicates that specialty stores in malls should emphasize moderately priced products. This may explain the historically low rate of failure in malls among such stores and the tendency of high-priced specialty shops to be located in only the prestigious malls or upscale nonenclosed shopping centers.[23] ■

# MULTICOLLINEARITY

Stepwise regression and multiple regression are complicated by the presence of multicollinearity. Virtually all multiple regression analyses done in marketing research involve predictors or independent variables that are related. However, *multicollinearity* arises when intercorrelations among the predictors are very high. Multicollinearity can result in several problems, including:

*multicollinearity*
A state of very high intercorrelations among independent variables.

1. The partial regression coefficients may not be estimated precisely. The standard errors are likely to be high.
2. The magnitudes as well as the signs of the partial regression coefficients may change from sample to sample.
3. It becomes difficult to assess the relative importance of the independent variables in explaining the variation in the dependent variable.
4. Predictor variables may be incorrectly included or removed in stepwise regression.

What constitutes serious multicollinearity is not always clear, although several rules of thumb and procedures have been suggested in the literature. Procedures of varying complexity have also been suggested to cope with multicollinearity.[24] A simple procedure consists of using only one of the variables in a highly correlated set of variables. Alternatively, the set of independent variables can be transformed into a new set of predictors that are mutually independent by using techniques such as principal components analysis (see Chapter 19). More specialized techniques, such as ridge regression and latent root regression, can also be used.[25]

# RELATIVE IMPORTANCE OF PREDICTORS

When multicollinearity is present, special care is required in assessing the relative importance of independent variables. In applied marketing research, it is valuable to determine the *relative importance of the predictors*. In other words, how important are the independent variables in accounting for the variation in the criterion or dependent variable?[26] Unfortunately, because the predictors are correlated, there is no unambiguous measure of relative importance of the predictors in regression analysis.[27] However, several approaches are commonly used to assess the relative importance of predictor variables.

1. *Statistical significance.* If the partial regression coefficient of a variable is not significant, as determined by an incremental $F$ test, that variable is judged to be unimportant. An exception to this rule is made if there are strong theoretical reasons for believing that the variable is important.
2. *Square of the simple correlation coefficient.* This measure, $r^2$, represents the proportion of the variation in the dependent variable explained by the independent variable in a bivariate relationship.
3. *Square of the partial correlation coefficient.* This measure, $R^2_{yx_i.x_jx_k}$, is the coefficient of determination between the dependent variable and the independent variable, controlling for the effects of the other independent variables.
4. *Square of the part correlation coefficient.* This coefficient represents an increase in $R^2$ when a variable is entered into a regression equation that already contains the other independent variables.
5. *Measures based on standardized coefficients or beta weights.* The most commonly used measures are the absolute values of the beta weights, $|B_i|$, or the squared values, $B_i^2$. Because they are partial coefficients, beta weights take into account the effect of the other independent variables. These measures become increasingly unreliable as the correlations among the predictor variables increase (multicollinearity increases).
6. *Stepwise regression.* The order in which the predictors enter or are removed from the regression equation is used to infer their relative importance.

Given that the predictors are correlated, at least to some extent, in virtually all regression situations, none of these measures is satisfactory. It is also possible that the different measures may indicate a different order of importance of the predictors.[28] Yet, if all the measures are examined collectively, useful insights may be obtained into the relative importance of the predictors.

# CROSS-VALIDATION

**cross-validation**
A test of validity that examines whether a model holds on comparable data not used in the original estimation.

Before assessing the relative importance of the predictors or drawing any other inferences, it is necessary to cross-validate the regression model. Regression and other multivariate procedures tend to capitalize on chance variations in the data. This could result in a regression model or equation that is unduly sensitive to the specific data used to estimate the model. One approach for evaluating the model for this, and other problems associated with regression, is cross-validation. **Cross-validation** examines whether the regression model continues to hold on comparable data not used in the estimation. The typical cross-validation procedure used in marketing research is as follows:

1. The regression model is estimated using the entire data set.
2. The available data are split into two parts, the *estimation sample* and the *validation sample*. The estimation sample generally contains 50 to 90 percent of the total sample.
3. The regression model is estimated using the data from the estimation sample only. This model is compared to the model estimated on the entire sample to determine the agreement in terms of the signs and magnitudes of the partial regression coefficients.
4. The estimated model is applied to the data in the validation sample to predict the values of the dependent variable, $\hat{Y}_i$, for the observations in the validation sample.
5. The observed values, $Y_i$, and the predicted values, $\hat{Y}_i$, in the validation sample are correlated to determine the simple $r^2$. This measure, $r^2$, is compared to $R^2$ for the total sample and to $R^2$ for the estimation sample to assess the degree of shrinkage.

**double cross-validation**
A special form of validation in which the sample is split into halves. One half serves as the estimation sample and the other as a validation sample. The roles of the estimation and validation halves are then reversed, and the cross-validation process repeated.

A special form of validation is called double cross-validation. In **double cross-validation,** the sample is split into halves. One half serves as the estimation sample, and the other is used as a validation sample in conducting cross-validation. The roles of the estimation and validation halves are then reversed, and the cross-validation is repeated.[29]

# REGRESSION WITH DUMMY VARIABLES

Cross-validation is a general procedure that can be applied even in some special applications of regression, such as regression with dummy variables. Nominal or categorical variables may be used as predictors or independent variables by coding them as dummy variables. The concept of dummy variables was introduced in Chapter 14. In that chapter, we explained how a categorical variable with four categories (heavy, medium, light, and nonusers) can be coded in terms of three dummy variables, $D_1$, $D_2$, and $D_3$, as shown.

| Product Usage Category | *Original Variable Code* | *Dummy Variable Code* | | |
|---|---|---|---|---|
| | | $D_1$ | $D_2$ | $D_3$ |
| Nonusers | 1 | 1 | 0 | 0 |
| Light users | 2 | 0 | 1 | 0 |
| Medium users | 3 | 0 | 0 | 1 |
| Heavy users | 4 | 0 | 0 | 0 |

Suppose the researcher was interested in running a regression analysis of the effect of attitude toward the brand on product use. The dummy variables $D_1$, $D_2$, and $D_3$ would be used as predictors. *Regression with dummy variables* would be modeled as:

$$\hat{Y}_i = a + b_1 D_1 + b_2 D_2 + b_3 D_3$$

In this case, "heavy users" has been selected as a reference category and has not been directly included in the regression equation. Note that for heavy users, $D_1$, $D_2$, and $D_3$ assume a value of 0, and the regression equation becomes:

$$\hat{Y}_i = a$$

For nonusers, $D_1 = 1$, and $D_2 = D_3 = 0$, and the regression equation becomes:

$$\hat{Y}_i = a + b_1$$

Thus the coefficient $b_1$ is the difference in predicted $\hat{Y}_i$ for nonusers, as compared to heavy users. The coefficients $b_2$ and $b_3$ have similar interpretations. Although "heavy users" was selected as a reference category, any of the other three categories could have been selected for this purpose.[30]

# ANALYSIS OF VARIANCE AND COVARIANCE WITH REGRESSION

Regression with dummy variables provides a framework for understanding the analysis of variance and covariance. Although multiple regression with dummy variables provides a general procedure for the analysis of variance and covariance, we show only the equivalence of regression with dummy variables to one-way analysis of variance. In regression with dummy variables, the predicted $\hat{Y}$ for each category is the mean of $Y$ for each category. To illustrate using the dummy variable coding of product use we just considered, the predicted $\hat{Y}$ and mean values for each category are as follows:

| Product Usage Category | Predicted Value $\hat{Y}$ | Mean Value $\overline{Y}$ |
|---|---|---|
| Nonusers | $a + b_1$ | $a + b_1$ |
| Light users | $a + b_2$ | $a + b_2$ |
| Medium users | $a + b_3$ | $a + b_3$ |
| Heavy users | $a$ | $a$ |

Given this equivalence, it is easy to see further relationships between dummy variable regression and one-way ANOVA.[31]

| Dummy Variable Regression | One-Way ANOVA |
|---|---|
| $SS_{res} = \sum_{i=1}^{n} (Y_i - \hat{Y}_i)^2$ | $= SS_{within} = SS\ error$ |
| $SS_{reg} = \sum_{i=1}^{n} (\hat{Y}_i - \overline{Y})^2$ | $= SS_{between} = SS_x$ |
| $R^2$ | $= \eta^2$ |
| Overall $F$ test | $= F$ test |

Thus we see that regression in which the single independent variable with $c$ categories has been recoded into $c - 1$ dummy variables is equivalent to one-way analysis of variance. Using similar correspondences, one can also illustrate how $n$-way analysis of variance and analysis of covariance can be performed using regression with dummy variables.

Regression analysis, in its various forms, is a widely used technique. The next example illustrates an application in the context of international marketing research, and the example after that shows how regression can be used in investigating ethics in marketing research.

## REAL RESEARCH

### *Frequent Fliers—Fly from the Clouds to the Clear*

Airline companies in Asia were facing uncertainty and tough competition from U.S. carriers for a long time. Asian airlines, hit by global recession and preemptive competitive deals, awakened to the realization of banding together to increase air patronage. Secondary data revealed that among the important factors leading to airline selection by consumers were price, on-time schedules, destinations, deals available, kitchen and food service, on-flight service, etc. Asian airlines offered these services at par if not better. In fact, research showed that in-flight and kitchen services may have been even better. So, why were they feeling the competitive pressure? Qualitative research in the form of focus groups revealed that the frequent flier program was a critical factor for a broad segment in general and the business segment in particular. A survey of international passengers was conducted and multiple regression analyses was used to analyze the data. The likelihood of flying and other choice measures served as the dependent variable and the set of service factors, including the frequent flier program, were the independent variables. The results indicated that frequent flier program, indeed, had a significant effect on the choice of an airline. Based on these findings, Cathay Pacific, Singapore International Airlines, Thai Airways International, and Malaysian Airline systems introduced a cooperative frequent flier program called Asia Plus available to all travelers. The program was the first time the Asian carriers offered free travel in return for regular patronage. A multimillion-dollar marketing and advertising campaign was started to promote Asia Plus. Frequent fliers, thus, flew from the clouds to the clear and the Asian airlines experienced increased passenger traffic. Although the frequent flier program proved successful for Asian airlines, the economic effects of September 11, 2001, have pushed them into a huge crisis having similar effects as the Asian economic recession. The Association of Asia Pacific Airlines (AAPA) said the current state of the industry was on the verge of hopelessness at its annual assembly. Despite the challenges ahead for Asian airlines in 2004, many believe that it will be possible to renew growth and restore profitability in the future. Director of the AAPA, General Richard Stirland, said, "The industry should seize the opportunity, think the unthinkable, and set a new course to establish a less fragmented and healthier industry."[32] ∎

### REAL RESEARCH

## *Reasons for Researchers Regressing to Unethical Behavior*

As of 2003, the Internet is being used more and more to conduct marketing research studies at an increasing rate. With that being said, it is crucial that the research community create an ethical code of standards to follow when researching in an online environment. Many online researchers are distressed at the way other researchers are abusing the Internet as a means of collecting data. Those who conduct online research in an ethical manner feel that an accepted code of ethics of online research and online marketing behavior must be established. Without such a code, dishonest marketing tactics will prevail and ultimately make online research an impractical means of collecting important consumer data. Not only does online marketing research raise ethical problems and concerns, but also traditional marketing research has been targeted as a major source of ethical problems within the discipline of marketing. In particular, marketing research has been charged with engaging in deception, conflict of interest, violation of anonymity, invasion of privacy, data falsifications, dissemination of faulty research findings, and the use of research as a guise to sell merchandise. It has been speculated that when a researcher chooses to participate in unethical activities, that decision may be influenced by organizational factors. Therefore, a study using multiple regression analysis was designed to examine organizational factors as determinants of the incidence of unethical research practices. Six organizational variables were used as the independent variables, namely: extent of ethical problems within the organization, top management actions on ethics, code of ethics, organizational rank, industry category, and organizational role. The respondent's evaluation of the incidence of unethical marketing research practices served as the dependent variable. Regression analysis of the data suggested that four of the six organization variables influenced the extent of unethical research practice: extent of ethical problems within the organization, top management actions on ethics, organizational role, and industry category. Thus, to reduce the incidence of unethical research practice, top management should take stern actions, clarify organizational roles and responsibilities for ethical violations, and address the extent of general ethical problems within the organization.[33] ∎

# INTERNET AND COMPUTER APPLICATIONS

The computer programs available for conducting correlation analysis are described in Exhibit 17.1. In SPSS, CORRELATE can be used for computing Pearson product moment correlations, PARTIAL CORR for partial correlations, and NONPAR CORR for Spearman's $\rho_s$ and Kendall's $\tau$. The SAS program CORR can be used for calculating Pearson, Spearman's, Kendall's, and partial correlations. In MINITAB, correlation can be computed using STAT>BASIC STATISTICS>CORRELATION function. It calculates Pearson's product moment. Spearman's ranks the columns first and then performs the correlation on the ranked columns. To compute partial correlation, use the menu commands STAT>BASIC STATISTICS>CORRELATION and STAT>REGRESSION>REGRESSION. Correlations can be determined in EXCEL by using the TOOLS>DATA ANALYSIS>CORRELATION

*EXHIBIT 17.1*
Computer Programs
for Correlations

*SPSS*

The CORRELATIONS program computes Pearson product moment correlations with significance levels. Univariate statistics, covariance, and cross-product deviations may also be requested. PARTIAL CORR computes partial correlations. The effects of one or more confounding variables can be controlled when describing the relationship between two variables. Significance levels are included in the output.

*SAS*

CORR produces metric and nonmetric correlations between variables, including Pearson's product moment correlation. It also computes partial correlations.

*MINITAB*

Correlation can be computed using STAT>BASIC STATISTICS>CORRELATION function. It calculates Pearson's product moment using all the columns. Spearman's ranks the columns first and then performs the correlation on the ranked columns.

To compute partial correlation, use the menu commands STAT> BASIC STATISTICS>CORRELATION and STAT>REGRESSION>REGRESSION. Partial correlations can also be calculated by using session commands.

*EXCEL*

Correlations can be determined in EXCEL by using the TOOLS>DATA ANALYSIS> CORRELATION function. Utilize the Correlation Worksheet function when a correlation coefficient for two cell ranges is needed. There is no separate function for partial correlations.

---

function. Utilize the Correlation Worksheet function when a correlation coefficient for two cell ranges is needed. There is no separate function for partial correlations.

As described in Exhibit 17.2, these packages contain several programs for performing regression analysis, calculating the associated statistics, performing tests for significance, and plotting the residuals. In SPSS, the main program is REGRESSION. In SAS, the most general program is REG. Other specialized programs such as RSREG, ORTHOREG, GLM, and NLIN are also available, but readers not familiar with the intricate aspects of regression analysis are advised to stick to REG when using SAS. In MINITAB, regression analysis under the STATS>REGRESSION function, can perform simple, polynomial, and multiple analysis. In EXCEL, regression can be assessed from the TOOLS>DATA ANALYSIS menu.

## SPSS Windows

The CORRELATE program computes Pearson product moment correlations and partial correlations with significance levels. Univariate statistics, covariance, and cross-product deviations may also be requested. Significance levels are included in the output. To select this procedure using SPSS for Windows, click:

Analyze>Correlate>Bivariate . . .
Analyze>Correlate>Partial . . .

Scatterplots can be obtained by clicking:

Graphs>Scatter . . . >Simple>Define

REGRESSION calculates bivariate and multiple regression equations, associated statistics, and plots. It allows for an easy examination of residuals. This procedure can be run by clicking:

Analyze>Regression>Linear . . .

*EXHIBIT 17.2*
Computer Programs
for Regression

### SPSS

REGRESSION calculates bivariate and multiple regression equations, associated statistics, and plots. It allows for an easy examination of residuals. Stepwise regression can also be conducted. Regression statistics can be requested with PLOT, which produces simple scattergrams and some other types of plots.

### SAS

REG is a general-purpose regression procedure that fits bivariate and multiple regression models using the least-squares procedure. All the associated statistics are computed and residuals can be plotted. Stepwise methods can be implemented. RSREG is a more specialized procedure that fits a quadratic response surface model using least-squares regression. It is useful for determining factor levels that optimize a response. The ORTHOREG procedure is recommended for regression when the data are ill conditioned. GLM uses the method of least squares to fit general linear models and can also be used for regression analysis. NLIN computes the parameters of a nonlinear model using least-squares or weighted least-squares procedures.

### MINITAB

Regression analysis, under the STATS>REGRESSION function can perform simple, polynomial, and multiple analysis. The output includes a linear regression equation, table of coefficients, $R$ square, $R$ squared adjusted, analysis of variance table, a table of fits and residuals that provide unusual observations. Other available features include stepwise, best subsets, fitted line plot, and residual plots.

### EXCEL

Regression can be assessed from the TOOLS>DATA ANALYSIS menu. Depending on the features selected, the output can consist of a summary output table, including an ANOVA table, a standard error of $y$ estimate, coefficients, standard error of coefficients, $R^2$ values, and the number of observations. In addition, the function computes a residual output table, a residual plot, a line fit plot, normal probability plot, and a two-column probability data output table.

## FOCUS ON BURKE

We are often faced with the situation in which we must mix dummy variables and interval-scaled variables in the same analysis. This presents us with an interesting way to present the results and raises issues of interpretation. We illustrate this from a project conducted by Burke but we will use a very simple data set. The respondents were asked how many credit cards they had in their possession at the time of the interview and to rate "the value of credit" to their lifestyle (on a scale ranging from essential to maintaining our lifestyle to not at all needed to maintain our lifestyle). The dummy variable $d$ indicates that the respondent lives in a rural area (1) or an urban area (0).

### THE DATA

| Number of Credit Cards | Rating on Value of Credit | Location of Respondent |
|:---:|:---:|:---:|
| $y$ | $x_1$ | $d_1$ |
| 2 | 1 | 1 |
| 4 | 2 | 1 |
| 6 | 3 | 1 |
| 4 | 4 | 0 |
| 5 | 5 | 0 |
| 6 | 6 | 0 |
| 2 | 1 | 1 |
| 3 | 2 | 1 |
| 4 | 3 | 1 |
| 5 | 4 | 0 |
| 6 | 5 | 0 |
| 8 | 6 | 0 |

*(Continued)*

The regression model was constructed and the criteria for inclusion of a variable was the 90% confidence level. Portions of the SPSS output from multiple regression follows:

## MODEL SUMMARY[c]

| Model | R | Adjusted R Square | Std. Error of the R Square Estimate | Change Statistics R Square Change | F Change | df$_1$ | Sig. F df$_2$ | Change |
|---|---|---|---|---|---|---|---|---|
| 1 | 0.872[a] | 0.761 | 0.737 | 0.9131 | 0.761 | 31.876 | 1 | 10 | 0.000 |
| 2 | 0.915[b] | 0.837 | 0.800 | 0.7964 | 0.075 | 4.146 | 1 | 9 | 0.072 |

[a]Predictors: (Constant), VALUE

[b]Predictors: (Constant), VALUE, LOCATION

[c]Dependent Variable: CARDS

## COEFFICIENTS[a]

| | Model | Unstandardized Coefficients B | Std. Error | Standardized Coefficients Beta | t | Sig. | 95% Confidence Interval for B Lower Bound | Upper Bound | Zero-order | Partial | Part |
|---|---|---|---|---|---|---|---|---|---|---|---|
| 1 | (Constant) | 1.533 | 0.601 | | 2.551 | 0.029 | 0.194 | 2.873 | | | |
| | VALUE | 0.871 | 0.154 | 0.872 | 5.646 | 0.000 | 0.528 | 1.215 | 0.872 | 0.872 | 0.872 |
| 2 | (Constant) | −1.208 | 1.445 | | −0.836 | 0.425 | −4.477 | 2.060 | | | |
| | VALUE | 1.375 | 0.282 | 1.377 | 4.883 | 0.001 | 0.738 | 2.012 | 0.872 | 0.852 | 0.658 |
| | LOCATION | 1.958 | 0.962 | 0.574 | 2.036 | 0.072 | −0.217 | 4.134 | −0.635 | 0.562 | 0.274 |

[a] Dependent Variable: CARDS

## EXCLUDED VARIABLES[b]

| Model | Beta In | t | Sig. | Partial Correlation | Collinearity Statistics Tolerance |
|---|---|---|---|---|---|
| 1   LOCATION | 0.574[a] | 2.036 | 0.072 | 0.562 | 0.229 |

[a]Predictors in the Model: (Constant), VALUE

[b]Dependent Variable: CARDS

In the preceding model we found:

$$\hat{Y} = -1.2083 + 1.375(X_1) + 1.9583(D_1)$$

Recall that $D_1$ was simply a zero or one code and if $D_1 = 0$, the respondent lived in a city. If $D_1 = 1$, the respondent lived in a rural area. You could write the model as two models. For those respondents living in a city, there is no contribution to $Y$ from the dummy code.

$$\text{City Model: } \hat{Y} = -1.2083 + 1.375(X_1)$$

For every respondent living in a rural area, the contribution to $Y$ was 1.9583. Therefore for these respondents, this is a constant value and can be added to the overall model constant of $-1.2081$ (e.g. $-1.2083 + 1.9583 = 0.75$). Now we have a separate model for rural respondents.

$$\text{Rural Model: } \hat{Y} = 0.7500 + 1.375(X_1)$$

One way to look at the difference between these two constant terms (the difference is, of course, the regression coefficient for $D_1$) is that it reflects the average difference between the rural respondents and the urban respondents holding the rating of credit constant.

What are the management implications of this? By modeling with a dummy variable as illustrated, you have made the assumption that the relationship between the number of credit cards and rating of credit is a constant for both urban and rural respondents. This can be tested by simply running a separate regression between rating of credit and number of credit cards by type of respondent. The two models can then be tested for different slopes. If the slopes are not different, then the one overall model

$$\hat{Y} = -1.2083 + 1.375(X_1) + 1.9583(D_1)$$

could be used.

If the slopes are not the same, different models should be constructed for rural and urban respondents.

# SUMMARY

The product moment correlation coefficient, $r$, measures the linear association between two metric (interval or ratio scaled) variables. Its square, $r^2$, measures the proportion of variation in one variable explained by the other. The partial correlation coefficient measures the association between two variables after controlling, or adjusting for, the effects of one or more additional variables. The order of a partial correlation indicates how many variables are being adjusted or controlled. Partial correlations can be very helpful for detecting spurious relationships.

Bivariate regression derives a mathematical equation between a single metric criterion variable and a single metric predictor variable. The equation is derived in the form of a straight line by using the least-squares procedure. When the regression is run on standardized data, the intercept assumes a value of 0, and the regression coefficients are called beta weights. The strength of association is measured by the coefficient of determination, $r^2$, which is obtained by computing a ratio of $SS_{reg}$ to $SS_y$. The standard error of estimate is used to assess the accuracy of prediction and may be interpreted as a kind of average error made in predicting $Y$ from the regression equation.

Multiple regression involves a single dependent variable and two or more independent variables. The partial regression coefficient, $b_1$, represents the expected change in $Y$ when $X_1$ is changed by one unit and $X_2$ through $X_k$ are held constant. The strength of association is measured by the coefficient of multiple determination, $R^2$. The significance of the overall regression equation may be tested by the overall $F$ test. Individual partial regression coefficients may be tested for significance using the $t$ test or the incremental $F$ test. Scattergrams of the residuals, in which the residuals are plotted against the predicted values, $\hat{Y}_i$, time, or predictor variables, are useful for examining the appropriateness of the underlying assumptions and the regression model fitted.

In stepwise regression, the predictor variables are entered or removed from the regression equation one at a time for the purpose of selecting a smaller subset of predictors that account for most of the variation in the criterion variable. Multicollinearity, or very high intercorrelations among the predictor variables, can result in several problems. Because the predictors are correlated, regression analysis provides no unambiguous measure of relative importance of the predictors. Cross-validation examines whether the regression model continues to hold true for comparable data not used in estimation. It is a useful procedure for evaluating the regression model.

Nominal or categorical variables may be used as predictors by coding them as dummy variables. Multiple regression with dummy variables provides a general procedure for the analysis of variance and covariance.

# KEY TERMS AND CONCEPTS

product moment correlation (r), *497*
covariance, *497*
partial correlation coefficient, *500*
part correlation coefficient, *501*
nonmetric correlation, *502*
regression analysis, *502*
bivariate regression, *503*
bivariate regression model, *503*
coefficient of determination, *503*
estimated or predicted value, *503*

regression coefficient, *503*
scattergram, *503*
standard error of estimate, *504*
standard error, *504*
standardized regression coefficient, *504*
sum of squared errors, *504*
t statistic, *504*
least-squares procedure, *505*
multiple regression, *511*
multiple regression model, *512*

adjusted $R^2$, *513*
coefficient of multiple determination, *513*
F test, *513*
partial F test, *513*
partial regression coefficient, *513*
residual, *517*
stepwise regression, *519*
multicollinearity, *521*
cross-validation, *522*
double cross-validation, *523*

# EXERCISES

## *Questions*

1. What is the product moment correlation coefficient? Does a product moment correlation of 0 between two variables imply that the variables are not related to each other?
2. What is a partial correlation coefficient?
3. What are the main uses of regression analysis?
4. What is the least-squares procedure?
5. Explain the meaning of standardized regression coefficients.
6. How is the strength of association measured in bivariate regression? In multiple regression?
7. What is meant by prediction accuracy?

8. What is the standard error of estimate?
9. What assumptions underlie bivariate regression?
10. What is multiple regression? How is it different from bivariate regression?
11. Explain the meaning of a partial regression coefficient. Why is it so called?
12. State the null hypothesis in testing the significance of the overall multiple regression equation. How is this null hypothesis tested?
13. What is gained by an examination of residuals?
14. Explain the stepwise regression approach. What is its purpose?

**15.** What is multicollinearity? What problems can arise because of multicollinearity?

**16.** What are some of the measures used to assess the relative importance of predictors in multiple regression?

**17.** Describe the cross-validation procedure. Describe the double cross-validation procedure.

**18.** Demonstrate the equivalence of regression with dummy variables to one-way ANOVA.

## Problems

**1.** A major supermarket chain wants to determine the effect of promotion on relative competitiveness. Data were obtained from 15 states on the promotional expenses relative to a major competitor (competitor expenses = 100) and on sales relative to this competitor (competitor sales = 100).

| State No. | Relative Promotional Expense | Relative Sales |
|---|---|---|
| 1 | 95 | 98 |
| 2 | 92 | 94 |
| 3 | 103 | 110 |
| 4 | 115 | 125 |
| 5 | 77 | 82 |
| 6 | 79 | 84 |
| 7 | 105 | 112 |
| 8 | 94 | 99 |
| 9 | 85 | 93 |
| 10 | 101 | 107 |
| 11 | 106 | 114 |
| 12 | 120 | 132 |
| 13 | 118 | 129 |
| 14 | 75 | 79 |
| 15 | 99 | 105 |

You are assigned the task of telling the manager whether there is any relationship between relative promotional expense and relative sales.

**a.** Plot the relative sales (*Y*-axis) against the relative promotional expense (*X*-axis), and interpret this diagram.

**b.** Which measure would you use to determine whether there is a relationship between the two variables? Why?

**c.** Run a bivariate regression analysis of relative sales on relative promotional expense.

**d.** Interpret the regression coefficients.

**e.** Is the regression relationship significant?

**f.** If the company matched the competitor in terms of promotional expense (if the relative promotional expense was 100), what would the company's relative sales be?

**g.** Interpret the resulting $r^2$.

**2.** To understand the role of quality and price in influencing the patronage of drugstores, 14 major stores in a large metropolitan area were rated in terms of preference to shop, quality of merchandise, and fair pricing. All the ratings were obtained on an 11-point scale, with higher numbers indicating more positive ratings.

| Store No. | Preference | Quality | Price |
|---|---|---|---|
| 1 | 6 | 5 | 3 |
| 2 | 9 | 6 | 11 |
| 3 | 8 | 6 | 4 |
| 4 | 3 | 2 | 1 |
| 5 | 10 | 6 | 11 |
| 6 | 4 | 3 | 1 |
| 7 | 5 | 4 | 7 |
| 8 | 2 | 1 | 4 |
| 9 | 11 | 9 | 8 |
| 10 | 9 | 5 | 10 |
| 11 | 10 | 8 | 8 |
| 12 | 2 | 1 | 5 |
| 13 | 9 | 8 | 5 |
| 14 | 5 | 3 | 2 |

**a.** Run a multiple regression analysis explaining store preference in terms of quality of merchandise and price.

**b.** Interpret the partial regression coefficients.

**c.** Determine the significance of the overall regression.

**d.** Determine the significance of the partial regression coefficients.

**e.** Do you think that multicollinearity is a problem in this case? Why or why not?

**3.** You come across a magazine article reporting the following relationship between annual expenditure on prepared dinners (*PD*) and annual income (*INC*):

$$PD = 23.4 + 0.003 \ INC$$

The coefficient of the *INC* variable is reported as significant.

**a.** Does this relationship seem plausible? Is it possible to have a coefficient that is small in magnitude and yet significant?

**b.** From the information given, can you tell how good the estimated model is?

**c.** What are the expected expenditures on prepared dinners of a family earning $30,000?

**d.** If a family earning $40,000 spent $130 annually on prepared dinners, what is the residual?

**e.** What is the meaning of a negative residual?

# INTERNET AND COMPUTER EXERCISES

**1.** Conduct the following analyses for the Nike data given in Internet and Computer Exercises 1 of Chapter 15.

**a.** Calculate the simple correlations between awareness, attitude, preference, intention, and loyalty toward Nike and interpret the results.

**b.** Run a bivariate regression with loyalty as the dependent variable and intention as the independent variable. Interpret the results.

**c.** Run a multiple regression with loyalty as the dependent variable and awareness, attitude, preference, and intention as the independent variables. Interpret the results. Compare the coefficients for intention obtained in bivariate and multiple regressions.

2. Conduct the following analyses for the outdoor lifestyle data given in Internet and Computer Exercises 2 of Chapter 15.
   a. Calculate the simple correlations between $V_1$ to $V_6$ and interpret the results.
   b. Run a bivariate regression with preference for an outdoor lifestyle ($V_1$) as the dependent variable and meeting people ($V_6$) as the independent variable. Interpret the results.
   c. Run a multiple regression with preference for an outdoor lifestyle as the dependent variable and $V_2$ to $V_6$ as the independent variables. Interpret the results. Compare the coefficients for $V_6$ obtained in the bivariate and the multiple regressions.

3. In a pretest, data were obtained from 20 respondents on preferences for sneakers on a seven-point scale, 1 = not preferred, 7 = greatly preferred ($V_1$). The respondents also provided their evaluations of the sneakers on comfort ($V_2$), style ($V_3$), and durability ($V_4$), also on seven-point scales, 1 = poor and 7 = excellent. The resulting data are given in the following.

| $V_1$ | $V_2$ | $V_3$ | $V_4$ |
|-------|-------|-------|-------|
| 6.00 | 6.00 | 3.00 | 5.00 |
| 2.00 | 3.00 | 2.00 | 4.00 |
| 7.00 | 5.00 | 6.00 | 7.00 |
| 4.00 | 6.00 | 4.00 | 5.00 |
| 1.00 | 3.00 | 2.00 | 2.00 |
| 6.00 | 5.00 | 6.00 | 7.00 |
| 5.00 | 6.00 | 7.00 | 5.00 |
| 7.00 | 3.00 | 5.00 | 4.00 |
| 2.00 | 4.00 | 6.00 | 3.00 |
| 3.00 | 5.00 | 3.00 | 6.00 |
| 1.00 | 3.00 | 2.00 | 3.00 |
| 5.00 | 4.00 | 5.00 | 4.00 |
| 2.00 | 2.00 | 1.00 | 5.00 |
| 4.00 | 5.00 | 4.00 | 6.00 |
| 6.00 | 5.00 | 4.00 | 7.00 |
| 3.00 | 3.00 | 4.00 | 2.00 |
| 4.00 | 4.00 | 3.00 | 2.00 |
| 3.00 | 4.00 | 3.00 | 2.00 |
| 4.00 | 4.00 | 3.00 | 2.00 |
| 2.00 | 3.00 | 2.00 | 4.00 |

   a. Calculate the simple correlations between $V_1$ to $V_4$ and interpret the results.
   b. Run a bivariate regression with preference for sneakers ($V_1$) as the dependent variable and evaluation on comfort ($V_2$) as the independent variable. Interpret the results.
   c. Run a bivariate regression with preference for sneakers ($V_1$) as the dependent variable and evaluation on style ($V_3$) as the independent variable. Interpret the results.
   d. Run a bivariate regression with preference for sneakers ($V_1$) as the dependent variable and evaluation on durability ($V_4$) as the independent variable. Interpret the results.
   e. Run a multiple regression with preference for sneakers ($V_1$) as the dependent variable and $V_2$ to $V_4$ as the independent variables. Interpret the results. Compare the coefficients for $V_2$, $V_3$, and $V_4$ obtained in the bivariate and the multiple regressions.

4. Use an appropriate microcomputer or mainframe program (SPSS, SAS, MINITAB, or EXCEL) to analyze the data for:
   a. Problem 1
   b. Problem 2
   c. Fieldwork exercise

# ACTIVITIES

## Fieldwork

1. Visit 10 different drug stores in your area. Evaluate each store in terms of its overall image and quality of in-store service using 11-point rating scales (1 = poor, 11 = excellent). Then analyze the data you have collected as follows:
   a. Plot the overall image ($Y$-axis) against relative in-store service ($X$-axis) and interpret this diagram.
   b. Which measure would you use to determine whether there is a relationship between the two variables? Why?
   c. Run a bivariate regression analysis of overall image on in-store service.
   d. Interpret the regression coefficients.
   e. Is the regression relationship significant?
   f. Interpret the resulting $r^2$.

## Group Discussion

1. As a small group, discuss the following statement: "Regression is such a basic technique that it should always be used in analyzing data."
2. As a small group, discuss the relationship between bivariate correlation, bivariate regression, multiple regression, and analysis of variance.

# Discriminant Analysis

## Objectives

After reading this chapter, the student should be able to:

1. Describe the concept of discriminant analysis, its objectives, and its applications in marketing research.
2. Outline the procedures for conducting discriminant analysis including the formulation of the problem, estimation of the discriminant function coefficients, determination of significance, interpretation, and validation.
3. Discuss multiple discriminant analysis and the distinction between two-group and multiple discriminant analysis.
4. Explain stepwise discriminant analysis and describe the Mahalanobis procedure.

"Often you have measured different groups of respondents on many metric variables. Discriminant analysis is a useful way to answer the questions . . . are the groups different? . . . . On what variables are they most different? . . . . Can I predict which group a person belongs to using these variables?"

*Jamie Baker-Prewitt,*
*vice president,*
*consulting & analytical,*
*Burke, Inc.*

## Overview

This chapter discusses the technique of discriminant analysis. We begin by examining the relationship of this procedure to regression analysis (Chapter 17) and analysis of variance (Chapter 16). We present a model and describe the general procedure for conducting discriminant analysis, with emphasis on formulation, estimation, determination of significance, interpretation, and validation of the results. The procedure is illustrated with an example of two-group discriminant analysis, followed by an example of multiple (three-group) discriminant analysis. The stepwise discriminant analysis procedure is also covered.

**ACTIVE RESEARCH** | DEPARTMENT STORE PROJECT

### *Two-Group Discriminant Analysis*

In the store project, two-group discriminant analysis was used to examine whether those respondents who were familiar with the stores, versus those who were unfamiliar, attached different relative importance to the eight factors of the choice criteria. The dependent variable was the two familiarity groups, and the independent variables were the importance attached to the eight factors of the choice criteria. The overall discriminant function was significant, indicating significant differences between the two groups. The results indicated that, as compared to the unfamiliar respondents, the familiar respondents attached greater relative importance to quality of merchandise, return and adjustment policy, service of store personnel, and credit and billing policies.

**REAL RESEARCH**

## *Rebate Redeemers*

A study of 294 consumers was undertaken to determine the correlates of rebate proneness, or the characteristics of consumers who respond favorably to rebate promotions. The predictor variables were four factors related to household shopping attitudes and behaviors, and selected demographic characteristics (sex, age, and income). The dependent variable was the respondent's degree of rebate proneness, of which three levels were identified. Respondents who reported no rebate-triggered purchases during the past 12 months were classified as nonusers; those who reported one or two such purchases as light users; and those with more than two purchases, frequent users of rebates. Multiple discriminant analysis was used to analyze the data.

Two primary findings emerged. First, consumers' perception of the effort/value relationship was the most effective variable in discriminating among frequent, light, and nonusers of rebate offers. Clearly, rebate-sensitive consumers associate less effort with fulfilling the requirements of the rebate purchase, and they are willing to accept a relatively smaller refund than other customers. Second, consumers who are aware of the regular prices of products, so that they recognize bargains, are more likely than others to respond to rebate offers.

These findings were utilized by DIRECTV, Inc. (www.directv.com) when it added the National Geographic Channel to its programming in 2001. As a way to promote their service, DIRECTV offered three levels of rebates for new customers. The company felt that this would encourage the rebate-sensitive new customers to choose DIRECTV service and was successful in promoting their service.[1] ■

In the department store example, there were two groups of respondents (familiar and unfamiliar), whereas the rebate proneness example examined three groups (nonusers, light users, and frequent users of rebates). In both studies, significant intergroup differences were found using multiple predictor variables. An examination of differences across groups lies at the heart of the basic concept of discriminant analysis.

# BASIC CONCEPT

*discriminant analysis*
A technique for analyzing marketing research data when the criterion or dependent variable is categorical and the predictor or independent variables are interval in nature.

*discriminant functions*
The linear combination of independent variables developed by discriminant analysis that will best discriminate between the categories of the dependent variable.

*Discriminant analysis* is a technique for analyzing data when the criterion or dependent variable is categorical and the predictor or independent variables are interval in nature.[2] For example, the dependent variable may be the choice of a brand of personal computer (brand A, B, or C) and the independent variables may be ratings of attributes of PCs on a seven-point Likert scale. The objectives of discriminant analysis are as follows:

1. Development of *discriminant functions*, or linear combinations of the predictor or independent variables, which will best discriminate between the categories of the criterion or dependent variable (groups)
2. Examination of whether significant differences exist among the groups, in terms of the predictor variables
3. Determination of which predictor variables contribute to most of the intergroup differences
4. Classification of cases to one of the groups based on the values of the predictor variables
5. Evaluation of the accuracy of classification

*two-group discriminant analysis*
Discriminant analysis technique where the criterion variable has two categories.

*multiple discriminant analysis*
Discriminant analysis technique where the criterion variable involves three or more categories.

Discriminant analysis techniques are described by the number of categories possessed by the criterion variable. When the criterion variable has two categories, the technique is known as *two-group discriminant analysis.* When three or more categories are involved, the technique is referred to as *multiple discriminant analysis.* The main distinction is that, in the two-group case, it is possible to derive only one discriminant function. In multiple discriminant analysis, more than one function may be computed.[3]

Examples of discriminant analysis abound in marketing research. This technique can be used to answer questions such as:

■ In terms of demographic characteristics, how do customers who exhibit store loyalty differ from those who do not?
■ Do heavy, medium, and light users of soft drinks differ in terms of their consumption of frozen foods?
■ What psychographic characteristics help differentiate between price-sensitive and non-price-sensitive buyers of groceries?
■ Do the various market segments differ in their media consumption habits?
■ In terms of lifestyles, what are the differences between heavy patrons of regional department store chains and patrons of national chains?
■ What are the distinguishing characteristics of consumers who respond to direct mail solicitations?

# RELATIONSHIP TO REGRESSION AND ANOVA

The relationship among discriminant analysis, analysis of variance (ANOVA), and regression analysis is shown in Table 18.1. We explain this relationship with an example in which the researcher is attempting to explain the amount of life insurance purchased in

| TABLE 18.1 | | | |
|---|---|---|---|
| **Similarities and Differences Among ANOVA, Regression, and Discriminant Analysis** | | | |
| | ANOVA | REGRESSION | DISCRIMINANT ANALYSIS |
| *Similarities* | | | |
| Number of dependent variables | One | One | One |
| Number of independent variables | Multiple | Multiple | Multiple |
| *Differences* | | | |
| Nature of the dependent variables | Metric | Metric | Categorical |
| Nature of the independent variables | Categorical | Metric | Metric |

terms of age and income. All three procedures involve a single criterion or dependent variable and multiple predictor or independent variables. However, the nature of these variables differ. In analysis of variance and regression analysis, the dependent variable is metric or interval scaled (amount of life insurance purchased in dollars), whereas in discriminant analysis it is categorical (amount of life insurance purchased classified as high, medium, or low). The independent variables are categorical in the case of analysis of variance (age and income are each classified as high, medium, or low) but metric in the case of regression and discriminant analysis (age in years and income in dollars, i.e., both measured on a ratio scale).

Two-group discriminant analysis, in which the dependent variable has only two categories, is closely related to multiple regression analysis. In this case, multiple regression, in which the dependent variable is coded as a 0 or 1 dummy variable, results in partial regression coefficients that are proportional to discriminant function coefficients (see the following section on the discriminant analysis model).

## DISCRIMINANT ANALYSIS MODEL

**discriminant analysis model**
The statistical model on which discriminant analysis is based.

The **discriminant analysis model** involves linear combinations of the following form:

$$D = b_0 + b_1 X_1 + b_2 X_2 + b_3 X_3 + \cdots + b_k X_k$$

where

$D$ = discriminant score
$b$s = discriminant coefficients or weights
$X$s = predictors or independent variables

The coefficients, or weights ($b$), are estimated so that the groups differ as much as possible on the values of the discriminant function. This occurs when the ratio of between-group sum of squares to within-group sum of squares for the discriminant scores is at a maximum. Any other linear combination of the predictors will result in a smaller ratio. The technical details of estimation are described in Appendix 18.1. Several statistics are associated with discriminant analysis.

## STATISTICS ASSOCIATED WITH DISCRIMINANT ANALYSIS

The important statistics associated with discriminant analysis include the following.

***Canonical correlation.*** Canonical correlation measures the extent of association between the discriminant scores and the groups. It is a measure of association between the single discriminant function and the set of dummy variables that define the group membership.

**Centroid.** The centroid is the mean values for the discriminant scores for a particular group. There are as many centroids as there are groups, as there is one for each group. The means for a group on all the functions are the *group centroids*.

**Classification matrix.** Sometimes also called *confusion* or *prediction matrix*, the classification matrix contains the number of correctly classified and misclassified cases. The correctly classified cases appear on the diagonal, because the predicted and actual groups are the same. The off-diagonal elements represent cases that have been incorrectly classified. The sum of the diagonal elements divided by the total number of cases represents the *hit ratio*.

**Discriminant function coefficients.** The discriminant function coefficients (unstandardized) are the multipliers of variables, when the variables are in the original units of measurement.

**Discriminant scores.** The unstandardized coefficients are multiplied by the values of the variables. These products are summed and added to the constant term to obtain the discriminant scores.

**Eigenvalue.** For each discriminant function, the eigenvalue is the ratio of between-group to within-group sums of squares. Large eigenvalues imply superior functions.

**F values and their significance.** These are calculated from a one-way ANOVA, with the grouping variable serving as the categorical independent variable. Each predictor, in turn, serves as the metric dependent variable in the ANOVA.

**Group means and group standard deviations.** These are computed for each predictor for each group.

**Pooled within-group correlation matrix.** The pooled within-group correlation matrix is computed by averaging the separate covariance matrices for all the groups.

**Standardized discriminant function coefficients.** The standardized discriminant function coefficients are the discriminant function coefficients and are used as the multipliers when the variables have been standardized to a mean of 0 and a variance of 1.

**Structure correlations.** Also referred to as *discriminant loadings*, the structure correlations represent the simple correlations between the predictors and the discriminant function.

**Total correlation matrix.** If the cases are treated as if they were from a single sample and the correlations computed, a total correlation matrix is obtained.

**Wilks' $\lambda$.** Sometimes also called the *U* statistic, Wilks' $\lambda$ for each predictor is the ratio of the within-group sum of squares to the total sum of squares. Its value varies between 0 and 1. Large values of $\lambda$ (near 1) indicate that group means do not seem to be different. Small values of $\lambda$ (near 0) indicate that the group means seem to be different.

The assumptions in discriminant analysis are that each of the groups is a sample from a multivariate normal population and all of the populations have the same covariance matrix. The role of these assumptions and the statistics just described can be better understood by examining the procedure for conducting discriminant analysis.

# CONDUCTING DISCRIMINANT ANALYSIS

The steps involved in conducting discriminant analysis consist of formulation, estimation, determination of significance, interpretation, and validation (see Figure 18.1). These steps are discussed and illustrated within the context of two-group discriminant analysis. Discriminant analysis with more than two groups is discussed later in this chapter.

## Formulate the Problem

The first step in discriminant analysis is to formulate the problem by identifying the objectives, the criterion variable, and the independent variables. The criterion variable must consist of two or more mutually exclusive and collectively exhaustive categories. When the dependent variable is interval or ratio scaled, it must first be converted into categories. For example, attitude toward the brand, measured on a seven-point scale, could be categorized as unfavorable (1, 2, 3), neutral (4), or favorable (5, 6, 7). Alternatively, one could plot the distribution of the dependent variable and form groups of equal size by determin-

Figure 18.1
Conducting Discriminant Analysis

Formulate the problem.

Estimate the discriminant function coefficients.

Determine the significance of the discriminant function.

Interpret the results.

Assess the validity of discriminant analysis.

ing the appropriate cutoff points for each category. The predictor variables should be selected based on a theoretical model or previous research, or, in the case of exploratory research, the experience of the researcher should guide their selection.

The next step is to divide the sample into two parts. One part of the sample, called the estimation or **analysis sample,** is used for estimation of the discriminant function. The other part, called the *holdout* or **validation sample,** is reserved for validating the discriminant function. When the sample is large enough, it can be split in half. One half serves as the analysis sample and the other is used for validation. The role of the halves is then interchanged and the analysis is repeated. This is called double cross-validation and is similar to the procedure discussed in regression analysis (Chapter 17).

Often the distribution of the number of cases in the analysis and validation samples follows the distribution in the total sample. For instance, if the total sample contained 50 percent loyal and 50 percent nonloyal consumers, then the analysis and validation samples would each contain 50 percent loyal and 50 percent nonloyal consumers. On the other hand, if the sample contained 25 percent loyal and 75 percent nonloyal consumers, the analysis and validation samples would be selected to reflect the same distribution (25% versus 75%).

Finally, it has been suggested that the validation of the discriminant function should be conducted repeatedly. Each time, the sample should be split into different analysis and validation parts. The discriminant function should be estimated and the validation analysis carried out. Thus, the validation assessment is based on a number of trials. More rigorous methods have also been suggested.[4]

**analysis sample**
Part of the total sample that is used for estimation of the discriminant function.

**validation sample**
That part of the total sample used to check the results of the estimation sample.

Two-group discriminant analysis can be used to determine the salient characteristics of families that have visited a vacation resort.

## TABLE 18.2

**Information on Resort Visits: Analysis Sample**

| No. | Resort Visit | Annual Family Income ($000) | Attitude Toward Travel | Importance Attached to Family Vacation | Household Size | Age of Head of Household | Amount Spent on Family Vacation |
|---|---|---|---|---|---|---|---|
| 1 | 1 | 50.2 | 5 | 8 | 3 | 43 | M (2) |
| 2 | 1 | 70.3 | 6 | 7 | 4 | 61 | H (3) |
| 3 | 1 | 62.9 | 7 | 5 | 6 | 52 | H (3) |
| 4 | 1 | 48.5 | 7 | 5 | 5 | 36 | L (1) |
| 5 | 1 | 52.7 | 6 | 6 | 4 | 55 | H (3) |
| 6 | 1 | 75.0 | 8 | 7 | 5 | 68 | H (3) |
| 7 | 1 | 46.2 | 5 | 3 | 3 | 62 | M (2) |
| 8 | 1 | 57.0 | 2 | 4 | 6 | 51 | M (2) |
| 9 | 1 | 64.1 | 7 | 5 | 4 | 57 | H (3) |
| 10 | 1 | 68.1 | 7 | 6 | 5 | 45 | H (3) |
| 11 | 1 | 73.4 | 6 | 7 | 5 | 44 | H (3) |
| 12 | 1 | 71.9 | 5 | 8 | 4 | 64 | H (3) |
| 13 | 1 | 56.2 | 1 | 8 | 6 | 54 | M (2) |
| 14 | 1 | 49.3 | 4 | 2 | 3 | 56 | H (3) |
| 15 | 1 | 62.0 | 5 | 6 | 2 | 58 | H (3) |
| 16 | 2 | 32.1 | 5 | 4 | 3 | 58 | L (1) |
| 17 | 2 | 36.2 | 4 | 3 | 2 | 55 | L (1) |
| 18 | 2 | 43.2 | 2 | 5 | 2 | 57 | M (2) |
| 19 | 2 | 50.4 | 5 | 2 | 4 | 37 | M (2) |
| 20 | 2 | 44.1 | 6 | 6 | 3 | 42 | M (2) |
| 21 | 2 | 38.3 | 6 | 6 | 2 | 45 | L (1) |
| 22 | 2 | 55.0 | 1 | 2 | 2 | 57 | M (2) |
| 23 | 2 | 46.1 | 3 | 5 | 3 | 51 | L (1) |
| 24 | 2 | 35.0 | 6 | 4 | 5 | 64 | L (1) |
| 25 | 2 | 37.3 | 2 | 7 | 4 | 54 | L (1) |
| 26 | 2 | 41.8 | 5 | 1 | 3 | 56 | M (2) |
| 27 | 2 | 57.0 | 8 | 3 | 2 | 36 | M (2) |
| 28 | 2 | 33.4 | 6 | 8 | 2 | 50 | L (1) |
| 29 | 2 | 37.5 | 3 | 2 | 3 | 48 | L (1) |
| 30 | 2 | 41.3 | 3 | 3 | 2 | 42 | L (1) |

To better illustrate two-group discriminant analysis, let us look at an example. Suppose we want to determine the salient characteristics of families that have visited a vacation resort during the last two years. Data were obtained from a pretest sample of 42 households. Of these, 30 households shown in Table 18.2 were included in the analysis sample and the remaining 12 shown in Table 18.3 were part of the validation sample. The households that visited a resort during the last two years are coded as 1; those that did not, as 2 (VISIT). Both the analysis and validation samples were balanced in terms of VISIT. As can be seen, the analysis sample contains 15 households in each category, whereas the validation sample has six in each category. Data were also obtained on annual family income (INCOME), attitude toward travel (TRAVEL, measured on a nine-point scale), importance attached to family vacation (VACATION, measured on a nine-point scale), household size (HSIZE), and age of the head of the household (AGE).

**TABLE 18.3**

**Information on Resort Visits: Holdout Sample**

| No. | Resort Visit | Annual Family Income ($000) | Attitude Toward Travel | Importance Attached to Family Vacation | Household Size | Age of Head of Household | Amount Spent on Family Vacation |
|-----|------|------|------|------|------|------|------|
| 1 | 1 | 50.8 | 4 | 7 | 3 | 45 | M (2) |
| 2 | 1 | 63.6 | 7 | 4 | 7 | 55 | H (3) |
| 3 | 1 | 54.0 | 6 | 7 | 4 | 58 | M (2) |
| 4 | 1 | 45.0 | 5 | 4 | 3 | 60 | M (2) |
| 5 | 1 | 68.0 | 6 | 6 | 6 | 46 | H (3) |
| 6 | 1 | 62.1 | 5 | 6 | 3 | 56 | H (3) |
| 7 | 2 | 35.0 | 4 | 3 | 4 | 54 | L (1) |
| 8 | 2 | 49.6 | 5 | 3 | 5 | 39 | L (1) |
| 9 | 2 | 39.4 | 6 | 5 | 3 | 44 | H (3) |
| 10 | 2 | 37.0 | 2 | 6 | 5 | 51 | L (1) |
| 11 | 2 | 54.5 | 7 | 3 | 3 | 37 | M (2) |
| 12 | 2 | 38.2 | 2 | 2 | 3 | 49 | L (1) |

## Estimate the Discriminant Function Coefficients

Once the analysis sample has been identified, as in Table 18.2, we can estimate the discriminant function coefficients. Two broad approaches are available. The ***direct method*** involves estimating the discriminant function so that all the predictors are included simultaneously. In this case, each independent variable is included, regardless of its discriminating power. This method is appropriate when, based on previous research or a theoretical model, the researcher wants the discrimination to be based on all the predictors. An alternative approach is the stepwise method. In ***stepwise discriminant analysis,*** the predictor variables are entered sequentially, based on their ability to discriminate among groups. This method, described in more detail later, is appropriate when the researcher wants to select a subset of the predictors for inclusion in the discriminant function.

The results of running two-group discriminant analysis on the data of Table 18.2 using a popular computer program are presented in Table 18.4. Some intuitive feel for the results may be obtained by examining the group means and standard deviations. It appears that the two groups are more widely separated in terms of income than other variables. There appears to be more of a separation on the importance attached to family vacation than on attitude toward travel. The difference between the two groups on age of the head of the household is small, and the standard deviation of this variable is large.

The pooled within-groups correlation matrix indicates low correlations between the predictors. Multicollinearity is unlikely to be a problem. The significance of the univariate $F$ ratios indicates that when the predictors are considered individually, only income, importance of vacation, and household size significantly differentiate between those who visited a resort and those who did not.

Because there are two groups, only one discriminant function is estimated. The eigenvalue associated with this function is 1.7862 and it accounts for 100 percent of the explained variance. The canonical correlation associated with this function is 0.8007. The square of this correlation, $(0.8007)^2 = 0.64$, indicates that 64 percent of the variance in the dependent variable (VISIT) is explained or accounted for by this model.

## Determine the Significance of Discriminant Function

It would not be meaningful to interpret the analysis if the discriminant functions estimated were not statistically significant. The null hypothesis that, in the population, the means of all discriminant functions in all groups are equal can be statistically tested. In SPSS, this

## TABLE 18.4

**Results of Two-Group Discriminant Analysis**

GROUP MEANS

| VISIT | INCOME | TRAVEL | VACATION | HSIZE | AGE |
|---|---|---|---|---|---|
| 1 | 60.52000 | 5.40000 | 5.80000 | 4.33333 | 53.73333 |
| 2 | 41.91333 | 4.33333 | 4.06667 | 2.80000 | 50.13333 |
| Total | 51.21667 | 4.86667 | 4.93333 | 3.56667 | 51.93333 |

GROUP STANDARD DEVIATIONS

| | | | | | |
|---|---|---|---|---|---|
| 1 | 9.83065 | 1.91982 | 1.82052 | 1.23443 | 8.77062 |
| 2 | 7.55115 | 1.95180 | 2.05171 | 0.94112 | 8.27101 |
| Total | 12.79523 | 1.97804 | 2.09981 | 1.33089 | 8.57395 |

POOLED WITHIN-GROUPS CORRELATION MATRIX

| | INCOME | TRAVEL | VACATION | HSIZE | AGE |
|---|---|---|---|---|---|
| INCOME | 1.00000 | | | | |
| TRAVEL | 0.19745 | 1.00000 | | | |
| VACATION | 0.09148 | 0.08434 | 1.00000 | | |
| HSIZE | 0.08887 | −0.01681 | 0.07046 | 1.00000 | |
| AGE | −0.01431 | −0.19709 | 0.01742 | −0.04301 | 1.00000 |

Wilks' $\lambda$ (U-statistic) and univariate $F$ ratio with 1 and 28 degrees of freedom

| VARIABLE | WILKS' $\lambda$ | $F$ | SIGNIFICANCE |
|---|---|---|---|
| INCOME | 0.45310 | 33.80 | 0.0000 |
| TRAVEL | 0.92479 | 2.277 | 0.1425 |
| VACATION | 0.82377 | 5.990 | 0.0209 |
| HSIZE | 0.65672 | 14.64 | 0.0007 |
| AGE | 0.95441 | 1.338 | 0.2572 |

CANONICAL DISCRIMINANT FUNCTIONS

| FUNCTION | EIGENVALUE | PERCENT OF VARIANCE | CUMULATIVE PERCENT | CANONICAL CORRELATION | | AFTER FUNCTION | WILKS' $\lambda$ | CHI-SQUARE | DF | SIG. |
|---|---|---|---|---|---|---|---|---|---|---|
| | | | | | : | 0 | 0.3589 | 26.130 | 5 | 0.0001 |
| 1* | 1.7862 | 100.00 | 100.00 | 0.8007 | : | | | | | |

*Marks the 1 canonical discriminant functions remaining in the analysis.

STANDARD CANONICAL DISCRIMINANT FUNCTION COEFFICIENTS

| | FUNC 1 |
|---|---|
| INCOME | 0.74301 |
| TRAVEL | 0.09611 |
| VACATION | 0.23329 |
| HSIZE | 0.46911 |
| AGE | 0.20922 |

STRUCTURE MATRIX

Pooled within-groups correlations between discriminating variables and canonical discriminant functions (variables ordered by size of correlation within function)

| | FUNC 1 |
|---|---|
| INCOME | 0.82202 |
| HSIZE | 0.54096 |
| VACATION | 0.34607 |
| TRAVEL | 0.21337 |
| AGE | 0.16354 |

*(Continued)*

## TABLE 18.4

### Results of Two-Group Discriminant Analysis *(Continued)*

UNSTANDARDIZED CANONICAL DISCRIMINANT FUNCTION COEFFICIENTS

|          | FUNC 1            |
|----------|-------------------|
| INCOME   | 0.8476710E-01     |
| TRAVEL   | 0.4964455E-01     |
| VACATION | 0.1202813         |
| HSIZE    | 0.4273893         |
| AGE      | 0.2454380E-01     |
| (constant) | −7.975476       |

CANONICAL DISCRIMINANT FUNCTIONS EVALUATED AT GROUP MEANS (GROUP CENTROIDS)

| GROUP | FUNC 1    |
|-------|-----------|
| 1     | 1.29118   |
| 2     | −1.29118  |

CLASSIFICATION RESULTS

| | | | PREDICTED GROUP MEMBERSHIP | | TOTAL |
|---|---|---|---|---|---|
| | | VISIT | 1 | 2 | |
| Original | Count | 1 | 12 | 3 | 15 |
| | | 2 | 0 | 15 | 15 |
| | % | 1 | 80.0 | 20.0 | 100.0 |
| | | 2 | 0.0 | 100.0 | 100.0 |
| Cross-validated | Count | 1 | 11 | 4 | 15 |
| | | 2 | 2 | 13 | 15 |
| | % | 1 | 73.3 | 26.7 | 100.0 |
| | | 2 | 13.3 | 86.7 | 100.0 |

[a] Cross-validation is done only for those cases in the analysis. In cross-validation, each case is classified by the functions derived from all cases other than that case.

[b] 90.0% of original grouped cases correctly classified.

[c] 80.0% of cross-validated grouped cases correctly classified.

CLASSIFICATION RESULTS FOR CASES NOT SELECTED FOR USE IN THE ANALYSIS (HOLDOUT SAMPLE)

| | ACTUAL GROUP | NO. OF CASES | PREDICTED GROUP MEMBERSHIP | |
|---|---|---|---|---|
| | | | 1 | 2 |
| Group | 1 | 6 | 4 | 2 |
| | | | 66.7% | 33.3% |
| Group | 2 | 6 | 0 | 6 |
| | | | 0.0% | 100.0% |

Percent of grouped cases correctly classified: 83.33%.

test is based on Wilks' $\lambda$. If several functions are tested simultaneously (as in the case of multiple discriminant analysis), the Wilks' $\lambda$ statistic is the product of the univariate $\lambda$ for each function. The significance level is estimated based on a chi-square transformation of the statistic. In testing for significance in the vacation resort example (see Table 18.4), it may be noted that the Wilks' $\lambda$ associated with the function is 0.3589, which transforms to a chi-square of 26.13 with 5 degrees of freedom. This is significant beyond the 0.05 level. In SAS, an approximate $F$ statistic, based on an approximation to the distribution of the likelihood ratio, is calculated. A test of significance is not available in MINITAB. If the null hypothesis is rejected, indicating significant discrimination, one can proceed to interpret the results.[5]

## Interpret the Results

The interpretation of the discriminant weights, or coefficients, is similar to that in multiple regression analysis. The value of the coefficient for a particular predictor depends on the other predictors included in the discriminant function. The signs of the coefficients are arbitrary, but they indicate which variable values result in large and small function values and associate them with particular groups.

Given the multicollinearity in the predictor variables, there is no unambiguous measure of the relative importance of the predictors in discriminating between the groups.[6] With this caveat in mind, we can obtain some idea of the relative importance of the variables by examining the absolute magnitude of the standardized discriminant function coefficients. Generally, predictors with relatively large standardized coefficients contribute more to the discriminating power of the function, as compared with predictors with smaller coefficients, and are, therefore, more important.

Some idea of the relative importance of the predictors can also be obtained by examining the structure correlations, also called *canonical loadings* or *discriminant loadings*. These simple correlations between each predictor and the discriminant function represent the variance that the predictor shares with the function. The greater the magnitude of a structure correlation, the more important the corresponding predictor. Like the standardized coefficients, these correlations must also be interpreted with caution.

An examination of the standardized discriminant function coefficients for the vacation resort example is instructive. Given the low intercorrelations between the predictors, one might cautiously use the magnitudes of the standardized coefficients to suggest that income is the most important predictor in discriminating between the groups, followed by household size and importance attached to family vacation. The same observation is obtained from examination of the structure correlations. These simple correlations between the predictors and the discriminant function are listed in order of magnitude.

The unstandardized discriminant function coefficients are also given. These can be applied to the raw values of the variables in the holdout set for classification purposes. The group centroids, giving the value of the discriminant function evaluated at the group means, are also shown. Group 1, those who have visited a resort, has a positive value (1.29118), whereas group 2 has an equal negative value. The signs of the coefficients associated with all the predictors are positive. This suggests that higher family income, household size, importance attached to family vacation, attitude toward travel, and age are more likely to result in the family visiting the resort. It would be reasonable to develop a profile of the two groups in terms of the three predictors that seem to be the most important: income, household size, and importance of vacation. The values of these three variables for the two groups are given at the beginning of Table 18.4.

The determination of relative importance of the predictors is further illustrated by the following example.

### REAL RESEARCH

### *Satisfied Salespeople Stay*

A survey conducted in 2001 asked business people about the concern of hiring and maintaining employees during the current harsh economic climate. It was reported that 85 percent of respondents were concerned about recruiting employees and 81 percent said they were concerned about retaining employees. When the economy is down, turnover is rapid. Generally speaking, if an organization wants to retain its employees, it must learn why people leave their jobs and why others stay and are satisfied with their jobs. Discriminant analysis was used to determine what factors explained the differences between salespeople who left a large computer manufacturing company and those who stayed. The independent variables were company rating, job security, seven job-satisfaction dimensions, four role-conflict dimensions, four role-ambiguity dimensions, and nine measures of sales performance. The dependent variable was the dichotomy between those who stayed and those who left. The canonical correlation, an index of discrimination ($R = 0.4572$), was significant (Wilks' $\lambda = 0.7909$, $F(26,173) = 1.7588$, $p = 0.0180$). This result indicated that the variables discriminated between those who left and those who stayed.

The results from simultaneously entering all variables in discriminant analysis are presented in the table. The rank order of importance, as determined by the relative magnitude of the structure correlations, is presented in the first column. Satisfaction with the job and promotional opportunities were the two most important discriminators, followed by job security. Those who stayed in the company found the job to be more exciting, satisfying, challenging, and interesting than those who left.[7]

Discriminant Analysis Results

| Variable | Coefficients | Standardized Coefficients | Structure Correlations |
|---|---|---|---|
| 1. Work[a] | 0.0903 | 0.3910 | 0.5446 |
| 2. Promotion[a] | 0.0288 | 0.1515 | 0.5044 |
| 3. Job security | 0.1567 | 0.1384 | 0.4958 |
| 4. Customer relations[b] | 0.0086 | 0.1751 | 0.4906 |
| 5. Company rating | 0.4059 | 0.3240 | 0.4824 |
| 6. Working with others[b] | 0.0018 | 0.0365 | 0.4651 |
| 7. Overall performance[b] | −0.0148 | −0.3252 | 0.4518 |
| 8. Time-territory mgmt.[b] | 0.0126 | 0.2899 | 0.4496 |
| 9. Sales produced[b] | 0.0059 | 0.1404 | 0.4484 |
| 10. Presentation skill[b] | 0.0118 | 0.2526 | 0.4387 |
| 11. Technical information[b] | 0.0003 | 0.0065 | 0.4173 |
| 12. Pay-benefits[a] | 0.0600 | 0.1843 | 0.3788 |
| 13. Quota achieved[b] | 0.0035 | 0.2915 | 0.3780 |
| 14. Management[a] | 0.0014 | 0.0138 | 0.3571 |
| 15. Information collection[b] | −0.0146 | −0.3327 | 0.3326 |
| 16. Family[c] | −0.0684 | −0.3408 | −0.3221 |
| 17. Sales manager[a] | −0.0121 | −0.1102 | 0.2909 |
| 18. Coworker[a] | 0.0225 | 0.0893 | 0.2671 |
| 19. Customer[c] | −0.0625 | −0.2797 | −0.2602 |
| 20. Family[d] | 0.0473 | 0.1970 | 0.2180 |
| 21. Job[d] | 0.1378 | 0.5312 | 0.2119 |
| 22. Job[c] | 0.0410 | 0.5475 | −0.1029 |
| 23. Customer[d] | −0.0060 | −0.0255 | 0.1004 |
| 24. Sales manager[c] | −0.0365 | −0.2406 | −0.0499 |
| 25. Sales manager[d] | −0.0606 | −0.3333 | 0.0467 |
| 26. Customer[a] | −0.0338 | −0.1488 | 0.0192 |

*Note:* Rank order of importance is based on the magnitude of the structure correlations.
[a] Satisfaction
[b] Performance
[c] Ambiguity
[d] Conflict

Note that in this example, promotion was identified as the second most important variable based on the structure correlations. However, it is not the second most important variable based on the absolute magnitude of the standardized discriminant function coefficients. This anomaly results from multicollinearity.

**characteristic profile**
An aid to interpreting discriminant analysis results by describing each group in terms of the group means for the predictor variables.

Another aid to interpreting discriminant analysis results is to develop a ***characteristic profile*** for each group by describing each group in terms of the group means for the predictor variables. If the important predictors have been identified, then a comparison of the group means on these variables can assist in understanding the intergroup differences. However, before any findings can be interpreted with confidence, it is necessary to validate the results.

## Assess Validity of Discriminant Analysis

Many computer programs, such as SPSS, offer a leave-one-out cross-validation option. In this option, the discriminant model is reestimated as many times as there are respondents in the sample. Each reestimated model leaves out one respondent and the model is used to predict for that respondent. When a large holdout sample is not possible, this gives a sense of the robustness of the estimate using each respondent, in turn, as a holdout.

As explained earlier, where possible, the data should be randomly divided into two subsamples. One, the analysis sample, is used for estimating the discriminant function; the validation sample is used for developing the classification matrix. The discriminant weights, estimated by using the analysis sample, are multiplied by the values of the predictor variables in the holdout sample to generate discriminant scores for the cases in the holdout sample. The cases are then assigned to groups based on their discriminant scores and an appropriate decision rule. For example, in two-group discriminant analysis, a case will be assigned to the group whose centroid is the closest. The **hit ratio,** or the percentage of cases correctly classified, can then be determined by summing the diagonal elements and dividing by the total number of cases.[8]

It is helpful to compare the percentage of cases correctly classified by discriminant analysis to the percentage that would be obtained by chance. When the groups are equal in size, the percentage of chance classification is 1 divided by the number of groups. How much improvement should be expected over chance? No general guidelines are available, although some authors have suggested that classification accuracy achieved by discriminant analysis should be at least 25 percent greater than that obtained by chance.[9]

Most discriminant analysis programs also estimate a classification matrix based on the analysis sample. Because they capitalize on chance variation in the data, such results are invariably better than leave-one-out classification or the classification obtained on the holdout sample.

Table 18.4, of the vacation resort example, also shows the classification results based on the analysis sample. The hit ratio, or the percentage of cases correctly classified, is $(12 + 15)/30 = 0.90$, or 90 percent. One might suspect that this hit ratio is artificially inflated, as the data used for estimation was also used for validation. Leave-one-out cross-validation correctly classifies only $(11 + 13)/30 = 0.80$ or 80 percent of the cases. Conducting classification analysis on an independent holdout set of data results in the classification matrix with a hit ratio of $(4 + 6)/12 = 0.833$, or 83.3 percent (see Table 18.4). Given two groups of equal size, by chance one would expect a hit ratio of $1/2 = 0.50$, or 50 percent. Hence, the improvement over chance is more than 25 percent, and the validity of the discriminant analysis is judged as satisfactory.

*hit ratio*

The percentage of cases correctly classified by the discriminant analysis.

## REAL RESEARCH

### *Home Bodies and Couch Potatoes*

Two-group discriminant analysis was used to assess the strength of each of five dimensions used in classifying individuals as TV users or nonusers. The procedure was appropriate for this use because of the nature of the predefined categorical groups (users and nonusers) and the interval scales used to generate individual factor scores.

Two equal groups of 185 elderly consumers, users and nonusers (total $n = 370$), were created. The discriminant equation for the analysis was estimated by using a subsample of 142 respondents from the sample of 370. Of the remaining respondents, 198 were used as a validation subsample in a cross-validation of the equation. Thirty respondents were excluded from the analysis because of missing values.

The canonical correlation for the discriminant function was 0.4291, significant at the $p < 0.0001$ level. The eigenvalue was 0.2257. The table summarizes the standardized canonical discriminant coefficients. A substantial portion of the variance is explained by the discriminant function. In addition, as the table shows, the home orientation dimension made a fairly strong contribution to classifying individuals as users or nonusers of television. Morale, security and health, and respect also contributed significantly. The social factor appeared to make little contribution.

The cross-validation procedure using the discriminant function from the analysis sample gave support to the contention that the dimensions aided researchers in discriminating between users and nonusers of television. As the table shows, the discriminant function was successful in classifying 75.76 percent of the cases. This suggests that consideration of the identified dimensions will help marketers understand the elderly market. Although it is very important for marketers to know and understand the elderly market, the Generation Xers (those born between 1961 and 1981) are also a group that should not be overlooked by marketers. Due to technological advances with the Internet and television, a revolutionary form of interactive TV (ITV) has been created. By 2003, ITV services will be fully deployed and operational and will combine the Internet and broadcasting with software programs and hardware components to give consumers Internet access, online shopping, music downloads, and an interactive broadcast program all through their television. By 2006, it is predicted that 61.5 million people will be interacting with their televisions through ITV. With such a prosperous looking forecast for ITV, who better to target this revolutionary form of television than Generation Xers? Discriminant analysis can again be used to determine who amongst Generation Xers are users or nonusers of ITV and to market ITV services successfully.[10]

Summary of Discriminant Analysis

**Standard Canonical Discriminant Function Coefficients**

| | |
|---|---|
| Morale | 0.27798 |
| Security & health | 0.39850 |
| Home orientation | 0.77496 |
| Respect | 0.32069 |
| Social | −0.01996 |

**Classification Results for Cases Selected for Use in the Analysis**

| | Number of | Predicted Group Membership | |
|---|---|---|---|
| **Actual Group** | **Cases** | **Nonusers** | **Users** |
| TV nonusers | 77 | 56 | 21 |
| | | 72.7% | 27.3% |
| TV users | 65 | 24 | 41 |
| | | 36.9% | 63.1% |

Percent of grouped cases correctly classified: 68.31%

**Classification Results for Cases Used for Cross-Validation**

| | Number of | Predicted Group Membership | |
|---|---|---|---|
| **Actual Group** | **Cases** | **Nonusers** | **Users** |
| TV nonusers | 108 | 85 | 23 |
| | | 78.7% | 21.3% |
| TV users | 90 | 25 | 65 |
| | | 27.8% | 72.2% |

Percent of grouped cases correctly classified: 75.76% ■

The extension from two-group discriminant analysis to multiple discriminant analysis involves similar steps.

# MULTIPLE DISCRIMINANT ANALYSIS

## Formulate the Problem

The data presented in Tables 18.2 and 18.3 can also be used to illustrate three-group discriminant analysis. In the last column of these tables, the households are classified into three categories, based on the amount spent on family vacation (high, medium, or low). Ten households fall in each category. The question of interest is whether the households that spend high, medium, or low amounts on their vacations (AMOUNT) can be differentiated in terms of annual family income (INCOME), attitude toward travel (TRAVEL), importance attached to family vacation (VACATION), household size (HSIZE), and age of the head of household (AGE).[11]

TABLE 18.5

**Results of Three-Group Discriminant Analysis**

GROUP MEANS

| AMOUNT | INCOME | TRAVEL | VACATION | HSIZE | AGE |
|---|---|---|---|---|---|
| 1 | 38.57000 | 4.50000 | 4.70000 | 3.10000 | 50.30000 |
| 2 | 50.11000 | 4.00000 | 4.20000 | 3.40000 | 49.50000 |
| 3 | 64.97000 | 6.10000 | 5.90000 | 4.20000 | 56.00000 |
| Total | 51.21667 | 4.86667 | 4.93333 | 3.56667 | 51.93333 |

GROUP STANDARD DEVIATIONS

| | INCOME | TRAVEL | VACATION | HSIZE | AGE |
|---|---|---|---|---|---|
| 1 | 5.29718 | 1.71594 | 1.88856 | 1.19722 | 8.09732 |
| 2 | 6.00231 | 2.35702 | 2.48551 | 1.50555 | 9.25263 |
| 3 | 8.61434 | 1.19722 | 1.66333 | 1.13529 | 7.60117 |
| Total | 12.79523 | 1.97804 | 2.09981 | 1.33089 | 8.57395 |

POOLED WITHIN-GROUPS CORRELATION MATRIX

| | INCOME | TRAVEL | VACATION | HSIZE | AGE |
|---|---|---|---|---|---|
| INCOME | 1.00000 | | | | |
| TRAVEL | 0.05120 | 1.00000 | | | |
| VACATION | 0.30681 | 0.03588 | 1.00000 | | |
| HSIZE | 0.38050 | 0.00474 | 0.22080 | 1.00000 | |
| AGE | −0.20939 | −0.34022 | −0.01326 | −0.02512 | 1.00000 |

Wilks' $\lambda$ (U-statistic) and univariate $F$ ratio with 2 and 27 degrees of freedom.

| VARIABLE | WILKS' LAMBDA | F | SIGNIFICANCE |
|---|---|---|---|
| INCOME | 0.26215 | 38.000 | 0.0000 |
| TRAVEL | 0.78790 | 3.634 | 0.0400 |
| VACATION | 0.88060 | 1.830 | 0.1797 |
| HSIZE | 0.87411 | 1.944 | 0.1626 |
| AGE | 0.88214 | 1.804 | 0.1840 |

CANONICAL DISCRIMINANT FUNCTIONS

| FCN | EIGENVALUE | % OF VARIANCE | CUM PCT | CANONICAL CORR | | AFTER FCN | WILKS' $\lambda$ | CHI-SQUARE | DF | SIG. |
|---|---|---|---|---|---|---|---|---|---|---|
| | | | | | : | 0 | 0.1664 | 44.831 | 10 | 0.00 |
| 1* | 3.8190 | 93.93 | 93.93 | 0.8902 | : | 1 | 0.8020 | 5.517 | 4 | 0.24 |
| 2* | 0.2469 | 6.07 | 100.00 | 0.4450 | : | | | | | |

*Marks the two canonical discriminant functions remaining in the analysis.

STANDARDIZED CANONICAL DISCRIMINANT FUNCTION COEFFICIENTS

| | FUNC 1 | FUNC 2 |
|---|---|---|
| INCOME | 1.04740 | −0.42076 |
| TRAVEL | 0.33991 | 0.76851 |
| VACATION | −0.14198 | 0.53354 |
| HSIZE | −0.16317 | 0.12932 |
| AGE | 0.49474 | 0.52447 |

STRUCTURE MATRIX

Pooled within-groups correlations between discriminating variables and canonical discriminant functions (variables ordered by size of correlation within function)

| | FUNC 1 | FUNC 2 |
|---|---|---|
| INCOME | 0.85556* | −0.27833 |
| HSIZE | 0.19319* | 0.07749 |
| VACATION | 0.21935 | 0.58829* |
| TRAVEL | 0.14899 | 0.45362* |
| AGE | 0.16576 | 0.34079* |

(Continued)

## TABLE 18.5

### Results of Three-Group Discriminant Analysis (*Continued*)

UNSTANDARDIZED CANONICAL DISCRIMINANT FUNCTION COEFFICIENTS

| | FUNC 1 | FUNC 2 |
|---|---|---|
| INCOME | 0.1542658 | −0.6197148E-01 |
| TRAVEL | 0.1867977 | 0.4223430 |
| VACATION | −0.6952264E-01 | 0.2612652 |
| HSIZE | −0.1265334 | 0.1002796 |
| AGE | 0.5928055E-01 | 0.6284206E-01 |
| (constant) | −11.09442 | −3.791600 |

CANONICAL DISCRIMINANT FUNCTIONS EVALUATED AT GROUP MEANS (GROUP CENTROIDS)

| GROUP | FUNC 1 | FUNC 2 |
|---|---|---|
| 1 | −2.04100 | 0.41847 |
| 2 | −0.40479 | −0.65867 |
| 3 | 2.44578 | 0.24020 |

CLASSIFICATION RESULTS

| | | | | PREDICTED GROUP MEMBERSHIP | | | |
|---|---|---|---|---|---|---|---|
| | | AMOUNT | 1 | 2 | 3 | TOTAL | |
| Original | Count | 1 | 9 | 1 | 0 | 10 | |
| | | 2 | 1 | 9 | 0 | 10 | |
| | | 3 | 0 | 2 | 8 | 10 | |
| | % | 1 | 90.0 | 10.0 | 0.0 | 100.0 | |
| | | 2 | 10.0 | 90.0 | 0.0 | 100.0 | |
| | | 3 | 0.0 | 20.0 | 80.0 | 100.0 | |
| Cross-validated | Count | 1 | 7 | 3 | 0 | 10 | |
| | | 2 | 4 | 5 | 1 | 10 | |
| | | 3 | 0 | 2 | 8 | 10 | |
| | % | 1 | 70.0 | 30.0 | 0.0 | 100.0 | |
| | | 2 | 40.0 | 50.0 | 10.0 | 100.0 | |
| | | 3 | 0.0 | 20.0 | 80.0 | 100.0 | |

[a] Cross-validation is done only for those cases in the analysis. In cross-validation, each case is classified by the functions derived from all cases other than that case.

[b] 86.7% of original grouped cases correctly classified.

[c] 66.7% of cross-validated grouped cases correctly classified.

CLASSIFICATION RESULTS FOR CASES NOT SELECTED FOR USE IN THE ANALYSIS

| | | | PREDICTED GROUP MEMBERSHIP | | |
|---|---|---|---|---|---|
| | ACTUAL GROUP | NO. OF CASES | 1 | 2 | 3 |
| Group | 1 | 4 | 3 | 1 | 0 |
| | | | 75.0% | 25.0% | 0.0% |
| Group | 2 | 4 | 0 | 3 | 1 |
| | | | 0.0% | 75.0% | 25.0% |
| Group | 3 | 4 | 1 | 0 | 3 |
| | | | 25.0% | 0.0% | 75.0% |

Percent of grouped cases correctly classified: 75.0%

## Estimate the Discriminant Function Coefficients

Table 18.5 presents the results of estimating three-group discriminant analysis. An examination of group means indicates that income appears to separate the groups more widely than any other variable. There is some separation on travel and vacation. Groups 1 and 2 are very close in terms of household size and age. Age has a large standard deviation relative to the separation between the groups. The pooled within-groups correlation matrix indicates some correlation of vacation and household size with income. Age has some negative correlation with travel. Yet, these correlations are on the lower side, indicating that although multi-collinearity may be of some concern, it is not likely to be a serious problem. The significance attached to the univariate $F$ ratios indicates that when the predictors are considered individually, only income and travel are significant in differentiating between the two groups.

In multiple discriminant analysis, if there are $G$ groups, $G - 1$ discriminant functions can be estimated if the number of predictors is larger than this quantity. In general, with $G$ groups and $k$ predictors, it is possible to estimate up to the smaller of $G - 1$ or $k$ discriminant functions. The first function has the highest ratio of between-groups to within-groups sum of squares. The second function, uncorrelated with the first, has the second highest ratio, and so on. However, not all the functions may be statistically significant.

Because there are three groups, a maximum of two functions can be extracted. The eigenvalue associated with the first function is 3.8190, and this function accounts for 93.93 percent of the explained variance. Because the eigenvalue is large, the first function is likely to be superior. The second function has a small eigenvalue of 0.2469 and accounts for only 6.07 percent of the explained variance.

## Determine the Significance of the Discriminant Function

To test the null hypothesis of equal group centroids, both the functions must be considered simultaneously. It is possible to test the means of the functions successively by first testing all means simultaneously. Then one function is excluded at a time, and the means of the remaining functions are tested at each step. In Table 18.5, the 0 below "After Function" indicates that no functions have been removed. The value of Wilks' $\lambda$ is 0.1644. This transforms to a chi-square of 44.831, with 10 degrees of freedom, which is significant beyond the 0.05 level. Thus, the two functions together significantly discriminate among the three groups. However, when the first function is removed, the Wilks' $\lambda$ associated with the second function is 0.8020, which is not significant at the 0.05 level. Therefore, the second function does not contribute significantly to group differences.

## Interpret the Results

The interpretation of the results is aided by an examination of the standardized discriminant function coefficients, the structure correlations, and certain plots. The standardized coefficients indicate a large coefficient for income on function 1, whereas function 2 has relatively larger coefficients for travel, vacation, and age. A similar conclusion is reached by an examination of the structure matrix (see Table 18.5). To help interpret the functions, variables with large coefficients for a particular function are grouped together. These groupings are shown with asterisks. Thus, income and household size have asterisks for function 1 because these variables have coefficients that are larger for function 1 than for function 2. These variables are associated primarily with function 1. On the other hand, travel, vacation, and age are predominantly associated with function 2, as indicated by the asterisks.

Figure 18.2 is a scattergram plot of all the groups on function 1 and function 2. It can be seen that group 3 has the highest value on function 1, and group 1 the lowest. Because function 1 is primarily associated with income and household size, one would expect the three groups to be ordered on these two variables. Those with higher incomes and higher household size are likely to spend large amounts of money on vacations. Conversely, those with low incomes and smaller household size are likely to spend small amounts on vacations. This interpretation is further strengthened by an examination of group means on income and household size.

Figure 18.2 further indicates that function 2 tends to separate group 1 (highest value) and group 2 (lowest value). This function is primarily associated with travel, vacation, and age. Given the positive correlations of these variables with function 2 in the structure matrix, we expect to find group 1 to be higher than group 2 in terms of travel, vacation, and age. This is indeed true for travel and vacation, as indicated by the group means of these variables. If families in group 1 have more favorable attitudes toward travel and attach more importance to family vacation than group 2, why do they spend less? Perhaps they would like to spend more on vacations but cannot afford it because they have low incomes.

A similar interpretation is obtained by examining a ***territorial map,*** as shown in Figure 18.3. In a territorial map, each group centroid is indicated by an asterisk. The group

*territorial map*
A tool for assessing discriminant analysis results that plots the group membership of each case on a graph.

**Figure 18.2**
All-Groups Scattergram

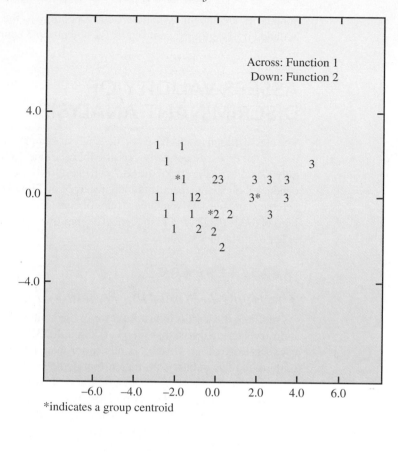

*indicates a group centroid

**Figure 18.3**
Territorial Map

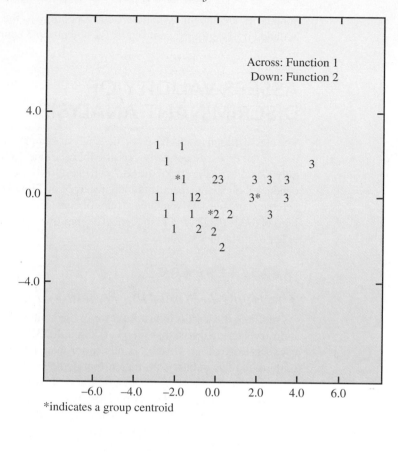

*indicates a group centroid

boundaries are shown by numbers corresponding to the groups. Thus, group 1 centroid is bounded by 1s, group 2 centroid by 2s, and group 3 centroid by 3s.

# ASSESS VALIDITY OF DISCRIMINANT ANALYSIS

The classification results based on the analysis sample indicate that $(9 + 9 + 8)/30 = 86.7$ percent of the cases are correctly classified. Leave-one-out cross-validation correctly classifies only $(7 + 5 + 8)/30 = 0.667$ or 66.7 percent of the cases. When the classification analysis is conducted on the independent holdout sample of Table 18.3, a hit ratio of $(3 + 3 + 3)/12 = 75$ percent is obtained. Given three groups of equal size, by chance alone one would expect a hit ratio of $1/3 = 0.333$ or 33.3 percent. The improvement over chance is 50 percent, indicating at least satisfactory validity.

## REAL RESEARCH

### *The Home Is Where the Patient's Heart Is*

As of 2003, the largest industry sector in the United States economy is the health services industry. During the next seven years through 2010, it is expected that spending on health care services will grow significantly faster than the economy. Contributing to the positive outlook for this industry are the current demographics, especially with demand for long-term care increasing as the population ages. It is expected that the number of Americans who are 85 and older will triple by 2020, and with such a large increase, it is crucial that the health care system be portrayed positively to this segment of the population. Consumers were surveyed to determine their attitudes toward four systems of health care delivery (home health care, hospitals, nursing homes, and outpatient clinics) along 10 attributes. A total of 102 responses were obtained, and the results were analyzed using multiple discriminant analysis (Table 1). Three discriminant functions were identified. Chi-square tests performed on the results indicated that all three discriminant functions were significant at the 0.01 level. The first function accounted for 63 percent of the total discriminative power, and the remaining two functions contributed 29.4 percent and 7.6 percent, respectively.

Table 1 gives the standardized discriminant function coefficients of the 10 variables in the discriminant equations. Coefficients ranged in value from $-1$ to $+1$. In determining the

Multiple discriminant analysis shows that nursing homes are perceived unfavorably on the dimensions of personalized care, quality of medical care, and value.

ability of each attribute to classify the delivery system, absolute values were used. In the first discriminant function, the two variables with the largest coefficients were comfort (0.53) and privacy (0.40). Because both related to personal attention and care, the first dimension was labeled "personalized care." In the second function, the two variables with the largest coefficients were quality of medical care (0.67) and likelihood of faster recovery (0.32). Hence, this dimension was labeled "quality of medical care." In the third discriminant function, the most significant attributes were sanitation (−0.70) and expense (0.52). Because these two attributes represent value and price, the third discriminant function was labeled "value."

The four group centroids are shown in Table 2. This table shows that home health care was evaluated most favorably along the dimension of personalized care, and hospitals least favorably. Along the dimension of quality of medical care, there was a substantial separation between nursing homes and the other three systems. Also, home health care received higher evaluations on the quality of medical care than did outpatient clinics. Outpatient clinics, on the other hand, were judged to offer the best value.

Classification analysis of the 102 responses, reported in Table 3, showed correct classifications ranging from 86 percent for hospitals to 68 percent for outpatient clinics. The misclassifications for hospitals were 6 percent each to nursing homes and outpatient clinics, and 2 percent to home health care. Nursing homes showed misclassifications of 9 percent to hospitals, 10 percent to outpatient clinics, and 3 percent to home health care. For outpatient clinics, 9 percent misclassifications were made to hospitals, 13 percent to nursing homes, and 10 percent to home health care. For home health care, the misclassifications were 5 percent to hospitals, 4 percent to nursing homes, and 13 percent to outpatient clinics. The results demonstrated that the discriminant functions were fairly accurate in predicting group membership.[12]

TABLE 1    Standardized Discriminant Function Coefficients

| Variable | Discriminant Function | | |
|---|---|---|---|
| | *1* | *2* | *3* |
| Safe | −0.20 | −0.04 | 0.15 |
| Convenient | 0.08 | 0.08 | 0.07 |
| Chance of medical complications[a] | −0.27 | 0.10 | 0.16 |
| Expensive[a] | 0.30 | −0.28 | 0.52 |
| Comfortable | 0.53 | 0.27 | −0.19 |
| Sanitary | −0.27 | −0.14 | −0.70 |
| Best medical care | −0.25 | 0.67 | −0.10 |
| Privacy | 0.40 | 0.08 | 0.49 |
| Faster recovery | 0.30 | 0.32 | −0.15 |
| Staffed with best medical personnel | −0.17 | −0.03 | 0.18 |
| Percentage of explained variance | 63.0 | 29.4 | 7.6 |
| Chi-square | 663.3[b] | 289.2[b] | 70.1[b] |

[a]These two items were worded negatively on the questionnaire. They were reverse coded for purposes of data analysis.
[b]$p < 0.01$.

TABLE 2    Centroids of Health Care Systems in Discriminant Space

| System | Discriminant Function | | |
|---|---|---|---|
| | *1* | *2* | *3* |
| Hospital | −1.66 | 0.97 | −0.08 |
| Nursing home | −0.60 | −1.36 | −0.27 |
| Outpatient clinic | 0.54 | −0.13 | 0.77 |
| Home health care | 1.77 | 0.50 | −0.39 |

TABLE 3    Classification Table

| | | Classification (%) | | |
| | | *Nursing* | *Outpatient* | *Home Health* |
| *System* | *Hospital* | *Home* | *Clinic* | *Care* |
|---|---|---|---|---|
| Hospital | 86 | 6 | 6 | 2 |
| Nursing home | 9 | 78 | 10 | 3 |
| Outpatient clinic | 9 | 13 | 68 | 10 |
| Home health care | 5 | 4 | 13 | 78 ■ |

# STEPWISE DISCRIMINANT ANALYSIS

Stepwise discriminant analysis is analogous to stepwise multiple regression (see Chapter 17) in that the predictors are entered sequentially based on their ability to discriminate between the groups. An *F* ratio is calculated for each predictor by conducting a univariate analysis of variance in which the groups are treated as the categorical variable and the predictor as the criterion variable. The predictor with the highest *F* ratio is the first to be selected for inclusion in the discriminant function, if it meets certain significance and tolerance criteria. A second predictor is added based on the highest adjusted or partial *F* ratio, taking into account the predictor already selected.

Each predictor selected is tested for retention based on its association with the other predictors selected. The process of selection and retention is continued until all predictors meeting the significance criteria for inclusion and retention have been entered in the discriminant function. Several statistics are computed at each stage. In addition, at the conclusion, a summary of the predictors entered or removed is provided. The standard output associated with the direct method is also available from the stepwise procedure.

The selection of the stepwise procedure is based on the optimizing criterion adopted. The **Mahalanobis procedure** is based on maximizing a generalized measure of the distance between the two closest groups. This procedure allows marketing researchers to make maximal use of the available information.[13]

**Mahalanobis procedure**
A stepwise procedure used in discriminant analysis to maximize a generalized measure of the distance between the two closest groups.

The Mahalanobis method was used to conduct a two-group stepwise discriminant analysis on the data pertaining to the visit variable in Tables 18.2 and 18.3. The first predictor variable to be selected was income, followed by household size and then vacation. The order in which the variables were selected also indicates their importance in discriminating between the groups. This was further corroborated by an examination of the standardized discriminant function coefficients and the structure correlation coefficients. Note that the findings of the stepwise analysis agree with the conclusions reported earlier by the direct method.

The next example gives an application of discriminant analysis in international marketing research, the example after that presents an application in ethics.

### REAL RESEARCH

## *Satisfactory Results of Satisfaction Programs in Europe*

These days, more and more computer companies are emphasizing customer service programs rather than their erstwhile emphasis on computer features and capabilities. Hewlett-Packard learned this lesson while doing business in Europe. Research conducted on the European market revealed that there was a difference in emphasis on service requirements across age segments. Focus groups revealed that customers above 40 years of age had a hard time with the technical aspects of the computer and greatly required the customer service programs. On the other hand, young customers appreciated the technical aspects of the product, which added to their satisfaction. Further research in the form of a large single cross-sectional survey was done to uncover the factors leading to differences in the two segments. A two-group discriminant analysis was conducted with satisfied and dissatisfied customers as the two groups and several independent variables such as technical information, ease of operation, variety and scope of customer service programs, etc. Results confirmed the fact that the variety and scope of customer satisfaction programs was indeed a strong differentiating factor. This was a crucial finding because HP could better handle dissatisfied customers by focusing more on customer services than technical details. Consequently, HP successfully started three programs on customer satisfaction—customer feedback, customer satisfaction surveys, and total quality control. This effort resulted in increased customer satisfaction. After seeing the successful results of these programs in Europe, HP Malaysia decided to launch a customer service program called HP Cares! in 2001. This program was developed in Malaysia as a part of HP's Total Customer Experience (TCE) initiative and will be rolled out worldwide by 2004. HP Malaysia's marketing and sales manager believes this program will allow HP to build brand value and to differentiate the company from its competitors. HP realizes that no matter how great their products may be, brand loyalty can be achieved only through continuous customer service.[14] ■

**REAL RESEARCH**

## *Discriminant Analysis Discriminates Ethical and Unethical Firms*

In order to identify the important variables that predict ethical and unethical behavior, discriminant analysis was used. Prior research suggested that the variables that impact ethical decisions are attitudes, leadership, the presence or absence of ethical codes of conduct, and the organization's size.

To determine which of these variables are the best predictors of ethical behavior, 149 firms were surveyed and asked to indicate how their firm operates in 18 different ethical situations. Of these 18 situations, nine related to marketing activities. These activities included using misleading sales presentations, accepting gifts for preferential treatment, pricing below out-of-pocket expenses, etc. Based on these nine issues, the respondent firms were classified into two groups: "never practice" and "practice."

An examination of the variables that influenced classification via two-group discriminant analysis indicated that attitudes and a company's size were the best predictors of ethical behavior. Evidently, smaller firms tend to demonstrate more ethical behavior on marketing issues. One particular company aimed at conducting ethical business practices is the Smile Internet Bank in the United Kingdom. In early 2002, Smile's marketing group launched six cartoon characters that focus on the bank's ethical position. Each cartoon character symbolizes one of six bad banking traits, and ultimately positions Smile as offering the opposite of these traits. This marketing strategy has been successful.[15] ■

# INTERNET AND COMPUTER APPLICATIONS

In the mainframe version of SPSS, the DISCRIMINANT procedure is used for conducting discriminant analysis. This is a general program that can be used for two-group or multiple discriminant analysis. Furthermore, the direct or the stepwise method can be adopted.

In SAS, the DISCRIM procedure can be used for performing two-group or multiple discriminant analysis. If the assumption of a multivariate normal distribution cannot be met, the NEIGHBOR procedure can be used. In this procedure, a nonparametric nearest neighbor rule is used for classifying the observations. CANDISC performs canonical discriminant analysis and is related to principal component analysis and canonical correlation. The STEPDISC procedure can be used for performing stepwise discriminant analysis. The mainframe and microcomputer versions are similar, except that the program NEIGHBOR is not available on the microcomputer version.

In MINITAB, discriminant analysis can be conducted using the Stats>Multivariate> Discriminate Analysis function. It computes both linear and quadratic discriminant analysis in the classification of observations into two or more groups. Discriminant analysis is not available in EXCEL.

# SPSS Windows

The DISCRIMINANT program performs both two-group and multiple discriminant analysis. To select this procedure using SPSS for Windows, click:

Analyze>Classify>Discriminant . . .

## FOCUS ON BURKE

As with multiple regression, the primary uses of discriminant analysis are prediction and determination of the relative importance of predictor variables. The key difference between these two techniques is the multiple regression requirement of an interval or ratio dependent variable, whereas discriminant analysis uses a dichotomous or categorical dependent variable. Whereas multiple regression might be used to predict degree of purchase interest, discriminant analysis would be used if one wanted only to predict group membership of purchasers verses nonpurchasers.

One of the issues for researchers to consider is the use of "natural groups" versus "created groups." For example, if you ask the age of respondents, you often collect the data in categories rather than measure the actual years of age. When you do this, the categories you used have determined the outcome of an analysis where the categories are to be used as the dependent variable. By pooling people into arbitrary age groups, you may obscure the differences between these people. Looking at the data in the most granular form allows you to make judgments about creating larger groups of respondents based on any particular measurement. In another situation, you may also collect data on whether the person lives in a single family residence, an apartment, condominium, etc. As nominal categories these are relatively "natural," it would be difficult to find categories describing the residence that were more interval in quality. Having confidence in the meaning of the groups allows further confidence in the validity of the conclusions.

In a Burke study, the following classification matrix resulted from a study of brand usage. Each respondent was asked if they had tried a certain brand. The discrimination was attempted based on the respondents' ratings of benefits desired in a product in this category. Every respondent was screened to be a category user. In the sample, 22.9 percent (60 respondents) had not tried the brand and 77.1 percent (202) had tried the brand. It is generally expected when the groups are disproportionate in the population, that the larger group will be predicted better than the smaller group. One way to think of this is that if random choice is used, you would correctly classify a brand trier 59.5 percent of the time ($0.771 \times 0.771$) and a nontrier 5.2 percent of the time ($0.229 \times 0.229$), and people would be misclassified 35.3 percent of the time ($0.229 \times 0.771 + 0.771 \times 0.229$). Although this model classified the smaller group (brand nontriers) less accurately than brand triers, it was better than what one would expect from random chance.

The cross-validation option in SPSS was used. In this situation, the cross-validation produced almost the same level of accuracy as the total model. Note that the cross-validation produced more errors in predicting to the smaller group.

Classification Results[b,c]

| | | | Predicted Group Membership | | |
|---|---|---|---|---|---|
| | | Have Tried Brand | No | Yes | Total |
| Original | Count | no | 35 | 25 | 60 |
| | | yes | 15 | 187 | 202 |
| | % | no | 58.3 | 41.7 | 100.0 |
| | | yes | 7.4 | 92.6 | 100.0 |
| Cross-validated[a] | Count | no | 33 | 27 | 60 |
| | | yes | 15 | 187 | 202 |
| | % | no | 55.0 | 45.0 | 100.0 |
| | | yes | 7.4 | 92.6 | 100.0 |

[a] Cross-validation is done only for those cases in the analysis. In cross-validation, each case is classified by the functions derived from all cases other than that case.

[b] 84.7% of original grouped cases correctly classified.

[c] 84.0% of cross-validated grouped cases correctly classified.

The typical output sometimes does not lend itself to the alternative ways management may want to interpret the model in light of its intended use. For example, management asks, "if you were to predict that a respondent was a nontrier, what is the estimated likelihood that you are correct?" In this situation (using the cross-validation results), Burke would say, "we would expect to predict a respondent to be nontrier about 18 percent of the time $((33 + 15)/262 = 0.183)$. When we do this, we would expect to be correct approximately 69 percent of the time $(33/48 = 0.688)$. The standard output is not laid out to allow management to immediately see this answer. Again, referring to random chance, Burke would tell management that "random selection would estimate about 23 (22.9) percent to be nontriers and be correct only 23 (22.9) percent of the time when this happens (i.e., proportion of sample randomly estimated to be nontriers is $0.229 \times 0.771 + 22.9 \times 0.229 = 0.229$; proportion correctly predicted $0.229 \times 0.229/(0.229 \times 0.229 + 0.229 \times 0.771) = 22.9$ percent). Just looking at the percent correctly classified does not tell the whole story.

# SUMMARY

Discriminant analysis is useful for analyzing data when the criterion or dependent variable is categorical and the predictor or independent variables are interval scaled. When the criterion variable has two categories, the technique is known as two-group discriminant analysis. Multiple discriminant analysis refers to the case when three or more categories are involved.

Conducting discriminant analysis is a five-step procedure. First, formulating the discriminant problem requires identification of the objectives and the criterion and predictor variables. The sample is divided into two parts. One part, the analysis sample, is used to estimate the discriminant function. The other part, the holdout sample, is reserved for validation. Estimation, the second step, involves developing a linear combination of the predictors, called discriminant functions, so that the groups differ as much as possible on the predictor values.

Determination of statistical significance is the third step. It involves testing the null hypothesis that, in the population, the means of all discriminant functions in all groups are equal. If the null hypothesis is rejected, it is meaningful to interpret the results.

The fourth step, the interpretation of discriminant weights or coefficients, is similar to that in multiple regression analysis. Given the multicollinearity in the predictor variables, there is no unambiguous measure of the relative importance of the predictors in discriminating between the groups. However, some idea of the relative importance of the variables may be obtained by examining the absolute magnitude of the standardized discriminant function coefficients and by examining the structure correlations or discriminant loadings. These simple correlations between each predictor and the discriminant function represent the variance that the predictor shares with the function. Another aid to interpreting discriminant analysis results is to develop a characteristic profile for each group, based on the group means for the predictor variables.

Validation, the fifth step, involves developing the classification matrix. The discriminant weights estimated by using the analysis sample are multiplied by the values of the predictor variables in the holdout sample to generate discriminant scores for the cases in the holdout sample. The cases are then assigned to groups based on their discriminant scores and an appropriate decision rule. The percentage of cases correctly classified is determined and compared to the rate that would be expected by chance classification.

Two broad approaches are available for estimating the coefficients. The direct method involves estimating the discriminant function so that all the predictors are included simultaneously. An alternative is the stepwise method, in which the predictor variables are entered sequentially, based on their ability to discriminate among groups.

In multiple discriminant analysis, if there are $G$ groups and $k$ predictors, it is possible to estimate up to the smaller of $G - 1$ or $k$ discriminant functions. The first function has the highest ratio of between-group to within-group sums of squares. The second function, uncorrelated with the first, has the second highest ratio, and so on.

# KEY TERMS AND CONCEPTS

discriminant analysis, *534*
discriminant functions, *534*
two-group discriminant analysis, *534*
multiple discriminant analysis, *534*
discriminant analysis model, *535*
canonical correlation, *535*
centroid, *536*
classification matrix, *536*

discriminant function coefficients, *536*
discriminant scores, *536*
eigenvalue, *536*
*F* values and their significance, *536*
group means and group standard
deviations, *536*
pooled within-group correlation
matrix, *536*

standardized discriminant function
coefficients, *536*
structure correlations, *536*
total correlation matrix, *536*
Wilks' λ, *536*
analysis sample, *537*
validation sample, *537*
direct method, *539*

# EXERCISES

## Questions

1. What are the objectives of discriminant analysis?
2. What is the main distinction between two-group and multiple discriminant analysis?
3. Describe the relationship of discriminant analysis to regression and ANOVA.
4. What are the steps involved in conducting discriminant analysis?
5. How should the total sample be split for estimation and validation purposes?
6. What is Wilks' $\lambda$? For what purpose is it used?
7. Define discriminant scores.
8. Explain what is meant by an eigenvalue.
9. What is a classification matrix?
10. Explain the concept of structure correlations.
11. How is the statistical significance of discriminant analysis determined?
12. Describe a common procedure for determining the validity of discriminant analysis.
13. When the groups are of equal size, how is the accuracy of chance classification determined?
14. How does the stepwise discriminant procedure differ from the direct method?

## Problems

1. In investigating the differences between heavy and light or nonusers of frozen foods, it was found that the two largest standardized discriminant function coefficients were 0.97 for convenience orientation and 0.61 for income. Is it correct to conclude that convenience orientation is more important than income when each variable is considered by itself?
2. Given the following information, calculate the discriminant score for each respondent. The value of the constant is 2.04.

| *Unstandardized Discriminant Function Coefficients* | |
| --- | --- |
| Age | 0.38 |
| Income | 0.44 |
| Risk taking | −0.39 |
| Optimistic | 1.26 |

| *Respondent ID* | *Age* | *Income* | *Risk Taking* | *Optimistic* |
| --- | --- | --- | --- | --- |
| 0246 | 36 | 43.7 | 21 | 65 |
| 1337 | 44 | 62.5 | 28 | 56 |
| 2375 | 57 | 33.5 | 25 | 40 |
| 2454 | 63 | 38.7 | 16 | 36 |

# INTERNET AND COMPUTER EXERCISES

1. Conduct a two-group discriminant analysis on the data given in Tables 18.2 and 18.3 using the SPSS, SAS, and MINITAB packages (microcomputer or mainframe). Compare the output from all the packages. Discuss the similarities and differences.
2. Conduct a three-group stepwise discriminant analysis on the data given in Tables 18.2 and 18.3 using the SPSS, SAS, or MINITAB package. Compare the results to those given in Table 18.5 for three-group discriminant analysis.
3. Analyze the Nike data given in Internet and Computer Exercises 1 of Chapter 15. Do the three usage groups differ in terms of awareness, attitude, preference, intention, and loyalty toward Nike when these variables are considered simultaneously?
4. Analyze the outdoor lifestyle data given in Internet and Computer Exercises 2 of Chapter 15. Do the three groups based on location of residence differ on the importance attached to enjoying nature, relating to the weather, living in harmony with the environment, exercising regularly, and meeting other people (V2 to V6) when these variables are considered simultaneously?
5. Conduct a two-group discriminant analysis on the data you obtained in Fieldwork exercise 1, using the SPSS, SAS, or MINITAB package. Is it possible to differentiate between graduate and undergraduate students using the four attitudinal measures?

# ACTIVITIES

## Fieldwork

1. Interview 15 graduate and 15 undergraduate students. Measure their attitudes towards college education (It is worthwhile getting a college degree), enjoyment in life (It is important to have fun in life), your university (I am not very happy that I chose to go to school here), and work ethic (In general, there is a lack of work ethic on the college campus). For each attitude, measure the degree of disagreement/agreement using a seven-point rating scale (1 = disagree, 7 = agree).

## Group Discussion

1. Is it meaningful to determine the relative importance of predictors in discriminating between the groups? Why or why not? Discuss as a small group.

# APPENDIX 18.1

## *Estimation of Discriminant Function Coefficients*

Suppose there are $G$ groups, $i = 1, 2, 3, \ldots, G$, each containing $n_i$ observations on $K$ independent variables, $X_1, X_2, \ldots, X_k$. The following notations are used.

$N$ = total sample size

$$= \sum_{i=1}^{G} n_i$$

$W_i$ = Matrix of mean corrected sum of squares and cross-products for the $i$th group

$W$ = Matrix of pooled within-groups mean corrected sum of squares and cross-products

$B$ = Matrix of between-groups mean corrected sum of squares and cross-products

$T$ = Matrix of total mean corrected sum of squares and cross products for all the $N$ observations ($= W + B$)

$\bar{X}_i$ = Vector of means of observations in the $i$th group

$\bar{X}$ = Vector grand means for all the $N$ observations

$\lambda$ = Ratio of between-groups to within-group sums of squares

$b$ = Vector of discriminant coefficients or weights

Then,

$$T = \sum_{i=1}^{G} \sum_{j=1}^{n_i} (X_{ij} - \bar{X})(X_{ij} - \bar{X})'$$

$$W_i = \sum_{j=1}^{n_i} (X_{ij} - \bar{X}_i)(X_{ij} - \bar{X}_i)'$$

$$W = W_1 + W_2 + W_3 + \cdots + W_G$$

$$B = T - W$$

Define the linear composite $D = b'_1 X$. Then, with reference to $D$, the between-groups and within-groups sums of squares are, respectively, given by $b'_1 Bb$ and $b'_1 Wb$. In order to maximally discriminate the groups, the discriminant functions are estimated to maximize the between-group variability. The coefficients $b$ are calculated to maximize $\lambda$, by solving

$$\text{Max } \lambda = \frac{b'Bb}{b'Wb}$$

Taking the partial derivative with respect to $\lambda$ and setting it equal to zero, with some simplification, yields:

$$(B - \lambda W)b = 0$$

To solve for $b$, it is more convenient to premultiply by $W^{-1}$ and solve the following characteristic equation:

$$(W^{-1}B - \lambda I)b = 0$$

The maximum value of $\lambda$ is the largest eigenvalue of the matrix $W^{-1}B$, and $b$ is the associated eigenvector. The elements of $b$ are the discriminant coefficients, or weights, associated with the first discriminant function. In general, it is possible to estimate up to the smaller of $G - 1$ or $k$ discriminant functions, each with its associated eigenvalue. The discriminant functions are estimated sequentially. In other words, the first discriminant function exhausts most of the between-group variability. The second function maximizes the between-group variation that was not explained by the first one, and so on.

# CHAPTER 19

# Factor Analysis

"Often among the many variables you measure, a few are more related to each other than they are to others. Factor analysis allows us to look at these groups of variables that tend to be related to each other and estimate what underlying reasons might cause these variables to be more highly correlated with each other."

*Jeff Miller, senior vice president, technology, Burke, Inc.*

## Objectives

After reading this chapter, the student should be able to:

1. Describe the concept of factor analysis and explain how it is different from analysis of variance, multiple regression, and discriminant analysis.
2. Discuss the procedure for conducting factor analysis including problem formulation, construction of the correlation matrix, selection of an appropriate method, determination of the number of factors, rotation, and interpretation of factors.
3. Understand the distinction between principal component factor analysis and common factor analysis methods.
4. Explain the selection of surrogate variables and their application, with emphasis on their use in subsequent analysis.
5. Describe the procedure for determining the fit of a factor analysis model using the observed and the reproduced correlations.

## Overview

In analysis of variance (Chapter 16), regression (Chapter 17), and discriminant analysis (Chapter 18), one of the variables is clearly identified as the dependent variable. We now turn to a procedure, factor analysis, in which variables are not classified as independent or dependent. Instead, the whole set of interdependent relationships among variables is examined. This chapter discusses the basic concept of factor analysis and gives an exposition of the factor model. We describe the steps in factor analysis and illustrate them in the context of principal components analysis. Next, we present an application of common factor analysis. To begin, we provide some examples to illustrate the usefulness of factor analysis.

---

**ACTIVE RESEARCH** | DEPARTMENT STORE PROJECT

### Factor Analysis

In the department store project, the respondents' ratings of 21 lifestyle statements were factor analyzed to determine the underlying lifestyle factors. Seven factors emerged: bank card versus store card preference, credit proneness, credit avoidance, leisure time orientation, credit card favorableness, credit convenience, and credit card cost consciousness. These factors, along with the demographic characteristics, were used to profile the segments formed as a result of clustering.

---

**REAL RESEARCH**

## Factor Analysis Earns Interest at Banks

How do consumers evaluate banks? Respondents in a survey were asked to rate the importance of 15 bank attributes. A five-point scale ranging from not important to very important was employed. These data were analyzed via principal components analysis.

A four-factor solution resulted, with the factors being labeled as traditional services, convenience, visibility, and competence. Traditional services included interest rates on loans, reputation in the community, low rates for checking, friendly and personalized service, easy-to-read monthly statements, and obtainability of loans. Convenience was comprised of convenient branch location, convenient ATM locations, speed of service, and convenient banking hours. The visibility factor included recommendations from friends and relatives, attractiveness of the physical structure, community involvement, and obtainability of loans. Competence consisted of employee competence and availability of auxiliary banking services. It was concluded that consumers evaluated banks using the four basic factors of traditional services, convenience, visibility, and competence and banks must excel on these factors to project a good image.[1] ■

# BASIC CONCEPT

**factor analysis**
A class of procedures primarily used for data reduction and summarization.

*Factor analysis* is a general name denoting a class of procedures primarily used for data reduction and summarization. In marketing research, there may be a large number of variables, most of which are correlated and which must be reduced to a manageable level. Relationships among sets of many interrelated variables are examined and represented in terms of a few underlying factors. For example, store image may be measured by asking respondents to evaluate stores on a series of items on a semantic differential scale. These item evaluations may then be analyzed to determine the factors underlying store image.

In analysis of variance, multiple regression, and discriminant analysis, one variable is considered as the dependent or criterion variable, and the others as independent or predictor variables. However, no such distinction is made in factor analysis. Rather, factor analysis is an **interdependence technique** in that an entire set of interdependent relationships is examined.[2]

**interdependence technique**
Multivariate statistical techniques in which the whole set of interdependent relationships is examined.

Factor analysis is used in the following circumstances:

**factors**
An underlying dimension that explains the correlations among a set of variables.

1. To identify underlying dimensions, or **factors,** that explain the correlations among a set of variables. For example, a set of lifestyle statements may be used to measure the psychographic profiles of consumers. These statements may then be factor analyzed to identify the underlying psychographic factors, as illustrated in the department store example.
2. To identify a new, smaller set of uncorrelated variables to replace the original set of correlated variables in subsequent multivariate analysis (regression or discriminant analysis). For example, the psychographic factors identified may be used as independent variables in explaining the differences between loyal and nonloyal consumers.
3. To identify a smaller set of salient variables from a larger set for use in subsequent multivariate analysis. For example, a few of the original lifestyle statements that correlate highly with the identified factors may be used as independent variables to explain the differences between the loyal and nonloyal users.

Factor analysis has numerous applications in marketing research. For example:

- It can be used in market segmentation for identifying the underlying variables on which to group the customers. New car buyers might be grouped based on the relative emphasis they place on economy, convenience, performance, comfort, and luxury. This might result in five segments: economy seekers, convenience seekers, performance seekers, comfort seekers, and luxury seekers.
- In product research, factor analysis can be employed to determine the brand attributes that influence consumer choice. Toothpaste brands might be evaluated in terms of protection against cavities, whiteness of teeth, taste, fresh breath, and price.
- In advertising studies, factor analysis can be used to understand the media consumption habits of the target market. The users of frozen foods may be heavy viewers of cable TV, see a lot of movies, and listen to country music.
- In pricing studies, it can be used to identify the characteristics of price-sensitive consumers. For example, these consumers might be methodical, economy minded, and home centered.

# FACTOR ANALYSIS MODEL

Mathematically, factor analysis is somewhat similar to multiple regression analysis, in that each variable is expressed as a linear combination of underlying factors. The amount of variance a variable shares with all other variables included in the analysis is referred to as *communality*. The covariation among the variables is described in terms of a small number of common factors plus a unique factor for each variable. These factors are not overtly observed. If the variables are standardized, the factor model may be represented as:

$$X_i = A_{i1}F_1 + A_{i2}F_2 + A_{i3}F_3 + \cdots + A_{im}F_m + V_iU_i$$

where

$X_i$ = *i*th standardized variable
$A_{ij}$ = standardized multiple regression coefficient of variable *i* on common factor *j*
$F$ = common factor
$V_i$ = standardized regression coefficient of variable *i* on unique factor *i*
$U_i$ = the unique factor for variable *i*
$m$ = number of common factors

The unique factors are uncorrelated with each other and with the common factors.[3] The common factors themselves can be expressed as linear combinations of the observed variables.

$$F_i = W_{i1}X_1 + W_{i2}X_2 + W_{i3}X_3 + \cdots + W_{ik}X_k$$

where

$F_i$ = estimate of *i*th factor
$W_i$ = weight or factor score coefficient
$k$ = number of variables

It is possible to select weights or factor score coefficients so that the first factor explains the largest portion of the total variance. Then a second set of weights can be selected, so that the second factor accounts for most of the residual variance, subject to being uncorrelated with the first factor. This same principle could be applied to selecting additional weights for the additional factors. Thus, the factors can be estimated so that their factor scores, unlike the values of the original variables, are not correlated. Furthermore, the first factor accounts for the highest variance in the data, the second factor the second highest, and so on. A technical treatment of the factor analysis model is presented in Appendix 19.1. Several statistics are associated with factor analysis.

# STATISTICS ASSOCIATED WITH FACTOR ANALYSIS

The key statistics associated with factor analysis are as follows:

***Bartlett's test of sphericity.*** Bartlett's test of sphericity is a test statistic used to examine the hypothesis that the variables are uncorrelated in the population. In other words, the population correlation matrix is an identity matrix; each variable correlates perfectly with itself ($r = 1$) but has no correlation with the other variables ($r = 0$).

***Correlation matrix.*** A correlation matrix is a lower triangle matrix showing the simple correlations, *r*, between all possible pairs of variables included in the analysis. The diagonal elements, which are all 1, are usually omitted.

***Communality.*** Communality is the amount of variance a variable shares with all the other variables being considered. This is also the proportion of variance explained by the common factors.

***Eigenvalue.*** The eigenvalue represents the total variance explained by each factor.

***Factor loadings.*** Factor loadings are simple correlations between the variables and the factors.

***Factor loading plot.*** A factor loading plot is a plot of the original variables using the factor loadings as coordinates.

***Factor matrix.*** A factor matrix contains the factor loadings of all the variables on all the factors extracted.

***Factor scores.*** Factor scores are composite scores estimated for each respondent on the derived factors.

***Kaiser-Meyer-Olkin (KMO) measure of sampling adequacy.*** The Kaiser-Meyer-Olkin (KMO) measure of sampling adequacy is an index used to examine the appropriateness of factor analysis. High values (between 0.5 and 1.0) indicate factor analysis is appropriate. Values below 0.5 imply that factor analysis may not be appropriate.

***Percentage of variance.*** This is the percentage of the total variance attributed to each factor.

***Residuals.*** Residuals are the differences between the observed correlations, as given in the input correlation matrix, and the reproduced correlations, as estimated from the factor matrix.

***Scree plot.*** A scree plot is a plot of the eigenvalues against the number of factors in order of extraction.

In the next section, we describe the uses of these statistics in the context of the procedure for conducting factor analysis.

# CONDUCTING FACTOR ANALYSIS

The steps involved in conducting factor analysis are illustrated in Figure 19.1. The first step is to define the factor analysis problem and identify the variables to be factor analyzed. Then a correlation matrix of these variables is constructed and a method of factor analysis selected. The researcher decides on the number of factors to be extracted and the method of rotation. Next, the rotated factors should be interpreted. Depending upon the objectives, the factor scores may be calculated, or surrogate variables selected, to represent the factors in subsequent multivariate analysis. Finally, the fit of the factor analysis model is determined. We discuss these steps in more detail in the following sections.[4]

## Formulate the Problem

Problem formulation includes several tasks. First, the objectives of factor analysis should be identified. The variables to be included in the factor analysis should be specified based on past research, theory, and judgment of the researcher. It is important that the variables be appropriately measured on an interval or ratio scale. An appropriate sample size should be used. As a rough guideline, there should be at least four or five times as many observations (sample size) as there are variables.[5] In many marketing research situations, the sam-

**Figure 19.1**
**Conducting Factor Analysis**

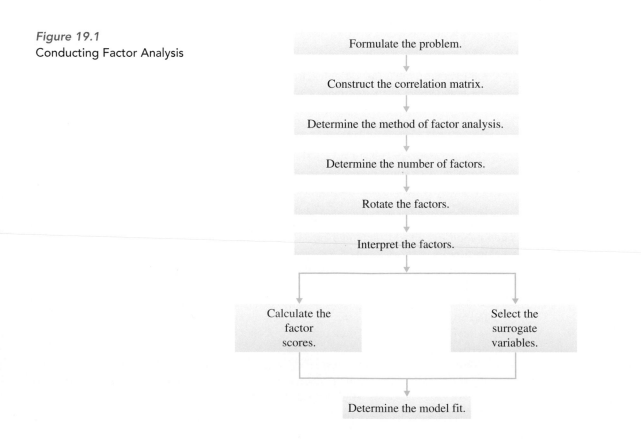

ple size is small and this ratio is considerably lower. In these cases, the results should be interpreted cautiously.

To illustrate factor analysis, suppose the researcher wants to determine the underlying benefits consumers seek from the purchase of a toothpaste. A sample of 30 respondents was interviewed using mall intercept interviewing. The respondents were asked to indicate their degree of agreement with the following statements using a seven-point scale (1 = strongly disagree, 7 = strongly agree):

$V_1$:   It is important to buy a toothpaste that prevents cavities.
$V_2$:   I like a toothpaste that gives shiny teeth.
$V_3$:   A toothpaste should strengthen your gums.
$V_4$:   I prefer a toothpaste that freshens breath.
$V_5$:   Prevention of tooth decay is not an important benefit offered by a toothpaste.
$V_6$:   The most important consideration in buying a toothpaste is attractive teeth.

The data obtained are given in Table 19.1. A correlation matrix was constructed based on these ratings data.

## TABLE 19.1

### Toothpaste Attribute Ratings

| RESPONDENT NUMBER | $V_1$ | $V_2$ | $V_3$ | $V_4$ | $V_5$ | $V_6$ |
|---|---|---|---|---|---|---|
| 1  | 7.00 | 3.00 | 6.00 | 4.00 | 2.00 | 4.00 |
| 2  | 1.00 | 3.00 | 2.00 | 4.00 | 5.00 | 4.00 |
| 3  | 6.00 | 2.00 | 7.00 | 4.00 | 1.00 | 3.00 |
| 4  | 4.00 | 5.00 | 4.00 | 6.00 | 2.00 | 5.00 |
| 5  | 1.00 | 2.00 | 2.00 | 3.00 | 6.00 | 2.00 |
| 6  | 6.00 | 3.00 | 6.00 | 4.00 | 2.00 | 4.00 |
| 7  | 5.00 | 3.00 | 6.00 | 3.00 | 4.00 | 3.00 |
| 8  | 6.00 | 4.00 | 7.00 | 4.00 | 1.00 | 4.00 |
| 9  | 3.00 | 4.00 | 2.00 | 3.00 | 6.00 | 3.00 |
| 10 | 2.00 | 6.00 | 2.00 | 6.00 | 7.00 | 6.00 |
| 11 | 6.00 | 4.00 | 7.00 | 3.00 | 2.00 | 3.00 |
| 12 | 2.00 | 3.00 | 1.00 | 4.00 | 5.00 | 4.00 |
| 13 | 7.00 | 2.00 | 6.00 | 4.00 | 1.00 | 3.00 |
| 14 | 4.00 | 6.00 | 4.00 | 5.00 | 3.00 | 6.00 |
| 15 | 1.00 | 3.00 | 2.00 | 2.00 | 6.00 | 4.00 |
| 16 | 6.00 | 4.00 | 6.00 | 3.00 | 3.00 | 4.00 |
| 17 | 5.00 | 3.00 | 6.00 | 3.00 | 3.00 | 4.00 |
| 18 | 7.00 | 3.00 | 7.00 | 4.00 | 1.00 | 4.00 |
| 19 | 2.00 | 4.00 | 3.00 | 3.00 | 6.00 | 3.00 |
| 20 | 3.00 | 5.00 | 3.00 | 6.00 | 4.00 | 6.00 |
| 21 | 1.00 | 3.00 | 2.00 | 3.00 | 5.00 | 3.00 |
| 22 | 5.00 | 4.00 | 5.00 | 4.00 | 2.00 | 4.00 |
| 23 | 2.00 | 2.00 | 1.00 | 5.00 | 4.00 | 4.00 |
| 24 | 4.00 | 6.00 | 4.00 | 6.00 | 4.00 | 7.00 |
| 25 | 6.00 | 5.00 | 4.00 | 2.00 | 1.00 | 4.00 |
| 26 | 3.00 | 5.00 | 4.00 | 6.00 | 4.00 | 7.00 |
| 27 | 4.00 | 4.00 | 7.00 | 2.00 | 2.00 | 5.00 |
| 28 | 3.00 | 7.00 | 2.00 | 6.00 | 4.00 | 3.00 |
| 29 | 4.00 | 6.00 | 3.00 | 7.00 | 2.00 | 7.00 |
| 30 | 2.00 | 3.00 | 2.00 | 4.00 | 7.00 | 2.00 |

## Construct the Correlation Matrix

The analytical process is based on a matrix of correlations between the variables. Valuable insights can be gained from an examination of this matrix. For the factor analysis to be appropriate, the variables must be correlated. In practice, this is usually the case. If the correlations between all the variables are small, factor analysis may not be appropriate. We would also expect that variables that are highly correlated with each other would also highly correlate with the same factor or factors.

Formal statistics are available for testing the appropriateness of the factor model. Bartlett's test of sphericity can be used to test the null hypothesis that the variables are uncorrelated in the population; in other words, the population correlation matrix is an identity matrix. In an identity matrix, all the diagonal terms are 1, and all off-diagonal terms are 0. The test statistic for sphericity is based on a chi-square transformation of the determinant of the correlation matrix. A large value of the test statistic will favor the rejection of the null hypothesis. If this hypothesis cannot be rejected, then the appropriateness of factor analysis should be questioned. Another useful statistic is the Kaiser-Meyer-Olkin (KMO) measure of sampling adequacy. This index compares the magnitudes of the observed correlation coefficients to the magnitudes of the partial correlation coefficients. Small values of the KMO statistic indicate that the correlations between pairs of variables cannot be explained by other variables and that factor analysis may not be appropriate. Generally, a value greater than 0.5 is desirable.

The correlation matrix, constructed from the data obtained to understand toothpaste benefits, is shown in Table 19.2. There are relatively high correlations among $V_1$ (prevention of cavities), $V_3$ (strong gums), and $V_5$ (prevention of tooth decay). We would expect these variables to correlate with the same set of factors. Likewise, there are relatively high correlations among $V_2$ (shiny teeth), $V_4$ (fresh breath), and $V_6$ (attractive teeth). These variables may also be expected to correlate with the same factors.[6]

The results of factor analysis are given in Table 19.3. The null hypothesis, that the population correlation matrix is an identity matrix, is rejected by the Bartlett's test of sphericity. The approximate chi-square statistic is 111.314 with 15 degrees of freedom, which is significant at the 0.05 level. The value of the KMO statistic (0.660) is also large (> 0.5). Thus, factor analysis may be considered an appropriate technique for analyzing the correlation matrix of Table 19.2.

## Determine the Method of Factor Analysis

Once it has been determined that factor analysis is an appropriate technique for analyzing the data, an appropriate method must be selected. The approach used to derive the weights or factor score coefficients differentiates the various methods of factor analysis. The two basic approaches are principal components analysis and common factor analysis. In ***principal components analysis,*** the total variance in the data is considered. The diagonal of the correlation matrix consists of unities, and full variance is brought into the factor matrix. Principal components analysis is recommended when the primary concern is to determine the minimum number of factors that will account for maximum variance in the data for use in subsequent multivariate analysis. The factors are called principal components.

***principal components analysis***
An approach to factor analysis that considers the total variance in the data.

**TABLE 19.2**

**Correlation Matrix**

| VARIABLES | $V_1$ | $V_2$ | $V_3$ | $V_4$ | $V_5$ | $V_6$ |
|---|---|---|---|---|---|---|
| $V_1$ | 1.00 | | | | | |
| $V_2$ | −0.053 | 1.00 | | | | |
| $V_3$ | 0.873 | −0.155 | 1.00 | | | |
| $V_4$ | −0.086 | 0.572 | −0.248 | 1.00 | | |
| $V_5$ | −0.858 | 0.020 | −0.778 | −0.007 | 1.00 | |
| $V_6$ | 0.004 | 0.640 | −0.018 | 0.640 | −0.136 | 1.00 |

**TABLE 19.3**

**Results of Principal Components Analysis**

Bartlett test of sphericity
Approx. chi-square = 111.314, df = 15, significance = 0.00000
Kaiser-Meyer-Olkin measure of sampling adequacy = 0.660

COMMUNALITIES

| VARIABLE | INITIAL | EXTRACTION |
|---|---|---|
| $V_1$ | 1.000 | 0.926 |
| $V_2$ | 1.000 | 0.723 |
| $V_3$ | 1.000 | 0.894 |
| $V_4$ | 1.000 | 0.739 |
| $V_5$ | 1.000 | 0.878 |
| $V_6$ | 1.000 | 0.790 |

INITIAL EIGENVALUES

| FACTOR | EIGENVALUE | % OF VARIANCE | CUMULATIVE % |
|---|---|---|---|
| 1 | 2.731 | 45.520 | 45.520 |
| 2 | 2.218 | 36.969 | 82.488 |
| 3 | 0.442 | 7.360 | 89.848 |
| 4 | 0.341 | 5.688 | 95.536 |
| 5 | 0.183 | 3.044 | 98.580 |
| 6 | 0.085 | 1.420 | 100.000 |

EXTRACTION SUMS OF SQUARED LOADINGS

| FACTOR | EIGENVALUE | % OF VARIANCE | CUMULATIVE % |
|---|---|---|---|
| 1 | 2.731 | 45.520 | 45.520 |
| 2 | 2.218 | 36.969 | 82.488 |

FACTOR MATRIX

| | FACTOR 1 | FACTOR 2 |
|---|---|---|
| $V_1$ | 0.928 | 0.253 |
| $V_2$ | −0.301 | 0.795 |
| $V_3$ | 0.936 | 0.131 |
| $V_4$ | −0.342 | 0.789 |
| $V_5$ | −0.869 | −0.351 |
| $V_6$ | −0.177 | 0.871 |

ROTATION SUMS OF SQUARED LOADINGS

| FACTOR | EIGENVALUE | % OF VARIANCE | CUMULATIVE % |
|---|---|---|---|
| 1 | 2.688 | 44.802 | 44.802 |
| 2 | 2.261 | 37.687 | 82.488 |

ROTATED FACTOR MATRIX

| | FACTOR 1 | FACTOR 2 |
|---|---|---|
| $V_1$ | 0.962 | −0.027 |
| $V_2$ | −0.057 | 0.848 |
| $V_3$ | 0.934 | −0.146 |
| $V_4$ | −0.098 | 0.854 |
| $V_5$ | −0.933 | −0.084 |
| $V_6$ | 0.083 | 0.885 |

*(Continued)*

**TABLE 19.3**

**Results of Principal Components Analysis** *(Continued)*

FACTOR SCORE COEFFICIENT MATRIX

|       | FACTOR 1 | FACTOR 2 |
|-------|----------|----------|
| $V_1$ | 0.358    | 0.011    |
| $V_2$ | $-0.001$ | 0.375    |
| $V_3$ | 0.345    | $-0.043$ |
| $V_4$ | $-0.017$ | 0.377    |
| $V_5$ | $-0.350$ | $-0.059$ |
| $V_6$ | 0.052    | 0.395    |

REPRODUCED CORRELATION MATRIX

|       | $V_1$      | $V_2$      | $V_3$      | $V_4$      | $V_5$      | $V_6$      |
|-------|-----------|-----------|-----------|-----------|-----------|-----------|
| $V_1$ | $0.926^*$ | 0.024     | $-0.029$  | 0.031     | 0.038     | $-0.053$  |
| $V_2$ | $-0.078$  | $0.723^*$ | 0.022     | $-0.158$  | 0.038     | $-0.105$  |
| $V_3$ | 0.902     | $-0.177$  | $0.894^*$ | $-0.031$  | 0.081     | 0.033     |
| $V_4$ | $-0.117$  | 0.730     | $-0.217$  | $0.739^*$ | $-0.027$  | $-0.107$  |
| $V_5$ | $-0.895$  | $-0.018$  | $-0.859$  | 0.020     | $0.878^*$ | 0.016     |
| $V_6$ | 0.057     | 0.746     | $-0.051$  | 0.748     | $-0.152$  | $0.790^*$ |

*The lower left triangle contains the reproduced correlation matrix; the diagonal, the communalities; the upper right triangle, the residuals between the observed correlations and the reproduced correlations.

---

**common factor analysis**
An approach to factor analysis that estimates the factors based only on the common variance.

In ***common factor analysis,*** the factors are estimated based only on the common variance. Communalities are inserted in the diagonal of the correlation matrix. This method is appropriate when the primary concern is to identify the underlying dimensions and the common variance is of interest. This method is also known as *principal axis factoring.*

Other approaches for estimating the common factors are also available. These include the methods of unweighted least squares, generalized least squares, maximum likelihood, alpha method, and image factoring. These methods are complex and are not recommended for inexperienced users.[7]

Table 19.3 shows the application of principal components analysis to the toothpaste example. Under "Communalities," "Initial" column, it can be seen that the communality for each variable, $V_1$ to $V_6$, is 1.0 as unities were inserted in the diagonal of the correlation matrix. The table labeled "Initial Eigenvalues" gives the eigenvalues. The eigenvalues for the factors are, as expected, in decreasing order of magnitude as we go from factor 1 to factor 6. The eigenvalue for a factor indicates the total variance attributed to that factor. The total variance accounted for by all the six factors is 6.00, which is equal to the number of variables. Factor 1 accounts for a variance of 2.731, which is (2.731/6) or 45.52 percent of the total variance. Likewise, the second factor accounts for (2.218/6) or 36.97 percent of the total variance, and the first two factors combined account for 82.49 percent of the total variance. Several considerations are involved in determining the number of factors that should be used in the analysis.

## Determine the Number of Factors

It is possible to compute as many principal components as there are variables, but in doing so, no parsimony is gained. In order to summarize the information contained in the original variables, a smaller number of factors should be extracted. The question is, how many? Several procedures have been suggested for determining the number of factors. These include a *priori* determination and approaches based on eigenvalues, scree plot, percentage of variance accounted for, split-half reliability, and significance tests.

**A Priori** *Determination.*   Sometimes, because of prior knowledge, the researcher knows how many factors to expect and thus can specify the number of factors to be extracted beforehand. The extraction of factors ceases when the desired number of factors have been extracted. Most computer programs allow the user to specify the number of factors, allowing for an easy implementation of this approach.

### Determination Based on Eigenvalues.

In this approach, only factors with eigenvalues greater than 1.0 are retained; the other factors are not included in the model. An eigenvalue represents the amount of variance associated with the factor. Hence, only factors with a variance greater than 1.0 are included. Factors with variance less than 1.0 are no better than a single variable, because, due to standardization, each variable has a variance of 1.0. If the number of variables is less than 20, this approach will result in a conservative number of factors.

### Determination Based on Scree Plot.

A scree plot is a plot of the eigenvalues against the number of factors in order of extraction. The shape of the plot is used to determine the number of factors. Typically, the plot has a distinct break between the steep slope of factors, with large eigenvalues and a gradual trailing off associated with the rest of the factors. This gradual trailing off is referred to as the scree. Experimental evidence indicates that the point at which the scree begins denotes the true number of factors. Generally, the number of factors determined by a scree plot will be one or a few more than that determined by the eigenvalue criterion.

### Determination Based on Percentage of Variance.

In this approach, the number of factors extracted is determined so that the cumulative percentage of variance extracted by the factors reaches a satisfactory level. What level of variance is satisfactory depends upon the problem. However, it is recommended that the factors extracted should account for at least 60 percent of the variance.

### Determination Based on Split-Half Reliability.

The sample is split in half and factor analysis is performed on each half. Only factors with high correspondence of factor loadings across the two subsamples are retained.

### Determination Based on Significance Tests.

It is possible to determine the statistical significance of the separate eigenvalues and retain only those factors that are statistically significant. A drawback is that with large samples (size greater than 200), many factors are likely to be statistically significant, although from a practical viewpoint many of these account for only a small proportion of the total variance.

In Table 19.3, we see that the eigenvalue greater than 1.0 (default option) results in two factors being extracted. Our *a priori* knowledge tells us that toothpaste is bought for two major reasons. The scree plot associated with this analysis is given in Figure 19.2. From the scree plot, a distinct break occurs at three factors. Finally, from the cumulative

**Figure 19.2**
Scree Plot

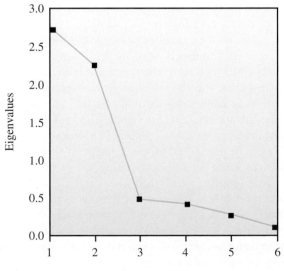

percentage of variance accounted for, we see that the first two factors account for 82.49 percent of the variance, and that the gain achieved in going to three factors is marginal. Furthermore, split-half reliability also indicates that two factors are appropriate. Thus, two factors appear to be reasonable in this situation.

The second column under "Communalities" in Table 19.3 gives relevant information after the desired number of factors have been extracted. The communalities for the variables under "Extraction" are different than under "Initial" because all of the variances associated with the variables are not explained unless all the factors are retained. The "Extraction Sums of Squared Loadings" give the variances associated with the factors that are retained. Note that these are the same as under "Initial Eigenvalues." This is always the case in principal components analysis. The percentage variance accounted by a factor is determined by dividing the associated eigenvalue with the total number of factors (or variables) and multiplying by 100. Thus, the first factor accounts for $(2.731/6) \times 100$ or 45.52 percent of the variance of the six variables. Likewise, the second factor accounts for $(2.218/6) \times 100$ or 36.969 percent of the variance. Interpretation of the solution is often enhanced by a rotation of the factors.

## Rotate Factors

An important output from factor analysis is the factor matrix, also called the *factor pattern matrix*. The factor matrix contains the coefficients used to express the standardized variables in terms of the factors. These coefficients, the factor loadings, represent the correlations between the factors and the variables. A coefficient with a large absolute value indicates that the factor and the variable are closely related. The coefficients of the factor matrix can be used to interpret the factors.

Although the initial or unrotated factor matrix indicates the relationship between the factors and individual variables, it seldom results in factors that can be interpreted, because the factors are correlated with many variables. For example, in Table 19.3, factor 1 is at least somewhat correlated with five of the six variables (absolute value of factor loading greater than 0.3). How should this factor be interpreted? In such a complex matrix it is difficult to interpret the factors. Therefore, through rotation, the factor matrix is transformed into a simpler one that is easier to interpret.

In rotating the factors, we would like each factor to have nonzero, or significant, loadings or coefficients for only some of the variables. Likewise, we would like each variable to have nonzero or significant loadings with only a few factors, if possible with only one. If several factors have high loadings with the same variable, it is difficult to interpret them. Rotation does not affect the communalities and the percentage of total variance explained. However, the percentage of variance accounted for by each factor does change. This is seen in Table 19.3. The variance explained by the individual factors is redistributed by rotation. Hence, different methods of rotation may result in the identification of different factors.

The rotation is called **orthogonal rotation** if the axes are maintained at right angles. The most commonly used method for rotation is the **varimax procedure.** This is an orthogonal method of rotation that minimizes the number of variables with high loadings on a factor, thereby enhancing the interpretability of the factors.[8] Orthogonal rotation results in factors that are uncorrelated. The rotation is called **oblique rotation** when the axes are not maintained at right angles, and the factors are correlated. Sometimes, allowing for correlations among factors can simplify the factor pattern matrix. Oblique rotation should be used when factors in the population are likely to be strongly correlated.

In Table 19.3, by comparing the varimax rotated factor matrix with the unrotated matrix (entitled Factor matrix), we can see how rotation achieves simplicity and enhances interpretability. Whereas five variables correlated with factor 1 in the unrotated matrix, only variables $V_1$, $V_3$, and $V_5$ correlate with factor 1 after rotation. The remaining variables, $V_2$, $V_4$, and $V_6$, correlate highly with factor 2. Furthermore, no variable correlates highly with both the factors. The rotated factor matrix forms the basis for interpretation of the factors.

---

**orthogonal rotation**
Rotation of factors in which the axes are maintained at right angles.

**varimax procedure**
An orthogonal method of factor rotation that minimizes the number of variables with high loadings on a factor, thereby enhancing the interpretability of the factors.

**oblique rotation**
Rotation of factors when the axes are not maintained at right angles.

## Interpret Factors

Interpretation is facilitated by identifying the variables that have large loadings on the same factor. That factor can then be interpreted in terms of the variables that load high on it. Another useful aid in interpretation is to plot the variables using the factor loadings as coordinates. Variables at the end of an axis are those that have high loadings on only that factor, and hence describe the factor. Variables near the origin have small loadings on both the factors. Variables that are not near any of the axes are related to both the factors. If a factor cannot be clearly defined in terms of the original variables, it should be labeled as an undefined or a general factor.

In the rotated factor matrix of Table 19.3, factor 1 has high coefficients for variables $V_1$ (prevention of cavities) and $V_3$ (strong gums), and a negative coefficient for $V_5$ (prevention of tooth decay is not important). Therefore, this factor may be labeled a health benefit factor. Note that a negative coefficient for a negative variable ($V_5$) leads to a positive interpretation that prevention of tooth decay is important. Factor 2 is highly related with variables $V_2$ (shiny teeth), $V_4$ (fresh breath), and $V_6$ (attractive teeth). Thus, factor 2 may be labeled a social benefit factor. A plot of the factor loadings, given in Figure 19.3, confirms this interpretation. Variables $V_1$, $V_3$, and $V_5$ (denoted by 1, 3, and 5, respectively) are at the end of the horizontal axis (factor 1), with $V_5$ at the end opposite to $V_1$ and $V_3$, whereas variables $V_2$, $V_4$, and $V_6$ (denoted by 2, 4, and 6) are at the end of the vertical axis (factor 2). One could summarize the data by stating that consumers appear to seek two major kinds of benefits from a toothpaste: health benefits and social benefits.

## Calculate Factor Scores

Following interpretation, factor scores can be calculated, if necessary. Factor analysis has its own stand-alone value. However, if the goal of factor analysis is to reduce the original set of variables to a smaller set of composite variables (factors) for use in subsequent multivariate analysis, it is useful to compute factor scores for each respondent. A factor is simply a linear combination of the original variables. The ***factor scores*** for the *i*th factor may be estimated as follows:

$$F_i = W_{i1}X_1 + W_{i2}X_2 + W_{i3}X_3 + \cdots + W_{ik}X_k$$

These symbols were defined earlier in the chapter.

The weights, or factor score coefficients, used to combine the standardized variables are obtained from the factor score coefficient matrix. Most computer programs allow you to request factor scores. Only in the case of principal components analysis is it possible to compute exact factor scores. Moreover, in principal component analysis, these scores are uncorrelated. In common factor analysis, estimates of these scores are obtained, and there is no guarantee that the factors will be uncorrelated with each other. The factor scores can be used instead of the original variables in subsequent multivariate analysis. For example, using the factor score coefficient matrix in Table 19.3, one could compute two factor scores for each respondent. The standardized

**factor scores**
Composite scores estimated for each respondent on the derived factors.

*Figure 19.3*
Factor Loading Plot

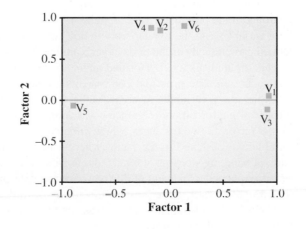

variable values would be multiplied by the corresponding factor score coefficients to obtain the factor scores.

## Select Surrogate Variables

Sometimes, instead of computing factor scores, the researcher wishes to select surrogate variables. Selection of substitute, or *surrogate variables*, involves singling out some of the original variables for use in subsequent analysis. This allows the researcher to conduct subsequent analysis and interpret the results in terms of original variables rather than factor scores. By examining the factor matrix, one could select for each factor the variable with the highest loading on that factor. That variable could then be used as a surrogate variable for the associated factor. This process works well if one factor loading for a variable is clearly higher than all other factor loadings. However, the choice is not as easy if two or more variables have similarly high loadings. In such a case, the choice between these variables should be based on theoretical and measurement considerations. For example, theory may suggest that a variable with a slightly lower loading is more important than one with a slightly higher loading. Likewise, if a variable has a slightly lower loading but has been measured more precisely, it should be selected as the surrogate variable. In Table 19.3, the variables $V_1$, $V_3$, and $V_5$ all have high loadings on factor 1, and all are fairly close in magnitude, although $V_1$ has relatively the highest loading and would therefore be a likely candidate. However, if prior knowledge suggests that prevention of tooth decay is a very important benefit, $V_5$ would be selected as the surrogate for factor 1. Also, the choice of a surrogate for factor 2 is not straightforward. Variables $V_2$, $V_4$, and $V_6$ all have comparable high loadings on this factor. If prior knowledge suggests that attractive teeth is the most important social benefit sought from a toothpaste, the researcher would select $V_6$.

## Determine the Model Fit

The final step in factor analysis involves the determination of model fit. A basic assumption underlying factor analysis is that the observed correlation between variables can be attributed to common factors. Hence, the correlations between the variables can be deduced or reproduced from the estimated correlations between the variables and the factors. The differences between the observed correlations (as given in the input correlation matrix) and the reproduced correlations (as estimated from the factor matrix) can be examined to determine model fit. These differences are called *residuals*. If there are many large residuals, the factor model does not provide a good fit to the data and the model should be reconsidered. In Table 19.3, we see that only five residuals are larger than 0.05, indicating an acceptable model fit.

### REAL RESEARCH

### *Manufacturing Promotion Components*

The objective of this study was to develop a rather comprehensive inventory of manufacturer-controlled trade promotion variables and to demonstrate that an association exists between these variables and the retailer's promotion support decision. Retailer or trade support was defined operationally as the trade buyer's attitude toward the promotion.

Factor analysis was performed on the explanatory variables with the primary goal of data reduction. The principal components method, using varimax rotation, reduced the 30 explanatory variables to eight factors having eigenvalues greater than 1.0. For the purpose of interpretation, each factor was composed of variables that loaded 0.40 or higher on that factor. In two instances, where variables loaded 0.40 or above on two factors, each variable was assigned to the factor where it had the highest loading. Only one variable, "ease of handling/stocking at retail," did not load at least 0.40 on any factor. In all, the eight factors explained 62 percent of the total variance. Interpretation of the factor loading matrix was straightforward. Table 1 lists the factors in the order in which they were extracted.

Stepwise discriminant analysis was conducted to determine which, if any, of the eight factors predicted trade support to a statistically significant degree. The factor scores for the

Principal components analysis reveals that item importance is the most important factor influencing the retailer's promotion support decision.

TABLE 1 Factors Influencing Trade Promotional Support

| Factor | Factor Interpretation (% variance explained) | Loading | Variables Included in the Factor |
|---|---|---|---|
| $F_1$ | Item importance (16.3%) | 0.77 | Item is significant enough to warrant promotion |
| | | 0.75 | Category responds well to promotion |
| | | 0.66 | Closest trade competitor is likely to promote item |
| | | 0.64 | Importance of promoted product category |
| | | 0.59 | Item regular (nondeal) sales volume |
| | | 0.57 | Deal meshes with trade promotional requirements |
| $F_2$ | Promotion elasticity (9.3%) | | Buyer's estimate of sales increase on the basis of: |
| | | 0.86 | Price reduction and display |
| | | 0.82 | Display only |
| | | 0.80 | Price reduction only |
| | | 0.70 | Price reduction, display, and advertising |
| $F_3$ | Manufacturer brand support (8.2%) | | Manufacturer's brand support in form of: |
| | | 0.85 | Coupons |
| | | 0.81 | Radio and television advertising |
| | | 0.80 | Newspaper advertising |
| | | 0.75 | Point-of-purchase promotion (e.g., display) |
| $F_4$ | Manufacturer reputation (7.3%) | 0.72 | Manufacturer's overall reputation |
| | | 0.72 | Manufacturer cooperates in meeting trade's promotional needs |
| | | 0.64 | Manufacturer cooperates on emergency orders |
| | | 0.55 | Quality of sales presentation |
| | | 0.51 | Manufacturer's overall product quality |
| $F_5$ | Promotion wearout (6.4%) | 0.93 | Product category is overpromoted |
| | | 0.93 | Item is overpromoted |
| $F_6$ | Sales velocity (5.4%) | −0.81 | Brand market share rank[a] |
| | | 0.69 | Item regular sales volume[a] |
| | | 0.46 | Item regular sales volume |
| $F_7$ | Item profitability (4.5%) | 0.79 | Item regular gross margin |
| | | 0.72 | Item regular gross margin[a] |
| | | 0.49 | Reasonableness of deal performance requirements |
| $F_8$ | Incentive amount (4.2%) | 0.83 | Absolute amount of deal allowances |
| | | 0.81 | Deal allowances as percent of regular trade cost[a] |
| | | 0.49 | Absolute amount of deal allowances[a] |

[a] Denotes objective (archival) measure

eight factors were the explanatory variables. The dependent variable consisted of the retail buyer's overall rating of the deal (Rating), which was collapsed into a three-group (low, medium, and high) measure of trade support. The results of the discriminant analyses are shown in Table 2. All eight entered the discriminant functions. Goodness-of-fit measures indicated that, as a group, the eight factors discriminated between high, medium, and low levels of trade support. Multivariate $F$ ratios, indicating the degree of discrimination between each pair of groups, were significant at $p < 0.001$. Correct classification into high, medium, and low categories was achieved for 65 percent of the cases. The order of entry into discriminant analysis was used to determine the relative importance of factors as trade support influencers, as shown in Table 3.[9]

TABLE 2    Discriminant Analysis Results: Analysis of Rating ($N = 564$)

| Factor | | Standardized Discriminant Coefficients Analysis of Rating | |
| --- | --- | --- | --- |
| | | Function 1 | Function 2 |
| $F_1$ | Item importance | 0.861 | −0.253 |
| $F_2$ | Promotion elasticity | 0.081 | 0.398 |
| $F_3$ | Manufacturer brand support | 0.127 | −0.036 |
| $F_4$ | Manufacturer reputation | 0.394 | 0.014 |
| $F_5$ | Promotion wearout | −0.207 | 0.380 |
| $F_6$ | Sales velocity | 0.033 | −0.665 |
| $F_7$ | Item profitability | 0.614 | 0.357 |
| $F_8$ | Incentive amount | 0.461 | 0.254 |
| | Wilks' λ (for each factor) | All significant at $p < 0.001$ | |
| | Multivariate $F$ ratios | All significant at $p < 0.001$ | |
| | % Cases correctly classified | 65% correct | |

TABLE 3    Relative Importance of Trade Support Influencers (As Indicated by Order of Entry into the Discriminant Analysis)

**Analysis of Rating**

| Order of Entry | Factor Name |
| --- | --- |
| 1 | Item importance |
| 2 | Item profitability |
| 3 | Incentive amount |
| 4 | Manufacturer reputation |
| 5 | Promotion wearout |
| 6 | Sales velocity |
| 7 | Promotion elasticity |
| 8 | Manufacturer brand support ■ |

# APPLICATIONS OF COMMON FACTOR ANALYSIS

The data of Table 19.1 were analyzed using the common factor analysis model. Instead of using unities in the diagonal, the communalities were inserted. The output, shown in Table 19.4, is similar to the output from principal components analysis presented in Table 19.3. Under "Communalities" under the "Initial" column, the communalities for the variables are no longer 1.0. Based on the eigenvalue criterion, again two factors are extracted. The variances, after extracting the factors, are different from the initial eigenvalues. The first factor accounts for 42.84 percent of the variance, whereas the second accounts for 31.13 percent, in each case a little less than what was observed in principal components analysis.

The values in the unrotated factor pattern matrix of Table 19.4 are a little different from those in Table 19.3, although the pattern of the coefficients is similar. Sometimes, however, the pattern of loadings for common factor analysis is different than that for principal components analysis, with some variables loading on different factors. The rotated factor matrix has the same pattern as that in Table 19.3, leading to a similar interpretation of the factors.

## TABLE 19.4

### Results of Common Factor Analysis

Bartlett test of sphericity
Approx. chi-square = 111.314, df = 15, significance = 0.00000
Kaiser-Meyer-Olkin measure of sampling adequacy = 0.660

COMMUNALITIES

| VARIABLE | INITIAL | EXTRACTION |
|---|---|---|
| $V_1$ | 0.859 | 0.928 |
| $V_2$ | 0.480 | 0.562 |
| $V_3$ | 0.814 | 0.836 |
| $V_4$ | 0.543 | 0.600 |
| $V_5$ | 0.763 | 0.789 |
| $V_6$ | 0.587 | 0.723 |

INITIAL EIGENVALUES

| FACTOR | EIGENVALUE | % OF VARIANCE | CUMULATIVE % |
|---|---|---|---|
| 1 | 2.731 | 45.520 | 45.520 |
| 2 | 2.218 | 36.969 | 82.488 |
| 3 | 0.442 | 7.360 | 89.848 |
| 4 | 0.341 | 5.688 | 95.536 |
| 5 | 0.183 | 3.044 | 98.580 |
| 6 | 0.085 | 1.420 | 100.000 |

EXTRACTION SUMS OF SQUARED LOADINGS

| FACTOR | EIGENVALUE | % OF VARIANCE | CUMULATIVE % |
|---|---|---|---|
| 1 | 2.570 | 42.837 | 42.837 |
| 2 | 1.868 | 31.126 | 73.964 |

FACTOR MATRIX

| | FACTOR 1 | FACTOR 2 |
|---|---|---|
| $V_1$ | 0.949 | 0.168 |
| $V_2$ | −0.206 | 0.720 |
| $V_3$ | 0.914 | 0.038 |
| $V_4$ | −0.246 | 0.734 |
| $V_5$ | −0.850 | −0.259 |
| $V_6$ | −0.101 | 0.844 |

ROTATION SUMS OF SQUARED LOADINGS

| FACTOR | EIGENVALUE | % OF VARIANCE | CUMULATIVE % |
|---|---|---|---|
| 1 | 2.541 | 42.343 | 42.343 |
| 2 | 1.897 | 31.621 | 73.964 |

ROTATED FACTOR MATRIX

| | FACTOR 1 | FACTOR 2 |
|---|---|---|
| $V_1$ | 0.963 | −0.030 |
| $V_2$ | −0.054 | 0.747 |
| $V_3$ | 0.902 | −0.150 |
| $V_4$ | −0.090 | 0.769 |
| $V_5$ | −0.885 | −0.079 |
| $V_6$ | 0.075 | 0.847 |

*(Continued)*

## TABLE 19.4

**Results of Common Factor Analysis** *(Continued)*

FACTOR SCORE COEFFICIENT MATRIX

|       | FACTOR 1 | FACTOR 2 |
|-------|----------|----------|
| $V_1$ | 0.628    | 0.101    |
| $V_2$ | −0.024   | 0.253    |
| $V_3$ | 0.217    | −0.169   |
| $V_4$ | −0.023   | 0.271    |
| $V_5$ | −0.166   | −0.059   |
| $V_6$ | 0.083    | 0.500    |

REPRODUCED CORRELATION MATRIX

|       | $V_1$ | $V_2$ | $V_3$ | $V_4$ | $V_5$ | $V_6$ |
|-------|-------|-------|-------|-------|-------|-------|
| $V_1$ | 0.928* | 0.022 | −0.000 | 0.024 | −0.008 | −0.042 |
| $V_2$ | −0.075 | 0.562* | 0.006 | −0.008 | 0.031 | 0.012 |
| $V_3$ | 0.873 | −0.161 | 0.836* | −0.051 | 0.008 | 0.042 |
| $V_4$ | −0.110 | 0.580 | −0.197 | 0.600* | −0.025 | −0.004 |
| $V_5$ | −0.850 | −0.012 | −0.786 | 0.019 | 0.789* | −0.003 |
| $V_6$ | 0.046 | 0.629 | −0.060 | 0.645 | −0.133 | 0.723* |

*The lower left triangle contains the reproduced correlation matrix; the diagonal, the communalities; the upper right triangle, the residuals between the observed correlations and the reproduced correlations.

## REAL RESEARCH

### *"Common" Rebate Perceptions*

Rebates are effective in obtaining new users, brand switching, and repeat purchases among current users. Microsoft deployed a rebate program as a means to draw new users to their MSN Internet service. Microsoft's intent behind this rebate plan was to acquire new users from rivals such as AOL Time Warner's American Online Service, who had 33 million subscribers in 2002. Under the rebate plan, Microsoft offered a cash-back option for new users who committed to two years of MSN service. What makes rebates effective?

A study was undertaken to determine the factors underlying consumer perception of rebates. A set of 24 items measuring consumer perceptions of rebates was constructed. Respondents were asked to express their degree of agreement with these items on five-point Likert scales. The data were collected by a one-stage area telephone survey conducted in the Memphis metropolitan area. A total of 303 usable questionnaires were obtained.

The 24 items measuring perceptions of rebates were analyzed using common factor analysis. The initial factor solution did not reveal a simple structure of underlying rebate perceptions. Therefore, items that had low loadings were deleted from the scale, and the factor analysis was performed on the remaining items. This second solution yielded three interpretable factors. The factor loadings and the reliability coefficients are presented in the table. The three factors contained four, four, and three items, respectively. Factor 1 seemed to capture the consumers' perceptions of the efforts and difficulties associated with rebate redemption (Efforts). Factor 2 was defined as a representation of consumers' faith in the rebate system (Faith). Factor 3 represented consumers' perceptions of the manufacturers' motives for offering rebates (Motives). The loadings of items on their respective factor ranged from 0.527 to 0.744.

Therefore, companies such as Microsoft that employ rebates should ensure that the effort and difficulties of consumers in taking advantage of the rebates are minimized. They should also try to build consumers' faith in the rebate system and portray honest motives for offering rebates.[10]

Common factor analysis reveals that three factors characterize consumers' perceptions of rebates: efforts associated with rebate redemption, faith in the rebate system, and manufacturers' motives for offering rebates.

Factor Analysis of Perceptions of Rebates

| Scale Items[a] | Factor Loading | | |
| --- | --- | --- | --- |
| | *Factor 1* | *Factor 2* | *Factor 3* |
| Manufacturers make the rebate process too complicated. | 0.194 | 0.671 | −0.127 |
| Mail-in rebates are not worth the trouble involved. | −0.031 | 0.612 | 0.352 |
| It takes too long to receive the rebate check from the manufacturer. | 0.013 | 0.718 | 0.051 |
| Manufacturers could do more to make rebates easier to use. | 0.205 | 0.616 | 0.173 |
| Manufacturers offer rebates because consumers want them.[b] | 0.660 | 0.172 | 0.101 |
| Today's manufacturers take a real interest in consumer welfare.[b] | 0.569 | 0.203 | 0.334 |
| Consumer benefit is usually the primary consideration in rebate offers.[b] | 0.660 | 0.002 | 0.318 |
| In general, manufacturers are sincere in their rebate offers to consumers.[b] | 0.716 | 0.047 | −0.033 |
| Manufacturers offer rebates to get consumers to buy something they don't really need. | 0.099 | 0.156 | 0.744 |
| Manufacturers use rebate offers to induce consumers to buy slow-moving items. | 0.090 | 0.027 | 0.702 |
| Rebate offers require you to buy more of a product than you need. | 0.230 | 0.066 | 0.527 |
| Eigenvalues | 2.030 | 1.344 | 1.062 |
| Percentage of explained variance | 27.500 | 12.200 | 9.700 |

[a]The response categories for all items were: strongly agree (1), agree (2), neither agree nor disagree (3), disagree (4), strongly disagree (5), and don't know (6). "Don't know" responses were excluded from data analysis.
[b]The scores of these items were reversed. ■

Note that in this example, when the initial factor solution was not interpretable, items that had low loadings were deleted and the factor analysis was performed on the remaining items. If the number of variables is large (greater than 15), principal components analysis and common factor analysis result in similar solutions. However, principal components analysis is less prone to misinterpretation and is recommended for the nonexpert user. The next example illustrates an application of principal components analysis in international marketing research, and the example after that presents an application in the area of ethics.

## Driving Nuts for Beetles

Generally, with time, consumer needs and tastes change. Consumer preferences for automobiles need to be continually tracked to identify changing demands and specifications. However, there is one car that is quite an exception—the Volkswagen Beetle. More than 22 million have been built since it was introduced in 1938. Surveys have been conducted in different countries to determine the reasons why people purchase Beetles. Principal components analyses of the variables measuring the reasons for owning Beetles have consistently revealed one dominant factor—fanatical loyalty. The company has long wished its natural death but without any effect. This noisy and cramped "bug" has inspired devotion in drivers. Now old bugs are being sought everywhere. "The Japanese are going absolutely nuts for Beetles," says Jack Finn, a recycler of old Beetles in West Palm Beach, Florida. Because of faithful loyalty for the "bug," VW reintroduced it in 1998 as the New Beetle. The New Beetle has proven itself as much more than a sequel to its legendary namesake. It has won several distinguished automotive awards, including the *Money* magazine Best Pick in the small car category for 2001. Due to the success of bringing back the Beetle, Volkswagen decided to unveil a new version of the VW classic love van called the Shaggin' Wagon II at the Detroit Auto Show. This new microbus is planned to launch in 2003 for an estimated $30,000. If the microbus proves successful, like the New Beetle has, Volkswagen may even introduce a micropickup truck to please the 4X4, off-road crowd.[11] ∎

## Factors Predicting Unethical Marketing Research Practices

In 2001, the U.S. Department of Commerce estimated that unethical employee behavior costs Corporate America nearly $60 billion a year. If companies want ethical employees, then they themselves must conform to high ethical standards. This also applies to the marketing research industry. In order to identify organizational variables that are determinants of the incidence of unethical marketing research practices, a sample of 420 marketing professionals were surveyed. These marketing professionals were asked to provide responses on several scales, and to provide evaluations of incidence of 15 research practices that have been found to pose research ethics problems.

One of these scales included 11 items pertaining to the extent ethical problems plagued the organization, and what top management's actions were toward ethical situations. A principal components analysis with varimax rotation indicated that the data could be represented by two factors.

Factor Analysis of Ethical Problems and Top Management Action Scales

| | *Extent of Ethical Problems Within the Organization (Factor 1)* | *Top Management Actions on Ethics (Factor 2)* |
|---|---|---|
| 1. Successful executives in my company make rivals look bad in the eyes of important people in my company. | 0.66 | |
| 2. Peer executives in my company often engage in behaviors that I consider to be unethical. | 0.68 | |
| 3. There are many opportunities for peer executives in my company to engage in unethical behaviors. | 0.43 | |
| 4. Successful executives in my company take credit for the ideas and accomplishment of others. | 0.81 | |
| 5. In order to succeed in my company, it is often necessary to compromise one's ethics. | 0.66 | |

| | Extent of Ethical Problems Within the Organization (Factor 1) | Top Management Actions on Ethics (Factor 2) |
|---|---|---|
| 6. Successful executives in my company are generally more unethical than unsuccessful executives. | 0.64 | |
| 7. Successful executives in my company look for a "scapegoat" when they feel they may be associated with failure. | 0.78 | |
| 8. Successful executives in my company withhold information that is detrimental to their self-interest. | 0.68 | |
| 9. Top management in my company has let it be known in no uncertain terms that unethical behaviors will not be tolerated. | | 0.73 |
| 10. If an executive in my company is discovered to have engaged in unethical behavior that results primarily in personal gain (rather than corporate gain), he/she will be promptly reprimanded. | | 0.80 |
| 11. If an executive in my company is discovered to have engaged in an unethical behavior that results primarily in corporate gain (rather than personal gain), he/she will be promptly reprimanded. | | 0.78 |
| Eigenvalue | 5.06 | 1.17 |
| % of Variance Explained | 46% | 11% |
| Coefficient Alpha | 0.87 | 0.75 |

To simplify the table, only varimax rotated loading of 0.40 or greater are reported.
Each was rated on a five-point scale with 1 = "strongly agree" and 5 = "strongly disagree."

These two factors were then used in a multiple regression along with four other predictor variables. They were found to be the two best predictors of unethical marketing research practices.[12] ■

# INTERNET AND COMPUTER APPLICATIONS

Computer programs are available to implement both of the approaches: principal components analysis and common factor analysis. The mainframe and microcomputer programs are similar for SPSS and SAS. In the SPSS packages, the program FACTOR may be used for principal components analysis as well as for common factor analysis. Some other methods of factor analysis are also available and factor scores are calculated.

In the SAS system, the program PRINCOMP performs principal components analysis and calculates principal component scores. To perform common factor analysis, the program FACTOR can be used. The FACTOR program also performs principal components analysis.

In MINITAB, factor analysis can be assessed using Multivariate>Factor analysis. Principal components or maximum likelihood can be used to determine the initial factor extraction. If maximum likelihood is used, specify the number of factors to extract. If a number is not specified with a principal component extraction, the program will set it equal to a number of variables in the data set. Factor analysis is not available in EXCEL.

## SPSS Windows

To select this procedure using SPSS for Windows, click:

Analyze>Data Reduction>Factor . . .

## FOCUS ON BURKE

Burke states its goal in using factor analysis in one word . . . simplify! In a typical interview, Burke asks many questions and groups of these questions are highly correlated with each other. Whether factor analysis is used for clarifying which questions tend to measure the same basic concepts or to aid in using the question responses as predictors in regression, Burke has to be careful in interpretation of the results.

A recent project conducted by Burke involved 16 questions (variables). The correlation matrix was subjected to principal components analysis. Five factors, or components, were retained. The varimax rotated solution shows that component 5 is essentially a "one question" component (we have omitted loadings less than 0.4 to make the picture clearer). Note the questions that load on the first rotated component.

Rotated Component Matrix[a]

| | Component | | | | |
|---|---|---|---|---|---|
| | *1* | *2* | *3* | *4* | *5* |
| V01 | | −0.649 | | | |
| V02 | 0.460 | | | 0.720 | |
| V03 | | | | | 0.873 |
| V04 | 0.553 | 0.675 | | | |
| V05 | | | 0.840 | | |
| V06 | | | 0.683 | | |
| V07 | | | 0.857 | | |
| V08 | | | | 0.881 | |
| V09 | 0.898 | | | | |
| V10 | 0.472 | | | | |
| V11 | | 0.697 | | | |
| V12 | 0.826 | | | | |
| V13 | 0.764 | | | | |
| V14 | 0.701 | | | | |
| V15 | | 0.860 | | | |
| V16 | 0.578 | 0.617 | | | |

Extraction Method: Principal Component Analysis.
Rotation Method: Varimax with Kaiser Normalization.
[a]Rotation converged in 6 iterations.

As a "one-question" component is not very parsimonious, we will find a four-component solution.

Note that V10 now appears to be somewhat related to variables 2, 8, and 14, where as it was previously somewhat more related to the questions in component 1. Variable 14 now appears to be less related to component 1 than seen in the first (five-component) solution. The structure of components 2 and 3 remain very stable in the two solutions. This leads to several practical considerations:

1. All questions will not necessarily be correlated enough with other questions to form a component. When this happens, it is often the case that the question is ambiguous or one in which everyone seems to give the same answer with only random variation among the responses. Take a look at the question and see if the question was a "good one."
2. The questions loading together can change when you rotate a different number of components. Look to the most stable ones for your interpretation of the results. Even a high loading on a component (look at V14 on the first, five-component, solution) does not mean that it will be a relationship that holds up under a different rotation.

**3.** As a last point, the questions that load together are a result of the relative size of the correlations between the questions, not the absolute size. You could divide all the correlations in this matrix by 10 and the same questions would load on the same components after rotation . . . the loadings would just be smaller. You must not assume that because questions load together on a component that they have a strong relationship. The strength of relationship is indicated by how much of the variance in the original variable is captured in the factor (the loading squared).

Rotated Component Matrix[a]

| | Component | | | |
|---|---|---|---|---|
| | *1* | *2* | *3* | *4* |
| V01 | | −0.651 | | |
| V02 | | | | 0.813 |
| V03 | | | | |
| V04 | 0.516 | 0.662 | | |
| V05 | | | 0.837 | |
| V06 | | | 0.672 | |
| V07 | | | 0.843 | |
| V08 | | | | 0.817 |
| V09 | 0.870 | | | |
| V10 | | | | 0.436 |
| V11 | | 0.679 | | |
| V12 | 0.734 | | | |
| V13 | 0.810 | | | |
| V14 | 0.589 | | | 0.4380 |
| V15 | | 0.860 | | |
| V16 | 0.550 | 0.604 | | |

Extraction Method: Principal Component Analysis.
Rotation Method: Varimax with Kaiser Normalization.
[a]Rotation converged in 5 iterations.

# SUMMARY

Factor analysis is a class of procedures used for reducing and summarizing data. Each variable is expressed as a linear combination of the underlying factors. Likewise, the factors themselves can be expressed as linear combinations of the observed variables. The factors are extracted in such a way that the first factor accounts for the highest variance in the data, the second the next highest, and so on. Additionally, it is possible to extract the factors so that the factors are uncorrelated, as in principal components analysis.

In formulating the factor analysis problem, the variables to be included in the analysis should be specified based on past research, theory, and the judgment of the researcher. These variables should be measured on an interval or ratio scale. Factor analysis is based on a matrix of correlation between the variables. The appropriateness of the correlation matrix for factor analysis can be statistically tested.

The two basic approaches to factor analysis are principal components analysis and common factor analysis. In principal components analysis, the total variance in the data is considered. Principal components analysis is recommended when the researcher's primary concern is to determine the minimum number of factors that will account for maximum variance in the data for use in subsequent multivariate analysis. In common factor analysis, the factors are estimated based only on the common variance. This method is appropriate when the primary concern is to identify the underlying dimensions, and when the common variance is of interest. This method is also known as principal axis factoring.

The number of factors that should be extracted can be determined a *priori* or based on eigenvalues, scree plots, percentage of variance, split-half reliability, or significance tests. Although the initial or unrotated factor matrix indicates the relationship between the factors and individual variables, it seldom results in factors that can be interpreted, because the factors are correlated with many variables. Therefore, rotation is used to transform the factor matrix into a simpler one that is easier to interpret. The most commonly used method of rotation is the varimax procedure, which results in orthogonal factors. If the factors are highly correlated in the population, oblique rotation can be utilized. The rotated factor matrix forms the basis for interpreting the factors.

Factor scores can be computed for each respondent. Alternatively, surrogate variables may be selected by examining the factor matrix and selecting for each factor a variable with the highest or near highest loading. The differences between the observed correlations and the reproduced correlations, as estimated from the factor matrix, can be examined to determine model fit.

## KEY TERMS AND CONCEPTS

factor analysis, *560*
interdependence technique, *560*
factors, *560*
Bartlett's test of sphericity, *561*
correlation matrix, *561*
communality, *561*
eigenvalue, *561*
factor loadings, *561*

factor loading plot, *561*
factor matrix, *561*
factor scores, *561*
Kaiser-Meyer-Olkin (KMO) measure of sampling adequacy, *561*
percentage of variance, *562*
residuals, *562*

scree plot, *562*
principal components analysis, *564*
common factor analysis, *566*
orthogonal rotation, *568*
varimax procedure, *568*
oblique rotation, *568*
factor scores, *569*

## EXERCISES

### Questions

1. How is factor analysis different from multiple regression and discriminant analysis?
2. What are the major uses of factor analysis?
3. Describe the factor analysis model.
4. What hypothesis is examined by Bartlett's test of sphericity? For what purpose is this test used?
5. What is meant by the term "communality of a variable"?
6. Briefly define the following: eigenvalue, factor loadings, factor matrix, and factor scores.
7. For what purpose is the Kaiser-Meyer-Olkin measure of sampling adequacy used?
8. What is the major difference between principal components analysis and common factor analysis?
9. Explain how eigenvalues are used to determine the number of factors.
10. What is a scree plot? For what purpose is it used?
11. Why is it useful to rotate the factors? Which is the most common method of rotation?
12. What guidelines are available for interpreting the factors?

13. When is it useful to calculate factor scores?
14. What are surrogate variables? How are they determined?
15. How is the fit of the factor analysis model examined?

### Problems

1. Complete the following portion of an output from principal component analysis:

| Variable | Communality | Factor | Eigenvalue | % of Variance |
|----------|-------------|--------|------------|---------------|
| $V_1$ | 1.0 | 1 | 3.25 | |
| $V_2$ | 1.0 | 2 | 1.78 | |
| $V_3$ | 1.0 | 3 | 1.23 | |
| $V_4$ | 1.0 | 4 | 0.78 | |
| $V_5$ | 1.0 | 5 | 0.35 | |
| $V_6$ | 1.0 | 6 | 0.30 | |
| $V_7$ | 1.0 | 7 | 0.19 | |
| $V_8$ | 1.0 | 8 | 0.12 | |

2. Draw a scree plot based on the data given in problem 1.
3. How many factors should be extracted in problem 1? Explain your reasoning.

## INTERNET AND COMPUTER EXERCISES

1. In a study of the relationship between household behavior and shopping behavior, data on the following lifestyle statements were obtained on a seven-point scale (1 = disagree, 7 = agree):

$V_1$   I would rather spend a quiet evening at home than go out to a party.
$V_2$   I always check prices, even on small items.
$V_3$   Magazines are more interesting than movies.
$V_4$   I would not buy products advertised on billboards.
$V_5$   I am a homebody.

$V_6$   I save and cash coupons.
$V_7$   Companies waste a lot of money advertising.

The data obtained from a pretest sample of 25 respondents are given below:

| No. | $V_1$ | $V_2$ | $V_3$ | $V_4$ | $V_5$ | $V_6$ | $V_7$ |
|-----|-------|-------|-------|-------|-------|-------|-------|
| 1 | 6 | 2 | 7 | 6 | 5 | 3 | 5 |
| 2 | 5 | 7 | 5 | 6 | 6 | 6 | 4 |
| 3 | 5 | 3 | 4 | 5 | 6 | 6 | 7 |

| No. | $V_1$ | $V_2$ | $V_3$ | $V_4$ | $V_5$ | $V_6$ | $V_7$ |
|-----|-------|-------|-------|-------|-------|-------|-------|
| 4   | 3     | 2     | 2     | 5     | 1     | 3     | 2     |
| 5   | 4     | 2     | 3     | 2     | 2     | 1     | 3     |
| 6   | 2     | 6     | 2     | 4     | 3     | 7     | 5     |
| 7   | 1     | 3     | 3     | 6     | 2     | 5     | 7     |
| 8   | 3     | 5     | 1     | 4     | 2     | 5     | 6     |
| 9   | 7     | 3     | 6     | 3     | 5     | 2     | 4     |
| 10  | 6     | 3     | 3     | 4     | 4     | 6     | 5     |
| 11  | 6     | 6     | 2     | 6     | 4     | 4     | 7     |
| 12  | 3     | 2     | 2     | 7     | 6     | 1     | 6     |
| 13  | 5     | 7     | 6     | 2     | 2     | 6     | 1     |
| 14  | 6     | 3     | 5     | 5     | 7     | 2     | 3     |
| 15  | 3     | 2     | 4     | 3     | 2     | 6     | 5     |
| 16  | 2     | 7     | 5     | 1     | 4     | 5     | 2     |
| 17  | 3     | 2     | 2     | 7     | 2     | 4     | 6     |
| 18  | 6     | 4     | 5     | 4     | 7     | 3     | 3     |
| 19  | 7     | 2     | 6     | 2     | 5     | 2     | 1     |
| 20  | 5     | 6     | 6     | 3     | 4     | 5     | 3     |
| 21  | 2     | 3     | 3     | 2     | 1     | 2     | 6     |
| 22  | 3     | 4     | 2     | 1     | 4     | 3     | 6     |
| 23  | 2     | 6     | 3     | 2     | 1     | 5     | 3     |
| 24  | 6     | 5     | 7     | 4     | 5     | 7     | 2     |
| 25  | 7     | 6     | 5     | 4     | 6     | 5     | 3     |

a. Analyze this data using principal components analysis, using the varimax rotation procedure.

b. Interpret the factors extracted.

c. Calculate factor scores for each respondent.

d. If surrogate variables were to be selected, which ones would you select?

e. Examine the model fit.

f. Analyze the data using common factor analysis, and answer questions b through e.

2. Conduct the following analysis on the Nike data given in Internet and Computer Exercises 1 of Chapter 15. Consider only the following variables: awareness, attitude, preference, intention, and loyalty toward Nike.

a. Analyze this data using principal components analysis, using the varimax rotation procedure.

b. Interpret the factors extracted.

c. Calculate factor scores for each respondent.

d. If surrogate variables were to be selected, which ones would you select?

e. Examine the model fit.

f. Analyze the data using common factor analysis, and answer questions b through e.

3. Conduct the following analysis on the outdoor lifestyle data given in Internet and Computer Exercises 2 of Chapter 15. Consider only the following variables: the importance attached to enjoying nature, relating to the weather, living in harmony with the environment, exercising regularly, and meeting other people ($V_2$ to $V_6$).

a. Analyze this data using principal components analysis, using the varimax rotation procedure.

b. Interpret the factors extracted.

c. Calculate factor scores for each respondent.

d. If surrogate variables were to be selected, which ones would you select?

e. Examine the model fit.

f. Analyze the data using common factor analysis, and answer questions b through e.

4. Conduct the following analysis on the sneakers data given in Internet and Computer Exercises 3 of Chapter 17. Consider only the following variables: evaluations of the sneakers on comfort ($V_2$), style ($V_3$), and durability ($V_4$).

a. Analyze this data using principal components analysis, using the varimax rotation procedure.

b. Interpret the factors extracted.

c. Calculate factor scores for each respondent.

d. If surrogate variables were to be selected, which ones would you select?

e. Examine the model fit.

f. Analyze the data using common factor analysis, and answer questions b through e.

5. Factor analyze the clothing psychographic and lifestyle data collected in Fieldwork exercise 1, using principal components analysis. Use the mainframe and microcomputer programs from SPSS, SAS, or MINITAB.

6. Factor analyze the leisure time data collected in Fieldwork exercise 2, using common factor analysis. Use SPSS, SAS, or MINITAB.

# ACTIVITIES

## Fieldwork

1. You are a marketing research analyst for a manufacturer of casual clothing. You have been asked to develop a set of 10 statements for measuring student psychographic characteristics and lifestyles, because they may relate to the use of casual clothing. The respondents will be asked to indicate their degree of agreement with the statements using a seven-point scale (1 = completely disagree, 7 = completely agree). Obtain data from 40 students on your campus.

2. You have been commissioned by a manufacturer of sporting goods to determine student attitudes toward leisure behavior.

Construct an eight-item scale for this purpose. Administer this scale to 35 students on the campus.

## Group Discussion

1. As a small group, identify the uses of factor analysis in each of the following major decision areas in marketing:

a. Market segmentation

b. Product decisions

c. Promotion decisions

d. Pricing decisions

e. Distribution decisions

# APPENDIX 19.1

## *Fundamental Equations of Factor Analysis*

In the factor analysis model, hypothetical components are derived that account for the linear relationship between observed variables.[1] The factor analysis model requires that the relationships between observed variables be linear and that the variables have nonzero correlations between them. The derived hypothetical components have the following properties:

1. They form a linearly independent set of variables. No hypothetical component is derivable from the other hypothetical components as a linear combination of them.
2. The hypothetical components' variables can be divided into two basic kinds of components: common factors and unique factors. These two components can be distinguished in terms of the patterns of weights in the linear equations that derive the observed variables from the hypothetical components' variables. A common factor has more than one variable with a nonzero weight or factor loading associated with the factor. A unique factor has only one variable with a nonzero weight associated with the factor. Hence, only one variable depends upon a unique factor.
3. Common factors are always assumed to be uncorrelated with the unique factors. Unique factors are also usually assumed to be mutually uncorrelated, but common factors may or may not be correlated with each other.
4. Generally, it is assumed that there are fewer common factors than observed variables. However, the number of unique factors is usually assumed to be equal to the number of observed variables.

The following notations are used.

$$X = \text{An } n \times 1 \text{ random vector of observed}$$
$$\text{random variables } X_1, X_2, X_3, \ldots X_n.$$

It is assumed that

$$E(X) = 0$$
$$E(XX') = R_{xx}, \text{ a correlation matrix with unities in the main}$$
$$\text{diagonal.}$$
$$F = \text{An } m \times 1 \text{ vector of } m \text{ common factors } F_1, F_2, \ldots,$$
$$F_m$$

It is assumed that

$$E(F) = 0$$
$$E(FF') = R_{ff}, \text{ a correlation matrix.}$$
$$U = \text{An } n \times 1 \text{ random vector of the } n \text{ unique factors}$$
$$\text{variables, } U_1, U_2, \ldots, U_n$$

It is assumed that

$$E(U) = 0, \text{ and}$$
$$E(UU') = I$$

The unique factors are normalized to have unit variances and are mutually uncorrelated.

$$A = \text{An } n \times m \text{ matrix of coefficients called the factor pattern}$$
$$\text{matrix}$$
$$V = \text{An } n \times n \text{ diagonal matrix of coefficients for the unique}$$
$$\text{factors}$$

The observed variables, which are the coordinates of $X$, are weighted combinations of the common factors and the unique factors. The fundamental equation of factor analysis can then be written as:

$$X = AF + VU$$

The correlations between variables in terms of the factors may be derived as follows.

$$\begin{aligned}
R_{xx} &= E(XX') \\
&= E\{(AF + VU)(AF + VU)'\} \\
&= E\{(AF + VU)(F'A' + U'V')\} \\
&= E(AFF'A' + AFU'V' + VUF'A' + VUU'V') \\
&= AR_{ff}A' + AR_{fu}V' + VR_{uf}A' + V^2
\end{aligned}$$

Given that the common factors are uncorrelated with the unique factors, we have:

$$R_{fu} = R'_{uf} = 0$$

Hence,

$$R_{xx} = AR_{ff}A' + V^2$$

Suppose we subtract the matrix of unique factor variance, $V^2$, from both sides. We then obtain:

$$R_{xx} - V^2 = AR_{ff}A'$$

$R_{xx}$ is dependent only upon the common factor variables, and the correlations among the variables are related only to the common factors. Let $R_c = R_{xx} - V^2$ be the reduced correlation matrix.

We have already defined the factor pattern matrix $A$. The coefficients of the factor pattern matrix are weights assigned to the common factors when the observed variables are expressed as linear combinations of the common and unique factors. We now define the factor structure matrix. The coefficients of the factor structure matrix are the covariances between the observed variables and the factors. The factor structure matrix is helpful in the interpreta-

---

[1] The material in this appendix has been drawn from Stanley A. Muliak, *The Foundations of Factor Analysis* (New York: McGraw-Hill, 1972).

tion of factors, as it shows which variables are similar to a common factor variable. The factor structure matrix, $A_s$, is defined as:

$$A_s = E(XF')$$
$$= E[(AF + VU)F']$$
$$= AR_{ff} + VR_{uf}$$
$$= AR_{ff}$$

Thus, the factor structure matrix is equivalent to the factor pattern matrix $A$ multiplied by the matrix of covariances among the factors $R_{ff}$. Substituting $A_s$ for $AR_{ff}$, the reduced correlation matrix becomes the product of factor structure and the factor pattern matrix.

$$R_c = AR_{ff}A'$$
$$= A_sA'$$

# CHAPTER 20

# Cluster Analysis

"We all believe that every population is made up of distinct segments. If we have measured the right variables, cluster analysis helps us to see if groups exist that are more like each other than they are like members of other groups."

*Tom Myers,*
*senior vice president,*
*Burke Customer*
*Satisfaction Associates,*
*Burke, Inc.*

## Objectives

After reading this chapter, the student should be able to:

1. Describe the basic concept and scope of cluster analysis and its importance in marketing research.
2. Discuss the statistics associated with cluster analysis.
3. Explain the procedure for conducting cluster analysis including formulating the problem, selecting a distance measure, selecting a clustering procedure, deciding on the number of clusters, and interpreting and profiling clusters.
4. Describe the purpose and methods for evaluating the quality of clustering results and assessing reliability and validity.
5. Discuss the applications of nonhierarchical clustering and clustering of variables.

## Overview

Like factor analysis (Chapter 19), cluster analysis examines an entire set of interdependent relationships. Cluster analysis makes no distinction between dependent and independent variables. Rather, interdependent relationships between the whole set of variables are examined. The primary objective of cluster analysis is to classify objects into relatively homogeneous groups based on the set of variables considered. Objects in a group are relatively similar in terms of these variables and different from objects in other groups. When used in this manner, cluster analysis is the obverse of factor analysis, in that it reduces the number of objects, not the number of variables, by grouping them into a much smaller number of clusters.

This chapter describes the basic concept of cluster analysis. The steps involved in conducting cluster analysis are discussed and illustrated in the context of hierarchical clustering by using a popular computer program. Then an application of nonhierarchical clustering is presented, followed by a discussion of clustering of variables.

---

**ACTIVE RESEARCH** | DEPARTMENT STORE PROJECT

### Cluster Analysis

In the department store project, respondents were clustered on the basis of self-reported importance attached to each factor of the choice criteria utilized in selecting a department store. The results indicated that respondents could be clustered into four segments. Differences among the segments were statistically tested. Thus, each segment contained respondents who were relatively homogeneous with respect to their choice criteria. The store choice model was then estimated separately for each segment. This procedure resulted in choice models that better represented the underlying choice process of respondents in specific segments.

---

### REAL RESEARCH

## Ice Cream Shops for "Hot" Regions

Häagen-Dazs Shoppe Co. (*www.haagen-dazs.com*), with more than 300 retail ice cream shops throughout the United States, was interested in expanding its customer base. The objective was to identify potential consumer segments that could generate additional sales. Geodemography, a method of clustering consumers based on geographic, demographic, and lifestyle characteristics, was employed for this purpose. Primary research was conducted to develop demographic and psychographic profiles of Häagen-Dazs Shoppe users, including frequency of purchase, time of the day they came in, day of the week, and other product use variables. The addresses and zip codes of the respondents were also obtained. The respondents were then assigned to 40 geodemographic clusters based on the clustering procedure developed by Claritas. For each geodemographic cluster, the profile of Häagen-Dazs customers was compared to the cluster profile to determine the degree of penetration. Using this information, Häagen-Dazs was also able to identify several potential customer groups from which to attract traffic. In addition to expanding Häagen-Dazs' customer base, product advertising was established to target new customers accordingly. In August 2001,

Häagen-Dazs increased its penetration by identifying geodemographic clusters offering potential for increased ice cream sales.

Häagen-Dazs launched a satirical advertising campaign that featured a self-help group talking to each other about the ultimate pleasure of the Häagen-Dazs sensual eating program. The tagline for this campaign was "Pleasure is the path to joy." This humorous take on the caring, group-supporting society of the late 1990s focused on targeting the 20-something crowd of the 2000s.[1] ■

The Häagen-Dazs example illustrates the use of clustering to arrive at homogeneous segments for the purpose of formulating specific marketing strategies. In the department store example, clustering was used to group respondents for subsequent multivariate analysis.

## BASIC CONCEPT

Cluster analysis is a class of techniques used to classify objects or cases into relatively homogeneous groups called *clusters*. Objects in each cluster tend to be similar to each other and dissimilar to objects in the other clusters. Cluster analysis is also called *classification analysis,* or *numerical taxonomy.*[2] We will be concerned with clustering procedures that assign each object to one and only one cluster.[3] Figure 20.1 shows an ideal clustering situation, in which the clusters are distinctly separated on two variables: quality consciousness (variable 1) and price sensitivity (variable 2). Note that each consumer falls into one cluster and there are no overlapping areas. Figure 20.2, on the other hand, presents a clustering situation that is more likely to be encountered in practice. In Figure 20.2, the boundaries for some of the clusters are not clear-cut, and the classification of some consumers is not obvious, as many of them could be grouped into one cluster or another.

*Figure 20.1*
An Ideal Clustering Situation

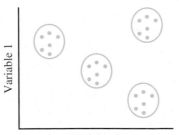

Variable 1

Variable 2

*Figure 20.2*
A Practical Clustering Situation

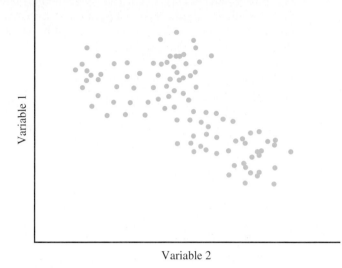

Variable 1

Variable 2

Both cluster analysis and discriminant analysis are concerned with classification. However, discriminant analysis requires prior knowledge of the cluster or group membership for each object or case included to develop the classification rule. In contrast, in cluster analysis there is no a *priori* information about the group or cluster membership for any of the objects. Groups or clusters are suggested by the data, not defined a *priori*.[4]

Cluster analysis has been used in marketing for a variety of purposes, including the following:[5]

■ *Segmenting the market:* For example, consumers may be clustered on the basis of benefits sought from the purchase of a product. Each cluster would consist of consumers who are relatively homogeneous in terms of the benefits they seek.[6] This approach is called *benefit segmentation.*

## REAL RESEARCH

### *The Vacationing Demanders, Educationalists, and Escapists*

In a study examining decision-making patterns among international vacationers, 260 respondents provided information on six psychographic orientations: psychological, educational, social, relaxational, physiological, and aesthetic. Cluster analysis was used to

Cluster analysis has revealed distinct market segments of international vacationers.

group respondents into psychographic segments. The results suggested that there were three meaningful segments based upon these lifestyles. The first segment (53%) consisted of individuals who were high on nearly all lifestyle scales. This group was called the "demanders." The second group (20%) was high on the educational scale and was named the "educationalists." The last group (26%) was high on relaxation and low on social scales and was named the "escapists." Specific marketing strategies were formulated to attract vacationers in each segment. A study conducted in 2000 examined 510 tourists' image of Thailand as an international travel destination. The study assessed the impact of the destination's image on the likelihood of the traveler returning to Thailand. The sample for this study was made up of international travelers who visited Thailand and were departing from Bangkok International Airport. The study involved the use of a three-stage sampling approach that included proportionate stratified, cluster, and systematic random sampling. Cluster sampling was used to randomly select departure flights from Bangkok International Airport. The results of this study revealed that Thailand has a negative image of environmental and social problems. At the same time, however, it has a positive image as a safe travel destination, associated with scenic natural beauty, culture, cuisine and hotels, and good shopping. Overall, most tourists, especially the "escapists," indicated that they would return to Thailand for a vacation. Thus, Thailand should make a special effort to reach the "escapists" segment, as the country would appeal the most to these vacationers.[7] ■

■ *Understanding buyer behaviors:* Cluster analysis can be used to identify homogeneous groups of buyers. Then the buying behavior of each group may be examined separately, as in the department store project, where respondents were clustered on the basis of self-reported importance attached to each factor of the choice criteria utilized in selecting a department store. Cluster analysis has also been used to identify the kinds of strategies automobile purchasers use to obtain external information.

■ *Identifying new product opportunities:* By clustering brands and products, competitive sets within the market can be determined. Brands in the same cluster compete more fiercely with each other than with brands in other clusters. A firm can examine its current offerings compared to those of its competitors to identify potential new product opportunities.

■ *Selecting test markets:* By grouping cities into homogeneous clusters, it is possible to select comparable cities to test various marketing strategies.

■ *Reducing data:* Cluster analysis can be used as a general data reduction tool to develop clusters or subgroups of data that are more manageable than individual observations. Subsequent multivariate analysis is conducted on the clusters rather than on the individual observations. For example, to describe differences in consumers' product usage behavior, the consumers may first be clustered into groups. The differences among the groups may then be examined using multiple discriminant analysis.

# STATISTICS ASSOCIATED WITH CLUSTER ANALYSIS

Before discussing the statistics associated with cluster analysis, it should be mentioned that most clustering methods are relatively simple procedures that are not supported by an extensive body of statistical reasoning. Rather, most clustering methods are heuristics, which are based on algorithms. Thus, cluster analysis contrasts sharply with analysis of variance, regression, discriminant analysis, and factor analysis, which are based upon an extensive body of statistical reasoning. Although many clustering methods have important statistical properties, the fundamental simplicity of these methods needs to be recognized.[8] The following statistics and concepts are associated with cluster analysis.

*Agglomeration schedule.* An agglomeration schedule gives information on the objects or cases being combined at each stage of a hierarchical clustering process.

***Cluster centroid.*** The cluster centroid is the mean values of the variables for all the cases or objects in a particular cluster.

***Cluster centers.*** The cluster centers are the initial starting points in nonhierarchical clustering. Clusters are built around these centers or *seeds*.

***Cluster membership.*** Cluster membership indicates the cluster to which each object or case belongs.

***Dendrogram.*** A dendrogram, or *tree graph*, is a graphical device for displaying clustering results. Vertical lines represent clusters that are joined together. The position of the line on the scale indicates the distances at which clusters were joined. The dendrogram is read from left to right. Figure 20.8 is a dendrogram.

***Distances between cluster centers.*** These distances indicate how separated the individual pairs of clusters are. Clusters that are widely separated are distinct, and therefore desirable.

***Icicle diagram.*** An icicle diagram is a graphical display of clustering results, so called because it resembles a row of icicles hanging from the eaves of a house. The columns correspond to the objects being clustered, and the rows correspond to the number of clusters. An icicle diagram is read from bottom to top. Figure 20.7 is an icicle diagram.

***Similarity/distance coefficient matrix.*** A similarity/distance coefficient matrix is a lower-triangle matrix containing pairwise distances between objects or cases.

# CONDUCTING CLUSTER ANALYSIS

The steps involved in conducting cluster analysis are listed in Figure 20.3. The first step is to formulate the clustering problem by defining the variables on which the clustering will be based. Then an appropriate distance measure must be selected. The distance measure determines how similar or dissimilar the objects being clustered are. Several clustering procedures have been developed and the researcher should select one that is appropriate for the problem at hand. Deciding on the number of clusters requires judgment on the part of the researcher. The derived clusters should be interpreted in terms of the variables used to cluster them and profiled in terms of additional salient variables. Finally, the researcher must assess the validity of the clustering process.

## Formulate the Problem

Perhaps the most important part of formulating the clustering problem is selecting the variables on which the clustering is based. Inclusion of even one or two irrelevant variables may distort an otherwise useful clustering solution. Basically, the set of variables selected should describe the similarity between objects in terms that are relevant to the marketing research problem. The variables should be selected based on past research, theory, or a consideration of the hypotheses being tested. In exploratory research, the researcher should exercise judgment and intuition.

*Figure 20.3*
Conducting Cluster Analysis

Formulate the problem.

↓

Select a distance measure.

↓

Select a clustering procedure.

↓

Decide on the number of clusters.

↓

Interpret and profile clusters.

↓

Assess the validity of clustering.

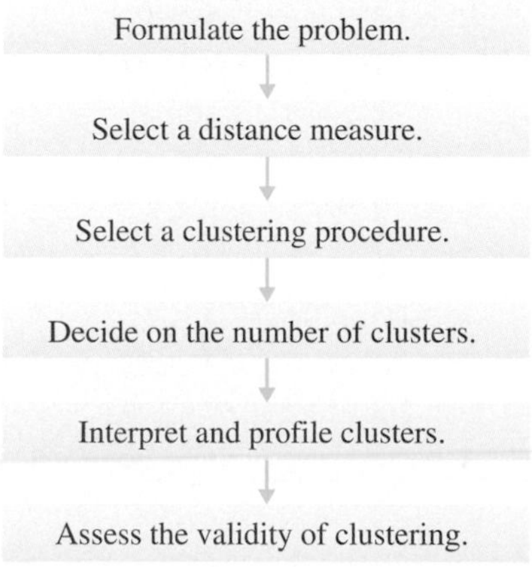

To illustrate, we consider a clustering of consumers based on attitudes toward shopping. Based on past research, six attitudinal variables were identified. Consumers were asked to express their degree of agreement with the following statements on a seven-point scale (1 = disagree, 7 = agree):

$V_1$: Shopping is fun.
$V_2$: Shopping is bad for your budget.
$V_3$: I combine shopping with eating out.
$V_4$: I try to get the best buys when shopping.
$V_5$: I don't care about shopping.
$V_6$: You can save a lot of money by comparing prices.

Data obtained from a pretest sample of 20 respondents are shown in Table 20.1. Note that, in practice, clustering is done on much larger samples of 100 or more. A small sample size has been used to illustrate the clustering process.

## Select a Distance or Similarity Measure

Because the objective of clustering is to group similar objects together, some measure is needed to assess how similar or different the objects are. The most common approach is to measure similarity in terms of distance between pairs of objects. Objects with smaller distances between them are more similar to each other than are those at larger distances. There are several ways to compute the distance between two objects.[9]

The most commonly used measure of similarity is the euclidean distance or its square. The ***euclidean distance*** is the square root of the sum of the squared differences in values for each variable. Other distance measures are also available. The *city-block* or *Manhattan distance* between two objects is the sum of the absolute differences in values for each variable. The *Chebychev distance* between two objects is the maximum absolute difference in values for any variable. For our example, we will use the squared euclidean distance.

**euclidean distance**
The square root of the sum of the squared differences in values for each variable.

**TABLE 20.1**

**Attitudinal Data for Clustering**

| Case No. | $V_1$ | $V_2$ | $V_3$ | $V_4$ | $V_5$ | $V_6$ |
|---|---|---|---|---|---|---|
| 1 | 6 | 4 | 7 | 3 | 2 | 3 |
| 2 | 2 | 3 | 1 | 4 | 5 | 4 |
| 3 | 7 | 2 | 6 | 4 | 1 | 3 |
| 4 | 4 | 6 | 4 | 5 | 3 | 6 |
| 5 | 1 | 3 | 2 | 2 | 6 | 4 |
| 6 | 6 | 4 | 6 | 3 | 3 | 4 |
| 7 | 5 | 3 | 6 | 3 | 3 | 4 |
| 8 | 7 | 3 | 7 | 4 | 1 | 4 |
| 9 | 2 | 4 | 3 | 3 | 6 | 3 |
| 10 | 3 | 5 | 3 | 6 | 4 | 6 |
| 11 | 1 | 3 | 2 | 3 | 5 | 3 |
| 12 | 5 | 4 | 5 | 4 | 2 | 4 |
| 13 | 2 | 2 | 1 | 5 | 4 | 4 |
| 14 | 4 | 6 | 4 | 6 | 4 | 7 |
| 15 | 6 | 5 | 4 | 2 | 1 | 4 |
| 16 | 3 | 5 | 4 | 6 | 4 | 7 |
| 17 | 4 | 4 | 7 | 2 | 2 | 5 |
| 18 | 3 | 7 | 2 | 6 | 4 | 3 |
| 19 | 4 | 6 | 3 | 7 | 2 | 7 |
| 20 | 2 | 3 | 2 | 4 | 7 | 2 |

If the variables are measured in vastly different units, the clustering solution will be influenced by the units of measurement. In a supermarket shopping study, attitudinal variables may be measured on a nine-point Likert-type scale; patronage, in terms of frequency of visits per month and the dollar amount spent; and brand loyalty, in terms of percentage of grocery shopping expenditure allocated to the favorite supermarket. In these cases, before clustering respondents, we must standardize the data by rescaling each variable to have a mean of zero and a standard deviation of unity. Although standardization can remove the influence of the unit of measurement, it can also reduce the differences between groups on variables that may best discriminate groups or clusters. It is also desirable to eliminate outliers (cases with atypical values).[10]

Use of different distance measures may lead to different clustering results. Hence, it is advisable to use different measures and compare the results. Having selected a distance or similarity measure, we can next select a clustering procedure.

## Select a Clustering Procedure

Figure 20.4 is a classification of clustering procedures. Clustering procedures can be hierarchical or nonhierarchical. ***Hierarchical clustering*** is characterized by the development of a hierarchy or tree-like structure. Hierarchical methods can be agglomerative or divisive. ***Agglomerative clustering*** starts with each object in a separate cluster. Clusters are formed by grouping objects into bigger and bigger clusters. This process is continued until all objects are members of a single cluster. ***Divisive clustering*** starts with all the objects grouped in a single cluster. Clusters are divided or split until each object is in a separate cluster.

Agglomerative methods are commonly used in marketing research. They consist of linkage methods, error sums of squares or variance methods, and centroid methods. ***Linkage methods*** include single linkage, complete linkage, and average linkage. The ***single linkage*** method is based on minimum distance or the nearest neighbor rule. The first

---

**hierarchical clustering**
A clustering procedure characterized by the development of a hierarchy or tree-like structure.

**agglomerative clustering**
Hierarchical clustering procedure where each object starts out in a separate cluster. Clusters are formed by grouping objects into bigger and bigger clusters.

**divisive clustering**
Hierarchical clustering procedure where all objects start out in one giant cluster. Clusters are formed by dividing this cluster into smaller and smaller clusters.

**linkage methods**
Agglomerative methods of hierarchical clustering that cluster objects based on a computation of the distance between them.

**single linkage**
Linkage method that is based on minimum distance or the nearest neighbor rule.

---

*Figure 20.4*
A Classification of Clustering Procedures

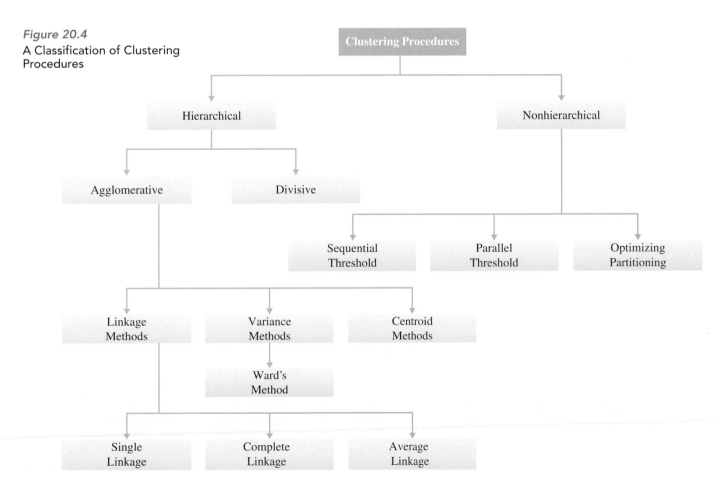

*Figure 20.5*
Linkage Methods of Clustering

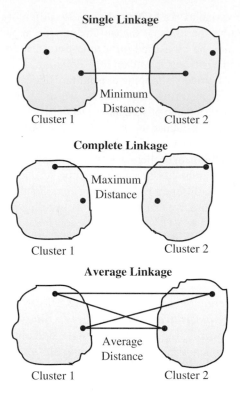

**Single Linkage**

Minimum Distance

Cluster 1          Cluster 2

**Complete Linkage**

Maximum Distance

Cluster 1          Cluster 2

**Average Linkage**

Average Distance

Cluster 1          Cluster 2

**complete linkage**
Linkage method that is based on maximum distance or the furthest neighbor approach.

**average linkage**
A linkage method based on the average distance between all pairs of objects, where one member of the pair is from each of the clusters.

**variance methods**
An agglomerative method of hierarchical clustering in which clusters are generated to minimize the within-cluster variance.

**Ward's procedure**
Variance method in which the squared euclidean distance to the cluster means is minimized.

**centroid methods**
A variance method of hierarchical clustering in which the distance between two clusters is the distance between their centroids (means for all the variables).

**nonhierarchical clustering**
A procedure that first assigns or determines a cluster center and then groups all objects within a prespecified threshold value from the center.

**sequential threshold method**
A nonhierarchical clustering method in which a cluster center is selected and all objects within a prespecified threshold value from the center are grouped together.

**parallel threshold method**
Nonhierarchical clustering method that specifies several cluster centers at once. All objects that are within a prespecified threshold value from the center are grouped together.

two objects clustered are those that have the smallest distance between them. The next shortest distance is identified, and either the third object is clustered with the first two, or a new two-object cluster is formed. At every stage, the distance between two clusters is the distance between their two closest points (see Figure 20.5). Two clusters are merged at any stage by the single shortest link between them. This process is continued until all objects are in one cluster. The single linkage method does not work well when the clusters are poorly defined. The **complete linkage** method is similar to single linkage, except that it is based on the maximum distance or the furthest neighbor approach. In complete linkage, the distance between two clusters is calculated as the distance between their two furthest points. The **average linkage** method works similarly. However, in this method, the distance between two clusters is defined as the average of the distances between all pairs of objects, where one member of the pair is from each of the clusters (Figure 20.5). As can be seen, the average linkage method uses information on all pairs of distances, not merely the minimum or maximum distances. For this reason, it is usually preferred to the single and complete linkage methods.

The **variance methods** attempt to generate clusters to minimize the within-cluster variance. A commonly used variance method is the **Ward's procedure.** For each cluster, the means for all the variables are computed. Then, for each object, the squared euclidean distance to the cluster means is calculated (Figure 20.6). These distances are summed for all the objects. At each stage, the two clusters with the smallest increase in the overall sum of squares within cluster distances are combined. In the **centroid methods,** the distance between two clusters is the distance between their centroids (means for all the variables), as shown in Figure 20.6. Every time objects are grouped, a new centroid is computed. Of the hierarchical methods, average linkage and Ward's methods have been shown to perform better than the other procedures.[11]

The second type of clustering procedures, the **nonhierarchical clustering** method, is frequently referred to as *k*-means clustering. These methods include sequential threshold, parallel threshold, and optimizing partitioning. In the **sequential threshold method,** a cluster center is selected and all objects within a prespecified threshold value from the center are grouped together. Then a new cluster center or seed is selected, and the process is repeated for the unclustered points. Once an object is clustered with a seed, it is no longer considered for clustering with subsequent seeds. The **parallel threshold method**

*Figure 20.6*
Other Agglomerative Clustering
Methods

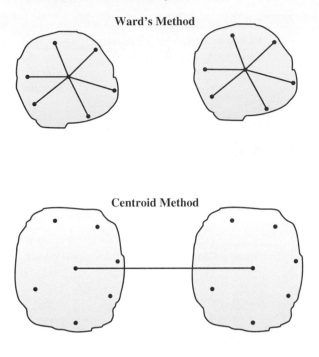

**Ward's Method**

**Centroid Method**

**optimizing partitioning method**
Nonhierarchical clustering method
that allows for later reassignment of
objects to clusters to optimize an
overall criterion.

operates similarly, except that several cluster centers are selected simultaneously, and objects within the threshold level are grouped with the nearest center. The ***optimizing partitioning method*** differs from the two threshold procedures in that objects can later be reassigned to clusters to optimize an overall criterion, such as average within-cluster distance for a given number of clusters.

Two major disadvantages of the nonhierarchical procedures are that the number of clusters must be prespecified and the selection of cluster centers is arbitrary. Furthermore, the clustering results may depend on how the centers are selected. Many nonhierarchical programs select the first $k$ ($k$ = number of clusters) cases without missing values as initial cluster centers. Thus, the clustering results may depend on the order of observations in the data. Yet nonhierarchical clustering is faster than hierarchical methods and has merit when the number of objects or observations is large. It has been suggested that the hierarchical and nonhierarchical methods be used in tandem. First, an initial clustering solution is obtained using a hierarchical procedure, such as average linkage or Ward's. The number of clusters and cluster centroids so obtained are used as inputs to the optimizing partitioning method.[12]

Choice of a clustering method and choice of a distance measure are interrelated. For example, squared euclidean distances should be used with the Ward's and centroid methods. Several nonhierarchical procedures also use squared euclidean distances.

We will use the Ward's procedure to illustrate hierarchical clustering. The output obtained by clustering the data of Table 20.1 is given in Table 20.2. Useful information is contained in the agglomeration schedule, which shows the number of cases or clusters being combined at each stage. The first line represents stage 1, with 19 clusters. Respondents 14 and 16 are combined at this stage, as shown in the columns labeled "Clusters Combined." The squared euclidean distance between these two respondents is given under the column labeled "Coefficients." The column entitled "Stage Cluster First Appears" indicates the stage at which a cluster is first formed. To illustrate, an entry of 1 at stage 6 indicates that respondent 14 was first grouped at stage 1. The last column, "Next Stage," indicates the stage at which another case (respondent) or cluster is combined with this one. Because the number in the first line of the last column is 6, we see that at stage 6, respondent 10 is combined with 14 and 16 to form a single cluster. Similarly, the second line represents stage 2 with 18 clusters. In stage 2, respondents 6 and 7 are grouped together.

Another important part of the output is contained in the icicle plot given in Figure 20.7. The columns correspond to the objects being clustered, in this case respondents labeled 1 through 20. The rows correspond to the number of clusters. This figure is read from bottom to top. At first, all cases are considered as individual clusters. Because there are 20 respondents, there are 20 initial clusters. At the first step, the two closest objects are combined, resulting in

## TABLE 20.2
### Results of Hierarchical Clustering

CASE PROCESSING SUMMARY[a,b]

| | CASES | | | | | |
|---|---|---|---|---|---|---|
| VALID | | MISSING | | | TOTAL | |
| N | Percent | N | Percent | | N | Percent |
| 20 | 100.0 | 0 | 0.0 | | 20 | 100.0 |

[a]Squared Euclidean Distance used
[b]Ward Linkage

WARD LINKAGE
AGGLOMERATION SCHEDULE

| | CLUSTER COMBINED | | | STAGE CLUSTER FIRST APPEARS | | |
|---|---|---|---|---|---|---|
| STAGE | CLUSTER 1 | CLUSTER 2 | COEFFICIENTS | CLUSTER 1 | CLUSTER 2 | NEXT STAGE |
| 1 | 14 | 16 | 1.000 | 0 | 0 | 6 |
| 2 | 6 | 7 | 2.000 | 0 | 0 | 7 |
| 3 | 2 | 13 | 3.500 | 0 | 0 | 15 |
| 4 | 5 | 11 | 5.000 | 0 | 0 | 11 |
| 5 | 3 | 8 | 6.500 | 0 | 0 | 16 |
| 6 | 10 | 14 | 8.167 | 0 | 1 | 9 |
| 7 | 6 | 12 | 10.500 | 2 | 0 | 10 |
| 8 | 9 | 20 | 13.000 | 0 | 0 | 11 |
| 9 | 4 | 10 | 15.583 | 0 | 6 | 12 |
| 10 | 1 | 6 | 18.500 | 0 | 7 | 13 |
| 11 | 5 | 9 | 23.000 | 4 | 8 | 15 |
| 12 | 4 | 19 | 27.750 | 9 | 0 | 17 |
| 13 | 1 | 17 | 33.100 | 10 | 0 | 14 |
| 14 | 1 | 15 | 41.333 | 13 | 0 | 16 |
| 15 | 2 | 5 | 51.833 | 3 | 11 | 18 |
| 16 | 1 | 3 | 64.500 | 14 | 5 | 19 |
| 17 | 4 | 18 | 79.667 | 12 | 0 | 18 |
| 18 | 2 | 4 | 172.667 | 15 | 17 | 19 |
| 19 | 1 | 2 | 328.600 | 16 | 18 | 0 |

CLUSTER MEMBERSHIP

| CASE | 4 CLUSTERS | 3 CLUSTERS | 2 CLUSTERS |
|---|---|---|---|
| 1 | 1 | 1 | 1 |
| 2 | 2 | 2 | 2 |
| 3 | 1 | 1 | 1 |
| 4 | 3 | 3 | 2 |
| 5 | 2 | 2 | 2 |
| 6 | 1 | 1 | 1 |
| 7 | 1 | 1 | 1 |
| 8 | 1 | 1 | 1 |
| 9 | 2 | 2 | 2 |
| 10 | 3 | 3 | 2 |
| 11 | 2 | 2 | 2 |
| 12 | 1 | 1 | 1 |
| 13 | 2 | 2 | 2 |
| 14 | 3 | 3 | 2 |
| 15 | 1 | 1 | 1 |
| 16 | 3 | 3 | 2 |
| 17 | 1 | 1 | 1 |
| 18 | 4 | 3 | 2 |
| 19 | 3 | 3 | 2 |
| 20 | 2 | 2 | 2 |

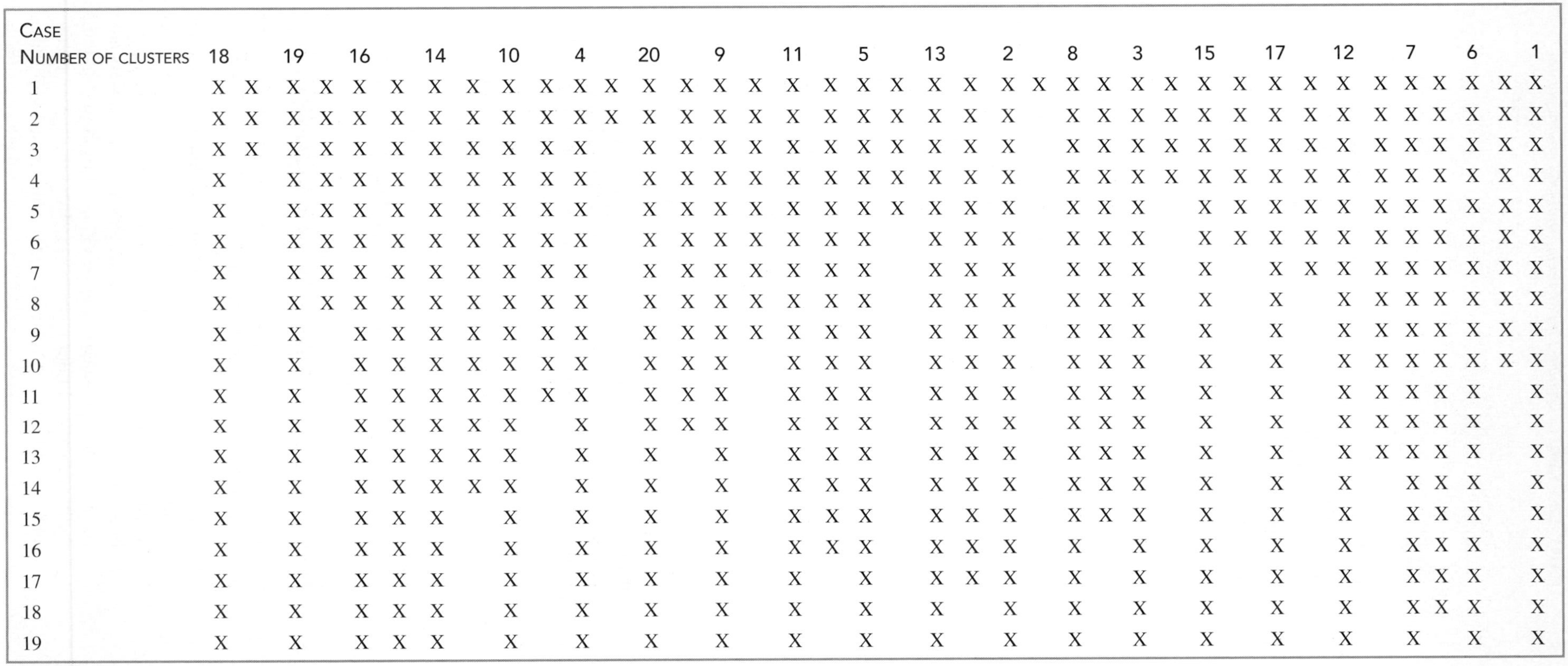

*Figure 20.7*
Vertical Icicle Plot Using Ward's Procedure

**Figure 20.8**
Dendrogram Using Ward's
Procedure

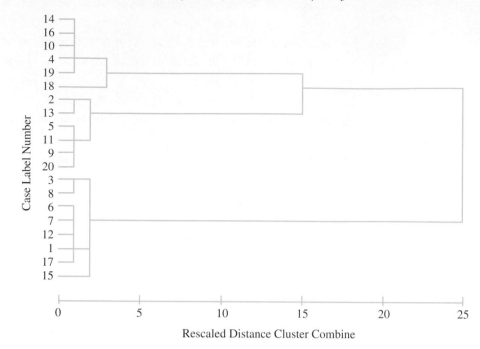

19 clusters. The last line of Figure 20.7 shows these 19 clusters. The two cases, respondents 14 and 16, that have been combined at this stage have between them all Xs in rows 1 through 19. Row number 18 corresponds to the next stage, with 18 clusters. At this stage, respondents 6 and 7 are grouped together. The column of Xs between respondents 6 and 7 has a blank in row 19. Thus, at this stage there are 18 clusters; 16 of them consist of individual respondents, and two contain two respondents each. Each subsequent step leads to the formation of a new cluster in one of three ways: (1) two individual cases are grouped together, (2) a case is joined to an already existing cluster, or (3) two clusters are grouped together.

Another graphic device that is useful in displaying clustering results is the dendrogram (see Figure 20.8). The dendrogram is read from left to right. Vertical lines represent clusters that are joined together. The position of the line on the scale indicates the distances at which clusters were joined. Because many of the distances in the early stages are of similar magnitude, it is difficult to tell the sequence in which some of the early clusters are formed. However, it is clear that in the last two stages, the distances at which the clusters are being combined are large. This information is useful in deciding on the number of clusters.

It is also possible to obtain information on cluster membership of cases if the number of clusters is specified. Although this information can be discerned from the icicle plot, a tabular display is helpful. Table 20.2 contains the cluster membership for the cases, depending on whether the final solution contains two, three, or four clusters. Information of this type can be obtained for any number of clusters and is useful for deciding on the number of clusters.

## Decide on the Number of Clusters

A major issue in cluster analysis is deciding on the number of clusters. Although there are no hard and fast rules, some guidelines are available:

1. Theoretical, conceptual, or practical considerations may suggest a certain number of clusters. For example, if the purpose of clustering is to identify market segments, management may want a particular number of clusters.
2. In hierarchical clustering, the distances at which clusters are combined can be used as criteria. This information can be obtained from the agglomeration schedule or from the dendrogram. In our case, we see from the agglomeration schedule in Table 20.2 that the value in the "Coefficients" column suddenly more than doubles between stages 17 (3 clusters) and 18 (2 clusters). Likewise, at the last two stages of the den-

drogram in Figure 20.8, the clusters are being combined at large distances. Therefore, it appears that a three-cluster solution is appropriate.

3. In nonhierarchical clustering, the ratio of total within-group variance to between-group variance can be plotted against the number of clusters. The point at which an elbow or a sharp bend occurs indicates an appropriate number of clusters. Increasing the number of clusters beyond this point is usually not worthwhile.

4. The relative sizes of the clusters should be meaningful. In Table 20.2, by making a simple frequency count of cluster membership, we see that a three-cluster solution results in clusters with eight, six, and six elements. However, if we go to a four-cluster solution, the sizes of the clusters are eight, six, five, and one. It is not meaningful to have a cluster with only one case, so a three-cluster solution is preferable in this situation.

## Interpret and Profile the Clusters

Interpreting and profiling clusters involves examining the cluster centroids. The centroids represent the mean values of the objects contained in the cluster on each of the variables. The centroids enable us to describe each cluster by assigning it a name or label. If the clustering program does not print this information, it may be obtained through discriminant analysis. Table 20.3 gives the centroids or mean values for each cluster in our example. Cluster 1 has relatively high values on variables $V_1$ (shopping is fun) and $V_3$ (I combine shopping with eating out). It also has a low value on $V_5$ (I don't care about shopping). Hence, cluster 1 could be labeled "fun-loving and concerned shoppers." This cluster consists of cases 1, 3, 6, 7, 8, 12, 15, and 17. Cluster 2 is just the opposite, with low values on $V_1$ and $V_3$ and a high value on $V_5$, and this cluster could be labeled "apathetic shoppers." Members of cluster 2 are cases 2, 5, 9, 11, 13, and 20. Cluster 3 has high values on $V_2$ (shopping upsets my budget), $V_4$ (I try to get the best buys when shopping), and $V_6$ (you can save a lot of money by comparing prices). Thus, this cluster could be labeled "economical shoppers." Cluster 3 comprises cases 4, 10, 14, 16, 18, and 19.

Often it is helpful to profile the clusters in terms of variables that were not used for clustering. These may include demographic, psychographic, product usage, media usage, or other variables. For example, the clusters may have been derived based on benefits sought. Further profiling may be done in terms of demographic and psychographic variables to target marketing efforts for each cluster. The variables that significantly differentiate between clusters can be identified via discriminant analysis and one-way analysis of variance.

## Assess Reliability and Validity

Given the several judgments entailed in cluster analysis, no clustering solution should be accepted without some assessment of its reliability and validity. Formal procedures for assessing the reliability and validity of clustering solutions are complex and not fully defensible.[13] Hence, we omit them here. However, the following procedures provide adequate checks on the quality of clustering results.

1. Perform cluster analysis on the same data using different distance measures. Compare the results across measures to determine the stability of the solutions.
2. Use different methods of clustering and compare the results.

| TABLE 20.3 | | | | | | |
| --- | --- | --- | --- | --- | --- | --- |
| **Cluster Centroids** | | | | | | |
| | | | MEANS OF VARIABLES | | | |
| CLUSTER NO. | $V_1$ | $V_2$ | $V_3$ | $V_4$ | $V_5$ | $V_6$ |
| 1 | 5.750 | 3.625 | 6.000 | 3.125 | 1.750 | 3.875 |
| 2 | 1.667 | 3.000 | 1.833 | 3.500 | 5.500 | 3.333 |
| 3 | 3.500 | 5.833 | 3.333 | 6.000 | 3.500 | 6.000 |

3. Split the data randomly into halves. Perform clustering separately on each half. Compare cluster centroids across the two subsamples.

4. Delete variables randomly. Perform clustering based on the reduced set of variables. Compare the results with those obtained by clustering based on the entire set of variables.

5. In nonhierarchical clustering, the solution may depend on the order of cases in the data set. Make multiple runs using different order of cases until the solution stabilizes.

We further illustrate hierarchical clustering with a study of differences in marketing strategy among American, Japanese, and British firms.

## REAL RESEARCH

### *It Is a Small World*

Data for a study of U.S., Japanese, and British competitors were obtained from detailed personal interviews with chief executives and top marketing decision makers for defined product groups in 90 companies. To control for market differences, the methodology was based upon matching 30 British companies with their major American and Japanese competitors in the U.K. market. The study involved 30 triads of companies, each composed of a British, American, and Japanese business that competed directly with one another.

Most of the data on the characteristics of the companies' performance, strategy, and organization were collected on five-point semantic differential scales. The first stage of the analysis involved factor analysis of variables describing the firms' strategies and marketing activities. The factor scores were used to identify groups of similar companies using Ward's hierarchical clustering routine. A six-cluster solution was developed.

Strategic Clusters

| Cluster | I | II | III | IV | V | VI |
|---|---|---|---|---|---|---|
| | | Quality | Price | Product | Mature | Aggressive |
| Name | Innovators | Marketeers | Promoters | Marketeers | Marketeers | Pushers |
| Size | 22 | 11 | 14 | 13 | 13 | 17 |
| Successful (%) | 55 | 100 | 36 | 38 | 77 | 41 |
| Nationality (%): | | | | | | |
| Japanese | 59 | 46 | 22 | 31 | 15 | 18 |
| American | 18 | 36 | 14 | 31 | 54 | 53 |
| British | 23 | 18 | 64 | 38 | 31 | 29 |

Membership in the six clusters was then interpreted against the original performance, strategy, and organizational variables. All the clusters contained some successful companies, although some contained significantly more than others. The clusters lent support to the hypothesis that successful companies were similar irrespective of nationality, because American, British, and Japanese companies were found in all the clusters. There was, however, a preponderance of Japanese companies in the more successful clusters and a predominance of British companies in the two least successful clusters. Apparently, Japanese companies do not deploy strategies that are unique to them; rather, more of them pursue strategies that work effectively in the British market.

The findings indicate that there are generic strategies that describe successful companies irrespective of their industry. Three successful strategies can be identified. The first is the Quality Marketeers strategy. These companies have strengths in marketing and research and development. They concentrate their technical developments on achieving high quality rather than pure innovation. These companies are characterized by entrepreneurial organizations, long-range planning, and a well-communicated sense of mission. The second generic strategy is that of the Innovators, who are weaker on advanced R & D but are entrepreneurial and driven by a quest for innovation. The last successful group is the Mature Marketeers, who are highly profit oriented and have in-depth marketing skills. All three appear to consist of highly marketing-oriented businesses. The United States, in 2000/2001, invested in close to 50 percent of all the British projects, and Japan also continues to be a key investor, especially in the automotive and electronics markets.[14] ■

# APPLICATIONS OF NONHIERARCHICAL CLUSTERING

We illustrate the nonhierarchical procedure using the data in Table 20.1 and an optimizing partitioning method. Based on the results of hierarchical clustering, a three-cluster solution was prespecified. The results are presented in Table 20.4. The initial cluster centers are the values of three randomly selected cases. In some programs, the first three cases are selected. The classification cluster centers are interim centers used for the assignment of cases. Each case is assigned to the nearest classification cluster center. The classification

## TABLE 20.4

### Results of Nonhierarchical Clustering

INITIAL CLUSTER CENTERS

|  | CLUSTER | | |
|---|---|---|---|
|  | 1 | 2 | 3 |
| $V_1$ | 4 | 2 | 7 |
| $V_2$ | 6 | 3 | 2 |
| $V_3$ | 3 | 2 | 6 |
| $V_4$ | 7 | 4 | 4 |
| $V_5$ | 2 | 7 | 1 |
| $V_6$ | 7 | 2 | 3 |

ITERATION HISTORY[a]

|  | CHANGE IN CLUSTER CENTERS | | |
|---|---|---|---|
| ITERATION | 1 | 2 | 3 |
| 1 | 2.154 | 2.102 | 2.550 |
| 2 | 0.000 | 0.000 | 0.000 |

[a]Convergence achieved due to no or small distance change. The maximum distance by which any center has changed is 0.000. The current iteration is 2. The minimum distance between initial centers is 7.746.

CLUSTER MEMBERSHIP

| CASE NUMBER | CLUSTER | DISTANCE |
|---|---|---|
| 1 | 3 | 1.414 |
| 2 | 2 | 1.323 |
| 3 | 3 | 2.550 |
| 4 | 1 | 1.404 |
| 5 | 2 | 1.848 |
| 6 | 3 | 1.225 |
| 7 | 3 | 1.500 |
| 8 | 3 | 2.121 |
| 9 | 2 | 1.756 |
| 10 | 1 | 1.143 |
| 11 | 2 | 1.041 |
| 12 | 3 | 1.581 |
| 13 | 2 | 2.598 |
| 14 | 1 | 1.404 |
| 15 | 3 | 2.828 |
| 16 | 1 | 1.624 |
| 17 | 3 | 2.598 |
| 18 | 1 | 3.555 |
| 19 | 1 | 2.154 |
| 20 | 2 | 2.102 |

*(Continued)*

## TABLE 20.4

**Results of Nonhierarchical Clustering *(Continued)***

FINAL CLUSTER CENTERS

| | CLUSTER | | |
|---|---|---|---|
| | 1 | 2 | 3 |
| $V_1$ | 4 | 2 | 6 |
| $V_2$ | 6 | 3 | 4 |
| $V_3$ | 3 | 2 | 6 |
| $V_4$ | 6 | 4 | 3 |
| $V_5$ | 4 | 6 | 2 |
| $V_6$ | 6 | 3 | 4 |

DISTANCES BETWEEN FINAL CLUSTER CENTERS

| CLUSTER | 1 | 2 | 3 |
|---|---|---|---|
| 1 | | 5.568 | 5.698 |
| 2 | 5.568 | | 6.928 |
| 3 | 5.698 | 6.928 | |

ANOVA

| | CLUSTER | | ERROR | | | |
|---|---|---|---|---|---|---|
| | MEAN SQUARE | DF | MEAN SQUARE | DF | F | SIG. |
| $V_1$ | 29.108 | 2 | 0.608 | 17 | 47.888 | 0.000 |
| $V_2$ | 13.546 | 2 | 0.630 | 17 | 21.505 | 0.000 |
| $V_3$ | 31.392 | 2 | 0.833 | 17 | 37.670 | 0.000 |
| $V_4$ | 15.713 | 2 | 0.728 | 17 | 21.585 | 0.000 |
| $V_5$ | 22.537 | 2 | 0.816 | 17 | 27.614 | 0.000 |
| $V_6$ | 12.171 | 2 | 1.071 | 17 | 11.363 | 0.001 |

The *F* tests should be used only for descriptive purposes because the clusters have been chosen to maximize the differences among cases in different clusters. The observed significance levels are not corrected for this and thus cannot be interpreted as tests of the hypothesis that the cluster means are equal.

NUMBER OF CASES IN EACH CLUSTER

| Cluster 1 | 6.000 |
|---|---|
| 2 | 6.000 |
| 3 | 8.000 |
| Valid | 20.000 |
| Missing | 0.000 |

centers are updated until the stopping criteria are reached. The final cluster centers represent the variable means for the cases in the final clusters. In SPSS WINDOWS, these are rounded to the nearest integer.

Table 20.4 also displays cluster membership and the distance between each case and its classification center. Note that the cluster memberships given in Table 20.2 (hierarchical clustering) and Table 20.4 (nonhierarchical clustering) are identical. (Cluster 1 of Table 20.2 is labeled cluster 3 in Table 20.4, and cluster 3 of Table 20.2 is labeled cluster 1 in Table 20.4.) The distances between the final cluster centers indicate that the pairs of clusters are well separated. The univariate *F* test for each clustering variable is presented. These *F* tests are only descriptive. Because the cases or objects are systematically assigned to clusters to maximize differences on the clustering variables, the resulting probabilities should not be interpreted as testing the null hypothesis of no differences among clusters.

The following example of hospital choice further illustrates nonhierarchical clustering.

**REAL RESEARCH**

## *Segmentation with Surgical Precision*

Cluster analysis was used to classify respondents who preferred hospitals for inpatient care to identify hospital preference segments. The clustering was based on the reasons respondents gave for preferring a hospital. The demographic profiles of the grouped respondents were compared to learn whether the segments could be identified efficiently.

Cluster analysis was used to classify consumers who preferred hospitals for inpatient care as old-fashioned, affluent, value conscious, and professional want-it-alls.

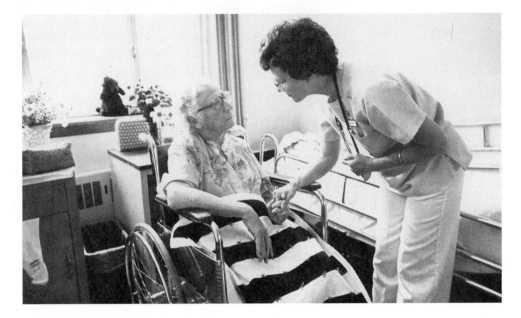

Quick Cluster (SPSS), a minimum variance clustering method, was used for grouping the respondents based on their answers to the hospital preference items. The squared euclidean distances between all clustering variables were minimized. Because different individuals perceive scales of importance differently, each individual's ratings were normalized before clustering. The results indicated that the respondents could best be classified into four clusters. The cross-validation procedure for cluster analysis was run twice, on halves of the total sample.

As expected, the four groups differed substantially by their distributions and average responses to the reasons for their hospital preferences. The names assigned to the four groups reflected the demographic characteristics and reasons for hospital preferences: Old-Fashioned, Affluent, Value Conscious, and Professional Want-It-Alls.[15] ∎

# CLUSTERING VARIABLES

Sometimes cluster analysis is also used for clustering variables to identify homogeneous groups. In this instance, the units used for analysis are the variables, and the distance measures are computed for all pairs of variables. For example, the correlation coefficient, either the absolute value or with the sign, can be used as a measure of similarity (the opposite of distance) between variables.

Hierarchical clustering of variables can aid in the identification of unique variables, or variables that make a unique contribution to the data. Clustering can also be used to reduce the number of variables. Associated with each cluster is a linear combination of the variables in the cluster, called the *cluster component*. A large set of variables can often be replaced by the set of cluster components with little loss of information. However, a given number of cluster components does not generally explain as much variance as the same number of principal components. Why, then, should the clustering of variables be used? Cluster components are usually easier to interpret than the principal components, even if the latter are rotated.[16] We illustrate the clustering of variables with an example from advertising research.

## Feelings—Nothing More Than Feelings

As of 2002, Polaroid was suddenly faced with increasing competition from digital cameras, so marketing executives decided to focus on the emotional potential of its core camera line. A $15 million campaign rolled out the new tagline, "Click, instantly" and implies that the Polaroid camera can change a feeling "right then and there." The ad campaign was designed to evoke emotional feelings in consumers when viewing the new Polaroid commercials.

Polaroid based this campaign on a study conducted to identify feelings that are precipitated by advertising. A total of 655 feelings were reduced to a set of 180 that were judged by respondents to be most likely to be stimulated by advertising. This group was clustered on the basis of judgments of similarity between feelings, resulting in 31 feeling clusters. These were divided into 16 positive and 15 negative clusters.[17]

| Positive Feelings | Negative Feelings |
|---|---|
| 1. Playful/childish | 1. Fear |
| 2. Friendly | 2. Bad/sick |
| 3. Humorous | 3. Confused |
| 4. Delighted | 4. Indifferent |
| 5. Interested | 5. Bored |
| 6. Strong/confident | 6. Sad |
| 7. Warm/tender | 7. Anxious |
| 8. Relaxed | 8. Helpless/timid |
| 9. Energetic/impulsive | 9. Ugly/stupid |
| 10. Eager/excited | 10. Pity/deceived |
| 11. Contemplative | 11. Mad |
| 12. Pride | 12. Disagreeable |
| 13. Persuaded/expectant | 13. Disgusted |
| 14. Vigorous/challenged | 14. Irritated |
| 15. Amazed | 15. Moody/frustrated |
| 16. Set/informed | |

Thus, 655 feeling responses to advertising were reduced to a core set of 31 feelings. As such, advertisers now have a manageable set of feelings for understanding and measuring emotional responses to advertising. When measured, these feelings can provide information on a commercial's ability to persuade the target consumers, as in the case of Polaroid camera. ■

Cluster analysis, particularly clustering of objects, is also frequently used in international marketing research (as in the next example) and could also be useful in researching ethical evaluations (as in the example after that).

## Perceived Product Parity—Once Rarity—Now Reality

How do consumers in different countries perceive brands in different product categories? Surprisingly, the answer is that the product perception parity rate is quite high. Perceived product parity means that consumers perceive all/most of the brands in a product category as similar to each other, or at par. A new study by BBDO Worldwide shows that two-thirds of consumers surveyed in 28 countries considered brands in 13 product categories to be at parity. The product categories ranged from airlines to credit cards to coffee. Perceived parity averaged 63 percent for all categories in all countries. The Japanese have the highest perception of parity across all product categories at 99 percent, and Colombians the lowest at 28 percent. Viewed by product category, credit cards have the highest parity perception at 76 percent, and cigarettes the lowest at 52 percent.

BBDO clustered the countries based on product parity perceptions to arrive at clusters that exhibited similar levels and patterns of parity perceptions. The highest perception parity figure came from Asia/Pacific region (83%) that included countries of Australia, Japan, Malaysia, South Korea, and France. It is no surprise that France was in this list because, for most products, they use highly emotional, visual advertising that is feelings oriented. The next cluster was U.S.-influenced markets (65%) that included Argentina, Canada, Hong Kong, Kuwait, Mexico, Singapore, and the United States. The third cluster, primarily European countries (60%) included Austria, Belgium, Denmark, Italy, the Netherlands, South Africa, Spain, the United Kingdom, and Germany.

What all this means is that in order to differentiate the product/brand, advertising can not focus just on product performance, but also must relate the product to the person's life in an important way. Also, much greater marketing effort will be required in the Asia/Pacific region and in France in order to differentiate the brand from competition and establish a unique image. A big factor in this growing parity is, of course, the emergence of the global market. A study conducted in 2001 explored the issues underlying the factual informational content of advertising under the conditions of product parity and product type. The data for this study were derived from content analysis from over 17,000 newspaper advertisements and 9,800 television advertisements. Analysis showed that advertisements for low-parity products contain more factual information than their counterparts. When the two conditions were seen together, parity influences factual informational content but not to the same degree as product type. The study revealed that overall, when it comes to including factual information in advertisements, advertisers respond more to product type than product parity.[18] ∎

## REAL RESEARCH

### Clustering Marketing Professionals Based on Ethical Evaluations

Cluster analysis can be used to explain differences in ethical perceptions by using a large multiitem, multidimensional scale developed to measure how ethical different situations are. One such scale was developed by Reidenbach and Robin. This scale has 29 items that compose five dimensions that measure how a respondent judges a certain action. For illustration, a given respondent will read about a marketing researcher that has provided proprietary information of one of his clients to a second client. The respondent is then asked to complete the 29-item ethics scale. For example, to indicate if this action is:

Just: \_\_\_:\_\_\_:\_\_\_:\_\_\_:\_\_\_:\_\_\_:\_\_\_: Unjust

Traditionally acceptable: \_\_\_:\_\_\_:\_\_\_:\_\_\_:\_\_\_:\_\_\_:\_\_\_: Unacceptable

Violates: \_\_\_:\_\_\_:\_\_\_:\_\_\_:\_\_\_:\_\_\_:\_\_\_: Does not violate an unwritten contract

This scale could be administered to a sample of marketing professionals. By clustering respondents based on these 29 items, two important questions should be investigated. First, how do the clusters differ with respect to the five ethical dimensions; in this case, Justice, Relativist, Egoism, Utilitarianism, and Deontology. Second, what types of firms compose each cluster? The clusters could be described in terms of North American Industry Classification System (NAICS) industrial category, firm size, and firm profitability. Answers to these two questions should provide insight into what types of firms use what dimensions to evaluate ethical situations. For instance, do large firms fall into a different cluster than small firms? Do more profitable firms perceive questionable situations more acceptable than less-profitable firms? An empirical study conducted in 2001 compared Taiwanese and U.S. perceptions of corporate ethics. A self-administered questionnaire was used that consisted of five measures. One of the measures, individual moral values, was measured using the Reidenbach and Robin scale. Results showed that in both national cultures, individual perceptions of corporate ethics appear to determine organizational commitment more than individual moral values.[19] ∎

# INTERNET AND COMPUTER APPLICATIONS

In SPSS, the main program for hierarchical clustering of objects or cases is CLUSTER. Different distance measures can be computed, and all the hierarchical clustering procedures discussed here are available. For nonhierarchical clustering, the QUICK CLUSTER program can be used. This program is particularly helpful for clustering a large number of cases. All the default options will result in a *k*-means clustering. To cluster variables, the distance measures should be computed across variables using the PROXIMITIES program. This proximity matrix can be read into CLUSTER to obtain a grouping of the variables.

In SAS, the CLUSTER program can be used for the hierarchical clustering of cases or objects. All the clustering procedures discussed here are available, as well as some additional ones. Nonhierarchical clustering of cases or objects can be accomplished using FASTCLUS. For clustering of variables, the VARCLUS program can be used. Dendrograms are not automatically computed but can be obtained using the TREE program.

IN MINITAB, cluster analysis can be assessed in the Multivariate>Cluster observation function. Also available are Clustering of Variables and Cluster K-Means. Cluster analysis is not available in EXCEL.

## SPSS Windows

To select this procedure using SPSS for Windows, click:

> Analyze>Classify>Hierarchical Cluster . . .
> Analyze>Classify>K-Means Cluster . . .

For clustering of variables, use Hierarchical Cluster and then select the variables option under cluster.

---

## FOCUS ON BURKE

When Burke presents the results of a cluster analysis to a client, the three big questions to be answered are:

1. What do the clusters tell me about my market?
2. What variables drive the clustering?
3. How different are the clusters?

*What do the clusters tell me about my market?*
To answer this question, Burke typically uses respondent data that was not included in the clustering procedure. For example, we might find four clusters of respondents based on their evaluations of product benefits. We also collected data on past purchase behavior and purchase intention for a new concept. If the clusters do not show any managerially significant differences on these behavioral and intentions measures, then it will be hard to justify to management that the clusters are useful. Because the purpose of clustering is to create groups that are as much alike as possible, there is no guarantee that they will be different in any way that has external value. We cannot simply accept that because the clusters were created, they are really different.

*What variables drive the clustering?*
If we use several variables to create the clustering, we have to be very careful that we do not create an implicit weighting system. For example, in working on a project for an automobile company, 20 questions about the benefits desired in a new automobile were proposed for use in clustering respondents. It was immediately clear that seven of the questions directly or indirectly were related to economy, eight of the questions were related to image, three questions were related to price/value, and two questions reflected speed/acceleration. Of course, a factor analysis was helpful in making these observations. You could predict that the questions that would impact the clustering the most would lead management to conclude "the clusters of respondents seem to heavily reflect economy and image." You would be amazed if this did not happen. When you calculate euclidean distance to examine the differences between respondents, the sum of squares would include 15 from economy

and image, with only five from either price/value or speed/acceleration. If these are all on comparable scales, the latter two categories have little opportunity to overcome the strength of the first two categories. It would be more reasonable to pare down the number of questions to come as close as possible to having the same number reflecting highly correlated groups of questions. If you do not do this, the number of questions you ask about a topic has the potential to have a stronger influence on your results than the topic itself.

### How different are the clusters?

In the first topic above, the notion of determining if the clusters are useful because of differences among external variables was discussed. We also need to examine if the clusters are actually "different" based on the variables used to create the clusters. You can put your data in a clustering algorithm and, if you tell it to stop at two clusters, you will have two clusters because of the nature of the process, not necessarily because of the logic or structure of differences that exist in the population. It becomes important to look at the clusters and see if the differences are of a magnitude and stability to evoke confidence.

1. It is not likely that the clusters will be different on all the questions you used as input for the clustering process. Although statistical procedures are not really valid when applied to systematically created clusters, they do offer insight as to how the clusters are formed. One-way ANOVA tells you if the individual questions are different across the clusters based on a statistic that would be appropriate for a probability sample (of course, that is not what you have . . . but it is a useful "index"). Using discriminant analysis is even more appealing, as it will show which of the questions would be potential discriminators between groups taking into account the collinearity between these predictors.

2. Managerial significance is a different issue. Suppose your clusters appear to be different on these statistical indices (ANOVA and discriminant analysis). That does not mean that the differences are large enough to be seen as useful by management. For example, a question for which the clusters are "different" was a rating of economy, and yet 90 percent of the ratings ranged between 6 and 9 on a 10-point scale. You would need additional supporting evidence to be able to support this as a meaningful difference to management. The ratings show different in degree of "positiveness," and not different in that some are high and some are low. This is a difficult issue and there is no cookbook answer for it. You have to be comfortable that you can interpret these numeric differences into meaningful management decisions.

# SUMMARY

Cluster analysis is used for classifying objects or cases, and sometimes variables, into relatively homogeneous groups. The groups or clusters are suggested by the data and are not defined a *priori*.

The variables on which the clustering is done should be selected based on past research, theory, the hypotheses being tested, or the judgment of the researcher. An appropriate measure of distance or similarity should be selected. The most commonly used measure is the euclidean distance or its square.

Clustering procedures may be hierarchical or nonhierarchical. Hierarchical clustering is characterized by the development of a hierarchy or tree-like structure. Hierarchical methods can be agglomerative or divisive. Agglomerative methods consist of linkage methods, variance methods, and centroid methods. Linkage methods are comprised of single linkage, complete linkage, and average linkage. A commonly used variance method is the Ward's procedure. The nonhierarchical methods are frequently referred to as *k*-means clustering. These methods can be classified as sequential threshold, parallel threshold, and optimizing partitioning. Hierarchical and nonhierarchical methods can be used in tandem. The choice of a clustering procedure and the choice of a distance measure are interrelated.

The number of clusters may be based on theoretical, conceptual, or practical considerations. In hierarchical clustering, the distances at which the clusters are being combined is an important criterion. The relative sizes of the clusters should be meaningful. The clusters should be interpreted in terms of cluster centroids. Often it is helpful to profile the clusters in terms of variables that were not used for clustering. The reliability and validity of the clustering solutions may be assessed in different ways.

# KEY TERMS AND CONCEPTS

agglomeration schedule, *588*
cluster centroid, *589*
cluster centers, *589*
cluster membership, *589*
dendrogram, *589*
distances between cluster centers, *589*
icicle diagram, *589*
similarity/distance coefficient matrix, *589*

euclidean distance, *590*
hierarchical clustering, *591*
agglomerative clustering, *591*
divisive clustering, *591*
linkage methods, *591*
single linkage, *591*
complete linkage, *592*
average linkage, *592*

variance methods, *592*
Ward's procedure, *592*
centroid methods, *592*
nonhierarchical clustering, *592*
sequential threshold method, *592*
parallel threshold method, *592*
optimizing partitioning method, *593*

# EXERCISES

## Questions

1. Discuss the similarity and difference between cluster analysis and discriminant analysis.
2. What are some of the uses of cluster analysis in marketing?
3. Briefly define the following terms: dendrogram, icicle plot, agglomeration schedule, and cluster membership.
4. What is the most commonly used measure of similarity in cluster analysis?
5. Present a classification of clustering procedures.
6. Why is the average linkage method usually preferred to single linkage and complete linkage?
7. What are the two major disadvantages of nonhierarchical clustering procedures?
8. What guidelines are available for deciding on the number of clusters?
9. What is involved in the interpretation of clusters?
10. What are some of the additional variables used for profiling the clusters?
11. Describe some procedures available for assessing the quality of clustering solutions.
12. How is cluster analysis used to group variables?

## Problems

1. Are the following statements true or false?
   a. Hierarchical and nonhierarchical clustering methods always produce different results.
   b. One should always standardize data before performing cluster analysis.
   c. Small distance coefficients in the agglomeration schedule imply that dissimilar cases are being merged.
   d. It does not matter which distance measure you use; the clustering solutions are essentially similar.
   e. It is advisable to analyze the same data set using different clustering procedures.

# INTERNET AND COMPUTER EXERCISES

1. Analyze the data in Table 20.1 using the following hierarchical methods: (a) single linkage (nearest neighbor), (b) complete linkage (furthest neighbor), and (c) method of centroid. Use SPSS, SAS, or MINITAB. Compare your results with those given in Table 20.2.
2. Conduct the following analysis on the Nike data given in Internet and Computer Exercises 1 of Chapter 15. Consider only the following variables: awareness, attitude, preference, intention, and loyalty toward Nike.
   a. Cluster the respondents based on the identified variables using hierarchical clustering. Use Ward's method and squared euclidean distances. How many clusters do you recommend and why?
   b. Cluster the respondents based on the identified variables using *k*-means clustering and the number of clusters identified in (a). Compare the results to those obtained in (a).
3. Conduct the following analysis on the outdoor lifestyle data given in Internet and Computer Exercises 2 of Chapter 15. Consider only the following variables: the importance attached to enjoying nature, relating to the weather, living in harmony with the environment, exercising regularly, and meeting other people ($V_2$ to $V_6$).
   a. Cluster the respondents based on the identified variables using hierarchical clustering. Use Ward's method and squared euclidean distances. How many clusters do you recommend and why?
   b. Cluster the respondents based on the identified variables using the following hierarchical methods: (a) single linkage (nearest neighbor), (b) complete linkage (furthest neighbor), and (c) method of centroid.
   c. Cluster the respondents based on the identified variables using *k*-means clustering and the number of clusters identified in (a). Compare the results to those obtained in (a).
4. Conduct the following analysis on the sneakers data given in Internet and Computer Exercises 3 of Chapter 17. Consider only the following variables: evaluations of the sneakers on comfort ($V_2$), style ($V_3$), and durability ($V_4$).
   a. Cluster the respondents based on the identified variables using hierarchical clustering. Use Ward's method and squared euclidean distances. How many clusters do you recommend and why?
   b. Cluster the respondents based on the identified variables using *k*-means clustering and the number of clusters identified in (a). Compare the results to those obtained in (a).

**5.** Analyze the data collected in the Fieldwork exercise to cluster the respondents, using the hierarchical and nonhierarchical methods. Use one of the software packages discussed in this chapter.

**6.** Analyze the data collected in the Fieldwork exercise to cluster the 15 variables measuring consumer attitude toward airlines and flying. Use one of the programs described in this chapter.

# ACTIVITIES

## *Fieldwork*

**1.** As a marketing research consultant to a major airline, you must determine consumers' attitudes toward airlines and flying. Construct a 15-item scale for this purpose. In a group of five students, obtain data on this scale and standard demographic characteristics from 50 male or female heads of households in your community. Each student should conduct 10 interviews. This data will be used to cluster respondents and to cluster the 15 variables measuring consumer attitudes toward airlines and flying.

## *Group Discussion*

**1.** As a small group, discuss the role of cluster analysis in analyzing marketing research data. Emphasize the ways in which cluster analysis can be used in conjunction with other data analysis procedures.

CHAPTER

# 21

# Multidimensional Scaling and Conjoint Analysis

"Often, relationships are easier to see if you can draw a picture or create a chart that illustrates the relationships . . . and that is the goal of multidimensional scaling. Conjoint analysis, on the other hand, helps us profile which attributes contribute most heavily to a person's choice among a variety of offerings made up of different combinations of these attributes."

*Michael Baumgardner, president, Burke, Inc.*

## Objectives

After reading this chapter, the student should be able to:

1. Discuss the basic concept and scope of multidimensional scaling (MDS) in marketing research and describe its various applications.
2. Describe the steps involved in multidimensional scaling of perception data including formulating the problem, obtaining input data, selecting an MDS procedure, deciding on the number of dimensions, labeling the dimensions and interpreting the configuration, and assessing reliability and validity.
3. Explain the multidimensional scaling of preference data and distinguish between internal and external analysis of preferences.
4. Explain correspondence analysis and discuss its advantages and disadvantages.
5. Understand the relationship between MDS, discriminant analysis, and factor analysis.
6. Discuss the basic concepts of conjoint analysis and contrast it with MDS and discuss its various applications.
7. Describe the procedure for conducting conjoint analysis including formulating the problem, constructing the stimuli, deciding the form of input data, selecting a conjoint analysis procedure, interpreting the results, and assessing reliability and validity.
8. Define the concept of hybrid conjoint analysis and explain how it simplifies the data-collection task.

This final chapter on data analysis presents two related techniques for analyzing consumer perceptions and preferences: multidimensional scaling (MDS) and conjoint analysis. We outline and illustrate the steps involved in conducting MDS and discuss the relationships among MDS, factor analysis, and discriminant analysis. Then we describe conjoint analysis and present a step-by-step procedure for conducting it. We also provide brief coverage of hybrid conjoint models.

**ACTIVE RESEARCH** | DEPARTMENT STORE PROJECT

### *Multidimensional Scaling*

In the department store project, respondents' evaluations of the 10 stores on each of the eight factors of the choice criteria were used to derive similarity measures between the stores. Euclidean distances were calculated between each pair of stores. These data were analyzed using multidimensional scaling to obtain spatial maps that represented the respondents' perceptions of the 10 stores. In one such map, the dimensions were identified as prestigious versus discount stores, and regional versus national store chains. Stores that competed directly with each other (e.g., JC Penney and Macy's) were located close together in the perceptual space. These perceptual maps were used to gain insights into the competitive positioning of the 10 department stores.

### REAL RESEARCH

## *Colas Collide*

In a survey, respondents were asked to rank-order all the possible pairs of 10 brands of soft drinks in terms of their similarity. These data were analyzed via multidimensional scaling and resulted in the following spatial representation of soft drinks.

From other information obtained in the questionnaire, the horizontal axis was labeled as "Cola Flavor." Tab was perceived to be the most cola flavored and 7-Up the least cola flavored. The vertical axis was labeled as "Dietness," with Tab being perceived to be the most dietetic and Dr. Pepper the most nondietetic. Note that Pepsi and Coke Classic were perceived to be very similar as indicated by their closeness in the perceptual map. Close similarity was also perceived between 7-Up and Slice, Diet 7-Up and Diet Slice, and Tab, Diet Coke, and Diet Pepsi. Note that Dr. Pepper is perceived to be relatively dissimilar to the other brands. Such MDS maps are very useful in understanding the competitive structure of the soft drink market. In a 2001 survey by Reader's Digest, the soft drinks Coca-Cola and Sprite were awarded "SuperBrand" status by Asian consumers. The survey was based on product quality, image, value, trustworthiness, and satisfaction from the consumer's perspective. Consumers

MDS has been used to understand consumers' perceptions of soft drinks and the competitive structure of the soft drink market.

rated Coca-Cola as "Platinum SuperBrand," and Sprite as "Gold SuperBrand." The Coca-Cola Company has utilized techniques such as MDS to understand how consumers perceive their products as well as those of competitors and, as a result, reaped rich rewards.[1] ∎

### REAL RESEARCH

## *Complete Credit Card Features Identified by Conjoint Analysis*

The Complete MasterCard—a "co-branded" card with SBC Communications, Inc. (*www.sbc.com*)—resulted from the adroit use of focus group research and conjoint analysis research. The Complete MasterCard became available to SBC's residential customers recently.

"With the increased competition in the calling card market, we needed to offer our customers the convenience of a multipurpose card in order to meet their expectations," Rich Bialek, director of SBC's credit card services said. "We wanted market research to help us determine what mix of features would make our card most appealing to customers."

In the first round of eight focus group sessions with users of both credit cards and calling cards, Wirthlin Worldwide (*www.wirthlin.com*) focused on the acceptance and expectations for the concept of a credit card with a calling card feature. In the second round of focus groups, Wirthlin researchers probed to identify a new card's features to be studied in the subsequent conjoint analysis phase.

During the conjoint analysis study, Wirthlin recruited 500 SBC customers to participate in a self-administered, computerized questionnaire taking 30 minutes. Wirthlin included 15 features of a credit and calling card, such as annual fee (four options), interest rate (three options), and card name (seven options). All questions gave the respondents two choices. For example, "What is more important—a card with no annual fee or a card that offers a variable interest rate?"

"By the time participants went through a series of 50 or so questions, they weren't sure what they wanted," Jamal Din, Wirthlin's conjoint designer said. "Conjoint analysis was able to assign relative values to the various features, based on each individual's answers, and then design the one card that would most likely be irresistible to that individual."

As a result of the study, the card received the name "SBC Complete MasterCard." The card featured no annual fee, and an annual automatic rebate of 10 percent—paid by the sponsoring bank—on most local and long-distance calls made with the card. In addition, the card included a tiered interest rate with a 25-day grace period. The usefulness of conjoint analysis in designing the SBC Complete MasterCard is demonstrated by the gratifying customer response to the card.[2] ■

The first two examples illustrate the derivation and use of perceptual maps, which lie at the heart of MDS. The SBC Complete MasterCard example involves trade-offs respondents make when evaluating alternatives. The conjoint analysis procedure is based on these trade-offs.

# BASIC CONCEPTS IN MULTIDIMENSIONAL SCALING (MDS)

*multidimensional scaling (MDS)*
A class of procedures for representing perceptions and preferences of respondents spatially by means of a visual display.

*Multidimensional scaling* (MDS) is a class of procedures for representing perceptions and preferences of respondents spatially by means of a visual display. Perceived or psychological relationships among stimuli are represented as geometric relationships among points in a multidimensional space. These geometric representations are often called spatial maps. The axes of the spatial map are assumed to denote the psychological bases or underlying dimensions respondents use to form perceptions and preferences for stimuli.[3] MDS has been used in marketing to identify:

1. The number and nature of dimensions consumers use to perceive different brands in the marketplace
2. The positioning of current brands on these dimensions
3. The positioning of consumers' ideal brand on these dimensions

Information provided by MDS has been used for a variety of marketing applications, including:

■ *Image measurement.* Compare the customers' and noncustomers' perceptions of the firm with the firm's perceptions of itself and thus identify perceptual gaps.
■ *Market segmentation.* Position brands and consumers in the same space and thus identify groups of consumers with relatively homogeneous perceptions.
■ *New product development.* To look for gaps in the spatial map, which indicate potential opportunities for positioning new products. Also, to evaluate new product concepts and existing brands on a test basis to determine how consumers perceive the new concepts. The proportion of preferences for each new product is one indicator of its success.
■ *Assessing advertising effectiveness.* Spatial maps can be used to determine whether advertising has been successful in achieving the desired brand positioning.
■ *Pricing analysis.* Spatial maps developed with and without pricing information can be compared to determine the impact of pricing.
■ *Channel decisions.* Judgments on compatibility of brands with different retail outlets could lead to spatial maps useful for making channel decisions.
■ *Attitude scale construction.* MDS techniques can be used to develop the appropriate dimensionality and configuration of the attitude space.

# STATISTICS AND TERMS ASSOCIATED WITH MDS

The important statistics and terms associated with MDS include the following:

***Similarity judgments.*** Similarity judgments are ratings on all possible pairs of brands or other stimuli in terms of their similarity using a Likert-type scale.

***Preference rankings.*** Preference rankings are rank orderings of the brands or other stimuli from the most preferred to the least preferred. They are normally obtained from the respondents.

***Stress.*** This is a lack-of-fit measure; higher values of stress indicate poorer fits.

***R-square.*** *R*-square is a squared correlation index that indicates the proportion of variance of the optimally scaled data that can be accounted for by the MDS procedure. This is a goodness-of-fit measure.

***Spatial map.*** Perceived relationships among brands or other stimuli are represented as geometric relationships among points in a multidimensional space called a spatial map.

***Coordinates.*** Coordinates indicate the positioning of a brand or a stimulus in a spatial map.

***Unfolding.*** The representation of both brands and respondents as points in the same space is referred to as unfolding.

# CONDUCTING MULTIDIMENSIONAL SCALING

Figure 21.1 shows the steps in MDS. The researcher must formulate the MDS problem carefully because a variety of data may be used as input into MDS. The researcher must also determine an appropriate form in which data should be obtained and select an MDS procedure for analyzing the data. An important aspect of the solution involves determining the number of dimensions for the spatial map. Also, the axes of the map should be labeled and the derived configuration interpreted. Finally, the researcher must assess the quality of the results obtained.[4] We describe each of these steps, beginning with problem formulation.

## Formulate the Problem

Formulating the problem requires that the researcher specify the purpose for which the MDS results would be used and select the brands or other stimuli to be included in the analysis. The number of brands or stimuli selected and the specific brands included determine the nature of the resulting dimensions and configurations. At a minimum, eight brands or stimuli should be included so as to obtain a well-defined spatial map. Including more than 25 brands is likely to be cumbersome and may result in respondent fatigue.

The decision regarding which specific brands or stimuli to include should be made carefully. Suppose a researcher is interested in obtaining consumer perceptions of automo-

*Figure 21.1*
Conducting Multidimensional Scaling

Formulate the problem.

Obtain input data.

Select an MDS procedure.

Decide on the number of dimensions.

Label the dimensions and interpret the configuration.

Assess reliability and validity.

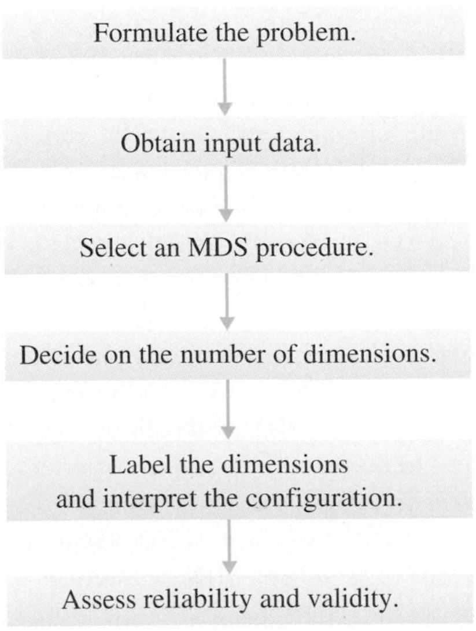

**Figure 21.2**
Input Data for Multidimensional
Scaling

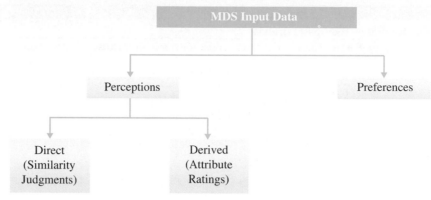

biles. If luxury automobiles are not included in the stimulus set, this dimension may not emerge in the results. The choice of the number and specific brands or stimuli to be included should be based on the statement of the marketing research problem, theory, and the judgment of the researcher.

Multidimensional scaling will be illustrated in the context of obtaining a spatial map for 10 toothpaste brands. These brands are Aqua-Fresh, Crest, Colgate, Aim, Gleem, Macleans, Ultra Brite, Close-Up, Pepsodent, and Dentagard. Given the list of brands, the next question, then, is: How should we obtain data on these 10 brands?

## Obtain Input Data

As shown in Figure 21.2, input data obtained from the respondents may be related to perceptions or preferences. Perception data, which may be direct or derived, is discussed first.

***Perception Data: Direct Approaches.*** In direct approaches to gathering perception data, the respondents are asked to judge how similar or dissimilar the various brands or stimuli are, using their own criteria. Respondents are often required to rate all possible pairs of brands or stimuli in terms of similarity on a Likert scale. These data are referred to as similarity judgments. For example, similarity judgments on all the possible pairs of toothpaste brands may be obtained in the following manner:

|  | *Very* *Dissimilar* |  |  |  |  |  | *Very* *Similar* |
|---|---|---|---|---|---|---|---|
| Crest vs. Colgate | 1 | 2 | 3 | 4 | 5 | 6 | 7 |
| Aqua-Fresh vs. Crest | 1 | 2 | 3 | 4 | 5 | 6 | 7 |
| Crest vs. Aim | 1 | 2 | 3 | 4 | 5 | 6 | 7 |
| . |  |  |  |  |  |  |  |
| . |  |  |  |  |  |  |  |
| . |  |  |  |  |  |  |  |
| Colgate vs. Aqua-Fresh | 1 | 2 | 3 | 4 | 5 | 6 | 7 |

The number of pairs to be evaluated is $n(n - 1)/2$, where $n$ is the number of stimuli. Other procedures are also available. Respondents could be asked to rank-order all the possible pairs from the most similar to the least similar. In another method, the respondent rank-orders the brands in terms of their similarity to an anchor brand. Each brand, in turn, serves as the anchor.

In our example, the direct approach was adopted. Subjects were asked to provide similarity judgments for all $45(10 \times 9/2)$ pairs of toothpaste brands, using a seven-point scale. The data obtained from one respondent are given in Table 21.1.[5]

***derived approaches***
In MDS, attribute-based approaches to collecting perception data requiring the respondents to rate the stimuli on the identified attributes using semantic differential or Likert scales.

***Perception Data: Derived Approaches.*** ***Derived approaches*** to collecting perception data are attribute-based approaches requiring the respondents to rate the brands or stimuli on the identified attributes using semantic differential or Likert scales. For example, the different brands of toothpaste may be rated on attributes such as these:

**TABLE 21.1**

**Similarity Ratings of Toothpaste Brands**

|  | AQUA-FRESH | CREST | COLGATE | AIM | GLEEM | MACLEANS | ULTRA BRIGHT | CLOSE-UP | PEPSODENT | DENTAGARD |
|---|---|---|---|---|---|---|---|---|---|---|
| Aqua-Fresh |  |  |  |  |  |  |  |  |  |  |
| Crest | 5 |  |  |  |  |  |  |  |  |  |
| Colgate | 6 | 7 |  |  |  |  |  |  |  |  |
| Aim | 4 | 6 | 6 |  |  |  |  |  |  |  |
| Gleem | 2 | 3 | 4 | 5 |  |  |  |  |  |  |
| Macleans | 3 | 3 | 4 | 4 | 5 |  |  |  |  |  |
| Ultra Brite | 2 | 2 | 2 | 3 | 5 | 5 |  |  |  |  |
| Close-Up | 2 | 2 | 2 | 2 | 6 | 5 | 6 |  |  |  |
| Pepsodent | 2 | 2 | 2 | 2 | 6 | 6 | 7 | 6 |  |  |
| Dentagard | 1 | 2 | 4 | 2 | 4 | 3 | 3 | 4 | 3 |  |

| | | |
|---|---|---|
| Whitens teeth | ___ __ __ __ __ __ __ __ __ __ | Does not whiten teeth |
| Prevents tooth decay | ___ __ __ __ __ __ __ __ __ __ | Does not prevent tooth decay |
| . | | |
| . | | |
| . | | |
| Pleasant tasting | ___ __ __ __ __ __ __ __ __ __ | Unpleasant tasting |

Sometimes an ideal brand is also included in the stimulus set. The respondents are asked to evaluate their hypothetical ideal brand on the same set of attributes. If attribute ratings are obtained, a similarity measure (such as euclidean distance) is derived for each pair of brands.

***Direct vs. Derived Approaches.***   Direct approaches have the advantage that the researcher does not have to identify a set of salient attributes. Respondents make similarity judgments using their own criteria, as they would under normal circumstances. The disadvantages are that the criteria are influenced by the brands or stimuli being evaluated. If the various brands of automobiles being evaluated are in the same price range, then price will not emerge as an important factor. It may be difficult to determine before analysis if and how the individual respondents' judgments should be combined. Furthermore, it may be difficult to label the dimensions of the spatial map.

The advantage of the attribute-based approach is that it is easy to identify respondents with homogeneous perceptions. The respondents can be clustered based on the attribute ratings. It is also easier to label the dimensions. A disadvantage is that the researcher must identify all the salient attributes, a difficult task. The spatial map obtained depends upon the attributes identified.

The direct approaches are more frequently used than the attribute-based approaches. However, it may be best to use both these approaches in a complementary way. Direct similarity judgments may be used for obtaining the spatial map, and attribute ratings may be used as an aid to interpreting the dimensions of the perceptual map. Similar procedures are used for preference data.

***Preference Data.***   Preference data order the brands or stimuli in terms of respondents' preference for some property. A common way in which such data are obtained is preference rankings. Respondents are required to rank the brands from the most preferred to the least preferred. Alternatively, respondents may be required to make paired comparisons and indicate which brand in a pair they prefer. Another method is to obtain preference ratings for the various brands. (The rank order, paired comparison, and rating scales were discussed in Chapters 8 and 9 on scaling techniques.) When spatial maps are based on preference data, distance implies differences in preference. The configuration derived from preference data may differ greatly from that obtained from similarity data. Two brands may be perceived as different in a similarity map yet similar in a preference map, and vice versa. For example, Crest and Pepsodent may be perceived by a group of respondents as very different brands and thus appear far apart on a perception map. However, these two brands may be about equally preferred and appear close together on a preference map. We will continue using the perception data obtained in the toothpaste example to illustrate the MDS procedure and then consider the scaling of preference data.

## Select an MDS Procedure

**nonmetric MDS**
A type of multidimensional scaling method that assumes that the input data are ordinal.

**metric MDS**
A multidimensional scaling method that assumes that input data are metric.

Selection of a specific MDS procedure depends upon whether perception or preference data are being scaled, or whether the analysis requires both kinds of data. The nature of the input data is also a determining factor. **Nonmetric MDS** procedures assume that the input data are ordinal, but they result in metric output. The distances in the resulting spatial map may be assumed to be interval scaled. These procedures find, in a given dimensionality, a spatial map whose rank orders of estimated distances between brands or stimuli best preserve or reproduce the input rank orders. In contrast, **metric MDS** methods assume that input data are metric. Because the output is also metric, a stronger relationship between the output and input data is maintained, and the metric (interval or ratio) qualities of the input data are preserved. The metric and nonmetric methods produce similar results.[6]

Another factor influencing the selection of a procedure is whether the MDS analysis will be conducted at the individual respondent level or at an aggregate level. In individual-level analysis, the data are analyzed separately for each respondent, resulting in a spatial map for each respondent. Although individual-level analysis is useful from a research perspective, it is not appealing from a managerial standpoint. Marketing strategies are typically formulated at the segment or aggregate level, rather than at the individual level. If aggregate-level analysis is conducted, some assumptions must be made in aggregating individual data. Typically, it is assumed that all respondents use the same dimensions to evaluate the brands or stimuli, but that different respondents weight these common dimensions differentially.

The data of Table 21.1 were treated as rank ordered and scaled using a nonmetric procedure. Because one respondent provided these data, an individual-level analysis was conducted. Spatial maps were obtained in one to four dimensions and then a decision on an appropriate number of dimensions was made. This decision is central to all MDS analyses; therefore, it is explored in greater detail in the following section.

## Decide on the Number of Dimensions

The objective in MDS is to obtain a spatial map that best fits the input data in the smallest number of dimensions. However, spatial maps are computed in such a way that the fit improves as the number of dimensions increases. Therefore, a compromise has to be made. The fit of an MDS solution is commonly assessed by the stress measure. Stress is a lack-of-fit measure; higher values of stress indicate poorer fits. The following guidelines are suggested for determining the number of dimensions.

**elbow criterion**
A plot of stress versus dimensionality used in MDS. The point at which an elbow or a sharp bend occurs indicates an appropriate dimensionality.

1. *A priori knowledge.* Theory or past research may suggest a particular number of dimensions.
2. *Interpretability of the spatial map.* Generally, it is difficult to interpret configurations or maps derived in more than three dimensions.
3. **Elbow criterion.** A plot of stress versus dimensionality should be examined. The points in this plot usually form a convex pattern, as shown in Figure 21.3. The point at which an elbow or a sharp bend occurs indicates an appropriate number of dimensions. Increasing the number of dimensions beyond this point is usually not worth the improvement in fit.
4. *Ease of use.* It is generally easier to work with two-dimensional maps or configurations than with those involving more dimensions.
5. *Statistical approaches.* For the sophisticated user, statistical approaches are also available for determining the dimensionality.[7]

*Figure 21.3*
Plot of Stress Versus
Dimensionality

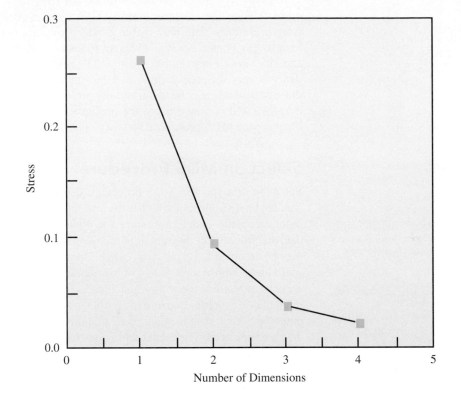

Based on the plot of stress versus dimensionality (Figure 21.3), interpretability of the spatial map, and ease-of-use criteria, it was decided to retain a two-dimensional solution. This is shown in Figure 21.4.

## Label the Dimensions and Interpret the Configuration

Once a spatial map is developed, the dimensions must be labeled and the configuration interpreted. Labeling the dimensions requires subjective judgment on the part of the researcher. The following guidelines can assist in this task:

1. Even if direct similarity judgments are obtained, ratings of the brands on researcher-supplied attributes may still be collected. Using statistical methods such as regression, these attribute vectors may be fitted in the spatial map (see Figure 21.5). The axes may then be labeled for the attributes with which they are most closely aligned.

*Figure 21.4*
A Spatial Map of
Toothpaste Brands

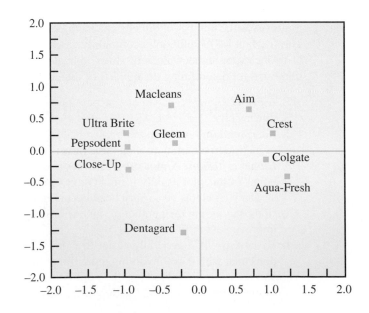

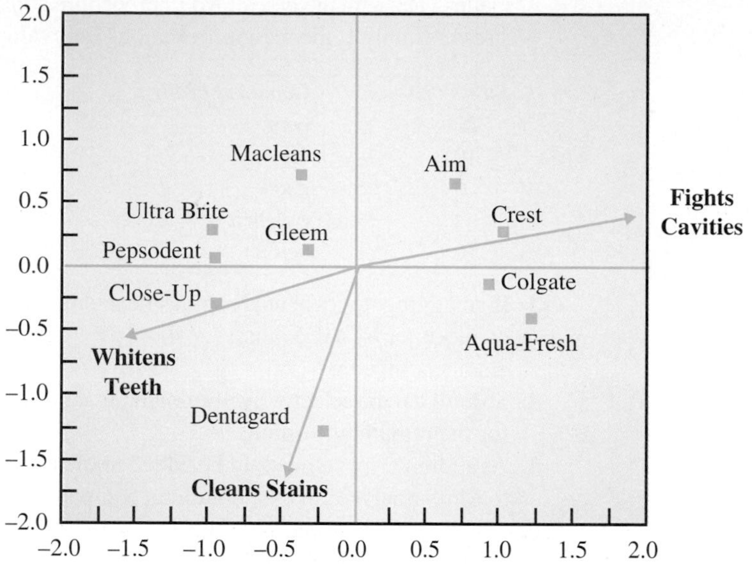

*Figure 21.5*
Using Attribute Vectors
to Label Dimensions

2. After providing direct similarity or preference data, the respondents may be asked to indicate the criteria they used in making their evaluations. These criteria may then be subjectively related to the spatial map to label the dimensions.
3. If possible, the respondents can be shown their spatial maps and asked to label the dimensions by inspecting the configurations.
4. If objective characteristics of the brands are available (e.g., horsepower or miles per gallon for automobiles), these could be used as an aid in interpreting the subjective dimensions of the spatial maps.

Often, the dimensions represent more than one attribute. The configuration or the spatial map may be interpreted by examining the coordinates and relative positions of the brands. For example, brands located near each other compete more fiercely. An isolated brand has a unique image. Brands that are farther along in the direction of a descriptor are stronger on that characteristic. Thus, the strengths and weaknesses of each product can be understood. Gaps in the spatial map may indicate potential opportunities for introducing new products.

In Figure 21.5, the horizontal axis might be labeled as cavity-fighting protection versus whiteness of teeth. Brands with high positive values on this axis include Aqua-Fresh, Crest, Colgate, and Aim (high cavity-fighting protection). Brands with large negative values on this dimension include Ultra Brite, Close-Up, and Pepsodent (high whiteness of teeth). The vertical axis may be interpreted as poor stain removal versus good stain removal. Note that Dentagard, known for its stain-removing ability, loads negatively on the vertical axis. The gaps in the spatial map indicate potential opportunities for a brand that offers high cavity protection as well as high stain removal.

## Assess Reliability and Validity

The input data, and consequently the MDS solutions, are invariably subject to substantial random variability. Hence, it is necessary that some assessment be made of the reliability and validity of MDS solutions. The following guidelines are suggested.

1. The index of fit, or $R$-square, should be examined. This is a squared correlation index that indicates the proportion of variance of the optimally scaled data that can be accounted for by the MDS procedure. Thus, it indicates how well the MDS model fits the input data. Although higher values of $R$-square are desirable, values of 0.60 or better are considered acceptable.
2. Stress values are also indicative of the quality of MDS solutions. Whereas $R$-square is a measure of goodness of fit, stress measures badness of fit, or the proportion of variance of the optimally scaled data that is not accounted for by the MDS model. Stress

values vary with the type of MDS procedure and the data being analyzed. For Kruskal's stress formula 1, the recommendations for evaluating stress values are as follows.[8]

| Stress (%) | Goodness of Fit |
|------------|-----------------|
| 20         | poor            |
| 10         | fair            |
| 5          | good            |
| 2.5        | excellent       |
| 0          | perfect         |

3. If an aggregate-level analysis has been done, the original data should be split into two or more parts. MDS analysis should be conducted separately on each part and the results compared.
4. Stimuli can be selectively eliminated from the input data and the solutions determined for the remaining stimuli.
5. A random error term could be added to the input data. The resulting data are subjected to MDS analysis and the solutions compared.
6. The input data could be collected at two different points in time and the test-retest reliability determined.

Formal procedures are available for assessing the validity of MDS. In the case of our illustrative example, the stress value of 0.095 indicates a fair fit. One brand, namely Dentagard, is different from the others. Would the elimination of Dentagard from the stimulus set appreciably alter the relative configuration of the other brands? The spatial map obtained by deleting Dentagard is shown in Figure 21.6. There is some change in the relative positions of the brands, particularly Gleem and Macleans. Yet the changes are modest, indicating fair stability.[9]

## ASSUMPTIONS AND LIMITATIONS OF MDS

It is worthwhile to point out some assumptions and limitations of MDS. It is assumed that the similarity of stimulus A to B is the same as the similarity of stimulus B to A. There are some instances where this assumption may be violated. For example, Mexico is perceived as more similar to United States than United States is to Mexico. MDS assumes that the distance (similarity) between two stimuli is some function of their partial similarities on each of several perceptual dimensions. Not much research has been done to test this assumption. When a spatial map is obtained, it is assumed that interpoint distances are ratio scaled and that the axes of the map are multidimensional interval scaled. A limitation of MDS is that dimension interpretation relating physical changes in brands or stimuli to changes in the perceptual map is difficult at best. These limitations also apply to the scaling of preference data.

**Figure 21.6**
Assessment of Stability
by Deleting One Brand

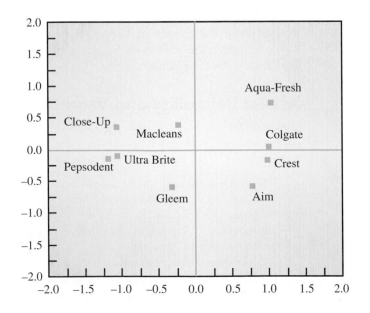

# SCALING PREFERENCE DATA

**internal analysis of preferences**
A method of configuring a spatial map such that the spatial map represents both brands or stimuli and respondent points or vectors and is derived solely from the preference data.

**external analysis of preferences**
A method of configuring a spatial map such that the ideal points or vectors based on preference data are fitted in a spatial map derived from perception data.

Analysis of preference data can be internal or external. In ***internal analysis of preferences,*** a spatial map representing both brands or stimuli and respondent points or vectors is derived solely from the preference data. Thus, by collecting preference data, both brands and respondents can be represented in the same spatial map. In ***external analysis of preferences,*** the ideal points or vectors based on preference data are fitted in a spatial map derived from perception (e.g., similarities) data. In order to perform external analysis, both preference and perception data must be obtained. The representation of both brands and respondents as points in the same space, by using internal or external analysis, is referred to as *unfolding.*

External analysis is preferred in most situations. In internal analysis, the differences in perceptions are confounded with differences in preferences. It is possible that the nature and relative importance of dimensions may vary between the perceptual space and the preference space. Two brands may be perceived to be similar (located close to each other in the perceptual space), yet, one brand may be distinctly preferred over the other (i.e., the brands may be located apart in the preference space). These situations cannot be accounted for in internal analysis. In addition, internal analysis procedures are beset with computational difficulties.[10]

We illustrate external analysis by scaling the preferences of our respondent into his spatial map. The respondent ranked the brands in the following order of preference (most preferred first): Colgate, Crest, Aim, Aqua-Fresh, Gleem, Pepsodent, Ultra Brite, Macleans, Close-Up, and Dentagard. These preference rankings, along with the coordinates of the spatial map (Figure 21.5), were used as input into a preference scaling program to derive Figure 21.7. Notice the location of the ideal point. It is close to Colgate, Crest, Aim, and Aqua-Fresh, the four most preferred brands and far from Close-Up and Dentagard, the two least preferred brands. If a new brand were to be located in this space, its distance from the ideal point, relative to the distances of other brands from the ideal point, would determine the degree of preference for this brand. Another application is provided by the following example.

**Figure 21.7**
External Analysis of Preference Data

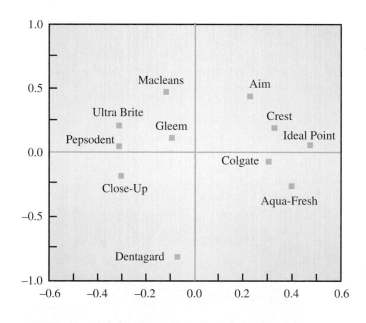

## REAL RESEARCH

### *Respondents Park in Different Spaces*

A study conducted in 2001 examined consumer perceptions of automobiles by using multidimensional scales. Subjects rated several automobile attributes and the effect those attributes had on final product choice. Ratings were conducted using a five-point scale, and each subject's responses were summed across each dimension. The five highest scoring attributes overall were price, braking, fuel economy, net horsepower, and acceleration. The use of multidimensional scaling can help automakers better understand what attributes are most important to consumers, and they can use that knowledge to leverage their positioning in the industry. An illustrative MDS map of selected automobile brands derived from similarity data is shown. In this spatial representation, each brand is identified by its distance from the other brands. The closer two brands are (e.g., Volkswagen and Chrysler), the more similar they are perceived to be. The further apart two brands are (e.g., Volkswagen and Mercedes), the less similar they are perceived to be. Small distance (i.e., similarity) may also indicate competition. To illustrate, Honda competes closely with Toyota but not with Continental or Porsche. The dimensions can be interpreted as economy/prestige versus sportiness/nonsportiness, and the position of each car on these dimensions can be determined.

The preference data consisted of a simple rank order of the brands according to consumers' preferences. Respondents' ideal points are also located in the same spatial representation. Each ideal point represents the locus of preference of a particular respondent. Thus, respondent 1 (denoted by I1) prefers the sporty cars: Porsche, Jaguar, and Audi. Respondent 2 (denoted by I2) on the other hand, prefers luxury cars: Continental, Mercedes, Lexus, and Cadillac.

Such analysis can be done at the individual-respondent level, enabling the researcher to segment the market according to similarities in the respondents' ideal points. Alternatively, the respondents can be clustered based on their similarity with respect to the original preference ranking and ideal points established for each segment.[11] ∎

**Joint Space Configuration of Automobile Brands and Consumer Preferences**

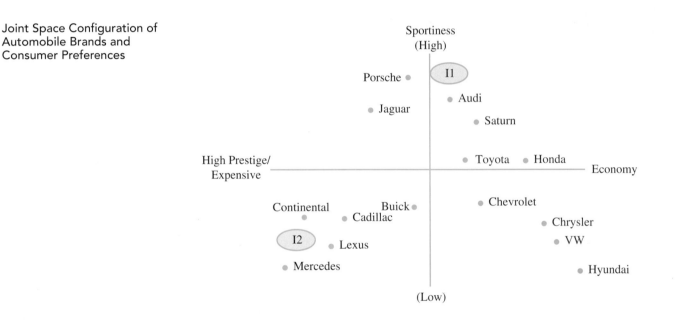

MDS has been used to identify consumers who prefer sporty cars, like Porsche.

Whereas, so far, we have considered only quantitative data, qualitative data can also be mapped using procedures such as correspondence analysis.

## CORRESPONDENCE ANALYSIS

*correspondence analysis*
A MDS technique for scaling qualitative data that scales the rows and columns of the input contingency table in corresponding units so that each can be displayed in the same low-dimensional space.

*Correspondence analysis* is an MDS technique for scaling qualitative data in marketing research. The input data are in the form of a contingency table indicating a qualitative association between the rows and columns. Correspondence analysis scales the rows and columns in corresponding units, so that each can be displayed graphically in the same low-dimensional space. These spatial maps provide insights into (1) similarities and differences within the rows with respect to a given column category; (2) similarities and differences within the column categories with respect to a given row category; and (3) relationship among the rows and columns.[12]

The interpretation of results in correspondence analysis is similar to that in principal components analysis (Chapter 19), given the similarity of the algorithms. Correspondence analysis results in the grouping of categories (activities, brands, or other stimuli) found within the contingency table, just as principal components analysis involves the grouping of the variables. The results are interpreted in terms of proximities among the rows and columns of the contingency table. Categories that are closer together are more similar in underlying structure.

The advantage of correspondence analysis, as compared to other multidimensional scaling techniques, is that it reduces the data-collection demands imposed on the respondents, because only binary or categorical data are obtained. The respondents are merely asked to check which attributes apply to each of several brands. The input data are the number of "yes" responses for each brand on each attribute. The brands and the attributes are then displayed in the same multidimensional space. The disadvantage is that between-set (i.e., between column and row) distances cannot be meaningfully interpreted. Correspondence analysis is an exploratory data analysis technique that is not suitable for hypothesis testing.[13]

MDS, including correspondence analysis, is not the only procedure available for obtaining perceptual maps. Two other techniques that we have discussed before, discriminant analysis (Chapter 18) and factor analysis (Chapter 19), can also be used for this purpose.

## RELATIONSHIP AMONG MDS, FACTOR ANALYSIS, AND DISCRIMINANT ANALYSIS

If the attribute-based approaches are used to obtain input data, spatial maps can also be obtained by using factor or discriminant analysis. In this approach, each respondent rates $n$ brands on $m$ attributes. By factor analyzing the data, one could derive for each respondent, $n$ factor scores for each factor, one for each brand. By plotting brand scores on the factors, a spatial map could be obtained for each respondent. If an aggregate map is desired, the factor score for each brand for each factor can be averaged across respondents. The dimensions would be labeled by examining the factor loadings, which are estimates of the correlations between attribute ratings and underlying factors.

The goal of discriminant analysis is to select the linear combinations of attributes that best discriminate between the brands or stimuli. To develop spatial maps by means of discriminant analysis, the dependent variable is the brand rated and the independent or predictor variables are the attribute ratings. A spatial map can be obtained by plotting the discriminant scores for the brands. The discriminant scores are the ratings on the perceptual dimensions, based on the attributes that best distinguish the brands. The dimensions can be labeled by examining the discriminant weights, or the weightings of attributes that make up a discriminant function or dimension.[14]

## BASIC CONCEPTS IN CONJOINT ANALYSIS

*conjoint analysis*
A technique that attempts to determine the relative importance consumers attach to salient attributes and the utilities they attach to the levels of attributes.

*Conjoint analysis* attempts to determine the relative importance consumers attach to salient attributes and the utilities they attach to the levels of attributes. This information is derived from consumers' evaluations of brands, or brand profiles composed of these attributes and their levels. The respondents are presented with stimuli that consist of combinations of attribute levels. They are asked to evaluate these stimuli in terms of their desirability. Conjoint procedures attempt to assign values to the levels of each attribute, so that the resulting values or utilities attached to the stimuli match, as closely as possible, the input evaluations provided by the respondents. The underlying assumption is that any set of stimuli, such as products, brands, or stores, is evaluated as a bundle of attributes.[15]

Like multidimensional scaling, conjoint analysis relies on respondents' subjective evaluations. However, in MDS, the stimuli are products or brands. In conjoint analysis, the stimuli are combinations of attribute levels determined by the researcher. The goal in MDS is to develop a spatial map depicting the stimuli in a multidimensional perceptual or preference space. Conjoint analysis, on the other hand, seeks to develop the part-worth or utility functions describing the utility consumers attach to the levels of each attribute. The two techniques are complementary.

Conjoint analysis has been used in marketing for a variety of purposes, including:

■ Determining the relative importance of attributes in the consumer choice process. A standard output from conjoint analysis consists of derived relative importance weights for all the attributes used to construct the stimuli used in the evaluation task. The relative importance weights indicate which attributes are important in influencing consumer choice.

■ Estimating market share of brands that differ in attribute levels. The utilities derived from conjoint analysis can be used as input into a choice simulator to determine the share of choices, and hence the market share, of different brands.

■ Determining the composition of the most preferred brand. The brand features can be varied in terms of attribute levels and the corresponding utilities determined. The brand features that yield the highest utility indicate the composition of the most preferred brand.

■ Segmenting the market based on similarity of preferences for attribute levels. The part-worth functions derived for the attributes may be used as a basis for clustering respondents to arrive at homogeneous preference segments.[16]

Applications of conjoint analysis have been made in consumer goods, industrial goods, financial, and other services. Moreover, these applications have spanned all areas of marketing. A survey of conjoint analysis reported applications in the areas of new product/concept identification, competitive analysis, pricing, market segmentation, advertising, and distribution.[17]

## STATISTICS AND TERMS ASSOCIATED WITH CONJOINT ANALYSIS

The important statistics and terms associated with conjoint analysis include:

*Part-worth functions.* The part-worth functions or *utility functions* describe the utility consumers attach to the levels of each attribute.

*Relative importance weights.* The relative importance weights are estimated and indicate which attributes are important in influencing consumer choice.

*Attribute levels.* The attribute levels denote the values assumed by the attributes.

*Full profiles.* Full profiles or complete profiles of brands are constructed in terms of all the attributes by using the attribute levels specified by the design.

*Pairwise tables.* In pairwise tables, the respondents evaluate two attributes at a time until all the required pairs of attributes have been evaluated.

*Cyclical designs.* Cyclical designs are designs employed to reduce the number of paired comparisons.

*Fractional factorial designs.* Fractional factorial designs are designs employed to reduce the number of stimulus profiles to be evaluated in the full profile approach.

*Orthogonal arrays.* Orthogonal arrays are a special class of fractional designs that enable the efficient estimation of all main effects.

*Internal validity.* This involves correlations of the predicted evaluations for the holdout or validation stimuli with those obtained from the respondents.

# CONDUCTING CONJOINT ANALYSIS

Figure 21.8 lists the steps in conjoint analysis. Formulating the problem involves identifying the salient attributes and their levels. These attributes and levels are used for constructing the stimuli to be used in a conjoint evaluation task. The respondents rate or rank the stimuli using a suitable scale and the data obtained are analyzed. The results are interpreted and their reliability and validity assessed.

## Formulate the Problem

In formulating the conjoint analysis problem, the researcher must identify the attributes and attribute levels to be used in constructing the stimuli. Attribute levels denote the values assumed by the attributes. From a theoretical standpoint, the attributes selected should be salient in influencing consumer preference and choice. For example, in the choice of an automobile brand, price, gas mileage, interior space, and so forth should be included. From a managerial perspective, the attributes and their levels should be actionable. To tell a manager that consumers prefer a sporty car to one that is conservative looking is not helpful, unless sportiness and conservativeness are defined in terms of attributes over which a manager has control. The attributes can be identified through discussions with management and industry experts, analysis of secondary data, qualitative research, and pilot surveys. A typical conjoint analysis study involves six or seven attributes.

Once the salient attributes have been identified, their appropriate levels should be selected. The number of attribute levels determines the number of parameters that will be estimated and also influences the number of stimuli that will be evaluated by the respondents. To minimize the respondent evaluation task, and yet estimate the parameters with reasonable accuracy, it is desirable to restrict the number of attribute levels. The utility or part-worth function for the levels of an attribute may be nonlinear. For example, a consumer may prefer a medium-sized car to either a small or large one. Likewise, the utility for price may be nonlinear. The loss of utility in going from a low to a medium price may be much smaller than the loss in utility in going from a medium to a high price. In these cases, at least three levels should be used. Some attributes, though, may naturally occur in binary form (two levels): a car does or does not have a sunroof.

The attribute levels selected will affect the consumer evaluations. If the price of an automobile brand is varied at $10,000, $12,000, and $14,000, price will be relatively unimportant. On the other hand, if the price is varied at $10,000, $20,000, and $30,000, it will be an important factor. Hence, the researcher should take into account the attribute levels prevalent in the marketplace and the objectives of the study. Using attribute levels that are beyond the range reflected in the marketplace will decrease the believability of the evaluation task, but it will increase the accuracy with which the parameters are estimated. The general guideline is to select attribute levels so that the ranges are somewhat greater

*Figure 21.8*
Conducting Conjoint Analysis

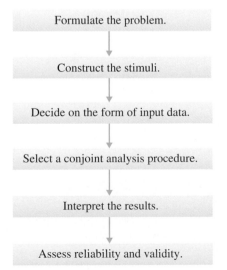

Formulate the problem.

Construct the stimuli.

Decide on the form of input data.

Select a conjoint analysis procedure.

Interpret the results.

Assess reliability and validity.

**TABLE 21.2**

**Sneaker Attributes and Levels**

| ATTRIBUTE | LEVEL NO. | DESCRIPTION |
|---|---|---|
| Sole | 3 | Rubber |
|  | 2 | Polyurethane |
|  | 1 | Plastic |
| Upper | 3 | Leather |
|  | 2 | Canvas |
|  | 1 | Nylon |
| Price | 3 | $30.00 |
|  | 2 | $60.00 |
|  | 1 | $90.00 |

than that prevalent in the marketplace but not so large as to adversely impact the believ-ability of the evaluation task.

We illustrate the conjoint methodology by considering the problem of how students evaluate sneakers. Qualitative research identified three attributes as salient: the sole, the upper, and the price.[18] Each was defined in terms of three levels, as shown in Table 21.2. These attributes and their levels were used for constructing the conjoint analysis stimuli. Note, to keep the illustration simple, we are using only a limited number, i.e., only three attributes. It has been argued that pictorial stimuli should be used when consumers' marketplace choices are strongly guided by the product's styling, such that the choices are heavily based on an inspection of actual products or pictures of products.[19]

## Construct the Stimuli

Two broad approaches are available for constructing conjoint analysis stimuli: the pairwise approach and the full-profile procedure. In the pairwise approach, also called *two-factor evaluations,* the respondents evaluate two attributes at a time until all the possible pairs of attributes have been evaluated. This approach is illustrated in the context of the sneaker example in Figure 21.9. For each pair, respondents evaluate all the combinations of levels

*Figure 21.9*

Pairwise Approach to Collecting Conjoint Data

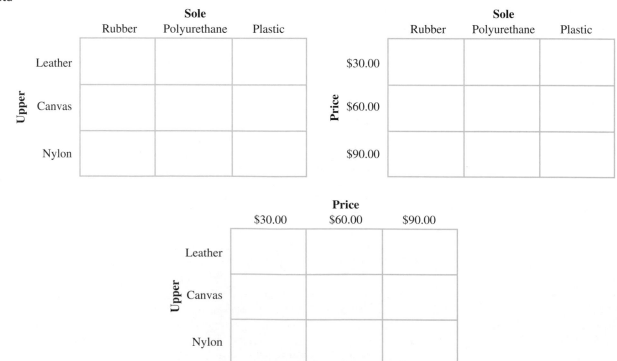

| TABLE 21.3 |  |
| --- | --- |
| **Full-Profile Approach to Collecting Conjoint Data** | |
| EXAMPLE OF A SNEAKER PRODUCT PROFILE | |
| Sole | Made of rubber |
| Upper | Made of nylon |
| Price | $30.00 |

of both the attributes, which are presented in a matrix. In the full-profile approach, also called *multiple-factor evaluations,* full or complete profiles of brands are constructed for all the attributes. Typically, each profile is described on a separate index card. This approach is illustrated in the context of the sneaker example in Table 21.3.

It is not necessary to evaluate all the possible combinations, nor is it feasible in all cases. In the pairwise approach, it is possible to reduce the number of paired comparisons by using cyclical designs. Likewise, in the full-profile approach, the number of stimulus profiles can be greatly reduced by means of fractional factorial designs. A special class of fractional designs, called orthogonal arrays, allows for the efficient estimation of all main effects. Orthogonal arrays permit the measurement of all main effects of interest on an uncorrelated basis. These designs assume that all interactions are negligible.[20] Generally, two sets of data are obtained. One, the *estimation set,* is used to calculate the part-worth functions for the attribute levels. The other, the *holdout set,* is used to assess reliability and validity.

The advantage of the pairwise approach is that it is easier for the respondents to provide these judgments. However, its relative disadvantage is that it requires more evaluations than the full-profile approach. Also, the evaluation task may be unrealistic when only two attributes are being evaluated simultaneously. Studies comparing the two approaches indicate that both methods yield comparable utilities, yet the full-profile approach is more commonly used.

The sneaker example follows the full-profile approach. Given three attributes, defined at three levels each, a total of $3 \times 3 \times 3 = 27$ profiles can be constructed. To reduce the respondent evaluation task, a fractional factorial design was employed and a set of nine profiles was constructed to constitute the estimation stimuli set (see Table 21.4). Another set of nine stimuli was constructed for validation purposes. Input data were obtained for both the estimation and validation stimuli. However, before the data could be obtained, it was necessary to decide on the form of the input data.

## Decide on the Form of Input Data

As in the case of MDS, conjoint analysis input data can be either nonmetric or metric. For nonmetric data, the respondents are typically required to provide rank order evaluations. For the pairwise approach, respondents rank all the cells of each matrix in terms of their desirability. For the full-profile approach, they rank all the stimulus profiles. Rankings involve relative evaluations of the attribute levels. Proponents of ranking data believe that such data accurately reflect the behavior of consumers in the marketplace.

In the metric form, the respondents provide ratings, rather than rankings. In this case, the judgments are typically made independently. Advocates of rating data believe that they are more convenient for the respondents and easier to analyze than rankings. In recent years, the use of ratings has become increasingly common.

In conjoint analysis, the dependent variable is usually preference or intention to buy. In other words, respondents provide ratings or rankings in terms of their preference or intentions to buy. However, the conjoint methodology is flexible and can accommodate a range of other dependent variables, including actual purchase or choice.

In evaluating sneaker profiles, respondents were required to provide preference ratings for the sneakers described by the nine profiles in the estimation set. These ratings were obtained using a nine-point Likert scale (1 = not preferred, 9 = greatly preferred). Ratings obtained from one respondent are shown in Table 21.4.

**TABLE 21.4**

**Sneaker Profiles and Their Ratings**

| PROFILE NO. | ATTRIBUTE LEVELS[a] | | | PREFERENCE RATING |
| | SOLE | UPPER | PRICE | |
| --- | --- | --- | --- | --- |
| 1 | 1 | 1 | 1 | 9 |
| 2 | 1 | 2 | 2 | 7 |
| 3 | 1 | 3 | 3 | 5 |
| 4 | 2 | 1 | 2 | 6 |
| 5 | 2 | 2 | 3 | 5 |
| 6 | 2 | 3 | 1 | 6 |
| 7 | 3 | 1 | 3 | 5 |
| 8 | 3 | 2 | 1 | 7 |
| 9 | 3 | 3 | 2 | 6 |

[a]The attribute levels correspond to those in Table 23.2

## Select a Conjoint Analysis Procedure

*conjoint analysis model*
The mathematical model expressing the fundamental relationship between attributes and utility in conjoint analysis.

The basic **conjoint analysis model** may be represented by the following formula:[21]

$$U(X) = \sum_{i=1}^{m} \sum_{j=1}^{k_i} \alpha_{ij} x_{ij}$$

where

$U(X)$ = overall utility of an alternative
$\alpha_{ij}$ = the part-worth contribution or utility associated with the $j$th level
   $(j, j = 1, 2, \ldots k_i)$ of the $i$th attribute $(i, i = 1, 2, \ldots m)$
$k_i$ = number of levels of attribute $i$
$m$ = number of attributes
$x_{ij}$ = 1 if the $j$th level of the $i$th attribute is present
   = 0 otherwise

Sneaker manufacturers like Nike have made use of conjoint analysis to develop sneakers with appealing features.

The importance of an attribute, $I_i$, is defined in terms of the range of the part-worths, $\alpha_{ij}$, across the levels of that attribute:

$$I_i = \{\max(\alpha_{ij}) - \min(\alpha_{ij})\}, \text{ for each } i$$

The attribute's importance is normalized to ascertain its importance relative to other attributes, $W_i$:

$$W_i = \frac{I_i}{\displaystyle\sum_{i=1}^{m} I_i}$$

so that

$$\sum_{i=1}^{m} W_i = 1$$

Several different procedures are available for estimating the basic model. The simplest, and one which is gaining in popularity, is dummy variable regression (see Chapter 17). In this case, the predictor variables consist of dummy variables for the attribute levels. If an attribute has $k_i$ levels, it is coded in terms of $k_i - 1$ dummy variables (see Chapter 14). If metric data are obtained, the ratings, assumed to be interval scaled, form the dependent variable. If the data are nonmetric, the rankings may be converted to 0 or 1 by making paired comparisons between brands. In this case, the predictor variables represent the differences in the attribute levels of the brands being compared. Other procedures that are appropriate for nonmetric data include LINMAP, MONANOVA, and the LOGIT model.[22]

The researcher must also decide whether the data will be analyzed at the individual-respondent or the aggregate level. At the individual level, the data of each respondent are analyzed separately. If an aggregate-level analysis is to be conducted, some procedure for grouping the respondents must be devised. One common approach is first to estimate individual-level part-worth or utility functions. The respondents are then clustered on the basis of the similarity of their part-worths. Aggregate analysis is then conducted for each cluster. An appropriate model for estimating the parameters should be specified.[23]

The data reported in Table 21.4 were analyzed using ordinary least-squares (OLS) regression with dummy variables. The dependent variable was the preference ratings. The independent variables or predictors were six dummy variables, two for each variable. The transformed data are shown in Table 21.5. Because the data pertain to a single respondent, an individual-level analysis was conducted. The part-worth or utility functions estimated for each attribute, as well the relative importance of the attributes, are given in Table 21.6.[24]

**TABLE 21.5**

**Sneaker Data Coded for Dummy Variable Regression**

| PREFERENCE RATINGS | | | ATTRIBUTES | | | |
|---|---|---|---|---|---|---|
| | SOLE | | UPPER | | PRICE | |
| Y | $X_1$ | $X_2$ | $X_3$ | $X_4$ | $X_5$ | $X_6$ |
| 9 | 1 | 0 | 1 | 0 | 1 | 0 |
| 7 | 1 | 0 | 0 | 1 | 0 | 1 |
| 5 | 1 | 0 | 0 | 0 | 0 | 0 |
| 6 | 0 | 1 | 1 | 0 | 0 | 1 |
| 5 | 0 | 1 | 0 | 1 | 0 | 0 |
| 6 | 0 | 1 | 0 | 0 | 1 | 0 |
| 5 | 0 | 0 | 1 | 0 | 0 | 0 |
| 7 | 0 | 0 | 0 | 1 | 1 | 0 |
| 6 | 0 | 0 | 0 | 0 | 0 | 1 |

**TABLE 21.6**

**Results of Conjoint Analysis**

| ATTRIBUTE | No. | LEVEL DESCRIPTION | UTILITY | IMPORTANCE |
|---|---|---|---|---|
| Sole | 3 | Rubber | 0.778 | |
| | 2 | Polyurethane | −0.556 | |
| | 1 | Plastic | −0.222 | 0.286 |
| Upper | 3 | Leather | 0.445 | |
| | 2 | Canvas | 0.111 | |
| | 1 | Nylon | −0.556 | 0.214 |
| Price | 3 | $30.00 | 1.111 | |
| | 2 | $60.00 | 0.111 | |
| | 1 | $90.00 | −1.222 | 0.500 |

The model estimated may be represented as:

$$U = b_0 + b_1X_1 + b_2X_2 + b_3X_3 + b_4X_4 + b_5X_5 + b_6X_6$$

where

$$X_1, X_2 = \text{dummy variables representing Sole}$$
$$X_3, X_4 = \text{dummy variables representing Upper}$$
$$X_5, X_6 = \text{dummy variables representing Price}$$

For Sole, the attribute levels were coded as follows:

| | $X_1$ | $X_2$ |
|---|---|---|
| Level 1 | 1 | 0 |
| Level 2 | 0 | 1 |
| Level 3 | 0 | 0 |

The levels of the other attributes were coded similarly. The parameters were estimated as follows:

$$b_0 = 4.222$$
$$b_1 = 1.000$$
$$b_2 = -0.333$$
$$b_3 = 1.000$$
$$b_4 = 0.667$$
$$b_5 = 2.333$$
$$b_6 = 1.333$$

Given the dummy variable coding, in which level 3 is the base level, the coefficients may be related to the part-worths. As explained in Chapter 17, each dummy variable coefficient represents the difference in the part-worth for that level minus the part-worth for the base level. For Sole, we have the following:

$$\alpha_{11} - \alpha_{13} = b_1$$
$$\alpha_{12} - \alpha_{13} = b_2$$

To solve for the part-worths, an additional constraint is necessary. The part-worths are estimated on an interval scale, so the origin is arbitrary. Therefore, the additional constraint that is imposed is of the form

$$\alpha_{11} + \alpha_{12} + \alpha_{13} = 0$$

These equations for the first attribute, Sole, are

$$\alpha_{11} - \alpha_{13} = 1.000$$
$$\alpha_{12} - \alpha_{13} = -0.333$$
$$\alpha_{11} + \alpha_{12} + \alpha_{13} = 0$$

Solving these equations, we get

$$\alpha_{11} = 0.778$$
$$\alpha_{12} = -0.556$$
$$\alpha_{13} = -0.222$$

The part-worths for other attributes reported in Table 21.6 can be estimated similarly. For Upper, we have

$$\alpha_{21} - \alpha_{23} = b_3$$
$$\alpha_{22} - \alpha_{23} = b_4$$
$$\alpha_{21} + \alpha_{22} + \alpha_{23} = 0$$

For the third attribute, Price, we have

$$\alpha_{31} - \alpha_{33} = b_5$$
$$\alpha_{32} - \alpha_{33} = b_6$$
$$\alpha_{31} + \alpha_{32} + \alpha_{33} = 0$$

The relative importance weights were calculated based on ranges of part-worths, as follows:

$$\text{Sum of ranges} = (0.778 - (-0.556)) + (0.445 - (-0.556))$$
$$\text{of part-worths} \quad + (1.111 - (-1.222))$$
$$= 4.668$$

$$\text{relative importance of Sole} = \frac{[0.778 - (-0.556)]}{4.668} = \frac{1.334}{4.668} = 0.286$$

$$\text{relative importance of Upper} = \frac{[0.445 - (-0.556)]}{4.668} = \frac{1.001}{4.668} = 0.214$$

$$\text{relative importance of Price} = \frac{[1.111 - (-1.222)]}{4.668} = \frac{2.333}{4.668} = 0.500$$

The estimation of the part-worths and the relative importance weights provides the basis for interpreting the results.

## Interpret the Results

For interpreting the results, it is helpful to plot the part-worth functions. The part-worth function values for each attribute given in Table 21.6 are graphed in Figure 21.10. As can be seen from Table 21.6 and Figure 21.10, this respondent has the greatest preference for a rubber sole when evaluating sneakers. Second preference is for a plastic sole, and a polyurethane sole is least preferred. A leather upper is most preferred, followed by canvas and nylon. As expected, a price of $30.00 has the highest utility and a price of $90.00 the lowest. The utility values reported in Table 21.6 have only interval-scale properties, and their origin is arbitrary. In terms of relative importance of the attributes, we see that Price is number one. Second most important is Sole, followed closely by Upper. Because price is by far the most important attribute for this respondent, this person could be labeled as price sensitive.

## Assessing Reliability and Validity

Several procedures are available for assessing the reliability and validity of conjoint analysis results.[25]

1. The goodness of fit of the estimated model should be evaluated. For example, if dummy variable regression is used, the value of $R^2$ will indicate the extent to which the model fits the data. Models with poor fit are suspect.
2. Test-retest reliability can be assessed by obtaining a few replicated judgments later in data collection. In other words, at a later stage in the interview, the respondents are asked to evaluate certain selected stimuli again. The two values of these stimuli are then correlated to assess test-retest reliability.

**Figure 21.10**
**Part-Worth Functions**

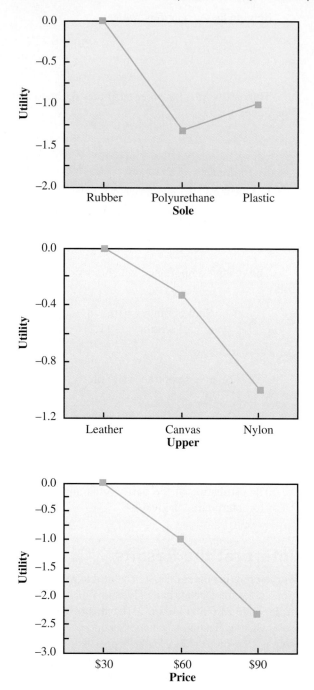

3. The evaluations for the holdout or validation stimuli can be predicted by the estimated part-worth functions. The predicted evaluations can then be correlated with those obtained from the respondents to determine internal validity.

4. If an aggregate-level analysis has been conducted, the estimation sample can be split in several ways and conjoint analysis conducted on each subsample. The results can be compared across subsamples to assess the stability of conjoint analysis solutions.

In running a regression analysis on the data of Table 21.5, an $R^2$ of 0.934 was obtained, indicating a good fit. The preference ratings for the nine validation profiles were predicted from the utilities reported in Table 21.6. These were correlated with the input ratings for these profiles obtained from the respondent. The correlation coefficient was 0.95, indicating good predictive ability. This correlation coefficient is significant at $\alpha = 0.05$.

**REAL RESEARCH**

## *Examining Microcomputer Trade-Offs Microscopically*

Consumers make trade-offs amongst various attributes when buying microcomputers.

Conjoint analysis was used to determine how consumers make trade-offs between various attributes when selecting microcomputers. Four attributes were chosen as salient. These attributes and their levels are:

**Input mode**
- Keyboard
- Mouse

**Screen size**
- 21 inch
- 15 inch

**Display monitor**
- CRT
- LCD (Flat Panel)

**Price level**
- $1,000
- $1,500
- $2,000

All possible combinations of these attribute levels result in 24 ($2 \times 2 \times 2 \times 3$) profiles of microcomputers. One such profile is as follows:

| | |
|---|---|
| Input mode: | Mouse |
| Display monitor: | LCD (Flat Panel) |
| Screen size: | 15″ |
| Price level: | $1,500 |

Respondents rank-ordered these profiles in terms of preferences. The data for each respondent can be utilized to develop preference functions. The preference functions for one individual are illustrated.

Consumer Preferences

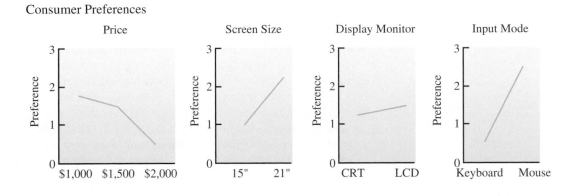

Based on the derived part-worth or preference functions, the relative importance of the various attributes in determining these consumer preferences can be estimated by comparing part-worths as follows:

Relative Importance

| Evaluative Criteria | Importance |
|---|---|
| Input mode | 35% |
| Display monitor | 15% |
| Screen size | 25% |
| Price level | 25% |

For this consumer, input mode is the most important feature and the mouse is the preferred option. Although price and screen size are also important, price becomes a factor only between $1,500 and $2,000. As expected, a screen size of 21″ is preferred. Whether the display monitor is CRT or LCD does not matter as much as the other factors. Information provided by the part-worth functions and relative importance weights can be used to cluster respondents to determine benefit segments for microcomputers.

Desktop and notebook computer makers such as Dell (*www.dell.com*) can make use of conjoint analysis as a way to find out whether consumers place more value on features such as speed, screen size, or disk space, or if consumers place more value on cost or weight. Anyway you look at it, conjoint analysis is continually being used by computer manufacturers and many other industries to deliver preferred products to consumers.[26] ■

# ASSUMPTIONS AND LIMITATIONS OF CONJOINT ANALYSIS

Although conjoint analysis is a popular technique, like MDS, it carries a number of assumptions and limitations. Conjoint analysis assumes that the important attributes of a product can be identified. Furthermore, it assumes that consumers evaluate the choice alternatives in terms of these attributes and make trade-offs. However, in situations where image or brand name is important, consumers may not evaluate the brands or alternatives in terms of attributes. Even if consumers consider product attributes, the trade-off model may not be a good representation of the choice process. Another limitation is that data collection may be complex, particularly if a large number of attributes are involved and the model must be estimated at the individual level. This problem has been mitigated to some extent by procedures such as interactive or adaptive conjoint analysis and hybrid conjoint analysis. It should also be noted that the part-worth functions are not unique.

# HYBRID CONJOINT ANALYSIS

**hybrid conjoint analysis**
A form of conjoint analysis that can simplify the data-collection task and estimate selected interactions as well as all main effects.

*Hybrid conjoint analysis* is an attempt to simplify the burdensome data-collection task required in traditional conjoint analysis. Each respondent evaluates a large number of profiles, yet usually only simple part-worths, without any interaction effects, are estimated. In the simple part-worths or main effects model, the value of a combination is simply the sum of the separate main effects (simple part-worths). In actual practice, two attributes may interact, in the sense that the respondent may value the combination more than the average contribution of the separate parts. Hybrid models have been developed to serve two main purposes: (1) simplify the data-collection task by imposing less of a burden on each respondent, and (2) permit the estimation of selected interactions (at the subgroup level) as well as all main (or simple) effects at the individual level.

In the hybrid approach, the respondents evaluate a limited number, generally no more than nine, conjoint stimuli, such as full profiles. These profiles are drawn from a large master design, and different respondents evaluate different sets of profiles, so that over a group of respondents, all the profiles of interest are evaluated. In addition, respondents directly evaluate the relative importance of each attribute and desirability of the levels of each attribute. By combining the direct evaluations with those derived from the evaluations of the conjoint stimuli, it is possible to estimate a model at the aggregate level and still retain some individual differences.[27]

MDS and conjoint analysis are complementary techniques and may be used in combination, as the following example shows.

## REAL RESEARCH

### Weeding Out the Competition

ICI Americas Agricultural Products did not know whether it should lower the price of Fusilade, its herbicide. It knew it had developed a potent herbicide, but it was not sure the weed killer would survive in a price-conscious market. So a survey was designed to assess the relative importance of different attributes in selecting herbicides and measure and map perceptions of major herbicides on the same attributes. Personal interviews were conducted with 601 soybean and cotton farmers who had at least 200 acres dedicated to growing these crops and who had used herbicides during the past growing season. First, conjoint analysis was used to determine the relative importance of attributes farmers use when selecting herbicides. Then multidimensional scaling was used to map farmers' perceptions of herbicides. The study showed that price greatly influenced herbicide selections, and respondents were particularly sensitive when costs were more than $18 an acre. But price was not the only determinant. Farmers also considered how much weed control the herbicide provided. They were willing to pay higher prices to keep the pests off their land. The study showed that herbicides that failed to control even one of the four most common weeds would have to be very inexpensive to attain a reasonable market share. Fusilade promised good weed control. Furthermore, multidimensional scaling indicated that one of Fusilade's competitors was considered to be expensive. Hence, ICI kept its original pricing plan and did not lower the price of Fusilade.

As of 2003, however, the agriculture industry has changed. One factor that has changed the industry is a shift in technology, especially biotechnology. Roundup Ready soybeans had a huge effect on the herbicide market, by making farmers switch from using traditional soybean herbicides to a new combined technology of Roundup and transgenic seed. The new technology cut the cost of per-acre herbicides in half and, as a result, competing chemical companies were forced to meet the price of the new technology. It is very important for companies to research consumer acceptance of technological innovations using techniques such as MDS and conjoint analysis to avoid being left by the wayside.[28] ■

Both MDS and conjoint analysis are useful in conducting international marketing research as illustrated by the next two examples. The example after that presents an application of MDS in researching ethical perceptions.

## REAL RESEARCH

### Herit-Age or Merit-Age in Europe?

European car manufacturers are increasingly focusing on an attribute that competitors will not be able to buy or build—it is heritage. For BMW, it is superior engineering. A. B. Volvo of Sweden has a reputation for safe cars. Italian Alfa Romeo rides on the laurels of engines that have won numerous races. The French Renault has savoir-faire. On the other hand, Japanese cars are advanced technologically but they do not have class or heritage. For example, Lexus and Infiniti are high-performance cars, but they lack class. Philip Gamba, VP-marketing at Renault, believes Japanese brands lack the "French touch" of that automaker's design and credibility. These days, Renault is building a car with a focus on comfort. BMW is trying to emphasize not the prestige of owning a luxury automobile but the "inner value" of its cars. To communicate value in cars is of growing importance. BMW has the edge of German heritage.

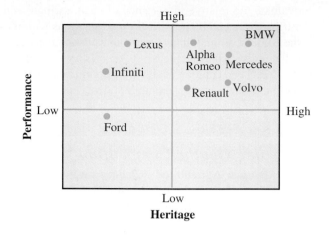

Because performance and heritage are important attributes or dimensions in automobile preferences of Europeans, the positioning of different European cars on these two dimensions is shown. Note that BMW has attained the best positioning on both these dimensions. Typical of most American and Japanese cars in the 2000s has been the emphasis on quality, reliability, and efficiency. However, to compete in the European market in the 21st century, Americans and Japanese are faced with the challenge of an added dimension—heritage. This calls for new marketing strategies by American and Japanese automakers. Due to the 2002 economic slowdown, it will be necessary for American automakers to employ new marketing strategies. For example, Ford introduced in 2003 a top-to-bottom evaluation of its overall marketing strategy in an effort to make the most of every dollar it spends for every brand and to compete effectively with European and Japanese brands.[29] ∎

## REAL RESEARCH

### *Fabs' Fabulous Foamy Fight*

Competition in the detergent market was brewing in Thailand. Superconcentrate detergent is fast becoming the prototype as of 2003. Market potential research in Thailand indicated that superconcentrates would continue to grow at a healthy rate, although the detergent market had slowed. In addition, this category had already dominated other Asian markets such as Taiwan, Hong Kong, and Singapore. Consequently, Colgate entered this new line of competition with Fab Power Plus with the objective of capturing 4 percent market share. The main players in the market were Kao Corp.'s Attack, Lever Brothers' Breeze Ultra and Omo, and Lion Corp.'s Pao Hand Force and Pao M. Wash. Based on qualitative research and secondary data, Colgate assessed the critical factors for the success of superconcentrates. Some of these factors were environmental appeal, hand washing and machine wash convenience, superior cleaning abilities, optimum level of suds for hand wash, and brand name. Market research also revealed that no brand had both hand and machine wash capabilities. Pao Hand Force was formulated as the hand washing brand. Pao M. Wash was the machine wash version. Lever's Breeze Ultra was targeted for machine use. Therefore, a formula that had both hand and machine wash capability was desirable. A conjoint study was designed and these factors varied at either two or three levels. Preference ratings were gathered from respondents and part-worths for the factors estimated both at the individual and the group level. Results showed that the factor on hand-machine capability had a substantial contribution supporting earlier claims. Based on these findings, Fab Power Plus was successfully introduced as a brand with both hand and machine wash capabilities.[30] ∎

## REAL RESEARCH

### *Ethical Perceptions of Marketing Research Firms*

In a refined scale to measure the degree a certain situation is ethical or unethical, three factors have been found to have acceptable validity and parsimony. Two of these dimensions

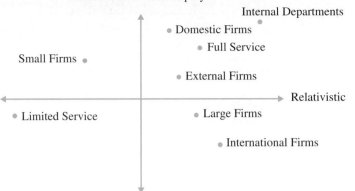

are particularly interesting. These are a broad-based moral equity dimension (factor 1), and a relativistic dimension (factor 2). Using multidimensional scaling, one can plot the perceived ethicalness of marketing research firms using these dimensions For example, an MDS plot might look like this.

In this example, internal marketing research departments are perceived to be the most ethical on both dimensions. Large marketing research firms are perceived to be more ethical on the relativistic dimension, whereas small firms are more ethical on the moral equity factor. International marketing research firms are more ethical on relativistic terms, whereas the domestic firms are higher on the moral equity dimension. Finally, full-service firms are perceived to be more ethical on both the dimensions as compared to the limited-service firms.

As of 2003, the marketing research industry was trying hard to portray that it maintained high ethical standards. These findings imply that marketing research firms (external firms) must convince the business world that their ethical standards are as high as those of internal marketing research departments of business firms. Also, if limited-service suppliers are to compete, then they must maintain and project the same ethical standards maintained by the full-service marketing research firms.[31] ■

# INTERNET AND COMPUTER APPLICATIONS

Over the years, several computer programs have been developed for conducting MDS analysis using microcomputers and mainframes. The ALSCAL program, available in the mainframe versions of both SPSS and SAS, incorporates several different MDS models and can be used for conducting individual or aggregate-level analysis. Other MDS programs are easily available and widely used. Most are available in both microcomputer and mainframe versions.

- MDSCAL 5M derives a spatial map of brands in a specified number of dimensions. Similarity data are used. A variety of input data formats and distance measures can be accommodated.
- KYST performs metric and nonmetric scaling and unfolding using similarity data.
- INDSCAL, denoting individual differences scaling, is useful for conducting MDS at the aggregate level. Similarity data are used as input.
- MDPREF performs internal analysis of preference data. The program develops vector directions for preferences and the configuration of brands or stimuli in a common space.
- PREFMAP performs external analysis of preference data. This program uses a known spatial map of brands or stimuli to portray an individual's preference data. PREFMAP2 performs both internal and external analysis.
- PC-MDS contains a variety of multidimensional scaling algorithms, including factor analysis, discriminant analysis, and some other multivariate procedures. It is available for the IBM PC and compatibles.

## FOCUS ON BURKE

A major role for Burke is advising clients in research design. Often clients will come to Burke with a request to execute the client's study design. It is our responsibility to advise the client if we see issues of application or interpretation. For example, in a full-profile conjoint for a cellular phone manufacturer, the following design was specified by the client.

**Factors: levels**

Power: 3 watts or 6 watts

Weight: 10 ounces or 14 ounces

Battery life: 30 minutes talk time; 1 hour talk time; 1.5 hours talk time; or 2 hours talk time

Brand: brand A; brand B

Price: Free with two-year subscription, $100, $200, or $250 (if you buy the phone, you can use
    any service you desire)

**Design Specifications:** Full factorial = 2 × 2 × 4 × 2 × 4 = 128 possible combinations

Because having a respondent evaluate 128 possible cellular phones was out of the question, a fractional factorial design (main effects only) using 16 profiles was selected. To see one of our objections to this design, a hypothetical respondent's answers are shown. The 16 profiles are:

|  | *Power* | *Weight* | *Talk Time* | *Brand* | *Price* |
|---|---|---|---|---|---|
| Profile 1: | 3 w | 10 oz. | 30 min | Brand B | Free |
| Profile 2: | 6 w | 10 oz. | 30 min | Brand B | $200 |
| Profile 3: | 6 w | 14 oz. | 30 min | Brand A | $250 |
| Profile 4: | 3 w | 14 oz. | 30 min | Brand A | $100 |
| Profile 5: | 6 w | 10 oz. | 1 hour | Brand A | $100 |
| Profile 6: | 3 w | 10 oz. | 1 hour | Brand A | $250 |
| Profile 7: | 3 w | 14 oz. | 1 hour | Brand B | $200 |
| Profile 8: | 6 w | 14 oz. | 1 hour | Brand B | Free |
| Profile 9: | 3 w | 14 oz. | 1.5 hours | Brand A | $200 |
| Profile 10: | 6 w | 14 oz. | 1.5 hours | Brand A | Free |
| Profile 11: | 6 w | 10 oz. | 1.5 hours | Brand B | $100 |
| Profile 12: | 3 w | 10 oz. | 1.5 hours | Brand B | $250 |
| Profile 13: | 6 w | 14 oz. | 2 hours | Brand B | $250 |
| Profile 14: | 3 w | 14 oz. | 2 hours | Brand B | $100 |
| Profile 15: | 3 w | 10 oz. | 2 hours | Brand A | Free |
| Profile 16: | 6 w | 10 oz. | 2 hours | Brand A | $200 |

- APM (Adaptive Perceptual Mapping) is an adaptive scaling program, available for the microcomputer, which can handle up to 30 brands and 50 attributes. There is no limit on the number of respondents per study or the number of computers that can be used to collect the data.
- MAPWISE by Market Action Research Software, Inc., is perceptual mapping software for conducting correspondence analysis. CORRESPONDENCE ANALYSIS by the Beaumont Organization Ltd. conducts correspondence analysis, what-if simulations, and ideal product analysis. Another program for correspondence analysis is SIMCA by Greenacre.

If OLS regression is used as the estimation procedure in conjoint analysis, these programs are universally available. In particular, the microcomputer and mainframe versions of SAS, SPSS, MINITAB, and EXCEL have several regression programs. These were dis-

One respondent's ratings on a 10-point purchase interest scale:

| | |
|---|---|
| Profile 1: 2 | Profile 9: 1 |
| Profile 2: 5 | Profile 10: 4 |
| Profile 3: 1 | Profile 11: 10 |
| Profile 4: 1 | Profile 12: 5 |
| Profile 5: 5 | Profile 13: 6 |
| Profile 6: 1 | Profile 14: 8 |
| Profile 7: 3 | Profile 15: 3 |
| Profile 8: 6 | Profile 16: 5 |

Subjecting this respondent's data to OLS regression, using the design matrix as predictor variables, the following results emerge.

| *Attribute* | *Utility Value* | *Relative Importance* |
|---|:---:|:---:|
| **Power** | | |
| 3 Watts | −1.12 | |
| 6 Watts | 1.12 | 18.8% |
| **Weight** | | |
| 10 oz. | 0.375 | |
| 14 oz. | −0.375 | 6.0% |
| **Battery Life** | | |
| 30 min. | −1.875 | |
| 1 hour | −0.375 | |
| 1.5 hours | 0.875 | |
| 2.0 hours | 1.375 | 27.1% |
| **Brand** | | |
| A | 1.5 | |
| B | −1.5 | 25.0% |
| **Price** | | |
| Free w/ 2 yr. sub. | −0.375 | |
| $100 | 1.875 | |
| $200 | −0.625 | |
| $250 | −0.875 | 22.9% |

Why would Burke question this design?

First, management wanted to understand the sensitivity to price. This model would assume that either both brands had the same price elasticity or management would gain the needed information from an "average" price elasticity for the two brands. When directly asked about this, the client had not considered that this "price sensitivity" may not actually fit either brand. Burke suggested a design that would examine the interaction between brand and price, as this is a way to examine the price elasticity of a brand (not an average of brands).

cussed in Chapter 17. Several specialized programs are also available for conjoint analysis. MONANOVA (Monotone Analysis of Variance) is a nonmetric procedure that uses full-profile data. For pairwise data, the TRADEOFF procedure can be used. TRADEOFF is also a nonmetric procedure that uses the rank ordering of preferences for attribute-level pairs. Both MONANOVA and TRADEOFF are available for the mainframe and microcomputers. Other popular programs include LINMAP and ACA (Adaptive Conjoint Analysis). ACA focuses on the attributes and levels most relevant for each individual respondent. PC-MDS also contains a program for conjoint analysis. Other useful programs include software by Bretton-Clark, including CONJOINT DESIGNER, CONJOINT ANALYZER, CONJOINT LINMAP, SIMGRAF, and BRIDGER. POSSE (Product Optimization and Selected Segmentation Evaluation) by Robinson Associates, Inc., is a generalized system for optimizing product and service designs using hybrid conjoint analysis and experimental design methods. It uses consumer choice simulators, response surface modeling, and optimization procedures to develop optimal product configurations. Choice-based conjoint (CBC) and multimedia conjoint programs that demonstrate product features rather than just describe them are also available, for example, from Sawtooth Technologies (*www.sawtooth.com*).

### SPSS Windows

The multidimensional scaling program allows individual differences as well as aggregate analysis using ALSCAL. The level of measurement can be ordinal, interval, or ratio. Both the direct and the derived approaches can be accommodated. To select multidimensional scaling procedures using SPSS for Windows, click:

Analyze>Scale>Multidimensional Scaling . . .

The conjoint analysis approach can be implemented using regression if the dependent variable is metric (interval or ratio). This procedure can be run by clicking:

Analyze>Regression>Linear . . .

## SUMMARY

Multidimensional scaling is used for obtaining spatial representations of respondents' perceptions and preferences. Perceived or psychological relationships among stimuli are represented as geometric relationships among points in a multidimensional space. Formulating the MDS problem requires a specification of the brands or stimuli to be included. The number and nature of brands selected influences the resulting solution. Input data obtained from the respondents can be related to perceptions or preferences. Perception data can be direct or derived. The direct approaches are more common in marketing research.

The selection of an MDS procedure depends on the nature (metric or nonmetric) of the input data and whether perceptions or preferences are being scaled. Another determining factor is whether the analysis will be conducted at the individual or aggregate level. The decision about the number of dimensions in which to obtain a solution should be based on theory, interpretability, elbow criterion, and ease-of-use considerations. Labeling of the dimensions is a difficult task that requires subjective judgment. Several guidelines are available for assessing the reliability and validity of MDS solutions. Preference data can be subjected to either internal or external analysis. If the input data are of a qualitative nature, they can be analyzed via correspondence analysis. If the attribute-based approaches are used to obtain input data, spatial maps can also be obtained by means of factor or discriminant analysis.

Conjoint analysis is based on the notion that the relative importance that consumers attach to salient attributes, and the utilities they attach to the levels of attributes, can be determined when consumers evaluate brand profiles that are constructed using these attributes and their levels. Formulating the problem requires an identification of the salient attributes and their levels. The pairwise and the full-profile approaches are commonly employed for constructing the stimuli. Statistical designs are available for reducing the number of stimuli in the evaluation task. The input data can be either nonmetric (rankings) or metric (ratings). Typically, the dependent variable is preference or intention to buy.

Although other procedures are available for analyzing conjoint analysis data, regression using dummy variables is becoming increasingly important. Interpretation of the results requires an examination of the part-worth functions and relative importance weights. Several procedures are available for assessing the reliability and validity of conjoint analysis results.

## KEY TERMS AND CONCEPTS

# EXERCISES

## Questions

1. For what purposes are MDS procedures used?
2. What is meant by a spatial map?
3. Describe the steps involved in conducting MDS.
4. Describe the direct and derived approaches to obtaining MDS input data.
5. What factors influence the choice of an MDS procedure?
6. What guidelines are used for deciding on the number of dimensions in which to obtain an MDS solution?
7. Describe the ways in which the reliability and validity of MDS solutions can be assessed.
8. What is the difference between internal and external analysis of preference data?
9. Briefly describe correspondence analysis.
10. What is involved in formulating a conjoint analysis problem?
11. Describe the full-profile approach to constructing stimuli in conjoint analysis.
12. Describe the pairwise approach to constructing stimuli in conjoint analysis.
13. How can regression analysis be used for analyzing conjoint data?
14. Graphically illustrate what is meant by part-worth functions.
15. What procedures are available for assessing the reliability and validity of conjoint analysis results?
16. Briefly describe hybrid conjoint analysis.

## Problems

1. Identify two marketing research problems where MDS could be applied. Explain how you would apply MDS in these situations.
2. Identify two marketing research problems where conjoint analysis could be applied. Explain how you would apply conjoint analysis in these situations.

# INTERNET AND COMPUTER EXERCISES

1. A respondent's ratings of nine luxury car brands on four dimensions are shown. Each brand was evaluated on each dimension (prestige, performance, luxury, and value) on a seven-point scale with 1 = poor and 7 = excellent. Using SPSS WINDOWS or alternative software, develop an MDS plot in two dimensions. Interpret the dimensions. Explain the plot.

| Brand | Prestige | Performance | Luxury | Value |
|-------|----------|-------------|--------|-------|
| Lexus | 5.00 | 7.00 | 5.00 | 7.00 |
| Infinity | 5.00 | 6.00 | 5.00 | 7.00 |
| BMW | 5.00 | 7.00 | 6.00 | 5.00 |
| Mercedes | 6.00 | 6.00 | 6.00 | 6.00 |
| Cadillac | 5.00 | 5.00 | 6.00 | 5.00 |
| Lincoln | 6.00 | 6.00 | 5.00 | 5.00 |
| Porsche | 5.00 | 6.00 | 5.00 | 4.00 |
| Bentley | 7.00 | 4.00 | 7.00 | 3.00 |
| Rolls | 7.00 | 5.00 | 7.00 | 1.00 |

2. Analyze the data of Table 21.1 using an appropriate MDS procedure. Compare your results to those given in the text.
3. Analyze the similarity judgments that you provided for the 12 bath soap brands in Fieldwork exercise 1. Use an appropriate MDS procedure, such as ALSCAL. Label the dimensions and interpret your own spatial map.
4. Use OLS regression to develop part-worth functions for the three sneaker attributes using the data you provided in Fieldwork exercise 2. How do your results compare with those reported in the text?

# ACTIVITIES

## Fieldwork

1. Consider the following 12 brands of bath soap: Jergens, Dove, Zest, Dial, Camay, Ivory, Palmolive, Irish Spring, Lux, Safeguard, Tone, and Monchel. Form all the possible 66 pairs of these brands. Rate these pairs of brands in terms of similarity, using a seven-point scale.
2. Construct the nine sneaker profiles given in Table 21.4. Rate these nine profiles in terms of your preference, using a nine-point rating scale.

## Group Discussion

1. As a small group, discuss the similarities and differences between MDS and conjoint analysis.
2. Discuss, as a small group, the similarities and differences between MDS, factor analysis, and discriminant analysis.

# Report Preparation and Presentation

"If your report doesn't make the information easy to understand, believable, and actionable . . . it is likely that management won't value your work."

*Nancy Bunn,
director, corporate
communications,
Burke, Inc.*

## Objectives

After reading this chapter, the student should be able to:

1. Discuss the basic requirements of report preparation including report format, report writing, graphs, and tables.
2. Discuss the nature and scope of the oral presentation and describe the "Tell 'Em" and "KISS 'Em" principles.
3. Describe the approach to the marketing research report from the client's perspective and the guidelines for reading the research report.
4. Explain the reason for follow-up with the client and describe the assistance that should be given to the client and the evaluation of the research project.
5. Understand the report preparation and presentation process in international marketing research.
6. Identify the ethical issues related to the interpretation and reporting of the research process and findings to the client and the use of these results by the client.
7. Explain the use of the Internet and computers in report preparation and presentation.

## Overview

Report preparation and presentation constitutes the sixth and final step in a marketing research project. It follows problem definition, approach development, research design formulation, fieldwork, and data preparation and analysis. This chapter describes the importance of this final step, as well as a process for report preparation and presentation. We provide guidelines for report preparation, including report writing and preparing tables and graphs. We discuss oral presentation of the report. Research follow-up, including assisting the client and evaluating the research process, is described. The special considerations for report preparation and presentation in international marketing research are discussed, and the relevant ethical issues identified. We conclude by explaining the role of the Internet and computers in report preparation and presentation.

**ACTIVE RESEARCH** | DEPARTMENT STORE PROJECT

### Report Preparation and Presentation

In the department store project, the formal report was prepared for the client's vice president of marketing. The first volume, the main body of the report, had a title page, table of contents, executive summary, and details of problem definition, approach, research design, methodology used to analyze the data, results, limitations of the project, and conclusions and recommendations. Volume II contained a title page, list of figures, and all the figures and graphs. Finally, all the statistical details, including all the tables, were given in Volume III. The writing of the report was influenced by the style preferences of the vice president for marketing and other key executives. Volume I had a nontechnical orientation and was easy to follow. In addition to the written report, an oral presentation of the entire project was made to the top management. Several of the recommendations made to management in the report were eventually implemented.

**REAL RESEARCH**

## Reporting the Friendly Skies

The task of Marketing Research is to assess information needs, to provide this information, and to help the decision maker in making the right decision. That is what United Airlines, the Chicago-based airline company, has understood with its ongoing in-flight customer satisfaction tracking program. Each month, 192,000 passengers among 900 flights are selected and surveyed, using a four-page scannable form. The survey covers the satisfaction of passengers on both "on-the-ground services" (flight reservation, airport service) and "in-the-air services" (flight attendants, meal, aircraft). The attendants distribute the forms early in the flight, so that passengers can take time to fill in the questionnaire.

Each month the internal department of marketing research of United issues a report, summarizing customer satisfaction. The report is also posted on the Internet and available online to United managers all over the world. Because of the large size of the sample, the data are very reliable (representative) and all departments of the company use the report:

- the marketing department to make strategic planning, product positioning, and target marketing decisions;
- the finance department to measure the success of its product investments;
- the airport department to evaluate ground service, including speed and efficiency of check-in (service representatives, waiting lines);
- the executive management to evaluate the performance of United, both internally achieving its goals, and externally compared to the competition.

The result of this high-powered customer satisfaction report is that all departments at United Airlines are customer oriented. This helps the company to differentiate itself in an environment where all companies have the same schedules, the same service, and the same fare. For example, based on the survey results, United recognized that airline food is an important component of travelers' satisfaction and consequently improved its meal service. The company also established brand partnership with some well-known food companies, such as Starbucks coffee and Godiva Chocolates, and advertised that as one more reason to fly the friendly skies. In winter 2003, United Airlines reduced the prices of many of its routes when its surveys showed that many passengers were looking for low fares in a slow economy.[1] ■

The department store example illustrates how the main body of the report follows the format of the earlier steps of the marketing research process. The United Airlines example highlights the importance of regular reporting.

# IMPORTANCE OF THE REPORT AND PRESENTATION

For the following reasons, the report and its presentation are important parts of the marketing research project:

1. They are the tangible products of the research effort. After the project is complete and management has made the decision, there is little documentary evidence of the project other than the written report. The report serves as a historical record of the project.
2. Management decisions are guided by the report and the presentation. If the first five steps in the project are carefully conducted but inadequate attention is paid to the sixth step, the value of the project to management will be greatly diminished.
3. The involvement of many marketing managers in the project is limited to the written report and the oral presentation. These managers evaluate the quality of the entire project based on the quality of the report and presentation.
4. Management's decision to undertake marketing research in the future or to use the particular research supplier again will be influenced by the perceived usefulness of the report and the presentation.

# THE REPORT PREPARATION AND PRESENTATION PROCESS

Figure 22.1 illustrates report preparation and presentation. The process begins by interpreting the results of data analysis in light of the marketing research problem, approach, research design, and fieldwork. Instead of merely summarizing the statistical results, the researcher should present the findings in such a way that they can be used directly as input into decision making. Wherever appropriate, conclusions should be drawn and recommendations made. Recommendations should be actionable. Before writing the report, the researcher should discuss the major findings, conclusions, and recommendations with the

*Figure 22.1*
The Report Preparation and
Presentation Process

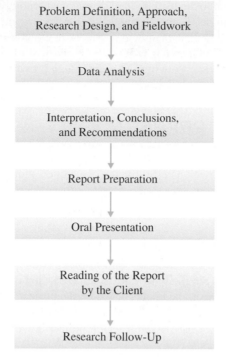

key decision makers. Discussions play a major role in ensuring that the report meets the client's needs and that the report is ultimately accepted. These discussions should confirm specific dates for the delivery of the written report and other data.

The entire marketing research project should be summarized in a single written report or in several reports addressed to different readers. Generally, an oral presentation supplements the written documents. The client should be given an opportunity to read the report. After that, the researcher should take necessary follow-up actions. The researcher should assist the client in understanding the report, implementing the findings, undertaking further research, and evaluating the research process in retrospect. The importance of the researcher being intimately involved in the report preparation and presentation process is highlighted by the following example.

### REAL RESEARCH

## *Focus Group Moderators' Ghostwriters Can Shortchange Clients*

Thomas Greenbaum, president of a market research company focusing on qualitative research, notes a disturbing trend in recent years in the focus group service sector. Greenbaum of Groups Plus, Inc. of Wilton, Connecticut, asserts that some moderators of focus groups misrepresent their work to clients because their reports are actually written by ghostwriters who did not participate in the focus group sessions.

According to Greenbaum, perhaps more than half of moderators use ghostwriters to develop their reports for clients. Often, junior researchers learning the business or part-time employees write these ghostwritten reports. Greenbaum criticizes such ghostwriting because the nonverbal reactions of focus group participants, or group synergy, cannot always be accurately reported by those who merely listen to audio tapes or view video tapes of focus group sessions. Greenbaum calls upon moderators to be forthright with clients about the authorship of focus group reports, and calls upon clients to be more demanding of their contracted research teams.

"Although some people in the industry defend ghostwriting by saying they always review the reports before they are sent to the client, or perhaps even write certain key sections, this practice must be looked at carefully by clients who use focus group research," Greenbaum said. "If the clients know in advance that their reports will be written by someone else, it is clearly less of a problem, but they still do not get the best effort from their research consultants."

In addition to the likelihood of degrading a report, Greenbaum observes that the ghost-writing system delays the submission of the final report. "Moderators who write their own reports try to complete them within a week or 10 days of the last group, so the information is still fresh in their minds when they do the writing," Greenbaum said. "However, most moderators (using ghostwriters) are not able to provide clients with final reports for three to four weeks after the last group, due to the process they use with ghostwriters."[2] ■

# REPORT PREPARATION

Researchers differ in the way they prepare a research report. The personality, background, expertise, and responsibility of the researcher, along with the decision maker (DM) to whom the report is addressed, interact to give each report a unique character. Yet, there are guidelines for formatting and writing reports and designing tables and graphs.[3]

# REPORT FORMAT

Report formats are likely to vary with the researcher or the marketing research firm conducting the project, the client for whom the project is being conducted, and the nature of the project itself. Hence, the following is intended as a guideline from which the researcher can develop a format for the research project at hand. Most research reports include the following elements:

    **I.** Title page
    **II.** Letter of transmittal
   **III.** Letter of authorization
   **IV.** Table of contents
    **V.** List of tables
   **VI.** List of graphs
  **VII.** List of appendices
 **VIII.** List of exhibits
   **IX.** Executive summary
      **a.** Major findings
      **b.** Conclusions
      **c.** Recommendations
    **X.** Problem definition
      **a.** Background to the problem
      **b.** Statement of the problem
   **XI.** Approach to the problem
  **XII.** Research design
      **a.** Type of research design
      **b.** Information needs
      **c.** Data collection from secondary sources
      **d.** Data collection from primary sources
      **e.** Scaling techniques
      **f.** Questionnaire development and pretesting
      **g.** Sampling techniques
      **h.** Fieldwork
 **XIII.** Data analysis
      **a.** Methodology
      **b.** Plan of data analysis
  **XIV.** Results
   **XV.** Limitations and caveats
  **XVI.** Conclusions and recommendations
 **XVII.** Exhibits
      **a.** Questionnaires and forms
      **b.** Statistical output
      **c.** Lists

This format closely follows the earlier steps of the marketing research process. The results may be presented in several chapters of the report. For example, in a national survey, data analysis may be conducted for the overall sample and then the data for each of the four geographic regions may be analyzed separately. If so, the results may be presented in five chapters instead of one.

## Title Page

The title page should include the title of the report, information (name, address, and telephone) about the researcher or organization conducting the research, the name of the client for whom the report was prepared, and the date of release. The title should indicate the nature of the project, as illustrated in the following example.

**REAL RESEARCH**

### *Elrick & Lavidge Guidelines on the Title Page*

Use client language in title—avoid "research-eze"

- "Practices Followed in Selecting Long-Distance Carriers"
  Better than "Long-Distance Service Study"
- "Customers' Reactions to an Expanded Financial/Insurance Relationship"
  Better than "Relationship Study"

© Copyright, Elrick & Lavidge, Inc. All rights reserved. Used by permission. ■

## Letter of Transmittal

A formal report generally contains a letter of transmittal that delivers the report to the client and summarizes the researcher's overall experience with the project, without mentioning the findings. The letter should also identify the need for further action on the part of the client, such as implementation of the findings or further research that should be undertaken.

## Letter of Authorization

A letter of authorization is written by the client to the researcher before work on the project begins. It authorizes the researcher to proceed with the project and specifies its scope and the terms of the contract. Often, it is sufficient to refer to the letter of authorization in the letter of transmittal. However, sometimes it is necessary to include a copy of the letter of authorization in the report.

## Table of Contents

The table of contents should list the topics covered and the appropriate page numbers. In most reports, only the major headings and subheadings are included. The table of contents is followed by a list of tables, list of graphs, list of appendices, and list of exhibits.

## Executive Summary

The executive summary is an extremely important part of the report, as this is often the only portion of the report that executives read. The summary should concisely describe the problem, approach, and research design that was adopted. A summary section should be devoted to the major results, conclusions, and recommendations. The executive summary should be written after the rest of the report has been completed.

## Problem Definition

This section of the report gives the background to the problem, highlights the discussions with the decision makers and industry experts, and discusses the secondary data analysis, the qualitative research that was conducted, and the factors that were considered. Moreover, it should contain a clear statement of the management decision problem and the marketing research problem (see Chapter 2).

## Approach to the Problem

This section should discuss the broad approach that was adopted in addressing the problem. This section should also contain a description of the theoretical foundations that guided the research, any analytical models formulated, research questions, hypotheses, and the factors that influenced the research design.

## Research Design

The section on research design should specify the details of how the research was conducted (see Chapters 3 to 13). This should include the nature of the research design adopted, information needed, data collection from secondary and primary sources, scaling techniques, questionnaire development and pretesting, sampling techniques, and fieldwork. These topics should be presented in a nontechnical, easy-to-understand manner. The technical details should be included in an appendix. This section of the report should justify the specific methods selected.

## Data Analysis

This section should describe the plan of data analysis and justify the data analysis strategy and techniques used. The techniques used for analysis should be described in simple, nontechnical terms.

## Results

This section is normally the longest part of the report and may comprise several chapters. Often, the results are presented not only at the aggregate level but also at the subgroup (market segment, geographical area, etc.) level. The results should be organized in a coherent and logical way. For example, in a health care marketing survey of hospitals, the results were presented in four chapters. One chapter presented the overall results, another examined the differences between geographical regions, a third presented the differences between for-profit and nonprofit hospitals, and a fourth presented the differences according to bed capacity. The presentation of the results should be geared directly to the components of the marketing research problem and the information needs that were identified. The details should be presented in tables and graphs, with the main findings discussed in the text.

## Limitations and Caveats

All marketing research projects have limitations caused by time, budget, and other organizational constraints. Furthermore, the research design adopted may be limited in terms of the various types of errors (see Chapter 3), and some of these may be serious enough to warrant discussion. This section should be written with great care and a balanced perspective. On one hand, the researcher must make sure that management does not overly rely on the results or use them for unintended purposes, such as projecting them to unintended populations. On the other hand, this section should not erode their confidence in the research or unduly minimize its importance.

## Conclusions and Recommendations

Presenting a mere summary of the statistical results is not enough. The researcher should interpret the results in light of the problem being addressed to arrive at major conclusions. Based on the results and conclusions, the researcher may make recommendations to the decision makers. Sometimes marketing researchers are not asked to make recommendations because they research only one area but do not understand the bigger picture at the client firm. If recommendations are made, they should be feasible, practical, actionable, and directly usable as inputs into managerial decision making. The following example contains guidelines on conclusions and recommendations.

## Elrick & Lavidge Guidelines on Conclusions and Recommendations

### Conclusions

- Conclusions
  Conclusions concerning, for example:
  - customer behavior
  - customer attitudes or perceptions
  - the nature of the markets studied

  Generally, in studies with samples designed to represent the market

  Avoid interesting results that are not relevant to the conclusions
- May be in the form of statement or paragraphs
- Use subheadings to identify conclusions covering different subjects or market segments

### Recommendations

- Recommendations regarding actions that should be taken or considered in light of the research results:

    Add/drop a product

    What to say in advertising—advertising positioning

    Market segments to select as primary targets

    How to price product

    Further research that should be considered
- Should be related to the stated purpose of the research
- Sometimes omitted—e.g.:

    Client staff members want to author the recommendations

    Study designed merely to familiarize client with a market
- Most clients are interested in our suggestions, in spite of the fact that we may not be familiar with internal financial issues and other internal corporate factors.

# REPORT WRITING

## Readers

A report should be written for a specific reader or readers: the marketing managers who will use the results. The report should take into account the readers' technical sophistication and interest in the project, as well as the circumstances under which they will read the report and how they will use it.

Technical jargon should be avoided. As expressed by one expert, "The readers of your reports are busy people; and very few of them can balance a research report, a cup of coffee, and a dictionary at one time."[4] Instead of technical terms such as maximum likelihood, heteroscedasticity, and nonparametric, use descriptive explanations. If some technical terms cannot be avoided, briefly define them in an appendix. When it comes to marketing research, people would rather live with a problem they cannot solve than accept a solution they cannot understand.

Often the researcher must cater to the needs of several audiences with different levels of technical sophistication and interest in the project. Such conflicting needs may be met by including different sections in the report for different readers, or by separate reports entirely.

## Easy to Follow

The report should be easy to follow.[5] It should be structured logically and written clearly. The material, particularly preparation body of the report, should be structured in a logical manner so that the reader can easily see the inherent connections and linkages. Headings should be used for different topics and subheadings for subtopics.

A logical organization also leads to a coherent report. Clarity can be enhanced by using well-constructed sentences that are short and to the point. The words used should express precisely what the researcher wants to communicate. Difficult words, slang, and clichés should be avoided. An excellent check on the clarity of a report is to have two or three people who are unfamiliar with the project read it and offer critical comments. Several revisions of the report may be needed before the final document emerges.

## Presentable and Professional Appearance

The appearance of a report is important. The report should be professionally reproduced with quality paper, typing, and binding. The typography should be varied. Variation in type size and skillful use of white space can greatly contribute to the appearance and readability of the report.

## Objective

Objectivity is a virtue that should guide report writing. Researchers can become so fascinated with their project that they overlook their scientific role. The report should accurately present the methodology, results, and conclusions of the project, without slanting the findings to conform to the expectations of management. Decision makers are unlikely to receive with enthusiasm a report that reflects unfavorably on their judgment or actions. However, the researcher must have the courage to present and defend the results objectively. The rule is, "Tell it like it is."

## Reinforce Text with Tables and Graphs

It is important to reinforce key information in the text with tables, graphs, pictures, maps, and other visual devices. Visual aids can greatly facilitate communication and add to the clarity and impact of the report. Guidelines for tabular and graphical presentation are discussed later.

## Terse

A report should be terse and concise. Anything unnecessary should be omitted. If too much information is included, important points may be lost. Avoid lengthy discussions of common procedures. Yet, brevity should not be achieved at the expense of completeness.

# GUIDELINES FOR TABLES

Statistical tables are a vital part of the report and deserve special attention. We illustrate the guidelines for tables using the data for U.S. automobile sales reported in Table 22.1. The numbers in parentheses in the following sections refer to the numbered sections of the table.

## Title and Number

Every table should have a number (1a) and title (1b). The title should be brief yet clearly descriptive of the information provided. Arabic numbers are used to identify tables so that they can be referred to in the text.[6]

## Arrangement of Data Items

The arrangement of data items in a table should emphasize the most significant aspect of the data. Thus, when the data pertain to time, the items should be arranged by appropriate time period. When order of magnitude is most important, the data items should be arranged in that order (2a). If ease of locating items is critical, an alphabetical arrangement is most appropriate.

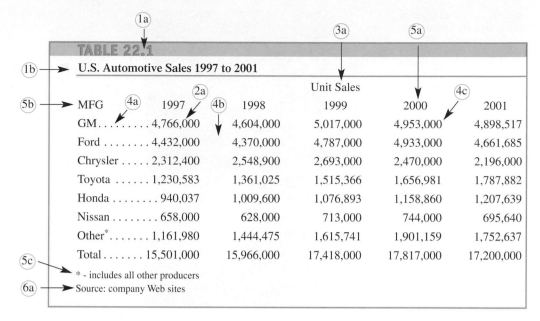

**TABLE 22.1**

**U.S. Automotive Sales 1997 to 2001**

|                  |            | Unit Sales |            |            |            |
| ---------------- | ---------- | ---------- | ---------- | ---------- | ---------- |
| MFG              | 1997       | 1998       | 1999       | 2000       | 2001       |
| GM . . . . . . . | 4,766,000  | 4,604,000  | 5,017,000  | 4,953,000  | 4,898,517  |
| Ford . . . . . . | 4,432,000  | 4,370,000  | 4,787,000  | 4,933,000  | 4,661,685  |
| Chrysler . . . . | 2,312,400  | 2,548,900  | 2,693,000  | 2,470,000  | 2,196,000  |
| Toyota . . . . . | 1,230,583  | 1,361,025  | 1,515,366  | 1,656,981  | 1,787,882  |
| Honda . . . . . . | 940,037   | 1,009,600  | 1,076,893  | 1,158,860  | 1,207,639  |
| Nissan . . . . . . | 658,000  | 628,000    | 713,000    | 744,000    | 695,640    |
| Other* . . . . . | 1,161,980  | 1,444,475  | 1,615,741  | 1,901,159  | 1,752,637  |
| Total . . . . . . | 15,501,000 | 15,966,000 | 17,418,000 | 17,817,000 | 17,200,000 |

\* - includes all other producers

Source: company Web sites

## Basis of Measurement

The basis or unit of measurement should be clearly stated (3a).

## Leaders, Rulings, and Spaces

*Leaders,* dots, or hyphens used to lead the eye horizontally, impart uniformity, and improve readability (4a). Instead of ruling the table horizontally or vertically, white spaces (4b) are used to set off data items. Skipping lines after different sections of the data can also assist the eye. Horizontal rules (4c) are often used after the headings.

## Explanations and Comments: Headings, Stubs, and Footnotes

Explanations and comments clarifying the table can be provided in the form of captions, stubs, and footnotes. Designations placed over the vertical columns are called headings (5a). Designations placed in the left-hand column are called stubs (5b). Information that cannot be incorporated in the table should be explained by footnotes (5c). Letters or symbols should be used for footnotes rather than numbers. The footnotes should come after the main table, but before the source note.

## Sources of the Data

If the data contained in the table are secondary, the source of data should be cited (6a).

# GUIDELINES FOR GRAPHS

As a general rule, graphic aids should be employed whenever practical. Graphical display of information can effectively complement the text and tables to enhance clarity of communication and impact. As the saying goes, a picture is worth a thousand words. The guidelines for preparing graphs are similar to those for tables. Therefore, this section focuses on the different types of graphical aids.[7] We illustrate several of these using the U.S. automobile sales data from Table 22.1.

Despite loss of sales and market share, General Motors remains the leader in automobiles.

## Geographic and Other Maps

Geographic and other maps, such as product-positioning maps, can communicate relative location and other comparative information. Geographic maps can pertain to countries, states, counties, sales territories, and other divisions. For example, suppose the researcher wanted to present information on the relative number of Coca-Cola Company bottlers versus the bottlers for PepsiCo and other competitors for each state in the United States. This information could be effectively communicated in a map in which each state was divided into three areas, proportionate to the number of Coca-Cola, PepsiCo, and other bottlers, with each area in a different color. Chapter 21 showed examples of product-positioning maps (e.g., Figure 21.4).

## Round or Pie Charts

**pie chart**
A round chart divided into sections.

In a **pie chart**, the area of each section, as a percentage of the total area of the circle, reflects the percentage associated with the value of a specific variable. A pie chart is not useful for displaying relationships over time or relationships among several variables. As a general guideline, a pie chart should not require more than seven sections.[8] Figure 22.2 shows a pie chart for U.S. automobile sales.

*Figure 22.2*
Pie Chart of Auto Sales by Manufacturer (2001)

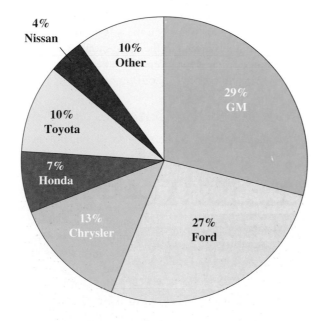

Burke gives its clients the best report graphics, bar none. Burke report showing bar chart.

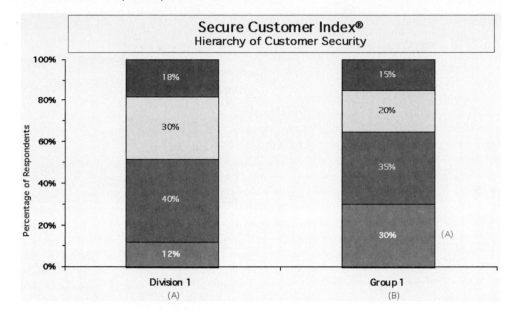

## Line Charts

A **line chart** connects a series of data points using continuous lines. This is an attractive way of illustrating trends and changes over time. Several series can be compared on the same chart, and forecasts, interpolations, and extrapolations can be shown. If several series are displayed simultaneously, each line should have a distinctive color or form (see Figure 22.3).[9]

A **stratum chart** is a set of line charts in which the data are successively aggregated over the series. Areas between the line charts display the magnitudes of the relevant variables (see Figure 22.4).

## Pictographs

A **pictograph** uses small pictures or symbols to display the data. As Figure 22.5 shows, pictographs do not depict results precisely. Hence, caution should be exercised when using them.[10]

## Histograms and Bar Charts

A **bar chart** displays data in various bars that may be positioned horizontally or vertically. Bar charts can be used to present absolute and relative magnitudes, differences, and change. The **histogram** is a vertical bar chart in which the height of the bars represents the relative or cumulative frequency of occurrence of a specific variable (see Figure 22.6).

**Figure 22.3**
Line Chart of Auto Sales by Manufacturer (1997 to 2001)

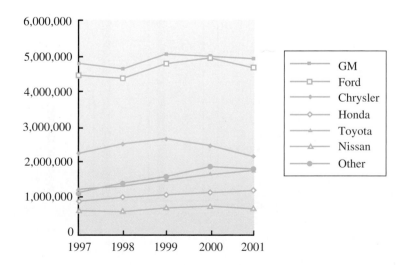

*Figure 22.4*
Stratum Chart of Auto Sales by Manufacturer (1997 to 2001)

20,000,000
18,000,000
16,000,000
14,000,000
12,000,000
10,000,000
8,000,000
6,000,000
4,000,000
2,000,000
0
1997
1998
1999
2000
2001
Other
Nissan
Toyota
Honda
Chrysler
Ford
GM

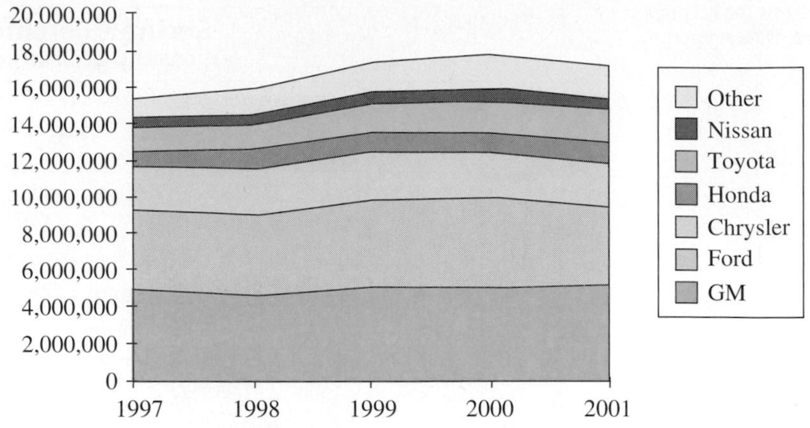

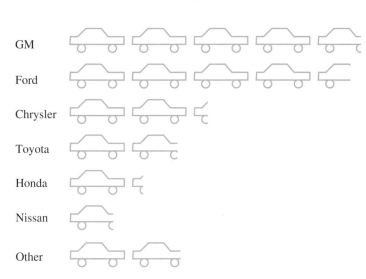

*Figure 22.5*
Pictograph of Auto Sales (2001)

Each Symbol Equals 1,000,000 Units
GM
Ford
Chrysler
Toyota
Honda
Nissan
Other

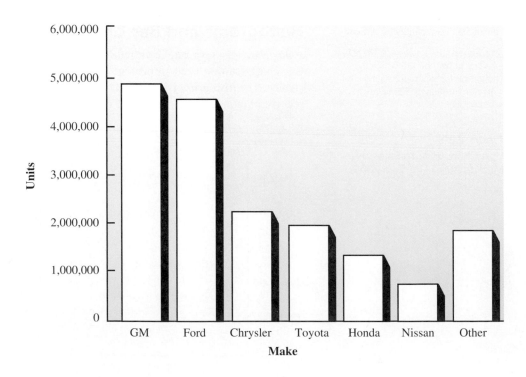

*Figure 22.6*
Histogram of Auto Sales by Manufacturer (2001)

6,000,000
5,000,000
4,000,000
3,000,000
2,000,000
1,000,000
0
Units
GM
Ford
Chrysler
Toyota
Honda
Nissan
Other
Make

## Schematic Figures and Flow Charts

Schematic figures and flow charts take on a number of different forms. They can be used to display the steps or components of a process, as in Figure 22.1. Another useful form of these charts is classification diagrams. Examples of classification charts for classifying secondary data were provided in Chapter 4 (Figures 4.1 to 4.4). An example of a flow chart for questionnaire design was given in Chapter 10 (Figure 10.2).[11]

# ORAL PRESENTATION

The entire marketing research project should be presented to the management of the client firm. This presentation will help management understand and accept the written report. Any preliminary questions that the management may have can be addressed in the presentation. Because many executives form their first and lasting impressions about the project based on the presentation, its importance cannot be overemphasized.[12]

The key to an effective presentation is preparation. A written script or detailed outline should be prepared following the format of the written report. The presentation must be geared to the audience. For this purpose the researcher should determine their backgrounds, interests, and involvement in the project, as well as the extent to which they are likely to be affected by it. The presentation should be rehearsed several times before it is made to the management.

Visual aids, such as tables and graphs, should be displayed with a variety of media. Chalkboards enable the researcher to manipulate numbers. They are particularly useful in communicating answers to technical questions. Although not as flexible, magnetic boards and felt boards allow for rapid presentation of previously prepared material. Flip charts are large pads of blank paper mounted on an easel. Visual aids are drawn on the pages in advance, and the speaker flips through the pages during the presentation. Overhead projectors can present simple charts as well as complex overlays produced by the successive additions of new images to the screen. Several computer programs are available for producing attractive overhead transparency (acetate sheet) masters. Color transparencies can also be prepared. Slides are useful for projecting photographs on the screen. Videotape equipment (VCRs) and large-screen projectors are particularly effective in presenting focus groups and other aspects of fieldwork that are dynamic in nature. Computer projectors attached to personal computers, which project the monitor image onto the screens, may also be employed. They can be used for making computer-controlled presentations or for presenting technical information such as analytical models.

It is important to maintain eye contact and interact with the audience during the presentation. Sufficient opportunity should be provided for questions, both during and after the presentation. The presentation should be made interesting and convincing with the use of appropriate stories, examples, experiences, and quotations. Filler words, such as "uh," "y'know," and "all right," should not be used. The ***"Tell 'Em" principle*** is effective for structuring a presentation. This principle states: (1) tell 'em what you're going to tell 'em, (2) tell 'em, and (3) tell 'em what you've told 'em. Another useful guideline is the ***"KISS 'Em" principle,*** which states: Keep It Simple and Straightforward (hence the acronym KISS).

Body language should be employed. Descriptive gestures are used to clarify or enhance verbal communication. Emphatic gestures are used to emphasize what is being said. Suggestive gestures are symbols of ideas and emotions. Prompting gestures are used to elicit a desired response from the audience. The speaker should vary the volume, pitch, voice quality, articulation, and rate while speaking. The presentation should terminate with a strong closing. To stress its importance, the presentation should be sponsored by a top-level manager in the client's organization, as in the following example.

*Tell 'Em principle*
An effective guideline for structuring a presentation. This principle states: (1) tell 'em what you're going to tell 'em, (2) tell 'em, and (3) tell 'em what you've told 'em.

*KISS 'Em principle*
A principle of report presentation that states: Keep It Simple and Straightforward.

**REAL RESEARCH**

*Taking It to the Top*

The importance of oral presentation cannot be overemphasized since many executives form their lasting impressions about the project based on it.

Elrick & Lavidge (*www.elavidge.com*) conducted a research project to measure the relative effectiveness of television, print, and radio as advertising media for a client firm. In addition, the effectiveness of 10 TV commercials, radio commercials, and print ads was assessed. Given the nature of the project, the oral presentation of the report was particularly important in communicating the findings. In addition to an overhead projector and slide projector, a VCR (for playing TV commercials), a tape recorder (for playing radio commercials), and a story board (for showing print ads) were utilized. The presentation was made to the client's top corporate officers, consisting of the president, all vice presidents, and all assistant vice presidents at one of their monthly meetings.[13] ■

After the presentation, key executives in the client firm should be given time to read the report in detail. Some guidelines are available for report reading.

# READING THE RESEARCH REPORT

Guidelines for reading the report and evaluating the marketing research project have been developed by the Advertising Research Foundation.[14]

## Addresses the Problem

The problem being addressed should be clearly identified and the relevant background information provided. The organization sponsoring the research, as well as the one conducting the research, should be clearly identified. The report should not assume that the reader has prior knowledge of the problem situation, but should give all the relevant information. A report that does not provide such information has missed the mark, as well as the readers.

## Research Design

The research design should be clearly described in nontechnical terms. If readers in the target audience of the report cannot understand the research design procedure, the fault lies with the researcher. The report should include a discussion of the information needs, data-collection methods, scaling techniques, questionnaire design and pretesting, sampling techniques, and fieldwork. Justification should be provided for the specific methods used. Reports that do not contain, or otherwise make available, methodological details should be viewed with caution.

## Execution of the Research Procedures

The reader should pay special attention to the manner in which the research procedures were executed. The people working on the project should be well qualified and properly trained. Proper supervision and control procedures should be followed. This is particularly important with respect to data collection, data preparation, and statistical analysis.

## Numbers and Statistics

Numbers and statistics reported in tables and graphs should be examined carefully by the reader. Inappropriate numbers and statistics can be highly misleading. Consider, for example, percentages based on small samples or means reported for ordinal data. Unfortunately, the occurrence of these types of misleading statistics in reports is not uncommon.

## Interpretation and Conclusions

The findings should be reported in an objective and candid way. The interpretation of the basic results should be differentiated from the results per se. Any assumptions made in interpreting the results should be clearly identified. The limitations of the research should be discussed. Any conclusions or recommendations made without a specification of the underlying assumptions or limitations should be treated cautiously by the reader.

## Generalizability

It is the responsibility of the researcher to provide evidence regarding the reliability, validity, and generalizability of the findings. The report should clearly identify the target population to which the findings apply. Factors that limit the generalizability of the findings, such as the nature and representativeness of the sample, mode and time of data collection, and various sources of error should be clearly identified. The reader should not attempt to generalize the findings of the report without explicit consideration of these factors.

## Disclosure

Finally, the reader should carefully examine whether the spirit in which the report was written indicates an honest and complete disclosure of the research procedures and results. It is particularly important that procedures, e.g., those used for the treatment of missing values, weighting, etc., that call for subjective judgment on the part of the researcher be made known. If any negative or unexpected findings were obtained, they should be reported. The reader should feel free to ask for any relevant information that is not contained in the report.

A careful reading of the report using these guidelines will help the client to effectively participate in research follow-up.

# RESEARCH FOLLOW-UP

The researcher's task does not end with the oral presentation. Two other tasks remain. The researcher should help the client understand and implement the findings and take follow-up action. Secondly, while it is still fresh in the researcher's mind, the entire marketing research project should be evaluated.

## Assisting the Client

After the client has read the report in detail, several questions may arise. Parts of the report, particularly those dealing with technical matters, may not be understood and the researcher should provide the help needed. Sometimes the researcher helps implement the findings. Often, the client retains the researcher to help with the selection of a new product or advertising agency, development of a pricing policy, market segmentation, or other marketing actions. An important reason for client follow-up is to discuss further research projects. For example, the researcher and management may agree to repeat the study after two years. Finally, the researcher should help the client firm make the information generated in the marketing research project a part of the firm's marketing (management) information system (MIS) or decision support system (DSS), as discussed in Chapter 1.

## Evaluation of the Research Project

Although marketing research is scientific, it also involves creativity, intuition, and expertise. Hence, every marketing research project provides an opportunity for learning, and the researcher should critically evaluate the entire project to obtain new insights and knowledge. The key question to ask is, "Could this project have been conducted more effectively or efficiently?" This question, of course, raises several more specific questions. Could the problem have been defined differently so as to enhance the value of the project to the client or reduce the costs? Could a different approach have yielded better results? Was the research design that was used the best? How about the mode of data collection? Should mall intercepts have been used instead of telephone interviews? Was the sampling plan employed the most appropriate? Were the sources of possible design error correctly anticipated and kept under control, at least in a qualitative sense? If not, what changes could have been made? How could the selection, training, and supervision of field workers be altered to improve data collection? Was the data analysis strategy effective in yielding information useful for decision making? Were the conclusions and recommendations appropriate and useful to the client? Was the report adequately written and presented? Was the project completed within the time and budget allocated? If not, what went wrong? The insights gained from such an evaluation will benefit the researcher and the subsequent projects conducted.

# INTERNATIONAL MARKETING RESEARCH

The guidelines presented earlier in the chapter apply to international marketing research as well, although report preparation may be complicated by the need to prepare reports for management in different countries and in different languages. In such a case, the researcher should prepare different versions of the report, each geared to specific readers. The different reports should be comparable, although the formats may differ. The guidelines for oral presentation are also similar to those given earlier, with the added proviso that the presenter should be sensitive to cultural norms. For example, making jokes, which is frequently done in the United States, is not appropriate in all cultures. Most marketing decisions are made from facts and figures arising out of marketing research. But these figures have to pass the test and limits of logic, subjective experience, and gut feelings of decision makers. The subjective experience and gut feelings of managers could vary widely across countries, necessitating that different recommendations be made for implementing the research findings in different countries. This is particularly important when making innovative or creative recommendations such as those pertaining to advertising campaigns.

### REAL RESEARCH

## *Camry Chicken Fries Ford*

The ad campaign designed for Toyota Camry in Australia was very different from the one used in Japan. "Why did the chicken cross the road?" Toyota asks in a continuing series of TV commercials aired recently in Australia. The answer: "To sell more Toyota Camrys, of course." The spots, showing an animated chicken trying to cross the road and getting its feathers blown off by a passing Camry, were created by Saatchi & Saatchi Advertising. When Bob Miller, Toyota's general manager for marketing, tried to explain the ad to their counterpart in Japan, they thought he was insane. Maybe so, but the commercial did unbelievably well. Hoary old joke that it was, the gag helped Toyota topple Ford's dominance in Australia. As a continuing series, the next ad showed the featherless chicken sitting on a pile of eggs in the middle of the road and hatching chicks as the Camry speeds past. Whereas such use of humor was offensive to the Japanese, it solicited a favorable response from the Australians.[15] By customizing its advertising and marketing efforts in each culture, the Toyota company remained a leader as of 2004 with some of the best selling cars such as the Camry. ■

Toyota launched a humorous advertising campaign to topple Ford's dominance in Australia. However, that campaign may not be successful in other countries.

# ETHICS IN MARKETING RESEARCH

Report preparation and presentation involves many issues pertaining to research integrity. These issues included defining the marketing research problem to suit hidden agendas, compromising the research design, deliberately misusing statistics, falsifying figures, altering research results, misinterpreting the results with the objective of supporting a personal or corporate point of view, and withholding information.[16] A survey of 254 marketing researchers revealed that 33 percent of the respondents considered the most difficult ethical problems they face encompass issues of research integrity. The researcher must address these issues when preparing the report and presenting the findings. The dissemination of the marketing research results to the client, and other stakeholders as may be appropriate, should be honest, accurate, and complete.

The researcher should be objective throughout all phases of the marketing research process. Some research procedures and analyses may not reveal anything new or significant. For example, the discriminant function may not classify better than chance (Chapter 18). Ethical dilemmas can arise in these instances if the researcher nevertheless attempts to draw conclusions from such analyses. Such temptations must be resisted to avoid unethical conduct.

Likewise, clients also have the responsibility for complete and accurate disclosure of the research findings and are obligated to use the research results in an ethical manner. For example, the public can be disadvantaged by a client who distorts the research findings to develop a biased advertising campaign that makes brand claims that have not been substantiated by marketing research. Such activities are condemned by the code of ethics of the American Marketing Association and other professional research associations (see Chapter 1).[17] Ethical issues also arise when client firms, such as tobacco companies, use marketing research findings to formulate questionable marketing programs.

## REAL RESEARCH

### *Tobacco Industry Is "Smoking Gun"*

Examination of secondary data sources uncovered the facts that tobacco smoking is responsible for 30 percent of all cancer deaths in the United States and is a leading cause of heart disease, along with being associated with problems such as colds, gastric ulcers, chronic bronchitis, emphysema, and other diseases. Do tobacco companies share an ethical responsibility for this situation? Is it ethical for these companies to employ marketing research to create glamorous images for cigarettes that have a strong appeal to the target market? It is estimated that advertising by the tobacco industry based on systematic research has a part in creating more than 3,000 teenage smokers each day in the United States. Advertising for Camel cigarettes through the Old Joe cartoon advertisements increased Camel's share of the illegal children's cigarette market segment from 0.5 percent to 32.8 percent—representing sales estimates at $476 million per year. These detrimental effects are not limited to the United States. Not only is the tobacco industry enticing children to smoke, but it also targets other less informed populations such as Third World countries because this is a way for tobacco companies to replace those smokers that quit or die.

In 1998, a multistate tobacco agreement was set forth between major cigarette manufacturers and 46 state governments in an effort to prohibit cigarette makers from targeting children in their advertisements. In 2002, however, R.J. Reynolds Tobacco Holdings, Inc. was sued by California's attorney general for allegedly targeting youth with their tobacco advertisements in magazines such as Rolling Stone and Sports Illustrated. Senior assistant attorney general, Dennis Eckhart said, "Kids shouldn't be targeted, and we want to prevent that from happening." The California attorney general demanded that Reynolds change its advertising practices and conduct business in an appropriate and ethical manner.[18] ∎

# INTERNET AND COMPUTER APPLICATIONS

Marketing research reports are being published or posted directly to the Web. Normally, these reports are not located in publicly accessible areas but in locations that are protected by passwords or on corporate intranets. The various word-processing, spreadsheet, and presentation packages have the capability to produce material in a format that can be posted directly to the Web, thus facilitating the process.

There are a number of advantages to publishing marketing research reports on the Web. These reports can incorporate all kinds of multimedia presentations including graphs, pictures, animation, audio, and full-motion video. The dissemination is immediate and the reports can be accessed by authorized persons online on a worldwide basis. These reports can be electronically searched to identify materials of specific interest. For example, a General Electric manager in Kuala Lumpur can electronically locate the portions of the report that pertain to Southeast Asia. Storage and future retrieval is efficient and effortless. It is easy to integrate these reports to become a part of the decision support system.

One good example of publishing marketing research reports on the Web is accutips.com. They have published many marketing research reports on the Web. The reports published online deal with many different categories within marketing, such as: Case Studies, Market Focus/Trends, Sales and Marketing, Data Selection and Mailing Lists, Creating Successful Direct Mail, Web Marketing, and E-marketing. You can easily go to their site at *www.accutips.com* and search in any of these categories. Furthermore, new Internet applications are allowing companies to share information with whom they choose to within their organization, as illustrated by the following example.

### REAL RESEARCH

## *Mom Was Right, Sharing Is Easy*

Companies such as General Electric are always looking for easier and better ways to share information and ideas. In many cases they have turned to new Internet applications to improve their channels of communication. Constant improvements have provided various options for sharing information. Some of the companies offering these solutions include Avistar (*www.avistar.com*), eRoom Technologies Inc. (*www.eroom.com*), Latitude Communications (*www.latitude.com*), PlaceWare (*www.placeware.com*), and Microsoft (*www.microsoft.com/netmeeting*). Avistar offers visual collaboration, which they tout as the next wave of collaborative commerce. eRoom Technologies offers a virtual eRoom where all users are able to share information in real time. Latitude Communications offers Meetingplace, which is a product that offers voice and web conferencing solutions. PlaceWare also provides conferencing along with PowerPoint presentations, whiteboard, web tours, and streaming video. Microsoft's Windows NetMeeting is a common online meeting application that is standard with most versions of Windows. While all of these companies offer different solutions, they all solve the same problem. They all offer companies the ability to share documents and presentations, as well as give the users an opportunity to communicate and hold meetings while being in different locations. These applications are constantly improving and their use is likely to increase over time, allowing companies to save time and money. ∎

In addition to a number of specialized programs, the mainframe and microcomputer versions of the major statistical packages have reporting procedures. In SPSS, the program REPORT can be used to present results in the desired format. TABLE(S) is particularly suited for formatting data for an on-page presentation. In SAS, the procedures PRINT, FORMS, CHARTS, PLOT, CALENDAR, and TIMEPLOT display information for reporting purposes. The tables and graphs produced from these packages can be directly incorporated into the report. MINITAB also has the capability to create graphs and charts and edit them for use in reports or professional presentations. Graphs can be created using GRAPH>PLOT, or GRAPH>CHART, or GRAPH>HISTOGRAM. Editing can be done using EDIT>EDIT LAST COMMAND DIALOG. EXCEL has extensive charting capabilities and, through Microsoft OFFICE, provides a direct link to WORD and POWERPOINT for report preparation and presentation.

## SPSS Windows

Whereas the normal graphs can be produced using the Base module of SPSS, for more extensive graphing, the DeltaGraph package can be used. This package has extensive graphing capabilities with 80+ chart types and 200+ chart styles.

Likewise, SPSS tables enables the researcher to create even complicated tables. For example, the results of multiple response tables can be condensed into a single table. The researcher can create a polished look by changing column width, adding boldface, drawing lines, or aligning.

SPSS OLAP cubes are interactive tables that enable you to slice your data in different ways for data exploration and presentation.

SmartViewer enables the researcher to distribute reports, graphs, tables, even pivotal report cubes, over the Web. Company managers can be empowered to interact with the results by putting a report cube on the Web, intranet, or extranet. Thus, they can answer their own questions by drilling down for more detail and creating new views of the data.

### FOCUS ON BURKE

Burke's philosophy and procedures for report preparation are very similar to those given in this chapter. Burke's guidelines for working with management place a great emphasis on the personal presentation as the most effective means of assuring that the research is understood, believed, and used. In some situations, a personal presentation is not asked for . . . push hard to be "invited." Keep pushing every time the opportunity arises. Getting an invitation is the first step, next comes managing the presentation and the audience. Listed below are many of Burke's key items to remember.

1. The real decision makers may be above the level that commissioned your work. Push to go higher with your personal presentation. If someone is to use the information . . . they should be in the presentation.

2. Always believe that you are the catalyst that will make the data come alive. You are more important to the presentation and the findings than a chart or picture.

3. Be willing to change your style. Many people are laid-back or low-key. It is said that many famous comedians are not at all funny off stage. Your role when giving the presentation is to be active, enthusiastic, and forceful. Maybe this is a "role" for you . . . but if you do not play the role . . . you will not be invited back.

4. Do not apologize to the audience or yourself: No one in the room knows the data and its meaning better than you do. At the moment of the presentation, you are the critical element. Do not apologize for not knowing a particular answer. Do not apologize if the room is not comfortable. Do not apologize if a piece of equipment does not work. Do not apologize if you have a cold. Do not apologize for anything. Just get on with the presentation.

5. Research your audience. Talk to the people "hosting" the meeting. Who will be there? What are their roles? What stake do they have in the results? What can you find out about positions they might take on the research? Prepare for those positions. How much do they already know about the subject of the meeting? You do not want to bore them with

*(Continued)*

information they already have. What are their styles? Is it a technical, detail-oriented group? Is it a generalist group, etc.?

6. Be prepared for skepticism. If you do not immediately have the answer . . . ask for a later meeting to discuss the issue and to determine how you and the questioner can arrive at an answer.

7. Do not stay on a topic more than five minutes unless your audience asks for you to do so with questions. The average attention span for a topic is about six minutes. After that time, people will start looking at their papers, thinking about other issues . . . you will be losing them.

8. Be on time, start on time, and do not go beyond your allotted time. No matter how interested you are and how interested the audience is, unless the senior host specifically requests it, stop exactly on time!

# SUMMARY

Report preparation and presentation is the final step in the marketing research project. This process begins with interpretation of data analysis results and leads to conclusions and recommendations. Next, the formal report is written and an oral presentation made. After management has read the report, the researcher should conduct a follow-up, assisting management and undertaking a thorough evaluation of the marketing research project.

In international marketing research, report preparation may be complicated by the need to prepare reports for management in different countries and in different languages. Several ethical issues are pertinent, particularly those related to the interpretation and reporting of the research process and findings to the client and the use of these results by the client. The use of microcomputers and mainframes can greatly facilitate report preparation and presentation.

# KEY TERMS AND CONCEPTS

pie chart, *650*
line chart, *651*
stratum chart, *651*

pictograph, *651*
bar char, *651*
histogram, *651*

"Tell 'Em" principle, *653*
"KISS 'Em" principle, *653*

# EXERCISES

## Questions

1. Describe the process of report preparation.
2. Describe a commonly used format for writing marketing research reports.
3. Describe the following parts of a report: title page, table of contents, executive summary, problem definition, research design, data analysis, conclusions, and recommendations.
4. Why is the "limitations and caveats" section included in the report?
5. Discuss the importance of objectivity in writing a marketing research report.
6. Describe the guidelines for report writing.
7. How should the data items be arranged in a table?
8. What is a pie chart? For what type of information is it suitable? For what type of information is it not suitable?
9. Describe a line chart. What kind of information is commonly displayed using such charts?
10. Describe the role of pictographs. What is the relationship between bar charts and histograms?

11. What is the purpose of an oral presentation? What guidelines should be followed in an oral presentation?
12. Describe the "Tell 'Em" and "KISS 'Em" principles.
13. Describe the evaluation of a marketing research project in retrospect.

## Problems

1. The following passage is taken from a marketing research report prepared for a group of printers and lithographers without much formal education who run a small family-owned business.

   To measure the image of the printing industry, two different scaling techniques were employed. The first was a series of semantic differential scales. The second consisted of a set of Likert scales. The use of two different techniques for measurement could be justified based on the need to assess the convergent validity of the findings. Data obtained using both these techniques were treated as interval scaled. Pearson product moment correlations were computed between the sets of ratings. The resulting correlations were high, indicating a high level of convergent validity.

Rewrite this paragraph so that it is suitable for inclusion in the report.

2. Graphically illustrate the consumer decision-making process described in the following paragraph:

The consumer first becomes aware of the need. Then the consumer simultaneously searches for information from several sources: retailers, advertising, word of mouth, and independent publications. After that, a criterion is developed for evaluating the available brands in the marketplace. Based on this evaluation, the most preferred brand is selected.

# INTERNET AND COMPUTER EXERCISES

1. For the data given in Table 22.1, use a graphics package or a spreadsheet, such as EXCEL, to construct the following graphs:
   a. Pie chart
   b. Line chart
   c. Bar chart

2. Using one of the report-generation programs discussed in this chapter or a similar package, write a report explaining the data and the charts constructed in exercise 1 of this section.

3. Visit *www.gallup.com* to identify a recent report prepared by this company. How does the format of this report compare to the one in the book?

# ACTIVITIES

## *Role Playing*

1. You are a researcher preparing a report for a high-tech firm on "The Demand Potential for Microcomputers in Europe." Develop a format for your report. How is it different from the one given in the book? Discuss your format with your boss (role enacted by a student in your class).

2. In Fieldwork question 2, suppose you were the researcher who wrote the report. Prepare an oral presentation of this report for senior marketing managers. Deliver your presentation to a group of students and ask them to critique it.

## *Fieldwork*

1. Make a trip to your library. Read the latest annual reports of three different companies that are known for effective marketing (e.g., Coca-Cola, P&G, GE). Identify the strong and weak points of these reports.

2. Obtain a copy of a marketing research report from your library or a local marketing research firm. (Many marketing research firms will provide copies of old reports for educational purposes). Critically evaluate this report.

## *Group Discussion*

1. As a small group, discuss the following statement: "All the graphical aids are really very similar; therefore, it does not matter which ones you use."

2. "Writing a report that is concise and yet complete is virtually impossible as these two objectives are conflicting." Discuss.

3. "Writing reports is an art. Presenting reports is an art. Reading reports is an art. It is all a matter of art." Discuss as a small group.

# CHAPTER 23

# International Marketing Research

## Objectives

After reading this chapter, the student should be able to:

1. Develop a framework for conducting international marketing research.
2. Explain in detail the marketing, governmental, legal, economic, structural, informational and technological, and sociocultural environmental factors and how they have an impact on international marketing research.
3. Describe the use of telephone, personal, and mail survey methods in different countries.
4. Discuss how to establish the equivalence of scales and measures including construct, operational, scalar, and linguistic equivalence.
5. Describe the processes of back translation and parallel translation in translating a questionnaire into a different language.
6. Discuss the ethical considerations in international marketing research.
7. Explain the use of the Internet and computers in international marketing research.

## Overview

This chapter discusses the environment in which international marketing research is conducted, focusing on the marketing, government, legal, economic, structural, informational and technological, and sociocultural environment.[1] Whereas discussions of how the six steps of the marketing research process should be implemented in an international setting took place in earlier chapters, here we present additional details on survey methods, scaling techniques, and questionnaire translation. The relevant ethical issues in international marketing research are identified and the use of the Internet and computers is discussed.

## REAL RESEARCH

### *In India, Familiarity Breeds Better Content*

Hewlett-Packard is using Linux as standard operating system (OS) in India after extensive market research. Through focus groups and survey research, the company found that many people in India felt that Linux is the fastest growing OS with about 10,000 users already. This is mainly due to the cost of the OS, which is free. Hewlett-Packard has publicly agreed to support Linux on its computers, hoping to grab market share in the international market's newest technology consumer powerhouse. In India, differences in culture and infrastructure had to be noted and respected when Hewlett-Packard was conducting research. The focus groups used to conduct this research on operating systems were designed with homogeneity in mind because of traditions held with regard to class, gender, and age. The focus groups were also conducted in hotels to make participants feel more comfortable. These focus groups helped Hewlett-Packard identify the OS that the Indian consumer preferred so they could position their product in accordance with these preferences.[2] ■

## REAL RESEARCH

### *Best in the West—And Around the World*

As of 2003, Best Western, with its more than 4,000 independently owned and operated hotels in 83 countries, is the world's largest chain in terms of number of hotels. As the following chart shows, business travelers make up 36 percent of the market, the largest single share. Best Western has found, through survey research, that business travelers often resist trying less expensive hotels and appreciate the security of a well-known brand. This information has helped the chain attract business travelers.

Through secondary data analysis and surveys, Best Western has learned the sources of hotel business in different regions of the world and geared its marketing strategy accordingly (see the following table). For example, the chain emphasizes domestic business in

Business travelers make up 36 percent of the hotel market, the single largest segment.

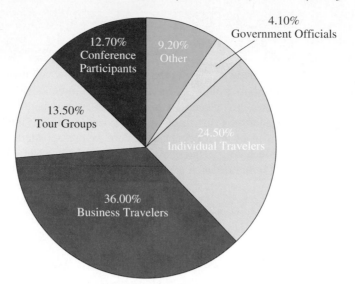

International marketing research has helped Best Western to become the world's largest hotel chain.

North America, focuses on both domestic and international business in Europe, and emphasizes foreign business in the Far East, Australia, Africa, and the Middle East. The use of marketing research continues to prove successful for Best Western.[3]

Sources of Worldwide Hotel Business by Region

| Source of Hotel Business | All Hotels Worldwide | Africa/Middle East | Asia/ Australia | North America | Europe |
|---|---|---|---|---|---|
| Domestic | 50.7% | 24.6% | 35.0% | 84.6% | 47.3% |
| Foreign | 49.3% | 75.4% | 65.0% | 15.4% | 52.7% |
| TOTAL | 100.0% | 100.0% | 100.0% | 100.0% | 100.0% |

Both these examples point to the fact that marketing research can contribute significantly to the formulation of successful international marketing strategies. The term international marketing research is used very broadly. It denotes research for true international products (international research), research carried out in a country other than the country of the research-commissioning organization (foreign research), research conducted in all or all important countries where the company is represented (multinational research), and research conducted in/across different cultures (cross-cultural research).

# MARKETING RESEARCH
# GOES INTERNATIONAL

In the 2000s, revenue generated outside the United States has become important to the top market research firms in the United States. Several of the top 50 research firms in the United States derive revenues from work through subsidiaries, branch offices, and/or affiliates that are located outside the United States.[4]

Because overseas expansion is a hot topic in the 2000s, many marketers will begin to expand into the overseas market. This expansion is primarily due to economic integration and the lowering of trade barriers. Overseas expansion will mean increased opportunities for market research companies inside and outside of the United States. When consumers outside of the United States begin to spend their money, they give far greater attention to price and quality rather than to the country of origin. To many firms, regional markets represent the "international order of the day."[5]

As attractive as foreign markets are, companies must realize that setting up for operations in these markets does not guarantee success. Many economists warn that the economic conditions are, at best, sluggish. Others argue "that it is unrealistic to expect aggressive consumerism in the near future even in markets with a taste for foreign concepts." The greatest problems that many firms will face in foreign markets is "red tape." Many governments have implemented laws and policies that will protect their countries' businesses.

Since the demise of the Cold War, the world's economy is no longer a simple three-way battle between the United States, Japan, and Germany. Stiffer competition will force many companies inside of the United States to try to gain competitive advantages outside of the United States. Three massive markets have developed since the end of the Cold War, some of which will require significant amounts of market research before entrance into that market can occur. The three markets are the Americas, Europe, and the Pacific Rim nations.

Since the passage of the North American Free Trade Agreement (NAFTA), a "veritable free-market revolution" has begun to take place in Mexico.[6] The passage of NAFTA created the world's largest market. In other Latin American countries, trade barriers are being reduced. Companies entering these changing markets will be forced to change the ways in which they do business. Quality standards will increase and prices will become more competitive due to greater selection. As product choices widen, consumer awareness and sophistication will increase. Latin Americans will become shoppers, and companies can no longer hide behind the protective barriers of their countries and will face more competition due to the greater selection in the marketplace. As a result, market researchers will be faced with two significant challenges. First, as manufacturing and markets assume a regional focus, service providers will be forced to do the same to achieve consistent results and quality. Researchers, both those internal to product operations and their outside suppliers, must follow this trend for a regional, quality approach. A top-down approach to marketing research will result in company executives becoming increasingly involved in marketing research. Secondly, marketing researchers must remain flexible to handle local conditions.[7]

With the number of U.S. products that are currently available in Europe, one can see that many manufacturers and researchers will not have to radically alter their marketing plans and objectives. The recently formed EC is perhaps the source of the greatest economic potential in the world. The western European market is roughly the size of the North American market, but the total size of the European market will increase due to the opening of the eastern bloc area of Europe. However, companies must remain cognizant of the fact that there is a significantly lower level of disposable income. Therefore, they must find ways in which to cope with this particular problem. A particular opportunity that should be explored is the potential for smaller and medium-sized companies to expand in the European market.

Many believe that the Asian rim is the fastest growing part of the world. This growth is paced by a rapid rate of investment and an abundance of trained human capital. Countries that are included in the Asian rim range from Australia to Indonesia to China. This region's average real economic growth is more than five percent per year and is expected to continue through this decade. China is being called the next great mecca for marketing research because it has a consumer population of over 1.2 billion. Recently, Gallup announced the formation of Gallup China, the first foreign marketing research firm in China. Gallup China will undoubtedly face many challenges in China, such as rapidly increasing competition, governmental regulation, and the forming of bonds with the Chinese people in order to be able to conduct successful research. Chinese research firms have begun to form within China, and American companies have begun to form alliances with these companies in order to penetrate the Chinese market. However, international marketing research can be very complex. We present a framework for understanding and dealing with the complexities involved.

# A FRAMEWORK FOR INTERNATIONAL MARKETING RESEARCH

Conducting international marketing research is much more complex than domestic marketing research.[8] Although the six-step framework for domestic marketing research (Chapter 1) is applicable, the environment prevailing in the countries, cultural units, or international markets that are being researched influences the way the six steps of the marketing research process should be performed. Figure 23.1 presents a framework for conducting international marketing research.

## The Environment

The differences in the environments of countries, cultural units, or foreign markets should be considered when conducting international marketing research. These differences may arise in the marketing environment, government environment, legal environment, economic environment, structural environment, informational and technological environment, and sociocultural environment, as shown in Figure 23.1.

## Marketing Environment

The role of marketing in economic development varies in different countries. For example, developing countries are frequently oriented toward production rather than marketing. Demand typically exceeds supply, and there is little concern about customer satisfaction, especially when the level of competition is low. In assessing the marketing environment, the researcher should consider the variety and assortment of products available, pricing policies, government control of media, the public's attitude toward advertising, the efficiency of the distribution system, the level of marketing effort undertaken, and the unsatisfied needs and behavior of consumers. For example, surveys conducted in the United States usually involve questions on the variety and selection of merchandise. These questions would be inappropriate in many countries, such as in eastern Europe, that are characterized by shortage economies. Likewise, questions about pricing may have to incorporate bargaining as an integral part of the exchange process. Questions about promotion should be modified as well. Television advertising, an extremely important promotion vehicle in the United States, is restricted or prohibited in some countries where TV stations are owned and operated by the government. Certain themes, words, and illustrations used in the United States are taboo in some countries. The types of retailers and intermediary institutions available, and the services these institutions offer, vary from country to country.

## Government Environment

An additional relevant factor is the government environment. The type of government has a bearing on the emphasis on public policy, regulatory agencies, government incentives and penalties, and investment in government enterprises. Some governments, particularly in developing countries, do not encourage foreign competition. High tariff barriers create

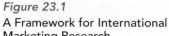

**Figure 23.1**
A Framework for International
Marketing Research

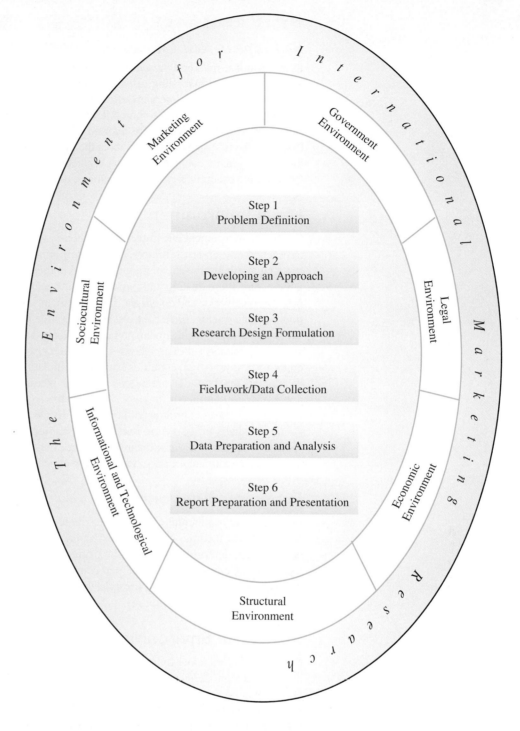

disincentives to the efficient use of marketing research approaches. Also, the role of government in setting market controls, developing infrastructure, and acting as an entrepreneur should be carefully assessed. The role of government is also crucial in many advanced countries, such as Germany and Japan, where government has traditionally worked with industry toward a common national industrial policy. At the tactical level, the government determines tax structures, tariffs, and product safety rules and regulations and often imposes special rules and regulations on foreign multinationals and their marketing practices. In many countries, the government may be an important member of the distribution channel. The government purchases essential products on a large scale and then sells them to the consumers, perhaps on a rationed basis. The following example shows how government may influence international marketing research.

*Red Tape in Red China*

In international marketing research, data collection and politics may go hand-in-hand. One Western industrial marketing researcher on a short, hurried trip through China learned this fact when attempting to interview officials of the Chinese automobile industry. Although they agreed to an interview, the automobile executives refused to answer any questions of substance. Instead, they continually referred the researcher to the Ministry of Foreign Affairs (MFA) as the first step in learning about the industry. After the researcher met with the MFA, they would grant a detailed interview. When the researcher became somewhat frustrated, the Chinese auto executives gave their assurance that this process would take only a few days.[9] ■

## Legal Environment

The legal environment encompasses common law, code law, foreign law, international law, transaction law, antitrust, bribery, and taxes. From the standpoint of international marketing research, particularly salient are laws related to the elements of the marketing mix. Product laws include those dealing with product quality, packaging, warranty and after-sales service, patents, trademarks, and copyright. Laws on pricing deal with price fixing, price discrimination, variable pricing, price controls, and retail price maintenance. Distribution laws relate to exclusive territory arrangements, type of channels, and cancellation of distributor or wholesaler agreements. Likewise, laws govern the type of promotional methods that can be employed. Although all countries have laws regulating marketing activities, some countries have only a few laws that are loosely enforced, whereas others have many complicated laws that are strictly enforced. In many countries, the legal channels are clogged and the settlement of court cases is prolonged. In addition, home-country laws may also apply while conducting business or marketing research in foreign countries. For example, a U.S. citizen is subject to certain U.S. laws regardless of the country where business is being done. These laws relate to national security, antitrust, and ethical considerations.

## Economic Environment

Economic environmental characteristics include economic size (GDP), level, source, and distribution of income, growth trends, and sectoral trends. A country's stage of economic development determines the size, the degree of modernization, and the standardization of its markets. Consumer, industrial, and commercial markets become more standardized and consumers' work, leisure, and lifestyles become more homogenized by economic development and advances in technology.

## Structural Environment

Structural factors relate to transportation, communication, utilities, and infrastructure. For example, telephone usage in Europe is much lower than in the United States, and many households do without telephones. Mail service is inefficient in many developing countries. Personal contact with respondents is difficult, as city people work during the day and rural residents are inaccessible. Block statistics and maps are not available or can be obtained only with great difficulty. Many dwelling units are unidentified.

## Informational and Technological Environment

Elements of the informational and technological environment include information and communication systems, computerization and the use of the Internet, use of electronic equipment, energy, production technology, science, and invention. For example, in India, South Korea, and many Latin American countries, advances in science and technology have not had a proportionate impact on the lifestyle of the common citizens. Computers, the Internet, and electronic information transfer have yet to make an impact in rural areas. Information handling and record keeping are performed in the traditional way. This, again, has an impact on the type of information and how it can be solicited from consumers, businesses, and other enterprises.

Differences in the marketing environment of countries should be considered when conducting international marketing research. Open-air markets, like this one in Paris, are quite common in France.

## Sociocultural Environment

Sociocultural factors include values, literacy, language, religion, communication patterns, and family and social institutions. Relevant values and attitudes toward time, achievement, work, authority, wealth, scientific method, risk, innovation, change, and the Western world should be considered. The marketing research process should be modified so that it does not conflict with the cultural values. In many developing countries, 60 percent or more of the population is illiterate. In tradition-directed, less developed societies, the ability of respondents to formulate opinions of their own seems to be all but absent; consequently, it is difficult to solicit information from these respondents. As a result, the sophisticated rating scales employed in the United States are not useful. Complexities are added by the fact that in a given nation or region there may be several distinct spoken languages and dialects.

A country with a homogeneous family structure is likely to be more culturally homogeneous than a country with multiple family structures. For example, Japan is culturally more homogeneous than either the United States or many African countries, which have many different kinds of family structures. The importance of designing products to be consistent with the sociocultural factors prevailing in a country is brought home by Universal Studios Japan.

### REAL RESEARCH

## *Universal Studios: Less Universal in Japan*

When Universal Studios (*www.universalstudios.com*) decided to build a Universal Studios in Osaka, Japan, they relied heavily on focus groups, depth interviews, and survey research to understand the sociocultural environment in Japan. The research was done by their business partner Dentsu (*www.dentsu.com*). The American and Japanese ways of doing business had to be combined.

Focus groups helped to decide on food items, which allowed them to take the Japanese culture into account. The portions of the food were made smaller to accommodate the traditional Japanese servings, whereas American foods such as hot dogs and pizzas were made larger to create the American image. Pies were made less sweet and the barbeque sauce was made sweeter.

Universal also found out about souvenirs and merchandise preferences through focus groups and depth interviews. The Japanese buy more souvenirs for friends and coworkers. Candy, household items, and stationery products are very popular. There is a great teenage girl population in the market who like items with cartoons on them. Clothing is not as important in Japan as it is other countries.

Universal Studios was able to adapt to the Japanese culture while keeping an American image. This has been a key to its success in Japan.

The focus group and depth interview findings were confirmed by survey research. Universal was able to adapt to the Japanese culture while keeping an American image. For example, the Wild Wild Wild West stunt show has all of the components of an American cowboy show, but the dialog is done in Japanese. The use of focus groups, depth interviews, and survey research helped Universal to launch successfully in Japan.[10] ■

Each country's environment is unique, so international marketing research must take into consideration the environmental characteristics of the countries or foreign markets involved. The previous chapters, 1 through 22, discussed how we can adapt the marketing research process to international situations. In the following sections, we provide additional details for implementing survey methods, scaling techniques, and questionnaire translation in international marketing research.[11]

# SURVEY METHODS

The following sections discuss the major interviewing methods in light of the challenges of conducting research in foreign countries, especially Europe and developing countries.[12]

## Telephone Interviewing and CATI

In the United States and Canada, the telephone has achieved almost total penetration of households. As a result, telephone interviewing is the dominant mode of questionnaire administration. The same situation exists in some of the European countries. In Sweden, the number of telephones per 1,000 inhabitants exceeds 900, and in Stockholm the figure is even higher.[13] This, along with the low cost, has led to a sharp increase in the use of telephone interviews, which now account for 46 percent of the interviews conducted and constitute the dominant interviewing method. In the countries such as the Netherlands, the number of telephone interviews exceeds the number of personal interviews.[14] Even in these countries, the sampling of respondents for telephone interviewing may pose serious problems. (See Chapter 6 for a discussion of the issues related to the selection of probability samples in telephone interviewing.)

In many of the other European countries, telephone penetration is still not complete. Telephone penetration in Great Britain is only about 80 percent, and many practitioners are still skeptical of the value of telephone interviewing, especially for voting-intention measurement. In Finland, only about 15 percent of interviews are administered over the telephone. In Portugal, telephone penetration is still low (about 40%), except in the Lisbon area (85%). For this reason, only 17 percent of interviews conducted are telephone interviews.[15]

In Hong Kong, 96 percent of households (other than on outlying islands and on boats) can be contacted by telephone. With some persistence, evening telephone interviewing can successfully achieve interviews with 70 to 75 percent of selected respondents. Residents are uninhibited about using telephones and relaxed about telephone interviews. Yet, given the culture, this is not the most important mode of data collection.

In developing countries, only very few households have telephones. Telephone incidence is low in Africa. India is a predominantly rural society where the penetration of telephones is less than 10 percent of households. In Brazil, the proportion of households with telephones is low (less than 50 percent in large cities).[16] Even in countries such as Saudi Arabia, where telephone ownership is extensive, telephone directories tend to be incomplete and outdated. In many developing countries, telephone interviewing may present additional problems. Daytime calls to households may be unproductive, as social customs may prohibit the housewife from talking with strangers. This situation can be somewhat alleviated by using female telephone interviewers, but the employment of women creates many obstacles in such countries. In many cultures, face-to-face relationships are predominant. These factors severely limit the use of telephone interviewing.

Telephone interviews are most useful with relatively upscale consumers who are accustomed to business transactions by phone or consumers who can be reached by phone and can express themselves easily. With the decline of costs for international telephone calls, multicountry studies can be conducted from a single location. This greatly reduces the time and costs associated with the organization and control of the research project in each country. Furthermore, international calls obtain a high response rate, and the results have been found to be stable (i.e., the same results are obtained from the first 100 interviews as from the next 200 or 500). It is necessary to find interviewers fluent in the relevant languages, but in most European countries, this is not a problem.

Computer-assisted telephone interviewing (CATI) facilities are well developed in the United States and Canada and in some European countries, such as Germany. As the use of telephone interviewing is growing, they are becoming popular in other countries.[17]

## In-Home Personal Interviews

In-home interviews require a large pool of qualified interviewers. Contractual arrangements with interviewers vary considerably. For example, in France, there are three categories of interviewers: interviewers with annual guarantee for a specified duration, interviewers with annual guarantee for an unspecified duration, and freelance interviewers with no salary guarantee. Overheads may also vary. In France, the employer and the interviewer must pay large social security contributions, in Belgium the interviewers are self-employed and pay their own social security contributions, whereas in the United Kingdom, although both the employer and the interviewer pay national insurance contributions, these tend to be small.

Due to high cost, the use of in-home personal interviews has declined in the United States and Canada, but this is the dominant mode of collecting survey data in many parts of Europe and the developing world. In-home personal interviewing is the dominant interviewing method in Switzerland.[18] In Portugal, face-to-face interviews are 77 percent of the total interviews conducted. The majority of the surveys are done door to door, whereas some quick sociopolitical polls are carried out in the street using accidental routes. Likewise, in-home interviews are popular in many Latin American countries.

### REAL RESEARCH

## *Coke Tops in Americas and Around the World*

In one of the research surveys conducted by the Gallup Organization, the objective was to assess consumers' recall of different ads they had seen in the past month. In-home personal surveys were conducted by Gallup and its affiliates in the United States, Canada, Uruguay, Chile, Argentina, Brazil, Mexico, and Panama. In all 7,498 people were surveyed. Unaided recall was used to get responses. Questions like, "what brands of soft drink advertisements seen in the past month first comes to mind?" were asked. Results show that Coca-Cola ads are the choice of a new generation of both North and South Americans. Coca-Cola ads were

International survey research shows that Coca-Cola ads are the choice of a new generation of both North and South Americans.

among the top six ads mentioned in seven of the eight Western Hemisphere nations and were cited the most often in four countries. Ads of archrival, Pepsi-Cola Co., were named among the top six in four countries, and McDonald's Corp., appeared in the top six in two countries. However, none of these three made it to the top six in Brazil. In 2002, Interbrand (*www.interbrand.com*), a brand consulting firm, named Coca-Cola the world's most valuable brand. Whereas Coca-Cola may be the soft drink of choice in both North and South America, according to this firm, Coca-Cola is the company of choice around the world.[19] ∎

## Mall Intercept and CAPI

In North America, many marketing research organizations have permanent facilities in malls, equipped with interviewing rooms, kitchens, observation areas, and other devices. Mall intercepts constitute about 15 percent of the interviews in Canada and 20 percent in the United States. Although mall intercepts are being conducted in some European countries, such as Sweden, they are not popular in Europe or developing countries. In contrast, central location/street interviews constitute the dominant method of collecting survey data in France and the Netherlands.

However, some interesting developments with respect to computer-assisted personal interviewing (CAPI) are taking place in Europe. Interviewing programs for the home computer have been developed and used in panel studies and at central locations using computer-assisted personal interviewing (CAPI).[20]

## Mail Interviews

Because of low cost, mail interviews continue to be used in most developed countries where literacy is high and the postal system is well developed. Mail interviews constitute 6.2 percent of the interviews in Canada and 7 percent in the United States. In countries where the education level of the population is extremely high (Denmark, Finland, Iceland, Norway, Sweden, and the Netherlands), mail interviews are common.[21] In Africa, Asia, and South America, however, the use of mail surveys and mail panels is low because of illiteracy and the large proportion of population living in rural areas. In Hong Kong, mail surveys have been tried with varied success. Mail surveys are, typically, more effective in industrial international marketing research, although it is difficult to identify the appropriate respondent within each firm and to personalize the address. Nevertheless, mail surveys are used internationally, as illustrated by the following example.

**REAL RESEARCH**

*Worldwide Achievers*

Global Scan is a detailed survey conducted annually by Bates Worldwide, the principal operating unit of Cordiant Communications Group plc (*www.cordiantww.com*), to measure the attitudes and behaviors of 15,000 respondents in 14 countries. The questionnaire contains 120 attitudinal statements and is customized for each country by insertion of attitudes, lifestyles, and purchases (both product and brands).

The questionnaire is administered by mail, with local country offices responsible for distribution, meeting sampling requirements, and then transcribing the returned questionnaires to computer tape, which is shipped to the home office in New York. Global Scan averages a 50 percent response rate.

Bates claims that 95 percent of the combined population of all countries surveyed can be assigned to five segments. Based on the data, five lifestyle segments have emerged and have remained constant over time: strivers (26 percent), achievers (22 percent), pressured (13 percent), adapters (18 percent), and traditionals (16 percent). Thus, marketers have a common set of attitudes and behaviors for defining consumers all over the world. For example, the similarities between achievers in the United States, England, Australia, and Finland are greater than those between achievers and strivers in the United States. Global Scan collects detailed brand and category information on more than 1,000 products. Marketers can then use this information to develop specific strategies. Financial services company Merrill Lynch targeted the achievers on a global basis in 2003 because they tend to be heavy investors.[22] ■

## Mail and Scanner Panels

Mail panels are extensively used in the United Kingdom, France, Germany, and the Netherlands. Mail and diary panels are also available in Finland, Sweden, Italy, Spain, and other European countries. Use of panels may increase with the advent of new technology. For example, in Germany, two agencies (ACNielsen and GfK-Nurnberg) have installed fully electronic scanner test markets, based on the Behavior Scan model from the United States. Nielsen will use on-the-air television; GfK, cable. Panels of this kind have not yet been developed in Hong Kong or most of the developing countries.[23]

## Electronic Surveys

In the United States and Canada, the use of e-mail and the Internet is growing by leaps and bounds. As such, the use of these methods for conducting surveys is growing not only with business and institutional respondents, but also with households. Both these methods have become viable for conducting surveys related to a wide range of product categories and scenarios. The popularity of both e-mail and Internet surveys is also growing overseas. Both these types of surveys are increasingly being used in western Europe, where access to the Internet is freely available. However, in some parts of eastern Europe and in other developing countries, e-mail access is restricted and Internet availability is even poorer. Hence, these methods are not suitable for surveying the general population in these countries. However, surveys with business and institutional respondents may still be attempted, particularly using e-mail. E-mail surveys use pure text (ASCII) to represent questionnaires, and can be received and responded to by anyone with an e-mail address, whether or not they have access to the Internet. As we illustrate in the section on Internet and Computer Applications later in the chapter, multinational firms are using both e-mail and the Internet to survey their employees worldwide.[24]

As was discussed and illustrated in Chapter 6, an important consideration in selecting the methods of administering questionnaires is to ensure equivalence and comparability across countries. Issues of equivalence are also salient in measurement and scaling.

# MEASUREMENT AND SCALING

In international marketing research, it is critical to establish the equivalence of scales and measures used to obtain data from different countries. As illustrated in Figure 23.2, this requires an examination of construct equivalence, operational equivalence, scalar equivalence, and linguistic equivalence.[25]

*Construct equivalence* deals with the question of whether the marketing constructs (for example, opinion leadership, variety seeking, brand loyalty) have the same meaning and significance in different countries. In many countries, the number of brands available in a given product category is limited. In some countries, the dominant brands have become generic labels symbolizing the entire product category. Consequently, a different perspective on brand loyalty may have to be adopted in these countries.

Construct equivalence is comprised of conceptual equivalence, functional equivalence, and category equivalence. *Conceptual equivalence* deals with the interpretation of brands, products, consumer behavior, and marketing effort. For example, promotional sales are an integral component of marketing effort in the United States. On the other hand, in countries with shortage economies, where the market is dominated by the sellers, consumers view sales with suspicion because they believe that the product being promoted is of poor quality. *Functional equivalence* examines whether a given concept or behavior serves the same role or function in different countries. For example, in many developing countries, bicycles are predominantly a means of transportation rather than of recreation. Marketing research related to the use of bicycles in these countries must examine different motives, attitudes, behaviors, and even different competing products than such research would in the United States. *Category equivalence* refers to the category in which stimuli like products, brands, and behaviors are grouped. In the United States, the category of the principal shopper may be defined as either the male or female head of household. This category may be inappropriate in countries where routine daily shopping is done by a domestic servant. Furthermore, the category "household" itself varies across countries.

*Operational equivalence* concerns how theoretical constructs are operationalized to make measurements. In the United States, leisure may be operationalized as playing golf, tennis, or other sports; watching television; or basking in the sun. This operationalization may not be relevant in countries where people do not play these sports or do not have round-the-clock TV transmission. Lying in the sun is not normal behavior in countries with hot climates or where people have brown skin. *Item equivalence,* which is closely connected to operational equivalence, presupposes both construct and operational equivalence. To establish item equivalence, the construct should be measured by the same instrument in different countries.

*Scalar equivalence,* also called metric equivalence, is established if the other types of equivalence have been attained. This involves demonstrating that two individuals from different countries with the same value on some variable, such as brand loyalty, will score at the same level on the same test. Scalar equivalence has two aspects. The specific scale or scoring procedure used to establish the measure should be equivalent. The equivalence of response to a given measure in different countries should be considered. For example,

---

**construct equivalence**
Construct equivalence deals with the question of whether the marketing constructs have the same meaning and significance in different countries.

**conceptual equivalence**
Construct equivalence issue that deals specifically with whether the interpretation of brands, products, consumer behavior, and the marketing effort is the same in different countries.

**functional equivalence**
Construct equivalence issue that deals specifically with whether a given concept or behavior serves the same role or function in different countries.

**category equivalence**
Construct equivalence issue that deals specifically with whether the categories in which brands, products, and behavior are grouped is the same in different countries.

**operational equivalence**
A type of equivalence that measures how theoretical constructs are operationalized in different countries to measure marketing variables.

**item equivalence**
Proposes that the same instrument should be used in different countries.

**scalar equivalence**
The demonstration that two individuals from different countries with the same value on some variable will score at the same level on the same test; also called metric equivalence.

---

**Figure 23.2**
Scaling and Measurement Equivalence in International Marketing Research

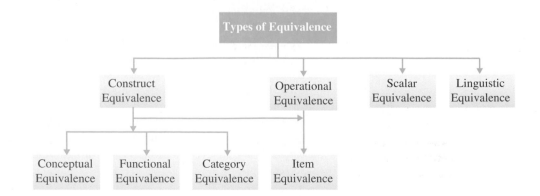

do the top-box or the top-two-boxes scores on a purchase-intent scale reflect similar likelihood of purchase in different countries? Finally, ***linguistic equivalence*** refers to both the spoken and the written language forms used in scales, questionnaires, and interviewing. The scales and other verbal stimuli should be translated so that they are readily understood by respondents in different countries and have equivalent meaning.[26]

# QUESTIONNAIRE TRANSLATION

The questions may have to be translated for administration in different cultures. Direct translation, in which a bilingual translator translates the questionnaire directly from a base language to the respondent's language, is frequently used. However, if the translator is not fluent in both languages and not familiar with both cultures, direct translation of certain words and phrases may be erroneous. Procedures such as back translation and parallel translation have been suggested to avoid these errors. In ***back translation,*** the questionnaire is translated from the base language by a bilingual speaker whose native language is the language into which the questionnaire is being translated. This version is then retranslated back into the original language by a bilingual whose native language is the initial or base language. Translation errors can then be identified. Several repeat translations and back translations may be necessary to develop equivalent questionnaires, and this process can be cumbersome and time consuming.[27]

An alternative procedure is ***parallel translation.*** A committee of translators, each of whom is fluent in at least two of the languages in which the questionnaire will be administered, discusses alternative versions of the questionnaire and makes modifications until consensus is reached. In countries where several languages are spoken, the questionnaire should be translated into the language of each respondent subgroup. It is important that any nonverbal stimuli (pictures and advertisements) also be translated using similar procedures. The following example underscores the importance of correct translation.

**REAL RESEARCH**

## *Researchers Can Get No Self-Respect in Germany*

A common questionnaire used to measure consumer values is the List of Values (LOV). In North America, it has revealed nine basic value segments of consumers. The most widely held values of Americans are self-respect, security, and warm relationships with others. To conduct a comparative study in Germany, the LOV had to be translated into a German version (GLOV). Through the process of translation and back translation, a suitable form was created; however, some inconsistencies remained. For example, it was very difficult to translate the English concepts of "warm relationships with others" and "self-respect" into German. As a result, the data revealed that significantly fewer Germans than Americans hold these as their most important values. The researchers concluded that the imprecise translation was more responsible for these results than actual differences in value orientations. The table shows the distribution of the top three values for each culture, with the rank in parentheses.

| *Values* | *Germany* | | *United States* | |
|---|---|---|---|---|
| Self-respect | 13% | (3) | 21% | (1) |
| Security | 24 | (2) | 21 | (2) |
| Warm relationships | 8 | (4) | 16 | (3) |
| Sense of belonging | 29 | (1) | 8 | (7) |

A similar study conducted in 2001 examined the significance of Chinese women's emerging roles. Data were collected via personal interviews from 1,000 women from mainland China. Based on six female role dimensions, the Chinese women were segmented into three groups. The groups were traditionalists, moderns, and ideologues and were found to have very different demographic and attitudinal characteristics. Among

---

**Sidebar definitions:**

*linguistic equivalence*
The equivalence of both spoken and written language forms used in scales and questionnaires.

*back translation*
A translation technique that translates a questionnaire from the base language by a translator whose native language is the one into which the questionnaire is being translated. This version is then retranslated back into the original language by a bilingual whose native language is the base language. Translation errors can then be identified.

*parallel translation*
A translation method in which a committee of translators, each of whom is fluent in at least two languages, discusses alternative versions of a questionnaire and makes modifications until consensus is reached.

these differences, consumption values associated with purchase decisions were one of the main differences.[28] ∎

# ETHICS IN MARKETING RESEARCH

Ethical responsibilities for marketing research conducted abroad are very similar to that conducted domestically. For each of the six stages of the marketing research design process, the same four stakeholders (client, researcher, respondent, and public) must act honorably and respect their responsibilities to one another. As the following example indicates, the ethical constraints facing marketing researchers abroad are fairly similar to those at home. For all the similarities, some ethical issues become more difficult. Conducting marketing research in a foreign country can easily become a political issue. Researchers must be careful to adopt the ethical guidelines of not only the domestic country but the host country as well.

## REAL RESEARCH

### *Europeans Legislate Data Privacy*

There is widespread implementation of data privacy laws in the European Union (EU). A prototype of the EU's data privacy laws is the United Kingdom's Data Protection Act (DPA) embodying eight guidelines.

1. Personal data will be obtained and processed fairly and lawfully.
2. Personal data will be held only for specified and lawful purposes.
3. Personal data will not be used for any reason other than the specified purpose.
4. Personal data for specified purposes will not be excessive in amount.
5. Personal data will be accurate and will be kept current.
6. Personal data will not be kept longer than necessary for the specified purpose.
7. Users of personal data must provide nondelayed access to personal data (at no expense) when individuals make requests to examine their personal data over reasonable intervals. Where appropriate, data users must correct or erase erroneous data.
8. Data users must take appropriate security measures against unauthorized access, alteration, disclosure, destruction, or loss of personal data.

In January 2001, the U.S. Department of Commerce launched the U.S Safe Harbor agreement with the European Union, which governed the transfer of personal data from member states of the EU to the United States. This negotiation followed the EC's 1998 Directive on Data, which forbids the transfer of personal data to non-EU nations that did not meet the protection standard established in the European data-privacy laws. As can be seen, the guidelines of the British DPA are similar to those espoused by the domestic codes of ethics.[29] ∎

# INTERNET AND COMPUTER APPLICATIONS

The Internet and computers can be extensively used in all phases of the international marketing research process. These uses parallel those discussed in the earlier chapters (1 through 22) and, therefore, will not be repeated here. The fact that the Internet can be used to communicate with respondents anywhere in the world has given a new dimension to international marketing research. For example, the online survey overcomes geographic boundaries by soliciting responses from around the world. The online survey also takes advantage of one interviewer (the computer) that can present the same survey in several different translations, as illustrated in the case of Hewlett Packard.

**REAL RESEARCH**

## Internet Surveys Pack Hewlett Packard's International Marketing Research Tool Box

Hewlett-Packard conducts online surveys to gather information about Internet users' perceptions about the HP Web site. Because HP customers are all over the world, the respondents get a choice of which language version of the surveys they wish to complete. Some other pages of the HP Web site are also available in several different translations. This approach recognizes the need to adapt marketing research tools as well as marketing communications to a more global environment.

As an example of one of the multilanguage surveys, the Web site contained an eight-page chemical analysis survey that first allowed the respondent to choose from six languages to complete the survey. The survey itself asked the respondents if having online information available in a local language is an advantage, compared to English.

Some parts of the survey were fixed-response alternative questions that asked the respondent to rate items on a scale of 1 to 5. This part of the survey was structured. There were other parts to the survey that were not as structured. For example, one objective of the survey was to determine how easy or difficult it is to find some information in the HP Chemical Analysis site. In this part of the survey, respondents were asked to search out information about two particular areas: the product features and benefits of the Mass Spectrometer Model HP 5973 and the application notes for the Gas Chromatograph Model HP 6890. Once the respondents looked for the information, they were instructed to return to the survey and answer questions about how easy it was to find the information on the Web site.

HP's Web site surveys collect data not only on the usefulness of its own Web site, but also information on how visitors to its site use the Internet overall. This helps HP keep up with trends in Internet usage as well as customer satisfaction. By monitoring how well received the Web site is in different languages, HP is also encouraging and nourishing global relationships. A 2001 international online survey was conducted to determine why online businesses lose sales from their Web sites. The study surveyed 1,264 experienced Internet shoppers in the United States, the United Kingdom, Japan, Sweden, France, and Germany. The findings of the study showed that 8 out of 10 attempted online purchases fail and purchasing attempts on the Internet are abandoned due to invasive information requests (52%), reluctance to enter credit card details (46%), Web site malfunction (42%), or failure to find the product (40%). This online international survey can help companies improve their Web sites and market their products successfully to the consumer in order to improve sales.[30] ■

Software programs that can facilitate cross-cultural research, such as INTERVIEWER, should become more widely available in the future to meet the challenges of international marketing research. INTERVIEWER by VOXCO of Montreal (Quebec), Canada (*www.voxco.com*) provides bilingual interviewing capability for computer-assisted telephone interviewing (CATI). With two keystrokes, operators can switch from a questionnaire written in English to the same questionnaire written in Spanish. This can even be done during the course of the interview in a matter of seconds. This feature markedly reduces the mental strain for bilingual interviewers. Such interviewing features prove useful in areas with nested cultures, such as in Miami, Los Angeles, or New York. In areas of the world where market areas spread beyond political or cultural boundaries, such as in Basel, Switzerland (near the three borders of Switzerland, France, and Germany), INTERVIEWER could be used with modification. Because of lower transnational telecommunication charges and political agreements permitting more open markets around the world, INTERVIEWER offered switching capability between nine languages as of 2003.

## FOCUS ON BURKE

Burke has had offices (either owned or licensed affiliates) in countries other than the United States for over 30 years. Among the many issues addressed relative to conducting research across cultural boundaries (as well as political boundaries) is the issue of creating a "common questionnaire" for different cultures.

Some researchers may initially approach a multicountry study as an issue of creating a questionnaire in their language and then working diligently to translate it accurately and with the proper tone into the language of another culture. This is required and necessary but not sufficient in many situations, as illustrated by the following projects.

A non-U.S. telephone company had their questionnaire translated into English to be administered in the United States by Burke's data-collection unit. Although the translation was very good, the questionnaire referred at many points to the U.S. National Telephone Company. The researcher had not done the simple secondary research to learn that the United States has hundreds of telephone companies and not a governmental national phone company as was true in the researcher's country. Dumb, you say? It happened.

A U.S. company wanted to do research on cooking chocolate in Mexico. The questionnaire was beautifully translated but failed to take into account the very different cooking behaviors and attitudes toward chocolate that were not present in the United States. For example, cooking chocolate in Mexico may be sold in large, loosely wrapped bars. If these bars are not exuding beads of oil on their surface, many cooks think they are not "natural and pure." The U.S. researcher had never heard of this, did not include this notion in the questionnaire, and completely missed why the product was not seen as acceptable.

The advice Burke gives to avoid such mistakes is: "Be concerned that you are asking about relevant issues in the culture before you worry about the translation!" The desire to have a common instrument cannot blind you to asking about issues that are culturally relevant in each country. In most situations, this requires local knowledge through local research professionals with access to secondary or primary research to aid in the "cultural translation" as well as the "language translation."

## SUMMARY

With the globalization of markets, international marketing research is burgeoning rapidly. The environment prevailing in the international markets being researched influences all six steps of the marketing research process. Important aspects of this environment include the marketing, government, legal, economic, structural, informational and technological, and sociocultural environment.

In collecting data from different countries, it is desirable to use survey methods with equivalent levels of reliability rather than the same method. It is critical to establish the equivalence of scales and measures in terms of construct

equivalence, operational equivalence, scalar equivalence, and linguistic equivalence. The questionnaire should be adapted to the specific cultural environment and should not be biased in favor of any one culture or language. Back translation and parallel translation are helpful in detecting translation errors.

The ethical concerns facing international marketing researchers are similar in many ways to the issues confronting domestic researchers. However, some of the responsibilities of the researchers become more difficult in the international arena. Specialized software has been developed to facilitate international marketing research.

## KEY TERMS AND CONCEPTS

construct equivalence, *674*
conceptual equivalence, *674*
functional equivalence, *674*
category equivalence, *674*

operational equivalence, *674*
item equivalence, *674*
scalar equivalence, *674*
linguistic equivalence, *675*

back translation, *675*
parallel translation, *675*

## EXERCISES

### Questions

1. Describe the aspects of the environment of each country that should be taken into account in international marketing research.

2. Describe the importance of considering the marketing environment in conducting international marketing research.

3. What is meant by the structural environment? How do the variables comprising the structural environment influence international marketing research?

4. What is meant by the informational and technological environment? How do the variables comprising the informational and technological environment influence international marketing research?

5. What is meant by the sociocultural environment? How do the variables comprising the sociocultural environment influence international marketing research?

6. Describe the status of telephone interviewing and CATI in foreign countries.

7. Describe the status of in-home personal interviewing in foreign countries.

8. Describe the status of mail interviewing in foreign countries.

9. How should the equivalence of scales and measures be established when the data are to be obtained from different countries or cultural units?

10. What problems are involved in the direct translation of a questionnaire into another language? How should these problems be addressed?

## Problems

1. Develop a short questionnaire to measure consumers' attitudes toward air travel. Have some foreign students do a direct translation to this questionnaire into their native language, and then do a back translation. What translation errors occurred? Correct these errors.

2. Formulate a research design for assessing consumer preferences for designer jeans in the United States, Sweden, Hong Kong, and China. Identify the sources of secondary data, decide whether any qualitative research should be carried out, recommend which survey method to use in each country, recommend one or more scaling techniques, develop a questionnaire in English, and suggest appropriate sampling procedures for use in each country.

# INTERNET AND COMPUTER EXERCISES

1. Identify several cultural issues pertaining to the Europeans by visiting *www.europa.eu.int*.

2. By visiting the Web site of Kodak (*www.kodak.com*), what can you learn about the company's international marketing efforts? Write a brief report.

3. You have to prepare a plan for marketing Coke in France. Visit *www.investinfrancena.org* or *www.afii.fr/NorthAmerica* to find the relevant information.

4. How can General Motors benefit from NAFTA? Visit *www.nafta-sec-alena.org/* to identify the relevant information.

5. Compile data on GDP, level of literacy, and percent of households with telephones for 20 different countries. Using SPSS, SAS, MINITAB, or EXCEL, run a regression analysis with GDP as the dependent variable and the other two variables as the independent variables. Interpret your results.

6. Compile data on consumption and expenditures for the following categories in 30 different countries: (1) food and beverages, (2) clothing and footwear, (3) housing and home operations, (4) household furnishings, (5) medical care and health, (6) transportation, and (7) recreation. Using SPSS, SAS, or MINITAB, determine if these variables are correlated. Run a factor analysis. Interpret your results.

7. Visit the Web site of a foreign firm and then visit the Web site of a competing U.S. firm. For example, visit the Web site of Unilever (U.K.) (*www.unilever.com/*) and P&G (U.S.) (*www.pg.com/*). Compare the two sites. Which site is more useful for a marketing researcher?

# ACTIVITIES

## Role Playing

1. You are the marketing research director for P&G for Europe. What challenges do you see in researching markets for household products in eastern European countries? Prepare a report for the P&G management in the United States. Make a presentation to a group of students representing P&G management.

2. You are a project manager in the international marketing research department of the Coca-Cola Company. Your boss, the director of the international marketing research department, has assigned you to a project designed to measure consumer preference for soft drinks in the United States, United Kingdom, Hong Kong, and Brazil. Your immediate task is to recommend survey methods to be used in this project and discuss them with your boss (who happens to be a student in your class).

## Fieldwork

1. Obtain the report of a marketing research project conducted in the United States from a local marketing research firm. Discuss how the research would be different if the same project were conducted in France.

2. Visit a local business with international operations. Discuss with them some possible international marketing research projects they could undertake.

## Group Discussion

1. Some scholars have argued that the same standardized marketing strategy should be adopted for all foreign markets. Does this imply that the marketing research process should also be standardized and the same procedures followed no matter where the research is being conducted? Discuss this question in a small group.

2. Discuss the impact of the globalization of markets on marketing research.

# CASES

# 3.1 Is Celebrity Advertising Worth Celebrating?

The theory behind the use of celebrities is that featuring stars in advertising has special cultural significance, born from the unique way they have constructed an image through various forms of media in the culture. In associating the star with the product, these special meanings are passed on to the products or brands. In a competitive market, a famous face can give a brand an added appeal and help it to stand out. Only a man playing John Houseman's roles in the way he played them could empower the Smith Barney slogan as Houseman did. Celebrities have particular configurations of meanings that cannot be found elsewhere.

Sports celebrities are often popular picks to be endorsers of everything from athletic apparel to vehicles. Nike has used basketball star Michael Jordan as an endorser and spokesperson since 1985. Nike continues to offer a line of athletic shoes under the Jordan name. In December of 2000, Venus Williams signed the most lucrative endorsement deal ever for a female athlete when she agreed to a three-year deal with Reebok International, reportedly worth more than $40 million. In 2000 and 2001, pro golfer Tiger Woods endorsed companies such as Buick, American Express, and Nike. Also, in 2001, Steve Young, former star quarterback for the San Francisco 49ers, appeared in commercial spots for Toyota, and Doug Flutie agreed to promote Sun Life Financial.

Another popular industry to draw celebrity endorsers from is the music industry. Soul singer Barry White appeared in commercials for Arby's in 2001 and R&B singer B.B. King continues to endorse Burger King in 2002. Britney Spears has been singing her way through Pepsi commercials to 2002. Along the same lines, companies often use actors, actresses, and supermodels to endorse their products. The state of California began using actors such as Clint Eastwood and Jack Nicholson at the end of 2001 in an attempt to boost tourism. Also in 2001, supermodel Christy Turlington endorsed Mayor's Jewelry and actresses Jennifer Aniston and Heather Locklear were used to promote L'Oreal's "Because You're Worth It" line of products. These are just a few of the many examples illustrating the recent usage of celebrities in advertising.

However, in addition to the exorbitant costs, there are risks and dangers associated with the use of celebrities in advertising. The best-laid plans can still backfire. Pepsi signed up Madonna for several million dollars in order to feature her in their campaign. The controversy over the religious imagery in Madonna's "Prayer" video led to the threat of a consumer boycott, and Pepsi lost $10 million. Actress Helena Bonham Carter admitted she did not wear make-up at the conference announcing her as the new face of Yardly. Cybill Shepherd's ad for the beef industry flopped when she publicly admitted that she rarely ate red meat. These examples are only a few of the problems with celebrity endorsements. Unfortunately, there have always been hidden dangers when using celebrities, as exemplified by the use of O. J. Simpson in Hertz advertising and the use of Lawrence Dallaglio (rugby player turned drug dealer) by Nike and Lloyds TSB. Other unforeseeable problems can arise. A celebrity's consumer appeal may fade if the celebrity "disappears from the media spotlight" before the end of their contract.

If so many dangers abound, why use celebrities? Many advertisers feel that celebrities make an advertisement more effective. Pepsi Cola and Revlon, for example, have boosted their products' images and sales by using Cindy Crawford in commercials. The use of celebrities has been demonstrated to lead to higher recall of an advertisement. Further evidence supporting the use of celebrities includes research showing that for attractiveness-related products, physically attractive celebrities elicit high credibility and attitude ratings for an ad. In early 2001, Revlon ceased using celebrity models and hired relative unknowns for their ad campaigns, thinking women wanted models with whom they could relate to more easily. In November 2001, they reversed this decision and started hiring celebrities such as Julianne Moore and Halle Berry after losing 10.6 percent of the cosmetics market share over the previous year. In 2000, it was estimated that around one-fourth of all commercials in the United States featured a celebrity.

However, there are mixed opinions about the affects that a celebrity has on brand sales. One research study done by Taylor Nelson Sofres in 2001 found surprising results about the effectiveness of celebrities in advertising. Of those polled, 91 percent said a celebrity had no effect on their decision to purchase a product. With research like this, many wonder why marketers shell out huge contracts to get celebrities to endorse their brands. One researcher, Michael Kamins, employed marketing research techniques in order to explore the effectiveness of celebrities in advertising and determine whether celebrity advertising is worth celebrating.

Kamins states that three processes of social influence determine whether an individual will adopt the attitude an advertiser is trying to convey: compliance, identification, and internalization. While the first of these factors is not relevant to Kamins' study, the last two hold considerable implications for celebrity advertising. Identification, where individuals try to imitate another person because they want to be like that person, is the most important factor determining a celebrity's influence in an advertisement. Internalization occurs when individuals imitate another because they perceive the other person to be sincere and to have values similar to their own. But this factor is not usually associated with celebrities.

However, Kamins inferred that if both identification and internalization could be achieved, the effectiveness of advertising would be increased. Therefore, he studied whether celebrities could increase the effectiveness of

advertising through the identification component, and whether so-called truth in advertising (operationalized as two-sided advertising, or advertising that included both positive and negative aspects of a product) could increase effectiveness through internalization. Furthermore, he wondered whether combining these two approaches resulted in even greater effectiveness.

In order to research this, a 2 × 2 factorial design was adopted. Sidedness (one-sided vs. two-sided) and type of spokesperson (celebrity vs. noncelebrity) were the two factors. Seventy-seven executives enrolled in an executive MBA program were randomly assigned to four groups: one-sided/noncelebrity, one-sided/celebrity, two-sided/noncelebrity, and two-sided/celebrity. Four ads corresponding to these criteria were made up, and each member of each group evaluated the appropriate ad on the basis of four variables: expectancy-value brand attitude (A), global brand attitude (B), global attitude toward the ad (C), and purchase intention (D). Expectancy-value brand attitude represented the degree to which the subject believed the product possessed an attribute the ad claimed it had.

## TABLE 1

### Means, Standard Deviations, and Number of Subjects

| VARIABLE EXPERIMENTAL CONDITION | | EXPECTANCY-VALUE BRAND ATTITUDE (A) | GLOBAL BRAND ATTITUDE (B) | GLOBAL ATTITUDE TOWARD THE AD (C) | PURCHASE INTENTION (D) |
|---|---|---|---|---|---|
| | (x) | 7.97 | 3.47 | 3.4 | 2.22 |
| | (sd) | 3.92 | 1.47 | 1.52 | 1.4 |
| One-sided | (n) | 38 | 40 | 40 | 40 |
| | (x) | 8.33 | 4.22 | 3.65 | 2.92 |
| | (sd) | 5.32 | 1.6 | 1.62 | 1.44 |
| Two-sided | (n) | 36 | 37 | 37 | 37 |
| | (x) | 8.04 | 3.5 | 3.65 | 2.55 |
| | (sd) | 4.73 | 1.55 | 1.46 | 1.38 |
| Noncelebrity | (n) | 38 | 40 | 40 | 40 |
| | (x) | 8.26 | 4.19 | 3.38 | 2.57 |
| | (sd) | 4.58 | 1.52 | 1.67 | 1.56 |
| Celebrity | (n) | 36 | 37 | 37 | 37 |
| | (x) | 7.89 | 3.45 | 3.55 | 2.4 |
| | (sd) | 4.48 | 1.57 | 1.39 | 1.5 |
| One-sided noncelebrity | (n) | 19 | 20 | 20 | 20 |
| | (x) | 8.04 | 3.5 | 3.25 | 2.05 |
| | (sd) | 3.4 | 1.4 | 1.65 | 1.32 |
| One-sided celebrity | (n) | 19 | 20 | 20 | 20 |
| | (x) | 8.18 | 3.55 | 3.75 | 2.7 |
| | (sd) | 5.09 | 1.57 | 1.55 | 1.26 |
| Two-sided noncelebrity | (n) | 19 | 20 | 20 | 20 |
| | (x) | 8.5 | 5 | 3.53 | 3.18 |
| | (sd) | 5.72 | 1.27 | 1.74 | 1.63 |
| Two-sided celebrity | (n) | 17 | 17 | 17 | 17 |

## TABLE 2

### ANOVA Results for the Dependent Measures

| VARIABLE | MAIN EFFECT FOR SIDEDNESS (E) | MAIN EFFECT FOR SPOKES-PERSON (S) | INTERACTION (E × S) |
|---|---|---|---|
| Expectancy-value brand attitude (A) | $F = 0.013$ | $F = 0.035$ | $F = 0.003$ |
| Global brand attitude (B) | $F = 10.876$[a] | $F = 4.355$[a] | $F = 4.233$[a] |
| Global attitude toward the ad (C) | $F = 0.209$ | $F = 0.276$ | $F = 0.001$ |
| Purchase intention (D) | $F = 4.845$[a] | $F = 0.050$ | $F = 1.868$ |

[a] indicates significance at $p = 0.05$.

Global brand attitude was a measure of how appealing the subjects found the product in the ad to be. Global attitude toward the ad was an evaluation of the ad's effectiveness. Purchase intention indicated how likely a subject was to purchase the product when an opportunity to do so came about.

Table 1 shows the mean (x) and standard deviation values (sd), along with the number of subjects (n), for each variable across each of the groups in Kamins' study. Note that the results from related groups can be combined to yield information on each of the four group characteristics (one-sided, two-sided, noncelebrity, and celebrity) separately. Table 2 contains the ANOVA results for the effect of the independent variables of sidedness (E) and type of spokesperson (S). These results provide valuable information about the effectiveness of celebrity spokespersons in advertisements.

## QUESTIONS

1. What kind of marketing research could businesses conduct to determine if their products would perform better with celebrity endorsements?
2. Discuss the role of MDS in the matching of a celebrity to the right product.
3. Could conjoint analysis be used to determine whether celebrities should be used and, if so, which celebrity should be selected? How could it be used?
4. What kinds of precautions or pretesting should the researcher engage in to ensure that the celebrities and two-sided ads used in the experiment were appropriate? What complications or contaminations might be present in the experimental results if these precautions were not taken?
5. Based on the results presented, do two-sided ads have an advantage over one-sided ads? Celebrity ads over noncelebrity ads?
6. Which type of ad is the most effective? The least effective? (Hint: look at the ANOVA results.)
7. Is analysis of variance an appropriate technique to use to analyze the data obtained in this study? Why or why not?
8. Could regression analysis be used to analyze the data obtained in this research? If so, how?

## REFERENCES

Nelson, Emily, "Revlon Changes Its Mind, Decides Celebrities Do Sell Makeup After All," *Wall Street Journal* (January 11, 2002): B1.

Mitchel Benson, "Here's Jack: California's Television Ads Use Famous Faces to Encourage Tourism," *Wall Street Journal* (December 18, 2001): B9.

Gregg Andrews, "Jewelry Chain Mayor's Taps Supermodel for Ad Campaign," *National Jeweler* 45 (22) (November 16, 2001): 6.

Dave Kovaleski, "Doug Flutie Carries Ball for Sun Life," *Pensions & Investments* 29 (22) (October 29, 2001): 8.

Suzy Bashford, "A Famous Face Is not Sufficient to Lure Consumers," *Marketing* (July 12, 2001): 5.

B. Zafer Erdogan, Michael J. Baker, Stephen Tagg, "Selecting Celebrity Endorsers: The Practitioner's Perspective," *Journal of Advertising Research* 41 (3) (May/June 2001): 39–48.

Kamins, Michael A., "An Investigation Into the 'Match-Up' Hypothesis in Celebrity Advertising: When Beauty May Be Only Skin Deep," *Journal of Advertising* 19 (1), (1990): 4–13.

Kamins, Michael A., "Celebrity and Noncelebrity Advertising in a Two-Sided Context," *Journal of Advertising Research* (June–July 1989): 34–42.

Kamins, M., M. Brand, S. Hoeke, and J. Moe, "Two-Sided Versus One-Sided Celebrity Endorsements: The Impact on Advertising Effectiveness and Credibility," *Journal of Advertising* 18 (2), (1989): 4–10.

# 3.2 The Demographic Discovery of the New Millennium

Many marketers are ill positioned to take advantage of one of the most important consumer segment groups to rise in the next 20 years: senior citizens. Senior households were responsible for one of every four dollars spent by U.S. households in 2000, and that percentage is expected to grow with the new millennium. The senior market consists of adults 55 years of age and older. According to Census 2000, there are 59,266,437 people over the age of 55 in the United States. The Census Bureau is expecting this number to grow at an estimated rate between 2.4 percent and 2.7 percent every year for the next decade. Below are two tables that show the 2000 senior population by age group and the future predictions of population in the 55 and older age group. The 50-plus generation accounts for one-third of the current population, and is expected to grow 42 percent over the next 15 years. This segment controls 42 percent of all after-tax income and 50 percent of all corporate stocks.

### Breakdown of 2000 Senior Population by Age Group

| 55–64 | 24,274,684 |
|-------|------------|
| 65–74 | 18,390,986 |
| 75–84 | 12,361,180 |
| 85+   | 4,239,587  |

### Estimated Population in the 55 + Age Group by Years (000)

| 2002 | 61,416 |
|------|--------|
| 2003 | 62,961 |
| 2004 | 64,499 |
| 2005 | 66,062 |
| 2006 | 67,688 |
| 2007 | 69,444 |
| 2008 | 71,248 |
| 2009 | 73,145 |
| 2010 | 75,144 |

The U.S. Census Bureau has also released information about the median income for the mature market segment, which is as follows.

### Median Income by Age Groups

| 55–64 | $44,993 |
|-------|---------|
| 65–69 | $30,880 |
| 70–74 | $25,085 |
| 75 +  | $18,873 |

Advertisers have not yet taken advantage of this nation's growing senior segment, and even though this group outspends many other segments of the market, advertisers are not producing large campaigns to attract senior customers. A useful classification for advertising purposes is based on attitudes toward advertising. These segments could then be profiled in terms of psychographic variables. A major concern of advertisers targeting the aged consumer has been the way in which the older population utilizes and evaluates information from advertising to make purchasing decisions.

One study by Davis and French explored aged consumers' use of advertising as a primary source of information in purchase decisions. The respondents were clustered based on attitudes toward advertising. Psychographic profiles were developed for each of the derived segments. A database of annual lifestyle surveys was used to obtain a sample of 217 married female respondents age 60 and over who were not employed outside the home. Respondents were asked to rate their degree of agreement with each of the 200 AIO (activities, interests, opinions) statements on the survey. Respondents were also asked to rate four attitudinal statements measuring information usage and beliefs about advertising, as well as the credibility of the source of advertising. Identical information obtained from a previous study was used for replication purposes by Davis and French.

The data on the four statements (shown in Table 1) measuring attitudes toward advertising was analyzed using Ward's method of clustering. Three clusters, Engaged, Autonomous, and Receptive consumers, were identified. Mean scores for each cluster are presented in Table 1. To test stability, replication of the cluster analysis was undertaken using the data obtained in the previous study. Ward's method of clustering was used to analyze the data from the previous study. Again, three clusters were obtained. Cluster means on each of the clustering variables for the replication sample (previous study) are also shown in Table 1 obtained by Davis and French.

To determine the psychographic differences among the three clusters, two additional steps were taken. First, one-way ANOVA was carried out to determine the discriminating variables. The three segments formed the grouping, or the independent variable, and each psychographic statement served as a dependent variable. Forty-one of the original 200 psychographic statements were found to be statistically significant. With the realization that some of these significant variables were probably measuring the same characteristics, a principal components factor analysis was carried out, with four factors (accounting for 60.3 percent of the variance) extracted in a varimax rotation. Factor scores were computed for each of the three segments by Davis and French, and Table 2 shows these scores, along with the variables that loaded highly on these factors and the variable means. This information can be used to provide psychographic profiles for each of the three segments identified in cluster analysis.

The results of this research and similar studies help marketers target the elderly, an especially promising group in light of the financial assets that they possess. By 2025, some

## TABLE 1

**Cluster Variable Scores by Segment**

| | | MEANS | |
|---|---|---|---|
| CLUSTER VARIABLE | SEGMENT | STUDY SAMPLE | REPLICATION |
| Advertising insults my intelligence. | Engaged | 5.24 (agree) | 4.35 (agree) |
| | Autonomous | 4.86 (agree) | 5.01 (agree) |
| | Receptive | 2.20 (disagree) | 2.10 (disagree) |
| Information from advertising helps me make better buying decisions. | Engaged | 4.69 (agree) | 4.88 (agree) |
| | Autonomous | 3.65 (agree) | 3.30 (disagree)[a] |
| | Receptive | 4.78 (agree) | 4.18 (agree) |
| I often seek out the advice of friends regarding brands and products. | Engaged | 4.55 (agree) | 4.21 (agree) |
| | Autonomous | 2.16 (disagree) | 1.87 (disagree) |
| | Receptive | 2.99 (disagree) | 3.02 (disagree) |
| I don't believe a company's ad when it claims that test results show its product to be better than competitive products. | Engaged | 4.78 (agree) | 4.25 (agree) |
| | Autonomous | 4.85 (agree) | 5.00 (agree) |
| | Receptive | 4.12 (agree) | 4.94 (agree) |

[a] 3.5 is the neutral point.

## TABLE 2

**Study Sample Mean Factor Scores by Cluster**

| FACTOR | ENGAGED | AUTONOMOUS | RECEPTIVE |
|---|---|---|---|
| Factor 1 | 0.45 | −0.11 | −0.21 |
| I am interested in the cultures of other countries. (loading = 0.58966) | 4.41 | 3.92 | 3.87 |
| I get personal satisfaction from using cosmetics. (loading = 0.48283) | 4.29 | 3.74 | 3.45 |
| I enjoy looking through fashion magazines. (loading = 0.41592) | 4.89 | 4.31 | 4.55 |
| Factor 2 | 0.29 | −0.32 | 0.17 |
| I like to bake. (loading = 0.70466) | 5.49 | 4.75 | 5.19 |
| I like to cook. (loading = 0.60793) | 5.28 | 4.63 | 5.01 |
| I always bake from scratch. (loading = 0.54404) | 3.76 | 3.15 | 3.62 |
| Factor 3 | 0.28 | −0.26 | 0.10 |
| I try to select foods that are fortified with vitamins and minerals. (loading = 0.49480) | 4.89 | 4.36 | 4.59 |
| I try to buy a company's products if they support educational TV. (loading = 0.43730) | 4.13 | 3.53 | 3.72 |
| I am usually among the first to try new products. (loading = 0.42521) | 3.47 | 2.81 | 3.19 |
| Factor 4 | 0.26 | 0.14 | −0.36 |
| Generally, manufacturers' warranties are not worth the paper they are printed on. (loading = 0.50313) | 3.31 | 3.47 | 2.82 |
| Most big companies are just out for themselves. (loading = 0.47638) | 4.25 | 4.50 | 3.93 |
| TV advertising is condescending toward women. (loading = 0.41031) | 4.25 | 4.24 | 3.55 |

113 million Americans—about 40 percent of the population—will be over 50. "Retirement used to be just a prelude to death, but now we live 20 plus years after retirement. People ought to think of their later years in terms of how they want to be productive," says Jim Denova, the director of a senior citizens center. Hence, the discovery of the mature market, the demographic discovery of the new millennium, represents a golden opportunity for marketers to target an old segment in a new way.

## QUESTIONS

1. Studies have found that the older (55 to 64 years), elderly (65 to 74 years), aged (75 to 84 years), and the very old (85 years and older) segments of the mature market need good supporting health services and facilities. Describe in detail how health maintenance organizations (HMOs) can effectively determine the differences in the health care needs of these segments. What kind of information should be obtained? Which statistical techniques should be used to analyze the data?

2. Do you think that the data analysis strategy adopted in the study reported in this case was appropriate? Why or why not?
3. Qualitatively describe each of the three clusters, based on the information in Table 1.
4. Interpret each factor in Table 2.
5. Do you think that the study reported in the case should have used discriminant analysis? If so, how?
6. Suggest an alternative data analysis strategy for the study reported.

## REFERENCES

Sid Ross, "Senior Webizens," *Adweek* 41 (48) (November 27, 2000): 46.

Erika Rasmusson, "The Age of Consumer Spending," *Sales and Marketing Management* 152 (04) (April 2000): 16.

B. Davis and W. French, "Exploring Advertising Usage Segments Among the Aged," *Journal of Advertising Research* (February–March 1989): 26.

# 3.3 Matsushita Retargets the U.S.A.

Matsushita (*www.matsushita.co.jp*), a large Japanese electronics producer renowned for its Panasonic, Quasar, and Technics brands, markets personal computers in the United States as a part of its overall program for the PC and PC peripherals market. A diversified conglomerate, its computer products include notebook computers, computer peripherals, multimedia products, displays, printers, scanners, and storage and networking devices. In 2001, Matsushita recorded annual sales of $61 billion, which is a 14 percent increase from the previous year. The Panasonic Industrial Company's office automation group managed this segment of the Japanese electronic giant's business (*www.panasonic.co.jp, www.panasonic.com*). In addition to manufacturing computers, printers, scanners, and CD-ROM drives, Matsushita also produces consumer products such as VCRs, CD and DVD players, TVs, and home appliances which account for 40 percent of their sales. The Matsushita group includes about 320 operating units in more than 45 countries. Its products are sold worldwide and Asia accounts for more than 70 percent of sales.

In 2001, Toshiba and Matsushita formed a joint venture company, called Toshiba Matsushita Display Technology Co., Ltd, in hopes of leveraging each other's technological strengths and diversifying beyond the PC and notebook LCD markets. They planned to produce products in emerging areas like organic light-emitting diodes (OLEDs), which is a very popular technology often used in the displays on personal digital assistants (PDAs) and cell phones. Analysts said that the combined revenue from the joint venture of Toshiba and Matsushita would place the new company among the top five suppliers of liquid crystal displays (LCDs). The joint venture company began operation on April 1, 2002. The sales forecast for the first fiscal year of operation, ending March 31, 2003, was Y340 billion.

With recent investment in flat panel displays and storage units, Matsushita has the marketing edge to propel itself further into the forefront of peripherals. The firm is a pioneer in DVD (digital video disc), a new wave in high-density data storage. The potential of this technology, which can store four hours of visual material on a single sided 12-cm disk, offers a wide range of applications. DVD-ROM drives give Tandy a strategic marketing point for Matsushita's DVD-supporting PCs. As its partner, Matsushita makes big steps towards expanding the horizons of multimedia applications, and Tandy can offer consumers the latest technologies. How did the Matsushita and Tandy alliance come about?

The Tandy-Panasonic alliance turned out to be strategic as computer retailing is becoming the biggest segment in consumer electronics, and is expected to dwarf the rest of the computer electronics industry. New capabilities, beyond just the breakthrough in storage technology, are expected to emerge at the fastest rate ever in the industry's history during the 2000s. As a result, PC companies will have to anticipate the needs of the consumer even more quickly and react to changes, as well as finding ways to support users of the new technology. Marketing research will help identify the needs of these new markets and give marketers ideas of how to satisfy these new needs which are likely to be different than those faced by PC and PC component marketers before.

Although some of Panasonic's products continue to be sold through Radio Shack retail outlets, the company also makes its products available through other means of distribution. Panasonic products, such as electronic batteries (for cell phones, PDAs, calculators, etc.), multimedia cards for digital devices, and phones can be purchased through Radio Shack stores. Panasonic has also internalized some of its distribution by allowing a wide range of consumer products to be purchased directly from its Web site. Including the above-mentioned items, the Panasonic Web page (*www.panasonic.com*) also offers computer peripherals, television accessories, and business equipment among other products. In addition, there are other authorized online dealers of Panasonic products including Best Buy, Circuit City, and Sears. Retailers selling Panasonic products include Office Max, Sears, and Comp USA, among others.

The marketing department of Panasonic's office automation group designed a promotional campaign for its new desktop and notebook computers (PCs). While the computers were suited for both the household and business markets, depending on the model, Panasonic wished to determine executives' willingness to buy Panasonic PCs. Management particularly wanted information in three areas: the reactions of businesses of various sizes; the impact of familiarity with Panasonic PCs on willingness to buy; and how American businesses were using PCs in the workplace. This led to the related question of whether sales of peripherals to technically competent PC users could be increased.

To address these issues, 1,080 companies throughout the United States were selected based on a stratified random sample and sent a questionnaire designed to uncover executives' willingness to purchase a Panasonic PC assuming they were in the market for a PC. The companies were stratified along three variables: company size, familiarity with Panasonic PCs, and business application of PCs. Each of these variables could assume one of three values as listed below.

| Variable | Value |
| --- | --- |
| Company Size | |
| Small/entrepreneurial | 1 |
| Medium/private | 2 |
| Division of major corporation | 3 |
| Familiarity with Panasonic PCs | |
| No experience | 1 |
| Has purchased peripherals/no knowledge of Panasonic PCs | 2 |
| Has purchased or is familiar with Panasonic PCs | 3 |
| Business Applications | |
| Individual use (word processing and data analysis) | 1 |
| Departmental use (functional computing, networking) | 2 |
| Corporate use (enterprise integration) | 3 |

Forty respondents were randomly assigned to each of the 27 possible combinations of variables (i.e., 40 respondents with Low-Low-Low ratings, 40 with Low-Low-Medium

ratings, etc.). The respondents' stated willingness to purchase a Panasonic PC was measured on an 11-point scale.

This design was chosen to allow for subsequent data analysis. Using SPSS, SAS, MINITAB, or EXCEL (or a similar statistical software package), you have been assigned to analyze the data using the following procedures.

1. Frequency distribution: Determine whether variables are appropriate for further analysis by running frequency distributions on all the variables.
2. Cross-tabulations: Recode the dependent variable, Willingness to Buy, into three relatively equal groups (low, medium, and high). Run cross-tabulations on the dependent variable with each of the independent variables (Company Size, Familiarity, and Business Application) for Panasonic PCs. Then, run cross-tabulations on the dependent variable with Familiarity with Panasonic PCs controlling for Business Application; on Company Size controlling for Business Application; and on Company Size controlling for Familiarity with Panasonic PCs. Interpret the results for management.
3. Regression: Regress the dependent variable on two dummy variables each for Company Size, Familiarity with Panasonic PCs, and Business Application. (Note that each independent variable has three categories and will therefore be represented by two dummy variables.) Interpret the results for management.
4. One-way analysis of variance: Explain the variation in the dependent variable by running three ANOVAs of the dependent variable with each of the predictor variables (Company Size, Familiarity with Panasonic PCs, and Business Application).
5. Three-way analysis of variance: Explain the variation in the dependent variable by running a three-way ANOVA to determine interaction effects between the predictor variables.
6. Discriminant analysis: Group the dependent variable into three relatively equal groups based on its distribution, run discriminant analysis on the grouped data with the dummy variables created for regression, and interpret the results for management.

The data for this case are provided on CD-ROM as well as the Web site. In the text (tab delimited) data file, the first variable represents the stated willingness to purchase a Panasonic PC. The next three variables, in the order listed in the case, represent the variables used to classify the companies. In addition, the data are also provided as an SPSS file and as an EXCEL file.

The principle consultant of your firm has asked you to analyze the data using a significance level of 0.05 and prepare a thorough report detailing the results of the analysis and offering recommendations for Panasonic management on their promotional program for the PCs. Remember that your target market is American business executives. Your mission, while not impossible, is a difficult one—help Panasonic penetrate this market and thus enable Matsushita to retarget the U.S.A.

## REFERENCES

Spencer Chin, "Toshiba, Matsushita Sign Strategic Pact," *EBN* 1285 (October 22, 2001): 3.

"Matsushita," *Forbes* 159 (1) (January 13, 1997): S7.

www.hoovers.com/co/capsule/3/0,2163,41873,00.html

Note: This case was prepared for class discussion purposes only and does not represent the views of Matsushita, Tandy, or their affiliates. The problem scenario is hypothetical and the data provided are simulated.

# 3.4 Pampers Develops a Rash — A Rash of Market Share

In 2001, the disposable diaper industry reached sales of $3.9 billion. Traditionally, the industry's top selling brand was Procter & Gamble's (*www.pg.com*) Pampers (*www.pampers. com*) line of diapers. Procter & Gamble dominated the market through the 1970s and into the 1980s with Pampers as its flagship offering. In the late 1970s, Luvs was added as a secondary offering to compete with Kimberly-Clark's (*www. kimberly-clark.com*) Huggies (*www.huggies.com*) brand. By 1985, Huggies controlled 32.6 percent of the market and was a major threat to P&G's industry leadership.

Beginning in 1994 and 1995, Huggies began to lead both Procter & Gamble brands in market share of the then $3.6 billion diaper industry. In 1996, Pampers and Luvs gave P&G a combined 36.9 percent share of the market while Huggies took 39.7 percent. While Huggies grabbed share in 1995, analysts stated that this share came at the expense of Pampers' market stake. Meanwhile, P&G undertook efforts to regain the top spot, by spending more promotional dollars and introducing new innovations. In 1996, P&G spent $48 million on diaper promotions. The company spent $8 million to add breathable side panels to its Pampers Premium brand. The panel strips allowed air to flow into the diaper without any leakage, and were supposed to lower the humidity in the diaper, thus reducing diaper rash.

In 1997, Huggies continued to lead the market, especially with Huggies' Pull-Up Training Pants holding a 10 percent market share. The Huggies brand was largely responsible for much of Kimberly-Clark's lead over Procter & Gamble. Kimberly-Clark's strategy was to segment the market with new niche products, and the strategy worked very well. Huggies Overnites, diapers for overnight use, and Huggies Pull-Ups GoodNites, diapers for older children who wet the bed, were new introductions that catered to specific segments of the market. The company was testing Huggies Little Swimmers Swim-pants, diapers designed to withstand swimming, and began nationwide marketing of the product in 1998.

In 1997, Procter & Gamble preceded its rival in introducing a product that addressed a new concern among consumers—skin care. P&G rolled out another innovation in diapers which was a diaper lining that was actually good for the baby's skin with Pampers Gentle Touch lining, backed by a $25 million promotional campaign. The lining contained a special blend of three skin-soothing chemicals that transfer to the baby's skin evenly. Pampers continued its focus on skincare with the introduction of Pampers Rash Guard in late 1999. Tests have shown that the formulation of zinc oxide and petrolatum used in the diaper lining reduces diaper rash without interfering with moving moisture away from the baby's skin. These innovations have proven very successful for P&G. Information Resources, Inc. listed Pampers Rash Guard as number nine on its list of the "top 10 best selling new products in the consumer packaged goods industry for 1999–2000." During the 52 weeks following the introduction of the product, sales reached $97.2 million. Likewise, P&G made new introductions under the Luvs brand. In 2000 Luvs Splashwear was introduced to provide consumers with a diaper babies could use in the pool. In 2001 Luvs Overnights were introduced for babies that needed improved leakage performance overnight. In 2002 SleepDrys from Luvs were introduced for children 4 and up that wet the bed.

In the beginning of 2002, both P&G and Kimberly-Clark had some unique product features that the competing brand was not offering. For example, Kimberly-Clark was marketing a Pull-Ups brand diaper that was targeting mothers with toddlers who were going through potty training. The disposable training diaper could be pulled on and off like regular underwear, but still had the absorbency features of a diaper. Kimberly-Clark was also offering GoodNites brand disposable underpants for older children who wet the bed. P&G had a unique hold on the skin care market with their Pampers Rash Guard Diaper, and had just introduced a Pampers Baby Dry brand with Quick Grip sides that could be fastened and re-fastened to get a perfect fit. Both Kimberly-Clark and Procter & Gamble were offering swimming diapers, overnight diapers with extra absorbency, diapers with added stretch for a better fit, and premium top-of-the-line diapers.

To remain on the cutting edge of customer needs, Procter & Gamble needs to continue to seek out and address exactly what consumers are searching for in a diaper before any rival, as the firm did by introducing the Pampers Gentle Touch lining. Thus, the use of marketing research may be the key to enabling P&G to regain leadership in the diaper market.

In this increasingly competitive diaper market, P&G's marketing department desired to formulate new approaches to the construction and marketing of Pampers to position them effectively against Huggies without cannibalizing Luvs. To

## TABLE 1

**Disposable Diaper Market Share (percent)**

|  | 1990 | 1991 | 1992 | 1993 | 1994 | 1995 | 1996 | 1997 | 1998 | 1999 | 2000 |
|---|---|---|---|---|---|---|---|---|---|---|---|
| Pampers | 24.4 | 27.2 | 29.2 | 28.0 | 24.9 | 26.8 | 25.6 | 25.1 | 18.6 | 24.2 | 23.4 |
| Luvs | 23.2 | 20.0 | 14.3 | 13.1 | 12.5 | 10.5 | 11.3 | 12.2 | 12.6 | 12.8 | 12.6 |
| TOTAL P&G | 47.6 | 47.2 | 43.5 | 41.1 | 37.4 | 37.3 | 36.9 | 37.3 | 31.2 | 37.0 | 36.0 |
| Huggies (K-C) | 30.9 | 36.3 | 37.2 | 38.4 | 38.9 | 39.6 | 39.7 | 39.6 | 38.0 | 42.7 | 44.0 |
| Private Label/Others | 21.5 | 16.5 | 19.3 | 20.5 | 23.7 | 23.1 | 23.4 | 23.1 | 30.8 | 20.3 | 20.0 |

do so, 300 mothers of infants were surveyed. Each was given a randomly selected brand of diaper (either Pampers, Luvs, or Huggies) and asked to rate that diaper on nine attributes and to give her overall preference for the brand. Preference was obtained on a seven-point Likert type scale (1 = Not at All Preferred; 7 = Greatly Preferred). Diaper ratings on the nine attributes were also obtained on seven-point Likert type scales (1 = Very Unfavorable; 7 = Very Favorable). The study was designed so that each of the three brands appeared 100 times. The goal of the study was to learn which attributes of diapers were most important in influencing purchase preference (Y). The nine attributes used in the study were:

| Variable | Attribute | Marketing Options |
|---|---|---|
| $X_1$ | Count per box | Desire large counts per box? |
| $X_2$ | Price | Pay a premium price? |
| $X_3$ | Value | Promote high value? |
| $X_4$ | Skincare | Offer high degree of skin care? |
| $X_5$ | Style | Prints/colors vs. plain diapers |
| $X_6$ | Absorbency | Regular vs. super absorbency |
| $X_7$ | Leakage | Narrow/tapered vs. regular crotch |
| $X_8$ | Comfort/size | Extra padding and form-fitting gathers? |
| $X_9$ | Taping | Resealable tape vs. regular tape |

Data were collected at a suburban mall using the mall intercept technique and are provided on CD-ROM as well as the Web site. In the text (tab delimited) data file, the first variable represents brand preference (Y). The next nine variables represent the ratings of the brands on the nine attributes in the order listed in the case ($X_1$ to $X_9$). In addition, the data are also provided as an SPSS file and as an EXCEL file.

## QUESTIONS

You must analyze the data and prepare a report for the marketing department. The one-page memo you received suggested that you use the following procedures:

1. Frequency distribution: Run a frequency distribution for each variable and show bar graphs of the first three variables.
2. Cross-tabulations: Group brand preference as low, medium, and high under the formula low = 1 or 2, medium = 3 to 5, and high = 6 or 7. Group all independent variables as either: low = 1 to 3, medium = 4, and high = 5 to 7. Run two-variable cross-tabulations of preference with each independent variable. Run the

following three-variable cross-tabulations: preference with count per box, controlling for price; preference with unisex, controlling for style; and preference with comfort, controlling for taping. Interpret these results for management.
3. Regression: Run a regression equation for brand preference that includes all independent variables in the model, and describe how meaningful the model is. Interpret the results for management.
4. One-way analysis of variance: Group all independent variables into low, medium, and high groups as you did for cross-tabulations. Run a one-way analysis of variance on each independent variable with brand preference. Explain the results to management.
5. Discriminant analysis: Group brand preference into two relatively equal groups based on its distribution. Run discriminant analysis on the grouped data and interpret the results for management. Repeat this analysis by grouping brand preference into three relatively equal groups.
6. Factor analysis: Determine any underlying factors inherent in the data by running a factor analysis using principle components extraction with varimax rotation. Print all available statistics. Save the factor scores and regress these on brand preference. Interpret these results for management.
7. Cluster analysis: Use a nonhierarchical procedure to cluster the respondents, based on the independent variables, into two, three, four, and five clusters. Also run a hierarchical procedure to obtain five clusters using Ward's method and creating a dendrogram. Interpret all these results for management.

Interpret the results of the survey and make recommendations based on your findings to the marketing department. They want your opinion about which of the nine attributes mothers value most highly, as well as your ideas for specific actions that can increase market share for Pampers in today's market. The marketing department is counting on your recommendations to provide them with ways to improve Pampers' image and cure the rash of market share loss.

## REFERENCES

Renee M. Kruger, "What Counts with Diapers," *Discount Merchandiser* 40 (3) (March 2000): 60–62.

Cheryl Guttman, "New Derm-Friendly Dandy Dominates Disposable Diapers," *Dermatology Times* 21 (3) (March 2000): 34.

"Cleaning Products and Convenient Foods Highlight IRI's List of Hottest New Products for 1999–2000" at www.infores.com/public/global/news/glo_new_j31topten.htm.

Note: This case was prepared for class discussion purposes only and does not represent the views of Procter & Gamble or their affiliates. The problem scenario is hypothetical and the data provided are simulated.

# 3.5 DaimlerChrysler Seeks a New Image

"I'd trade in my Corvette convertible in a minute to buy this car," exclaimed an excited observer at an advance showing of the then Chrysler Motors Corporation's (now DaimlerChrysler, *www.daimlerchrysler.com*) design ideas for the 1990s. Since battling back from the brink of bankruptcy in the late 1970s, Chrysler continued to run a distant third to GM and Ford in the American automobile market, and even that position was challenged by Honda in 1990 (see Table 1). Chrysler dramatically rebounded in the early 1980s and gained almost two percentage points over the first five years of the 1980s by adding more economical, middle-class cars to its line of luxury sedans. However, increased competition from Japanese imports, poor product quality, and unimaginative design led to falling market share in the latter half of the decade.

Chrysler did, however, succeed with its minivan. Because of their triumph with the minivan, Chrysler was even more determined to succeed in the car market, so engineers and managers tried to design automobiles that fit the stylish, high-quality image Chrysler needed. Chrysler continued to maintain its business strategy of focusing on profit instead of market share, avoiding global alliances, and thriving on a shortage of capital. In 1989, Chrysler held an advance showing of concept cars for the 1990s that included a V-10 engine for both trucks and cars. Two stylish, yet pragmatic concepts were released, including the Chrysler Millennium and the tiny Plymouth Speedster. Both cars featured eye-catching design but failed to deliver performance because underneath they were based on the traditional Chrysler platform and powertrain. The reviewers, however, did take note of the rear-drive two-seat sports car, made available in 1992, which incorporated the V-10 engine. Code-named the Dodge TBD (To Be Determined) and later named the Dodge Viper, it looked like a Chevrolet Corvette — but carried a price tag of $55,000. Since the introduction of the Viper (*www.dodge.com/viper*), Chrysler raised the starting price several times. At the beginning of 2002, Chrysler added a four-figure price hike bringing the price to a starting value of $75,500 for the RT/10 Roadster model and $76,000 for the GTS Coupe model. The Viper was positioned to restore Chrysler's reputation for designing exciting cars.

Even though some call the Dodge Viper the "sexiest yet silliest" car around, it appears that the introduction of the Dodge Viper was a success. Recently, Chrysler Corporation President John Lutz stated that the company will keep Viper production lower than the number of Vipers that are demanded, estimated as approximately 2000 cars per year. Chrysler also revealed that it would offer the Viper in two new colors, emerald green and yellow. Previously, the first 250 cars were red, and the rest were painted black. Improvements are also planned for the interior of the Viper. Chrysler also introduced a coupe version of the Viper, the Viper GTS, which featured a roof instead of a soft convertible top. In April 2002, Dodge planned to end the production of the GTS coupe with a limited Final Edition production run. The Final Edition GTS will be painted an eye-catching red and have white racing stripes. It will feature other unique touches such as a black leather steering wheel and shift knob embellished with red stitching. Only 360 of the Final Edition GTS models will be produced. In May 2002, Dodge planned to begin production on the 2003 Dodge Viper SRT-10, which will be available exclusively in convertible form.

For continued success the Viper must attract the yuppie crowd—the highly educated, affluent baby boomers—that tend to prefer imported vehicles. Because this group would be the prime target group for such a high-performance car, Chrysler needed to ensure that it could compete in a market traditionally dominated by Corvette, Mazda Miata, Porsche Boxster, Porsche 911/96, and Mitsubishi 3000GT. Primary concerns for Chrysler were overcoming its boxcar image with this group, determining if they should offer incentives on the Dodge Viper, the importance of styling and prestige when promoting to this market, and how to exploit its merger with Daimler-Benz to the advantage of Viper.

To address these concerns, 30 statements were constructed to measure attitudes towards these factors and to classify the respondents. The respondents used a nine-point Likert scale (1 = definitely disagree, 9 = definitely agree). The respondents were obtained from the mailing lists of Car and Driver, Business Week, and Inc. magazines and they were telephoned at their homes by an independent surveying company. The statements used in the survey of 400 respondents are listed below:

1. I am in very good physical condition.
2. When I must choose between the two, I usually dress for fashion, not comfort.
3. I have more stylish clothes than most of my friends.

### TABLE 1

**U.S. Automobile Market Shares (%)**

| Year | Chrysler | Ford | G.M. | Honda | Other |
|------|----------|------|------|-------|-------|
| 1980 | 10.7 | 16.6 | 46.8 | 4.3 | 21.6 |
| 1985 | 12.5 | 18.8 | 42.5 | 5.0 | 21.2 |
| 1990 | 9.3 | 23.9 | 35.5 | 9.4 | 21.9 |
| 1993 | 15.0 | 26.0 | 34.0 | 5.0 | 20.0 |
| 1996 | 15.9 | 25.1 | 32.1 | 5.5 | 21.4 |
| 2001 | 12.8 | 27.1 | 28.5 | 7.0 | 24.6 |

4. I want to look a little different from others.
5. Life is too short not to take some gambles.
6. I am not concerned about the ozone layer.
7. I think the government is doing too much to control pollution.
8. Basically, society today is fine.
9. I don't have time to volunteer for charities.
10. Our family is not too heavily in debt today.
11. I like to pay cash for everything I buy.
12. I pretty much spend for today and let tomorrow bring what it will.
13. I use credit cards because I can pay the bill off slowly.
14. I seldom use coupons when I shop.
15. Interest rates are low enough to allow me to buy what I want.
16. I have more self-confidence than most of my friends.
17. I like to be considered a leader.
18. Others often ask me to help them out of a jam.
19. Children are the most important thing in a marriage.
20. I would rather spend a quiet evening at home than go out to a party.
21. American-made cars can't compare with foreign-made cars.
22. The government should restrict imports of products from Japan.
23. Americans should always try to buy American products.
24. I would like to take a trip around the world.
25. I wish I could leave my present life and do something entirely different.
26. I am usually among the first to try new products.
27. I like to work hard and play hard.
28. Skeptical predictions are usually wrong.
29. I can do anything I set my mind to.
30. Five years from now, my income will be a lot higher than it is now.

In addition, the criterion variable, attitude towards Dodge Viper, was measured by asking each person to respond to the statement, "I would consider buying the Dodge Viper made by DaimlerChrysler." This statement was measured on the same nine-point scale as the 30 predictor statements.

The data for the case are provided on CD-ROM as well as the Web site. In the text (tab delimited) data file, the first variable represents attitude toward a Chrysler sports car. The next 30 variables, in the order listed in the case, represent the ratings of the lifestyle statements. In addition, the data are also provided as an SPSS file and as an EXCEL file.

## QUESTIONS

The director of marketing for Chrysler is interested in knowing the psychological characteristics of the yuppies to configure the Dodge Viper program. You have been presented with the responses from the survey outlined above. Analyze the data according to the following guidelines:

1. Frequency distribution: Ensure that each variable is appropriate for analysis by running a frequency distribution for each variable.
2. Regression: Using a stepwise regression analysis, locate those variables that best explain the criterion variable. Evaluate the strength of the model and assess the impact of each variable included on the criterion variable.
3. Factor analysis: Determine the underlying psychological factors that characterize the respondents by means of factor analysis of all 30 independent variables. Use principle component extraction with varimax rotation for ease of interpretation. Save the factor scores and then regress them on the criterion variable, forcing all predictor variables to be included in the analysis. Evaluate the strength of this model and compare it with the initial regression. Use the factor scores to cluster the respondents into three groups. Discuss the significance of the groups based on the underlying factors. Repeat this cluster analysis for four groups.
4. Cluster analysis: Cluster the respondents on the original variables into three and four clusters. Which is a better model? Compare these cluster results with the cluster results on the factor scores. Which is easier to interpret, and which explains the data better?

Based on the analysis, prepare a report to management explaining the yuppie consumer and offering recommendations on the design of the Dodge Viper. Your recommendations should aid DaimlerChrysler in achieving what they seek: a new image for the Viper that is attractive to the yuppie market and that helps them outperform the competition in the performance car market.

## REFERENCES

Jeffrey McCracken, "Dodge's SRT-4 Aims Speed at 20-ish Set," *Knight Ridder Tribune Business News* (January 4, 2002): 1.
John K. Teahen, Jr., "Dodge Viper Gets 4-Digit Price Hike," *Automotive News* 76 (5959) (November 26, 2001): 42.
*www.activemedia-guide.com*

# VIDEO CASES

## 3.1 The Mayo Clinic: Staying Healthy with Marketing Research

William and Charles Mayo began practicing medicine in the 1880s in Rochester, Minnesota. They were quickly recognized as extremely talented surgeons, and the number of their patients increased so much that they were forced to think about the expansion of their practice. Around the turn of the century the Mayo brothers began inviting others to join their practice.

The Mayos had a new vision for practicing medicine and they thought partnerships with other individuals who had varying expertise would further enhance the care of their patients. Dr. William Mayo had the vision that medicine could be "a cooperative science; the clinician, the specialist, and the laboratory worker united for the good of the patient, each assisting in the elucidation of the problem at hand, and each dependent upon the other for support." The idea was unique and the balance of practice, research, and education is what helped the Mayo Clinic excel. The partnerships that the Mayos entered into created one of the first private group practices of medicine in the United States. In 1919, the Mayo brothers turned their partnership into a not-for-profit, charitable organization known as the Mayo Foundation. All proceeds beyond operating expenses were to be contributed to education, research, and patient care. The Mayo Clinic has been operating in this fashion ever since.

Today, the Mayo Clinic employs more than 45,000 physicians, scientists, nurses, and staff. It encompasses four hospitals and three clinics in Minnesota, Florida, and Arizona. Over six million people have received treatment at the Mayo Clinic since it was founded approximately 100 years ago.

Philanthropy is a big part of the Mayo Clinic. From the Mayo's donations in 1919, philanthropy has been deeply rooted in the Mayo Clinic's functionality. In 2001, 46,340 donors provided $146.3 million in contributions, private grants, and endowments. These donations are used heavily in research and education, and Mayo's capital expansion depends on these investments.

Revenues for 2001 were $4.1 billion, up from $3.7 billion in 2000. Income from current activities was $53.2 million for 2001, up from $16 million in 2000. The Mayo Clinic operated on a 1.3 percent margin. Patient care is the largest form of revenue. Despite the increase in revenues, the Mayo Clinic had a net loss of $59.1 million in 2001. The main cause for this was a loss in investments, which reflected the overall market for the year. The Mayo Clinic will be increasingly looking to develop relationships with foundations, benefactors, government, and industry to help meet their objectives in the future. The Mayo Clinic continues to donate huge amounts of money to education and research. In 2001, Mayo contributed $104.3 million to education and $127.9 million to research. This was in addition to the amounts donated by outside sources.

The Mayo Clinic brand was born through building the practice. The majority of its business is brought in through the positive experiences that patients have at the Mayo Clinic. Satisfied patients are the key to the Clinic's success. The brand's existence is due to the popularity of the Clinic, which is a result of the care it provides as well as the environment it has created. Collaboration throughout the practice has resulted in excellent care, better methods, and innovation. Mayo has done this while also being mindful of the environment in which the care takes place. Marketing research revealed that the Clinic environment is an important part of the patient's experience. Therefore, Mayo breaks the mold of a plain, static look with the addition of soothing music and elaborate art. Mayo believes that this adds to the patients' experience and helps them heal faster. Over the years, the Mayo Clinic has become a name that the public trusts despite the lack of any advertising. It has a strong reputation as a research center, a specialty care provider, and a school of medicine.

In the mid 1980s, the Mayo Clinic expanded to three locations and thus began the process of expanding and leveraging its brand. It created a marketing department to help with the management of the brand. Despite spending only 0.25 percent of its budget on marketing, the Mayo Clinic has been able to maintain its strong brand. What helps Mayo achieve this is its emphasis on marketing research.

A significant portion of marketing research is devoted to brand management. Marketing research is used to continuously monitor consumer perceptions and evaluations of the Mayo Clinic. The Mayo Clinic's Office of Brand Management serves two basic functions. The first is operating as a clearinghouse for external perception. The second function is to provide the physicians with an understanding of the brand as they branch out into new areas. A brand equity research project found that the Mayo Clinic was thought of as the best practice in the country. It also found that 84 percent of the public is aware of the Mayo Clinic, and that the public associates words such as excellence, care, and compassion with the clinic. Thus, a large part of its branding strategy is to protect and preserve this perception. Mayo does this by continuing to deliver excellent service and providing the ultimate experience to patients and obtaining feedback by conducting marketing research.

The other part of the Clinic's strategy is the enhancement of the brand. Moving the brand forward can be difficult because the brand is intangible. Mayo must be delicate with its brand because people do not think of the Mayo Clinic as a typical brand. The Clinic has to take extra care in its marketing and partnerships so it does not change that perception. To accomplish this, the Mayo Clinic relies on marketing research to monitor the perceptions of the patients, the public, the donors, the medical staff, and its other constituencies. A recent marketing research study revealed that consumers' choice of a health care organization is determined by their evaluation of the alternative health care organizations on the following salient attributes: (1) doctors, (2) medical technology, (3) nursing care, (4) physical facilities, (5) management, and (6) ethics. Since then, the Mayo Clinic has sought to emphasize these factors. Thus, marketing research helps the Mayo Clinic to stay healthy by maintaining and enhancing its brand.

## QUESTIONS

1. In a survey, consumers are asked to express their degree of agreement with the statement "the Mayo Clinic provides excellent health care" using a standard Likert scale. They also expressed their degree of agreement using the same scale with the following six statements selected as independent variables: Mayo Clinic has excellent (1) doctors, (2) medical technology, (3) nursing care, (4) physical facilities, (5) management, and (6) ethics. Which statistical technique(s) will you use to answer the following questions?

   a. Is the rating of the Mayo Clinic as an excellent health care provider associated individually with each of the six independent variables?

   b. Considered collectively, which independent variables best explain the rating of the Mayo Clinic as an excellent health care provider?

   c. For the sample as a whole, do the ratings on medical technology differ significantly from the ratings on nursing care?

   d. The sample is divided into two groups: those with a favorable (ratings of 4 or 5) and those with an unfavorable or neutral (ratings of 1, 2, or 3) response to the Mayo Clinic as an excellent health care provider. Do the two groups differ in their ratings of each of the six independent variables?

   e. Do the two groups of question d differ in terms of the ratings of all six independent variables when these variables are considered collectively?

   f. The sample is divided into three groups: those with a favorable (ratings of 4 or 5), those with a neutral (rating of 3), and those with an unfavorable (ratings of 1 or 2) response to the Mayo Clinic as an excellent health care provider. Do the three groups differ in their ratings of each of the six independent variables?

   g. Do the three groups of question f differ in terms of the ratings of all six independent variables when these variables are considered collectively?

   h. Can the ratings of the Mayo Clinic on (1) doctors, (2) medical technology, (3) nursing care, (4) physical facilities, (5) management, and (6) ethics be represented by a smaller set of dimensions that capture the respondents underlying perceptions?

   i. Can the respondents be divided into relatively homogeneous groups based on their ratings of the Mayo Clinic on (1) doctors, (2) medical technology, (3) nursing care, (4) physical facilities, (5) management, and (6) ethics? If so, into how many groups?

## REFERENCES

www.mayoclinic.com

Misty Hathaway and Kent Seltman, "International Market Research at the Mayo Clinic," *Marketing Health Services* (2001 Winter): 19.

Daniel Fell, "Taking U.S. Health Services Overseas," *Marketing Health Services* (2002 Summer): 21.

# CASES

# 4.1 Astec: Regaining the Top Spot

Astec America, Inc. (*www.astecpower.com*) is one of the world's largest suppliers of industrial power supply products. In 1989, Emerson Electric Company (*www.gotoemerson. com*) bought a 50 percent stake in Astec and due to that massive business transaction, five of Emerson's power supply companies were rolled into Astec. In 1999, Astec became wholly owned by Emerson; however, those companies retained Astec names but became independently managed under Emerson. Astec's parent company, Emerson Electric, completed a $725 million purchase of Ericsson Energy Systems in Spring 2000.

Astec was the first company to enter AC/DC switching power supplies, which included both low power and custom switches. Given its dominance in this niche in the market, Astec historically had no reason to rely on a marketing orientation in order to sell its products. However, the industry was becoming more and more competitive. When Unitech Plc. acquired Lambda Electronics it sent a definite signal that the industry was entering its competitive, mature stage. In an industry in which it was estimated that more than 1,000 power-related companies were involved, no one supplier had more than a 7 percent share of the market. In addition, Unitech's acquisition of Lambda was a blow to Astec since Unitech, ranked tenth in market share prior to the acquisition, suddenly catapulted to number one in the industry with its acquisition of Lambda. By 1998, however, Astec had slipped to third in sales of power supplies, behind Lucent Technologies and Ericsson. Additionally, the market was rapidly growing. U.S. sales of AC/DC power switches exceeded $10 billion by 2001. In order to keep even with its current market share, Astec had to nearly double its sales. It seemed as though the industry was heading for a competitive shake-up.

In 2000, 37 percent (nearly $600 million) of Astec's sales came from the communications sector of the power supply market. Astec is continuing to rely on growth in this area to fuel future sales. Although the communications industry has been experiencing an economic downturn, Howard Lance (former Chief Executive of Astec and current Vice President at Emerson) believed that Astec was "well positioned to grow as fast or faster than the market." Lance also predicted that the Electronics and Telecommunications sector of Emerson, of which Astec is a part, would grow about 15 percent per year through 2002. The sales and revenues for the Electronics and Telecommunications sectors of Emerson are presented in the following table. This sector consists of four subsidiaries of Emerson: Astec, ASCO, HIROSS, and Liebert.

|          | 2001  | 2000  | 1999  |
|----------|-------|-------|-------|
| **Sales**    | 3,590 | 3,289 | 2,072 |
| **Earnings** | 359   | 447   | 234   |

All figures in millions.

One of the major changes Astec believed it needed to make was to improve its marketing. Astec, like most members of the industry, had maintained a production focus since it entered this heavily engineer-driven industry. Traditionally, power supply vendors' livelihoods depended on selling mechanisms to manufacturers that provided power to radios, televisions, computers, and other electronic goods. In the past, the industry had been run by engineers who started their businesses in back rooms or garages. Recently, however, the electronic goods industry underwent rapid changes that required its suppliers to change as well—in order to keep up with foreign and domestic competition. As such, the industry became known as the weak link in the electronics chain. The once engineering driven industry had to change lanes and move into a market driven orientation. Marketing was needed in order to keep potential customers up-to-date with technology and to enable manufacturers to better understand what the future needs of the industry would be.

In order to improve its position with its customers, Astec felt it needed to offer more reliable products, create stronger long-term relationships with suppliers, and develop closer ties with customers by assisting in design of components and increasing the quality of their power supply products through increased testing. In addition, Astec developed interests in expanding its product base by offering standard as well as custom products. A reflection of this new marketing interest is evident, in that Astec has an ever-increasing advertising budget.

In 1999, Astec restructured its sales and marketing divisions. Prior to the restructuring, Astec focused on two separate market groups: standard products and custom products. In an attempt to target more key markets, Astec reorganized the sales and marketing division into four separate groups. The first group, the Computer Solutions Segment, focuses on reducing costs and expanding available product lines for PC, notebook, and server applications. The second group focuses on the Networking, Imaging, and Mobile Communications Segment of the power supply market. The third group, the Standard Product Solutions group, attempts to meet the needs of small and midsize distributors. The fourth and final group, the Power Module Solutions unit, caters to customers with more customized needs.

In an effort to tap into a new market, Astec developed a strong position in the South American communications market. At the end of 2000, nearly $11 billion was spent on building Brazil's telecom infrastructure. Astec's regional manager for Brazil, Marco Prado, states, "Our presence in Brazil enables us to work closely with customers throughout South America, to understand their needs, and to provide them with complete end-to-end power solutions for their communications networks."

Many companies such as Ericsson, Lucent, and Nortel have sold off their captive power-supply businesses, which has created huge opportunities for power-supply companies like Astec. As a result of these business sell-offs, Astec has seen a tremendous acceleration in DC/DC product demand. Due to technological changes in centralized power systems, Astec branched out into new products. Only several years ago, a centralized power supply consisted of 80 percent AC/DC power and 20 percent DC/DC power; however, in 2002 the power supply consisted of nearly 50 percent of both. In addition, the power-supply market is also getting a boost from the data-communications industry, which is also seeing explosive growth. For 2003, Astec expected to see a 20 percent increase in power sales resulting from these new opportunities.

Having slipped to number three in the industry, Astec desired to regain the top position. The company knows that it needs to be more consumer driven in order to have a successful marketing program. It is well aware of the fact that customers have been willing to buy from one of the hundreds of small power supply producers which compete on price, but Astec also believes that there is a growing demand for both higher quality products with expanded deluxe features and more customer service among its clients. While new product designs will take some time to develop, new service programs can be easily launched. The difficulty is that Astec does not know which services are in demand from their clients. The marketing manager wants to know if new service programs will be beneficial in increasing Astec's sales and which service programs should be launched. He wants the information within two months in order to develop the programs for the next major trade show. With its competitors' growing awareness that reaching out to customers is the way to grow as the market matures, Astec must play by the new rules if it is to regain the top spot.

## QUESTIONS

### Chapter 1

1. Marketing research involves the identification, collection, analysis, and dissemination of information. Explain how each of these phases of marketing research applies to Astec's problem.
2. Is the problem facing Astec a case of problem identification research or problem solution research? Explain.

3. What ethical considerations does the researcher face in this project?

### Chapter 2

1. Identify two items that relate to each of the following factors to be considered in the environmental context of the problem.

   Past information and forecasts

   Resources and constraints

   Objectives

   Buyer behavior

   Legal environment

   Economic environment

   Marketing and technological skills
2. What is the management decision problem facing Astec?
3. What is the marketing research problem facing Astec?
4. Break down the general marketing research problem statement into component parts.
5. What theoretical findings can assist in developing an approach to the problem?
6. Develop three suitable research questions and hypotheses for the marketing research problem.

### Chapter 3

1. Can exploratory research be used in this case? How?
2. Can descriptive research be used in this case? How?
3. Can causal research be used in this case? How?
4. What types of non-sampling error is industrial research particularly prone to? Why?
5. Is a cross-sectional design or a longitudinal design most preferable in this case?

### Chapter 4

1. What internal sources of secondary data can you identify which would be helpful?
2. What published sources of secondary data can you identify which would be helpful?
3. What information can be obtained from the Internet?
4. Why are syndicated sources likely to be helpful in this case? Which sources would you consider using?
5. Assess the possible bias in the sources of secondary data that you have identified.

### Chapter 5

1. Which qualitative research techniques would you recommend and why?
2. Develop a list of topics for the depth interviews that will assess industrial preferences for power supply generators.
3. Which techniques would you recommend for the depth interviews?
4. Devise a story completion exercise to be used during a depth interview.
5. Design sentence completion techniques to uncover underlying motives.

### Chapter 6

1. Which of the following criteria for selecting survey methods are most important in this case? Check all that apply.

Use of physical stimuli _____

Quantity of data _____

Obtaining sensitive information _____

Speed _____

Diversity of questions _____

Sample control _____

Response rate _____

Cost _____

Flexibility of data collection _____

Control of field force _____

Social desirability _____

Potential for interviewer bias _____

Control of data collection environment _____

Perceived anonymity of respondent _____

2. Which survey method would you recommend to Astec to conduct descriptive research? Why? What are the limitations of this mode?

3. Can observational methods be used to collect data? How? What are the limitations of your method?

## Chapter 7

1. Classify each of the following as one of the conditions of causality that need to be demonstrated in the relationship between sales of power supply generators and level of service.

   Using an experimental design to ensure that no other variables affect purchase of power supply generators except for level of service.

   _____

   Purchases of power supply generators increasing with changes in level of service.

   _____

   The changes in the level of service occur before changes in purchases of power supply generators.

   _____

2. Is causal research necessary in this case? If so, which experimental designs would you recommend and why? If not, devise a scenario in which it would be.

3. What extraneous variables are threats to the internal and external validity in the design you have selected?

4. Suppose Astec created three different service programs (A, B, & C) and wanted to know how both the level of technology and the fiscal size of the company affect attitudes towards a service program. Customers are classified as high-tech, mid-tech, and low-tech, and companies as large, medium, and small. If Astec is not concerned about interaction effects, what would be the most feasible design?

5. Suppose service program A is rated highest in the experiment in the above question (4). How can a test market be conducted to determine its acceptance by the market? Explain.

## Chapters 8 & 9

1. Will the use of scales differ for industrial research as opposed to consumer research?

2. What types of comparative scales can be used to gather the information needed on knowledge, attitudes, intentions, and preferences? Design these scales.

3. What types of noncomparative scales can be used to gather the information needed on knowledge, attitudes, intentions, and preferences? Design these scales.

4. In designing scales for the survey, which scales do you recommend?

5. How would you determine the reliability of the scales?

6. How would you assess the validity of the scales?

## Chapter 10

1. Are each of the following questions well formulated? If not, what is the error?

   a. Do you think power supply generator producers should offer services and deluxe features on their generators?

   Yes _____

   No _____

   b. How often do you order power supply generators?

   Occasionally _____

   Sometimes _____

   Often _____

   Regularly _____

   c. Would you like power supply producers to increase services to you?

   Yes _____

   No _____

   d. How often did you order power supply generators last year?

   _____

2. Design a questionnaire to be used in a survey.

## Chapter 11

Answer questions 1 through 4 assuming that a mail survey is being conducted.

1. What is the target population for this study?

2. What sampling frame can you use?

3. What sampling technique do you recommend for this study? Why?

4. What non-response issues must be considered and how can they be overcome?

## Chapter 12

1. Astec is interested in offering the guaranteed distribution program. Astec believes that companies which order power supplies every month are good candidates for this program. It is estimated that the program will be worthwhile if only 20 percent of the companies order power supplies each month. The management wants to be 99 percent sure that they are within 2 percent. How large of a sample do they need to survey?

2. In the problem above (1), does your result seem feasible? If not, what recommendations would you make to management in conducting the study to achieve a feasible sample size?

## Chapter 13

1. How should the fieldwork process given in the book be modified for mail surveys?

## Chapter 14

1. Suppose the following responses appeared on a completed mail survey that you as the supervisor of the project are editing. How would you correct for the respondent skipping question Q10, assuming that the number of respondents with incomplete responses is small?

**Q5.** I would like assistance in designing my products from a power supply generator producer

| Strongly Disagree | | | Neutral | | Strongly Agree | |
|---|---|---|---|---|---|---|
| 1 | 2 | 3 | 4 | 5 | X | 7 |

**Q6.** A program that would guarantee delivery is important to me

| Strongly Disagree | | | Neutral | | Strongly Agree | |
|---|---|---|---|---|---|---|
| 1 | 2 | 3 | 4 | 5 | X | 7 |

**Q10.** Suppose you are purchasing power supply generators. Please rate the relative importance of the factors you would consider in selecting a power supply generator on a 1 to 7 scale where 1 means "Not so Important" and 7 means "Very Important."

| | Not so Important | | | | | Very Important | |
|---|---|---|---|---|---|---|---|
| 1. Quality of components | 1 | 2 | 3 | 4 | 5 | 6 | 7 |
| 2. Mfr. design assistance | 1 | 2 | 3 | 4 | 5 | 6 | 7 |
| 3. Product warranty | 1 | 2 | 3 | 4 | 5 | 6 | 7 |
| 4. Cutting-edge technology | 1 | 2 | 3 | 4 | 5 | 6 | 7 |
| 5. Price | 1 | 2 | 3 | 4 | 5 | 6 | 7 |
| 6. Made by a well-known company | 1 | 2 | 3 | 4 | 5 | 6 | 7 |
| 7. Reliable distribution | 1 | 2 | 3 | 4 | 5 | 6 | 7 |

**Q12.** Please rate the following services on a 1 to 7 scale where 1 means "Not at All Important to Me" and 7 means "Critical to Me."

| | Not at All Important to Me | | | | Critical to Me | | |
|---|---|---|---|---|---|---|---|
| 1. Product design assistance | 1 | 2 | 3 | 4 | 5 | X | 7 |
| 2. Assembly assistance | 1 | 2 | 3 | 4 | X | 6 | 7 |
| 3. Distribution guarantee | 1 | 2 | 3 | 4 | 5 | X | 7 |
| 4. Technical explanations | 1 | 2 | 3 | 4 | X | 6 | 7 |

2. Develop a codebook for questions 10 through 15 in the questionnaire constructed in Chapter 10.
3. In editing the completed surveys, you are told that management wants to know if there are differences between high-tech, mid-tech, and low-tech companies. Develop a scheme for analyzing the data within this paradigm.

## Chapter 15

1. Suppose you administered the questionnaire designed in Chapter 10 and collected data. As a marketing analyst for Astec, you must analyze the resulting data sets and make recommendations to your boss. The data sets were the result of diligent efforts from dozens of persons in your department who helped conduct the mail survey of Astec customers' purchasing agents during the previous two weeks. After screening the results of the survey, the information was coded and entered into the two data matrices of 230 cases you now possess. Up to this point, your firm has devoted 300 man-hours to this project over the last three weeks. The CEO wants a preliminary report on the findings of this research effort.
   a. Run frequency distributions on all variables with all accompanying descriptive statistics.
   b. Use the crosstabs procedure to produce contingency tables for analysis of whether relationships exist between pairs of variables. Of interest will be the types of PSGs purchased (Q8), sources of PSG purchased (Q9), receptivity to additional services (Q16), frequency of ordering PSGs (Q17), needs being met by PSG producers (Q18), and demographic variables regarding the agents and their firms (Q19–Q23).

## Chapter 16

1. Use the analysis of variance procedure to compare the means of Q1 to Q7, Q10, and Q11 when grouped on Q17's four possible responses. These groups represent the frequency of ordering PSGs per quarter. Use multiple range tests to determine which groups differ in their mean values.

## Chapter 17

1. Run a multiple regression with Q5 as the dependent variable and Q 15 (a to d) as the independent variables. Interpret the results.

## Chapter 18

1. Use discriminant analysis to determine what variables would best predict the grouping of cases into the existing group who would be likely to buy PSGs with additional services (Yes = group 1) and those who would not (No = group 2) (Q16). Perform discriminant analysis of Q16 on the remaining variables.
2. Use the same discriminant analysis approach used in Question 1 above to determine if "current services offered by PSG producer meets your needs" (Q18). Be sure not to include Q2 as a predictor variable. (Q2 is Q18 merely restated in another form.)

## Chapters 19–20

1. Analyze the importance of factors used in selecting PSGs (Q10) by using factor analysis to identify a reduced set of factors from the seven available. In this case, use the principal components method for extracting factors. Follow this analysis with quick clustering, discriminant analysis (to check the model constructed through quick clustering), and then run crosstabs on cluster membership by suppliers of PSGs last year (Q9), and appeal of product with additional services (Q16).

## Chapter 21

1. Use multidimensional scaling (of similarity data obtained in Q13) to visualize the relationship between potential services to be offered.

## Chapter 22

1. Prepare an oral presentation for management that explains your research results and provides an answer for their management decision problem.

## Chapter 23

1. Suppose, due to its low market share in the U.S., Astec feels that it should turn to international markets to solidify a leading position in the power supply industry. What are some strategies Astec could pursue, and what considerations would they have to take into account to conduct marketing research internationally?

## Questions on Ethics

1. ABC Marketing Research Company completed a marketing research study for Zytec Corporation (a competitor of Astec) focusing on customer profiles and desires. Astec hires ABC Company. Under what circumstances could ABC use the data from the Zytec research in the new Astec research project?

2. Astec offers the marketing research project to a small research firm. Astec says they will use the company in the future if they conduct this project at cost. Under what circumstances would this be ethical?

3. XYZ Marketing Research, Inc. specializes in gathering and compiling data for industry-wide statistics. Astec asks XYZ to conduct primary research for its study. What are some of the possible ethical considerations in this relationship?

4. What are the ethical considerations for detailed data gathered on individuals for this research project?

5. A focus group is conducted to determine perceptions of AC/DC switches and Astec. The focus group is videotaped. What are some of the ethical implications for the use of this tape?

## REFERENCES

Spencer Chin, "Astec Looks to Supply More Power—Focus Put On New Products, Inventory Management," *EBN* (1256) (April 2, 2001): 4.

Robert Bellinger, "Artesyn Reclaims Growth Track—Focus on Internet, Wireless Leads to Strong Turnaround," *Electronic Buyers' News* (1229) (September 18, 2000): 44.

Bettyann Liotta, "Power Supplies," *Electronic Buyers' News* (1229) (September 18, 2000): 52.

Arthur Zaczkiewicz, "Astec Moves Power Devices Deeper Into South America," *Electronic Buyers' News* (1210) (May 8, 2000): 62.

Bettyann Liotta, "Astec, now Subsidiary of Emerson, Reorganizes — Power-Supply Maker Creates Four Marketing Groups, Appoints Top Execs," *Electronic Buyers News* (1156) (April 19, 1999): 5.

## CASE 4.1–ASTEC QUESTIONNAIRE

Please answer ALL the questions listed below.

### Part A

Please indicate your agreement with each of the following statements (Q1 to Q7).

1. Power supply generators are an important part of my operation.

| Strongly Disagree | | | Neutral | | Strongly Agree | |
|---|---|---|---|---|---|---|
| 1 | 2 | 3 | 4 | 5 | 6 | 7 |

2. The service of power supply generator producers meets my needs.

| Strongly Disagree | | | Neutral | | Strongly Agree | |
|---|---|---|---|---|---|---|
| 1 | 2 | 3 | 4 | 5 | 6 | 7 |

3. Power supply generators are all alike.

| Strongly Disagree | | | Neutral | | Strongly Agree | |
|---|---|---|---|---|---|---|
| 1 | 2 | 3 | 4 | 5 | 6 | 7 |

4. I have no difficulty understanding the technical designs of power supply generators.

| Strongly Disagree | | | Neutral | | Strongly Agree | |
|---|---|---|---|---|---|---|
| 1 | 2 | 3 | 4 | 5 | 6 | 7 |

5. I would like assistance in designing my products from a power supply generator producer.

| Strongly Disagree | | | Neutral | | Strongly Agree | |
|---|---|---|---|---|---|---|
| 1 | 2 | 3 | 4 | 5 | 6 | 7 |

6. A program that would guarantee delivery is important to me.

| Strongly Disagree | | | Neutral | | Strongly Agree | |
|---|---|---|---|---|---|---|
| 1 | 2 | 3 | 4 | 5 | 6 | 7 |

7. I need assistance in placing the power supply generators in my products.

| Strongly Disagree | | | Neutral | | Strongly Agree | |
|---|---|---|---|---|---|---|
| 1 | 2 | 3 | 4 | 5 | 6 | 7 |

8. What types of power supply generators have you purchased in the past year?

_____

_____

_____

9. From which companies have you purchased power supply generators in the past year?

_____

_____

_____

### Part B

10. Suppose you are purchasing power supply generators. Please rate the relative importance of the factors you would consider in selecting a power supply generator on a 1 to 7 scale where 1 means "Not so Important" and 7 means "Very Important."

| | Not so Important | | | | | Very Important | |
|---|---|---|---|---|---|---|---|
| a. Quality of components | 1 | 2 | 3 | 4 | 5 | 6 | 7 |
| b. Assistance from the manufacturer | 1 | 2 | 3 | 4 | 5 | 6 | 7 |
| c. Product warranty | 1 | 2 | 3 | 4 | 5 | 6 | 7 |
| d. Cutting-edge technology | 1 | 2 | 3 | 4 | 5 | 6 | 7 |
| e. Price | 1 | 2 | 3 | 4 | 5 | 6 | 7 |
| f. Made by a well-known company | 1 | 2 | 3 | 4 | 5 | 6 | 7 |
| g. Reliable distribution | 1 | 2 | 3 | 4 | 5 | 6 | 7 |

11. How likely would you be to order power supply generators because of customer service programs?

| Not so Likely | | | Maybe/Maybe Not | | Very Likely | |
|---|---|---|---|---|---|---|
| 1 | 2 | 3 | 4 | 5 | 6 | 7 |

12. Please rate the following services on a 1 to 7 scale where 1 means "Not at All Important to Me" and 7 means "Critical to Me."

| | Not at All Important to Me | | | | | Critical to Me | |
|---|---|---|---|---|---|---|---|
| a. Product design | 1 | 2 | 3 | 4 | 5 | 6 | 7 |
| b. Assembly assistance | 1 | 2 | 3 | 4 | 5 | 6 | 7 |
| c. Distribution guarantee | 1 | 2 | 3 | 4 | 5 | 6 | 7 |
| d. Technical explanations | 1 | 2 | 3 | 4 | 5 | 6 | 7 |

**13.** We would like you to evaluate the following power supply producers on the service they provide to you. Compare the row company to the column company. Please write 1 if the row company provides better service or 0, otherwise.

| | Astec | Unitech | PCA | Lite-On | Vicor | Zenith |
|---|---|---|---|---|---|---|
| Astec | XXXX | XXXX | XXXX | XXXX | XXXX | XXXX |
| Unitech | | XXXX | XXXX | XXXX | XXXX | XXXX |
| PCA | | | XXXX | XXXX | XXXX | XXXX |
| Lite-On | | | | XXXX | XXXX | XXXX |
| Vicor | | | | | XXXX | XXXX |
| Zenith | | | | | | XXXX |

**14.** Please rank the various services listed below in your order of preference. Assign the brand you like most a 1, second most a 2, and so on until all 4 services have been ranked.

| Service | Rank |
|---|---|
| Product design assistance | _____ |
| Assembly assistance | _____ |
| Technical explanations | _____ |
| Guaranteed distribution | _____ |

**15.** Please rate the quality of the following services:
   a. Production design assistance

| Very Low Quality | | | | | | Very High Quality |
|---|---|---|---|---|---|---|
| 1 | 2 | 3 | 4 | 5 | 6 | 7 |

   b. Assembly assistance

| Very Low Quality | | | | | | Very High Quality |
|---|---|---|---|---|---|---|
| 1 | 2 | 3 | 4 | 5 | 6 | 7 |

   c. Technical explanations

| Very Low Quality | | | | | | Very High Quality |
|---|---|---|---|---|---|---|
| 1 | 2 | 3 | 4 | 5 | 6 | 7 |

   d. Guaranteed distribution

| Very Low Quality | | | | | | Very High Quality |
|---|---|---|---|---|---|---|
| 1 | 2 | 3 | 4 | 5 | 6 | 7 |

**16.** If a company were to offer additional service programs to assist you, do you think you would be more likely to use that supplier?

Yes _____

No _____

Why or why not?

_____

_____

**17.** How many times per quarter do you order power supply generators?

_____ Less than once per quarter

_____ 2 times per quarter

_____ 3 times per quarter

_____ 4 or more times per quarter

**18.** Do the current services offered by power supply producers meet your needs?

_____ Yes

_____ No

Why or why not?

_____

_____

*Part C*

**19.** Your job title?
   1. _____ Manager
   2. _____ Purchasing Agent

**20.** Your age:
   1. _____ 18–24
   2. _____ 25–40
   3. _____ 41–60
   4. _____ 60+

**21.** Company sales
   1. _____ Less than $1 million
   2. _____ $1 million to $4.999 million
   3. _____ $5 million to $9.999 million
   4. _____ $10 million or more

**22.** Level of technology
   1. Low _____
   2. Medium _____
   3. High _____

**23.** Which one of the following best describes your primary category of manufacturing?

   1. Computer _____
   2. Small appliances _____
   3. Large appliances _____
   4. Electronics _____
   5. Other _____

Thank you for your participation.

_____

# 4.1 Astec Coding Sheet

Note: Fill variable column(s) with "9" if no response marked on questionnaire.

| Column | Question/Number Code Name | Variable Name | Coding Instructions |
|---|---|---|---|
| 1–3 | Obs | observation number | 001-099 with leading zeros |
| 4–5 | | blank | |
| 6 | Q1 | importance of PSG to my product | code circled number |
| 7 | Q2 | service for PSGs meets needs | " |
| | | | " |
| 8 | Q3 | PSGs are all alike | " |
| 9 | Q4 | PSG designs understood | " |
| 10 | Q5 | want aid in product design | " |
| 11 | Q6 | guaranteed delivery important | " |
| 12 | Q7 | need aid to put PSG in product | " |
| 13–14 | Q8 | types of PSG bought last year | 00 = Type A;<br>01 = Type B;<br>10 = Type C; |
| 15–19 | Q9 | source of purchase for PSG | 00000 = Co. L;<br>00001 = Co. M;<br>00010 = Co. N;<br>00100 = Co. O;<br>01000 = Co. P;<br>10000 = Co. Q; |
| 20 | Q10a | importance of quality components | code circled number |
| 21 | Q10b | "      " mfr. assistance | " |
| 22 | Q10c | "      " product warranty | " |
| 23 | Q10d | "      " newest technology | " |
| 24 | Q10e | "      " price | " |
| 25 | Q10f | "      " well-known mfr. | " |
| 26 | Q10g | "      " reliable distribution | " |
| 27 | Q11 | significance of cust. svc. program | " |
| 28 | Q12a | importance of production design svcs. | " |
| 29 | Q12b | "      " assembly assistance svc. | " |
| 30 | Q12c | "      " distribution guarantee | " |
| 31 | Q12d | "      " technical explanation | " |
| 32 | Q15a | rating of product design assist. | " |
| 33 | Q15b | "      " assembly assistance | " |
| 34 | Q15c | "      " technical explanation | " |
| 35 | Q15d | "      " guarantee distribution | " |
| 36 | Q16 | more likely to use co. with add. svcs. | No = 0; Yes =1 |
| 37–39 | Q17 | frequency of ordering PSGs | 000 = quarterly or less<br>100 = twice quarterly<br>010 = 3 times per qtr.<br>001 = 4 or more times per quarter |
| 40 | Q18 | needs met by current svcs. | No = 0; Yes = 1 |
| 41 | Q19 | job | manager = 0;<br>purchasing agent = 1 |

| Column | Question/Number Code Name | Variable Name | Coding Instructions |
|---|---|---|---|
| 42–44 | Q20 | age | 000 = 20–35; <br> 001 = 36–50; <br> 010 = 51–65; <br> 100 = 65+ |
| 45–47 | Q21 | annual company sales | 000 = less than $1 mill. <br> 001 = $1 to $4.99 mill. <br> 010 = $5 to $9.99 mill. <br> 100 = $10 million+ |
| 48–49 | Q22 | level of technology | 00 = low; 01 = med.; <br> 10 = high |
| 50–53 | Q23 | primary category of manufacturing | 0000 = computer; <br> 0001 = small appliance; <br> 0010 = large appliance; <br> 0100 = electronics; <br> 1000 = other |

(Note: Q13 & Q14 will be coded into a separate data file)

### Astec Question 13

(File - ASINSCAL.DAT)

Note: Responses form the lower left triangle of a square matrix.

| Column | Line | Variable | Coding Instructions |
|---|---|---|---|
| 1–3 | 1 | Respondent ID | Take number from top of questionnaire |
| 1 | 2 | Co. Service Comparison | Enter number marked |
| 1–2 | 3 | " | " |
| 1–3 | 4 | " | " |
| 1–4 | 5 | " | " |
| 1–5 | 6 | " | " |

### Astec Question 14

(File - ASUNFOLD.DAT)

| Column | Variable | | Coding Instructions |
|---|---|---|---|
| 1 | Rank of Product design assistance | | Enter no. marked |
| 2 | " | Assembly assistance | " |
| 3 | " | Technical explanations | " |
| 4 | " | Guaranteed distribution | " |

# 4.2 Is Marketing Research the Cure for Norton Healthcare Kosair Children's Hospital's Ailments?

Traditionally, the primary concern of hospitals has been producing services, rather than servicing markets. However, due to increased competition, alternate delivery systems, and the recognition of the usefulness of marketing as a tool, the industry has begun to explore the potential of marketing research. This trend began when Medicare started reimbursing hospitals by way of DRGs (diagnostic-related groups of illnesses), rather than on the basis of costs, and thus paved the way for other insurance companies to use DRGs. This had a severe effect on hospital revenue, since it meant that only a set fee was paid for each category of DRG—affecting 40 percent of hospital revenue. Thus, hospitals faced the harsh reality of becoming more efficient or losing money. This loss of revenue has been further increased due to the glut of doctors and hospital beds.

In 1997 and 1998, hospital occupancy hovered around the 70 percent mark nationwide, according to the American Hospital Association's report. In 1999, the average hospital occupancy rate in the United States was 66.1 percent. It is expected that hospital occupancy will be reduced to 59 percent by the year 2005 and that "the aggressive interventions of health plans that have driven much activity out of the inpatient setting will continue, but at a relatively slower pace." It is also predicted that 13 percent of hospitals will close by 2010. Analysts are predicting that occupancy rates will continue to decrease based, in part, on the trend toward outpatient and fast recovery services and away from treatment and procedures that require long hospital stays. Therefore, it has become necessary for health care marketers to evaluate consumer preferences, since the successful hospital marketer must target the key decision maker and make them aware of services that the hospital provides which are of crucial importance to the decision maker in the selection process.

The problems of low occupancy rates have turned health care into a buyer's market. Instead of physicians deciding where patients are going for treatment, 70 percent of patients decide where they will go for treatment. Surprisingly enough, there is even an indication that patients are not basing their decisions on quality of treatment (i.e. medical technology or adequacy in staffing), rather they are making buying decisions on the way they are treated (i.e., the room, the food, difficulty in parking, and whether people are friendly). Therefore, hospitals have begun to engage in advertising, to offer customized and specialized services, and, in general, learn that people are markets and markets have needs that must be addressed if hospitals expect to stay in business. In short, the health care industry has developed a customer-service orientation. One of the ways in which children's hospitals are making marketing improvements is with improved building designs and interiors that are visually more appealing to parents and children.

Since numerous markets are served by health care organizations: patients, payers, caregivers, regulators, and the surrounding community, the organization has some latitude regarding which market to target. Especially since each of these markets represents market share potential, and a customer base on which to conduct market research. However, most hospital marketing programs have centered on patients and potential patients (i.e. a customer oriented approach). In particular, birthing centers are often the focus of patient oriented marketing programs. This is because routine obstetrical services often play the role of loss leaders. In other words, they are priced below cost—in order to build up hospital image and attract future, more profitable business.

Decreasing revenue and loss of occupancy is the dilemma of Norton Healthcare Kosair Children's Hospitals, Inc. (NHKCH) of Louisville, Kentucky. The hospital is the only full service children's hospital in Kentucky and serves as the primary children's referral center for Kentucky and Southern Indiana. The 253-bed hospital is part of Norton Healthcare (*www.nortonhealthcare.com*), a non-profit organization that operates Norton Hospital and the Norton Healthcare Pavilion in the Louisville Medical Center. This hospital ranks sixth in awareness of local residents out of the nine hospitals in its market. It feels that one way to increase awareness, and thus business, is through the implementation of an aggressively marketed maternity care program. In particular, it is of the opinion that it could be successful in this venture if it employed a product-line marketing approach—packaging a service such as maternity care and promoting elements of that service (i.e. a birthing center: labor, delivery, and recovery—all in the same room to avoid moving the new mother unnecessarily; or a more expansive line that would include other inpatient services such as: cosmetic surgery, breast screening, and infertility, in addition to the birthing center—all in the same location).

Norton Healthcare Kosair Children's Hospital renovated its facilities in 2000 and enhanced the existing pediatric intensive care and transitional care units. It created a "child-friendly" environment that enhanced their facility by offering red wagons for child transportation, a book and video library, and playrooms on all patient floors. Most of the patient rooms are private and include an extra bed so a parent can stay overnight with the child. The hospital understands that children are often uneasy in the hospital and the presence of a loved one is very reassuring.

In 1999, the chaplain at Kosair Children's Hospital began a new outreach program to comfort the families and friends of children who died from traumatic injuries. Research showed that there were far fewer programs designed for these families than for the families of children with cancer or other terminal illnesses. The program has had a lot of success in helping families and friends to deal with the bereavement associated with losing a child to a traumatic injury.

In June of 2000, a new program at Kosair Children's Hospital planned to facilitate and improve the inpatient care of the Department of Pediatrics' general medical patients. Pediatricians and other physicians that admitted children to Kosair Children's Hospital were able to leave their patients in the care of the "Just for Kids" hospitalists. The program was a service of the University Pediatric Foundation and was supported by a generous grant from the Children's Hospital Foundation. The hospitalists are responsible for all aspects of inpatient care management including daily patient rounds, after hours telephone consultations, communication with family members and coordinating consultants, as well as teaching students and residents. In 2003, Kosair Children's Hospital also employed Child Life Specialists to help reduce the stress on the patients. The specialists use distraction techniques, deep breathing, guided imagery, art, play, and counseling to help young patients to relax and make it through difficult tests and procedures.

Norton Healthcare, the parent company of Kosair Children's Hospital, made great progress in 2003 to increase the market share of its hospitals. Overall, the company experienced double-digit increases in customer satisfaction levels, and increased employee satisfaction levels by 14 percent. The company also posted 70 percent increases in revenues for fiscal year 2000, which lead to improvements in overall operating margins by more than 100 percent.

The senior vice president of corporate development for Kosair Children's Hospital, Mr. Galvagni, wonders how extensive the maternity care product line should be to capitalize on the local market, and to maximize hospital revenue. He is certain that the hospital has the capability to establish a maternity care line that potential patients will like, but is uncertain how to market the maternity line. He would like to undertake marketing research believing that marketing research is the cure for Norton Healthcare Kosair Children's Hospital's ailments.

## QUESTIONS

### Chapter 1

1. Marketing research involves the identification, collection, analysis, and dissemination of information. Explain how each of these phases of marketing research applies to NHKCH's problem.
2. Is the problem facing NHKCH a case of problem identification research or problem solution research? Explain.
3. Could NHKCH use DSS or marketing research suppliers to help them in their study? If so, describe how they could be used.

### Chapter 2

1. In the hospital industry scenario, you first want to analyze environmental factors before attempting to define the problem. How would you acquire information on objectives, buyer behavior, legal environment, and marketing and technical skills? Specify what information you would want with respect to the hospital industry scenario for each of the listed environmental factors.
2. State the management decision problem.
3. State the marketing research problem:
   a. Broad statement
   b. Specific components
4. How would you go about approaching the problem that faces NHKCH?
5. If you wished to conduct a case study, how might you go about it? A simulation?
6. In approaching the problem, what kind of outputs do you think you would get for:
   a. Analytical models
   b. Research questions and hypotheses
   c. Identification of information needed

### Chapter 3

1. In light of the information uncovered in defining the problem (Chapter 2), what are some examples of exploratory research that could be conducted for NHKCH? Descriptive research? Causal research?
2. Specify the six W's of NHKCH's research project.

### Chapter 4

1. What are the criteria for evaluating secondary data, and how might they be applied to NHKCH's marketing research problem?
2. Discuss internal and external sources of secondary data in the context of NHKCH.

### Chapter 5

1. What are the two types of direct techniques in qualitative research? Discuss how the researcher might utilize each of these techniques for NHKCH.
2. Give examples of each of the four projective techniques in the context of NHKCH's marketing research problem.

### Chapter 6

1. What are the two types of descriptive research designs? Which mode of each of these techniques would be appropriate for NHKCH? Why?
2. What are the advantages and disadvantages of each of the two types of descriptive research and each of the primary modes you selected in your answer to question 1?

### Chapter 7

1. What are the conditions for causality with respect to NHKCH's hypothesis that a specialized maternity care line will bring about high awareness for the hospital?
2. Define an experiment. Does the telephone survey proposed for NHKCH constitute an experiment? Why or why not?
3. Can this survey be used to infer causality?

## Chapter 8

1. Identify the measurement scales that are commonly used in marketing research for both comparative and noncomparative techniques. How might you employ each of these scales to collect data that are useful for NHKCH's marketing researcher?
2. What are the comparative scaling techniques? Give an example of each in the context of NHKCH's marketing research problem and comment on the properties of the data obtained from each of the techniques.

## Chapter 9

1. What are the two types of noncomparative techniques? Give an example of how each type of technique might be applied in the context of NHKCH's marketing research problem.
2. What kinds of decisions did you have to make when designing the itemized scales in Question 1? Why did you make the decisions you did?
3. Is the characteristic of hospital awareness better represented as a single or multi-item scale? Briefly explain why you chose the answer you did.
4. How would you evaluate the awareness scale of Question 3?

## Chapter 10

1. Specify the information needed and type of interviewing method you would use if you wanted to administer a questionnaire that addresses NHKCH's marketing research problem.
2. Chapter 10 stresses the importance of carefully designing a questionnaire so that the data obtained are relevant to the marketing research problem, as well as internally consistent and able to be coherently analyzed. Often in practice, designing a questionnaire in such a manner is difficult; therefore, it is important to be able to identify potential problems in questionnaire items. For the following questions, discuss what is wrong or could be improved about them, and how you would correct or improve them.

   a. What is the approximate combined annual income of your household before taxes?
      1. $10,000 or less _____
      2. $10,000 to 20,000 _____
      3. $20,000 to 30,000 _____
      4. $30,000 to 40,000 _____
      5. $40,000 to 60,000 _____
      6. $60,000 and over _____

   b. Please rate the relative importance of the factors you considered in selecting a hospital for delivery.

| | Not so Important | | | Very Important | | |
|---|---|---|---|---|---|---|
| a. Reputation of hospital | 1 | 2 | 3 | 4 | 5 | 6 |
| b. Quality of care | 1 | 2 | 3 | 4 | 5 | 6 |
| c. Distance from home | 1 | 2 | 3 | 4 | 5 | 6 |
| d. Advice from doctor | 1 | 2 | 3 | 4 | 5 | 6 |
| e. Advice from friends | 1 | 2 | 3 | 4 | 5 | 6 |
| f. Advertisements | 1 | 2 | 3 | 4 | 5 | 6 |
| g. Friendliness of staff | 1 | 2 | 3 | 4 | 5 | 6 |
| h. State-of-the-art maternity facilities | 1 | 2 | 3 | 4 | 5 | 6 |
| i. State-of-the-art nursery facilities | 1 | 2 | 3 | 4 | 5 | 6 |
| j. Maternity insurance | 1 | 2 | 3 | 4 | 5 | 6 |

3. Design a questionnaire to address NHKCH's marketing research problem.

## Chapter 11

1. If we choose to use a telephone survey of parents, what is the target population? The sampling frame? The sample size?
2. What type of sampling technique would be appropriate for carrying out the telephone survey mentioned in Question 1?
3. What kind of nonresponse issues should we anticipate if we carry out a telephone survey in the previously defined manner? How might we reduce the effects of these types of nonresponse?

## Chapter 12

1. Suppose that the researcher for NHKCH takes a simple random sample of 100 couples who delivered a child in a local hospital within the last three months, in order to determine the average expense for delivery services. If the average expense is $10,000, and past studies indicate that the population standard deviation is $1,500, what is the 95 percent confidence interval for the population mean?
2. After examining the confidence interval obtained in the previous problem, the researcher does not feel that he needs the confidence interval to be that exact. Furthermore, he wonders if perhaps he broadens the interval, so that it is within $500 of the true population value, can he save time and money by reducing the sample size? What sample size should he use to get within $500 of the true population value, if a 95 percent confidence interval is desired?
3. Suppose that the standard deviation of $1,500, given in Question 1, was not the population standard deviation, but an estimate. Further suppose that a sample of 100 was used and yielded an average of $10,000 in delivery expenses with a sample standard deviation of $1,000. What would the revised 95 percent confidence interval be?

## Chapter 13

1. Of the qualifications that field workers should possess, which characteristics would be of importance in selecting interviewers for NHKCH's telephone survey and why?
2. Discuss how the use of telephone interviewing as a fieldwork procedure affects the supervision of field workers and validation processes.

## Chapter 14

1. What are the reasons for not accepting a questionnaire from the field?
2. How would you code the following question from the questionnaire in Chapter 10?

   Q5. In your opinion, what services should a perfect maternity facility offer?

   _____

   _____

3. Suppose it is necessary to determine the effect of the respondent's involvement in the survey on the responses. To do this, the five items of Q9 are added together to give one score. How can this score be used to distinguish low involvement, medium involvement, and high involvement participants?

## Chapter 15

During a one-week period, 270 persons in the greater Louisville community responded to the survey designed in Chapter 10. Editing the data for completeness and correctness of entries, along with entering the data into matrix form for analysis by a computer statistical package, consumed another week (see Appendix for details).

1. Run frequency distributions for each variable with all accompanying descriptive statistics.
2. To determine the nature of the relationship between the variable for services offered by a perfect maternity facility (Q5) and the demographic variables (Q10 to Q14), run a cross-tabulation analysis of Q5 on each of the demographic variables.

## Chapter 16

1. Run separate one-way ANOVAs using questions Q2 and Q6 as a dependent variable, and hospital selected in forced choice as the grouping variable (Q4).

## Chapter 17

1. Run a multiple regression with Q8a as the dependent variable and Q6 (a to e) as the independent variables. Interpret the results.

## Chapter 18

1. To see how factors rated as being important in selecting a hospital for delivery would do in assigning respondents to four different groups, run a four-group discriminant analysis of Q1 on all questions comprising Q2. Form the four groups according to the respondents' frequency of use for maternity services as follows: Group 1 should correspond to hospitals B, C, and F; Group 2 should correspond to the NHKCH Hospital; Group 3 should be comprised of hospitals E, G, and H; and Group 4 should consist of hospitals D and I.

## Chapters 19 & 20

1. Use factor analysis to determine if a reduced set of variables can be derived from the 10 hospital selection factors (Q2A-J). This reduced set can then be used for clustering to determine if respondents can be clustered into groups according to their responses on the new set of variables. Cross-tabulation analysis can then be performed using cluster membership as one variable along with the composite variable above used for past visits to hospitals (Q1).
2. To assess whether the five dimensions of hospitals asked about in Q6 can be used to assign cases to the clusters developed after the factor analysis of Q2, run a four-group discriminant analysis of Q2 clusters on the five variables of Q6.

## Chapter 21

1. To determine if any hidden reasons exist for the reputation hospitals carry in the mind of the public, run multidimensional scaling (internal unfolding analysis) using the ALSCAL procedure on the rankings provided by respondents in Q7.

## Chapter 22

1. Prepare an executive summary of the results from the study.

## Chapter 23

1. Suppose NHKCH or another hospital was interested in conducting business on an international level. Choose a country (other than the U.S.) and discuss environmental factors that would have to be considered and possible opportunities in light of these environmental factors.

### Questions on Ethics

1. Describe two forms of unethical behavior that might be conducted by a hospital that is contracting with an outside research firm to conduct research on a new maternity care line.
2. Describe three unethical behaviors of a marketing researcher in the context of this case.

## REFERENCES

*American Hospital Association Hospital Statistics* (2001–2 Edition).

Anonymous, "Report Predicts Oversupply of Physicians, Minimal Hospital Closings in Next 10 Years," *Health Care Strategic Management* 18 (6) (June 2000): 7–8.

Jim Montague, "Unmasking A Dirty Secret," *Hospitals & Health Networks* 71 (4) (February 20, 1997): 34–36.

## CASE 4.2—NORTON HEALTHCARE KOSAIR CHILDREN'S HOSPITAL QUESTIONNAIRE

### Hospital Maternity Services Survey

Please answer ALL the questions.

### Part A

1. Which, if any, of the following hospitals have you ever used for maternity services? Please check as many as apply.

   a. ____ NHKC   b. ____ Hospital B   c. ____ Hospital C
   d. ____ Hospital D   e. ____ Hospital E   f. ____ Hospital F
   g. ____ Hospital G   h. ____ Hospital H   i. ____ Hospital I

2. Please rate the relative importance of the factors you considered in selecting a hospital for delivery.

|  | Not so Important | | | Very Important | | |
|---|---|---|---|---|---|---|
| a. Reputation of hospital | 1 | 2 | 3 | 4 | 5 | 6 |
| b. Quality of care | 1 | 2 | 3 | 4 | 5 | 6 |
| c. Distance from home | 1 | 2 | 3 | 4 | 5 | 6 |
| d. Advice from doctor | 1 | 2 | 3 | 4 | 5 | 6 |
| e. Advice from friends | 1 | 2 | 3 | 4 | 5 | 6 |
| f. Advertisements | 1 | 2 | 3 | 4 | 5 | 6 |
| g. Friendliness of staff | 1 | 2 | 3 | 4 | 5 | 6 |
| h. State-of-the-art maternity facilities | 1 | 2 | 3 | 4 | 5 | 6 |
| i. State-of-the-art nursery facilities | 1 | 2 | 3 | 4 | 5 | 6 |
| j. Maternity insurance | 1 | 2 | 3 | 4 | 5 | 6 |

3. How familiar are you with the features of maternity services offered by hospitals?

|  | Not<br>Familiar |  |  |  | Very<br>Familiar |
|---|---|---|---|---|---|
|  | 1 | 2 | 3 | 4 | 5 | 6 |

**4.** If you had to choose a hospital for delivery which one of the following hospitals would you prefer? Please choose only one.

| _____ NHKC | _____ Hospital B | _____ Hospital C |
|---|---|---|
| _____ Hospital D | _____ Hospital E | _____ Hospital F |
| _____ Hospital G | _____ Hospital H | _____ Hospital I |

**5.** In your opinion, what services should a perfect maternity facility offer?

_____

_____

**6.** Please indicate your degree of agreement with the following statements. The more you agree with a statement, the higher the number you should give it.

|  | Little<br>Agreement |  |  |  | High<br>Agreement |
|---|---|---|---|---|---|
| a. We feel a high degree of loyalty towards the hospital we used for delivery. | 1 2 3 4 5 6 |
| b. We like the convenience of having many related services offered in a maternity care line. | 1 2 3 4 5 6 |
| c. Our hospital should offer a full line of maternity services. | 1 2 3 4 5 6 |
| d. Our hospital offers high quality care. | 1 2 3 4 5 6 |
| e. Our hospital is very convenient. | 1 2 3 4 5 6 |

## Part B

**7.** Please rank each of the hospitals below (with a number between 1 and 9) to indicate your preference for the hospital (1 = most preferred and 9 = least preferred; use each number only once).

| _____ NHKC | _____ Hospital F |
|---|---|
| _____ Hospital B | _____ Hospital G |
| _____ Hospital C | _____ Hospital H |
| _____ Hospital D | _____ Hospital I |
| _____ Hospital E | |

**8.** How many times in the last year have you received treatment from:

a. NHKC _____

b. Hospital B _____

c. Hospital C _____

d. Hospital D _____

e. Hospital E _____

f. Hospital F _____

g. Hospital G _____

h. Hospital H _____

i. Hospital I _____

## Part C

**9.** Please answer the following questions as they relate to the way in which you have answered this survey.

|  | Not so<br>Interested |  |  |  | Very<br>Interested |
|---|---|---|---|---|---|
| a. How interested were you? | 1 | 2 | 3 | 4 | 5 | 6 |

|  | Not so<br>Committed |  |  |  | Very<br>Committed |
|---|---|---|---|---|---|
| b. How committed were you? | 1 | 2 | 3 | 4 | 5 | 6 |

|  | Not much<br>Effort |  |  |  | Much<br>Effort |
|---|---|---|---|---|---|
| c. How much effort did you use? | 1 | 2 | 3 | 4 | 5 | 6 |

|  | Not so<br>Motivated |  |  |  | Very<br>Motivated |
|---|---|---|---|---|---|
| d. How motivated were you? | 1 | 2 | 3 | 4 | 5 | 6 |

|  | Not so<br>Involved |  |  |  | Very<br>Involved |
|---|---|---|---|---|---|
| e. How involved were you? | 1 | 2 | 3 | 4 | 5 | 6 |

## Part D

**10.** Your gender

1. _____ Male
2. _____ Female

**11.** Marital Status

1. _____ Married
2. _____ Never Married
3. _____ Divorced/Separated/Widowed

**12.** Your age

1. _____ 25 or under
2. _____ 26–40
3. _____ 41–55
4. _____ 56 & over

**13.** Your formal education

1. Less than High School _____      3. Some College _____
2. High School Graduate _____      4. College Graduate _____

**14.** What is the approximate combined annual income of your household before taxes?

1. less than $10,000 _____      4. $30,000 to 39,999 _____
2. $10,000 to 19,999 _____      5. $40,000 to 59,999 _____
3. $20,000 to 29,999 _____      6. $60,000 and over _____

Thank you for your participation.

_____

Note: Questions 8, 9, and 14 have been deleted from the student data file to reduce the number of variables.

# 4.2 Norton Healthcare Kosair Children's Hospital Coding Sheet

Note: Fill variable column(s) with "9" if no response on questionnaire.

| Column | Question/Number Code Name | Variable Name | Coding Instructions |
|---|---|---|---|
| 1–3 | Obs | observation number | 001–099 with leading zeros |
| 4–5 | | blank | |
| 6 | Q1a | NHKCH maternity service used | No = 0; Yes = 1 |
| 7 | Q1b | Hospital B | "    "    " " |
| 8 | Q1c | Hospital C | "    "    " " |
| 9 | Q1d | Hospital D | "    "    " " |
| 10 | Q1e | Hospital E | "    "    " " |
| 11 | Q1f | Hospital F | "    "    " " |
| 12 | Q1g | Hospital G | "    "    " " |
| 13 | Q1h | Hospital H | "    "    " " |
| 14 | Q1i | Hospital I | "    "    " " |
| 15 | Q2a | importance of hosp. rep. | code circled number |
| 16 | Q2b | "    quality of care | " |
| 17 | Q2c | "    distance from home | " |
| 18 | Q2d | "    advice from doctor | " |
| 19 | Q2e | "    advice from friends | " |
| 20 | Q2f | "    advertisements | " |
| 21 | Q2g | "    friendliness of staff | " |
| 22 | Q2h | "    modern maternity facility | " |
| 23 | Q2i | "    modern nursery | " |
| 24 | Q2j | "    maternity insurance | " |
| 25 | Q3 | familiarity with maternity svcs | " |
| 26–33 | Q4 | hospital forced choice | 00000000 = NHKCH; <br> 10000000 = B; <br> 01000000 = C; <br> 00100000 = D; <br> 00010000 = E; <br> 00001000 = F; <br> 00000100 = G; <br> 00000010 = H; <br> 00000001 = I |
| 34–36 | Q5 | svcs of perfect maternity facility | 000 = personal attention; <br> 100 = integrated ops; <br> 010 = pre-birth classes; <br> 001 = post-birth classes |
| 37 | Q6a | loyalty for delivery hosp. | code circled number |
| 38 | Q6b | like for convenience of related services | "    "    " |
| 39 | Q6c | our hosp. should offer full maternity svcs. | "    "    " |
| 40 | Q6d | our hosp. offers high quality care | "    "    " |
| 41 | Q6e | our hosp. is very convenient | "    "    " |

(Note: Q7 will be entered in a separate data file)

| Column | Question/Number Code Name | Variable Name | Coding Instructions |
|---|---|---|---|
| 42 | Q8a | use of NHKCH last year | code circled number |
| 43 | Q8b | "    Hospital B | "    "    " |
| 44 | Q8c | "    Hospital C | "    "    " |
| 45 | Q8d | "    Hospital D | "    "    " |
| 46 | Q8e | "    Hospital E | "    "    " |
| 47 | Q8f | "    Hospital F | "    "    " |
| 48 | Q8g | "    Hospital G | "    "    " |
| 49 | Q8h | "    Hospital H | "    "    " |
| 50 | Q8i | "    Hospital I | "    "    " |
| 51 | Q9a | interest in survey | code circled number |
| 52 | Q9b | commitment of answers | " |
| 53 | Q9c | level of effort | " |
| 54 | Q9d | "    motivation | " |
| 55 | Q9e | "    involvement | " |
| 56 | Q10 | gender | 0 = Female; 1 = Male |
| 57–58 | Q11 | marital status | 00 = married; 10 = never married; 01 = other |
| 59–61 | Q12 | age | 000 = 25 & under; 100 = 26–40; 010 = 41–55; 001 = 55+ |
| 62–64 | Q13 | formal education | 000 = some HS; 100 = HS grad; 010 = some coll.; 001 = coll. grad |
| 65–69 | Q14 | annual pre-tax household income | 00000 = $10,000 or less; 10000 = $10,001–20,000; 01000 = $20,001–30,000; 00100 = $30,001–40,000; 00010 = $40,001–60,000; 00001 = $60,001 and over |

Note: Questions 8, 9, and 14 have been deleted from the student data file to reduce the number of variables.

## NHKCH Question 7

(File - HPPREF.DAT)

| Column | Variable | | | Coding Instructions |
|---|---|---|---|---|
| 1 | Preference rank NHKCH | | | Enter no. marked |
| 2 | "    " | Hospital | B | " |
| 3 | "    " | " | C | " |
| 4 | "    " | " | D | " |
| 5 | "    " | " | E | " |
| 6 | "    " | " | F | " |
| 7 | "    " | " | G | " |
| 8 | "    " | " | H | " |
| 9 | "    " | " | I | " |

# 4.1 Subaru: "Mr. Survey" Monitors Customer Satisfaction

Subaru (*www.subaru.com*) is the automobile division of Fuji Heavy Industries (FHI). Subaru has been operating in the United States since 1968 when they began selling the 360 Minicar. Subaru has offered many different cars over the years, but they currently sell five different brands in the United States. These brands each have a variety of different models. The five main brands are Outback, Forester, Legacy, Impreza, and Baja. One of the unique things about Subaru is that 100 percent of their models come with all-wheel drive. The Outback and Forester fall in to the sport-utility category, whereas the Legacy and Impreza fall in to the more traditional four-door car category. The Impreza was remodeled most recently in 2001, and this has led to an 85 percent increase in the sales of the Impreza. Particularly popular is the award-winning WRX model of the Impreza, which is a new sports car model that Subaru is beginning to market in the United States. This increase helped Subaru set a record in 2001 with 185,944 units sold.

Subaru's strategy is apparent in one of its key players, Joe Barstys. Joe has been with Subaru for 18 years, and he spends his time there worrying about customer satisfaction. Joe and people like him are the backbone of Subaru. These people help Subaru focus on the customers and cater to the wants and needs of these customers by conducting marketing research. Joe has incorporated the use of customer surveys into his practice, and for this he has gained the title of "Mr. Survey." Joe's goal is to develop a customer satisfaction level that will help build a certain level of loyalty in Subaru's customers. This loyalty is extremely important in the car business because it has historically been much lower than other industries. In fact, although approximately 90 percent of customers are pleased with their automobile purchase, only 40 percent are loyal enough to buy the same brand again. This is a result of the short-term approach that has been traditionally used by the auto industry. Subaru hopes to avoid this approach by making the entire experience of owning a Subaru an enjoyable one.

Surveys are a very valuable tool to Subaru in its quest for customer loyalty. It received surveys from about 50 percent of its approximately 180,000 customers last year. These surveys provided important feedback, allowing Subaru to adjust its approach to the demands of the consumer. An example of the importance of adjustments can be found in the case of the female consumer. Through surveying, Subaru found out that it needed to adjust its marketing to include female consumers, who are becoming an increasingly large part of the market. It was important for Subaru to understand what types of things would appeal to women in order to offer a more desirable product for them.

Another benefit of marketing research is that Subaru has been able to identify what types of people are more likely to buy its automobiles. Subaru believes that the typical Subaru owner is different from the average consumer. Subaru's average consumer is highly intelligent, highly independent, and somebody that is outside the mainstream crowd. Thus, Subaru tries to market its automobiles to these types of people and attempts to distinguish itself from its larger, more mainstream competitors.

Subaru is ambitiously aiming for U.S. sales of 250,000 units in 2005. This would be a 34 percent increase over 2001 numbers. Subaru hopes that with the help of marketing research it will be able to achieve this goal. Subaru believes that listening to the customers and adapting its practices to meet their concerns will provide its customers with a higher level of satisfaction and ultimately lead to a higher level of loyalty. Subaru's marketing research staff, like "Mr. Survey," will be critical to this endeavor.

## QUESTIONS

1. Discuss the role that marketing research can play in helping Subaru understand the devotion of consumers to its brands.
2. In order to continue to grow, Subaru must foster and build the loyalty of its customers. Define the management decision problem.
3. Define an appropriate marketing research problem based on the management decision problem you have identified.
4. In what way can Subaru make use of Census 2000 data? What are the limitations of these data? How can these limitations be overcome?
5. What type of data available from syndicate marketing research firms will be useful to Subaru?
6. Discuss the role of qualitative research in understanding the devotion of consumers to a particular automobile brand. Which qualitative research technique(s) should be used and why?

7. If a survey is to be conducted to understand consumer preferences for various automobile brands, which survey method should be used and why?

8. Design a questionnaire to measure consumers' evaluation of Subaru brands.

9. Develop a sampling plan for the survey of question 7.

10. Qualitative research has indicated that the following factors influence the willingness of consumers to purchase an automobile brand (dependent variable): (1) reliability, (2) performance, (3) gas mileage, (4) repair and maintenance, (5) price, (6) image, and (7) features (independent variables). In a survey, consumers were asked to state their willingness to purchase an automobile brand by Subaru, Toyota, Honda, and Nissan using five-point scales with 1 = not at all willing, and 5 = very willing. The respondents were also asked to evaluate each of these major brands (Subaru, Toyota, Honda, and Nissan) on the seven independent variables, again using five-point scales with 1 = very poor, and 5 = very good. What statistical analyses will you perform to answer the following questions?

   a. Is the willingness to purchase an automobile brand related to each of the seven independent variables when the variables are considered individually?

   b. Is the willingness to purchase an automobile brand related to all the seven independent variables when the variables are considered simultaneously?

   c. Do the respondents rate Subaru brands higher on reliability than image?

   d. Are Toyota brands perceived as more reliable than Subaru brands?

   e. Do the evaluations of Subaru on the seven independent variables differ for those who have purchased and those who have not purchased a Subaru brand?

   f. Are men more willing to purchase Subaru brands than women?

   g. Respondents were classified into four age groups: less than 25, 26 to 45, 46 to 65, and 66 or older. Do the four groups differ in their willingness to purchase Subaru brands?

   h. Willingness to purchase Toyota brands was classified into three categories: unwilling (ratings of 1 and 2), neutral (rating of 3), and willing (ratings of 4 and 5). Do the four age groups of question g differ in their willingness to purchase Toyota brands?

   i. Do the never married, currently married, and divorced/separated/widowed groups differ in their willingness to purchase Subaru brands?

   j. Do the never married, currently married, and divorced/separated/widowed groups differ in their willingness to purchase Toyota brands as classified in question h?

   k. Can the willingness to purchase Toyota brands as classified in question h be explained in terms of the evaluations of Toyota on the seven independent variables?

   l. Can the seven independent variables be reduced to a smaller set of underlying variables?

   m. Can the respondents be divided into relatively homogeneous groups based upon their ratings of Subaru on the seven independent variables? If so, into how many groups?

11. If Subaru were to conduct marketing research to determine consumer willingness to purchase automobile brands in Germany, how would the research process be different?

12. Discuss the ethical issues involved in researching consumer willingness to purchase automobile brands.

## REFERENCES

www.subaru.com

Alicia Griswold, "Subaru Changes Creative Course; Rugged Individualism Gives Way to Owner Values in Temerlin Ads," *AdWeek* (June 20, 2002).

Laura Clark Geist, "Licensing Links Brands, People with Goods," *Automotive News* (September 16, 2002): 2M.

# 4.2 Procter & Gamble: Using Marketing Research to Build Brands

Procter & Gamble delivers products under more than 250 brands to nearly five billion consumers in more than 130 countries around the world. P&G employs over 105,000 employees in approximately 80 countries worldwide. The company began operations in the United States in 1837 and has continued to expand its global operations, most recently to Algeria in 2001. The stated purpose of the company is to "provide products and services of superior quality and value that improve the lives of the world's consumers."

P&G is the number one U.S. maker of household products, with nearly 300 brands in five main categories: baby, feminine, and family care; fabric and home care; beauty care; heath care; and food and beverage. P&G also makes pet food and water filters and produces the soap operas *Guiding Light* and *As the World Turns*. Twelve of P&G's brands are billion-dollar sellers (Always/Whisper, Ariel, Bounty, Charmin, Crest, Downy/Lenor, Folgers, Iams, Pampers, Pantene, Pringles, and Tide). The company recently purchased hair care giant Clairol (Nice & Easy, Herbal Essences, Aussie) from Bristol-Myers Squibb in 2001.

Over time, Proctor & Gamble has proven to be an innovator in creating brands and understanding consumers by making extensive use of marketing research. Building brands has been a cornerstone of P&G's success. The marketers at P&G undertake marketing research to determine a brand's equity and then make sure everyone understands it because that drives every decision made about the brand.

P&G thinks of marketing in many of the same ways that it used to. It has always thought about the consumer and why the product would be relevant to the consumer. P&G believes in catering to the experience of the consumer. Its principles of marketing haven't changed, but its methods of targeting and identifying consumers have changed to meet the increasingly complicated consumer base. In the early days, P&G would mass market through television and other sources because this was effective at the time. It has changed its key strategy from mass marketing to consumer targeting. Marketing research has revealed targeting as the future of brand marketing and brand management. P&G believes this takes much more than a focus group, and it wants to spend time with consumers and understand their behaviors. P&G's market research is so extensive that it even develops new products based on research to meet the demands of a consumer. P&G's innovative approach puts the consumer at the center of everything it does. P&G has also aligned its business to go along with each brand. It has integrated all departments under each brand because it wants the consumer to think of the brand as a unified entity and to provide an integrated experience.

One of the areas that P&G researches constantly is the in-store experience of the consumer. P&G sees this as another way of connecting with consumers and making their experiences better. One of the ways P&G enhances this is by partnering with retailers and developing the in-store experience to please its consumers. Pleasing the consumers has become more difficult today because the consumer has less time and more expectations. Packaging is also important in conveying a message to the consumer. It is a key challenge because labeling has become more complex and consumers are demanding more.

The Internet is also becoming an important marketing research tool for P&G. The company has increased the services it provides on the Internet in order to reach out to more consumers. This has proven effective, and P&G has even used the Internet as its sole source for some marketing campaigns. It also uses the Internet to gain new ideas and share them throughout the company.

P&G marketing has been innovative and pioneering over the years, and one would expect the same in the future. P&G is constantly using marketing research to solve the problems of today and to build brands that will continue to be leaders tomorrow.

## QUESTIONS

1. Discuss the role that marketing research can play in helping P&G build its various brands.
2. P&G is considering further increasing its market share. Define the management decision problem.
3. Define an appropriate marketing research problem based on the management decision problem you have identified.
4. Use the Internet to determine the market shares of the major toothpaste brands for the last calendar year.
5. What type of syndicate data will be useful in addressing the marketing research problem?
6. Discuss the role of qualitative research in helping P&G to increase its share of the toothpaste market.
7. P&G has developed a new toothpaste that provides tooth and gum protection for 24 hours after each brushing. It would like to determine consumers' response to this new toothpaste before introducing it in the marketplace. If a survey is to be conducted to determine consumer preferences, which survey method should be used and why?
8. Develop a questionnaire for assessing consumer preferences for toothpaste brands.
9. What sampling plan should be adopted for the survey of question 7?
10. According to P&G vice president of marketing, cavity and gum protection, whiteness of teeth, taste, fresh breath, and price are all independent variables that affect the preference for a toothpaste brand. Assume that in a survey, each of the leading toothpaste brands is evaluated on each of the independent variables using a seven-point scale with 1 = poor and 7 = excellent. Preference for toothpaste brands is also measured on a seven-point scale with 1 = not at all preferred and 7 = greatly preferred. Each respondent rates Crest and three competing toothpaste brands on all the independent variables as well as brand preference. What statistical technique(s) would you use to answer the following questions?
    a. Is brand preference related to each of the independent variables considered individually? What is the nature of the relationship you expect?
    b. Is brand preference related to all the independent variables considered simultaneously?
    c. Do the respondents evaluate the toothpaste more favorably on cavity and gum protection than they do on whiteness of teeth?
    d. The sample is divided into two groups: regular users of Crest and users of other brands. Do these two groups differ in terms of their ratings of Crest on price?
    e. The sample is divided in three groups: heavy, medium, and light users of toothpaste. Do the three groups differ in terms of preference for Crest?
    f. Can the three groups of heavy, medium, and light users be differentiated in terms of their evaluations of Crest on cavity and gum protection, whiteness of teeth, taste, fresh breath, and price, when these variables are considered together?
    g. Can the evaluations of Crest and its competitors on cavity and gum protection, whiteness of teeth, taste, fresh breath, and price be represented by a few underlying dimensions?
    h. Can the respondents be divided into relatively homogeneous groups based on their ratings of Crest on the five factors? If so, into how many groups?
11. If marketing research to determine consumer preferences for toothpaste brands were to be conducted in Latin America, how would the research process be different?
12. Discuss the ethical issues involved in researching consumer preferences for toothpaste brands.

## REFERENCES

*www.pg.com.*

Alan Mitchell, "Supermarkets Get the Message," *Financial Times* (London) (May 17, 2002) (Inside Track): 16.

Jack Neff, "Humble Try: P&G's Stengel Studies Tactics of Other Advertisers—and Moms—in Bid to Boost Marketing Muscle," *Advertising Age* (February 18, 2002): 3.

# Appendix

## Statistical Tables

### TABLE 1

**Simple Random Numbers**

| LINE/COL. | (1) | (2) | (3) | (4) | (5) | (6) | (7) | (8) | (9) | (10) | (11) | (12) | (13) | (14) |
|---|---|---|---|---|---|---|---|---|---|---|---|---|---|---|
| 1 | 10480 | 15011 | 01536 | 02011 | 81647 | 91646 | 69179 | 14194 | 62590 | 36207 | 20969 | 99570 | 91291 | 90700 |
| 2 | 22368 | 46573 | 25595 | 85393 | 30995 | 89198 | 27982 | 53402 | 93965 | 34095 | 52666 | 19174 | 39615 | 99505 |
| 3 | 24130 | 48390 | 22527 | 97265 | 76393 | 64809 | 15179 | 24830 | 49340 | 32081 | 30680 | 19655 | 63348 | 58629 |
| 4 | 42167 | 93093 | 06243 | 61680 | 07856 | 16376 | 39440 | 53537 | 71341 | 57004 | 00849 | 74917 | 97758 | 16379 |
| 5 | 37570 | 39975 | 81837 | 16656 | 06121 | 91782 | 60468 | 81305 | 49684 | 60072 | 14110 | 06927 | 01263 | 54613 |
| 6 | 77921 | 06907 | 11008 | 42751 | 27756 | 53498 | 18602 | 70659 | 90655 | 15053 | 21916 | 81825 | 44394 | 42880 |
| 7 | 99562 | 72905 | 56420 | 69994 | 98872 | 31016 | 71194 | 18738 | 44013 | 48840 | 63213 | 21069 | 10634 | 12952 |
| 8 | 96301 | 91977 | 05463 | 07972 | 18876 | 20922 | 94595 | 56869 | 69014 | 60045 | 18425 | 84903 | 42508 | 32307 |
| 9 | 89579 | 14342 | 63661 | 10281 | 17453 | 18103 | 57740 | 84378 | 25331 | 12568 | 58678 | 44947 | 05585 | 56941 |
| 10 | 85475 | 36857 | 53342 | 53988 | 53060 | 59533 | 38867 | 62300 | 08158 | 17983 | 16439 | 11458 | 18593 | 64952 |
| 11 | 28918 | 69578 | 88231 | 33276 | 70997 | 79936 | 56865 | 05859 | 90106 | 31595 | 01547 | 85590 | 91610 | 78188 |
| 12 | 63553 | 40961 | 48235 | 03427 | 49626 | 69445 | 18663 | 72695 | 52180 | 20847 | 12234 | 90511 | 33703 | 90322 |
| 13 | 09429 | 93969 | 52636 | 92737 | 88974 | 33488 | 36320 | 17617 | 30015 | 08272 | 84115 | 27156 | 30613 | 74952 |
| 14 | 10365 | 61129 | 87529 | 85689 | 48237 | 52267 | 67689 | 93394 | 01511 | 26358 | 85104 | 20285 | 29975 | 89868 |
| 15 | 07119 | 97336 | 71048 | 08178 | 77233 | 13916 | 47564 | 81056 | 97735 | 85977 | 29372 | 74461 | 28551 | 90707 |
| 16 | 51085 | 12765 | 51821 | 51259 | 77452 | 16308 | 60756 | 92144 | 49442 | 53900 | 70960 | 63990 | 75601 | 40719 |
| 17 | 02368 | 21382 | 52404 | 60268 | 89368 | 19885 | 55322 | 44819 | 01188 | 65255 | 64835 | 44919 | 05944 | 55157 |
| 18 | 01011 | 54092 | 33362 | 94904 | 31273 | 04146 | 18594 | 29852 | 71685 | 85030 | 51132 | 01915 | 92747 | 64951 |
| 19 | 52162 | 53916 | 46369 | 58586 | 23216 | 14513 | 83149 | 98736 | 23495 | 64350 | 94738 | 17752 | 35156 | 35749 |
| 20 | 07056 | 97628 | 33787 | 09998 | 42698 | 06691 | 76988 | 13602 | 51851 | 46104 | 88916 | 19509 | 25625 | 58104 |
| 21 | 48663 | 91245 | 85828 | 14346 | 09172 | 30163 | 90229 | 04734 | 59193 | 22178 | 30421 | 61666 | 99904 | 32812 |
| 22 | 54164 | 58492 | 22421 | 74103 | 47070 | 25306 | 76468 | 26384 | 58151 | 06646 | 21524 | 15227 | 96909 | 44592 |
| 23 | 32639 | 32363 | 05597 | 24200 | 13363 | 38005 | 94342 | 28728 | 35806 | 06912 | 17012 | 64161 | 18296 | 22851 |
| 24 | 29334 | 27001 | 87637 | 87308 | 58731 | 00256 | 45834 | 15398 | 46557 | 41135 | 10307 | 07684 | 36188 | 18510 |
| 25 | 02488 | 33062 | 28834 | 07351 | 19731 | 92420 | 60952 | 61280 | 50001 | 67658 | 32586 | 86679 | 50720 | 94953 |
| 26 | 81525 | 72295 | 04839 | 96423 | 24878 | 82651 | 66566 | 14778 | 76797 | 14780 | 13300 | 87074 | 79666 | 95725 |
| 27 | 29676 | 20591 | 68086 | 26432 | 46901 | 20849 | 89768 | 81536 | 86645 | 12659 | 92259 | 57102 | 80428 | 25280 |
| 28 | 00742 | 57392 | 39064 | 66432 | 84673 | 40027 | 32832 | 61362 | 98947 | 96067 | 64760 | 64584 | 96096 | 98253 |
| 29 | 05366 | 04213 | 25669 | 26422 | 44407 | 44048 | 37937 | 63904 | 45766 | 66134 | 75470 | 66520 | 34693 | 90449 |
| 30 | 91921 | 26418 | 64117 | 94305 | 26766 | 25940 | 39972 | 22209 | 71500 | 64568 | 91402 | 42416 | 07844 | 69618 |
| 31 | 00582 | 04711 | 87917 | 77341 | 42206 | 35126 | 74087 | 99547 | 81817 | 42607 | 43808 | 76655 | 62028 | 76630 |
| 32 | 00725 | 69884 | 62797 | 56170 | 86324 | 88072 | 76222 | 36086 | 84637 | 93161 | 76038 | 65855 | 77919 | 88006 |
| 33 | 69011 | 65795 | 95876 | 55293 | 18988 | 27354 | 26575 | 08625 | 40801 | 59920 | 29841 | 80150 | 12777 | 48501 |
| 34 | 25976 | 57948 | 29888 | 88604 | 67917 | 48708 | 18912 | 82271 | 65424 | 69774 | 33611 | 54262 | 85963 | 03547 |
| 35 | 09763 | 83473 | 73577 | 12908 | 30883 | 18317 | 28290 | 35797 | 05998 | 41688 | 34952 | 37888 | 38917 | 88050 |
| 36 | 91567 | 42595 | 27958 | 30134 | 04024 | 86385 | 29880 | 99730 | 55536 | 84855 | 29088 | 09250 | 79656 | 73211 |
| 37 | 17955 | 56349 | 90999 | 49127 | 20044 | 59931 | 06115 | 20542 | 18059 | 02008 | 73708 | 83517 | 36103 | 42791 |
| 38 | 46503 | 18584 | 18845 | 49618 | 02304 | 51038 | 20655 | 58727 | 28168 | 15475 | 56942 | 53389 | 20562 | 87338 |
| 39 | 92157 | 89634 | 94824 | 78171 | 84610 | 82834 | 09922 | 25417 | 44137 | 48413 | 25555 | 21246 | 35509 | 20468 |
| 40 | 14577 | 62765 | 35605 | 81263 | 39667 | 47358 | 56873 | 56307 | 61607 | 49518 | 89656 | 20103 | 77490 | 18062 |
| 41 | 98427 | 07523 | 33362 | 64270 | 01638 | 92477 | 66969 | 98420 | 04880 | 45585 | 46565 | 04102 | 46880 | 45709 |
| 42 | 34914 | 63976 | 88720 | 82765 | 34476 | 17032 | 87589 | 40836 | 32427 | 70002 | 70663 | 88863 | 77775 | 69348 |

(Continued)

TABLE 1—*continued*

**Simple Random Numbers**

| Line/Col. | (1) | (2) | (3) | (4) | (5) | (6) | (7) | (8) | (9) | (10) | (11) | (12) | (13) | (14) |
|---|---|---|---|---|---|---|---|---|---|---|---|---|---|---|
| 43 | 70060 | 28277 | 39475 | 46473 | 23219 | 53416 | 94970 | 25832 | 69975 | 94884 | 19661 | 72828 | 00102 | 66794 |
| 44 | 53976 | 54914 | 06990 | 67245 | 68350 | 82948 | 11398 | 42878 | 80287 | 88267 | 47363 | 46634 | 06541 | 97809 |
| 45 | 76072 | 29515 | 40980 | 07391 | 58745 | 25774 | 22987 | 80059 | 39911 | 96189 | 41151 | 14222 | 60697 | 59583 |
| 46 | 90725 | 52210 | 83974 | 29992 | 65831 | 38857 | 50490 | 83765 | 55657 | 14361 | 31720 | 57375 | 56228 | 41546 |
| 47 | 64364 | 67412 | 33339 | 31926 | 14883 | 24413 | 59744 | 92351 | 97473 | 89286 | 35931 | 04110 | 23726 | 51900 |
| 48 | 08962 | 00358 | 31662 | 25388 | 61642 | 34072 | 81249 | 35648 | 56891 | 69352 | 48373 | 45578 | 78547 | 81788 |
| 49 | 95012 | 68379 | 93526 | 70765 | 10592 | 04542 | 76463 | 54328 | 02349 | 17247 | 28865 | 14777 | 62730 | 92277 |
| 50 | 15664 | 10493 | 20492 | 38301 | 91132 | 21999 | 59516 | 81652 | 27195 | 48223 | 46751 | 22923 | 32261 | 85653 |
| 51 | 16408 | 81899 | 04153 | 53381 | 79401 | 21438 | 83035 | 92350 | 36693 | 31238 | 59649 | 91754 | 72772 | 02338 |
| 52 | 18629 | 81953 | 05520 | 91962 | 04739 | 13092 | 97662 | 24822 | 94730 | 06496 | 35090 | 04822 | 86774 | 98289 |
| 53 | 73115 | 35101 | 47498 | 87637 | 99016 | 71060 | 88824 | 71013 | 18735 | 20286 | 23153 | 72924 | 35165 | 43040 |
| 54 | 57491 | 16703 | 23167 | 49323 | 45021 | 33132 | 12544 | 41035 | 80780 | 45393 | 44812 | 12515 | 98931 | 91202 |
| 55 | 30405 | 83946 | 23792 | 14422 | 15059 | 45799 | 22716 | 19792 | 09983 | 74353 | 68668 | 30429 | 70735 | 25499 |
| 56 | 16631 | 35006 | 85900 | 98275 | 32388 | 52390 | 16815 | 69293 | 82732 | 38480 | 73817 | 32523 | 41961 | 44437 |
| 57 | 96773 | 20206 | 42559 | 78985 | 05300 | 22164 | 24369 | 54224 | 35083 | 19687 | 11052 | 91491 | 60383 | 19746 |
| 58 | 38935 | 64202 | 14349 | 82674 | 66523 | 44133 | 00697 | 35552 | 35970 | 19124 | 63318 | 29686 | 03387 | 59846 |
| 59 | 31624 | 76384 | 17403 | 53363 | 44167 | 64486 | 64758 | 75366 | 76554 | 31601 | 12614 | 33072 | 60332 | 92325 |
| 60 | 78919 | 19474 | 23632 | 27889 | 47914 | 02584 | 37680 | 20801 | 72152 | 39339 | 34806 | 08930 | 85001 | 87820 |
| 61 | 03931 | 33309 | 57047 | 74211 | 63445 | 17361 | 62825 | 39908 | 05607 | 91284 | 68833 | 25570 | 38818 | 46920 |
| 62 | 74426 | 33278 | 43972 | 10119 | 89917 | 15665 | 52872 | 73823 | 73144 | 88662 | 88970 | 74492 | 51805 | 99378 |
| 63 | 09066 | 00903 | 20795 | 95452 | 92648 | 45454 | 69552 | 88815 | 16553 | 51125 | 79375 | 97596 | 16296 | 66092 |
| 64 | 42238 | 12426 | 87025 | 14267 | 20979 | 04508 | 64535 | 31355 | 86064 | 29472 | 47689 | 05974 | 52468 | 16834 |
| 65 | 16153 | 08002 | 26504 | 41744 | 81959 | 65642 | 74240 | 56302 | 00033 | 67107 | 77510 | 70625 | 28725 | 34191 |
| 66 | 21457 | 40742 | 29820 | 96783 | 29400 | 21840 | 15035 | 34537 | 33310 | 06116 | 95240 | 15957 | 16572 | 06004 |
| 67 | 21581 | 57802 | 02050 | 89728 | 17937 | 37621 | 47075 | 42080 | 97403 | 48626 | 68995 | 43805 | 33386 | 21597 |
| 68 | 55612 | 78095 | 83197 | 33732 | 05810 | 24813 | 86902 | 60397 | 16489 | 03264 | 88525 | 42786 | 05269 | 92532 |
| 69 | 44657 | 66999 | 99324 | 51281 | 84463 | 60563 | 79312 | 93454 | 68876 | 25471 | 93911 | 25650 | 12682 | 73572 |
| 70 | 91340 | 84979 | 46949 | 81973 | 37949 | 61023 | 43997 | 15263 | 80644 | 43942 | 89203 | 71795 | 99533 | 50501 |
| 71 | 91227 | 21199 | 31935 | 27022 | 84067 | 05462 | 35216 | 14486 | 29891 | 68607 | 41867 | 14951 | 91696 | 85065 |
| 72 | 50001 | 38140 | 66321 | 19924 | 72163 | 09538 | 12151 | 06878 | 91903 | 18749 | 34405 | 56087 | 82790 | 70925 |
| 73 | 65390 | 05224 | 72958 | 28609 | 81406 | 39147 | 25549 | 48542 | 42627 | 45233 | 57202 | 94617 | 23772 | 07896 |
| 74 | 27504 | 96131 | 83944 | 41575 | 10573 | 03619 | 64482 | 73923 | 36152 | 05184 | 94142 | 25299 | 94387 | 34925 |
| 75 | 37169 | 94851 | 39117 | 89632 | 00959 | 16487 | 65536 | 49071 | 39782 | 17095 | 02330 | 74301 | 00275 | 48280 |
| 76 | 11508 | 70225 | 51111 | 38351 | 19444 | 66499 | 71945 | 05422 | 13442 | 78675 | 84031 | 66938 | 93654 | 59894 |
| 77 | 37449 | 30362 | 06694 | 54690 | 04052 | 53115 | 62757 | 95348 | 78662 | 11163 | 81651 | 50245 | 34971 | 52974 |
| 78 | 46515 | 70331 | 85922 | 38329 | 57015 | 15765 | 97161 | 17869 | 45349 | 61796 | 66345 | 81073 | 49106 | 79860 |
| 79 | 30986 | 81223 | 42416 | 58353 | 21532 | 30502 | 32305 | 86482 | 05174 | 07901 | 54339 | 58861 | 74818 | 46942 |
| 80 | 63798 | 64995 | 46583 | 09785 | 44160 | 78128 | 83991 | 42865 | 92520 | 83531 | 80377 | 35909 | 81250 | 54238 |
| 81 | 82486 | 84846 | 99254 | 67632 | 43218 | 50076 | 21361 | 64816 | 51202 | 88124 | 41870 | 52689 | 51275 | 83556 |
| 82 | 21885 | 32906 | 92431 | 09060 | 64297 | 51674 | 64126 | 62570 | 26123 | 05155 | 59194 | 52799 | 28225 | 85762 |
| 83 | 60336 | 98782 | 07408 | 53458 | 13564 | 59089 | 26445 | 29789 | 85205 | 41001 | 12535 | 12133 | 14645 | 23541 |
| 84 | 43937 | 46891 | 24010 | 25560 | 86355 | 33941 | 25786 | 54990 | 71899 | 15475 | 95434 | 98227 | 21824 | 19535 |
| 85 | 97656 | 63175 | 89303 | 16275 | 07100 | 92063 | 21942 | 18611 | 47348 | 20203 | 18534 | 03862 | 78095 | 50136 |
| 86 | 03299 | 01221 | 05418 | 38982 | 55758 | 92237 | 26759 | 86367 | 21216 | 98442 | 08303 | 56613 | 91511 | 75928 |
| 87 | 79626 | 06486 | 03574 | 17668 | 07785 | 76020 | 79924 | 25651 | 83325 | 88428 | 85076 | 72811 | 22717 | 50585 |
| 88 | 85636 | 68335 | 47539 | 03129 | 65651 | 11977 | 02510 | 26113 | 99447 | 68645 | 34327 | 15152 | 55230 | 93448 |
| 89 | 18039 | 14367 | 61337 | 06177 | 12143 | 46609 | 32989 | 74014 | 64708 | 00533 | 35398 | 58408 | 13261 | 47908 |
| 90 | 08362 | 15656 | 60627 | 36478 | 65648 | 16764 | 53412 | 09013 | 07832 | 41574 | 17639 | 82163 | 60859 | 75567 |
| 91 | 79556 | 29068 | 04142 | 16268 | 15387 | 12856 | 66227 | 38358 | 22478 | 73373 | 88732 | 09443 | 82558 | 05250 |
| 92 | 92608 | 82674 | 27072 | 32534 | 17075 | 27698 | 98204 | 63863 | 11951 | 34648 | 88022 | 56148 | 34925 | 57031 |
| 93 | 23982 | 25835 | 40055 | 67006 | 12293 | 02753 | 14827 | 23235 | 35071 | 99704 | 37543 | 11601 | 35503 | 85171 |
| 94 | 09915 | 96306 | 05908 | 97901 | 28395 | 14186 | 00821 | 80703 | 70426 | 75647 | 76310 | 88717 | 37890 | 40129 |

(*Continued*)

TABLE 1—*continued*

**Simple Random Numbers**

| LINE/COL. | (1) | (2) | (3) | (4) | (5) | (6) | (7) | (8) | (9) | (10) | (11) | (12) | (13) | (14) |
|---|---|---|---|---|---|---|---|---|---|---|---|---|---|---|
| 95 | 59037 | 33300 | 26695 | 62247 | 69927 | 76123 | 50842 | 43834 | 86654 | 70959 | 79725 | 93872 | 28117 | 19233 |
| 96 | 42488 | 78077 | 69882 | 61657 | 34136 | 79180 | 97526 | 43092 | 04098 | 73571 | 80799 | 76536 | 71255 | 64239 |
| 97 | 46764 | 86273 | 63003 | 93017 | 31204 | 36692 | 40202 | 35275 | 57306 | 55543 | 53203 | 18098 | 47625 | 88684 |
| 98 | 03237 | 45430 | 55417 | 63282 | 90816 | 17349 | 88298 | 90183 | 36600 | 78406 | 06216 | 95787 | 42579 | 90730 |
| 99 | 86591 | 81482 | 52667 | 61582 | 14972 | 90053 | 89534 | 76036 | 49199 | 43716 | 97548 | 04379 | 46370 | 28672 |
| 100 | 38534 | 01715 | 94964 | 87288 | 65680 | 43772 | 39560 | 12918 | 80537 | 62738 | 19636 | 51132 | 25739 | 56947 |

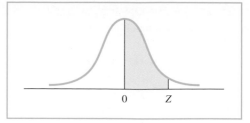

TABLE 2

**Area Under the Normal Curve**

| Z | .00 | .01 | .02 | .03 | .04 | .05 | .06 | .07 | .08 | .09 |
|---|-----|-----|-----|-----|-----|-----|-----|-----|-----|-----|
| 0.0 | .0000 | .0040 | .0080 | .0120 | .0160 | .0199 | .0239 | .0279 | .0319 | .0359 |
| 0.1 | .0398 | .0438 | .0478 | .0517 | .0557 | .0596 | .0636 | .0675 | .0714 | .0753 |
| 0.2 | .0793 | .0832 | .0871 | .0910 | .0948 | .0987 | .1026 | .1064 | .1103 | .1141 |
| 0.3 | .1179 | .1217 | .1255 | .1293 | .1331 | .1368 | .1406 | .1443 | .1480 | .1517 |
| 0.4 | .1554 | .1591 | .1628 | .1664 | .1700 | .1736 | .1772 | .1808 | .1844 | .1879 |
| 0.5 | .1915 | .1950 | .1985 | .2019 | .2054 | .2088 | .2123 | .2157 | .2190 | .2224 |
| 0.6 | .2257 | .2291 | .2324 | .2357 | .2389 | .2422 | .2454 | .2486 | .2518 | .2549 |
| 0.7 | .2580 | .2612 | .2642 | .2673 | .2704 | .2734 | .2764 | .2794 | .2823 | .2852 |
| 0.8 | .2881 | .2910 | .2939 | .2967 | .2995 | .3023 | .3051 | .3078 | .3106 | .3133 |
| 0.9 | .3159 | .3186 | .3212 | .3238 | .3264 | .3289 | .3315 | .3340 | .3365 | .3389 |
| 1.0 | .3413 | .3438 | .3461 | .3485 | .3508 | .3531 | .3554 | .3577 | .3599 | .3621 |
| 1.1 | .3643 | .3665 | .3686 | .3708 | .3729 | .3749 | .3770 | .3790 | .3810 | .3830 |
| 1.2 | .3849 | .3869 | .3888 | .3907 | .3925 | .3944 | .3962 | .3980 | .3997 | .4015 |
| 1.3 | .4032 | .4049 | .4066 | .4082 | .4099 | .4115 | .4131 | .4147 | .4162 | .4177 |
| 1.4 | .4192 | .4207 | .4222 | .4236 | .4251 | .4265 | .4279 | .4292 | .4306 | .4319 |
| 1.5 | .4332 | .4345 | .4357 | .4370 | .4382 | .4394 | .4406 | .4418 | .4429 | .4441 |
| 1.6 | .4452 | .4463 | .4474 | .4484 | .4495 | .4505 | .4515 | .4525 | .4535 | .4545 |
| 1.7 | .4554 | .4564 | .4573 | .4582 | .4591 | .4599 | .4608 | .4616 | .4625 | .4633 |
| 1.8 | .4641 | .4649 | .4656 | .4664 | .4671 | .4678 | .4686 | .4693 | .4699 | .4706 |
| 1.9 | .4713 | .4719 | .4726 | .4732 | .4738 | .4744 | .4750 | .4756 | .4761 | .4767 |
| 2.0 | .4772 | .4778 | .4783 | .4788 | .4793 | .4798 | .4803 | .4808 | .4812 | .4817 |
| 2.1 | .4821 | .4826 | .4830 | .4834 | .4838 | .4842 | .4846 | .4850 | .4854 | .4857 |
| 2.2 | .4861 | .4864 | .4868 | .4871 | .4875 | .4878 | .4881 | .4884 | .4887 | .4890 |
| 2.3 | .4893 | .4896 | .4898 | .4901 | .4904 | .4906 | .4909 | .4911 | .4913 | .4916 |
| 2.4 | .4918 | .4920 | .4922 | .4925 | .4927 | .4929 | .4931 | .4932 | .4934 | .4936 |
| 2.5 | .4938 | .4940 | .4941 | .4943 | .4945 | .4946 | .4948 | .4949 | .4951 | .4952 |
| 2.6 | .4953 | .4955 | .4956 | .4957 | .4959 | .4960 | .4961 | .4962 | .4963 | .4964 |
| 2.7 | .4965 | .4966 | .4967 | .4968 | .4969 | .4970 | .4971 | .4972 | .4973 | .4974 |
| 2.8 | .4974 | .4975 | .4976 | .4977 | .4977 | .4978 | .4979 | .4979 | .4980 | .4981 |
| 2.9 | .4981 | .4982 | .4982 | .4983 | .4984 | .4984 | .4985 | .4985 | .4986 | .4986 |
| 3.0 | .49865 | .49869 | .49874 | .49878 | .49882 | .49886 | .49889 | .49893 | .49897 | .49900 |
| 3.1 | .49903 | .49906 | .49910 | .49913 | .49916 | .49918 | .49921 | .49924 | .49926 | .49929 |
| 3.2 | .49931 | .49934 | .49936 | .49938 | .49940 | .49942 | .49944 | .49946 | .49948 | .49950 |
| 3.3 | .49952 | .49953 | .49955 | .49957 | .49958 | .49960 | .49961 | .49962 | .49964 | .49965 |
| 3.4 | .49966 | .49968 | .49969 | .49970 | .49971 | .49972 | .49973 | .49974 | .49975 | .49976 |
| 3.5 | .49977 | .49978 | .49978 | .49979 | .49980 | .49981 | .49981 | .49982 | .49983 | .49983 |
| 3.6 | .49984 | .49985 | .49985 | .49986 | .49986 | .49987 | .49987 | .49988 | .49988 | .49989 |
| 3.7 | .49989 | .49990 | .49990 | .49990 | .49991 | .49991 | .49992 | .49992 | .49992 | .49992 |
| 3.8 | .49993 | .49993 | .49993 | .49994 | .49994 | .49994 | .49994 | .49995 | .49995 | .49995 |
| 3.9 | .49995 | .49995 | .49996 | .49996 | .49996 | .49996 | .49996 | .49996 | .49997 | .49997 |

Entry represents area under the standard normal distribution from the mean to $Z$

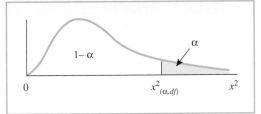

TABLE 3

## Chi-Square Distribution

| DEGREES OF FREEDOM | UPPER TAIL AREAS ($\alpha$) | | | | | | | | | | | |
|---|---|---|---|---|---|---|---|---|---|---|---|---|
| | .995 | .99 | .975 | .95 | .90 | .75 | .25 | .10 | .05 | .025 | .01 | .005 |
| 1 | — | — | 0.001 | 0.004 | 0.016 | 0.102 | 1.323 | 2.706 | 3.841 | 5.024 | 6.635 | 7.879 |
| 2 | 0.010 | 0.020 | 0.051 | 0.103 | 0.211 | 0.575 | 2.773 | 4.605 | 5.991 | 7.378 | 9.210 | 10.597 |
| 3 | 0.072 | 0.115 | 0.216 | 0.352 | 0.584 | 1.213 | 4.108 | 6.251 | 7.815 | 9.348 | 11.345 | 12.838 |
| 4 | 0.207 | 0.297 | 0.484 | 0.711 | 1.064 | 1.923 | 5.385 | 7.779 | 9.488 | 11.143 | 13.277 | 14.860 |
| 5 | 0.412 | 0.554 | 0.831 | 1.145 | 1.610 | 2.675 | 6.626 | 9.236 | 11.071 | 12.833 | 15.086 | 16.750 |
| 6 | 0.676 | 0.872 | 1.237 | 1.635 | 2.204 | 3.455 | 7.841 | 10.645 | 12.592 | 14.449 | 16.812 | 18.548 |
| 7 | 0.989 | 1.239 | 1.690 | 2.167 | 2.833 | 4.255 | 9.037 | 12.017 | 14.067 | 16.013 | 18.475 | 20.278 |
| 8 | 1.344 | 1.646 | 2.180 | 2.733 | 3.490 | 5.071 | 10.219 | 13.362 | 15.507 | 17.535 | 20.090 | 21.955 |
| 9 | 1.735 | 2.088 | 2.700 | 3.325 | 4.168 | 5.899 | 11.389 | 14.684 | 16.919 | 19.023 | 21.666 | 23.589 |
| 10 | 2.156 | 2.558 | 3.247 | 3.940 | 4.865 | 6.737 | 12.549 | 15.987 | 18.307 | 20.483 | 23.209 | 25.188 |
| 11 | 2.603 | 3.053 | 3.816 | 4.575 | 5.578 | 7.584 | 13.701 | 17.275 | 19.675 | 21.920 | 24.725 | 26.757 |
| 12 | 3.074 | 3.571 | 4.404 | 5.226 | 6.304 | 8.438 | 14.845 | 18.549 | 21.026 | 23.337 | 26.217 | 28.299 |
| 13 | 3.565 | 4.107 | 5.009 | 5.892 | 7.042 | 9.299 | 15.984 | 19.812 | 22.362 | 24.736 | 27.688 | 29.819 |
| 14 | 4.075 | 4.660 | 5.629 | 6.571 | 7.790 | 10.165 | 17.117 | 21.064 | 23.685 | 26.119 | 29.141 | 31.319 |
| 15 | 4.601 | 5.229 | 6.262 | 7.261 | 8.547 | 11.037 | 18.245 | 22.307 | 24.996 | 27.488 | 30.578 | 32.801 |
| 16 | 5.142 | 5.812 | 6.908 | 7.962 | 9.312 | 11.912 | 19.369 | 23.542 | 26.296 | 28.845 | 32.000 | 34.267 |
| 17 | 5.697 | 6.408 | 7.564 | 8.672 | 10.085 | 12.792 | 20.489 | 24.769 | 27.587 | 30.191 | 33.409 | 35.718 |
| 18 | 6.265 | 7.015 | 8.231 | 9.390 | 10.865 | 13.675 | 21.605 | 25.989 | 28.869 | 31.526 | 34.805 | 37.156 |
| 19 | 6.844 | 7.633 | 8.907 | 10.117 | 11.651 | 14.562 | 22.718 | 27.204 | 30.144 | 32.852 | 36.191 | 38.582 |
| 20 | 7.434 | 8.260 | 9.591 | 10.851 | 12.443 | 15.452 | 23.828 | 28.412 | 31.410 | 34.170 | 37.566 | 39.997 |
| 21 | 8.034 | 8.897 | 10.283 | 11.591 | 13.240 | 16.344 | 24.935 | 29.615 | 32.671 | 35.479 | 38.932 | 41.401 |
| 22 | 8.643 | 9.542 | 10.982 | 12.338 | 14.042 | 17.240 | 26.039 | 30.813 | 33.924 | 36.781 | 40.289 | 42.796 |
| 23 | 9.260 | 10.196 | 11.689 | 13.091 | 14.848 | 18.137 | 27.141 | 32.007 | 35.172 | 38.076 | 41.638 | 44.181 |
| 24 | 9.886 | 10.856 | 12.401 | 13.848 | 15.659 | 19.037 | 28.241 | 33.196 | 36.415 | 39.364 | 42.980 | 45.559 |
| 25 | 10.520 | 11.524 | 13.120 | 14.611 | 16.473 | 19.939 | 29.339 | 34.382 | 37.652 | 40.646 | 44.314 | 46.928 |
| 26 | 11.160 | 12.198 | 13.844 | 15.379 | 17.292 | 20.843 | 30.435 | 35.563 | 38.885 | 41.923 | 45.642 | 48.290 |
| 27 | 11.808 | 12.879 | 14.573 | 16.151 | 18.114 | 21.749 | 31.528 | 36.741 | 40.113 | 43.194 | 46.963 | 49.645 |
| 28 | 12.461 | 13.565 | 15.308 | 16.928 | 18.939 | 22.657 | 32.620 | 37.916 | 41.337 | 44.461 | 48.278 | 50.993 |
| 29 | 13.121 | 14.257 | 16.047 | 17.708 | 19.768 | 23.567 | 33.711 | 39.087 | 42.557 | 45.722 | 49.588 | 52.336 |
| 30 | 13.787 | 14.954 | 16.791 | 18.493 | 20.599 | 24.478 | 34.800 | 40.256 | 43.773 | 46.979 | 50.892 | 53.672 |
| 31 | 14.458 | 15.655 | 17.539 | 19.281 | 21.434 | 25.390 | 35.887 | 41.422 | 44.985 | 48.232 | 52.191 | 55.003 |
| 32 | 15.134 | 16.362 | 18.291 | 20.072 | 22.271 | 26.304 | 36.973 | 42.585 | 46.194 | 49.480 | 53.486 | 56.328 |
| 33 | 15.815 | 17.074 | 19.047 | 20.867 | 23.110 | 27.219 | 38.058 | 43.745 | 47.400 | 50.725 | 54.776 | 57.648 |
| 34 | 16.501 | 17.789 | 19.806 | 21.664 | 23.952 | 28.136 | 39.141 | 44.903 | 48.602 | 51.966 | 56.061 | 58.964 |
| 35 | 17.192 | 18.509 | 20.569 | 22.465 | 24.797 | 29.054 | 40.223 | 46.059 | 49.802 | 53.203 | 57.342 | 60.275 |
| 36 | 17.887 | 19.233 | 21.336 | 23.269 | 25.643 | 29.973 | 41.304 | 47.212 | 50.998 | 54.437 | 58.619 | 61.581 |
| 37 | 18.586 | 19.960 | 22.106 | 24.075 | 26.492 | 30.893 | 42.383 | 48.363 | 52.192 | 55.668 | 59.892 | 62.883 |
| 38 | 19.289 | 20.691 | 22.878 | 24.884 | 27.343 | 31.815 | 43.462 | 49.513 | 53.384 | 56.896 | 61.162 | 64.181 |
| 39 | 19.996 | 21.426 | 23.654 | 25.695 | 28.196 | 32.737 | 44.539 | 50.660 | 54.572 | 58.120 | 62.428 | 65.476 |
| 40 | 20.707 | 22.164 | 24.433 | 26.509 | 29.051 | 33.660 | 45.616 | 51.805 | 55.758 | 59.342 | 63.691 | 66.766 |

*(Continued)*

TABLE 3—*continued*

## Chi-Square Distribution

| DEGREES OF FREEDOM | .995 | .99 | .975 | .95 | .90 | UPPER TAIL AREAS ($\alpha$) .75 | .25 | .10 | .05 | .025 | .01 | .005 |
|---|---|---|---|---|---|---|---|---|---|---|---|---|
| 41 | 21.421 | 22.906 | 25.215 | 27.326 | 29.907 | 34.585 | 46.692 | 52.949 | 56.942 | 60.561 | 64.950 | 68.053 |
| 42 | 22.138 | 23.650 | 25.999 | 28.144 | 30.765 | 35.510 | 47.766 | 54.090 | 58.124 | 61.777 | 66.206 | 69.336 |
| 43 | 22.859 | 24.398 | 26.785 | 28.965 | 31.625 | 36.436 | 48.840 | 55.230 | 59.304 | 62.990 | 67.459 | 70.616 |
| 44 | 23.584 | 25.148 | 27.575 | 29.787 | 32.487 | 37.363 | 49.913 | 56.369 | 60.481 | 64.201 | 68.710 | 71.893 |
| 45 | 24.311 | 25.901 | 28.366 | 30.612 | 33.350 | 38.291 | 50.985 | 57.505 | 61.656 | 65.410 | 69.957 | 73.166 |
| 46 | 25.041 | 26.657 | 29.160 | 31.439 | 34.215 | 39.220 | 52.056 | 58.641 | 62.830 | 66.617 | 71.201 | 74.437 |
| 47 | 25.775 | 27.416 | 29.956 | 32.268 | 35.081 | 40.149 | 53.127 | 59.774 | 64.001 | 67.821 | 72.443 | 75.704 |
| 48 | 26.511 | 28.177 | 30.755 | 33.098 | 35.949 | 41.079 | 54.196 | 60.907 | 65.171 | 69.023 | 73.683 | 76.969 |
| 49 | 27.249 | 28.941 | 31.555 | 33.930 | 36.818 | 42.010 | 55.265 | 62.038 | 66.339 | 70.222 | 74.919 | 78.231 |
| 50 | 27.991 | 29.707 | 32.357 | 34.764 | 37.689 | 42.942 | 56.334 | 63.167 | 67.505 | 71.420 | 76.154 | 79.490 |
| 51 | 28.735 | 30.475 | 33.162 | 35.600 | 38.560 | 43.874 | 57.401 | 64.295 | 68.669 | 72.616 | 77.386 | 80.747 |
| 52 | 29.481 | 31.246 | 33.968 | 36.437 | 39.433 | 44.808 | 58.468 | 65.422 | 69.832 | 73.810 | 78.616 | 82.001 |
| 53 | 30.230 | 32.018 | 34.776 | 37.276 | 40.308 | 45.741 | 59.534 | 66.548 | 70.993 | 75.002 | 79.843 | 83.253 |
| 54 | 30.981 | 32.793 | 35.586 | 38.116 | 41.183 | 46.676 | 60.600 | 67.673 | 72.153 | 76.192 | 81.069 | 84.502 |
| 55 | 31.735 | 33.570 | 36.398 | 38.958 | 42.060 | 47.610 | 61.665 | 68.796 | 73.311 | 77.380 | 82.292 | 85.749 |
| 56 | 32.490 | 34.350 | 37.212 | 39.801 | 42.937 | 48.546 | 62.729 | 69.919 | 74.468 | 78.567 | 83.513 | 86.994 |
| 57 | 33.248 | 35.131 | 38.027 | 40.646 | 43.816 | 49.482 | 63.793 | 71.040 | 75.624 | 79.752 | 84.733 | 88.236 |
| 58 | 34.008 | 35.913 | 38.844 | 41.492 | 44.696 | 50.419 | 64.857 | 72.160 | 76.778 | 80.936 | 85.950 | 89.477 |
| 59 | 34.770 | 36.698 | 39.662 | 42.339 | 45.577 | 51.356 | 65.919 | 73.279 | 77.931 | 82.117 | 87.166 | 90.715 |
| 60 | 35.534 | 37.485 | 40.482 | 43.188 | 46.459 | 52.294 | 66.981 | 74.397 | 79.082 | 83.298 | 88.379 | 91.952 |

For a particular number of degrees of freedom, entry represents the critical value of $\chi^2$ corresponding to a specified upper tail area, $\alpha$

For larger values of degrees of freedom (DF) the expression $z = \sqrt{2\chi^2} - \sqrt{2(DF) - 1}$ may be used and the resulting upper tail area can be obtained from the table of the standardized normal distribution.

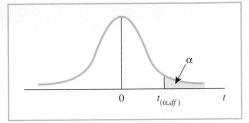

TABLE 4

## *t* Distribution

| DEGREES OF FREEDOM | UPPER TAIL AREAS | | | | | |
|---|---|---|---|---|---|---|
| | .25 | .10 | .05 | .025 | .01 | .005 |
| 1 | 1.0000 | 3.0777 | 6.3138 | 12.7062 | 31.8207 | 63.6574 |
| 2 | 0.8165 | 1.8856 | 2.9200 | 4.3027 | 6.9646 | 9.9248 |
| 3 | 0.7649 | 1.6377 | 2.3534 | 3.1824 | 4.5407 | 5.8409 |
| 4 | 0.7407 | 1.5332 | 2.1318 | 2.7764 | 3.7469 | 4.6041 |
| 5 | 0.7267 | 1.4759 | 2.0150 | 2.5706 | 3.3649 | 4.0322 |
| 6 | 0.7176 | 1.4398 | 1.9432 | 2.4469 | 3.1427 | 3.7074 |
| 7 | 0.7111 | 1.4149 | 1.8946 | 2.3646 | 2.9980 | 3.4995 |
| 8 | 0.7064 | 1.3968 | 1.8595 | 2.3060 | 2.8965 | 3.3554 |
| 9 | 0.7027 | 1.3830 | 1.8331 | 2.2622 | 2.8214 | 3.2498 |
| 10 | 0.6998 | 1.3722 | 1.8125 | 2.2281 | 2.7638 | 3.1693 |
| 11 | 0.6974 | 1.3634 | 1.7959 | 2.2010 | 2.7181 | 3.1058 |
| 12 | 0.6955 | 1.3562 | 1.7823 | 2.1788 | 2.6810 | 3.0545 |
| 13 | 0.6938 | 1.3502 | 1.7709 | 2.1604 | 2.6503 | 3.0123 |
| 14 | 0.6924 | 1.3450 | 1.7613 | 2.1448 | 2.6245 | 2.9768 |
| 15 | 0.6912 | 1.3406 | 1.7531 | 2.1315 | 2.6025 | 2.9467 |
| 16 | 0.6901 | 1.3368 | 1.7459 | 2.1199 | 2.5835 | 2.9208 |
| 17 | 0.6892 | 1.3334 | 1.7396 | 2.1098 | 2.5669 | 2.8982 |
| 18 | 0.6884 | 1.3304 | 1.7341 | 2.1009 | 2.5524 | 2.8784 |
| 19 | 0.6876 | 1.3277 | 1.7291 | 2.0930 | 2.5395 | 2.8609 |
| 20 | 0.6870 | 1.3253 | 1.7247 | 2.0860 | 2.5280 | 2.8453 |
| 21 | 0.6864 | 1.3232 | 1.7207 | 2.0796 | 2.5177 | 2.8314 |
| 22 | 0.6858 | 1.3212 | 1.7171 | 2.0739 | 2.5083 | 2.8188 |
| 23 | 0.6853 | 1.3195 | 1.7139 | 2.0687 | 2.4999 | 2.8073 |
| 24 | 0.6848 | 1.3178 | 1.7109 | 2.0639 | 2.4922 | 2.7969 |
| 25 | 0.6844 | 1.3163 | 1.7081 | 2.0595 | 2.4851 | 2.7874 |
| 26 | 0.6840 | 1.3150 | 1.7056 | 2.0555 | 2.4786 | 2.7787 |
| 27 | 0.6837 | 1.3137 | 1.7033 | 2.0518 | 2.4727 | 2.7707 |
| 28 | 0.6834 | 1.3125 | 1.7011 | 2.0484 | 2.4671 | 2.7633 |
| 29 | 0.6830 | 1.3114 | 1.6991 | 2.0452 | 2.4620 | 2.7564 |
| 30 | 0.6828 | 1.3104 | 1.6973 | 2.0423 | 2.4573 | 2.7500 |
| 31 | 0.6825 | 1.3095 | 1.6955 | 2.0395 | 2.4528 | 2.7440 |
| 32 | 0.6822 | 1.3086 | 1.6939 | 2.0369 | 2.4487 | 2.7385 |
| 33 | 0.6820 | 1.3077 | 1.6924 | 2.0345 | 2.4448 | 2.7333 |
| 34 | 0.6818 | 1.3070 | 1.6909 | 2.0322 | 2.4411 | 2.7284 |
| 35 | 0.6816 | 1.3062 | 1.6896 | 2.0301 | 2.4377 | 2.7238 |
| 36 | 0.6814 | 1.3055 | 1.6883 | 2.0281 | 2.4345 | 2.7195 |
| 37 | 0.6812 | 1.3049 | 1.6871 | 2.0262 | 2.4314 | 2.7154 |
| 38 | 0.6810 | 1.3042 | 1.6860 | 2.0244 | 2.4286 | 2.7116 |
| 39 | 0.6808 | 1.3036 | 1.6849 | 2.0227 | 2.4258 | 2.7079 |
| 40 | 0.6807 | 1.3031 | 1.6839 | 2.0211 | 2.4233 | 2.7045 |
| 41 | 0.6805 | 1.3025 | 1.6829 | 2.0195 | 2.4208 | 2.7012 |
| 42 | 0.6804 | 1.3020 | 1.6820 | 2.0181 | 2.4185 | 2.6981 |
| 43 | 0.6802 | 1.3016 | 1.6811 | 2.0167 | 2.4163 | 2.6951 |

*(Continued)*

TABLE 4—*continued*

## *t* Distribution

| DEGREES OF FREEDOM | UPPER TAIL AREAS | | | | | |
|---|---|---|---|---|---|---|
| | .25 | .10 | .05 | .025 | .01 | .005 |
| 44 | 0.6801 | 1.3011 | 1.6802 | 2.0154 | 2.4141 | 2.6923 |
| 45 | 0.6800 | 1.3006 | 1.6794 | 2.0141 | 2.4121 | 2.6896 |
| 46 | 0.6799 | 1.3002 | 1.6787 | 2.0129 | 2.4102 | 2.6870 |
| 47 | 0.6797 | 1.2998 | 1.6779 | 2.0117 | 2.4083 | 2.6846 |
| 48 | 0.6796 | 1.2994 | 1.6772 | 2.0106 | 2.4066 | 2.6822 |
| 49 | 0.6795 | 1.2991 | 1.6766 | 2.0096 | 2.4049 | 2.6800 |
| 50 | 0.6794 | 1.2987 | 1.6759 | 2.0086 | 2.4033 | 2.6778 |
| 51 | 0.6793 | 1.2984 | 1.6753 | 2.0076 | 2.4017 | 2.6757 |
| 52 | 0.6792 | 1.2980 | 1.6747 | 2.0066 | 2.4002 | 2.6737 |
| 53 | 0.6791 | 1.2977 | 1.6741 | 2.0057 | 2.3988 | 2.6718 |
| 54 | 0.6791 | 1.2974 | 1.6736 | 2.0049 | 2.3974 | 2.6700 |
| 55 | 0.6790 | 1.2971 | 1.6730 | 2.0040 | 2.3961 | 2.6682 |
| 56 | 0.6789 | 1.2969 | 1.6725 | 2.0032 | 2.3948 | 2.6665 |
| 57 | 0.6788 | 1.2966 | 1.6720 | 2.0025 | 2.3936 | 2.6649 |
| 58 | 0.6787 | 1.2963 | 1.6716 | 2.0017 | 2.3924 | 2.6633 |
| 59 | 0.6787 | 1.2961 | 1.6711 | 2.0010 | 2.3912 | 2.6618 |
| 60 | 0.6786 | 1.2958 | 1.6706 | 2.0003 | 2.3901 | 2.6603 |
| 61 | 0.6785 | 1.2956 | 1.6702 | 1.9996 | 2.3890 | 2.6589 |
| 62 | 0.6785 | 1.2954 | 1.6698 | 1.9990 | 2.3880 | 2.6575 |
| 63 | 0.6784 | 1.2951 | 1.6694 | 1.9983 | 2.3870 | 2.6561 |
| 64 | 0.6783 | 1.2949 | 1.6690 | 1.9977 | 2.3860 | 2.6549 |
| 65 | 0.6783 | 1.2947 | 1.6686 | 1.9971 | 2.3851 | 2.6536 |
| 66 | 0.6782 | 1.2945 | 1.6683 | 1.9966 | 2.3842 | 2.6524 |
| 67 | 0.6782 | 1.2943 | 1.6679 | 1.9960 | 2.3833 | 2.6512 |
| 68 | 0.6781 | 1.2941 | 1.6676 | 1.9955 | 2.3824 | 2.6501 |
| 69 | 0.6781 | 1.2939 | 1.6672 | 1.9949 | 2.3816 | 2.6490 |
| 70 | 0.6780 | 1.2938 | 1.6669 | 1.9944 | 2.3808 | 2.6479 |
| 71 | 0.6780 | 1.2936 | 1.6666 | 1.9939 | 2.3800 | 2.6469 |
| 72 | 0.6779 | 1.2934 | 1.6663 | 1.9935 | 2.3793 | 2.6459 |
| 73 | 0.6779 | 1.2933 | 1.6660 | 1.9930 | 2.3785 | 2.6449 |
| 74 | 0.6778 | 1.2931 | 1.6657 | 1.9925 | 2.3778 | 2.6439 |
| 75 | 0.6778 | 1.2929 | 1.6654 | 1.9921 | 2.3771 | 2.6430 |
| 76 | 0.6777 | 1.2928 | 1.6652 | 1.9917 | 2.3764 | 2.6421 |
| 77 | 0.6777 | 1.2926 | 1.6649 | 1.9913 | 2.3758 | 2.6412 |
| 78 | 0.6776 | 1.2925 | 1.6646 | 1.9908 | 2.3751 | 2.6403 |
| 79 | 0.6776 | 1.2924 | 1.6644 | 1.9905 | 2.3745 | 2.6395 |
| 80 | 0.6776 | 1.2922 | 1.6641 | 1.9901 | 2.3739 | 2.6387 |
| 81 | 0.6775 | 1.2921 | 1.6639 | 1.9897 | 2.3733 | 2.6379 |
| 82 | 0.6775 | 1.2920 | 1.6636 | 1.9893 | 2.3727 | 2.6371 |
| 83 | 0.6775 | 1.2918 | 1.6634 | 1.9890 | 2.3721 | 2.6364 |
| 84 | 0.6774 | 1.2917 | 1.6632 | 1.9886 | 2.3716 | 2.6356 |
| 85 | 0.6774 | 1.2916 | 1.6630 | 1.9883 | 2.3710 | 2.6349 |
| 86 | 0.6774 | 1.2915 | 1.6628 | 1.9879 | 2.3705 | 2.6342 |
| 87 | 0.6773 | 1.2914 | 1.6626 | 1.9876 | 2.3700 | 2.6335 |
| 88 | 0.6773 | 1.2912 | 1.6624 | 1.9873 | 2.3695 | 2.6329 |
| 89 | 0.6773 | 1.2911 | 1.6622 | 1.9870 | 2.3690 | 2.6322 |
| 90 | 0.6772 | 1.2910 | 1.6620 | 1.9867 | 2.3685 | 2.6316 |
| 91 | 0.6772 | 1.2909 | 1.6618 | 1.9864 | 2.3680 | 2.6309 |
| 92 | 0.6772 | 1.2908 | 1.6616 | 1.9861 | 2.3676 | 2.6303 |
| 93 | 0.6771 | 1.2907 | 1.6614 | 1.9858 | 2.3671 | 2.6297 |
| 94 | 0.6771 | 1.2906 | 1.6612 | 1.9855 | 2.3667 | 2.6291 |

(*Continued*)

TABLE 4—*continued*

## *t* Distribution

| Degrees of Freedom | Upper Tail Areas | | | | | |
|---|---|---|---|---|---|---|
| | .25 | .10 | .05 | .025 | .01 | .005 |
| 95 | 0.6771 | 1.2905 | 1.6611 | 1.9853 | 2.3662 | 2.6286 |
| 96 | 0.6771 | 1.2904 | 1.6609 | 1.9850 | 2.3658 | 2.6280 |
| 97 | 0.6770 | 1.2903 | 1.6607 | 1.9847 | 2.3654 | 2.6275 |
| 98 | 0.6770 | 1.2902 | 1.6606 | 1.9845 | 2.3650 | 2.6269 |
| 99 | 0.6770 | 1.2902 | 1.6604 | 1.9842 | 2.3646 | 2.6264 |
| 100 | 0.6770 | 1.2901 | 1.6602 | 1.9840 | 2.3642 | 2.6259 |
| 110 | 0.6767 | 1.2893 | 1.6588 | 1.9818 | 2.3607 | 2.6213 |
| 120 | 0.6765 | 1.2886 | 1.6577 | 1.9799 | 2.3578 | 2.6174 |
| 130 | 0.6764 | 1.2881 | 1.6567 | 1.9784 | 2.3554 | 2.6142 |
| 140 | 0.6762 | 1.2876 | 1.6558 | 1.9771 | 2.3533 | 2.6114 |
| 150 | 0.6761 | 1.2872 | 1.6551 | 1.9759 | 2.3515 | 2.6090 |
| $\infty$ | 0.6745 | 1.2816 | 1.6449 | 1.9600 | 2.3263 | 2.5758 |

For a particular number of degrees of freedom, entry represents the critical value of *t* corresponding to a specified upper tail area $\alpha$.

## TABLE 5

**F Distribution**

$\alpha = .05$

$F_{(\alpha, df_1, df_2)}$

| DENOMINATOR DF₂ | NUMERATOR DF₁ | | | | | | | | | | | | | | | | | | |
|---|---|---|---|---|---|---|---|---|---|---|---|---|---|---|---|---|---|---|---|
| | 1 | 2 | 3 | 4 | 5 | 6 | 7 | 8 | 9 | 10 | 12 | 15 | 20 | 24 | 30 | 40 | 60 | 120 | ∞ |
| 1 | 161.4 | 199.5 | 215.7 | 224.6 | 230.2 | 234.0 | 236.8 | 238.9 | 240.5 | 241.9 | 243.9 | 245.9 | 248.0 | 249.1 | 250.1 | 251.1 | 252.2 | 253.3 | 254.3 |
| 2 | 18.51 | 19.00 | 19.16 | 19.25 | 19.30 | 19.33 | 19.35 | 19.37 | 19.38 | 19.40 | 19.41 | 19.43 | 19.45 | 19.45 | 19.46 | 19.47 | 19.48 | 19.49 | 19.50 |
| 3 | 10.13 | 9.55 | 9.28 | 9.12 | 9.01 | 8.94 | 8.89 | 8.85 | 8.81 | 8.79 | 8.74 | 8.70 | 8.66 | 8.64 | 8.62 | 8.59 | 8.57 | 8.55 | 8.53 |
| 4 | 7.71 | 6.94 | 6.59 | 6.39 | 6.26 | 6.16 | 6.09 | 6.04 | 6.00 | 5.96 | 5.91 | 5.86 | 5.80 | 5.77 | 5.75 | 5.72 | 5.69 | 5.66 | 5.63 |
| 5 | 6.61 | 5.79 | 5.41 | 5.19 | 5.05 | 4.95 | 4.88 | 4.82 | 4.77 | 4.74 | 4.68 | 4.62 | 4.56 | 4.53 | 4.50 | 4.46 | 4.43 | 4.40 | 4.36 |
| 6 | 5.99 | 5.14 | 4.76 | 4.53 | 4.39 | 4.28 | 4.21 | 4.15 | 4.10 | 4.06 | 4.00 | 3.94 | 3.87 | 3.84 | 3.81 | 3.77 | 3.74 | 3.70 | 3.67 |
| 7 | 5.59 | 4.74 | 4.35 | 4.12 | 3.97 | 3.87 | 3.79 | 3.73 | 3.68 | 3.64 | 3.57 | 3.51 | 3.44 | 3.41 | 3.38 | 3.34 | 3.30 | 3.27 | 3.23 |
| 8 | 5.32 | 4.46 | 4.07 | 3.84 | 3.69 | 3.58 | 3.50 | 3.44 | 3.39 | 3.35 | 3.28 | 3.22 | 3.15 | 3.12 | 3.08 | 3.04 | 3.01 | 2.97 | 2.93 |
| 9 | 5.12 | 4.26 | 3.86 | 3.63 | 3.48 | 3.37 | 3.29 | 3.23 | 3.18 | 3.14 | 3.07 | 3.01 | 2.94 | 2.90 | 2.86 | 2.83 | 2.79 | 2.75 | 2.71 |
| 10 | 4.96 | 4.10 | 3.71 | 3.48 | 3.33 | 3.22 | 3.14 | 3.07 | 3.02 | 2.98 | 2.91 | 2.85 | 2.77 | 2.74 | 2.70 | 2.66 | 2.62 | 2.58 | 2.54 |
| 11 | 4.84 | 3.98 | 3.59 | 3.36 | 3.20 | 3.09 | 3.01 | 2.95 | 2.90 | 2.85 | 2.79 | 2.72 | 2.65 | 2.61 | 2.57 | 2.53 | 2.49 | 2.45 | 2.40 |
| 12 | 4.75 | 3.89 | 3.49 | 3.26 | 3.11 | 3.00 | 2.91 | 2.85 | 2.80 | 2.75 | 2.69 | 2.62 | 2.54 | 2.51 | 2.47 | 2.43 | 2.38 | 2.34 | 2.30 |
| 13 | 4.67 | 3.81 | 3.41 | 3.18 | 3.03 | 2.92 | 2.83 | 2.77 | 2.71 | 2.67 | 2.60 | 2.53 | 2.46 | 2.42 | 2.38 | 2.34 | 2.30 | 2.25 | 2.21 |
| 14 | 4.60 | 3.74 | 3.34 | 3.11 | 2.96 | 2.85 | 2.76 | 2.70 | 2.65 | 2.60 | 2.53 | 2.46 | 2.39 | 2.35 | 2.31 | 2.27 | 2.22 | 2.18 | 2.13 |
| 15 | 4.54 | 3.68 | 3.29 | 3.06 | 2.90 | 2.79 | 2.71 | 2.64 | 2.59 | 2.54 | 2.48 | 2.40 | 2.33 | 2.29 | 2.25 | 2.20 | 2.16 | 2.11 | 2.07 |
| 16 | 4.49 | 3.63 | 3.24 | 3.01 | 2.85 | 2.74 | 2.66 | 2.59 | 2.54 | 2.49 | 2.42 | 2.35 | 2.28 | 2.24 | 2.19 | 2.15 | 2.11 | 2.06 | 2.01 |
| 17 | 4.45 | 3.59 | 3.20 | 2.96 | 2.81 | 2.70 | 2.61 | 2.55 | 2.49 | 2.45 | 2.38 | 2.31 | 2.23 | 2.19 | 2.15 | 2.10 | 2.06 | 2.01 | 1.96 |
| 18 | 4.41 | 3.55 | 3.16 | 2.93 | 2.77 | 2.66 | 2.58 | 2.51 | 2.46 | 2.41 | 2.34 | 2.27 | 2.19 | 2.15 | 2.11 | 2.06 | 2.02 | 1.97 | 1.92 |
| 19 | 4.38 | 3.52 | 3.13 | 2.90 | 2.74 | 2.63 | 2.54 | 2.48 | 2.42 | 2.38 | 2.31 | 2.23 | 2.16 | 2.11 | 2.07 | 2.03 | 1.98 | 1.93 | 1.88 |
| 20 | 4.35 | 3.49 | 3.10 | 2.87 | 2.71 | 2.60 | 2.51 | 2.45 | 2.39 | 2.35 | 2.28 | 2.20 | 2.12 | 2.08 | 2.04 | 1.99 | 1.95 | 1.90 | 1.84 |
| 21 | 4.32 | 3.47 | 3.07 | 2.84 | 2.68 | 2.57 | 2.49 | 2.42 | 2.37 | 2.32 | 2.25 | 2.18 | 2.10 | 2.05 | 2.01 | 1.96 | 1.92 | 1.87 | 1.81 |
| 22 | 4.30 | 3.44 | 3.05 | 2.82 | 2.66 | 2.55 | 2.46 | 2.40 | 2.34 | 2.30 | 2.23 | 2.15 | 2.07 | 2.03 | 1.98 | 1.94 | 1.89 | 1.84 | 1.78 |
| 23 | 4.28 | 3.42 | 3.03 | 2.80 | 2.64 | 2.53 | 2.44 | 2.37 | 2.32 | 2.27 | 2.20 | 2.13 | 2.05 | 2.01 | 1.96 | 1.91 | 1.86 | 1.81 | 1.76 |
| 24 | 4.26 | 3.40 | 3.01 | 2.78 | 2.62 | 2.51 | 2.42 | 2.36 | 2.30 | 2.25 | 2.18 | 2.11 | 2.03 | 1.98 | 1.94 | 1.89 | 1.84 | 1.79 | 1.73 |
| 25 | 4.24 | 3.39 | 2.99 | 2.76 | 2.60 | 2.49 | 2.40 | 2.34 | 2.28 | 2.24 | 2.16 | 2.09 | 2.01 | 1.96 | 1.92 | 1.87 | 1.82 | 1.77 | 1.71 |
| 26 | 4.23 | 3.37 | 2.98 | 2.74 | 2.59 | 2.47 | 2.39 | 2.32 | 2.27 | 2.22 | 2.15 | 2.07 | 1.99 | 1.95 | 1.90 | 1.85 | 1.80 | 1.75 | 1.69 |
| 27 | 4.21 | 3.35 | 2.96 | 2.73 | 2.57 | 2.46 | 2.37 | 2.31 | 2.25 | 2.20 | 2.13 | 2.06 | 1.97 | 1.93 | 1.88 | 1.84 | 1.79 | 1.73 | 1.67 |
| 28 | 4.20 | 3.34 | 2.95 | 2.71 | 2.56 | 2.45 | 2.36 | 2.29 | 2.24 | 2.19 | 2.12 | 2.04 | 1.96 | 1.91 | 1.87 | 1.82 | 1.77 | 1.71 | 1.65 |
| 29 | 4.18 | 3.33 | 2.93 | 2.70 | 2.55 | 2.43 | 2.35 | 2.28 | 2.22 | 2.18 | 2.10 | 2.03 | 1.94 | 1.90 | 1.85 | 1.81 | 1.75 | 1.70 | 1.64 |
| 30 | 4.17 | 3.32 | 2.92 | 2.69 | 2.53 | 2.42 | 2.33 | 2.27 | 2.21 | 2.16 | 2.09 | 2.01 | 1.93 | 1.89 | 1.84 | 1.79 | 1.74 | 1.68 | 1.62 |
| 40 | 4.08 | 3.23 | 2.84 | 2.61 | 2.45 | 2.34 | 2.25 | 2.18 | 2.12 | 2.08 | 2.00 | 1.92 | 1.84 | 1.79 | 1.74 | 1.69 | 1.64 | 1.58 | 1.51 |
| 60 | 4.00 | 3.15 | 2.76 | 2.53 | 2.37 | 2.25 | 2.17 | 2.10 | 2.04 | 1.99 | 1.92 | 1.84 | 1.75 | 1.70 | 1.65 | 1.59 | 1.53 | 1.47 | 1.39 |
| 120 | 3.92 | 3.07 | 2.68 | 2.45 | 2.29 | 2.17 | 2.09 | 2.02 | 1.96 | 1.91 | 1.83 | 1.75 | 1.66 | 1.61 | 1.55 | 1.50 | 1.43 | 1.35 | 1.25 |
| ∞ | 3.84 | 3.00 | 2.60 | 2.37 | 2.21 | 2.10 | 2.01 | 1.94 | 1.88 | 1.83 | 1.75 | 1.67 | 1.57 | 1.52 | 1.46 | 1.39 | 1.32 | 1.22 | 1.00 |

(Continued)

# TABLE 5—continued

## F Distribution

$\alpha = .025$

$F_{(\alpha, df_1, df_2)}$

| DENOMINATOR DF$_2$ | NUMERATOR DF$_1$ | | | | | | | | | | | | | | | | | | |
|---|---|---|---|---|---|---|---|---|---|---|---|---|---|---|---|---|---|---|
| | 1 | 2 | 3 | 4 | 5 | 6 | 7 | 8 | 9 | 10 | 12 | 15 | 20 | 24 | 30 | 40 | 60 | 120 | ∞ |
| 1 | 647.8 | 799.5 | 864.2 | 899.6 | 921.8 | 937.1 | 948.2 | 956.7 | 963.3 | 968.6 | 976.7 | 984.9 | 993.1 | 997.2 | 1001 | 1006 | 1010 | 1014 | 1018 |
| 2 | 38.51 | 39.00 | 39.17 | 39.25 | 39.30 | 39.33 | 39.36 | 39.37 | 39.39 | 39.40 | 39.41 | 39.43 | 39.45 | 39.46 | 39.46 | 39.47 | 39.48 | 39.49 | 39.50 |
| 3 | 17.44 | 16.04 | 15.44 | 15.10 | 14.88 | 14.73 | 14.62 | 14.54 | 14.47 | 14.42 | 14.34 | 14.25 | 14.17 | 14.12 | 14.08 | 14.04 | 13.99 | 13.95 | 13.90 |
| 4 | 12.22 | 10.65 | 9.98 | 9.60 | 9.36 | 9.20 | 9.07 | 8.98 | 8.90 | 8.84 | 8.75 | 8.66 | 8.56 | 8.51 | 8.46 | 8.41 | 8.36 | 8.31 | 8.26 |
| 5 | 10.01 | 8.43 | 7.76 | 7.39 | 7.15 | 6.98 | 6.85 | 6.76 | 6.68 | 6.62 | 6.52 | 6.43 | 6.33 | 6.28 | 6.23 | 6.18 | 6.12 | 6.07 | 6.02 |
| 6 | 8.81 | 7.26 | 6.60 | 6.23 | 5.99 | 5.82 | 5.70 | 5.60 | 5.52 | 5.46 | 5.37 | 5.27 | 5.17 | 5.12 | 5.07 | 5.01 | 4.96 | 4.90 | 4.85 |
| 7 | 8.07 | 6.54 | 5.89 | 5.52 | 5.29 | 5.12 | 4.99 | 4.90 | 4.82 | 4.76 | 4.67 | 4.57 | 4.47 | 4.42 | 4.36 | 4.31 | 4.25 | 4.20 | 4.14 |
| 8 | 7.57 | 6.06 | 5.42 | 5.05 | 4.82 | 4.65 | 4.53 | 4.43 | 4.36 | 4.30 | 4.20 | 4.10 | 4.00 | 3.95 | 3.89 | 3.84 | 3.78 | 3.73 | 3.67 |
| 9 | 7.21 | 5.71 | 5.08 | 4.72 | 4.48 | 4.32 | 4.20 | 4.10 | 4.03 | 3.96 | 3.87 | 3.77 | 3.67 | 3.61 | 3.56 | 3.51 | 3.45 | 3.39 | 3.33 |
| 10 | 6.94 | 5.46 | 4.83 | 4.47 | 4.24 | 4.07 | 3.95 | 3.85 | 3.78 | 3.72 | 3.62 | 3.52 | 3.42 | 3.37 | 3.31 | 3.26 | 3.20 | 3.14 | 3.08 |
| 11 | 6.72 | 5.26 | 4.63 | 4.28 | 4.04 | 3.88 | 3.76 | 3.66 | 3.59 | 3.53 | 3.43 | 3.33 | 3.23 | 3.17 | 3.12 | 3.06 | 3.00 | 2.94 | 2.88 |
| 12 | 6.55 | 5.10 | 4.47 | 4.12 | 3.89 | 3.73 | 3.61 | 3.51 | 3.44 | 3.37 | 3.28 | 3.18 | 3.07 | 3.02 | 2.96 | 2.91 | 2.85 | 2.79 | 2.72 |
| 13 | 6.41 | 4.97 | 4.35 | 4.00 | 3.77 | 3.60 | 3.48 | 3.39 | 3.31 | 3.25 | 3.15 | 3.05 | 2.95 | 2.89 | 2.84 | 2.78 | 2.72 | 2.66 | 2.60 |
| 14 | 6.30 | 4.86 | 4.24 | 3.89 | 3.66 | 3.50 | 3.38 | 3.29 | 3.21 | 3.15 | 3.05 | 2.95 | 2.84 | 2.79 | 2.73 | 2.67 | 2.61 | 2.55 | 2.49 |
| 15 | 6.20 | 4.77 | 4.15 | 3.80 | 3.58 | 3.41 | 3.29 | 3.20 | 3.12 | 3.06 | 2.96 | 2.86 | 2.76 | 2.70 | 2.64 | 2.59 | 2.52 | 2.46 | 2.40 |
| 16 | 6.12 | 4.69 | 4.08 | 3.73 | 3.50 | 3.34 | 3.22 | 3.12 | 3.05 | 2.99 | 2.89 | 2.79 | 2.68 | 2.63 | 2.57 | 2.51 | 2.45 | 2.38 | 2.32 |
| 17 | 6.04 | 4.62 | 4.01 | 3.66 | 3.44 | 3.28 | 3.16 | 3.06 | 2.98 | 2.92 | 2.82 | 2.72 | 2.62 | 2.56 | 2.50 | 2.44 | 2.38 | 2.32 | 2.25 |
| 18 | 5.98 | 4.56 | 3.95 | 3.61 | 3.38 | 3.22 | 3.10 | 3.01 | 2.93 | 2.87 | 2.77 | 2.67 | 2.56 | 2.50 | 2.44 | 2.38 | 2.32 | 2.26 | 2.19 |
| 19 | 5.92 | 4.51 | 3.90 | 3.56 | 3.33 | 3.17 | 3.05 | 2.96 | 2.88 | 2.82 | 2.72 | 2.62 | 2.51 | 2.45 | 2.39 | 2.33 | 2.27 | 2.20 | 2.13 |
| 20 | 5.87 | 4.46 | 3.86 | 3.51 | 3.29 | 3.13 | 3.01 | 2.91 | 2.84 | 2.77 | 2.68 | 2.57 | 2.46 | 2.41 | 2.35 | 2.29 | 2.22 | 2.16 | 2.09 |
| 21 | 5.83 | 4.42 | 3.82 | 3.48 | 3.25 | 3.09 | 2.97 | 2.87 | 2.80 | 2.73 | 2.64 | 2.53 | 2.42 | 2.37 | 2.31 | 2.25 | 2.18 | 2.11 | 2.04 |
| 22 | 5.79 | 4.38 | 3.78 | 3.44 | 3.22 | 3.05 | 2.93 | 2.84 | 2.76 | 2.70 | 2.60 | 2.50 | 2.39 | 2.33 | 2.27 | 2.21 | 2.14 | 2.08 | 2.00 |
| 23 | 5.75 | 4.35 | 3.75 | 3.41 | 3.18 | 3.02 | 2.90 | 2.81 | 2.73 | 2.67 | 2.57 | 2.47 | 2.36 | 2.30 | 2.24 | 2.18 | 2.11 | 2.04 | 1.97 |
| 24 | 5.72 | 4.32 | 3.72 | 3.38 | 3.15 | 2.99 | 2.87 | 2.78 | 2.70 | 2.64 | 2.54 | 2.44 | 2.33 | 2.27 | 2.21 | 2.15 | 2.08 | 2.01 | 1.94 |
| 25 | 5.69 | 4.29 | 3.69 | 3.35 | 3.13 | 2.97 | 2.85 | 2.75 | 2.68 | 2.61 | 2.51 | 2.41 | 2.30 | 2.24 | 2.18 | 2.12 | 2.05 | 1.98 | 1.91 |
| 26 | 5.66 | 4.27 | 3.67 | 3.33 | 3.10 | 2.94 | 2.82 | 2.73 | 2.65 | 2.59 | 2.49 | 2.39 | 2.28 | 2.22 | 2.16 | 2.09 | 2.03 | 1.95 | 1.88 |
| 27 | 5.63 | 4.24 | 3.65 | 3.31 | 3.08 | 2.92 | 2.80 | 2.71 | 2.63 | 2.57 | 2.47 | 2.36 | 2.25 | 2.19 | 2.13 | 2.07 | 2.00 | 1.93 | 1.85 |
| 28 | 5.61 | 4.22 | 3.63 | 3.29 | 3.06 | 2.90 | 2.78 | 2.69 | 2.61 | 2.55 | 2.45 | 2.34 | 2.23 | 2.17 | 2.11 | 2.05 | 1.98 | 1.91 | 1.83 |
| 29 | 5.59 | 4.20 | 3.61 | 3.27 | 3.04 | 2.88 | 2.76 | 2.67 | 2.59 | 2.53 | 2.43 | 2.32 | 2.21 | 2.15 | 2.09 | 2.03 | 1.96 | 1.89 | 1.81 |
| 30 | 5.57 | 4.18 | 3.59 | 3.25 | 3.03 | 2.87 | 2.75 | 2.65 | 2.57 | 2.51 | 2.41 | 2.31 | 2.20 | 2.14 | 2.07 | 2.01 | 1.94 | 1.87 | 1.79 |
| 40 | 5.42 | 4.05 | 3.46 | 3.13 | 2.90 | 2.74 | 2.62 | 2.53 | 2.45 | 2.39 | 2.29 | 2.18 | 2.07 | 2.01 | 1.94 | 1.88 | 1.80 | 1.72 | 1.64 |
| 60 | 5.29 | 3.93 | 3.34 | 3.01 | 2.79 | 2.63 | 2.51 | 2.41 | 2.33 | 2.27 | 2.17 | 2.06 | 1.94 | 1.88 | 1.82 | 1.74 | 1.67 | 1.58 | 1.48 |
| 120 | 5.15 | 3.80 | 3.23 | 2.89 | 2.67 | 2.52 | 2.39 | 2.30 | 2.22 | 2.16 | 2.05 | 1.94 | 1.82 | 1.76 | 1.69 | 1.61 | 1.53 | 1.43 | 1.31 |
| ∞ | 5.02 | 3.69 | 3.12 | 2.79 | 2.57 | 2.41 | 2.29 | 2.19 | 2.11 | 2.05 | 1.94 | 1.83 | 1.71 | 1.64 | 1.57 | 1.48 | 1.39 | 1.27 | 1.00 |

(*Continued*)

## TABLE 5—continued

### F Distribution

For a particular combination of numerator and denominator degrees of freedom, entry represents the critical values of F corresponding to a specified upper tail area α.

**DENOMINATOR**

**NUMERATOR DF₁**

| DF₂ | 1 | 2 | 3 | 4 | 5 | 6 | 7 | 8 | 9 | 10 | 12 | 15 | 20 | 24 | 30 | 40 | 60 | 120 | ∞ |
|---|---|---|---|---|---|---|---|---|---|---|---|---|---|---|---|---|---|---|---|
| 1 | 4052 | 4999.5 | 5403 | 5625 | 5764 | 5859 | 5928 | 5982 | 6022 | 6056 | 6106 | 6157 | 6209 | 6235 | 6261 | 6287 | 6313 | 6339 | 6366 |
| 2 | 98.50 | 99.00 | 99.17 | 99.25 | 99.30 | 99.33 | 99.36 | 99.37 | 99.39 | 99.40 | 99.42 | 99.43 | 99.45 | 99.46 | 99.47 | 99.47 | 99.48 | 99.49 | 99.50 |
| 3 | 34.12 | 30.82 | 29.46 | 28.71 | 28.24 | 27.91 | 27.67 | 27.49 | 27.35 | 27.23 | 27.05 | 26.87 | 26.69 | 26.60 | 26.50 | 26.41 | 26.32 | 26.22 | 26.13 |
| 4 | 21.20 | 18.00 | 16.69 | 15.98 | 15.52 | 15.21 | 14.98 | 14.80 | 14.66 | 14.55 | 14.37 | 14.20 | 14.02 | 13.93 | 13.84 | 13.75 | 13.65 | 13.56 | 13.46 |
| 5 | 16.26 | 13.27 | 12.06 | 11.39 | 10.97 | 10.67 | 10.46 | 10.29 | 10.16 | 10.05 | 9.89 | 9.72 | 9.55 | 9.47 | 9.38 | 9.29 | 9.20 | 9.11 | 9.02 |
| 6 | 13.75 | 10.92 | 9.78 | 9.15 | 8.75 | 8.47 | 8.26 | 8.10 | 7.98 | 7.87 | 7.72 | 7.56 | 7.40 | 7.31 | 7.23 | 7.14 | 7.06 | 6.97 | 6.88 |
| 7 | 12.25 | 9.55 | 8.45 | 7.85 | 7.46 | 7.19 | 6.99 | 6.84 | 6.72 | 6.62 | 6.47 | 6.31 | 6.16 | 6.07 | 5.99 | 5.91 | 5.82 | 5.74 | 5.65 |
| 8 | 11.26 | 8.65 | 7.59 | 7.01 | 6.63 | 6.37 | 6.18 | 6.03 | 5.91 | 5.81 | 5.67 | 5.52 | 5.36 | 5.28 | 5.20 | 5.12 | 5.03 | 4.95 | 4.86 |
| 9 | 10.56 | 8.02 | 6.99 | 6.42 | 6.06 | 5.80 | 5.61 | 5.47 | 5.35 | 5.26 | 5.11 | 4.96 | 4.81 | 4.73 | 4.65 | 4.57 | 4.48 | 4.40 | 4.31 |
| 10 | 10.04 | 7.56 | 6.55 | 5.99 | 5.64 | 5.39 | 5.20 | 5.06 | 4.94 | 4.85 | 4.71 | 4.56 | 4.41 | 4.33 | 4.25 | 4.17 | 4.08 | 4.00 | 3.91 |
| 11 | 9.65 | 7.21 | 6.22 | 5.67 | 5.32 | 5.07 | 4.89 | 4.74 | 4.63 | 4.54 | 4.40 | 4.25 | 4.10 | 4.02 | 3.94 | 3.86 | 3.78 | 3.69 | 3.60 |
| 12 | 9.33 | 6.93 | 5.95 | 5.41 | 5.06 | 4.82 | 4.64 | 4.50 | 4.39 | 4.30 | 4.16 | 4.01 | 3.86 | 3.78 | 3.70 | 3.62 | 3.54 | 3.45 | 3.36 |
| 13 | 9.07 | 6.70 | 5.74 | 5.21 | 4.86 | 4.62 | 4.44 | 4.30 | 4.19 | 4.10 | 3.96 | 3.82 | 3.66 | 3.59 | 3.51 | 3.43 | 3.34 | 3.25 | 3.17 |
| 14 | 8.86 | 6.51 | 5.56 | 5.04 | 4.69 | 4.46 | 4.28 | 4.14 | 4.03 | 3.94 | 3.80 | 3.66 | 3.51 | 3.43 | 3.35 | 3.27 | 3.18 | 3.09 | 3.00 |
| 15 | 8.68 | 6.36 | 5.42 | 4.89 | 4.56 | 4.32 | 4.14 | 4.00 | 3.89 | 3.80 | 3.67 | 3.52 | 3.37 | 3.29 | 3.21 | 3.13 | 3.05 | 2.96 | 2.87 |
| 16 | 8.53 | 6.23 | 5.29 | 4.77 | 4.44 | 4.20 | 4.03 | 3.89 | 3.78 | 3.69 | 3.55 | 3.41 | 3.26 | 3.18 | 3.10 | 3.02 | 2.93 | 2.84 | 2.75 |
| 17 | 8.40 | 6.11 | 5.18 | 4.67 | 4.34 | 4.10 | 3.93 | 3.79 | 3.68 | 3.59 | 3.46 | 3.31 | 3.16 | 3.08 | 3.00 | 2.92 | 2.83 | 2.75 | 2.65 |
| 18 | 8.29 | 6.01 | 5.09 | 4.58 | 4.25 | 4.01 | 3.84 | 3.71 | 3.60 | 3.51 | 3.37 | 3.23 | 3.08 | 3.00 | 2.92 | 2.84 | 2.75 | 2.66 | 2.57 |
| 19 | 8.18 | 5.93 | 5.01 | 4.50 | 4.17 | 3.94 | 3.77 | 3.63 | 3.52 | 3.43 | 3.30 | 3.15 | 3.00 | 2.92 | 2.84 | 2.76 | 2.67 | 2.58 | 2.49 |
| 20 | 8.10 | 5.85 | 4.94 | 4.43 | 4.10 | 3.87 | 3.70 | 3.56 | 3.46 | 3.37 | 3.23 | 3.09 | 2.94 | 2.86 | 2.78 | 2.69 | 2.61 | 2.52 | 2.42 |
| 21 | 8.02 | 5.78 | 4.87 | 4.37 | 4.04 | 3.81 | 3.64 | 3.51 | 3.40 | 3.31 | 3.17 | 3.03 | 2.88 | 2.80 | 2.72 | 2.64 | 2.55 | 2.46 | 2.36 |
| 22 | 7.95 | 5.72 | 4.82 | 4.31 | 3.99 | 3.76 | 3.59 | 3.45 | 3.35 | 3.26 | 3.12 | 2.98 | 2.83 | 2.75 | 2.67 | 2.58 | 2.50 | 2.40 | 2.31 |
| 23 | 7.88 | 5.66 | 4.76 | 4.26 | 3.94 | 3.71 | 3.54 | 3.41 | 3.30 | 3.21 | 3.07 | 2.93 | 2.78 | 2.70 | 2.62 | 2.54 | 2.45 | 2.35 | 2.26 |
| 24 | 7.82 | 5.61 | 4.72 | 4.22 | 3.90 | 3.67 | 3.50 | 3.36 | 3.26 | 3.17 | 3.03 | 2.89 | 2.74 | 2.66 | 2.58 | 2.49 | 2.40 | 2.31 | 2.21 |
| 25 | 7.77 | 5.57 | 4.68 | 4.18 | 3.85 | 3.63 | 3.46 | 3.32 | 3.22 | 3.13 | 2.99 | 2.85 | 2.70 | 2.62 | 2.54 | 2.45 | 2.36 | 2.27 | 2.17 |
| 26 | 7.72 | 5.53 | 4.64 | 4.14 | 3.82 | 3.59 | 3.42 | 3.29 | 3.18 | 3.09 | 2.96 | 2.81 | 2.66 | 2.58 | 2.50 | 2.42 | 2.33 | 2.23 | 2.13 |
| 27 | 7.68 | 5.49 | 4.60 | 4.11 | 3.78 | 3.56 | 3.39 | 3.26 | 3.15 | 3.06 | 2.93 | 2.78 | 2.63 | 2.55 | 2.47 | 2.38 | 2.29 | 2.20 | 2.10 |
| 28 | 7.64 | 5.45 | 4.57 | 4.07 | 3.75 | 3.53 | 3.36 | 3.23 | 3.12 | 3.03 | 2.90 | 2.75 | 2.60 | 2.52 | 2.44 | 2.35 | 2.26 | 2.17 | 2.06 |
| 29 | 7.60 | 5.42 | 4.54 | 4.04 | 3.73 | 3.50 | 3.33 | 3.20 | 3.09 | 3.00 | 2.87 | 2.73 | 2.57 | 2.49 | 2.41 | 2.33 | 2.23 | 2.14 | 2.03 |
| 30 | 7.56 | 5.39 | 4.51 | 4.02 | 3.70 | 3.47 | 3.30 | 3.17 | 3.07 | 2.98 | 2.84 | 2.70 | 2.55 | 2.47 | 2.39 | 2.30 | 2.21 | 2.11 | 2.01 |
| 40 | 7.31 | 5.18 | 4.31 | 3.83 | 3.51 | 3.29 | 3.12 | 2.99 | 2.89 | 2.80 | 2.66 | 2.52 | 2.37 | 2.29 | 2.20 | 2.11 | 2.02 | 1.92 | 1.80 |
| 60 | 7.08 | 4.98 | 4.13 | 3.65 | 3.34 | 3.12 | 2.95 | 2.82 | 2.72 | 2.63 | 2.50 | 2.35 | 2.20 | 2.12 | 2.03 | 1.94 | 1.84 | 1.73 | 1.60 |
| 120 | 6.85 | 4.79 | 3.95 | 3.48 | 3.17 | 2.96 | 2.79 | 2.66 | 2.56 | 2.47 | 2.34 | 2.19 | 2.03 | 1.95 | 1.86 | 1.76 | 1.66 | 1.53 | 1.38 |
| ∞ | 6.63 | 4.61 | 3.78 | 3.32 | 3.02 | 2.80 | 2.64 | 2.51 | 2.41 | 2.32 | 2.18 | 2.04 | 1.88 | 1.79 | 1.70 | 1.59 | 1.47 | 1.32 | 1.00 |

# Notes

## Chapter 1

1. Anonymous, "IBM Unveils Linux-Driven Mainframe," (January 25, 2002); and Joseph Rydholm, "A Global Enterprise," *Quirk's Marketing Research Review* (November 1997).

2. Joe Flint, "How NBC Defies Network Norms—To Its Advantage," *Wall Street Journal* (May 20, 2002): A1, A10; Michael Freeman, "NBC: No Laughing Matter," *Electronic Media,* 21 (1) (January 7, 2002); and Jack Neff, "Marketers Use Recipio to Tap Users' View," *Advertising Age,* 72 (7) (February 12, 2001): 24.

3. Barbara Benson, "Market Researcher Wins Clients with Documentaries," *Crain's New York Business,* 17 (17) (April 23, 2001): 31.

4. Jack Neff, "P&G Targets Teen Via Tremor, Toejam Sites," *Advertising Age,* 72 (10) (March 5, 2001): 12; and *www.pg.com.*

5. For the strategic role of marketing research, see Denise Jarratt and Ramzi Fayed, "The Impact of Market and Organizational Challenges On Marketing Strategy Decision Making," *Journal of Business Research,* 51 (01) (January 2001): 61–72; and Lexis F. Higgins, "Applying Principles of Creativity Management to Marketing Research Efforts in High-Technology Markets," *Industrial Marketing Management,* 28 (3) (May 1999): 305–317.

6. The AMA definition is reported in "New Marketing Research Definition Approved," *Marketing News,* 21 (January 2, 1987). See also Michelle Wirth Fellman, "An Aging Profession," *Marketing Research,* Chicago (Spring 2000): 33–35; and Lawrence D Gibson, "Quo Vadis, Marketing Research?" *Marketing Research,* Chicago (Spring 2000): 36–41.

7. For a historical discussion and an assessment of marketing research, see Stephen Brown, "Always historicize! Researching Marketing History in a Post Historical Epoch," *Marketing Theory,* 1 (1) (September 2001): 49–89; L. McTier Anderson, "Marketing Science: Where's the Beef?" *Business Horizons,* 37 (January/February 1994): 8–16; Alvin J. Silk, "Marketing Science in a Changing Environment," *Journal of Marketing Research,* 30 (November 1993): 401–404; and Frank M. Bass, "The Future of Research in Marketing: Marketing Science," *Journal of Marketing Research,* 30 (February 1993): 1–6.

8. Gordon A Wyner, "Learn and Earn Through Testing on the Internet," *Marketing Research* (Fall 2000): 3; and Jerry W. Thomas, "How, When, and Why to do Market Research," *Nation's Restaurant News,* 31 (19) (May 12, 1997): 84, 136.

9. Peter H. Gray, "A Problem-Solving Perspective on Knowledge Management Practices," *Decision Support Systems,* Amsterdam; (May 2001): 87; and Barry de Ville, "Intelligent Tools for Marketing Research: Case-Based Reasoning," *Marketing Research: A Magazine of Management & Applications,* 9 (2) (Summer 1997): 38–40.

10. Anonymous, "Kellogg's Brings Olympic Spirit to America's Breakfast Table," *PRNewswire* (December 6, 2001); Anonymous, "Kellogg's Crunchy Nut Gets Ready for Adult Breakfast," *Grocer,* 224 (7524) (October 6, 2001): 53; and *www.kelloggs.com.*

11. Rayna Katz, "Marriott Establishing a Substantial Presence Across the State," *Meeting News,* 26 (5) (April 8, 2002): 19; and Sanjit Sengupta, Robert E. Krapfel and Michael A. Pusateri, "The Marriott Experience," *Marketing Management,* 6 (2) (Summer 1997): 33.

12. For relationship among information processing, marketing decisions, and performance, see William D. Neal, "Advances in Marketing Segmentation," *Marketing Research,* Chicago, (Spring 2001): 14–18.

13. "Motrin," *Advertising Age,* 72 (11) (March 12, 2001): 44; and "J.J. Unit Purchases St. Joseph's Aspirin of Schering-Plough," *Wall Street Journal,* 236 (120) (December 20, 2000): 20.

14. For the role of marketing research in marketing management, see Naresh K. Malhotra, "The Past, Present, and Future of the Marketing Discipline," *Journal of the Academy of Marketing Science,* 27 (Spring 1999): 116–119; Naresh K. Malhotra, Mark Peterson, and Susan Kleiser, "Marketing Research: A State-of-the-Art Review and Directions for the Twenty-First Century," *Journal of the Academy of Marketing Science,* 27 (Spring 1999): 160–183; and Siva K. Balasubramanian, "The New Marketing Research Systems—How to Use Strategic Database Information for Better Marketing," *Journal of the Academy of Marketing Science,* 24 (2) (Spring 1996): 179–181.

15. Naresh K. Malhotra and Mark Peterson, "Marketing Research in the New Millennium: Emerging Issues and Trends," *Market Intelligence and Planning,* 2001, 19 (4) (2001): 216–235; David Smith and Andy Dexter, "Whenever I Hear the Word 'Paradigm' I Reach for my Gun: How to Stop Talking and Start Walking: Professional Development Strategy and Tactics for the 21st Century Market Researcher," *International Journal of Market Research,* 43 (3) (Third Quarter 2001): 321–340; and Naresh K. Malhotra, "Shifting Perspective on the Shifting Paradigm in Marketing Research," *Journal of the Academy of Marketing Science,* 20 (Fall 1992): 379–387.

16. Alex Taylor, "Can the Germans Rescue Chrysler?" *Fortune,* 143 (09) (April 30, 2001): 106; and Jean Halliday, "Chrysler Group Restructures," *Advertising Age,* 72 (13) (March 26, 2001): 41.

17. Stephanie Thompson, "Oscar Mayer Hams It Up for New Lunch Meat Line," *Advertising Age,* 71 (32) (July 31, 2000): 14; and Charlie Etmekjian and John Grede, "Marketing Research in a Team-Oriented Business: The Oscar Mayer Approach," *Marketing Research: A Magazine of Management & Applications* (December 1990): 6–12.

18. A complete listing and description of the individual firms in the marketing research industry is provided in *The GreenBook International Directory of Marketing Research Companies and Services* (New York Chapter, American Marketing Association, annually). See the Web site *www.greenbook.org.*

19. Jack Honomichl, "Honomichl Top 50: Annual Business Report on the Marketing Research Industry," *Marketing News* (June 10, 2002): H1–H43.

20. For a historical note and future directions in syndicated services, see Mike Penford, "Continuous Research—Art Nielsen to AD 2000," *Journal of the Market Research Society,* 36 (January 1994): 19–28; and the ACNielsen website (*www.acnielsen.com*).

21. Joe Nicholson, "Baxter Ads Fuel New Recruitment Trend," *Editor and Publisher,* New York (September 25, 2000): 36;

Robert Gray, "High Gloss Boost to Customer Titles," *Marketing,* London (October 12, 2000): 25–26; and Thomas C. Kinnear and Ann R. Root, *1988 Survey of Marketing Research,* Chicago: American Marketing Association.

22. Sarah Nonis and Gail Hudson, "The Second Course in Business Statistics and Its Role in Undergraduate Marketing Education," *Journal of Marketing Education,* 21 (December 1999): 232–241; and Ralph W. Giacobbe and Madhav N. Segal, "Rethinking Marketing Research Education: A Conceptual, Analytical, and Empirical Investigation," *Journal of Marketing Education,* 16 (Spring 1994): 43–58.

23. Richard Burnett, "BP Plans to Build Up-Scale Convenience Stores in Orlando, Fla., Area," *Knight Ridder Tribune Business News* (January 19, 2002): 1, "AMR Interviews Abdul Azhari, On Today and the Future of Marketing Research at a Major Corporation," *Applied Marketing Research* (Spring 1989): 3–8; and *www.bpamoco.com.*

24. O. I. Larichev, A. V. Kortnev, and D. Yu Kochin, "Decision Support System for Classification of a Finite Set of Multicriteria Alternatives," *Decision Support Systems,* 33 (1) (May 2002): 13–21.

25. Sanjay K. Rao, "A Marketing Decision Support System for Pricing New Pharmaceutical Products," *Marketing Research,* Chicago (Winter 2000): 22–29.

26. R. Jeffery Thieme, "Artificial Neural Network Decision Support Systems for New Product Development Project Selection," *Journal of Marketing Research* (November 2000): 499–507.

27. Anonymous, "FedEx Ground Receives Wireless Industry Award for New System That Captures Digital Signatures At Package Delivery," *Businesswire* (December 10, 2001); Aisha Williams, "FedEx Delivers Information Right To Customers' Hands," *Information Week* (March 19, 2001): 33; and *www.fedex.com.*

28. Allyson Stewart, "Do Your International Homework First," *Marketing News,* 33 (01) (January 4, 1999): 25.

29. Vanessa O'Connell, "Unilever To Run Some TV Spots, Digitized, Online," *Wall Street Journal,* 237 (43) (March 2, 2001): 1; and David Kilburn, "Thai Recipe for Haircare Growth," *Marketing Week,* 20 (2) (April 10, 1997).

30. Naresh K. Malhotra and Gina Miller, "Social Responsibility and the Marketing Educator: A Focus on Stakeholders, Ethical Theories, and Related Codes of Ethics," *Journal of Business Ethics,* 19 (1999): 211–224.

31. Information about the software cited in this book, if not referenced, can be obtained from recent issues of *Marketing News and Marketing Research: A Magazine of Management & Applications,* published by the American Marketing Association, or from a software vendor directory.

# Chapter 2

1. Marilyn Alva, "Hog Maker Gets (Financial) Motor Running," *Investor's Business Daily* (Monday, January 28, 2002): A9; Ian Murphy, "Aided by Research, Harley Goes Whole Hog," *Marketing News* (December 2, 1996): 16–17; and *www.harleydavidson.com.*

2. Jagdish N. Sheth and Rajendra S. Sisodia, "Marketing Productivity: Issues and Analysis," *Journal of Business Research,* 55 (5) (May 2002): 349; and Patrick Butler, "Marketing Problem: From Analysis to Decision," *Marketing Intelligence & Planning,* 12 (2) (1994): 4–12.

3. Molly Inhofe Rapert, "The Strategic Implementation Process: Evoking Strategic Consensus Through Communication,"

*Journal of Business Research,* 55 (4) (April 2002): 301; and David Smith and Andy Dexter, "Quality in Marketing Research: Hard Frameworks for Soft Problems," *Journal of the Market Research Society,* 36 (2) (April 1994): 115–132.

4. Greg W. Marshall, "Selection Decision Making by Sales Managers and Human Resource Managers: Decision Impact, Decision Frame and Time of Valuation," *The Journal of Personal Selling and Sales Management* (Winter 2001): 19–28; and Berend Wierenga and Gerrit H. van Bruggen, "The Integration of Marketing Problem Solving Modes and Marketing Management Support Systems," *Journal of Marketing,* 61 (3) (July 1997): 21–37.

5. Anonymous, "How to Decide Who Should Get What Data," *HR Focus* (May 2001): 7; and Mary J. Cronin, "Using the Web to Push Key Data to Decision Makers," *Fortune,* 36 (6) (September 29, 1997): 254.

6. Neil A. Morgan, "Marketing Productivity, Marketing Audits, and Systems for Marketing Performance Assessment: Integrating Multiple Perspectives," *Journal of Business Research,* 55 (5) (May 2002): 363; Merrilyn Astin Tarlton, "Quick Marketing Audit," *Law Practice Management,* 23 (6) (September 1997): 18, 63; and Leonard L. Berry, Jeffrey S. Conant, and A. Parasuraman, "A Framework for Conducting a Services Marketing Audit," *Journal of the Academy of Marketing Science,* 19 (Summer 1991): 255–268.

7. Ram Charan, "Conquering a Culture of Indecision," *Harvard Business Review* (April 2001): 74; and Saviour L. S. Nwachukwu and Scott J. Vitell, Jr., "The Influence of Corporate Culture on Managerial Ethical Judgments," *Journal of Business Ethics,* 16 (8) (June 1997): 757–776.

8. Tobi Elkin, "Cingular Believes in Self," *Advertising Age,* Midwest region edition, 72 (26) (June 25, 2001): 39; and Joe Zibell, "Velocity Chosen by Cingular to Maximize Sports Sponsorships," *The Business Times,* 23 (8) (August 1, 2001): 9.

9. Keith Malo, "Corporate Strategy Requires Market Research," *Marketing News,* 36 (2) (January 21, 2002): 14; Ruth Winett, "Guerilla Marketing Research Outsmarts the Competition," *Marketing News,* 29 (1) (January 2, 1995): 33; and J. Scott Armstrong, "Prediction of Consumer Behavior by Experts and Novices," *Journal of Consumer Research,* 18 (September 1991): 251–256.

10. Matthew Arnold, "Can New Flavours Help Coke Get Back Its Fizz?" *Marketing* (April 11, 2002): 15; Karen Benezra, "Diet Cherry Coke Apes Full-Cal Sister," *Brandweek* (May 11, 1998); and Hank Kim, "Freeman Sets Goals for Cherry Coke," *Adweek* (August 24, 1998).

11. Arlene Weintraub and Gerry Khermouch, "Chairman of the Board; How Shoemaker Vans Turned Itself into Skateboarders' Fave," *Business Week,* Industrial/Technology Edition (3734) (May 28, 2001): 96; Becky Ebenkamp, "Van's Board Room Battle," *Brandweek,* 41 (12) (March 20, 2000): 17–20.

12. Anonymous, "Movers, Shakers, and Decision Makers 2002," *Financial Planning* (January 1, 2002): 1; and, Mary T. Curren, Valerie S. Folkes, and Joel H. Steckel, "Explanations for Successful and Unsuccessful Marketing Decisions: The Decision Maker's Perspective," *Journal of Marketing,* 56 (April 1992): 18–31.

13. Michael J. Hennel, "Forecasting Demand Begins with Integration," *B to B,* 87 (11) (November 11): 9; and C. L. Jain, "Myths and Realities of Forecasting," *Journal of Business Forecasting,* 9 (Fall 1990): 18–22.

14. Tania Mason, "Pizza Hut Boss Moves to Concepts Role in U.S.," *Marketing* (January 17, 2002): 1; and Johnson, Kemba, "Brown Baggin' It," *American Demographics,* 23 (1) (January 2001): 12.

15. Ray Suutari, "Playing the Decision-Making Game," *CMA Management,* 75 (7), (October 2001): 14–17; Lehman Benson III and Lee Roy Beach, "The Effect of Time Constraints on the Prechoice Screening of Decision Options," *Organizational Behavior & Human Decision Processes,* 67 (2) (August 1996): 222–228; and Ron Sanchez and D. Sudharshan, "Real-Time Market Research," *Marketing Intelligence and Planning,* 11 (1993): 29–38.

16. Based on a marketing research project conducted by the author. See also Darren W. Dahl, "The Influence and Value of Analogical Thinking During New Product Ideation," *Journal of Marketing Research,* 39 (1) (February 2002): 47–60.

17. Jennifer Sabe, "Advertising Agency of the Year 2000," *MC Technology Marketing Intelligence,* 20 (4) (April 2000): 44; Hillary Chura and Stephanie Thompson, "Bozell Moving Beyond Mustaches in Milk Ads," *Advertising Age,* 70 (43) (October 18, 1999): 81; and *www.gotmilk.com/story.html,* 16 January 2001.

18. R. Jeffery Thieme, "Artificial Neural Network Decision Support Systems for the New Product Development Project Selection," *Journal of Marketing Research,* Chicago (Nov 2000): 499–507; and Stephen M. Heyl, "Decision Matrix Points the Way to Better Research ROI," *Marketing News,* 31 (19) (September 15, 1997): 18, 30.

19. *www.tennis.com/external.cfm?articleid= 2141,* January 13, 2002; Tony Lance, Telephone interview (212.636.2731), January 12, 2002; Mark Adams, "Court Marshal," *Mediaweek,* 6 (12) (March 18, 1996): 22.

20. Gary L. Lilien, "Bridging the Marketing Theory," *Journal of Business Research,* 55 (2) (February 2002): 111; and Shelby D. Hunt, "For Reason and Realism in Marketing," *Journal of Marketing,* 56 (April 1992): 89–102.

21. A positivist perspective on research is used here. Positivism encompasses logical positivism, logical empiricism, and all forms of falsificationism. This is the dominant perspective adopted in commercial marketing research. More recently, a relativist perspective has been offered. See, for example, Jillian Dawes and Reva Berman Brown, "Postmodern Marketing: Research Issues for Retail Financial Services," *Qualitative Market Research,* 3 (2) (2000): 90–98; and Shelby D. Hunt, *A General Theory of Competition* (Thousand Oaks, CA: Sage Publishing Co., 2000).

22. Mika Boedeker, "New-Type and Traditional Shoppers: A Comparison of Two Major Consumer Groups," *International Journal of Retail & Distribution Management,* 23 (3) (1995) 17–26; and Naresh K. Malhotra, "A Threshold Model of Store Choice," *Journal of Retailing* (Summer 1983): 3–21.

23. Naresh K. Malhotra and Lan Wu, "Decision Models and Descriptive Models: Complementary Roles," *Marketing Research,* 13 (4) (December 2001): 43–44; and Peter S. H. Leeflang, "Building Models for Marketing Decisions: Past, Present and Future," *International Journal of Research in Marketing* (September 2000): 105.

24. The integrated role of theory, models, research questions, and hypotheses in marketing research can be seen in Arne Nygaard and Robert Dahlstrom, "Role Stress and Effectiveness in Horizontal Alliances," *Journal of Marketing,* 66 (April 2002): 61–82; and Joseph C. Nunes, "A Cognitive Model of People's Usage Estimations," *Journal of Marketing Research,* 37 (4) (November 2000): 397–409.

25. Deepak Sirdeshmukh, "Consumer Trust, Value, and Loyalty in Relational Exchanges," *Journal of Marketing,* 66 (1) (January 2002): 15–37.

26. Brian Wansink and Cynthia Sangerman, "The Taste of Comfort," *American Demographics,* 22 (7) (July 2000): 66–67; and Anonymous, "Comfort Food," *Potentials,* 35 (1) (January 2002): 12.

27. Nancy Dillon, "United Airlines to Rehire Customer Service, Other Staffers," *Knight Ridder Tribune Business News* (March 23, 2002): 1; "Marketing Key for Air Giants," *Advertising Age,* 72 (03) (January 15, 2001): 22; and Karen Schwartz and Ian P. Murphy, "Marketers Improve Menus to Please Passengers," *Marketing News,* 31 (21) (October 13, 1997): 1, 10.

28. Sonia Reyes, "Heinz Builds on EZ Squirt Success with Adult-Skewing Kick'rs Line," *Brandweek,* 43 (3) (January 21, 2002): 4; and "ConAgra, Heinz Rule Mexican Frozens," *Frozen Food Age,* 45 (11) (June 1997): 16.

29. Paul Westhead, "International Market Selection Strategies Selected by 'Micro' and 'Small' Firms," *Omega,* 30 (1) (February 2002): 51; and Susan P. Douglas and C. Samuel Craig, *International Marketing Research* (Englewood Cliffs, NJ: Prentice-Hall, 1983).

30. Sonoo Singh, "Unilever Picks Global Brand Director for Surf," *Marketing Week* (March 7, 2002): 7; and David Kilburn, "Unilever Struggles with Surf in Japan," *Advertising Age,* May 6, 1991.

31. J. Pierre Brans, "Ethics and Decisions," *European Journal of Operational Research,* 136 (2) (January 16, 2002): 340; and G. R. Laczniak and P. E. Murphy, *Ethical Marketing Decisions, the Higher Road* (Boston, MA: Allyn and Bacon, 1993).

# Chapter 3

1. Anonymous, "Environmental Groups Unveil Eco-friendly Coffee Guidelines," *Gourmet News,* 66 (7) (July 2001): 5; and Marianne Wilson. "More Than Just Causes," *Business and Industry,* 76 (August 2000): 37–54.

2. I. M. Halman, "Evaluating Effectiveness of Project Start-ups: An Exploratory Study," *International Journal of Project Management,* 20 (1) (January 2002): 81; and Thomas T. Semon, "Marketing Research Needs Basic Research," *Marketing News,* 28 (6) (March 14, 1996): 12.

3. John W. Creswell, *Research Design: Qualitative, Quantitative, and Mixed Method Approaches,* 2nd ed. (Thousand Oaks, CA: Sage Publications, 2002); Hanjoon Lee, Jay D. Lindquist, and Frank Acito, "Managers' Evaluation of Research Design and Its Impact on the Use of Research: An Experimental Approach," *Journal of Business Research,* 39 (3) (July 1997): 231–240; and R. Dale Wilson, "Research Design: Qualitative and Quantitative Approaches," *Journal of Marketing Research,* 33 (2) (May 1996): 252–255.

4. For examples of exploratory research, see Paul Ellis and Anthony Pecotich, "Social Factors Influencing Export Initiation in Small- and Medium-Sized Enterprises," *Journal of Marketing Research,* 38 (1) (February 2001): 119–130; and Ellen Bolman Pullins, "An Exploratory Investigation of the Relationship of Sales Force Compensation and Intrinsic Motivation," *Industrial Marketing Management,* 30 (5) (July 2001): 403.

5. Eyal Rabinovitch, "360 Degrees: Microsoft Publisher 2002," *Fortune Small Business,* 11 (10) (January 2002): 79; Robert W. Scott, "The Small Biz Wars," *Accounting Technology,* 17 (3) (April 2001): 18–21; Microsoft's Web site: *www. microsoft.com;* and *www.sba.gov/advo/stats/sbfaq.pdf.*

6. For an example of descriptive research, see William T. Robinson, "Is the First to Market the First to Fail?" *Journal of Marketing Research,* 39 (1) (February 2002): 120–128.

7. Jeff Goldsmith, "Integrating Care: A Talk with Kaiser Permanente's David Lawrence," *Health Affairs,* 21 (1)

(January/February 2002): 39–48; and Julie T. Chyna, "Is Your Culture e-Compatible?" *Healthcare Executive*, 17 (1) (January/February 2002): 53.

8. John Creswell, *Research Design: Qualitative, Quantitative, and Mixed Method Approaches*, 2nd ed. (Thousand Oaks, CA: Sage Publications, 2002); Ranjita Misra and B. Panigrahi, "Changes in Attitudes Toward Women: A Cohort Analysis," *International Journal of Sociology & Social Policy*, 15 (6) (1995): 1–20; and Norval D. Glenn, *Cohort Analysis* (Beverly Hills: Sage Publications, 1981).

9. Joseph O. Rentz, Fred D. Reynolds, and Roy G. Stout, "Analyzing Changing Consumption Patterns with Cohort Analysis," *Journal of Marketing Research*, 20 (February 1983): 12–20. See also Joseph O. Rentz and Fred D. Reynolds, "Forecasting the Effects of an Aging Population on Product Consumption: An Age-Period-Cohort Framework," *Journal of Marketing Research* (August 1991): 355–360.

10. David Teel, "Anheuser-Busch Replaces Virginia Men's Golf Tournament with Women's Event," *Knight Ridder Tribune Business News* (March 2, 2002): 1; and Anonymous, "Ways to Use Golf," *Incentive* (January 2001): 2–7.

11. For recent applications of panel data, see Jack K. H. Lee, K. Sudhir, and Joel H. Steckel, "A Multiple Ideal Point Model: Capturing Multiple Preference Effects from within an Ideal Point Framework," *Journal of Marketing Research*, 39 (1) (February 2002): 73–86. For a basic treatment, see Gregory B. Markus, *Analyzing Panel Data* (Beverly Hills: Sage Publications, 1979).

12. Table 3.6 can also be viewed as a transition matrix. It depicts the brand-buying changes from period to period. Knowing the proportion of consumers who switch allows for early prediction of the ultimate success of a new product or change in market strategy.

13. Kurt Brannas, "A New Approach to Modeling and Forecasting Monthly Guest Nights in Hotels," *International Journal of Forecasting*, 18 (1) (January-March 2002): 19; and Seymour Sudman and Robert Ferber, *Consumer Panels* (Chicago: American Marketing Association, 1979): 19–27.

14. Toon W. Taris, *A Primer in Longitudinal Data Analysis* (Thousand Oaks, CA: Sage Publications, 2001); G. J. Van Den Berg, M. Lindeboom, and G. Ridder, "Attrition in Longitudinal Panel Data and the Empirical Analysis of Dynamic Labour Market Behaviour," *Journal of Applied Econometrics*, 9 (4) (October-December 1994): 421–435; and Russell S. Winer, "Attrition Bias in Econometric Models Estimated with Panel Data," *Journal of Marketing Research*, 20 (May 1983): 177–186.

15. Jack K. H. Lee, K. Sudhir, and Joel H. Steckel, "A Multiple Ideal Point Model: Capturing Multiple Preference Effects from within an Ideal Point Framework," *Journal of Marketing Research*, 39 (1) (February 2002): 73–86; and Laszlo Maytas and Patrick Sevestre, eds., *The Econometrics of Panel Data, A Handbook of the Theory With Applications* (Norwell, MA: Kluwer Academic Publishers, 1996).

16. Grant F. Gould and James L. Gould, *Chance and Causation: To Experimental Design and Statistica* (New York: W. H. Freeman & Company, 2001); John Hulland, Yiu Ho, and Shunyin Lam, "Use of Causal Models in Marketing Research: A Review," *International Journal of Research in Marketing*, 13 (2) (April 1996): 181–197.

17. Russell S. Winer, "Experimentation in the 21st Century: The Importance of External Validity," *Journal of the Academy of Marketing Science* (Summer 1999): 349–358.

18. Anonymous, "Mead, Westvaco Join Forces," *Printing Impressions*, 44 (4A) (October 1, 2001): 1–2; and *www.meadwestvaco.com/consumer.html*. April 11, 2002.

19. Jack Willoughby, "Exit Citigroup Smiling," *Barron's*, 82 (11) (March 18, 2002): 1; and Sabra Brock, Sara Lipson, and Ron Levitt, "Trends in Marketing Research and Development at Citicorp/Citibank," *Marketing Research: A Magazine of Management and Applications*, 1 Number 4 (December 1989).

20. Eunkyu Lee, "Are Consumer Survey Results Distorted? Systematic Impact of Behavioral Frequency and Duration on Survey Response Errors," *Journal of Marketing Research*, (February 2000): 125–133; and Solomon Dutka and Lester R. Frankel, "Measuring Response Error," *Journal of Advertising Research*, 37 (1) (January/February 1997): 33–39.

21. Alison Stein Wellner, "The American Family in the 21st Century," *American Demographics*, 23 (8) (August 2001): 20; Rebecca P. Heath, "Life on Easy Street," *American Demographics*, 19 (4) (April 1997): 32–38; and *Marketing News* (April 10, 1987): 3.

22. Pritbhushan Sinha, "Determination of Reliability of Estimations Obtained with Survey Research: A Method of Simulation," *International Journal of Market Research*, 42 (3) (Summer 2000): 311–318; Margret R. Rollere, "Control is Elusive in Research Design," *Marketing News*, 31 (19) (September 15, 1997): 17; and Tom Corlett, "Sampling Errors in Practice," *Journal of Market Research Society*, 38 (4) (October 1996): 307–318.

23. I. M. Premachandra, "An Approximation of the Activity Duration Distribution in PERT," *Computers and Operations Research*, New York (April 2001): 443; and Zedan Hatush and Martin Skitmore, "Assessment and Evaluation of Contractor Data Against Client Goals Using PERT Approach," *Construction Management & Economics*, 15 (4) (July 1997): 327–340.

24. Carl Rohde and Ole Christensen, "Understanding European Youth," *Quirk's Marketing Research Review* (November 2000), article number 0630 online at *www.quirks.com/articles/article_print.asp?arg_articleid= 630*.

25. Neil C. Herndon, Jr., " An Investigation of Moral Values and the Ethical Content of the Corporate Culture: Taiwanese versus U.S. Sales People," *Journal of Business Ethics*, 30 (1) (March 2001): 73–85; and Betsy Peterson, "Ethics Revisited," *Marketing Research: A Magazine of Management & Applications*, 8 (4) (Winter 1996): 47–48.

26. Anonymous, "Bright Ideas," *Internet World*, 7 (3) (February 1, 2001): 11.

27. Sou-Sen Leu, "A Genetic Algorithm-based Optimal Resource-constrained Scheduling Simulation Model," *Construction Management and Economics*, 20 (2) (March 2002): 131–141; Pritbhushan Sinha, "Determination of Reliability of Estimations Obtained with Survey Research: A Method of Simulation," *International Journal of Market Research*, 42 (3) (Summer 2000): 311–318; Naresh K. Malhotra, "An Approach to the Measurement of Consumer Preferences Using Limited Information," *Journal of Marketing Research*, 23 (February 1986): 33–40; and Naresh K. Malhotra, "Analyzing Marketing Research Data with Incomplete Information on the Dependent Variable," *Journal of Marketing Research*, 24 (February 1987): 74–84.

## Chapter 4

1. Niall Ó. Dochartaigh, *The Internet Research Handbook: A Practical Guide for Students and Researchers in the Social Sciences* (Thousand Oaks, CA: Sage Publications, 2002); Stephen B. Castleberry, "Using Secondary Data in Marketing

Research: A Project that Melds Web and Off-Web Sources," *Journal of Marketing Education*, 23 (3) (December 2001): 195–203; and Gordon L. Patzer, *Using Secondary Data in Marketing Research* (Westport: Greenwood Publishing Group, 1995).

2. Anonymous, "HMR: Designed to Beat Eating Out," *Grocer*, 224 (7505) (May 26, 2001): 52–53. *www.bostonmarket.com/4_company/news_110601.htm.*

3. Steven M. Barney, "A Changing Workforce Calls for Twenty-First Century Strategies," *Journal of Healthcare Management*, 47 (2) (March/April 2002): 81–84; and *www.elotouch.com/pdfs/marcom/regal.pdf.*

4. For recent applications of secondary data, see Masaaki Kotabe, "Using Euromonitor Database in International Marketing Research," *Journal of the Academy of Marketing Science*, 30 (2) (Spring 2002): 172; and Paul A. Bottomley and Stephen J. S. Holden, "Do We Really Know How Consumers Evaluate Brand Extensions? Empirical Generalizations Based on Secondary Analysis of Eight Studies," *Journal of Marketing Research*, 38 (4) (November 2001): 494–500.

5. Anonymous, "Nielsen Ratings," *Adweek*, 43 (4) (January 21, 2002): B1; Claude Brodesser, "Nielsen Under Fire on Hispanic Sample," *Mediaweek* (July 21, 1997): 15; and *www.acnielsen.com/services/media/trad/.* January 26, 2002.

6. Antonio A. Prado, "E-Tail Revenue Numbers Seldom Add Up," *Investor's Business Daily*, 18 (201) (January 25, 2002): A6.

7. Terry Maxon, "American Airlines to Join Swiss Air Lines in Marketing Partnership," *Knight Ridder Tribune Business News*, (March 27, 2002): 1; Peter Keating, "The Best Airlines to Fly Today," *Money* (November 1997): 118–128.

8. Ronald G. Drozdenko and Perry D. Drake, *Optimal Database Marketing* (Thousand Oaks, CA: Sage Publications, 2002); and Drayton Bird, "Database Marketing Gets Vote Over Management Consultants," *Marketing* (March 7, 2002): 18.

9. Jean Halliday, "Carmakers Learn to Mine Databases," *Advertising Age* (April 2000): S6–S8; and *www.daimlerchrysler.com/company/company_e.htm.* January 27, 2002.

10. Jeremy White, "KFC Seeks a Modern Identity Beyond the Animated Colonel," *Campaign* (January 18, 2002): 14; "The Colonel's Bold Campaign," *Chain Store Age* (June 1997): A12–A13; and *www.kfc.com/about/kfcfacts.htm.* January 28, 2002.

11. Keith Malo, "Corporate Strategy Requires Market Research," *Marketing News*, 36 (2) (January 21, 2002): 14.

12. Bob Brewin, "U.S. Census Bureau Plans for First Paperless Tally in 2010," *Computerworld*, 36 (12) (March 18, 2002): 5; Cynthia Etkin, "Historical United States Census Data Browser," *Library Journal*, 125 (7) (April 15, 2000): 58; and *www.census.gov.*

13. Katarzyna Dawidowska, "The Census Bureau Century," *American Demographics*, 24 (3) (March 2002): 12.

14. One such firm is Claritas (*www.claritas.com*). See David Wren, "San Diego's Claritas Studies Myrtle Beach, SC, Demographics by ZIP Code," *Knight Ridder Tribune Business News* (May 7, 2002): 1.

15. Robert J. Samuelson, "Can America Assimilate?" *Newsweek*, 137 (15) (April 9, 2001): 42; and *www.census.gov.* January 28, 2002.

16. Ephraim Schwartz, "Dawn of a New Database," *InfoWorld*, 24 (11) (March 18, 2002): 32; Carol Post, "Marketing Data Marts Help Companies Stay Ahead of the Curve and in Front of the Competition," *Direct Marketing*, 59 (12) (April 1997): 42–44.

17. Darla Martin Tucker, "Technology: Online Database Set to Debut This Summer," *The Business Press* (March 18, 2002): 8.

18. Jody Dodson, "Dos, Don'ts of Online Research," *Advertising Age's Business Marketing* (August 1999): 8.

19. Anonymous, "infoUSA.com Provides Fee Internet Database," *Direct Marketing* (January 2000): 15–16; and Mary Ellen Bates, "American, Business Information: Here, There, and Everywhere," *Database*, 20 (2) (April/May 1997): 45–50.

20. Carol Tenopir, "Links and Bibliographic Databases," *Library Journal*, 126 (4) (March 1, 2001): 34–35; and Greg R. Notess, "The Internet as an Online Service: Bibliographic Databases on the Net," *Database*, 19 (4) (August/September 1996): 92–95.

21. For applications of PIMS database, see David Besanko, David Dranove, and Mark Shanley, "Exploiting a Cost Advantage and Coping with a Cost Disadvantage," *Management Science*, 47 (2) (February 2001): 221; and Venkatram Ramaswamy, Hubert Gatignon, and David J. Reibstein, "Competitive Marketing Behavior," *Journal of Marketing*, 58 (April 1994): 45–56.

22. "The MonitorTM Service," brochure prepared by Yankelovich and Partners (*www.yankelovich.com*); and Gail Pitts, "Too Bad We Can't Eat the Campbell's Soup Web Site," *Knight Ridder Tribune Business News* (February 6, 2002): 1.

23. Julie Napoli, "The Net Generation: An Analysis of Lifestyles, Attitudes, and Media Habits," *Journal of International Consumer Marketing* (2001): 21; and Leon G. Schiffman and Leslie Lazar Kanuk, *Consumer Behavior*, 7th ed. (Upper Saddle River, NJ: Prentice Hall, Inc., 1999).

24. William D. Wells, "Recognition, Recall, and Rating Scales," *Journal of Advertising Research*, 40 (6) (November/December 2000): 14–20.

25. "NPD Fashion Word Reveals that Women Secretly Like Shopping for Swimwear: Two New NPDFashionworld Reports Examine the Swimwear Market and Shopping Experience" at *www.npd.com* (January 23, 2002).

26. Allison Romano, "New to Nielsen's Numbers," *Broadcasting and Cable*, 132 (5) (February 4, 2002): 29; and Steve Wilcox, "Sampling and Controlling a TV Audience Measurement Panel," *International Journal of Market Research*, 42 (4) (Winter 2000): 413–430.

27. Anonymous, "Over Half of All U.S. Citizens are Online According to New Commerce Department Report," *Internet Business News* (February 2002).

28. Anonymous, "Arbitron Tweaks Race Methodology," *Mediaweek*, 12 (2) (January 14, 2002): 24.

29. Eunkyu Lee, Michael Y. Hu, and Rex S. Toh, "Are Consumer Survey Results Distorted? Systematic Impact of Behavioral Frequency and Duration on Survey Response Errors," *Journal of Marketing Research*, 37 (1) (February 2000): 125–133; "Why Consumer Mail Panel Is the Superior Option" (Chicago: Market Facts, Inc., undated); and John H. Parfitt and B. J. K. Collins, "Use of Consumer Panels for Brand-Share Predictions," *Journal of Market Research Society*, 38 (4) (October 1996): 341–367.

30. Kevin J. Clancy, "Brand Confusion," *Harvard Business Review*, 80 (3) (March 2002): 22; and Seymour Sudman, "On the Accuracy of Recording of Consumer Panels II," *Learning Manual* (New York: Neal-Schumen Publishers, 1981).

31. Harald J. Van Heerde, "The Estimation of Pre- and Post-Promotion Dips with Store Level Scanner Data," *Journal of Marketing Research*, 37 (3) (August 2000): 383–396. A study investigating the accuracy of UPC scanner pricing systems found that both underring and overring rates were significantly higher than retailers' expectations: Ronald C. Goodstein, "UPC Scanner Pricing Systems: Are They Accurate?" *Journal of Marketing*, 58 (April 1994): 20–30.

32. Martin Natter, "Real World Performance of Choice-Based Conjoint Models," *European Journal of Operational Research,* 137 (2) (March 1, 2002): 448; and Marcel Corstjens and Rajiv Lal, "Building Store Loyalty Through Store Brands," *Journal of Marketing Research,* 37 (3) (August 2000): 281–291.

33. It is possible to combine store-level scanner data with scanner panel data to do an integrated analysis. See Tulin Erdem, Glenn Mayhew, and Baohong Sun, "Understanding Reference-Price Shoppers: A Within- and Cross-Category Analysis," *Journal of Marketing Research,* 38 (4) (November 2001): 445–457; and Gary J. Russell and Wagner A. Kamakura, "Understanding Brand Competition Using Micro and Macro Scanner Data," *Journal of Marketing Research,* 31 (May 1994): 289–303.

34. Jack K. H. Lee, K. Sudhir, and Joel H. Steckel, "A Multiple Ideal Point Model: Capturing Multiple Preference Effects from within an Ideal Point Framework," *Journal of Marketing Research,* 39 (1) (February 2002): 73–86; and Anonymous, "Cereals: A Key Meal—But When?" *Grocer,* 224 (7507) (June 9, 2001): 72.

35. Examples of recent applications of scanner data include Katherine W. Lemon and Stephen M. Nowlis, "Developing Synergies Between Promotions and Brands in Different Price-Quality Tiers," *Journal of Marketing Research,* 39 (2) (May 2002): 171–185; and Pradeep K. Chintagunta, "Investigating Category Pricing Behavior at a Retail Chain," *Journal of Marketing Research,* 39 (2) (May 2002): 141–154.

36. Anonymous, "Study of Online Shopping in U.S. Released by ComScore Networks," *Internet Business News* (January 21, 2002); and *www.ashford.com.*

37. For applications of single source data, see Bruce Fox, "Retailers Integrate Space Planning with Key Business Functions," *Stores,* 83 (12) ( December 2001): 59–60; Michael Darkow, "Compatible or Not? Results of a Single Source Field Experiment within a TV Audience Research Panel,"*Marketing & Research Today,* 24 (3) (August 1996): 150–161; and John Deighton, Caroline M. Henderson, and Scott A. Neslin, "The Effects of Advertising on Brand Switching and Repeat Purchasing," *Journal of Marketing Research,* 31 (February 1994): 28–43.

38. Stephanie Thompson, "Diet V8 Splash Carves Niche in Juice Category for Adults," *Advertising Age,* 71 (13) (March 27, 2000): 24; Joanne Lipman, "Single-Source Ad Research Heralds Detailed Look at Household Habits," *Wall Street Journal,* (February 16, 1988): 39; *www.cbs.com*; and *www.v8juice.com.*

39. Jonathan W. Lowe, "GIS Meets the Mapster," *Geospatial Solutions,* 12 (2) (February 2002): 46–48.

40. For an example of international marketing research based on secondary data, see Sherriff T. K. Luk, "The Use of Secondary Information Published by the PRC Government," *Market Research Society, Journal of the Market Research Society* (July 1999): 355–365.

41. Peter M. Chisnall, "Marketing Research: State of the Art Perspectives," *International Journal of Market Research,* 44 (1) (First Quarter 2002): 122–125.

42. Daniel Joelson, "Latin America Set for ATM Spike; Consumer Demand is Making Latin Banks Reassess Their ATM Strategies," *Bank Technology News,* 15 (1) (January 2002): 7–8.

43. Dan Trigoboff, "Saying No to Nielsen," *Broadcasting & Cable,* 132 (5) (February 4, 2002): 33; and Alan Bunce, "Faced with Lower Ratings, Networks Take Aim at Nielsen; The Big Three Consider a Competing Ratings Service," *Christian Science Monitor* (March 20, 1997).

44. Len Strazewski, "Fine Tune Your Agency Web Site," *Rough Notes,* 145 (1) (January 2002): 102–105; and *www.nytimes.com,* January 31, 2002.

# Chapter 5

1. Rick Popely and Jim Mateja, "General Motors Takes Lead in Introduction of New Models, Show Cars," *Knight Ridder Tribune Business News* (February 7, 2002); and Joseph Rydholm, "Igniting the Sunfire," *Quirk's Marketing Research Review* (March, 1995).

2. Kenneth Wade, "Focus Groups' Research Role Is Shifting," *Marketing News,* 36 (5) (March 4, 2002): 47; and Rana Dogar, "Marketing to the Sense," *Working Woman* (April, 1997): 32–35.

3. Kathryn C. Rentz, "Reflexive Methodology: New Vistas for Qualitative Research," *The Journal of Business Communication,* 39 (1) (January 2002): 149–156; and David J. Carson, Audrey Gilmore, Chad Perry, and Kjell Gronhaug, *Qualitative Marketing Research* (Thousand Oaks, CA: Sage Publications, 2001).

4. Gill Ereaut, Mike Imms, and Martin Callingham, *Qualitative Market Research: Principle & Practice: Seven Volume Set* (Thousand Oaks, CA: Sage Publications, 2002); and Shay Sayre, *Qualitative Methods for Marketplace Research* (Thousand Oaks, CA: Sage Publications, 2001).

5. A positivist perspective on research is being adopted here. Positivism encompasses logical positivism, logical empiricism, and all forms of falsificationism. This is the dominant perspective in commercial marketing research. A relativist perspective has been offered. See, for example, Richard R. Wilk, "The Impossibility and Necessity of Re-Inquiry: Finding Middle Ground in Social Science," *Journal of Consumer Research,* 28 (2) (September 2001): 308–312; and Shelby D. Hunt, *A General Theory of Competition* (Thousand Oaks, CA: Sage Publications, 2000).

6. Sara Eckel, "Cheese Whiz," *American Demographics,* 23 (3) (March 2001): S14.

7. Gill Ereaut, Mike Imms, and Martin Callingham, *Qualitative Market Research: Principle & Practice: Seven Volume Set* (Thousand Oaks, CA: Sage Publications, 2002); and John Gill and Phil Johnson, *Research Methods for Managers,* 3rd ed. (Thousand Oaks, CA: Sage Publications, 2002).

8. Michael Bloor, Jane Frankland, Michelle Thomas, and Kate Robson, *Focus Groups in Social Research* (Thousand Oaks, CA: Sage Publications, 2001).

9. Richard A. Krueger and Mary Anne Casey, *Focus Groups: A Practical Guide for Applied Research,* 3rd ed. (Thousand Oaks, CA: Sage Publications, 2000).

10. The group size of 8 to 12 is based on rules of thumb. For more discussion, see Edward F. Fern, *Advanced Focus Group Research* (Thousand Oaks, CA: Sage Publications, 2001); and Robert Blackburn, "Breaking Down the Barriers: Using Focus Groups to Research Small- and Medium-Sized Enterprises," *International Small Business Journal,* 19 (1) (October–December 2000): 44–67.

11. Catherine Forrest, "Research with a Laugh Track," *Marketing News,* 36 (5) (March 4, 2002): 48; Gloria F. Mazella, "Show-and-Tell Focus Groups Reveal Core Boomer Values," *Marketing News,* 31 (12) (June 9, 1997): H8.

12. Colin MacDougall, "Planning and Recruiting the Sample for Focus Groups and In-Depth Interviews," *Qualitative Health Research,* 11 (1) (January 2001): 117–126; and Hazel Kahan, "A Professional Opinion," *American Demographics (Tools Supplement)* (October 1996): 14–19.

13. Jonathan Hall, "Moderators Must Motivate Focus Group," *Marketing News,* 34 (9) (September 11, 2000): 26–27; and Thomas L. Greenbaum, *Moderating Focus Groups: A Practical Guide for Group Facilitation* (Thousand Oaks, CA: Sage Publications,

1999). Adapted from Donald A. Chase, "The Intensive Group Interviewing in Marketing," *MRA Viewpoints,* 1973.

14. Edward F. Fern, *Advanced Focus Group Research* (Thousand Oaks, CA: Sage Publications, 2001); and Richard A. Krueger, *Developing Questions for Focus Groups* (Newbury Park, CA: Sage Publications, 1997).

15. Becky Ebenkamp, "The Focus Group Has Spoken," *Brandweek,* 42 (17) (April 23, 2001): 24; and David L. Morgan, *The Focus Group Guidebook* (Newbury Park, CA: Sage Publications, 1997).

16. Anonymous, "Focus Groups: A Practical Guide for Applied Research," *International Journal of Public Opinion Research,* 13 (1) (Spring 2001): 85; and Richard A. Krueger and Mary Anne Casey, *Focus Groups: A Practical Guide for Applied Research,* 3rd ed. (Thousand Oaks, CA: Sage Publications, 2000).

17. Joan Raymond, "All Smiles," *American Demographics,* 23 (3) (March 2001): S18; and Stephanie Thompson, "Kraft Does the 'Twist'," *Advertising Age,* 72 (4) (January 22, 2001): 8.

18. Edward F. Fern, *Advanced Focus Group Research* (Thousand Oaks, CA: Sage Publications, 2001); and Anonymous, "Research Reports: Efficiency Through Telephone Focus Groups," *Agri Marketing,* Skokie (June 2000): 17.

19. Ronald E. Goldsmith, "The Focus Group Research Handbook," *The Service Industries Journal,* 20 (3) (July 2000): 214–215; and Thomas L. Greenbaum, *The Handbook for Focus Group Research* (Newbury Park, CA: Sage Publications, 1997).

20. Anonymous, "Focus Group Warning," *Marketing News,* 34 (6) (March 13, 2000): 6; Howard Furmansky, "Debunking the Myth About Focus Groups," *Marketing News,* 31 (13) (June 23, 1997): 22; and Jack Edmonston, "Handle Focus Group Research with Care," *Business Marketing,* 79 (6) (June 1994): 38.

21. Don Akchin, "Quick & Dirty Research," *Nonprofit World,* Madison (May/June 2001): 32–33; and "How Nonprofits Are Using Focus Groups," *Nonprofit World,* 14 (5) (September/ October 1996): 37.

22. Poppy Brech, "Research Proves the Obvious," *Marketing,* (March 21, 2002): 48.

23. Shay Sayre, *Qualitative Methods for Marketplace Research* (Thousand Oaks, CA: Sage Publications, 2001); and "Looking for a Deeper Meaning," *Marketing* (Market Research Top 75 Supplement) (July 17, 1997): 16–17.

24. Edward C. Baig, "One Smart Card for All Your Debts," *USA Today* (February 6, 2002): D7.

25. Gwendolyn Bounds, "Psychology of Marketing: Marketers Tread Precarious Terrain—Ads Alluding to Sept. 11 Risk Taint of Commercializing Tragedy to Push Products," *Wall Street Journal* (February 5, 2002): B1; and Klaus G. Grunert and Suzanne C. Grunert, "Measuring Subjective Meaning Structures by Laddering Method: Theoretical Considerations and Methodological Problems,"*International Journal of Research in Marketing,* 12 (3) (October 1995): 209–225. This example is derived from Jeffrey F. Durgee, "Depth-Interview Techniques for Creative Advertising," *Journal of Advertising Research,* 25 (December 1985/January 1986): 29–37.

26. R. Kenneth Wade, "Focus Groups' Research Role Is Shifting," *Marketing News,* 36 (5) (March 4, 2002): 47; Brian Wansink, "New Techniques to Generate Key Marketing Insights," *Marketing Research,* 12 (2) (Summer 2000): 28–36; and Richard A. Feder, "Depth Interviews Avoid Turmoil of Focus Groups," *Advertising Age,* 68 (16) (April 21, 1997): 33.

27. Robert A. Guth, "PlayStation 2 Helps Sony Beat Forecasts," *Wall Street Journal* (January 28, 2002): A12; and Brian Wansink, "New Techniques to Generate Key Marketing Insights," *Marketing Research,* 12 (Summer 2000): 28–36.

28. Gill Ereaut, Mike Imms, and Martin Callingham, *Qualitative Market Research: Principle & Practice: Seven Volume Set* (Thousand Oaks, CA: Sage Publications, 2002); and H. H. Kassarjian, "Projective Methods," in R. Ferber, Ed., *Handbook of Marketing Research* (New York: McGraw-Hill, 1974), 3.85–3.100.

29. Judith Lynne Zaichowsky, "The Why of Consumption: Contemporary Perspectives and Consumer Motives, Goals, and Desires," *Academy of Marketing Science,* 30 (2) (Spring 2002): 179; and Sidney J. Levy, "Interpreting Consumer Mythology: Structural Approach to Consumer Behavior Focuses on Story Telling," *Marketing Management,* 2 (4) (1994): 4–9.

30. Miriam Catterall, "Using Projective Techniques in Education Research," *British Educational Research Journal,* 26 (2) (April 2000): 245–256; Marilyn M. Kennedy, "So How'm I Doing?" *Across the Board,* 34 (6) (June 1997): 53–54; and G. Lindzey, "On the Classification of Projective Techniques," *Psychological Bulletin* (1959): 158–168.

31. Kerri Walsh, "Soaps and Detergents," *Chemical Week,* 164 (3) (January 23, 2002): 24–26; and "Interpretation is the Essence of Projective Research Techniques," *Marketing News* (September 28, 1984): 20.

32. J. Dee Hill, "7-Eleven Hopes Hosiery Has Legs," *Adweek,* 22 (42) (October 16, 2000): 12; and Ronald B. Lieber, "Storytelling: A New Way to Get Close to Your Customer," *Fortune Magazine* (February 3, 1997); and *www.dupont.com.*

33. Amy Zuber, "McD Unveils New Brands, Tries to Reverse 'McSlide'," *Nation's Restaurant News,* 35 (46) (November 12, 2001): 1–2; David Kilburn, "Haagen-Dazs Is Flavor of Month," *Marketing Week,* 20 (23) (September 4, 1997): 30; and S. Bhargava, "Gimme a Double Shake and a Lard on White," *Business Week* (March 1, 1993): 59.

34. Debby Andrews, "Playing a Role," *Business Communication Quarterly,* 64 (1) (March 2001): 7–8; "Role Playing for Better Service," *Lodging Hospitality,* 53 (2) (February 1997): 16.

35. Kevin Smith, "Apartment, Townhouse Area Offers Upscale Living in Rancho Cucamonga, Calif.," *Knight Ridder Tribune Business News* (May 17, 2002): 1; and Jerome R. Corsi, "Adapting to Fit the Problem: Impact Research Takes a Different Approach to Marketing," *Rocky Mountain Business Journal,* 36 (26) (March 25, 1985): 1.

36. Edward H. Phillips, "Fear of Flying," *Aviation Week & Space Technology,* 154 (3) (January 15, 2001): 419; "Fear of Flying" *Economist,* 339 (7966) (May 18, 1996): 30; *www.airlines.org;* and *www.airsafe.com.*

37. Gill Ereaut, Mike Imms, and Martin Callingham, *Qualitative Market Research: Principle & Practice: Seven Volume Set* (Thousand Oaks, CA: Sage Publications, 2002); David Bakken, "State of the Art in Qualitative Research," *Marketing Research: A Magazine of Management & Applications,* 8 (2) (Summer 1996): 4–5; Elaine Cibotti and Eugene H. Fram, "The Shopping List Studies and Projective Techniques: A 40-Year View," *Marketing Research: A Magazine of Management & Applications,* 3 (4) (December 1991): 14–22; and Maison Haire, "Projective Techniques in Marketing Research," *Journal of Marketing,* 14 (April 1950): 649–656.

38. John Gill and Phil Johnson, *Research Methods for Managers,* 3rd ed. (Thousand Oaks, CA: Sage Publications, 2002); and Sajeev Varki, Bruce Cooil, and Roland T. Rust, "Modeling Fuzzy Data in Qualitative Marketing Research," *Journal of Marketing Research,* 37 (4) (November 2000): 480–489.

39. Alan S. Zimmerman and Michael Szenberg, "Implementing International Qualitative Research: Techniques and Obstacles,"

*Qualitative Market Research,* 3 (3) (2000): 158–164; and Jeffery S. Nevid, "Multicultural Issues in Qualitative Research," *Psychology & Marketing* (July 1999): 305–325.

40. Thomas L. Greenbaum, "Understanding Focus Group Research Abroad," *Marketing News,* 30 (12) (June 3, 1996): H14, H36.

41. Richa Mishra, "India: Whirlpool to Continue with New Marketing Initiative," *Businessline* (November 6, 2001): 1; and Hal Daume, "Making Qualitative Research Work in the Pacific Rim," *Marketing News,* 31 (May 12, 1997): 13.

42. Connie Rate Bateman, "Framing Effects Within the Ethical Decision-Making Process of Consumers," *Journal of Business Ethics,* 36 (1/2) (March 2002): 119–138.

43. Evan Thomas, "Calling All Swing States," *Newsweek,* 136 (21) (November 20, 2000): 110–120.

44. Robert V. Kozinets, "The Field Behind the Screen: Using Netnography for Marketing Research Online Communities," *Journal of Marketing Research,* 39 (1) (February 2002): 61–72; Thomas L Greenbaum, "Focus Groups vs. Online," *Advertising Age,* Chicago (February 14, 2000): 34; and Judith Langer, "'On' and 'Offline' Focus Groups: Claims, Questions," *Marketing News,* 34 (12) (June 5, 2000): H38

45. Chuck Moozakis, "Nissan Wants to Be like Dell—Automaker Says It Can Achieve Build-to-Order Via the Web in 18 Months; Experts Are Skeptical," *InternetWeek* (January 7, 2002): 11; Jean Halliday, "Makers Use Web to Help Design Cars," *Automotive News* (5860) (February 7, 2001): 22; and *www.nissandriven.com.*

# Chapter 6

1. Humphrey Taylor, John Bremer, Cary Overmeyer, Jonathan W. Siegel, and George Terhanian, "Using Internet Polling to Forecast the 2000 Elections," *Marketing Research,* 13 (Spring 2001): 26–30.

2. Anonymous, "Canon Logs Record Profit, Sales in '01," *Jiji Press English News Service* (January 31, 2002): 1; and Johnny K. Johansson and Ikujiro Nonaka, "Market Research the Japanese Way," *Harvard Business Review* (May/June 1987): 16–18.

3. Surveys are commonly used in marketing research. See, for example, Naresh K. Malhotra and Daniel McCort, "A Cross-Cultural Comparison of Behavioral Intention Models: Theoretical Consideration and an Empirical Investigation," *International Marketing Review,* 18 (3) (2001): 235–269.

4. Rajesh Nakwah, "Getting Good Feedback," *Quirk's Marketing Research Review* (November 2000).

5. David W. Glasscoff, "Measuring Clinical Performance: Comparison and Validity of Telephone Survey and Administrative Data," *Marketing Health Services,* 22 (1) (Spring 2002): 43–44; and Niki Thurkow, "The Effects of Group and Individual Monetary Incentives on Productivity of Telephone Interviewers," *Journal of Organizational Behavior Management,* 20 (2) (2000): 3.

6. Leigh Dyer, "Maya Angelou Sells Lines to Hallmark," *Knight Ridder Tribune Business News* (February 1, 2002): 1.

7. *www.roperasw.com.* See also Floyd J. Fowler, Jr., *Survey Research Methods,* 3rd ed. (Thousand Oaks, CA: Sage Publications, 2001).

8. Karen V. Fernandez, "The Effectiveness of Information and Color in Yellow Pages Advertising," *Journal of Advertising,* 29 (2) (Summer 2000): 61–73; and A. J. Bush and J. F. Hair, Jr., "An Assessment of the Mall Intercept as a Data Collection Method," *Journal of Marketing Research* (May 1985): 158–67.

9. Rebecca Gardyn, "Same Name, New Number," *American Demographics,* 23 (3) (March 2001): 6.

10. Anonymous, "Comerica Bank, KeyCorp, Bank One Rank in Top 15 with Their Internet Sites," *Michigan Banker,* 12 (7) (July 2000): 29; Nicolaos E. Synodinos and Jerry M. Brennan, "Computer Interactive Interviewing in Survey Research," *Psychology and Marketing,* 5 (Summer 1988): 117–138; and *www.bankone.com/about/profile/description.*

11. Mail surveys are common in institutional and industrial marketing research. See, for example, H. L. Brossard, "Information Sources Used by an Organization During a Complex Decision Process: An Exploratory Study," *Industrial Marketing Management,* 27 (1) (January 1998): 41–50.

12. Jack Schmid, "Assigning Value to Your Customer List," *Catalog Age,* 18 (5) (April 2001): 69; and Rob Yoegei, "List Marketers Head to Cyberspace," *Target Marketing,* 20 (8) (August 1997): 54–55.

13. Michael Straus, "Charlotte Art Museum Uses Research to Light Path to 21st Century," *Quirks* (February 1998) (*www.quirks.com/articles/article.asp?arg_ArticleId= 311*); and *www.mintmuseum.org/mmcd/index.htm.*

14. Matthew Schwartz, "Postal and E-mail 'Combos' Gain Favor with Marketers," *B to B,* 87 (2) (February 11, 2002): 25; and Jim Stevens and John Chisholm, "An Integrated Approach: Technology Firm Conducts Worldwide Satisfaction Research Survey Via E-Mail, Internet," *Quirk's Marketing Research Review,* 11 (8) (October 1997): 12–13, 64–65.

15. John W. Gorman, "An Opposing View of Online Surveying," *Marketing News* (April 24, 2000).

16. Steven K. Thompson, *Sampling* (New York: John Wiley & Sons, 2002); and Terry L. Childers and Steven J. Skinner, "Theoretical and Empirical Issues in the Identification of Survey Respondents," *Journal of the Market Research Society,* 27 (January 1985): 39–53.

17. Gregory B. Murphy, "The Effects of Organizational Sampling Frame Selection," *Journal of Business Venturing,* 17 (3) (May 2002): 237; and Wayne Smith, Paul Mitchell, Karin Attebo, and Stephen Leeder, "Selection Bias from Sampling Frames: Telephone Directory and Electoral Rolls Compared to Door-to-Door Population Census: Results from the Blue Mountain Eye Study," *Australian and New Zealand Journal of Public Health,* 21 (2) (April 1997): 127–133.

18. Timothy R. Graeff, "Uninformed Response Bias in Telephone Surveys," *Journal of Business Research,* 55 (3) (March 2002): 251; and Scott Keeter, "Estimating Telephone Noncoverage Bias with a Telephone Survey," *Public Opinion Quarterly,* 59 (2) (Summer 1995): 196–217.

19. Anonymous, "Random Sampling," *Marketing News,* 36 (3) (February 4, 2002): 7; Dana James, "Old, New Make Up Today's Surveys," *Marketing News* (June 5, 2000): 4; David Wilson, "Random Digit Dialing and Electronic White Pages Samples Compared: Demographic Profiles and Health Estimates," *Australian and New Zealand Demographic Profiles and Health Estimates,* 23 (6) (December 1999): 627–633; Johnny Blair and Ronald Czaja, "Locating a Special Population Using Random Digit Dialing," *Public Opinion Quarterly,* 46 (Winter 1982): 585–590; and E. L. Landon, Jr., and S. K. Banks, "Relative Efficiency and Bias of Plus-One Telephone Sampling," *Journal of Marketing Research,* 14 (August 1977): 294–299.

20. Sherry Chiger, "Benchmark 2002: Lists and E-lists," *Catalog Age,* 19 (3) (March 1, 2002): 41–45; David O. Schwartz,

"Mailing List Owners and the Millennium," *Marketing News,* 31 (11) (May 26, 1997): 4; Paul M. Biner and Deborah L. Barton, "Justifying the Enclosure of Monetary Incentives in Mail Survey Cover Letters," *Psychology and Marketing* (Fall 1990): 153–162; and "Lists Make Targeting Easy," *Advertising Age* (July 9, 1984): 20.

21. B. Zafer Erdogan, "Increasing Mail Survey Response Rates from an Industrial Population: A Cost Effectiveness Analysis of Four Follow-Up Techniques," *Industrial Marketing Management,* 31 (1) (January 2002): 65; Jack Edmonston, "Why Response Rates are Declining," *Advertising Age's Business Marketing,* 82 (8) (September 1997): 12; Raymond Hubbard and Eldon L. Little, "Promised Contributions to Charity and Mail Survey Responses: Replications with Extension," *Public Opinion Quarterly,* 52 (Summer 1988): 223–230; and Paul L. Erdos and Robert Ferber, Ed., "Data Collection Methods: Mail Surveys," *Handbook of Marketing Research* (New York: McGraw-Hill, 1974): 102.

22. Floyd J. Fowler, Jr., *Survey Research Methods,* 3rd ed. (Thousand Oaks, CA: Sage Publications, 2001); Pamela G. Guengel, Tracy R. Berchman, and Charles F. Cannell, *General Interviewing Techniques: A Self-Instructional Workbook for Telephone and Personal Interviewer Training* (Ann Arbor, MI: Survey Research Center, University of Michigan, 1983).

23. Eunkyu Lee, "Are Consumer Survey Results Distorted? Systematic Impact of Behavioral Frequency and Duration on Survey Response Errors," *Journal of Marketing Research,* 37 (1) (February 2000): 125–133.

24. Lee Murphy, "Survey Software Gets Simpler, More Effective," *Marketing News,* 35 (3) (January 29, 2001): 4–5; and Karen Fletcher, "Jump on the Omnibus," *Marketing* (June 15, 1995): 25–28.

25. Jamie Smith, "How to Boost DM Response Rates Quickly," *Marketing News,* 35 (9) (April 23, 2001): 5; Richard Colombo, "A Model for Diagnosing and Reducing Nonresponse Bias," *Journal of Advertising Research,* (January/April 2000): 85–93; Barbara Bickart, "The Distribution of Survey Contact and Participation in the United States: Constructing a Survey-Based Estimate," *Journal of Marketing Research,* Chicago, (May 1999): 286–294; William L. Nicholls, II, "Highest Response," *Marketing Research: A Magazine of Management & Applications,* 8 (1) (Spring 1996): 5–7; Jeannine M. James and Richard Bolstein, "The Effect of Monetary Incentives and Follow-Up Mailings on the Response Rate and Response Quality in Mail Surveys," *Public Opinion Quarterly,* 54 (Fall 1990): 346–361; and Julie Yu and Harris Cooper, "A Quantitative Review of Research Design Effects on Response Rates to Questionnaires," *Journal of Marketing Research,* 20 (February 1983): 36–44.

26. Bruce Keillor, "A Cross-Cultural/Cross-National Study of Influencing Factors and Socially Desirable Response Biases," *International Journal of Market Research,* 43 (1) (First Quarter 2001): 63–84; Maryon F. King, "Social Desirability Bias: A Neglected Aspect of Validity Testing," *Psychology & Marketing,* New York (Feb 2000): 79; Deniz Ones, Angelika D. Reiss, and Chockalingam Viswesvaran, "Role of Social Desirability in Personality Testing for Personnel Selection: The Red Herring," *Journal of Applied Psychology,* 81 (6) (December 1996): 660–679.

27. Anonymous, "Random Sampling: Homework—Yeah Right," *Marketing News,* 36 (6) (March 18, 2002): 4; Gerald Vinten, "The Threat in the Question," *Credit Control,* 18 (1) (1997):

25–31; and Priya Raghubir and Geeta Menon, "Asking Sensitive Questions: The Effects of Type of Referent and Frequency Wording in Counterbiasing Method," *Psychology & Marketing,* 13 (7) (October 1996): 633–652.

28. Timothy R. Graeff, "Uninformed Response Bias in Telephone Surveys," *Journal of Business Research,* 55 (3) (March 2002): 251; Eleanor Singer, "Experiments with Incentives in Telephone Surveys," *Public Opinion Quarterly,* 64 (2) (Summer 2000): 171–188; Charles F. Cannell, Peter U. Miller, Lois Oksenberg, and Samuel Leinhardt, Eds., "Research on Interviewing Techniques," *Sociological Methodology* (San Francisco: Jossey-Bass, 1981); and Peter U. Miller and Charles F. Cannell, "A Study of Experimental Techniques for Telephone Interviewing," *Public Opinion Quarterly,* 46 (Summer 1982): 250–269.

29. Duane P. Bachmann, John Elfrink, and Gary Vazzana, "E-mail and Snail Mail Face Off in Rematch," *Marketing Research,* 11 (Winter 1999/Spring 2000): 10–15.

30. Mark McMaster, "E-Marketing Poll Vault," *Sales and Marketing Management,* 153 (8) (August 2001): 25; and Arlene Fink, *A Survey Handbook* (Thousand Oaks, CA: Sage Publications, 1995).

31. Jon Martin Denstadli, "Analyzing Air Travel: A Comparison of Different Survey Methods and Data Collection Procedures," *Journal of Travel Research,* 39 (1) (August 2000): 4–10; Hybrid methods that combine the features of these basic methods are also being employed. For example, the disk-by-mail (DBM) involves mailing the questionnaire on a disk to the respondents. This method is growing in popularity, as it offers the benefits of both computer-assisted and mail surveys. Anonymous, "Disk-by-Mail Data Collection: A Researcher's Notes," *Sawtooth News,* 10 (Winter 1994/1995): 3–4. See also David Chaudron, "The Right Approach to Employee Surveys," *HR Focus,* 74 (3) (March 1997): 9–10.

32. Cihan Cobanoglu, Bill Warde, and Patrick J. Moreo, "A Comparison of Mail, Fax, and Web-Based Survey Methods," *International Journal of Market Research,* 43 (4) (Fourth Quarter 2001): 441–452; Sophie K. Turley, "A Case of Response Rate Success," *Journal of the Market Research Society* (July 1999): 301–309; and Stanley L. Payne, "Combination of Survey Methods," *Journal of Marketing Research* (May 1964): 62.

33. Don Bruzzone and Lizabeth L. Reyer, "Using Recognition-Based Tracking to Compare the ROI of Print, Radio and TV," *Quirk's Marketing Research Review,* March 1999, online at *www.qmrr.com/articles/article.asp?arg_ArticleId= 469.*

34. Andrew J. Milat, "Measuring Physical Activity in Public Open Space—An Electronic Device Versus Direct Observation," *Australian and New Zealand Journal of Public Health,* 26 (1) (February 2002): 1; Stephen B. Wilcox, "Trust, But Verify," *Appliance Manufacturer,* 46 (1) (January 1998): 8, 87; Langbourne Rust, "How to Reach Children in Stores: Marketing Tactics Grounded in Observational Research," *Journal of Advertising Research,* 33 (November/December 1993): 67–72.

35. Beth Kurcina, "Use Videos to Obtain Crucial POP Info," *Marketing News,* 34 (24) (November 20, 2000): 16; A. V. Seaton, "Unobtrusive Observational Measures as a Qualitative Extension of Visitor Surveys at Festivals and Events: Mass Observation Revisited," *Journal of Travel Research,* 35 (4) (Spring 1997): 25–30; and Fred N. Kerlinger, *Foundations of Behavioral Research,* 3rd ed. (New York: Holt, Rinehart & Winston, 1986): 538.

36. Joseph Rydholm, "Extending Excellence," (January 1998), *www.quirks.com,* Article 0297.

37. Erwin Ephron, "Nielsen's Secret Passive Meter," *Mediaweek,* 10 (36) (September 18, 2000): 32; Laurence N. Gold, "Technology in Television Research: The Meter," *Marketing Research: A Magazine of Management & Applications,* 6 (1) (Winter 1994): 57–58.

38. Rik Pieters, Edward Rosbergen, and Michel Wedel, "Visual Attention to Repeated Print Advertising: A Test of Scanpath Theory," *Journal of Marketing Research,* 36 (4) (November 1999): 424–438; and J. Edward Russo and France Leclerc, "An Eye-Fixation Analysis of Choice Processes for Consumer Nondurables," *Journal of Consumer Research,* 21 (September 1994): 274–290.

39. For applications of GSR, see Gary H. Anthes, "Smile, You're on Candid Computer," *Computerworld,* 35 (49) (December 3, 2001): 50; Priscilla A. LaBarbera and Joel D. Tucciarone, "GSR Reconsidered: A Behavior-Based Approach to Evaluating and Improving the Sales Potency of Advertising," *Journal of Advertising Research,* 35 (5) (September/October 1995): 33–53; and Piet Vanden Abeele and Douglas L. Maclachlan, "Process Tracing of Emotional Responses to TV Ads: Revisiting the Warmth Monitor," *Journal of Consumer Research,* 20 (March 1994): 586–600.

40. N'Gai Croal, "Moviefone Learns to Listen," *Newsweek,* 135 (19) (May 8, 2000): 84; S. Gregory, S. Webster, and G. Huang, "Voice Pitch and Amplitude Convergence as a Metric of Quality in Dyadic Interviews," *Language & Communication,* 13 (3) (July 1993): 195–217; and Glen A. Buckman, "Uses of Voice-Pitch Analysis," *Journal of Advertising Research,* 20 (April 1980): 69–73.

41. Rinus Haaijer, "Response Latencies in the Analysis of Conjoint Choice Experiments," *Journal of Marketing Research* (August 2000): 376–382; Nicholas Vasilopoulos, "The Influence of Job Familiarity and Impression Management on Self-Report Measure Scale Scores and Response Latencies," *Journal of Applied Psychology,* 85 (1) (February 2000): 50; John N. Bassili and B. Stacey Scott, "Response Latency as a Signal to Question Problems in Survey Research," *Public Opinion Quarterly,* 60 (3) (Fall 1996): 390–399; and David A. Aaker, Richard P. Bagozzi, James M. Carman, and James M. MacLachlan, "On Using Response Latency to Measure Preference," *Journal of Marketing Research,* 17 (May 1980): 237–244.

42. Joseph Rydholm, "Design Inspiration," *Marketing Research Review* (January 2000); and *www.newellrubbermaid.com,* June 3, 2001.

43. Kimberly A. Neuendorf, *The Content Analysis Guidebook* (Thousand Oaks, CA: Sage Publications, 2002); and Cheng Lu Wang, "A Content Analysis of Connectedness vs. Separateness Themes Used in U.S. and PRC Print Advertisements," *International Marketing Review,* 18 (2) (2001): 145.

44. Laurel Wentz, "2002 Lookout: Global," *Advertising Age,* 23 (1) (January 7, 2002): 8; Michael Maynard, "Girlish Images Across Cultures: Analyzing Japanese Versus U.S. Seventeen Magazine Ads," *Journal of Advertising,* 28 (1) (Spring 1999): 39–48; Subir Sengupta, "The Influence of Culture on Portrayals of Women in Television Commercials: A Comparison Between the United States and Japan," *International Journal of Advertising,* 14 (4) (1995): 314–333; Charles S. Madden, Marjorie J. Caballero, and Shinya Matsukubo, "Analysis of Information Content in U.S. and Japanese Magazine Advertising," *Journal of Advertising,* 15, 3 (1986): 38–45; and *adv.asahi.com.*

45. Dan Verton, "SafeWeb Users Vulnerable," *Computerworld,* 36 (8) (February 18, 2002): 6; and Ruby Bayan, "Privacy Means Knowing Your Cookies," *Link-Up,* 18 (1) (January/February 2001): 22–23.

46. Gerald Berstell and Denise Nitterhouse, "Looking 'Outside the Box'," *Marketing Research: A Magazine of Management & Applications,* 9 (2) (Summer 1997): 4–13.

47. Kendra Parker, "How Do You Like Your Beef?" *American Demographics,* 22 (1) (January 2000): 35–37; and *www.beef.org.*

48. Bruce Keillor, "A Cross-Cultural/Cross-National Study of Influencing Factors and Socially Desirable Response Bias," *International Journal of Market Research* (First Quarter 2001): 63–84; C. L. Hung, "Canadian Business Pursuits in the PRC, Hong Kong, and Taiwan, and Chinese Perception of Canadians as Business Partners," *Multinational Business Review,* 6 (1) (Spring 1998): 73–82; and C. Min Han, Byoung-Woo Lee, Kong-Kyun Ro, "The Choice of a Survey Mode in Country Image Studies," *Journal of Business Research,* 29 (2) (February 1994): 151–162.

49. Richard Linnett, "Reebok Re-Brands for Hip-Hop Crowd," *Advertising Age,* 73 (4) (January 28, 2002): 3–4.

50. Steve Jarvis, "CMOR Finds Survey Refusal Rate Still Rising," *Marketing News,* 36 (3) (February 4, 2002): 4.

51. Marla Royne Stafford and Thomas F. Stafford, "Participant Observation and the Pursuit of Truth: Methodological and Ethical Considerations," *Journal of the Market Research Society,* 35 (January 1993): 63–76.

52. Guilherme D. Pires, "Ethnic Marketing Ethics," *Journal of Business Ethics,* 36 (1/2) (March 2002): 111–118; and C. N. Smith and J. A. Quelch, *Ethics in Marketing* (Homewood, IL: Richard D. Irwin, 1993).

53. Anonymous, "In-Stat Market Snapshot," *Wireless Week,* 8 (4) (January 28, 2002): 15; Deborah Mendez-Wilson, "PCIA Report Predicts Mobile Usage," *Wireless Week,* 8 (5) (February 4, 2002): 18; and Adam Creed, "AOL to Put Instant Messenger in Mobile Phones," *Newsbytes* (February 19, 2002).

# Chapter 7

1. Booth Moore, "Fashion Notes: Those '70s Bags Are Back in LeStyle, with a New Range of Looks," *The Los Angeles Times,* Record Edition (December 21, 2001): E.2; "LeSportsac Announces Latest International Expansion," *Showcase,* 20 (6) (December 1995): 67; "Surveys Help Settle Trade Dress Infringement Case," *Quirk's Marketing Research Review,* (October/November 1987): 16, 17, 33.

2. Anonymous, "In-Store Promo Drives Soda Sales, Study Says," *Drug Store News,* 23 (18) (December 17, 2001): 81; Robert Dwek, "Prediction of Success," *Marketing* (POP & Field Marketing Supplement) (April 17, 1997): XII–XIII; and "POP Radio Test Airs the Ads In Store," *Marketing News* (October 24, 1986): 16.

3. Michael Sobel, "Causal Inference in the Social Sciences," *Journal of the American Statistical Association,* 95 (450) (June 2000): 647–651; and R. Barker Bausell, *Conducting Meaningful Experiments* (Thousand Oaks, CA: Sage Publications, Inc., 1994).

4. Grant F. Gould and James L. Gould, *Chance and Causation: To Experimental Design and Statistica* (New York: W. H. Freeman & Company, 2001); and Robert F. Boruch, *Randomized Experiments for Planning and Evaluation* (Thousand Oaks, CA: Sage Publications, Inc., 1994).

5. Thomas Lee, "Experts Say Point-of-Purchase Advertising Can Influence Shoppers' Choices," *Knight Ridder Tribune Business*

*News* (January 19, 2002): 1; and Michele Witthaus, "POP Stars," *Marketing Week,* 20 (16) (July 17, 1997): 37–41.

6. John Liechty, Venkatram Ramaswamy, and Steven H. Cohen, "Choice Menus for Mass Customization: An Experimental Approach for Analyzing Customer Demand with an Application to a Web-Based Information Service," *Journal of Marketing Research,* 38 (2) (May 2001): 183–196; Gordon A. Wyner, "Experimental Design," *Marketing Research: A Magazine of Management & Applications,* 9 (3) (Fall 1997): 39–41; and Steven R. Brown and Lawrence E. Melamed, *Experimental Design and Analysis* (Newbury Park, CA: Sage Publications, 1990).

7. Paul W. Farris, "Overcontrol in Advertising Experiments," *Journal of Advertising Research* (November/December 2000): 73–78.

8. "CPGs Change Coupon Media Mix & Purchase Requirements," *NCH Marketing Services Press Release* (March 15, 2002): 1–4; John Fetto, "Redeeming Value," *American Demographics,* 23 (10) (October 2001): 25; Uri Ben-Zion, "The Optimal Face Value of a Discount Coupon," *Journal of Economics and Business,* 51 (2) (March/April 1999): 159–164; and Robert W. Shoemaker and Vikas Tibrewala, "Relating Coupon Redemption Rates to Past Purchasing of the Brand," *Journal of Advertising Research,* 25 (October/November 1985): 40–47.

9. In addition to internal and external validity, there also exist construct and statistical conclusion validity. Construct validity addresses the question of what construct, or characteristic, is in fact being measured and is discussed in Chapter 9 on measurement and scaling. Statistical conclusion validity addresses the extent and statistical significance of the covariation that exists in the data and is discussed in the chapters on data analysis. See Richard R. Klink and Daniel C. Smith, "Threats to the External Validity of Brand Extension Research," *Journal of Marketing Research,* 38 (3) (August 2001): 326–335.

10. Gilles Laurent, "Improving the External Validity of Marketing Models: A Plea for More Qualitative Input," *International Journal of Research in Marketing,* 17 (2) (September 2000): 177; Prashant Bordia, "Face-to-Face Computer-Mediated Communication: A Synthesis of the Experimental Literature," *Journal of Business Communication,* 34 (1) (January 1997): 99–120; and David M. Bowen, "Work Group Research: Past Strategies and Future Opportunities," *IEEE Transactions on Engineering Management,* 42 (1) (February 1995): 30–38; and John G. Lynch, Jr., "On the External Validity of Experiments in Consumer Research," *Journal of Consumer Research,* 9 (December 1982): 225–244.

11. Russell Winer, "Experimentation in the 21st Century: The Importance of External Validity," *Academy of Marketing Science,* 27 (3) (Summer 1999): 349–358; Chris Argyris, "Actionable Knowledge: Design Causality in the Service of Consequential Theory," *Journal of Applied Behavioral Science,* 32 (4) (December 1966): 390–406; John G. Lynch, Jr., "The Role of External Validity in Theoretical Research," B. J. Calder, L. W. Phillips, and Alice Tybout, "Beyond External Validity," and J. E. McGrath and D. Brinberg, "External Validity and the Research Process," *Journal of Consumer Research* (June 1983): 109–111, 112–114, and 115–124.

12. Paul Berger and Robert Maurer, *Experimental Design with Applications in Management, Engineering and the Sciences* (Boston: Boston University Press, 2002).

13. Paul R. Rosenbaum, "Attributing Effects to Treatment in Matched Observational Studies," *Journal of the American Statistical Association,* 97 (457) (March 2002): 183–192; and Lloyd S. Nelson, "Notes on the Use of Randomization in Experimentation," *Journal of Quality Technology,* 28 (1) (January 1996): 123–126.

14. Paul R. Rosenbaum, "Attributing Effects to Treatment in Matched Observational Studies," *Journal of the American Statistical Association,* 97 (457) (March 2002): 183–192; Marcus Selart, "Structure Compatability and Restructuring in Judgment and Choice," *Organizational Behavior & Human Decision Processes,* 65 (2) (February 1996): 106–116; and R. Barker Bausell, *Conducting Meaningful Experiments* (Thousand Oaks, CA: Sage Publications, Inc., 1994).

15. Beomsoo Kim, "Virtual Field Experiments for a Digital Economy: A New Research Methodology for Exploring an Information Economy," *Decision Support Systems,* 32 (3) (January 2002): 215; Eleni Chamis, "Auto Dealers Test Online Sales in 90-Day Experiment," *Washington Business Journal,* 19 (54) (May 11, 2001): 15; Betsy Spethmann, "Choosing a Test Market," *Brandweek,* 36 (19) (May 8, 1995): 42–43; and Andrew M. Tarshis, "Natural Sell-in Avoids Pitfalls of Controlled Tests," *Marketing News* (October 24, 1986): 14.

16. Other experimental designs are also available. See Connie M. Borror, "Evaluation of Statistical Designs for Experiments Involving Noise Variables," *Journal of Quality Technology,* 34 (1) (January 2002): 54–70; and Donald T. Campbell and M. Jean Russo, *Social Experimentation* (Thousand Oaks, CA: Sage Publications, 1999).

17. For an application of the Solomon four-group design, see Joe Ayres, "Are Reductions in CA an Experimental Artifact? A Solomon Four-Group Answer," *Communication Quarterly,* 48 (1) (Winter 2000): 19–26.

18. Duncac Simester, "Implementing Quality Improvement Programs Designed to Enhance Customer Satisfaction: Quasi Experiments in the United States and Spain," *Journal of Marketing Research,* 37 (1) (February 2000): 102–112; C. Moorman, "A Quasi Experiment to Assess the Consumer and Informational Determinants of Nutrition Information-Processing Activities—The Case of the Nutrition Labeling and Education Act," *Journal of Public Policy and Marketing,* 15 (1) (Spring 1996): 28–44.

19. Fred S. Zufryden, "Predicting Trial, Repeat, and Sales Response from Alternative Media Plans," *Journal of Advertising Research,* 40 (6) (November/December 2000): 65–72; Leonard M. Lodish, Magid M. Abraham, Jeanne Livelsberger, Beth Lubetkin, et al, "A Summary of Fifty-Five In-Market Experimental Estimates of the Long-Term Effects of TV Advertising," *Marketing Science* (Summer 1995): G133–G140; and Lakshman Krishnamurthi, Jack Narayan, and S. P. Raj, "Intervention Analysis of a Field Experiment to Assess the Buildup Effect of Advertising," *Journal of Marketing Research,* 23 (November 1986): 337–345.

20. See, for example, Anthony Vagnoni, "Fear of Funny Abating," *Advertising Age,* 73 (10) (March 11, 2002): 8–9; and M. G. Weinberger, H. Spotts, L. Campbell, and A. L. Parsons, "The Use and Effect of Humor in Different Advertising Media," *Journal of Advertising Research,* 35 (3) (May/June 1995): 44–56.

21. For a recent application of factorial designs, see Jaideep Sengupta and Gerald J. Gorn, "Absence Makes the Mind Grow Sharper: Effects of Element Omission on Subsequent Recall," *Journal of Marketing Research,* 39 (2) (May 2002): 186–201.

22. Michelle L. Roehm, Ellen Bolman Pullins, and Harper A. Roehm, Jr., "Designing Loyalty-Building Programs for

Packaged Goods Brands," *Journal of Marketing Research,* 39 (2) (May 2002): 202–213.

23. Niraj Dawar, "Impact of Product Harm Crises on Brand Equity: The Moderating Role of Consumer Expectations," *Journal of Marketing Research,* 37 (2) (May 2000): 215–226.

24. Vicki R. Lane, "The Impact of Ad Repetition and Ad Content on Consumer Perceptions of Incongruent Extensions," *Journal of Marketing* (Apr 2000): 80–91; J. Perrien, "Repositioning Demand Artifacts in Consumer Research," *Advances in Consumer Research,* 24 (1997): 267–271; and T. A. Shimp, E. M. Hyatt, and D. J. Snyder, "A Critical Appraisal of Demand Artifacts in Consumer Research," *Journal of Consumer Research,* 18 (3) (December 1991): 272–283.

25. Chezy Ofir and Itamar Simonson, "In Search of Negative Customer Feedback: The Effect of Expecting to Evaluate on Satisfaction Evaluations," *Journal of Marketing Research,* 38 (2) (May 2001): 170–182; and Gilles Laurent, "Improving the External Validity of Marketing Models: A Plea for More Qualitative Input," *International Journal of Research in Marketing,* 17 (2,3) (September 2000): 177.

26. Karen Blumenschein, "Hypothetical Versus Real Willingness to Pay in the Health Care Sector: Results from a Field Experiment," *Journal of Health Economics,* 20 (3) (May 2001): 441; and Richard M. Alston and Clifford Nowell, "Implementing the Voluntary Contribution Game: A Field Experiment," *Journal of Economic Behavior & Organization,* 31 (3) (December 1996): 357–368.

27. Grant F. Gould and James L. Gould, *Chance and Causation: To Experimental Design and Statistica* (New York: W. H. Freeman & Company, 2001); Hurbert M. Blalock, Jr., *Causal Inferences in Nonexperimental Research* (Chapel Hill: University of North Carolina Press, 1964).

28. In some situations, surveys and experiments can complement each other and may both be used. For example, the results obtained in laboratory experiments may be further examined in a field survey.

29. Cynthia Vinarsky, "Test Market for Smokeless Tobacco," *Knight Ridder Tribune Business News* (March 11, 2002): 1; Peter Romeo, "Testing, Testing," *Restaurant Business,* 97 (2) (January 15, 1998): 12.

30. Keith Lawrence, "Owensboro, Kentucky Could Be Next Test Market for New McDonald's Eatery Concept," *Knight Ridder Tribune Business News* (February 7, 2002): 1; Stephanie Thompson, "Tetley Tests Higher-Value Pitches," *Brandweek,* 38 (47) (December 15, 1997): 8; and Ed Rubinstein, "7-Eleven Tests Internet Kiosks in Seattle Market," *Nation's Restaurant News,* 31 (42) (October 20, 1997): 24.

31. Anonymous, "P&G Wields Axe on Failing Brands," *Grocer,* 224 (7509) (June 23, 2001): 18; and Tara Parker-Pope, "Frito-Lay to Begin Selling Wow! Chips Made with Olestra Later This Month," *The Wall Street Journal* (February 10, 1998): B2.

32. Anonymous, "Vaseline to Back Dermacare with Llm Ads Activity," *Marketing* (January 10, 2002): 4; and Sean Mehegan, "Vaseline Ups Ante via AntiBacterial," *Brandweek,* 38 (21) (May 26, 1997): 1, 6.

33. Anonymous, "Simulated Test Marketing," *Sloan Management Review,* 36 (2) (Winter 1995): 112.

34. Frank S. Costanza, "Exports Boost German Jewelry Industry," *National Jeweler,* 45 (8) (April 16, 2001): 57; and David Woodruff and Karen Nickel, "When You Think Deluxe, Think East Germany," *Business Week,* May 26, 1997: 124E2.

35. Anonymous, "The Disclosure Dilemma," *Workspan,* 45 (1) (January 2002): 72; and Bernd H. Schmitt, "Contextual Priming of Visual Information in Advertisements," *Psychology & Marketing,* 11 (1) (January/February 1994): 1–14.

36. Marlene de Laine, *Fieldwork, Participation and Practice: Ethics and Dilemmas in Qualitative Research* (Thousand Oaks, CA: Sage Publications, 2001); and Betsy Peterson, "Ethics, Revisited," *Marketing Research: A Magazine of Management & Applications,* 8 (4) (Winter 1996): 47–48.

37. Jim Milliot, "Barnes & Noble.com to Integrate Fatbrain," *Publishers Weekly,* 249 (5) (February 4, 2002): 9; Dan Verton, "Barnes & Noble Takes Popular Literature Digital," *Computerworld,* 35 (2) (January 8, 2001): 14; and Isabelle Sender, "Internet Coupons Driving Store Traffic," *Chain Store Age,* 73 (9) (September, 1997).

# Chapter 8

1. *www.fortune.com/lists/mostadmired/index.html*. April 3, 2002.

2. Stephen J. Newell, "The Development of a Scale to Measure Perceived Corporate Credibility," *Journal of Business Research* (June 2001): 235; Ken Gofton, "If it Moves, Measure It," *Marketing* (Marketing Technique Supplement (September 4, 1997): 17; and Jum C. Nunnally, *Psychometric Theory,* 2nd ed. (New York: McGraw-Hill, 1978), p. 3.

3. Subabrata Bobby Banerjee, "Corporate Environmentalism: The Construct and Its Measurement," *Journal of Business Research,* 55 (3) (March 2002): 177; and Stanley S. Stevens, "Mathematics, Measurement and Psychophysics," in Stanley S. Stevens, Ed., *Handbook of Experimental Psychology* (New York: John Wiley, 1951).

4. Helen M. Moshkovich, "Ordinal Judgments in Multiattribute Decision Analysis," *European Journal of Operational Research,* 137 (3) (March 16, 2002): 625; Wade D. Cook, Moshe Kress, and Lawrence M. Seiford, "On the Use of Ordinal Data in Data Envelopment Analysis," *Journal of the Operational Research Society,* 44 (2) (February 1993): 133–140; and William D. Perreault, Jr. and Forrest W. Young, "Alternating Least Squares Optimal Scaling: Analysis of Nonmetric Data in Marketing Research," *Journal of Marketing Research,* 17 (February 1980): 1–13.

5. Merja Halme, "Dealing with Interval Scale Data in Data Envelopment Analysis," *European Journal of Operational Research,* 137 (1) (February 16, 2002): 22; and Michael Lynn and Judy Harris, "The Desire for Unique Consumer Products: A New Individual Difference Scale," *Psychology & Marketing,* 14 (6) (September 1997): 601–616.

6. *www.fifa.com/index_E.html*. April 1, 2002.

7. For a discussion of these scales, refer to Delbert C. Miller and Neil J. Salkind, *Handbook of Research Design and Social Measurement,* 6th ed. (Thousand Oaks, CA: Sage Publications, 2002); Taiwo Amoo, "Overall Evaluation Rating Scales: An Assessment," *International Journal of Market Research* (Summer 2000): 301–311; and C. H. Coombs, "Theory and Methods of Social Measurement," L. Festinger and D. Katz, Eds., *Research Methods in the Behavioral Sciences* (New York: Holt, Rinehart & Winston, 1953).

8. However, there is some controversy regarding this issue. See Donald T. Campbell and M. Jean Russo, *Social Measurement* (Thousand Oaks, CA: Sage Publications, 2001); and T. Amoo, "Do the Numeric Values Influence Subjects' Responses to Rating Scales," *Journal of International Marketing and Marketing Research* (Feb 2001): 41.

9. Anonymous, "Competition Between Coca-Cola and Pepsi to Start," *Asiainfo Daily China News* (March 19, 2002): 1; Leah

Rickard, "Remembering New Coke," *Advertising Age,* 66 (16) (April 17, 1995): 6; and "Coke's Flip-Flop Underscores Risks of Consumer Taste Tests," *Wall Street Journal* (July 18, 1985): 25.

10. However, it is not necessary to evaluate all possible pairs of objects. Procedures such as cyclic designs can significantly reduce the number of pairs evaluated. A treatment of such procedures may be found in Albert C. Bemmaor and Udo Wagner, "A Multiple-Item Model of Paired Comparisons: Separating Chance from Latent Performance," *Journal of Marketing Research,* 37 (4) (November 2000): 514–524; and Naresh K. Malhotra, Arun K. Jain, and Christian Pinson, "The Robustness of MDS Configurations in the Case of Incomplete Data," *Journal of Marketing Research,* 25 (February 1988): 95–102.

11. For an advanced application involving paired comparison data, see Albert C. Bemmaor and Udo Wagner, "A Multiple-Item Model of Paired Comparisons: Separating Chance from Latent Performance," *Journal of Marketing Research,* 37 (4) (November 2000): 514–524.

12. Donald T. Campbell and M . Jean Russo, *Social Measurement* (Thousand Oaks, CA: Sage Publications, 2001); Rensis Likert, Sydney Roslow, and Gardner Murphy, "A Simple and Reliable Method of Scoring the Thurstone Attitude Scales," *Personnel Psychology,* 46 (3) (Autumn 1993): 689–690; L. L. Thurstone, *The Measurement of Values* (Chicago: University of Chicago Press, 1959). For an application of the case V procedure, see Naresh K. Malhotra, "Marketing Linen Services to Hospitals: A Conceptual Framework and an Empirical Investigation Using Thurstone's Case V Analysis," *Journal of Health Care Marketing,* 6 (March 1986): 43–50.

13. Anonymous, "Cranberry Juice in a Can," *Grocer,* 225 (7538) (January 26, 2002): 64; and The Beverage Network; *www.bevnet.com.*

14. Paul A. Bottomley, "Testing the Reliability of Weight Elicitation Methods: Direct Rating Versus Point Allocation," *Journal of Marketing Research,* 37 (4) (November 2000): 508–513; and Michael W. Herman and Waldemar W. Koczkodaj, "A Monte Carlo Study of Pairwise Comparison," *Information Processing Letters,* 57 (1) (January 15, 1996): 25–29.

15. *www.corebrand.com/brandpower/index.html.* April 1, 2002.

16. Tony Siciliano, "Magnitude Estimation," *Quirk's Marketing Research Review* (November 1999); Noel M. Noel and Nessim Hanna, "Benchmarking Consumer Perceptions of Product Quality with Price: An Exploration," *Psychology & Marketing,* 13 (6) (September 1996): 591–604; and Jan-Benedict E. M. Steenkamp and Dick R. Wittink, "The Metric Quality of Full-Profile Judgments and the Number of Attribute Levels Effect in Conjoint Analysis," *International Journal of Research in Marketing,* 11 (3) (June 1994): 275–286.

17. Roger Calantone, "Joint Ventures in China: A Comparative Study of Japanese, Korean, and U.S. Partners," *Journal of International Marketing,* 9 (1) (2001): 1–22; Joseph Marinelli and Anastasia Schleck, "Collecting, Processing Data for Marketing Research Worldwide," *Marketing News* (August 18, 1997): 12, 14; and Naresh K. Malhotra, "A Methodology for Measuring Consumer Preferences in Developing Countries," *International Marketing Review,* 5 (Autumn 1988): 52–66.

18. Anonymous, "Sales Down but Profits Up for Nissan," *Northern Echo* (January 31, 2002): 14.

19. Gael McDonald, "Cross-Cultural Methodological Issues in Ethical Research," *Journal of Business Ethics,* 27 (1/2) (September 2000): 89–104; and I. P. Akaah, "Differences in Research Ethics Judgments Between Male and Female Marketing Professionals," *Journal of Business Ethics,* 8 (1989): 375–381. See also Anusorn Singhapakdi, Scott J. Vitell, Kumar C. Rallapalli, and Kenneth L. Kraft, "The Perceived Role of Ethics and Social Responsibility: A Scale Development," *Journal of Business Ethics,* 15 (11) (November 1996): 1131–1140.

20. Amy Zuber, "Pizza Chains Top Customer Satisfaction Poll," *Nation's Restaurant News,* 36 (9) (March 4, 2002): 4–5; and *www.dominos.com.* April 1, 2002.

## Chapter 9

1. Anonymous, "Planned Rail Projects Still Moving Forward," *New York Construction News* (March 20, 2002): 10; Heidi Tolliver, "A Tale of Four Cities: How Paris, London, Florence and New York Measure—and React—to What Riders Want," *Mass Transit,* XXII (2) (March/April 1996): 22–30, 107; and *www.mta.nyc.ny.us/nyct/index.html.* April 14, 2002.

2. Bob Sperber, "McDonald's Targets Adults with 'Trust' Effort," *Brandweek,* 43 (14) (April 8, 2002): 6; William Murphy and Sidney Tang, "Continuous Likeability Measurement," *Marketing Research: A Magazine of Management & Applications,"* 10 (2) (Summer 1998): 28–35; and *www.perceptionanalyzer.com.*

3. Taiwoo Amoo and Hershey H. Friedman, "Overall Evaluation Rating Scales: An Assessment," *International Journal of Market Research,* 42 (3) (Summer 2000): 301–310; G. Albaum, "The Likert Scale Revisited—An Alternate Version," *Journal of the Market Research Society,* 39 (2) (April 1997): 331–348; C. J. Brody and J. Dietz, "On the Dimensionality of 2-Question Format Likert Attitude Scales," *Social Science Research,* 26 (2) (June 1997): 197–204; and Rensis Likert, "A Technique for the Measurement of Attitudes," *Archives of Psychology,* 140 (1932).

4. However, when the scale is multidimensional, each dimension should be summed separately. See Jeffrey M. Stanton, "Issues and Strategies for Reducing the Length of Self-Report Scales," *Personnel Psychology,* 55 (1) (Spring 2002): 167–194; and Jennifer L. Aaker, "Dimensions of Brand Personality," *Journal of Marketing Research,* 34 (August 1997): 347–356.

5. Jeongkoo Yoon, "A Dual Process Model of Organizational Commitment: Job Satisfaction and Organizational Support," *Work and Occupations,* 29 (1) (February 2002): 97–125; John P. Walsh and Shu-Fen Tseng, "The Effects of Job Characteristics on Active Effort at Work," *Work & Occupations,* 25 (1) (February 1998): 74–96; and George H. Lucas, Jr., A. Parasuraman, Robert A. Davis, and Ben M. Enis, "An Empirical Study of Salesforce Turnover," *Journal of Marketing,* 51 (July 1987): 34–59.

6. Rajesh Sethi, Daniel C. Smith, and C. Whan Park, "Cross-Functional Product Development Teams, Creativity, and the Innovativeness of New Consumer Products," *Journal of Marketing Research,* 38 (1) (February 2001): 73–85; and T. A. Chandler and C. J. Spies, "Semantic Differential Comparisons of Attributions and Dimensions Among Respondents from 7 Nations," *Psychological Reports,* 79 (3 pt 1) (December 1996): 747–758.

7. Delbert C. Miller and Neil J. Salkind, *Handbook of Research Design and Social Measurement,* 6th ed. (Thousand Oaks, CA: Sage Publications, 2002); and William O. Bearden and Richard G. Netemeyer, *Handbook of Marketing Scales: Multi-Item Measures for Marketing and Consumer Behavior Research* (Thousand Oaks, CA: Sage Publications, 1999).

8. Naresh K. Malhotra, "A Scale to Measure Self-Concepts, Person Concepts and Product Concepts," *Journal of Marketing Research,* 18 (November 1981): 456–464. See also Aron

O'Cass, "A Psychometric Evaluation of a Revised Version of the Lennox and Wolfe Revised Self-Monitoring Scale," *Psychology & Marketing* (May 2000): 397.

9. However, there is little difference in the results based on whether the data are ordinal or interval. See Shizuhiko Nishisato, *Measurement and Multivariate Analysis* (New York: Springer-Verlag, New York, 2002); and John Gaiton, "Measurement Scales and Statistics: Resurgence of an Old Misconception," *Psychological Bulletin,* 87 (1980): 564–567.

10. Chezy Ofir, "In Search of Negative Customer Feedback: The Effect of Expecting to Evaluate on Satisfaction Evaluations," *Journal of Marketing Research,* Chicago (May 2001): 170–182; Timothy H. Reisenwitz and G. Joseph Wimbish, Jr., "Over-the-Counter Pharmaceuticals: Exploratory Research of Consumer Preferences Toward Solid Oral Dosage Forms," *Health Marketing Quarterly,* 13 (4) (1996): 47–61; and S. Malhotra, S. Van Auken, and S. C. Lonial, "Adjective Profiles in Television Copy Testing," *Journal of Advertising Research* (August 1981): 21–25.

11. Michael K. Brady, "Performance Only Measurement of Service Quality: A Replication and Extension," *Journal of Business Research,* 55 (1) (January 2002): 17; Jan Stapel "About 35 Years of Market Research in the Netherlands," *Markonderzock Kwartaalschrift,* 2 (1969): 3–7.

12. Eugene W. Anderson, "Foundations of the American Customer Satisfaction Index," *Total Quality Management,* 11 (7) (September 2000): 5869–5882; A. M. Coleman, C. E. Norris, and C. C. Peterson, "Comparing Rating Scales of Different Lengths—Equivalence of Scores from 5-Point and 7-Point Scales," *Psychological Reports,* 80 (2) (April 1997): 355–362; Madhubalan Viswanathan, Mark Bergen, and Terry Childers, "Does a Single Response Category in a Scale Completely Capture a Response?" *Psychology & Marketing,* 13 (5) (August 1996): 457–479; and Eli P. Cox, III, "The Optimal Number of Response Alternatives for a Scale: A Review," *Journal of Marketing Research,* 17 (November 1980): 407–422.

13. Yadolah Dodge, "On Asymmetric Properties of the Correlation Coefficient in the Regression Setting," *The American Statistician,* 55 (1) (February 2001): 51–54; D. F. Alwin, "Feeling Thermometers Versus 7-Point Scales—Which Are Better," *Sociological Methods & Research,* 25 (3) (February 1997): 318–340; M. M. Givon and Z. Shapira, "Response to Rating Scales: A Theoretical Model and Its Application to the Number of Categories Problem," *Journal of Marketing Research* (November 1984): 410–419; and D. E. Stem, Jr., and S. Noazin, "The Effects of Number of Objects and Scale Positions on Graphic Position Scale Reliability," in R. F. Lusch, et al., *1985 AMA Educators' Proceedings* (Chicago: American Marketing Association, 1985): 370–372.

14. Bradford S. Jones, "Modeling Direction and Intensity in Semantically Balanced Ordinal Scales: An Assessment of Congressional Incumbent Approval," *American Journal of Political Science,* 44 (1) (January 2000): 174; D. Watson, "Correcting for Acquiescent Response Bias in the Absence of a Balanced Scale—An Application to Class-Consciousness," *Sociological Methods & Research,* 21 (1) (August 1992): 52–88; and H. Schuman and S. Presser, *Questions and Answers in Attitude Surveys* (New York: Academic Press, 1981), pp. 179–201.

15. Palmer Morrel-Samuels, "Getting the Truth into Workplace Surveys," *Harvard Business Review,* 80 (2) (February 2002): 111; and G. J. Spagna, "Questionnaires: Which Approach Do

You Use?" *Journal of Advertising Research,* (February/March 1984): 67–70.

16. Janet McColl-Kennedy, "Measuring Customer Satisfaction: Why, What and How," *Total Quality Management,* 11 (7) (September 2000): 5883–5896; Kathy A. Hanisch, "The Job Descriptive Index Revisited: Questions About the Question Mark," *Journal of Applied Psychology,* 77 (3) (June 1992): 377–382; and K. C. Schneider, "Uninformed Response Rate in Survey Research," *Journal of Business Research* (April 1985): 153–162.

17. T. Amoo, "Do Numeric Values Influence Subjects' Responses to Rating Scales," *Journal of International Marketing and Market Research* (February 2001): 41; K. M. Gannon and T. M. Ostrom, "How Meaning Is Given to Rating Scales—The Effects of Response Language on Category Activation," *Journal of Experimental Social Psychology,* 32 (4) (July 1996): 337–360; and H. H. Friedman and J. R. Leefer, "Label Versus Position in Rating Scales," *Journal of the Academy of Marketing Science,* (Spring 1981): 88–92.

18. D. F. Alwin, "Feeling Thermometers Versus 7-Point Scales—Which Are Better," *Sociological Methods & Research,* 25 (3) (February 1997): 318–340.

19. For recent constructions of multiitem scales, see Tom Brown, "The Customer Orientation of Service Workers: Personality Trait Effects on Self- and Supervisor-Performance Ratings," *Journal of Marketing Research,* 39 (1) (February 2002): 110–119; and Charla Mathwick, Naresh K. Malhotra, and Edward Rigdon, "Experiential Value: Conceptualization, Measurement and Application in the Catalog and Internet Shopping Environment," *Journal of Retailing,* 77 (2001): 39–56.

20. For example, see Leisa Reinecke Flynn and Dawn Pearcy, "Four Subtle Sins in Scale Development: Some Suggestions for Strengthening the Current Paradigm," *International Journal of Market Research,* 43 (4) (Fourth Quarter 2001): 409–423; and Maryon F. King, "Social Desirability Bias: A Neglected Aspect of Validity Testing," *Psychology & Marketing,* 17 (2) (February 2000): 79.

21. Stephania H. Davis, "Smart Products for Smart Marketing," *Telephony,* 234 (9) (March 2, 1998): 66; and Erin Anderson, Wujin Chu, and Barton Weitz, "Industrial Purchasing: An Empirical Exploration of the Buyclass Framework," *Journal of Marketing,* 51 (July 1987): 71–86.

22. Walter C. Borman, "An Examination of the Comparative Reliability, Validity, and Accuracy of Performance Ratings Made Using Computerized Adaptive Rating Scales," *Journal of Applied Psychology,* 86 (5) (October 2001): 965; and Eric A. Greenleaf, "Improving Rating Scale Measures by Detecting and Correcting Bias Components in Some Response Styles," *Journal of Marketing Research,* 29 (May 1992): 176–188.

23. Bruce Thompson, *Score Reliability: Contemporary Thinking on Reliability Issues* (Thousand Oaks, CA: Sage Publications, 2002); Pritibhushan Sinha, "Determination of Reliability of Estimations Obtained with Survey Research: A Method of Simulation," *International Journal of Market Research,* 42 (3) (Summer 2000): 311–317; E. J. Wilson, "Research Design Effects on the Reliability of Rating Scales in Marketing—An Update on Churchill and Peter," *Advances in Consumer Research,* 22 (1995): 360–365; William D. Perreault, Jr. and Laurence E. Leigh, "Reliability of Nominal Data Based on Qualitative Judgments," *Journal of Marketing Research,* 25 (May 1989): 135–148; and J. Paul Peter, "Reliability: A Review

of Psychometric Basics and Recent Marketing Practices," *Journal of Marketing Research,* 16 (February 1979): 6–17.

24. Donald T. Campbell and M . Jean Russo, *Social Measurement* (Thousand Oaks, CA: Sage Publications, 2001); Simon S. K. Lam and Ka S. Woo, "Measuring Service Quality: A Test-Retest Reliability Investigation of SERVQUAL," *Journal of the Market Research Society,* 39 (2) (April 1997): 381–396.

25. David Hunt, *Measurement and Scaling in Statistics* (London, UK: Edward Arnold, 2001); David Armstrong, Ann Gosling, John Weinman, and Theresa Marteau, "The Place of Inter-Rater Reliability in Qualitative Research: An Empirical Study," *Sociology: The Journal of the British Sociological Association,* 31 (3) (August 1997): 597–606; and M. N. Segal, "Alternate Form Conjoint Reliability," *Journal of Advertising Research,* 4 (1984): 31–38.

26. Tom J. Brown, John C. Mowen, D. Todd Donavan, and Jane W. Licata, "The Customer Orientation of Service Workers: Personality Trait Effects on Self- and Supervisor-Performance Ratings," *Journal of Marketing Research,* 39 (1) (February 2002): 110–119; Robert A. Peterson, "A Meta-Analysis of Chronbach's Coefficient Alpha," *Journal of Consumer Research,* 21 (September 1994): 381–391; and L. J Cronbach, "Coefficient Alpha and the Internal Structure of Tests," *Psychometrika,* 16 (1951): 297–334.

27. Patrick Y. K. Chau and Kai Lung Hui, "Identifying Early Adopters of New IT Products: A Case of Windows 95," *Information & Management,* 33 (5) (May 28, 1998): 225–230.

28. Gilad Chen, "Validation of a New General Self-Efficacy Scale," *Organizational Research Methods,* 4 (1) (January 2001): 62–83; D. G. Mctavish, "Scale Validity–A Computer Content-Analysis Approach," *Social Science Computer Review,* 15 (4) (Winter 1997): 379–393; and J. Paul Peter, "Construct Validity: A Review of Basic Issues and Marketing Practices," *Journal of Marketing Research,* 18 (May 1981): 133–145.

29. For further details on validity, see Bruce Keillor, "A Cross-Cultural/Cross-National Study of Influencing Factors and Socially Desirable Response Biases," *International Journal of Market Research* (First Quarter 2001): 63–84; M. Joseph Sirgy, Dhruv Grewal, Tamara F. Mangleburg, Jae-ok Park et al., "Assessing the Predictive Validity of Two Methods of Measuring Self-Image Congruence," *Journal of the Academy of Marketing Science,* 25 (3) (Summer 1997): 229–241; and Rosann L. Spiro and Barton A. Weitz, "Adaptive Selling: Conceptualization, Measurement, and Nomological Validity," *Journal of Marketing Research,* 27 (February 1990): 61–69.

30. For a discussion of generalizability theory and its applications in marketing research, see Karen L. Middleton, "Socially Desirable Response Sets: The Impact of Country Culture," *Psychology and Marketing* (February 2000): 149; Shuzo Abe, Richard P. Bagozzi, and Pradip Sadarangani, "An Investigation of Construct Validity and Generalizability of the Self-Concept: Self-Consciousness in Japan and the United States," *Journal of International Consumer Marketing,* 8 (3, 4) (1996): 97–123; and Joseph O. Rentz, "Generalizability Theory: A Comprehensive Method for Assessing and Improving the Dependability of Marketing Measures," *Journal of Marketing Research,* 24 (February 1987): 19–28.

31. Matthew Myers, "Academic Insights: An Application of Multiple-Group Causal Models in Assessing Cross-Cultural Measurement Equivalence," *Journal of International Marketing,* 8 (4) (2000): 108–121; and Timothy R. Hinkin, "A Review of Scale Development Practices in the Study of Organizations," *Journal of Management,* 21 (5) (1995): 967–988.

32. Alan Page Fiske, "Using Individualism and Collectivism to Compare Cultures—A Critique of the Validity and Measurement of the Constructs: Comment on Oyserman," *Psychological Bulletin,* 128 (1) (January 2002): 78; Michael R. Mullen, George R. Milne, and Nicholas M. Didow, "Determining Cross-Cultural Metric Equivalence in Survey Research: A New Statistical Test," *Advances in International Marketing,* 8 (1996): 145–157; and E. Gencturk, T. L. Childers, and R. W. Ruekert, "International Marketing Involvement—The Construct, Dimensionality, and Measurement," *Journal of International Marketing,* 3 (4) (1995): 11–37.

33. Alan L. Unikel, "Imitation Might Be Flattering, but Beware of Trademark Infringement," *Marketing News,* 21 (19) (September 11, 1997): 20021; and Betsy Mckay, "Xerox Fights Trademark Battle," *Advertising Age International* (April 27, 1992).

34. Denny Hatch, "How Truthful Is Your Offer?" *Target Marketing,* 24 (4) (April 2001): 94.

35. Naresh K. Malhotra, Sung S. Kim, and James Agarwal, "Internet Users' Information Privacy Concerns (IUIPC): The Construct, the Scale, and a Nomological Framework," Working Paper, Georgia Institute of Technology, 2002.

# Chapter 10

1. Patricia Kelly, "Questionnaire Design, Printing, and Distribution," *Government Information Quarterly,* 17 (2) (2000): 147.

2. S.L. Payne, *The Art of Asking Questions* (Princeton, NJ: Princeton University Press, 1951): 141. See also Michael Schrage, "Survey Says," *Adweek Magazines' Technology Marketing,* 22 (1) (January 2002): 11; and Bill Gillham, *Developing a Questionnaire* (New York: Continuum International Publishing Group, 2000).

3. These guidelines are drawn from several books on questionnaire design. See, for example, Marco Vriens, "Split-Questionnaire Designs: A New Tool in Survey Design and Panel Management," *Marketing Research,* 13 (2) (Summer 2001): 14–19; Stephen Jenkins, "Automating Questionnaire Design and Construction," *Journal of the Market Research Society* (Winter 1999–2000): 79–95; Bill Gillham, *Developing a Questionnaire* (New York: Continuum International Publishing Group, 2000); Robert A. Peterson, *Constructing Effective Questionnaires* (Thousand Oaks, CA: Sage Publications, 2000); Howard Schuman and Stanley Presser, *Questions & Answers in Attitude Survey* (Thousand Oaks, CA: Sage Publications, Inc., 1996); Arlene Fink, *How to Ask Survey Questions* (Thousand Oaks, CA: Sage Publications, Inc., 1995); and Floyd J. Fowler, Jr., *Improving Survey Questions* (Thousand Oaks, CA: Sage Publications, Inc., 1995).

4. Darlene B. Bordeaux, "Interviewing—Part II: Getting the Most Out of Interview Questions," *Motor Age,* 121 (2) (February 2002): 38–40; Thomas T. Semon, "Better Questions Means More Honesty," *Marketing News,* 34 (17) (August 14, 2000): 10; and Thomas T. Semon, "Asking 'How Important' Is Not Enough," *Marketing News,* 31 (16) (August 4, 1997): 19.

5. Jennifer Hess, "The Effects of Person-Level Versus Household-Level Questionnaire Design on Survey Estimates and Data Quality," *Public Opinion Quarterly,* 65 (4) (Winter 2001): 574–584.

6. Timothy R. Graeff, "Uninformed Response Bias in Telephone Surveys," *Journal of Business Research,* 55 (3) (March 2002): 251; Rachel Miller, "Counting the Cost of Response Rates," *Marketing* (January 18, 2001): 37–38; Arthur Sterngold, Rex H.

Warland, and Robert O. Herrmann, "Do Surveys Overstate Public Concerns?" *Public Opinion Quarterly,* 58 (20 (Summer 1994): 255–263; and D. I. Hawkins and K. A. Coney, "Uninformed Response Error in Survey Research," *Journal of Marketing Research* (August 1981): 373.

7. Barbel Knauper, "Filter Questions and Question Interpretation: Presuppositions at Work," *Public Opinion Quarterly,* 62 (1) (Spring 1998): 70–78; and George F. Bishop, Robert W. Oldendick, and Alfred J. Tuchfarber, "Effects of Filter Questions in Public Opinion Surveys," *Public Opinion Quarterly,* 46 (Spring 1982): 66–85.

8. Timothy R. Graeff, "Uninformed Response Bias in Telephone Surveys," *Journal of Business Research,* 55 (3) (March 2002): 251.

9. Eunkyu Lee, Michael Y. Hu, and Rex S. Toh, "Are Consumer Survey Results Distorted? Systematic Impact of Behavioral Frequency and Duration on Survey Response Errors," *Journal of Marketing Research,* 37 (1) (February 2000): 125–133; Solomon Dutka and Lester R. Frankel "Measuring Response Error," *Journal of Advertising Research,* 37 (1) (January/February 1997): 33–39; and Terry Haller, *Danger: Marketing Researcher at Work* (Westport, CT: Quorum Books, 1983): 149.

10. George D. Gaskell, "Telescoping of Landmark Events: Implications for Survey Research," *Public Opinion Quarterly,* 64 (1) (Spring 2000): 77–89; Geeta Menon, Priya Raghubir, and Norbert Schwarz, "Behavioral Frequency Judgments: An Accessibility-Diagnosticity Framework," *Journal of Consumer Research,* 22 (2) (September 1995): 212–228; and William A. Cook, "Telescoping and Memory's Other Tricks," *Journal of Advertising Research* (February/March 1987): 5–8.

11. Mike France, "Why Privacy Notices Are a Sham," *Business Week* (June 18, 2001): 82; R. P. Hill, "Researching Sensitive Topics in Marketing—The Special Case of Vulnerable Populations," *Journal of Public Policy & Marketing,* 14 (1) (Spring 1995): 143–148.

12. Patrick Hanrahan, "Mine Your Own Business," *Target Marketing* (Feb 2000): 32; Roger Tourangeau and Tom W. Smith, "Asking Sensitive Questions: The Impact of Data-Collection Mode, Question Format, and Question Context," *Public Opinion Quarterly,* 60 (20) (Summer 1996): 275–304; and Kent H. Marquis et al., *Response Errors in Sensitive Topic Survey: Estimates, Effects, and Correction Options* (Santa Monica, CA: Rand Corporation, 1981).

13. Hans Baumgartner and Jan-Benedict E. M. Steenkamp, "Response Styles in Marketing Research: A Cross-National Investigation," *Journal of Marketing Research,* 38 (2) (May 2001): 143–156; and Priya Raghubir and Geeta Menon, "Asking Sensitive Questions: The Effects of Type of Referent and Frequency Wording in Counterbiasing Methods," *Psychology & Marketing,* 13 (7) (October 1996): 633–652.

14. For applications, see Ernest R. Larkins, Evelyn C. Hume, and Bikramjit S. Garcha, "The Validity of the Randomized Response Method in Tax Ethics Research," *Journal of Applied Business Research,* 13 (3) (Summer 1997): 25–32; Brian K. Burton and Janet P. Near, "Estimating the Incidence of Wrongdoing and Whistle-Blowing: Results of a Study Using Randomized Response Technique," *Journal of Business Ethics,* 14 (January 1995): 17–30; and D. E. Stem, Jr. and R. K. Steinhorst, "Telephone Interview and Mail Questionnaire Applications of the Randomized Response Model," *Journal of the American Statistical Association* (September 1984): 555–564.

15. Mildred L. Patten, *Questionnaire Research: A Practical Guide* (Los Angeles: Pyrczak Publishing, 2001); and Lynn M. Newman, "That's a Good Question," *American Demographics,* (Marketing Tools) (June 1995): 10–13.

16. Roel Popping, *Computer-Assisted Text Analysis* (Thousand Oaks, CA: Sage Publications, 2000); and Serge Luyens, "Coding Verbatims by Computers," *Marketing Research: A Magazine of Management & Applications,* 7 (2) (Spring 1995): 20–25.

17. Based on a marketing research project conducted by the author. See also Steven G. Rogelberg, "Attitudes Toward Surveys: Development of a Measure and Its Relationship to Respondent Behavior," *Organizational Research Methods,* 4 (1) (January 2001): 3–25.

18. Anne-Marie Pothas, "Customer Satisfaction: Keeping Tabs on the Issues That Matter," *Total Quality Management,* 12 (1) (January 2001): 83; and Kevin W. Mossholder, Randall P. Settoon, Stanley G. Harris, and Achilles A. Armenakis, "Measuring Emotion in Open-Ended Survey Responses: An Application of Textual Data Analysis," *Journal of Management,* 21 (2) (1995): 335–355.

19. Debra Javeline, "Response Effects in Polite Cultures," *Public Opinion Quarterly,* 63 (1) (Spring 1999): 1–27; and Jon A. Krosnick and Duane F. Alwin, "An Evaluation of a Cognitive Theory of Response-Order Effects in Survey Measurement," *Public Opinion Quarterly* (Summer 1987): 201–219. Niels J. Blunch, "Position Bias in Multiple-Choice Questions," *Journal of Marketing Research,* 21 (May 1984): 216–220, has argued that position bias in multiple-choice questions cannot be eliminated by rotating the order of the alternatives. This viewpoint is contrary to the common practice.

20. Eleanor Singer, "Experiments with Incentives in Telephone Surveys," *Public Opinion Quarterly,* 64 (2) (Summer 2000): 171–188; and Howard Schuman and Stanley Presser, *Questions & Answers in Attitude Survey* (Thousand Oaks, CA: Sage Publications, Inc., 1996).

21. Karen Blumenschein, "Hypothetical Versus Real Willingness to Pay in the Health Care Sector: Results from a Field Experiment," *Journal of Health Economics,* 20 (3) (May 2001): 441; Joseph A. Herriges and Jason F. Shogren, "Starting Point Bias in Dichotomous Choice Valuation with Follow-Up Questioning," *Journal of Environmental Economics & Management,* 30 (1) (January 1996): 112–131; and R. W. Mizerski, J. B. Freiden, and R. C. Green, Jr., "The Effect of the 'Don't Know' Option on TV Ad Claim Recognition Tests," *Advances in Consumer Research,* 10 (Association for Consumer Research, 1983): 283–287.

22. Frederick G. Conrad, "Clarifying Question Meaning in a Household Telephone Survey," *Public Opinion Quarterly,* 64 (1) (Spring 2000): 1–27; Michael McBurnett, "Wording of Questions Affects Responses to Gun Control Issue," *Marketing News,* 31 (1) (January 6, 1997): 12; and M. Wanke, N. Schwarz, and E. Noelle-Neumann, "Asking Comparative Questions: The Impact of the Direction of Comparison," *Public Opinion Quarterly,* 59 (3) (Fall 1995): 347–372.

23. Joseph Rydholm, "Syndicated Survey Monitors Airline Performance Around the World," *Quirk's Marketing Research Review* (November, 2000), online at *www.quirks.com/articles/article_print.asp?arg_articleid=623,* March 23, 2001.

24. Richard Colombo, "A Model for Diagnosing and Reducing Nonresponse Bias," *Journal of Advertising Research,* 40 (1/2) (January/April 2000): 85–93; G. S. Omura, "Correlates of Item Nonresponse," *Journal of the Market Research Society* (October 1983): 321–330; and S. Presser, "Is Inaccuracy on Factual Survey Items Item-Specific or Respondent-Specific?" *Public Opinion Quarterly* (Spring 1984): 344–355.

25. Christopher R. Bollinger, "Estimation with Response Error and Nonresponse: Food-Stamp Participation in the SIPP," *Journal of Business & Economic Statistics,* 19 (2) (April 2001): 129–141; and Nancy Johnson Stout, "Questionnaire Design Workshop Helps Market Researchers Build Better Surveys," *Health Care Strategic Management,* 12 (7) (July 1994): 10–11.

26. Bill Gillham, *Developing a Questionnaire* (New York: Continuum International Publishing Group, 2000); and Lida C. Saltz, "How to Get Your News Release Published,"*Journal of Accountancy,* 182 (5) (November 1996): 89–91.

27. Mick P. Couper, "Web Surveys: A Review of Issues and Approaches," *Public Opinion Quarterly,* 64 (4) (Winter 2000): 464–494; Brad Edmondson, "How to Spot a Bogus Poll," *American Demographics,* 8 (10) (October 1996): 10–15; and John O'Brien, "How Do Market Researchers Ask Questions?" *Journal of the Market Research Society,* 26 (April 1984): 93–107.

28. Peter M. Chisnall, "Marketing Research: State of the Art Perspectives," *International Journal of Market Research,* 44 (1) (First Quarter 2002): 122–125; and Paul R. Abramson and Charles W. Ostrom, "Question Wording and Partisanship," *Public Opinion Quarterly,* 58 (1) (Spring 1994): 21–48.

29. Bob Becker, "Take Direct Route When Data Gathering," *Marketing News,* 33 (20) (September 27, 1999): 29–30; and "Don't Lead: You May Skew Poll Results," *Marketing News,* 30 (12) (June 3, 1996): H37.

30. Bill Gillham, *Developing a Questionnaire* (New York: Continuum International Publishing Group, 2000); Raymond J. Adamek, "Public Opinion and Roe v. Wade: Measurement Difficulties," *Public Opinion Quarterly,* 58 (3) (Fall 1994): 409–418; and E. Noelle-Neumann and B. Worcester, "International Opinion Research," *European Research* (July 1984): 124–131.

31. Ming Ouyand, "Estimating Marketing Persistence on Sales of Consumer Durables in China," *Journal of Business Research,* 55 (4) (April 2002): 337; Jacob Jacoby and George J. Szybillo, "Consumer Research in FTC Versus Kraft (1991): A Case of Heads We Win, Tails You Lose?" *Journal of Public Policy & Marketing,* 14 (1) (Spring 1995): 1–14; and E. D. Jaffe and I. D. Nebenzahl, "Alternative Questionnaire Formats for Country Image Studies," *Journal of Marketing Research* (November 1984): 463–471.

32. Howard Schuman and Stanley Presser, *Questions & Answers in Attitude Survey* (Thousand Oaks, CA: Sage Publications, Inc., 1996); and Jon A. Krosnick and Duane F. Alwin, "An Evaluation of a Cognitive Theory of Response-Order Effects in Survey Measurement," *Public Opinion Quarterly* (Summer 1987): 201–219.

33. Rating a brand on specific attributes early in a survey may affect responses to a later overall brand evaluation. For example, see Larry M. Bartels, "Question Order and Declining Faith in Elections," *Public Opinion Quarterly,* 66 (1) (Spring 2002): 67–79; and Barbara A Bickart, "Carryover and Backfire Effects in Marketing Research," *Journal of Marketing Research,* 30 (February 1993): 52–62.

34. Peter D. Watson, "Adolescents' Perceptions of a Health Survey Using Multimedia Computer-Assisted Self-Administered Interview," *Australian and New Zealand Journal of Public Health,* 25 (6) (December 2001): 520; Fern K. Willits and Bin Ke, "Part-Whole Question Order Effects: Views of Rurality," *Public Opinion Quarterly,* 59 (3) (Fall 1995): 392–403; and Donald J. Messmer and Daniel J. Seymour, "The Effects of Branching on Item Nonresponse," *Public Opinion Quarterly,* 46 (Summer 1982): 270–277.

35. David Zatz, "Create Effective E-Mail Surveys," *HRMagazine,* 45 (1) (January 2000): 97–103; and George R. Milne, "Consumer Participation in Mailing Lists: A Field Experiment," *Journal of Public Policy & Marketing,* 16 (2) (Fall 1997): 298–309.

36. Jon Van, "New Technology, Fast Internet Connections Give Researchers Easy Data Access," *Knight Ridder Tribune Business News* (February 3, 2002): 1; "A World Press Model Debuts," *Graphic Arts Monthly,* 66 (6) (June 1994): 66.

37. Frederick G. Conrad, "Clarifying Questions Meaning in a Household Telephone Survey," *Public Opinion Quarterly,* 64 (1) (Spring 2000): 1–27; E. Martin and A. E. Polivka, "Diagnostics for Redesigning Survey Questionnaires—Measuring Work in the Current Population Survey," *Public Opinion Quarterly,* 59 (4) (Winter 1995): 547–567; and Adamantios Diamantopoulos, Nina Reynolds, and Bodo B. Schlegelmilch, "Pretesting in Questionnaire Design: The Impact of Respondent Characteristics on Error Detection," *Journal of the Market Research Society,* 36 (October 1994): 295–314.

38. Bill Gillham, *Developing a Questionnaire* (New York: Continuum International Publishing Group, 2000); Nina Reynolds, A. Diamantopoulos, and Bodo B. Schlegelmilch, "Pretesting in Questionnaire Design: A Review of the Literature and Suggestions for Further Research," *Journal of the Market Research Society,* 35 (April 1993): 171–182.

39. Donald J. MacLaurin and Tanya L. MacLaurin, "Customer Perceptions of Singapore's Theme Restaurants," *Cornell Hotel and Restaurant Administration Quarterly* (June 2000) 41 (3): 75–85; and *www.tourismsingapore.com/frameset.asp*

40. Mark A. Davis, "Measuring Ethical Ideology in Business Ethics: A Critical Analysis of the Ethics Position Questionnaire," *Journal of Business Ethics,* 32 (1) (July 2001): 35–53; and R. W. Armstrong, "An Empirical Investigation of International Marketing Ethics: Problems Encountered by Australian Firms," *Journal of Business Ethics,* 11 (1992): 161–171.

41. Raquel Benbunan-Fich, "Using Protocol Analysis to Evaluate the Usability of a Commercial Web Site," *Information & Management,* 39 (2) (December 2001): 151; and Marshall Rice, "What Makes Users Revisit a Web Site?" *Marketing News,* 31 (March 17, 1997): 12.

42. H. Lee Murphy, "Survey Software Gets Simpler, More Effective," *Marketing News,* 35 (January 29, 2001): 4–6.

# Chapter 11

1. Joseph Rydholm, "Focus Groups Shape Ads Designed to Expand Market for Federal Duck Stamp Program," *Quirk's Marketing Research Review* (March 2000), online at *www.quirks.com/articles/article_print.asp?arg_articleid= 566,* January 30, 2002.

2. Anonymous, "Random Sampling," *Marketing News* (Jul 16, 2001): 10; Steve Wilcox, "Sampling and Controlling a TV Audience Measurement Panel," *International Journal of Market Research,* 42 (4) (Winter 2000): 413–430; V. Verma and T. Le, "An Analysis of Sampling Errors for the Demographic and Health Surveys," *International Statistical Review,* 64 (3) (December 1966): 265–294; and H. Assael and J. Keon, "Nonsampling vs. Sampling Errors in Sampling Research," *Journal of Marketing* (Spring 1982): 114–123.

3. Bob Brewin, "U.S. Census Bureau Plans for First Paperless Tally in 2010," *Computerworld,* 36 (12) (March 18, 2002): 5; Simon Marquis, "I'm a Research Addict but Even I Can See the Census Is a Waste," *Marketing* (May 10, 2001): 22; and "Frequently Asked Questions About Census 2000," *Indiana Business Review,* 72 (8) (Summer 1997): 10.

4. Anonymous, "Random Sampling: Bruised, Battered, Bowed," *Marketing News,* 36 (5) (March 4, 2002): 12; Arlene Fink, *How to Sample in Surveys* (Thousand Oaks, CA: Sage Publications, Inc, 1995); Martin R. Frankel, "Sampling Theory," in Peter H. Rossi, James D. Wright, and Andy B. Anderson, Eds., *Handbook of Survey Research* (Orlando, FL: Academic Press, 1983): 21–67; and R. M. Jaeger, *Sampling in Education and the Social Sciences* (New York: Longman, 1984): 28–29.

5. Jerome P. Reiter, "Topics in Survey Sampling/Finite Population Sampling and Inference: A Prediction Approach," *Journal of the American Statistical Association,* 97 (457) (March 2002): 357–358; Gary T. Henry, *Practical Sampling* (Thousand Oaks, CA: Sage Publications, Inc, 1995); and Seymour Sudman, "Applied Sampling," in Peter H. Rossi, James D. Wright, and Andy B. Anderson, Eds., *Handbook of Survey Research* (Orlando, FL: Academic Press, 1983): 145–194.

6. Mick P. Couper, "Web Surveys: A Review of Issues and Approaches," *Public Opinion Quarterly,* 64 (4) (Winter 2000): 464–494; and Wayne Smith, Paul Mitchell, Karin Attebo, and Stephen Leeder, "Selection Bias from Sampling Frames: Telephone Directory and Electoral Roll Compared with Door-to-Door Population Census: Results from the Blue Mountain Eye Study," *Australian & New Zealand Journal of Public Health,* 21 (2) (April 1997): 127–133.

7. For the effect of sample frame error on research results, see Gregory B. Murphy, "The Effects of Organizational Sampling Frame Selection," *Journal of Business Venturing,* 17 (3) (May 2002): 237; and Kelly E. Fish, James H. Barnes, and Benjamin F. Banahan III, "Convenience or Calamity: Pharmaceutical Study Explores the Effects of Sample Frame Error on Research Results," *Journal of Health Care Marketing,* 14 (Spring 1994): 45–49.

8. Sean Mussenden, "Florida Tourism Leaders Say Industry is Recovering Slowly," *Knight Ridder Tribune Business News* (March 22, 2002): 1; "The Many Faces of Florida," *Association Management* (A Guide to Florida Supplement) (April 1997): 3; and "Florida Travel Habits Subject of Phone Survey," *Quirk's Marketing Research Review* (May 1987): 10, 11, 31, 56, 60.

9. Linda Ritchie, "Empowerment and Australian Community Health Nurses Work with Aboriginal Clients: The Sociopolitical Context," *Qualitative Health Research,* 11 (2) (March 2001): 190–205.

10. Kate Maddox, "XIX Winter Olympics: Marketing Hot Spot," *B to B,* 87 (2) (February 11, 2002): 1–2.

11. Steven K. Thompson, *Sampling* (New York: John Wiley & Sons, 2002); Seymour Sudman "Sampling in the Twenty-First Century," *Academy of Marketing Science Journal,* 27 (2) (Spring 1999): 269–277; and Leslie Kish, *Survey Sampling* (New York: John Wiley, 1965): 552.

12. Patricia M. Getz, "Implementing the New Sample Design for the Current Employment Statistics Survey," *Business Economics,* 35 (4) (October 2000): 47–50; "Public Opinion: Polls Apart," *Economist,* 336 (7927) (August 12, 1995): 48; and Seymour Sudman, "Improving the Quality of Shopping Center Sampling," *Journal of Marketing Research,* 17 (November 1980): 423–431.

13. For a recent application of snowball sampling, see Lisa Maher, "Risk Behaviors of Young Indo-Chinese Injecting Drug Users in Sydney and Melbourne," *Australian and New Zealand Journal of Public Health* (February 2001): 50–54; Gary L. Frankwick, James C. Ward, Michael D. Hutt, and Peter H. Reingen, "Evolving Patterns of Organizational Beliefs in the Formation of Strategy," *Journal of Marketing,* 58 (April 1994): 96–110.

14. If certain procedures for listing members of the rare population are followed strictly, the snowball sample can be treated as a probability sample See S. Sampath, *Sampling Theory and Methods* (Boca Raton, FL: CRC Press, 2000); Gary T. Henry, *Practical Sampling* (Thousand Oaks, CA: Sage Publications, Inc, 1995); and Graham Kalton and Dallas W. Anderson, "Sampling Rare Populations," *Journal of the Royal Statistical Association* (1986): 65–82.

15. Lisa Maher, "Risk Behaviors of Young Indo-Chinese Injecting Drug Users in Sydney and Melbourne," *Australian and New Zealand Journal of Public Health* (February 2001): 50–54.

16. When the sampling interval, $i$, is not a whole number, the easiest solution is to use as the interval the nearest whole number below or above $i$. If rounding has too great an effect on the sample size, add or delete the extra cases.

17. For recent applications of systematic random sampling, see Phyllis MacFarlane, "Structuring and Measuring the Size of Business Markets," *International Journal of Market Research,* 44 (1) (First Quarter 2002): 7–30; Hailin Qu and Isabella Li, "The Characteristics and Satisfaction of Mainland Chinese Visitors to Hong Kong," *Journal of Travel Research,* 35 (4) (Spring 1997): 37–41; and Goutam Chakraborty, Richard Ettenson, and Gary Gaeth, "How Consumers Choose Health Insurance," *Journal of Health Care Marketing,* 14 (Spring 1994): 21–33.

18. Ed Garsten, "Poll: Phone Ban Support Tepid," *Chicago Tribune* (July 23, 2001): 9.

19. For a recent application of stratified random sampling, see Gunnar Kjell, "The Level-Based Stratified Sampling Plan," *Journal of the American Statistical Association,* 95 (452) (December 2000): 1185–1191; and Samaradasa Weerahandi and Soumyo Moitra, "Using Survey Data to Predict Adoption and Switching for Services," *Journal of Marketing Research,* 32 (February 1995): 85–96.

20. Anonymous, "Charge, Losses Stifle Growth," *Business Insurance,* 36 (6) (February 11, 2002): 2; and Joanne Gallucci, "Employees with Home Internet Access Want Online Retirement Plans CIGNA Retirement & Investment Services Study Reveals," *PR Newswire,* June 27, 2000.

21. "Jeff D. Opdyke and Carrick Mollenkamp, "Yes, You Are 'High Net Worth,' " *The Wall Street Journal* (May 21, 2002): D1, D3; and Thomas J. Stanley and Murphy A. Sewall, "The Response of Affluent Consumers to Mail Surveys," *Journal of Advertising Research* (June/July 1986): 55–58.

22. Geographic clustering of rare populations, however, can be an advantage. See Poduri S. Rao, *Sampling Methodologies with Applications* (Boca Raton, FL: CRC Press, 2001); John B. Carlin, "Design of Cross-Sectional Surveys Using Cluster Sampling: An Overview with Australian Case Studies," *Australian and New Zealand Journal of Public Health,* 23 (5) (October 1999): 546–551; James C. Raymondo, "Confessions of a Nielsen Household," *American Demographics,* 19 (3) (March 1997): 24–27; and Seymour Sudman, "Efficient Screening Methods for the Sampling of Geographically Clustered Special Populations," *Journal of Marketing Research,* 22 (February 1985): 20–29.

23. J. Walker, "A Sequential Discovery Sampling Procedure," *The Journal of the Operational Research Society,* 53 (1) (January 2002): 119; June S. Park, Michael Peters, and Kwei Tang, "Optimal Inspection Policy in Sequential Screening," *Management Science,* 37 (8) (August 1991): 1058–1061; and E. J. Anderson, K. Gorton, and R. Tudor, "The Application of Sequential Analysis in Market Research," *Journal of Marketing Research,* 17 (February 1980): 97–105.

24. For more discussion of double sampling, see Ken Brewer, *Design and Estimation in Survey Sampling* (London, UK: Edward Arnold, 2001); John Shade, "Sampling Inspection Tables: Single and Double Sampling," *Journal of Applied Statistics,* 26 (8) (December 1999): 1020; David H. Baillie, "Double Sampling Plans for Inspection by Variables When the Process Standard Deviation Is Unknown," *International Journal of Quality & Reliability Management,* 9 (5) (1992): 59–70; and Martin R. Frankel and Lester R. Frankel, "Probability Sampling," in Robert Ferber, Ed., *Handbook of Marketing Research* (New York: McGraw-Hill, 1974): 2–246.

25. Charles J. Whalen, "Jobs: The Truth Might Hurt," *Business Week,* 3725 (March 26, 2001): 34.

26. For the use of different nonprobability and probability sampling techniques in cross-cultural research, see Naresh K. Malhotra and Mark Peterson, "Marketing Research in the New Millennium: Emerging Issues and Trends," *Market Intelligence and Planning,* 19 (4) (2001): 216–235; Naresh K. Malhotra, James Agarwal, and Mark Peterson, "Cross-Cultural Marketing Research: Methodological Issues and Guidelines," *International Marketing Review,* 13 (5) (1996): 7–43; and Samiee Saeed and Insik Jeong, "Cross-Cultural Research in Advertising: An Assessment of Methodologies," *Journal of the Academy of Marketing Science,* 22 (Summer 1994): 205–215.

27. Sunil Erevelles, "The Use of Price and Warranty Cues in Product Evaluation: A Comparison of U.S. and Hong Kong Consumers," *Journal of International Consumer Marketing,* 11 (3) (1999): 67; Taylor Humphrey, "Horses for Courses: How Survey Firms in Different Countries Measure Public Opinion with Different Methods," *Journal of the Market Research Society,* 37 (3) (July 1995): 211–219; and B. J. Verhage, U. Yavas, R. T. Green, and E. Borak, "The Perceived Risk Brand Loyalty Relationship: An International Perspective," *Journal of Global Marketing,* 3 (3) (1990): 7–22.

28. Aileen Smith, "Ethics-Related Responses to Specific Situation Vignettes: Evidence of Gender-Based Differences and Occupational Socialization," *Journal of Business Ethics,* 28 (1) (November 2000): 73–86; Satish P. Deshpande, "Managers' Perception of Proper Ethical Conduct: The Effect of Sex, Age, and Level of Education," *Journal of Business Ethics,* 16 (1) (January 1997): 79–85; and I. P. Akaah, "Differences in Research Ethics Judgments Between Male and Female Marketing Professionals," *Journal of Business Ethics,* 8 (1989): 375–381.

29. Shane Schick, "IT Managers Stress Skills Help," *Computer Dealer News,* 17 (3) (February 2, 2001): 1–2; and *www.surveysite. com/newsite/docs/profile.htm.* April 25, 2002.

# Chapter 12

1. *Bicycling* Magazine, *Bicycling Magazine's 2002 Semiannual Study of U.S. Retail Bicycle Stores.*

2. A discussion of the sampling distribution may be found in any basic statistics textbook. For example, see Mark L. Berenson, David M. Levine, and Timothy Krehbiel, *Basic Business Statistics: Concepts and Applications,* 8th ed. (Englewood Cliffs, NJ: Prentice Hall, 2002).

3. Other statistical approaches are also available. However, a discussion of these is beyond the scope of this book. The interested reader is referred to Marion R. Reynolds, Jr., "EWMA Control Charts with Variable Sample Sizes and Variable Sampling Intervals," *IIE Transactions,* 33 (6) (June 2001): 511–530; S. Sampath, *Sampling Theory and Methods* (Boca Raton, FL:

CRC Press, 2000); L. Yeh and L. C. Van, "Bayesian Double-Sampling Plans with Normal Distributions," *Statistician,* 46 (2) (1997): 193–207; W. G. Blyth and L. J. Marchant, "A Self-Weighing Random Sampling Technique," *Journal of the Market Research Society,* 38 (4) (October 1996): 473–479; Clifford Nowell and Linda R. Stanley, "Length-Biased Sampling in Mall Intercept Surveys," *Journal of Marketing Research,* 28 (November 1991): 475–479; and Raphael Gillett, "Confidence Interval Construction by Stein's Method: A Practical and Economical Approach to Sample Size Determination," *Journal of Marketing Research,* 26 (May 1989): 237.

4. Steven K. Thompson, *Sampling* (New York: John Wiley & Sons, 2002); Melanie M. Wall, "An Effective Confidence Interval for the Mean with Samples of Size One and Two," *The American Statistician,* Alexandria (May 2001): 102–105; and Siu L. Chow, *Statistical Significance* (Thousand Oaks, CA: Sage Publications, 1996).

5. Richard L. Valliant, Alan H. Dorfman, and Richard M. Royall, *Finite Population Sampling and Inference: A Prediction Approach* (New York: John Wiley & Sons, 2000).

6. "City of Los Angeles Internet Services Project: Market Analysis and Best Practices Report," *e-Government Services Project Reports,* October 29, 1999: Online at *www.ci.la.ca.us/ 311/ marketanalysis.pdf,* April 8, 2001.

7. See, for example, S. Sampath, *Sampling Theory and Methods* (Boca Raton, FL: CRC Press, 2000); Nigel Bradley, "Sampling for Internet Surveys: An Examination of Respondent Selection for Internet Research," *Market Research Society,* 41 (4) (October 1999): 387–395; C. J. Adcock, "Sample Size Determination—A Review," *Statistician,* 46 (2) (1997): 261–283; and Seymour Sudman, "Applied Sampling," in Peter H. Rossi, James D. Wright, and Andy B. Anderson, Eds., *Handbook of Survey Research* (Orlando, FL: Academic Press, 1983): 145–194.

8. Adjusting for incidence and completion rates is discussed in Poduri S. Rao, *Sampling Methodologies with Applications* (Boca Raton, FL: CRC Press, 2001); Barbara Bickart, "The Distribution of Survey Contact and Participation in the United States: Constructing a Survey-Based Estimate," *Journal of Marketing Research,* 36 (2) (May 1999): 286–294; Don A. Dillman, Eleanor Singer, Jon R. Clark, and James B. Treat, "Effects of Benefits Appeals, Mandatory Appeals, and Variations in Statements of Confidentiality on Completion Rates for Census Questionnaires," *Public Opinion Quarterly,* 60 (3) (Fall 1996): 376–389; and Louis G. Pol and Sukgoo Pak, "The Use of Two-Stage Survey Design in Collecting Data from Those Who Have Attended Periodic or Special Events," *Journal of the Market Research Society,* 36 (October 1994): 315–326.

9. Judith Green, "Jacksonville Symphony Sets Big Anniversary Fest," *The Atlanta Journal, The Atlanta Constitution* (February 20, 2000): K7; Nevin J. Rodes, "Marketing a Community Symphony Orchestra," *Marketing News,* 30 (3) (January 29, 1996): 2; and "Sales Makes Sweet Music," *Quirk's Marketing Research Review* (May 1988): 10–12.

10. Patrick Van Kenhove, "The Influence of Topic Involvement on Mail-Survey Response Behavior," *Psychology & Marketing,* 19 (3) (March 2002): 293; M. R. Fisher, "Estimating the Effect of Nonresponse Bias on Angler Surveys," *Transactions of the American Fisheries Society,* 125 (1) (January 1996): 118–126; and Charles Martin, "The Impact of Topic Interest on Mail Survey Response Behaviour," *Journal of the Market Research Society,* 36 (October 1994): 327–338.

11. Simone M. Cummings, "Reported Response Rates to Mailed Physician Questionnaires," *Health Services Research,* 35 (6) (February 2001): 1347–1355; A. Hill, J. Roberts, P. Ewings, and D. Gunnell, "Nonresponse Bias in a Lifestyle Survey,"*Journal of Public Health Medicine,* 19 (2) (June 1997): 203–207; and Stephen W. McDaniel, Charles S. Madden, and Perry Verille, "Do Topic Differences Affect Survey Nonresponse?" *Journal of the Market Research Society* (January 1987): 55–66.

12. For minimizing the incidence of nonresponse and adjusting for its effects, see Richard Colombo, "A Model for Diagnosing and Reducing Nonresponse Bias," *Journal of Advertising Research,* 40 (1/2) (January/April 2000): 85–93; H. C. Chen, "Direction, Magnitude, and Implications of Nonresponse Bias in Mail Surveys," *Journal of the Market Research Society,* 38 (3) (July 1996): 267–276; and Michael Brown, "What Price Response?" *Journal of the Market Research Society,* 36 (July 1994): 227–244.

13. Steve Jarvis, "CMOR Finds Survey Refusal Rate Still Rising," *Marketing News,* 36 (3) (February 4, 2002): 4; Artur Baldauf, "Examining Motivations to Refuse in Industrial Mail Surveys," *Journal of the Market Research Society,* 41 (3) (July 1999): 345–353; Reg Baker, "Nobody's Talking," *Marketing Research: A Magazine of Management & Applications,* 8 (1) (Spring 1996): 22–24; and Jolene M. Struebbe, Jerome B. Kernan, and Thomas J. Grogan, "The Refusal Problem in Telephone Surveys," *Journal of Advertising Research* (June/July 1986): 29–38.

14. Van Kenhove, "The Influence of Topic Involvement on Mail-Survey Response Behavior," *Psychology & Marketing,* 19 (3) (March 2002): 293; Robert M. Groves, "Leverage-Saliency Theory of Survey Participation: Description and an Illustration," *Public Opinion Quarterly,* 64 (3) (Fall 2000): 299–308; S. A. Everett, J. H. Price, A. W. Bedell, and S. K. Telljohann," The Effect of a Monetary Incentive in Increasing the Return Rate of a Survey of Family Physicians," *Evaluation and the Health Professions,* 20 (2) (June 1997): 207–214; and J. Scott Armstrong and Edward J. Lusk, "Return Postage in Mail Surveys: A Meta-Analysis," *Public Opinion Quarterly* (Summer 1987): 233–248; and Julie Yu and Harris Cooper, "A Quantitative Review of Research Design Effects on Response Rates to Questionnaires," *Journal of Marketing Research,* 20 (February 1983): 36–44.

15. Steven G. Rogelberg, "Attitudes Toward Surveys: Development of a Measure and Its Relationship to Respondent Behavior," *Organizational Research Methods,* 4 (1) (January 2001): 3–25; and Edward F. Fern, Kent B. Monroe, and Ramon A. Avila, "Effectiveness of Multiple Request Strategies: A Synthesis of Research Results," *Journal of Marketing Research,* 23 (May 1986): 144–153.

16. Michael J. Shaw, "The Use of Monetary Incentives in a Community Survey: Impact on Response Rates, Date, Quality, and Cost," *Health Services Research,* 35 (6) (February 2001): 1339–1346; Sheldon Wayman, "The Buck Stops Here When It Comes to Dollar Incentives," *Marketing News,* 31 (1) (January 6, 1997): 9; and Paul M. Biner and Heath J. Kidd, "The Interactive Effects of Monetary Incentive Justification and Questionnaire Length on Mail Survey Response Rates," *Psychology & Marketing,* 11 (5) (September/October 1994): 483–492.

17. B. Zafer Erdogan, "Increasing Mail Survey Response Rates from an Industrial Population: A Cost-Effectiveness Analysis of Four Follow-up Techniques," *Industrial Marketing Management,* 31 (1) (January 2002): 65.

18. John Byrom, "The Effect of Personalization on Mailed Questionnaire Response Rates," *International Journal of Market Research* (Summer 2000): 357–359; D. A. Dillman, E. Singer, J. R. Clark, and J. B. Treat, "Effects of Benefits Appeals, Mandatory Appeals, and Variations in Statements of Confidentiality on Completion Rates for Census Questionnaires," *Public Opinion Quarterly,* 60 (3) (Fall 1996): 376–389; P. Gendall, J. Hoek, and D. Esslemont, "The Effect of Appeal, Complexity, and Tone in a Mail Survey Covering Letter," *Journal of the Market Research Society,* 37 (3) (July 1995): 251–268; and Thomas V. Greer and Ritu Lohtia, "Effects of Source and Paper Color on Response Rates in Mail Surveys," *Industrial Marketing Management,* 23 (February 1994): 47–54.

19. Jamie Smith, "How to Boost DM Response Rates Quickly," *Marketing News,* 35 (9) (April 23, 2001): 5; James D. Peacock, "Yes, You Can Raise Response Rates," *Journal of Advertising Research,* 36 (1) (January 1996): RC7–RC10.

20. Scott Keeter, "Consequences of Reducing Nonresponse in a National Telephone Survey," *Public Opinion Quarterly,* 64 (2) (Summer 2000): 125–148; G. L. Bowen, "Estimating the Reduction in Nonresponse Bias from Using a Mail Survey as a Backup for Nonrespondents to a Telephone Interview Survey," *Research on Social Work Practice,* 4 (1) (January 1994): 115–128; and R. A. Kerin and R. A. Peterson, "Scheduling Telephone Interviews," *Journal of Advertising Research* (May 1983): 44.

21. Richard Colombo, "A Model for Diagnosing and Reducing Nonresponse Bias," *Journal of Advertising Research* (January/April 2000): 85–93; and M. L. Rowland and R. N. Forthofer, "Adjusting for Nonresponse Bias in a Health Examination Survey," *Public Health Reports* 108 (3) (May/June 1993): 380–386.

22. Michael D. Larsen, "The Psychology of Survey Response," *Journal of the American Statistical Association,* 97 (457) (March 2002): 358–359; and E. L. Dey, "Working with Low Survey Response Rates—The Efficacy of Weighting Adjustments," *Research in Higher Education,* 38 (2) (April 1997): 215–227.

23. Kevin J. Flannelly, "Reducing Undecided Voters and Other Sources of Error in Election Surveys," *International Journal of Market Research,* 42 (2) (Spring 2000): 231–237; and John Maines, "Taking the Pulse of the Voter," *American Demographics* (November 1992): 20.

24. Jing Qin, "Estimation with Survey Data Under Nonignorable Nonresponse or Informative Sampling," *Journal of the American Statistical Association,* 97 (457) (March 2002): 193–200; R. C. Kessler, R. J. Little, and R. M. Grover, "Advances in Strategies for Minimizing and Adjusting for Survey Nonresponse," *Epidemiologic Reviews,* 17 (1) (1995): 192–204; and James C. Ward, Bertram Russick, and William Rudelius, "A Test of Reducing Callbacks and Not-at-Home Bias in Personal Interviews by Weighting At-Home Respondents," *Journal of Marketing Research,* 2 (February 1985): 66–73.

25. Ken Brewer, *Design and Estimation in Survey Sampling* (London: Edward Arnold, 2001); Jun Sao, "Variance Estimation for Survey Data with Composite Imputation and Nonnegligible Sampling Fractions," *Journal of American Statistical Association* (Mar 1999): 254–265; and J. W. Drane, D. Richter, and C. Stoskopf, "Improved Imputation of Nonresponse to Mailback Questionnaires," *Statistics in Medicine,* 12 (3–4) (February 1993): 283–288.

26. Ben Dolven, "The Best Little Airline in China," *Far Eastern Economic Review,* 165 (2) (January 17, 2002): 32–35; and

"Another Chinese Take-Off," *The Economist* (December 19, 1992).

27. Anne-Wil Harzing, "Cross-National Industrial Mail Surveys; Why Do Response Rates Differ Between Countries?" *Industrial Marketing Management,* 29 (3) (May 2000): 243–254.

28. Humphrey Taylor, "Using Internet Polling to Forecast the 2000 Elections," *Marketing Research,* 13 (1) (Spring 2001): 26–30; Vicki G. Morwitz and Carol Pluzinski, "Do Polls Reflect Opinions or Do Opinions Reflect Polls? The Impact of Political Polling on Voters' Expectations, Preferences, and Behavior," *Journal of Consumer Research,* 23 (1) (June 1996): 53–67.

# Chapter 13

1. Steve Jarvis, "CMOR Finds Survey Refusal Rate Still Rising," *Marketing News* (February 4, 2002): 4; Reg Baker, "Nobody's Talking," *Marketing Research: A Magazine of Management & Applications,* 8 (1) (Spring 1996): 22–24; and "Study Tracks Trends in Refusal Rates," *Quirk's Marketing Research Review* (August/September 1989): 16–18, 42–43.

2. Carolyn Folkman Curasi, "A Critical Exploration of Face-to-Face Interviewing vs. Computer-Mediated Interviewing," *International Journal of Market Research,* 43 (4) (Fourth Quarter 2001): 361–375; Gale D. Muller and Jane Miller, "Interviewers Make the Difference," *Marketing Research: A Magazine of Management & Applications,* 8 (1) (Spring 1996): 8–9; and "JDC Interviews Michael Redington," *Journal of Data Collection,* 25 (Spring 1985): 2–6.

3. Jaber F. Gubrium and James A. Holstein, *Handbook of Interview Research: Context and Method* (Thousand Oaks, CA: Sage Publications, 2001); and James H. Frey and Sabine M. Oishi, *How to Conduct Interviews by Telephone and in Person* (Thousand Oaks, CA: Sage Publications, 1995).

4. Susan C. McCombie, "The Influences of Sex of Interviewer on the Results of an AIDS Survey in Ghana," *Human Organization,* 61 (1) (Spring 2002): 51–55; Joseph A. Catina, Diane Binson, Jesse Canchola, Lance M. Pollack, et al., "Effects of Interviewer Gender, Interviewer Choice, and Item Wording on Responses to Questions Concerning Sexual Behavior," *Public Opinion Quarterly,* 60 (3) (Fall 1996): 345–375; Philip B. Coulter, "Race of Interviewer Effects on Telephone Interviews," *Public Opinion Quarterly,* 46 (Summer 1982): 278–284; and Eleanor Singer, Martin R. Frankel, and Marc B. Glassman, "The Effect of Interviewer Characteristics and Expectations on Response," *Public Opinion Quarterly,* 47 (Spring 1983): 68–83.

5. Jessica Clark Newman, "The Differential Effects of Face-to-Face and Computer Interview Models," *American Journal of Public Health,* 92 (2) (February 2002): 294–297; Darren W. Davis, "Nonrandom Measurement Error and Race of Interviewer Effects Among African Americans," *Public Opinion Quarterly,* 61 (1) (Spring 1997): 183–207; and Raymond F. Barker, "A Demographic Profile of Marketing Research Interviewers," *Journal of the Market Research Society* (UK) (July 29, 1987): 279–292.

6. Anonymous, "Dextra Hands Out Vital Interview Advice," *Management Services,* 46 (2) (February 2002): 6; M. K. Kacmar and W. A. Hochwarter, "The Interview as a Communication Event: A Field Examination of Demographic Effects on Interview Outcomes," *Journal of Business Communication,* 32 (3) (July 1995): 207–232; and Martin Collins and Bob Butcher, "Interviewer and Clustering Effects in an Attitude Survey," *Journal of the Market Research Society* (UK) 25 (January 1983): 39–58.

7. Anonymous, "Renewing Your Interviewing Skills," *Healthcare Executive,* 17 (1) (January/February 2002): 29; Pamela Kiecker and James E. Nelson, "Do Interviewers Follow Telephone Survey Instructions?" *Journal of the Market Research Society,* 38 (2) (April 1996): 161–176; and P. J. Guenzel, T. R. Berkmans, and C. F. Cannell, *General Interviewing Techniques* (Ann Arbor, MI: Institute for Social Research, 1983).

8. Brent Robertson, "The Effect of an Introductory Letter on Participation Rates Using Telephone Recruitment," *Australian and New Zealand Journal of Public Health,* 24 (5) (October 2000): 552; Karl Feld, "Good Introductions Save Time, Money," *Marketing News,* 34 (5) (February 28, 2000): 19–20; and Mick P. Couper, "Survey Introductions and Data Quality," *Public Opinion Quarterly* (Summer 1997): 317–338.

9. This procedure is similar to that followed by Burke Marketing Research, Cincinnati.

10. Darlene B. Bordeaux, "Interviewing—Part II: Getting the Most out of Interview Questions," *Motor Age,* 121 (2) (February 2002): 38–40; "Market Research Industry Sets Up Interviewing Quality Standards," *Management-Auckland,* 44 (2) (March 1997): 12; and "JDC Interviews Michael Redington," *Journal of Data Collection,* 25 (Spring 1985): 2–6.

11. This section follows closely the material in *Interviewer's Manual,* rev. ed. (Ann Arbor, MI: Survey Research Center, Institute for Social Research, University of Michigan) and P. J. Guenzel, T. R. Berkmans, and C. F. Cannell, *General Interviewing Techniques* (Ann Arbor, MI: Institute for Social Research).

12. For an extensive treatment of probing, see Jaber F. Gubrium and James A. Holstein, *Handbook of Interview Research: Context and Method* (Thousand Oaks, CA: Sage Publications, 2001); and *Interviewer's Manual:* 15–19.

13. *Interviewer's Manual,* rev. ed. (Ann Arbor, MI: Survey Research Center, Institute for Social Research, University of Michigan): 16.

14. Ara C. Trembly, "Poor Data Quality: A $600 Billion Issue," *National Underwriter,* 106 (11) (March 18, 2002): 48; "Market Research Industry Sets Up Interviewing Quality Standards," *Management-Auckland,* 44 (2) (March 1997): 12; and Jean Morton-Williams and Wendy Sykes, "The Use of Interaction Coding and Follow-Up Interviews to Investigate Comprehension of Survey Questions," *Journal of the Market Research Society,* 26 (April 1984): 109–127.

15. Jaber F. Gubrium and James A. Holstein, *Handbook of Interview Research: Context and Method* (Thousand Oaks, CA: Sage Publications, 2001); John Anderson, *Behavioral Risk Factors Surveillance System User's Guide* (Atlanta: U.S. Department of Health and Human Services, Centers for Disease Control and Prevention, 1998).

16. John Pallister, "Navigating the Righteous Course: A Quality Issue," *Journal of the Market Research Society,* 41 (3) (July 1999): 327–343; and Martin Collins and Bob Butcher, "Interviewer and Clustering Effects in an Attitude Survey," *Journal of the Market Research Society* (UK) 25 (January 1983): 39–58.

17. Nigel G. Fielding, *Interviewing: Four Volume Set* (Thousand Oaks, CA: Sage Publications, 2003); and Donald S. Tull and Larry E. Richards, "What Can Be Done About Interviewer Bias," in Jagdish Sheth, Ed., *Research in Marketing* (Greenwich, CT: JAI Press, 1980): 143–162.

18. Carla Johnson, "Making Sure Employees Measure Up," *HRMagazine,* 46 (3) (March 2001): 36–41; and Elaine D. Pulakos, Neal Schmitt, David Whitney, and Matthew Smith,

"Individual Differences in Interviewer Ratings: The Impact of Standardization, Consensus Discussion, and Sampling Error on the Validity of a Structured Interview," *Personnel Psychology,* 49 (1) (Spring 1996): 85–102.

19. Jamie Smith, "How to Boost DM Response Rates Quickly," *Marketing News,* 35 (9) (April 23, 2001): 5; Sophie K. Turley, "A Case of Response Rate Success," *Journal of Market Research Society,* 41 (3) (July 1999): 301–309; and Jack Edmonston, "Why Response Rates Are Declining," *Advertising Age's Business Marketing,* 82 (8) (September 1997): 12.

20. Carter Dougherty, "European Union Asks U.S. to Follow Rules, End Exports Spat," *Knight Ridder Tribune Business News,* (January 26, 2002): 1; Laurel Wentz, "Poll: Europe Favors U.S. Products," *Advertising Age* (September 23, 1991); and *www.npes.org/membersonly/INTERNATIONAL-TRADE-FAX-2001.pdf.*

21. Stephanie Stahl, "Ethics and the No-Fear Generation," *Information Week* (880) (March 18, 2002): 8; and James E. Nelson and Pamela L. Kiecker, "Marketing Research Interviewers and Their Perceived Necessity of Moral Compromise," *Journal of Business Ethics,* 15 (10) (October 1996): 1107–1117.

22. *www.gallup.com.*

# Chapter 14

1. Ara C. Trembly, "Poor Data Quality: A $600 Billion Issue," *National Underwriter,* 106 (11) (March 18, 2002): 48; Kevin T. Higgins, "Never Ending Journey," *Marketing Management,* 6 (1) (Spring 1997): 4–7; and Joann Harristhal, "Interviewer Tips," *Applied Marketing Research,* 28 (Fall 1988): 42–45.

2. Bruce Keillor, Deborah Owens, and Charles Pettijohn, "A Cross-Cultural/Cross-National Study of Influencing Factors and Socially Desirable Response Biases," *International Journal of Market Research,* 43 (1) (First Quarter 2001): 63–84; Kofi Q. Dadzie, "Demarketing Strategy in Shortage Marketing Environment," *Journal of the Academy of Marketing Science* (Spring 1989): 157–165. See also Shizuhiko Nishisato, *Measurement and Multivariate Analysis* (New York: Springer-Verlag, New York, 2002).

3. Stephen Jenkins, "Automating Questionnaire Design and Construction," *Journal of the Market Research Society,* 42 (1) (Winter 1999–2000): 79–95; Arlene Fink, *How to Analyze Survey Data* (Thousand Oaks, CA: Sage Publications, 1995); Pamela L. Alreck and Robert B. Settle, *The Survey Research Handbook,* 2nd ed. (Homewood, IL: Irwin Professional Publishing, 1994).

4. Ide Kearney, "Measuring Consumer Brand Confusion to Comply with Legal Guidelines," *International Journal of Market Research,* 43 (1) (First Quarter 2001): 85–91; Serge Luyens, "Coding Verbatims by Computer," *Marketing Research: A Magazine of Management & Applications,* 7 (2) (Spring 1995): 20–25.

5. Yvette C. Hammett, "Voters in Hillsborough County, Florida, Try Out Touch-Screen Voting Machines," *Knight Ridder Tribune Business News* (April 3, 2002): 1; Tim Studt, "Exclusive Survey Reveals Move to High-Tech Solutions," *Research & Development,* 43 (3) (March 2001): 37–38; and Norman Frendberg, "Scanning Questionnaires Efficiently," *Marketing Research: A Magazine of Management & Applications,* 5 (2) (Spring 1993): 38–42.

6. Joseph Rydholm, "Scanning the Seas," *Marketing Research Review* (May 1993); and *www.princess.com* (May 23, 2002).

7. SPSS, Inc. Staff, *SPSS 11.0 Guide to Data Analysis* (Paramus, NJ: Prentice Hall, 2002); SPSS, Inc. Staff, *SPSS 11.0 for Windows: Student Version* (Paramus, NJ: Prentice Hall, 2001); Brian C. Cronk, *How to Use SPSS: A Step-by-Step Guide to Analysis and Interpretation* (Los Angeles, CA: Pyrczak Publishing, 2002); SAS Institute Staff, *SAS/ACCESS Interface to R/3: User's Guide, Release 8* (Cary, NC: SAS Publishing, 2002); Rick Aster, *Professional SAS Programming Shortcuts: Over 1000 Ways to Improve Your SAS Programs* (Phoenixville, PA: Breakfast Communications, 2002); Allan J. Rossman, Beth L. Chance, and Minitab Staff, *Workshop Statistics: Discovery with Data and Minitab + Minitab Software* (Oakland, CA: Key Curriculum Press, 2001); Terry Sincich, David M. Levine, David Stephan, and Mark Berenson, *Practical Statistics by Example Using Microsoft Excel and Minitab* (Paramus, NJ: Prentice Hall, 2002); Barbara F. Ryan and Brian L. Joiner, *Minitab Handbook* (Pacific Grove, CA: Duxbury, 2002); Bernard V. Liengme, *Guide to Microsoft Excel 2000 for Business and Management* (Woburn, MA: Butterworth-Heinemann, 2002); Michael R. Middleton, *Data Analysis Using Microsoft Excel: Updated for Office XP* (Pacific Grove, CA: Duxbury, 2002).

8. Paul D. Allison, *Missing Data* (Thousand Oaks, CA: Sage Publications, 2001); Byung-Joo Lee, "Sample Selection Bias Correction for Missing Response Observations," *Oxford Bulletin of Economics and Statistics,* 62 (2) (May 2000): 305; and Naresh K. Malhotra, "Analyzing Marketing Research Data with Incomplete Information on the Dependent Variable," *Journal of Marketing Research,* 24 (February 1987): 74–84.

9. A meaningful and practical value should be imputed. The value imputed should be a legitimate response code. For example, a mean of 3.86 may not be practical if only single-digit response codes have been developed. In such cases, the mean should be rounded to the nearest integer.

10. Kevin M. Murphy, "Estimation and Inference in Two-Step Econometric Models," *Journal of Business & Economic Statistics,* 20 (1) (January 2002): 88–97; Ali Kara, Christine Nielsen, Sundeep Sahay, and Nagaraj Sivasubramaniam, "Latent Information in the Pattern of Missing Observations in Global Mail Surveys," *Journal of Global Marketing,* 7 (4) (1994): 103–126; and Naresh K. Malhotra, "Analyzing Marketing Research Data with Incomplete Information on the Dependent Variable," *Journal of Marketing Research,* 24 (February 1987): 74–84.

11. Some weighting procedures require adjustments in subsequent data analysis techniques. See David J. Bartholomew, *The Analysis and Interpretation of Multivariate Data for Social Scientists* (Boca Raton, FL: CRC Press, 2002); Llan Yaniv, "Weighting and Trimming: Heuristics for Aggregating Judgments Under Uncertainty," *Organizational Behavior & Human Decision Processes,* 69 (3) (March 1997): 237–249; and Humphrey Taylor, "The Very Different Methods Used to Conduct Telephone Surveys of the Public," *Journal of the Market Research Society,* 39 (3) (July 1997): 421–432.

12. Anonymous, "Nielsen Ratings," *Adweek,* 43 (10) (March 4, 2002): CT3; and Rajiv M. Rao, "Nielsen's Internet Survey: Does It Carry Any Weight?" *Fortune,* 133 (5) (March 18, 1996): 24.

13. Michael Bradford, "Health Care Access Services for Expats Gain in Popularity," *Business Insurance,* 36 (1) (January 7, 2002): 19–20; Arch G. Woodside, Robert L. Nielsen, Fred Walters, and Gale D. Muller, "Preference Segmentation of Health Care Services: The Old-Fashioneds, Value Conscious,

Affluents, and Professional Want-It-Alls," *Journal of Health Care Marketing* (June 1988): 14–24. See also Rama Jayanti, "Affective Responses Toward Service Providers: Implications for Service Encounters," *Health Marketing Quarterly,* 14 (1) (1996): 49–65.

14. See Richard Arnold Johnson and Dean W. Wichern, *Applied Multivariate Statistical Analysis* (Paramus, NJ: Prentice Hall, 2001); B. Swift, "Preparing Numerical Data," in Roger Sapsford and Victor Jupp, Eds., *Data Collection and Analysis* (Thousand Oaks, CA: Sage Publications, 1996); and Ronald E. Frank, "Use of Transformations," *Journal of Marketing Research* (August 1966): 247–253, for specific transformations frequently used in marketing research.

15. Dan Vesset, "Trends in the Market for Analytic Applications," *KM World,* 11 (4) (April 2002): 14; Fred Davidson, *Principles of Statistical Data Handling* (Thousand Oaks, CA: Sage Publications, 1996). For a similar data analysis strategy, see Naresh K. Malhotra, "Modeling Store Choice Based on Censored Preference Data," *Journal of Retailing* (Summer 1986): 128–144.

16. Bivariate techniques have been included here with multivariate techniques. Whereas bivariate techniques are concerned with pairwise relationships, multivariate techniques examine more complex simultaneous relationships among phenomena.

17. Wayne S. DeSarbo, "The Joint Spatial Representation of Multiple Variable Batteries Collected in Marketing Research," *Journal of Marketing Research,* 38 (2) (May 2001): 244–253; J. Douglass Carroll and Paul E. Green, "Psychometric Methods in Marketing Research: Part II: Multidimensional Scaling," *Journal of Marketing Research,* 34 (2) (May 1997): 193–204.

18. Anonymous, "For a Scoop of Their Own," *Businessline* (January 17, 2002): 1; David Kilburn, "Haagen-Dazs Is Flavor of Month," *Marketing Week,* 20 (23) (September 4, 1997): 30; Mark Maremont, "They're All Screaming for Haagen Dazs," *Business Week* (October 14, 1991); and *www.dairyfoods.com/articles/2001/0901/0901market.htm.*

19. Gael McDonald, "Cross-Cultural Methodological Issues in Ethical Research," *Journal of Business Ethics,* 27 (1/2) (September 2000): 89–104; Pertti Alasuutari, *Researching Culture* (Thousand Oaks, CA: Sage Publications, 1995); and C. T. Tan, J. McCullough, and J. Teoh, "An Individual Analysis Approach to Cross-Cultural Research," in Melanie Wallendorf and Paul Anderson, Eds., *Advances in Consumer Research,* Vol. 14 (Provo, UT: Association for Consumer Research, 1987): 394–397.

20. See, for example, Robert G. Tian, "Cross-Cultural Issues in Internet Marketing," *Journal of American Academy of Business,* 1 (2) (March 2002): 217–224; Lisa D. Spiller and Alexander J. Campbell, "The Use of International Direct Marketing by Small Businesses in Canada, Mexico, and the United States: A Comparative Analysis," *Journal of Direct Marketing,* 8 (Winter 1994): 7–16; and Meee-Kau Nyaw and Ignace Ng, "A Comparative Analysis of Ethical Beliefs: A Four-Country Study," *Journal of Business Ethics,* 13 (July 1994): 543–556.

21. Willie E. Hopkins and Shirley A. Hopkins; "The Ethics of Downsizing: Perception of Rights and Responsibilites," *Journal of Business Ethics,* 18 (2) (January 1999): 145–154.

# Chapter 15

1. Jami A. Fullerton and Alice Kendrick, "Portrayal of Men and Women in U.S. Spanish-Language Television Commercials," *Journalism and Mass Communication Quarterly,* 77 (1) (Spring 2000): 128–142; Laura M. Milner, "Sex-Role Portrayals and the Gender of Nations," *Journal of Advertising,* 29 (1) (Spring 2000): 67–79; and Mary C. Gilly, "Sex Roles in Advertising: A Comparison of Television Advertisements in Australia, Mexico, and the United States," *Journal of Marketing,* 52 (April 1988): 75–85.

2. Charla Mathwick, Naresh K. Malhotra, and Edward Rigdon, "The Effect of Dynamic Retail Experiences on Experiential Perceptions of Value: An Internet and Catalog Comparison," *Journal of Retailing,* 78 (2002): 51–60; and Troy A. Festervand, Don R. Snyder, and John D. Tsalikis, "Influence of Catalog vs. Store Shopping and Prior Satisfaction on Perceived Risk," *Journal of the Academy of Marketing Science* (Winter 1986): 28–36.

3. Lisa Deply Neirotti, Heather A. Bosetti, and Kenneth C. Teed, "Motivation to Attend the 1996 Summer Olympic Games," *Journal of Travel Research,* 39 (3) (February 2001): 327–331.

4. See any introductory statistics book for a more detailed description of these statistics, for example, Mark L. Berenson, David M. Levine, and Timothy Krehbiel, *Basic Business Statistics: Concepts and Applications,* 8th ed. (Englewood Cliffs, NJ: Prentice Hall, 2002).

5. For our purposes, no distinction will be made between formal hypothesis testing and statistical inference by means of confidence intervals.

6. Excellent discussions of ways to analyze cross-tabulations can be found in Bryan E. Denham, "Advanced Categorical Statistics: Issues and Applications in Communication Research," *Journal of Communication,* 52 (1) (March 2002): 162; and O. Hellevik, *Introduction to Causal Analysis: Exploring Survey Data by Crosstabulation* (Beverly Hills, CA: Sage Publications, 1984).

7. Ran Kivetz and Itamar Simonson, "Earning the Right to Indulge: Effort as a Determinant of Customer Preferences Toward Frequency Program Rewards," *Journal of Marketing Research,* 39 (2) (May 2002): 155–170; Lawrence F. Feick, "Analyzing Marketing Research Data with Association Models," *Journal of Marketing Research,* 21 (November 1984): 376–386. For a recent application, see Wagner A. Kamakura and Michel Wedel, "Statistical Data Fusion for Cross-Tabulation," *Journal of Marketing Research,* 34 (4) (November 1997): 485–498.

8. Daniel B. Wright, *First Steps in Statistics* (Thousand Oaks, CA: Sage Publications, 2002); and R. Mark Sirkin, *Statistics for the Social Sciences,* 2nd ed. (Thousand Oaks, CA: Sage Publications, 1999).

9. James J. Higgins, *Introduction to Modern Nonparametric Statistics* (Pacific Grove, CA: Duxbury, 2002); and Marjorie A. Pett, *Nonparametric Statistics for Health Care Research* (Thousand Oaks, CA: Sage Publications, 1997). For a more extensive treatment, see H. O. Lancaster, *The Chi-Squared Distribution* (New York: John Wiley, 1969).

10. Mark L. Berenson, David M. Levine, and Timothy Krehbiel, *Basic Business Statistics: Concepts and Applications,* 8th ed. (Englewood Cliffs, NJ: Prentice Hall, 2002).

11. Some statisticians, however, disagree. They feel that a correction should not be applied. See, for example, John E. Overall, "Power of Chi-Square Tests for $2 \times 2$ Contingency Tables with Small Expected Frequencies," *Psychological Bulletin* (January 1980): 132–135.

12. Significance tests and confidence intervals are also available for either lambda-asymmetric or lambda-symmetric. See L. A. Goodman and W. H. Kruskal, "Measures of Association for

Cross-Classification: Appropriate Sampling Theory," *Journal of the American Statistical Association,* 88 (June 1963): 310–364.

13. John M. Hoenig, "The Abuse of Power: The Pervasive Fallacy of Power Calculation for Data Analysis," *The American Statistician,* 55 (1) (February 2001): 19–24; and Michael Cowles and Caroline Davis, "On the Origins of the 0.05 Level of Statistical Significance," *American Psychologist* (May 1982): 553–558.

14. Technically, a null hypothesis cannot be accepted. It can be either rejected or not rejected. This distinction, however, is inconsequential in applied research.

15. The condition when the variances cannot be assumed to be equal is known as the Behrens-Fisher problem. There is some controversy over the best procedure in this case. For a recent example, see Carrie M. Heilman, Kent Nakamoto, and Ambar G. Rao, "Pleasant Surprises: Consumer Response to Unexpected In-Store Coupons," *Journal of Marketing Research,* 39 (2) (May 2002): 242–252.

16. Susan Chandler, "Some Retailers Begin to Cater to Growing Group of Aging Shoppers," *Knight Ridder Tribune Business News* (March 17, 2001): 1; and James R. Lumpkin and James B. Hunt, "Mobility as an Influence on Retail Patronage Behavior of the Elderly: Testing Conventional Wisdom," *Journal of the Academy of Marketing Science* (Winter 1989): 1–12.

17. Amy Harmon, "Skip-the-Ads TV Has Madison Ave. Upset," *New York Times* (May 23, 2002): A1; Larry Dunst, "Is It Possible to Get Creative in 15 Seconds?" *Advertising Age,* 64 (50) (November 29, 1993): 18; and Jerry A. Rosenblatt and Janet Mainprize, "The History and Future of 15-Second Commercials: An Empirical Investigation of the Perception of Ad Agency Media Directors," in William Lazer, Eric Shaw, and Chow-Hou Wee, Eds., *World Marketing Congress, International Conference Series,* Vol. IV (Boca Raton, FL: Academy of Marketing Science, 1989): 169–177.

18. Gopal K. Kanji, *100 Statistical Tests: new edition* (Thousand Oaks, CA: Sage Publications, 1999); and Donald L. Harnett, *Statistical Methods,* 3rd ed. (Reading, MA: Addison-Wesley, 1982).

19. James J. Higgins, *Introduction to Modern Nonparametric Statistics* (Pacific Grove, CA: Duxbury, 2002); and Marjorie A. Pett, *Nonparametric Statistics for Health Care Research* (Thousand Oaks, CA: Sage Publications, 1997).

20. There is some controversy over whether nonparametric statistical techniques should be used to make inferences about population parameters.

21. The $t$ test in this case is equivalent to a chi-square test for independence in a $2 \times 2$ contingency table. The relationship is $\chi^2_{0.95(1)} = t^2_{0.05(n_1 + n_2 - 2)}$. For large samples, the $t$ distribution approaches the normal distribution and so the $t$ test and the $z$ test are equivalent.

22. David Swaddling, "Good Data Still Worth the Investment," *Marketing News,* 35 (2) (January 15, 2001): 20–21; and James R. Krum, Pradeep A. Rau, and Stephen K. Keiser, "The Marketing Research Process: Role Perceptions of Researchers and Users," *Journal of Advertising Research* (December/ January 1988): 9–21.

23. Reinhard Bergmann, "Different Outcomes of the Wilcoxon-Mann-Whitney Test from Different Statistics Packages," *The American Statistician,* 54 (1) (February 2000): 72–77.

24. Marjorie A. Pett, *Nonparametric Statistics for Health Care Research* (Thousand Oaks, CA: Sage Publications, 1997); and J. G. Field, "The World's Simplest Test of Significance," *Journal of the Market Research Society* (July 1971): 170–172.

25. Louella Miles, "Finding a Balance in Global Research," *Marketing* (November 29, 2001): 33; and Leslie de Chernatony, Chris Halliburton, and Ratna Bernath, "International Branding: Demand or Supply Driven," *International Marketing Review,* 12 (2) (1995): 9–21.

26. Mark Dolliver, "Keeping Honest Company" *Adweek,* 41 (28) (July 10, 2000): 29; Lawrence B. Chonko, *Ethical Decision Making in Marketing* (Thousand Oaks, CA: Sage Publications, 1995); and G. R. Laczniak and P. E. Murphy, "Fostering Ethical Marketing Decisions," *Journal of Business Ethics,* 10 (1991): 259–271.

27. SPSS, Inc. Staff, *SPSS 11.0 Guide to Data Analysis* (Paramus, NJ: Prentice Hall, 2002); SPSS, Inc. Staff, *SPSS 11.0 for Windows: Student Version* (Paramus, NJ: Prentice Hall, 2001); Brian C. Cronk, *How to Use SPSS: A Step-by-Step Guide to Analysis and Interpretation* (Los Angeles: Pyrczak Publishing, 2002); SAS Institute Staff, *SAS/ACCESS Interface to R/3: User's Guide, Release 8* (Cary, NC: SAS Publishing, 2002); Rick Aster, *Professional SAS Programming Shortcuts: Over 1000 Ways to Improve Your SAS Programs* (Phoenixville, PA: Breakfast Communications, 2002); Allan J. Rossman, Beth L. Chance, and Minitab Staff, *Workshop Statistics: Discovery with Data and Minitab + Minitab Software* (Oakland, CA: Key Curriculum Press, 2001); Terry Sincich, David M. Levine, David Stephan, and Mark Berenson, *Practical Statistics by Example Using Microsoft Excel and Minitab* (Paramus, NJ: Prentice Hall, 2002); Barbara F. Ryan and Brian L. Joiner, *Minitab Handbook* (Pacific Grove, CA: Duxbury, 2002); Bernard V. Liengme, *Guide to Microsoft Excel 2000 for Business and Management* (Woburn, MA: Butterworth-Heinemann, 2002); and Michael R. Middleton, *Data Analysis Using Microsoft Excel: Updated for Office XP* (Pacific Grove, CA: Duxbury, 2002).

# Chapter 16

1. Seyhmus Balogluand Mehmet Mangaloglu, "Tourism Destination Images of Turkey, Egypt, Greece, and Italy as Perceived by U.S.-Based Tour Operators and Travel Agents," *Tourism Management,* 22 (1) (February 2001): 1–9.

2. Anthony D. Miyazaki, "Consumer Perceptions of Privacy and Security Risks for Online Shopping," *The Journal of Consumer Affairs,* 35 (1) (Summer 2001): 27; Richard Burnett, "As Internet Sales Rise, So Do Shoppers' Complaints," *Knight Ridder Tribune Business News* (December 20, 2001): 1; and Pradeep Korgaonkar and George P. Moschis, "The Effects of Perceived Risk and Social Class on Consumer Preferences for Distribution Outlets," in Paul Bloom, Russ Winer, Harold H. Kassarjian, Debra L. Scammon, Bart Weitz, Robert Spekman, Vijay Mahajan, and Michael Levy, Eds., *Enhancing Knowledge Development in Marketing,* Series No. 55 (Chicago: American Marketing Association (1989): 39–43.

3. For a recent application of ANOVA, see Jaideep Sengupta and Gerald J. Gorn, "Absence Makes the Mind Grow Sharper: Effects of Element Omission on Subsequent Recall," *Journal of Marketing Research,* 39 (2) (May 2002): 186–201.

4. Denis G. Janky, "Sometimes Pooling for Analysis of Variance Hypothesis Tests: A Review and Study of a Split-Plot Model," *The American Statistician,* 54 (4) (November 2000): 269–279; Wade C. Driscoll, "Robustness of the ANOVA and Tukey-Kramer Statistical Tests," *Computers & Industrial Engineering,* 31 (1, 2) (October 1996): 265–268; and Richard K. Burdick,

"Statement of Hypotheses in the Analysis of Variance," *Journal of Marketing Research* (August 1983): 320–324.

5. The *F*-test is a generalized form of the *t* test. If a random variable is *t* distributed with *n* degrees of freedom, then $t^2$ is *F* distributed with 1 and *n* degrees of freedom. Where there are two factor levels or treatments, ANOVA is equivalent to the two-sided *t* test.

6. Although computations for the fixed-effects and random-effects models are similar, interpretations of results differ. A comparison of these approaches is found in J. Rick Turner and Julian Thayer, *Introduction to Analysis of Variance: Design, Analysis, and Interpretation* (Thousand Oaks, CA: Sage Publications, 2001); Amir Erez, Matthew C. Bloom, and Martin T. Wells, "Using Random Rather Than Fixed Effects Models in Meta-Analysis: Implications for Situational Specificity and Validity Generalization," *Personnel Psychology,* 49 (2) (Summer 1996): 275–306. See also J. Rick Turner and Julian F. Thayer, *Introduction to Analysis of Variance: Design, Analysis, and Interpretation* (Thousand Oaks, CA: Sage Publications, 2001).

7. Anonymous, "Why Video Direct Marketing Works," *Adweek* (2000): 12; and Denise T. Smart, James E. Zemanek, Jr., and Jeffrey S. Conant, "Videolog Retailing: How Effective Is This New Form of Direct Mail Marketing?" in Paul Bloom, Russ Winer, Harold H. Kassarjian, Debra L. Scammon, Bart Weitz, Robert Spekman, Vijay Mahajan, and Michael Levy, Eds., *Enhancing Knowledge Development in Marketing,* Series No. 55 (Chicago: American Marketing Association, 1989): 85.

8. We consider only the full factorial designs, which incorporate all possible combinations of factor levels.

9. Jaideep Sengupta and Gerald J. Gorn, "Absence Makes the Mind Grow Sharper: Effects of Element Omission on Subsequent Recall," *Journal of Marketing Research,* 39 (2) (May 2002): 186–201; James Jaccard, *Interaction Effects in Factorial Analysis of Variance* (Thousand Oaks, CA: Sage Publications, 1997); Jerome L. Mayers, *Fundamentals of Experimental Design,* 3rd ed. (Boston: Allyn & Bacon, 1979).

10. Shizuhiko Nishisato, *Measurement and Multivariate Analysis* (New York: Springer-Verlag New York, 2002).

11. Kalpesh Kaushik Desai, "The Effects of Ingredient Branding Strategies on Host Brand Extendibility," *Journal of Marketing,* 66 (1) (January 2002): 73–93; and Paul Chao, "The Impact of Country Affiliation on the Credibility of Product Attribute Claims," *Journal of Advertising Research* (April/May 1989): 35–41.

12. Although this is the most common way in which analysis of covariance is performed, other situations are also possible. For example, covariate and factor effects may be of equal interest, or the set of covariates may be of major concern. For a recent application, see Michel Tuan Pham and A. V. Muthukrishnan, "Search and Alignment in Judgment Revision: Implications for Brand Positioning," *Journal of Marketing Research,* 39 (1) (February 2002): 18–30.

13. For a more detailed discussion, see J. Rick Turner and Julian Thayer, *Introduction to Analysis of Variance: Design, Analysis, and Interpretation* (Thousand Oaks, CA: Sage Publications, 2001); Stanton A. Glantz and Bryan K. Slinker, *Primer of Applied Regression and Analysis of Variance* (Blacklick, OH: McGraw-Hill, 2000); and A. R. Wildt and O. T. Ahtola, *Analysis of Covariance* (Beverly Hills, CA: Sage, 1978).

14. See Shi Zhang and Bernd H. Schimitt, "Creating Local Brands in Multilingual International Markets," *Journal of Marketing Research,* 38 (3) (August 2001): 313–325; U. N. Umesh, Robert A. Peterson, Michelle McCann-Nelson, and Rajiv Vaidyanathan,

"Type IV Error in Marketing Research: The Investigation of ANOVA Interactions," *Journal of the Academy of Marketing Science,* 24 (1) (Winter 1996): 17–26; William T. Ross, Jr., and Elizabeth H. Creyer, "Interpreting Interactions: Raw Means or Residual Means," *Journal of Consumer Research,* 20 (2) (September 1993): 330–338; and J. H. Leigh and T. C. Kinnear, "On Interaction Classification," *Educational and Psychological Measurement,* 40 (Winter 1980): 841–843.

15. James Jaccard, *Interaction Effects in Factorial Analysis of Variance* (Thousand Oaks, CA: Sage Publications, 1997).

16. This formula does not hold if repeated measurements are made on the dependent variable. See Edward F. Fern and Kent B. Monroe, "Effect-Size Estimates: Issues and Problems in Interpretation," *Journal of Consumer Research,* 23 (2) (September 1996): 89–105; and David H. Dodd and Roger F. Schultz, Jr., "Computational Procedures for Estimating Magnitude of Effect for Some Analysis of Variance Designs," *Psychological Bulletin* (June 1973): 391–395.

17. The $\omega^2$ formula is attributed to Hays. See W. L. Hays, *Statistics for Psychologists* (New York: Holt, Rinehart & Winston, 1963).

18. Richard Arnold Johnson and Dean W. Wichern, *Applied Multivariate Statistical Analysis* (Paramus, NJ: Prentice Hall, 2001); Edward F. Fern and Kent B. Monroe, "Effect-Size Estimates: Issues and Problems in Interpretation," *Journal of Consumer Research,* 23 (2) (September 1996): 89–105; and Jacob Cohen, *Statistical Power Analysis for the Behavioral Sciences* (Mahwah, NJ: Lawrence Erlbaum Associates, 1988).

19. J. Rick Turner and Julian F. Thayer, *Introduction to Analysis of Variance: Design, Analysis, and Interpretation* (Thousand Oaks, CA: Sage Publications, 2001); John W. Neter, *Applied Linear Statistical Models,* 4th ed. (Burr Ridge, IL: Irwin, 1996); and B. J. Winer, Donald R. Brown, and Kenneth M. Michels, *Statistical Principles in Experimental Design,* 3rd ed. (New York: McGraw-Hill, 1991).

20. It is possible to combine between-subjects and within-subjects factors in a single design. See, for example, Rohini Ahluwalia, H. Rao Unnava, and Robert E. Burnkrant, "The Moderating Role of Commitment on the Spillover Effect of Marketing Communications," *Journal of Marketing Research,* 38 (4) (November 2001): 458–470.

21. See Michelle L. Roehm, Ellen Bolman Pullins, and Harper A. Roehm, Jr., "Designing Loyalty-Building Programs for Packaged Goods Brands," *Journal of Marketing Research,* 39 (2) (May 2002): 202–213; J. H. Bray and S. E. Maxwell, *Multivariate Analysis of Variance* (Beverly Hills, CA: Sage, 1985). For a recent application of MANOVA, see Nigel F. Piercy, "Sales Manager Behavior Control Strategy and Its Consequences: The Impact of Gender Differences," *The Journal of Personal Selling & Sales Management,* 21 (1) (Winter 2001): 39–49.

22. Allan J. Kimmel and N. Craig Smith, "Deception in Marketing Research: Ethical, Methodological, and Disciplinary Implications," *Psychology and Marketing,* 18 (7) (July 2001): 663–689; and Ishmael P. Akaah, "A Cross-National Analysis of the Perceived Commonality of Unethical Practices in Marketing Research," in William Lazer, Eric Shaw, and Chow-Hou Wee, Eds., *World Marketing Congress,* International Conference Series, Vol. IV (Boca Raton, FL: Academy of Marketing Science, 1989): 2–9.

23. Dane Peterson, Angela Rhoads, and Bobby C. Vaught, "Ethical Beliefs of Business Professionals: A Study of Gender, Age and External Factors," *Journal of Business Ethics,* 31 (3) (June 2001): 1; and Ishmael P. Akaah, "Differences in Research Ethics Judgments Between Male and Female Marketing Professionals," *Journal of Business Ethics,* 8 (1989): 375–381.

# Chapter 17

1. Christine Bittar, "Avon Refreshed 'Let's Talk' Campaign—Goes Global for Skincare Line Debut," *Brandweek*, 43 (7) (February 18, 2002): 4; Joanne Wojcik, "Avon's Benefits Booklet Presents Easily Understood Information to all Levels of the Corporation," *Business Insurance*, 35 (47) (November 19, 2001): 14; and Cyndee Miller, "Computer Modeling Rings the Right Bell for Avon," *Marketing News* (May 9, 1988): 14.

2. Jeanette Brown, Heather Green, and Wendy Zellner, "Shoppers Are Beating a Path to the Web," *Business Week*, (3763) (December 24, 2001): 41; and Pradeep K. Korgaonkar and Allen E. Smith, "Shopping Orientation, Demographic, and Media Preference Correlates of Electronic Shopping," in Kenneth D. Bahn, Ed., *Developments in Marketing Science*, Vol. 11 (Blacksburg, VA: Academy of Marketing Science, 1988): 52–55.

3. Peter Y. Chen and Paula M. Popovich, *Correlation: Parametric and Nonparametric Measures* (Thousand Oaks, CA: Sage Publications, 2002); Philip Bobko, Philip L. Roth, and Christopher Bobko, "Correcting the Effect Size of *d* for Range Restriction and Unreliability," *Organizational Research Methods*, 4 (1) (January 2001): 46–61; Michael E. Doherty and James A. Sullivan, "rho: = p," *Organizational Behavior & Human Decision Processes*, 43 (1) (February 1989): 136–144; W. S. Martin, "Effects of Scaling on the Correlation Coefficient: Additional Considerations," *Journal of Marketing Research*, 15 (May 1978): 304–308; and K. A. Bollen and K. H. Barb, "Pearson's *R* and Coarsely Categorized Measures," *American Sociological Review*, 46 (1981): 232–239.

4. Trevor Cox and Joao Branco, *Introduction to Multivariate Analysis* (New York: Oxford University Press, 2002).

5. Although the topic is not discussed here, partial correlations can also be helpful in locating intervening variables and making certain types of causal inferences.

6. Joan E. Harvey, "Home Shopping 'NET' work," *Business First*, 18 (30) (February 22, 2002): 27; Ronald E. Goldsmith, "The Impact of Corporate Credibility and Celebrity Credibility on Consumer Reaction to Advertisements and Brands," *Journal of Advertising*, 29 (3) (Fall 2000): 43–54; "Bates Saatchi & Saatchi, Budapest: Accounting for Change," *Accountancy*, 116 (224) (August 1995): 31; and Ken Kasriel, "Hungary's Million-Dollar Slap," *Advertising Age* (June 8, 1992).

7. Another advantage to tau is that it can be generalized to a partial correlation coefficient. James J. Higgins, *Introduction to Modern Nonparametric Statistics* (Pacific Grove, CA: Duxbury, 2002); Marjorie A. Pett, *Nonparametric Statistics for Health Care Research* (Thousand Oaks, CA: Sage Publications, 1997); and Sidney Siegel and N. J. Castellan, *Nonparametric Statistics*, 2nd ed. (New York: McGraw-Hill, 1988).

8. In a strict sense, the regression model requires that errors of measurement be associated only with the criterion variable and that the predictor variables be measured without error. For serially correlated errors, see Eugene Canjels and Mark W. Watson, "Estimating Deterministic Trends in the Presence of Serially Correlated Errors," *Review of Economics and Statistics*, 79 (2) (May 1997): 184–200. See also Philip Bobko, *Correlation and Regression: Applications for Industrial/Organizational Psychology and Management*, 2nd ed. (Thousand Oaks, CA: Sage Publications, 2001).

9. See any text on regression, such as M. A. Goldberg, *Introduction to Regression Analysis* (South Hampton, UK: WIT Press, 2002); and Leo H. Kahane, *Regression Basics* (Thousand Oaks, CA: Sage Publications, 2001).

10. Technically, the numerator is $b - \beta$. However, because it has been hypothesized that $\beta = 0.0$, it can be omitted from the formula.

11. The larger the SEE, the poorer the fit of the regression.

12. The assumption of fixed levels of predictors applies to the "classical" regression model. It is possible, if certain conditions are met, for the predictors to be random variables. However, their distribution is not allowed to depend on the parameters of the regression equation. See Jeremy Miles and Mark Shevlin, *Applying Regression and Correlation: A Guide for Students and Researchers* (Thousand Oaks, CA: Sage Publications, 2001); N. R. Draper and H. Smith, *Applied Regression Analysis*, 3rd ed. (New York: John Wiley, 1998).

13. For an approach to handling the violations of these assumptions, see Arnold Zellner, "Further Results on Baysian Method of Moments Analysis of the Multiple Regression Model," *International Economic Review*, 42 (1) (February 2001): 121–140; Gary S. Dispensa, "Use Logistic Regression with Customer Satisfaction Data," *Marketing News*, 31 (1) (January 6, 1997): 13; and S. K. Reddy, Susan L. Holak, and Subodh Bhat, "To Extend or Not to Extend: Success Determinants of Line Extensions," *Journal of Marketing Research,* 31 (May 1994): 243–262.

14. Ying Fan, "The National Image of Global Brands," *Journal of Brand Management*, 9 (3) (January 2002): 180–192; Naveen Donthu, Sungho Lee, and Boonghee Yoo, "An Examination of Selected Marketing Mix Elements and Brand Equity," *Academy of Marketing Science*, 28 (2) (Spring 2000): 195–211; and Nancy Giges, "Europeans Buy Outside Goods, But Like Local Ads," *Advertising Age International* (April 27, 1992).

15. For other recent applications of multiple regression, see Klaus Wertenbroch and Bernd Skiera, "Measuring Consumers' Willingness to Pay at the Point of Purchase," *Journal of Marketing Research*, 39 (2) (May 2002): 228–241; and Julie R. Irwin, "Misleading Heuristics and Moderated Multiple Regression Models," *Journal of Marketing Research*, 38 (1) (February 2001): 100–109.

16. Yet another reason for adjusting $R^2$ is that, as a result of the optimizing properties of the least-squares approach, it is a maximum. Thus, to some extent, $R^2$ always overestimates the magnitude of a relationship.

17. If $R^2_{pop}$ is zero, then the sample $R^2$ reflects only sampling error, and the $F$ ratio will tend to be equal to unity.

18. Another approach is the hierarchical method, in which the variables are added to the regression equation in an order specified by the researcher.

19. Julie R. Irwin and Gary H. McClelland, "Misleading Heuristics and Moderated Multiple Regression Models," *Journal of Marketing Research,* 38 (1) (February 2001): 100–109; A. C. Atkinson, S. J. Koopman, and N. Shephard, "Detecting Shocks: Outliers and Breaks in Time Series," *Journal of Econometrics*, 80 (2) (October 1997): 387–422; George C. S. Wang and Charles K. Akabay, "Autocorrelation: Problems and Solutions in Regression Modeling," *Journal of Business Forecasting Methods & Systems*, 13 (4) (Winter 1994–1995): 18–26; David Belsley, *Conditioning Diagnostics: Collinearity and Weak Data in Regression* (New York: John Wiley, 1980); and David Belsley, Edwin Kuh, and Roy E. Walsh, *Regression Diagnostics* (New York: John Wiley, 1980).

20. The Durbin-Watson test is discussed in virtually all regression textbooks. See also Francesc Marmol, "Near Observational Equivalence and Fractionally Integrated Processes," *Oxford Bulletin of Economics and Statistics*, 61 (2) (May 1999): 283;

Hiroyuki Hisamatsu and Koichi Maekawa, "The Distribution of the Durbin-Watson Statistic in Integrated and Near-Integrated Models," *Journal of Econometrics*, 61 (2) (April 1994): 367–382; and N. R. Draper and H. Smith, *Applied Regression Analysis*, 3rd ed. (New York: John Wiley, 1998).

21. Martin A. Koschat and William P. Putsis, Jr., "Audience Characteristics and Bundling: A Hedonic Analysis of Magazine Advertising Rates," *Journal of Marketing Research*, 39 (2) (May 2002): 262–273; and Lawrence Soley and R. Krishnan, "Does Advertising Subsidize Consumer Magazine Prices?" *Journal of Advertising*, 16 (Spring, 1987): 4–9.

22. Neal Schmitt, "Estimates for Cross-Validity for Stepwise Regression and with Predictor Selection," *Journal of Applied Psychology*, 84 (1) (February 1999): 50; and Shelby H. McIntyre, David B. Montgomery, V. Srinivasan, and Barton A. Weitz, "Evaluating the Statistical Significance of Models Developed by Stepwise Regression," *Journal of Marketing Research*, 20 (February 1983): 1–11.

23. Murray Forseter and David Q. Mahler, "The Roper Starch Report" *Drug Store News* (2000): 46–63; and Glen R. Jarboe and Carl D. McDaniel, "A Profile of Browsers in Regional Shopping Malls," *Journal of the Academy of Marketing Science*, (Spring 1987): 46–53.

24. Possible procedures are given in Rajesh Sethi, Daniel C. Smith, and C. Whan Park, "Cross-Functional Product Development Teams, Creativity, and the Innovations of New Consumer Products," *Journal of Marketing Research*, 38 (1) (February 2001): 73–85; Terry Grapentine, "Path Analysis vs. Structural Equation Modeling," *Marketing Research*, 12 (3) (Fall 2000): 12–20; George C. S. Wang, "How to Handle Multicollinearity in Regression Modeling," *Journal of Business Forecasting Methods & Systems*, 15 (1) (Spring 1996): 23–27; Charlotte H. Mason and William D. Perreault, Jr., "Collinearity, Power, and Interpretation of Multiple Regression Analysis," *Journal of Marketing Research*, 28 (August 1991): 268–280; R. R. Hocking, "Developments in Linear Regression Methodology: 1959–1982," *Technometrics*, 25 (August 1983): 219–230; and Ronald D. Snee, "Discussion," *Technometrics*, 25 (August 1983): 230–237.

25. Nedret Billor, "An Application of the Local Influence Approach to Ridge Regression," *Journal of Applied Statistics*, 26 (2) (February 1999): 177–183; R. James Holzworth, "Policy Capturing with Ridge Regression," *Organizational Behavior & Human Decision Processes*, 68 (2) (November 1996): 171–179; Albert R. Wildt, "Equity Estimation and Assessing Market Response," *Journal of Marketing Research,* 31 (February 1994): 437–451; and Subhash Sharma and William L. James, "Latent Root Regression: An Alternative Procedure for Estimating Parameters in the Presence of Multicollinearity," *Journal of Marketing Research* (May 1981): 154–161.

26. Only relative importance can be determined, because the importance of an independent variable depends upon all the independent variables in the regression model.

27. McKee J. McClendon, *Multiple Regression and Causal Analysis* (Prospect Heights, IL: Waveland Press, 2002); Robert Rugimbana, "Predicting Automated Teller Machine Usage: The Relative Importance of Perceptual and Demographic Factors," *International Journal of Bank Marketing*, 13 (4) (1995): 26–32; Paul E. Green, J. Douglas Carroll, and Wayne S. DeSarbo, "A New Measure of Predictor Variable Importance in Multiple Regression," *Journal of Marketing Research* (August 1978): 356–360; and Barbara Bund Jackson, "Comment on 'A New Measure of Predictor Variable Importance in Multiple

Regression,'" *Journal of Marketing Research* (February 1980): 116–118.

28. In the rare situation in which all the predictors are uncorrelated, simple correlations = partial correlations = part correlations = betas. Hence, the squares of these measures will yield the same rank order of the relative importance of the variables.

29. Neal Schmitt, "Estimates for Cross-Validity for Stepwise Regression and with Predictor Selection," *Journal of Applied Psychology*, 84 (1) (February 1999): 50; X. Michael Song and Mark E. Perry, "The Determinants of Japanese New Product Success," *Journal of Marketing Research,* 34 (February 1997): 64–76; and Bruce Cooil, Russell S. Winer, and David L. Rados, "Cross-Validation for Prediction," *Journal of Marketing Research* (August 1987): 271–279.

30. For further discussion on dummy variable coding, see Stanton A. Glantz and Bryan K. Slinker, *Primer of Applied Regression and Analysis of Variance* (Blacklick, OH: McGraw-Hill, 2000); and Jacob Cohen and Patricia Cohen, *Applied Multiple Regression Correlation Analysis for the Behavioral Sciences*, 2nd ed. (Hillsdale, NJ: Lawrence Erlbaum Associates, 1983): 181–222.

31. Stanton A. Glantz and Bryan K. Slinker, *Primer of Applied Regression and Analysis of Variance* (Blacklick, OH: McGraw-Hill, 2000). For an application, see Sonya A. Grier and Rohit Deshpande, "Social Dimensions of Consumer Distinctiveness: The Influence of Social Status on Group Identity and Advertising Persuasion," *Journal of Marketing Research*, 38 (2) (May 2001): 216–224.

32. Jens Flottau, "Asian Carriers Advised to Seek New Formulas," *Aviation Week & Space,* 155 (23) (December 3, 2001): 45; and Andrew Geddes, "Asian Airlines Try Loyalty Offers," *Advertising Age* (December 14, 1992).

33. Denise E. DeLorme, George M. Zinkhan, and Warren French, "Ethics and the Internet: Issues Associated with Qualitative Research," *Journal of Business Ethics*, 33 (4) (October 2001): 2; and I. P. Akaah and E. A. Riordan, "The Incidence of Unethical Practices in Marketing Research: An Empirical Investigation," *Journal of the Academy of Marketing Science*, 18 (1990): 143–152.

# Chapter 18

1. Anonymous, "DirecTv Adds National Geographic Channel," *Satellite News,* 24 (3) (January 15, 2001): 1; Donald R. Lichtenstein, Scot Burton, and Richard G. Netemeyer, "An Examination of Deal Proneness Across Sales Promotion Types: A Consumer Segmentation Perspective," *Journal of Retailing,* 73 (2) (Summer 1997): 283–297; and Marvin A. Jolson, Joshua L. Wiener, and Richard B. Rosecky, "Correlates of Rebate Proneness," *Journal of Advertising Research* (February/March 1987): 33–43.

2. A detailed discussion of discriminant analysis may be found in E. K. Kemsley, *Discriminant Analysis and Class Modeling of Spectroscopic Data* (New York: John Wiley & Sons, 1998); Jacques Tacq, *Multivariate Analysis Techniques in Social Science Research* (Thousand Oaks, CA: Sage Publications, 1997); and P. A. Lachenbruch, *Discriminant Analysis* (New York: Hafner Press, 1975). For a recent application, see Vipin Gupta, Paul J. Hanges, and Peter Dorfman, "Cultural Clusters: Methodology and Findings," *Journal of World Business,* 37 (1) (Spring 2002): 11.

3. See Richard Arnold Johnson and Dean W. Wichern, *Applied Multivariate Statistical Analysis* (Paramus, NJ: Prentice Hall,

2001); and W. R. Klecka, *Discriminant Analysis* (Beverly Hills, CA: Sage, 1980).

4. Philip Hans Franses, "A Test for the Hit Rate in Binary Response Models," *International Journal of Market Research,* 42 (2) (Spring 2000): 239–245; Vincent-Watne Mitchell, "How to Identify Psychographic Segments: Part 2," *Marketing Intelligence & Planning,* 12 (7) (1994): 11–16; and M. R. Crask and W. D. Perreault, Jr., "Validation of Discriminant Analysis in Marketing Research," *Journal of Marketing Research,* 14 (February 1977): 60–68.

5. Strictly speaking, before testing for the equality of group means, the equality of group covariance matrices should be tested. Box's M test can be used for this purpose. If the equality of group covariance matrices is rejected, the results of discriminant analysis should be interpreted with caution. In this case, the power of the test for the equality of group means decreases.

6. See Nessim Hanna, "Brain Dominance and the Interpretation of Advertising Messages," *International Journal of Commerce & Management,* 9 (3/4) (1999): 19–32; Lillian Fok, John P. Angelidis, Nabil A. Ibrahim, and Wing M. Fok, "The Utilization and Interpretation of Multivariate Statistical Techniques in Strategic Management," *International Journal of Management,* 12 (4) (December 1995): 468–481; and D. G. Morrison, "On the Interpretation of Discriminant Analysis," *Journal of Marketing Research,* 6 (May 1969): 156–163.

7. Robert J. Sahl, "Retention Reigns as Economy Suffers Drought," *Workspan,* 44 (11) (November 2001): 6–8; Jon M. Hawes, C. P. Rao, and Thomas L. Baker, "Retail Salesperson Attributes and the Role of Dependability in the Selection of Durable Goods," *Journal of Personal Selling & Sales Management,* 13 (4) (Fall 1993): 61–71; Edward F. Fern, Ramon A. Avila, and Dhruv Grewal, "Salesforce Turnover: Those Who Left and Those Who Stayed," *Industrial Marketing Management* (1989): 1–9.

8. For the validation of discriminant analysis, see Werner J. Reinartz and V. Kumar, "On the Profitability of Long-Life Customers in a Noncontractual Setting: An Empirical Investigation and Implications for Marketing," *Journal of Marketing,* 64 (4) (October 2000): 17–35.

9. Joseph F. Hair, Jr., Ralph E. Anderson, Ronald L. Tatham, and William C. Black, *Multivariate Data Analysis with Readings,* 5th ed. (Englewood Cliffs, NJ: Prentice-Hall, Inc., 1998). See also J. J. Glen, "Classification Accuracy in Discriminant Analysis: A Mixed Integer Programming Approach," *The Journal of the Operational Research Society,* 52 (3) (March 2001): 328.

10. Anonymous, "Interactive TV Growth Set to Erupt over Next Five Years," *Satellite News,* 24 (2) (January 8, 2001): 1; and Don R. Rahtz, M. Joseph Sirgy, and Rustan Kosenko, "Using Demographics and Psychographic Dimensions to Discriminate Between Mature Heavy and Light Television Users: An Exploratory Analysis," in Kenneth D. Bahn, Ed., *Developments in Marketing Science,* Vol. 11 (Blacksburg, VA: Academy of Marketing Science, 1988): 2–7.

11. Richard A. Johnson and Dean W. Wichern, *Applied Multivariate Statistical Analysis,* 5th ed. (Upper Saddle River, NJ: Prentice-Hall, 2002). For a recent application, see Werner J. Reinartz and V. Kumar, "On the Profitability of Long-Life Customers in a Noncontractual Setting: An Empirical Investigation and Implications for Marketing," *Journal of Marketing,* 64 (4) (October 2000): 17–35.

12. Jan Tudor, "Valuation of the Health Services Industry," *Weekly Corporate Growth Report,* (1133) (March 26, 2001):

11237–11238; Kathryn H. Dansky and Diane Brannon, "Discriminant Analysis: A Technique for Adding Value to Patient Satisfaction Surveys," *Hospital & Health Services Administration,* 41 (4) (Winter 1996): 503–513; and Jeen-Su Lim and Ron Zallocco, "Determinant Attributes in Formulation of Attitudes Toward Four Health Care Systems," *Journal of Health Care Marketing* (June 1988): 25–30.

13. Richard A. Johnson and Dean W. Wichern, *Applied Multivariate Statistical Analysis,* 5th ed. (Upper Saddle River, NJ: Prentice-Hall, 2002); Joseph F. Hair, Jr., Ralph E. Anderson, Ronald L. Tatham, and William C. Black, *Multivariate Data Analysis with Readings,* 5th ed. (Englewood Cliffs, NJ: Prentice-Hall, Inc., 1998).

14. Prasanna Raman, "Taking Customer Service a Step Ahead," *Computimes* (October 22, 2001): 1; and Charlotte Klopp and John Sterlicchi, "Customer Satisfaction Just Catching on in Europe," *Marketing News* (May 28, 1990).

15. Suzy Bashford, "Smile in Ethics Push with Cartoon Icons," *Marketing* (January 10, 2002): 1; and Paul R. Murphy, Jonathan E. Smith, and James M. Daley, "Executive Attitudes, Organizational Size and Ethical Issues: Perspectives on a Service Industry," *Journal of Business Ethics,* 11 (1992): 11–19.

# Chapter 19

1. Barbara R. Lewis and Sotiris Spyrakopoulos, "Service Failures and Recovery in Retail Banking: The Customers' Perspective," *The International Journal of Bank Marketing,* 19 (1) (2001): 37–48; and James M. Sinukula and Leanna Lawtor, "Positioning in the Financial Services Industry: A Look at the Decomposition of Image," in Jon M. Hawes and George B. Glisan, Eds., *Developments in Marketing Science,* Vol. 10 (Akron, OH: Academy of Marketing Science, 1987): 439–442.

2. For a detailed discussion of factor analysis, see Jacques Tacq, *Multivariate Analysis Techniques in Social Science Research* (Thousand Oaks, CA: Sage Publications, 1997); George H. Dunteman, *Principal Components Analysis* (Newbury Park, CA: Sage Publications, 1989).

3. See A. Adam Ding, "Prediction Intervals, Factor Analysis Models, and High-Dimensional Empirical Linear Prediction," *Journal of the American Statistical Association,* 94 (446) (June 1999): 446–455; and W. R. Dillon and M. Goldstein, *Multivariate Analysis: Methods and Applications* (New York: John Wiley, 1984): 23–99.

4. For a recent application of factor analysis, see Nick Johns and Szilvia Gyimothy, "Market Segmentation and the Prediction of Tourist Behavior: The Case of Bornholm, Denmark," *Journal of Travel Research,* 40 (3) (February 2002): 316–327.

5. David J. Bartholomew and Martin Knott, *Latent Variable Models and Factor Analysis* (London, UK: Edward Arnold Publishers, 1999); Joseph F. Hair, Jr., Ralph E. Anderson, Ronald L. Tatham, and William C. Black, *Multivariate Data Analysis with Readings,* 5th ed. (Upper Saddle River, NJ: Prentice-Hall, Inc., 1998); and Alexander Basilevsky, *Statistical Factor Analysis & Related Methods: Theory & Applications* (New York: John Wiley, 1994).

6. Factor analysis is influenced by the relative size of the correlations rather than the absolute size.

7. See Wagner A. Kamakura and Michel Wedel, "Factor Analysis and Missing Data," *Journal of Marketing Research,* 37 (4) (November 2000): 490–498; Sangit Chatterjee, Linda Jamieson, and Frederick Wiseman, "Identifying Most Influential Observations in Factor Analysis," *Marketing Science* (Spring

1991): 145–160; and Frank Acito and Ronald D. Anderson, "A Monté Carlo Comparison of Factor Analytic Methods," *Journal of Marketing Research,* 17 (May 1980): 228–236.

8. Other methods of orthogonal rotation are also available. The quartimax method minimizes the number of factors needed to explain a variable. The equamax method is a combination of varimax and quartimax.

9. Jorge M. Silva-Risso, Randolph E. Bucklin, and Donald G. Morrison, "A Decision Support System for Planning Manufacturers' Sales Promotion Calendars," *Marketing Science,* 18 (3) (1999): 274; Ronald C. Curhan, and Robert J. Kopp, "Obtaining Retailer Support for Trade Deals: Key Success Factors," *Journal of Advertising Research* (December 1987–January 1988): 51–60.

10. Anonymous, "Microsoft to Discontinue MSN Rebate Promotion," *The Los Angeles Times* (February 3, 2001): C1; and Peter Tat, William A. Cunningham III, and Emin Babakus, "Consumer Perceptions of Rebates," *Journal of Advertising Research* (August/September 1988): 45–50.

11. Bret Begun, Susannah Meadows, and Katherine Stroup, "Now Playing: 'Dude, Where's My Microbus?" *Newsweek,* 137 (4) (January 22, 2001): 9; and "Return of the Beetle," *The Economist,* 346 (8050) (January 10, 1998).

12. Erin Stout, "Are Your Salespeople Ripping You Off?" *Sales and Marketing Management,* 153 (2) (February 2001): 56–62; David J. Fritzsche, "Ethical Climates and the Ethical Dimension of Decision Making," *Journal of Business Ethics,* 24 (2) (March 2000): 125–140; and Ishmael P. Akaah and Edward A. Riordan, "The Incidence of Unethical Practices in Marketing Research: An Empirical Investigation," *Journal of the Academy of Marketing Science,* 18 (1990): 143–152.

# Chapter 20

1. Emma Reynolds, "Is Haagen-Dazs Shrewd to Drop Its Sexy Image?" *Marketing* (September 6, 2001): 17; Liz Stuart, "Haagen-Dazs Aims to Scoop a Larger Share," *Marketing Week,* 19 (46/2) (February 21, 1997): 26; Dwight J. Shelton, "Birds of a Geodemographic Feather Flock Together," *Marketing News* (August 28, 1987): 13.

2. For recent applications of cluster analysis, see Wendy W. Moe and Peter S. Fader, "Modeling Hedonic Portfolio Products: A Joint Segmentation Analysis of Music Compact Disc Sales," *Journal of Marketing Research,* 38 (3) (August 2001): 376–388; and George Arimond, "A Clustering Method for Categorical Data in Tourism Market Segmentation Research," *Journal of Travel Research,* 39 (4) (May 2001): 391–397.

3. Overlapping clustering methods that permit an object to be grouped into more than one cluster are also available. See Anil Chaturvedi, J. Douglass Carroll, Paul E. Green, and John A. Rotondo, "A Feature-Based Approach to Market Segmentation via Overlapping K-Centroids Clustering," *Journal of Marketing Research,* 34 (August 1997): 370–377.

4. Excellent discussions on the various aspects of cluster analysis may be found in Brian S. Everitt, Sabine Landau, and Morven Leese, *Cluster Analysis,* 4th ed. (Oxford, UK: Oxford University Press, 2001); and H. Charles Romsburg, *Cluster Analysis for Researchers* (Melbourne: Krieger Publishing Company, 1990).

5. Jafar Ali, "Micro-Market Segmentation Using a Neural Network Model Approach," *Journal of International Consumer Marketing* (2001): 7; Vicki Douglas, "Questionnaires Too Long? Try Variable Clustering," *Marketing News,* 29 (5)

(February 27, 1995): 38; Girish Punj and David Stewart, "Cluster Analysis in Marketing Research: Review and Suggestions for Application," *Journal of Marketing Research,* 20 (May 1983): 134–148.

6. For use of cluster analysis for segmentation, see George Arimond, "A Clustering Method for Categorical Data in Tourism Market Segmentation Research," *Journal of Travel Research,* 39 (4) (May 2001): 391–397; William D. Neal, "Advances in Market Segmentation," *Marketing Research* (Spring 2001): 14–18; and Mark Peterson and Naresh K. Malhotra, "A Global View of Quality of Life: Segmentation Analysis of 165 Countries," *International Marketing Review,* 17 (1) (2000): 56–73.

7. Tom J. Brown, Hailin Qu, and Bongkosh Ngamsom Rittichainuwat, "Thailand's International Travel Image: Mostly Favorable," *Cornell Hotel and Restaurant Administration Quarterly,* 42 (2) (April 2001): 85–95; Chul-Min Mo, Mark E. Havitz, and Dennis R. Howard, "Segmenting Travel Markets with the International Tourism Role (ITR) Scale," *Journal of Travel Research,* 33 (1) (Summer 1994): 24–31; George P. Moschis and Daniel C. Bello, "Decision-Making Patterns Among International Vacationers: A Cross-Cultural Perspective," *Psychology & Marketing* (Spring 1987): 75–89.

8. Brian S. Everitt, Sabine Landau, and Morven Leese, *Cluster Analysis,* 4th ed. (Oxford, UK: Oxford University Press, 2001).

9. For a detailed discussion on the different measures of similarity and formulas for computing them, see Eric T. Bradlow, "Subscale Distance and Item Clustering Effects in Self-Administered Surveys: A New Metric," *Journal of Marketing Research* (May 2001): 254–261; Victor Chepoi and Feodor Dragan, "Computing a Median Point of a Simple Rectilinear Polygon," *Information Processing Letters,* 49 (6) (March 22, 1994): 281–285; and H. Charles Romsburg, *Cluster Analysis for Researchers* (Melbourne: Krieger Publishing Company, 1990).

10. For further discussion of the issues involved in standardization, see H. Charles Romsburg, *Cluster Analysis for Researchers* (Melbourne: Krieger Publishing Company, 1990).

11. Brian Everitt, Sabine Landau, and Morven Leese, *Cluster Analysis,* 4th ed. (Oxford, UK: Oxford University Press, 2001); and G. Milligan, "An Examination of the Effect of Six Types of Error Perturbation on Fifteen Clustering Algorithms," *Psychometrika,* 45 (September 1980): 325–342.

12. Brian Everitt, Sabine Landau, and Morven Leese, *Cluster Analysis,* 4th ed. (Oxford, UK: Oxford University Press, 2001).

13. For a formal discussion of reliability, validity, and significance testing in cluster analysis, see Michael J. Brusco, J. Dennis Cradit, and Stephanie Stahl, "A Simulated Annealing Heuristic for a Bicriterion Partitioning Problem in Market Segmentation," *Journal of Marketing Research,* 39 (1) (February 2002): 99–109; Hui-Min Chen, "Using Clustering Techniques to Detect Usage Patterns in a Web-Based Information System," *Journal of the American Society for Information Science and Technology,* 52 (11) (September 2001): 888; S. Dibbs and P. Stern, "Questioning the Reliability of Market Segmentation Techniques," *Omega,* 23 (6) (December 1995): 625–636; G. Ray Funkhouser, "A Note on the Reliability of Certain Clustering Algorithms," *Journal of Marketing Research,* 30 (February 1983): 99–102; T. D. Klastorin, "Assessing Cluster Analysis Results," *Journal of Marketing Research,* 20 (February 1983): 92–98; and S. J. Arnold, "A Test for Clusters," *Journal of Marketing Research,* 16 (November 1979): 545–551.

14. William Pedder, "Annual Report," *Invest UK Web Site* (March 31, 2001) (*www.invest.uk.com/investing/annual.cfm?d=ar_cereport&*

*action=pdisp*); John Saunders, Rosalind H. Forrester, "Capturing Learning and Applying Knowledge: An Investigation of the Use of Innovation Teams in Japanese and American Automotive Firms," *Journal of Business Research*, 47 (1) (January 2000): 35; Peter Doyle, John Saunders, and Veronica Wong, "International Marketing Strategies and Organizations: A Study of U.S., Japanese, and British Competitors," in Paul Bloom, Russ Winer, Harold H. Kassarjian, Debra L. Scammon, Bart Weitz, Robert E. Spekman, Vijay Mahajan, and Michael Levy, Eds., *Enhancing Knowledge Development in Marketing*, Series No. 55 (Chicago: American Marketing Association, 1989): 100–104.

15. Alfred Lin, Leslie A. Lenert, Mark A. Hlatky, Kathryn M. McDonald, et al., "Clustering and the Design of Preference-Assessment Surveys in Healthcare," *Health Services Research*, 34 (5) (December 1999): 1033–1045; Edward J. Holohean, Jr., Steven M. Banks, and Blair A. Maddy, "System Impact and Methodological Issues in the Development of an Empirical Typology of Psychiatric Hospital Residents," *Journal of Mental Health Administration*, 22 (2) (Spring 1995): 177–188; and Arch G. Woodside, Robert L. Nielsen, Fred Walters, and Gale D. Muller, "Preference Segmentation of Health Care Services: The Old-Fashioneds, Value Conscious, Affluents, and Professional Want-It-Alls," *Journal of Health Care Marketing* (June 1988): 14–24.

16. Brian Everitt, Sabine Landau, and Morven Leese, *Cluster Analysis*, 4th ed. (Oxford, UK: Oxford University Press, 2001); and Vicki Douglas, "Questionnaire Too Long? Try Variable Clustering," *Marketing News*, 29 (5) (February 27, 1995): 38.

17. Aaron Baar, "Polaroid Ads Play Up Emotion," *Adweek*, 42 (15) (April 9, 2001): 2; Thorolf Helgesen, "The Power of Advertising Myths and Realities," *Marketing & Research Today*, 24 (2) (May 1996): 63–71; David A. Aaker, Douglas M. Stayman, and Richard Vezina, "Identifying Feelings Elicited by Advertising," *Psychology & Marketing* (Spring 1988): 1–16.

18. Gergory M. Pickett, "The Impact of Product Type and Parity on the Informational Content of Advertising," *Journal of Marketing Theory and Practice*, 9 (3) (Summer 2001): 32–43; Fred Zandpour and Katrin R. Harich, "Think and Feel Country Clusters: A New Approach to International Advertising Standardization," *International Journal of Advertising*, 15 (4) (1996): 325–344; and Nancy Giges, "World's Product Parity Perception High," *Advertising Age* (June 20, 1988).

19. John P. Fraedrich, Neil C. Herndon, Jr., and Quey-Jen Yeh, "An Investigation of Moral Values and the Ethical Content of the Corporate Culture," *Journal of Business Ethics*, 30 (1) (March 2001): 73–85; Ishmael P. Akaah, "Organizational Culture and Ethical Research Behavior," *Journal of the Academy of Marketing Science*, 21 (1) (Winter 1993): 59–63; and R. E. Reidenbach and D. P. Robin, "Some Initial Steps Toward Improving the Measurement of Ethical Evaluations of Marketing Activities," *Journal of Business Ethics*, 7 (1988): 871–879.

# Chapter 21

1. Anonymous, "Soft Drink Product Tops Survey," *Businessworld*, (August 14, 2001): 1; and Paul E. Green, Frank J. Carmone, Jr., and Scott M. Smith, *Multidimensional Scaling: Concepts and Applications* (Boston: Allyn and Bacon, 1989): 16–17.

2. Ali Kara, Erdener Kaynak, and Orsay Kucukemiroglu, "Credit Card Development Strategies for the Youth Market: The Use of Conjoint Analysis," *International Journal of Bank Marketing*, 12 (6) (1994): 30–36; and Mary Tonnenberger, "In Search of the Perfect Plastic," *Quirk's Marketing Research Review*, 5 (May 1992): 6–7, 37.

3. For a review of MDS studies in marketing research, see Tammo H. A. Bijmolt and Michel Wedel, "A Comparison of Multidimensional Scaling Methods for Perceptual Mapping," *Journal of Marketing Research*, 36 (2) (May 1999): 277–285; J. Douglass Carroll and Paul E. Green, "Psychometric Methods in Marketing Research: Part II, Multidimensional Scaling," *Journal of Marketing Research*, 34 (February 1997): 193–204; and Lee G. Cooper, "A Review of Multidimensional Scaling in Marketing Research," *Applied Psychological Measurement*, 7 (Fall 1983): 427–450.

4. An excellent discussion of the various aspects of MDS may be found in Tammo H. A. Bijmolt, "A Comparison of Multidimensional Methods for Perceptual Mapping," *Journal of Marketing Research*, 36 (2) (May 1999): 277–285; and Mark L. Davison, *Multidimensional Scaling* (Melbourne: Krieger Publishing Company, 1992).

5. The data are commonly treated as symmetric. For an asymmetric approach, see Wayne S. Desarbo and Ajay K. Manrai, "A New Multidimensional Scaling Methodology for the Analysis of Asymmetric Proximity Data in Marketing Research," *Marketing Science*, 11 (1) (Winter 1992): 1–20. For other approaches to MDS data, see Kim Juvoung, "Incorporating Context Effects in the Multidimensional Scaling of 'Pick Any/N' Choice Data," *International Journal of Research in Marketing*, 16 (1) (February 1999): 35–55; and Tammo H. A. Bijmolt and Michel Wedel, "The Effects of Alternative Methods of Collecting Similarity Data for Multidimensional Scaling," *International Journal of Research in Marketing*, 12 (4) (November 1995): 363–371.

6. See Trevor F. Cox and Michael A. Cox, *Multidimensional Scaling*, 2nd ed. (New York: Chapman & Hall, 2000); Jan-Benedict SteenKamp and Hans C. M. van Trijp, "Task Experience and Validity in Perceptual Mapping: A Comparison of Two Consumer-Adaptive Techniques," *International Journal of Research in Marketing*, 13 (3) (July 1996): 265–276; and Naresh K. Malhotra, Arun K. Jain, and Christian Pinson, "The Robustness of MDS Configurations in the Case of Incomplete Data," *Journal of Marketing Research*, 25 (February 1988): 95–102.

7. See Trevor F. Cox and Michael A. Cox, *Multidimensional Scaling*, 2nd ed. (New York: Chapman & Hall, 2000).

8. Kruskal's stress is probably the most commonly used measure for lack of fit. See Ingwer Borg and Patrick J. Groenen, *Modern Multidimensional Scaling Theory and Applications* (New York: Springer-Verlag, 1996). For the original article, see J. B. Kruskal, "Multidimensional Scaling by Optimizing Goodness of Fit to a Nonmetric Hypothesis," *Psychometrika*, 29 (March 1964): 1–27.

9. Wayne S. DeSarbo, "The Joint Spatial Representation of Multiple Variable Batteries Collected in Marketing Research," *Journal of Marketing Research*, 38 (2) (May 2001): 244–253; J. Douglass Carroll and Paul E. Green, "Psychometric Methods in Marketing Research: Part II, Multidimensional Scaling," *Journal of Marketing Research*, 34 (February 1997): 193–204; and Naresh K. Malhotra, "Validity and Structural Reliability of Multidimensional Scaling," *Journal of Marketing Research*, 24 (May 1987): 164–173.

10. See, for example, Jack K. H. Lee, K. Sudhir, and Joel H. Steckel, "A Multiple Ideal Point Model: Capturing Multiple Preference Effects from Within an Ideal Point Framework," *Journal of Marketing Research*, 39 (1) (February 2002): 73–86; Wayne S. DeSarbo, M. R. Young, and Arvind Rangaswamy, "A Parametric Multidimensional Unfolding Procedure for

Incomplete Nonmetric Preference/Choice Set Data Marketing Research," *Journal of Marketing Research,* 34 (4) (November 1997): 499–516; and David B. Mackay, Robert F. Easley, and Joseph L. Zinnes, "A Single Ideal Point Model for Market Structure Analysis," *Journal of Marketing Research,* 32 (4) (November 1995): 433–443.

11. Jeff Sweat, "Keep 'em Happy," *Information Week,* 873 (January 28, 2002): 55–58; and Ian P. Murphy, "Downscale Luxury Cars Drive to the Heart of Baby Boomers," *Marketing News,* 30 (21) (October 1997): 1, 19.

12. For recent applications of correspondence analysis, see Naresh K. Malhotra and Betsy Charles, "Overcoming the Attribute Prespecification Bias in International Marketing Research by Using Nonattribute Based Correspondence Analysis," *International Marketing Review,* 19 (1) 2002, 65–79; and Ken Reed, "The Use of Correspondence Analysis to Develop a Scale to Measure Workplace Morale from Multi-Level Data," *Social Indicators Research,* 57 (3) (March 2002): 339.

13. See Jorg Blasius and Michael L. Greenacre, *Visualization of Categorical Data* (McLean, VA: Academic Press, 1998); Michael J. Greenacre, *Correspondence Analysis in Practice* (New York: Academic Press, 1993); Michael J. Greenacre, "The Carroll-Green-Schaffer Scaling in Correspondence Analysis: A Theoretical and Empirical Appraisal," *Journal of Marketing Research,* 26 (August 1989): 358–365; Michael J. Greenacre, *Theory and Applications of Correspondence Analysis* (New York: Academic Press, 1984); and Donna L. Hoffman and George R. Franke, "Correspondence Analysis: Graphical Representation of Categorical Data in Marketing Research," *Journal of Marketing Research,* 23 (August 1986): 213–227.

14. Tammo H. A. Bijmolt and Michel Wedel, "A Comparison of Multidimensional Scaling Methods for Perceptual Mapping," *Journal of Marketing Research,* 36 (2) (May 1999): 277–285; and John R. Hauser and Frank S. Koppelman, "Alternative Perceptual Mapping Techniques: Relative Accuracy and Usefulness," *Journal of Marketing Research,* 16 (November 1979): 495–506. Hauser and Koppelman conclude that factor analysis is superior to discriminant analysis. See also Ingwer Borg and Patrick J. Groenen, *Modern Multidimensional Scaling Theory and Applications* (New York: Springer-Verlag, 1996).

15. For applications and issues in conjoint analysis, see Rick L. Andrews, Asim Ansari, and Imran S. Currim, "Hierarchical Bayes Versus Finite Mixture Conjoint Analysis Models: A Comparison of Fit, Prediction, and Partworth Recovery," *Journal of Marketing Research,* 39 (1) (February 2002): 87–98; V. Srinivasan and Chan Su Park, "Surprising Robustness of the Self-Explicated Approach to Customer Preference Structure Measurement," *Journal of Marketing Research,* 34 (May 1997): 286–291; and Paul E. Green and Abba M. Krieger, "Segmenting Markets with Conjoint Analysis," *Journal of Marketing,* 55 (October 1991): 20–31.

16. Marco Vriens, "Linking Attributes, Benefits, and Consumer Values," *Marketing Research,* 12 (3) (Fall 2000): 4–10; and Judith Thomas Miller, James R. Ogden, and Craig A. Latshaw, "Using Trade-Off Analysis to Determine Value-Price Sensitivity of Custom Calling Features," *American Business Review,* 16 (1) (January 1998): 8–13. For an overview of conjoint analysis in marketing, see J. Douglass Carroll and Paul E. Green, "Psychometric Methods in Marketing Research: Part I, Conjoint Analysis," *Journal of Marketing Research,* 32 (November 1995): 385–391; and Paul E. Green and V. Srinivasan, "Conjoint Analysis in Marketing: New Developments with Implications for Research and Practice," *Journal of Marketing,* 54 (October 1990): 3–19.

17. Zsolt Sandor and Michel Wedel, "Designing Conjoint Choice Experiments Using Managers' Prior Beliefs," *Journal of Marketing Research,* 38 (4) (November 2001): 430–444; V. Srinivasan, "Predictive Validation of Multiattribute Choice Models," *Marketing Research,* 11 (4) (Winter 1999/Spring 2000): 28–34; Dick R. Wittink, Marco Vriens, and Wim Burhenne, "Commercial Uses of Conjoint Analysis in Europe: Results and Critical Reflections," *International Journal of Research in Marketing,* 11 (1) (January 1994): 41–52; Dick R. Wittink and Philippe Cattin, "Commercial Use of Conjoint Analysis: An Update," *Journal of Marketing,* 53 (July 1989): 91–97. For using conjoint analysis to measure price sensitivity, see "Multistage Conjoint Methods to Measure Price Sensitivity," *Sawtooth News,* 10 (Winter 1994/1995): 5–6.

18. These three attributes are a subset of attributes identified in the literature. See Chuck Stogel, "It's Easier Being Green (If You're Nike)," *Brandweek,* 43 (4) (January 28, 2002): 16–19; and Hilary Cassidy, "Adidas & New Balance: Passing Shots," *Brandweek,* 42 (47) (December 17, 2001): 1.

19. Martin Wetzels, "Measuring Service Quality Trade-Offs in Asian Distribution Channels: A Multilayer Perspective," *Total Quality Management,* 11 (3) (May 2000): 307–318; Gerard H. Loosschilder, Edward Rosbergen, Marco Vriens, and Dick R. Wittink, "Pictorial Stimuli in Conjoint Analysis to Support Product Styling Decisions," *Journal of the Market Research Society,* 37 (January 1995): 17–34.

20. See Paul E. Green, Abba M. Krieger, and Yoram Wind, "Thirty Years of Conjoint Analysis: Reflections and Prospects," *Interfaces,* 31 (3) (May/June 2001): S56; J. Douglass Carroll and Paul E. Green, "Psychometric Methods in Marketing Research: Part I, Conjoint Analysis," *Journal of Marketing Research,* 32 (November 1995): 385–391; Warren F. Kuhfeld, Randall D. Tobias, and Mark Garratt, "Efficient Experimental Designs with Marketing Applications," *Journal of Marketing Research,* 31 (November 1994): 545–557; Sidney Addleman, "Orthogonal Main-Effect Plans for Asymmetrical Factorial Experiments," *Technometrics,* 4 (February 1962): 21–36; and Paul E. Green, "On the Design of Choice Experiments Involving Multifactor Alternatives," *Journal of Consumer Research,* 1 (September 1974): 61–68.

21. Rinus Haaijer, Wagner Kamakura, and Michel Wedel, "Response Latencies in the Analysis of Conjoint Choice Experiments," *Journal of Marketing Research,* 37 (3) (August 2000): 376–382; J. Douglass Carroll and Paul E. Green, "Psychometric Methods in Marketing Research: Part I, Conjoint Analysis," *Journal of Marketing Research,* 32 (November 1995): 385–391.

22. Zsolt Sandor and Michel Wedel, "Designing Conjoint Choice Experiments Using Managers' Prior Beliefs," *Journal of Marketing Research,* 38 (4) (November 2001): 430–444; and Arun K. Jain, Franklin Acito, Naresh K. Malhotra, and Vijay Mahajan, "A Comparison of the Internal Validity of Alternative Parameter Estimation Methods in Decompositional Multiattribute Preference Models," *Journal of Marketing Research* (August 1979): 313–322.

23. Neeraj Arora and Greg M. Allenby, "Measuring the Influence of Individual Preference Structures in Group Decision Making," *Journal of Marketing Research,* 36 (4) (November 1999): 476–487; J. Douglass Carroll and Paul E. Green, "Psychometric Methods in Marketing Research: Part I, Conjoint Analysis," *Journal of Marketing Research,* 32 (November 1995): 385–391; and Frank J. Carmone and Paul. E. Green, "Model Misspecification in Multiattribute Parameter Estimation," *Journal of Marketing Research,* 18 (February 1981): 87–93.

24. For a recent application of conjoint analysis using OLS regression, see Rinus Haaijer, Wagner Kamakura, and Michel Wedel, "The 'No-Choice' Alternative to Conjoint Choice Experiments," *International Journal of Market Research,* 43 (1) (First Quarter 2001): 93–106; Amy Ostrom and Dawn Iacobucci, "Consumer Trade-Offs and the Evaluation of Services," *Journal of Marketing,* 59 (January 1995): 17–28; and Peter J. Danaher, "Using Conjoint Analysis to Determine the Relative Importance of Service Attributes Measured in Customer Satisfaction Surveys," *Journal of Retailing,* 73 (2) (Summer 1997): 235–260.

25. Rick L. Andrews, "Hierarchical Bayes Verus Finite Mixture Conjoint Analysis: A Comparison of Fit, Prediction and Partworth Recovery," *Journal of Marketing Research,* 39 (1) (February 2002): 87–98; J. Douglass Carroll and Paul E. Green, "Psychometric Methods in Marketing Research: Part I, Conjoint Analysis," *Journal of Marketing Research,* 32 (November 1995): 385–391; Naresh K. Malhotra, "Structural Reliability and Stability of Nonmetric Conjoint Analysis," *Journal of Marketing Research,* 19 (May 1982): 199–207; Thomas W. Leigh, David B. MacKay, and John O. Summers, "Reliability and Validity of Conjoint Analysis and Self-Explicated Weights: A Comparison," *Journal of Marketing Research,* 21 (November 1984): 456–462; and Madhav N. Segal, "Reliability of Conjoint Analysis: Contrasting Data Collection Procedures," *Journal of Marketing Research,* 19 (February 1982): 139–143.

26. Jay Palmer, "The Best Notebook Computers," *Barron's,* 80 (46) (November 13, 2000): V16–V17; William L. Moore, "Using Conjoint Analysis to Help Design Product Platforms," *The Journal of Product Innovation Management,* 16 (1) (January 1999): 27–39; Del I. Hawkins, Roger J. Best, and Kenneth A. Coney, *Consumer Behavior Implications for Marketing Strategy,* 7th ed. (Boston: McGraw Hill, 1998).

27. Frenkel Ter Hofstede, Youngchan Kim, and Michel Wedel, "Bayesian Prediction in Hybrid Conjoint Analysis," *Journal of Marketing Research,* 39 (2) (May 2002): 253–261; Terry G. Vavra, Paul E Green, and Abba M Krieger, "Evaluating EZPass," *Marketing Research,* 11 (2) (Summer 1999): 4–14; Clark Hu and Stephen J. Hiemstra, "Hybrid Conjoint Analysis as a Research Technique to Measure Meeting Planners Preferences in Hotel Selection," *Journal of Travel Research,* 35 (2) (Fall 1996): 62–69; Paul E. Green and Abba M. Krieger, "Individualized Hybrid Models for Conjoint Analysis," *Management Science,* 42 (6) (June 1996): 850–867; Paul E. Green, "Hybrid Models for Conjoint Analysis: An Expository Review," *Journal of Marketing Research,* 21 (May 1984): 155–169.

28. Kevin J. Boyle, "A Comparison of Conjoint Analysis Response Formats," *American Journal of Agricultural Economics,* 83 (2) (May 2001): 441–454; Dale McDonald, "Industry Giants," *Farm Industry News,* 34 (3) (February 2001): 6; and Diane Schneidman, "Research Method Designed to Determine Price for New Products, Line Extensions," *Marketing News,* (October 23, 1987): 11.

29. Will McSheehy, "Think Globally, Act Locally," *Corporate Location* (July/August 2001): 12; Michael McCarthy, "Marketers Reduce National Ad Spending," *USA Today,* (April 17, 2001): B3; and "Luxury Car Makers Assemble World View," *Corporate Location* (January/February 1997): 4.

30. Sukanya Jitpleecheep, "Thailand's Detergent Market Growth Rate Slows," *Knight Ridder Tribune Business News* (May 24, 2002): 1; Linda Grant, "Outmarketing P & G," *Fortune,* 137 (1) (January 12, 1998): 150–152; and David Butler, "Thai Superconcentrates Foam," *Advertising Age* (January 18, 1993).

31. Dane Peterson, Angela Rhoads, and Bobby C. Vaught, "Ethical Beliefs of Business Professionals: A Study of Gender, Age and External Factors," *Journal of Business Ethics,* 31 (3) (June 2001): 1; and S. J. Vitell and F. N. Ho, "Ethical Decision Making in Marketing: A Synthesis and Evaluation of Scales Measuring the Various Components of Decision Making in Ethical Situations," *Journal of Business Ethics,* 16 (7) (May 1997): 699–717.

# Chapter 22

1. Christine Tatum, "United Airlines Banks on New Network, Customer Data to Fill More Seats," *Knight Ridder Tribune Business News* (April 1, 2002): 1; and Joseph Rydholm, "Surveying the Friendly Skies," *Marketing Research* (May 1996).

2. Gill Ereaut, Mike Imms, and Martin Callingham, *Qualitative Market Research: Principle & Practice: Seven Volume Set* (Thousand Oaks, CA: Sage Publications, 2002); Thomas L. Greenbaum, *The Handbook for Focus Group Research* (Thousand Oaks, CA: Sage Publications, 1997); and Thomas L. Greenbaum, "Using 'Ghosts' to Write Reports Hurts Viability of Focus Group," *Marketing News,* 27 (19) (September 13, 1993): 25.

3. Anonymous, "Research Reports," *Barron's,* 82 (14) (April 8, 2002): 30; Edward R. Tufte, *Visual Explanations: Images and Quantities, Evidence and Narrative* (Cheshire, CT: Graphic Press, 1997); and Arlene Fink, *How to Report on Surveys* (Thousand Oaks, CA: Sage Publications, 1995).

4. Harry F. Wolcott, *Writing Up Qualitative Research,* 2nd ed. (Thousand Oaks, CA: Sage Publications, 2001); S. H. Britt, "The Writing of Readable Research Reports," *Journal of Marketing Research* (May 1971): 265. See also Simon Mort, *Professional Report Writing* (Brookfield Vermont: Ashgate Publishing Company, 1995); and David I. Shair, "Report Writing," *HR Focus,* 71 (2) (February 1994): 20.

5. George S. Low, "Factors Affecting the Use of Information in the Evaluation of Marketing Communications Productivity," *Academy of Marketing Science Journal,* 29 (1) (Winter 2001): 70–88; and Ann Boland, "Got Report-O-Phobia?: Follow These Simple Steps to Get Those Ideas onto Paper," *Chemical Engineering,* 103 (3) (March 1996): 131–132.

6. Gabriel Tanase, "Real-Life Data Mart Processing," *Intelligent Enterprise,* 5 (5) (March 8, 2002): 22–24; L. Deane Wilson, "Are Appraisal Reports Logical Fallacies," *Appraisal Journal,* 64 (2) (April 1996): 129–133; John Leach, "Seven Steps to Better Writing," *Planning,* 59 (6) (June 1993): 26–27; and A. S. C. Ehrenberg, "The Problem of Numeracy," *American Statistician,* 35 (May 1981): 67–71.

7. Joshua Dean, "High-Powered Charts and Graphs," *Government Executive,* 34 (1) (January 2002): 58; and Neal B. Kauder, "Pictures Worth a Thousand Words," *American Demographics* (Tools Supplement) (November/December 1996): 64–68.

8. Ann Michele Gutsche, "Visuals Make the Case," *Marketing News,* 35 (20) (Sept 24, 2001): 21–22; and Sue Hinkin, "Charting Your Course to Effective Information Graphics," *Presentations,* 9 (11) (November 1995): 28–32.

9. Michael Lee, "It's All in the Charts," *Malaysian Business* (February 1, 2002): 46; Mark T. Chen, "An Innovative Project Report," *Cost Engineering,* 38 (4) (April 1996): 41–45; and Gene Zelazny, *Say It with Charts: The Executive's Guide to Visual Communication,* 3rd ed. (Burr Ridge, IL: Irwin Professional Publishing, 1996).

10. N. I. Fisher, "Graphical Assessment of Dependence: Is a Picture Worth 100 Tests?" *The American Statistician,* 55 (3) (August

2001): 233–239; and Patricia Ramsey and Louis Kaufman, "Presenting Research Data: How to Make Weak Numbers Look Good," *Industrial Marketing,* 67 (March 1982): 66, 68, 70, 74.

11. Anonymous, "Flow Chart," *B-to-B,* 87 (4) (April 8, 2002): 16; and Sharon Johnson and Michael Regan, "A New Use for an Old Tool," *Quality Progress,* 29 (11) (November 1996): 144. For a recent example, see Naresh K. Malhotra and Daniel McCort, "An Information Processing Model of Consumer Behavior: Conceptualization, Framework and Propositions," *Asian Journal of Marketing,* 8 (2) (2000–2001): 5–32.

12. Lori Desiderio, "At the Sales Presentation: Ask and Listen," *ID,* 38 (4) (April 2002): 55; and Charles R. McConnell, "Speak Up: The Manager's Guide to Oral Presentations," *The Health Care Manager,* 18 (3) (March 2000): 70–77.

13. Information provided by Roger L. Bacik, senior vice president, Elrick & Lavidge, Atlanta.

14. Janet Moody, "Showing the Skilled Business Graduate: Expanding the Tool Kit," *Business Communication Quarterly,* 65 (1) (March 2002): 21–36; David Byrne, *Interpreting Quantitative Data* (Thousand Oaks, CA: Sage Publications, 2002); and Lawrence F. Locke, Stephen Silverman, and Wannen W. Spirduso, *Reading and Understanding Research* (Thousand Oaks, CA: Sage Publications, 1998).

15. Anonymous, "Toyota Camry," *Consumer Reports,* 67 (4) (April 2002): 67; Ross Garnaut, "Australian Cars in a Global Economy," *Australian Economic Review,* 30 (4) (December 1997): 359–373; and Geoffrey Lee Martin, "Aussies Chicken Fries Ford," *Advertising Age* (January 18, 1993).

16. Milton Liebman, "Beyond Ethics: Companies Deal with Legal Attacks on Marketing Practices," *Medical Marketing and Media,* 37 (2) (February 2002): 74–77; Ralph W. Giacobbe, "A Comparative Analysis of Ethical Perceptions in Marketing Research: USA vs. Canada," *Journal of Business Ethics,* 27 (3) (October 2000): 229–245.

17. Mark Dolliver, "Ethics, or the Lack Thereof," *Adweek,* 43 (14) (April 1, 2002): 29; and Andrew Crane, "Unpacking the Ethical Product," *Journal of Business Ethics,* 30 (4) (April 2001): 361–373.

18. Gordon Fairclough, "Case on Children and Tobacco Ads Commences Today," *Wall Street Journal* (April 22, 2002): B8; and S. Rapp, "Cigarettes: A Question of Ethics," *Marketing News* (November 5, 1992): 17.

# Chapter 23

1. See Naresh K. Malhotra, "Cross-Cultural Marketing Research in the Twenty-First Century," *International Marketing Review,* 18 (3) (2001): 230–234; Susan P. Douglas, "Exploring New Worlds: The Challenge of Global Marketing," *Journal of Marketing,* 65 (1) (January 2001): 103–107; Naresh K. Malhotra, James Agarwal, and Mark Peterson, "Cross-Cultural Marketing Research: Methodological Issues and Guidelines," *International Marketing Review,* 13 (5) (1996): 7–43; Naresh K. Malhotra, "Administration of Questionnaires for Collecting Quantitative Data in International Marketing Research," *Journal of Global Marketing,* 4 (2) (1991): 63–92; and Naresh K. Malhotra, "Designing an International Marketing Research Course: Framework and Content," *Journal of Teaching in International Business,* 3 (1992): 1–27.

2. Melissa LeHardy, "In India, Familiarity Breeds Better Content," *Marketing News,* 35 (9) (April 23, 2001): 40.

3. Anonymous, "Best Western Grows to 4,000," *Arizona Business Gazette* (August 16, 2001): 2; Anonymous, "Best Western Quantifies Guest Quality Measures," *Lodging Hospitality,* 57 (3) (March 1, 2001): 34; "Hotel Chains Capitalize on International Travel Market," *Hotels and Restaurants International* (June 1989): 81S–86S; and "Target Marketing Points to Worldwide Success," *Hotels and Restaurants International* (June 1989): 87S.

4. Jack Honomichl, "Honomichl Top 50: Annual Business Report on the Marketing Research Industry," *Marketing News* (June 10, 2002): H1–H43.

5. Dave Crick, "Small High-Technology Firms and International High-Technology Markets," *Journal of International Marketing,* 8 (2) (2000): 63–85; Associated Press, "Regional Markets Are International Order of the Day," *Marketing News* (March 1, 1993): IR–10; and Thomas T. Semon, "Red Tape Is Chief Problem in Multinational Research," *Marketing News* (March 1, 1993): 7.

6. Doreen Hemlock, "Mexican Companies Establish Offices in United States Due to NAFTA," *Knight Ridder Tribune Business News* (January 24, 2002): 1.

7. See Naresh K. Malhotra, "Cross-Cultural Marketing Research in the Twenty-First Century," *International Marketing Review,* 18 (3) (2001): 230–234.

8. For recent examples of international marketing research, see Naresh K. Malhotra and Betsy Charles, "Overcoming the Attribute Prespecification Bias in International Marketing Research by Using Nonattribute Based Correspondence Analysis," *International Marketing Review,* 19 (1) (2002): 65–79; and Naresh K. Malhotra and Daniel McCort, "A Cross-Cultural Comparison of Behavioral Intention Models: Theoretical Consideration and an Empirical Investigation," *International Marketing Review,* 18 (3) (2001): 235–269.

9. Ming Ouyang, "Estimating Marketing Persistence on Sales of Consumer Durables in China," *Journal of Business Research,* 55 (4) (April 2002): 337; Tanya Clark, "China's Challenges," *Industry Week,* 246 (19) (October 20, 1997): 126–134.

10. Natasha Emmons, "Universal Studios Japan Employs Aid of Focus Groups for Cultural Ideas," *Amusement Business,* 113 (12) (March 26, 2001): 28.

11. See Dana James, "Dark Clouds Should Part for International Marketers," *Marketing News,* 36 (1) (January 7, 2002): 9–10.

12. Naresh K. Malhotra, "Cross-Cultural Marketing Research in the Twenty-First Century," *International Marketing Review,* 18 (3) (2001): 230–234; Susan P. Douglas, "Exploring New Worlds: The Challenge of Global Marketing," *Journal of Marketing,* 65 (1) (January 2001): 103–107; Naresh K. Malhotra, James Agarwal, and Mark Peterson, "Cross-Cultural Marketing Research: Methodological Issues and Guidelines," *International Marketing Review,* 13 (5) (1996): 7–43.

13. Robert F. Belli, "Event History Calendars and Question List Surveys: A Direct Comparison of Interviewing Methods," *Public Opinion Quarterly,* 65 (1) (Spring 2001): 45–74; Thomas T. Semon, "Select Local Talent When Conducting Research Abroad," *Marketing News,* 31 (19) (September 15, 1997): 28.

14. Michael A. Einhorn, "International Telephony: A Review of the Literature," *Information Economics and Policy,* 14 (1) (March 2002): 51; Humphrey Taylor, "The Very Different Methods Used to Conduct Telephone Surveys of the Public," *Journal of the Market Research Society,* 39 (3) (July 1997): 421–432.

15. Peter M. Chisnall, "International Market Research," *International Journal of Market Research,* 42 (4) (Winter 2000): 495–497; Clive Fletcher, "Just How Effective Is a Telephone Interview," *People Management,* 3 (13) (June 26, 1997): 49; and Minoo Farhangmehr and Paula Veiga, "The Changing Consumer in

Portugal," *International Journal of Research in Marketing,* 12 (5) (December 1995): 485–502.

16. Norman Lerner, "Latin America and Mexico: A Change in Focus," *Telecommunications,* 34 (3) (March 2000): 51–54; Peter H. Wertheim and Dayse Abrantes, "Brazil: New Take on Telecom," *Data Communications,* 26 (5) (April 1997): 42; and P. Pinheiro de Andrade, "Market Research in Brazil," *European Research* (August 1987): 188–197.

17. Brad Frevert, "Is Global Research Different?" *Marketing Research,* 12 (1) (Spring 2000): 49–51; and Karen Fletcher, "Jump on the Omnibus," *Marketing* (June 15, 1995): 25–28.

18. Anonymous, "Searching for the Pan-European Brand (Part 1 of 2)," *Funds International* (March 1, 1999): 8; and Naresh K. Malhotra, James Agarwal, and Mark Peterson, "Cross-Cultural Marketing Research: Methodological Issues and Guidelines," *International Marketing Review,* 13 (5) (1996): 7–43.

19. Anonymous, "Coca-Cola Listed as One of 10 Most Respected Firms," *Businessworld* (January 23, 2002): 1; Jonathan Holburt, "Global Tastes, Local Trimmings," *Far Eastern Economic Review,* 160 (1) (December 26, 1996–January 2, 1997): 24; and Julie Skur Hill, "Coke Tops in Americas," *Advertising Age* (November 12, 1990).

20. Ase Hedberg, "The Rise of the Technophile," *Marketing Week,* 23 (49) (January 25, 2001): 40; and Peter Jones and John Polak, "Computer-Based Personal Interviewing: State-of-the-Art and Future Prospects," *Journal of Market Research Society,* 35 (3) (July 1993): 221–223.

21. Cihan Cobanoglu, "A Comparison of Mail, Fax, and Web-Based Survey Methods," *International Journal of Market Research,* 43 (4) (Fourth Quarter 2001): 441–454; Paul Lewis, "Do Your Homework!" *Successful Meetings,* 46 (3) (March 1997): 120–121; T. Vahvelainen, "Marketing Research in the Nordic Countries," *European Research* (April 1985): 76–79; and T. Vahvelainen, "Marketing Research in Finland," *European Research* (August 1987): 62–66.

22. Mark Peterson and Naresh K. Malhotra, "A Global View of Quality of Life: Segmentation Analysis of 165 Countries," *International Marketing Review,* 17 (1) (2000): 56–73; Lewis C. Winters, "International Psychographics," *Marketing Research: A Magazine of Management & Applications,* 4 (3) (September 1992): 48–49; "We Are the World," *American Demographics* (May 1990): 42–43.

23. Kai Arzheimer, "Research Note: The Effect of Material Incentives on Return Rate, Panel Attrition and Sample Composition of a Mail Panel Survey," *International Journal of Public Opinion Research,* 11 (4) (Winter 1999): 368–377; Kevin J. Clancy, "Brand Confusion," *Harvard Business Review,* 80 (3) (March 2002): 22; Jorge Zamora, "Management of Respondents' Motivation to Lower the Desertion Rates in Panels in Emerging Countries: The Case of Talca, Chile," *Marketing & Research*

*Today,* 25 (3) (August 1997): 191–198; and "TSMS and AGB Set Up Ad Effectiveness Panel," *Marketing Week,* 18 (27) (September 22, 1995): 15.

24. Anonymous, "DMA Survey Examines Popularity of Email Marketing," *Telecomworldwire* (April 8, 2002): NA.

25. Matthew B. Myers, "Academic Insights: An Application of Multiple-Group Causal Models in Assessing Cross-Cultural Measurement Equivalence," *Journal of International Marketing,* 8 (4) (2000): 108–121; Naresh K. Malhotra, James Agarwal, and Mark Peterson, "Cross-Cultural Marketing Research: Methodological Issues and Guidelines," *International Marketing Review,* 13 (5) (1996): 7–43.

26. Linda Thorne, "The Sociocultural Embeddedness of Individuals' Ethical Reasoning in Organizations (Cross Cultural Ethics)," *Journal of Business Ethics,* 35 (1) (January 2002): 1–13; and Gael McDonald, "Cross-Cultural Methodological Issues in Ethical Research," *Journal of Business Ethics,* 27 (1/2) (September 2000): 89–104.

27. Orlando Behling and Kenneth S. Law, *Translating Questionnaires and Other Research Instruments: Problems and Solutions* (Thousand Oaks, CA: Sage Publications, 2000); Naresh K. Malhotra and Daniel McCort, "A Cross-Cultural Comparison of Behavioral Intention Models: Theoretical Consideration and an Empirical Investigation," *International Marketing Review,* 18 (3) (2001): 235–269; and Naresh K. Malhotra, James Agarwal, and Mark Peterson, "Cross-Cultural Marketing Research: Methodological Issues and Guidelines," *International Marketing Review,* 13 (5) (1996): 7–43.

28. Leo Yat-ming Sin and Oliver Hon-ming Yau, "Female Role Orientation and Consumption Values: Some Evidence from Mainland China," *Journal of International Consumer Marketing,* 13 (2) (2001): 49–75; John Shannon, "National Values Can be Exported," *Marketing Week,* 19 (45) (February 7, 1997): 20; and S. C. Grunert and G. Scherhorn, "Consumer Values in West Germany: Underlying Dimensions and Cross-Cultural Comparison with North America," *Journal of Business Research,* 20 (1990): 97–107. See also H. C. Triandis, *Culture and Social Behavior* (New York: McGraw-Hill, Inc., 1994).

29. Heather R. Goldstein, "International Personal Data Safe Harbor Program Launched," *Intellectual Property & Technology Law Journal,* 13 (4) (April 2001): 24–25; Rebecca Sykes, "Privacy Debates Get More Complicated Overseas," *InfoWorld,* 19 (44) (November 3, 1997): 111; and Simon Chadwick, "Data Privacy Legislation All the Rage in Europe," *Marketing News,* vol. 27, 17 (August 16, 1993): A7.

30. Anonymous, "HP Measures Across Countries, Product Lines for Competitive Edge," *PR News* (May 27, 2002): 1; Hewlett Packard Web site: *www.hp.com.* HP's Chemical Analysis survey (English): *www.hp.com/chem_survey/english/index.html.*

# Index

## Name Index

# Credits

## Chapter 1
**2** NKM Photo/Naresh K. Malhotra; **4** Courtesy of IBM Global Financial Services Sector; **5** Frank LaBua/Pearson Education/PH College; **13** Courtesy of DaimlerChrysler Corporation; **22** Mary Katz/The Image Works; **23** Sears, Roebuck & Co.

## Chapter 2
**30** NKM Photo/Naresh K. Malhotra; **32** Ron Kimball Photography; **36** Cingular Wireless; **38** Spencer Grant/PhotoEdit; **46** NKM Photo/Naresh K. Malhotra; **52** Pan American World Airways.

## Chapter 3
**72** NKM Photo/Naresh K. Malhotra; **74** Jon Anderson/Black Star; **77** Microsoft Corporation; **83** Fotopic/Omni-Photo Communications, Inc.; **86** Bill Aron/PhotoEdit; **88** John Lei/Stock Boston; **94** AP/Wide World Photos.

## Chapter 4
**100** NKM Photo/Naresh K. Malhotra; **102** Boston Chicken, Inc.; **118** AP/Wide World Photos; **119** Nielsen Media Research; **125 (top)** Frank LaBua/Pearson Education/PH College; **125 (bottom)** National Decision Systems; **127** AP/Wide World Photos.

## Chapter 5
**134** NKM Photo/Naresh K. Malhotra; **139** Elrick & Lavidge, Inc.; **148** Susan Van Etten/PhotoEdit; **154** Getty Images, Inc.- Taxi; **155** The Terry Wild Studio, Inc.

## Chapter 6
**166** NKM Photo/Naresh K. Malhotra; **171** NKM Photo/Naresh K. Malhotra; **172** Elrick & Lavidge, Inc.; **173** AT&T Archives; **175 (top)** Elrick & Lavidge, Inc.; **175 (bottom)** Sean Bucher/Mint Museum of Art.

## Chapter 7
**202** NKM Photo/Naresh K. Malhotra; **204** Eckerd Corporation; **208** Pearson Education/PH College; **225** Frank LaBua/Pearson Education/PH College; **229** Lee Snider/The Image Works.

## Chapter 8
**234** NKM Photo/Naresh K. Malhotra; **236** General Electric Company; **238** David Madison/Getty Images, Inc. – Stone Allstock; **244** Frank LaBua/Pearson Education/PH College; **246** Frank LaBua/Pearson Education/PH College.

## Chapter 9
**253** Courtesy of New York City Transit; **254** NKM Photo/Naresh K. Malhotra; **257** MSInteractive Multimedia Services; **259** Rhoda Sidney; **271** Jeff Greenberg/PhotoEdit.

## Chapter 10
**278** NKM Photo/Naresh K. Malhotra; **280** Spencer Grant/PhotoEdit; **283** Steve Hall/Hedrick Blessing/Nike Town; **293** Bob Daemmrich/The Image Works; **294** Susan Van Etten/PhotoEdit.

## Chapter 11
**312** NKM Photo/Naresh K. Malhotra; **314** Courtesy of U.S. Fish and Wildlife Service; **319** Corbis RF; **322** AP/Wide World Photos, Inc.; **324** Margot Granitsas/Photo Researchers, Inc.; **330** Gary Russ/Getty Images, Inc. – Image Bank.

## Chapter 12
**340** NKM Photo/Naresh K. Malhotra; **341** Jean-Claude LeJeune/ Stock Boston; **346** Courtesy of New York Convention & Visitors Bureau; **353** Courtesy of Jacksonville Symphony Orchestra; **359** ChromoSohm/ Unicorn Stock Photos.

## Chapter 13
**386** NKM Photo/Naresh K. Malhotra; **388** Courtesy of CMOR.

## Chapter 14
**400** NKM Photo/Naresh K. Malhotra; **412** James Leynse/Corbis/SABA Press Photos, Inc.; **418** Felicia Martinez/PhotoEdit.

## Chapter 15
**424** NKM Photo/Naresh K. Malhotra; **426** Six-Cats Research, Inc.; **459** Colgate-Palmolive Company.

## Chapter 16
**466** NKM Photo/Naresh K. Malhotra; **468** Michael Justice/The Image Works; **482** Douglas C. Pizac/RCA/Thomson Multimedia.

## Chapter 17
**494** NKM Photo/Naresh K. Malhotra; **496** Frank LaBua/Pearson Education/PH College; **519** Teri Stratford/Pearson Education/PH College; **520** Laima E. Druskis/Pearson Education/PH College.

## Chapter 18
**532** NKM Photo/Naresh K. Malhotra; **537** R. Ford Smith/Corbis/Stock Market; **550** Peter Menzel/Stock Boston.

## Chapter 19
**558** NKM Photo/Naresh K. Malhotra; **571** Bic Corporation; **575** Jeff Chistensen/Corbis.

## Chapter 20

**584** NKM Photo/Naresh K. Malhotra; **586** Robert Frerck/Getty Images, Inc. – Stone Allstock; **587** Getty Images, Inc. – Stone Allstock; **601** Cathy Cheny/Stock Boston.

## Chapter 21

**608** NKM Photo/Naresh K. Malhotra; **610** Frank LaBua/Pearson Education/PH College; **620** AP/Wide World Photos; **626** Dwayne Newton/PhotoEdit; **631** Courtesy of Dell Computer Corporation.

## Chapter 22

**640** NKM Photo/Naresh K. Malhotra; **650** Pascal Le Segretain/Getty Images, Inc. – Liaison; **651** Burke, Inc.; **654** NKM Photo/Naresh K. Malhotra; **657** Courtesy of Toyota Motor Corporation.

## Chapter 23

**662** NKM Photo/Naresh K. Malhotra; **664** Tom Prettyman/PhotoEdit; **669** Stuart Cohen/Comstock Images; **670** AP/Wide World Photos; **672** Hugh Rogers/Hugh Rogers; **677** Courtesy of Hewlett-Packard Company.